THE OXFORD HANDBOOK OF

THE SELF

THE OXFORD HANDBOOK OF

THE SELF

Edited by

SHAUN GALLAGHER

OXFORD

UNIVERSITY PRESS

OXFORD
UNIVERSITY PRESS

Great Clarendon Street, Oxford OX2 6DP

Oxford University Press is a department of the University of Oxford.
It furthers the University's objective of excellence in research, scholarship,
and education by publishing worldwide in

Oxford New York

Auckland Cape Town Dar es Salaam Hong Kong Karachi
Kuala Lumpur Madrid Melbourne Mexico City Nairobi
New Delhi Shanghai Taipei Toronto

With offices in

Argentina Austria Brazil Chile Czech Republic France Greece
Guatemala Hungary Italy Japan Poland Portugal Singapore
South Korea Switzerland Thailand Turkey Ukraine Vietnam

Oxford is a registered trade mark of Oxford University Press
in the UK and in certain other countries

Published in the United States
by Oxford University Press Inc., New York

British Library Cataloguing in Publication Data

Data available

Library of Congress Cataloging in Publication Data

Data available

Typeset by SPI Publisher Services, Pondicherry, India
Printed in Great Britain
on acid-free paper by
MPG Books Group, Bodmin and King's Lynn

ISBN 978–0–19–954801–9

1 3 5 7 9 10 8 6 4 2

CONTENTS

VI SELF PATHOLOGIES

VII THE SELF IN DIVERSE CONTEXTS

List of contributors

James R. Anderson, Psychology Department, University of Stirling, Scotland [jra1@stir.ac.uk]

John Barresi, Psychology Department, Dalhousie University, Canada [jbarresi@dal.ca]

José Luis Bermúdez, Dean of Liberal Arts, Texas A&M University, USA [jbermudez@tamu.edu]

John Campbell, Department of Philosophy, University of California Berkeley, USA [jcampbell@berkeley.edu]

Quassim Cassam, Department of Philosophy, University of Warwick, UK [q.Cassam@warwick.ac.uk]

Marcia Cavell, New York City, USA [mcavell@earthlink.net]

Lorraine Code, Department of Philosophy, York University, Canada [codelb@yorku.ca]

Shaun Gallagher, Philosophy and Cognitive Sciences, University of Central Florida USA; School of Humanities, University of Hertfordshire, UK [gallaghr@mail.ucf.edu]

Gordon G. Gallup, Jr, Department of Psychology, SUNY-Albany, USA [gallup@albany.edu]

Kenneth J. Gergen, Department of Psychology, Swarthmore College, USA [kgergen1@swarthmore.edu]

Aaron Henry, Philosophy Department, University of Toronto, Canada [aaron.henry@utoronto.ca]

Hubert J. M. Hermans, Psychology Department, Radboud University, Nijmegen, The Netherlands [hhermans@psych.ru.nl]

Peter R. Hobson, Tavistock Clinic and University College London, UK [r.hobson@ih.ucl.ac.uk]

Leonard Lawlor, Department of Philosophy, Pennsylvania State University, USA [lul19@psu.edu]

DOROTHÉE LEGRAND, Centre de Recherche en Epistémologie Appliqué (CREA), Paris, France [dorothee.legrand@polytechnique.edu]

RAYMOND MARTIN, Philosophy Department, Union College, USA [martnr@union.edu]

ALFRED R. MELE, Department of Philosophy, Florida State University, USA [amele@fsu.edu]

RICHARD MENARY, Philosophy Department, University of Wollongong, Australia [rmenary@uow.edu.au]

THOMAS METZINGER, Philosophisches Seminar, Johannes Gutenberg-Universität, Germany [metzinge@uni-mainz.de]

ELISABETH PACHERIE, Institut Jean Nicod, Paris, France [pacherie@ens.fr]

DEREK PARFIT, All Souls College, Oxford University, UK [derek.parfit@all-souls.ox.ac.uk]

JOSEF PARNAS MD, Danish National Research Foundation's Center for Subjectivity Research, University of Copenhagen and Psychiatric Center Hvidovre, Copenhagen, Denmark [jpa@hum.ku.dk]

JOHN PERRY, Philosophy Department, University of California Riverside [johnperry43@gmail.com]

STEVEN M. PLATEK, Psychology Department, Georgia Gwinnett College, USA [splatek@ggc.edu]

ELSPETH PROBYN, Gender & Cultural Studies and The Hawke Research Institute, The University of South Australia, Australia [Elspeth.Probyn@unisa.edu.au]

JENNIFER RADDEN, Philosophy Department, University of Massachusetts Boston, USA [Jennifer.Radden@umb.edu]

PHILIPPE ROCHAT, Psychology Department, Emory University, USA [psypr@emory.edu]

LOUIS A. SASS, Department of Clinical Psychology, Rutgers University, USA [louissass@aol.com]

MARYA SCHECHTMAN, Department of Philosophy, University of Illinois, Chicago, USA [marya@uic.edu]

DAVID W. SHOEMAKER, Department of Philosophy and Murphy Institute, Tulane University, USA [dshoemak@tulane.edu]

SYDNEY SHOEMAKER, Sage School of Philosophy, Cornell University, USA [ss56@corn ell.edu]

MARK SIDERITS, Department of Philosophy, Seoul National University, Korea [msideri@ilstu.edu]

GALEN STRAWSON, Philosophy Department, University of Reading, UK [gstrawson@mac.com]

EVAN THOMPSON, Department of Philosophy, University of Toronto, Canada [evan.thompson@utoronto.ca]

MANOS TSAKIRIS, Department of Psychology, Royal Holloway, University of London, UK [manos.tsakiris@rhul.ac.uk]

KAI VOGELEY, Department of Psychiatry, University of Cologne, Germany [kai.vogeley@uk-koeln.de]

DAN ZAHAVI, Danish National Research Foundation, Center for Subjectivity Research, and Department of Media, Cognition and Communication, University of Copenhagen, Denmark [danzahavi@gmail.com]

INTRODUCTION
A DIVERSITY OF SELVES

SHAUN GALLAGHER

RESEARCH and publications on the topic of the self have increased significantly in recent years across a number of disciplines, including philosophy, psychology, and neuroscience. This increase of interest in the concept of self has been motivated by a number of factors in different disciplines. In philosophy and some areas of cognitive science, the emphasis on embodied cognition has fostered a renewed interest in rethinking mind–body dualism and conceptions of the self that remain too Cartesian. Poststructuralist deconstructions of traditional metaphysical conceptions of subjectivity have led to debates about whether there are any grounds (moral if not metaphysical) for the reconstruction of the notion of self. Recent interest in Buddhist conceptions of no-self has motivated questions about whether such a thing as self even exists. In light of new understandings of dynamic and distributed processing in the brain, philosophers and neuroscientists are exploring similar questions about whether the self might be an illusion. With respect to the self, understood as an agent, similar questions arise in experimental psychology. Advances in developmental psychology have pushed to the forefront questions about the ontogenetic origin of self-experience, while studies of psychopathology suggest that concepts like self and agency are central to explaining important

Thanks to research grants from the École Normale Supérieure de Lyon and from CNRS for support of SG's work on this introduction while a visiting professor at the ENS in Lyon, and visiting researcher at the Centre de Recherche en Epistémelogie Appliquée, École Polytechnique, Paris.

aspects of pathological experience. Finally, an increase of interest in narrative has also played a role in generating renewed interest in how we understand, not only '*the* self', but also how we understand *our*selves in social and cultural contexts.

This volume explores a number of these recent developments, and is not limited to any one approach. It is meant to introduce the reader to the complexity of the concept (or plurality of concepts) of self and to the many different approaches to its (their) analysis. It includes essays by leading representatives from areas such as analytic philosophy of mind, phenomenology, pragmatism, Buddhist studies, psychology and psychiatry, neuroscience, feminism, and postmodernism. These various analyses do not necessarily have the same target. Some critically focus on the notion of self as it has been constructed in social and cultural arrangements; others conceive of the self in terms of psychological continuity; others as a bodily manifestation. Some of the authors explore how certain aspects of self are constituted in brain processes, narratives, or actions; others explore how some aspects of self come apart in anomalous experiences, experiments, or pathologies.

In this introduction I will try to provide a map of this broad area of research by summarizing the problems and the conclusions that we find in the following chapters. The details of analyses and arguments are developed in the relevant chapters, and the reader can find them there.

MAKING A START

The first part, 'Self: Beginnings and Basics', covers a number of large areas, including questions of development and neural underpinnings. We start, however, with the history of the notions of self and person. *John Barresi* and *Raymond Martin*, a psychologist and a philosopher respectively, review ancient, medieval, and modern ideas about the self and focus on a central issue of whether the self is something spiritual (an immaterial substance), and therefore beyond any natural scientific analysis, or something that can be explained naturalistically. In the twentieth century the development of this issue is reflected in the fact that, with respect to the self, 'during the first half of the century [philosophy] labored to separate itself from science and in the last half to reintegrate itself with science'. History also shows us that many of the ideas about the self that we explore today were foreshadowed by past thinkers, from fission examples in the eighteenth- and nineteenth-century writings of Clarke, Collins, Priestley, Hazlitt, and Bradley, to the idea that the self may be a fiction, in Hume and Nietzsche, or that it originates in social relations, as suggested in writings by Hartley, Reid, and Hazlitt. As such ideas have developed in the late twentieth and early twenty-first century, the challenge,

Barresi and Martin suggest, is to provide an integrated theory of selves that makes sense out of their *experiential, ontological,* and *social* dimensions.

An important question that may help us to address these different dimensions and to sort out what we mean by self is to ask when and how something like self, or self-consciousness, emerges. Ontogenetically, can we say that something like a self is present in the newborn, or is the self something that emerges as the child develops? Even to attempt an answer to these questions, we need to distinguish between different aspects of self. While William James (1890) distinguished between the material self, social self, and spiritual self, Ulrich Neisser's (1988) distinctions between ecological, interpersonal, extended, private, and conceptual dimensions of the self are perhaps more directly relevant to the developmental question. Although it may be clear that newborns lack episodic memory required for an extended self, or the ability to entertain a self-concept, this does not mean that they are necessarily without self or self-awareness.

Philippe Rochat, from the perspective of developmental psychology, reviews the evidence for such self-awareness in newborns, specifically a minimal and phenomenal self-awareness in the context of feeling, perception, and action. In this regard, Neisser's concepts of *ecological* and, importantly, *interpersonal* aspects of the self are most relevant. There is good evidence that what some philosophers call the 'minimal self' or minimal self-awareness is already operative in newborn humans, if we understand it to include embodied ecological and interpersonal aspects. Rochat is especially interested to explore the phenomenal and emotional aspects of this self-awareness, how organized the experience of the body is in infants, and the role of intersubjective interaction. Over the course of the first months of life, however, and especially in contexts of intersubjective interaction, self and self-awareness develop to the significant point of an objective and conceptually born self-recognition. The notion of self-recognition, however, is itself complex, ranging from primitive non-conscious bodily processes (as in the immune system) to sophisticated aspects of self-consciousness in human adults.

Gordon Gallup, James Anderson, and *Steven Platek* focus on one of these more developed aspects of self-consciousness, namely, mirror self-recognition, the ability to recognize one's own image in a mirror. Gallup (1970) provided the first experimental report of mirror self-recognition. He showed that chimpanzees are able to learn that the chimps they see in the mirror are not other chimps, but themselves, as evidenced by self-directed behavior. There is evidence (some more convincing and some less so) that this phenomenon can be found in elephants, dolphins, magpies, some gorillas, chimpanzees, and human infants starting around fifteen months. Gallup, Anderson, and Platek suggest that this ability correlates to large brain size (relative to the animal's body size), and they review evidence for a neural network for self-recognition and self–other differentiation. They cite evidence that frontal cortex and cortical midline structures are implicated in self-recognition tasks.

Again it seems important to ask precisely what aspects of self and self-processing are being considered in the various experiments and tasks that inform any conclusions about self and self-consciousness. This is equally so in regard to determining what neural processes and brain areas might be involved. Although a large number of studies point to frontal and cortical midline structures as important for self-specific experience, *Kai Vogeley* and *Shaun Gallagher* reconsider this idea in light of several recent reviews of the neuroscience literature on this point. Depending on the precise nature of the questions being asked, there seems to be overwhelming evidence that the self is both everywhere and nowhere in the brain. A widely cited review by Gillihan and Farah (2005) suggests that there is no specialized or common area responsible for self-related representations; when the entire survey of self-related tasks is considered, the entire cortex seems to be involved. As LeDoux suggests, 'different components of the self reflect the operation of different brain systems, which can be but are not always in sync' (2002: 31).

In other words, frontal cortex and the cortical midline structure are *not* the only areas involved in self-related tasks. In addition, however, these areas may be involved not because the tasks are self-specific, but because they are tasks that involve a specific kind of cognitive operation, namely, reflective evaluation (Legrand and Ruby 2009). The question is then whether these areas are activated because they are self-specific, or because the experimental tasks used to test self-recognition, for example, involve reflective evaluation. The question of how self and brain are related, however, is not localized in one chapter; it is distributed across a number of other essays in this volume (Chapters 3 and 7 especially).

On some conceptions, what we call self may be nothing other than the product of brain processes. On other conceptions, what we call self involves a larger system that includes the whole body and the environment. The second part of this volume, 'Bodily Selves', explores questions about how bodily processes contribute to self. *Quassim Cassam*, in his chapter on the embodied self, focuses on three questions: the metaphysical question about the relation between body and self; the phenomenological question about the nature of our awareness of our own body; and the epistemological question of whether anything is special about the knowledge we have of our own bodies. Although these questions can be treated separately, they are also knotted together and, as such, in various ways they weave through a number of the chapters in this section, and the next two sections, which deal with phenomenological, metaphysical, and epistemological problems. Cassam considers various arguments for and against the claim that I (the person) am identical with my body, demonstrating how unsettled the various answers are. He also considers answers to the question of whether bodily awareness is a form of *self*-awareness, showing that it may depend on whether bodily awareness targets the body qua object or the body qua subject. This distinction is central for anyone who considers the question of bodily self-awareness and its status with respect to the possibility of misidentification. Cassam thus begins a discussion of the principle of immunity to error through misidentification (IEM) that is continued in a number of the following chapters.

IEM

The idea of immunity to error through misidentification can be traced back to Wittgenstein (1958), but was explored more fully by Sydney Shoemaker (1968) and subsequent thinkers. IEM characterizes judgments about self, and the information sources on which such judgments are based, *iff* the information source can be only about the self *as subject*. When, for example, I use the first-person pronoun *as subject* I cannot be mistaken in regard to whom it refers. If I happen to have a toothache, Wittgenstein suggests, it would be nonsensical to ask: 'someone has a toothache, is it I?' I may be wrong about it being a toothache—it may be some kind of referred pain. But I cannot misidentify who it is who is experiencing it. My use of the first-person pronoun in this case ('I have a toothache'), my judgment, and the nocioceptive information source that is the basis for my judgment, are IEM. In contrast, uses of the first-person pronoun *as object*, that is, in judgments based on sources of information that deliver only objective knowledge about ourselves, are not IEM. For example, when I look at a live video it is possible that I mistakenly identify the person in the video as myself when it is actually someone else.

John Perry, in his chapter on self-knowledge, considers the possibility that the first-person pronoun has this characteristic of IEM because it refers to something special, for example, a Cartesian ego. He, in agreement with Elizabeth Anscombe and Sydney Shoemaker, rejects this idea, not because, as Anscombe (1975) famously argued, the 'I' does not refer at all, but because the way of referring, rather than the referent itself, is special. 'I' is an indexical that follows the rule of a reflexive reference (the token-reflexive rule): the word 'I', without any further intention accompanying the utterance, refers to the speaker of that utterance. It's not clear, however, that this rule reflects the difference Wittgenstein noted between the use of 'I' as-subject, and 'I' as-object. It also motivates questions, pursued by *Peter Hobson*, about what happens to the use of the first-person pronoun in some pathologies.

A number of different positions are staked out in various chapters when it comes to the question of extending IEM to proprioception (bodily position sense which allows one to know where one's limbs are), an extension originally suggested by Gareth Evans (1982). Cassam argues, in agreement with Evans, that bodily self-ascriptions based on proprioception are IEM, but IEM *per se* is not the thing that guarantees that proprioceptive awareness, or any other form of self-consciousness is awareness of one's self qua subject, because some judgments (e.g. demonstrative judgments) about things that are not self are IEM. In the case of making a judgement about an object, for example, a new car, when it is perceptually present, and I refer to it as *that* car, my reference to it cannot involve misidentification. Cassam goes on to make the further point that if a judgment is IEM it is because it is based on a source of information that is IEM.

In contrast, *José Bermúdez* turns this around and suggests that an information source is only derivatively IEM, based on the fact that judgments based on it are IEM. That is, the property of IEM is primarily a property of judgments rather than information sources. It is not clear, however, that this would reduce the reliability of the self-experience of the agent, or, as *Elizabeth Pacherie* suggests, that it implies a high reliability for judgments about self-agency. Bermúdez agrees, however, that, like introspection, proprioception (including what Gibson calls 'visual proprioception', that is, information about the bodily self originating in the visual modality and linked to our bodily position or movement through the environment) is IEM. On the one hand, this is a kind of non-conceptual awareness that has implications for agency which are constitutive for self-consciousness and are 'grounded in the IEM property'. On the other hand, IEM is not sufficient for something to count as self-*consciousness*, since some non-conscious sources of information (e.g. vestibular system processes) are IEM.

IEM, then, is said to apply to the use of pronouns and demonstratives, the judgments that include those uses, and the information sources on which those judgments are based. There are debates about various issues concerning IEM, but there is general agreement that if an information source or a judgment is IEM, then it is highly reliable with respect to the kind of self-consciousness that may be associated with it. As we'll see later, this may include our awareness of ourselves as agents. It may also apply to the sense of body ownership insofar as it is based on proprioception.

BODY OWNERSHIP AND SOME PHENOMENOLOGICAL DETAILS

The question of body ownership is explored in the chapters by *José Bermúdez* and *Manos Tsakiris*, from two very different perspectives. Bermúdez pursues a philosophical analysis of the concept. He reviews deflationary and inflationary conceptions of the sense of ownership and rejects the strong (inflationary) claim that the sense of ownership is a distinct and phenomenologically salient dimension of bodily awareness. On the deflationary view, ownership is not a first-order sense (a feeling or experience) at all, but simply a fact about or a label for a certain aspect of bodily experience. Although it seems clear that one can distinguish between a first-order experience of one's body, and a second-order judgment about that experience, it is not so clear that there is an important difference between saying that the experience of bodily ownership derives from a particular fact about bodily experience (e.g. the spatial content of bodily sensations), and that the sense of ownership is an implicit feature of bodily experience. On the inflationary view, the issue may simply be a question of how implicit (recessive) or explicit (phenomenologically salient) it is, and that may depend on circumstances and individual differences. On the deflationary view, there is no feeling of ownership over and beyond the judgments of ownership and the facts about bodily experiences that ground them.

Tsakiris follows the more inflationary view and reviews a growing body of empirical research on the sense of body ownership that suggests that the latter depends on the integration of somatosensory signals. The latter may include proprioceptive, kinaesthetic, tactile, visual, and vestibular signals generated as feedback from our movements or actions. In experimental settings, the distinction between a reflective attribution or judgment of ownership and the first-order experience of ownership is also important. The Rubber Hand Illusion (RHI), which is the focus of much of the research on body ownership, involves the experiential level, and not just the level of judgment. When one sees a rubber hand being tactilely stroked in synchrony with tactile stimulation of one's own unseen hand, one begins to feel the rubber hand to be part of one's own body (Botvinick and Cohen, 1998). In other words, the sense of ownership extends to the rubber hand. Tsakiris argues that this depends not simply on bottom–up somatosensory integration, but also on top–down modulation effected by a pre-established representational model of the body.

Beyond rubber hand experiments, Tsakiris discusses recent research on out-of-body experiences (OBE). He shows that the neurocognitive processes involved in the RHI (and thus for body parts) are also involved in OBE (and thus for the body as a whole). Accordingly, multisensory integration together with the modulation of internal models of the body generate the experience of the body as being one's own as well as the experienced discrimination between one's body and other objects. This experience of bodily ownership may, Tsakiris suggests, be a critical component of self-specificity as defined by Legrand and Ruby (2009; see Vogeley and Gallagher, in Chapter 4 below).

In her chapter on the phenomenological dimensions of bodily self-consciousness *Dorothée Legrand* explores in detail our awareness of the bodily self-as-subject. She starts with the central distinction between self-as-object and self-as-subject, and goes on to show its relationship to the transitivity and non-transitivity of self-consciousness. Consciousness of myself-as-object, for example, in my reflective evaluation of my posture, is transitive in so far as it considers my body as an intentional object. Consciousness of myself-as-subject is intransitive in the sense that this form of self-awareness does not take my body as an intentional object. When I reach for a hammer, for example, I am transitively aware of the hammer (I may have to consciously look for and locate the hammer to successfully complete the action of grasping it), and, at the same time, intransitively aware of my movement (in a way that I do not have to look for and locate, or keep track of, my hand). Accordingly, my intransitive awareness of my body has the characteristic of experiential transparency within the same consciousness of an object (usually other than my body).

Legrand goes on to show that even this transparent and intransitive awareness of one's own body includes some details about the experienced volume, location, and orientation of one's body. In this regard the experiencing subject is more than a perspectival zero-point; she is, phenomenologically, something > 0 as perspectival origin, likely because experienced bodily volume and location is something > 0. Moreover, Legrand's analysis shows that the bodily self is self-conscious, not in spite of the fact that it is intentionally oriented towards the world, but thanks to this intentional orientation. Thanks to this intentional orientation, and the working of kinaesthesis, I experience myself located in a peripersonal space that extends beyond my body's boundaries. Other aspects of experienced embodiment are opened up by different sensory modalities, and even through intersubjective experiences. Without contradiction to the experiential transparency of my body in perception and action, the modality of touch introduces a sense of opacity into the experienced volume of my body. Furthermore, when others direct their gaze at me, the fact that I experience embarrassment or comfort introduces other dimensions into my bodily experience of self. Throughout her analysis, just in such details, Legrand builds up a rich phenomenological description of the body-as-self.

Self Versus Non-Self

A number of chapters turn on questions that run from phenomenological to metaphysical issues concerning the existential status of the self—questions about whether there is a self, and if there is, how much more than some minimal or basic set of characteristics we should bestow on it. On one side some theorists, influenced by Indian and Buddhist philosophies, argue that there is no self (e.g. Albahari 2006, discussed in chapters by Henry and Thompson, Siderits, and Zahavi). This is a view that challenges the view of self as embodied (Bermúdez, Cassam, Legrand), as well as views that emphasize the self as a socially and narratively constituted entity (e.g. Schechtman, Hermans, Gergen). In no case, however, does anyone defend the substantial spirit of the Cartesian self. Indeed, a number of theorists, reacting against just such an idea, posit no more than a minimal self (Strawson, Henry and Thompson), and, in one case, something less than a minimal self (Metzinger).

Aaron Henry and *Evan Thompson*, in agreement with Legrand that self is a bodily subject, argue against the no-self or nonegological account. They find in the phenomenological concept of pre-reflective bodily self-awareness, which entails a basic experience of boundedness, something more than just the experience of subjectivity, namely a distinction between body and world that constitutes a basic sense of self/non-self discrimination. This is a minimal bodily and experiential sense of self that involves a phenomenal 'mineness', or what Bermúdez and Tsakiris call a sense of ownership. For Henry and Thompson, the mineness of experience is based on an intransitive, non-observational, pre-reflective self-awareness which is part of the structure of intentional consciousness (as such, it is what Bermúdez calls an inflationary sense of ownership, i.e. something that manifests itself phenomenologically). This self-awareness, at a minimum, helps to account for the first-person perspective that characterizes our experience of the world, and amounts to a 'minimal self' (also see Zahavi, Chapter 13). Although this idea of the minimal self is close to a nonegological conception of the sort found in Albahari (2006), Henry and Thompson argue that the difference hinges on the status of the body, which, for the former view, is constitutive, and for the latter view, merely an accompaniment. On the constitutive view, the body is experienced as subject and as bounded, which involves a fundamental distinction between self and other.

Other conceptions of the minimal self, however, are not so closely tied to bodily experience. *Galen Strawson* is concerned with both the metaphysics and phenomenology of the self or subject of experience. Although he posits no inconsistency between an understanding of the minimal subject as belonging to the metaphysics of mind or consciousness, on the one hand, and bodily conceptions of the self, on the other, the phenomenological description of the minimal subject requires no reference to body, environment, or social relations. The thought is not that the body is the subject who has experience, but that 'the subject is identical with its experience'. Rather than a 'thick' conception of subjectivity, which would include the body as constitutive, Strawson argues for a 'thin' conception which equates the subject with the experience itself. No experience, no subject. Accordingly, on this minimal conception, the subject does not exist if the person (or human animal) is asleep (unconscious). What one can say about the subject is that it exists in a living moment of an indeterminably short amount of time; that it has a unitary singleness amid the rich and complex, but unified, experiential field; that it is a material process (a neural synergy) located in the brain—where or what process that is is open to empirical investigation.

For Strawson the profound metaphysical question about experience, and therefore experiential selves, is whether experience is limited to certain types of physical processes, or is characteristic of all physical processes, which would entail panpsychism. One does not need to answer this question, however, to know, as Strawson suggests at the end of his essay, that as human beings we are more than minimal selves.

On the other hand, is it possible that we are less than a minimal self? *Thomas Metzinger* further explores the 'no-self alternative' and, as he suggests, takes it not to be an 'alternative' but rather the default position since, on his view, there is neither evidence for, nor convincing argument that there is, something that we should call 'the self'. Even what Strawson calls a minimal subject is a little too much—something that, if not a thing or object or substance, is still, nonetheless, some instance of a real material individual rather than a theoretical entity or conceptual fiction. Metzinger can accept the general parameters of the phenomenological analyses of Legrand, Henry and Thompson, and Zahavi, for instance, that there is a distinct *phenomenology of singularity* in bodily self-consciousness, but in contrast to someone like Strawson (1997) who suggested that 'metaphysics must wait on phenomenology', for Metzinger, phenomenology does not constrain metaphysics. If science does (i.e. constrain metaphysics), then it doesn't do so in a way that would lead us to think that there is anything that we would call a self. The closest we could come via neuroscience, for example, is to talk about a set of functional mechanisms that would integrate individual property-representations into a unified 'self-representation' or self-model, which is not equivalent to a self in any real sense.

Metzinger outlines several different anti-realist arguments about the self and then goes on to explain why the idea that there are no selves is counter-intuitive. In the process he shows why the intuitions of phenomenology are traceable to the contingent fact about the causal structure of our brains, which induces in each of us a first-person perspective that makes it difficult to deny the existence of selves. Even if the phenomenological evidence is overwhelmingly in favor of our intuitions about self, such that it makes it difficult, if not impossible, not to have an intuition about the existence of a self, this is so only because our phenomenology is generated by the kinds of brains that we have. According to Metzinger, this neuroscientific fact pulls the rug out from under phenomenology.

Buddhism is also associated with a no-self position. As *Mark Siderits* shows, however, there are various Buddhist versions of this position. Distinguishing between the concepts of self and person, Siderits takes *self* to mean one part of the psychophysical complex, whereas *person* is the whole of the psychophysical complex. The Buddhist anti-realist or reductionist position denies that the self exists, and considers the person to be a conceptual fiction. We may think of the self as something that has permanence over time; but if there is no permanence in the psychophysical complex, then, on that concept, there is no self. Why then does it seem to us that we are in fact enduring entities? It is an illusion, or a fiction, albeit a strong one, and perhaps a practical one. It is practical to think of ourselves as an enduring entity insofar as it may help us to plan for our own future happiness and to avoid practices that may impede our future welfare. Discourse about persons can include concepts such as moral responsibility, self-interest, and so forth. If understanding ourselves as persons can be beneficial in this respect, it can also lead to problems and the kind of suffering associated with alienation, frustration, and despair. That there can be a valid discourse about the person at this practical or conventional level is not denied by the Buddhist reductionist; but the idea that this kind of discourse reflects something true at the ultimate, metaphysical level is ruled out.

As Siderits points out, however, not all Buddhists are reductionists in this sense. Buddhist personalists hold something close to an emergentist view, which suggests that, although the self does not have real existence, the person does. One objection to reductionist accounts, which we might call the phenomenological objection, seems to support this view. Namely, that if the reductionist holds that it merely seems to us as though we are persons when there are really just psychophysical elements arranged person-wise, then to *whom* does it seem to be that there are persons? Another way to put this might be that only a *person* could be a reduction-ist. To answer this objection the reductionist appeals to consciousness as an impermanent (apparently unified, but truly not unified) and impersonal (non-self) subject of experience, itself a concept of practical use, but not one that references something ultimately real.

The phenomenological objection to this Buddhist no-self view is renewed by *Dan Zahavi* in his defense of the minimal self. Zahavi, like Henry and Thompson, considers the distinction made by Albahari (2006) between two forms of the sense of ownership: personal ownership and perspectival ownership. Personal owner-ship, where I identify myself as the owner of my experiences ('these are my experiences'), on the Buddhist view, is what leads to the illusion of the self and the establishment of a felt boundary between self and other. Perspectival ownership is simply the fact that I experience what I experience from a certain perspective. These different senses of ownership can come apart in pathologies like deperson-alization where the subject experiences a thought or feeling, but without the sense that this is his own thought or feeling. On Albahari's Buddhist view, there is no self in reality; the manifolds of thoughts, emotions, perceptions, and so forth, have existence, as a perspectival or 'witness' consciousness. This consciousness may produce a sense of self, but there is no reality to self; it is a constructed illusion.

For Zahavi there is an important contrast between this Buddhist conception and the phenomenological conception of nonegological consciousness as found, for example, in the early Husserl and Sartre. For Husserl, as for Sartre, the self (ego) is a product of the self-constituting, self-unifying temporal flow of consciousness, but this does not mean that it isn't real. Husserl and Sartre go different ways on this point. For Husserl the self is a transcendental ego; for Sartre, it is nothing more than an empirical ego. One possibility, as Sartre suggested, is that in first-order experience neither of these selves exists, and that they are more the product of reflection than the product of a temporal synthesis. In that case, there may be little difference between the Buddhist view and the phenomenological view; the ego would have a false reality. But, as Zahavi shows, the difference is more apparent at the pre-reflective, first-order level of experience. That level, which is the level of what Albahari calls a perspectival witness consciousness, turns out not to be impersonal. Experiences, as Strawson suggests, always involve an *experiencer*, and as such they are for-someone. That is, even the simplest perspectival experience of pain or emotion or perception is, in Sartre's terms, for-itself. My experience is inescapably for me. Within one stream of consciousness, the difference between one experience and the next experience is not of the same sort as the difference between my current experience and the current experience of somebody else. This quality of 'mineness' is not something added on to experience as an extra kind of personal ownership, nor is it part of the content that I experience; rather, Zahavi argues, it is inescapably part of the structure of experience. Experience, in its very structure, involves the first-person perspective. This brings us back to the minimal notion of self.

A LARGER AND MORE SUSTAINED NOTION
OF SELF: PERSONAL IDENTITY

Debates about minimal or less than minimal selves cannot be the full story about the self or person. The notion of the minimal self tends to be synchronic or very near synchronic—happening, if not in one or more chronons (see Strawson, Chapter 10) or on the order of the neuroscientist's milliseconds, then in what James calls the specious present, which is on the order of seconds. Because we live our lives in the larger time frames of the everyday, however, we need to be able to say something about our *selves* in that more extended period. Since the time of John Locke there has been an ongoing discussion of personal identity, conceived as an identity over an extended time. *John Campbell's* chapter starts the discussion of this more extended self.

Campbell identifies two issues that are central to the question of personal identity: one concerns causality, and the other concerns the notion of first person. Any object, as well as any person, has a kind of internal or what Shoemaker (Chapter 15) calls 'immanent' causality: the set of properties it has now will determine how it behaves later under varying conditions, and what sort of properties it will have then. One can understand this in terms of an interventionist conception of causality. An intervention now, changing the properties I have now (whether physical properties or psychological properties), will have an effect on properties that I have later. In this regard there is no quarantine of physical changes from psychological changes: getting a tattoo now may make me happy now and unhappy later. In any case, this kind of causality is measured by the counterfactual. Causality is at play if we can say that, given an intervention on a person's earlier condition, there would have been a difference in the person's later condition. On some interpretations, this internal causality is constitutive of what the object is, or, in this case, what the person is. If we adopt that view, however, as Campbell suggests, it becomes clear that the causal complexity of a person stands in the way of getting a clear conception of the identity of the person. What, for example, does it take for us to have the same human being or person later as we had earlier? (see Parfit, Chapter 18, for more on this question). Since the complexity is both physical and psychological, and may add up to an even more complex psychophysical unit, the question of personal identity is a difficult one, especially when some theorists tend to look for identity in only the biological or embodied existence of the person, and others tend to look for it exclusively in psychological existence.

Issues surrounding the notion of the first person, however, also introduce some uncertainty into our conception of personal identity. Start with the first-person pronoun. Pragmatically, the problem of reference for 'I' is solved by the token-reflexive rule: any token of 'I' refers to whoever produced it. Epistemologically, in some cases, we have immunity to error through misidentification (see discussion of IEM, above). Beyond that, however, problems abound, since, as many of the other chapters make clear, the metaphysical status of the speaker to whom 'I' refers is unclear: a body, a mind, a soul, a self, a non-self? Campbell points out that it is also not clear how the use of 'I' can capture or transcend the complex causal happenings that make up the person. Nonetheless, the importance of the first-person perspective (and the use of the first-person pronoun) in our understanding of the world seems essential for action. Here Campbell sides with Perry (1979), who shows that an impersonal description (without the ability to use 'I') would never motivate action or responsibility, against Parfit (1984; and Chapter 18), who suggests that we could gain in the moral realm (perhaps along the line of an ethics of care) if we were able to drop the use of the first-person pronoun. These are issues explored in several later chapters.

Sydney Shoemaker takes up one of these questions: should identity be sought only in the biological or embodied existence of the person, or exclusively in psychological existence—or, more generally, what determines the nature of a person? Whatever the answer turns out to be, Shoemaker suggests, it involves causality. Successor states and the diachronic unity of one individual can be explained in terms of the immanent causality of its properties, and especially properties that belong to the thing because it is of a certain kind (Shoemaker calls these 'thick' properties). What a thing *is*, is constituted by what thick properties it is capable of having. These properties are the ones that determine its persistence conditions. So if we are asking what kind of things persons are, we can answer that question by specifying what sorts of properties persons have and, most importantly, what thick properties persons have. Shoemaker argues against the animalist view, and defends the classical neo-Lockean view by arguing that the thick properties of person are psychological or mental ones, and that a person persists through psychological continuity.

Psychological continuity is defined in terms of immanent causality. This is not to deny that persons also have physical properties, but the physical properties that are relevant to the question of personhood are just those physical properties that instantiate mental properties. Mental properties are primary and defining even for body ownership. *My* body is the body whose states cause my perceptual and sensory states, and whose behavior is the product of my volitional states.

Campbell indicated two areas of difficulty when it came to personal identity: causality and the first person. While Shoemaker addresses the topic of causality, *John Perry* starts with the issue of how we use the first-person pronoun. In thinking about the special way that the word 'I' refers, Perry suggests that what we call the self plays a certain role, similar to the role that the present day plays in relation to the word 'today' and to our knowledge about today. To know about the present day, the methods I use involve the present day playing a role. For example, I can look out the window to see whether it is raining or not. The methods I use today to find out about today are different from the methods I use today to find out about past or future days. I can't look out the window today to see whether it was raining on 4 July 1776. In this literal way today's methods are always different from tomorrow's when today is the object of knowledge. In knowing about the person I am, the self plays a role similar to the role that the present day plays in knowing about today.

Self-based inquiry includes reflection, introspection, and perception. Perception gives me knowledge not only about the object perceived, but also about the perceiver. Serving this role, the self presents no difficulty; it is not something that I have independent epistemological worries about. For the present day to function the way it does in my ability to know things about it, I do not have to take today itself as an object (as I might do if I were researching it years from now); and for the self to function the way it does in my ability to know things about it (or about myself), I do not have to take the self as an object.

For example, in my appointment book I might find the following note: 'SG has an appointment to meet John Perry in Palo Alto on April 7'. For SG to keep the appointment it is not enough for me (SG) to know just the fact that I have the appointment. I have to know when 7 April is, relative to today, and especially if it is today. I have to know that Palo Alto is here, where I am, or there where I am not. And I have to know that I am SG. The latter depends on a first-person knowledge source, an ability to identify myself. But this ability depends, according to Perry, on a self-notion—the idea that I have of myself that 'controls the use of the first person'. Luckily, on the one hand, the self is not difficult to keep track of—indeed I don't need to keep track of it in the way that I have to keep track of what day it is. It is always the same, in the sense that, as Perry suggests, it is a role that is always played by the same person. The concept of role in this case, and as Perry uses it, is a functional one. On the other hand, the idea of a narrative self is just the idea that keeping track of the self across time is what constitutes the self as something more than a minimal self. In this case the role becomes a character role.

Marya Schechtman tells the story of the narrative self. The strongest versions of the narrative approach hold that both a person's sense of self and a person's life are narrative in structure. Schechtman calls this the hermeneutical narrative theory; it takes the self to be a self-interpreting being. Human behavior is not tied simply to the moment, nor is it understandable completely in its physical facts; insofar as it has meaning it is related to the agent's past and future intentions and to a set of intersecting contexts. These things are best expressed in narrative form, and only in narrative form is the meaning made clear. The self is a character that plays a role in that narrative. Dennett (1992) defends a more abstract view of the narrative self: the self as the 'center of narrative gravity'. On this account, the self has no existential reality; it is a fictional abstraction generated in the various narratives that we tell about ourselves. The self is no more than the functional role that it plays in these stories; it is the narrated more than the narrator, and the latter role Dennett assigns to the brain. Even in these narrative conceptions, then, the debates between proponents of no-self, minimal self, and something 'thicker' than the minimal self are played out.

Schechtman herself defends the view that the self constitutes itself in narrative. She argues for something less than the hermeneutical view insofar as the narrative is less agency-oriented and without an overarching thematic unity, and something more than Dennett's view insofar as the self constituted in narrative is something more real than a fictional abstraction. All three of these views contrast with those that simply focus on the fact that as humans we have narrative capacities that we sometimes deploy to make sense of our actions. Narrative capacities make us narrators, but not necessarily products of or characters in our narratives. These learned capacities enable us to understand ourselves as extended over time and to draw more robust distinctions between self and other. Insofar as our capacity to narrate gives us a certain ability to plan and control our lives, however, narrative is not simply a retrospective shadow that follows the self; rather it helps us to shape what we will become and thereby contribute to our self-identities. As David Velleman (2006) puts it, this narrative capacity makes us agents in a strong sense. This notion of agency, and Schechtman's discussion of narrative as involving strong intersubjective connections, points us in the direction of accounts of self that enter a moral dimension. Narratives enable us to make our actions intelligible and to provide reasons for our actions, to ourselves and to others.

Narrative identity can be distinguished from personal identity following a distinction made both by Paul Ricoeur (1994) and *Derek Parfit* in this volume. Parfit distinguishes between numerical identity and qualitative identity, which corresponds to Ricoeur's use of the Latin terms *idem* and *ipse*, respectively. *Idem* or numerical identity signifies that a thing (e.g. a person) just is identical with itself, and that there is only one instance of its existence. Most accounts of personal identity, starting with John Locke, are about numerical identity. *Ipse* or qualitative identity allows for the possibility that something in the thing (or person) changes. Derek Parfit is numerically the same person who published *Reasons and Persons* in 1984, but qualitatively he is no longer identical with that person since he, like everyone else, has changed. Narrative identity attempts to track this kind of qualitative change in self.

Parfit, like most philosophers who think about personal identity, focuses on numerical identity. Also, like many philosophers who write about personal identity, Parfit follows a tradition started by John Locke, namely, appealing to thought experiments that help to get at the issues of numerical identity. One issue is just this: is the person I am today the same (numerically identical to the) person I was yesterday, or will be next year? Another issue is: does it matter? Parfit is interested in the criteria that we use to answer the first question. The standard criteria, as we see discussed in the chapter by Sydney Shoemaker, are bodily continuity and psychological continuity. While Shoemaker opts for psychological continuity, Parfit defends constitutional reductionism. A person is reducible to but not identical to bodily and psychological events. If I want to know anything about a person I must look to the various bodily and psychological events that constitute her life. Parfit then uses thought experiments (science fiction cases) to show that in many instances we are unable to decide about the identity of the person. The question, then, is whether this matters.

MORAL DIMENSIONS OF SELF

The question of whether identity matters starts us on a set of moral considerations that involve questions about agency, freedom, and responsibility. As Parfit notes, ideas of personal identity come along with implications for living and acting one way rather than another, and for responsibility, and desert. As Thomas Reid once put it, personal identity forms 'the foundation of all rights and obligations, and of all accountableness' (Reid 1785: 112). The idea that identity does not matter, then, seemingly challenges our normal concerns with these moral phenomena. Why should I be concerned to deliberate and to act in a certain prudential way today if in fact it is not clear that I will be the one to benefit from the results of those actions tomorrow? Why should agency matter if identity doesn't? The idea that personal identity may not matter challenges us to explain how we can decide moral responsibility. Many narrative theories of the self, we note, meet this challenge by denying the sort of constitutional reductionism that Parfit defends; for such narrative theories, the self is more than the purely physical and psychological events that add up to human behaviors. Rather, narrative accounts for the person in terms of her intentions and actions.

It is often said that *what we do* makes us *who we are*, and that action involves self-discovery. *Elisabeth Pacherie* explores this close relationship between self and agency. Where focus on the sense of ownership (see Chapters 6 and 7) can tell us something important about how our embodied experience is structured, the sense of self-agency is important for understanding the relation between self and action. The contemporary debate about agency raises questions about the role of consciousness in controlling action, and considers the possibility that the sense of agency is epiphenomenal or, even worse, an illusion, if we are led to believe that we have some control over our actions (see e.g. Wegner 2002).

Pacherie reviews empirical evidence that supports various theories that explain the sense of agency in either higher level cognitive (and sometimes narrative) terms or lower level sensorimotor terms. Reflecting a recent view in the literature, she argues for a more integrative model that acknowledges the contribution of multiple (higher and lower level) factors to a complex sense of agency, unified by the same principle: that the sense of agency on every level is based on comparisons between intended goal, predicted movement or action, and actual end states. Along these lines, the analysis of the sense of agency is conducted in terms of representational content (e.g. bodily movement, accomplished goal, reasons for acting), mode (experiential or cognitive), structure (directive or descriptive), and temporality. Questions about the reliability of our sense of agency naturally lead into questions about the nature of free will and moral responsibility. For Pacherie, responses to the latter questions will depend on how metaphysically loaded the conception of free will is. That we at least sometimes consciously deliberate and act on our deliberations, however, defeats any overly generalized dismissal of free will.

Alfred Mele takes this fact of conscious deliberation as a starting point to develop a neo-Aristotelian conception of self-control, a concept that seems essential to what it means to be a mature human person. That we sometimes succeed and sometimes fail to act in accordance with our best-laid plans is worth considering. What happens when we lose self-control, a moral condition known as *akrasia*? To understand self-control or the lack of it, one needs to understand the conception of self that underpins it. Aristotle regarded the human self to be primarily rational, where reason is taken in a strong sense. Mele suggests a more holistic conception of the self, where to act out of passion may not mean that one is acting without self-control. This means that the kind of inner conflict associated with *akrasia* should not be explained purely in terms of rational versus irrational forces. The evaluations that support our rational decisions are often driven by emotional factors rather than cold logic. For any action there may be both rational and non-rational motivations involved, but one can find both on the supporting or opposing side of self-control.

That the self in self-control may be something other than a purely rational agent conceived in terms of the standard model of mental causation (my mental states directing my body to move in certain ways to accomplish an action) addresses certain worries mentioned by both Pacherie and Mele. On both phenomenological and metaphysical grounds one can object to the standard model. Just as I don't experience my brain as causing my actions, I don't experience my mental states *per se* as causing my actions; rather I experience myself as controlling my actions. It is not the brain that acts; nor is it the mind that acts; it is the person that I am who engages in action. As Mele and others (Nagel 1986; Velleman 1992) suggest, the person, as agent, tends to disappear in many of the standard causal accounts that draw a line from mental states through bodily movement to worldly action. Mele proposes a place for the more holistic conception of self insofar as someone, not just some brain state, and not just some mental state, must be motivated to exercise self-control, must care how she conducts herself, must be a practically concerned individual. Without giving up on causal theories entirely, it is this overarching conception of caring about how one's life goes that brings the dimension of personhood back into play.

The practically concerned individual is the one responsible for her own actions. *David Shoemaker* sets out to show that what makes an action the person's own (what keeps the agent in the picture) with regard to responsibility is better expressed in terms of practical identity than in terms of personal identity. A standard view is that moral responsibility presupposes personal identity. This view would send us back to questions about criteria for personal identity, for example, psychological continuity versus biological continuity (animalism), and to the problem Parfit raises with regard to whether personal identity matters. David Shoemaker shows that all such criteria of personal identity (psychological, biological, narrative) fail to provide a sufficient account of how a person can be morally responsible for an action. Specifically he shows that action ownership, which is important for moral responsibility, does not entail identity. Ownership is a person-to-action relation whereas identity is a person-to-person relation. Accordingly, identity doesn't matter for moral responsibility.

This does not solve the issue of how self is related to the question of responsibility, however. Shoemaker thus examines the model of the 'Real Self View' (RSV) concerning ownership of action and moral responsibility, and various objections that have been raised against it. The RSV states that an action is one's own if it is governed by a will consistent with one's system of valuation, where the idea of having a valuation system is similar to Mele's idea of caring. To maintain the RSV, Shoemaker indicates that it must be open to an approach based on attributable responsibility (where one can be attributed responsibility as a person, often accompanied by significant reactive, and usually emotional, attitudes) rather than an accountable responsibility (where one is held responsible to the extent that one has normative competency). In the former case, an action is judged to be an expression of some aspect (e.g. a character flaw) of the person, and not just caused by the person.

Shoemaker here makes clear the distinction between attributability and accountability using the example of the psychopath. We may want to attribute moral responsibility to the psychopath insofar as we want to judge his actions cruel, or manipulative, even if we don't want to hold him accountable since he lacks the ability to grasp and apply moral reasons. In a number of ways the questions about the moral dimensions of self point to issues concerning normalcy and pathology. Are some pathologies, such as psychopathy, pathologies of the self?

PATHOLOGIES OF THE SELF

Part VI of this volume, on pathologies of the self, is very much a fractal image of the previous parts. It covers much the same ground—issues pertaining to development, embodied self, minimal self, personal and narrative identities, and moral dimensions of the self. This time these issues are run against the foil of psychopathology, which allows us to question everything all over again.

The idea that all psychopathologies involve the self can be taken in a thoroughly trivial sense that they all happen to someone. But in a non-trivial sense there are certain pathologies that are self-specific insofar as they are devastating or disruptive for the person's self-experience. Schizophrenia is a clear but complex example of this. *Josef Parnas* and *Louis Sass* focus on the phenomenology of schizophrenia and its disruption of *ipseity*, the basic (minimal) self-experience. There are two important lessons we can learn from their analysis. First, our self-experience is not neutral with respect to the metaphysical status of the self. The existence of the self is in some large part constituted in its experience, and if that experience is significantly disrupted, it threatens the self in its existence. The second point follows from the first. To understand schizophrenia, one must carefully attend to the experience of the subject. It is, perhaps, the lack of such attention that explains why the concept of self is not mentioned in the standard diagnostic criteria for schizophrenia (DSM-IV 2000; ICD 10 n.d.).

Parnas and Sass appeal to large-scale, clinically based empirical studies, informed by phenomenology, to establish the basic fact that subjects within the schizophrenic spectrum suffer from self-specific disorders, namely, 'disorders *that affect the articulation and functioning of minimal or core self*'. The disturbance includes two main features: (1) hyper-reflexivity: an exaggerated self-consciousness, where the subject directs focal, objectifying attention toward processes that would normally remain tacit in experience; (2) diminished self-affection: a decline in the experienced sense of existing as a living and unified subject of awareness. The result is variable disruptions in the sense of self-presence, first-person perspective, the phenomenality (the what-it-is-like) of experience, and intentionality (including the subject's sense of reality). Disruptions of this sort directly affect the minimal self, but as Parnas and Sass note, they also have implications for the narrative self (see Gallagher 2003).

In her account of the narrative self, Schechtman, following Dennett, mentioned Multiple Personality Disorder (recently renamed Dissociative Identity Disorder, DID) as a pathology that involves non-intersecting narratives. *Jennifer Radden* takes a closer look at DID in her chapter on multiple selves. She considers recent approaches to the self, including embodied, agentive, and narrative approaches, and suggests that while none rule out the possibility of multiple selves (ranging from non-pathological to the pathological cases of DID), the idea of rational agency, following the work of Carol Rovane (1998), is perhaps the most appropriate for explaining these types of multiplicity. That is, in the realm of agency, within one human being, one may find separate sets of practical commitments and small-scale, incommensurable projects. This approach, however, doesn't account for the distinct (and often non-communicating) centers of apperception in DID, a feature that is explained in Stephen Braude's (1995) account. Radden attempts to introduce this latter feature of multiple centers of apperception into the agentive account, thus offering a more adequate explanation for the possibility of DID. To do this she introduces the idea that personality traits, which easily mesh with agentive patterns, may be a place to start. This construes self as involving dispositions or traits that are manifested, with some degree of continuity, over time. Together with epistemic or amnesic barriers that can lead to dissociated awareness, as discussed by Braude, we can get a better picture of DID. Still, the picture is often blurred by the fact that each of these factors admits of degree.

Discussions of DID may be clarifying for questions about our normative conceptions of self-unity. It seems possible that we are not as unified as we sometimes think, even if we do not reach degrees of pathology. Whether unity is an ideal to aim for, or, as Radden suggests, the lack of unity, the sometimes contradictory and sometimes confusing agentive roles that we play, is a valuable part of human nature, is a good question to keep in mind as we think about the nature of the self. It also has implications for therapy, and it forces us to consider whether and to what degree unity is to be aimed for in terms of treating pathological subjects. Clearly some relatively strong degree of self-unity is expressed in the normative preferences of most societies, but whether such norms should be imposed in therapy is a question similar to the one raised by Strawson concerning the moral claim that it is a good thing to experience one's life as a narrative (see Chapter 17).

Peter Hobson, in his chapter on autism, draws on developmental psychopathology to gain insight into the self. This involves, first, focusing on evidence about complementary aspects in the seemingly unified phenomena of the self that may be distinguishable factors in development; and, second, understanding that what we may regard as familiar distinctions in mental life may originate as indissoluble aspects in early experience, for example, cognition and emotion. Hobson is interested in the question of how we, especially as infants, enter into, and sometimes fail to enter into, a shared form of life (Wittgenstein 1958; also see Rochat, Chapter 2). Amid the multitude of problems that autistic individuals have in regard to social relations, there are clues that such problems have an effect on how they relate to themselves. In this regard, Hobson suggests that autism is not only a disorder in self–other relations but also in self-awareness.

Hobson reviews evidence that autistic children have, among other problems, difficulties in using the personal pronouns, confusing 'I', 'you', 'she', and so forth, one among many things that reflect the lack of coherency in their practices of self-reference, or in co-reference between self and other. This problem isn't simply on the grammatical level, of course; it extends deep into their bodily capacities for movement and interaction with others and in some cases (e.g. in some instances of imitating another's action) affects their ability to adopt the appropriate spatial (egocentric) perspective; in other cases their ability to adopt appropriate psychological or emotional perspective *vis-à-vis* others. Autistic children thus have trouble experiencing and understanding themselves as selves in relation to other people with selves of their own. At the conceptual level, Hobson suggests, the notion of self is operative in both self-ascription and other-ascription; to learn what 'self' means is to learn that it applies to oneself and to others, who are also selves.

The importance of this co-constitutive relation between self and other is also something to be found in the psychoanalytic relation, as *Marcia Cavell* makes clear. In the therapeutic relation, the struggle for self-expression helps create the thing to be expressed, and in some sense the self comes to be in its attempt to be understood by the other. The same can be said about the self in regard to action, as well as in regard to artistic expression. More generally Cavell emphasizes the point that Hobson and Rochat also emphasized: that the self is generated from the beginning in its social relations. For Cavell, however, there is no self at first; it emerges in our relations with others; it then grows, 'leads a life', with some continuity; but it can also fragment and come apart in ways that can be either pathological or creative.

The coming apart of the self is not always pathological. One can find it in self-deception and denial, which are often part of our normal everyday life. Here we find intra-psychic conflict. Repression and dissociation may lead further toward pathology. The first, repression, Cavell indicates, is vertical—the self coming apart in layers, leaving some important layer of meaning in the dark; the second, dissociation, is horizontal—some set of experiences (part of an idea, an action, a feeling, an experience, a memory) setting up their own shop with a different person behind the counter, as in DID. But some forms of dissociation can be creative and can be integrated—or not integrated—with the self. Art, literature, and our creative encounters with others can count here.

THE SELF IN DIVERSE CONTEXTS

In the last part of this book the reader will find other fractal elements—repeating and reinforcing themes, yet on different scales and in different contexts, and often reviewing from a critical perspective the positions that have been staked out in previous chapters. We can find, for example, ideas about the formation of self in habits and as developing in social interaction in the work of the pragmatists—Peirce, James, Dewey and Mead—as *Richard Menary* makes clear in his extended discussion of a pragmatic conception of self. This conception reinforces the agentive idea that what we do makes us who we are: I am what I do. As such, there is no pre-established certainty in the self; it is marked by fallibility and I come to know myself only through my interactions with physical and social environments. My self-awareness develops only by attending to the continuities and habitualities in my practices, which are already permeated by the gestures of others, which I internalize to form what I call my self. All of these actions and interactions and self-formations shape a moral dimension in which we have to negotiate our freedom, since we are neither absolutely free nor absolutely determined.

Menary takes this pragmatic account to support an externalist conception of the self. We construct our selves out in the world, among things, with people, in institutions, all of which operate as scaffolds in this process. To the extent that the environment affords regular structures, including those that are shaped on the bodies of others—gestures, words and facial expressions—our habits become regularized. Yet, they do not become rigid, and the environments themselves are not entirely predictable or stable. The self, then, is not something 'in the head', the Cartesian ego, a mental structure, or the brain; it is distributed through embodied practices into the environment. Here we can find good support in John Dewey, noting his proximity to recent conceptions of extended cognition. In complete contrast to what we normally take to be the Cartesian self, Dewey states: 'Thinking, or knowledge getting, [and here we would insert 'self'] is far from being the armchair thing it is often supposed to be. The reason it is not an armchair thing is that it is not an event going on exclusively within the cortex. . . . Hands and feet, apparatus and appliances of all kinds are as much a part of it as changes within the brain.' (1916: 13–14).

This kind of externalist view opens up the question pursued by *Kenneth Gergen*—is the self socially constructed? A social constructionist approach to the self is critical insofar as it targets many of the traditional conceptions of self under discussion in this volume. At the same time, a point of departure for the social constructionist is something mentioned numerous times before: that self and self-knowledge find their origins in human—social, cultural—relationships. This social orientation, however, is set as the compass for truth and falsity, objectivity and subjectivity, the scientific and the mythical, the rational and the irrational, and so forth. That is, these categories, and the power that they have over our philosophical ideas as well as our everyday practices, are brought into being through historically and culturally situated social processes. The social constructionist thus challenges the concept of the individual autonomous self, the rational, self-directing, morally centered agent of action.

Gergen targets the primary use of the term 'self' in psychological and mental discourse, suggesting many ways in which the sources of knowledge about the realm of the mental, for example, introspection, behavioral observation, are open to question. Perhaps more positively, looking at how we use language—or how language allows us to build up conceptions of the self through, for example, the uses of personal pronouns—we can see how a notion of the self is generated. Not grammar alone, however, but conversational and narrative practices, especially, seem to be well-established sources for the fashioning and fabrication of our sense of self. The analyses of such practices, however, simply reinforce the movement of focus away from purely mental or psychological conceptions of self. Furthermore, the practices themselves have a certain power insofar as they establish vocabularies of the self that legitimize the concept, and that in turn rationalize and sustain these very practices. Here Gergen cites the work of Foucault and others who develop a sustained critique of what may be the 'dark side' of the construction of the self as an autonomous, alienated entity differentiated from the other, laying the ground for organizing a world characterized by separation, distrust, and self-gain. Such relations then get reflected in disciplines like psychology and economics, and psychiatry, which then reinforce the normative divisions that define contemporary conceptions of self in theory and practice.

Alternative conceptions of the self, which acknowledge a certain primacy of the social over the individual, hold some promise, according to Gergen, and can be found in various theorists, including the pragmatism of Mead and the work of Bakhtin on dialogicality. These are just the thinkers that *Hubert Hermans* takes to be foundational for the theory of the dialogical self, which he construes as a combination of American pragmatism and Russian dialogism. This theory views the other not as external to self, but as part of the self and constitutive of it. The self is intrinsically social, a micro-society within the larger society to which it belongs.

Hermans introduces the notion of *positioning* as a further articulation of the dialogical self situated in time and space. The idea is that the self is not organized around one center or core, but distributed over social relations. Insofar as an individual is immersed in dialogical interactions (relations, conversations, cooperative or competitive projects) with others in the social world, the self is distributed in those relations, playing perhaps very different roles or occupying different positions in each one. These different positions are themselves in dialogue with each other within the comprehensive set of relations that we call self. The self fluctuates across these different positions which are sometimes and imperfectly collected together as a set of differences. These differences are given voice as different characters, or different roles to be played out in different times and places, generating a set of complex, intersecting narratives that reflect and are reflected in the self-structure. These differences can be defined in terms of relative dominance positions of speakers in interaction, or in terms of socially defined power differences tied to class, race, gender, religion, age, etc., all of which can be reflected in a person's self-perception and self-understanding. What defines me as an intellectual or a factory worker does not define me as a sexual partner or as a parent. Such positions may come in contact, informing each other, or may not. A self is a unique map of these different positions.

This conception of the dialogical self has implications for a variety of investigations, and Hermans traces some of these out. For example, one can employ the concept in an attempt to understand pathological conditions such as DID and other dissociations discussed by Radden and Cavell. He notes that self-positions are not constituted in abstract terms, but in embodied practices and spatially situated circumstances. There is also a developmental story to be told about the dialogical self, one that would reinterpret the interactive aspects of development iterated by Rochat. In this regard, for example, one can think that the infant rehearses the *positions* previously experienced in her embodied relationship with others in her pre-sleep (proto-) conversations with herself (see the case of Sarah in Garvey 1984, discussed by Hermans). Hermans's notion of positions can also fruitfully inform feminist or poststructuralist analyses, a possibility that is suggested by *Elspeth Probyn*'s concept of gender positions.

Probyn considers the possibility that young women, with few resources for fashioning a strong sense of self, specifically because of their gender positions, use anorexia as a mode of negotiating societal strictures. Her notion of gender position is closely tied to a psychoanalytic (Lacan)–Marxist (Althusser)–poststructuralist (Foucault) conception of subjectification. The institutional imprinting of a certain image, and a certain kind of third-person observation (a 'regime of visibility') imposed on the girls/patients/anorexics is just such an exercise of subjectification. What is the self like if it is intensively inspected as an object—a medical patient for example—if it is so much the object of inspection that it feels, in the words of one anorexic, like she were made of glass? What happens when the subject becomes a subject of research, which is to say, an object of research?

Furthermore, Probyn asks, what happens to the researcher when certain emotions manifest themselves in connection with the research—something that is not unusual when not only the researchers, but also the research subjects, are human? Such emotion belongs to the subjectivity of the researcher. It belongs to her *self.* Let's say that the emotional dimension defines an essential aspect of self. Does the researcher simply leave this dimension of herself behind, for example, when the subject matter of research is the self itself? How *heavily* (i.e. *emotionally*) invested is the researcher in her research, or the position that she stakes out and defends, such that, even if she fails to mention the emotional dimension of the self, it is lurking there between the lines?

The reader will notice that the questions of power and subjectification are ones that have arisen only in these last three chapters (Gergen, Hermans, Probyn), without having come up at all in the first twenty-six. The general question posed by these chapters, positioned as they are for critical reflection in this volume, posed one might say against not only the traditional conceptions of self, but against even the most contemporary ones, is the critical question of whether these social, cultural, institutional power structures, these forces of subjectification, can qualify everything that has already been said about the self. Probyn makes this question clear in regard to research on anorexic subjects and the formation of a research discourse that will classify those subjects, and more generally. This motivates a similar question about the theoretical stakes associated with this volume. What does it mean, in terms of practical effect, to inspect the self and to develop a vocabulary, or a set of vocabularies, about the self? This is not, of course, the subjectification of a person. The self is not our patient. But if we are setting a vocabulary, and a system of classification where we can decide between minimal and narrative selves, embodied and psychological selves, and the various categories that have been used to specify self and to talk of action, moral responsibility, pathological behaviour, etc., and if we have any expectations that this will change our way of thinking about selves—about our *selves*—should we not think critically about what that means in terms of the practical effect that it may have? At the very least, raising such questions motivates, I think, self-reflection on the set of projects that constitute this volume.

Postmodern thought also poses a set of critical questions about the self. *Leonard Lawlor* guides us through these questions. For the postmodern, the self is heterogeneous, which means that it is multiple (a theme we also find in Gergen and Hermans). Rather than an 'I' or a 'me', there is a 'we'. But even the 'we' lacks unity and is thus more like a political collective characterized by differences instead of identities. Rather than a dialogical 'we', the 'we' is agonistic. Thus Lawlor looks to the political as a helpful metaphor for understanding the self. The postmodern political, in contrast to a social bond, however, is not something that can be brought into unity or under the control of a narrative. Rather, an economic discourse of performance and efficiency (just as it characterizes the political today) seems better able to position the self within the larger system. Here it is not so much that self is observed and disciplined (as Probyn suggests), but that self is measured, commodified, bought and sold, within a system that is dominated by a totalizing (totalitarian), global capitalistic set of values (where values are simply quantifications). What is the self worth; what is its cash value?

This description, which tries to capture the real situation of postmodern selves, is meant as a critique, which at the very least raises the question of what we are doing to ourselves. The political, then, is no longer a metaphor. Rather, the question about the self is just as pressing as (and not disconnected from), for example, environmental politics.

What are we doing to ourselves? Lawlor sets out a response in terms of imagining the right kind of literature that would express and constitute the non-totalitarian self, without pretending that this would be a 'we' that exists in consensus or as otherwise unified. He turns to the analysis of the temporality of experience, in Husserl and Bergson, which then, on a postmodern reading, shows that at base the self is caught in a tension (or is the tension) between an element that goes against time (ana-chronism), and a powerlessness to escape time. Being against time, however, is being against the efficiency imposed by the economic system (where time is of great value: 'time is money'). It suggests that the economic discourse doesn't really fit the self, as it tries to fit the self into the efficiency of the system. The alternative to the varieties of totalizing connected with narrative or economic calculation is to accept a powerlessness in the face of the passage of time—to be 'friends' of this passage, and to refrain from imposing on it the narrative strictures or the economic structures that characterize our time. This is also to refrain from imposing identity on the self, and is rather to treat the self as a constant possibility, which is never completed.

Lorraine Code carries these kind of postmodern or poststructuralist themes into a feminist analysis of self. The ideas of positioning and being positioned within power structures, or linguistic structures, or the 'social imaginary' that define the subject, often as a thin, decontextualized, abstract self, have implications for epistemological, moral, and political philosophies. For Code, a viable feminist analysis of self needs to recognize that selves/subjects are always embodied and situated—which means, always gendered, raced, and identified in various ways. To understand real selves, one needs to understand their particular positions and how, as such, they are thrown together into the complex, rich, and challenging world. This is what she calls the 'subjectivity' of the self—subjectivity not in the sense of phenomenological subject, but in the sense of the particular social and political subject that anyone actually is.

Science and philosophy can study *what* the self is; in doing so, they tend to ignore *who* we are; the focus on numerical identity fails to recognize the qualitative aspects that define our lives. Narrative accounts seem to have a place for the *who*, but narrative theorists nonetheless spend much of their time debating about the *what*: are we narrative animals, are we abstract centers of gravity, are narratives constitutive of the self, and so on? Of course scientists and philosophers are not meant to be biographers, but they should not ignore the strongly situated aspects of their subjects. Is personal identity a universal that does not change across cultures? Across genders? Across economic classes? Perhaps science and philosophy need to be balanced with history and literature in order to get an adequate picture of what selves can be. The danger here, as Code points out, is that the Others will be defined as such, as meeting or failing to meet criteria of personal identity already sorted out in terms of white, male, western, abstract, autonomous, affluently academic standards.

Code cites Annette Baier (1985: 84) as indicating one possible way to shift the center of the discussion: 'A person, perhaps, is best seen as one who was long enough dependent upon other persons to acquire the essential arts of personhood. Persons essentially are *second* persons.' The point is that philosophical analyses that suppress intersubjectivity in favour of the detached first-person individual self (analyses that are philosophically autistic) conceive of 'the self' as quite removed from how human beings actually are. A second-person orientation opens up possible ways of rethinking autonomy and exploring the kind of ideas that can be found in pragmatist philosophers and dialogical approaches (see Menary and Hermans, respectively), as well as in feminist ethics. Code's conception of understanding selves as differing as they are positioned across differing ecologies helps to break the lines that have been drawn too tightly around standard philosophical conceptions of self.

Where does this leave us? In the various chapters that compose this volume the reader can trace different conceptions of the self, some set in opposition to others— minimal, narrative, real, not real, existing, illusory, reduced, irreducible, embodied, psychological, social, pathological, socially constructed, and deconstructed. This disparity, which is both problematic and productive, is directly related to the variety of methodological approaches taken within philosophy and in related interdisciplinary studies of the self. They include introspection, phenomenological analysis, linguistic analysis, the use of thought experiments, empirical research in cognitive and brain sciences, developmental studies and studies of exceptional and pathological behavior, ethical, social and political analyses. One question is whether different characterizations of self signify diverse aspects of some unitary phenomenon, or whether they pick out different and unrelated phenomena. Regardless of how one answers this question, however, the variety of approaches and definitions found in studies of the self productively reinforces the idea that this concept involves complex and varied aspects that are not easily reducible to one set of principles. As a result, it seems imperative to keep methodological options open and to explore different conceptions of self and non-self in the analyses of philosophy of mind, moral and social philosophy, psychology, psychopathology, phenomenology, neuroscience, psychoanalysis, history, literature, narrative theory, ethnology, cross cultural studies, and so on. What we can be certain about, as we'll see in the following pages, is that we are not all on the same page when it comes to conceptions of self.

REFERENCES

ALBAHARI, M. (2006). *Analytical Buddhism: The Two-Tiered Illusion of Self* (New York: Palgrave Macmillan).

ANSCOMBE, G. E. M. (1975). 'The First Person', in S. Guttenplan (ed.), *Mind and Language* (Oxford: Oxford University Press). Reprinted in Cassam (1994: 140–59).

BAIER, A. (1985). *Postures of the Mind: Essays on Minds and Morals* (Minneapolis: University of Minnesota Press).

BOTVINICK, M., and COHEN, J. (1998). 'Rubber Hands "Feel" Touch that Eyes See', *Nature*, 391: 756.

BRAUDE, S. E. (1995). 'Multiple Personality and Moral Responsibility', *Philosophy, Psychiatry and Psychology*, 3: 37–54.

Cassam, Q. (ed.) (1994). *Self-Knowledge* (Oxford: Oxford University Press).

DENNETT, D. (1992). 'The Self as a Center of Narrative Gravity', in F. S. Kessel, P. M. Cole, and D. L. Johnson (eds), *Self and Consciousness: Multiple Perspectives* (Hillsdale, NJ: Lawrence Erlbaum Associates), 103–15.

DEWEY, J. (1916). *Essays in Experimental Logic* (New York: Dover).

DSM-IV (2000). American Psychiatric Association, *Diagnostic and Statistical Manual of Mental Disorders*, 4th edn, text revision (Washington, DC: American Psychiatric Association).

EVANS, G. (1982). *The Varieties of Reference* (Oxford: Oxford University Press).

GARVEY, C. (1984). *Children's Talk* (Cambridge, Mass.: Harvard University Press).

GALLAGHER, S. (2003). 'Self-Narrative in Schizophrenia', in A. S. David and T. Kircher (eds), *The Self in Neuroscience and Psychiatry* (Cambridge: Cambridge University Press), 336–57.

GALLUP, G. G. (1970). 'Chimpanzees: Self-Recognition', *Science*, 167(3914), 86–7.

GILLIHAN, S. J., and FARAH, M. J. (2005). 'Is Self Special? A Critical Review of Evidence from Experimental Psychology and Cognitive Neuroscience', *Psychological Bulletin*, 131: 76–97.

ICD 10 (n.d.). World Health Organization, *International Statistical Classification of Diseases and Related Health Problems*, 10th revision (http://apps.who.int/classifications/apps/icd10online/).

JAMES, W. (1890). *The Principles of Psychology* (Cambridge, Mass.: Harvard University Press).

LEDOUX, J. (2002). *The Synaptic Self* (New York: Penguin Putnam).

LEGRAND, D., and RUBY, P. (2009). 'What is Self-Specific? Theoretical Investigation and Critical Review of Neuroimaging Results', *Psychological Review*, 116: 252–82.

NAGEL, T. (1986). *The View from Nowhere* (New York: Oxford University Press).

NEISSER, U. (1988). 'Five Kinds of Self-Knowledge', *Philosophical Psychology*, 1: 35–59.

PARFIT, D. (1984). *Reasons and Persons* (Oxford: Oxford University Press).

PERRY, J. (1979). 'The Essential Indexical', *Philosophical Review*, 86: 874–97.

RICOEUR, P. (1994). *Oneself as Another*, tr. K. Blamey (Chicago: University of Chicago Press).

REID, T. (1785). *Essays on the Intellectual Powers of Man* (Cambridge: John Bartlett, 1850).

ROVANE, C. (1998). *The Bounds of Agency* (Princeton: Princeton University Press).

SHOEMAKER, S. (1968). 'Self-Reference and Self-Awareness', *Journal of Philosophy*, 65: 555–67.

STRAWSON, G. (1997). 'The Self', *Journal of Consciousness Studies*, 4(5/6): 405–28.

VELLEMAN, J. D. (1992). 'What Happens When Someone Acts?', *Mind*, 101: 461–81.

——(2006). *Self to Self: Selected Essays* (Cambridge: Cambridge University Press).

WEGNER, D. (2002). *The Illusion of Conscious Will* (Cambridge, Mass.: MIT Press).

WITTGENSTEIN, L. (1958). *The Blue and Brown Books* (Oxford: Oxford University Press).

PART I

SELF

BEGINNINGS AND
BASICS

··

CHAPTER 1

HISTORY AS PROLOGUE

WESTERN THEORIES
OF THE SELF

··

JOHN BARRESI
RAYMOND MARTIN

In philosophical theory, as well as in common parlance, the words *self* and *person* are often used interchangeably, usually, but not always, in an effort to express the same idea. For instance, John Locke, in one of the most consequential discussions relating these terms, declared that: 'PERSON, as I take it, is the name for . . . self. Wherever a man finds what he calls himself, there, I think, another may say is the same person.' But when Locke actually defines *person* and *self* he defines *self* as 'that conscious thinking thing, whatever substance made up of (whether spiritual or material, simple or compounded, it matters not), which is sensible, or conscious of pleasure and pain, capable of happiness or misery, and so is concerned for itself, as far as that consciousness extends'. By contrast, he defines *person* as 'a thinking intelligent being, that has reason and reflection, and can consider itself as itself,

---

This brief historical survey of theories of self in Western thought is based in part on our earlier work, especially, Martin and Barresi (2000, 2006). For a fuller appreciation of this history, we recommend reading these works as well as Sorabji (2006) for the ancient period, Seigel (2005) for the modern period, and Taylor (1989) for a full history but with a somewhat different emphasis.

the same thinking thing in different times and places; which it does only by that consciousness which is inseparable from thinking, and, as it seems to me, essential to it.' (Locke 1694/1979: 346, 341, 335). Yet, despite these differing definitions, Locke bases identity over time of both self and person on consciousness. In the present chapter, we use the terms *self* and *person* interchangeably, to express the same idea.

SELF AS SPIRITUAL SUBSTANCE: PLATONISM

In the *Phaedo* of Plato (429–347 BCE), Socrates equated his essential self with his *psyche*, or soul. Earlier Greek thinkers, such as Homer, thought that the psyche or life principle separated from the body at death and went to Hades as a shade. But individuals did not identify with their shades. By taking the soul to be one's essential self, Plato turned a new leaf on this traditional belief. He argued for the immortality of each person's soul, which he took to be 'immaterial' and akin to the divine. In his view, the soul's simplicity ensures both personal survival of bodily death and each person's 'pre-existence' prior to incarnation into a body. It also ensures personal survival of changes undergone while one is alive and embodied.

Plato did not ask what accounts for the unity of the self at any given time. Had he raised this question, he might have answered that the soul's immateriality and, hence, its indivisibility, accounts for its unity. Six centuries later Plotinus (c.204–70) did raise this question and answered that unity of experience would be impossible if the soul were matter, because matter is inherently divisible in a way that would destroy its own and also the mind's unity. While conceding that the soul too is divisible, he argued that its divisibility is different: '[The soul] does not consist of separate sections; its divisibility lies in its presence at every point in the recipient, but it is indivisible as dwelling entire in any part.' If the soul 'had the nature of body', he continued, 'it would consist of isolated members each unaware of the conditions of each other'. In that case, he wrote, 'there would be a particular soul—say, a soul of the finger—answering as a distinct and independent entity to every local experience'; hence, 'there would be a multiplicity of souls administering each individual'. Since the mental lives of such individuals, he pointed out, would be unlike our own mental lives, each of us cannot be administered by a multiplicity of (equal) souls. 'Without a dominant unity,' he concluded, our lives would be 'meaningless' (Plotinus 1952: 140). So far as is known, no one had entertained such thoughts before.

Plato's view that one's soul is immaterial, provoked, for the first time, the problem of explaining the relationship of this immaterial essence—one's true self—to the body, and hence that of explaining how, in general, dualism as a philosophy of nature is possible. Plotinus later provided one such account, which involved an elaborate cosmology with gradations of being, including immaterial substances, material substances, and activities. Later still, Descartes, in whose view consciousness would play a central role, provided a different account—one which distinguished more sharply between mental and material substances. In spite of the problems raised by dualism, the view that the soul is an immaterial substance proved to be remarkably persistent, mainly because it was endorsed by the Church, but also partly because it has seemed to many that each of us has a kind of mental unity that could not be explained if we were wholly material. When, in the twentieth century, self and personal identity thinkers en masse finally did embrace materialism the question of how unified we are mentally and how whatever mental unity we have can be explained came to the fore.

Self as Hylomorphic Substance: Aristotelianism

Aristotle (384–322 BCE), in opposing Plato's dualism, showed little interest in individual selves. In his view, the soul is related to body as 'form' to 'matter', which are integrated into a unified whole—the individual organism. While this form is the same in all humans, matter varies with the individual. Aristotle's interest was not in particular persons, but in human nature. Thus, he shifted the focus from the self as a special part of the human organism to human nature in general and to individuals only as particular instances of human nature. In his view, every living thing has a psyche, or soul, which is its vital principle—that is, what it is about it that accounts for its being alive. For plants and most animals, the soul is inseparable from the body that it informs. However, Aristotle seems to have held that for humans, the soul's rational part—*nous*—is separable, although some scholars dispute whether he really held this view. Assuming that he did hold it, it is not clear whether it was also part of his view that *nous* can retain personal individuality when it is separate from a body. When, in the late middle ages and early Renaissance, Aristotle achieved among Christian scholars an authoritative status almost equal to divine revelation, the implications of his view of the psyche for personal survival of bodily death became a contentious issue, with some thinkers even suggesting that his true view must have been that no parts of the soul, not even *nous*, are separable from the body.

SELF AS MATERIAL SUBSTANCE:
EPICUREANISM ATOMISM

In addition to the tradition in Greek thought that went through Plato and Aristotle, then to Plotinus, and afterwards to the church fathers, there was in classical Greece and Rome a tradition of materialistic atomism that was sparked by Leucippus (fl. 440 BCE) and Democritus (460?–370? BCE) and included the Epicureans and Stoics, who developed atomist metaphysics into a philosophy of life. Epicurus (341–270 BCE), for instance, taught that pleasure is the only good, pain the only evil, and fear of death a needless source of human distress. The problem posed by death, he claimed, is not death itself but the fear of death, and the way to resolve that problem is to accept death for exactly what it is, the physical coming apart of the complex of atoms that is one's self, resulting in the cessation of any subject that can experience pleasure or pain.

In his Epicurean poem, *De Rerum Natura*, Lucretius (95?–54? BCE) denied both the existence of an immaterial soul and personal survival of bodily death. In the context of his making the point that we have nothing to fear from bodily death, he argued that 'if any feeling remains in mind or spirit after it has been torn from body, that is nothing to us, who are brought into being by the wedlock of body and spirit, conjoined and coalesced'. He then considered the possibility that 'the matter that composes us should be reassembled by time after our death and brought back into its present state'. He claimed that, even if this were to happen—that is, were we, in effect, to be resurrected—it would be of no concern to us 'once the chain of our identity had been snapped' (Lucretius 1951: 121).

Why of no concern? Lucretius's answer seems to have been, first, that whatever parts of us may survive, we cease at our bodily deaths and, second, that our persisting—that is, our continuing as the same people we now are—is a precondition of any egoistic concern we might have for the experiences of any parts of ourselves that survive our bodily deaths. What is impressive in these thoughts is not so much his answer to the question of what matters in a person's apparently self-interested desire to survive (his view was that what matters presupposes personal identity) but rather his asking the question in the first place. No one previously, at least in the West, had asked it. Because Lucretius was so widely read into the modern period, he introduced into the discussion of self the question of *what matters* in survival, that is, in one's egoistic concern to survive.

CHRISTIANITY AND THE RESURRECTION OF SELF

So far as one can tell, most people in classical Greek and Roman culture did not have a deep, self-interested longing to survive bodily death. Of course, they did not want to die in the first place, but that is a different matter. By contrast, in today's Western industrialized cultures many people are not only curious about whether they themselves will survive, but *long* to survive, particularly in some way that is better than their earthly lives. Such attitudes, which are foreign to Greek philosophy, seem to owe their prevalence, if not also their very origin, to Christianity.

According to Christian scripture, not only do people survive their bodily deaths, but they survive them in a bodily way. And the very same people, and bodies, that lived on Earth are rewarded or punished in the afterlife. But most people, when they die, are in bad shape physically. Critics questioned how it could be a good thing that the bodies that people have in the afterlife are the ones they had at the times of their deaths.

In reply, the Church Fathers went out of their way to make the case that the body which is resurrected, while identical to the earthly body, is somehow spiritualized, glorified, or at least repaired. Such claims provoked questions. From what parts is the body that dies reconstructed? What happens if the matter of the previous body is subsequently shared by more than one body, as, for instance, in cannibalism? And how is the reconstruction of the body compatible with its being the very same body as the one that died?

From the first through the twelfth centuries Christian philosophers offered answers to these questions from the perspective of Neoplatonism. In considering their answers, it is helpful to distinguish among three views about personal identity: first, that it depends only on the continuation of an immaterial soul; second, that it depends on the continuation of both an immaterial soul and a material body; and third, that it depends only on the continuation of a material body (which was thought by those Church Fathers who were materialists to include a material soul). Some Christian thinkers, such as Origen (185?–254), who had a Platonic view of survival, adopted something like the first of these options; others, like Tertullian (160?–230?), who in accordance with his commitment to Stoicism was a materialist, adopted something like the third. Eventually, due importantly to the influence of Augustine (354–430), most gravitated toward the second: that personal immortality requires the continuation of the very same immaterial soul and the very same material body. This view then became an integral and enduring dogma of Christianity.

Augustine was among the first to become self-conscious about the problem of explaining the relation of the soul-substance to the body. Plato had maintained, in effect, that the soul is related to the body like a pilot to his ship. In his view, the soul at death always leaves forever the specific body with which it had been associated, and when sufficiently purified eventually leaves body itself forever. Augustine's view, in contrast, was that the dogma of bodily resurrection requires that soul and body together form an intimate unit: 'A soul in possession of a body does not constitute two persons, but one man' (Augustine 1995: 259).

THE ARISTOTELIAN SYNTHESIS

In the early middle ages the only works of (and on) Aristotle that had been translated and so were available to Latin philosophers were his *Categories* and *De Interpretatione*, together with Boethius' (480–525?) commentaries on them. From the mid-twelfth to the mid-thirteenth centuries, most of the remaining works of Aristotle were translated and became available. These newly translated works, which in the thirteenth century would stimulate and confuse European intellectuals, provoked novel questions and cast old ones in a new light. So far as the self and personal identity are concerned, the essential problem was that since the third century most Latin philosophers had become accustomed to thinking that each human has just one soul, which is a simple, incorporeal substance that somehow inhabits the body. On the views inspired by Aristotle's *De Anima*, there is not just one soul per human, but several, each of which is more intimately related to the body. The trick, for Christian European thinkers struggling to assimilate Aristotle, was to explain the relationship of Aristotelian souls to each other and to the body in an account that preserved the Christian dogma of personal immortality. For the first time in Europe since Christian Neoplatonism had become the received view, the soul was undergoing a process of naturalization. In the seventeenth and eighteenth centuries, it would happen again, only more radically, until eventually a self that is a product of the brain displaced the soul altogether.

CARTESIAN DUALISM

The sixteenth- and seventeenth-century rise of modern science, spearheaded by Johannes Kepler (1571–1630), Galileo Galilei (1564–1642), and René Descartes (1596–1650) spawned theories in which there was no place either for substantial forms or teleology, both of which were central to Aristotelian science. Instead, the universe and its parts were conceptualized as if they were clocks, pushed along by springs and pulleys, which—as efficient causes—have no prevision of the ends they might achieve.

Descartes was the first major thinker to start using the word mind (Latin, *mens*) as an alternative to the word soul (*anima*). In his view, the self is the mind, which is an unextended substance whose essence is thinking. Although he thereby freed the Platonic soul from its Aristotelian accretions, he also inadvertently exposed its scientific irrelevance, a consequence that would not become apparent to most philosophers until the end of the eighteenth century. Insofar as the self was concerned, there was one main question for both Descartes and his critics: how does the self as immaterial substance fit into an otherwise wholly material world governed by mechanistic laws?

Descartes answered that, independently of the immaterial self, the neural organization of the brain accounts for sensation, perception, and imagination, and that in non-human animals this entirely mechanical system is all that there is. According to his theory, during sensation 'animal spirits' in the sense-organs of non-human animals are stimulated mechanically by the sizes, shapes, and motions of the matter impinging on their organs, thereby transmitting physiologically to the brain, and eventually to the pineal gland in the brain, decodable information about objects external to the organism. This information in the pineal gland is then redirected to some other region of the brain or body. In the case of humans, the process works much the same, with two exceptions: what humans sense and imagine is directly experienced by the immaterial self; and the immaterial self's thoughts are its own mental acts, which remain in that substance and are not coded in the brain at all. Nevertheless, through the pineal gland thoughts do sometimes causally affect, and are affected by, the motion of the animal spirits and hence the behavior of the organism.

It seemed to some of Descartes's critics that, on his view, the mind should be related to the body as a pilot to his ship. In response, Descartes seems to have tried to say that individual non-material minds and their associated bodies form one substance in virtue of their unity as a causal mechanism. In other words, they systematically affect each other, but not other things, in ways that make the two of them together function as if they were one.

NATURALIZATION OF THE SOUL

The seventeenth century ended with the dazzling theories of Isaac Newton (1642–1727), who showed once and for all that there could be a natural philosophy of the external world. Quick on the heels of his triumph came an unprecedented confidence in human reason. Thinkers at the forefront of progressive developments wanted to do for 'moral philosophy', that is, the science of human nature, what Newton had done for 'natural philosophy'. In the early seventeenth century, rationalists, such as Descartes, had been at the forefront of this progressive extension of natural science. By the end of the century empiricism's time had arrived, nowhere more consequentially than in the work of Newton's contemporary, John Locke (1632–1704).

So far as self and personal identity are concerned, Locke had two main ideas, one negative and one positive. His negative idea was that the persistence of selves and persons cannot be understood as parasitic upon the persistence of any underlying substance, or substances, out of which persons might be composed. His positive idea was that the persistence of selves and persons could be understood in terms of the unifying role of consciousness:

For since consciousness always accompanies thinking, and it is that which makes every one to be what he calls self, and thereby distinguishes himself from all other thinking things; in this alone consists personal identity, i.e. the sameness of a rational being: And as far as this consciousness can be extended backwards to any past action or thought, so far reaches the identity of that person; it is the same self now it was then; and it is by the same self with this present one that now reflects on it, that that action was done. (Locke 1694/1979: 335)

Locke thereby motivated the decisive break with substance accounts of the self, or person, toward relational accounts, according to which each self, or person, is a complex composed of physical and/or mental elements that persists as long as the elements in the complex are properly related.

When in the context of talking about personal identity Locke talked about consciousness, most of the time he meant memory. His eighteenth-century critics invariably took him to mean this. They, thus, attributed to him the view that a person at one time and one at another have the same consciousness, and hence are the same person, just in case the person at the later time remembers having experienced and done what the person at the earlier time experienced and did. Whether or not this was Locke's view, his critics were right in thinking that it is vulnerable to decisive objections. However, almost all of them wanted to defeat the memory view of personal identity in order to retain the view that personal identity depends on the persistence of an immaterial soul. They failed to see that even the memory view that they attributed to Locke was riding the crest of a wave of naturalization that was about to engulf them. As the century wore on, their vision improved.

Personal Identity vs. What Matters in Survival

The first extended discussion of fission examples, in which one thing multiplies, in connection with personal identity occurred between 1706 and 1709 when Samuel Clarke (1675–1729) and Anthony Collins (1676–1729) confronted each other in a six-part written debate in which Clarke argued that it is not possible for a system of mere matter to think, and Collins argued that matter does think. In this debate, Clarke introduced fission examples as a way of objecting to Collins's (and Locke's) relational view of personal identity. He did this by pointing out that if God in the afterlife can make one being with the same consciousness as someone who had lived on Earth, then God could make many such beings, which on Collins's view would be the same person. Clarke took it as obvious that such multiple fission-descendants would be different people. Subsequently he and Collins discussed fission examples several times. Because their debate was well-known, both fission examples and the idea that they have implications for personal identity theory were brought to the attention of eighteenth-century theorists.

During most of the eighteenth century fission examples were used to argue in support of an immaterial substance view of self. But Joseph Priestley (1733–1804), toward the end of the century, and William Hazlitt (1778–1830), at the beginning of the nineteenth century, used fission examples in more progressive ways. Hazlitt, for instance, not only conceded but embraced and celebrated the idea that fission examples implied that it is 'wild and absurd' to believe in 'absolute, metaphysical identity' between our present and any future self (Hazlitt, 1805/1969: 6). And in his view, fission examples have the further implication that people have no special ('self-interested') reason to value their future selves. At least to his own satisfaction, and in a way that anticipated the work of Derek Parfit and others in our own times, he then tried to explain how the idea that the notion of an identical continued self is a fiction, far from being destructive to theories of rationality and morality, actually makes them better. In the process, he sowed the seeds, albeit on barren ground, of a modern psychology of the acquisition of self-concepts and of a modern approach to separating the traditional philosophical problem of personal identity from the question of what matters in survival. Toward the end of the nineteenth century, F. H. Bradley (1846–1924) returned to the consideration of the implications of fission examples for theories of personal identity. However, after Bradley, a serious discussion of fission would have to await the latter third of the twentieth century, when it would help revolutionize personal identity theory.

Around 1970, the discussion of fission examples, together with puzzles provoked by the high-visibility experimentation done on split brain patients, precipitated two major developments. One of these is that the intrinsic relations view of personal identity was superseded by the extrinsic relations (closest-continuer, externalist) view. According to the older intrinsic relations view, what determines whether a person at different times is identical is just how the two are physically and/or psychologically related to each other. According to extrinsic relations views, what determines it is not just how the two are physically and/or psychologically related to each other, but also how they are related to others. For instance, in the memory version of Locke's intrinsic relations view, you right now are the same person as someone who existed yesterday if you remember having experienced or having done things which that person of yesterday experienced or did. In an extrinsic relations version of Locke's memory view, one would have to take into account not only whether you remember having experienced or having done things which that person of yesterday experienced or did, but also whether, besides you, anyone else remembers having experienced or having done them.

In the 1970s, fission examples also provided grist for a second major development in personal identity theory. Philosophers began again to question whether something other than personal identity might be what matters primarily in survival. That is, they faced the possibility that people might cease and be continued by others whose existences they would value as much as their own and in pretty much the same ways as they would value their own. Derek Parfit, perhaps the leading analytic personal identity theorist of the twentieth century, has a neo-Lockean view of personal identity and what matters in survival, according to which what binds the different stages of us into the individual people that we are is not just memory but psychological relations generally (including beliefs, intentions, character traits, anticipations, and so on). And, unlike in Locke's view, but similar to Collins's, Parfit holds that it is not necessary for each stage of us to be directly related to every other stage, as long as each is indirectly related through intermediate stages. Parfit also claims that it ought to matter less to us whether our identical self persists into the future than that our psychological continuity is maintained in what might be a non-identical continuer.

SELF AS FICTION AND THE ORIGINS
OF SOCIAL PSYCHOLOGY

In ancient Western philosophy, the question of whether the self is a fiction did not arise. Locke's view pushed it to the fore. Subsequently, while the notion of soul continued to have a life in religious thought and in ethical theory, for scientific purposes it was all but dead. It was replaced by the notion of a unified self. However, there was a major difference in the history of these two notions. When the notion of the soul was introduced as a scientifically useful notion, it was posited as a real thing. There was never any suggestion that it might merely be a useful fiction. Not so in the case of the notion of self/person. In the second edition of Locke's *Essay*, this notion plays a theoretically prominent role in his relational account of personal identity alongside the suggestion that it is 'a forensic term', which suggested to some readers, but may not have been Locke's intention, that selves and persons are not real entities but only useful fictions.

Subsequently David Hume (1711–76) argued, in *A Treatise of Human Nature*, that the idea of a substantial, persisting self is an illusion. In his view, since all ideas arise from impressions and there is no impression of a 'simple and continu'd' self, there is no idea of such a self. He formulated his alternative 'bundle' conception of the self and compared the mind to a theater in which none of the actors—the 'perceptions [that] successively make their appearance'—are either 'simple' at a time or, strictly speaking, identical over time. Beyond this succession of perceptions, Hume claimed, humans do not even have minds, except as fictional constructions. Thus, in his view, there is no site for the mental performance, at least none of which we have knowledge; rather, there 'are the successive perceptions only, that constitute the mind; nor have we the most distant notion of the place, where these scenes are represented, or of the materials, of which it is compos'd.' (Hume 1739/1888: 253).

Hume then turned to the tasks of explaining why people are so susceptible to the illusion of self and to explaining how certain dynamic mentalistic systems in which we represent ourselves to ourselves, as well as to others, actually work. When Hume moved on to these largely psychological concerns he became deeply involved in what today we would call social psychology of the self. He, thus, completed a transition from skeptical philosophy to the most general sorts of associational issues, and then to specific psychological hypotheses about how self-representations function in our mental economy, as for instance in his explanation of how sympathy works. He thereby shifted the emphasis from conceptually analyzing the notion of personal identity to empirically accounting, first, for how it arises and, second, for its functional role.

In the case of many, if not most, eighteenth-century thinkers, it is difficult to tell whether they are employing the notion of the self merely pragmatically, as a useful fiction, or as a realistically understood scientific postulate. Hume often seems to have had a foot in both camps. By the end of the nineteenth century, in the case of some thinkers, it was no longer difficult to tell. Friedrich Nietzsche (1844–1900), for instance, having publicly proclaimed 'God is dead', privately noted the perhaps deeper truth that the self also is dead. 'The concept of substance', he wrote, 'is a consequence of the concept of the subject: not the reverse! If we relinquish the soul, "the subject," the precondition for "substance" in general disappears. One acquires degrees of being, one loses that which has being.' The subject, he said, is but a 'term for our belief in a unity underlying all the different impulses of the highest feeling of reality'. But, he claimed, there is no such unity, only 'the fiction that many similar states in us are the effect of one substratum: but it is we who first created the "similarity" of these states; our adjusting them and making them similar is the fact, not their similarity, which ought rather to be denied' (Nietzsche 1901/1968: 268–9). There is neither subject nor object, he concluded. Both are fictions.

Nietzsche claimed that, rather than unity of consciousness, we have 'only a semblance of Unity'. To explain this semblance, rather than a single subject, we could do as well by postulating 'a multiplicity of subjects, whose interaction and struggle is the basis of our thought and our consciousness in general'. We have no reason to believe that there is a dominant subject overseeing this multiplicity. Philosophers have bought into the fiction of self, he continued, by supposing that if there is thinking, there must be something that thinks. But the thought that 'when there is thought there has to be something "that thinks" is simply a formulation of our grammatical custom that adds a doer to every deed'. Intellectual culture, he wrote, has made several 'tremendous blunders', including an 'absurd overestimation of consciousness' in which it has been transformed 'into a unity, an entity: "spirit," "soul," something that feels, thinks, wills'. We have been victimized by our language, he concluded, by 'our bad habit' of taking a mnemonic, an abbreviative formula, to be not only an entity, but also a cause, as when we say of lightning that 'it flashes' (Nietzsche 1901/1968: 270, 268, 285–6, 294).

THE DEVELOPMENTAL AND SOCIAL ORIGIN OF SELF-CONCEPTS

As commonsensical as the idea of a developmental account of the acquisition of self-concepts may seem to us today, that idea did not begin to emerge until the middle of the eighteenth century. David Hartley (1705–57), one of the first to turn in this direction, had a developmental, associational account of the mind, but focused on the development of the passions and did not consider the acquisition of self-concepts. Thomas Reid (1710–96), late in the century, had a developmental psychology, but because of his commitment to the immateriality of the soul and to the reflexive nature of consciousness (if I am aware, then necessarily I am aware that I am aware), he may actually have made an exception in the case of the idea of self. Priestley, largely under the influence of Hartley, did think that a developmental account could be extended to the acquisition of self-concepts, but he did not elaborate.

Toward the beginning of the nineteenth century, Hazlitt distinguished three developmental stages in the acquisition of self-concepts: first, young children acquire an idea of themselves as beings who are capable of experiencing pleasure and pain; second, and almost 'mechanically' (since physiology insures that children remember only their own pasts), children include their own pasts in their notions of themselves; finally, they include what they imagine to be their own futures. Hazlitt then raised the question of how a child's formation of self-concepts is related to its development of empathy and sympathy. No one previously had asked this question. With the exception of Hazlitt, no British thinker until Alexander Bain (1811–77), late in the century, considered either how self-concepts are actually acquired or the impact of social context on their acquisition. German and French theorists did somewhat better on these issues.

In Germany, Johann Friedrich Herbart (1776–1841) wrote several works that were primarily psychological, in which he claimed that initially the idea of self comes from humans' experience of their bodily activities, which provides them with information about themselves as well as objects in the world with which they interact. Subsequently, as they more thoughtfully relate past to present thoughts, they come to identify more with their ideas than with their bodies. Thereby, they develop a notion of an ego or subject of their thoughts, which they then generalize as an abstract ego, or identical subject of experience, that persists throughout their lives.

In France, Maine de Biran (1766–1824) described the human self as developing through a purely sensitive, animal phase, to a phase of will and freedom which finally culminates in spiritual experiences that transcend humanity. As a developmental psychologist, he was concerned especially with the active or voluntary self, which infants first notice in experiencing the resistance of the world to their desires. He claimed that the continuity of voluntary agency provides children with a basis for their concept of themselves as extended over time.

Somewhat later, in America, James Mark Baldwin (1861–1934) said that soul theorists seemed to have assumed that 'the man is father of the child', that is, that 'if the adult consciousness shows the presence of principles not observable in the child consciousness, we must suppose, nevertheless, that they are really present in the child consciousness beyond the reach of our observation'. The proper procedure ('the genetic idea'), Baldwin claimed, is precisely the opposite of this (1894: 2–4).

In Baldwin's view, rather than first becoming aware of themselves as persons, children become aware of others. Later, by becoming aware of their trying to imitate others, they become aware of their own 'subjective' activity. Next, they come to understand what others feel by 'ejecting' their own inner states onto others: 'The subjective becomes ejective; that is, other people's bodies, says the child to himself, have experiences in them such as mine has. They also have me's.' In this last phase, Baldwin concludes, 'the social self is born' (1897: 8). Yet, while Baldwin's developmental account in bringing in the social succeeded in relating self to other, it under-emphasized the role of recognition by the other in self-consciousness.

Georg W. F. Hegel (1770–1831), in his *Phenomenology of the Spirit* (1807), had earlier famously claimed that self-consciousness arises in an individual not through an act of introspection and not in isolation from others, but by means of a dynamic process of reciprocal relationships in which each recognizes the other as a self-conscious being, becomes aware of that recognition of himself in the other, and ultimately becomes dependent on the other for his self-consciousness. The notion that self-consciousness arises from our reaction to recognition by others played an important role in the twentieth century both in the existential phenomenology of Jean-Paul Sartre (1905–80) as well as in the social-developmental psychology of George Herbert Mead (1863–1931), and through them on many subsequent theorists both in philosophy and psychology. In Sartre's account, for instance, there is a pre-reflective self-consciousness that precedes objective self-awareness—an idea going back to Fichte (1762–1814)—but a more developed self-consciousness requires the 'gaze' of the other, so is essentially a social product.

A Self for Science, Religion, Morality, and Politics

Immanuel Kant (1724–1804), in his *Critique of Pure Reason* (1781), focused on an understanding of the operations of the mind, particularly with respect to the limits of human knowledge. He there posited a distinction between the noumenal and phenomenal world, which was not only the key to his project of making a secure place both for knowledge and for faith, but provided him with a theoretical framework for understanding the self.

On one interpretation of Kant's view, there are two selves, one phenomenal and one noumenal. The phenomenal self is extended temporally and perhaps also spatially and is capable of being experienced both subjectively and objectively. The noumenal self lacks spatial and temporal extension and is not capable of being experienced. On another interpretation, there is only one self which is capable of being considered either noumenally or phenomenally. On either of these interpretations, the task of accounting for the phenomenal self is no different in principle from that of accounting for any other object or event that exists in space and time, such as planets or atoms. Thus, the phenomenal self is part of the subject matter of what today we would call the science of psychology. The noumenal self, on the other hand, cannot be known. Even so, Kant held that it affects the way the phenomenal self is structured in experience.

Personal identity over time concerns only the phenomenal self. Locke thought that personal identity could be known empirically if it consists in sameness of consciousness. Kant disagreed. He thought that in principle the consciousnesses of two people could be qualitatively identical. Delusions of memory, which Locke acknowledged may occur, are an obvious case in point. Kant concluded that if personal identity is to be known, rather than its consisting solely in sameness of consciousness, it must consist, at least in part, in some sort of physical continuity.

In Kant's view, there can be no experience which is not the experience of a subject. This can sound like the view that thought requires a thinker, which is more or less the move that Descartes made in attempting to prove the existence of a substantial self. The difference, however, is that by *thinker* Kant doesn't mean substantial self, but something more intimately connected with experience. He tried to explain what this 'something' is by saying that 'in the synthetic original unity of apperception, I am conscious of myself, not as I appear to myself, nor as I am in myself, but only that I am. This representation is a thought, not an intuition' (Kant 1781/1965: 168). Hence, accompanying every experience is the conscious thought, 'I think', which is the logical subject of the experience. What Kant meant by these dark remarks is a matter of scholarly dispute.

There is another side to Kant's thoughts about the self, which has to do with the self as a source of autonomous agency and meaning. This other side appears in Kant's practical and moral philosophy, where he celebrated what all rational beings have in common, in the process giving birth to a dominant strain in modern liberalism according to which the principle of equal respect requires that people be treated equally, in a way that is blind to their differences. In the latter half of the twentieth century, this sort of one-size-fits-all approach to the self became contentious. A number of theorists, convinced that an oppressive dominant majority has ignored, overlooked, and repressed what is distinctive about the marginalized groups with which they identified, turned their attention to what differentiates people from each other. Various groups—women, gays, lesbians, ethnic minorities, and others—articulated their own accounts, each indexed to their particular marginalized group, of what it is to be a self and to have an identity.

The Quest for an Integrated
Theory of the Self

In the nineteenth century, philosophical views of the self and personal identity were dominated by the philosophies of Kant and Hegel. Concurrently there was a growing spirit of naturalized science, typified by Charles Darwin (1809–82), but independently including inquiry into the development of self-concepts, mental diseases such as dissociative disorders, and the physiology of the brain. The

American philosopher and psychologist William James (1842–1910) integrated this naturalizing impulse into psychology by proposing a scientific philosophy of the self.

James's general empirical approach, in his *Principles of Psychology* (1890), is primarily a 'study of the mind from within'. Hence, in his account of self the experience of self is primary. He describes the properties of consciousness from a first-person point of view, arguing that each of us is, or has, a 'personal conscious-ness' and that we experience only the content that occurs within it. We have no first-person experience of the content of any other personal consciousness: 'My thought belongs with my other thoughts, and your thought with your other thoughts' (James 1890: i. 224–5).

However, after claiming that no psychology that hopes to stand can question the existence of a 'personal self', James immediately conceded that in cases of dissocia-tion an individual human could have more than one personal self. Moreover, he continued, each personal self may be regarded both as an object and as a subject (a *me* and an *I*). The self as object may be further divided into the *material self*, the *social self*, and the *spiritual self*, each of which can be still further divided. For instance, James said that 'a man has as many social selves' as there are individuals and groups 'who recognize him and carry an image of him in their mind'. He further said that a person's spiritual self may be regarded as a set of 'psychic dispositions', including the abilities to argue and discriminate and to have 'moral sensibility', 'conscience', and an 'indomitable will'. Alternatively, he elaborated, one's spiritual self can be seen as 'the entire stream of our personal consciousness', or more narrowly as the 'present "segment" or "section" of that stream'. When James speaks of the *I*, he further parceled the stream into thoughts, adding that the *I*, a thought, is at each moment a different thought 'from that of the last moment, but appropriative of the latter, together with all that the latter called its own' (James 1890: i. 294, 296, 401).

On James's account it is the passing mental state, 'the real, present onlooking, remembering, "judging thought" or identifying "section" of the stream', that is the active agent in unifying past and present selves. It is the thought that takes note of past thoughts as having the same feeling of warmth as the present feeling and thereby unifies them through a process of ownership that he calls appropriation. The subjective phenomena of consciousness do not need any reference to 'any more simple or substantial agent than the present Thought or "section" of the stream'. The immaterial soul, he said, 'explains nothing'. According to James, the core of personhood is 'the incessant presence of two elements, an objective person, known by a passing subjective Thought and recognized as continuing in time' (James 1890: i. 338, 344, 346, 371).

James resolved to use the word *me* for 'the empirical person' and *I* for 'the judging Thought'. Since the 'me' is constantly changing: 'the identity found by the I in its me is only a loosely construed thing, an identity "on the whole," just like that which any outside observer might find in the same assemblage of facts'. But while the 'me' is 'an empirical aggregate of things objectively known', the 'I' which 'knows them cannot itself be an aggregate'. Rather, 'it is a Thought, at each moment different from that of the last moment, but appropriative of the latter, together with all that the latter called its own' (James 1890: i. 373, 400–1). In other words, what one calls 'the I' is constantly changing and the I as a persisting thing is relegated to fiction. In James's view, one doesn't have to settle metaphysical or ontological questions in order to give a scientific account of the self. Getting clear about the empirical relations between one's experience, one's brain, and one's social relations is enough. A generalized version of this idea resonates strongly with some philosophers in our own times (see, for instance, van Fraassen 2002).

The Stream Divides

From the beginning of the twentieth century (after James) until the 1960s, no important philosopher of the self took the view that philosophy properly done is continuous with empirical science. That idea, which among analytic philosophers is so widespread today, owes its popularity to the ascendancy of analytic pragmatism. So, one way of thinking about the philosophy of the self in the twentieth century is that during the first half of the century it labored to separate itself from science and in the last half to reintegrate itself with science. The relevant sciences were biology, psychology, and sociology. In addition, in both analytic philosophy and phenomenology, but earlier in phenomenology, the idea caught on that immediate experience is suspect. Rather than a basis on which a view of the world, but particularly of the relations between self and other, could be securely constructed, it became commonplace to suppose that immediate experience must be understood as a product of social and historical influences and, hence, may need to be cleansed of misleading accretions.

In the phenomenological tradition, the influence of Hegel and Marx, together with the demise of foundationalism in epistemology, gave rise to a greatly heightened interest in social conceptions of the self. Max Scheler (1874–1928) began to examine social attitudes, such as empathy and sympathy. Martin Heidegger (1889–1976) and later Jean-Paul Sartre stressed that the idea of an individual isolated from social and worldly involvements is an abstraction. And, in the analytic tradition, ordinary language philosophy, inspired by 'the later Wittgenstein' (1889–1951), stressed such themes as the impossibility of a 'private language' and the epistemological significance of collectively shared 'forms of life'. While all of this was going on, psychology, for its part, became a discipline of its own, the main focus of which was provided by experimentalists—in the early part of the century, introspectionists, and then later, from the 1920s until after the Second World War, behaviorists. Neither group of experimental psychologists had much to say about the self and nothing to say about it of lasting importance. That job was left to empirical theorists from three different traditions: depth psychology, humanistic psychology, and social and developmental psychology.

Born in the nineteenth century, depth psychology grew to maturity in the work of Sigmund Freud (1856–1939), who proposed a radically new way of understanding human psychological development and of treating mental abnormality. Freud's view included new understandings of the unconscious, of infantile sexuality, and of repression. Previously, most theorists had understood the self in terms of consciousness, including rationality, free will, and self-reflection. A few, like Nietzsche, had claimed that there is an irrational, unconscious part of the mind that dominates the rational. But Freud had a much more elaborate theory of how this happens, for which he claimed support from psychotherapeutic and historical case studies, as well as from his analyses of dreams and mental slips.

In the 1930s, what came to be called existential psychology tended to look for inspiration not to depth psychologists, but to phenomenologists, especially to Heidegger. What these two approaches had in common was the goal of discovering deeper recesses of the self hidden below the surface of normal experience. In the case of Freud and other depth psychologists, this search led to the exploration of unconscious motives, rooted in the past and in human biology, that determined present behavior. In the case of existential and humanistic psychologists, the focus was not on uncovering historical and biological determinants of behavior, but on realizing in the present one's most developed and authentic self. These approaches, together with most of the phenomenology which preceded them, tended to share two underlying assumptions—that there is a real self beneath the surface of expressed personality, and that knowing who one is requires uncovering this real self.

THE SELF IN FRAGMENTS

In the modern history of theories of the self, the Second World War is a watershed. Prior to the war, the seeds of dissolution of the self had been sown and had even begun to sprout. Yet, while some approaches demoted the self, none dismantled it. Across disciplines, the self had fragmented. Within disciplines, it was still intact. As a consequence, by mid-century the self may have been challenged, but it was not dethroned. That task was left to the second half of the century.

After the war many theorists began to think of the self more as a product of culture than as its creator. The last half of the century witnessed rampant unintegrated scientific specialization, the withering philosophical critiques of deconstruction and postmodernism, the penetrating attack in analytic philosophy on the very concept and importance of personal identity, and newfound perspectives spawned by feminism, post-colonialism, gender/sexual/ethnic awareness, and by technological development. As a consequence, the self, which began the century looking unified—the master of its own house—ended it looking fragmented—a byproduct of social and psychological conditions.

Currently, in the science of psychology, when the notion of self shows up, it tends to be in one of its many hyphenated roles, such as self-image, self-conception, self-discovery, self-confidence, self-esteem, self-knowledge, self-acceptance, self-reference, self-modeling, self-consciousness, self-interest, self-control, self-denial, self-deception, self-narrative, and self-actualization. To some extent, the notion of identity has suffered a similar fate, as notions of racial identity, ethnic identity, sexual identity, gender identity, social identity, political identity, and so on have come even in scientific contexts to take prominence over the notion of personal identity.

The ontological status of these various hyphenated notions of self and identity is often unspecified. Psychologists rarely explain whether the self-notions they employ are supposed to be interpreted realistically or as explanatory fictions, such as the notion of a center of gravity. Moreover, even as theories that employ hyphenated self-notions in an individually manageable way have proliferated, there has been no concerted attempt to unify self-theories with one another. And the proliferation of competing, or at least well insulated, accounts of the self is not confined to the science of psychology. By the end of the century, virtually every discipline that took cognizance of human nature, including biology, sociology, anthropology, political science, and even neuroscience joined the fray. Their accounts, while making enormous progress with respect to limited questions about the self, increasingly separated the questions to be asked and the kinds of answers that could count as reasonable to each question. The result has been runaway fragmentation.

So, where does that leave us? The notion of a unified self was introduced into scientific theory in the seventeenth century, particularly in the theories of Descartes and Locke, as a replacement for the notion of soul, which had fallen on hard times. But eventually the notion of a unified self fell onto hard times of its own. Its demise was gradual, but by the end of the twentieth century the unified self had died the death if not of a thousand qualifications, then of a thousand hyphenations.

Of course, researchers working in different traditions or on different aspects of the self have continued to share a common focus of inquiry in that they all study the behavior of the human organism. But, lacking a refined understanding of how the human organism unifies hyphenated self-behaviors and self-phenomena, researchers lost touch with anything that deserves to be called a unified self.

Surprisingly, it has not seemed to matter. In order to get on with their research, psychologists have found little need to relate hyphenated self-behaviors and self-phenomena to a unified self, as James had tried so heroically to do. The same seems to be true of researchers in other traditions, such as neuroscience. As a result, the unified self, if indeed there ever was such a thing, has receded from view. Those who seek it today in both the philosophical and scientific literatures soon discover that none but the carefully initiated can wade into the waters of theoretical accounts of the self without soon drowning in a sea of symbols, technical distinctions, and empirical results, the end result of which is that the notion of the unified self has faded from view.

So ended the twentieth century. Prior to the Second World War, the self seemed to be a unified subject of investigation. Theorists did not agree on what to say about it, but they seemed to agree that it was something about which they had something to say. When they talked about the self, it was as if they agreed that in talking about it they were talking about the same thing, and about just one thing. By the end of the century, there was no such presupposition. What once had seemed so unified, now lay in fragments.

Prospects for Theoretical Integration

In an article published in 1999, Eric Olson surveyed a variety of definitions of the self only to conclude that they and the ideas involved in them are so different from and unrelated to each other that there is no hope of developing an adequate single definition of self to answer the variety of issues involved in the use of the term. He proposed that 'self' as a term should be dropped from our vocabulary and that particular questions that once involved that term should go their separate ways.

Olson, in his later book *What are we?* (2007), divides his title question, which he takes to be metaphysical, into a number of 'smaller questions': 'What are we made of?'; 'What parts have we?'; 'Are we abstract or concrete?'; 'Do we persist through time?'; 'Which of our properties are essential to us and which are accidental?' (Olson 2007: 3–6). He suggests that the best answers to these questions lead us in different directions and that no single account of what we are is likely to give the best answer to all of them.

However, even with all the questions and answers considered in his book, Olson leaves aside other important questions about the self. For instance, he explicitly puts aside the question of 'what we take ourselves to be' (2007: 14). Because we might be quite wrong in our self-conceptions he views this as a question of 'anthropology', not metaphysics. He's right, of course, that it is not a metaphysical or ontological question, but, even so, for other theories of self, whether in anthropology or not, as well as for humanistic self-understanding in which the main goal is not so much to understand the self, but ourselves, this question is a major concern. Even if our self-conceptions are wrong, if they are persistent and ubiquitous, they are an important part of who we are, and hence part of what needs to be understood in order to understand ourselves.

Olson's project and that of providing an integrated account of what we are that is not just an account of what the words *we* and *I* refer to are not in competition with each other. Both can be pursued. As we have seen, before theories of the self began to fragment at the beginning of the twentieth century, William James worked heroically to put together an integrated account of the self. In light of specialized progress in different approaches to self made since James's time, we can see that there are problems with his account. Is there any prospect for an integrated theory that avoids these problems?

It seems to us that an integrated theory of the self, were one feasible, would have to consider three major dimensions of selves, which we will call the *experiential* dimension, the *ontological* dimension, and the *social* dimension (see Martin and Barresi 2006: esp. chs. 12–14; Seigel 2005; Wiggins 1987). Each of these dimensions focuses on an aspect of self that can be viewed as independent of the others, but can also be seen to be interdependent. Each typically plays a central and sometimes singular role in theories of self, often in different disciplines.

The focus of the experiential dimension is on the first-person experience of self, not with regard to what we can infer about what sort of thing, other than experience, the self might be, but on what our experience of the self is actually like. For whatever else we are, within a common culture, and to a great extent even across cultures, people tend to experience themselves in certain characteristic ways, almost always ones that differ dramatically from the ways that non-human animals experience themselves. An integrated account of the self should take note of these characteristic ways in which humans experience themselves. What is important in such an account is not whether one acknowledges *metaphysically* the existence of experience, or even whether one concludes ultimately that the self itself is real or illusory, but whether one explains what human experiences of self are like and the role that they play in human lives.

The ontological dimension focuses not on experience but on what kind of thing or process the self is, if it exists at all. Descartes's answer was that we are a thinking, immaterial substance—the soul of Christian tradition. Subsequent theorists about mind often agreed with him that the self is a thinking thing, but they viewed the self or mind as a material substance, or as a function or process of a material substance. Currently, in our view, the human self is most appropriately thought of as something that is either an organism or constituted by an organism.

The third dimension is the social dimension. Individual humans relate socially to each other in unique ways unparalleled in any other species. How? And to what effect, so far as the humans and their conception of themselves are concerned? Included in this dimension will be the general role that social interaction beginning in infancy plays in self-awareness and in the developmental origins of self-concepts. But it also deals with narrative accounts of self-identity, social responsibilities, practical ethical principles, and ideals of the good life that we eventually form as adults. Ultimately, the social dimension is essential to our understanding of ourselves as selves and as persons and is the basis for the rich understanding of self that is unique to our species.

Most current theorists are materialists and think of the organism and its brain as the basis for all experience of self. For those who accept this view as their starting point, it is not necessary for the purpose of providing an integrated view of the self to determine whether the self should be analyzed ontologically in a neo-Lockean or materialist way, but rather how the experiential and social dimensions connect to the material basis of self in the organism.

This new question is not the traditional mind–body problem, but one that already presupposes an integration of the experiential and social in an embodied self. The self is taken here as a unified organic individual extended in time, and the question is more about how that individual experiences its selfhood, including identification of the brain and body mechanisms that produce these experiences, insofar as we can figure this out through cognitive science and neuroscience. It also includes how the first-person perspective of self develops in the individual's life history. Important, with respect to this latter issue, is the role that social existence and other individuals play in the development of self-consciousness.

In the hints toward a theoretical framework that we are proposing, the human organism should be acknowledged to be the primary source of unity for human selves. Under normal circumstances the life history of the biological individual gives the self not only an objectively verifiable unique identity that persists through time, but a site for a variety of processes involving the other two dimensions of self to occur. This cannot be said for the other two dimensions. Under normal conditions both the experiential and social dimensions of self depend on the existence of organic individuals as the basis for the self as defined by these other dimensions.

In addition, the issue of self-unity is less of a problem if the organic dimension is taken as primary than if the experiential or social dimensions are taken as primary. The issue of the identity of self over time is a problem regardless of which dimension is taken as primary. But the issue of identity over time can await the provision of an integrated theory of the self. An integrated theory does not presuppose an answer to the hypothetical puzzles that bedevil the question of self-identity over time. And an answer to those questions does not yield an integrated theory. So, the two projects can proceed apace, aware of developments in the other, but not dependent on the resolution of all puzzles in the other.

There may be better ways to define the dimensions of self that need to be brought together to form an integrated theory of self, and the dimensions that we have proposed might be reduced to eliminate the non-essential or expanded to be more inclusive. Our aim has merely been to show that there is nothing inevitable about the theoretical fragmentation of the notion of self. Admittedly theorizing in the last half of the twentieth century made it seem as if fragmentation were the only game in town. But it seems to us that integration is also an option.

Even so, it should be conceded that if one steps back and looks at Western theorizing about the self and personal identity as a whole and asks what it means that theory took the course that it did, from the earliest beginnings of theory in the West, what seems clear is that until the last half of the twentieth century most thinkers tried to elevate the self—the 'I'—to an exalted status. The soul was created importantly for this purpose, and when the soul ceased to be useful, the unified self was called in to fill the void. Seemingly very different notions, but essentially the same game: to show that the self—the I—is a demigod of sorts, reigning unopposed over its domain, the human person. From a selfish point of view, much of what matters most to humankind was linked to this demigod: one's essence, free will, consciousness, personal survival, the defeat of death. What the history of theory makes all too apparent is that there has been a persistent effort, from beginning to end, to make this case—to show that a unified self is a secure repository of many of humankind's most glorious conceits and aspirations. And what that history also shows is that, in the face of continuing scientific development, the case for many of these conceits and aspirations cannot be made.

In the seventeenth and eighteenth centuries, science undermined the soul. The self was recruited to take its place, including providing unity and direction to the human person, as well as being the vehicle for persistence both during life and after bodily death. In effect, science took the I, as soul, out of heaven and in the guise of a unified self brought it down to earth. Like the soul, the self was to be the source of unity, power, freedom, control, and persistence. But the fly in the ointment was analysis. So, soon enough what had been one—the I—became many. What had been real became fiction. And what had been a source of explanations became itself in need of explanation. Analysis has been the self's undoing. In sum, the story of Western theorizing about the self and personal identity is both the story of humankind's attempt to elevate itself above the rest of the natural world and the story of how that attempt has failed. It is another saga, as if another were needed, of how pride goeth before the fall.

As a fragmented, explained, and illusory phenomenon, the self can no longer regain its elevated status. Even so, the notion of self is too important for personal and social purposes to just go away. The question, it seems to us, is not how best to get along without it, but how best to think about it—that is, not how best to think about it *instead of* the ways theorists in various disciplines are thinking about it, but how best to *integrate* what is central in those ways.

REFERENCES

AUGUSTINE (1995). *City of God*, in Philip Schaff (ed.) and Marcus Dods (tr.), *Nicene and Post-Nicene Fathers*, ii, 1st ser. (Peabody, Mass.: Hendrickson).

BALDWIN, JAMES MARK (1894). *Mental Development in the Child and the Race* (New York: Macmillan).

——(1897). *Social and Ethical Interpretations* (New York: Macmillan).

HAZLITT, WILLIAM (1805/1969). *An Essay on the Principles of Human Action and some Remarks on the Systems of Hartley and Helvetius*. Reprint, intro. J. R. Nabholtz (Gainesville, Fla.: Scholars' Facsimiles & Reprints).

HUME, DAVID (1739/1888). *Treatise of Human Nature*, ed. L. A. Selby-Bigge (Oxford: Clarendon Press).

JAMES, WILLIAM (1890). *Principles of Psychology*, 2 vols. (New York: Henry Holt).

KANT, IMMANUEL (1781/1787/1965). *Critique of Pure Reason*, ed. and tr. Norman Kemp Smith (New York: St Martin's Press).

LOCKE, JOHN (1690–4/1979). *An Essay Concerning Human Understanding*, ed. Peter H. Nidditch (Oxford: Oxford University Press, paperback edn.).

LUCRETIUS (1951). *On the Nature of Things*, tr. R. E. Latham (Harmondsworth: Penguin).

MARTIN, RAYMOND, and BARRESI, JOHN (2000). *Naturalization of the Soul: Self and Personal Identity in the Eighteenth Century* (London: Routledge).

——(2006). *The Rise and Fall of Soul and Self: An Intellectual History of Personal Identity* (New York: Columbia University Press).

NIETZSCHE, FRIEDRICH (1901/1968). *The Will to Power*, tr. Walter Kaufmann (New York: Vintage).

OLSON, ERIC (1999). 'There is No Problem of the Self', in Shaun Gallagher and Jonathan Shear (eds), *Models of the Self* (Exeter: Imprint Academic), 49–61.

——(2007). *What are we? A Study in Personal Ontology* (New York: Oxford University Press).

PLOTINUS (1952). *Ennead*, in *Great Books of the Western World* (Chicago: Encyclopedia Britannica), xvii.

SEIGEL, JERROLD (2005). *The Idea of the Self: Thought and Experience in Western Europe since the Seventeenth Century* (Cambridge: Cambridge University Press).

SORABJI, RICHARD (2006). *Self: Ancient and Modern Insights about Individuality, Life, and Death* (Oxford: Oxford University Press).

TAYLOR, CHARLES (1989). *Sources of the Self: The Making of the Modern Identity* (Cambridge: Cambridge University Press).

VAN FRAASSEN, BAS C. (2002). *The Empirical Stance* (New Haven: Yale University Press).

WIGGINS, DAVID (1987). 'The Person as Object of Science, as Subject of Experience, and as Locus of Value', in Arthur Peacocke and Grant Gillett (eds), *Persons and Personality: A Contemporary Inquiry* (Oxford: Basil Blackwell), 56–74.

C H A P T E R 2

WHAT IS IT LIKE TO BE A NEWBORN?

PHILIPPE ROCHAT

IN this chapter, we are interested in what might constitute the first manifestation of consciousness in the life of an individual. The focus is on the subjective starting state of newborns: what it might be like to be newly born in *this* world and *that* body; and whether we can refer to any of this subjective experience as a 'self'.

In general, it is easier to determine when consciousness ends than when it begins. If we shy away from dualism or any form of metaphysical transcendence, consciousness can be said to end with the absence of bodily vital signs, to the extent that consciousness is necessarily embodied. In Sartre's existentialist jargon, with biological death, *the body turns into the in-itself of inanimate things.*

Even if we believe in some form of afterlife, the awareness of what it is like to be alive *now*, in *that* particular living body, necessarily has to vanish with that body. Experience is indeed rooted in the body, existing in a relation of mutual exclusivity with it, one defining the other, thus both passing at the same time. Even in a coma, still with vital signs, and even if assisted by a ventilator, no one can say for sure that consciousness is totally gone, hence the ongoing debate as to when it is ethically acceptable to terminate care, a profound philosophical dilemma. The debate will

Ideas contained in this chapter, in particular those regarding the minimal self and newborns' sense of sameness, are also discussed, in a different theoretical context and with a different spin, in contingent contributions by the author to other edited volumes: A. Fotopoulou, S. Pfaff, and M. A. Conway (eds), *From the Couch to the Lab: Psychoanalysis, Neuroscience and Cognitive Psychology in Dialogue* (Oxford University Press, in press), as well as in Philip D. Zelazo (ed.), *Oxford Handbook of Developmental Psychology* (Oxford University Press, in press).

continue despite progress in the neurosciences, brain imaging techniques, and the biological account of conscious states. We can only approximate whether explicit awareness is a prerequisite of consciousness or whether particular brain regions need to be active in order to be conscious. However, despite all these difficulties, when the body stops showing any vital signs, unaided or aided artificially, consciousness can be said to have necessarily ended. Death brings absolute resolution to the question.

In French, a funeral undertaker or mortician goes by the name of *croque-mort*, literally a 'dead-biter'. It is so because up to a couple of centuries ago, the *croque-mort* was the official individual in a community who determined whether the dying was still alive, forcefully biting his or her big toe on the deathbed. If the corpse remained inert, with no reaction, it could be legally buried. The acid test of physical death was thus measured by the absence of pain awareness and its obligatory reactive (behavioral) symptoms of excruciating pain (the biting of one's big toe is indeed very painful). The implicit rationale behind such cultural practice is that, with the death of our body, its decay, and the certainty of its physical dissipation, dies also our subjective 'embodied' experiential point of view of what it is like to be *Me* including the experience of *My* pain which depends on *that* body.

As a case in point, I do remember now dead persons that I have known, through the memory representations stored in my living body. I will probably be able to do so as long as it (my body) shows vital signs. The truth is that these persons cannot remember themselves because their consciousness or experience of what it is like vanished with their body some years ago. That is that.

In reverse, there are no decisive criteria as to when consciousness might begin in a living individual, newly born in particular. No absolute criteria exist regarding the beginning limits of *what it is like to be me*: is it already in the womb, at birth, or only when children start to utter personal pronouns? What qualifies living individuals (children or other animals) to possess self-awareness by having some minimal experience of what it is like to be?

In this chapter, I try to bring to bear some recent infancy research findings on the beginning limit question, once the child is born. My goal is to develop some approximation of what it might be like to be a newborn. I will present evidence demonstrating that we are born with some minimal self-awareness, a kind of awareness that might even be present in fetuses depending on what criteria we use. The focus is on what might be considered as the starting state consciousness of newborns (i.e. what it is like to be a newborn) and the mechanisms that might account for how self-awareness quickly evolves from being minimal and phenomenal in the context of sensation, perception, and action, to become within months explicit and conceptual *as well*.

I will first discuss what it might be like to be a newborn at a sensuous level: the level of feelings and emotion within the context of extreme dependence from the generous care of others (*general affective and survival context*). I will then turn to empirical evidence suggesting that newborns express a minimal self-awareness, in particular an awareness of their own body as unified and organized (*facts from infancy research*). Finally, I will present what I see as a major mental process underlying this awareness that I identify as the innate propensity of newborns to detect *sameness* in the experience of things that surround them, people in particular, but also to detect *sameness* in the subjective, embodied experience of being in the world as a feeler, perceiver, and an actor (i.e. self-experience). Based on empirical findings, I identify two putative mechanisms that would support an innate propensity to detect sameness: synesthesia and the vicariousness of experience.

1. GENERAL AFFECTIVE AND SURVIVAL CONTEXT OF THE NEWBORN

For centuries the question of the origins and development of subjectivity intrigued philosophers, moralists, educators, biologists, and more recently psychologists and neuroscientists: from St Augustine, Rabelais, Rousseau, Darwin, to Freud and Piaget. All speculated how the experience of being in the world comes into place and is shaped in the early days of psychic life, from the moment infants come out from the obligatory, in appearance lethargic and silent nine months' gestation in the womb. Over sixteen centuries ago, for example, in what is often considered the first self-narrative in the history of Western thought, St Augustine in his *Confessions* expresses the idea that the origins of what one knows about the self are primarily social. Self-knowledge would be learned from others, particularly women, because of the primal maternal bond:

I give thanks to you, lord of heaven and earth . . . For you have granted to man that he should come to self-knowledge through the knowledge of others, and that he should believe many things about himself on the authority of the womenfolk. Now, clearly, I had life and being; and, as my infancy closed, I was already learning signs by which my feelings could be communicated to others. (Augustine 2007: 1. 6. 10)

Primordial submission to the authority of maternal cares

St Augustine's intuition that we first learn about ourselves through contact with 'the womenfolk' reflects a basic fact to which any speculation on early subjective experience should indeed refer: that infants rely on others to live and survive. Necessary submission to the cares of others, the mother in particular, is the point of psychic origin. If neonates do their share to survive—breathing, eating, as well as orienting, approaching, and avoiding—they are nonetheless born is a profound state of helplessness and dependence. This is the bottom line, particularly pronounced in the human infant who is 'born too soon' after nine months of relatively slow gestation (Rochat 2001).

The human birth creates a unique ecology of behavioral growth compared to other animal species, an ecology of protracted 'extero-gestation', hence a particularly long and marked dependence due to immaturity (Montagu 1961; Bruner 1972). It is an ecology that has been constrained, among other contingent and cascading factors, by the evolution of bi-pedal locomotion. After nine months in the womb, the head circumference of the normally developing fetus becomes dangerously large for the mother and for itself.

Disproportionately big compared to other primate species, it also reaches a growth limit in relation to the birth canal of humans that evolved to be narrower with changes in pelvic bone configuration, reflecting itself the bi-pedal locomotion evolved by the *Homo* genus (Montagu 1961; Gould 1977; Trevarthan 1987).

Human protracted extero-gestation creates a unique case of altriciality in the animal kingdom, an unusual need for care from others and an exacerbated dependence on others to survive beyond the third year (when most children of all cultures today expand the circle of close care takers to socialize on their own with peers in the more formal circle of school).

This state of protracted dependence is the specific context in which human consciousness and the human psyche take roots in their development. That is the original bath that we need to consider if we want to figure what it is like to be a newborn: it is first and foremost the experience of relying on generous caregivers, themselves conscious and reflective, willing to give freely and abundantly attention and care. It defines human experience at the outset. Attachment and dependence are evident in other animals. However, what is unique in comparison to any other mammalian species is that human dependence is (1) protracted, and (2) engages explicitly conscious (as opposed to just minimally conscious) others that have beliefs and communicate 'symbolically' with one another.

In this primary context, how might it feel to be a newborn? What kind of sensuous experience might arise in such a great state of immaturity and dependence?

In *The Family Idiot*, his biography of nineteenth-century writer Gustave Flaubert, Sartre (1971/1981) speculates at length and in remarkable depth on this question. In the first part of this long essay ('the constitution'), Sartre describes at length the initial experiential state of total abandon to the cares of others. Sartre speculates that it is in this early submission to specific maternal gestures, attitudes, and attention that one can find the roots of Flaubert's apparent passivity as a child and subjective disconnection as an adult, possibly also the source of his genius as inventor of the modern novel: 'Gustave as a child is not *made* to act; what he feels is dizzying submission to this constitutive nature experienced within him as the product of *others*' (Sartre 1971/1981: 48; my translation from French). Sartre goes on a few pages later:

The newborn, molded everyday by dispensed cares, internalizes the maternal activity of his own passive 'being there', in other words the infant internalizes the maternal care activity as the passivity that conditions all the pulsions, and all the internal rhythms of desires, speeds, accumulated storms, schemas that reveal at the same time organic constancies and unspeakable wishes—in brief that his own mother, buried deep into that body, becomes the *pathetic* structure of affectivity. (Ibid. 58)

Sartre insists on the inescapable determinant of the mother as a whole person that determines the affective core experience of cared newborns. Maternal constitution, relative sensitivity, and life story are inescapably reflected in the kind of care, attention, and gestures mothers are able to dispense to their infant. Indeed, in the experiential life of newborns that revolves primarily in the passive reception of cares molded by others, there is more than the serving of basic survival needs such as food, warmth, and hygiene. There is also, as Sartre points out, the transmission of unique transgenerational idiosyncrasies or family truth:

when the mother breastfeeds or cleans her infant, she expresses herself, like anybody else, in her personal truth, which, naturally, sums up in it all her life, from her own birth; in the meantime, she realizes a rapport that changes depending on circumstances and people—for which she is the *subject* and that we can call maternal love. . . . But, at the same time, by this love and through it, by that person, skillful or unskillful, rough or tender, the way her history made her, the child is manifested to himself. (Ibid. 57)

In summary, from Sartre the philosopher, at the end of his life, wearing the hat of psychoanalysis that for years he tended to dismiss, these reflections suggest that experiential awareness of what it might be like to be a newborn is highly dependent on the subjective experience of others. It would be, in large part, socially determined and intersubjective to start with, in the context of dispensed cares. In other words, it would depend primarily on the interaction of a mother–infant experiential point of view, from which each partner would extract their own mutually defining meanings, not unlike the dialectic of master and slave: the newborn would extract a sense of imposed passivity and submission, the mother would extract a sense of duty and fulfillment in the instinctive call for maternal love and protection.

But aside from this basic *rapport* of force that is clearly expressed at birth, certainly contributing in the determination of crucial aspects of what it might be like to be a newborn, couldn't neonates experience themselves as more than passive recipients, once they are fed and clean, alert and content, laying alone in their crib and looking around, as they all do at some point? Or what is it like to be newborn during the period that precedes care, when the infant screams his lungs out in apparent pain, discomfort, or hunger? What are those feeling experiences made of?

Early private experience

Until a few years ago, the Zeitgeist was to deny infants any form of worthwhile phenomenal awareness. This was not just an intellectual innuendo. In the 1940s and 1950s, surgery without anesthesia was routinely performed on infants and young children. Modern surgeons conveniently paralyzed squirming infants by injection of Curare or similar paralytic agents. Under such circumstances, adults recalled excruciating pain during surgery, but patients were not believed and the practice went on for twenty years. As pointed out by Dennett (1981: 201): 'The fact that most of the patients were infants and small children may explain this credibility gap.'

Less dramatic, but still revealing of the mainstream outlook on early affective life, until a few years ago (and probably still today at some hospitals) local anesthetics were not automatically applied prior to routine painful procedures on newborns such as heel prick and circumcision, even by pediatricians practicing in state of the art maternity hospitals.

Despite the fact that from birth infants cry when hungry or smile after a good feed, historically there has been a formidable resistance to attribute the rich affective and mindful life that we now know infants do have from birth, and even prior to birth during the last four weeks of gestation (see Rochat 2001 for a review of empirical evidence accumulated in the past thirty years).

Based on empirical facts from the past forty years in the booming field of infancy research, we have now more empirical ammunition to speculate about what it might be like to encounter the world by seeing, feeling, or hearing at the origins of life. Not only do we better understand the experience of newborns from the perspective of psychophysics (what range of stimulus thresholds they detect across the various sense modalities), but also what attracts them in their exploration of objects in the environment, and what information they appear to pick up, store, and eventually retrieve, as newborns, but also as fetuses during the last two trimesters of gestation. We know that newborns see colors, use dynamic information, preferring things that move, rather than things that are static. We also know that infants are innately attracted to particular configurations like moving faces, regions of high contrast on a visual display, high-pitch sounds, and human voices with particular contours ('mothereese'). We know that they crave sugar and why, why they appear to innately savor sweet tastes, show repulsion and strong rejection of bitter tastes.

Topping all of these well-established empirical facts, there is now a vast amount of habituation and other operant conditioning studies with newborns showing that infants from birth are fully attuned to novel as opposed to familiar experiences. Striking, and arguably among the major discoveries in developmental psychology over the past thirty years, is the fact that most of what is demonstrated in newborns is also shown in healthy fetuses during the last trimester of gestation: they habituate, learn, store experiential information, demonstrate comparable thresholds across sensory modalities. Furthermore, what they learn in the womb is readily transferable *ex utero*. Facts show that few-hour-old newborns prefer to suck in certain ways on a pacifier, to hear the voice of their mother over the voice of a female stranger (DeCasper and Fifer 1980). They orient significantly more, showing preference in smelling a gauze impregnated with the mother's amniotic fluid over the fluid of a stranger that just gave birth (Marlier *et al.* 1998*a*, 1998*b*).

What can be safely inferred from these now well recognized and numerous facts is that not only are newborns sophisticated learners, perceivers, and even knowers but also that they have from the start a very rich affective and emotional life. We are not born affectively 'neutral' but on the contrary alive with forces pushing and pulling us around: born with strong desires and untamed affective needs, as Freud speculated in a highly controversial book over a century ago (Freud 1905). This rich and untamed affective life cannot, however, be reduced to an early sensory experience that would be undifferentiated and disorganized. What newborns experience of the world is not a blob of chaotic multimodal sensations that would be the source of an initial 'a blooming, buzzing, confusion', confusion taken to mean 'chaos' and not the literal sense of con-fusion or *fusion with* that suggests some harmony of experience (see a suggestion of a different meaning of William James's famous claim in section 3 of this chapter).

We now know that newborn experience is anything but chaos. Neonates are quick to learn, they attend and respond to specific physical events felt in and out of the body, manifest emotions (in the literal sense of 'moving out' feelings via screams and other clearly readable 'basic' facial expressions that are innate). In all, this experience is not an affectively neutral experience that would be mainly attached to the functioning of automatic reflexes. This is not the case since learning is involved from the start, infants acting rather than responding in a world that has values: comfort, pain, relief, and an intense orientation toward particular affective states linked to satiety, specific odors and tastes, dim lights, contrasted visual contours or high-pitch speech sounds. This experience rests on an embodied semantics of approach and avoidance, dangers and strong attractors or pulls.

Because of learning, newborns' experience is not repetitive but rather cumulative: a present experience is influenced by what happened prior. It can be therefore assumed that if successive experiences might be homologous, they are never absolutely the same. This inference simply means that newborn experience does not rest on the feelings that might accompany automatic reflexes, as for example the feeling of something hitting my knee and the proprioceptive sensation of my knee automatically jerking forward. Such machine-like experience does exist in newborns, in the same way it persists in adults with the feeling experience that accompanies non-volitional responses like a knee jerk or the obligatory chill one feels running down the spine while stepping on what was thought to be a piece of dead wood, but in fact is a snake.

However, what it is like to be a neonate cannot be reduced to the sensations that arise from such responses. Infants at birth are more than reflex machines: from the outset they desire. They are fast to learn, showing unmistakable orientation toward specific and meaningful experiences: food, comfort, and an optimum level of stimulation (e.g. not too loud, not too bright, but with a lot of contrast and movement).

Daniel Stern (1991), in an unusual book entitled *Diary of a Baby: What your Child Sees, Feels, and Experiences*, took on the task of imagining what it is like to be a young child from six weeks to four years of age. Stern writes from the perspective of the child and reconstructs what it must feel like to be hungry, to wake up, or to stare at a moving spot of light. Stern infers the world of sensations of a fictive newborn (named Joey), based on what we now know about perception, learning, and affect regulation in infancy. The world of Joey at six weeks is for Stern a world of sensations. Although this world is nameless and non-objectified, not yet explicit or conceptualized, it is a world rich in motion and moving impressions, where pieces of space are contrasted, detached, move, meet, overlap, vanish. It is a world made of rhythms and changes of pace in which the infant detects forces expressed in movements: acceleration, deceleration, shrinking and looming of forms and shapes that are more or less capturing the attention of the child like magnets of various forces that wax and wane. The world that Stern describes has phenomenal 'qualities'. It is experienced from a particular embodied point of view, the first-person perspective that Stern tries to capture. It is a world of sensations, but a world with a point of experiential origin that is the body, the referential point in space where sensations arise while the infant experiences being awake and alive in the world via multiple sensory channels that are *all open at the same time*, either actively when the infant is on his own, or more passively while cared for and manipulated by others (see Sartre above). This in-unison working of the senses does not however entail chaos, but rather a pull toward a primitive harmonious order (of phenomenal awareness) that will become eventually objectified, brought to explicit cognitive coherence and scrutiny (consciousness proper), a phenomenal consciousness that has, in addition, cognitive accessibility (see the recent discussion and distinction proposed by Block 2007).

Stern's assumption, in his speculation, is that the world of sensations of the newborn is not just undifferentiated or diffuse. It is a world of experiences with distinct qualities and values that are anchored in the body, lived from within and therefore carrying with them a subjective perspective.

We will see next that such speculation regarding what it must be like to be a newborn finds support in numerous research studies pointing to a minimal *self-awareness* at birth, therefore evidence that even neonates have subjectivity and the propensity to experience the world from their own embodied perspective. We will review empirical evidence strongly suggesting that from birth infants express a sense of their own feeling body as a differentiated entity among other entities.

Among all the existing speculations on what might animate the psychic life of newborns, assuming that there is one prior to language, which was not easily accepted until fairly recently, ideas emerging from Freud's psychoanalytical approach have been the most prolific as well as the most controversial. Freud (1905) was the first to place desire in the instinctive behaviors expressed by newborns, and the first to identify early embodied sensory experience as being the cradle of the person, with its often debilitating characteristics emerging in development. To introduce the notion of infantile sexuality was a revolutionary act of courage at the time, and still is to a large extent.

Freud's 'pulsion theory' of psychosexual development outlined in *Three Essays on the Theory of Sexuality* (1905/2000) was a paradigm shift. With it he took on the taboo idea that infants from birth might be driven by erotic desires that quickly extend and transcend survival instincts evolved by the species. In the history of ideas, *de facto*, Freud offered with his pulsion theory the most comprehensive account of what might drive behavior at birth, aside from conditioning.

Obviously, Freud's theory was not the first published account on the questions of early experience and what it might be like to be an infant (see St Augustine above) but Freud's account was the most thorough and inquisitive to be proposed on what might constitute the psycho-affective forces driving behavior at birth. This account opened a whole new vista on what might be the constitutive elements of subjective life.

Although Freud's pulsion theory and the theoretical concepts inferred continue to be criticized, it was the first to ground subjective life, from the outset, in the experience of the body as we perceive and act in the world, an 'embodiment' of psychic life, its somatic grounding that is now routinely vindicated by current research in the cognitive and affective neurosciences (for a review see Barsalou 2008; Damasio 1995; Gallese 2007; Gazzaniga *et al.* 1998).

The important contribution of Freud's pulsion theory is that it grounds psychic life in the feeling of the body, particularly certain bodily regions (oral, anal, genital) invested successively by the young child in his or her development. At the core of this theory, there is the pleasurable quest for bodily feelings (excitability) and its control (search and suppression): a drive reduction account that remains a powerful causal account of what might motivate psychic life at the outset. There is also the general, rightful intuition that, at birth, the body is the primordial locus of exploration and meaning making.

However, the concepts of 'auto-eroticism' and primary narcissism expressed by the infant, both at the core of Freud's 1905 pulsion theory, need serious revision in light of recent progress in infancy research. This will be demonstrated in the next section of this chapter focusing on empirical evidence of minimal self-awareness in the young child, from birth.

As we will see, the Freudian idea of a first drive toward 'auto-eroticism' and the view that early psychic life primarily revolves around a basic form of narcissism are now problematic. Auto-eroticism as a primary drive reduces early experience of being in the world to some sort of blind, circular, non-objectified and autistic quest toward bodily excitation and suppression. We now know that there is much more than blind auto-eroticism in the life of newborns: there is minimal self-awareness.

2. THE MINIMAL SELF OF NEWBORNS

The infancy literature provides an abundance of empirical observations demonstrating the existence of an early, if not innate experience of the body as an entity perceived by the infant as unified. These observations refute the chaotic view typically associated with the original blooming buzzing confusion of neonates proposed by William James over a century ago (James 1890; but see section 3 below for a different understanding of James's statement).

We now know that infants are not born in a state of un-differentiation and disorganization with respect to perceiving the world but rather show signs that they perceive their own body as well as non-self entities as unified discrete things. Based on selected research findings, I review next some of the content of the presumed unified and meaningful self-perception and action expressed at birth, or shortly after birth. These findings indicate that newborns' perception of their own body in action is anything but disorganized, meaningless, or confused. It appears that there are innate frames to self-perception and experience. These frames correspond to biologically prescribed propensities that are embodied in action systems (i.e. feeding, orienting, avoiding), above and beyond the collection of reflexes structuring behavior at birth (Amiel-Tison and Grenier 1980; Reed 1982; Rochat and Senders 1991; Rochat 2001).

The strong behavioral propensities expressed at birth and already in the womb during the last trimester of gestation (e.g. bringing hand to mouth followed by sucking and swallowing, see Prechtl 1984) constrain subjective experience from the start, in particular the embodied proprioceptive sense of the own body as a distinct entity among other discrete entities in the environment. It also constrains what develops in relation to this minimal, perceptual sense of self. But what is the evidence in support of such assertion?

Looking at the research literature, we can extract characteristics of the *minimal self* expressed at birth and in the course of the first weeks of life, long before children begin to show signs of self-objectification, or the explicit sense of themselves as object thoughts, the next layer of conceptualizing discussed later.

These characteristics pertain to the content of subjective or self-experience at the outset, a 'proto' experience that is implicit but seen here as a first level of self-conceptualizing in the generic sense of seizing the essence of selfhood: what it consists of and the *gist* of its meaning, as implicit as this meaning might be (see the affective and survival context in section 1).

These characteristics do not have to be construed as innate representational modules, probably more accurately as primary representations that are *emergent* from the innate structure of the body and its propensities to act. It also means that these representations are not fixed but subject to enrichment based on learning and experience.

Subjectivity and body schema at birth

The basic emotions expressed at birth and reliably identifiable by caretakers as pain, joy, disgust, interest, or anger, are symptomatic of a rich affective life. Newborns express these emotions with their whole body, becoming spastic and tense in particular ways, emitting particular sound pitches and contours, when for example crying out of pain as opposed to hunger. A rich palette of distinct affective motives underlies newborns' bodily movements. For example, a drop of sucrose on their tongue leads them to calm down and systematically bring hand to the mouth in the most direct trajectory, coming to closure after oral biting and sucking (Rochat *et al.* 1988). The drop of sucrose engages the feeding or appetitive system of the infant that in turn mobilizes her whole body in orienting and rooting activities. These functionally purposeful activities come to rest only when something solid such as a finger or a nipple comes in appropriate contact with the face, eventually finding its way into the mouth for sucking (Blass *et al.* 1989).

In relation to the body as a whole, hand–mouth coordination is closely associated with the engagement of the feeding system, as in this case of the drop of sucrose on the tongue of the infant. In itself, it is suggestive that newborns do possess rudiments of a body schema (Gallagher and Meltzoff 1996). Such coordination implies some mapping of the body whereby regions and parts of the own body are actively and systematically (as opposed to just randomly) put in contact with each other, in this case hands and mouth with a coordinated spatio-temporal trajectory (hand movements, head orientation, and mouth opening, often in anticipation of hand contact).

Neonatal imitation of tongue protrusion, but also of hand clasping or head rotation (Meltzoff and Moore 1977), is another expression of a body schema whereby the sight of active bodily regions in another person (the model) is mapped onto homologous regions of the own body. Other evidence of body schema at birth is demonstrated in neonates who are turned to the side in their crib and plunged into the dark with just a thin beam of light cutting across their visual field. Newborns observed in this condition tend to bring systematically their ipsilateral hand and arm into the beam of light for active visual exploration (Van der Meer and Lee 1995).

In all, body schema and the active propensity of neonates to bring sense modalities and regions of their own body in relation with each other are now well documented. This, in itself, supports the idea that infants sense their own body from birth as an *invariant spatial structure*, as rudimentary and in need of further refinement as this spatial structure might be. This structure is obviously not Euclidean in the sense of not synthesized (represented) in the mind of the young infant as a precise map of accurate spatial co-ordinates and configurations. It does not yet entail that the infant has already a recognizable image of her own body (a body image). This structure is essentially *topological* in the sense that it is made of focal attractor regions on the body surface that have great degrees of freedom and a high concentration of sensory receptors such as mouth and fingers. This topology is embodied in action systems that are functional from birth and drive early behavior.

Evidence of a body schema at birth provides some theoretical ground for the ascription of basic selfhood from the outset. Other recent research shows that neonates behave in relation to their own body in ways that are different, when compared to how they behave in relation to other physical bodies that exist independently of their own. They feel and unquestionably demonstrate from birth a distinct sensitivity to their own bodily movements via *proprioception* and internal (*vestibular*) receptors in the inner ears. Both proprioceptive and vestibular sensitivities are well developed and operational at birth. They are sense modalities of the self par excellence.

Differentiated 'ecological' self at birth

Research shows, for example, that neonates root significantly more with head and mouth toward a tactile stimulation from someone else's finger than from their own hand touching their cheek (Rochat and Hespos 1997). Other studies report that newborns do pick up visual information that specifies ego-motion or movements of their own body while they, in fact, remain stationary. These studies indicate that neonates experience the illusion of moving, adjusting their bodily posture according to changes in direction of an optical flow that is presented in the periphery of their visual field (Jouen and Gapenne 1995). These observations point to the fact that, from birth, infants are endowed with the perceptual qua intermodal capacity to pick up and process meaningfully *self-specifying* information.

Questions remain as to what might be actually synthesized or represented as an outcome of the self-specifying perceptual capacity manifested at birth. What might be the experience of selfhood in neonates? What is the subjective experience of the own body considering that selfhood is first embodied, only later becoming recognized as 'Me'?

Neonates experience the body as an invariant locus of pleasure and pain, with a particular topography of hedonic attractors, the mouth region being the most powerful of all, as noted by Freud (1905) in his account of the primitive oral stage of psychosexual development. Within hours after birth, in relation to this topography, infants learn and memorize sensory events that are associated with pleasure and novelty: they selectively orient to odors associated with the pleasure of feeding and they show basic discrimination of what can be expected from familiar events that unfold over time and that are situated in a space that is embodied, structured within a body schema. But if it is legitimate to posit an a priori 'embodied' spatial and temporal organization of self-experience at birth, what might be the content of this experience aside from pleasure, pain and the sheer excitement of novelty?

Neonates do have an a priori proprioceptive sense of their own body in the way they act and orient to meaningful affordances of the environment, as well as in the way they detect visual information that specifies ego motion, adjusting their posture appropriately in direction and amplitude to compensate for surreptitious changes in gravitational forces (Jouen and Gapenne 1995).

The proprioceptive sense of the body appears to be a necessary correlate of most sensory experiences of the world, that is, from birth on. As proposed by James Gibson (1979), to perceive the world is to *co-perceive* oneself in this world. In this process, proprioception, or the muscular and skeletal sense of the body in reference to *itself*, is indeed the sense modality of the self 'par excellence'.

From birth, proprioception alone or in conjunction with other sense modalities, specifies the own body as a differentiated, situated, and eventually also agent entity among other entities in the world. This corresponds to what Ulric Neisser (1988, 1991) first termed the 'ecological self', a self that can be ascribed to infants from birth.

Bounded and substantial embodied self

As pointed out by Neisser (1995), criteria for the ascription of an ecological self rest on the behavioral expression by the individual both of an awareness of the environment in terms of a layout with particular affordances for action, and of its body as a motivated agent to explore, detect, and use these affordances.

Newborns fill the criteria proposed by Neisser for such awareness. In addition, however, I would like to add that they also seem to possess an a priori awareness that their own body is a distinct entity that is bounded and substantial, as opposed to disorganized and 'airy'.

Newborns perform self-oriented acts by systematically bringing hand to mouth, as already mentioned. In these acts, the mouth tends to open in anticipation of manual contact and the insertion of fingers into the oral cavity for chewing and sucking (Blass *et al.* 1989; Watson 1995). What is instantiated in such systematic acts is, once again, an *organized body schema*. These acts are not just random and cannot be reduced to reflex arcs. They need to be construed as functionally self-oriented acts proper. Because they bring body parts in direct relation to one another, as in the case of hand–mouth coordination, they provide neonates with invariant sensory information specifying the own body's quality as *bounded substance*, with an inside and an outside, specified by particular texture, solidity, temperature, elasticity, taste, and smell.

The a priori awareness of the own body as a bounded substantial entity is evident in neonates' postural reaction and gestures when experiencing the impending collision with a looming visual object, an event that carries potentially life-threatening information.

Years ago, Ball and Tronick (1971) showed that neonates aged two to eleven weeks manifest head withdrawal and avoidant behavior when exposed to the explosive expansion of an optic array that specifies the impending collision of an object. Infants do not manifest any signs of upset or avoidant behavior when viewing expanding shadows specifying an object either receding or on a miss path in relation to them. Consonant with Ball and Tronick's findings, Carroll and Gibson (1981) report that by three months, when facing a looming object with a large aperture in the middle, as an open window in a façade, they do not flinch or show signs of withdrawal as they do with a full textured solid object. Instead, they tend to lean forward to look through the aperture.

In all, the detection of such affordances in the looming object indicates that there is an a priori awareness that the own body is organized and substantial. There is an innate sense that the own body occupies space and can be a physical obstacle to other objects in motion.

In summary, I briefly reviewed empirical observations that warrant the ascription of an innate sense of self in perception and action. What is proposed here is that it corresponds to a first implicit and minimal self-awareness. It is a perceptual awareness of the body that is framed by innate propensities to act in particular ways. It includes the early characteristics that infants perceive of their own body in perception and action as *bounded, organized, differentiated*, and *substantial*, but also *situated* (e.g. in the early detection of reachable objects) and *containing* (e.g. food ingestion and digestion, early transport of suck-able objects to the mouth).

In the generic sense used here, it is also infants' implicit awareness of the body as an agentive entity: sucking to hear a sound and obtain food, kicking in a certain way to set a mobile in motion. It is as well the awareness of the own body as a specific bounded spatial *locus* of fluctuating emotions with a permanent address in space and where from the outset a rich affective life made of pleasure and pain is experienced: the locus of a continuous string of *embodied* satisfaction and frustration.

Stating that newborns have minimal self-awareness is tantamount to saying that this awareness is 'innate', hence possibly modular, corresponding to a 'system' evolved by the species and that infants are born equipped with such a system. Alternatively, I suggested earlier that minimal self-awareness does not have to be construed as any kind of innate representational module. It is probably more accurate to construe minimal self-awareness expressed from birth as primary representations that are *emergent* from the innate structure of the body and its propensities to act. Accordingly, these representations are not fixed but subject to enrichment based on learning and experience.

We turn now to the wide open and crucial question of what might be the mechanism that allows infants to maintain unity in their embodied experience of the world (including the self), an experience that is constantly changing with learning and physical maturation, leading infants within months to becoming explicit and meta-cognizant of themselves when for example they begin to recognize themselves in mirrors by twenty months or become self-conscious with shame, embarrassment, humor, and self-deprecation starting the third year (see Rochat 2009).

I propose next that this mechanism is the innate propensity to detect sameness in things and people, but also in the embodied self-experience from which minimal self-awareness would arise.

3. Newborn Sense of Sameness

Throughout our lives we try to establish what can be counted on and relied upon to survive and make sense of being alive in this world. This quest is already embodied in the neonate, and that is the built-in focus on what can be expected and trusted in a world that is by definition constantly changing, associated to a subjective experience that is fundamentally dynamic and changing.

If there is one thing that we have learned in recent years by studying babies, and there has been a huge wave of interest in studying infants in the past thirty years (Rochat, 2001), it is the fact that from birth, infants are active in processing invariant information over changes. In their inclination to scrutinize novelty hides a deep look for 'sameness'. They avidly look for regularities in the environment and this is the name of the game from the outset: we are born and built in a way that what we are primarily preoccupied with is the detection of what remains the same in the midst of many changes.

Throughout our lives we try to establish what can be counted on and relied upon to survive and make sense of being alive in this world. This quest is already embodied in the neonate, and that is the built-in focus on what can be expected and trusted in a world that is by definition constantly changing, associated to a subjective experience that is fundamentally dynamic.

It is important to insist that the focus on *sameness* in the environment that I take as a core aspect of infant psychological development remains a core aspect of the human mind all through the life span. As William James wrote over a century ago: 'The mind can always intend, and know when it intends, to think of the Same . . . This sense of sameness is the very keel and backbone of our thinking' (James 1890: 459).

The question is: what mechanisms might jumpstart the sense of sameness expressed by infants at birth? What might drive newborns to focus their attention and learning on what remains the same in the midst of constant changes? On what rests the minimal self-awareness they express from birth?

Based on recent discoveries in behavioral neurosciences, I will identify two possible mechanisms that would jumpstart the innate sense of sameness expressed by newborns: (1) a starting experiential state of acute *synesthesia*; (2) the innate capacity for direct *vicarious experience* with the world. I review these processes in turn, based on recent supporting evidence.

Starting experiential state of acute synesthesia

Synesthesia corresponds to the spontaneous, implicit 'metaphorical' experience of a sensation or percept in one modality that is simultaneously experienced in another. For example, one might experience the particular timbre or pitch of a sound with the vivid experience of a specific color, the experience of time duration corresponding to the obligatory experience of a particular spatial layout or form (Simner *et al.* 2006).

Neuroscientists have now established the embodied (neurobiological) reality of such 'synesthesic' experiences that, according to existing surveys, are part of the life of approximately 5 per cent of all adults (Hubbard *et al.* 2005; Spector and Maurer 2009).

What is of interest to us here is the idea recently proposed and tentatively documented with infancy research by Spector and Maurer (2009) that adult cases of synesthesia might in fact be remnant and magnifying cases of inter-sensory connections that are present at birth, pruned and somehow inhibited in the course of typical perceptual development. But these connections are expressed in 'muted forms' in *all adults*, as Spector and Maurer put it. Accordingly, synesthesia could be the natural starting state of our subjective sensory experience. We would indeed start off with a 'conflation' of all sensory modalities as suggested by William James in his statement about blooming, buzzing, confusion. Here is what James had to say:

The physiological condition of (the) first sensible experience is probably nerve-currents coming in from many peripheral organs at once. . . . In a new-born brain, this gives rise to an absolutely pure sensation. But the experience leaves its 'unimaginable touch' on the matter of the convolutions, and the next impression which a sense organ transmits, produces a cerebral reaction in which the awakened vestige of the last impression plays its part. Another sort of feeling and a higher grade of cognition are the consequences; and the complication goes on increasing till the end of life, no two successive impressions falling on an identical brain, and no two successive thoughts being exactly the same. (James 1890: 7–8)

This experiential conflation or 'pure sensory experience' elegantly described by James, is, I would suggest, the symptom of a major competence, and not an incompetence as it has been taken by most infancy researchers (including myself), over the past thirty years.

Infants are born with the ready-made opportunity to link experiences from the various sense modalities, experiences that co-occur and tend to be qualitatively linked, corresponding to particular feeling tones and profiles.

From the start, intermodal systems might exist that allow these sensory experiences to coalesce into the 'affective' core of subjective experience that ultimately gives it *values*: values in rudimentary polarized terms such as pleasure or displeasure, stress or calm, soothing or enhancing, attunement or disharmony, bonding or estrangement. All these represent affective meanings (good or bad feelings) that are at the core of subjective experience, particularly in early development.

In my view this affective core cannot be simply dissociated from subjective experience, as abstract and rational as such experience might be later in development: as for example in the epistemic pleasures and satisfactions in discovering a theorem, in the building of a coherent argument, or in the reaching of an agreement with others.

But what kind of empirical evidence is there that supports the assertion of a rich primitive sensory conflation, a conflation that would harmonize rather than confuse early experience?

In relation to *synesthesia*, there is an abundance of empirical evidence showing that infants from birth are readily able to process information across sensory modalities. One-month-old infants are reported to discriminate an object they see projected on a screen based on the previous experience of an analogous object explored with their mouth only (i.e. a smooth spherical pacifier or a bumpy spherical pacifier with a knobee texture, Meltzoff and Moore 1977). In another series of highly controlled, careful psychophysical studies on newborns in the early 1980s, Lewkowiz and Turkewitz (1980) demonstrated that neonates transfer learning from the auditory to the visual modality. Following visual habituation to either a bright or a dimmed light, they responded differently to corresponding soft or intense sounds in the auditory domain.

In support of such unitary or common functioning of the senses at the outset, an even older neurobehavioral study by Wolff and collaborators (1974) shows that if the tactile stimulation of the newborn's wrist evokes activation of the somatosensory cortex, this activity is significantly enhanced when the infant hears also a white noise. Such auditory-tactile interaction is not found in adults, a phenomenon that appears to be specific to the perceptual experience of newborns.

As additional developmental evidence on an early unitary functioning of the senses, let me mention the work of Neville and collaborators showing that if infants respond to spoken language with, as expected, enhanced activity in the auditory cortex, unlike adults and children, they also respond with enhanced activity in the visual cortex (Neville 1995).

Finally, in support of the natural primacy of synesthetic experience, Mondloch and Maurer (2004) show in a series of studies that 2–3-year-old children tend to be naturally inclined to perceive the same pitch–lightness, color–letters, or sound–shape correspondences typically expressed by synesthetic adults (but also, to some extent, by nonsynesthetic adults). Young toddlers tend, for example, to systematically perceive that a higher pitch sound goes with a brighter color; a nonsense word made of rounded vowels goes with a jagged shape (e.g. te-ta-ke goes with a sharp edged form), or that the letter A goes with the color red).

In all, these few empirical examples taken from the developmental literature on synesthesia, and there are many others, support the idea of a highly organized intermodal and resonating experience at birth. Early perceptual experience is made of rich sensory correspondences and implicit 'a-modal' representations that can be said to be metaphorical because they transcend the particularities of the sense modalities as singular perceptual systems. It is, and this is important, an experience that carries rich conflation and correspondences, not the cognitive confusion that has been assumed by many infancy researchers, including myself, since James's misconstrued 'blooming, buzzing confusion'.

Let us turn now to another set of findings in the neuroscience, the recent discovery of *mirror neuron systems*, which has contributed to changing the view on the nature of early experience, in particular what might characterize phenomenal experience at birth.

Innate and direct vicarious experience of being in the world

There is now abundant empirical evidence and even precise animal models that would substantiate the possibility of an experiential (phenomenological) equivalence between the observation and the execution of actions. As a quick reminder, in the original experiments, Rizzolatti and his team from Parma found that the responses of single nerve cells recorded in area F5 of the pre-motor frontal cortex of the macaque monkey discharge equally when the monkey itself performs a specific action (e.g. reaching for a peanut), or the same monkey observes another monkey—or another person—performing the same action (Rizzolatti *et al.* 1996). These cells are thus multimodal by nature, activated when a particular action is performed by the individual or seen performed by another.

This discovery has had much resonance as it might provide (although many are still skeptical) some biological validation to the idea that there might be a deeply rooted system matching self and others' representations, a mirroring system that could be the constitutive element of higher order phenomena like empathy, language learning, and in general, basic embodied intersubjectivity, as defined at the beginning of the chapter.

Plausible, *yet indirect*, behavioral evidence of mirror systems functional at birth is provided by the numerous research on facial imitation in neonates, the 'matching' reproduction of facial expression, tongue gestures, or emotional displays, actions that are seen repetitively being performed by an adult model at close visible range and that are systematically reproduced by the infant (e.g. Meltzoff and Moore 1977, 1997).

Such imitative responses in neonates suggest that we are born with the necessary mechanism that would allow for the experience of an equivalence between the perception and the execution of actions (Lepage and Théoret 2007).

In William James's terminology from the quote at the opening of this third section of the chapter, infants would be born with the opportunity to experience the '*sameness*' of what is done by the self or what is seen done by somebody else, or vice versa.

Rather than in a state of cognitive confusion, infants would thus be able from the start to experience and exploit in future learning, the *analogical link* between the products of two different agents: something self-generated and the same thing generated by others, in the same way that they would be able to experience the analogical link between the varieties of sensory experiences in their incipient *synesthesia*.

It is worth noting that the importance placed here on an innate sense of sameness expressed by neonates is also at the root of analogical reasoning and processing, the mechanism by which novel situations are understood in reference to what is familiar ('the same'), and that developmental psychologists view as a core mechanism of cognitive development (see Gentner *et al.* 2001).

4. CONCLUSIONS AND SUMMARY

So, what is it like to be a newborn? Many speculations have been made by philosophers, educators, theologians, and more recently by psychoanalysts, developmental psychologists, and neuroscientists. Beyond these interesting, often astute, and inspiring speculations, there is now an abundance of new infancy research providing more reliable facts on the question.

In the second section, I reviewed some of the empirical evidence suggesting that infants are not born in a state of chaotic mental confusion. Newborns are oriented rather than disoriented, organized rather than disorganized. We are not born experientially incoherent. I tried to show that infants from birth, and possibly even before, manifest *minimal self-awareness*: a sense of themselves as differentiated and situated entities among other entities in the world. They appear very early on to have a sense of being embodied and substantial, occupying space in an environment in which they are agent. This minimal self-awareness is expressed in spite of the passive submission to the cares of others that is dictated by the prolonged immaturity of the human infant, a unique feature of the species. This latter human feature indicates further that early minimal self-awareness is infused with meaning arising from interaction with others. Early minimal self-awareness encompasses both an interpersonal and an ecological sense of self (Neisser 1988, 1991).

In section 3 I suggested that the minimal self-awareness expressed by newborns might rest on innate mechanisms by which infants are from the start particularly attuned to 'sameness', what is familiar as opposed to unfamiliar. The attunement to sameness might jumpstart self-awareness in newborns, infants wired from birth to pick up what is the same in their successive embodied experiences, thus also, *mutatis mutandis*, wired to pick up what deviates from the familiar. I reviewed evidence of a starting experiential state of acute synesthesia as well as the plausibility of an innate and direct vicarious experience of being in the world.

Research shows that infants are born with mechanisms of inter-sensory integration and the probable existence of mirror neuron systems at birth. These mechanisms would cause both acute synestheses and the possibility of vicarious experience from the outset. They would play a major role in scaffolding and jumpstarting the sense of sameness in the context of embodied self-experience: unifying sensations originating simultaneously from the various sense modalities and providing equivalence across experiences that originate from within and without the body, movements that are either self-experienced or detected in others.

I proposed that these putative mechanisms are at the root of the minimal self-awareness expressed by newborns: ultimately what it is like to be a newborn. Obviously, these speculations need further validation; still, existing empirical evidence in the field of infancy research demonstrates that there is an exciting new avenue for empirical research on the ontogenetic origins of self-awareness, the beginning limit question of consciousness.

REFERENCES

AMIEL-TISON, C., and GRENIER, A. (1980). *Evaluation neurologique du nouveau-né et du nourrisson* (Neurological evaluation of the newborn and the young infant) (Paris: Masson).

AUGUSTINE (397/2007). *Confessions* (New York: Barnes & Noble Classics).

BALL, W., and TRONICK, E. (1971). 'Infant Responses to Impending Collision: Optical and Real', *Science*, 171: 818–20.

BARSALOU, L. W. (2008). 'Grounded Cognition', *Annual Review of Psychology*, 59: 617–45.

BLASS, E. M., FILLION, T. J., ROCHAT, P., HOFFMEYER, L. B., and METZGER, M. A. (1989) 'Sensorimotor and Motivational Determinants of Hand–Mouth Coordination in 1–3-day-old Human Infants', *Developmental Psychology*, 25(6): 963–75.

BLOCK, N. (2007). 'Consciousness, Accessibility, and the Mesh between Psychology and Neuroscience', *Brain and Behavioral Sciences*, 30: 481–548.

BRUNER, J. S. (1972). 'Nature and Uses of Immaturity', *American Psychologist*, 27(8): 687–708.

CARROLL, J. J., and GIBSON, E. J. (1981). 'Differentiation of an Aperture from an Obstacle under Conditions of Motion by 3-month-old Infants', paper presented at the Meetings of the Society for Research in Child Development, Boston, Mass.

DECASPER, A. J., and FIFER, W. P. (1980). 'Of Human Bonding: Newborns Prefer their Mothers' Voices', *Science*, 208: 1174–6.

DAMASIO, A. R. (1995). *Descartes' Error: Emotion, Reason and the Human Brain* (New York: Avon Publishers).

DENNETT, D. C. (1981). *Brainstorms: Philosophical Essays on Mind and Psychology* (Cambridge, Mass.: MIT Press, Bradford Books Series).

FREUD, S. (1905/2000). *Three Essays on the Theory of Sexuality* (New York: Basic Books, Classics series).

GALLAGHER, S., and MELTZOFF, A. (1996). 'The Earliest Sense of Self and Others: Merleau-Ponty and Recent Developmental Studies', *Philosophical Psychology*. 9: 213–36.

GALLESE, V. (2007). 'Before and Below 'Theory of Mind': Embodied Simulation and the Neural Correlates of Social Cognition', *Philosophical Transactions of the Royal Society, Biological Sciences* (29 Apr.), 362/1480: 659–69.

GAZZANIGA, M., MANGUN, G., and IVRY, R. (1998). *Cognitive Neuroscience: The Biology of the Mind* (New York: Norton).

GENTNER, D., HOLYOAK, K. J., and KOKINOV, B. (eds) (2001). *The Analogical Mind: Perspectives from Cognitive Science* (Cambridge, Mass.: MIT Press).

GIBSON, J. J. (1979). *The Ecological Approach to Visual Perception* (Boston: Houghton-Mifflin Co.).

GOULD, S. J. (1977). *Ontogeny and Phylogeny* (Cambridge, Mass.: Harvard University Press).

HUBBARD, E. M., ARMAN, A. C., RAMACHANDRAN, V. S., and BOYNTON, G. M. (2005). 'Individual Differences among Grapheme–Color Synesthetes: Brain–Behavior Correlations', *Neuron*, 45: 975–85.

JAMES, W. (1890). *The Principles of Psychology* (New York: Henry Holt & Co.).

JOUEN, F., and GAPENNE, O. (1995). 'Interactions between the Vestibular and Visual Systems in the Neonate', in P. Rochat (ed.), *The Self in Infancy: Theory and Research* (Amsterdam: North-Holland, Elsevier Publishers), 277–302.

LEPAGE, J. P., and THÉORET, H. (2007). 'The Mirror Neuron System: Grasping Others' Actions from Birth?', *Developmental Science*, 10/5: 513–29.

LEWKOWICZ, D. J., and TURKEWITZ, G. (1980). 'Cross-Modal Equivalence in Early Infancy: Auditory–Visual Intensity Matching', *Developmental Psychology*, 16: 597–607.

MARLIER, L., SCHAAL, B., and SOUSSIGNAN, R. (1998a). 'Neonatal Responsiveness to the Odor of Amniotic and Lacteal Fluids: A Test of Perinatal Chemosensory Continuity', *Child Development*, 69/3: 611–23.

———and ——(1998b). 'Bottle-Fed Neonates Prefer an Odor Experienced in Utero to an Odor Experienced Postnatally in the Feeding Context', *Developmental Psychobiology*, 33: 133–45.

MELTZOFF, A. N., and BORTON, R. W. (1979). 'Intermodal Matching by Human Neonates', *Nature*, 282: 403–4.

——and MOORE, M. K. (1977). 'Imitation of Facial and Manual Gestures by Human Neonates', *Science*, 198: 75–8.

MONDLOCH, C., and MAURER, D. (2004). 'Do Small White Balls Squeak? Pitch–Object Correspondences in Young Children', *Cognitive, Affective, and Behavioral Neuroscience*, 4: 133–6.

MONTAGU, A. (1961). 'Neonatal and Infant Immaturity in Man', *Journal of the American Medical Association*, 178/23: 56–7.

NEISSER, U. (1988). 'Five Kinds of Self-Knowledge', *Philosophical Psychology*, 1: 35–59.

——(1991). 'Two Perceptually Given Aspects of the Self and their Development', *Developmental Review*, 11/3: 197–209.

——(1995). 'Criteria for an Ecological Self', in P. Rochat (ed.), *The Self in Infancy: Theory and Research* (Advances in Psychology, 112; Amsterdam: North-Holland/Elsevier Science Publishers), 17–34.

NEVILLE, H. (1995). 'Developmental Specificity in Neurocognitive Development in Humans', in M. Gazzaniga (ed.), *The Cognitive Neurosciences* (Cambridge, Mass.: Bradford), 219–31.

PRECHTL, H. F. R. (ed.) (1984). *Continuity of Neural Functions from Prenatal to Postnatal Life* (Oxford: Blackwell Scientific Publications).

REED, E. S. (1982). 'An Outline of a Theory of Action Systems', *Journal of Motor Behavior*, 14: 98–134.

RIZZOLATTI, G., FADIGA, L., GALLESE, V., and FOGASSI, L. (1996). 'Premotor Cortex and the Recognition of Motor Actions', *Brain Research, Cognitive Brain Research*, 3/2: 131–41.

ROCHAT, P. (2001). *The Infant's World* (Cambridge, Mass.: Harvard University Press).

——(2009) *Others in Mind:—Social Origins of Self-Consciousness* (New York and Cambridge: Cambridge University Press).

——and HESPOS, S. J. (1997). 'Differential Rooting Response by Neonates: Evidence of an Early Sense of Self', *Early Development and Parenting*, 6(3/4): 105–12.

——and SENDERS, S. J. (1991). 'Active Touch in Infancy: Action Systems in Development', in M. J. Weiss and P. R. Zelazo (eds), *Infant Attention: Biological Constraints and the Influence of Experience* (Norwood, NJ: Ablex Publishers), 412–42.

—— BLASS, E. M., and HOFFMEYER, L. B. (1988). 'Oropharyngeal Control of Hand–Mouth Coordination in Newborn Infants', *Developmental Psychology*, 24(4): 459–63.

SARTRE, J.-P. (1971/1981). *The Family Idiot: Gustave Flaubert 1821–1857*. i, tr. Carol Cosman (Chicago: University of Chicago Press).

SIMNER, J., SAGIV, N., MULVENNA, C., TSAKANIKOS, E., WITHERBY, S., FRASER, C., et al. (2006). 'Synesthesia: The Prevalence of Atypical Cross-Modal Experiences', *Perception*, 35: 1024–33.

SPECTOR, F., and MAURER, D. (2009). 'Synesthesia: A New Approach to Understanding the Development of Perception', *Developmental Psychology*, 45/1: 175–89.

STERN, D. (1991). *The Diary of a Baby: What your Child Sees, Feels, and Experiences* (London: Fontana Press).

TREVARTHAN, W. R. (1987). *Human Birth: An Evolutionary Perspective* (Hawthorne, NY: Aldine de Gruyter).

VAN DER MEER, A., and LEE, D. (1995). 'The Functional Significance of Arm Movements in Neonates', *Science*, 267: 693–5.

WATSON, J. S. (1995). 'Self-Orientation in Early Infancy: The General Role of Contingency and the Specific Case of Reaching to the Mouth', in P. Rochat (ed.), *The Self in Infancy: Theory and Research* (Advances in Psychology, 112; Amsterdam: North-Holland/Elsevier Science Publishers).

WOLFF, P., MATSUMIYA, Y., ABROHMS, I. F., VAN VELZER, C., and LOMBROSO, C. T. (1974). 'The Effect of White Noise on the Somatosensory Evoked Responses in Sleeping Newborn Infants', *Electroencephalography and Clinical Neurophysiology*, 37: 269–74.

....

CHAPTER 3

SELF-RECOGNITION

....

GORDON G. GALLUP, JR.
JAMES R. ANDERSON
STEVEN M. PLATEK

SELF-RECOGNITION can be expressed in several ways. The immune system represents a primitive form of self-recognition. In order to function appropriately the immune system needs to distinguish between the biochemistry of self versus other (e.g. pathogens). Autoimmune reactions, where the immune system begins to attack parts of the person's own body (such as the cartilage in joints in the case of arthritis), represent a failure to show immunogenic self-recognition.

At another level of analysis some people seem incapable of identifying the source of their own behavior. When shown an image of their hand and the hand of another person on a television monitor in real time, schizophrenics are often unable to tell which hand is theirs—even if they are instructed to move their hand while they watch the results on the screen (for more details see Gallup *et al.* 2003*a*). You get the same effect in human patients when the right cortical hemisphere is anesthetized. Not only do they fail to recognize themselves in mirrors (Keenan *et al.* 2000), they fail to recognize their own hands (Meador *et al.* 2000). Rhesus monkeys appear likewise incapable of locating hidden food by monitoring the position of their hand in a mirror (Menzel *et al.* 1985). Even following extended exposure to mirrors, as their hand approaches the food that can only be seen in the mirror they vocalize and threaten the image as if it were the hand of another monkey.

In this chapter we will focus on mirror self-recognition, the ability to recognize one's own image in a mirror. If self-awareness is the ability to become the object of your own attention, then mirrors can be used to measure and objectify this capacity. In front of a mirror you are the object of your own attention. When you look at yourself in a mirror you are an audience to your own behavior. Unlike most (but not all) humans in the presence of mirrors, many species act as if they were seeing other organisms and often persist in treating the image as another animal (Gallup 1968). Therefore, from a scientific perspective, the question is whether an observer is capable of recognizing the dualism implicit in mirrors and realizing that its own behavior is the source of the behavior depicted in the reflection.

RESEARCH METHODS

Claims for and against self-recognition in different species can be based on strong evidence, weak evidence, inconclusive evidence, or wishful thinking. Research on animal self-recognition is contentious and hotly debated, but the literature is no better than the evidence upon which it is based. All too often claims for self-recognition have been made on the basis of intuitions and impressionistic observations rather than on solid, experimental, and reproducible evidence. For instance, holding a young child in front of a mirror and asking who it sees has often been used to infer self-recognition in children. But just because a child can correctly label the reflection does not mean that it recognizes itself. Many children are held up in front of mirrors over and over by parents and others as they repeat the child's name. As a consequence children may learn to associate the image in the mirror with their name. But that does not necessarily mean that they realize they are seeing themselves. Consistent with this interpretation, children at eighteen months of age are as likely to say their own name when viewing the image of another child or an image of themselves (Johnson 1983).

In the first experimental report of mirror self-recognition (Gallup 1970) chimpanzees were individually exposed to themselves in a mirror for ten days. Initially they reacted as though they were seeing another chimpanzee and engaged in social behavior directed toward the reflection. With time these other-directed responses began to subside and were replaced by the emergence of self-directed behavior, where rather than responding to the mirror as such the apes began to use the mirror to respond to themselves: that is, using the mirror to manipulate and examine parts of the body they could not otherwise see (such as the inside of their mouths or ano-genital areas). After the last day of mirror exposure the chimpanzees were anesthetized and removed from their cages. Once they were unconscious a bright red, odorless, alcohol soluble, non-irritating dye was applied to the upper portion of an eyebrow ridge and the top half of the opposite ear of each chimpanzee. The animals were then returned to their individual cages and allowed to recover in the absence of the mirror.

There are three special properties of this procedure. First, since the chimpanzees were under deep anesthesia they would have no information about the application of the marks. Second, the dye was carefully chosen to be free from any residual, tell-tale odor or tactile properties. Finally, the marks were applied to facial features that the chimpanzees could not see without a mirror.

Following recovery from anesthesia the chimpanzees were given access to food and water and their behavior was monitored individually for thirty minutes to determine how often the marks were contacted in the absence of the mirror. After establishing a very low baseline of spontaneous face touching, the mirror was reintroduced as an explicit test of self-recognition. Upon seeing themselves with red marks on their faces the chimpanzees reached up, touched, and made repeated attempts to investigate these marks that could only be seen in the mirror.

Several comparable chimpanzees without the benefit of prior mirror exposure were also anesthetized and marked, but upon recovery from anesthesia failed to discover the location of the marks. These control data demonstrate that the discovery and investigation of the facial marks was a consequence of prior experience with mirrors, and that the results were not an artifact of either anesthetization or residual cues left by the dye. The use of the pre-exposure baseline period following recovery from anesthesia also demonstrates that the mark-directed responses shown by mirror-experienced chimpanzees on the test trial were in fact conditional upon seeing themselves in the mirror.

It is important to compare this approach with one that Amsterdam (1972) developed several years later for use with children, where mothers were instructed to place a spot of rouge on their child's nose before the child was tested with a mirror. While some people have argued that these are parallel techniques (Mitchell 1994), consider the following important differences. Unlike chimpanzees that are rendered unconscious before applying the facial marks, the children in Amsterdam's study were fully awake. As a consequence the application of rouge was not only accompanied by tactile and visual cues provided unwittingly by the mother as she touched the child's nose, but rouge is often scented and could have been a source of confounding olfactory cues. To make matters worse, rather than being applied to parts of the child's face that could not be seen without a mirror, the rouge was placed on the side of the child's nose, which is one of the few facial features that can be seen directly. As a consequence all of the infants in Amsterdam's study were provided with extensive information about the presence of the facial mark prior to seeing themselves in the mirror, and since none of the children was given a pretest to determine the incidence of spontaneous face touching it is impossible to know whether they were actually using the mirror to locate the mark (for more details see Gallup 1994).

HABITUATION OF SOCIAL BEHAVIOR

Upon seeing themselves in mirrors most animals act as if they were seeing another animal and engage in a variety of species-specific social responses directed toward their reflected image (Gallup 1968). Among those that never learn to recognize themselves in mirrors it is not uncommon for social responses to the mirror to eventually diminish over time. Some people have taken the position that this is evidence in and of itself for a form of self-recognition (de Waal *et al.* 2005). While it may be a necessary condition for self-recognition, the absence of social behavior is not sufficient. In a series of studies conducted a number of years ago on a pair of rhesus monkeys that had received thousands of hours of mirror exposure, it was discovered that a simple change in the position of the mirror or briefly removing and replacing the mirror both led to a dramatic, short-term reinstatement of social and aggressive responses directed toward the mirror (Suarez and Gallup 1986; Gallup and Suarez 1991).

CONTINGENCY TESTING

It is not uncommon to see animals intently watching and monitoring their behavior in mirrors. Sometimes this takes the form of what has been called 'contingency testing' where the animal seems to move repeatedly in front of the mirror in an apparent attempt to confirm/identify the relationship between its behavior and the reflection in the mirror. Some people claim that instances of this so-called contingency testing in the presence of mirrors can be taken as evidence of self-recognition. But simply making quick and repeated body movements while watching the reflection is not compelling evidence for contingency testing. Repetitive instances of behavior in front of a mirror could occur for a variety of reasons (e.g. trying to get the 'other' monkey to reciprocate rather than mimic). What is typically lacking in such claims is an objective methodology for identifying the intentional stance required to make the claim that repetitive instances of behavior qualify as contingency testing.

ROBOT SELF-RECOGNITION

On the basis of programming a robot to distinguish between contingent and non-contingent movements, Gold and Scassellati (2009) claim to have simulated an instance of robotic self-recognition. Programming a robot to identify contingent movements of its arm in a mirror is not fundamentally different from training a pigeon to peck at a blue dot on its breast that can only be seen in a mirror (Epstein *et al.* 1980). Although the methods differ, programming robots and training pigeons are analogous operations. With less effort and sophistication, you could also program a robot or teach a pigeon to pick the correct answers on an answer sheet to the questions on the Graduate Record Exam. But would that provide a compelling account of the performance of college seniors taking that test? And if the robot got a combined verbal and quantitative score of 1500 would it qualify for admission to the doctoral program in computer science at Yale University? What you get out of a set of programming or training operations is no more that what you put in (see Suarez and Gallup 1986). Just because you can simulate a naturally occurring instance of behavior does not mean that the underlying mediating mechanisms are the same, or even similar. Gold and Scassellati are quick to point out that 'this result is an engineering solution for a robot, and not a model of human, or animal mirror self-recognition'. But if it is not a serious attempt to model human or animal cognition it seems rather trivial.

Contingency recognition is not self-recognition. Contingency recognition may be a necessary condition for self-recognition, but it is hardly sufficient. In terms of learning and problem-solving, rhesus monkeys are pretty sophisticated creatures. However, a pair of rhesus monkeys given a lifetime of exposure to mirrors never showed even the faintest evidence of being able to recognize their reflections (Gallup and Suarez 1991). It was not because they were unable to understand the dualism implicit in mirrors. Upon entering the room where they were housed if they caught sight of you in the mirror they would immediately turn to confront you directly. Most people not only appreciate the mimicry inherent in mirrors, they have also come to realize that their behavior is the source of the behavior being seen in a mirror. Unlike people, rhesus monkeys are unable to identify the source of their own behavior. Mirror self-recognition not only requires contingency recognition, it requires the ability to identify the source of the behavior depicted in the reflection.

MIRROR NEURONS: WHAT'S IN A NAME?

The discovery of neurons in the motor cortex that are activated when macaque monkeys see other monkeys engaged in particular behaviors led to the designation 'mirror neurons' (Rizzolatti *et al.* 2001). This has prompted some people to speculate that these neurons may be an important component to mirror self-recognition (e.g. Gold and Scassellati 2009). It is important to note, however, that in spite of many ingenious attempts at repeated testing, prompting and the use of incentives, neither macaques nor any other monkeys have ever shown any compelling evidence for self-recognition. There are no mirror neurons for self-awareness, consciousness, or mental states.

INDIVIDUAL DIFFERENCES IN SELF-RECOGNITION

In an effort to impugn and call into question the significance of self-recognition some critics have paid particular attention to the fact that not all chimpanzees recognize themselves in mirrors (e.g. Swartz and Evans 1991). It is important to realize, however, that chimpanzees are not unique in this respect. Not all humans recognize themselves in mirrors (Gallup 1997). Prior to eighteen to twenty-four months of age most children react to themselves in mirrors as if they were seeing other children, and self-recognition is further delayed or even absent in mentally retarded youngsters and autistic children. The same is true for schizophrenics, certain patients with brain damage to the frontal cortex, and people suffering from the advanced stages of Alzheimer's disease (see Gallup *et al.* 2003*b*). Given that there are over 6 billion people alive today, a conservative estimate would be that there are 400–600 million humans who would fail the mark test because of developmental and cognitive constraints.

There is, however, at least one important difference between chimpanzees and humans. Self-recognition in chimpanzees is developmentally delayed. Most children begin to show evidence of self-recognition between eighteen and twenty-four months of age. In contrast, the onset of self-recognition in chimpanzees does not typically occur until later in childhood or early adolescence, and the loss of self-recognition appears to be accelerated as animals grow older (Povinelli *et al.* 1993). Despite some extreme claims that only a few chimpanzees show self-recognition (e.g. Swartz and Evans 1991), actually about 75 per cent of those tested between 8 and 15 years of age pass the mark test (Povinelli *et al.* 1993).

In the context of these individual differences attempts have also been made to trace the evolutionary origins of this trait. Most of the available evidence suggests that chimpanzees, orangutans, gorillas and humans are all descended from a single common ancestor, who by implication may have been self-aware (see Povinelli and Cant 1995). Rather than being the odd man out, it is possible that the reason gorillas do not usually show mirror self-recognition is because the capacity in this species has diminished as a consequence of changes in socio-ecology and reproductive competition, and chimpanzees may not be far behind (see Gallup 1997).

RETENTION OF SELF-RECOGNITION

The existence of individual differences in self-recognition also raises some potentially important methodological questions. Is the variance in performance on the mark test simply a consequence of inherent unreliability of the test? Or do these differences relate to real and important underlying differences in the means by which individuals process mirrored information about themselves? One way of resolving these problems is to examine the stability of the trait over time. Do chimpanzees that either pass or fail the mark test during adolescence continue to show comparable results when retested later as adults? It is not only a question of whether mirror self-recognition exists in different individuals, it is also important to determine whether the differences in the expression of this trait are enduring, reliable features that persist over time.

To address this issue de Veer *et al.* (2003) conducted a detailed longitudinal study of mirror self-recognition in a sample of the chimpanzees tested previously by Povinelli *et al.* (1993). The 1993 study based on ninety-two chimpanzees is the largest and most comprehensive cross-sectional study of mirror self-recognition conducted to date. Whereas Povinelli *et al.* found that relatively few chimpanzees younger than 8 years of age or older than 15 showed compelling evidence of self-recognition, 75 per cent of those between 8 and 15 years of age did. Eight years after this study was completed, twelve subjects from the original 8–15-year-old group were retested by de Veer *et al.* Nine of these chimpanzees showed compelling evidence for self-recognition in 1992, one was classified as ambiguous, and two failed the test. Upon being retested in 2000 with little or no intervening mirror exposure, six out of the nine that originally tested positive continued to show compelling evidence for self-recognition, and two of the remaining three showed suggestive evidence. The concordance rate for those that tested negative was even better: none of the three chimpanzees that were classified as ambiguous or failed the original test showed any evidence of self-recognition on the retest. Thus, in the absence of any explicit intervening mirror experience the individual differences in mirror self-recognition remained strikingly constant over a span of eight years and therefore, mirror self-recognition in chimpanzees (or the lack thereof) appears to be a reliable, stable trait.

THE SELF-FACE REACTION TIME PARADIGM

A number of years ago Keenan *et al.* (1999) pioneered the development of a self-face reaction time paradigm in humans. Adults were shown facial photographs of different individuals on a computer monitor. The subject's task was to press an appropriate key on the keyboard as fast as they could for each photo to indicate whether it was their picture, the picture of a friend, a stranger, or a famous person. When subjects were instructed to respond with their right hand, Keenan *et al.* found no differences in reaction time latencies to self or other faces. However, when subjects responded with their left hand, reaction times to self-faces were signifi-cantly faster than to other faces. Because of hemispheric contra-lateral control (the right side of the brain largely controls movement on the left side of the body and vice versa), these results have been taken as evidence that self-face processing occurs in the right cortical hemisphere.

This left-hand, self-face reaction time advantage has been replicated a number of times in different contexts (e.g. Platek and Gallup 2002) and extended to a self-trait identification paradigm. In this instance, rather than being shown faces, subjects were shown individual self-descriptive adjectives (e.g. honest, intelligent, lazy) on a computer screen and asked to indicate by pressing one of two keys whether or not it was one of their traits. Just as with self-face reaction times, there was a significant left-hand reaction time advantage for identifying self-descriptive traits (Platek *et al.* 2003*a*). Whereas self-recognition has heretofore been treated as an all or nothing trait, the unique feature of these self-face/self-trait reaction time paradigms is that they can be used to measure and quantify underlying individual differences in sensory and cognitive self-processing.

SELF-PROCESSING IN OTHER MODALITIES

Incorporating the use of priming procedures into the self-face reaction time paradigm can be used to measure the impact of cross-modal processing of infor-mation about the self. That is, priming procedures can be used to determine if the way people process information about the self in one modality is affected by the presentation of information about the self in other modalities. Platek *et al.* (2004) found that if subjects were first shown or heard their own names in contrast to the names of other people, it facilitated (i.e. sped up) self-face identification. The same positive priming effect on self-face recognition was found for exposure to self-odor in comparison to body odor samples taken from other people.

These results have several important implications. If animals seem incapable of recognizing their own image in a mirror would it still be possible for them to recognize their own odor, or their own vocalizations? Conversely, if organisms can recognize themselves in different modalities would that mean they have separate self-concepts (e.g. a visual self, an auditory self, and/or an olfactory concept of self)?

We think these are mistaken questions. If you close your eyes, hold your nose, or cover your ears, your sense of self does not change or become fundamentally altered. Rather than being modality specific, your sense of self allows you to integrate information about yourself across different modalities and as such enables you to match information about yourself from different sensory domains and achieve intermodal equivalence about the self as it relates to input from diverse sources. This point is nicely illustrated by the Platek *et al.* (2004) priming study noted above. Briefly presenting someone with the printed image of their name, a tape recording of someone speaking their name, or a sample of their own body odor all produced the same effect; they enhanced self-face processing and promoted significantly faster self-face reaction times, suggesting the existence of an underlying, unitary self-processing system. In other words, perceptions of self in the visual, auditory, and olfactory domains are not mutually exclusive, but combine to promote integrative self-processing.

These results have important implications for several recent attempts to discredit/diminish the cognitive significance of self-recognition. If self-recognition has nothing to do with self-awareness, as Swartz (1998) and Morin (2002) claim, and if mirror self-recognition involves little more that matching motor cues to mirror feedback, as Mitchell (1993) and Povinelli (1995) argue, then information about the self in other sensory domains ought to leave visual self-recognition unaffected. In stark contrast to these arguments, the fact that presenting information about the self in other modalities affects self-face identification clearly shows that self-recognition is an expression of an integrated, multi-modal self-processing system.

MENTAL STATE ATTRIBUTION

Some time ago a model was formulated that stipulates self-awareness as a necessary condition for being able to make inferences about mental state in others (Gallup 1982). According to this model, inferential knowledge of mental states in others builds on the existence and awareness of mental states in oneself. Organisms that can become the object of their own attention (i.e. recognize themselves in mirrors) are in a unique position to use their experience as a means of modeling/inferring comparable experiences in others. Because humans share similar receptor mechanisms and brains that are organized in roughly the same way, there is bound to be considerable overlap between their experiences. Moreover, people who have access to their own mental states and take note of the relationship between these and various external events have a means of making inferences about mental states in others. Knowledge of self, in other words, paves the way for achieving an inferential knowledge of mental states in others.

Since the ability to recognize oneself in a mirror varies as a function of species, age, neurological status, and mental illness (Gallup *et al.* 2003*b*), this model can be tested in each of these domains. According to the model, variation in mirror self-recognition ought to predict comparable variation in the ability to take into account how others feel, and variation in being able to accurately infer what they want, know, or intend to do. In instances in which self-recognition is deficient or absent there should be a corresponding deficiency or absence of mental state attribution and when it comes to developmental status, brain damage, and mental illness most of the available evidence is consistent with these predictions (e.g. Gallup and Platek 2001).

Newly Discovered 'Self-Recognizing' Species

How animals react to mirrors remains a popular research topic in comparative psychology. Since our last overview of research on self-recognition (Gallup *et al.* 2003*b*) several additional claims for self-recognition have emerged. Some of the results have important implications for our understanding of the phylogenetic origins of self-awareness.

In one case there is a report of a captive Asian elephant showing appropriate use of its reflection to investigate an otherwise invisible mark on its body (Plotnik *et al.* 2006). Specifically, the elephant reached toward the mark with its trunk while looking at the mirror, whereas a sham mark used as a control did not elicit similar interest. It should be noted, however, that the same elephant failed to repeat the performance when retested, and two other elephants in the same zoo-housed group never showed strong evidence of understanding that the reflection was an image of themselves. Other attempts to demonstrate self-recognition in elephants have also produced negative results (Povinelli 1989; Nissani and Hoefler Nissani 2007). Clearly, the issue requires further investigation; confirmation that at least some elephants are capable of self-recognition would complement other lines of evidence for advanced cognitive abilities in these highly socially complex, large-brained mammals, which are known to use tools and are thought to show apparent instances of empathic behavior toward others (Hart *et al.* 2001; Bates and Byrne 2008).

If elephants are admitted to an expanding 'self-recognition club' then it follows that the capacity underlying this cognitive achievement has most probably evolved independently in at least three vastly different mammalian groups: ancestral hominoid primates, cetaceans (Reiss and Marino 2001)[1] and elephants. Of course these species differ enormously in terms of biological structure and the environments in which they evolved. But they do share some characteristics that appear important, including large body size, complex social lives and, presumably crucial, large brains with neocortical expansion.

In this context another recent study stands out because it claims the capacity for self-recognition in a vastly different type of animal: the magpie (Prior *et al.* 2008). Magpies are birds of the corvid family, which includes crows and ravens. They are known for storing food, a behavior that is influenced by the presence of conspecifics and the experience of pilfering other individuals' caches. They are also reported to reach the final stage of the Piagetian object-permanence sequence, and can use tools to extract food items that would otherwise be impossible to access. When shown their reflection, two of five magpies spontaneously showed 'contingency testing', that is, they made repeated head- or whole-body movements back and forth while monitoring their reflection. The birds were subsequently given formal self-recognition tests, which consisted of placing a brightly colored small dot (a paper sticker) on the bird's throat. The dot was visible to the magpie only when it looked in the mirror, whereas a black dot placed in the same area was not readily visible even in the mirror because of the bird's black throat feathers. Over two tests, one of the two contingency-testing birds and one other showed significantly more mark-directed responses (either with the beak or a foot) than responses to other parts of the body; this difference did not emerge in either the black dot tests or control tests with colored marks but no mirror present. The authors relate the evidence for self-recognition to the capacity for perspective-taking, but perhaps the most impressive aspect of this work is that it concerns animals with a brain weighing less than 6 grams. As a percentage of body weight, the magpie brain is actually much bigger than that of humans, chimpanzees, and Asian elephants (by a factor of almost 20, in the latter case), but the small absolute amount of neural tissue available raises important questions about the neural architecture and networks underpinning the ability to show self-recognition.

---

[1] Like the elephant study, the cetacean study only found suggestive evidence for self-recognition in one dolphin. As a consequence such effects must be treated as tentative. Replication is the cornerstone of science.

Mirror Self-Recognition in Nonhuman Primates: Recent Studies

Like elephants and dolphins, self-recognition in corvids clearly requires replication/confirmation, but we welcome this work as a vast improvement on a previous study of self-recognition in birds, an attempt (never fully replicated) that used operant conditioning procedures to explicitly train pigeons to peck at a colored dot on their breast (Epstein *et al.* 1980). Although the end product of that work was unconvincing as evidence of self-recognition in pigeons (Suarez and Gallup 1986), a recent study followed the same approach by using reinforcement and successive approximation to shape mark touching in capuchin monkeys (Roma *et al.* 2007). In fact the reasoning behind this approach—that monkeys may be naturally non-inquisitive about marks on their bodies—appears unfounded, as directly visible marks (e.g. on the wrist or belly) have been used for many years to confirm spontaneous interest in changes to animals' normal physical appearance (e.g. Gallup *et al.* 1980). Even so, the three monkeys tested by Roma *et al.* failed to generalize the shaped response of touching an orange mark in various locations in the test cage to a mark placed on their forehead while they looked in a mirror with which they were familiarized. Subsequently, in a procedure similar to the 'sequential marking' procedure first described by Anderson (1984), the monkeys were trained by successive approximation to touch marks located on various parts of their bodies. Again, no monkey touched its marked forehead while looking in the mirror. In a final assessment, the monkeys were marked at the neck/upper chest region so that the mark could not be seen directly by looking down but could be seen in the mirror (this approximates marking the breast or neck region in studies with birds). No monkeys used the mirror to locate the body mark, which is in agreement with another recent description of the absence of mirror-guided self-exploration in capuchin monkeys given mirrors of various sizes, shapes, and colors (Paukner *et al.* 2004).

Typically, when first exposed to their mirror image, animals react by emitting responses that would be shown to another member of their species (Anderson 1994). In chimpanzees and orangutans, these social responses diminish and give way to appropriate use of the mirror to investigate parts of the body that cannot otherwise be seen. However, neither monkeys nor birds, nor indeed most other animals, make this transition from social to self-directed responding in front of the mirror. Although many people view the results of the mark test as definitive evidence for the presence or absence of self-recognition (hence the belief of some that animals might be trained up to do something that looks like passing the mark test), Gallup has long emphasized that the mark test should only be seen as confirming what is clear from the self-recognizing individual's spontaneous mirror-guided self-exploration, that is, the correct understanding of the source of the reflection.

Evidence for self-recognition is strongest if both spontaneous mirror-guided self-exploration and a positive result on the mark test are observed. This was the outcome of the latest report concerning self-recognition in the gorilla, the great ape for which the literature is most contradictory. Unlike in many other cases when zoo-housed gorillas are exposed to their reflection (e.g. Shillito et al. 1999), the adult male lowland gorilla studied by Posada and Colell (2007) appeared interested, calm, and relaxed on looking into a 100 × 150 cm mirror placed just 0.2 m from his cage; he showed little sign of gaze aversion. Instead, he would sometimes stick his tongue out and move it around while staring into the mirror, and pull his upper lip upward. These kinds of self-referred behaviors increased on day 5 of mirror exposure. Following sixteen sessions of less than two hours with the mirror, the gorilla was marked with paint on the forehead. No mark-directed responses were observed in a 30-minute period in the absence of the mirror, but reintroduction of the mirror prompted a marked increase in prolonged staring at his reflection, sometimes accompanied by lateral head movements as if trying to see his profile. After 30 minutes had elapsed he moved away from the mirror and started to touch the marked area on his forehead; he frequently looked at and sniffed his hand, then he repeated the sequence while looking in the mirror; this behavior continued until the mark had been totally removed.

This study provides evidence that some gorillas may show explicit self-recognition under some circumstances. But it also raises some interesting methodological issues. First, after the initial discovery of the paint on his forehead, the gorilla's continued investigation of the mark was probably being reinforced each time some of the paint came away in his hand; looking in the mirror at this stage may have been coincidental. Also, following a procedure introduced by Lin et al. (1992) and used with increasingly frequency, no anesthestic was used to ensure that the subject was unaware of the marking procedure. Instead, a sham marking procedure using only water was used to habituate the gorilla to the general manipulation involved in marking, but responses to the sham marking procedure are not presented.

Although anesthetizing the subject and allowing the mark to dry completely might be considered as offering the tightest experimental control, general anesthesia is not risk-free, and many laboratories and zoos are unwilling to permit this procedure for research.[2] A couple of recent studies have addressed whether attempts to conceal the marking procedure are in fact necessary. Bard et al. (2006) took no special precautions when marking the faces of nine young chimpanzees (twenty-four to thirty-two months of age) with cosmetics other than applying the mark unobtrusively while grooming their faces; there was no sham marking

[2] One way of dealing with this limitation is to sequence the mark test with the need to perform routine anesthetization for purposes such as tuberculosis testing.

control procedure. Even so, the chimpanzees did not show mirror-mediated mark-directed responses until the age of twenty-eight months, largely replicating the earlier finding of Lin *et al.* (1992). As part of the same study, Bard *et al.* (2006) also got human mothers to explicitly tell their children (fifteen or twenty-four months of age) that they were putting makeup on them just before marking them on the forehead, but this did not lead to inflated mark-directed responses; no fifteen-month-olds passed the mark test whereas all twenty-four-month-olds did, as expected from the literature.

Another recent variant of the mark test aimed to dispel any doubts about whether failure to respond to the mark might be due to a lack of motivation, rather than a lack of self-recognition. Heschl and Burkart (2006) first tested common marmosets after marking them with a soluble odorless green dye following several days of habituation to sham marking. No monkey showed convincing signs of using the mirror to investigate the mark. Then the authors marked the monkeys using familiar brown chocolate cream, reasoning that this would increase the motivation to locate the now edible and highly prized mark. However, this did not lead to any of the monkeys finding the mark by looking in the mirror; in fact in this condition seven of the ten monkeys repeatedly tried to lick the chocolate mark on the monkey they saw in the mirror!

THE REFLECTION AS A STRANGE CONSPECIFIC

Notably, the marmosets tested for self-recognition by Heschl and Burkart (2006) had learned that reflected information about the environment could be used to locate hidden targets that were only visible in the mirror. Yet like other monkeys who learned to do this (see Anderson 1986; Anderson and Marchal 1994), they failed to show that they understood the source of the monkey who appears in the mirror. In another study, a group of talapoin monkeys was exposed to a large mirror and showed a range of social behaviors including aggressive acts (threat faces, hitting the mirror). Although some individuals appeared to compare real and reflected parts of their bodies, no individual used the mirror for self-exploration and none passed the mark test (Posada and Colell 2005). In other words, the talapoin monkeys reacted to their reflection as if confronted with a 'strange conspecific' (Anderson 1994). This is not to imply that responses to a mirror image are exactly the same as toward another individual; differences were shown many years ago (Anderson and Chamove 1986). But whereas some authors take the existence of differences in responding to one's reflection and a live conspecific to imply some degree of understanding of the source of the image (e.g. de Waal *et al.* 2005), we suggest that this is simply a consequence of the unusual stimulus properties of mirrors. In fact, it is conceivable that the mimicking behavior of the reflection is partly responsible for the calming effect of a mirror, once the initial social phase of responding has peaked. A mirror as a surrogate companion has been shown to alleviate separation distress in macaques (Anderson 1983) and behavioral indices of transportation stress in horses (Kay and Hall 2008). Individually caged rabbits strongly preferred the half of their cage that contained a mirror as environmental enrichment (Dalle Zotte *et al.* 2008).

SELF-RECOGNITION: OTHER MEDIA

One of the most striking things about a mirror is the perfect temporal contingency between the viewing individual's movements and those of the reflection. Indeed it is thought that understanding this one-to-one correspondence is critical for the emergence of self-recognition. Some investigators have asked whether self-recognition can emerge in the absence of the mimicry inherent in mirrors. It is known that chimpanzees recognize live television images of themselves; they can use the image of their hand to search for targets visible only via the monitor (Menzel *et al.* 1985), and they show self-exploration much as they do with a reflection (Hirata 2007). Although there have been studies of self-recognition in human children using delayed video images of themselves, this has not yet been done systematically with great apes. Recently, however, Anderson *et al.* (2009) explored capuchin monkeys' responses to live and 1-sec delayed video images of their own behavior. Face-on live and delayed images elicited facial expressions that are usually shown to other monkeys, and when presented with two screens, one showing the monkey's live image and the other showing the same image 1 sec later, the monkeys clearly differentiated between the two. None of the monkeys showed any signs of explicit self-recognition, but their behavior indicated recognition of the correspondence between their movements and the live image on the screen. Interestingly, like chimpanzees, macaques are able to recognize when somebody is imitating them (Paukner *et al.* 2005). These studies suggest that monkeys have at least *some* sense of agency and expectations about the environmental consequences of their behavior.

Cheney and Seyfarth (2007) give an interesting account of the baboon's sense of self. They suggest that, for a baboon, 'self' is equated with 'kin'. In other words, baboons are egocentric to the point that a fight or a predation event involving one of their kin is so salient that the baboon itself will show behavioral and physiological reactions much as if it was directly involved. Events involving non-kin do not give rise to the same effects. What baboons, and probably most other animals, do not seem to have, however, is the capacity to conceive of themselves as distinct, temporally continuous entities in their environment. It is this metacognitive ability that is crucial for the capacity to show self-recognition, and it is precisely this that is lacking in most animals, and all robots.

NEURAL CORRELATES OF SELF-RECOGNITION

In the first neuropsychological investigation of self-recognition in humans, Preilowski (1977) measured the galvanic skin response in split-brain patients and demonstrated that the right cortical hemisphere played a greater role in self-face recognition than the left (see also Sperry *et al.* 1979). Turk *et al.* (2002), however, worked with a split-brain patient and presented varying levels of morphed images of self and familiar-other faces to the right and left hemispheres and found the opposite effect.

The first attempts to investigate the neural correlates of self-recognition using modern neuroimaging and psychophysical techniques were conducted by Keenan *et al.* (1999, 2000). They developed a task that measured reaction times to one's own face as opposed to other faces that were either familiar or novel. They found a left-hand advantage (faster reaction times) when subjects responded to self-faces, but not to other faces. A second experiment asked subjects to stop a movie of a morphed face that transitioned between a famous face and self-face when they thought the image looked more like themselves than the famous person. Keenan *et al.* (2000) found that subjects stopped the movies sooner when responding with the left hand; that is, they were more likely to stop the movie when it had less self in the morph (i.e. more sensitive to self) with the left hand rather than with the right hand. Because of contralateral motor control, they interpreted these findings as implicating right hemisphere dominance for self-face recognition (see also Platek and Gallup 2002; Platek *et al.* 2003*a*, 2003*b*, 2004).

Keenan *et al.* (2001) went on to show that the right hemisphere is implicated in self-face recognition by utilizing the WADA (sodium amobarbital) technique (Wada 1949) to selectively deactivate one or the other of the two cortical hemispheres. Using patients with intractable epilepsy, they measured reactions to the self-face morphed 50 per cent with a famous face, and found that when the right hemisphere was anesthetized patients were more likely to report that the face was famous (i.e. not self), but when the left hemisphere was anesthetized they were more likely to report that the face looked like themselves.

Further evidence for right hemisphere localization of self-face recognition comes from case studies of delusional misidentification, particularly mirrored self-misidentification. Such patients typically show extensive right hemisphere damage (e.g. Feinberg 2000; Breen *et al.* 2001; Feinberg and Keenan 2005; Spangenberg *et al.* 1998). Recently, Platek and colleagues (Platek *et al.* 2004, 2006; Platek and Kemp, 2009) and others (Devue *et al.* 2007; Sugiura *et al.* 2000, 2005) have replicated the right-hemisphere activation when viewing one's own face.

Platek *et al.* (2004) measured BOLD (blood oxygen level dependent) signal response while subjects saw their own face, the face of a stranger, or the face of someone famous. When comparing activation associated with viewing self-faces as opposed to famous and novel faces, they found that the right hemisphere was selectively active; that is, self-face recognition preferentially activated the right frontal lobes. Using personally familiar gender and age matched control faces, Platek *et al.* (2006) found a distributed bilateral network involved in self-face recognition that included right superior frontal gyrus, right inferior parietal lobe, bilateral medial frontal lobe, and left anterior middle temporal gyrus (see Figure 3.1). Kircher and his colleagues (2000, 2001) also found a distributed bilateral network that included left prefrontal regions and right temporal lobe regions. However, in a reanalysis of Kircher *et al.*'s (2001) data, Keenan (personal communication) noted a slightly greater amount of right hemisphere activation in the self-face condition. These inconsistencies may be partially explained by differences in methodology (Gillihan and Farah 2005).

Sugiura *et al.* (2005) contrasted self-faces with a prelearned novel face (i.e. a face they had been trained to remember for a memory experiment) with two personally familiar faces, and found activation in left fusiform gyrus, right frontal operculum, and right occipitotemporoparietal junction. The personally familiar faces activated regions in the right occipitotemporoparietal junction as well, suggesting that the right frontal operculum and left fusiform gyrus are critical regions involved in self-face recognition.

Uddin *et al.* (2005) presented subjects with varying levels of morphed images and found activation in right superior frontal and inferior parietal lobes. They suggest that this activation to 'self' represents activation of a self–other frontal-parietal mirror network. That is, they speculate that the way in which one discriminates self from other is by recruiting a mirror neuron like network that compares self to other (but, as noted previously, because mirror neurons only fire in response to seeing others move this is a questionable interpretation).

More recently, Devue *et al.* (2007) contrasted self-face with a familiar colleague and found activation in the right inferior frontal lobe and right insula. Additionally, they found activation in anterior (right medial and frontal) regions when distinguishing self-body from non-self body. They suggest that there is a posterior–anterior stream of processing whereby posterior regions serve as first-level structural characterization of faces and bodies. They speculate that anterior regions

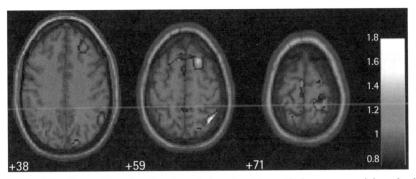

Figure 3.1 Distributed bilateral network involved in self–face recognition, including right superior frontal gyrus, right inferior parietal lobe, bilateral medial frontal lobe, and left anterior middle temporal gyrus. From Platek *et al.* (2006).

serve to differentiate self from other at a higher level of processing and perhaps at an abstract level of knowledge about the self.

A DISTRIBUTED SELF–OTHER NETWORK?

The frontal lobes are developing rapidly between the first and third years of life (Thatcher 1999; Semendeferi 1999), which is the period when children are also developing the capacities to represent self and other (see Amsterdam 1972; Lewis 2003). This has led to suggestions of a frontal lobe localization theory of self-awareness and theory of mind (Frith and Frith 1998; Gallup 1982; Keenan *et al.* 2000, 2003; Stuss and Anderson 2004). Additionally, the frontal cortex/prefrontal cortex (PFC) appears to be the most recently evolved portion of the neocortex (Rakic 1995) and is a highly intricate multi-modal information-processing center (Gibson 2002). Neuropsychologists have known for decades that damage to the PFC produces drastic changes in personality and behavior (Weinberger 1993). It is interesting that among non-human primates, chimpanzees, one of three non-human species who show evidence of self-recognition and self-awareness, have the most developed frontal cortex (Semendeferi *et al.* 1997). In contrast, the gorilla, the outlier great ape species that has not consistently shown evidence for mirror self-recognition or theory of mind, appears to have the least developed frontal lobes (Semendeferi 1999) and may also be the least anatomically lateralized in terms of the two cortical hemispheres (LeMay and Geschwind 1975). The frontal lobes may thus be a necessary substrate for the capacity to engage in self-processing (Gallup 1998).

It is now apparent, however, that several other substrates besides the frontal lobes are involved in self-referential processing. For instance, recent evidence has shown that the inferior parietal lobes and left anterior temporal lobe may also be involved in self-face recognition (Platek *et al.* 2006, 2008). Similarly, cortical midline structures such as the precuneus and cingulate gyrus appear to be involved in self-referent information processing and discriminating self- from other-descriptive words/ phrases (Fossati *et al.* 2003, 2004; Kelley *et al.* 2002; Lou *et al.* 2004; Macrae *et al.* 2004; Northoff and Bermpohl 2004; Seger *et al.* 2004). The medial parietal lobes, posterior cingulate and precuneus have also been associated with autobiographical memory retrieval (Maddock *et al.* 2001), engaging in self-generated actions and self-monitoring (Blakemore *et al.* 1998), self-reference in morphed faces (Platek *et al.* 2008), and discriminating between theory of mind stories and 'physical' stories (Fletcher *et al.* 1995; see also Vogeley *et al.* 2001). This again suggests a major role for midline cortical structures in the capacity to be self-aware.

Keenan *et al.* (2003) summarize a number of neuropsychological studies which show both right hemispheric lateralization and localization of self-recognition in the prefrontal cortex (see also Feinberg 2000). There is also the suggestion that self-other processing is subserved by processes associated with mirroring others' action—the so-called mirror neuron system (Gallese *et al.* 2004; Iacoboni 2004; Decety and Chaminade 2003), localized to the left inferior frontal lobe and left inferior parietal lobe (see also Uddin *et al.* 2005), but again in response to static photographs there is no basis for mirror neurons to be activated.

Self and Mind in Neuropsychiatric Disorders: Selective Deficits in Self-Processing

The growing evidence that individuals with autism, schizophrenia, and related, but milder, disturbances such as Asperger's syndrome and schizotypy perform less well on self-processing tasks further implicates the frontal lobes, since these conditions have been linked to deficits in frontal lobe functioning (Baron-Cohen *et al.* 1985; Baron-Cohen 1997; Corcoran *et al.* 1997; Doody *et al.* 1998; Frith and Corcoran 1996; Langdon and Coltheart 1999; Pickup and Frith 2001; Ellis and Gunter 1999; Mattay *et al.* 1999). See Callicot *et al.* 2000; Craig *et al.* 2004 for discussions of frontal lobe functioning and autism, Asperger's, and schizophrenia.

People who score high on the Schizotypal Personality Questionnaire, which measures schizotypal personality traits (premorbid schizophrenic-like tendencies), show impairments in self-face recognition (Platek and Gallup 2002) and self-descriptive adjective processing (Platek *et al.* 2003*b*). There is mounting evidence that schizophrenia is associated with frontal lobe pathology (e.g. Frith 1997) and, consistent with a connection between self processing and theory of mind (Gallup 1982), individuals with schizophrenia show pronounced mental state attribution deficits (e.g. Frith and Corcoran 1996; Besche *et al.* 1997; Sarfati *et al.* 1999).

Schizophrenics often see their own reflections in mirrors as independently alive, alien, or sinister (Harrington *et al.* 1989). They also have been observed talking and laughing at their mirrored reflection as if it were another person (Rosenzweig and Shakow 1937). In a now classic series of studies, Traub and Orbach (1964; Orbach *et al.* 1966) showed that schizophrenics had difficulty with a task that involved self-referent mirror use. The task involved rectifying a distorted mirror image of the subject, or an inanimate object using remote motorized controls attached to a metal mirror. Although schizophrenics were as good as the controls at adjusting the image of the inanimate object (a door), unlike controls, they were unable to adjust the mirror to appropriately represent themselves. This suggests that, rather than involving a deficit in mirror understanding, schizophrenia involves a deficit in self-processing.

Additionally, Frith and his colleagues (Frith 1992; Blakemore *et al.* 2000) have shown that schizophrenics occasionally report seeing nothing in their mirrored reflection (negative autoscopy) and are also unable to realize when behaviors such as speech are self-initiated. Frith (1992) has conceptualized schizophrenia as a disorder of mental states. He suggests that certain psychotic symptoms associated with schizophrenia may impair the ability to reason about other people's mental states. This inability can then lead to social withdrawal, inappropriate social behaviors, and affective blunting. The literature has been fairly consistent in showing that schizophrenics perform worse on theory of mind tasks than non-psychiatric and psychiatric controls, as well as patients in remission (Garety and Freeman 1999). For instance, Corcoran *et al.* (1995) found that patients with schizophrenia perform poorer on a simple social inference task than normal and non-psychotic psychiatric control groups. Brunet *et al.* (2003) used PET to investigate brain activation during a nonverbal theory of mind task. While control subjects showed significant cerebral activation in the right prefrontal cortex, these activations were not found in the schizophrenia group.

Platek and colleagues recently investigated the hypothesis that self-processing and mental state attribution are part of a shared behavioral and neurocognitive network that is impaired in schizophrenia-spectrum disorders (Irani *et al.* 2006). They found that unaffected first-degree relatives of patients with schizophrenia take longer than controls to recognize their own face, but are more accurate in making self vs. other judgments. This was related to the level of schizotypy shown by the family members. Additionally, patients were more likely to misattribute self to unfamiliar faces; that is, when they made errors at classifying a novel face, they were more likely to indicate that it was a self-face.

In children suffering from autistic-spectrum disorders, mirror self-recognition is developmentally delayed and sometimes even absent (Spiker and Ricks 1984). A series of studies have shown that only between 50 and 70 per cent of children with autism pass a modified version of the Gallup mark test (Dawson and McKissick 1984; Spiker and Ricks 1984). Those that eventually pass the test do so at a developmentally delayed age of 5–7 years while most children pass between eighteen and twenty-four months of age. Similarly to schizophrenics, children with autism perform poorly on theory of mind tasks (Baron-Cohen *et al.* 1985, 1986, 1995, 1997b, 1999, 2001; Latham and Platek, under review).

Patients with damage to the frontal cortex are not only impaired in their ability to recognize their own faces, but they show corollary deficits in self-evaluation and autobiographical memory (e.g. Keenan *et al.* 2003). Additionally, when patients have the anterior portion of the temporal lobe removed in order to treat intractable seizures associated with epilepsy, this impairs the ability to recognize their own face (slower reaction time and more errors) compared to personally familiar and famous faces (Platek *et al.*, unpublished data). This finding, while inconsistent with a simple right hemispheric model for self-processing, supports our recent fMRI data (Platek *et al.* 2006) showing a larger, distributed network for self-processing that involves the anterior middle temporal gyrus (Platek, Scheiser, Glosser, Schneider, Irani, and Panyavin, unpublished data). Thus, the brain disorder data support the idea that self-recognition is impaired by deficiencies in frontal lobe processing that may be localized to specific regions (e.g. superior or inferior frontal gyri, as well as anterior temporal regions).

Neuropsychology of Self-Awareness and Contagious Yawning

The fact that self-processing, mental state attribution, and autobiographical memories share similar brain regions in common is not only consistent with the suggestion that self-awareness and mental state attribution are functionally related (Gallup 1982), but it has interesting implications for contagious yawning. The tendency to yawn when someone witnesses (or even thinks about) another person yawning is termed contagious yawning. We have evidence that this phenomenon may be linked to primitive empathic mechanisms related to mental state attribution. For example, in contrast to those who are unaffected, we found that people who show contagious yawning recognize their own faces more quickly, score higher on tests of mental state attribution, and show fewer schizotypal personality characteristics (Platek *et al.* 2003a). Using functional magnetic resonance imaging we also found that witnessing someone yawn uniquely activates the posterior cingulate and the precuneus (Platek *et al.* 2004), both areas of the human brain that are related to self-referential processing, theory of mind, and autobiographical memories.

There is additional support for a connection between contagious yawning, self-awareness, and mental state attribution. Consistent with predictions that follow from this model, Anderson, Myowa-Yamakoshi and Matsuzawa (2004) have found clear evidence of contagious yawning in several chimpanzees that were shown videoclips of other chimpanzees yawning. In contrast, recent research shows that autistic children, who are impaired at self-recognition and mental state attribution, fail to show evidence of contagious yawning (Senju, Maeda, Kikuchi, Hasegawa, Tojo and Osanai 2007).

REFERENCES

AMSTERDAM, B. (1972). 'Mirror Self-Image Reactions Before the Age of Two', *Developmental Psychobiology*, 5: 297–305.

ANDERSON, J. R. (1983). 'Mirror-Image Stimulation and Short Separations in Stumptail Monkeys', *Animal Learning and Behavior*, 11: 138–43.

——(1984). 'Monkeys with Mirrors: Some Questions for Primate Psychology', *International Journal of Primatology*, 5: 81–98.

——(1986). 'Mirror-Mediated Finding of Hidden Food by Monkeys (*Macaca tonkeana* and *M. fascicularis*)'. *Journal of Comparative Psychology*, 100: 237–42.

——(1994). 'The Monkey in the Mirror: A Strange Conspecific', in R. W. Mitchell, S. T. Parker, and M. L. Boccia (eds), *Self-Awareness in Animals and Humans: Developmental Perspectives* (New York: Cambridge University Press), 315–29.

——and CHAMOVE, A. S. (1986). 'Infant Stumptailed Macaques Reared with Mirrors or Peers: Social Responsiveness, Attachment, and Adjustment', *Primates*, 27: 63–82.

ANDERSON, J. R., and GALLUP, G. G., JR. (1999). 'Self-Recognition in Nonhuman Primates: Past and Future Challenges', in M. Haug and R. E. Whalen (eds), *Animal Models of Human Emotion and Cognition* (Washington, DC: American Psychological Association), 175–94.

——KUROSHIMA, H., PAUKNER, A., and FUJITA, K. (2009). 'Capuchin Monkeys (Cebus apella) Respond to Video Images of Themselves', *Animal Cognition*, 12: 55–62.

——and MARCHAL, P. (1994). 'Capuchin Monkeys and Confrontations with Mirrors', in J.-J. Roeder, B. Thierry, J. R. Anderson, and N. Herrenschmidt (eds), *Current Primatology: Social Development, Learning and Behaviour* (Strasbourg: University Louis Pasteur), 371–80.

ANDERSON, J. R., MYOWA-YAMAKOSHI, M., and MATSUZAWA, T. (2004). 'Contagious Yawning in Chimpanzees', *Proceedings of the Royal Society: B*, 271: 468–70.

BAARS, B., RAMSOY, T., and LAUREYS, S. (2003). 'Brain, Conscious Experience and the Observing Self', *Trends in Neurosciences*, 26: 671–5.

BARD, K. A., TODD, B. K., BERNIER, C. K., LOVE, J., and LEAVENS, D. A. (2006). 'Self-Awareness in Human and Chimpanzee Infants: What is Measured and What is Meant by the Mark and Mirror Test?', *Infancy*, 9: 185–213.

BARON-COHEN, S. (1997). 'Hey! It was Just a Joke! Understanding Propositions and Propositional Attitudes by Normally Developing Children and Children with Autism', *Israel Journal of Psychiatry*, 34: 174–8.

——and CROSS, P. (1995). 'Reading the Eyes: Evidence for the Role of Perception in the Development of a Theory of Mind', in M. Davies and M. Stone (eds), *The Stimulation Theory Debate* (Oxford: Blackwells).

——LESLIE, A. M., and FRITH, U. (1985). 'Does the Autistic Child have a "Theory of Mind"?', *Cognition*, 21: 37–46.

——and ——(1986). 'Mechanical, Behavioural, and Intentional Understanding of Picture Stories in Autistic Children', *British Journal of Developmental Psychology*, 4: 113–25.

——JOLLIFFE, T., MORTIMORE, C., and ROBERTSON, M. (1997*a*). 'Another Advanced Test of Theory of Mind: Evidence from Very High Functioning Adults with Autism or Asperger's Syndrome', *Journal of Child Psychology and Psychiatry and Allied Disciplines*, 38: 813–22.

——O'RIORDAN, M., JONES, R., STONE, V., and PLAISTED, K. (1999). 'A New Test of Social Sensitivity: Detection of Faux Pas in Normal Children and Children with Asperger's Syndrome', *Journal of Autism and Developmental Disorders*, 29: 407–18.

——WHEELWRIGHT, S., HILL, J., RASTE, Y., and PLUMB, I. (2001). 'The "Reading the Mind in the Eyes" Test Revised Version: A Study with Normal Adults, and Adults with Asperger Syndrome or High-Functioning Autism', *Journal of Child Psychology and Psychiatry*, 42: 241–51.

——WHEELWRIGHT, S., and JOLLIFFE, T. (1997*c*). 'Is there a Language of the Eyes? Evidence from Normal Adults and Adults with Autism or Asperger's Syndrome', *Visual Cognition*, 4: 311–31.

BATES, J., and BYRNE, R. W. (2008). 'Do Elephants Show Empathy?', *Journal of Consciousness Studies*, 15: 204–25, 241–52.

BESCHE, C., PASSERIEUX, C., SEGUI, J., SARFATI, Y., LAURENT, J. P., and HARDY-BAYLE, M. C. (1997). 'Syntactic and Semantic Processing in Schizophrenic Patients Evaluated by Lexical Decision Tasks', *Neuropsychology*, 11: 498–505.

BLAKEMORE, S. J., SMITH, J., STEEL, R., JOHNSTONE, E., and FRITH, C. D. (2000). 'The Perception of Self-Produced Sensory Stimuli in Patients with Auditory Hallucinations and Passivity Experiences: Evidence for a Breakdown in Self-Monitoring', *Psychological Medicine*, 30: 1131–9.

——WOLPERT, D. M., and FRITH, C. D. (1998). 'Central Cancellation of Self-Produced Tickle Sensation', *Nature Neuroscience*, 1: 635–40.

BREEN, N., CAINE, D., and COLTHEART, M. (2001). 'Mirrored-Self Misidentification: Two Cases of Focal Onset Dementia', *Neurocase*, 7(3): 239–54.

BRUNET, E., SARFATI, Y., HARDY-BAYLE, M. C., and DECETY, J. (2003). 'Abnormalities of Brain Function during a Nonverbal Theory of Mind Task in Schizophrenia', *Neuropsychologia*, 41(12): 1574–82.

CALLICOT, J. H., BERTOLINO, A., EGAN, M. F., MATTAY, V. S., LANGHEIM, F. J., and WEINBERGER, D. R. (2000). 'Selective Relationship between Prefrontal N-Acetylaspartate Measures and Negative Symptoms in Schizophrenia', *American Journal of Psychiatry*, 157: 1646–51.

CHENEY, D. L., and SEYFARTH, R. M. (2007). *Baboon Metaphysics: The Evolution of a Social Mind* (Chicago: University of Chicago Press).

CORCORAN, R., CAHILL, C., and Frith C. D. (1997). 'The Appreciation of Visual Jokes in People with Schizophrenia: A Study of "Mentalizing" Ability', *Schizophrenia Research*, 24: 319–27.

——MERCER, G., and FRITH, C. D. (1995). 'Schizophrenia, Symptomatology and Social Inference: Investigating "Theory of Mind" in People with Schizophrenia', *Schizophrenia Research*, 17: 5–13.

CRAIG, J. S., HATTON, C., CRAIG, F. B., and BENTALL, R. P. (2004). 'Persecutory Beliefs, Attributions and Theory of Mind: Comparison of Patients with Paranoid Delusions, Asperger's Syndrome and Healthy Controls', *Schizophrenia Research*, 69: 29–33.

DALLE ZOTTE, A., PRINCZ, Z., MATICS, Z., GERENCSER, Z., METZGER, S., and SZENDRO, Z. (2008). 'Rabbit Preference for Cages and Pens with or without Mirrors', *Applied Animal Behaviour Science*, 116: 273–8.

DAWSON, G., and MCKISSICK, F. C. (1984). 'Self-Recognition in Autistic Children', *Journal of Autism and Developmental Disorders*, 17: 383–94.

DECETY, J., and CHAMINADE, T. (2003). 'Neural Correlates of Feeling Sympathy', *Neuropsychologia* (Special issue on Social Cognition), 41: 127–38.

DEN OUDEN, H. E., FRITH, U., FRITH, C., and BLAKEMORE, S. J. (2005). 'Thinking about Intentions', *Neuroimage*, 28: 787–96.

DE VEER, M. W., GALLUP, G. G., JR., THEALL, L. A., VAN DEN BOS, R., and POVINELLI, D. J. (2003). 'An Eight-Year Longitudinal Study of Mirror Self-Recognition in Chimpanzees (Pan troglodytes)', *Neuropsychologica*, 41: 229–34.

DEVUE, C., COLLETTE, F., BALTEAU, E., DEGUELDRE, C., LUXEN, A., MAQUET, P., and BRÉDART, S. (2007). 'Here I am: The Cortical Correlates of Visual Self-Recognition', *Brain Research*, 1: 169–82.

DE WAAL, F. B. M., DINDO, M., FREEMAN, C. A., and HALL, M. J. (2005). 'The Monkey in the Mirror: Hardly a Stranger', *Proceedings of the National Academy of Sciences*, 102: 11140–7.

DOODY, G. A., GOETZ, M., JOHNSON, E. C., FRITH, C. D., and CUNNIGHAM-OWENS, D. G. (1998). 'Theory of Mind and Psychoses', *Psychological Medicine*, 28: 397–405.

DUNBAR, R. I. M. (1998). 'The Social Brain Hypothesis', *Evolutionary Anthropology*, 6(5): 178–90.

ELLIS, H. D., and GUNTER, H. L. (1999). 'Asperger Syndrome: A Simple Matter of White Matter?', *Trends in Cognitive Sciences*, 3: 192–200.

EPSTEIN, R., LANZA, R. P., and SKINNER, B. F. (1980). '"Self-Awareness" in the Pigeon', *Science*, 212: 695–6.

FEINBERG, T. E. (2000). *Altered Egos: How the Brain Creates the Self* (New York: Oxford University Press).

——and KEENAN, J. P. (2005). 'Where in the Brain is the Self?', *Consciousness and Cognition*, 14/4: 661–78.

FLETCHER, P. C., HAPPE, F., FRITH, U., BAKER, S. C., DOLAN, R. J., FRACKOWIAK, R. S. J., and FRITH, C. D. (1995). 'Other Minds in the Brain: A Functional Imaging Study of "Theory of Mind" in Story Comprehension', *Cognition*, 57: 109–28.

FOSSATI, P., HEVENOR, S. J., GRAHAM, S. J., GRADY, C., KEIGHTLEY, M. L., CRAIK, F., and MAYBERG, H. (2003). 'In Search of the Emotional Self: An FMRI Study Using Positive and Negative Emotional Words', *American Journal of Psychiatry*, 60: 1938–45.

Fossati, P., Hevenor, S. J., Lepage, M., Graham, S. J., Gradya, C., Keightley, M. L., Craika, F., and Mayberg, H. (2004). 'Distributed Self in Episodic Memory: Neural Correlates of Successful Retrieval of Self-Encoded Positive and Negative Personality Traits', *Neuroimage*, 22: 1596–1604.

Fox, P. T., Parsons, L. M., and Lancaster, J. L. (1998). 'Beyond the Single Study: Function/ Location Metanalysis in Cognitive Neuroimaging', *Current Opinion in Neurobiology*, 8(2): 178–87.

Frith, C. D. (1992). *The Cognitive Neuropsychology of Schizophrenia* (Hillsdale, NJ: Lawrence Erlbaum Associates).

——(1997) 'Functional Brain Imaging and the Neuropathology of Schizophrenia', *Schizophrenia Bulletin*, 23: 525–7.

——and Corcoran, R. (1996). 'Exploring "Theory of Mind" in People with Schizophrenia', *Psychological Medicine*, 26: 521–30.

Frith, U., and Frith, C. (1998). 'Modularity of Mind and Phonological Deficit', in C. Von Euler, I. Lundberg, and R. Llinas (eds), *Basic Mechanisms in Cognition and Language* (New York: Elsevier Science), 3–17.

Gallese, V., Keysers, C., and Rizzolatti, G. (2004). 'A Unifying View of the Basis of Social Cognition', *Trends in Cognitive Science*, 8: 396–403.

Gallup, G. G., Jr. (1968). 'Mirror-Image Stimulation', *Psychological Bulletin*, 70: 782–93.

——(1970). 'Chimpanzees: Self-Recognition', *Science*, 167(3914): 86–7.

——(1982). 'Self-Awareness and the Emergence of Mind in Primates', *American Journal of Primatology*, 2(3): 237–48.

——(1994). 'Self-Recognition: Research Strategies and Experimental Design', in S. Parker, R. Mitchell, and M. Boccia (eds), *Self-Awareness in Animals and Humans* (Cambridge: Cambridge University Press), 35–50.

——(1997). 'On the Rise and Fall of Self-Conception in Primates', *Annals of the New York Academy of Sciences*, 818: 73–84.

——(1998). 'Can Animals Empathize: Yes?' *Scientific American Presents*, 9: 66–71.

——and Platek, S. M. (2001). 'Cognitive Empathy Presupposes Self-Awareness: Evidence from Phylogeny, Ontogeny, Neuropsychology, and Mental Illness', *Behavioral and Brain Sciences*, 25: 36–7.

——and Suarez, S. D. (1991). 'Social Responding to Mirrors in Rhesus Monkeys (Macaca mulatta): Effects of Temporary Mirror Removal', *Journal of Comparative Psychology*, 105: 376–9.

——Anderson, J. R., and Platek, S. M. (2003a). 'Self-Awareness, Social Intelligence, and Schizophrenia', in T. Kircher and A. S. David (eds), *The Self in Neuroscience and Psychiatry* (Cambridge: Cambridge University Press), 147–65.

——Anderson, J. R., and Shillito, D. J. (2003b). 'The Mirror Test', in M. Bekoff, C. Allen, and G. M. Burghardt (eds), *The Cognitive Animal* (Cambridge, Mass.: MIT Press), 325–33.

——Wallnau, L. B., and Suarez, S. D. (1980). 'Failure to Find Self-Recognition in Mother–Infant and Infant–Infant Rhesus Monkey Pairs', *Folia Primatologica*, 33: 210–19.

Garety, P. A., and Freeman, D. (1999). 'Cognitive Approaches to Delusions: A Critical Review of Theories and Evidence', *British Journal of Clinical Psychology*, 38/2: 113–54.

Gazzaniga, M. S. (1998). 'The Split-Brain Revisited', *Scientific America*, 279/6: 51–5.

Gibson, K. R. (2002). 'Evolution of Human Intelligence: The Roles of Brain Size and Mental Construction', *Brain, Behavior, and Evolution*, 59: 10–20.

GILLIHAN, S., and FARAH, M. J. (2005). 'Is Self-Related Processing Special? A Critical Review', *Psychological Bulletin*, 131: 76–97.

GOBBINI, M. I., and HAXBY, J. V. (2006). 'Neural Response to the Visual Familiarity of Faces', *Brain Research Bulletin*, 71: 76–82.

GOLD, B., and SCASSELLATI, B. (2009). 'Using Probalistic Reasoning over Time to Self-Recognize', *Robotics and Autonomous Systems*, 57: 384–92.

GU, X., and HAN, S. (2007). 'Attention and Reality Constraints on the Neural Processes of Empathy for Pain', *Neuroimage*, 36: 256–67.

GUSNARD, D. A., and RAICHLE, M. E. (2001). 'Searching for a Baseline: Functional Imaging and the Resting Human Brain', *Nature Reviews Neuroscience*, 2: 685–94.

——AKBUDAK, E., SHULMAN, G. L., and RAICHLE, M. E. (2001). 'Medial Prefrontal Cortex and Self-Referential Mental Activity: Relation to a Default Mode of Brain Function', *Proceedings of the National Academy of Sciences USA*, 98: 4259–64.

HARRINGTON, A., OEPEN, G., and MANFRED, S. (1989). 'Disordered Recognition and Perception of Human Faces in Acute Schizophrenia and Experimental Psychosis', *Comprehensive Psychiatry*, 30: 376–84.

HART, B. L., HART, L. A., McCOY, M., and SARATH, C. R. (2001). 'Cognitive Behaviour in Asian Elephants: Use and Modification of Branches for Fly Switching', *Animal Behaviour*, 62: 839–47.

HESCHL, A., and BURKART, J. (2006). 'A New Mark Test for Mirror Self-Recognition in Primates', *Primates*, 47: 187–98.

HIRATA, S. (2007). 'A Note on the Responses of Chimpanzees (*Pan troglodytes*) to Live Self-Images on Television Monitors', *Behavioural Processes*, 75: 85–90.

IACOBONI, M. (2004). 'Understanding Others: Imitation, Language, Empathy', in S. Hurley and N. Chater (eds), *Perspectives on Imitation: From Cognitive Neuroscience to Social Science*, i. *Mechanisms of Imitation and Imitation in Animals* (Cambridge, Mass.: MIT Press).

IRANI, F., PLATEK, S. M., BUNCE, S., RUOCCO, A. C., and CHUTE, D. (2007). 'Functional Near Infrared Spectroscopy (fNIRS): An Emerging Neuroimaging Technology with Important Applications for the Study of Brain Disorders', *Clinical Neuropsychology*, 21: 9–37.

——PANYAVIN, I. S., CALKINS, M. E., KOHLER, C., SIEGEL, S. J., SCHACHTER, M., GUR, R. E., and GUR, R. C. (2008). 'Self-Race Recognition and Theory of Mind in Patients with Schizophrenia and First-Degree Relatives', *Schizophrenia Research*, 88: 151–60.

——RUOCCO, A. C., BUNCE, S. B., and CHUTE, D. L. (in press). 'Current and Potential Applications of Functional Near Infrared Spectroscopy (fNIRS) to Psychiatric and Neurological Disorders', *The Clinical Neuropsychologist*, Special issue, 'Emerging Technologies:—Imaging for Dummies, Who Also Happen to be Neuropsychologists'.

JOHNSON, D. B. (1983). 'Self-Recognition in Infants', *Infant Behavior and Development*, 6: 211–22.

KANWISHER, N., McDERMOTT, J., and CHUN, M. M. (1997). 'The Fusiform Face Area: A Module in Human Extra-Striate Cortex Specialized for Face Perception', *Journal of Neuroscience*, 17: 4302–11.

KAY, R., and HALL, C. (2008). 'The Use of a Mirror Reduces Isolation Stress in Horses Being Transported by Trailer', *Applied Animal Behaviour Science*, 116: 237–43.

KEENAN, J. P., FREUND, S., HAMILTON, R. H., GANIS, G., and PASCUAL-LEONE, A. (2000). 'Hand Response Differences in a Self-Face Identification Task', *Neuropsychologia*, 38: 1047–53.

KEENAN, J. P., GALLUP, G. G., and FALK, D. (2003). *The Face in the Mirror: The Search for the Origins of Consciousness* (New York: HarperCollins/Ecco).

——McCUTCHEON, B., FREUND, S., GALLUP, G. G., JR., SANDERS, G., and PASCUAL-LEONE, A. (1999). 'Left Hand Advantage in a Self-Face Recognition Task', *Neuropsychologia*, 37: 1421–5.

——NELSON, A., O'CONNOR, M., and PASCUAL-LEONE, A. (2001). 'Self-Recognition and the Right Hemisphere', *Nature*, 409: 305.

——WHEELER, M., and EWERS, M. (2003). 'The Neural Correlates of Self-Awareness and Self-Recognition', in Tilo Kircher and Anthony David (eds), *The Self in Neuroscience and Psychiatry* (Cambridge: Cambridge University Press), 166–79.

KELLEY, W., MACRAE, C., WYLAND, C., CAGLAR, S., INATI, S., and HEATHERTON, T. (2002). 'Finding the Self? An Event-Related FMRI Study', *Journal of Cognitive Neuroscience*, 14: 785–94.

KIRCHER, T. T. J., BRAMMER, M., BULLMORE, E., SIMMONS, A., BARTELS, M., and DAVID, A. S. (2002). 'The Neural Correlates of Intentional and Incidental Self Processing', *Neuropsychologia*, 40/6: 683–92.

——SENIOR, C., PHILLIPS, M. L., BENSON, P. J., BULLMORE, E. T., BRUMMER, M., SIMMONS, A., WILLIAMS, S. C., BARTELS, M., and DAND, A. J. (2000). 'Towards a Functional Neuroanatomy of Self-Processing: Effects of Faces and Words', *Cognitive Brain Research*, 10: 133–44.

——SENIOR, C., PHILLIPS, M., RABE-HESKETH, S., BENSON, P., BULLMORE, E., BRAMMER, M., SIMMONS, A., BARTELS, M., and DAVID, A. (2001). 'Recognizing One's Own Face', *Cognition*, 78: 1–15.

LANGDON, R., and COLTHEART, M. (1999). 'Mentalising, Schizotypy, and Schizophrenia', *Cognition*, 71: 43–71.

LATHAM, J. R., and PLATEK, S. M. (submitted). 'Inhibitory Control is Not a Necessary Executive Function for Theory of Mind: A Pilot Investigation into High Functioning Autistic and Healthy Control Children'. *Evolutionary Psychology*.

LeMAY, M., and GESCHWIND, N. (1975). 'Hemispheric Differences in the Brains of Great Apes', *Brain, Behavior, and Evolution*, 11: 48–52.

LEWIS, M. (2003). 'The Emergence of Consciousness and its Role in Human Development', *Annals of the New York Academy of Sciences*, 1001: 104–33.

LIN, A. C., BARD, K. A., and ANDERSON, J. R. (1992). 'Development of Self-Recognition in Chimpanzees (*Pan troglodytes*)', *Journal of Comparative Psychology*, 106: 120–7.

LOU, H. C, LUBER, B., CRUPAIN, M., KEENAN, J. P., NOWAK, M., KJAER, T. W., SACKEIM, H. A., and LISANBY, S. H. (2004). 'Parietal Cortex and Representation of the Mental Self', *Proceedings of the National Academy of Sciences* (USA), 101: 6827–32.

MACRAE, C. N., MORAN, J. M., HEATHERTON, T. F., BANFIELD, J. F., and KELLEY, W. M. (2004). 'Medial Prefrontal Activity Predicts Memory for Self', *Cerebral Cortex*, 14: 647–54.

MADDOCK, R. J., GARRETT, A. S., and BUONOCORE, M. H. (2001). 'Remembering Familiar People: The Posterior Cingulate Cortex and Autobiographical Memory Retrieval', *Neuroscience*, 104/3: 667–76.

MATTAY, V. S., BACHEVALIER, J., FRANK, J. A., EGAN, M., and WEINBERGER, D. R. (1999). 'The Relationship between Dorsolateral Prefrontal N-Acetylaspartate Measure and Striatal Dopamine Activity in Schizophrenia', *Biological Psychiatry*, 45: 660–7.

MAZOYER, B., ZAGO, L., MELLET, E., BRICOGNE, S., ETARD, O., HOUDÉ, O., CRIVELLO, F., JOLIOT, M., PETIT, L., and TZOURIO-MAZOYER, N. (2001). 'Cortical Networks for

Working Memory and Executive Functions Sustain the Conscious Resting State in Man', *Brain Research Bulletin*, 54: 287–98.

MEADOR, K. J., LORING, D. W., FEINBERG, T. E., LEE, G. P., and NICHOLS, M. E. (2000). 'Anosognosia and Asomatognosia during Intracarotid Amobarbital Inactivation', *Neurology*, 55: 816–20.

MENZEL, E. W., JR., SAVAGE-RUMBAUGH, E. S., and LAWSON, J. (1985). 'Chimpanzee (*Pan troglodytes*) Spatial Problem Solving with the Use of Mirrors and Televised Equivalents of Mirrors', *Journal of Comparative Psychology*, 99: 211–17.

MITCHELL, R. W. (1993). 'Mental Modes of Mirror Self-Recognition: Two Theories', *New Ideas in Psychology*, 11: 295–325.

——(1994). 'Multiplicities of Self', in S. Parker, R. W. Mitchell, and M. L. Boccia (eds), *Self-Awareness in Animals and Humans* (New York: Cambridge University Press), 81–107.

MORIN, A. (2002). 'Right Hemisphere Self-Awareness: A Critical Assessment', *Consciousness and Cognition*, 112: 396–401.

NISSANI, M., and HOEFLER-NISSANI, D. (2007). 'Absence of Mirror Self-Referential Behavior in Two Asian Elephants', *Journal of Veterinary Science*, 1/1: www.scientificjournals.org/journals2007/articles/1043.htm.

NORTHOFF, G., and BERMPOHL, F. (2004). 'Cortical Midline Structures and the Self', *Trends in Cognitive Sciences*, 8: 102–7.

——HEINZEL, A., DE GRECK, M., BERMPOHL, F., DOBROWOLNY, H., and PANKSEPP, J. (2006). 'Self-Referential Processing in our Brain—A Meta-Analysis of Imaging Studies on the Self', *Neuroimage*, 31: 440–57.

ORBACH, J., TRAUB A. C., and OLSON, R. (1966). 'Psychological Studies of Body-Image: II Normative Data on the Adjustable Body-Distorting Mirror', *Archives of General Psychiatry*, 14: 41–7.

PATTERSON, F. G. P., and COHN, R. H. (1994). In S. T. Parker, R. W. Mitchell, and M. L. Boccia (eds), *Self-Awareness in Animals and Humans: Developmental Perspectives* (Cambridge and New York: Cambridge University Press), 273–90.

PAUKNER, A., ANDERSON, J. R., BORELLI, A., VISALBERGHI, E., and FERRARI, P. (2005). 'Macaques (*Macaca nemestrina*) Recognize When they are Being Imitated', *Biology Letters*, 1: 219–22.

——ANDERSON, J. R., and FUJITA, K. (2004). 'Reactions of Capuchin Monkeys (*Cebus apella*) to Multiple Mirrors', *Behavioural Processes*, 66: 1–6.

PICKUP, G. J., and FRITH, C. D. (2001). 'Schizotypy, Theory of Mind and Weak Central Coherence', *Schizophrenia Research*, 49/1–2 suppl.: 118.

PLATEK, S. M., and GALLUP, G. G., JR. (2002). 'Self-Face Recognition is Affected by Schizotypal Personality Traits', *Schizophrenia Research*, 57: 311–15.

——and KEMP, S. M. (2009). 'Is Family Special to the Brain? An Event-Related FMRI Study of Familiar, Familial, and Self-Face Recognition', *Neuropsychologia*, 47: 849–58.

——CRITTON, S. R., MYERS, T. E., and GALLUP, G. G., JR. (2003a). 'Contagious Yawning: The Role of Self-Awareness and Mental State Attribution', *Cognitive Brain Research*, 17: 223–7.

——IRANI, F., SCHEISER, D., SCHNEIDER, J., and GLOSSER, G. (accepted). 'Effect of Anterior Temporal Lobectomy on Self-Face Recognition', *Social Neuroscience*.

——KEENAN, J. P., GALLUP, G. G., JR., and MOHAMED, F. B. (2004). 'Where am I? The Neurological Correlates of Self and Other', *Cognitive Brain Research*, 19: 114–22.

PLATEK, S. M., LOUGHEAD, J. W., GUR, R. C., BUSCH, S., RUPAREL, K., PHEND, N., PANYAVIN, I. S., and LANGLEBEN, D. D. (2006). 'Neural Substrates for Functionally Discriminating Self-Face from Personally Familiar Faces', *Human Brain Mapping*, 27/2: 91–8.

——MYERS, T. E., CRITTON, S. R., and GALLUP, G. G., JR. (2003*b*). 'A Left-Hand Advantage for Self-Description and the Effects of Schizotypal Personality Traits', *Schizophrenia Research*, 65/2–3: 147–51.

——THOMPSON, J. W., and GALLUP, G. G., JR. (2004). 'Cross-Modal Self-Recognition: The Role of Visual, Auditory, and Olfactory Primes', *Consciousness and Cognition*, 13: 197–210.

——WATHNE, K., TIERNEY, N. G., and THOMSON, J. W. (2008). 'Neural Correlations of Self-Face Recognition: An Effect-Location Meta-analysis', *Brain Research*, 1232: 173–84.

PLOTNIK, J. M., DE WAAL, F. B. M., and REISS, D. (2006). 'Self-Recognition in an Asian Elephant', *Proceedings of the National Academy of Sciences of the United States of America*, 103/45: 17053–7.

POSADA, S., and COLELL, M. (2005). 'Mirror Responses in a Group of *Miopithecus talapoin*'. *Primates*, 46: 165–72.

——and ——(2007). 'Another Gorilla (*Gorilla gorilla gorilla*) Recognizes himself in a Mirror', *American Journal of Primatology*, 69: 576–83.

POVINELLI, D. J. (1989). 'Failure to Find Self-Recognition in Asian Elephants (*Elephas maximus*) in Contrast to their Use of Mirror Cues to Discover Hidden Food', *Journal of Comparative Psychology*, 103: 122–31.

——(1995). 'The Unduplicated Self', in P. Rochat (ed.), *The Self in Early Infancy* (Amsterdam: North-Holland-Elsevier), 161–92.

——and CANT, J. G. H. (1995). 'Arboreal Clambering and the Evolution of Self-Conception', *Quarterly Review of Biology*, 70: 393–421.

——RULF, A. B., LANDAU, K. R., and BIERSCHWALE, D. T. (1993). 'Self-Recognition in Chimpanzees: Distribution, Ontogeny, and Patterns of Emergence', *Journal of Comparative Psychology*, 107: 347–72.

PREILOWSKI, B. (1977). 'Self-Recognition as a Test of Consciousness in Left and Right Hemisphere of "Split-Brain" Patients', *Activas Nervosa Superior*, 19/suppl. 2: 343–4.

PRIOR, H., SCHWARZ, A., and GUNTURKUN, O. (2008). 'Mirror-Induced Behavior in the Magpie (*Pica pica*): Evidence of Self-Recognition', *Public Library of Science Biology*, 6/8: e202.

RAICHLE, M. E., MacLEOD, A. M., SNYDER, A. Z., POWERS, W. J., GUSNARD, D. A., and SHULMAN, G. L. (2001). 'A Default Mode of Brain Function', *Proceedings of the National Academy of Sciences USA*, 98: 676–82.

RAKIC, P. (1995). 'A Small Step for the Cell, a Giant Leap for Mankind: A Hypothesis of Neocortical Expansion during Evolution', *Trends Neurosci*, 18/9: 383–8.

REISS, D., and MARINO, L. (2001). 'Mirror Self-Recognition in the Bottlenose Dolphin: A Case of Cognitive Convergence', *Proceedings of the National Academy of Sciences of the United States of America*, 98(10): 5937–42.

RIZZOLATTI, G., FOGASSI, L., and GALLESE, V. (2001). 'Neurophysiological Mechanisms Underlying the Understanding and Imitation of Action', *Nature Reviews Neuroscience*, 2: 661–70.

ROMA, P. G., SILBERBERG, A., HUNTSBERRY, M. E., CHRISTENSEN, C. J., RUGGERIO, A. M., and SUOMI, S. J. (2007). 'Mark Tests for Mirror Self-Recognition in Capuchin Monkeys (*Cebus apella*) Trained to Touch Marks', *American Journal of Primatology*, 898–1000.

ROSENZWEIG, S., and SHAKOW, D. (1937). 'Mirror Behavior in Schizophrenic and Normal Individuals', *Journal of Nervous and Mental Disease*, 86: 166–74.

SARFATI, Y., HARDY-BAYLÉ, M. C., BRUNET, E., and WIDLÖCHER, D. (1999). 'Investigating Theory of Mind in Schizophrenia: Influence of Verbalization in Disorganized and Non-Disorganized Patients', *Schizophrenia Research*, 37: 183–90.

SEGER, C. A., STONE, M., and KEENAN, J. P. (2004). 'Cortical Activations during Judgements about the Self and Another Person', *Neuropsychologia*, 42: 1168–77.

SEMENDEFERI, K. (1999). 'The Frontal Lobes of the Great Apes with a Focus on the Gorilla and the Orangutan', in R. W. Parker, H. L. Miles, and S. Taylor Parker (eds), *The Mentalities of Gorillas and Orangutans* (Cambridge: Cambridge University Press), 70–97.

——DAMASIO, H., FRANK, R., and VAN HOESEN, G. W. (1997). 'The Evolution of the Frontal Lobes: A Volumetric Analysis Based on Three-Dimensional Reconstructions of Magnetic Resonance Scans of Human and Ape Brains', *Journal of Human Evolution*, 32 (4): 375–88.

SENJU, A., MAEDA, M., KIKUCHI, Y., HASEGAWA, T., TOJO, Y., and OSANAI, H. (2007). 'Absence of Contagious Yawning in children with Autism Spectrum Disorder', *Biology Letters*, 22: 706–8.

SHILLITO, D. J., GALLUP, G. G., JR., and BECK, B. B. (1999). 'Factors Effecting Mirror Behavior in Western Lowland Gorillas, *Gorilla gorilla*', *Animal Behavior*, 57: 999–1004.

SHULMAN, G. L., McAVOY, M. P., COWAN, M. C., ASTAFIEV, S. V., TANSY, A. P., and CORBETTA, M. (2003). 'A Quantitative Analysis of Attention and Detection Signals during Visual Search', *Journal of Neurophysiology*, 90: 3384–97.

SPANGENBERG, K., WAGNER, M. T., and BACHMAN, D. L. (1998). 'Neuropsychological Analysis of a Case of Abrupt Onset Following a Hypotensive Crisis in a Patient with Vascular Dementia', *Neurocase*, 4: 149–54.

SPERRY, R. (1982). 'Some Effects of Disconnecting the Cerebral Hemispheres', *Science*, 217: 1223–6.

——ZAIDEL, E., and ZAIDEL, D. (1979). 'Self Recognition and Social Awareness in the Deconnected Minor Hemisphere', *Neuropsychologia*, 17: 153–66.

SPIKER, D., and RICKS, M. (1984). 'Visual Self-Recognition in Autistic Children: Developmental Relationships', *Child Development*, 55: 214–25.

SUAREZ, S. D., and GALLUP, G. G. (1981). 'Self-Recognition in Chimpanzees and Orangutans, But Not Gorillas', *Journal of Human Evolution*, 10(2): 175–88.

——and ——(1986). 'Social Responding to Mirrors in Rhesus Macaques (Macaca mulatta): Effects of Changing Mirror Location', *American Journal of Primatology*, 11: 239–44.

SUGIURA, M., KAWASHIMA, R., NAKAMURA, K., OKADA, K., KATO, T., NAKAMURA, A., HATANO, K., ITOH, K., KOJIMA, S., and FUKUDA, H. (2000). 'Passive and Active Recognition of One's Own Face', *Neuroimage*, 11: 36–48.

——SASSA, Y., JEONGB, H., MIURAB, N., AKITSUKIB, Y., HORIED, K., SATOD, S., and KAWASHIMA, R. (2006). 'Multiple Brain Networks for Visual Self-Recognition with Different Sensitivity for Motion and Body Part', *Neuroimage*, 32: 1905–17.

——WATANABE, J., MAEDA Y., MATSUE, Y., FUKUDA, H., and KAWASHIMA, R. (2005). 'Cortical Mechanisms of Visual Self-Recognition', *Neuroimage*, 24: 143–9.

SWARTZ, K. B. (1998). 'Self-Recognition in Nonhuman Primates', in G. Greenberg and M. Haraway (eds), *Comparative Psychology: A Handbook* (New York: Garland), 849–55.

——and EVANS, S. (1991). 'Not All Chimpanzees Show Self-Recognition', *Primates*, 32: 483–96.

TALAIRACH, J., and TOURNOUX, P. (1988). *Co-Planar Stereotaxic Atlas of the Human Brain: An Approach to Medical Cerebral Imaging* (Stuttgart and New York: Thieme Medical Publishers).

THATCHER, R. W. (1999). 'EEG Database-Guided Neurotherapy', in J. R. Evans and A. Abarbanel (eds), *Introduction to Quantitative EEG and Neurofeedback* (New York: Academic Press).

TRAUB, A. C., and ORBACH, J. (1964). 'Psychophysical Studies of Body Image I. The Adjustable Body-Distorting Mirror', *Archives of General Psychiatry*, 11: 53–66.

TURK, D. J., HEATHERTON, T. F., KELLEY, W. M., FUNNELL, M. G., GAZZANIGA, M. S., and NEIL MACRAE, C. (2002). 'Mike or Me? Self-Recognition in a Split-Brain Patient', *Nature Neuroscience*, 5(9): 841–2.

UDDIN, L.Q., KAPLAN, J. T., MOLNAR-SZAKACS, I., ZAIDEL, E., and IACOBONI, M. (2005). 'Self-Face Recognition Activates a Frontoparietal "mirror" Network in the Right Hemisphere: An Event-Related FMRI Study', *Neuroimage*, 25: 926–35.

VOGELEY, K., BUSSFELD, P., NEWEN, A., HAPPE, F., FALKAI, P., MAIER, W., SHAH, N. J., FINK, G. R., and ZILLES K. (2001). 'Mind Reading: Neural Mechanisms of Theory of Mind and Self-Perspective', *Neuroimage*, 14: 170–81.

WADA, J. (1949). 'A New Method for the Determination of the Side of Cerebral Speech Dominance: A Preliminary Report of the Intra-Carotid Injection of Sodium Amytal in Man', *Igaku to Seibutsugaki*, 14: 221–2.

WALRAVEN, V., VANELSACKER, L., and VERHEYEN, R. (1995). 'Reactions of a Group of Pygmy Chimpanzees (Pan-Paniscus) to their Mirror-Images: Evidence of Self-Recognition', *Primates*, 36/1: 145–50.

WEINBERGER, D. R. (1993). 'A Connectionist Approach to the Prefrontal Cortex', *Journal of Neuropsychiatry and Clinical Neurosciences*, 5: 241–53.

CHAPTER 4

....

SELF IN THE BRAIN

....

KAI VOGELEY

SHAUN GALLAGHER

1. INTRODUCTION

....

In 1977 the philosopher Karl Popper and the Nobel Prize-winning neuroscientist John Eccles published *The Self and its Brain*, one of the first contributions in modern neurophilosophy. In that book they defended a dualism that viewed the self as an autonomous entity that interacted with, and in fact controlled, brain processes. This view, which Eccles (1989, 1994) further defended and developed, was not at all representative of either the philosophical or neuroscientific communities of the time, and it was, in terms of its general, non-reductionist philosophical position, comparable to Descartes's famous doctrine of the pineal gland as the site of interaction between mind and brain. According to Popper, 'the action of the mind on the brain may consist in allowing certain fluctuations to

Shaun Gallagher's work on this chapter was, in part, supported by the National Science Foundation under Grant No. 0639037, and the European Science Foundation's Eurocore program: *Consciousness in a Natural and Cultural Context*, BASIC project. Any opinions, findings, and conclusions or recommendations expressed in this chapter are those of the authors and do not necessarily reflect the views of NSF or ESF.

lead to the firing of neurones' (Popper and Eccles 1985: 541). Eccles, famous for his work on synaptic mechanisms, proposed that the probabilistic operations of synaptic connections could be the place of interaction. 'The self-conscious mind acts upon . . . neural centres, modifying the dynamic spatio-temporal patterns of the neural events' (ibid. 495).

The work by Popper and Eccles motivated a debate in the journal *Neuroscience* between the philosopher Mario Bunge, who defended an emergentist view, and the neuroscientist Donald McKay, who staked out a position between materialism and dualism (Bunge 1977, 1979; McKay 1978, 1979, 1980). McKay argued that we should 'start from our immediate experience of what it is like to be a person' (McKay 1978: 601). He proposed that since each change in our experience corresponds to a change in brain activity, we have both first-person data and third-person data about the same entity, the conscious self, but that one set of data is not reducible to the other set, despite the high, possibly even perfect, degree of correlation. It is, he suggested, like the relation between a computer and a mathematical equation being solved by the operations of the computer. Without being able to identify the precise part of the computer in which an equation interacts with the mechanism, we can nonetheless say that the nature of the equation determines what the computer will do, while the laws of physics that govern the processes of the computer chip will determine the solution to the equation.

It is important to notice that in these discussions the concept of self was not clearly defined, and this is one thing that leads these theorists into the murky metaphysical corners of dualism and materialism. If, since 1977, cognitive neuroscience has significantly advanced our understanding of certain brain functions, during the same time philosophy has further clarified and complicated the notion of the self, as one can see from the chapters in this present volume. If one were to oversimplify things and to define self as having three clearly distinct aspects, for instance A, B, and C, or to define *n* clearly distinct conceptions of self (1, 2, . . . n), then it is an important principle for work in the neuroscience of self to say precisely which aspect or conception of self is at stake when we go looking in the brain for 'the self'. Our intention in this chapter is not to provide an exhaustive review of recent work on the neuroscience of self (given the amount of recent research in this area, this is likely an impossible task), but in part to show why this principle is important and that it potentially allows the operationalization of key features of the self (Vogeley *et al.* 1999; Gallagher 2000).

2. CONCEPTUAL ISSUES: THE SELF IN THE BRAIN—EVERYWHERE AND NOWHERE

Joseph LeDoux (2002: 31) points out that theories of the self 'are not usually framed in ways that are compatible with our understanding of brain function'.[1] Indeed, it is frequently the case that the neuroscience of self stays on a very general level by including in the concept of self a variety of different self-related aspects. For example, autobiographical knowledge, personal beliefs, self-conceptions, and the recognition of our own face have been grouped together as related to left hemisphere activity (Turk *et al.* 2003; see also Kircher *et al.* 2000). Alternatively, Platek *et al.* (2003: 147) claim that there 'is growing evidence that processing of self-related information (e.g., autobiographical memory, self face identification, theory of mind) is related to activity in the right frontal cortex' (see also Devinksy 2000; Miller *et al.* 2001). Representation of both the physical and phenomenological aspects of self and 'self-representation in general' apparently involve the right lateral parietal cortex (Lou *et al.* 2004: 6831), while the 'self model . . . a theoretical construct comprising essential features such as feelings of continuity and unity, experience of agency, and body-centered perspective' (Fossati *et al.* 2003: 1943) involves activation of the medial prefrontal cortex in both hemispheres.

Functional neuroimaging and neuropsychological studies have recently revealed the importance of cortical midline structures (CMS) for processing information related to the self. In particular, activation of the ventromedial prefrontal cortex (VMPFC) has been repeatedly observed when subjects think about themselves (Northoff and Bermpohl 2004; Northoff *et al.* 2006) and specifically when they make judgements regarding their own personality traits (D'Argembeau *et al.* 2007; Gutchess *et al.* 2007; Heatherton *et al.* 2006; Johnson *et al.* 2002; Kelley *et al.* 2002; Ruby *et al.* 2009). In addition, lesion studies suggest that damage to the VMPFC leads to deficits in self-awareness (Stuss *et al.* 2001*a*, 2001*b*).

Other studies that explore the cerebral areas associated with self-referential processing in normal aging observe that younger and older adults engaged the VMPFC to a similar extent when judging personality traits in reference to the self versus another person (Gutchess *et al.* 2007). The only cerebral differences between the groups in self versus other personality assessment were found in somatosensory and motor-related areas.[2]

---

[1] Northoff *et al.* (2006: 453) put it this way: 'Neither the historical nor modern psychological approaches are obviously isomorphic with any known brain analysis.'

[2] Ruby *et al.* (2009) explored the neural substrate of self-personality assessment from different perspectives. Young and older adults evaluated personality traits in reference to the self versus a close friend or relative. Moreover, they were asked to make those judgments from either their own (first-person) perspective or the perspective of their friend or relative (third-person perspective).

On the one hand, on the basis of such studies, some theorists posit a unitary system responsible for all self-related phenomena. For example Northoff has argued for a self-system in the CMS (Northoff *et al.* 2006; Northoff and Bermpohl 2004). We note, however, that this putative self-system corresponding to CMS covers a quite large set of brain regions (including ventro- and dorsomedial prefrontal, anterior and posterior cingulate, retrosplenial and medial parietal cortices) and involves, in addition, the multitude of connections between CMS and subcortical areas, and the possible role of subcortical areas in a sense of embodied self (see Northoff and Panksepp 2008). On the other hand, the widespread nature of CMS seems to suggest that there is no specialized brain area responsible for generating the self, just as there is no candidate region or system at hand that could be made fully responsible for the constitution of consciousness. In a number of recent reviews, a variety of conceptual and methodological issues have been highlighted that qualify any claims for the notion of an overall, consistent self-system in the brain.[3]

Gillihan and Farah (2005) demonstrate that even when studies focus on a specific self-related representation, such as self-face recognition (judged in contrast with another person's face, or morphed faces), different methodologies and different subject groups will identify different areas of the brain for this function:

- right hemisphere (Platek and Gallup 2002, in neurologically intact subjects; Preilowski 1979; Keenan *et al.* 2003, in studies of split-brain patients; Keenan *et al.* 1999, 2000; Keenan *et al.* 2001, using TMS in normal subjects and the 'Wada test' in patients undergoing epilepsy surgery)
- left hemisphere (Turk *et al.* 2003, in studies of split-brain patients)
- left anterior insula, putamen, and pulvinar, the right anterior cingulate cortex, and globus pallidus, in subjects asked to identify a picture of their own face from a series of photos (Sugiura *et al.* 2000, using PET);
- left fusiform gyrus, anterior cingulate cortex, right supramarginal gyrus, superior parietal lobule, and precuneus (Sugiura *et al.* 2000, using PET); right middle, superior, and inferior frontal gyri (Platek *et al.* 2004, using fMRI); and right insula, hippocampal formation, and lenticular and subthalamic

---

[3] Complications in the interpretation of the data are quite common in this literature. For example, Northoff *et al.* (2006) cite the study by Kelley *et al.* (2002) as showing that the medial prefrontal cortex is involved in processing self-related stimuli. Gillihan and Farah (2005), in contrast, citing that study along with others, claim that processing of the traits of others also activated this area and that may signify that it is involved in 'person processing' rather than specifically self-processing. The question is further complicated, as noted by Kelley *et al.* and Northoff *et al.*, by the fact that the MPFC normally deactivates (relative to baseline) in contexts of task-dependent activities and external stimulation. The MPFC is part of what Raichle *et al.* (2001) call the 'default mode' of brain function. Kelley *et al.* (2002) suggest that the normal baseline activation of the MPFC might be interpreted as a region responsible for a default self-referentiality when the person is not engaged in some task or attending to some stimulus. See below for further discussion.

nuclei, the left prefrontal cortex (inferior and middle frontal gyri), right middle temporal gyrus, left cerebellum, as well as parietal lobe and lingual gyrus (Kircher *et al.* 2000, using fMRI), in subjects asked to judge orientation in a set of photos that include their own.

Using a similar diversity of methods, studies of *self-agency* show the involvement of a further variety of brain areas. For example, when the sense of self-agency fails, as in cases of schizophrenic delusions of control, studies show hyperactivation of the right parietal cortex (Spence *et al.* 1997). If non-pathological subjects are asked to imagine themselves acting, however, we find activation in left inferior parietal, posterior insula, post-central gyrus, and inferior occipital gyrus, bilaterally (Ruby and Decety 2001). When subjects are asked to distinguish actions that are self-generated (accompanied by a sense of self-agency) from actions generated by others, activation is seen in the right inferior parietal area for our actions (Chaminade and Decety 2002) as well as in the anterior insula bilaterally (Farrer and Frith 2002).

In their review Gillihan and Farah (2005) show that studies of self-trait descriptions (part of what they refer to as the psychological component of self) yielded no clear results for specialized brain areas because of various confounds. For example, although in a number of studies the medial prefrontal cortex was activated for self-judgments, the same area was also activated for other-judgments. 'It is therefore possible that medial PFC plays a role in person processing in general . . . [or that] it is possible that the activation of these areas is a function of amount and type of knowledge rather than self versus other knowledge per se' (2005: 89). Other confounds prevent any clear results from studies of autobiographical memory.

On various definitions of first-person perspective, experiments show activation of different areas of the brain. (1) Often in psychology and cognitive neuroscience first-person perspective simply means that the object of my attention is myself rather than someone else (e.g. Ruby and Decety 2001). For example, first-person perspective may be operationalized in terms of a narrative perspective as what I can say when I occupy the role of self-narrator. While narrating about self or another person activates the right prefrontal cortex, narrating about self but not the other activates the right temporoparietal junction and bilateral anterior cingulate cortex (Vogeley *et al.* 2001). (2) In philosophy, first-person perspective is frequently thought of as the view from the place of the observer (whether in introspection or in perception). Accordingly, if I describe the world from the perspective of an observer in the egocentric spatial framework, then I am taking a first-person perspective; likewise if I give a phenomenological report on my own experience. In this sense, processing in early sensory areas may be considered correlated to first-person experience (Gillihan and Farah 2005: 92; Vogeley and Fink 2003). When subjects are asked to report on their own emotional reactions to stimuli, in contrast to objective spatial properties of the stimuli, significantly more

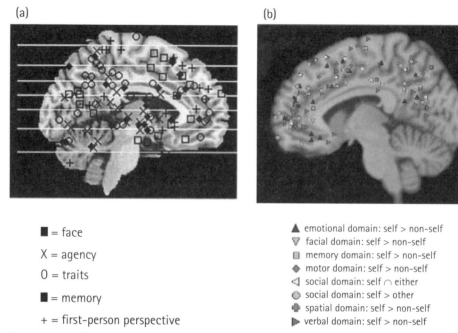

(a)   (b)

■ = face
X = agency
0 = traits
■ = memory
+ = first-person perspective

▲ emotional domain: self > non-self
▼ facial domain: self > non-self
▣ memory domain: self > non-self
◆ motor domain: self > non-self
◁ social domain: self ∩ either
◕ social domain: self > other
◆ spatial domain: self > non-self
▶ verbal domain: self > non-self

Figure 4.1 (A) Self–related activation in a 'glass brain' view (all areas of activation are visible regardless of whether they fall on the midline). From Gillihan and Farah (2005). (B) Activation in CMS observed in imaging studies during self–related tasks in different domains (from Northoff *et al.* 2006)

activation can be found in the anterior cingulate cortex (Lane *et al.* 1997) or medial prefrontal areas (Gusnard *et al.* 2001).[4]

It thus looks like the entire cortex is specialized for self-referential processing, or, in other words, as the review by Gillihan and Farah (2005) demonstrates, there is no specialized or common area responsible for self-related representations.[5] Even theorists like Northoff who set out to identify a circumscribed self-system end up pointing to an extensive set of brain areas that come close to the diversity summarized by Gillihan and Farah (see Figure 4.1). Thus, LeDoux seems correct to maintain that 'different components of the self reflect the operation of different brain systems, which can be but are not always in sync' (2002: 31). Perhaps a more critically pessimistic view on the general inconsistency of results is summarized by Craik *et al.* (1999: 30): 'every significant activation in the [self condition] was also found in either the

[4] As Gillihan and Farah (2005) point out, although both the Lane and Gusnard studies involve first-person reports on affective experience, the third-person conditions involve no affective component, so the contrast results of brain activation may be emotion-related rather than precisely for first-person perspective.

[5] 'The different ways in which the self–non-self distinction is confounded with other distinctions across studies are likely to account for the different patterns of activation in different studies . . . even when the same aspect of the self is under study' (Gillihan and Farah 2005: 94).

[other person condition] or the [general semantic] condition, or both' (cited by Gillihan and Farah 2005: 94). One issue that needs to be resolved in this regard is whether we should think of the self exclusively in terms of self-referential processing. It could be argued that the self is not exhausted in just such processing, since even as I respond to stimuli that are not self-referential, my response is itself always self-specific. For example, my response is made on the basis of information that is already framed from the perspective in which I perceive the stimulus—a first-person (ego-centric) perspective. In this case, it is not the self as an object of reference (e.g. I report on recognizing my own photo, or judging whether I think or feel thus and thus) but the self-as-subject (as the one doing the reporting in ways that may not be self-referential) that is at stake. Legrand and Ruby (2009) have followed up on just this idea in a clarifying way.

In a meta-analysis of neuroimaging studies, Legrand and Ruby (2009) detected a certain pattern, the so-called 'E-network' ('evaluation network'), within the variety of differential self-related activations. They point out that four brain areas are repeatedly activated in self versus non-self contrasts: medial prefrontal cortex, precuneus/posterior cingulate gyrus, temporoparietal junction, and temporal pole. Rather than conclude that this network is a self-network, however, they raise another question. They note that since the areas of this network are activated in tasks that involve a contrast between self and non-self, they are not really self-specific, that is, specialized only for self. Numerous studies in fact show that the areas of the E-network are also the areas activated in 'theory of mind' (ToM) tasks which require the modeling of the internal experiences or mental states of others (see below). Thus, 'the main brain regions recruited for others' mind representa-tion are also and precisely the main brain regions reported in self studies and . . . this overlap extends beyond the brain areas usually pointed out, that is, it com-prises the medial prefrontal cortex, the precuneus/posterior cingulate, the tempor-oparietal junction, and the temporal pole' (2009: 254–8). Legrand and Ruby go on to postulate and to cite multiple studies that show that the lowest common denominator involved in all of the tasks designed for self-referential or other-referential activation is inferential processing using memory recall, which they term 'evaluation'. Thus, the brain areas in the E-network are activated for certain cognitive processes that apply not just to self, but to other persons, and even to objects. They are not specialized for self-referential processing. For example, fMRI studies by Fangmeier et al. (2006) and Fonlupt (2003) show very clearly that the medial prefrontal cortex is activated in logical (deductive reasoning) processes that involve premise integration where the premises are not about self or other, but about an array of single letters, billiard-ball causality, or color.[6]

---

[6] Activation of the medial prefrontal cortex (MPFC) for evaluative inference would be consistent with data cited by both Northoff et al. (2006) and Gillihan and Farah (2005) without deciding the issue about self-reference. Legrand and Ruby point to a different interpretation of the default mode

It might seem at this point that we are making only little progress in identifying any consistent brain-related activity responsible for self. First, rather than finding a common, well-circumscribed brain area of self-referential activation, we found a large number of diverse areas activated for a variety of self-related experience. Now, however, on the Legrand–Ruby interpretation, the diverse areas implicated in self-referential experience are in fact not areas of activation exclusively for self. At first it seemed the self was almost everywhere in the brain; now it seems to be nowhere.

3. KEY ASPECTS OF SELF

Self-agency and self-ownership

This perplexity about the brain's role in self-specific processes may stem from the lack of any clear correspondence between theoretical conceptions of self and how cognitive neuroscience operationalizes such conceptions. To get a grasp on the difficulties involved in this, let's take a look at one area in which a seemingly clear distinction with regard to self-experience helps to structure experimental design. Gillihan and Farah suggest that some of the most clear and specialized instances of self-specified brain functions have to do with body ownership and agency for action. They suggest that asomatognosia (the lack of recognition of one's body, e.g. following stroke) 'demonstrates both the functional independence and the neural localization of limb ownership; our sense of a limb as being our own is distinct from our sense that other people's limbs belong to them. [In addition] studies of the experience of agency in limb movements indicate a similar functional independence and neural localization' (2005: 93).

One important and widely cited experimental brain-imaging study cited by Gillihan and Farah, as well as by Norhoff, and Legrand and Ruby, is Farrer and Frith (2002). The study by Farrer and Frith, like a number of other studies (e.g. Chaminade and Decety 2002; Farrer *et al.* 2003; Tsakiris and Haggard 2005), refers to a phenomenological distinction between the sense of ownership and the sense of agency (Gallagher 2000).

The distinction is made as part of a delineation of what a number of theorists call the minimal or core self. The minimal self is constituted by a pre-reflective

---

activation of the MPFC. Rather than self-specific activity, the MPFC may be busy inferring or predicting future events. Bar (2007) makes this proposal, which 'posits that rudimentary information is extracted rapidly from the input to derive analogies linking that input with representation in memory. The linked stored representations then activate the associations that are relevant in the specific context, which provides focused predictions' (p. 280).

consciousness of oneself as an immediate, embodied subject of experience, and is distinguished from the narrative (extended) self, the 'more or less coherent self (or self-image) that is constituted with a past and a future in the various stories that we and others tell about ourselves' (Gallagher 2000: 16). The minimal self involves a number of aspects, including the *sense of ownership (SoO)*—the sense that I am the one who is undergoing an experience, for example, the sense that my body is moving, regardless of whether the movement is voluntary or involuntary—and the *sense of agency (SoA)*—the sense that I am the one who is causing or generating an action. These are pre-reflective, implicit, or tacit aspects of our experience. That is, one's SoA, for example, is not something generated in reflective or conceptual thinking about what I am doing. Rather, it is built into the doing, the action, itself (Marcel 2003; Gallagher and Marcel 1999).

Recent conceptual developments distinguish between different levels in the phenomenology of agency comprising an implicit or first-order level of an experiential feeling of agency as opposed to an explicit higher level of judgment or attribution of agency (Gallagher 2007; Synofzik *et al.* 2008). As such, SoO and SoA are distinguished from a reflective level of intention formation or attribution that may be involved in reporting about or evaluating our actions. Thus, Stephens and Graham (2000) make a corresponding distinction on the reflective level between attributions of subjectivity (ownership) and attributions of agency. Whereas SoO and SoA are first-order (phenomenal) experiences related to my bodily movement and action, attributions are reflective judgments that I make about my actions. If someone asks me whether I bought a car yesterday, my affirmative response is an attribution of agency to myself. As such, attributions of ownership ('this happened to me') or agency ('I did it') involve the narrative self, although they may normally be reports on, or based on, my actual pre-reflective experience of agency or ownership (Gallagher 2010).

It may be a helpful oversimplification to think of the SoA as generated in efferent signals or motor control processes that occur just prior to or in the initial stages of the action. The SoO may be tied to sensory feedback, its attenuation or cross-modal integration (see e.g. Tsakiris and Haggard 2005; Chapter 7 below). SoA is missing in the case of involuntary movement where there is no efferent motor command, but the SoO is still present ('My body moved'). One can also think of pathologies that may involve a loss of the SoA (as in schizophrenic delusions of control or anarchic hand) or SoO (as in asomatognosia following stroke, or alien hand syndrome).

The fMRI study by Farrer and Frith sets out to identify the neural correlates of the SoA, which they distinguish from the SoO.

Subjects manipulated a joystick [to drive a colored circle moving on a screen to specific locations on the screen]. Sometimes the subject caused this movement and sometimes the experimenter. This paradigm allowed us to study the sense of agency without any confounding from the sense of ownership. To achieve this, subjects were requested to execute an action during all the different experimental conditions. By doing so the effect related to the sense of ownership (I am performing an action) would be present in all conditions and would be canceled in the various contrasts. (2003: 597)

One might wonder why the SoA varies across tasks in this experiment, since in each case the subject is required to move the joystick. If one conceives of the SoA as a pre-reflective experience that is built into action, perhaps tied to efferent motor commands, then one would expect that the subject's action of moving the joystick would be accompanied by SoA for that action. Farrer and Frith, however, although citing the distinction between SoA and SoO as defined above, operationalize the SoA according to a different definition. In the experiment the SoA is not tied to motor control processes, but to what is accomplished by the action. Does my action have an effect in the world, or, in this case, on the computer screen? If so, then I have a sense of agency for that action. We will refer to this as a SoA tied to action consequence.

One should, in fact, welcome this as a useful clarification of the SoA, although it is not presented as such in the study. That is, the suggestion that the SoA may involve more than just motor control processes, and that it may include aspects tied to intentional fulfillment of the action (action consequence) is important, especially for fully embodied and embedded versions of cognitive experience (see Gallagher 2008, 2010). Farrer and Frith, however, fail to note their shift of definition or the complexity involved in the SoA.

But things are more complicated than this. In some trials the subject is informed ahead of each task whether the movement will be his or not his, and he is asked to perform the task regardless of this. In the cases when the action represented on the computer screen is not the subject's action, and because the subject knows it, one might suspect that his SoA short-circuits in the control of the joystick. That is, if he does not have SoA tied to the intentional aspect of the task, his SoA may be redirected specifically to his bodily movement in a way that would be consistent with the original definition of SoA. In the case where the subject is not the agent for the task represented on the computer screen, the right inferior parietal cortex (IPC) is activated. Consistent with other studies (Spence *et al.* 1997; Ruby and Decety 2001), Farrer and Frith interpret this to mean that the IPC activation correlates to a sense of other-agency, rather than to the subject's own SoA for control of the joystick. When the subject does know that he is causing the action on the screen, his anterior insula is activated bilaterally. Thus, the experimenters identify activation in the anterior insula as the correlate of SoA.

If we set aside some of these complexities and accept the operational definition of SoA in terms of the experiment, another problem appears when Farrer and Frith turn to theoretical considerations about why the anterior insula should be involved in generating SoA. In effect, they revert from the definition of SoA in terms of action consequences to the original definition in terms of motor control.

Why should the parietal lobe have a special role in attributing actions to others while the anterior insula is concerned with attributing actions to the self? The sense of agency (i.e., being aware of causing an action) occurs in the context of a body moving in time and space. Damasio (1999) has suggested that the sense of agency critically depends upon the experience of such a body. There is evidence that both the inferior parietal lobe and the anterior insula are representations of the body.... the anterior insula, in interaction with limbic structures, is also involved in the representation of body schema.... One aspect of the experience of agency that we feel when we move our bodies through space is the close correspondence between many different sensory signals. In particular there will be a correspondence between three kinds of signal: somatosensory signals directly consequent upon our movements, visual and auditory signals that may result indirectly from our movements, and last, the corollary discharge associated with motor commands that generated the movements. A close correspondence between all these signals helps to give us a sense of agency. (Farrer and Frith 2003: 601–2)

A number of things can be said about this explanation. (1) Note the introduction of the issue of attribution, that is, judging rather than experiencing agency. Indeed, although starting with the distinction between the pre-reflective, experiential SoO and SoA, the authors state: 'The main purpose of this experiment was to compare brain activity associated with attributing an action to oneself and attributing an action to another person' (597). As part of the protocol, the subjects, who were informed prior to the task that they would be controlling the icon or someone else would be, were asked, in the former case, 'to drive the circle, to be aware that they drove the circle, and thus to mentally attribute the visualized action to themselves' (597). As a result we could rightly ask whether the results reflected a pre-reflective SoA tied to motor control, a pre-reflective SoA tied to action consequence, or a reflective attribution of agency. (2) Farrer and Frith, while asking why the insula might be responsible for *attribution* of self-agency, go on to decide this issue on theoretical grounds that are more related to SoA understood in terms of motor control—that is, it seems tied to a body-schematic, pre-reflective experience of the body and sensory feedback integration with 'corollary discharge associated with motor commands'. One interpretation that might make sense out of this is to say that attribution of agency is based on (is a report on) the pre-reflective SoA tied to motor control, which is associated with increased neural activation of the insula. Yet the experiment was set up to ignore the SoA as tied to motor control, and to focus on the SoA as tied to action consequence. (3) The mention of the integration of 'somatosensory signals directly consequent upon our movements, [and] visual and auditory signals that may result indirectly from our movements' may suggest some involvement of the SoO if the latter is based on such integration. This raises a further question about how Farrer and Frith explain the attribution of agency to the other person and activation of the IPC. They cite well-known evidence that suggests the IPC may be responsible for SoO: 'Lesions in the right parietal cortex have been associated with disturbances in the feeling of belonging of the patient's limbs.... patients with right parietal lesion do not recognize their limbs as their own and perceive them as belonging to others' (2003: 601). So one question that remains unanswered is whether IPC can be involved in both the SoO for one's body, and the sense of other-agency.

We can learn some valuable lessons about research on the self from this kind of study. First, experimental brain-imaging can help to clarify the meaning of concepts like the sense of agency. Theoretical models may suggest that SoA is closely tied to motor control; but when operationalizing SoA in the context of an experiment, we can start to see that it may be a much more complex concept. Second, if we are to obtain any clear results from such experiments, we definitely have to make careful distinctions between reflective and pre-reflective aspects of the self.

Self in action

The predominant account on explaining the SoA of our own actions has been the 'central monitoring theory' or 'comparator model' as a theory of motor learning and motor control (Frith 1992; von Holst and Mittelstaedt 1950; Wolpert *et al.* 1995). Two types of internal models are implemented in the central motor system: so-called inverse and forward models. The sense of agency particularly hinges on the forward model which uses an efference copy, that is, a copy of a motor command, to predict its sensory consequences. We are usually unaware of the results of this comparison as long as the desired state is successfully achieved (Blakemore and Frith 2003). As outlined above a good opportunity to study this phenomenon is the capacity to monitor one's own movement to false visual feedback without being aware of the adjustment (David *et al.* 2007, 2008; Farrer and Frith 2003; Fourneret and Jeannerod 1998). In pathological states in which patients experience so-called delusions of control by attributing their own actions to external sources (Daprati *et al.* 1997; Franck *et al.* 2001; Haggard *et al.* 2003) the central monitoring mechanisms might be disturbed (Blakemore *et al.* 2002) or errors might arise from a disturbed judgment or attribution of agency (e.g. Fourneret *et al.* 2001). The posterior parietal cortex (PPC) represents a very likely candidate for providing reference to the agent of an action as this region seems to monitor the concordance between self-produced actions and their visual consequences, being especially involved in the detection of visual-motor incongruence (Chaminade and Decety 2002; Farrer *et al.* 2003; Farrer and Frith 2003; Fink *et al.* 1999). Similarly, the cerebellum has been implicated in signaling discrepancies between predicted and actual sensory consequences of movements (e.g. an associated tone; Blakemore *et al.* 2001). Recently, a region in visual association cortex called the *extrastriate body area* (EBA) has been reported to show greater activity during self-generated movements (Peelen and Downing 2005). This finding opened the possibility that the EBA may also be involved in the SoA, as suggested by Jeannerod (2004). Indeed, activity in the EBA could be shown to be differentially modulated by a manipulation of agency responding to the perception of visuo-motor incongruence. Furthermore, the EBA showed a similar response pattern as the PPC as well as an increased functional connectivity to the PPC underlining a close functional relationship between them (David *et al.* 2007).

Another account was presented by Haggard and colleagues with the phenom-enon of so-called 'intentional binding' showing that voluntary—but not involun-tary or passive—movements and movement consequences are temporally bound together in conscious awareness. Subjects judged the perceived time of voluntary movements as occurring later and the sensory consequences as earlier than was actually the case (Haggard *et al.* 2002; Haggard and Clark 2003; Tsakiris and Haggard 2003). The phenomenon of intentional binding appears to be related to increased activation of the SMA or pre-SMA and insula. Recruitment of these regions has specifically been associated with awareness and execution of self-generated actions, action preparation, and the subject's own intention-to-act (Cunnington *et al.* 2006; Farrer *et al.* 2003; Farrer and Frith 2003; Haggard and Clark 2003; Haggard and Whitford 2004; Lau *et al.* 2006).

In summary, findings from cognitive neuroscience suggest that essentially the brain regions of ventral premotor cortex (vPMC), the supplementary motor area (SMA and pre-SMA), the cerebellum and the dorsolateral prefrontal cortex (DLPFC), the posterior parietal cortex (PPC), the posterior segment of the superi-or temporal sulcus (pSTS), and the insula are associated with experiences of agency (Blakemore *et al.* 2001; Farrer *et al.* 2003; Farrer and Frith 2003; Fink *et al.* 1999; Jeannerod 2004). This list of brain regions appears to subserve a network of sensorimotor transformations and motor control, whereas a second component represents heteromodal association cortices associated with a variety of cognitive functions (e.g. prefrontal cortex; Fuster 1997, 2001). One could speculate that motor system-related regions may subserve 'executive' functions whereas hetero-modal associative regions subserve 'supervisory' functions (David *et al.* 2008). At the current stage, a multifactorial and multilevel model appears to provide the most helpful and comprehensible framework for integrating divergent theories and findings (Synofzik *et al.* 2008; Wegner and Sparrow 2004).

Self in space

In the context of spatial cognition the self refers to the experience of the centered-ness of the subjective multidimensional and multimodal experiential space upon one's own body. During spatial cognition, as 'a means of representing the locations of entities in space' (Klatzky 1998), we operate in an egocentric reference frame, constituted by subject-to-object relations. Egocentric reference frames can be differentiated with respect to the midline of the visual field, the head, the trunk, or the longitudinal axis of the limb involved in the execution of a certain action (Behrmann 1999). In contrast, an allocentric reference frame, sometimes also referred to as 'exocentric' or 'geocentric', is constituted by object-to-object relations (best described in a Cartesian co-ordinate system). It refers to a framework that is independent of the agent's position (Klatzky 1998; Aguirre and D'Esposito 1999; Vogeley and Fink 2003).

Cognitive operations when perceiving a visual scene from one's own perspective (1PP) differ from taking a view of the same scene from another person's viewpoint (3PP), although both tasks are centered on the body of the respective agent, the self or the other. To clearly separate these two levels of descriptions, the perspective-related terms 1PP and 3PP indicate the phenomenal level, whereas the terms egocentric and allocentric reference frames refer to the cognitive or neural level as conceptualized by the onlooking (scientific) observer. The crucial difference between 1PP and 3PP is that 3PP necessitates a translocation of the egocentric viewpoint.

A number of studies have focused on the issue of perspective taking in space. Taking 1PP appears to rely at least in part on temporo-parietal processing as assessed in navigational tasks (Maguire *et al.* 1998, 1999; Zacks 2008). For example, Maguire *et al.* (1998) demonstrated that a right inferior parietal region was activated whenever egocentric calculations (i.e. computing body turns toward the target) were necessary in addition to the processing of allocentric spatial information (mediated via the hippocampus). Subtracting a static condition from 'ego-movement' conditions including trail-following or way-finding also involved bilateral medial parietal cortex (Maguire *et al.* 1998). These findings have been corroborated by other studies (Maguire *et al.* 1999).

A simple spatial cognitive task to be solved from 1PP and 3PP was employed in a 3D-visuospatial task in which a virtual scene consisting of a virtual character surrounded by red objects was presented. Subjects were asked to assess the number of red balls as seen from either their own (1PP) or the virtual character's perspective (3PP). Both conditions were based on egocentric operations, as the objects have to be located in relation to an agent in both conditions, either the test person or the virtual character. In the case of 3PP, however, additional use of allocentric operations is necessary to generate egocentric coordinates for the agent. Neural correlates revealed differentially increased neural activity during 1PP (as opposed to 3PP) in the left medial prefrontal cortex and the posterior cingulate cortex bilaterally. In contrast, 3PP was associated with differentially increased neural activity in the region of the superior parietal lobe bilaterally, predominantly on the right side, and right premotor cortex (Vogeley *et al.* 2004). The relevance of the right parietal cortex for spatial cognition can also be inferred from lesion studies exploring patients with right parietal lesions leading to extinction or spatial neglect

(Behrmann 1999; Marshall and Fink 2001) and from mental rotation tasks (Vogeley and Fink 2003; Zacks 2008; Wolbers and Hegarty 2010).

It has been hypothesized that 1PP generates a spatial model of one's own body in the brain, upon which the experiential space is centered (Berlucchi and Aglioti 1997). This conjecture is in good accordance with reports on increased neural activity of right inferior parietal cortex involving visuo-spatial attention not only in navigation tasks (Maguire *et al.* 1998) but also the assessment of the subjective mid-sagittal plane (Vallar *et al.* 1999; Galati *et al.* 2001). Another important source of information of bodily states is obviously the reference to a gravitational vertical of upright orientation as primary reference. Andersen *et al.* (1999) reviewed evidence for the fact that vestibular information is used by the posterior parietal cortex for the perception of self-motion. A highly relevant study in this respect was performed by Ruby and Decety (2001) who studied perspective taking in a motor imagery task. Subjects were asked to imagine that either themselves (1PP) or the experimenter (3PP) manipulates an object. During 1PP simulation of action, only regions in the left hemisphere were activated, including the inferior parietal lobe, precentral gyrus, superior frontal gyrus, occipito-temporal junction and anterior insula. During 3PP simulation of action, the right hemisphere was activated, namely the inferior parietal cortex, precuneus, posterior cingulate and frontopolar cortex.

Social self

Studies on the neural mechanisms of self-related processes and social cognitive processes have become a key topic in cognitive neuroscience over the past decade. More recently, social (cognitive) neuroscience has emerged as a new subdiscipline in neuroscience, and has recently developed into an autonomous scientific discipline (Cacioppo *et al.* 2004). Social neuroscience focuses on processes that are related to the adequate ascription of mental states to others for the purpose of successful communication or interaction between personal agents. A key constituent is the capacity to distinguish between one's own and others' mental states, and this seems to involve some form of self-consciousness (Newen and Vogeley 2000, 2009).

Closely related to the ability to attribute and maintain a self-perspective is the capacity to discriminate between self and other in intersubjective interaction. The ability to attribute mental states (beliefs, desires, intentions) to others is often referred to as 'mindreading' (e.g. Baron-Cohen 1995). This ability has been studied extensively in so-called 'theory of mind' (ToM) paradigms (e.g. Fletcher *et al.* 1995; Premack and Woodruff 1978), in which mental states or propositional attitudes of an agent are inferred or simulated. The concept of ToM is used to refer to both the attribution of mental states to oneself and to others.

In a typical ToM paradigm, a subject has to model the knowledge, attitudes, or beliefs of another person. ToM capacities may be related to the ability to assign and maintain a self-perspective. In classical ToM paradigms (e.g. Fletcher *et al.* 1995), in which mental states or propositional attitudes of an agent need to be modeled (e.g. 'Person A knows, believes, etc., that p' with p being a physical event), self-perspective refers to the special situation, in which I am the agent myself (e.g. 'I know, believe, etc., that p'), and to the subjective experiential multidimensional space centered around one's own person. These studies have repeatedly demonstrated increased neural activity associated with ToM conditions in the anterior cingulate cortex. Vogeley *et al.* (2001) were able to replicate these findings and to demonstrate additional differential brain activation when the test persons themselves were involved as an agent in a particular story. The capacity for taking 1PP in such ToM contexts showed differential activation in the right temporo-parietal junction and the medial aspects of the superior parietal lobe, that is, the precuneus (Vogeley *et al.* 2001). Neural activations common to 1PP and 3PP in ToM contexts were observed, however, in the anterior cingulate cortex. Similar activation patterns were also found in two other studies involving self-referential processing. Anterior cingulate activations were found during judgments about trait adjectives that were related to oneself as opposed to others (Kelley *et al.* 2002) and during a study in which volunteers were asked to think intensely on how they would describe the personality traits and physical appearance of themselves as opposed to others (Kjaer *et al.* 2002).

Ruby and Decety (2003) studied perspective taking by asking subjects to respond to a list of health-related questions, either from one's own or someone else's perspective. During 1PP the postcentral gyrus was activated, whereas 3PP relevant activations comprised the anterior medial prefrontal cortex, the left superior temporal sulcus and temporal pole and the right inferior parietal lobe. The results of this particular study are somewhat different from the studies reported above as the right inferior parietal lobule is activated during 3PP but not during 1PP. This could be integrated in the hypothesis that the right temporo-parietal region is crucial for the successful differentiation between 1PP and 3PP.

However, the fact that differential brain loci in different brain lobes are activated in association with the attribution of 1PP relative to 'mind-reading' (reviewed in Gallagher and Frith 2003), or ascription of trait adjectives to others, suggests that these components constitute distinct psychological processes.

Note on the default mode of brain function

Empirical evidence for the recruitment of medial cortical activation sites during experiences of self-reference is provided by the concept of a so-called 'default mode of the brain' put forward recently (Gusnard *et al.* 2001; Raichle *et al.* 2001). According to this hypothesis, resting states, stimulus-independent thoughts, and the like, which are experienced as a 'state of self', correlate with 'the default mode of the brain' characterized by certain cortical activation patterns, predominantly in the anterior and posterior cingulate and medial parietal cortices. If a cognitive activity requires a higher demand, neural activation is 'shifted' towards the re-cruited neuronal network; medial frontal and parietal regions in turn then tend to decrease their activity (Raichle *et al.* 2001). According to the speculative inter-pretation of Gusnard *et al.* (2001), this is not merely a noisy signal, but might reflect a 'continuous simulation of behavior' or 'an inner rehearsal as well as an optimi-zation of cognitive and behavioral serial programs for the individual's future', in short, a state of the 'multifaceted self' (p. 4263). What appears as 'state of self' on the phenomenal level appears as 'default brain state' on the neuronal level. Simi-larly, Andreasen *et al.* (1995) described a posterior cingulate deactivation during situations in which subjects were not engaged in a focused cognitive task, attribut-ing this deactivation to spontaneous, probably purely associative, mentation pro-cesses. This ongoing purely associative mentation would then be suspended when the subject becomes engaged in an experimental task requiring specific cognitive activities. In the same sense, Burgess *et al.* (2001) argue that the precuneus supports the inspection of internal images.

The association of the default mode of the brain with self-related mentation processes, however, is controversial. The resting state is not well described in cognitive terms. Furthermore, the areas involved in the default network overlap with the E-network (Legrand and Ruby 2009), and the absence of external stimu-lation tells us nothing about what kind of cognitive operations may be taking place. They may be self-related or non-self-related, ruminating or forward-looking, reflective or day-dreamy.

LEVELS OF PROCESSING: REFLECTIVE AND PRE-REFLECTIVE ASPECTS OF SELF

To understand individual behavior requires a conceptualization of the self in the context of perceiving and acting in its environment. This relation of the subject itself with surrounding objects and pragmatic contexts was conceptualized as the 'core self' by Damasio (1999), and postulated to be a transient relation, in need of reinstantiation from moment to moment, a process which in turn constantly refers to the so-called 'proto self', which remains unconscious and represents bodily states. Medial cortical regions are hypothetically recruited if such a state of 'core self' is instantiated, a prediction in accord with medial cortical activation sites, which comprise anterior medial prefrontal, medial parietal and posterior cingulate cortex (Damasio 1999).

Gillihan and Farah 2005, reflecting broad trends in the literature, take a 'commonsensical approach to the meaning of *self*' and include three broad categories of self-related information under this heading: (1) physical self, which focuses on either specific body parts, including one's own face, or the body as a whole; (2) psychological self, which includes conceptual knowledge about oneself, autobiographical memory, semantic memory (facts about oneself), first-person perspective, and self-other differentiation; (3) agency, which combines 'elements of the physical and the psychological, in that agency concerns the role of the psychological self in causing the actions of the physical self' (p. 77). We can see that these distinctions cut across others made between minimal and narrative aspects of self, as well as pre-reflective and reflective. Getting clear on this latter distinction, however, suggests a different way of thinking about the relation between brain and self.

It is possible to challenge what seems to be the primacy of explicit self-referential processing in the neuroscientific experimental studies of self. Self-referential processing involves the kind of evaluation that is involved in most experimental tasks in studies of the self—'e.g., one refers to "this face" as one's own by evaluating the resemblance of this face to one's representation of one's face' (Legrand and Ruby 2009: 271). Such tasks, however, are clearly reflective tasks that require subjects to reflectively evaluate information about themselves. In such tasks, the self operates as an intentional object that comes under attentive consideration. My concern, or my task, is about, or is directed to, my self. In many, if not most, of one's everyday experiences, however, this is not the case. My attention is most often directed at the environment, at others, at accomplishing some task that does not call for any explicit self-consciousness or attention to the self. If we think of it in terms of reflective regard, then we can say that the connection between the self-as-subject, that is, the one who is doing the reflecting (or who is engaged in the task of reflecting), and the self-as-object, that is, the self that is reflected on or referred to (the self as intentional object), or, more generally, whatever I learn or can report about myself, is neither exclusive nor non-contingent, and is therefore not self-specific, in the sense of the term defined by Legrand and Ruby.[7] The one aspect that they define as self-specific is the embodied first-person perspective, which constitutes being the self-as-subject. That is, a first-person perspective is something only selves have; and absent a first-person perspective there is no self. First-person perspective is basic for the

---

[7] 'We define the notion of self-specificity according to the two criteria of *exclusivity* and *noncontingency.* . . . a given self S is constituted by a self-specific component C only if C characterizes S exclusively (i.e., C does not characterize non-S) and noncontingently (i.e., changing or losing C would amount to changing or losing the distinction between S and non-S)' (Legrand and Ruby 2009: 272).

self/non-self distinction, is the point of orientation for every perception and action, and is to be taken in a constitutive sense.[8]

The first-person perspective is relational or intentional insofar as having a first-person perspective on anything relates that thing (some object in the world, another person, even the self-as-object) to the experiencing subject. Legrand and Ruby (2009) thus suggest that this concept can be cashed out at a basic neurophysiological level, namely, the level of sensorimotor integrative processes involving efference and reafference. The fact that one can find activation in sensorimotor areas not only when one is perceiving and acting, but also in tasks related to language, emotion, and intersubjectivity, strengthens their suggestion. One challenge is to discover any activity that involves first-person perspective that does not activate such areas.

What, however, does the first-person perspective amount to? One possibility is that it is an ecological phenomenon, in the Gibsonian sense. Neisser's (1988) conception of the ecological aspect of self suggests that any perception or action engaged in by the subject always provides some information about the subject, as well as about the perceived or acted upon object or environment. In terms of perception and action, at least, this embodied, ecological, pre-reflective self-awareness is more basic (and developmentally more primary) than any form of self-recognition (see Chapter 2 above, for the developmental evidence; and Chapter 3, for the neural correlates of self-recognition).

CONCLUSION

To achieve clarity in neuroscientific studies of self it is incumbent on researchers to define the precise aspect of self under study. Selves are experiential, ecological, and agentive; they are often engaged in reflective evaluations and judgments; they are capable of various forms of self-recognition, self-related cognition, self-narrative, and self-specific perception and movement. In many of these activities, selves are more 'in-the-world' than 'in-the-brain', and they are in-the-world *as-subject* more so than *as-object*. In this regard we endorse Dennett's warning: 'it is a

---

[8] We offer the phrase 'in a constitutive sense' to avoid a certain ambiguity in Legrand and Ruby's account. One may have the impression that when they discuss the self/non-self distinction they may mean the usual relative distinction between one's self and everything else. In that respect, another person would count as part of the non-self. But in a constitutive sense the distinction between self/non-self means that there are certain aspects that define what would count as a self—e.g. first-person perspective—and fail to define everything that is not a self. In that case another person counts as a self (rather than non-self) because they also have a first-person perspective.

category mistake to start looking around for [selves] in the brain' (1992: 109). The project rather should be the study of what happens in the brain when the self-as-subject is engaged in the world, in specific actions and in specific social contexts. This requires not only the sophisticated tools of the neuroimaging lab, and the brilliant experiments of neuropsychology, but also the subtle conceptual tools of philosophy.

REFERENCES

AGUIRRE, G. K., and D'ESPOSITO, M. D. (1999). 'Topographical Disorientation: A Synthesis and Taxonomy', *Brain*, 122: 1613–28.

ANDERSEN, R. A., SHENOY, K. V., SNYDER, L. H., BRADLEY, D. C., and CROWELL, J. A. (1999). 'The Contributions of Vestibular Signals to the Representations of Space in Posterior Parietal Cortex', *Annals of the New York Academy of Science*, 871: 282–92.

ANDREASEN, N. C., O'LEARY, D. S., CIZADLO, T., ARNDT, S., REZAI, K., WATKINS, G. L., PONTO, L. L., and HICHWA, R. D. (1995). 'II. PET Studies of Memory: Novel versus Practiced Free Recall of Word Lists', *Neuroimage*, 2: 296–305.

BAR, M. (2007). 'The Proactive Brain: Using Analogies and Associations to Generate Predictions', *Trends in Cognitive Sciences*, 11/7: 280–9.

BARON-COHEN, S. (1995). *Mindblindness: An Essay on Autism and Theory of Mind* (Cambridge, Mass., and London: MIT Press).

BEHRMANN, M. (1999). 'Spatial Reference Frames and Hemispatial Neglect', in M. Gazzaniga (ed.), *The New Cognitive Neurosciences* (Cambridge, Mass.: MIT Press), 651–66.

BERLUCCHI, G., and AGLIOTI, S. (1997). 'The Body in the Brain: Neural Bases of Corporeal Awareness', *Trends in Neuroscience*, 20: 560–4.

BLAKEMORE, S. J., and FRITH, C. (2003). 'Self-Awareness and Action', *Current Opinions in Neurobiology*, 13/2: 219–24.

——and WOLPERT, D. M. (2001). 'The Cerebellum is Involved in Predicting the Sensory Consequences of Action', *Neuroreport*, 12/9: 1879–84.

——WOLPERT, D. M., and FRITH, C. D. (2002). 'Abnormalities in the Awareness of Action', *Trends in Cognitive Science*, 6(6): 237–42.

BUNGE, M. (1977). 'Emergence and the Mind', *Neuroscience*, 2: 501–10.

——(1979). 'The Mind-Body Problem, Information Theory, and Christian Dogma', *Neuroscience*, 4: 453.

BURGESS, N., MAGUIRE, E. A., SPIERS, H. J., and O'KEEFE, J. (2001). 'A Temporoparietal and Prefrontal Network for Retrieving the Spatial Context of Lifelike Events', *Neuroimage*, 14: 439–53.

CACIOPPO, J. T., LORIG, T. S., NUSBAUM, H. C., and BERNTSON, G. G. (2004). 'Social Neuroscience: Bridging Social and Biological Systems', in C. Sansone, C. C. Morf, and A. T. Panter (eds), *The Sage Handbook of Methods in Social Psychology* (Thousand Oaks, CA: SAGE), 383–404.

CHAMINADE, T., and DECETY, J. (2002). 'Leader or Follower? Involvement of the Inferior Parietal Lobule in Agency', *Neuroreport*, 13/1528: 1975–8.

CRAIK, F. I. M., MOROZ, T. M., MOSCOVITCH, M., STUSS, D. T., WINOCUR, G., TULVING, E., and KAPUR, S. (1999). 'In Search of the Self: A Positron Emission Tomography Study', *Psychological Science*, 10: 26–34.

CUNNINGTON, R., WINDISCHBERGER, C., ROBINSON, S., and MOSER, E. (2006). 'The Selection of Intended Actions and the Observation of Others' Actions: A Time-Resolved FMRI Study', *NeuroImage*, 29/4: 1294–1302.

DAMASIO, A. R. (1999). *The Feeling of What Happens. Body and Emotion in the Making of Consciousness* (New York: Harcourt Brace).

DAPRATI, E., FRANCK, N., GEORGIEFF, N., PROUST, J., PACHERIE, E., DALERY, J., and JEANNEROD, M. (1997). 'Looking for the Agent: An Investigation into Consciousness of Action and Self-Consciousness in Schizophrenic Patients', *Cognition*, 65(1): 71–86.

D'ARGEMBEAU, A., RUBY, P., COLLETTE, F., DEGUELDRE, C., BALTEAU, E., LUXEN, A., MAQUET, P., and SALMON, E. (2007). 'Distinct Regions of the Medial Prefrontal Cortex are Associated with Self-Referential Processing and Perspective-Taking', *Journal of Cognitive Neuroscience*, 19: 935–44.

DAVID, N., COHEN, M. X., NEWEN, A., BEWERNICK, B. H., SHAH, N. J., FINK, G. R., and VOGELEY, K. (2007). 'The Extrastriate Cortex Distinguishes between the Consequences of One's Own and Others' Behaviour', *Neuroimage*, 36: 1004–14.

——NEWEN, A., and VOGELEY, K. (2008). 'The 'Sense of Agency' and its Underlying Cognitive and Neural Mechanisms', *Consciousness and Cognition*, 17: 523–34.

DENNETT, D. (1992). 'The Self as a Center of Narrative Gravity', in F. S. Kessel, P. M. Cole, and D. L. Johnson (eds), *Self and Consciousness: Multiple Perspectives* (Hillsdale, NJ: Lawrence Erlbaum Associates), 103–15.

DEVINSKY, O. (2000). 'Right Cerebral Hemisphere Dominance for a Sense of Corporeal and Emotional Self', *Epilepsy and Behavior*, 1: 60–73.

ECCLES, J. C. (1989). *Evolution of the Brain, Creation of the Self* (London: Routledge).

——(1994). *How the Self Controls its Brain* (Berlin: Springer-Verlag).

FANGMEIER, T., KNAUFF, M., RUFF, C. C., and SLOUTSKY, V. (2006). 'FMRI Evidence for a Three-Stage Model of Deductive Reasoning', *Journal of Cognitive Neuroscience*, 18/3: 320–34.

FARRER, C., and FRITH, C. D. (2002). 'Experiencing Oneself vs. Another Person as Being the Cause of an Action: The Neural Correlates of the Experience of Agency', *NeuroImage*, 15: 596–603.

——GEORGIEFF, N., FRITH, C. D., DECETY, J., and JEANNEROD, M. (2003). 'Modulating the Experience of Agency: A Positron Emission Tomography Study', *NeuroImage*, 18: 324–33.

FINK, G. R., MARSHALL, J. C., HALLIGAN, P. W., FRITH, C. D., DRIVER, J., FRACKOWIAK, R. S. J., and DOLAN, R. J. (1999). 'The Neural Consequences of Conflict between Intention and the Senses', *Brain*, 122/3: 497–512.

FLETCHER, P., HAPPÉ, F., FRITH, U., BAKER, S. C., DOLAN, R. J., FRACKOWIAK, R. S. J., and FRITH, C. D. (1995). 'Other Minds in the Brain: A Functional Imaging Study of "Theory of Mind" in Story Comprehension', *Cognition*, 57: 109–28.

FONLUPT, P. (2003). 'Perception and Judgement of Physical Causality Involve Different Brain Structures', *Brain Research Cognitive Brain Research*, 17/2: 248–54.

FOURNERET, P., and JEANNEROD, M. (1998). 'Limited Conscious Monitoring of Motor Performance in Normal Subjects', *Neuropsychologia*, 36: 1133–40.

FOURNERET, P., FRANCK, N., SLACHEVSKY, A., and JEANNEROD, M. (2001). 'Self-Monitoring in Schizophrenia Revisited', *Neuroreport*, 12/6: 1203–8.

FOSSATI, P., HEVENOR, S. J., GRAHAM, S. J., GRADY, C., KEIGHTLEY, M. L., CRAIK, F., and MAYBERG, H. (2003). 'In Search of the Emotional Self: An FMRI Study Using Positive and Negative Emotional Words', *American Journal of Psychiatry*, 160: 1938–45.

FRANCK, N., FARRER, C., GEORGIEFF, N., MARIE-CARDINE, M., DALÉRY, J., d'AMATO, T., and JEANNEROD, M. (2001). 'Defective Recognition of One's Own Actions in Patients with Schizophrenia', *American Journal of Psychiatry*, 158: 454–9.

FRITH, C. D. (1992). *The Cognitive Neuropsychology of Schizophrenia* (Hillsdale, NJ: Lawrence Erlbaum Associates).

FUSTER, J. M. (1997). *The Prefrontal Cortex: Anatomy, Physiology and Neuropsychology of the Frontal Lobe* (Philadelphia: Lippincott-Raven).

——(2001). 'The Prefrontal Cortex an Update: Time is of the Essence', *Neuron*, 30: 319–33.

GALATI, G. *et al.* (2001). 'Spatial Coding of Visual and Somatic Sensory Information in Body-Centred Coordinates', *European Journal of Neuroscience*, 14: 737–46.

GALLAGHER, H. L., and FRITH, C. D. (2003). 'Functional Imaging of 'Theory of Mind'', *Trends in Cognitive Science*, 7/2: 77–83.

GALLAGHER, S. (2000). 'Philosophical Conceptions of the Self: Implication for Cognitive Science', *Trends in Cognitive Sciences*, 4: 14–21.

——(2007). 'The Natural Philosophy of Agency', *Philosophy Compass*. 2 (http://www.blackwell-synergy.com/doi/full/10.1111/j.1747-9991.2007.00067.x).

——(2008). 'Self-Agency and Mental Causality', in J. Parnas and Kenneth S. Kendler (eds), *Philosophical Issues in Psychiatry: Natural Kinds, Mental Taxonomy and the Nature of Reality* (Baltimore: Johns Hopkins University Press), 286–312.

——(2010). 'Multiple Aspects of Agency', *New Ideas in Psychology* (doi:10.1016/j.newideapsych.2010.03.003).

——and MARCEL, A. J. (1999). 'The Self in Contextualized Action', *Journal of Consciousness Studies*, 6/4: 4–30.

GILLIHAN, S. J., and FARAH, M. J. (2005). 'Is Self Special? A Critical Review of Evidence from Experimental Psychology and Cognitive Neuroscience', *Psychology Bulletin*, 131/1: 76–97.

GUSNARD, D. A., AKBUDAK, E., SHULMAN, G. L., and RAICHLE, M. E. (2001). 'Medial Prefrontal Cortex and Self-Referential Mental Activity: Relation to a Default Mode of Brain Function', *Proceedings of the National Academy of Sciences, USA*, 98: 4259–64.

GUTCHESS, A. H., KENSINGER, E. A., YOON, C., and SCHACTER, D. L. (2007). 'Ageing and the Selfreference Effect in Memory', *Memory*, 15: 822–37.

HAGGARD, P., and CLARK, S. (2003). 'Intentional Action: Conscious Experience and Neural Prediction', *Conscious Cognition*, 12: 695–707.

——and WHITFORD, B. (2004). 'Supplementary Motor Area Provides an Efferent Signal for Sensory Suppression', *Brain Research Cognitive Brain Research*, 19/1: 52–8.

——CLARK, S., and KALOGERAS, J. (2002). 'Voluntary Action and Conscious Awareness', *Nature Neuroscience*, 5/4: 382–5.

——MARTIN, F., TAYLOR-CLARKE, M., JEANNEROD, M., and FRANCK, N. (2003). 'Awareness of Action in Schizophrenia', *Neuroreport*, 14/7: 1081–5.

HEATHERTON, T. F., WYLAND, C. L., MACRAE, C. N., DEMOS, K. E., DENNY, B. T., and KELLEY, W. M. (2006). 'Medial Prefrontal Activity Differentiates Self from Close Others', *Social Cognitive and Affective Neuroscience*, 1: 18–25.

JEANNEROD, M. (2004). 'Visual and Action Cues Contribute to the Self–Other Distinction', *Nature Neuroscience*, 7: 422–3.

JOHNSON, S. C., BAXTER, L. C., WILDER, L. S., PIPE, J. G., HEISERMAN, J. E., and PRIGATANO, G. P. (2002). 'Neural Correlates of Self-Reflection', *Brain*, 125: 1808–14.

KEENAN, J. P., FREUND, S., HAMILTON, R. H., GANIS, G., and PASCUAL-LEONE, A. (2000). 'Hand Response Differences in a Self-Face Identification Task', *Neuropsychologia*, 38: 1047–53.

——McCUTCHEON, B., FREUND, S., GALLUP, G. G., SANDERS, G., and PASCUAL-LEONE, A. (1999). 'Left Hand Advantage in a Self-Face Recognition Task', *Neuropsychologia*, 37: 1421–5.

——NELSON, A., O'CONNOR, M., and PASCUAL-LEONE, A. (2001). 'Neurology: Self-Recognition and the Right Hemisphere', *Nature*, 409 (18 Jan.): 305.

——WHEELER, M., PLATEK, S. M., LARDI, G., and LASSONDE, M. (2003). 'Self-Face Processing in a Callosotomy Patient', *European Journal of Neuroscience*, 18: 2391–5.

KELLEY, W. M., MACRAE, C. N., WYLAND, C. L., CAGLAR, S., INATI, S., and HEATHERTON, T. F. (2002). 'Finding the Self? An Event-Related FMRI Study', *Journal of Cognitive Neuroscience*, 14: 785–94.

KIRCHER, T. T. J., SENIOR, C., PHILLIPS, M. L., BENSON, P. J., BULLMORE, E. T., BRAMMER, M., SIMMONS, A., WILLIAMS, S. C. R., BARTELS, M., and DAVID, A. S. (2000). 'Towards a Functional Neuroanatomy of Self Processing: Effects of Faces and Words', *Cognitive Brain Research*, 10: 133–44.

KJAER, T. W., NOWAK, M., and LOU, H. C. (2002). 'Reflective Self-Awareness and Conscious States: PET Evidence for a Common Midline Parietofrontal Core', *NeuroImage*, 17: 1080–6.

KLATZKY, R. L. (1998). 'Allocentric and Egocentric Spatial Representations: Definitions, Distinctions, and Interconnections', in C. Freksa and C. Habel (eds), *Spatial Cognition: An Interdisciplinary Approach to Representing and Processing Spatial Knowledge* (Heidelberg: Springer), 1–17.

LANE, R. D., FINK, G. R., CHAU, P. M.-L., and DOLAN, R. J. (1997). 'Neural Activation during Selective Attention to Subjective Emotional Responses', *NeuroReport*, 8: 3969–72.

LAU, H. C., ROGERS, R. D., and PASSINGHAM R. E. (2006). 'On Measuring the Perceived Onsets of Spontaneous Actions', *Journal of Neuroscience*, 26/27: 7265–71.

LEDOUX, J. (2002). *The Synaptic Self* (New York: Penguin Putnam).

LEGRAND, D., and RUBY, P. (2009). 'What is Self Specific? A Theoretical Investigation and a Critical Review of Neuroimaging Results', *Psychological Review*, 116/1: 252–82.

LOU, H. C., LUBER, B., CRUPAIN, M., KEENAN, J. P., NOWAK, M., KJAER, T. W., *et al.* (2004). 'Parietal Cortex and Representation of the Mental Self', *Proceedings of the National Academy of Sciences, USA*, 101: 6827–32.

McKAY, D. M. (1978). 'Selves and Brains', *Neuroscience*, 3: 599–606.

——(1979). 'Reply to Bunge', *Neuroscience*, 4: 454.

——(1980). 'The Interdependence of Mind and Brain', *Neuroscience*, 5: 1389–91.

MAGUIRE, E. A., BURGESS, N., DONNETT, J. G., FRACKOWIAK, R. S. J., FRITH, C. D., and O'KEEFE, J. (1998). 'Knowing Where and Getting There: A Human Navigation Network', *Science*, 280: 921–4.

——and O'KEEFE, J. (1999). 'Human Spatial Navigation: Cognitive Maps, Sexual Dimorphism, and Neural Substrates', *Current Opinions in Neurobiology*, 9: 171–7.

MARCEL, A. (2003). 'The Sense of Agency: Awareness and Ownership of Action', in J. Roessler and N. Eilan (eds), *Agency and Awareness* (Oxford: Oxford University Press), 48–93.

MARSHALL, J. C., and FINK, G. R. (2001). 'Spatial Cognition: Where we were and Where we are', *NeuroImage*, 14: S2–7.

MILLER, B. L., SEELEY, W. W., MYCHACK, P., ROSEN, H. J., MENA, I., and BOONE, K. (2001). 'Neuroanatomy of the Self: Evidence from Patients with Frontotemporal Dementia', *Neurology*, 57: 817–21.

NEISSER, U. (1988). 'Five Kinds of Self-Knowledge', *Philosophical Psychology*, 1: 35–59.

NEWEN, A., and VOGELEY, K. (eds) (2000). *Selbst und Gehirn* (Paderborn: Mentis Verlag).

——and ——(2003). 'Self Representation: Searching for a Neural Signature of Self Consciousness', *Consciousness and Cognition*, 12: 529–43.

——and ——(2009). 'The Definition and the Constitution of Mental Disorders and the Role of Neural Dysfunctions', in S. Wood, N. Allen, and C. Pantelis (eds.), *The Neuropsychology of Mental Illness* (Cambridge: Cambridge University Press), 414–20.

NORTHOFF, G., and BERMPOHL, F. (2004). 'Cortical Midline Structures and the Self', *Trends in Cognitive Sciences*, 8: 102–7.

——and PANKSEPP, J. (2008). 'The Trans-Species Concept of Self and the Subcortical–Cortical Midline System', *Trends in Cognitive Sciences*, 12/7: 259–64.

——HEINZEL, A., de Greck M., Bermpohl, F., Dobrowolny, H., and Panksepp, J. (2006). 'Self-Referential Processing in our Brain: A Meta-Analysis of Imaging Studies on the Self', *NeuroImage*, 31: 440–57.

PEELEN, M. V., and DOWNING, P. E. (2005). 'Is the Extrastriate Body Area Involved in Motor Actions?', *Nature Neuroscience*, 8/125 (doi:10.1038/nn0205-125a).

PLATEK, S. M., and GALLUP, G. G. (2002). 'Self-Face Recognition is Affected by Schizotypal Personality Traits', *Schizophrenia Research*, 57: 81–5.

——KEENAN, J. P., GALLUP, G. G., and MOHAMED, F. B. (2004). 'Where am I? The Neurological Correlates of Self and Other', *Cognitive Brain Research*, 19: 114–22.

——MYERS, T. E., CRITTON, S. R., and GALLUP, G. G. (2003). 'A Left-Hand Advantage for Self-Description: The Impact of Schizotypal Personality Traits', *Schizophrenia Research*, 65: 147–51.

POPPER, K. R., and ECCLES, J. C. (1985). *The Self and its Brain: An Argument for Interactionism* (New York: Springer International).

PREILOWSKI, B. (1979). 'Consciousness After Complete Surgical Section of the Forebrain Commissures in Man', in I. S. Russell, M. W. van Hoff, and G. Berlucchi (eds), *Structure and Function of Cerebral Commissures* (London: Macmillan Press), 411–20.

PREMACK, D., and WOODRUFF, G. (1978). Does the chimpanzee have a theory of mind? *Behavioural and Brain Sciences*, 1: 515–26.

RAICHLE, M. E., MACLEOD, A. M., SNYDER, A. Z., POWERS, W. J., GUSNARD, D. A., and SHULMAN, G. L. (2001). 'A Default Mode of Brain Function', *Proceedings of the National Academy of Sciences, USA*, 98: 676–82.

RUBY, P., and DECETY, J. (2001). 'Effect of Subjective Perspective Taking during Simulation of Action: A PET Investigation of Agency', *Nature Neuroscience*, 4: 546–50.

——and ——(2003). 'What you Believe versus What you Think they Believe: A Neuroimaging Study of Conceptual Perspective-Taking', *European Journal of Neuroscience*, 17/11: 2475–80.

——Collette, F., D'Argembeau, A., Peters, F., Degueldre, C., Balteau, E., Luxen, A., Maquet, P., and Salmon, E. (2009). 'Perspective Taking to Assess Self-Personality: What's Modified in Alzheimer's Disease?', *Neurobiology of Aging*, 30: 1637–51.

Spence, S. A., Brooks, D. J., Hirsch, S. R. *et al.* (1997). 'A PET Study of Voluntary Movement in Schizophrenic Patients Experiencing Passivity Phenomena (Delusions of Alien Control)', *Brain*, 120: 1997–2011.

Stephens, G. L., and Graham, G. (2000). *When Self-Consciousness Breaks: Alien Voices and Inserted Thoughts.* (Cambridge, Mass.: MIT Press).

Stuss, D. T., Gallup, G. G., Jr., and Alexander, M. P. (2001*a*). 'The Frontal Lobes are Necessary for 'Theory of Mind'', *Brain*, 124: 279–86.

——Picton, T. W., and Alexander, M. P. (2001*b*). 'Consciousness, Self-Awareness and the Frontal Lobes', in S. Salloway, P. Malloy, and J. Duffy (eds), *The Frontal Lobes and Neuropsychiatric Illness* (Washington, DC: American Psychiatric Press), 101–9.

Sugiura, M., Kawashima, R., Nakamura, K., Okada, K., Kato, T., Nakamura, A., *et al.* (2000). 'Passive and Active Recognition of One's Own Face', *NeuroImage*, 11: 36–48.

Synofzik, M., Vosgerau, G., and Newen, A. (2008). 'Beyond the Comparator Model: A Multifactorial Two-Step Account of Agency', *Consciousness and Cognition*, 17/1: 219–39.

Tsakiris, M., and Haggard, P. (2003). 'Awareness of Somatic Events Associated with a Voluntary Action', *Experimental Brain Research*, 149/4: 439–46.

——and ——(2005). 'Experimenting with the Acting Self', *Cognitive Neuropsychology*, 22/3–4: 387–407.

Turk, D. J., Heatherton, T. F., Macrae, C. N., Kelley, W. M., and Gazzaniga, M. S. (2003). 'Out of Contact, Out of Mind: The Distributed Nature of the Self', *Annals of the New York Academy of Science*, 1001: 65–78.

Vallar, G., Lobel, E., Galati, G., Berthoz, A., Pizzamiglia, L., LeBihan, D. (1999). 'A Fronto-Parietal System for Computing the Egocentric Spatial Frame of Reference in Humans', *Experimental Brain Research*, 124: 281–6.

Vogeley, K., and Fink, G. (2003). 'Neural Correlates of the First-Person-Perspective', *Trends in Cognitive Science*, 7: 38–42.

——and Newen, A. (2009). 'Consciousness of Oneself and Others in Relation to Mental Disorders', in S. Wood, N. Allen, and C. Pantelis (eds), *The Neuropsychology of Mental Illness* (Cambridge: Cambridge University Press), 408–13.

——Bussfeld, P., Newen, A., Herrmann, S., Happé, F., Falkai, P., Maier, W., Shah, N. J., Fink, G. R., and Zilles, K. (2001). 'Mind Reading: Neural Mechanisms of Theory of Mind and Self-Perspective', *NeuroImage*, 14: 170–81.

——Kurthen, M., Falkai, P., and Maier, W. (1999). 'Essential Functions of the Human Self Model are Implemented in the Prefrontal Cortex', *Consciousness and Cognition*, 8: 343–63.

——May, M., Ritzl, A., Falkai, P., Zilles, K., and Fink, G. R. (2004). 'Neural Correlates of First-Person-Perspective as one Constituent of Human Self-Consciousness', *Journal of Cognitive Neuroscience*, 16: 817–27.

von Holst, E. (1954). 'Relations between the Central Nervous System and the Peripheral Organs', *British Journal of Animal Behavior*, 2: 89–94.

——and Mittelstaedt, H. (1950). 'Das Reafferenzprinzip: Wechselwirkungen zwischen Zentralnervensystem und Peripherie', *Naturwissenschaften*, 37: 464–76.

Wegner, D., and Sparrow, B. (2004). 'Authorship Processing', in M. S. Gazzaniga (ed.), *The New Cognitive Neurosciences* (3rd edn. Cambridge, Mass.: MIT).

WOLBERS, T., and HEGARTY, M. (2010). 'What Determines our Navigational Abilities?', *Trends in Cognitive Science*, 14/3: 138–46.

WOLPERT, D. M., GHAHRAMANI, Z., and JORDAN, M. I. (1995). 'An Internal Model for Sensorimotor Integration', *Science*, 269: 1880–2.

ZACKS, J. M. (2008). 'Neuroimaging Studies of Mental Rotation: A Meta-Analysis and Review', *Journal of Cognitive Neuroscience*, 20/1: 1–19.

PART II

BODILY SELVES

CHAPTER 5

....

THE EMBODIED SELF

....

QUASSIM CASSAM

1. INTRODUCTION

....

Descartes thought that he was distinct from his body and could exist without it. The self that is distinct from its body is, according to Descartes, an immaterial substance. This immaterial self possesses a body and is so intimately conjoined with its body that it forms a union with it. The relation between self and body is, Descartes insists, unlike the relation between a pilot and his vessel. If one were in one's body like a pilot in a vessel one would not feel pain when one's body is hurt. Nevertheless, the fact remains that each of us is, strictly speaking, distinct from his or her body. The self is a thinking and unextended thing. The body is an extended and unthinking thing.[1]

The question to which Cartesian dualism is a response is, first and foremost, a metaphysical question, namely:

(M) What is the relation between a person and his or her body?

To talk about the 'person' is, in the context of (M), to talk about the thinking, experiencing self. It is this self or soul that, according to the dualist, is distinct from

---

[1] Descartes sets out his views on the relation between mind (self) and body in his *Meditations on First Philosophy* (Descartes 1996). See, especially, the Sixth Meditation, where he makes the point that the relation between self and body is unlike the relation between a pilot and his vessel.

its body. At the other end of the scale from dualism is a form of materialism according to which, far from being distinct from its body, self and body are in fact identical. On this account, the only sense in which each of us *has* a body is that each of us *is* a body.[2] A third view is constitutionalism. This says that a (human) person is constituted by a human body without being identical to the constituting body. For the constitutionalist, the relation between person and body is like the relation between Michelangelo's *David* and the piece of marble that constitutes it.[3]

Both dualists and constitutionalists think that the identity conditions for persons are different from those for bodies and that it is metaphysically possible for a person to have different bodies at different times. If this is a genuine possibility then an obvious question is: what makes a particular body mine? To answer this question is to specify criteria of embodiment. On one account, the criteria of embodiment are both volitional and sensory. A person is volitionally embodied in a particular body B only if his or her volitions produce movements in B that fulfil or conform to those volitions. A person is sensorily embodied in B 'to the extent that the interactions of that body with its surroundings produce in the person sense-experiences corresponding to, and constituting veridical perceptions of, aspects of those surroundings' (Shoemaker 1984*a*: 117).

A related consideration is that people are normally aware of their own bodies 'from the inside', in a way that they are not aware of any other person's body.[4] One might think that one's own body just is the body that one is aware of from the inside.[5] More cautiously, it might be proposed that for a body to be one's own body it is at least necessary that one is aware of it from the inside. This criterion of embodiment faces some serious challenges. If, as seems plausible, proprioceptive awareness of one's present bodily position and posture is a key element of one's awareness of one's own body from the inside then what are we to make of those unfortunate individuals who, as a result of illness of injury, have lost much of their proprioceptive awareness of their own bodies?[6] In such cases, there is little inclination to say that the body that the individual used to be aware of from the inside is no longer her body.

Even if one is not satisfied by the idea that awareness of one's body from the inside is a criterion of embodiment or regards the search for such criteria as misconceived, it is still an interesting question how such awareness should be

---

[2] For a defence of this view see Williams 1973; Thomson 1997.

[3] See Baker 2000 for an exposition and defence of constitutionalism or what she calls the 'Constitution View'.

[4] Cassam 1995 and Martin 1995 both contain detailed discussions of this form of bodily awareness.

[5] In the terminology of Cassam 1995 this would be an 'idealist' conception of body ownership. Locke appears to be an idealist in this sense in bk. 2, ch. 27, of his *Essay Concerning Human Understanding* (Locke 1975).

[6] See the case study in Cole 1991.

characterized. The issue here is phenomenological rather than metaphysical. The question is:

(P) What is the nature of the awareness that each of us has of his or her own body from the inside?

One issue is whether bodily awareness is a form of perceptual awareness. A related issue is whether it is awareness of one's body as an object, as a subject, or both. From the premise that one's body *is* an object in space it does not follow immediately that awareness of one's body from the inside is awareness of it *as* an object. Nevertheless, it is clear on reflection that there is much to be said for the idea that bodily awareness is awareness of one's body as a bounded spatial object. Does this mean that one cannot be aware of one's body as a subject or, to put it another way, that bodily awareness is not self-awareness? The assumption that awareness of something as an object is incompatible with awareness of it as a subject is open to question but even without this assumption the proposal that bodily awareness is self-awareness runs into serious difficulties. What is hard to dispute, however, is that to be aware of a particular body from the inside is to be aware of it as one's own body. This sense of ownership is something that a satisfactory response to (P) might be expected to acknowledge and explain.

To talk about the nature of bodily awareness is to invite questions about the nature of bodily knowledge. In its most general form, the epistemological question is:

(E) What, if anything, is special about the knowledge we have of our own bodies?

One suggestion is that we have ways of gaining knowledge of our own physical states and properties that give rise to the phenomenon of immunity to error through misidentification relative to the first person.[7] To get a fix on this phenomenon, suppose that I feel pain and judge on this basis that I am in pain. The sense in which this judgement is immune to error through misidentification is that the following is not possible: I know that someone is in pain but my judgement is mistaken because, and only because, the person I know to be in pain is not me. Now compare the proprioceptively based judgement 'My legs are crossed'. It is not possible that this judgement is expressive of the knowledge that *someone's* legs are crossed but is mistaken because, and only because, the individual whose legs I know to be crossed is not me. One of the major challenges facing a philosophical account of our bodily knowledge will be to explain the immunity to error through misidentification of such bodily self-ascriptions.[8]

---

[7] The idea that some first-person judgements are immune to error in this sense is associated, above all, with Sydney Shoemaker. Shoemaker 1994 contains the classic account of this phenomenon. See Pryor 1999 and Campbell 2004 for further discussion.

[8] The claim that some bodily self-ascriptions are immune to error through misidentification relative to the first person is associated, above all, with Gareth Evans. See Evans 1982: 220–4.

While (M), (P), and (E) are not unconnected, we will proceed by considering each of them in more depth in the next three sections. In the concluding section, the focus will be on the importance of embodiment. The issue here is whether cognition can properly be understood as anything other than embodied. It seems compelling that 'embodiment plays a central role in structuring experience, cognition, and action' (Gallagher 2005: 136). Indeed, one might go further and claim that embodiment is what makes cognition possible. If this is right then it tells us something important about the 'self'. For if the self is that which perceives, acts, and thinks, and perceiving, acting, and thinking must be understood in bodily terms, then the metaphysical lesson is obvious: the self is, first and foremost, an embodied self.

2. THE BODY AND THE SELF

Am I identical with my body? If not, can I exist without having a body? Descartes thinks that the answer to both questions is 'yes'. Many philosophers who are not dualists still believe that Descartes is right on both counts. On the distinctness of self and body, consider the following simple argument: when I die I cease to exist but my body does not cease to exist.[9] So I am not identical with my body, and the continued existence of my body is not sufficient for my own continued existence. Call this the *argument from death* for the thesis that I and my body are not identical. It is also plausible, many believe, that the continued existence of my body is not necessary for my continued existence. Suppose that my brain is removed from my body, which is subsequently destroyed, and transplanted into my best friend's debrained body. The resulting person would not just be (let us assume) psychologically continuous with me. The resulting person would *be* me, but I would have a different body from the one I had previously. What was once my body (the one from which my brain was removed) no longer exists but I still exist, so I could not have been identical with that body and am not identical with my new body. Call this the *argument from bodily transfer* for the non-identity of self and body.[10] Now consider this variation on the argument from bodily transfer: my brain is removed from my skull and kept alive and conscious in a vat of nutrients. My body is

---

[9] Unless my death is extremely violent.

[10] See bk. 2, ch. 27, of Locke's *Essay* for a version of this argument. Shoemaker's 'Brownson' case makes the same point. If Brown's brain is removed from Brown's body and transplanted into Robinson's debrained skull in such a way that the resulting person—Brownson—is psychologically continuous with Brown it is hard to resist the conclusion that Brownson is the same person as Brown even though they have different bodies. See Shoemaker 1984b: 78.

destroyed. On one view, I still exist even though I no longer have a body. In this scenario, I can truly think 'I no longer have a body'.[11] So it is not just that the continued existence of my body is not necessary for my continued existence. It is also the case that I can exist without having a body. Call this the *brain in a vat argument* for the possibility of disembodied existence.

Cartesian dualism explains the alleged fact that an embodied person is not identical with his body and can exist without a body on the basis that the person, or at any rate the self, is an immaterial substance, a soul. The coherence of this approach has been questioned on the basis that it is not possible to specify criteria of singularity and identity for souls and that this makes all talk of such entities unacceptable.[12] In response, Descartes might question the claim that it is illegitimate to posit souls in the absence of informative general criteria of singularity or identity. As long as each of us is directly aware of his or own singularity and identity the absence of criteria does not matter. It is questionable, however, that there is any such consciousness of one's own identity as an immaterial thinking substance. In addition, the positing of souls might be questioned on the basis that if we think of the world as causally closed then there will not be any room in it for a 'separate realm of mental substance that exerts its own influence on physical processes' (Chalmers 1996: 124–5).

If we are satisfied that Cartesian dualism is no longer a serious option how can we still agree that a person is distinct from his body and can exist without it or, indeed, without any body? As Shoemaker observes, any account of personal identity which allows for the possibility of bodily transfer is incompatible with the view that a person is simply identical with his body, but the thesis that a person is not identical to his body 'gives no support to dualism and is in fact perfectly compatible with a materialist view of the world' (1984*b*: 106). It is perfectly compatible with the view that mental states are realized in, or at least supervenient on, states of the brain. Neither the argument from bodily transfer nor the brain in a vat argument implies that I am an immaterial thing or that a person's mental states are realized in states of an immaterial substance.

What, then, is the relation between a person and his or her body? Constitutionalism holds that this relation is 'simply an instance of a very general relation: constitution' (Baker 2000: 27). A human person is constituted by a human body, and if x constitutes y at any time, then x is not identical to y. The constitution view is still a form of materialism. It can 'agree to many claims dear to dualists' (Baker 2000: 217) without positing immaterial souls. On the issue of whether a human person is identical to his or own body and whether such a person can survive a complete change of body the constitutionalist and the dualist are in complete agreement, even though they explain

---

[11] This example is taken from Peacocke 2008: 98.
[12] This is Strawson's objection to Cartesian dualism. See Strawson 1974 and Cassam 2008 for further discussion.

the non-identity of person and body and the possibility of bodily transfer in quite different ways. Constitutionalism is a form of materialism.[13]

It is only an argument in favour of the constitution view that it can give dualists so much of what they say they want if dualism's desiderata are reasonable. Those who think that people are identical with their bodies do not accept these desiderata and are sceptical about the various arguments in favour of the view that a person is not identical to his or her body. Take the argument from death. Unless my death is extremely violent my body will not go out of existence when I die. It only follows that I am not identical with my body *if* it is true that *I* will go out of existence when I die. But is this true? As Judith Jarvis Thomson asks:

Don't people who die in bed just become dead people at the time of their deaths? Cats who die in bed become dead cats at the time of their deaths; why should it be thought otherwise in the case of people? Can't there be some dead people as well as dead cats after the roof falls in? The answer is surely that there can be. (1997: 202)

If there is anything in what Thomson says in this passage then the argument from death is inconclusive.

The same goes for the argument from bodily transfer. Suppose that scientists invent a brain-state transfer device which can record the state of one brain and imposes that state on a second brain.[14] One day my wife is kidnapped by someone who, having access to a brain-state transfer device, records the state of his own brain and imposes it on my wife's brain. There is then a shoot-out in which, as we would say before we know the full facts of the situation, the kidnapper is killed and my wife is rescued. Even if the person who was rescued thinks that she is the kidnapper would we really say, even after discovering what happened with the brain-state transfer device, that this person is the kidnapper in my wife's body? Would we not think that my wife survived and that, as a result of what the kidnapper did to her, she is under the illusion that she is the kidnapper?[15] In this case, there is no brain transplantation but if the fact that the rescued individual is psychologically continuous with the kidnapper does not make it true that she is the kidnapper then it is not at all clear why we should take a different view of the case in which this psychological continuity obtains as the result of a brain transplant. If my wife has had her brain removed from her skull and the brain of the kidnapper transplanted into her skull then I might reasonably think that something quite terrible has happened to her but deny that the terrible thing that has happened to her is that she has been killed. She has been psychologically mutilated but when she says after the rescue that she kidnapped someone yesterday she says

[13] According to Baker, 'although it may be empirically impossible for me to have a complete change of body, the Constitution View raises no theoretical barrier to a human person's having a complete change of body' (2000: 218).

[14] The idea of a brain-state transfer device is used by Shoemaker (1984b: 108–11) to make a point about personal identity.

[15] Paul Snowdon makes substantially the same point (1995: 77).

something false. She is the victim rather than the perpetrator of the crime; the kidnapper has not survived in my wife's body.

Animalism is the view that we are identical with certain human animals.[16] The sense in which I am identical with a certain human animal H is not that I share my matter with H but that I am identical with H. On this account, the sense in which it is my wife rather than the kidnapper who has survived the shoot-out is that the animal with which my wife is identical has survived the shoot-out. The fact that an animal's brain has been tampered with by a brain-state transfer device does not mean that the animal no longer exists. If I am an animal, and it is true that an animal cannot change bodies, then I cannot change bodies. If animals cannot be disembodied then I cannot be disembodied. If my brain is removed from my skull and kept alive in a vat of nutrients while the rest of my body is destroyed the animal that is located where I am presently located ceases to exist. If that animal ceases to exist then I cease to exist. Even if it makes sense to suppose that my disembodied brain can think, the survival of my brain is insufficient for my survival.

As P. F. Snowdon observes, 'it is an open question what the relation is between an animal and its body' (1995: 71). While even animalists may be reluctant to say that an animal is identical with its body, there is little doubt that certain bodily continuities are sufficient for the survival of the animal. The hard question for the animalist is whether bodily continuity is necessary for the survival of the animal and, if so, what kind of bodily continuity. In the case in which my brain is transplanted into my friend's debrained body, with the rest of my body being destroyed, it looks as though this amounts to the destruction of the animal with which I am identical. The survival of this animal requires more than the survival of one of its organs, its brain. The animalist must therefore resist the characterization of such cases as ones in which the person goes with the brain. From an animalist perspective, the intuition that we can change bodies is deviant unless human animals can change bodies.[17] We are, in fact, bodily beings and, as Descartes recognized, we are presented to ourselves as such. The next question, therefore, is: what is involved in our being aware of ourselves as bodily beings?

3. BODILY AWARENESS

What is the nature of the awareness that each of us has of his or her own body? To see oneself in a mirror is to be aware of one's own body but this is not the kind of bodily awareness that led Descartes to say that the experienced relation between

---

[16] Snowdon 1990 is a classic paper in defence of animalism.
[17] See Snowdon 1991 for further discussion of this point.

body and self is not like the relation between a pilot and his ship. To make sense of
Descartes's remark it has to be recognized that each of us is normally aware of his or
her own body from the inside. Such awareness takes many different forms. For
example, most of us can tell, without looking, whether we are moving or not, or
whether our legs are crossed. The source of this kind of non-visual knowledge of
bodily posture and movement is proprioception.[18] In Gallagher's terminology,
subpersonal proprioceptive *information* updates the motor system with respect
to the body's posture and movement and is the basis for proprioceptive *awareness*.
The latter is a 'self-referential, but normally pre-reflective, awareness of one's own
body' (2005: 73; see Chapter 6 below). The body of which one is proprioceptively
aware is given to one as one's own body. In being proprioceptively aware that one's
legs are crossed one is not normally aware of the position of a pair of legs in a way
that leaves it open whether the legs in question are one's own. Proprioceptive
awareness of one's body is awareness of it 'from the inside'. It is a cognitive relation
to one's body that is not like the relation between pilot and ship.

Bodily sensation is another important aspect of bodily awareness. To feel a pain
in one's foot is to perceive one's own body.[19] It is my foot that feels a certain way
when I feel a pain in my foot, and in feeling a pain in my foot I am aware of the foot
as a part of my own body. A sense of ownership is built into the phenomenology of
this type of bodily awareness, and one question that has been raised is whether
everything that one feels in this way must be a part of one's own body. M. G. F.
Martin draws a useful contrast in this connection between what he calls the 'sole-
object' and the 'multiple-object' views of bodily awareness. The former says that
'bodily sensations, together with kinaesthesia, proprioception, and the vestibular
sense, amount to an awareness of one's body that is only of one's own body and its
parts' (1995: 273). In contrast, while the multiple-object view grants that sensation
gives one awareness of body parts it maintains that 'it is merely a contingent matter
that one comes to be aware only of one's own body parts in this way and that it is
quite conceivable that one could be aware of parts of others' bodies in the same
way' (1995: 274).

Consider the following argument in support of the multiple-object view: imagine that it feels to me as if there is a pain in my left hand but that, when asked where
it hurts, I indicate my neighbour's hand. This would surely be a case in which
sensation is providing me with awareness from the inside of a part of someone
else's body. If such a thing is conceivable, then we might conclude that what the
multiple-object view is right to insist is that it is merely contingent that sensation
only gives us awareness of our own body parts. The question, however, is whether

---

[18] 'Proprioception is the bodily sense that allows us to know how our body and limbs are
positioned' (Gallagher 2005: 43).

[19] This assumes the correctness of a perceptual model of sensation. See Martin 1995 for further
discussion and references.

in the example just given it would be correct to say that one should be regarded as having genuinely *perceptual* awareness of a body part that is not one's own. On the sole-object view I do not count as perceiving my neighbour's hand in the case described even if I am hooked up to it by a radio transmitter. The proposal is that bodily experiences of parts of other people's bodies are illusory or hallucinatory and that it is a necessary condition for a subject to perceive a body part that the part in question is a part of the subject's body.[20]

A further potential difficulty for the sole-object view is suggested by Shoe-maker's observation that 'ordinary modes of perception admit our perceiving, successively or simultaneously, a multiplicity of different objects, all of which are on a par as non-factual objects of perception' (1994*b*: 126). Given that one's own body is the only body that one can be aware of from the inside, how can it be right to characterize such awareness as genuinely perceptual? More generally, isn't the very idea of sole-object perception absurd? Only if what Shoemaker says is true of ordinary modes of perception is necessarily true of any form of awareness that deserves to be called perceptual. On a more liberal conception, perceptual aware-ness is fundamentally a sort of awareness in which objects are presented; it provides knowledge of the presented object, and the knowledge that it provides is grounded in sensation. On each of these counts, bodily awareness comes out as a form of perceptual awareness even if the fact that it is restricted to one object means that it is not perception in the ordinary sense.

The sense in which bodily awareness involves the presentation of an object is not just that one's body is an object but that one is aware of it *as* an object. It is presumably a sufficient condition for one to be aware of something 'as an object' that one is aware of it as a material object. To be aware of something as a material object is to be aware of it as having shape, extension and solidity. In Locke's terms, it is to be aware of it as possessing primary qualities. The first thing to notice about the awareness we have of our own bodies is that it involves having a sense of the shape of our bodies. To have a sense of the shape of one's body is, in turn, to have a sense of its boundaries, a sense of where it ends and the rest of the world begins. In addition, awareness of one's own body from the inside is awareness of it as extended in space, as three-dimensional. Finally, there is also the sense of one's body as solid, that is, as occupying a region of space. Touch and movement provide us with access to the solidity of other bodies, and are bound up with a sense of the solidity of one's own body. There is no better way of becoming aware of the solidity of one's own body than literally to bump into someone else or something else. In each of these respects, awareness of one's own body from the inside is awareness of it as an object.

---

[20] This proposal is defended in Martin 1995.

Is bodily awareness a form of self-awareness? If self and body are identical then it follows that awareness of one's body is in fact awareness of oneself. However, this is not what those who think that bodily awareness is self-awareness have in mind. Their idea is that bodily awareness is self-awareness to the extent that it is awareness of one's body qua subject.[21] Specifically, the suggestion is that bodily awareness fulfils the necessary and sufficient conditions for a form of awareness to count as awareness of something *qua* subject. Suppose that the conditions for awareness of something qua subject are that it is:

(*a*) awareness of it as one's point of view on the world;
(*b*) awareness of it as the bearer of one's sensations and other mental states;
(*c*) a form of awareness which does not allow for misidentification.

If it is true that these conditions are sufficient and that bodily awareness satisfies all of them then there would be no reason not to count such awareness as self-awareness.[22] The problem is that it is doubtful whether the proposed conditions are sufficient and it is not clear, in any case, that bodily awareness satisfies all of them.

A way of defending (*a*) would be to stress the perspectival nature of perception. When one perceives objects other than oneself one perceives them as standing in spatial relations to one's body. The spatial content of perception is, in this sense, egocentric, and one's body 'functions as the absolute point about which spatial relations are experienced as orientated' (Bell 1990: 210).[23] It might be held that for one's body to function in this way just is for one to be aware of it as one's point of view on the world. In vision, however, it is only a part of the body—the head—that serves as the point about which spatial relations are experienced as orientated, and a different story will need to be told about the egocentric spatial content of tactile perception. In addition, the fact that objects are perceived as standing in spatial relations to a specific body part does not seem sufficient to justify the claim that one is aware of that part as one's point of view on the world, especially if that body part can itself be perceived. When one perceives a part of one's own body one is aware of it not as one's point of view on the world but rather as something on which one has a point of view.

The most that can be said in favour of (*b*) is that we are conscious of our sensations as having bodily locations. As Brewer writes, 'we cannot get away from the fact that bodily sensations immediately appear as determinately located not only in egocentric space but also in specific body parts filling those locations' (1995: 299). Does this mean that one is aware of one's body as a 'bearer of sensations' (Husserl 1989: 168)? One might think that there is a gap between the idea that one's

---

[21] See Cassam 1997 for a defence of this view.
[22] This is the basis on which Cassam 1997 argues for the view that bodily awareness is self-awareness.
[23] Bell is here describing Husserl's view. See Husserl 1989: 166.

sensations present themselves as having a bodily location and the idea that one's body is their presented subject. Even if no such gap exists there is still the question of whether the body is the apparent bearer of other mental states. Whatever there is to be said for the idea that the body is the presented subject of sensation it is harder to make anything of the proposal that it is the presented subject of belief. Beliefs do not appear to have bodily locations in the way that sensations do, and this puts further pressure on the idea that bodily awareness is awareness of one's body qua subject.

The issue of immunity to error through misidentification will be taken up below. If bodily self-ascriptions that are based on awareness of one's body from the inside enjoy this kind of immunity[24] then (c) looks in somewhat better shape than either (a) or (b). However, the significance of this point should not be exaggerated. For the immunity to error through misidentification of some bodily self-ascriptions is not sufficient to justify the proposal that the awareness on which they are based is awareness of one's body qua subject. Immunity to error through misidentification is a relatively widespread phenomenon. Demonstrative judgements like 'This is red' enjoy such immunity even though the perceptual awareness on which such judgements are based is not awareness of anything qua subject.

Even if bodily awareness could be shown to satisfy (a), (b), and (c) there would still be doubts about the idea that bodily awareness is self-awareness. As Martin notes, 'if it is at least open to the subject to wonder whether the object that she is presented with in bodily sensation is not herself but rather only an object closely associated with herself, then that object cannot be presented to her as being the self' (1995: 284). It makes sense for one to wonder whether the object one is presented with in bodily sensation is oneself because even if the two coincide they do not coincide a priori. To make this vivid, suppose that object of bodily sensation or awareness includes an artificial limb. In this case the question whether the object of one's bodily awareness is oneself would not be confused. Indeed, if one is identical with one's physical body then the answer to this question is actually 'no', at least on the reasonable assumption that a prosthetic limb is not strictly speaking a part of one's physical body.

A related consideration is this: suppose that awareness of one's own body from the inside is, as the discussion so far suggests, awareness of it as an object. In that case, it might be thought to follow almost immediately that it is not awareness of one's body qua subject. This assumes that awareness of something as an object and awareness of it qua subject are incompatible modes of awareness.[25] We might call this position *incompatibilism*. On this account, 'bodily awareness can be of both kinds—awareness qua subject, awareness as an object' but 'it cannot be both at

---

[24] For further discussion of the immunity to error through misidentification of demonstrative judgements see Evans 1982: 179–91.

[25] For further discussion see Cassam 1997: 68–73.

once' (Longuenesse 2006: 296). To put it another way, the body is either 'a thing among other things, or it is that by which things are revealed to me' but 'it cannot be both at the same time' (Sartre 1989: 304).

In contrast, *compatibilism* is the view that one can be simultaneously aware of one's body both as subject as an object. To be aware of one's body in both of these modes is, in Merleau-Ponty's suggestive terminology, to be aware of it as a 'subject-object' (1989: 95).[26] The body that is the presented subject of experience and sensation is not a mere body, a piece of inanimate physical matter, but an animated, living body, a point of occupancy for psychological properties.[27] A mere body can neither be, nor be presented as being, a self or subject. But once we think in terms of the living body, the idea that such a thing can appear in consciousness both as subject and as object should begin to strike us as less mysterious.

One way of arguing for incompatibilism would be to note that the sort of awareness in which objects are presented involves the exercise of 'a capacity to *keep track* of a single thing over a period of time—that is, an ability, having perceived an object, to identify later perceptions involving the same object over a continuous period of observation' (Evans 1982: 175). In contrast, awareness of oneself qua subject does not involve the exercise of any such ability. Suppose that I judge that 'I am now F' and judge a few moments later 'I was F'. If this transition is to be expressive of awareness of oneself qua subject, one would expect 'the later dispositions to judge to flow out of the earlier dispositions to judge without the need for any *skill* or *care* (not to lose something) on the part of the subject' (Evans 1982: 237). Since it cannot be the case that a given form of awareness both does and does not involve keeping track there can be no such thing as awareness of something qua subject as an object.[28]

Now imagine that I am disposed to judge at one time that I am standing up and disposed to judge a few moments later that I was standing up. Assuming that the present-tense judgement is proprioceptively based should the later disposition to judge be regarded as flowing out of the earlier disposition without my needing to keep track of my body? This is, in a way, quite plausible. One does not keep track of one's own body in the way that one keeps track of other bodies, and one is not liable to lose track of one's own body in the way in which one is liable to lose track of other bodies. From an incompatibilist perspective this makes it difficult to think of proprioceptive awareness as awareness of one's body as an object and correspondingly easier to think of it as awareness of one's body qua subject. Yet there are also conditions on awareness of the self qua subject that bodily awareness does not satisfy. Strictly speaking, therefore, bodily awareness is neither awareness of oneself

---

[26] Cassam 1997 defends a form of compatibilism.

[27] The distinction between a mere body and a living body corresponds to Husserl's distinction between *der Körper* and *der Leib*. For a useful account of this distinction see the Translators' Introduction to Husserl 1989: p. xiv.

[28] See Longuenesse 2006 for further discussion.

as an object nor awareness qua subject. This puts paid to compatibilism: if bodily awareness is neither awareness of oneself as an object nor awareness of oneself qua subject then it can hardly be both awareness of oneself as an object and awareness of oneself qua subject. Bodily awareness is *sui generis*, and this accounts for the failure of attempts to assimilate it to other more familiar forms of awareness.

4. Knowing One's Own Body

According to Descartes, the mind is better known than the body. Introspective knowledge of one's mental properties is epistemically privileged in ways that distinguish it from the knowledge that one may have of one's physical properties. Among the supposed epistemic privileges of introspection are infallibility and incorrigibility. If I judge that I am in pain then my judgement is immune to error and to correction. In addition, introspective knowledge is knowledge of facts that are in some sense self-intimating. I cannot be in pain without realizing that I am in pain, at least on the assumption that I am attentive and have the concept of pain. So when it comes to introspective knowledge of one's own mind both error and ignorance are ruled out. In contrast, neither error nor ignorance is ruled out in relation to one's bodily properties, whether the properties in question are properties of one's own body or of a body that is not one's own. For example, my judgement that my legs are bent can be mistaken, and my legs can be bent without my realizing it. I might wake up from an operation in which my legs have been amputated and mistakenly judge that my legs are bent because it feels as if they are. In this case, there is no question here of my judgement being either infallible or incorrigible.

   One question that has been raised about these claims is whether they exaggerate the epistemic privileges of introspective knowledge. We can agree that this kind of knowledge has a special authority without agreeing that it is infallible or incorrigible, or that mental properties are self-intimating.[29] A more pertinent question for present purposes is whether the Cartesian picture of self-knowledge underestimates the epistemic privileges of bodily self-knowledge. When I judge that my legs are bent, it can happen that my judgement is mistaken because my legs are not bent. Can it happen that my judgement is mistaken because, although I know that someone's legs are bent, the person whose legs I know to be bent is not me? If the judgement is based on vision then such a mistake cannot be ruled out. In contrast, if the judgement is based on proprioception then there is a strong case for thinking

---

[29] We might think e.g. that the special authority of self-knowledge consists in its not being based on evidence. See Moran 2001; McDowell 2006.

that it is immune to immune to error through misidentification relative to the first-person pronoun. As Evans remarks:

[W]e cannot think of the kinaesthetic and proprioceptive system as gaining knowledge of truths about the condition of a body which leave the question of the identity of the body open. If the subject does not know that *he* has his legs bent (say) on this basis ... then he does not know *anything* on this basis (To judge that *someone* has his legs bent would be a wild shot in the dark). (1982: 221)

We can see the force of this observation by considering the possibility that my brain is hooked up to someone else's body in such a way that I am registering information from that other body. When that body's legs are bent it feels to me as if my legs are bent. If I then judge on this basis that my legs are bent is my judgement at least expressive of the knowledge that *someone's* legs are bent, even if I am not the person whose legs I know to be bent? If, as suggested above, bodily experiences of parts of other people's bodies are illusory, then we should resist this characterization of the case. I cannot be said to know that someone's legs are bent on the basis of an illusion. So the fact that such illusions are possible does not show that proprioceptively based bodily self-ascriptions are not immune to error through misidentification.

What explains this immunity? One explanation is that it is a condition or criterion of embodiment in body B that (i) one has proprioceptive and other ways of coming to know about the position and movement of B, and (ii) these ways of coming to know give rise to first-person judgements that are immune to error through misidentification relative to the first person. On this account, 'my body is the one of which I gain knowledge in the non-inferential ways described by Evans' (Peacocke 2008: 100). This approach will appeal to those who think that body and self are not identical, and that it is a genuine question what makes a particular body mine. If I am identical to my body then this question does not arise in the same way. In that case, an alternative explanation of immunity to error through misidentification would be one that sees this phenomenon as a reflection of the constraints on first-person thought rather than as flowing from supposed conditions on 'ownership' of a particular body. First-person thinking requires the conception of oneself as a bodily being, and to have this conception is for one to have ways of gaining knowledge of one's bodily properties that do not leave open the question of the identity of the body.

5. THE SIGNIFICANCE OF EMBODIMENT

Can cognition properly be understood as anything other than embodied? If not there would be no better way of bringing out the significance of embodiment for a proper understanding of cognition. The claim that cognition must be understood as embodied can be defended by focusing on the idea that perception must be embodied. For if there is no such thing as disembodied perception, then there is no such thing as disembodied cognition, at least on the assumption that perception is the most basic form of cognition. What is now needed, therefore, is an answer to two questions: in what sense is perception embodied, and what is wrong with the idea of disembodied cognition?

A controversial answer to both questions is suggested by what Alva Noë calls the 'enactive approach to perception'. This says that perceiving is something we do rather than something that happens to us. The world 'makes itself available to the perceiver through physical movement and interaction' (2004: 1). Only a creature with bodily skills can be a perceiver, and perception is not a process in the brain but 'a kind of skilful activity on the part of the animal as a whole' (2004: 2). If perception is constituted by our possession and exercise of bodily skills then it may also depend on our possession of the sort of bodies that can encompass or sustain such skills: 'to perceive like us, it follows, you must have a body like ours' (2004: 25).

One argument for the enactive approach appeals to the phenomenon of experiential blindness. This type of blindness is not due to the absence of sensation but to an inability to integrate sensory stimulation with patterns of movement and thought. The existence of experiential blindness provides evidence for the enactive approach because it shows that in order to see one needs 'implicit practical knowledge of the ways movement gives rise to changes in stimulation' (2004: 8). A creature that lacks this sensorimotor knowledge is to all intents and purposes blind in the experiential sense. This is not to claim that paralysis is a form of blindness. Quadriplegics can see but then they also have the pertinent skills. They can still move their eyes and head, and their condition does not deprive them of a practical understanding of the significance of movement for stimulation.

On one reading of the enactive approach, the dependence of perception on bodily skills or sensorimotor knowledge is merely causal. On a stronger reading, the dependence is constitutive.[30] On this reading, perception *is* a skilful activity. Either way, perception depends on embodiment. To conceive of a disembodied being is to conceive of a being with no sensorimotor knowledge and no bodily skills. Such a being could not be a perceiver and its knowledge of the world could not be perceptual knowledge. More cautiously, it would not be possible for a disembodied being to perceive the world in anything like the way that we perceive the world.

Another way of bringing out the significance of embodiment for perception and so for cognition more generally would be to adopt Gallagher's distinction between

---

[30] See Block 2005 for a discussion of the importance of distinguishing clearly between these two versions of the enactive approach.

body image and *body schema*. There are at least two questions in relation to which this distinction serves a useful purpose:

1. To what extent, and in what way, does one's body appear as part of one's perceptual field?
2. To what extent, and in what way, does one's body constrain or shape the perceptual field?

The concept of the body image bears on the first of these questions whereas the concept of the body schema bears on the second. A body image 'consists of a system of perceptions, attitudes, and beliefs pertaining to one's own body' (Gallagher 2005: 24). The body image includes one's perceptual experience of one's body, one's conceptual understanding of bodies in general, and one's emotional attitude towards one's own body. The body schema, in contrast, is not a set of perceptions, beliefs, or attitudes. It is a 'system of sensory-motor capacities that function without awareness or the necessity of perceptual monitoring' (2005: 24). It structures consciousness without showing up in the contents of consciousness. It is responsible for processing new information about posture and movement and can also be seen as a set of motor programmes or habits, such as those involved in walking, reaching, and swallowing. It is one's body schema rather than one's body image that allows one to walk beneath a low-hanging tree branch without bumping one's head.

The value of the distinction between body image and body schema can be brought out by considering cases in which the two become dissociated. On the one hand, there are cases of unilateral neglect in which a stroke patient disowns, say, an arm which continues to be used to dress, walk, and eat. In this case the patient's body schema is intact but there are problems with the body image. On the other hand, there are cases of deafferentation in which the patient has no sense of touch or proprioception below the neck. Here it is the body schema rather than the body image which has gone missing. In one well-documented case, the patient was still capable of controlled movement but only by means of a 'partial and imperfect functional substitution of body image for body schema' (Gallagher 2005: 44).[31]

These reflections on the significance of embodiment for perception and action tell us something important about 'the self'. They suggest that the fantasy of a disembodied self is just that: a fantasy. For it is important to remember that 'self' is not normally used as a sortal noun. We might ask how many people there are in a particular room but not how many selves there are. 'Self' is, in this respect, more like a formal concept, and the point of talking about the self or subject is to identify a locus of thought, perception, and action. Yet perception and action require embodiment, and thought is inseparable from perception and action. So if the self is that which perceives, thinks, and acts then the self is, above all, an embodied self.

---

[31] This is the case of Ian Waterman, vividly described in Cole 1991.

REFERENCES

BAKER, L. (2000). *Persons and Bodies: A Constitution View* (Cambridge: Cambridge University Press).

BELL, D. (1990). *Husserl* (London: Routledge).

BERMÚDEZ, J., MARCEL A., and EILAN, N. (1995). *The Body and the Self* (Cambridge, Mass.: MIT Press).

BLOCK, N. (2005). 'Review of Alva Noë, *Action in Perception*', *Journal of Philosophy*, 102: 259–72.

BREWER, B. (1995). 'Bodily Awareness and the Self', in Bermúdez *et al.* (1995: 291–309).

CAMPBELL, J. (2004). 'The First Person, Embodiment, and the Certainty that one Exists', *The Monist*, 87: 475–88.

CASSAM, Q. (ed.) (1994). *Self-Knowledge* (Oxford: Oxford University Press).

——(1995). 'Introspection and Bodily Self-Ascription', in Bermúdez *et al.* (1995: 311–36).

——(1997). *Self and World* (Oxford: Clarendon Press).

——(2008). 'Contemporary Reactions to Descartes's Philosophy of Mind', in J. Broughton and J. Carriero (eds), *A Companion to Descartes* (Oxford: Blackwell), 482–95.

CHALMERS, D. (1996). *The Conscious Mind: In Search of a Fundamental Theory* (Oxford: Oxford University Press).

CLARK, A. (1997). *Being There: Putting Brain, Body, and World Together Again* (Cambridge, Mass.: MIT Press).

COLE, J. (1991). *Pride and a Daily Marathon* (London: Duckworth).

DAMASIO, A. (1999). *The Feeling of What Happens: Body and Emotion in the Making of Consciousness* (New York: Harcourt Brace & Co.).

DESCARTES, R. (1996). *Meditations on First Philosophy with Selections from the Objections and Replies*, ed. J. Cottingham (Cambridge: Cambridge University Press).

EVANS, G. (1982). *The Varieties of Reference*, ed. J. McDowell (Oxford: Oxford University Press).

GALLAGHER, S. (2005). *How the Body Shapes the Mind* (Oxford: Clarendon Press).

HUSSERL, E. (1989). *Ideas Pertaining to a Pure Phenomenology and to a Phenomenological Philosophy, Second Book*, tr. R. Rojcewicz and A. Shuwer (Dordrecht: Kluwer Academic Publishers).

LOCKE, J. (1975). *An Essay Concerning Human Understanding*, ed. P. Nidditch (Oxford: Clarendon Press).

LONGUENESSE, B. (2006). 'Self-Consciousness and Consciousness of One's Body: Variations on a Kantian Theme', *Philosophical Topics*, 34: 283–309.

McDOWELL, J. (2006). 'Response to Cynthia Macdonald', in C. Macdonald and G. Macdonald (eds), *McDowell and his Critics* (Oxford: Blackwell Publishing), 89–94.

MARTIN, M. G. F. (1995). 'Bodily Awareness: A Sense of Ownership', in Bermúdez *et al.* (1995: 267–89).

MERLEAU-PONTY, M. (1989). *Phenomenology of Perception*, tr. C. Smith (London: Routledge).

MORAN, R. (2001). *Authority and Estrangement: An Essay on Self-Knowledge* (Princeton and Oxford: Princeton University Press).

NOË, A. (2004). *Action in Perception* (Cambridge, Mass.: MIT Press).

PEACOCKE, C. (2008). *Truly Understood* (Oxford: Oxford University Press).

PRYOR, J. (1999). 'Immunity to Error through Misidentification', *Philosophical Topics*, 26: 271–304.

SARTRE, J.-P. (1989). *Being and Nothingness: An Essay on Phenomenological Ontology*, tr. H. Barnes (London: Routledge).

SHOEMAKER, S. (1984*a*). 'Embodiment and Behaviour', in *Identity, Cause and Mind* (Cambridge: Cambridge University Press), 113–38.

——(1984*b*). 'Personal Identity: A Materialist's Account', in S. Shoemaker and R. Swinburne, *Personal Identity* (Oxford: Basil Blackwell), 67–132.

——(1994*a*). 'Self-Reference and Self-Awareness', in Cassam (1994: 80–93).

——(1994*b*). 'Introspection and the Self', in Cassam (1994: 118–39).

SNOWDON, P. F. (1990). 'Persons, Animals and Ourselves', in C. Gill (ed.), *The Person and the Human Mind: Issues in Ancient and Modern Philosophy* (Oxford: Clarendon Press), 83–107.

——(1991). 'Personal Identity and Brain Transplants', in D. Cockburn (ed.), *Human Beings* (Cambridge: Cambridge University Press), 109–26.

——(1995). 'Persons, Animals, and Bodies', in Bermúdez *et al.* (1995: 71–86).

STRAWSON, P. F. (1974). 'Self, Mind and Body', in *Freedom and Resentment and Other Essays* (London: Methuen), 169–77.

THOMSON, J. J. (1997). 'People and their Bodies', in J. Dancy (ed.), *Reading Parfit* (Oxford: Blackwell), 202–29.

VARELA, F. J., THOMPSON, E., and ROSCH, E. (1991). *The Embodied Mind: Cognitive Science and Human Experience* (Cambridge, Mass.: MIT Press).

WILLIAMS, B. (1973). 'Are Persons Bodies?', in *Problems of the Self* (Cambridge: Cambridge University Press), 64–81.

....

CHAPTER 6

BODILY AWARENESS AND SELF-CONSCIOUSNESS

....

JOSÉ LUIS BERMÚDEZ

WE are embodied, and we are aware of our bodies 'from the inside' through different forms of bodily awareness. But what is the relation between these two facts? Are these forms of bodily awareness types of self-consciousness, on a par, say, with introspection? In this chapter I argue that bodily awareness is a basic form of self-consciousness, through which perceiving agents are directly conscious of the bodily self.

The first two sections clarify the nature of bodily awareness. We get information about our bodies in many different ways. Some are conscious; others non-conscious. Some are conceptual; others nonconceptual. Some are first-personal; others third-personal. Section 1 taxonomizes these different types of body-relative information. Some philosophers have claimed that we have a 'sense of ownership' of our own bodies. In section 2 I evaluate, and ultimately reject, a strong reading of this claim, on which the sense of ownership is a distinct and phenomenologically salient dimension of bodily awareness.

In sections 3 to 5 I explore how bodily awareness functions as a form of self-consciousness. Section 3 discusses the significance of certain forms of bodily awareness sharing an important epistemological property with canonical forms of self-consciousness such as introspection. This is the property of being immune to error through misidentification relative to the first person pronoun. I explain why having the immunity property qualifies those types of bodily awareness as forms of self-consciousness (subject to two further requirements that I spell out). In section 4 I consider, and remain unconvinced by, an argument to the effect that bodily awareness cannot have first-person content (and hence cannot count as a form of self-consciousness). Finally, section 5 sketches out an account of the spatial content of bodily awareness and explores the particular type of awareness of the bodily self that it provides.

1. Types of Bodily Awareness

Normal subjects have many different ways of finding out how things are with their bodies. Unfortunately, there is little consistency in the philosophical, psychological, or physiological literatures on how to label and conceptualize them. This section offers a general taxonomy and explains how it relates to discussions of proprioception within psychology and physiology.

The body is a physical object and we can be aware of it in much the same ways that we can be aware of any other physical object. The body can be the object of vision, smell, or touch, for example. I will call these *third-person forms of bodily awareness*. These forms of bodily awareness involve the normal exercise of our ordinary, outward-directed sensory modalities. At the same time, we have special ways of finding out how things are with our bodies—ways that do not extend to any other physical object. Each of us is aware of their body 'from the inside', as it is standardly put. There are several different forms of awareness here. I will term them collectively *first-person forms of bodily awareness*.

As I am using the terms, 'awareness' is synonymous with 'consciousness'. Both first- and third-person bodily awareness are conscious phenomena, although they may of course be recessive. We have many ways of finding out about our bodies that are not conscious. Successfully executing most actions, for example, depends upon constantly updated and very fine-grained information about the position of the relevant limbs and often the orientation of the body as a whole. This updating, and the information upon which it is based, typically takes place below the threshold of consciousness.

This type of information falls on the first-person rather than the third-person side of the distinction. The systems that generate this type of information operate only within the confines of one's own body. So, the general category of body-relative information needs to be organized as in Figure 6.1.

In the first decade of the twentieth century the physiologist Charles Sherrington introduced the concept of proprioception (Sherrington 1907). Sherrington

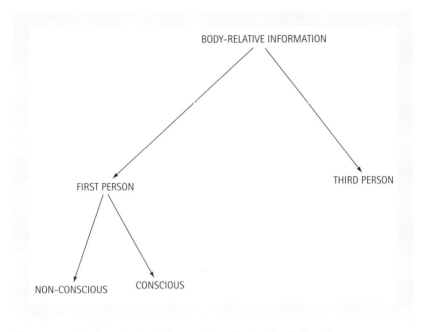

BODY-RELATIVE INFORMATION

FIRST PERSON

THIRD PERSON

NON-CONSCIOUS   CONSCIOUS

Figure 6.1 Body–relative information: the basic distinctions

distinguished proprioception both from *exteroception* (the five, outwardly directed sensory modalities) and from *interoception* (our awareness of the internal states of our bodily organs, as in the sensations of hunger, thirst, and subcutaneous pain). For Sherrington, the function of proprioception is to provide information about limb position and movement and, through the vestibular system, about balance and related whole-body properties.

Proprioception, in Sherrington's sense, has both conscious and non-conscious elements. The vestibular system, which monitors balance and spatial orientation, is typically non-conscious (although disturbances of the vestibular system, such as motion sickness, certainly make their presence felt within consciousness). In contrast, we typically do have conscious awareness of how our limbs are distributed and whether they are moving. This awareness is coarser grained than the non-conscious information exploited in the online control of action.

Sherrington's reasons for separating out interoception and proprioception are primarily physiological. Interoception and proprioception are subserved by different neural systems. From my perspective, however, interoception counts as a form of first-person bodily awareness. Bodily sensations certainly provide one of the ways in which we are aware of our bodies from the inside. So interoception needs to be added to the taxonomy of body-relative information—under the first-person, conscious branch.

The non-conscious branch needs to include information about body morphology—information about the overall shape and size of the body. This sort of information is indispensable for planning and executing action. It is constantly changing during childhood and adolescence and remains plastic during adulthood. It can be modified by tool use (Cardinali *et al.* 2009), and also changes in response to drastic changes in the body (such as amputation) as well as to neuropsychological disorders such as hemi-spatial neglect (when patients ignore one side of their body).

Let me draw attention to a form of first-person conscious bodily awareness that has not received as much attention from philosophers as the somatosensory varieties. The psychologist J. J. Gibson gave the name *visual proprioception* to forms of self-specifying information that can be derived from the visual field of view. Vision presents the world in a fundamentally egocentric and perspectival way. The embodied self appears in visual perception as the origin of the field of view. This is secured through several features of the phenomenology of vision, including self-specifying structural invariants (such as the property one's limbs have of only being able to subtend a narrow range of visual solid angles); visual kinesthesis (the way in which changing patterns in the optic array specify the perceiver's movement through the environment); and the perception of affordances (higher order invariants in the visual field that specify the organism's possibilities for acting in the environment). For more details on how visual proprioception counts as a form of bodily awareness see Gibson (1979) and Bermúdez (1998).

There are various additional ways in which the body is represented at the conscious level. People have an awareness of their body with strong evaluative and affective dimensions, for example. I will term this the affective body image. Disorders such as bulimia and anorexia seem to be pathologies of the affective body image. The affective body image is a paradigmatically first-person phenomenon. But it has a third-person analog in the general beliefs that many people have about both the structure and function of different body parts. Some of these beliefs, particularly those tied to emotions such as shame, have a strong cultural dimension. A related but distinct type of body-relative information is semantic—semantic knowledge of the names of body parts. This is also third-person, rather than first-person.

I have organized the taxonomy of body-relative information up to now in terms of two distinctions—the first person/third person distinction and the distinction between conscious and non-conscious information. There is a further distinction to take into account. This is the distinction between conceptual and non-conceptual information about the body. The distinction between conceptual and nonconceptual content is not easy to pin down precisely (see Bermúdez 2007 and Bermúdez and Cahen 2008 for reviews of the extensive literature), but for present purposes I use it simply to mark the difference between representations of the body that are integrated with the propositional attitude system (and hence with reflection, planning, and emotional responses), on the one hand, and representations that are more closely tied to the online control of action, on the other.

In the light of all this I propose the taxonomy of body-relative information depicted in Figure 6.2. There is much more to be said about the different elements

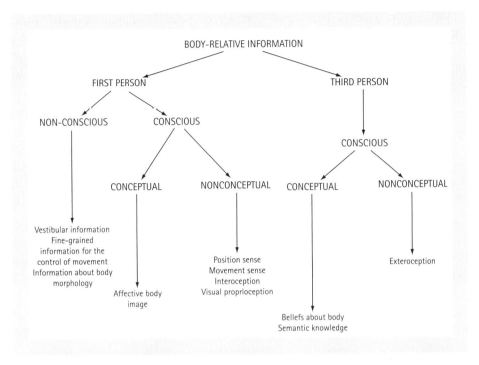

Figure 6.2 Body–relative information: a taxomomy

of this taxonomy. It would be useful to map out the different sources of each type of body-relative information. What is the source, for example, of non-conscious information about body morphology? Where in the brain does it get processed? How is it integrated with other types of body-relative information in the control of action? But fortunately answers to these questions (which are a long way from being settled) are not required to explore how bodily awareness counts as a form of self-consciousness.

2. A 'SENSE' OF OWNERSHIP?

Many of the types of body-relative information identified in section 1 form part of our conscious experience. We are consciously aware of our bodily sensations (through interoception) and of the general disposition of our limbs. These forms of bodily awareness are all, one might say, phenomenologically salient. This section explores the relation between these phenomenologically salient forms of bodily awareness and what is often called the 'sense of ownership' of one's own body.

There are two rather different conceptions of the sense of ownership current in the literature (although they are often not clearly distinguished). I will call them the deflationary and inflationary conceptions. They differ according to whether or not they make the sense of ownership phenomenologically salient—according to whether or not they hold there to be a positive phenomenology of ownership.

Here is a statement of the deflationary conception from Jérôme Dokic:

Bodily experience gives us a *sense of ownership*. Whatever property we can be aware of 'from the inside' is instantiated in our own apparent body. Bodily experience seems to be necessarily short-sighted, so to speak, since it cannot extend beyond the boundaries of one's body. The very idea of *feeling* a pain in a limb which does not seem to be ours is difficult to frame, perhaps unintelligible. (Dokic 2003: 325; emphasis in the original)

As presented in this passage, the sense of ownership is really just a label for a higher order property of somatosensation—the fact that the objects of proprioception and interoception are experienced within the confines of the body. This is a descriptive fact about the phenomenology of bodily awareness—a descriptive fact that a number of authors have partially analyzed in terms of the content of bodily sensations (e.g. Martin 1995; Bermúdez 1998; as well as Dokic himself). If, as these authors maintain, bodily sensations are experienced as representing the state of the body at particular locations, then it is not surprising that they should have this higher order property.

And one would expect, as Dokic points out, that this feature of somatosensation would lead to people finding bizarre the idea of feeling a pain in someone else's limb—and to other fairly standard features of how we *think* about the body and bodily sensations. On the deflationary conception of ownership the sense of ownership consists, first, in certain facts about the phenomenology of bodily sensations and, second, in certain fairly obvious judgments about the body (which we can term judgments of ownership).

Certainly, it is a long way from these basic phenomenological facts and judgments of ownership to what I term the inflationary conception of the sense of ownership. Here is a statement of the inflationary conception from Shaun Gallagher.

In non-observational self-awareness I do not require the mediation of a perception or judgment to recognize myself as myself. I do not need to reflectively ascertain that my body is mine, or that it is *my* body that is in pain or that is experiencing pleasure. *In normal experience, this knowledge is already built into the structure of experience.* (Gallagher 2005: 29; my emphasis)

As I read this passage, it states that bodily awareness incorporates a specific feeling of 'myness'. For Gallagher this feeling of 'myness' is present both in bodily awareness and in introspection. Later on in his book he describes the sense of ownership as 'a sense that it is I who am experiencing the movement or thought' (2005: 173) and emphasizes that this is a 'first-order phenomenal aspect of experience' (p. 174 n. 1).

One possible way of thinking about the relation between the deflationary and inflationary conceptions of the sense of ownership would be to hold that the basic facts about bodily awareness highlighted in the deflationary conception are what ground the feeling of 'myness' identified in the inflationary conception. This view has in fact been canvassed by Frédérique de Vignemont (2007), who claims both that there is a positive phenomenology of the sense of ownership and that this positive phenomenology is grounded in the spatial content of bodily sensations.

Certainly, if there were a phenomenologically salient sense of ownership, then this could be a plausible way to try to explain where it comes from. But are there any reasons to accept the inflationary description of the phenomenology?

One strategy would be to argue from pathological cases of 'disownership'. In alien hand syndrome, for example, patients deny that their hand is their own (Feinberg *et al.* 1998). This 'disownership' is certainly phenomenologically salient. Perhaps what patients with alien hand syndrome are experiencing is the absence of the normal feeling of ownership? I suspect that something like this reasoning is behind the inflationary conception of ownership. It is not very compelling, however. There are all sorts of reasons why a patient might report that their hand does not feel their own. There is no particular reason for understanding a feeling of disownership as the absence of a feeling of ownership—at least, not without prior reasons for thinking that there is such a thing as the feeling of ownership.

De Vignemont offers two arguments. One is derived from the normal case.

Imagine the following situation. You close your eyes and someone takes your hand. Nothing in your experience tells you who is holding your hand. Yet, you feel this anonymous hand holding *your own* hand and nobody else's hand. There seems to be a phenomenological difference between your experience of someone else's hand and your experience, which could be explained by a sense of ownership. (de Vignemont 2007)

I am not sure that is very clearly expressed, however. A basic starting-point here is that we do *not* experience someone else's hand. So it is not clear what the phenomenological difference is that the sense of ownership is being called upon to explain. Do we need a feeling of myness to explain what is going on when I feel the pressure of someone else's hand upon mine? If we do, then we need it to explain what is going on when I feel the pressure of the table on my hand. But I am not sure that we have anything here beyond the descriptive fact emphasized in the deflationary conception of ownership—namely, that sensations are typically experienced within the confines of the body.

A second argument comes from introspective reports of amputees wearing prostheses. Some amputees feel their artificial limb as their own. Others do not. We can make sense of this difference, according to de Vignemont, by assuming that the first group has a sense of ownership, while the second does not. This is not very compelling, however. The sense of ownership, on the inflationary view, is phenomenologically salient. It is a feeling of 'myness'. So we are entitled to ask: where do amputees with prostheses feel this feeling of myness?

There are three possibilities. It might be felt in the prosthesis. It might be felt at a determinate location elsewhere in the body. Or it might be a non-localizable feeling (comparable to the feeling of depression, for example). None of these is very plausible. It seems unlikely that they feel a feeling of myness in their prostheses. This would contravene the descriptive fact that feelings and sensations are experienced only within the confines of the body. And it is most unclear how either of the other two would work. What would it be like to have a feeling of myness in my elbow, say, that made it the case that I felt my prosthetic leg to be my own? It would presumably have to be a feeling *that* my prosthetic leg is part of me. This seems to be a suspiciously determinate content for a feeling (as opposed to a judgment, for example). But even assuming that there could be such a feeling, it is hard to imagine what it would be like to feel it in one's elbow—or somehow diffused through one's whole body. I find it hard to make sense of this proposal.

So, the arguments in support of the inflationary conception of the sense of ownership are not convincing. But are there any good arguments against it? I think that a line of argument canvassed by Elizabeth Anscombe in her paper 'On Sensations of Position' (1962) can be adapted to show that the inflationary view is not sustainable.

Anscombe argues for the thesis that our knowledge of how our limbs are disposed and whether or not they are moving (position sense and movement sense) is 'knowledge without observation', on a par with our knowledge of our own actions and intentions. The claim here is not simply that position sense and movement sense are forms of what I am terming first-person bodily awareness. That would hardly require argument. Nor is she denying that there are sensations of position and movement. That would quite simply be false. Her position, rather, is that our knowledge of limb position and movement is not based on proprioceptive and kinesthetic sensations. That is, we do not have proprioceptive and kinesthetic sensations and then, on that basis, arrive at conclusions about how our limbs are disposed and whether or not they are moving.

Anscombe is prepared to grant that we can speak of having the sensation of one's legs being crossed, but she thinks that this way of talking is ambiguous.

If we are considering an expression of the form 'sensation of X', we need to ask whether the words 'of X' are a description of the sensation content, or whether the sensation has some different content and X is what produces or always goes with it, etc. The sensation of going down in a lift is a sensation of sudden lightness and as it were of one's stomach's lurching upwards; 'of going down in a lift' is not the internal description of the sensation. (Anscombe 1962: 56)

According to Anscombe, if proprioceptive and kinesthetic sensations ground knowledge of limb position and movement, then this can only be because their internal description stands in the right relation to the knowledge that they are being claimed to ground. And this, in turn, depends upon the internal description being suitably independent of (or, as she puts it, separable from) the description of the fact known. We can know, through having the sensation of going down in a lift, that we are in fact going down in a lift because the sensation can be described in a way that makes no mention of lifts or downward motion—and, moreover, the occurrence of that sensation is a good (although not infallible) guide that one is going down in a lift.

The problem Anscombe identifies is that the vast majority of proprioceptive and kinaesthetic sensations are not like the sensation of going down in a lift. They can only be internally described in very general terms, if at all—in terms of sensations of contact, muscle stretch, and so on. These internal descriptions completely underdetermine any conclusions that one might try to draw from them about how one's body is configured. They are simply not reliable guides in the required sense. Alternatively, bodily sensations can be, as she puts it, non-separably described (as, for example, the sensation of having one's legs crossed). But under the non-separable description they cannot ground our knowledge that our legs are crossed.

The issue here is not one of vocabulary, it should be emphasized. She is not claiming that we lack the descriptive tools to characterize a perfectly determinate sensation. We can capture the spirit of Anscombe's position without talking about descriptions at all. The claim, rather, is that there is really nothing interesting in common between all the different sensory experiences that we might have when our legs are crossed, say—other than that they are the sensations of having our legs crossed. There is no distinctive 'my legs are crossed' qualitative feel that we might use as a sign that our legs are crossed. There is simply the sensation of one's legs being crossed, which might or might not be accompanied by any one of a whole range of 'qualitative feels'.

However it is formulated, I find this argument that proprioception and kinesthesia give us knowledge without observation very compelling. But be that as it may, the argument is completely devastating against the inflationary conception of the sense of ownership. According to the inflationary conception, there is a feeling of myness that explains some of the judgments that we make about the body—what I have termed judgments of ownership. Anscombe's argument shows us that this view is fatally flawed.

To the best of my knowledge nobody has claimed that the feeling of myness can be internally described in Anscombe's sense. As emphasized, this is not a vocabulary issue. It is not that we lack the conceptual or linguistic apparatus to describe the feeling of myness. What I am (and, I think, everyone else is) denying is that there is a perfectly determinate 'quale' associated with the feeling of myness that we can identify and consider independently of the myness that it is communicating.

Given this, what work can the feeling of myness do? It is called upon to do the job of grounding and underwriting what I have called judgments of ownership. But I think that Anscombe would be exactly right to object that a feeling of myness that can only be characterized or experienced in those very terms is not suitable for that job. It is not sufficiently independent of the fact that it is being claimed to justify.

The upshot of all this, I submit, is that the inflationary conception of the sense of ownership is neither supported by the considerations offered on its behalf, nor capable of doing the work it is called upon to do. We would be most unwise to go beyond the deflationary conception. There are facts about the phenomenology of bodily awareness (about position sense, movement sense, and interoception) and there are judgments of ownership, but there is no additional feeling of ownership. The remainder of this chapter will focus on exploring the relation between the phenomenology and the judgments, in order to elucidate how bodily awareness qualifies as a form of self-consciousness.

3. BODILY AWARENESS AS A FORM OF SELF-CONSCIOUSNESS: IMMUNITY TO ERROR THROUGH MISIDENTIFICATION

Why should we think that (first-person) bodily awareness is a form of self-consciousness? In *The Paradox of Self-Consciousness* (Bermúdez 1998) I discussed what I termed the simple argument.

(1) The self is embodied.
(2) First person bodily awareness provides perceptions of bodily properties.
(3) First person bodily awareness is a form of self-perception.
(4) Therefore, first person bodily awareness is a form of self-consciousness.

The crucial step here is the step from (3) to (4)—although there are some interesting issues concerning the precise relation between bodily awareness and the exteroceptive sense modalities (for further discussion see Shoemaker 1994 and Bermúdez 1998: section 6.3). The simple fact that bodily awareness involves perceiving something that happens to be the self is plainly not enough for it to count as an interesting form of self-consciousness. Self-perception falls short of self-consciousness, since one can perceive oneself without being aware that it is oneself that one is perceiving.

How do we get from self-perception to self-consciousness? One popular strategy, pioneered by Gareth Evans (1982), is to stress that first-person bodily awareness shares an important epistemological property with canonical forms of self-consciousness, such as introspection and autobiographical memory. This is the property, originally highlighted by Wittgenstein and subsequently labeled and explored more systematically by Sydney Shoemaker, of being *immune to error through misidentification relative to the first-person pronoun* (Shoemaker 1968)—henceforth the IEM property.[1]

The IEM property is a property of judgments—of the judgment, for example, that my legs are crossed. It holds relative to the information on which those judgments are made. A particular judgment can have the IEM property when based on one type of information, while lacking the property when based on a different type of information. The information-sources that give rise to judgments with the IEM property all have the following feature. They provide information only about the self. These sources of information are such that, if we know from them that somebody has a particular property, we *ipso facto* know that we ourselves have that property. For the remainder of this chapter I will say that an information-source has the IEM property when it gives rise to judgments that have the IEM property.

Introspection is an example of such an information-source. If I know through introspection that someone is currently thinking about Southern Arizona, then I know that I am thinking about Southern Arizona. Introspection cannot provide information about anybody other than me. This does not mean that introspection (and other comparable sources of information) cannot be mistaken. They certainly can be mistaken. I might really be thinking about Eastern New Mexico, for example. But there is a certain type of error that they do not permit. Judgments made on the basis of them cannot be mistaken about who it is who has the property in question. It wouldn't make sense, for example, to think: someone is thinking about Southern Arizona, but is it me?

In Chapter 7 of *Varieties of Reference* Gareth Evans observed that certain types of first-person bodily awareness give rise to judgments with the IEM property. He concluded that position sense, interoception, and movement sense all count as primitive forms of self-consciousness. I have argued elsewhere that the same holds for visual proprioception (Bermúdez 2003). So, all four of the nonconceptual first-person types of body-relative information have the IEM property.[2] Can we conclude from this that they are types of self-consciousness? Everything depends upon the importance attached to the IEM property as an index of self-consciousness. It is certainly true that judgments with the IEM property are typically self-conscious. But that may simply be because they are typically expressed with the first-person pronoun—as opposed to reflecting special characteristics of the information-sources from which they are derived.

It is also true that judgments with the IEM property play a foundational role in our thoughts about ourselves. Judgments with the IEM property reflect ways of finding out about ourselves that are exclusively about the self and that do not

---

[1] There has been much discussion of the precise way to formulate the IEM property. See e.g. Pryor 1999; Campbell 1999; Peacocke 1999; and the essays in Prosser forthcoming.

[2] Anyone skeptical about this is directed to ch. 2 of Cassam 1997, esp. sections 6 and 7.

require identifying an object *as* the self. Self-conscious judgments that are susceptible to error through misidentification must ultimately be grounded in judgments
that do have the IEM property. This is because judgments lacking the IEM property
involve identifying an object as the self, and any such identification must be
immune to error through misidentification on pain of regress.

But again we are not entitled to draw conclusions from this about information-
sources with the IEM property. Some of these information-sources are plainly
forms of self-consciousness. It would be hard to deny that introspection is a form
of self-consciousness, for example. But there are enough differences between
introspection and bodily awareness to cast doubt upon any quick extrapolation
from the former to the latter.

A more plausible approach is via functional role. The distinctive functional role
of self-conscious thoughts is relatively well understood thanks to the work of
Castañeda (1966, 1969) and Perry (1979), among others. As these authors have
brought out, a thought expressed with the sentence 'I am F' has immediate
implications for action not necessarily present in a thought expressible as '*a* is F',
even when 'I' and '*a*' are co-referential (pick out the same individual). Castañeda
and Perry make a powerful case that these implications for action are (partly)
constitutive of self-conscious thought. The absence of any gap between thought
and action is an important part of what makes self-conscious thought self-conscious. It is, moreover, ultimately grounded in the IEM property, since there will
always be a potential gap between thought and action whenever thoughts are
identification-involving in a way that is not ultimately discharged in a thought
with the IEM property.

This gives a powerful reason for thinking that first-person bodily awareness is a
form of self-consciousness, because it has similarly immediate implications for
action. This is true of self-directed actions. There is no gap between feeling an itch
in a certain place and knowing where to scratch. It also holds for actions whose
target is not the body. There tends not to be a gap between knowing how one's
limbs are distributed and knowing which reaching movement to make to a
particular extra-bodily location. It is true that visual calibration is typically required in order to fix the end-point of the movement. But this itself reflects a form
of bodily awareness, since the perspectival nature of vision provides relational
information about the world on an egocentric co-ordinate frame. This is part of
visual proprioception, as analyzed by J. J. Gibson and his colleagues and students.

There are two further respects in which visual proprioception has immediate
implications for action. The first is the phenomenon of *looming* (of particular
interest to Gibson, much of whose research into vision was inspired by his service
as head of the Air Force Research Unit during the Second World War). Imagine that
you are a pilot landing an airplane. You are looking ahead at the point on the
runway where you anticipate landing. As you approach, the landing point remains
stationary, but the magnification of the visual solid angle it subtends accelerates. At

the same time, the field of view contains textured surfaces around the stationary aiming point. These surfaces radiate outwards in what Gibson calls patterns of optic flow, expanding in a law-like manner as the landing point approaches. These perceptual invariants give the pilot direct feedback and in effect control over the adjustments that he makes to the landing pattern. Looming and optic flow are key determinants in the control of almost every type of movement.

Affordances are another aspect of visual proprioception with immediate implications for action. The theory of affordances is a key part of Gibson's theory that the fundamentals of perceptual experience are dictated by the organism's need to act in the environment. Affordances are forms of information in the field of view that specify the organism's possibilities for action and reaction. They are properties that objects and surfaces have relative to the organisms that perceive them. According to Gibson, they are directly perceived, rather than learnt or inferred. Nonetheless, while having immediate implications for action seems necessary for something to count as a form of self-consciousness, it cannot be sufficient (even in conjunction with the IEM property). If it were sufficient then we would have the puzzling result that there are non-conscious forms of self-consciousness. This is because the workings of the vestibular system, for example, both have the IEM property and have immediate implications for action—but are typically non-conscious (except in cases of motion sickness, and so forth).

So, what else is required for self-consciousness? We could, of course, simply stipulate a consciousness requirement. But this would be unsatisfactory without some principled reason for imposing the requirement. Here is one suggestion, developing the earlier discussion of information-sources with the IEM property. We have seen that information-sources have the IEM property derivatively. They derive it from the IEM status of the judgments derived from them. The notion of a judgment being based on an information-source has been left unexplained up to now. There are several forms the basing relation can take. One way of thinking about it is in terms of the thinker taking the deliverances of the information-source as *evidence* for the judgment.

It seems clear that the basing relation does not always work like this. I might judge that I am in balance without that judgment being based on evidence. This could be a case where the deliverances of my vestibular system issue directly in thought (as opposed to my feeling in balance, through some sort of sensation of equilibrium). In this sort of circumstance we might say: I just know that I am not in balance. I claim that this is not based on evidence because there is no aspect of my conscious life to which I can point as the source of the judgment. I would suggest, then, that body-relative information-sources only count as forms of self-consciousness when they generate conscious phenomenology that can be taken as evidence for first-person judgments with the IEM property. This immediately generates a consciousness requirement and produces the required result that all forms of bodily self-consciousness do indeed have to be conscious. It is a corollary that, for these purposes, we will have to separate out the conscious deliverances of the vestibular system from the non-conscious deliverances. Both can give rise to first-person judgments with the IEM property, but only the former qualify as instances of self-consciousness.

4. Objections?

Some authors have objected to thinking of different types of bodily awareness as forms of self-consciousness. Not all of these criticisms are directly relevant to the line of reasoning that I have been canvassing. Anne Newstead, for example, has taken issue with Evans's insistence that a proper understanding of bodily awareness is, as he puts it, 'the most powerful antidote to a Cartesian conception of the self' (Evans 1982: 220). She interprets Evans as trying to argue directly from the IEM status of bodily awareness to the truth of some form of materialism about the self (Newstead 2006). Unsurprisingly, she thinks that any such line of argument would be question-begging. The argument hinges upon the IEM nature of bodily self-ascriptions, but this requires assuming that bodily self-ascriptions are immune to error through misidentification *relative to 'I'*. But this of course is precisely what is at issue between the materialist and the Cartesian. The Cartesian will accept that bodily self-ascriptions are IEM, but deny that they are IEM relative to 'I' (as opposed to being IEM relative to 'my body', say).

Newstead seems to me to be right in thinking that the prospects are dim for a direct argument from bodily awareness to materialism about the self (but see Cassam 1997, particularly chapter 2, for a more subtle argument to the effect that self-conscious thinkers have to be intuitively aware of themselves qua subjects as physical objects). Like almost everyone else (including, I think, Evans), I am simply taking it for granted that Cartesianism about the self is false—and hence that bodily awareness is awareness of the embodied self. The question I am interested in is whether this counts as a self-conscious awareness of the embodied self.

Joel Smith has argued that bodily awareness cannot be self-conscious awareness of the self in this sense. His argument is unusual in resting neither upon the metaphysics of the self nor upon the epistemology of self-consciousness. Instead he argues (rather imaginatively) from the nature of imagination. Smith claims that it follows from two theses about imagination that the experiential content of bodily awareness is not first-personal—or, to put it another way, that bodily awareness does not present the body to me as my bodily self, and so cannot count as a form of self-consciousness.

The first thesis on which Smith's argument rests is:

The dependency thesis
When I imagine a bodily sensation (or other instance of bodily awareness) I imagine experiencing that sensation.

The dependency thesis stands opposed, on the one hand, to the view that one cannot imagine a bodily sensation without having that sensation and, on the other, to the view that imagining a bodily sensation is a cognitive achievement rather than an experiential one. According to the dependency thesis, to imagine some form of bodily awareness is to imagine an experience. This is something that one can do without undergoing that experience, but nonetheless is sufficiently close to undergoing the experience that one can derive conclusions about experiential content from imaginative content—and vice versa.

The second thesis is:

The imagination thesis
When I imagine something about someone else I am not imagining anything about myself.

The imagination thesis rests upon a positive account of what it is to imagine someone else (S) having an experience. This imaginative project has two components.

(*a*) I (experientially) imagine from the inside.
(*b*) I (suppositionally) imagine that the subject of the experience is S.

Smith introduces the distinction between experiential and suppositional imagining with an example from Christopher Peacocke (1985). There is no difference in experiential imagination between imagining a suitcase and imagining a suitcase with a cat behind it. But there is a difference in suppositional imagination—in the second case but not the first we suppositionally imagine a cat behind the experientially imagined suitcase.

Smith ingeniously applies these two theses to bodily awareness. I can imagine someone else having a particular bodily sensation—feeling a pain in their tooth, for example. By the imagination thesis, I imagine the experience of toothache from the inside. The other person only enters the imaginative project at the level of suppositional imagination. As far as the experiential content of the imagining is concerned there is just the toothache. This means that the imagined experience has to be impersonal, because otherwise we could not imagine someone else having it. But, by the dependency thesis, the content of the imagining is structurally analogous to the content of the original experience (namely, the toothache). Since the imagined experience is impersonal, the original experience must be impersonal also.

The argument is summarized in the following passage:

When I imagine being Napoleon having a pain, the very same piece of sensory imagination would serve equally well to imagine being Goldilocks having a pain. The difference between the two is a difference in what is suppositionally imagined, i.e. whose experience it is. This means that the occurrence of the experience in the imagination leaves open, fails to determine, the identity of the imagined experiencer. But this means that the imagined experience does not have first person content, for the first person concept serves precisely to determine the identity of the experiencer. First personal states have as their object the subject whose states they are. Once again, the conclusion is that neither imagined, nor actual, bodily awareness has first person content. My body is not presented to me as myself. (Smith 2006: 57)

The argument depends critically upon how Smith interprets the consequences of applying the dependency thesis to imagining someone else's bodily awareness. The dependency thesis requires that, if the relevant bodily experience has a first-person content, then that first-person content will carry over to the content of imagining. He thinks that there are two ways in which this might occur.

(i) 'I imagine myself having a pain and then suppose that I am identical to Napoleon' (Smith 2006: 58).
(ii) 'The occurrence of the first person in the imagined experience has, not me, but Napoleon as its object' (ibid.).

He is quite right to reject (i). We need to look more closely at the discussion of (ii), however.

Smith rejects (ii) on the grounds that it conflicts with the following principle.

(*) 'If I am in a state that has first person content, then that state has me as its object' (ibid.).

Principle (*) seems to be an analog at the level of thought of the token-reflexive rule governing the first-person pronoun. And so it inherits the (considerable) plausibility of the rule. An initial reaction to (*), however, might be that it is incompatible with the concept of *quasi-memory* (q-memories) introduced by Sydney Shoemaker (1970). Shoemaker observes that it is at least conceptually possible (and, for all we know, perhaps nomologically possible) for a thinker's apparent memories to be causally derived from someone else's experiences.[3] We can imagine, in fact, a situation in which this is a widespread but intermittent practice, so that a thinker confronted with an apparent memory cannot immediately determine whether it is a genuine memory or a q-memory.

Shoemaker claims that in this sort of situation autobiographical memory would no longer be an information-source with the IEM property. He is surely right in this (although wrong, I suspect, to extend this claim to autobiographical memory in the normal case[4]). But we should not follow Parfit in drawing the further conclusion that the possibility of q-memory shows that autobiographical memories

---

[3] The discussion here is confined to what psychologists would typically call autobiographical episodic memories.

[4] For further discussion see Evans 1982: section 7.5.

do not have first-person contents (Parfit 1971).[5] Q-memories are first-person states. The *q*-remembering subject has an apparent memory of she herself doing something. The problem that she faces is working out whether or not to take that apparent memory at face value—or, to put it in Smith's terms, whether or not she herself is the object of the first-person content.

So, principle (*) seems questionable in the case of quasi-memory. But it would certainly be unwise to extrapolate from quasi-memory to bodily awareness. Quite apart from any doubts about the ultimate coherence of *q*-memories, there are significant disanalogies between memory and bodily awareness as information-sources. The content of memory remains poorly understood, but it might be thought to contain a significant doxastic element that it is lacking in bodily awareness. Are there any more directly experiential apparent counter-examples to principle (*)? Vision seems to me to fit the bill. The first step in seeing why is to appreciate how deeply figurative it is to talk about the first person occurring in an experience. Neither the first-person pronoun nor the first-person concept appear in an experience. It would be more accurate to say that experiences have certain features that warrant certain types of first-person judgment.[6] Experiences are properly described as first-person when they have those features. In the case of vision, these are the features that collectively make it correct to describe visual experiences as perspectival. We have already looked at some of them in the context of Gibson's notion of visual proprioception. The important point for the moment, though, is simply this. To say that the content of vision is perspectival is not to say that the content of visual experience specifies whose perspective it is. That is an external fact about the experience, rather than an internal fact about the content of the experience. By analogy, the meaning of the first-person pronoun specifies that it refers to the person responsible for a particular token utterance. It does not specify who that person actually is—which is a feature of the utterance's context, rather than of its meaning.

So, it is not just the possibility of quasi-memory that casts doubt upon principle (*). It is also suspect in the case of vision. This surely weakens Smith's argument significantly. But it will not be conclusive to anyone who thinks that there are enough disanalogies between vision and the types of bodily awareness that Smith is

---

[5] Parfit writes: 'When I seem to remember an experience, I do indeed seem to remember *having* it. But it cannot be a part of what I seem to remember about this experience that I, the person who now seems to remember it, am the person who had this experience. That is something I automatically assume. (My apparent memories sometimes come to me simply as the belief that *I* had a certain experience.) But it is something that I am justified in assuming only because I do not in fact have *q*-memories of other people's experiences' (Parfit 1971: 15). Evans rebuts this view convincingly (1982: 246–8).

[6] The issues here are, I take it, orthogonal to discussions over whether the content of experience is conceptual or nonconceptual. A conceptualist about the content of experience can (and should!) deny that the first-person concept features in the conceptual content of experience.

considering for principle (*) to apply in the latter cases, even if not in the former. I end this section by arguing that the argument does not go through even if principle (*) is accepted.

The problem emerges when we ask: to which state does principle (*) apply? Smith's argument rests upon applying principle (*) to the imagined bodily sensation—to the experience that Napoleon (or Goldilocks) is imagined to be undergoing. This, he thinks, is what forces the choice between (i) and (ii) above. But, by his own lights, we do not ourselves experience bodily sensations that we imagine. And so there is no sense in which we are in the state of pain, say, that we are imagining Napoleon being in. Hence there is nothing in the domain of bodily awareness to which principle (*) can apply.

So, what state are we in? The answer is obvious. We are in a state of imagining—the state of imagining that Napoleon is in pain. Is this a first-person state? I can see arguments both ways, but for present purposes it doesn't really matter.[7] The state of imagining is either first-person or not. If not, then there is plainly no problem and principle (*) falls completely out of the picture. But if it is first-personal, on the other hand, there are no difficulties accommodating principle (*)—the state of imagining, construed first-personally, certainly has me as its object.

I conclude, then, that Smith's argument fails. The thesis that bodily awareness can serve a form of self-consciousness is still standing. More needs to be said, though, about exactly how we are aware of ourselves in bodily awareness. We turn to this in the next section.

5. THE CONTENT OF BODILY AWARENESS

The upshot of the discussion so far is that we should think about bodily awareness as a form of self-consciousness. The nonconceptual, first-person forms of body-relative information identified in section 1 have two key features in virtue of which they qualify as forms of self-consciousness. They have the IEM property in a way that allows the outputs of those information-sources to serve as evidence for first-person judgments. And they have the immediate implications for action characteristic of self-consciousness. But we have so far said little about the sort of awareness of the bodily self that bodily awareness provides. That is the subject of this final section.

---

[7] We need to distinguish the state of imagining that Napoleon is in pain from the state of imagining oneself as Napoleon in pain. The latter is definitely first-personal, but (as we have seen from the discussion of the dependency thesis) Smith is focusing on the former and here the issues are less clear.

Let me begin by mentioning two very general ways in which bodily awareness counts as a form of self-consciousness. The first is that bodily awareness offers a direct, experiential way of grasping the structure and limits of the embodied self—and, as a direct consequence, of the boundary between self and non-self. The second is that several different types of bodily awareness are directly implicated in the control of action, thereby offering a way of grasping the body as the unique object that is directly responsive to the will. But how exactly do these emerge from the structure of bodily awareness? And what other forms of consciousness of the bodily self does bodily awareness provide?

I begin tackling these questions with the observation that bodily awareness is a form of spatial awareness. It is spatial awareness because it provides information about the properties of the spatially extended body. This seemingly trivial observation holds the key to many of the distinctive properties of bodily awareness. As a spatially extended thing, the body is a physical object just like any other physical object. From the point of view of the embodied self, however, the experienced body is a very peculiar type of object. The distinctiveness of embodied experience has led some philosophers to drastic conclusions. Merleau-Ponty, for example, often seems to describe the experienced body (or, as he puts it, the phenomenal body) as standing outside the physical world (see, in particular, part 1 of Merleau-Ponty 1962).

Considered from the perspective of metaphysics, this approach is unlikely to garner much support. But, from an epistemological point of view, it seems an accurate description of the relation in which we stand to our bodies 'from the inside'. The challenge, then, is to provide an account of the spatiality of bodily awareness that does justice both to the distinctive phenomenology of bodily awareness and to how it provides information about the spatially extended body. In previous work I have proposed an account that tries to do this (Bermúdez 1998, 2003). I sketch the basic framework here.

Since bodily awareness is a form of spatial awareness, we must be aware of our bodies relative to a particular frame of reference. I claim that much of what is distinctive about the phenomenology of bodily awareness is directly derived from the distinctiveness of that frame of reference. Our experience of bodily space is fundamentally different from our experience of non-bodily space. Spatial awareness always requires a frame of reference and we are typically aware of objects in non-bodily space relative to egocentric frames of reference. When we perceive objects we perceive them in terms of their distance and bearing from a point of origin (on what mathematicians call a system of polar co-ordinates).[8] There are many different egocentric frames of reference. These vary according to the point of origin. An egocentric frame of reference might have its origin in the eye, for example, or in the hand. Different frames of reference will be useful for different

---

[8] For a helpful tutorial on frames of reference in a cognitive context see Klatzky 1998.

tasks and much of the computational challenge of acting within the world is coordinating and integrating these different frames of reference.

This challenge is made all the greater because acting within the world requires coordinating information about the spatial layout of the world with information (derived from bodily awareness) about the spatial layout of the body. And, I claim, the frame of reference for bodily awareness is of a fundamentally different type. We do not experience our bodies on an egocentric frame of reference. There is no privileged point in the body that counts as *me*, serving as the point of origin relative to which the distance and bearing of, say, bodily sensations are fixed. We experience events within our bodies as spatial events, but the spatiality of bodily experience is fundamentally different from the spatiality of our experience of the world.

So, how do we experience bodily space? There are, I suggest, two different ways of thinking about locations in bodily space, which I term A-location and B-location respectively. Imagine the following two cases:

(i) I have an itch at a point in my right ankle when I am standing up and my right foot is resting on the ground in front of me.

(ii) I have an itch at the same point in my ankle when I am sitting down and my right ankle is resting on my left knee.

The itch is experienced at the same A-location in (i) and (ii)—that is, it is experienced in the same bodily location (my right ankle). But it is experienced at a different B-location, because my right ankle has moved relative to other body-parts. Neither A-location nor B-location can be mapped on to location in objective space, since both are body-relative. The itch's B-location, for example, would be the same if my body were located at a different point in space.

A-location and B-location are fixed relative to similar frames of reference. The frame of reference is given by the body's articulation into moveable and immoveable body-parts. The human body is an immoveable torso to which are appended moveable limbs—the head, arms, and legs. Within the moveable limbs there are small-scale body-parts that are moveable (such as the fingers, the toes, and the lower jaw) and others that are not (such as the base of the skull). A joint is a body-part that affords the possibility of moving a further body-part, such as the neck, the elbow or the ankle. In the human body, the relatively immoveable torso is linked by joints to five moveable limbs (the head, two legs and two arms), each of which is further segmented by means of further joints. These joints provide the fixed points in terms of which the particular A-location and B-location of individual body-parts at a time can be given.

A particular bodily A-location is given relative to the joints that bound the body-part within which it is located. A particular point in the forearm is specified relative to the elbow and the wrist. It is the point that lies on the surface of the skin at such-and-such a distance and direction from the wrist and such-and-such a distance and direction from the elbow. This ensures that a given point within a given body-part will have the same A-location irrespective of how the body as a whole moves, or of how the relevant body-part moves relative to other body-parts.

A-location and B-location often coincide for points within the relatively immoveable torso (although not in the parts of the torso that can be bent, for example). But in any case B-location is fixed relative to A-location, in the following way. If a sensation, say, has an A-location within a moveable limb, then its B-location is fixed recursively relative to the joints that lie between it and the immoveable torso. The B-location is given by the angle of the relevant joints, which might be rotational (as in the elbow) or translational (as in the knee).

So, there are fundamental differences between the frame of reference relative to which we experience our bodies and the frames of reference exploited in perceiving every other physical object. These differences go a long way towards explaining what is so distinctive about our experience of our own bodies—both the general sense of distinctiveness that led Merleau-Ponty to claim that the phenomenal body is not part of the objective world, and certain specific features of the phenomenology of bodily awareness.

So, for example, it explains what was earlier described as the descriptive fact underlying the sense of ownership (in its deflationary construal). It is part of the phenomenology of bodily awareness that sensations are always experienced within the limits of the experienced body (which may not always coincide with the real body, as we see in phantom limb and other illusions). This is exactly what one would expect given the coding in terms of A-location and B-location. There are no points in (non-pathological) body-space that do not fall within the body. In contrast, it would be mysterious if we thought about the spatial content of bodily awareness in terms of distance and bearing from a point of origin. Such way of representing the location of bodily events provides no basis for the distinction between bodily space and extra-bodily space. Moreover, it explains the phenomenological fact that we do not experience body parts in isolation, but rather as attached to other body-parts. Part of what it is to experience my foot, say, as located at a particular place is to experience the disposition of leg-segments in virtue of which it is at that place. This is exactly what one would expect, if the B-location of the foot were part of the content of bodily awareness. Again, it would be mysterious if the spatiality of bodily awareness were given in terms of co-ordinates relative to an origin.

So, by way of summary, let us return to the two modes of self-consciousness identified at the beginning of this section. I suggested that bodily awareness (a) provides a direct, experiential way of grasping the structure and limits of the embodied self, and (b) presents the body as the unique physical object that is directly responsive to the will. I hope to have made clear how closely connected (a) and (b) are with the distinctive spatial content of bodily awareness.

REFERENCES

ANSCOMBE, G. E. M. (1962). 'On Sensations of Position', *Analysis*, 22: 55–8.

BERMÚDEZ, J. L. (1998). *The Paradox of Self-Consciousness* (Cambridge Mass.: MIT Press).

——(2003). 'The Elusiveness Thesis, Immunity to Error through Misidentification, and Privileged Access', in B. Gertler (ed.), *Self-Knowledge and Privileged Access* (Aldershot: Ashgate), 213–31.

——(2007). 'What is at Stake in the Debate about Nonconceptual Content?', *Philosophical Perspectives*, 21: 55–72.

——, and CAHEN, A. (2008). 'Mental Content, Nonconceptual', *Stanford Encyclopedia of Philosophy* (plato.stanford.edu).

CAMPBELL, J. (1999). 'Immunity to Error through Misidentification and the Meaning of a Referring Term', *Philosophical Topics*, 29: 89–104.

CARDINALI, L., FRASSINETTI, F., BOZZOLI, C., URQUIZAR, C., ROY, A. C., and FARNE, A. (2009). 'Tool-Use Induces Morphological Updating of the Body-Schema', *Current Biology*, 19: R478–R479.

CASSAM, Q. (1997). *Self and World* (Oxford: Oxford University Press).

CASTAÑEDA, H.-N. (1966). '"He": A Study in the Logic of Self-Consciousness', *Ratio*, 8: 130–57.

——(1969/1994). 'On the Phenomeno-Logic of the I', in Q. Cassam (ed.), *Self-Knowledge* (Oxford: Oxford University Press), 160–6.

DE VIGNEMONT, F. (2007). 'Habeas Corpus: The Sense of Ownership of One's Own Body', *Mind and Language*, 22: 427–49.

DOKIC, J. (2003). 'The Sense of Ownership: An Analogy between Sensation and Action', in J. Roessler and N. Eilan (eds), *Agency and Self-Awareness* (Oxford: Oxford University Press), 321–44.

EVANS, G. (1982). *The Varieties of Reference* (Oxford: Oxford University Press).

FEINBERG, T. E., ROANE, D. M., and COHEN, J. (1998). 'Partial Status Epilepticus Associated with Asomatognosia and Alien Hand-Like Behaviors', *Archive of Neurology*, 55: 1574–7.

GALLAGHER, S. (2005). *How the Body Shapes the Mind* (New York: Oxford University Press).

GIBSON, J. J. (1979). *The Ecological Approach to Visual Perception* (Boston: Houghton Mifflin).

KLATZKY, R. L. (1998). 'Allocentric and Egocentric Spatial Representations: Definitions, Distinctions, and Interconnections', in C. Freksa, C. Habel, and K. F. Wender (eds), *Spatial Cognition: An Interdisciplinary Approach to the Representation and Processing of Spatial Knowledge* (Berlin: Springer-Verlag), 1–17.

MARTIN, M. (1995). 'Bodily Awareness: A Sense of Ownership', in J. L. Bermúdez, A. J. Marcel, and N. Eilan (eds), *The Body and the Self* (Cambridge, Mass.: MIT Press), 267–89.

MERLEAU-PONTY, M. (1968). *The Phenomenology of Perception* (London: Routledge).

NEWSTEAD, A. (2006). 'Evans's Anti-Cartesian Argument: A Critical Evaluation', *Ratio*, NS 19: 214–28.

PARFIT, D. (1971). 'Personal Identity', *Philosophical Review*, 80: 3–27.

PEACOCKE, C. (1985). 'Imagination, Possibility, and Experience: A Berkeleian View Defended', in J. Foster and H. Robinson (eds), *Essays on Berkeley: A Tercentennial Celebration* (Oxford: Oxford University Press), 19–35.

——(1999). *Being Known* (Oxford: Oxford University Press).

PERRY, J. (1979). 'The Essential Indexical', *Philosophical Review*, 86: 874–97.

PRYOR, J. (1999). 'Immunity to Error through Misidentification', *Philosophical Topics*, 26: 271–304.

SHERRINGTON, C. S. (1907). 'On the Proprioceptive System, Especially in its Reflex Aspect', *Brain: A Journal of Neurology*, 29: 467–82.

SHOEMAKER, S. (1968). 'Self-Reference and Self-Awareness', *Journal of Philosophy*, 65/19: 555–67.

——(1970). 'Persons and their Pasts', *American Philosophical Quarterly*, 7: 269–85.

——(1994). 'Self-Knowledge and Inner Sense', *Philosophy and Phenomenological Research*, 54: 249–314.

SMITH, J. (2006). 'Bodily Awareness, Imagination, and the Self', *European Journal of Philosophy*, 14: 49–68.

SPEAKS, J. (2005). 'Is there a Problem about Nonconceptual Content?', *Philosophical Review*, 114: 359–98.

CHAPTER 7

··

THE SENSE OF
BODY OWNERSHIP

··

MANOS TSAKIRIS

1. EXPERIMENTING WITH BODY OWNERSHIP
···

Current approaches on the sense of self operationalize the self as a physical entity underpinned by the processing of multisensory and motor signals that generate the experiences of ownership over her body and agency over her actions (Gallagher 2000). Recent approaches stemming from this emphasis on sensorimotor processing and its relevance for higher cognition have attempted to explain two basic senses of one's body: the sense of agency and the sense of body ownership. The senses of body ownership and agency jointly constitute a minimal, bodily, sense of self, but their exact relation remains unknown. It is not the purpose of this chapter to discuss the interactions between body ownership and agency (for a discussion see Synofzik *et al.* 2008; Tsakiris *et al.* 2007; see also Chapter 19 below). Instead, the focus will be on the sense of body ownership, that is, on 'how to justify the fact that a certain physical body is called my own body (*corpus meum*)' (Waldenfels 2004: 235). In essence, the main research question is about the foundations of the experience of one's *own* body: 'What grounds my experience of my body as my own? The body that one experiences is always one's own, but it does not follow that one always experiences it as one's own' (de Vignemont 2007: 427).

Acknowledgments: ESRC First Grant RES-061-25-0233.

Empirical research on the bodily self has only recently started to investigate how the link between a body and the experience of this body as *mine* is developed, maintained, or disturbed. In neurocognitive terms, the focus is on the processing and integration of the appropriate body-related signals that provide a coherent experience of one's body. Body ownership refers to the special perceptual status of one's own body, which makes bodily sensations seem unique to oneself, that is, the feeling that 'my body' belongs to me, and is ever present in my mental life. Body ownership gives somatosensory signals a special phenomenal quality, and it is fundamental to self-consciousness: the relation between my body and 'me' differs from both the relation between my body and other people's bodies and the relation between me and external objects.

William James noted that contrary to the perception of an object, which can be perceived from different perspectives or even cease to be perceived, we experience 'the feeling of the same old body always there' (James 1890: 242). Echoing James, Merleau-Ponty (1962: 90) wrote that 'the permanence of my own body is entirely different in kind...Its permanence is not a permanence in the world, but a permanence on my part'. This seemingly inescapable permanence of the body raises interesting methodological problems in our attempt to study body ownership scientifically. Classical experimental designs in psychology involve the direct comparison between conditions where the phenomenon under investigation is either present or absent. The experimental isolation of body ownership by direct manipulations that make the body present in one experimental condition but absent in another would seem problematic, if not impossible. Early studies on the bodily self have focused mainly on self-recognition in human and non-human primates (see Chapter 3 above). Jeannerod and colleagues performed a series of experiments on self-recognition of bodily movements (for a review see Jeannerod, 2003). In most studies of self-recognition, participants see a body-part, which may or may not be related to their own body. The task is to judge whether what they see is their own body-part or not. The information available to support this judgment is systematically varied across conditions, for example by moving the hand (Daprati *et al.* 1997; Sirigu *et al.* 1999; Tsakiris *et al.* 2005), by introducing delays between the movement and the visual feedback (Franck *et al.* 2001), or by rotating the hand image (Van den Bos and Jeannerod 2002). Self-recognition requires the monitoring and integration of various sources of information such as intention, efferent and afferent signals in a short time-window. The tasks require an explicit self-recognition judgment: the participant's body-part is *objectified*, that is, a body-part is presented like an external object projected on a screen, and the research focus is on the conditions under which this body-part will be *judged* as infallibly *me*. Therefore, these experiments involve explicit judgments of agency (e.g. 'was that your action?') and body ownership (e.g. 'was that your hand?'), rather than the feeling of agency and body ownership *per se* (see also Synofzik *et al.* 2008). Experimentation with the *feeling* of body ownership becomes possible when one uses multisensory stimulation as a means of altering the experience of the body: the experience of body ownership being present in one condition, and absent in another.

The Rubber Hand Illusion (RHI) is an experimental paradigm that allows the controlled manipulation of body ownership. In brief, watching a rubber hand being stroked synchronously with one's own unseen hand causes the rubber hand to be attributed to one's own body, to 'feel like it's my hand' (Botvinick and Cohen 1998). This illusion does not occur when the rubber hand is stroked asynchronously with respect to the subject's own hand. One behavioral correlate of the RHI is an induced change in the perceived location of the participant's own hand towards the rubber hand. Botvinick and Cohen (1998) showed that, after synchronous visuo-tactile stimulation of the rubber hand and the participant's hand, participants perceived the position of their hand to be closer to the rubber hand than it really was. Interestingly, the prevalence of illusion over time (Botvinick and Cohen 1998) and the subjective intensity of the experience of body ownership (Longo *et al.* 2008) are positively correlated with drifts in the felt location of the subject's own hand toward the rubber hand. The successful manipulation of body ownership during the RHI has been demonstrated in several replications (Armel and Ramachandran 2003; Ehrsson *et al.* 2004; Longo *et al.* 2008; Tsakiris and Haggard 2005; Tsakiris *et al.* 2007) and modifications of the classic paradigm (Austen *et al.* 2004; Durgin *et al.* 2007; Ehrsson 2007; Ehrsson *et al.* 2007, 2008; Hägni *et al.* 2008; Kammers *et al.* 2009; Lenggenhager *et al.* 2007; Petkova and Ehrsson 2008; Schutz-Bosbach *et al.* 2006; Slater *et al.* 2008; Tsakiris *et al.* 2006) since the original study (Botvinick and Cohen 1998).

The RHI paradigm allows for an external object to be treated, rather than simply recognized, as part of my body, or not, under experimental control, and for that reason it is one of the few viable ways of investigating body ownership scientifically. The RHI paradigm can be used as a model instance of embodiment and, therefore, be contrasted to the neurological syndrome of somatoparaphrenia (i.e. the belief that limbs contralateral to the side of the lesion belong to someone else, see Bisiach *et al.* 1991; Halligan *et al.* 1995; Nightingale 1982; Vallar and Ronchi 2009, for a review).

2. TRUSTING THE SUBJECT: WHAT IS THE EXPERIENCE OF BODY OWNERSHIP LIKE?

Phenomenology has provided rich descriptive characterizations of embodiment (e.g. Merleau-Ponty 1962). However, psychological research has often been reluctant to produce operational working definitions and measures needed for rigorous empirical research on the *experience* of embodiment. A first step towards this approach was taken by Longo *et al.* (2008) who applied psychometric methods to structured introspective reports of the conscious experience of embodiment as found in the RHI. If embodiment is a coherent psychological construct, rigorous measurement and analysis should clarify what it is, and what its subcomponents are. A large sample study (Longo *et al.* 2008) investigated the subjective experience during the RHI by asking participants to complete a twenty-seven-item questionnaire after each of the synchronous and asynchronous blocks of visuo-tactile stimulation. A Principal Component Analysis (PCA) revealed that the subjective experience of ownership of the rubber hand consists of distinct dissociable components present in both synchronous and asynchronous conditions (Longo *et al.* 2008): *ownership* (e.g. rubber hand as part of one's body); *location* (i.e. the rubber hand and one's own hand were in the same place; also this applies to sensations of causation between the seen and felt touches); and *agency* (i.e. being able to move the rubber hand and have control over it). A further analysis focused on the relation between the component scores and the behavioral proxy of the RHI used in this study (i.e. proprioceptive drift obtained with the method described in Tsakiris and Haggard 2005).

Embodiment of rubber hand in general significantly predicted the proprioceptive displacement. Given that embodiment of rubber hand as a whole is significantly related to proprioceptive displacement, in the RHI, Longo *et al.* (2008) also investigated which of its subcomponents are driving this effect: the *location* subcomponent was a significant predictor of proprioceptive displacement, as well as the *ownership* subcomponent. A follow-up study (Longo *et al.* 2009) showed how the experience of ownership of the rubber hand can alter the physical similarity that participants perceive between their own hand and the rubber hand. Participants who experienced the RHI perceived their hand and the rubber hand as significantly more similar than participants who did not experience the illusion, suggesting that ownership leads to perceived similarity, but perceived similarity does not lead to ownership.

These studies aptly demonstrate that the model instance of embodiment induced in RHI induces a complex yet structured experience of body ownership with identifiable components. Overall, it seems that three main aspects of embodiment are successfully manipulated during RHI: the sense of ownership of the rubber hand, the perceived location of the participant's own hand, and the perceived similarity of appearance of body-parts. A fourth, and perhaps the most intriguing, component that could be involved in RHI is a change in the experience of one's own body during this illusion of body ownership. In other words, the interest here is in whether the experienced ownership over a new body-part will subsequently alter the experience of my body. One possibility is that the rubber hand is simply added as a third supernumerary limb to one's body, without actually affecting the experience of one's hand. Alternatively, the rubber hand may replace the participant's own hand and, in turn, alter the experience of one's hand.

Consistent introspective and behavioral measures suggest that the rubber hand is not simply added as a third limb, but instead it replaces the real hand, in terms of both phenomenal experience and physiological regulation. Participants deny that they felt as if they had three hands, while they accepted the statement that they felt as if their own hand had disappeared, and that their own hand was in the location where the rubber hand was, significantly more after synchronous compared to asynchronous visuo-tactile stimulation (Longo *et al.* 2008). Therefore, accounts of the subjective experience during RHI suggest that incurred changes do not consist of an addition or extension of one's body, but instead they cause incorporation and moreover replacement of one's own hand. Interestingly, physiological data corroborate this observation; the experience of ownership during RHI is accompanied by significant changes in the homeostatic regulation of the real hand (Moseley *et al.* 2008). In particular, skin temperature of the real hand decreased when participants experienced the RHI, and the magnitude of the decrease in skin temperature on the participant's own hand was positively correlated with the vividness of the illusion. Importantly, this effect was absent in the mere presence of synchronous visual and tactile stimulation (see experiment 5 in Moseley *et al.* 2008), but occurred only as a result of the experience of ownership. Thus, experienced ownership over a new body-part has direct consequences for real body-parts that occur once participants experience the RHI, implying that cognitive processes that disrupt the awareness of our physical self may in turn disrupt the physiological regulation of the self (Moseley *et al.* 2008). The changes caused in the physiological regulation of the self as a result of the experience of body ownership over and above multisensory integration suggest that processes other than multisensory integration may be involved in generating, maintaining, or disrupting the awareness of the bodily self.

3. THE BOTTOM–UP ACCOUNT OF BODY OWNERSHIP: THE ROLE OF INTERMODAL MATCHING

Why and how is the rubber hand experienced as part of one's body, or more generally, how is body ownership developed and maintained? In brief, the RHI reflects the malleability of the representation of the body caused by multisensory processing. Multisensory processing aims at the integration of sensory signals and the resolution of potential conflicts to generate a coherent representation of the world and the body on the basis of sensory stimulation. During integration, different senses have different weights, and the RHI reflects a three-way interaction between vision, touch, and proprioception: vision of tactile stimulation on the rubber hand captures the tactile sensation on the participant's own hand, and this visual capture results in a mislocalization of the felt location of one's own hand towards the spatial location of the visual percept. Botvinick and Cohen (1998) put forward a bottom–up explanation of the RHI by suggesting that intermodal matching between vision and touch is *sufficient* for self-attribution of the rubber hand. The first RHI studies showed the presence of synchronized visual and tactile stimulation to be a *necessary* condition for the inducement of the RHI, since RHI did not occur after asynchronous stimulation (Botvinick and Cohen 1998; Ehrsson *et al.* 2004; Tsakiris and Haggard 2005). But does this make intermodal matching sufficient for the experience of body ownership?

Armel and Ramachandran (2003) held a strong version of the Botvinick and Cohen view by arguing that visuo-tactile correlation is both a necessary and sufficient condition for the RHI: any object can be experienced as part of one's body if the appropriate intermodal matching is present. They showed that if, after the synchronous visuo-tactile stimulation period, the experimenter 'injured' the rubber hand (e.g. the experimenter bent one of the rubber fingers backwards), Skin Conductance Responses (SCRs) measured from the subject's unstimulated hand were significantly higher compared to the control asynchronous condition. Similar differences, albeit smaller in magnitude, between SCRs for synchronous and asynchronous conditions were found when participants observed a table, instead of a rubber hand, being stroked while tactile stimulation was delivered on the participant's own hand. According to Armel and Ramachandran (2003), both the rubber hand and the table, and in principle any other object, can be self-attributed, provided that strong visuo-tactile correlations are present. Therefore, the illusion that 'the fake hand/table is my hand', and more generally the sense of body ownership, is the result of a bottom–up mechanism, which associates synchronous visuo-tactile events: any object can become part of 'me', simply because strong statistical correlations between different sensory modalities are both necessary and sufficient conditions for body ownership.

Indeed, the possibility that body ownership arises in a bottom–up fashion, as an accumulative effect of frequent and recurring multisensory correlations during ontogeny, cannot be excluded. Developmental studies suggest that intermodal matching is a prerequisite for self-identification (Rochat and Striano 2000; see Chapter 2 above). At the same time, developmental studies also suggest that at least some body representations seem to be innate, facilitating intermodal matching. For example, Morgan and Rochat (1997) showed that three-month-old infants, with relatively little experience of seeing their legs, are sensitive to left–right reversal of their own legs shown on a screen and to differences in the relative movements and/or the featural characteristics of the legs (i.e. the relative bending of the legs at the knees and ankles), supporting the idea of innate representations of the anatomical and structural features of a normative body. The extent to which multisensory input is the sole driver of body ownership or not is a controversial issue at the heart of the neurocognitive understanding of body ownership in particular, and of body-representations more generally (Berlucchi and Aglioti 1997; de Vignemont *et al.* 2005; Dijkerman and de Haan 2007; Graziano and Botvinick 2001; Carruthers 2008; Holmes and Spence 2006; Sirigu *et al.* 1991; Tsakiris and Fotopoulou 2008).

4. TOP–DOWN MODULATIONS: THE EVIDENCE AGAINST THE BOTTOM–UP ACCOUNT

Is the effect of multisensory stimulation on body ownership simply a passive stimulus-driven process, or does it depend on the modulatory influence of representations of the body that are not primarily sensory in nature (Graziano and Botvinick 2001; de Vignemont *et al.* 2005)? As broadly defined by Graziano and Botvinick (2001) body representations involve the interpretation of peripheral inputs in the context of a rich internal model of the body's structure; body-related percepts are not simply correlated, but they are integrated against a set of background conditions that preserve the coherence of bodily experience. These background conditions would require different types of body-representations that modulate in a top–down manner the integration of current multisensory input. On this latter view, intermodal matching may not be sufficient for the experience of body ownership.

If body ownership was driven by synchronous multisensory stimulation as a sufficient condition, then we would expect to induce a sense of body ownership over objects that do not resemble body-parts. Accumulating evidence suggests that the RHI is not induced when the rubber hand is replaced by a neutral non-corporeal object such as a wooden stick (i.e. coding of visual form representations of body-parts, Haans *et al.* 2008; Tsakiris and Haggard 2005; Tsakiris *et al.* 2008; see also Holmes *et al.* 2006; Graziano *et al.* 2000; but cf. Armel and Ramachandran 2003). Instead the viewed object should match a visual representation of the tactually stimulated body-part for the synchronous visuo-tactile stimulation to elicit a sense of body ownership. Following on the work of Graziano *et al.* (2000) on bimodal neurons in monkeys and Tsakiris and Haggard (2005) on RHI, Haans *et al.* (2008) revisited the hypothesis that any object can be self-attributed if strong statistical correlations between vision and touch are present. Haans *et al.* (2008) assessed the strength of the RHI in a factorial design where a viewed object that could have a hand shape or not, with a natural-skin texture or not, was stimulated in synchrony with the participant's own hand. The results, contrary to what Armel and Ramachandran (2003) predicted, showed that a hand-shaped object induced a stronger RHI as measured with a questionnaire than a non-hand-shaped object (see also Tsakiris and Haggard 2005). These findings further support the hypothesis that no experience of ownership is induced when the viewed object does not resemble the human hand, even if its texture is hand-like.

Other experiments have shown that the RHI is abolished when the rubber hand is placed in an incongruent anatomical posture with respect to one's own hand (i.e. coding of postural representations of body-parts, see Costantini and Haggard 2007; Tsakiris and Haggard 2005, see also Graziano *et al.* 2000; Pavani *et al.* 2000; but cf. Armel and Ramachandran 2003), or when the rubber hand is of a different laterality with respect to one's own stimulated hand (i.e. coding of anatomical representations of body-parts, see Tsakiris and Haggard 2005). Two elegant studies (Costantini and Haggard 2007; Lloyd 2007) have used parametric designs to investigate in greater detail the role of postural and spatial relations between the rubber hand and the participant's own hand in inducing the RHI.

Lloyd (2007) systematically varied the distance between the rubber hand and the participant's own hand to quantify the spatial boundaries over which referred tactile sensations can be felt on a rubber hand. Introspective evidence showed that the strongest ratings of the illusion were collected when the distance between the two hands was closest (17.5 cm), while ratings of the RHI decayed significantly when the distance exceeded 30cm, because the visual representation of the rubber hand fell outside the visual receptive field that surrounds the tactile receptive field of the participant's own hand. Costantini and Haggard (2007) investigated the effects of directional mismatch between the stimulation of the two hands, and equivalent mismatches between the postures of the two hands, either by adjusting stimulation or posture of the participant's hand, or by adjusting stimulation or posture of the rubber hand. RHI survived small changes in the participant's hand posture, but disappeared when the same posture transformations were applied to the rubber hand, while a mismatch between the direction of stimulation delivered to the participant's hand and the rubber hand abolished completely the RHI. According to Costantini and Haggard (2007), first a transformation aligns the rubber hand with the subject's own hand and then the correlation between visual and tactile stimulation is computed.

Converging evidence from RHI studies (Costantini and Haggard 2007; Lloyd 2007; Ehrsson *et al.* 2004; Pavani *et al.* 2000; Tsakiris and Haggard 2005), studies on visuo-tactile extinction on neuropsychological patients (Ladavas *et al.* 1998), and neurophysiological studies on monkeys (Graziano *et al.* 2000) suggests that correlated multisensory stimulation and spatial proximity are necessary but not sufficient for the integration of a visual stimulus to peripersonal space or for the experience of ownership during the RHI. Anatomical and postural correspondence between the visually stimulated body part and the tactually stimulated body-part are also necessary for body ownership. These consistent findings suggest that factors other than the mere correlation between synchronized visual and tactile events modulate the experience of body ownership.

5. BODY OWNERSHIP AS AN INTERACTION BETWEEN CURRENT MULTISENSORY INPUT AND INTERNAL MODELS OF THE BODY: A NEUROCOGNITIVE MODEL OF BODY OWNERSHIP

Makin *et al.* (2008) put forward a parsimonious account of RHI based on processes of multi-sensory integration in peri-hand space (Maravita *et al.* 2003), without the need of top–down modulation by body-representations. On their account, RHI occurs when the following two conditions are met: first, the rubber hand should be situated in an anatomically plausible position, and second, the synchronous visual and tactile events should be both located near to the visible hand. Even though all the aforementioned modulations of RHI take place within peripersonal space and exploit mechanisms of multisensory hand-centered representations of space (Lloyd 2007; Makin *et al.* 2008), it seems unlikely that a full account of the experience of ownership during the RHI can be given solely on the basis of these mechanisms and their neural underpinnings. Note that this account does not make any explicit predictions about the occurrence of RHI when the rubber hand is placed in an anatomically plausible position but one that is incongruent to the participant's own hand (see Costantini and Haggard 2007), or when the viewed object is not a body-part (e.g. a neutral non-corporeal object). Even small incongruencies at the postural level abolish the RHI (Costantini and Haggard 2007). Mechanisms of hand-centered multisensory integration operate during body extension after use of non-corporeal objects (e.g. tool-use, see Maravita and Iriki 2004) as well as during incorporation (Ehrsson *et al.* 2004), suggesting that they perform a basic computational process that is not unique to body ownership. In fact, the mechanisms of peri-hand multisensory integration implicated by Makin *et al.* (2008) in the experience of body ownership are present even if there is a postural incongruency between the participant's own hand and the rubber hand: for example, the preference for a stimulus approaching the rubber hand is similar in the posterior part of the intraparietal sulcus to that shown for the real hand (Makin *et al.* 2007), suggesting that viewing visual stimuli near a rubber hand is sufficient to change the representation of hand position in peri-hand brain areas. In addition, lesions in brain areas that underpin these processes such as the ventral premotor cortex and intraparietal sulcus (Makin *et al.* 2008) do not result in denial of body ownership (Baier and Karnath, 2008). Makin *et al.* (2008) cite two studies by Arzy *et al.* (2006) and Berti *et al.* (2005) to support the hypothesis that lesions in premotor cortex result in deficits in body ownership. Arzy *et al.* (2006: 1022) report a case study of a patient who, following two small confined lesions in the right premotor and motor cortices, 'felt that parts of her left arm had disappeared. Much to her surprise she could see the table on which she had rested her left arm as if she could see the table through the arm, and saw her left arm only above her elbow, with a clear-cut border'. The patient described by Arzy *et al.* (2006) displayed asomatognosia (i.e. loss of awareness of one body-half (which may or may be not paralyzed, see Critchley 1953), but not somatoparaphrenia, that is, the patient did not report any experience of dis-ownership (at least not as the case is reported). Similarly, the study by Berti *et al.* (2005) focused on a patient with anosognosia for hemiplegia, a syndrome that is dissociable from somatoparaphrenia (Vallar and Ronchi 2009). Finally, there are behavioral changes that occur after participants experience the RHI (see Moseley *et al.* 2008, and the discussion in section 2) that cannot be solely accounted for by multisensory integration in peri-hand space, without considering other higher-order representations of the body.

The aforementioned processes postulated by Makin *et al.* (2008) are indeed necessary for the experience of body ownership. However, the studies reviewed in section 4 converge on the hypothesis that multisensory integration in peri-personal hand space by itself is not sufficient for body ownership. Instead, other factors, such as the visual form congruency between the viewed object and the felt body-part (Tsakiris and Haggard 2005; Haans *et al.* 2008; see also Holmes *et al.* 2006), the anatomical congruency between viewed and felt body-part (Tsakiris and Haggard 2005; Graziano *et al.* 2000; Pavani *et al.* 2000), the volumetric congruency between the viewed and the felt body-part (Pavani and Zampini 2007), the postural congruency between the viewed and felt body-part (Austen *et al.* 2004; Tsakiris and Haggard 2005; Costantini and Haggard 2007; Ehrsson *et al.* 2004; Pavani *et al.* 2000), and the spatial relation between viewed and felt body-part (Lloyd 2007), modulate the inducement of the RHI and the experience of body ownership. Figure 7.1 proposes a preliminary neurocognitive model of body ownership that can account for the majority of the empirical findings to date and generate testable hypotheses for future research.

In the first critical comparison, the visual form of the viewed object is compared against a pre-existing body model that contains a reference description of the visual, anatomical, and structural properties of the body (Tsakiris *et al.*, 2008; Costantini and Haggard 2007; Tsakiris and Haggard 2005) that are diachronic, in contrast to the body schema which is continuously updated as the body moves (Wolpert *et al.*

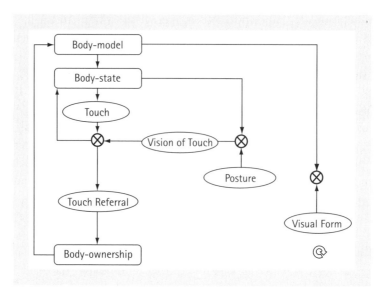

Figure 7.1 A neurocognitive model of body-ownership during the Rubber Hand Illusion. In the first critical comparison, the visual form of the viewed object is compared against a preexisting body model that contains a reference description of the visual, anatomical and structural properties of the body. The rTPJ has been shown to be involved in this comparison (Tsakiris *et al.* 2008). The second critical comparison takes place between the current state of the body and the postural and anatomical features of the body-part that is to be experienced as mine. This comparison is underpinned by activity in anterior parietal areas such as the primary and secondary somatosensory cortices (see Press *et al.* 2007; Tsakiris *et al.* 2007). The third comparison is between the current sensory inputs, that is, between the vision of touch and the felt touch and their respective reference frames. The PPC underpins this third comparison by resolving the conflict between visual and tactile information and recalibrating the visual and tactile coordinate systems (Ehrsson *et al.* 2004; Makin *et al.* 2008). This recalibration will result in the touch referral underpinned by activity in the premotor cortex (Ehrsson *et al.* 2004). Finally, the subjective experience of ownership, underpinned by activity in the right posterior insula (Tsakiris *et al.* 2007), will update the body model, resulting in the incorporation of hand and subsequent physiological regulation of the body (Moseley *et al.* 2008). The crossed circle represents a comparator. The recycling arrow denotes a loop.

1998). Other authors have suggested the existence of a stored and not stimulus-evoked body-structural description that would contain representations about (*a*) the shape and contours of the human body, (*b*) a detailed plan of the body surface, (*c*) the location of body-parts, the boundaries between them, and their internal part relation (de Vignemont *et al.* 2005; Schwoebel and Coslett 2005). Schwoebel and

Coslett (2005) suggested that this body-structural description is view-independent or even allocentric, but what seems to be important for the sense of body ownership induced during the RHI is that the body-model operates offline and more interestingly it seems to be normative (de Preester and Tsakiris 2009) or egopetal (Longo *et al.* 2009) for one's own body, because its modulatory influence allows for an external body-part to be considered as a potential part of *my* body or not. This first critical comparison will test the fitness for incorporeability of the viewed object. Objects that do not pass this test will not be experienced as part of one's body even if visuo-tactile stimulation is synchronous (Haans *et al.* 2008; Tsakiris *et al.* 2008; Tsakiris and Haggard 2005; but see Armel and Ramachandran 2003). The model predicts that the more the viewed object matches the structural appearance of the body-part's form, the stronger the experience of body ownership will be. Features such as skin color do not seem to enter into this comparison (see Longo *et al.* 2009) and this is a further argument why this body-model should not be equated with a conscious body-image.

The second critical comparison takes place between the current state of the body and the postural and anatomical features of the body-part that is to be attributed. Body schematic processes (e.g. current postural configuration), as well as current reafferent information (as shown in the connection between touch and vision and body state in Figure 7.1) will be informing this current state of the body. If there is incongruency between the postures of felt and seen hands, the seen hand will not be experienced as part of one's own body, even if the multisensory stimulation between the two hands suggests otherwise (Costantini and Haggard 2007; Ehrsson *et al.* 2004; Tsakiris and Haggard 2005). The model predicts that discrepancies at the postural and anatomical level will reduce the experience of ownership. The third comparison is between current sensory inputs, that is, between the vision of touch and the felt touch and their reference frames. For large discrepancies in tactile and visual reference frames (Lloyd 2007), the RHI will not occur. Similarly, temporal asynchrony between vision of touch and felt touch will not induce the subjective referral of touch to the rubber hand and the eventual feeling of body ownership (Botvinick and Cohen 1998; Tsakiris and Haggard 2005) that updates the body-model. The model predicts that discrepancies at the directional or temporal parameters of visuo-tactile stimulation will impede the recalibration of their reference frames and the subsequent touch referral, preventing, thus, the inducement of the experience of ownership.

On the basis of the empirical findings reviewed above, body ownership as studied in the RHI arises as an interaction between multisensory input and modulations exerted by stored and online internal models of the body (Tsakiris and Haggard 2005; Tsakiris 2007). As shown in the following sections, this functional interaction between multisensory integration and body models has identifiable neural signatures.

6. MY BODY IN MY BRAIN: A NEURAL NETWORK FOR BODY OWNERSHIP

....

The body-model: the contribution of rTPJ

How does the brain decide on the compatibility and eventual 'incorporeability' of an external object? The behavioral (Tsakiris and Haggard 2005) and electrophysiological (Press *et al.* 2008) data suggest that the process of filtering what may or may not become part of one's body is not the same as the process of multisensory integration that drives the RHI. Tsakiris *et al.* (2008) suggested that current sensory stimuli are processed and finally tested-for-fit against an abstract body-model that maintains a coherent sense of one's body as distinct from other non-corporeal objects (see Figure 7.1, comparison 1). Neuropsychological and neuroimaging studies suggest that the right temporal and parietal lobes may underpin this reference model of one's body. Lesions in this region may result in denial of ownership of the contralateral hand (Bottini *et al.* 2002), neglect of the left side of the body (Mort *et al.* 2003), anosognosia for hemiplegia (Berlucchi and Aglioti 1997; Fotopoulou *et al.* 2008), impaired self-recognition for body-parts (Frassinetti *et al.* 2009), while direct electrical stimulation of the right temporo-parietal junction (rTPJ) may elicit 'out-of-body experiences', and illusory transformations of the arms and legs (Blanke *et al.* 2002). Tsakiris *et al.* (2008) hypothesized that disrupting activity in the rTPJ would impair the test-for-fit process that underpins the distinction between corporeal and non-corporeal objects on the basis of visuo-tactile evidence. Single-pulse transcranial magnetic stimulation (TMS) was delivered 350ms after synchronous visuo-tactile stimulation of the participant's own hand and a rubber hand, or the participant's own hand and a neutral object. Proprioceptive drift was used as a behavioral proxy of the RHI. Overall, TMS over rTPJ reduced the extent to which the rubber hand was incorporated into the mental representation of one's own body, while it increased the incorporation of a neutral object, as measured by the proprioceptive drift towards or away from the viewed object. An object (i.e. a rubber hand) that would normally have been perceived as part of the subject's own body was no longer significantly distinguished from a clearly neutral object, suggesting that the disruption of neural activity over rTPJ blocked the contribution of the body-model in the assimilation of current sensory input, making the discrimination between what may or may not be part of one's body ambiguous.

This effect of TMS over rTPJ seems to have impaired a body/non-body discrimination process. This specific test-for-fit process can be used to filter visual and tactile events that may be assigned to one's own body from sensory events that produce a mismatch. This view also resonates with a recent hypothesis about the computational process implemented in the rTPJ. Decety and Lamm (2007) suggested that the rTPJ may underpin a single computational mechanism that is used by multiple cognitive processes (e.g. self-recognition, agency, theory of mind, attention reorientation, and perspective-taking); this mechanism involves the comparison of internal states (e.g. prediction and representations of the body or the self more generally) with external sensory events. This basic computational mechanism would be important for self–world interactions (e.g. detection of multisensory mismatch, agency), but also for higher cognitive functions involved in self–other interactions.

The body state: the role of somatosensory cortices

Tsakiris *et al.* (2007) used a Positron Emission Tomography (PET) protocol to investigate the correlation between brain activity and a behavioral proxy of the RHI during conditions where participants either experience ownership of the external hand or not. A negative correlation between the proprioceptive measure of the illusion and rCBF was observed in the contralateral (right) primary and secondary somatosensory cortices. A small or negative proprioceptive drift in the RHI studies indicates that the rubber hand was not experienced as part of one's body (Botvinick and Cohen 1998; Longo *et al.* 2008). In these situations, the representation of the current state of the body is not captured by visual input because of the discrepancy. A possible role of somatosensory cortex activation relates to the saliency of the representation of the subject's own hand when the pattern of multisensory stimulation does not support the incorporation of the rubber hand: for example, when the visuo-tactile stimulation is asynchronous or when the rubber hand is anatomically incongruent with respect to the participant's hand. The maintenance of the current state of the body in the somatosensory cortex would prevent the inducement of RHI by making the participant's hand representation salient so that it becomes resistant to multisensory stimulation. Somatosensory cortex activations are sensitive to handedness (i.e. left- vs. right-hand manipulation) and related anatomic constraints (see also Costantini *et al.* 2005), and to the kinesthetic proprioceptive space (i.e. proprioceptive drift). Thus, the somatosensory cortex may be involved in the processing of the current body state that includes anatomical and postural representations. This type of functional engagement would make the contribution of associative sensory (see Tsakiris *et al.* 2007 for a discussion) areas critical for the comparison between the body's current state and the postural, spatial, and anatomical features of the rubber hand (see Figure 7.1, comparison 2).

Body-related multisensory integration: the contribution of parietal and premotor cortices

If the external object passes the test-for-fit with the body-model and the matching process with the current body-state (see Costantini and Haggard 2007; Tsakiris *et al.* 2007), then synchronized visuo-tactile stimulation will drive the inducement of the

RHI as a necessary condition. If there is a congruency between the posture and spatial location of the two hands, processes of multisensory integration in peri-hand space will allow for the recalibration of the visual and tactile co-ordinate systems, leading to the eventual referral of the tactile sensation on the vision of touch delivered on the rubber hand (see Figure 7.1, comparison 3). Ehrsson and colleagues (2004, 2005, 2007) showed bilateral neural activity in the ventral premotor cortex (PMv) and posterior parietal cortex (PPC) in the conditions that induced the RHI. Consistent findings in three fMRI studies suggest different roles for posterior parietal cortex and PMv during the RHI. According to Makin *et al.* (2008), the PPC seems to integrate multisensory information with respect to the rubber hand. This integration starts before the onset of the RHI (<11.3, ± 7.0 sec, from Erhsson *et al.* 2004), suggesting that PPC is involved in the resolution of the conflict between the incoming visual and tactile information, and the resulting recalibration of the visual and tactile coordinate systems (see Figure 7.1, comparison 3).

Regarding the contribution of premotor cortex, as Makin *et al.* (2008) note, the PMv shows additional multisensory responses during the period when people ex-perience the illusion (between 11.3 and 42 sec). This supra-additive activation can be accounted for by the enhancement of the responses of bimodal neurons once their reference frame is centered on the rubber hand, and participants start referring the touch to the rubber hand as a result of binding the visual and tactile events in hand-centered coordinates in the PPC. Thus, when the illusion starts, the hand-centered reference frames shift from the participant's hidden hand to the rubber hand. This shift is accompanied by a recalibration of the participant's hand position (i.e. prop-rioceptive drifts), and it results in the referral of the tactile sensation to the rubber hand. Note, however, that visuo-tactile correlation generates particularly strong proprioceptive drifts towards the rubber hand during the first 60 sec, implying that the hand-centred reference frames continue to shift towards the rubber hand, and that the referred sensations are enhanced during that period. After 1 minute of stimulation, the recalibration of hand position increases in a less exponential manner for up to 3 min (see experiment 4 in Tsakiris and Haggard 2005). It therefore remains unknown whether activity in the PMv between 11.3 and 42 sec in Ehrsson *et al.* (2004) reflects this rapid recalibration of hand position or the referral of tactile sensation on the rubber hand which should in principle arise as an effect of the recalibration.

The subjective experience of body ownership (and dis-ownership): the role of the right insular lobe

The experience of ownership of the rubber hand as measured by proprioceptive drifts was positively correlated with activity in the right posterior insula (Tsakiris *et al.* 2007). The roles of the insular lobe for body awareness in general (Craig 2002,

2009), and of the right posterior insula in particular for egocentric representation (Fink *et al.* 2003), agency (Farrer *et al.* 2003), and body ownership (Baier and Karnath 2008) are well supported by recent studies. The hypothesis that the right posterior insula is linked to the experience of body ownership is specifically supported by the available evidence on somatoparaphrenia. Somatoparaphrenia is a neurological condition, which is usually related to anosognosia for hemiplegia, and occurs after predominantly right hemispheric lesions. Patients with somatoparaphrenia believe that their limbs contralateral to the side of the lesion belong to someone else (Bisiach *et al.* 1991; Halligan *et al.* 1995; Nightingale 1982), and the disorder is often accompanied by the inability to feel tactile sensations in the 'non-belonging' part of the body (see Bottini *et al.* 2002). A first lesion mapping study suggested that the right posterior insula is commonly damaged in patients with anosognosia for hemiplegia (AHP), but is significantly less involved in hemiplegic patients without AHP (Karnath *et al.* 2005; see also Cereda *et al.* 2002; Berti *et al.* 2005). However, the extent to which these patients exhibited somatoparaphrenic symptoms was not formally assessed in these studies. A more recent lesion mapping study that focused specifically on patients with somatoparaphrenic symptoms (Baier and Karnath 2008) revealed that the right posterior insula is indeed the critical structure involved in phenomena of 'disturbed sensation of limb ownership'. Two further insights from the literature on somatoparaphrenia are particularly relevant for the understanding of induced body ownership in RHI. As the review by Vallar and Ronchi (2009) suggests, patients with spared proprioception do not exhibit somatoparaphrenia. The hypothesis that proprioceptive impairment plays a central role in breakdowns of ownership is particularly interesting in relation to the behavioral measure used to quantify ownership in the RHI.[1] Second, Vallar and Ronchi (2009) point to the fact that, on the basis of the available case studies to date, one main feature of somatoparaphrenia may be a blurred distinction between corporeal and extra-corporeal objects. This observation points to the critical role of the body-model in maintaining a coherent sense of one's body.

A neural network for body ownership

The brain processes that produce the sense of body ownership depend both on current sensory integration and the contribution of internal models of the body. The right temporoparietal junction may underpin the assimilation of novel multi-sensory signals by maintaining a pre-existing reference representation of one's own body. The rTPJ may underpin decisions about the incorporeability of the visual

---

[1] Obviously, loss of proprioception by itself is by no means sufficient for breakdowns in body ownership as the literature on deafferented patients suggests.

form of the viewed object with a reference body-model (Tsakiris *et al.* 2008). The primary and associative somatosensory cortices seem to maintain online anatomical and postural representations of the current state of the body against which the anatomical and postural features of the stimulated object are compared. Body-related sensory integration linked to the onset of body ownership during the RHI is related to activity in the posterior parietal cortex and the ventral premotor cortex (Ehrsson *et al.* 2004, 2007; Kammers *et al.* 2008). The effect of multisensory integration and recalibration of hand position, namely the experience of body ownership of the rubber hand, is correlated with activity in the right posterior insula (Tsakiris *et al.* 2007; see also Baier and Karnath 2008). Other authors have also suggested that the insula is concerned with higher-order somatosensory processing of the body that is related to a subjective awareness and affective processing of bodily signals (Craig 2002, 2009; Dijkerman and de Haan 2007). The available imaging evidence on the RHI is consistent with the view that SII and the insula are responsible for conscious somatosensory perception, with the right posterior parietal cortex contributing to spatio-temporal integration (Dijkerman and de Haan 2007). Circuitry and connectivity analyses demonstrate both the afferent and efferent connectivity of the insula with SII, the temporoparietal area and the premotor cortex (Augustine 1996; see also Dijkerman and de Haan 2007). These structures may form a network that plays a fundamental role in linking current sensory stimuli to one's own body, and thus also in self-awareness.

7. BEYOND MY HAND: MY BODY AND MYSELF

This chapter has focused on experimental paradigms and neuropsychological cases that investigate the necessary conditions for the experience of a body-*part* as belonging to my body. Blanke and Metzinger (2009) rightly comment on the need to investigate a more 'global' sense of body ownership for the whole body. Two recent studies employed the main experimental manipulation to investigate the extent to which phenomena similar to the RHI can be induced for whole bodies. Ehrsson (2007) used synchronous or asynchronous visuo-tactile stimulation while participants were looking at their back with the perspective of a person sitting behind them with stereoscopic vision. Synchronous but not asynchronous visuo-tactile stimulation induced a shift in the first-person perspective such that participants experienced being located at some distance behind the visual image of their own body as if they were looking at someone else. In Lenggenhager *et al.* (2007), participants viewed the backs of their bodies filmed from a distance of 2 m and projected onto a three-dimensional (3D) video head-mounted display. The participants' backs were stroked either synchronously or asynchronously with respect to the virtually seen body. Questionnaire ratings and a behavioral measure analogous to proprioceptive drift in RHI showed that only after synchronous stimulation did participants feel as if the virtual body was their body. Similar results were obtained when participants saw a virtual fake body (e.g. a mannequin), but not when participants saw a virtual non-corporeal object, replicating other studies reporting an abolishment of the illusion of ownership for non-corporeal objects (see Haans *et al.* 2008; Tsakiris and Haggard 2005). Interestingly, the necessary conditions for the experience of ownership over a body-part seem to be the same as the ones involved in the experience of ownership for full bodies. The question of whether ownership for body-parts is functionally different from ownership for the whole body has not been directly addressed in the empirical literature. However, the available empirical findings from the two domains suggest that very similar neurocognitive processes are involved independently for ownership of body-parts and bodies.

Two further manipulations of the whole-body studies resulted in the illusion of body-swapping (Petkova and Ehrsson 2008) and changes in self-face recognition (Tsakiris 2008). Petkova and Ehrsson (2008) fitted two small cameras on the head of a mannequin directed downwards. The image from the two cameras was projected to a head-mounted display worn by the participant. When the participant looked downwards, she saw the mannequin's body, where she would normally expect to see her own. Synchronous visuo-tactile stimulation induced the illusion of being this other body (i.e. the mannequin's body), suggesting that multisensory stimulation can induce not only an analogue of out-of-body experiences (Ehrsson 2007; Lenggenhager *et al.* 2007), but also an illusion of being in another body and a dramatic change in embodied perspective. These manipulations demonstrate the efficiency of current multisensory input in determining the experience of a minimal first-person perspective (Ehrsson 2007), self-location (Lenggenhager *et al.* 2007), and self-identification (Petkova and Ehrsson 2008), three conditions that are critical for the experience of selfhood (Blanke and Metzinger 2009).

To further investigate the extent to which current multisensory input may influence the sense of self-identity, Tsakiris (2008) extended the paradigm of multisensory integration to self-face recognition. Participants were stroked on their face while they were looking at a morphed face being touched in synchrony or asynchrony. Before and after the visuo-tactile stimulation participants performed a self-recognition task. The results showed that synchronized multisensory signals had a significant effect on self-face recognition. Synchronous tactile stimulation while watching another person's face being similarly touched produced a bias in recognizing one's own face, in the direction of the other person included in the morphed representation of one's own face. This effect provides direct evidence that our mental representation of our self, including the self-face representation, is not solely derived from stable mnemonic representations, but instead these representations are susceptible to current multisensory evidence. Multisensory integration can update cognitive representations of one's body, such as the sense of ownership of body-parts (Longo *et al.* 2008), or whole body (Ehrsson 2007; Lenggenhager *et al.* 2007; Petkova and Ehrsson 2008), the physical appearance of one's body (Longo *et al.* 2009), and the representation of one's identity in relation to other people (Tsakiris 2008).

8. CONCLUSION

One of the key questions in the neurocognitive study of self is that of specificity (Gillihan and Farah 2005; Legrand and Ruby 2009). Gillihan and Farah (2005) point to the fact that there is not a self-specific neural system or a single sense of self. Legrand and Ruby (2009) suggest that 'self-specificity characterizes the subjective perspective, which is not intrinsically self-evaluative but rather relates any represented object to the representing subject', by means of multisensory processing and sensorimotor integration. The present review focused on multisensory processing and its role for body ownership only (for the role of sensorimotor integration for body ownership, see Tsakiris *et al.* 2008). In particular, it considered how multisensory integration together with internal models of the body modulate the experience of the body as being one's own as well as the demarcation or distinction between one's body and other objects. The experience of body ownership may represent a critical component of self-specificity as evidenced by the different ways in which multisensory integration in interaction with internal models of the body can actually manipulate important physical and psychological aspects of the self. Future studies should further investigate the neurocognitive processes that bridge the physical and psychological dimensions of the self to create a coherent sense of self-identity.

REFERENCES

ARMEL, K. C., and RAMACHANDRAN, V. S. (2003). 'Projecting Sensations to External Objects: Evidence from Skin Conductance Response', *Proceedings of the Royal Society London B Biological Sciences*, 270: 1499–1506.

ARZY, S., OVERNEY, L. S., LANDIS, T., and BLANKE, O. (2006). 'Neural Mechanisms of Embodiment: Asomatognosia due to Premotor Cortex Damage', *Archives of Neurology*, 63: 1022–5.

AUGUSTINE, J. R. (1996). 'Circuitry and Functional Aspects of the Insular Lobe in Primates Including Humans', *Brain Research: Brain Research Reviews*, 22: 229–44.

AUSTEN, E. L., SOTO-FARACO, S., ENNS, J. T., and KINGSTONE, A. (2004). 'Mislocalisation of Touch to a Fake Hand', *Cognitive, Affective, and Behavioral Neuroscience*, 4: 170–81.

BAIER, B., and KARNATH, H. O. (2008). 'Tight Link between our Sense of Limb Ownership and Self Awareness of Actions', *Stroke*, 39: 486–8.

BERLUCCHI, G., and AGLIOTI, S. (1997). 'The Body in the Brain: Neural Bases of Corporeal Awareness', *Trends in Neuroscience*, 20: 560–4.

BERTI, A., BOTTINI, G., GANDOLA, M., PIA, L., SMANIA, N., STRACCIARI, A., CASTIGLIONI, I., VALLAR, G., and PAULESU, E. (2005). 'Shared Cortical Anatomy for Motor Awareness and Motor Control', *Science*, 309: 488–91.

BISIACH, E., RUSCONI, M. L., and VALLAR, G. (1991). 'Remission of Somatoparaphrenic Delusion through Vestibular Stimulation', *Neuropsychologia*, 29/10: 1029–31.

BLANKE, O., and METZINGER, T. (2009). 'Full-Body Illusions and Minimal Phenomenal Selfhood', *Trends in Cognitive Sciences*, 13: 7–13.

——ORTIGUE, S., LANDIS, T., and SEECK, M. (2002). 'Stimulating Illusory Own-Body Perceptions', *Nature*, 419: 269.

BOTTINI, G., BISIACH, E., STERZI, R., and VALLAR, G. (2002). 'Feeling Touches in Someone Else's Hand', *Neuroreport*, 13: 249–52.

BOTVINICK, M., and COHEN, J. (1998). 'Rubber Hands "Feel" Touch that Eyes See', *Nature*, 391: 756.

BUXBAUM, L. J., and COSLETT, H. B. (2001). 'Specialised Structural Descriptions for Human Body Parts: Evidence from Autotopagnosia', *Cognitive Neuropsychology*, 18: 289–306.

CARRUTHERS, G. (2008). 'Types of Body Representation and the Sense of Embodiment', *Consciousness and Cognition*, 17: 1302–16.

CEREDA, C., GHIKA, J., MAEDER, P., and BOGOUSSLAVSKY, J. (2002). 'Strokes Restricted to the Insular Cortex', *Neurology*, 59: 1950–5.

CRAIG, A. D. (2002). 'How do you Feel? Interoception: The Sense of the Physiological Condition of the Body', *Nature Reviews Neuroscience*, 3: 655–66.

——(2009). 'How do you Feel—Now? The Anterior Insula and Human Awareness', *Nature Reviews Neuroscience*, 10: 59–70.

CRITCHLEY, M. (1953). *The Parietal Lobes* (New York: Hafner).

COSTANTINI, M., and HAGGARD, P. (2007). 'The Rubber Hand Illusion: Sensitivity and Reference Frame for Body Ownership', *Consciousness and Cognition*, 16: 229–40.

——GALATI, G., FERRETTI, A., CAULO, M., TARTARO, A., ROMANI, G. L., and AGLIOTI, S. M. (2005). 'Neural Systems Underlying Observation of Humanly Impossible Movements: An FMRI Study', *Cerebral Cortex*, 15: 1761–7.

DAPRATI, E., FRANCK, N., GEORGIEFF, N., PROUST, J., PACHERIE, E., DALERY, J., and JEANNEROD, M. (1997). 'Looking for the Agent: An Investigation into Consciousness of Action and Self-Consciousness in Schizophrenic Patients', *Cognition*, 65: 71–86.

DECETY, J., and LAMM, C. (2007). 'The Role of the Right Temporoparietal Junction in Social Interaction: How Low-Level Computational Processes Contribute to Metacognition', *The Neuroscientist: A Review Journal Bringing Neurobiology, Neurology and Psychiatry*, 13: 580–93.

DE PREESTER, H., and TSAKIRIS, M. (2009). 'Body-Extension versus Body-Incorporation: Is there a Need for a Body-Model?', *Phenomenology and Cognitive Sciences*, 8: 307–19.

DE VIGNEMONT, F. (2007). 'Habeas Corpus: The Sense of Ownership of One's Own Body', *Mind and Language*, 22: 427–49.

——TSAKIRIS, M., and HAGGARD, P. (2005). 'Body Mereology', in G. Knoblich, I. Thornton, M. Grosjean, and M. Shiffrar (eds), *Human Body Perception from the Inside Out* (New York: Oxford University Press).

DIJKERMAN, H. C., and DE HAAN, E. H. (2007). 'Somatosensory Processes Subserving Perception and Action', *Behavioural Brain Science*, 30: 189–201.

DURGIN, F. H., EVANS, L., DUNPHY, N., KLOSTERMANN, S., and SIMMONS, K. (2007). 'Rubber Hands Feel the Touch of Light', *Psychological Science*, 18: 152–7.

EHRSSON, H. H. (2007). 'The Experimental Induction of Out-of-Body Experiences', *Science*, 317: 1048.

——HOLMES, N. P., and PASSINGHAM, R. E. (2005). 'Touching a Rubber Hand: Feeling of Body Ownership is Associated with Activity in Multisensory Brain Areas', *Journal of Neuroscience*, 25: 10564–73.

——ROSÉN, B., STOCKSELIUS, A., RAGNÖ, C., KÖHLER, P., and LUNDBORG, G. (2008). 'Upper Limb Amputees can be Induced to Experience a Rubber Hand as their own', *Brain*, 131: 3443–52.

——SPENCE, C., and PASSINGHAM, R. E. (2004). 'That's My Hand! Activity in Premotor Cortex Reflects Feeling of Ownership of a Limb', *Science*, 305: 875–7.

——WIECH, K., WEISKOPF, N., DOLAN, R. J., and PASSINGHAM, R. E. (2007). 'Threatening a Rubber Hand that you Feel is Yours Elicits a Cortical Anxiety Response', *Proceedings of the National Academy of Sciences*, 104: 9828–33.

FARRER, C., FRANCK, N., GEORGIEFF, N., FRITH, C. D., DECETY, J., and JEANNEROD, M. (2003). 'Modulating the Experience of Agency: A Positron Emission Tomography Study', *NeuroImage*, 18: 324–33.

FINK, G. R., MARSHALL, J. C., WEISS, P. H., STEPHAN, T., GREFKES, C., SHAH, N. J., ZILLES, K., and DIETERICH, M. (2003). 'Performing allocentric Visuospatial Judgments with Induced Distortion of the Egocentric Reference Frame: An FMRI Study with Clinical Implications', *NeuroImage*, 20: 1505–17.

FOTOPOULOU, A., TSAKIRIS, M., HAGGARD, P., VAGOPOULOU, A., RUDD, A., and KOPELMAN, M. (2008). 'The Role of Motor Intention in Motor Awareness: An Experimental Study on Anosognosia for Hemiplegia', *Brain*, 131: 3432–42.

FRANCK, N., FARRER, C., GEORGIEFF, N., MARIE-CARDIN, M., DALERY, J., D'AMATO, T., and JEANNEROD, M. (2001). 'Defective Recognition of One's Own Actions in Patients with Schizophrenia', *American Journal of Psychiatry*, 158: 454–9.

FRASSINETTI, F., MAINI, M., ROMUALDI, S., GALANTE, E., and AVANZI, S. (2009). 'Is it Mine? Hemispheric Asymmetries in Corporeal Self-Recognition', *Journal of Cognitive Neuroscience*, 20: 1507–16.

GALLAGHER, S. (2000). 'Philosophical Concepts of the Self: Implications for Cognitive Sciences', *Trends in Cognitive Sciences*, 4: 14–21.

GILLIHAN, S. J., and FARAH, M. J. (2005). 'Is Self Special? A Critical Review of Evidence from Experimental Psychology and Cognitive Neuroscience', *Psychological Bulletin*, 131: 76–97.

GRAZIANO, M. S. A., and BOTVINIK, M. M. (2001). 'How the Brain Represents the Body: Insights from Neurophysiology and Psychology', in W. Prinz and B. Hommel (eds), *Common Mechanisms in Perception and Action, Attention and Performance XIX* (Oxford and New York: Oxford University Press).

——COOKE, D. F., and TAYLOR, C. S. (2000). 'Coding the Location of the Arm by Sight', *Science*, 290: 1782–6.

HAANS, A., IJSSELSTEIJN, W. A., and DE KORT, Y. A. (2008). 'The Effect of Similarities in Skin Texture and Hand Shape on Perceived Ownership of a Fake Limb', *Body Image*, 5/4: 389–94.

HÄGNI, K., ENG, K., HEPP-REYMOND, M. C., HOLPER, L., KEISKER, B., SIEKIERKA, E., and KIPER, D. C. (2008). 'Observing Virtual Arms that you Imagine are Yours Increases the Galvanic Skin Response to an Unexpected Threat', *PLoS ONE*, 3(8): e3082.

HALLIGAN, P. W., MARSHALL, J. C., and WADE, D. T. (1995). 'Unilateral Somatoparaphrenia After Right Hemisphere Stroke: A Case Description', *Cortex*, 31/1: 173–82.

HOLMES, N. P., and SPENCE, C. (2006). 'Beyond the Body Schema: Visual, Prosthetic, and Technological Contributions to Bodily Perception and Awareness', in G. Knoblich, I. Thornton, M. Grosjean, M. Shiffrar (eds), *Human Body Perception from the Inside Out* (Oxford: Oxford University Press), 15–64.

——SNIJDERS, H. J., and SPENCE, C. (2006). 'Reaching with Alien Limbs: Visual Exposure to Prosthetic Hands in a Mirror Biases Proprioception without Accompanying Illusions of Ownership', *Perception and Psychophysics*, 68: 685–701.

JAMES, W. (1890). *The Principles of Psychology* (Cambridge, Mass.: Harvard University Press).

JEANNEROD, M. (2003). 'The Mechanism of Self-Recognition in Humans', *Behavioural Brain Research*, 142: 1–15.

KAMMERS, M. P., DE VIGNEMONT, F., VERHAGEN, L., and DIJKERMAN, H. C. (2009). 'The Rubber Hand Illusion in Action', *Neuropsychologia*, 47: 204–11.

——VERHAGEN, L., DIJKERMAN, H. C., HOGENDOORN, H., DE VIGNEMONT, F., and SCHUTTER, D. J. (2008). 'Is This Hand for Real? Attenuation of the Rubber Hand Illusion by Transcranial Magnetic Stimulation over the Inferior Parietal Lobule', *Journal of Cognitive Neuroscience* [Epub ahead of print].

KARNATH, H. O., BAIER, B., and NAGELE, T. (2005). 'Awareness of the Functioning of One's Own Limbs Mediated by the Insular Cortex?', *Journal Neuroscience*, 25: 7134–8.

KEENAN, J. P., RUBIO, J., RACIOPPI, C., JOHNSON, A., and BARNACZ, A. (2005). 'The Right Hemisphere and the Dark Side of Consciousness', *Cortex*, 41: 695–704.

LADAVAS, E., DI PELLEGRINO, G., FARNE, A., and ZELONI, G. (1998). 'Neuropsychological Evidence of an Integrated Visuotactile Representation of Peripersonal Space in Humans', *Journal of Cognitive Neuroscience*, 10: 581–9.

LEGRAND, D., and RUBY, P. (2009). 'What is Self-Specific? Theoretical Investigation and Critical Review of Neuroimaging Results', *Psychological Review*, 116: 252–82.

LENGGENHAGER, B., TADI, T., METZINGER, T., and BLANKE, O. (2007). 'Video Ergo Sum: Manipulating Bodily Self-Consciousness', *Science*, 317: 1096–9.

LLOYD, D. M. (2007). 'Spatial Limits on Referred Touch to an Alien Limb may Reflect Boundaries of Visuo-Tactile Peripersonal Space Surrounding the Hand', *Brain and Cognition*, 64: 104–9.

LONGO, M., SCHÜÜR, F., KAMMERS, M. P. M., TSAKIRIS, M., and HAGGARD, P. (2008). 'What is Embodiment? A Psychometric Approach', *Cognition*, 107: 978–98.

————————and ——(2009). 'Self Awareness and the Body Image', *Acta Psychologica*, 32: 166–72.

MAKIN, T. R., HOLMES, N. P., and EHRSSON, H. H. (2008). 'On the Other Hand: Dummy Hands and Peripersonal Space', *Behavioral Brain Research*, 191: 1–10.

——HOLMES, N. P., and ZOHARY, E. (2007). 'Is that Near my Hand? Multisensory Representation of Peripersonal Space in Human Intraparietal Sulcus', *Journal of Neuroscience*, 27: 731–40.

MARAVITA, A., and IRIKI, A. (2004). 'Tools for the Body (Schema)', *Trends in Cognitive Sciences*, 8: 79–86.

——SPENCE, C., and DRIVER, J. (2003). 'Multisensory Integration and the Body Schema: Close to Hand and within Reach', *Current Biology*, 13: R531–R539.

MERLEAU-PONTY, M. (1962). *The Phenomenology of Perception*, tr. C Smith (London: Routledge).

MORGAN, R., and ROCHAT, P. (1997). 'Intermodal Calibration of the Body in Early Infancy', *Ecological Psychology*, 9: 1–24.

MORT, D. J., MALHOTRA, P., MANNAN, S. K., RORDEN, C., PAMBAKIAN, A., KENNARD, C., and HUSAIN, M. (2003). 'The Anatomy of Visual Neglect', *Brain*, 126: 1986–97.

MOSELEY, G. L., OLTHOF, N., VENEMA, A., DON, S., WIJERS, M., GALLACE, A., and SPENCE, C. (2008). 'Psychologically Induced Cooling of a Specific Body Part Caused by the Illusory Ownership of an Artificial Counterpart', *Proceedings of the National Academy of Sciences*, 105: 13169–73.

NIGHTINGALE, S. (1982). 'Somatoparaphrenia: A Case Report', *Cortex*, 18: 463–7.

PAVANI, F., and ZAMPINI, M. (2007). 'The Role of Hand Size in the Fake-Hand Illusion Paradigm', *Perception*, 36: 1547–54.

——SPENCE, C., and DRIVER, J. (2000). 'Visual Capture of Touch: Out-of-the-Body Experiences with Rubber Gloves', *Psychological Science*, 11: 353–9.

PETKOVA, V. I., and EHRSSON, H. H. (2008). 'If I were you: Perceptual Illusion of Body Swapping', *PLoS ONE*, 3(12): e3832.

PRESS, C., HEYES, C., HAGGARD, P., and EIMER, M. (2008). 'Visuotactile Learning and Body Representation: An ERP Study with Rubber Hands and Rubber Objects', *Journal of Cognitive Neuroscience*, 20: 312–23.

ROCHAT, P., and STRIANO, T. (2000). 'Perceived Self in Infancy', *Infant Behavior and Development*, 23: 513–30.

SCHÜTZ-BOSBACH, S., MANCINI, B., AGLIOTI, S. M., and HAGGARD, P. (2006). 'Self and Other in the Human Motor System', *Current Biology*, 16: 1830–4.

SCHWOEBEL, J., and COSLETT, H. B. (2005). 'Evidence for Multiple, Distinct Representations of the Human Body', *Journal of Cognitive Neuroscience*, 17: 543–53.

SIRIGU, A., DAPRATI, D., PRADAT-DIEHL, P., FRANCK, N., and JEANNEROD, M. (1999). 'Perception of Self-Generated Movement Following Left Parietal Lesion', *Brain*, 122/10: 1867–74.

——GRAFMAN, J., BRESSLER, K., and SUNDERLAND, T. (1991). 'Multiple Representations Contribute to Body Knowledge Processing: Evidence from a Case of Autotopagnosia', *Brain*, 114: 629–42.

SLATER, M., PEREZ-MARCOS, D., EHRSSON, H. H., and SANCHEZ-VIVES, M. V. (2008). 'Towards a Digital Body: The Virtual Arm Illusion', *Frontiers in Human Neuroscience*, 2: 6.

SYNOFZIK, M., VOSGERAU, G., and NEWEN, A. (2008). 'I Move, Therefore I am: A New Theoretical Framework to Investigate Agency and Ownership', *Consciousness and Cognition*, 17: 411–24.

TSAKIRIS, M. (2008). 'Looking for Myself: Current Multisensory Input Alters Self-Face Recognition', *PLoS ONE* 3(12): e4040.

——and FOTOPOULOU, A. (2008). 'Is my Body the Sum of Online and Offline Body-Representations?', *Consciousness and Cognition*, 17: 1317–20; discussion 1321–3.

——and HAGGARD, P. (2005). 'The Rubber Hand Illusion Revisited: Visuotactile Integration and Self-Attribution', *Journal of Experimental Psychology: Human Perception and Performance*, 31: 80–91.

——COSTANTINI, M., and HAGGARD, P. (2008). 'The Role of the Right Temporoparietal Junction in Maintaining a Coherent Sense of One's Body', *Neuropsychologia*, 46: 3014–18.

——HAGGARD, P., FRANCK, N., MAINY, N., and SIRIGU, A. (2005). 'A Specific Role for Efferent Information in Self-Recognition', *Cognition*, 96: 215–31.

——HESSE, M., BOY, C., HAGGARD, P., and FINK, G. R. (2007). 'Neural Correlates of Body-Ownership: A Sensory Network for Bodily Self-Consciousness', *Cerebral Cortex*, 17: 2235–44.

——PRABHU, G., and HAGGARD, P. (2006). 'Having a Body versus Moving your Body: How Agency Structures Body-Ownership', *Consciousness and Cognition*, 15: 423–32.

——SCHÜTZ-BOSBACH, S., and GALLAGHER, S. (2007). 'On Agency and Body-Ownership: Phenomenological and Neurocognitive Reflections', *Consciousness and Cognition*, 16: 645–60.

VALLAR, G., and RONCHI, R. (2009). 'Somatoparaphrenia: A Body Delusion. A Review of the Neuropsychological Literature', *Experimental Brain Research*, 192: 533–51.

VAN DEN BOS, E., and JEANNEROD, M. (2002). 'Sense of Body and Sense of Action Both Contribute to Self-Recognition', *Cognition*, 85: 177–87.

WALDENFELS, B. (2004). 'Bodily Experience between Selfhood and Otherness', *Phenomenology and Cognitive Sciences*. 3: 235–48.

WOLPERT, D. M., GOODBODY, S. J., and HUSAIN, M. (1998). 'Maintaining Internal Representations: The Role of the Human Superior Parietal Lobe', *Nature Neuroscience*, 1: 529–33.

CHAPTER 8

....

PHENOMENOLOGICAL DIMENSIONS OF BODILY SELF-CONSCIOUSNESS

....

DOROTHÉE LEGRAND

1. INTRODUCTION

....

This chapter concerns the multidimensionality of self-consciousness. Starting from the distinction between the self-as-subject and the self-as-object, I intend to argue that each act of consciousness is adequately characterized by two modes of givenness, the intentional mode of givenness by which the subject is conscious of intentional objects and the subjective mode of givenness by which the subject is conscious of intentional objects as experienced by himself. The latter corresponds to the consciousness of the self-as-subject and will be the focus of the present analysis. In particular, I intend to clarify in which ways the self-as-subject is consciously experienced, and will do so by investigating the co-constitution of the subjective and intentional modes of givenness of consciousness: how is subjectivity both constitutive of and constituted by intentionality? I will tackle this

I acknowledge the support of the European Platform for Life Sciences, Mind Sciences, and the Humanities grant by the Volkswagen Stiftung for the 'Body-Project: interdisciplinary investigations on bodily experiences'.

general question by considering how the bodily self is constituted as being a bodily-subject-in-the-world.

2. SELF-AS-SUBJECT AND SELF-AS-OBJECT

Intentionality and subjectivity

When investigating self-consciousness, a crucial point concerns the distinction between the self-as-subject and the self-as-object (Zahavi 2005; Legrand 2006, 2007b, 2007c). In the present account, the *self-as-object* corresponds to the intentional object of my experience, for example to the one I evaluate (e.g. as being nice), remember (e.g. as being healthy), perceive (e.g. as being tall). The *self-as-subject* corresponds to the subject of the experience, the evaluating, remembering, or perceiving subject. This subject can experience either himself or things in the world, that is, the intentional object of this subject's experience can be either the *self-as-object* (e.g. the perceived self-image) or not. For example, when looking in a mirror, a subject perceives the appearance of his face by taking the latter as an intentional object (of visual perception). While looking at the frame surrounding the mirror, he remains a perceiving self-as-subject but perceives a thing in the world (the frame).

This distinction between self-as-subject and self-as-object is not ontological but phenomenological; it primarily concerns how self-consciousness is structured: each intentional act of consciousness can be adequately described as having two poles, a subjective pole and an objective pole, and the subject can be conscious of either of these two poles, thereby being conscious of himself either as-subject or as-object. To phrase it differently, each act of consciousness is adequately characterized by two modes of givenness, the *intentional* mode of givenness by which the subject is conscious of intentional objects and the *subjective* mode of givenness by which the subject is conscious of intentional objects as experienced by himself. The former corresponds to consciousness of the self-as-object when the intentional object is oneself and the latter corresponds to consciousness of the self-as-subject.

Importantly, intentionality and subjectivity are two non-dissociable aspects of experience: acts of consciousness 'are self-aware because in the very event of presenting an x they are present to themselves. In grasping the object, the act returns to itself' (Welton 2004: 6). In this view, 'we can no longer treat self-awareness in isolation, as if being-self-conscious were not being-self-consciously-experiencing-x' (ibid.). In a representationalist view, a comparable idea has been phrased in the following way: 'in any given experience there must always be a mode of presentation that cannot, in that experience, be made into an object of awareness. In any experience, there must always be a component of that experience of which we cannot be aware' (Rowlands 2008: 293). I agree with the first of these sentences which argues for the 'non-eliminability' of what I call here the self-as-subject; however, I disagree with the second of these sentences and intend to clarify in which ways the self-as-subject is consciously experienced.

Transitivity and intransitivity

To better understand the distinction between the self-as-subject and the self-as-object, it is relevant to differentiate transitive and non-transitive forms of consciousness (see also Legrand 2009). Consciousness of the self-as-object is a form of transitive self-consciousness while consciousness of the self-as-subject is a form of intransitive self-consciousness. A *transitive* verb is one that takes a direct object (e.g. to dream about something); it expresses an action undertaken by a subject towards an object. By contrast, an *intransitive* verb is one that cannot take a direct object (e.g. to sleep). Sometimes transitivity is silent. For example, any time I state the seemingly intransitive 'I read', I silently imply the transitive 'I read something'. Distinguishing tacit transitivity (transitive verbs with implied objects) from intransitivity is usually fairly easy: it is enough to check whether or not it makes sense to ask the 'what' question. When the 'what' is not specified but could be specified, it makes sense to ask about it, and the verb is implicitly transitive: 'I dreamed . . .'—'*What* did you dream about?' When there is no 'what', no object albeit unspecified, the verb is intransitive. With 'I sleep' it does not make sense to ask '*what* did you sleep?'

These basic grammatical rules are relevant here because they help clarify the difference between consciousness of the self-as-subject and consciousness of the self-as-object. 'Being conscious' is ambitransitive: it can be used either transitively or intransitively. Transitively, one refers to state-consciousness saying e.g. 'I am conscious of being sad today', 'He is conscious of his mistake'. One can also refer to creature-consciousness saying 'I am conscious', by opposition to situations where one is not conscious. This is a case of tacit transitivity, since it does make sense to ask '*what* are you conscious of'. Now, one may be tempted (but it would be a mistake) to end the story here, and to assume that consciousness is either explicitly transitive or tacitly transitive. Indeed, any time I report 'I am conscious', I silently report the transitive consciousness 'I am conscious of something'. This is just another way to say that consciousness is intentional, that is, constitutively directed at something. However, and this is the crucial point, stating that consciousness is transitively intentional, even stating that consciousness is necessarily transitively intentional, does not allow one to state that consciousness is *only* transitively intentional.

All there is to consciousness is not its intentional, transitive mode of givenness. In addition to explicit and implicit transitive states, the *intransitive* mode of givenness of consciousness is irreducible to transitive states and must be considered for its own sake. What I named above consciousness of the self-as-subject corresponds to the intransitive mode of givenness of consciousness. To see what this means, let us consider the following example. Imagine you are perceiving a picture as subtly blurry. You then realize that you forgot to put your glasses on and that in fact the picture is not blurry, only your perception is. At the beginning, you take the picture as object of your experience and experience it as blurry. In the end, you experience your *experience* of the picture as blurry. Importantly for the point at stake here, what remains present from the beginning to the end of this scenario is the intransitive consciousness of yourself-as-subject: you experience the picture as experienced by *you*, and you experience your experience of the picture (e.g. your blurry perception) as experienced by *you*. Considering 'only' the two intentional *objects* of consciousness (e.g. the picture and your visual perception taken as objects of consciousness) would leave aside the distinction between two modes of givenness of consciousness itself, i.e. the transitive mode of givenness of consciousness when an experience is itself taken as an object of consciousness (e.g. I experience my vision of the picture as being blurry) and the intransitive mode of givenness of consciousness (e.g. I experience the picture as experienced *by me*). In the former (transitive) case, it makes sense to detail *what* I experience when I experience my experience; for example, I experience blurriness. In the latter (intransitive) case, this '*what*' question cannot be appropriately asked about my involvement as experiencing subject.

Notice that these considerations lead to an interesting change in the frame of investigation of self-consciousness. The most common question asked when investigating self-consciousness is 'who': who are you conscious of, yourself or not? Here, the framework is different and involves checking whether the 'what' question can be asked meaningfully. If yes, then the transitive consciousness at stake may be a form of self-consciousness or not, and asking the 'who' question becomes relevant only then. Conversely, if the 'what' question cannot be asked meaningfully, then the form of consciousness involved is intransitive and the 'who' question is just as irrelevant as the 'what' question. What needs to be emphasized is that here 'the question of self-awareness is not primarily a question of a specific what, but of a unique how. It does not concern the specific content of an experience, but its unique mode of givenness' (Zahavi 2005: 204).

The investigation of the self-as-subject is paved with a number of difficulties. One is to keep clear the distinction between consciousness of the self-as-object and consciousness of the self-as-subject. The discussion of this issue in terms of transitive and intransitive forms of consciousness is meant to clarify this point. It allows considering that consciousness is (transitively) intentional but not only: it is also irreducibly (intransitively) subjective. This distinction, however, opens up other difficulties. In the remaining parts of the present investigation, I will take the distinction between the subjective and intentional modes of givenness as a disquieting starting-point rather than as a satisfactory achievement. Indeed, differentiation is not separation and once subjectivity and intentionality are differentiated from each other, the difficulty is to show how they constitute a single experience. The co-constitution of subjectivity and intentionality thus needs to be clarified. In particular, *how is the subjective aspect of consciousness, i.e. the intransitive consciousness of oneself-as-subject, both constitutive of and constituted by intentionality?* In the following, I will tackle this issue by considering more specifically *bodily* self-consciousness. Before starting, this focus on the body needs justification.

3. THE SELF AND THE BODY

Constitutive embeddedness

The subject is constitutively bodily. To see why, let us first consider what the self is supposed to be in order for intentional consciousness to be possible. A traditional way to phrase this issue is to ask: 'what is the ground of intentional consciousness or what founds subjective experience?', and to answer: 'the self'. This view comes at a high price as it involves (1) the idea that the appearance of the world is grounded on a foundation that is exterior to the world itself, that is, the idea that consciousness of the world needs to be constituted from outside of the world, as no *constituted* phenomenon could possibly be constitutive of phenomenality; and (2) the notion of a 'foundational self' that would ground its subjective experience of the world. It is only by being its own foundation that the self can *constitute* consciousness of the world rather than being *constituted* in the world.

This 'foundationalist' view of the self, in an idealist vein, privileges the constitutive role of the experiencing subject, to the detriment of the transcendence of the experienced object. The realist counter-reaction conversely preserves the transcendence of the experienced object to the detriment of the constitutive role of the experiencing subject (Barbaras 2008a: 80). Either way, these two antagonist positions fail to account for the *inseparability* of the constituting self and the constituted intentional object (Zahavi 2003: 106; 2005: 124).

To adequately consider such inseparability, 'selfhood has to be conceived outside of (or "beyond") the ground-grounded relation' (Mensch 2001: 13). In particular, what needs to be understood is that the self needs to be *in* the world for this world to appear (Barbaras, 2008a: 14–15): 'the apparition of the world is the counterpart of the immersion of the subject' (ibid. 79). The world can appear only for a subject who is embedded in the very world which is experienced (ibid. 91): 'the constitution of the world implies a mundanization of the constituting subject' (Zahavi 2009: 260). This view points to the 'the necessity of [the subject's] concrete and contingent existence in the midst of the world' (Sartre 1943/1956: 359) and straightforwardly contradicts the foundationalist idea of 'the fundamental detachability of the entire natural world from the domain of consciousness' (Husserl 1913/1952: i. 87). Rather, the constituting subject belongs to the world. Nonetheless, it remains that the subject is unlike any thing in the world (Barbaras 2008*a*: 41). The task is thus to understand the specificity of the belongingness to the world of this constitutive subjectivity, i.e. to understand the 'paradox of human subjectivity': 'being a subject for the world and at the same time being an object in the world' (Husserl 1934–7/1970: §53).

Constitutive embodiment

For the self to belong to the world, there is no other way than being corporeal. Not only being an experiencing subject, but more specifically being an experiencing *body* is necessary for there to be an experienced world at all. Moreover, one appears to oneself as belonging to the world: 'my being-in-the-world, by the sole fact that it *realizes* a world, causes itself to be indicated to itself as a being-in-the-midst-of-the-world by the world which it realizes' (Sartre 1943/1956: 318). My body as it is for me 'is therefore in no way a contingent addition to my soul; on the contrary it is a permanent structure of my being and a permanent condition of possibility for my consciousness as consciousness *of* the world' (ibid. 328).

Accordingly, we must provide a characterization of the body which allows the full-fledged consideration of the 'paradox of human subjectivity': on the one hand, the body is lived subjectively as 'one's own' while this bodily self-consciousness is not reduced to inner experiences but lived as the bodily belonging to the world of the subject, among other worldly things; on the other hand, the body that belongs to the world cannot be reduced to any other worldly thing but must encompass a lived subjectivity, including the ability to experience worldly things (Barbaras 2008*a*: 38).

Describing the body in a way that does justice to this 'paradox' is not easy and is threatened by a vicious circularity: how can the body be constitutive of the appearance of objects in the world when it is itself an object in the world (Zahavi 2003: 101)? Phenomenologists' considerations of the body often focus on the distinction between the physical body considered in its objectivity (*Körper*) and the body lived in its subjectivity (*Leib*). However, merely underlining that the latter is irreducible to the former does not help here, notably because this opens up a 'body–body' problem (Hanna and Thompson 2003), that is, the problem of understanding how 'our lived body is a performance of our living body, something our body enacts in living' (Thompson 2007: 237). Here, we find ourselves back to our initial problem: on the basis of the distinction between the subjective and intentional modes of givenness of consciousness, we concluded that we needed to understand their co-constitution, i.e. to understand the self as being constitutively a subject-in-the-world. Given that, as just argued, the self is bodily, we now need to consider how the body itself is experienced as a bodily-subject-in-the-world.

The subjective body

Maine de Biran is often considered as one of the first 'philosophers of the *body*'. He argues that the self is not a 'pure abstract concept'. He adds that the experience of self resides neither in desire, need, malaise, nor in any general capacity to *sense*. Rather, it is constituted in one's individual power to *act* (1852/1952: 208–42). Given this accentuation of action over and against sensation, it might be more relevant to qualify Maine de Biran as a philosopher of *agency*: The feeling of our very existence, the origin of 'me', coincides with the feeling of 'active force' (ibid. 207). Maine de Biran describes the experience of voluntary effort as composed of two elements: (i) the feeling of the force which produces the movement and (ii) the sensory effect of muscular contraction. The sensory effect is common to both voluntary movement and passive, automatic, compulsory movements (like the heartbeat). The force, by contrast, is specific of voluntary movements, and for that reason, it is specific of my movements felt as *my own*, felt as being under *my* control (ibid. 147). This feeling of force is not received in any way, but is self-generated, and as such, it is the origin of self-consciousness (ibid. 173). By contrast, sensations are founded on material organization from which I am foreign, and can thus be reduced to matter (ibid. 174). Maine de Biran thus argues that the sense of self is constituted as a sense of being a subject of effort (ibid. 234–5), by our effortful movement determined willfully. Open your eyes in the dark, prick up your ears in silence, contract your muscles in rest: suspend all impression from the outside, and you'll get a 'pure personal element' (p. 243). By contrast, maintain sensations but suppress all self-generated action, and the person would then be only 'virtual' (p. 243).

On the basis of his reading of Maine de Biran, Michel Henry (1965) developed a philosophy and phenomenology of the body and defined a 'subjective body'. He argued that the fact that a subject has a body is not merely a contingent fact (ibid. 2); and he defended this view by defining the very nature of the body as subjective: 'In fact, our body is originally neither a biological body, nor a living body, nor a human body, it belongs to a radically different ontological region which is the one of absolute subjectivity' (ibid. 11). This ontology defines the 'real body, and not only the idea of the body' as a 'subjective being' (ibid. 78). In this sense, Henry, following Maine de Biran, intended to 'undermine materialism in its very foundation' (ibid. 15). Indeed, this view requires a 'rigorous dissociation' between, on the one hand, the subjective body felt as one's own (as oneself) and, on the other hand, the body characterized as a muscular mass (ibid. 90).

This quick description of Henry's position should suffice to underline the contrast between two ways to acknowledge the subjectivity of the body. One view would follow Henry's ontological dissociation between the biological and subjective body. Since this view deprives the 'subjective body' of its materiality, since it dissociates the living and the lived body, subjectivity can be considered as bodily only in a metaphorical sense (Barbaras 2008a: 9). In fact, in a radical inversion,

Henry defines the body as what is traditionally opposed to it, that is, immanent subjectivity (ibid. 35). But Henry himself underlined the opposition between his view and another one which he attributes to Merleau-Ponty: in the second edition of his *Philosophie et phénoménologie du corps* (1987), Henry warns that

> the content of this first work does not owe anything to contemporary research from Merleau-Ponty, which I was unaware of at this time. It differs from it totally. If the body is subjective, its nature depends on that of subjectivity. On this point my conceptions are radically opposed to those of German and French phenomenology... today, I haven't changed anything in the text. It is on this essential basis that my later research has developed.

In sharp contrast with Henry, Merleau-Ponty rejects the dissociation between the lived and the living body while acknowledging their differentiation. Following this line of thought, the bodily self is not reducible to 'pure auto-affection but rather contains a relation to exteriority' (Barbaras 2008b: 7–8). It is with this latter idea that the present investigation concurs, in the attempt to characterize the self-as-subject as non-metaphorically bodily.

The bodily template of the world

In Husserl's phenomenology, the body contributes to the constitution of perceptual appearances via kinesthesis (from the Ancient Greek *cineå*, to put in motion and *aesthåsis*, sensation), the experience of one's bodily movements. Kinesthesis is conceived by Husserl as the condition of possibility for the constitution of an object as one, across the variation of its apparitions. This position is grounded on the view that an appearing object never appears all at once: it always transcends its current appearance. To be experienced as such, that is, to be experienced as one over and above the collection of its appearances, the object must be experienced from various perspectives. This variation of perspective, however, cannot in itself suffice for the constitution of the unified identity of the object. This is where kinesthesis comes into play: kinesthesis ensures the continuity of one's subjective perspective across its variations, and in turn allows the unification of the appearances of the object, by linking the different profiles of an object to each other, thanks to their respective anchoring to the perceiving subject's kinesthesis. Kinesthesis therefore somehow prefigures the variations of appearing objects: 'Perceptual intentionality is a movement that can only be effectuated by an embodied subject' (Zahavi 1994: 68).

On this basis, it has been argued that 'every worldly experience is mediated by and made possible by our embodiment' (Zahavi 2003: 98–9). It may be tempting but misleading to associate this view to another one, according to which 'A sense of one's own spatial organization can become a sense of the spatial order of things around one: the body is a template to measure things in the world . . . The arrangement of one's body mirrors that of the object touched; in being aware of the former one can attend to the latter' (Martin 1992: 205–6). This view is however profoundly misleading if it assumes the equivalence of body-consciousness and world-consciousness. Superficially, it may seem that body and world are experienced equivalently, because touch is taken as the paradigm of bodily-consciousness and because 'in touch we directly appeal to the tactile properties of our own bodies by investigating the self-same tactile properties of other bodies . . . the space and solidity of our bodies provides the access to the space and solidity of other bodies' (O'Shaughnessy 1989: 38). By contrast with this view, and in line with the mode of givenness of the self-as-subject described above, I will further develop below (section 5) the idea that the body is experienced as-subject and as such it is experienced as a transparency through which the world appears. At this level, it is not experienced as an object which would provide a template for the experience of correlated things experienced (touched) in the world. Rather than considering that body-consciousness is the template of world-consciousness, which involves two different, successive but equivalent events of consciousness, it is important to consider how body- and world-consciousness (at this level) belong to one and a single act of consciousness, constituted by two irreducible but inseparable modes of givenness (the bodily subjectivity and the intentionality of this experience): 'external perception and the perception of one's own body vary in conjunction because they are the two facets of one and the same act . . . every external perception is immediately synonymous with a certain perception of my body' (Merleau-Ponty 1945/1962: 237–8). Note that this 'synonymy' implies that we do not first experience our body and from it infer states of the world, or the other way around: 'the consciousness of the world is not based on self-consciousness: they are strictly contemporary' (ibid. 345). This view has also been defended by Husserl who considered that 'the body is not first given for us and subsequently used to investigate the world. On the contrary, the world is given to us as bodily investigated, and the body is revealed to us in this exploration of the world' (Zahavi 2003: 105; see also Zahavi 1998: 4, 7; 1994: 79). In the rest of this chapter, I will describe different forms of bodily self-consciousness in order to provide some experiential clarification of such self–world intertwining.

Words of caution

In the following sections, I will propose a number of distinctions, notably the distinction between the extension and materiality (Husserl's terms) of the bodily self. It should be clear that the point of these distinctions is not to argue that one aspect (e.g. extension) can come along without others (e.g. materiality). The point is rather to argue that, even if they factually or constitutively accompany each other, these aspects cannot be reduced to each other.

Moreover, different perceptual modalities (e.g. touch and vision) participate in their own way in different forms of bodily self-consciousness. Nonetheless, it is important to remember throughout this investigation that the relevant distinctions here concern different modes of givenness of bodily self-consciousness, not different modalities of body-related information. To put it differently, the present account is not primarily about how different modalities participate differently in the sense of being a bodily self but is rather primarily about how a given modality can be experienced in multiple ways, thereby phenomenally constituting different modes of givenness of the bodily self.

4. FOUR FORMS OF BODILY CONSCIOUSNESS

If the self is bodily in a non-metaphorical sense, then bodily self-consciousness always involves the intermingling of subjective and intentional aspects. To clarify the multiple forms that this intermingling can take in one's experience, I will now describe a simple example, which unfolds in four steps:

(1) I see a rose within reaching distance.
(2) I reach out, my hand moves towards the rose.
(3) Getting closer, I remember that roses are delicate but thorns are sharp, I thus pay attention to the movement of my hand so that I damage neither the rose nor my hand. I touch the rose, squeeze its stem and feel a sudden pain at the tip of my finger.
(4) I scrutinize the skin of my finger in the attempt to detect a hidden thorn.

This simple scenario is characterized by four different forms of bodily self-consciousness. Notice that some or all of them are paradigmatically lived in conjunction with each other but here I present them successively to better analyze their specific characteristics.

1. When I experience the rose as being in front of me, within reaching distance, I don't take myself as an intentional object but I experience myself, specifically *as-subject*. In particular, I experience the anchoring of my perspective in my body, and the orientation of my body towards the rose (see section 5).

2. When I experience my moving hand while attending to the rose, I take neither my hand nor my movements as intentional objects, but again I experience *myself-as-subject*. The difference from the previous moment of the scenario is that I am not only conscious of the localization and orientation of my body towards an

object of the world (the rose). Rather, I am also conscious of my body itself; for example, I experience the contraction of my muscles, the velocity of my moving hand, the touch of my skin on rose leaves, etc. (see section 6).

3. When I pay attention to my movement, I experience myself in a different way, namely, by explicitly, overtly taking myself (my moving hand) *as-object*. Nonetheless, in this case, I experience the intentional object in its *subjectivity*, namely, I experience subjective control. When I touch the rose stem and experience pain, my attention is directed to my painful finger tip. I explicitly, overtly take myself *as-object* and experience this peculiar intentional object in its *subjectivity*, namely, its painfulness (see section 7).

4. When I scrutinize my finger in the attempt to detect a hidden thorn, I take myself as an *object* of experience but this case importantly differs from the aforementioned one. Indeed, by taking my finger as an object of *scrutiny*, I do *not* specifically access it in its subjectivity. On the contrary, I experience it in its objectivity: as it is penetrable and penetrated by another object (the thorn), it deploys its belongingness to the physical realm, and I could adopt the same scrutinizing observation to find a thorn in *your* finger. In this sense, even if this is the most explicit and most commonly studied form of self-consciousness, it is also the least subjective: this mode of access is not specific to myself (see section 8).

In the rest of this chapter, I will detail these four forms of bodily self-consciousness and argue that they are not reducible to each other and that each of them is bodily in a non-metaphorical sense. I will specifically exploit the descriptions of these four forms of bodily self-consciousness to shed light on what it means to be a bodily-subject-in-the-world, that is, what it means that one's subjectivity is intentional. For this reason, I will focus on cases (1) and (2), while cases (3) and (4) won't be detailed at length here.

5. THE SELF-AS-SUBJECT AS A LOCALIZED AND ORIENTED VOLUME

Orientation

Let us start with the most subtle form of self-consciousness (first step of the above scenario), for instance the experience of an element in the world as being located relative to oneself. Husserl allows the generalization of this point:

each thing that appears has *eo ipso* an orienting relation to the Body, and this refers not only to what actually appears but to each thing that is supposed to be able to appear. If I am imagining a centaur I cannot help but imagine it as in a certain orientation and in a particular relation to my sense organs: it is 'to the right' of me; it is 'approaching' me or 'moving away;' it is 'revolving,' turning toward or away from 'me'—from me, i.e., from my Body, from my eye, which is directed at it. (Husserl 1913/1952: pii. 61–2)

Given this characterization, it is also relevant to mention that the eye, the eye qua seeing, the eye-as-subject, is not itself seen: 'The eye does not appear visually . . . Naturally, one would not say that I see my eye in the mirror. For my eye, the seeing qua seeing, I do not perceive' (ibid. 155). The seeing body is thus *transparent* in the sense that one experiences the world *through* it. This notion of transparency, however, can be understood in at least two concurrent ways (Legrand 2005).

Transparency

Transparency as invisibility and pre-noetic embodiment

In a first understanding, transparency is interpreted as invisibility. This leads to the idea that at this level, one's subjective perspective is factually anchored to one's body, while this anchoring dimension of the body is not experienced at all by the subject. According to Shaun Gallagher, this would be a pre-noetic form of embodiment which concerns 'aspects of the structure of consciousness that are . . . hidden, those that may be . . . difficult to get at because they happen *before we know it*' (2005: 2). What matters here is thus not bodily experience. Rather, what matters is that the self and mental states are shaped '*prenoetically* by the fact that they are embodied' (idid.). Such factual, non-experiential, pre-noetic embodiment is certainly a very important and interesting one, but it doesn't address the point at stake here, since the present investigation focuses on bodily self-*consciousness*.

Transparency vs. invisibility

A second and concurrent interpretation of transparency underlines that transparency is *not* invisibility. As Merleau-Ponty says (1945/1962: 345) about consciousness, we operate here at a level where the subject is neither posited nor ignored. Rather, the subject is 'not concealed' from experience, which means that perceptual experience in some way announces the bodily subject, even when the body is not itself taken as a perceptual object. The important point here is that the subject is transparent as it is absent-as-object but it remains non-invisible as it is experienced specifically as subject.

The elusive body

We are operating here with a very subtle form of bodily consciousness. Indeed, the body here is not taken as an intentional object of experience, and it is not even experienced in the background or periphery of one's attentional field. This is precisely what it means to be transparent: it is not looked at, not even peripherally. However, if the anchoring body is not itself taken as an object of perception at this level, if all we get is the experience of a transparent subject, is it justified to claim that the subjective perspective is *experientially* (and not only factually) anchored to the body, or are we left with a subjective perspective which is transparently experienced but which is not experienced as *bodily*?

Voluminosity

Husserl characterizes the body in a way that helps to clarify the mode of givenness of the transparent subject as bodily. In particular, he distinguishes between bodies which are extended and mental states which are not extended. To avoid any confusion potentially linked to the notion of extension used in various contexts, I will use here the notion of voluminosity: the body is voluminous in a way mental states are not. Given this characteristic, it is relevant to consider whether the transparent subject can be adequately said to be voluminous. If yes, then it is bodily in a non-metaphorical sense; if no, then it is not bodily or only metaphorically so.

Capturing the specificity of voluminosity, Husserl argues the following:

Even the ghost necessarily has its ghostly Body . . . the case would be thinkable (and an actual ghost would result) that a psychic being would appear and be actual while lacking a *material* Body . . . But this still does not imply that a Body in every sense is lacking or would be lacking . . . A ghost is characterized by the fact that its Body is a pure 'spatial phantom' with no material properties at all . . . A psychic subject without a material Body is indeed thinkable, i.e. as a ghost instead of a natural animal being, but *in no way without a Body of some kind.* (1913/1952: ii. 100–1; my emphasis)

To avoid any confusing talk about non-material bodies, instead of contrasting extension to materiality, I will rather contrast voluminosity to the localization of sensations in/on one's skin boundary. I take Husserl's characterization of the ghostly body as a thought-experiment illustrating the thinkable possibility of characterizing the body by its voluminosity, independently of bodily sensations: the ghost would have the former but not the latter. This thought-experiment allows characterizing the subtle form of bodily self-consciousness that I intend to describe here: one's transparent subjectivity is experienced as bodily voluminous and this experiential dimension is irreducible to (is not necessarily mediated by) bodily sensations.

Husserl conceives of the body as characterized both by its voluminosity and by bodily sensations but argues that the body is *experienced* only thanks to bodily sensations while voluminosity would not be experienced. Here, I follow Husserl's distinction between voluminosity and sensations but propose that one's voluminosity is *experienced* in its specificity. This implies that experiencing bodily sensations is not the only way to experience one's body. Rather, the bodily self experiences itself as a volume localized in space and oriented relative to things in the world. As described above, in vision, we do not see the seeing; nonetheless, we experience ourselves as the seeing subject, as anchoring the visual field. Moreover, we experience this seeing subject as a voluminous subject. This volume may not be experienced as 'this specific volume', and voluminosity may not be experientially contrasted with 'thinness' or 'flatness'. Rather, what matters at this level is that one experiences oneself as a volume *by experiencing one's location and orientation in space*: through his vision of an object in front of him, the seeing subject experiences himself as having a back and front, a right and left, a down and up. In seeing in front of you, you do experience the very fact that you do not see behind your head. In other terms, the seeing subject experiences the very fact that he has a voluminous, localized, and oriented body structured in such a way that only forward-looking is possible. This position contrasts with the claim that 'vision offers a view of the world that is seemingly uncorrupted by the body' (Ratcliffe 2008: 300). Rather, one must acknowledge the bodily presence of the invisible in the experience of the voluminosity, location, and orientation of one's body: *the experienced spatiality of the world is correlational to the experienced voluminosity-location-orientation of one's body.*

Voluminosity vs. zero-point of orientation

Among the main contributions of the body to the constitution of perceptual appearances, phenomenologists classically mention the body as the necessary anchoring point of one's perspective on the world. It is the 'here' from where anything is experienced: 'Every perspectival appearance presupposes that the experiencing subject is himself given in space. However, since the subject only possesses a spatial location due to its embodiment, Husserl claims that spatial objects can only appear for and be constituted by *embodied subjects*' (Zahavi 1994: 65). Pace Husserl, however, the body-anchoring subjective perspective would be better characterized as an *orienting volume* than as 'the bearer of the zero point of orientation' (1913/1952: ii. 61–2).

The characterization of bodily self-consciousness as involving the basic experience of one's body as an orienting volume presents the advantage of being both genuinely subjective and genuinely bodily. On the one hand, it is genuinely bodily because I am here conscious of an aspect which is specific of bodies: voluminosity. On the other hand, this form of bodily self-consciousness is genuinely subjective because I experience this volume as oriented subjectively by an act of consciousness. Moreover, I experience this subjective orientation without taking it as an intentional object of my experience. All together, I thus experience myself as a bodily subject at this level. Such bodily self-consciousness proceeds by a 'detour' through the outer world, but there is in fact no shorter way towards oneself than one's exteriorization in the world (Barbaras 2008a: 111). In this view, the subject is bodily self-conscious not despite the fact that he is intentionally oriented towards the outer world but thanks to this intentional orientation: directing one's objectifying gaze/touch away from oneself is the very condition to be conscious of oneself specifically as being a bodily subject. Notice that, given the transparency of the subject here, this form of experience is particularly elusive, but also particularly pervasive. At this level, 'there is a world for me because I am not unaware of myself, and I am not concealed from myself because I have a world' (Merleau-Ponty 1945/1962: 347).

Bodily self-consciousness beyond one's skin boundary

Voluminosity, location, and orientation are not experienced only as modalities of bodily sensations. The important point here is that the body is experienced as located in a space that extends beyond its boundaries, rather than being merely experienced thanks to the localization of sensations in/on its own boundaries. Here, bodily self-consciousness goes beyond the skin boundary of the body proper, as it corresponds to the experience of the world as disclosed by the body, to the 'center of reference which things indicate' (Sartre 1943/1956: 320). At this level, one is transitively conscious of objects in the world, and by the same token, one is intransitively conscious of one's bodily subjectivity. In this sense, experiencing one's body here amounts to experiencing the space around one's body and, in particular, the bodily orientation of this space.

This last phrasing opens up the consideration of the role of the 'world' in constituting bodily self-consciousness. From the description given up to now, it appears that one is conscious of oneself as one relates to the world beyond oneself. Going one step further, one may be tempted to eradicate any asymmetry between the subject and the world he is living in. In such a view, 'there can be no talk of a privileged localization of one's lived-body ... The objectively appearing formation of the perceived world erects its own center for itself' (Holenstein 1999: 60). The way the subject stands in front of various objects in the world is not left to 'our own power' (ibid. 81). Rather, it is due to the arrangement of things themselves. Accordingly, 'the lived body of the perceiving subject behaves no differently than any perceived object, as far as its localization is concerned' (ibid. 58). Given the present account, it is surely interesting to reinforce the consideration of the very structure of the world and objects. However, I think that there is a relevant way to acknowledge that the subject has no 'dominating role' in that the world/objects are intrinsically structured, while keeping the subject as the anchoring point of his own perspective. In particular, the structure of the world/objects appears only from a subjective perspective which has to be bodily anchored and experienced as such. Moreover, the 'zero-point of orientation' is in any case not the 'I' determined by a 'grasp on ourselves and our psychic abilities' criticized by Holenstein (1999: 81). Rather, according to the above argumentation, it is the voluminous-located-oriented body anchoring one's perspective on the world extending beyond one's boundary, and this is compatible with the consideration of the objective structure of the world. Even in a view where 'a complex perception gives itself polycentrically' (ibid.), it must be considered that there remains an asymmetry between self and world. Indeed, 'we can only perceive perspectivally' (ibid. 82): the perspective is given by and to a subject; it does not exist if there is no subject since objects do not have perspective on each other. Therefore, the consideration of the world-embeddedness of bodily self-consciousness and the implied co-foundational view of the self does not require 'a distinctive phenomenology that can explore "an intentionality of a wholly different type . . . an "inversion" of intentionality' (Westphal 2007: 168). Rather, such a view does not prevent acknowledging an asymmetry such that subject and intentional object are irreducible and irreversible (ibid. 184). The specificity of the subject notably consists of its bodily anchoring of a subjective perspective.

6. The Self-as-Subject as the Bearer of Bodily Sensations

What distinguishes human bodies from hypothetical ghosts is bodily sensations which the subject experiences by localizing sensations in/on his body (see step 2 of the 'rose' scenario described above, section 4), that is, the body as 'a bearer of sensations' (Husserl 1913/1952: ii. 161). Notice again that such bodily sensations are not constitutive of the aforementioned form of bodily self-consciousness (the self-as-subject as a localized and oriented volume).

Touching and touched: the voluptuous body

Bodily sensations like touch become relevant here. For example, I experience my touching hand when I explore an object to evaluate its texture. In this case, I do not take myself as an intentional object but I experience myself-as-subject by experiencing touch. In particular, I experience my touching hand in a specific way which is not available for any other object, hence the characterization of this experience as a form of consciousness of the self-as-subject. This form of self-consciousness gives me a sense of the opacity of my body, over and above the transparency of its voluminosity, localization, and orientation described above.

Note that the self-as-subject is not only the active touching subject, but also the receptive touched subject, for example when your skin is touched by a crawling spider, by the hand of your lover, or more prosaically by the edge of a table. What such receptive touch offers is the experience of the opacity of my subjectivity in a way that does not objectify it, that is, in a way that fully preserves subjectivity by avoiding turning it into an intentional object. An intentional object is surely present in the experience (the spider, the hand of your lover, the table), but the self is not objectified even if it is touched.

'Don't give me that look': touched by your gaze

The experience of myself as the 'bearer of sensations' is not restricted to the tactile modality. Indeed, I can experience myself not only as being touched, but also as being seen. Again, this experience has multiple dimensions. First, as developed by Sartre, 'with the appearance of the Other's look I experience the revelation of my being-as-object' (Sartre 1943/1956: 351). But this objectivation of my body when others look at it cannot be all there is to the experience of being seen by others.

In fact the other's gaze transforms me into an object, and mine him, only if both of us withdraw into the core of our thinking nature, if we both make ourselves into an inhuman gaze, if each of us feels his actions to be not taken up and understood, but observed as if they were an insect's. . . . A dog's gaze directed towards me causes me no embarrassment. (Merleau-Ponty 1945/1962: 420)

I'll leave aside the dog's gaze to take up the embarrassment which I feel when others look at me. Embarrassment, or comfort, etc. are among the sensations which are, like touch, immediately localized in/on my body, and are elicited when I am seen by others. Such experiences thus also deploy the opacity of my subjectivity by eliciting bodily sensations, and without necessarily objectifying it. This deployment of one's subjective opacity derives from the experience of sensations in/on one's body (Husserl 1913/1952: ii) but is nonetheless basic.

Under my skin and beyond

'Is it cold here or is it just me?': feeling the world out there

The discussion that precedes contrasts the experience of the self-as-subject as a bodily volume localized and oriented in a space that extends beyond its own skin and the experience of the self-as-subject as the bearer of bodily sensations localized in/on one's skin boundary. This contrast, however, should not give the misleading impression that, in the latter case, bodily experiences shrink the subject's experience to his skin limits. Bodily sensations should not be thought of as being 'non-intentional bodily sensations, but rather crucial carriers of world-directed intentionality' (Slaby, 2008: 430), that is, 'feelings which are intentionally direc-ted not just at one's body and its physiological changes, but rather at the world beyond the body' (ibid. 434). Similarly, Goldie argues that 'bodily feelings, includ-ing the bodily feelings involved in emotional experience, can tell you things not just about the condition of your body and the sort of emotion you are experiencing, but also about other parts of the world beyond the surface of your body (and what comes into physical contact with it)' (2002: 238). Furthermore, Goldie also defines 'feelings towards' which are feelings directly directed towards objects in the world. Accordingly, both the transparent voluminous-located-oriented body and opaque bodily sensations relate the subject to the external world. However, they do so in fundamentally different ways, as the next section will further develop.

'Don't be so touchy': the necessity of pre-tactile bodily self-consciousness

In philosophical considerations of the constitution of the lived body, the experience of the voluminous-located-oriented body is neglected, in favor of the experience of the body as the bearer of bodily sensations. This, however, is a mistake. It is classically thought that 'the capacity for tactile-sense [and] the capacity for body-sense, i.e. immediate body-awareness . . . rigorously require one another' (O'Shaughnessy 1989: 40) and that 'body-sense is blind in the following sense: that it is not made for accord with sight, since it is itself pre-visual and has nothing to do with sight, being so to say born in the dark' (ibid. 55). I disagree with both claims: bodily self-consciousness is primarily constituted through the experience of the structure of the (visual) percep-tual field, and before the localization of (tactile) sensations on the body. This is what the preceding sections intended to describe at the experiential level. In the current section, I intend to argue that the experience of bodily sensations and their embedding material world presupposes the experience of the transparency of the voluminous-located-oriented body: 'our bodily experience would by far exceed the experience of the body. In a way similar to how, in Husserl's view, our experience of time presup-poses the temporality of experience itself, the experience of our body would presup-pose the corporeality of experience itself' (Waldenfels 2004: 236). This consideration is fully coherent with the present proposal which emphasizes that bodily self-conscious-ness does not arise from a unique property of touch (or double touch, see section 7) but is pervasive in perception, even in perceptual acts which do not involve the localization of sensations on/in the body.

Following Carman's work, the issue at stake here can be framed as a debate between Husserl and Merleau-Ponty. According to Husserl, 'The body as such can be constituted originally *only in tactuality* and in everything localized within the sensations of touch, such as warmth, cold, pain, and the like' (1913/1952: ii. 150). Carman underlines that on Merleau-Ponty's account, this view 'amounts instead to a kind of privative modification of our prior bodily self-understanding' (1945/1962:

222). The body experienced through bodily sensations is 'a kind of quasi-objective thing with which I identify thanks to the localization in it of my subjective sensations' (Carman 1999: 222–3). However, such experience presupposes that I already experience myself as bodily in a more primary manner: the very possibility to localize sensations on *my* body presupposes a form of bodily self-consciousness which does not rely on the identification of bodily properties as mine, nor on the identification of bodily feelings as carried by me. As argued for by Shoemaker (1968), self-consciousness cannot rely only on object-identification: I do not first experience a neutral or anonymous experience, then ask the question 'Whose experience is this actually?' to finally find myself as the subject of these experiences (Legrand 2007*a*). This holds as well for identification of one's body as one's own (Legrand 2006): the identification of one's body as the bearer of one's bodily sensations cannot ground consciousness of the bodily subject (Legrand 2007*b*). Before being, and for becoming the 'bearer of sensations' (Husserl 1913/1952: ii. 161), the body is 'our general means of having a world' (Merleau-Ponty, 1945/1962: 146) and it is experienced as such.

Another, complementary, way to argue for this view goes as follows. To be non-metaphorically a bodily self, one needs to experience oneself as a body in a space extending beyond oneself. For that, there must be a form of bodily self-consciousness that is not restricted to the location of sensations in/on one's body. Let me unpack these claims. First, by its physicality, the body belongs to the physical world and experiencing the body thus involves experiencing its embeddedness in the physical world: 'we are aware of ourselves as bounded and limited within a world that extends beyond us' (Martin 1992: 201). Moreover, anything experienced in the way one's body is experienced is experienced as being one's body: 'anything which one feels in this way is taken to be part of one's body' (ibid.). It follows that, for experiencing the body as such, it is not enough to localize sensations in/on one's body: this would prevent the experience of the physical world embedding the body, that is, it would prevent the experience of the world-embeddedness of the physical body, which is an intrinsic feature of the body as physical without which it would make only metaphorical sense to say that one experiences oneself as a bodily subject:

one feels oneself to have a certain shape and size in a space which contains one and extends beyond one. This space, which extends beyond one's body, cannot be a place where one feels a limb or sensation to be since then it would no longer appear to be somewhere which falls outside one's body but would come to appear to be part of it. (Ibid. 202)

According to Martin 'the sensations can only feel to be internal to the body where one has a sense of a space extending beyond possible locations of sensations and hence beyond any such sensory field' (ibid. 209). I'm adding that this sense of space extending beyond one's bodily limits is itself correlative to a form of bodily self-consciousness, described above as the experience of the body as a volume located and oriented in space.

7. THE SUBJECTIVE ACCESS TO THE SELF-AS-OBJECT

We just differentiated two forms of bodily consciousness of the self-as-subject which are irreducible to each other and are both bodily in a non-metaphorical sense. An equivalent investigation must be done with consciousness of the self-as-object: is it uni- or multi-form? Because the present focus is on the self-as-subject, this issue will be addressed much more concisely. In particular, the question here is whether the subject necessarily ends experiencing its bodily subjectivity the moment the body is taken as an intentional object of experience. Is perceiving one's body necessarily equivalent to perceiving anything in the world?

Touching myself

For Husserl, one of the reasons why touch is primordial for the constitution of the lived body is because it is extended in a way that allows double touch: my left hand can touch my right one. What matters here is 'the way my Body as touched is something touching which is touched' (Husserl 1913/1952: ii. 155). By contrast with this identification of the touching and touched body, Merleau-Ponty rather acknowledges that double touch gives me two irreducible experiences: the hand as touching which I experience as subject, and the hand as touched which I experience as object (1945/1962: 105): '[in double touch] what we have is neither the perception of two objects (O'Shaughnessy) nor the perception of one object that can be attended to in two different ways (Martin). Instead, touch is the relationship between touching and touched' (Ratcliffe 2008: 309).

It is surely important to retain that these two experiences are not reducible to each other. However, it is also important to underline that the touched hand does not lose its subjectivity altogether (see step 3 of the 'rose' scenario described above, section 4): it cannot be reduced to a set of muscles and bones. Rather, the self-touched hand 'gives itself in exteriority without being developed as an object' (Barbaras 2008b: 7–8): what is special in double touch is that the two hands are experienced as subjective but in different ways. The touching hand is experienced as-subject, and the touched hand is taken as-object without losing its subjectivity. In double touch, I thus experience the opening of my subjectivity to itself without the intermediary of any objectifying experience. I do not experience my touched hand by reading the world, by discovering a special object in the world. Rather, in double touch, I experience myself as a touched subject, leading to the aforementioned opacity of subjectivity (also accessible in passive single touch) *without any detour through the external objectified world* (unlike other modalities, and unlike single touch).

Bodily reflectivity

Double touch does not only bring the experience of sensations localized in/on one's body. Single receptive touch is sufficient for that. More specifically, double touch also opens the different aspects of subjectivity to each other (by linking the touched to the touching subject). Accordingly, perceiving oneself is not reducible to perceiving an object (Legrand and Ravn 2009). Interestingly, this form of experience of the body's subjectivity is perceptual but not reifying: the body can be experienced as subjective, while being taken as the attentional/intentional object of perception: 'Although our inspection of the body implies its objectivation, it does not imply a total suspension of its subjectivity' (Zahavi 1994: 72).

Such self-perception can be characterized as a form of reflective self-consciousness, if the term 'reflective' refers to a structure of experience where one accesses oneself as such. Double touch would thus provide some bodily roots to reflectivity. This latter point interestingly echoes Merleau-Ponty when he says that: 'the body . . . tries to touch itself while being touched, and initiates "a kind of reflection" which is sufficient to distinguish it from objects' (1945/1962: 107). Following the terminology used by Varela *et al.* (1991: 27), this form of self-consciousness can also be called 'embodied reflection', that is, a form of reflection 'in which body and mind have been brought together'. Following the terminology used by Gallagher and Marcel (1999: 25), it may also be called 'embedded reflection', that is, 'a first-person reflective consciousness that is embedded in a pragmatically or socially contextualized intentional attitude and the corresponding actions'.

8. THE ANALYTIC ACCESS TO THE SELF-AS-OBJECT

It is important to underline that not every type of perceptual experience avoids reifying subjectivity (see step 4 of the 'rose' scenario described above, section 4). The paradigmatic form of spontaneous perception does. However, such perception importantly differs from scrutinizing observation. The difference is not a matter of attention but of reification. Both perception and scrutiny can be attentively focused, but only scrutinizing involves a reification of the intentional object. This is the case whenever you 'fix your gaze' and adopt an 'analytical attitude' (Merleau-Ponty 1945/1962: 262) in order to scrutinize, for example, the wrinkles at the corner of your friend's eyes or a scar on your finger. It is not paradigmatically the case, however, when you perceive (even attentively) your friend's facial expression while talking to him, or the scar on your finger while trying on a new ring. The point here is that, even if subjectivity can be expressed bodily, in a way that makes it accessible directly in perception, it would nonetheless be alienated by the reification involved in scrutiny.

Here it is worth noting that it is problematic that both empirical and phenomenological investigations of bodily consciousness primarily focus either on pathological movements disrupted in their adaptation to the task/environment or disrupted in their fluidity, or on very simple and rather isolated everyday movements like holding a cup or pointing to one's nose. Such investigations neglect important components which are evidently present in whole-body movements and spontaneous actions. The latter are best suited for the investigation of the perceivability of bodily subjectivity as they do not impose any scrutinizing/reifying attitude (Legrand and Ravn 2009).

9. SUMMARIZING CONCLUSION

The experience of the body-as-intentional-object is an 'aberrant type of appearance' (Sartre 1943/1956: 357) as it does not give us 'the body as it acts and perceives but only as it is acted on and perceived' (ibid. 358). It is however important to recognize that this 'aberrant' type of consciousness is constitutive of the experience of oneself as being bodily in a non-metaphorical sense. Indeed, the body is constitutively opaque, thus visible, touchable, perceivable, that is, take-able as intentional object of perceptual experience. As we saw above, there are two ways to experience one's body at this level: one way disrupts the body's subjectivity (section 8) while the other doesn't (section 7). Moreover, and more generally, intentionality is not an 'aberrant' aspect of subjective experience. Quite on the contrary, the experience of oneself-as-subject involves the experience of oneself as oriented towards intentional objects from one's first-person perspective (section 5) and the experience of oneself as in contact with intentional objects through one's bodily feelings (section 6).

The present investigation is intended to show that it is partly misleading to claim that one's body most of the time 'disappears' from one's consciousness (Leder 1990). Indeed, such a claim should not hide the fact that we constantly experience our body in a rich and complex manner, even if not explicitly. Moreover, *all* the forms of self-consciousness described here are bodily in a non-metaphorical manner and illustrate how subjectivity and intentionality are co-constitutive of the bodily self: the physical body can be taken as intentional object and be experienced as expressing its subjectivity (section 7); it can also be taken as intentional object and be experienced as fully belonging to the physical world in which it is embedded (section 8); the subject can be experienced specifically as-subject, while being experienced through its bodily dimensions of voluminosity-location-orientation (section 5) and opacity (section 6).

REFERENCES

BARBARAS, R. (2008a). *Introduction à une phénoménologie de la vie* (Paris: Vrin).

——(2008b). 'Life, Movement and Desire', *Research in Phenomenology*, 38: 3–17.

CARMAN, T. (1999). 'The Body in Husserl and Merleau-Ponty', *Philosophical Topics*, 27/2: 205–26.

GALLAGHER, S. (2005). *How the Body Shapes the Mind* (Oxford: Oxford University Press).

——and MARCEL, A. J. (1999). 'The Self in Contextualized Action', *Journal of Consciousness Studies*, 6/4: 4–30.

GOLDIE, P. (2002). 'Emotions, Feelings and Intentionality', *Phenomenology and the Cognitive Sciences*, 1: 235–54.

HANNA, R., and THOMPSON, E. (2003). 'The Mind–Body–Body Problem', *Theoria et Historia Scientiarum*, 7/1/200: 23–42.

HENRY, M. (1965). *Philosophie et phénoménologie du corps: Essai sur l'ontologie Biranienne* (Paris: Presse Universitaire de France).

HOLENSTEIN, E. (1999). 'The Zero-Point of Orientation: The Placement of the I in Perceived Space', in D. Welton, *The Body: Classic and Contemporary Readings* (Oxford: Blackwell), 57–94.

HUSSERL, E. (1913/1952). *Ideas Pertaining to a Pure Phenomenology and to a Phenomenological Philosophy* (Ideen zu einer reinen Phänomenologie und phänomenologischen Philosophie), tr. R. Rojcewicz and A. Schuwer (Dordrecht: Kluwer Academic Publishers).

——(1934-7/1970). *The Crisis of European Science and Transcendental Phenomenology: An Introduction to Phenomenological Philosophy*, tr. D. Carr (Evanston, Ill.: Northwestern University Press).

LEDER, D. (1990). *The Absent Body* (Chicago: University of Chicago Press).

LEGRAND, D. (2005). 'Transparently Oneself: A Commentary on Metzinger, *Being No One*', *Psyche*, 11(5): 1–23.

——(2006). 'The Bodily Self: The Sensori-Motor Roots of Pre-Reflexive Self-Consciousness', *Phenomenology and the Cognitive Sciences*, 5: 89–118.

——(2007a). 'Naturalizing the Acting Self: Subjective vs. Anonymous Agency', *Philosophical Psychology*, 20/4: 457–78.

——(2007b). 'Pre-Reflective Self-as-Subject from Experiential and Empirical Perspectives', *Consciousness and Cognition*, 16/3: 583–99.

——(2007c). 'Subjectivity and the Body: Introducing Basic Forms of Self-Consciousness', *Consciousness and Cognition*, 16/3: 577–82.

——(2009). 'Two Senses for "Givenness of Consciousness": Commentary on Lyyra' *Phenomenology and the Cognitive Sciences*, 8: 89–94.

——and RAVN, S. (2009). 'Perceiving Subjectivity in Movement: The Case of Dancers', *Phenomenology and the Cognitive Sciences*, 8/3: 389–408.

MAINE DE BIRAN, P. (1852/1952). *Sur la décomposition de la pensée* (Paris: Presse Universitaire de France).

MARTIN, M. (1992). 'Sight and Touch', in Tim Crane (ed.), *The Contents of Experience* (New York: Cambridge University Press), 199–201.

MENSCH, J. R. (2001). *Postfoundational Phenomenology: Husserlian Reflections on Presence and Embodiment* (University Park, Pa.: Pennsylvania State University Press).

MERLEAU-PONTY, M. (1945/1962). *Phenomenology of Perception*, tr. C. Smith (London and New York: Routledge).

O'SHAUGHNESSY, B. (1989). 'The Sense of Touch', *Australasian Journal of Philosophy*, 67/1: 37–58.

RATCLIFFE, M. (2008). 'Touch and Situatedness', *International Journal of Philosophical Studies*, 16/3: 299–322.

ROWLANDS, M. (2008). 'From the Inside: Consciousness and the First-Person Perspective', *International Journal of Philosophical Studies*, 16/3: 281–97.

SARTRE, J.-P. (1943/1956). *Being and Nothingness*, tr. H. E. Barnes (New York: Philosophical Library).

SHOEMAKER, S. (1968). 'Self-Reference and Self-Awareness', *Journal of Philosophy*. 65: 556–79.

SLABY, J. (2008). 'Affective Intentionality and the Feeling Body', *Phenomenology and the Cognitive Sciences*, 7: 429–44.

THOMPSON, E. (2007). *Mind in Life: Biology, Phenomenology and the Sciences of the Mind* (Cambridge, Mass.: Harvard University Press).

VARELA, F. J., THOMPSON, E., and ROSCH, E. (1991). *The Embodied Mind: Cognitive Science and Human Experience* (Cambridge, Mass.: MIT Press).

WALDENFELS, B. (2004). 'Bodily Experience between Selfhood and Otherness', *Phenomenology and the Cognitive Sciences*, 3: 235–48.

WELTON, D. (1999). 'Soft, Smooth Hands: Husserl's Phenomenology of the Lived-Body', in D. Welton, *The Body: Classic and Contemporary Readings* (Oxford: Blackwell), 38–56.

——(2004). 'Affectivity and Body: Prolegomena to a Theory of Incarnate Existence', revision of a lecture given in the Philosophy Dept, Northwestern University, 2 Apr. (www.stonybrook.edu/philosophy/faculty/dwelton/Lecture.6D_with_Bibliogr90AFF2.pdf).

WESTPHAL, M. (2007). 'The Prereflective Cogito as Contaminated Opacity', *Southern Journal of Philosophy*, 45/suppl.: 152–77.

ZAHAVI, D. (1994). 'Husserl's Phenomenology of the Body', *Études Phénoménologiques*, 19: 63–84.

——(1998). 'The Fracture in Self-Awareness', in D. Zahavi (ed.), *Self-Awareness, Temporality and Alterity* (Dordrecht: Kluwer Academic Publishers), 21–40.

——(2003). *Husserl's Phenomenology: Cultural Memory in the Present* (Stanford, Calif.: Stanford University Press).

——(2005). *Subjectivity and Selfhood: Investigating the First-Person Perspective* (Cambridge, Mass.: Bradford Books, MIT Press).

——(2009). 'Philosophy, Psychology, Phenomenology', in S. Heinämaa and M. Reuter (eds.), *Psychology and Philosophy: Inquiries into the Soul from Late Scholasticism to Contemporary Thought* (Dordrecht: Springer), 247–62.

CHAPTER 9

WITNESSING FROM HERE:

SELF-AWARENESS FROM A BODILY VERSUS EMBODIED PERSPECTIVE

AARON HENRY

EVAN THOMPSON

Is every conscious experience characterized by a sense of self or are there experiences that lack this feature? Does the sense of self entail the reality of a self or might the self be an illusion? Although the first question is phenomenological and the second one metaphysical, it is common to give the same answer to both. Aaron Gurwitsch's classic distinction between egological versus nonegological theories of consciousness clearly displays this broad tendency (Gurwitsch 1966). Egological theories affirm that every conscious experience fundamentally includes the awareness of an ego as the subject of the experience. Nonegological theories deny this claim and maintain that unreflective conscious experience is fundamentally ownerless or anonymous or impersonal. Both sides agree, however, that an answer to the metaphysical question of the self's existence presupposes an answer to the phenomenological question about how experience is structured. In this way, phenomenology is taken to guide metaphysics.[1]

---

[1] Cf. Galen Strawson (1997): 'Here I think there is a fundamental dependence: metaphysical investigation of the nature of the self is subordinate to phenomenological investigation of the sense of

Egological and nonegological theories come in various forms. For example, Kant argued that in order to account for the unity of experience, we must posit a non-experiential ego whose synthetic activity confers unity upon an otherwise hetero-geneous and chaotic stream of experience. Such an argument is transcendental; it claims that the concept of self is a presupposition for meaningfully structured experience. John Searle (2000) has recently advanced a similar argument: in his view, the unity of consciousness and the logical form of explanations of volitional action require the postulation of an irreducible self in addition to the sequence of experiences. Nonegological theorists, most notably Sartre (1991) in his *Transcendence of the Ego*, have responded to these kinds of considerations by rejecting the inference to an experience-transcendent principle of unity. Sartre argued that experience has no need of such an external principle of organization. Following Husserl, he maintained that consciousness as a temporal flow is self-unifying and that it is precisely this feature of consciousness that obviates an appeal to a transcendental ego.[2] The ego, according to Sartre, rather than being an ever-present *subject* of experience, appears only as an *object* of reflection. When unreflectively immersed in an activity, experience involves no awareness of an ego; in this way, experience is ownerless and impersonal.

In recent years, a growing number of philosophers have become interested in how these themes from Western philosophy, arising especially from phenomenology, intersect with themes concerning selfhood and consciousness from Indian philosophy (Siderits, Thompson & Zahavi 2011). In this chapter, we aim to contribute to this cross-cultural analysis. Our approach here will be to assess critically, from the perspective of a Western phenomenological treatment of bodily subjectivity, one recent presentation of a nonegological view of consciousness inspired by early Indian Buddhism.

In an important and innovative study, Miri Albahari (2006) offers an original and forceful defense of a nonegological view of consciousness. Drawing on a novel and controversial interpretation of early Indian Buddhism, Albahari argues that the self we habitually take ourselves to be is an illusion. Our everyday sense of self is that of a bounded subject that is a personal owner of experiences and a controlling agent of actions, but in reality there is no self that possesses these attributes of ownership and executive control. Rather, the impression of self arises from a process of identification with transitory mental and bodily experiences as 'me' or 'mine'. In contrast with standard interpretations of early Indian Buddhism,

the self. There is a strong phenomenological constraint on any acceptable answer to the metaphysical question which can be expressed by saying that the factual question "Is there such a thing as the mental self?" is equivalent to the question "Is any (genuine) sense of the self an accurate representation of anything that exists?" '

2 Husserl had himself maintained a nonegological theory in his *Logical Investigations* but then later revised his account of consciousness to include the transcendental ego as an invariant structure of the stream of intentional experiences. For discussion, see Zahavi (2005: 32–36, 130–132).

however, and unlike other no-self theorists, Albahari affirms the experiential reality of a 'witnessing subject'. She thus distinguishes between a mere 'subject' of experience and a full-blown 'self'. The self, in her view, is a specific *kind* of subject that exhibits the property of 'boundedness', where 'boundednes' refers to the condition of being ontologically distinct with a unique personal identity that separates it from all other things (Albahari 2006: 90–91). Whereas being a subject of experience is simply a matter of instantiating an impersonal perspectival awareness of the world, the experience of selfhood additionally involves a sense of unique 'personal ownership' or 'my-ness'. It is this sense of being an ontologically distinct personal owner of experiences that Albahari argues is an illusion generated by desire-driven identification. If one could remove the deep-seated psychological 'craving' for me and mine that drives the process of identification, one would thereby remove the illusion of selfhood and realize the inherently ownerless structure of experience.

In what follows, we propose an account of consciousness that challenges this kind of nonegological view, in particular its sharp distinction between subject and self. Given the notion of a subject of experience—understood minimally as the instantiation of a perspectival awareness of the world—we need to investigate the relation such a subject bears to the *body* as the phenomenal locus of that awareness. Two broad options seem available. On the one hand, we can view the body as an object that belongs, in some special way, to an essentially mental subject. On the other hand, we can view the body as *constituting* the subject of experience. As Dorothée Legrand (2006) notes, whereas the first view can allow that the subject of experience is *embodied*, the second view holds that the subject is constitutively *bodily*.

With Legrand (2006, this volume), we contend that the subject of experience is a bodily subject and not merely an embodied one. This commitment underlies our evaluation of Albahari's nonegological position. Specifically, we will argue that in order to be a subject of experience even in the minimal sense of 'witnessing-from-a-perspective', one must be prereflectively aware of oneself as a living body, i.e., one must be a bodily subject (Thompson 2007). If this view is correct, then it casts doubt on Albahari's proposed distinction between subject and self. The phenomenon of prereflective bodily self-awareness entails a basic experience of boundedness between one's subjective body and the phenomenal world with which one is bodily engaged. Consequently, by Albahari's own criteria, simply being a subject of experience will involve a basic sense of self.

In challenging Albahari's account, we intend to defend the necessary presence of a minimal bodily sense of self as a constitutive feature of perspectival awareness of the world. Dan Zahavi (2005, this volume) has recently argued that the distinctive first-personal way experiences are subjectively given and lived-through reveals them immediately as *mine* or *for-me*. According to Zahavi, this ubiquitous structural feature of experience, which pertains to *how* experience is given rather than *what* it is about, suffices to establish the experiential reality of a minimal self. Related to this line of thought, our argument will be (i) transcendental, in that it will aim to identify a structural feature of consciousness without which experience of the world could not occur, and (ii) phenomenological, insofar as the self whose existence we will be affirming is one given in bodily experience of the world. Focusing on the nature of prereflective bodily self-awareness, we will argue that the processes responsible for one's egocentric bodily perspective on the world are simultaneously responsible for the formation of a minimal bounded self in the form of a living bodily subject of experience.

One final introductory remark is in order. Our aim here is not to defend an egological account of consciousness if that means an account according to which the unity of consciousness requires the postulation of an unconstructed ego (an ego not constructed by the stream of intentional experiences).[3] Rather, our concern is to show that perspectival awareness of the world already involves a kind of prereflective bodily self-awareness and hence bodily selfhood that Albahari's non-egological account misses. If our account is correct, then although the experience of being a bounded self may not be unconstructed, it is not therefore an illusion.

THE 'TWO-TIERED ILLUSION OF SELF'

One of the distinctive features of Albahari's study is that she offers a detailed analysis of the self we normally and unreflectively take ourselves to be. According to her analysis, we habitually assume that we are "a conscious subject that is unified, happiness-seeking, unbrokenly persisting, [an] ontologically distinct or bounded 'me' who is an owner of experiences, thinker of thoughts, and agent of actions" (2006: 2). So understood, the self is fundamentally a *subject* of experience; it is that to which objects of experience are phenomenally presented, where 'object' is understood as anything upon which one can direct attention. A number of additional features, however, characterize the kind of subject we habitually take the self to be. As an experiential subject, the self is '*elusive* to its own attentive purview' (2006: 110–111, our emphasis). Because the self is the attending subject, it cannot show up fully as an object of attention. Nevertheless, we implicitly regard this

---

[3] At least on Zahavi's reading, Husserl's transcendental ego would not fit this notion of an unconstructed ego: 'although the ego must be distinguished from the experiences in which it lives and functions, it cannot exist in any way independently of them. It is a transcendence, but in Husserl's now famous phrase, it is a *transcendence in the immanence*' (2005: 131). Zahavi goes on to interpret this phrase as involving the following idea: 'Whereas we live through a number of different experiences, the dimension of first-personal experiencing remains the same. In short, although the self, as an experiential dimension, does not exist in separation from the experiences, and is identified by the very first-personal givenness of the experiences, it may still be described as the invariant dimension of first-personal givenness throughout the multitude of changing experiences' (2005: 132).

elusive subject as having a definite *boundary*, i.e., as being 'ontologically distinct' and separate from everything that is not experienced as part of the self (2006: 90). We also take this bounded subject to be *unified* in all of its experiences and roles (as agent, thinker, owner, and so on). In other words, there appears to be only *one* point of view to which a multitude of experiences are presented, both at a time (synchronically) and over time (diachronically) (2006: 111–112). We also assume the self to be both *unbroken*—numerically identical through changing experiences— and *invariable*—qualitatively the same over time (2006: 113, 117). Finally, we habitually assume the self to be *unconstructed* (2006: 118). In other words, we believe that our self exists prior to and stands apart from particular experiences, that the self is their precedent rather than their product. In this way, the phenomenal content belonging to our sense of self seems 'unborrowed' and not 'contributed to' by the intentional objects of experience.

Although Albahari regards the self as a whole to be illusory, she does not regard all of its features as illusory. In her view, many of the properties mistakenly attributed to the self are intrinsic to nonegological consciousness. These properties include elusiveness, unity, unbrokenness, invariability, and unconstructedness.[4] To appreciate this distinctive version of the nonegological conception of consciousness, we need to examine Albahari's distinction between 'subject' and 'self' as well as the related distinctions between different kinds of ownership.

Albahari defines a subject as 'witnessing as it presents from a psycho-physical (hence spatiotemporal) perspective' (Albahari 2006: 8). 'Witnessing' refers to an invariant property of apprehension or observation that she argues is present in all experience. Witnessing is modality-neutral, i.e., it is not tied to a particular mode of cognition, and it has its own phenomenal character, i.e., there is something it is like simply to be aware.[5] All conscious experiences, according to Albahari, share this feature of witnessing presence or awareness. Thus the phenomenal content of an experience is not exhausted by the objects of which we are aware, whether focally or peripherally (2006: 143–145). Moreover, with the exception of boundedness, witness consciousness truly exhibits all of the features that we mistakenly attribute to the self, including elusiveness, unity, unbrokenness, invariability, and unconstructedness (2006: 166).

---

[4] Albahari presents this aspect of her view as an (unorthodox) interpretation of Theravada Buddhism, but we would argue it is much closer to the later Indian school of Advaita Vedanta than to early Indian Buddhism.

[5] In *Analytical Buddhism*, Albahari distinguishes between witness consciousness and awareness, where the former refers only to 'the mode-neutral awareness' present in all acts of phenomenal apprehension and the latter incorporates the dimension of intrinsic phenomenal character. In a more recent paper (Albahari 2009), she collapses the distinction so that witness consciousness is now the same as what she called awareness in her book. We will follow her in treating them synonymously. For more on the Indian philosophical origin and development of the concept of witness consciousness, see Gupta (1998).

Albahari also discusses the role of ownership and distinguishes between 'perspectival ownership' and 'personal ownership'.[6] For a subject to own something perspectivally is for it to appear to the subject in a way that it does not appear to any other subject. When I have a toothache, for example, it presents itself to my perspective in a distinctive way. In the case of outer objects of perception, what is perspectivally owned is not the object, but the specific manner through which the object appears to the subject (2006: 53). Personal ownership, however, occurs when one *identifies with* an experience or experienced object *as* the owner of that experience or object. Personal ownership involves the reflexive assumption, made by the witnessing subject, that various psychophysical attributes either belong to or constitute it as a subject. In this way, these attributes appear as part of the subject rather than as objects within the subject's attentive purview (2006: 56). In making this assumption, one comes to regard these attributes as *mine* or as part of *me*. Albahari also conjectures that this process of identification induces and is induced by emotions of craving, which represent a bounded self as part of their content (2006: 205).

It is with the onset of feelings of personal ownership, Albahari maintains, that one also finds a sense of self (2006: 73). Once one identifies with an object of experience, such that it is perceived as *belonging to* or as *part of* the subject, a felt boundary emerges between what is self (what is felt to be mine) and what is other (what is felt to be not-mine). This felt sense of boundedness, created by identification with objects of experience, transforms the impersonal subject of experience into a subject that experiences itself as a 'substantial personal thing', i.e., a self (2006: 94). As a consequence, the features proper to witnessing awareness—elusiveness, unity, unbrokenness, invariability, and unconstructedness—that are nonillusory in themselves are 'imported' into the sense of self. In conjunction with identification and emotions of self-concern, such importation creates the impression of a bounded personal owner who possesses the features of awareness (2006: 140).

Albahari's account thus proposes two 'feeders' that create a 'two-tiered' illusion of self: (i) a subject's awareness purports to be essentially bounded when it is not (the experience of boundedness can drop away); and (ii) the bounded self, in reality a cognitive and emotional construction, purports to harbour features that in reality belong to the unconstructed awareness. As a result, the self does not have the ontological status it purports to have, namely, being bounded or ontologically distinct as well as being the possessor of features that belong instead to the egoless awareness (2006: 72).

[6] Albahari also distinguishes these from 'possessive ownership', which refers to social conventions governing personal property. We will be concerned only with perspectival and personal ownership.

PERSPECTIVAL OWNERSHIP AND PREREFLECTIVE
SELF-AWARENESS

Important similarities can be found between Albahari's account of subjectivity as 'perspectival ownership' and Western phenomenological accounts of subjectivity as 'prereflective self-awareness' (see Zahavi 2005; this volume). Here we call attention to these similarities in order to zero in on a crucial difference, which we discuss in the next two sections.

One of the central theses found in the phenomenological tradition is that intentionality (the object-directedness of consciousness) essentially involves self-awareness. The kind of self-awareness at issue, however, is not the reflective self-awareness that consists in a higher-order mental state taking a distinct, first-order mental state as its intentional object. Rather, it is a prereflective self-awareness by which every conscious experience manifests to itself as a conscious experience. Because this kind of self-disclosure or self-manifestation does not consist in relating to the experience as an intentional object, the self-experience is described as a prereflective and intransitive self-consciousness. Zahavi (2005) proposes that this feature of consciousness accounts for the 'first-person givenness' of conscious experience: regardless of *what* I am conscious *of* (the intentional object of my conscious state), my conscious experience manifests immediately as *mine* or *for-me*. According to this conception, phenomenal consciousness is necessarily characterized by a prereflective sense of self or by what Sartre called 'ipseity' (selfhood). For Zahavi, this kind of selfhood—a prereflective selfhood prior to and more fundamental than the ego of reflection—amounts to a 'minimal self' as the subject (or subjectivity) of intentional consciousness (2005: 106).

There is thus a significant convergence between Albahari's Buddhist-inspired view of consciousness and Western phenomenological views. Both reject the 'object-knowledge thesis', according to which 'all knowledge and experience must be derived from the object side of the apparent subject/object dichotomy (remembering that objects are, in principle, able to be attended to)' (Albahari 2006: 107). For Albahari (2006: 168), awareness contributes to the phenomenal content of an experience by being reflexively about itself but without being an object of attention (2006: 168). Similarly, phenomenologists maintain, in being intentionally directed toward objects, we are also prereflectively aware of the experiences through which those objects are given (see Thompson 2007: chapter 10). Finally, according to both viewpoints, the most fundamental mode of self-awareness is not to be understood as any kind of transitive or object-directed consciousness. Rather, the subject is self-aware in a tacit and non-object-directed manner in and through its being aware of the world.

Given these similarities, it is tempting to regard Albahari's notion of the subject or 'witnessing as it presents from a perspective' as basically equivalent to the phenomenological notion of ipseity, or more precisely to Zahavi's interpretation of ipseity as a 'minimal self'. According to this reading, the 'for-me-ness' of conscious experience is a matter of being a perspectival owner of experience (as opposed to a personal owner); it is simply the observation that all subjective experiences are presented from the first-person perspective. Hence one might conclude that the disagreement between Albahari and Zahavi over the status of the self—or between other Buddhist no-self viewpoints and Husserlian phenomenology (Siderits, Thompson, and Zahavi 2010)—is largely terminological: the notion of self Albahari rejects as illusory is not the notion of self described and defended by phenomenologists. Yet, as we will now see, there is another phenomenological thesis about subjectivity that can be used to highlight an important difference between these views.

DISTINGUISHING THE BODILY SUBJECT FROM THE (MERELY) EMBODIED SUBJECT

In a famous passage of *Meditation VI*, Descartes states that the mental subject of experience (the thinking ego) and its body are 'very closely joined' and 'intermingled,' 'so that I and the body form a unit' (Descartes 1986: 56). On this view, although the subject of experience can be said to be *embodied*, it is not constitutively *bodily*; rather, the subject is conceived as an essentially mental being, one that simply happens to be united to *this* particular body rather than some other.

Some philosophers deny the Cartesian claim that a mental subject can exist without being embodied, yet still hold that the subject appears to introspective self-awareness as distinctively mental. In other words, they would argue that although the self is necessarily embodied, one is nonetheless presented to oneself in introspective self-awareness as a mental subject and not as a bodily one. For example, Sydney Shoemaker writes, 'we are not presented with ourselves in introspection as bodily entities' (Shoemaker 1986), and, 'when one is introspectively aware of one's thoughts, feelings, beliefs, and desires, one is not presented to oneself as a flesh and blood person, and one does not seem to be presented to one as an object at all' (Shoemaker 1984: 102).

In contrast, many phenomenologists, most notably Merleau-Ponty (1962), would reject this view.[7] The subject is not merely *embodied* but *bodily*: 'But I am not in

[7] See also Cassam (1999; this volume), although his discussion does not differentiate between the body as subject and the body as object in the way we do here.

front of my body, I am in my body, or rather I am my body' (Merleau-Ponty 1962: 150). Yet Merleau-Ponty refuses to understand the proposition 'I am my body' in a materialist way, as meaning that I am (or my self is) nothing more than a certain physical *object*. Instead, he maintains the original position that I am a *bodily subject*.

This view involves several crucial ideas that depart from the conception of the subject as merely embodied. First, introspective self-awareness is not our primary mode of self-awareness; rather, we are prereflectively self-aware in world-directed perception, action, and feeling. Second, introspective self-awareness is not the only mode of self-experience that can be nonobservational, i.e., not based on being presented to oneself as an object. On the contrary, prereflective self-awareness presents the *body* not as an *object* of inner or outer perception, but rather as the *subject* of perception, action, and feeling (Legrand 2006; this volume). Finally, therefore, self-experience in its most basic nonobservational form presents oneself as a *living bodily subject* and not as a purely mental one (Thompson 2007).

Merleau-Ponty's sentence quoted above expresses these ideas. 'I am not in front of my body' means that I cannot experience my body simply as an object of outer perception: 'I observe external objects with my body, I handle them, examine them, walk round them, but my body itself is a thing which I do not observe; in order to be able to do so, I should need the use of a second body which itself would be unobservable' (Merleau-Ponty 1962: 104). Of course, I can, for example, look down at my hands or see my reflection in mirror, but I cannot completely objectify my body, for 'I am in my body.' Yet the crucial point here is not that what makes my body different from other objects is that I also happen to experience my body from within (interoceptively or proprioceptively). Rather, it is that I prereflectively and nonobservationally experience my body as the *subject* of my perspectival awareness of the world (including my body as an object). As Zahavi writes:

Whereas I can approach or move away from any object in the world, the body itself is always present as my very perspective on the world. That is, rather than being simply yet another perspectivally given object, the body itself is exactly that which allows me to perceive objects perspectivally... The body is present, not as a permanent perceptual object, but as myself. Originally, I do not have any consciousness *of* my body as an intentional object. I am not perceiving it, *I am it*... Thus, my *original* body-awareness is not a type of object-consciousness, is *not* a perception of the body as an object, but a form of immediate, prereflective, self-awareness (Zahavi 2002: 21).

In summary, according to this phenomenological line of thought, the subject of experience is a bodily subject. Bodily self-awareness, however, does not happen only when one experiences one's body as an object of inner or outer perception. On the contrary, the primary form of body awareness is not a type of transitive consciousness of the body-as-object. Rather, the primary form of body awareness is the body's intransitive self-experience as a perceiving, acting, and feeling subject—the body-as-subject (see Legrand, this volume, for further discussion).

BODILY SUBJECTIVITY AND PERSPECTIVAL WITNESSING

Returning now to Albahari's nonegological view, we need to ask about the status of the body in relation to the subject of experience. Does the body belong constitutively to the unified and impersonal conscious awareness? Or is the body an inessential accompaniment of a witness consciousness that is essentially mental? In short, is the subject of experience constitutively bodily or merely embodied?

We will now present evidence to suggest that Albahari understands the subject of experience as being *merely* embodied. According to her view, witness consciousness is not intrinsically tied to a psychophysical perspective, for she wishes to allow for the psychological possibility of a completely perspectiveless and thus subjectless witness consciousness (2006: 9–10). On her reading, the consciousness proper to the fully liberated state of nirvana ('nibbanic consciousness') would be such a witness consciousness, i.e., a form of pure awareness that lacks any intentional object and is unconditioned by space and time (2006: 46). Albahari makes clear that her aim is not to *argue* for the psychological possibility of a pure subjectless witnessing unconditioned by spatiotemporal perspective. Instead, her concern is to describe the nature of the ordinary consciousness that harbours a sense of self ('pre-nibbanic consciousness') and to defend the possibility of a consciousness ridden of the sense of self but that still functions as a perspectival owner of experience ('proximate-nibbanic consciousness'). Nevertheless, the fact that she wishes to leave open the possibility of pure witnessing awareness indicates that the phenomenal character of witnessing, as it occurs in the context of the impersonal perspectival awareness (absent a sense of self), will not be inherently bodily.

Albahari might wish to say that although pure witness consciousness is not bodily in nature, the subject of experience *is* bodily. Recall that she defines the subject as 'witnessing as it presents from a psycho-physical (hence spatiotemporal) perspective' (2006: 8). One might therefore claim that the subject, by definition, is bodily. For example, one might understand the subject as the conjoining of a witnessing awareness, itself prior to the subject-object distinction, with a bodily perspective. As a result of this union, experience would take on a subject-object structure with witnessing awareness being phenomenally located on the subject-side of experience (as Albahari says, witnessing is the '*modus operandi*' of the subject). This combination would appear to generate a bodily subject insofar as the subject is partly constituted by the specific bodily perspective from which witnessing appears to emanate. Consequently, one might think that subject and body are one, not two.

Yet other considerations make this interpretation untenable. Recall that, for Albahari, an 'object' is anything that can, in principle, be attended to by a witnessing subject, such that whatever attention targets will be experienced as standing over and against the subject. Included in what can be a focus of attention are not only external objects, i.e., ones we experience as transcending our particular point of view, but also 'perspective-lending' aspects or features of experience, such as sensations, feelings, and qualities of awareness (e.g., drowsy or alert), which determine the subject's unique egocentric perspective on external objects (2006: 11, 14, 57–58). Thus the subject has different kinds of 'objects' available to it. On the one hand, perspective-lending objects are ones whose features pertain to the subject's phenomenal perspective; on the other hand, non-perspective-lending or external objects pertain to the world as experienced by the subject.

Given Albahari's distinction between perspective-lending and external objects, it seems to follow that a subject that is free of the self-illusion (e.g., the *arahant* or enlightened person) will have an entirely objectified experience of its body. At various points in the text, Albahari describes the subject's experience of its body as both a perspective-lending object and an external object (2006: 11, 14, 58). On the one hand, the body is perspective-lending in the sense that our experience of it serves to relate us to external objects; for example, bodily sensation (tactile, proprioceptive, visual, and so on) provides us with information about our relation to the external world. On the other hand, the body can also be experienced as an object belonging to the world, as when one touches oneself or sees oneself in a mirror. Albahari treats both kinds of bodily experience as experience of the body as an object: 'The central point of relevance is that the object is anything that can be attended to by a witnessing subject, whether *through* channels that are mental, visual, auditory, gustatory, olfactory, tactile, proprioceptive, or pertaining *to* those channels, to the very qualia *associated with* each sensory or mental modality' (2006: 11, emphasis in original). Furthermore, witnessing awareness, which is the *modus operandi* of the subject, is distinct from any such object: 'Our core concept of awareness thus conveys a type of experience—a subjective sense of presence—that is unmediated by any specific quality pertaining to objects, outer or inner. In our concept, this subjective sense of presence intrinsically qualifies the witness-consciousness that is the *modus operandi* of a subject' (2006: 144). Consequently, it would seem impossible for the subject to be constitutively bodily, because the body is given fundamentally as an object. As that which is aware of any such object, the subject must be essentially body-transcendent.

Albahari confirms her conception of the subject as body-transcendent when she discusses an especially subtle and 'primal' mode of identification in which the subject assumes itself to be essentially (rather than contingently) confined to its unique 'hemmed-in' perspective (2006: 58–59). She writes: '"The self", in this context, would thus refer to those perspective-lending *khandhas* [psychophysical factors] as assimilated with the witnessing that shows through them' (2006: 58). Consequently, to regard one's perspective-lending *body* as part of the subject involves one in the illusion of subjectively *being* what, in reality, is a transient object within one's attentive purview. This assessment can be seen clearly in Albahari's analysis of the statement, 'I feel healthy today.' On her interpretation, the proposition expressed by this statement betrays the subject's identification with a healthy-feeling body as self. As a result, the body is felt as belonging to the subject: 'a single entity in which subject and body are fused . . . The "I" that claims to feel healthy seems to be a hybrid, namely the *body-as-subject*' (2006: 58, emphasis in original). It follows that one who is free of the sense of self can only be an *embodied* subject but not a *bodily* one. Thus, according to Albahari's view, although the experience of the body may contribute to defining the confines of one's perspectival awareness, it is not intrinsically part of that subjective awareness.[8]

We have now arrived at a basic disagreement between Albahari's nonegological view and the phenomenological conception of bodily subjectivity. As we have seen, phenomenologists from Husserl onward regard the original form of bodily experience not as a consciousness of the body as intentional object but rather as an intransitive (non-object-directed) and prereflective bodily self-awareness. In other words, phenomenologists regard bodily self-experience as belonging on the subject-side of the subject–object distinction. In order for it to be possible to perceive a world of objects (including the body-as-object), one must be a bodily subject. According to Albahari's account, however, such body-as-subject awareness is symptomatic of a particularly subtle form of identification with the body as the self. Such an awareness reflects the fact that the body as perspective-lending object has been illicitly appropriated to the witnessing subject, such that the body's status *as an object* has been rendered invisible (Albahari 2006: 63, 118). According to Albahari, witnessing without a sense of self will still occur from a perspective (so long as the experience is object-involving), but it will not assume this bodily perspective to be inherent to itself (2006: 58). Another way to put this disagreement is that, on Albahari's view, the phenomenological tradition is mistaken in regarding the body as prereflectively self-aware, that is, as nonobservationally and intransitively self-aware. Rather, on her view, the perspective-lending body that we live

---

[8] It is intriguing that Albahari chooses to describe the phenomenal character of witness-consciousness as a 'subjective sense of presence' (2006: 144). She points out that 'presence' conveys both a spatial and a temporal connotation: 'present' can mean the sense of both a spatial *here* and a temporal *now*. In our view, such a characterization of witness consciousness would be perfectly appropriate *if* witnessing were inherently bodily. If that were the case, then one would expect witness consciousness to be centered or rooted in a feeling of 'here' and 'now'; both express a lived bodily presence. It is, however, unclear whether Albahari intends this description to apply only to pre-nibbanic consciousness (which harbors a sense of self) or would *also* regard it as an apt description of proximate-nibbanic consciousness (i.e., the consciousness of a *arahant* or enlightened person). Put differently, would witness consciousness be associated with the spatiotemporal experience of the 'here and now' for someone liberated from the self-illusion or is this experience simply a manifestation of the habitual tendency to identify with and thus appropriate the experience of one's bodily perspective to witness consciousness?

through in our experience of the world would rather have the status of a marginal or unattended-to object of awareness.

One reason this disagreement matters is that if it turns out that the subject is constitutively bodily, then it would follow that the subject is also bounded. (As we will discuss in the conclusion, however, it would not follow that its boundaries are static and fixed rather than dynamic and flexible.) As long as the body is experienced as subject, there will be a fundamental experiential distinction between self and other. Hence a sense of boundedness would be implicit in both personal and perspectival ownership; having a perspective on the world would entail a distinction between the subjective body, which one nonintentionally lives through in world-directed experience, and the objective world, toward which one is intentionally related via one's bodily self-experience. This nonillusory sense of distinctness would count against Albahari's account, according to which any experience of boundedness is illusory.

ARGUING FOR THE BODILY SUBJECT

We will now consider why perspectival ownership requires being a bodily subject. Specifically, we will present a modified version of Sydney Shoemaker's argument that self-awareness must be based on a nonobservational awareness of oneself as subject (Shoemaker 1968).

According to Shoemaker (1968), the awareness that I have of myself as the subject of experience is not based on the perception of an object whose observed properties serve to identify it to me as myself. In order to identify an object as myself, I must find something true of the observed object that I already hold to be true of myself. In particular, I would need to have prior knowledge of a distinguishing property the observation of which allows me to identify something as myself. Such a judgment therefore presupposes some prior acquaintance with myself. Consequently, according to Shoemaker, it is impossible to claim that all instances of self-knowledge are grounded on judgments of identification without generating an infinite regress of such judgments. It is therefore not the case that one first encounters a neutral or anonymous mental state and then asks, 'to whom does this mental state belong?' Instead, one's mental states are known immediately and nonobservationally as one's own. Thus, the awareness that I have of myself as the *subject* of experience is not based on perception or observation.

In its original form, Shoemaker's argument does not apply to Albahari, for two reasons. First, 'identification' is used differently by the two authors. By 'identification', Albahari means the act of *appropriating* what is in reality an object of experience to the subject of experience, such that it appears as assimilated with the subject's perspective on the world. Roughly, by 'identification', Shoemaker means a judgment, made on the basis of observation and inference, in which an identity is asserted between the subject of the judgment and the bearer of the property figuring in the predicate of the judgment. For example, I judge that it is John who is running, given that I know someone is running and that I identify that individual as John. Second, Albahari would grant that the subject's awareness of itself is not based on the observation of an object (Albahari 2006: 144–145, 167–169). As we mentioned above, she rejects the 'object-knowledge thesis', according to which 'all knowledge and experience must be derived from the object side of the apparent subject/object dichotomy (remembering that objects are, in principle, able to be attended to)' (2006: 107). In her nonegological view (2006: 168), the witnessing subject contributes to the phenomenal content of an experience by being reflexively about itself but without being an object of attention (2006: 168). Thus, her account is compatible with Shoemaker's argument.

Nevertheless, we can formulate an argument in terms of perspectival-ownership and the body that does apply to Albahari.[9] Specifically, we can ask the following question: How is it possible for the witnessing awareness to know that it is witnessing from a perspective? To answer this question, Albahari would appeal to her distinction between perspective-lending objects and external-objects. Specifically, according to her account, it is through awareness of the former that there can be awareness of the latter. In this way, perspective-lending objects provide the subject's access to the world; they constitute the medium for world-directed experience.

The trouble with this explanation is that it is difficult to understand how witness consciousness could ever acquire the understanding that what it apprehends in experience is a perspective on an objective world and hence that it occupies the role of a subject of experience. We contend that it is only if the witnessing awareness *already* knew itself to be a perspective-holder, specifically a body in relation to which external objects are egocentrically situated, that it would be possible to identify *which* aspects of experience are distinctively perspective-lending. The subject's ability to identify some item of experience as perspective-lending presupposes a prior prereflective awareness of itself as located *here* in *this* lived body. If awareness did not include an immediate and non-observational bodily-self-acquaintance, then it is unclear why it would be experienced as emanating from a psychophysical perspective at all. We contend that only if witness consciousness is experientially

---

[9] Shoemaker would probably not agree with this modification of his argument; in his view, although mental predicates are absolutely immune to error through misidentification relative to the first-person pronoun, bodily predicates are merely *de facto* immune. For further discussion of this issue, see Legrand (2006); Chen (2009); Cassam (this volume); Bermúdez (this volume).

anchored to the body as an ordering frame of reference for perception and action can there be anything specifically subjective or perspectival in awareness.

Let us put this argument in a more Shoemaker-style form. To identify (in Shoemaker's sense) an object as perspective-lending requires finding something true of that object that one already holds true of one's perspective on the world (some distinguishing property that identifies the object as pertaining to one's unique perspective). Such object-identification, however, presupposes knowledge of the perspective in question. To avoid an infinite regress, one must have some nonobservational, prereflective awareness of oneself as the relevant perspective-holder, most fundamentally as a bodily subject. Hence nonobservational bodily awareness must belong originally to the subject of experience.

If our view is correct, then it poses a problem for Albahari's proposed distinction between subject and self, as well as the distinction between perspectival owner and personal owner. Prereflective bodily self-awareness entails an experience of bound-edness, i.e., it entails a basic distinction within experience between one's subjective body (self) and one's phenomenal world (other). Consequently, by Albahari's proposed criteria, merely being a subject of experience will involve a basic sense of self. If the body belongs constitutively to the nature of perspectival awareness, then when the subject *qua* witnessing-from-a-psychophysical-perspective experiences the world, it does so as a 'natively unified' bodily subject.

In light of this point, let us consider some of the empirical considerations Albahari draws on to support her view. An important case study to which she appeals to support her distinction between perspectival and personal ownership is the pathology of somatoparaphrenia.[10] Here the patient personally disowns a body part (say, the left arm) but still perspectivally owns the experience of the arm insofar as the arm appears in her visual field (2006: 55–56). The patient can recognize, with puzzlement, that the arm is joined to the rest of her body, while nevertheless denying that it is *her* arm.

Albahari sees in this pathology evidence for the possibility of dissociating perspectival from personal ownership. In our view, however, such pathologies constitute a breakdown of not only personal ownership but also perspectival ownership. To the extent that the patient no longer perceives the world with and through her personally disowned arm, the pathology includes a partial breakdown of the patient's subjective perspective on the world. As a consequence

---

[10] Albahari refers to the pathology as anosognosia, but from her description of the symptoms it seems that somatopharaprenia is the precise condition she has in mind. Anosognosia is a patient's denial of her paralysis or disability, but is not usually accompanied by the denial that her arm is hers or part of her body. The patient will typically correctly assert that it is her arm, but will incorrectly assert that it is functioning perfectly when in fact it is paralyzed. Somatoparaphrenia occurs when the patient denies that the arm is hers and is usually accompanied by the claim that it belongs to someone else.

of this impairment, certain affordances within her environment will no longer be present to the patient; for example, the teacup just to her left will no longer present to her as graspable-from-the-left. Although the arm will still be given in experience as an object (it will still appear as an object within her visual field), it will not be appropriately integrated into the sensorimotor capabilities of the body as subject and consequently no longer be part of her subjective perspective on the world.

Albahari (2006: 161) also contends that one can conceive of a global condition of depersonalization, in which the body continues to function properly, unlike limb paralysis in anosognosia. In such a case, she claims, one's whole body would be experienced as an object, rather than as integrated with the subject, and moreover the subject would still be able to interact with the world in the capacity of a perspectival owner.

Yet it is precisely the possibility of this scenario of global depersonalization that we mean to challenge with the above argument. Without one's body being experienced prereflectively as that in relation to which objects are situated, it would be impossible for a subject to experience a world of objects as external to one's subjective perspective (an ability that Albahari maintains is preserved in perspectival ownership). Therefore, to be a subject of experience even in the minimal sense of witnessing-from-a-perspective requires being prereflectively aware of oneself as a bodily subject.

This line of thought implies that perspectival ownership involves an experience of the body as belonging constitutively to the subject rather than as an object appropriated to the subject's witnessing perspective. Therefore, one's awareness of the body as belonging to the subject cannot be the result of the process of appropriation that Albahari describes. Identification-as-appropriation cannot occur at the level of the body-as-subject because the body is not given in experience originally as an object. Hence the primary metaphors Albahari uses to conceptualize the process of identification-as-appropriation seem inapt for understanding the nature of the body-as-subject. She states that appropriated objects present 'a reflexive aspect' to the subject's experience and hence that one comes to view 'the world through the lens of that aspect, such that its filter seems to become a part of the subject's first-person perspective' (2006: 93). Although the body is that by which the world shows up or comes into focus for a subject, it would be wrong to construe the body as an instrument through which one perceives the world. Such an image implies the problematic distinction between the observing subject and its body, and moreover is too disembodied and spectatorial to capture the lived body and its distinctive mode of transparency in world-directed experience (see Legrand 2007, this volume).

Might it be the case that we identify with the body-as-subject in some other way? We will return to this question in our conclusion.

SUBJECTIVITY AND BOUNDEDNESS

One might object that we have moved too quickly from the conclusion that the body is fundamentally part of the subject of experience to the conclusion that all subjective experience is characterized by a sense of *boundedness*. After all, Albahari proposes that one can be free of the self-illusion, yet still be able to perceive and navigate the world as a perspectival owner. Although one might grant that prereflective awareness of one's body-as-subject is necessary for perspectival ownership, one might still deny that this kind of self-awareness implies boundedness in the sense that Albahari regards as constitutive of the self-illusion. To put the point another way, perhaps Albahari's notion of boundedness differs from the mere distinction in experience between bodily subject and worldly object—a distinction that would be preserved when the illusory sense of self is removed.

To meet this objection, we need to distinguish between a weak sense of boundedness and a strong sense of boundedness. Weak boundedness consists in the experiential distinction between one's bodily perspective and whatever is perceived from that perspective. Strong boundedness consists in the experiential distinction evinced by Albahari's four modes of self-identification—'this-importance-of-being-this-very-thing', 'agency', 'consistent self-concern', and 'personal ownership' (Albahari 2006: 94). These modes of self-identification, she conjectures, co-arise with the mindset of 'craving' and emotional investment. Consequently, each possesses an emotional valence (2006: 107–109). It is thus the differential value placed on being 'this very thing' that is symptomatic of a sense of self.

Let us note first that the way Albahari defines boundedness favours the weak sense. She states that boundedness consists in the property of being ontologically unique or distinct from everything else (2006: 90–91). This definition, however, is too inclusive for her purpose of showing that the self is an illusion whereas the subject is not, for just as there appears to be an ontological distinction between self and other, so too there is an experiential distinction between the perspectival subject and its intentional objects. Albahari states that she does not intend boundedness to be an attribute of the witnessing subject as such, but only of the witnessing subject that harbours a sense of personal selfhood (2006: 90). Nevertheless, if we understand 'boundedness' minimally as ontological distinctness or uniqueness, then despite her claim to the contrary, a (bodily) subject would seem as conceptually and experientially bounded as a self.

Albahari might reply that an experiential distinction between subject and object does not determine whether the subject in itself is bounded or unbounded. Specifically, she might argue that the subject–object distinction is extrinsic to the witnessing subject (witness consciousness), whereas a self would have to be intrinsically characterized by its ontological distinctness from everything else.

Given that the subject is a bodily subject, however, boundedness cannot be extrinsic to the witnessing subject. Suppose we allow for purposes of argument the possibility of a pure witness consciousness with no sense of boundedness. Although boundedness would then be extrinsic to *witnessing as such*, it does not follow that boundedness would be extrinsic to *witnessing qua subject*. Defining 'subject' in terms of a psychophysical perspective (as Albahari does) implies that there is something that is perspectivally owned (one cannot have a point of view without something appearing within one's field of view). In this way, subject and object are constituted in relation to each other. Consequently, boundedness is intrinsic to the subject–object relation and therefore to the role of perspectival ownership.

This reasoning depends on the premise that the subject is constitutively bodily and not merely embodied. If one holds, however, that the subject is distinct from the body, then one could also hold, as Albahari apparently does, that a subject can have a completely impersonal awareness of its psychophysical perspective and hence that the experiential distinction between that perspective and what appears from that perspective is not a distinction inherent to the subject itself. Instead, this distinction would reside within the appearances that are given to the witnessing subject. Moreover, if there were a condition of pure objectless (and thus subject-less) witnessing (as is putatively the case in nibbanic consciousness), then, upon returning to one's life as a perspectival owner, the witnessing subject would have a sense that its status as a subject is a merely contingent one and hence recognize that it is not intrinsically confined to this role. Albahari appears to conceive of the subject's unboundedness in this way (2006; 57–58).[11]

Suppose now that what Albahari means by boundedness is not captured by her definition (which is too weak) but instead corresponds to what we have called strong boundedness. In other words, boundedness does not consist in the mere distinction between subject and object, but rather in the fundamentally evaluative distinction between a differentially important self and the rest of the world.

---

[11] One might nevertheless object that conceptualizing the subject as unbounded in the weak sense remains problematic. Specifically, even if we put aside the issue of whether or not the subject is constitutively bodily or merely embodied, one might claim that there will still remain a straightforward distinction between the witnessing subject and the experiences that are given to it. Consider that Albahari (2009) argues for a 'radical ontological distinction' between the stream of experience and the witnessing subject to which the stream of experience presents. If boundedness, however, refers simply to ontological distinctness, then calling the witnessing subject 'separate' and 'distinct' from the stream of experience will conflict with the thesis that the subject is inherently unbounded. Once again, although witnessing *per se* might be unbounded, witnessing *qua subject* would be inherently bounded, i.e., distinct in relation to that which is witnessed. Although this objection points to a weakness in Albahari's definition of boundedness, we do not intend to stress this point. It seems to us that the boundedness that one finds in the context of the bodily subject is more robust and a source of more substantive disagreement between us than the mere distinction between witness consciousness and the stream of experience that is witnessed.

According to this interpretation, boundedness arises when the pre-existing non-evaluative boundary between one's subjective perspective and what is perceived from that perspective becomes distorted or exaggerated as a result of self-identification and 'craving'.

This interpretation captures much of what seems to motivate Albahari's differentiation of the subject as unbounded from the self as bounded. Consider her discussion of the mere perceptual differentiation between oneself and an emotionally neutral object, such as a blade of grass:

> I still identify myself as something decisively separate from the blade of grass. It is reasonable to suppose that if the Buddhist theory is correct, then the ongoing mindset of *tanha* [emotional investment/craving], involving a constant (although not exclusive) lookout for 'number one', will be enough to create a general perceptual *tropism*, such that we involuntarily view even emotionally neutral items in our perceptual purview as decisively 'other' from the 'self' that perceives them. *Tanha* will thus, on the Buddhist position, fuel the subject's overall disposition to identify itself with the perspectival owner of its perceptions, such that the perceptions are felt as personally 'belonging' to the subject. (Albahari 2006: 181–182)

We find two lines of thought in tension here. According to the first, perceptual experience comprises a distinction between one's subjective perspective and whatever objects are perceived from that perspective, but this distinction gets accentuated and distorted through the process of craving-driven identification-as-appropriation. The repeated use of 'decisively' in the passage above ("decisively separate" and "decisively other") suggests that what is illusory in the experience is not the separation between self and other *per se*, but rather the *nature* of the separation. The kind of boundedness in play here is strong boundedness: the experience of being a self results from one's disposition to imbue the self–world distinction with differential value and emotional significance, and thereby to reify what is actually a fluid boundary. According to the second, the basic differentiation in perception between one's subjective perspective and what appears from that perspective is already the result of object-appropriation and emotions of self-concern. The problem with this line of thought, however, is that it conflicts with Albahari's thesis that one would still be able to perceive and act effectively in the world without a sense of self. If removing the sense of self entails removing the perceptual distinction between perceiver and perceived, then it will also eliminate perspectival ownership.

In summary, the concept of boundedness does not seem to provide a clear way of distinguishing between subject and self and establishing that the self is an illusion. Our overall impression from Albahari is that she conceives the experience of boundedness as something quite minimal, namely, the sense of being ontologically distinct from the surrounding world. But it is difficult to accept that what is primarily responsible for this minimal sense of distinctness is the same as what generates the four modes of evaluative self-identification ('this-ness', 'agency', 'consistent self-concern', and 'personal ownership'). Instead, the sense of being a bounded self seems more intimately connected to the experience of having a first-person perspective that is constitutively related to the subjective experience of the lived body. Although the phenomenological boundary between self and other may be exaggerated or distorted as a result of a craving mind-set, it seems misleading to assert that experiences lacking this feature involve no sense of boundedness whatsoever. It seems more accurate to say that the boundary separating self and other, though still phenomenally manifest, is no longer reified.

CONCLUSION

We have argued that in order to be a subject of experience, in Albahari's sense of 'witnessing from a psychophysical perspective', one must be prereflectively aware of oneself as a living body, i.e., one must be a bodily subject. The argument we have given focuses on the ability to identify something as a perspective-lending object; we have suggested that this ability presupposes a more fundamental and distinctly subjective awareness of the living body as the locus of perspectival awareness. According to this line of thought, an object's status as 'perspective-lending' pre-supposes a prior prereflective and non-object-directed awareness of oneself as the perspective-holder. If this point is correct, then one's subjective bodily awareness is identification-free in both Albahari's and Shoemaker's senses. One does not iden-tify one's body on the basis of observation and identification (in Shoemaker's sense); rather, one's body is known prereflectively and nonobservationally. Con-sequently, the body-as-subject cannot be the result of identification (in Albahari's sense), because the body is not given fundamentally an object of experience.

We have also argued that being a perspectival owner of experience suffices for a certain sense of boundedness. Prereflective bodily self-awareness comprises an experience of the basic distinction between one's subjective body and the phenom-enal world. Consequently, according to Albahari's criterion, merely being a subject of experience involves a basic sense of self.

Although we have argued that the subject is bounded and hence a self, we do not thereby affirm that the self is a separately existing *entity* or *thing* (Albahari 2006: 90–91). Albahari frequently uses these words to convey that our everyday assump-tion of selfhood is substantialist in nature, i.e., that we implicitly take the self to be a thing whose nature is 'unconstructed' and that exists independently of its experiences and the rest of the world. Yet such a conception is hardly the only way to understand the self.

On our view, the distinction between self and world is best understood as a mutually specifying relation that is enacted in the process of living (Thompson 2007). The selfhood of the living body is one that is continually reaffirmed through its bodily comportment within a milieu, an environment upon which it vitally depends and toward which it is of necessity normatively directed. Consequently, the self should not be conceived as a being that exists independently of its world, for neither self nor world exist or can be understood in abstraction from the other. Moreover, in arguing for the boundedness of the subject, we do not assume that this boundary is fixed or inflexible. On the contrary, as phenomenologists and cognitive scientists have discussed, the felt boundary between subject and world is plastic and fluidly adaptive (Di Paolo 2009; Thompson and Stapleton 2009).

Hans Jonas's remarks about the organism as a living being can equally be applied to the self: 'organisms are entities whose being is their own doing . . . the being that they earn from this doing is not a possession they then own in separation from the activity by which it was generated, but is the continuation of that very activity itself' (Jonas, 1996: 88; see also Thompson 2007). As Mackenzie (2009) has recently argued, there is a connection between Jonas's conception of living being as a continuous activity of self-production and the Buddhist claim that the self arises from a process of self-appropriation (and, moreover, is nothing *beyond* this appropriative activity). Given this connection, a form of identification or 'I-making' will be an ineliminable condition of living being. Moreover, this biological self-appropriation will be reflected phenomenologically in prereflective self-awareness as the experience of sentience or the feeling of being alive (Thompson 2007).

In conclusion, although we disagree with Albahari's account of *how* we come to identify with the body-as-subject (namely, as the result of object-appropriation), we do not deny that we identify with this body and that this identification is the outcome of processes of self-appropriation or self-constitution. Indeed, we agree that the lived body is something that we have a sense of being and that this kind of identification with the body is crucial for successful perspectival ownership. Although the selfhood of the bodily subject may be *constructed* through ongoing processes of self-appropriation, it does not follow that its status as a self is an *illusion*.

REFERENCES

ALBAHARI, M. (2006). *Analytical Buddhism: The Two-Tiered Illusion of Self* (New York: Palgrave Macmillan).
——(2009). 'Witness Consciousness: Its Definition, Appearance, and Reality'. *Journal of Consciousness Studies*, 16/1: 62–84.
CASSAM, Q. (1999). *Self and World* (Oxford: Oxford University Press).

CHEN, C. (2009). 'Bodily Awareness and Immunity to Error through Misidentification'. *European Journal of Philosophy* (DOI: 10.1111/j.1468-0378.2009.00363.x).

DESCARTES, R. (1986). *Meditations on First Philosophy, with Selections from the Objections and Replies,* tr. J. Cottingham (Cambridge: Cambridge University Press).

DI PAOLO, E. (2009). 'Extended Life', *Topoi,* 28: 9–21.

GUPTA, B. (1998). *The Disinterested Witness: A Fragment of Advaita Vedanta Phenomenology* (Evanston, Ill.: Northwestern University Press).

GURWITSCH, A. (1966). 'A Nonegological Conception of Consciousness', in A. Gurwitsch, *Studies in Phenomenology and Psychology* (Evanston, Ill.: Northwestern University Press), 287–300.

JONAS, H. (1996). *Mortality and Morality: A Search for the Good After Auschwitz* (Evanston, Ill.: Northwestern University Press).

LEGRAND, D. (2006). 'The Bodily Self: The Sensori-Motor Roots of Pre-Reflexive Self-Consciousness', *Phenomenology and the Cognitive Sciences* 5: 89–118.

——(2007). 'Pre-Reflective Self-Consciousness: On Being Bodily in the World', *Janus Head* 9/1: 493–519.

MACKENZIE, M. (2009). 'Enacting the Self: Buddhist and Enactivist Approaches to the Emergence of the Self', *Phenomenology and the Cognitive Sciences* (DOI 10.1007/s11097-009-9132-8).

MERLEAU-PONTY, M. (1962). *Phenomenology of Perception,* tr. Colin Smith (London: Routledge Press).

SARTRE, J.-P. (1991). *The Transcendence of the Ego* (New York: Hill & Wang).

SEARLE, J. (2000). 'Consciousness, Free Action, and the Brain'. *Journal of Consciousness Studies,* 7/10: 3–22.

SHOEMAKER, S. (1968). 'Self-Reference and Self-Awareness', *Journal of Philosophy,* 65: 555–67.

——(1984). 'Personal Identity: A Materialist's Account. in S. Shoemaker and R. Swinburne (eds), *Personal Identity* (Oxford: Basil Blackwell).

——(1986). 'Introspection and the self', *Midwest Studies in Philosophy* 10: 101–20.

SIDERITS, M., THOMPSON, E., and ZAHAVI, D. (eds) (2010). *Self, No-Self? Perspectives from Analytical, Phenomenological, and Indian Traditions* (Oxford: Clarendon Press).

STRAWSON, G. (1997). 'The self', *Journal of Consciousness Studies,* 4/5–6: 405–28.

THOMPSON, E. (2007). *Mind in Life: Biology, Phenomenology, and the Sciences of Mind* (Cambridge, Mass.: Harvard University Press).

——and STAPLETON, M. (2009). 'Making Sense of Sense-Making: Reflections on Enactive and Extended Mind Theories', *Topoi,* 28: 23–30.

ZAHAVI, D. (2002). 'First-Person Thoughts and Embodied Self-Awareness: Some Reflections on the Relation between Recent Analytical Philosophy and Phenomenology', *Phenomenology and the Cognitive Sciences,* 1: 7–26.

——(2005). *Subjectivity and Selfhood: Investigating the First-Person Perspective* (Cambridge, Mass.: MIT Press, Bradford Books).

PART III

PHENOMENOLOGY AND METAPHYSICS OF SELF

CHAPTER 10

··

THE MINIMAL
SUBJECT

··

GALEN STRAWSON

1. INTRODUCTION

··

Consider a subject of experience as it is present and alive in the living moment of experience. Consider its experience—where by the word 'experience' I mean the experiential-qualitative character of experience, experiential 'what-it's-likeness', and absolutely nothing else. Strip away in thought everything other than the being of this experience.

When you do this, the subject remains. You can't get rid of the subject of experience, in taking a portion of experience or experiential what-it's-likeness and stripping away everything other than the existence of that experience. Concretely occurring experience can't possibly exist without a subject of experience existing. If you strip away the subject, you haven't got experience any more. You can't get things down to concretely occurring experiential content[1] existing at a given time without an experiencer existing at that time. This is the *Experience/Experiencer Thesis*:

(1) Experience is impossible without an experiencer.[2]

One shouldn't think that stripping away everything other than the being of experience can somehow leave something less than a complete subject of experience,

---

[1] Experiential content wholly 'internalistically' conceived: everything experiential that you have in common with your philosophical Twin on 'Twin Earth'.

[2] See Frege 1918: 27. Hume knew this well, and section 1.4.6 of his *Treatise* has been much misinterpreted.

something that has, as such, no right to the full title 'subject'. Experience is experienc*ing*: whatever remains if experience remains, something that is correctly called a subject must remain. One can reach this conclusion without endorsing any view about the ontological category of this subject, or indeed of experience.

I'll call the subject that must remain when everything but experience has been stripped away the 'minimal' subject. The fact that I'm calling it 'minimal' doesn't mean that there's any respect in which it isn't a genuine subject, a whole subject of experience. In a fully articulated metaphysics of mind, the minimal subject may turn out to be the best candidate for being called 'the subject' *tout court*: it is arguable that the propriety of calling organisms like human beings 'subjects of experience' is wholly grounded in the fact that the existence of such organisms involves the existence of minimal subjects. And whether this is so or not, the attempt to isolate the minimally viable notion of the subject is I think necessary in a thoroughgoing metaphysics of mind.[3]

The minimal subject, then, remains when one has stripped away everything other than the being of experience. A minimal subject needn't be self-conscious—it may be very primitive, experientially speaking. It may last for only a very short time. It may be of no interest to ethics as ordinarily understood. Its place is in the metaphysics of mind, and in particular the metaphysics of consciousness (using 'consciousness' to mean experience in the sense defined above). There's no tension between the claim that minimal subjects exist and the best scientific psychology and neurology, or the current stress in philosophy of mind on the profoundly environmentally embedded, embodied, 'enactive', 'ecological', or (for short) *EEE* aspects of our experiential predicament as organic and social beings situated in a physical world. To think that there is is to have misunderstood the present project.

I'm not going to argue for the minimal subject. I'm going to describe it. I'm going to give an account of what I think it comes to, given certain assumptions. It certainly exists as defined, because experience certainly exists, and the existence of the minimal subject is given with the existence of experience: experience is experiencing, and experiencing is impossible without an experiencer.

The next four sections prepare the ground.

2. TOS

—The use of the count noun 'minimal subject' amounts in effect to an assumption about the ontological category of minimal subjects. It strongly inclines us to think that minimal subjects must be things or objects or substances of some kind.

---

[3] Compare Dainton's different notion of the minimal subject (2008: 249–51).

I've explicitly cancelled any such assumption. I think, in fact, that to assert the existence of a subject of experience must in the end be to assert the existence of something that has at least as good a claim to be considered as a Thing or Object or Substance—a 'TOS', for short—as anything else.[4] That said, I accept the increasingly widely held view that all concretely existing TOSs are best thought of as processes that all matter is well thought of as 'process-stuff', relative to whatever conception of time is correct. More dramatically, I reject—with Descartes, Spinoza, Leibniz, Kant, Nietzsche, Russell, Whitehead, Ramsey, and many others—the view that there is a fundamental ontological categorial distinction between the being of a TOS like a human being or a chair, considered at any time, and the being of its propertiedness, considered at that time.[5]

The reduction of 'thing or object or substance' to 'TOS' is an attempt to damp down some of the many different theoretical associations these three words have in philosophy. For x to be a TOS, I propose, is, most fundamentally, just for x to be a unity of a certain kind, a dynamic unity, in Leibnizian phrase, a 'strong activity-unity' (where the word 'activity' carries no implication of intentional agency). On this view, it doesn't matter how x classifies according to the traditional object/process/property/state/event cluster of metaphysical distinctions so long as it can be seen to qualify as a strong unity in the required manner. Unity alone—activity-unity—is the key notion. Those who wish can read 'TOS' as 'strong activity-unity' in what follows.

One model for such unity is an electron, or perhaps the entity that is a pair of entangled electrons, or a human being or other living thing, or (among the ontologically more liberal) a table or chair. Spinoza argues powerfully that only the whole universe can really qualify as such a unity. I'm going to leave tables and chairs on the list of candidate TOSs for purposes of discussion, although they come pretty low on the list according to Feynman, and fail the test altogether according to many others, including Nāgārjuna, Descartes, Spinoza, Leibniz, and van Inwagen.[6]

---

[4] This view is compatible with the view that there aren't any TOSs, and with the view that there aren't any TOSs even though there are subjects of experience.

[5] For argument see e.g. Strawson 2008*a* (revised in Strawson 2009: 304–17). The word 'property' is fine and valuable for many philosophical purposes, but there are areas of philosophical enquiry in which it contains almost irresistible incentives to metaphysical misunderstanding; one difficulty is that the fact that the word works fine in many philosophical contexts leads many to think that it must be fine in all contexts.

[6] See e.g. van Inwagen 1990.

3. MATERIALISM, NATURALISM, AND EXPERIENCE

In offering a description of the minimal subject, I'm going to assume that materialism or equivalently physicalism is true—that (briefly) every real, concrete phenomenon in this universe is physical.[7] I'm also going to assume for argument, although without great enthusiasm, that physical reality is made up of tiny something-or-others which I'll call 'ultimates' or 'u-fields' ('u' for 'ultimate'), and that everything that concretely exists is a u-field or an interaction of u-fields.[8] I take the term 'u-field' to be neutral as between traditional ontological categories or modes of being. I've already remarked that individual u-fields may be good candidates for being TOSs, given the unity criterion for TOSity. I'm mindful, though, of Russell's remark, long before such discoveries as the discovery that protons are composed of quarks, that 'to treat an electron or a proton as a single entity has become as wrong-headed as it would be to treat the population of London or New York as a single entity' (1927: 254).

I assume materialism, then, but I take 'material' and 'physical' to be natural-kind terms, in a sense that will become clearer in section 11, and by 'materialism' I mean *real materialism*. Real materialists are outright realists about experience. They're outright realists about the experiential-qualitative character of consciousness, experiential what-it's-likeness.[9] All philosophers before about 1915, and almost all philosophers since, are outright realists about experience, but various forms of irrealism about experience have been fashionable in the last hundred years, under such names as 'behaviourism', 'functionalism', and 'representationalism'. The fashion is absurd, but it is so insistent that it is worth listing Block, Chalmers, Fodor, Jackson (pre-2000), Lockwood, Levine, McGinn, Nagel, Kripke, Parfit, and Searle as clear recent representatives of outright realism about experience.

There's so much terminological wreckage in present-day analytic philosophy of mind that it is close to collapse as a shared enterprise. So let me add that by 'experience' (experiential-qualitative character, what-it's-likeness) I mean *real* experience, and that by 'realism about experience' I mean *real* realism about experience. What is real realism about experience? Consider basic examples of experience: pain, itching, blue colour-experience, tasting blood. One way to convey what is to be a real realist about experience is to say that it is to continue to take colour experience or taste experience or experience of pain to be what one took it to be—knew it to be—quite unreflectively, before one did any philosophy, for

[7] I use 'phenomenon' as a completely general word for any sort of concrete existent without regard to ontological category.

[8] Wilson 2004 calls this 'smallism'.

[9] This is what the word 'materialism' always meant until unreal materialism arrived in the 20th century. Only then did the word become, for some, the name of a position that denies the existence of the most certainly known thing: the experiential-qualitative character of conscious experience.

example when one was 5.[10] However many new and surprising facts real realists about experience learn from scientists—about the neurophysiology of experience, say, or the 'filling-in' that characterizes visual experience, or 'change blindness', or 'inattentional blindness'[11]—their basic grasp of what colour experience or pain experience (etc.) is remains exactly the same as it was before they did any philosophy. It remains, in other words, correct, grounded in the fact that to have experience at all is already to know what experience is, however little one reflects about it. *The having is the knowing*. It is knowledge 'by acquaintance'. To taste pineapple, in Locke's old example, is sufficient, as well as necessary, for knowing what it is like to taste pineapple.[12]

This way of saying what I mean by 'experience', and hence by 'realist about experience', guarantees that anyone who claims not to know what I mean is being disingenuous (the last paragraph would be unnecessary if philosophers like Dennett hadn't looking-glassed the term 'consciousness' or 'experience').[13]

Real materialism, then, incorporates real realism about experience. It accepts that all mental goings on, including crucially all experiential goings on, are wholly physical goings on. It doesn't take it to follow that there must somehow be less to experience than we thought before we did philosophy. On the contrary, it concludes that there must be more to the physical than we thought before we did philosophy—assuming that we then took the physical to be something essentially non-experiential in nature. Real materialism is adductive, not reductive. If materialism is true, it says, there must be more to the physical than we thought, for experience is real and must be wholly physical if materialism is true. Real materialists don't (can't) set up the terms 'mental' and 'physical' in opposition to each other, except when talking loosely, because they hold that everything that concretely exists is physical. Instead they distinguish the mental physical from the non-mental physical, the experiential physical from the non-experiential physical; for everything that exists, on their view, and once again, is physical.

All this is part of *real* naturalism, which I take to be the same as real materialism. Real naturalism is serious, hard-nosed naturalism, naturalism that starts from the most certainly known natural fact, the fact of experience, the fact of the existence of experience, as fully comprehended by (e.g.) 5-year-olds. To this it adds a commitment to materialism, and this delivers real materialism. Real naturalism is in

[10] One doesn't need to attribute a general conception of experience to 5-year-olds to make the point, but one shouldn't underestimate 5-year-olds (some of them wonder whether others see colours the way they do themselves).

[11] See e.g. Pessoa and De Weerd 2003; Simons and Levin 1997; Chun and Marois 2002.

[12] Locke 1689–1700: 2. 1. 6. I put aside the point that different people may have different taste-experiences in tasting pineapple.

[13] To looking-glass a term is to define it in such a way that whatever one means by it excludes what the term means.

direct conflict with the wildly anti-naturalist doctrine now commonly known as 'naturalism', which tries to turn its first (or at least equal first) datum into its greatest problem, and then deal with it by denying its existence!

4. EXPERIENCE IS EXPERIENCE-*FOR*

Experience is necessarily experience-*for*—experience for someone or something. I intend this only in the sense in which it is necessarily true, and without commitment to any particular account of the metaphysical nature of the someone-or-something.

To claim that experience is necessarily experience-for, experience-for-someone-or-something, is to claim that it is necessarily experience on the part of a subject of experience. Again I intend this only in the sense in which it is a necessary truth, and certainly without any commitment to the idea that subjects of experience are persisting things. This is the Experience/Experiencer Thesis.

Some say one can't infer the existence of a subject from the existence of experience (see e.g. Stone 1988, 2005), only the existence of subjectivity, but I understand the notion of the subject in a maximally ontologically non-committal way: in such a way that the presence of subjectivity is already sufficient for the presence of a subject, so that 'there is subjectivity, but there isn't a subject' can't possibly be true.

Consider pain, a well known experience. It is, essentially, a feeling, and a feeling is just that, a *feeling*, i.e. a feel-ing, a being-felt, and a feel-ing or being-felt can't possibly exist without there being a feel-er. Again I'm only interested in the sense in which this is a necessary truth. The noun 'feeler' doesn't import any metaphysical commitment additional to the noun 'feeling'. It simply draws one's attention to the full import of 'feeling'. The sense in which it's necessarily true that there's a feel*ing*, and hence a feel*er*, of pain, if there is pain at all, is the sense in which it's necessarily true that there's a subject of experience if there is experience, and hence subjectivity, at all. These truths are available prior to any particular metaphysics of object or property or process or event or state.[14]

---

[14] Descartes is very clear about this: 'I know that I exist; the question is, what is this I that I know?' I do not know.' I do not know that I am not just a 'human body', or 'some thin vapour which permeates my limbs—a wind, fire, air, breath'. 'But whatever I suppose, and whatever the truth is, for all that I am still something' (1648/1976: 18).

5. SUBJECTIVITY AND SUBJECT–OBJECT STRUCTURE

There are at least two notions of subjectivity in circulation, so let me briefly try to clarify the one I have in mind. John Dunne follows a venerable tradition when he claims that subjectivity always involves experience having a 'subject–object structure'. This, however, leads him to hold that the subjectivity of experience is at its lowest ebb in cases like the experience of orgasm,[15] and this in turn puts him at odds with what is I think the most common understanding of the notion of subjectivity in philosophy of mind, according to which subjectivity is in no way diminished in the case of orgasm.[16] I favour the second understanding of subjectivity, and take 'subjectivity' to be synonymous with 'experientiality', i.e., with 'experience' (mass term) as defined in section 1, experiencing, the phenomenon of experiential-qualitative character, experiential 'what-it's-likeness'.

This is not to reject the venerable tradition. There's a sense in which all subjectivity necessarily has subject–object structure. All experience has subject–object structure simply insofar as all experience necessarily has experiential content, experiential content which is (of course) experienced by the subject of experience and which to that extent 'stands over against' the subject as object to subject. In this sense, 'object' means nothing more than 'experiential content'; it carries no trace of any implication that anything external to experience exists.[17]

To say that all experience has subject–object structure in this sense is not to say that all experience necessarily has subject–object structure phenomenologically speaking—i.e., that the (necessary) subject-object structure of experience is always somehow experienced as such by the experiencer.[18] Nor is it to say that all experience has subject–object structure in any metaphysical sense that involves the idea that the subject of experience is irreducibly ontologically distinct from the content of experience. I think that there's a metaphysically crucial notion of what the subject of experience is—which is, precisely, the notion of the minimal subject—given which there's no real distinction between the subject of experience and that which is the object of experience, in the sense of the content of the

---

[15] Dunne forthcoming.

[16] Some claim that it's increased, but it isn't a matter of degree.

[17] Or at least that any concrete external thing exists (I add the qualification for those who take it that there's an abstract entity corresponding to every possible experiential content). Note that I accept the implication that all experience, in necessarily having an object, is necessarily intentional, for reasons given in Montague 2009. All experience has experiential content (a necessary truth), and there's a fundamental sense of 'intentional' according to which the existence of experiential content is sufficient for the existence of intentionality.

[18] It's not clear that one needs to say this even if one holds, along with many phenomenologists, that all experience—even in the simplest organisms—involves some sort of sense of self.

experience (internalistically understood). In fact I endorse the *Experience/Experi-encer Identity Thesis*, along with Descartes, Kant, William James, and others, according to which

(2) The subject is identical with its experience.[19]

This, though, is a very difficult idea, at least on first acquaintance. It's immediately tripped up by Leibniz's Law, a device that is massively misapplied in philosophy (most of its uses amount to an insistence on the validity of ordinary thought categories or ordinary language use, masquerading as a killer metaphysical objection). In fact Leibniz's Law has no real force against the Experience/Experiencer Identity Thesis; nevertheless I'll put the thesis aside. It certainly isn't forced on us by the Experience/Experiencer Thesis, the 'obvious conceptual truth that an experiencing is necessarily an experiencing by a subject of experience, and involves that subject as intimately as a branch-bending involves a branch' (Shoemaker 1986: 10), for this, so far, allows the (minimal) subject to be ontically distinct from—non-identical with—the experience.

6. THIN SUBJECTS

Consider Louis, a representative human being, a subject of experience. Louis is a portion of reality that I will—for purposes of discussion—take to be neatly separable off from the rest of reality. We're familiar with the *thick* conception of the subject, according to which the subject is the whole organism, e.g., the whole human being. We're no less familiar with the *traditional inner* conception of the subject, according to which the subject is a persisting entity which isn't the same thing as the whole human being, a particular persisting complex brain-system, say, or an immaterial soul (an immaterial soul isn't strictly speaking inner, but the idea is clear). In both the thick and the traditional case it is standardly supposed that the subject can continue to exist when there's no experience that it is the subject of. The existence of Louis as subject of experience isn't thought to be put in question by the fact that Louis is now in a dreamless sleep. (The same goes for immaterial subjects as conceived by Locke and many others, although not for Cartesian immaterial subjects.)

According to the *thin inner* conception of the subject of experience, by contrast, a subject of experience is something that exists only if experience exists that it is the subject of. A thin subject is essentially experientially 'live', it can't have merely

---

[19] Descartes 1648: 15; Kant 1772: 75; James 1890: i. 191; Strawson 2008*b*, 2009: 405–19.

dispositional being; if there's no experience/experiencing, there's no subject of experience. And we may now invoke the Experience/Experiencer Thesis (if there's no subject of experience, then there's no experience) to add an 'if' to this 'only if', to get

(3) A thin *subject of experience* exists if and only if *experience* exists that it is the *subject of.*

The thin conception of the subject isn't currently popular. The idea that subjects continue to exist when there's no experience is deeply engrained in the currently standard use of 'subject of experience', not only among those who assume that the subject is the whole organism, or a persisting neural structure, but also among radical Daintonian 'C-theorists', who hold that subjects are simply 'collections of experiential powers', things that can exist without ever being the source or site of any actual experience.[20] I don't think it's possible to get far in the metaphysics of the subject without having the notion of the thin subject in play, whether or not one chooses to endorse it (along with Descartes, Leibniz, Spinoza, Kant in 1772, Fichte, James, and Husserl, among others).[21] But I'm not going to defend it. I'm simply going to use it to the exclusion of the other two. When I talk about subjects, then, I mean thin subjects. It's perfectly acceptable to call a whole human being a subject of experience, on this view, but the reason it's acceptable is that the existence of the whole human being involves the existence of an inner subject. And when we try to say exactly why any traditional, persisting, *non*-thin candidate for being an inner subject qualifies as a subject, we are eventually led, so I believe, to the notion of the thin subject.

Thin subjects certainly exist, whatever their ontological category or mode of being, for experience certainly exists, and to speak of a thin subject is (by definition) just to speak in a certain way of a feature of reality that certainly exists given that experience exists. It's to speak of a feature of reality that is part of what it is for experience to exist, for experience is experiencing, and the existence of a thin subject is guaranteed by the fact that there is experiencing. It is, if you like, the *live subjectivity phenomenon* that certainly exists if experience exists, and (equally certainly) exists only if experience exists. There's nothing 'anti-naturalistic' about the notion of the thin subject (even in the bad sense of 'naturalistic' rejected in section 3). To think that there is is, again, to misunderstand the present project. You may think that the cut in reality that the notion of the thin subject makes isn't philosophically significant. For the moment it's enough that you allow that it makes a cut that yields a genuine portion of reality, a portion of reality that we can give a name like 'thin subject' to—whether or not you think that such portions of

[20] Dainton 2008.

[21] Hume holds that it's the only positively empirically warranted conception of the subject, but he doesn't endorse it. His clearly stated position is that 'the essence of the mind [is] unknown' (1739–40: introduction, §8).

reality are good candidates for being TOSs in the way that human beings or persisting complex brain-systems are supposed to be.

Given this definition of 'thin subject', my proposal is that

(4) All minimal subjects are thin subjects.

Minimal subjects certainly exist as initially defined, given that experience exists, for experience is sufficient for their existence. They're now further defined by the condition that they exist only if experience exists. Part of what it is for them to be *minimal* subjects is for them to have no being of such a kind that they could exist without experience existing.

The converse of (4), i.e.

(5) All thin subjects are minimal subjects

completes the definition, and the merging of the terms 'thin' and 'minimal'. A thin or minimal subject is a portion of live subjectivity. If there are constant, short, unnoticed gaps in the experience of an ordinary human being during the normal waking day, as I suspect there are, then the existence of a human being during a normal waking day involves the existence of many thin or minimal subjects, although we (or most of us) normally think of it as involving the existence of a single continuing subject.

Note that the thin notion of the subject doesn't exclude the use of other notions, even if one accords it a certain metaphysical primacy.

7. THE LIVING MOMENT OF EXPERIENCE

We have the minimal subject as it is present and alive in the living moment of experience. But what is the living moment of experience? It isn't a durationless instant, because there can't be any experience at a durationless instant, so it is at least a short temporal interval. I propose to characterize it as follows.

(6) The living moment of experience is the shortest period of time in which experience can be going on at all.

It is an empirical question how long this is (it may possibly vary from species to species), but I take it that it is in any case a much shorter period of time than the so-called 'specious present', which Dainton estimates to last for up to a third of a second.

If time is 'dense' in the mathematical sense, and there is between any two moments (temporal intervals) always a third, and if there are periods of experience that are truly temporally continuous, as we ordinarily assume, then living moments of experience are indefinitely short. In this case the term 'living moment of experience' denotes a theoretical abstraction from the concrete continuum. It's not a real measure, something which allows us to say 'This living moment of experience ends here and this one begins here'. If on the other hand time isn't dense, but has a grainy structure at the very small scale, as some suppose, then living moments of experience may indeed be discrete entities. Some call the fundamental units of time 'chronons' (perhaps there are about 10^{43} a second). One proposal may then be that each living moment of experience lasts for one chronon.

The question is not one for neurology or experimental psychology. These disciplines have their own interesting questions—about the shortest stimuli that we can detect in any given sensory modality, about the temporally closest stimuli that we can temporally order, and so on. They may even definitively inform us, one day, that experience comes in short bursts, lasting 20 ms, say, or 50 ms. It won't be possible to identify these 20 ms or 50 ms bursts with the living moment of experience, however, for although it may then be true that experience can't go on at all unless there is at least 20 ms of it, it won't be true that 20 ms is the shortest period of time in which experience can be going on, so long as it is true that experience is going on throughout the 20 ms in question.

8. STRONG ACTIVITY-UNITY: AN EXAMPLE

Consider an experiencing subject in the living moment of experience, a human being, say. Consider the totality of its experience at that moment, its 'total experiential field', the total content of its experiential field at that moment, and ask whether it could fail to be experientially single or unified in being what it is.

To ask the question is to see the fundamental sense in which the answer is No. The total experiential field involves many things—rich interoceptive (somatosensory) and exteroceptive sensation, mood-and-affect-tone, deep conceptual animation, and so on. It has, standardly, a particular focus, and more or less dim peripheral areas, and it is, no doubt, and overall, quite extraordinarily complex in content. But it is for all that a unity, and essentially—necessarily—so. It is fundamentally unified, utterly indivisible, as the particular concrete phenomenon it is, simply in being, indeed, *a* total experiential field; or, equivalently, simply in being *the* content of the experience of a single subject at that moment.[22] The unity

---

[22] I don't want to rule out the possibility that there can be more than one total experiential field in a human being at a given time. If there can, the present point about necessary singleness will apply to each one individually.

or singleness of the (thin) subject of the total experiential field in the living moment of experience and the unity or singleness of the total experiential field are aspects of the same thing. They're necessarily dependent on each other even if they aren't the same thing.

I think, in fact, that there's only a conceptual distinction between them, not a 'real' distinction in Descartes's sense, for neither can conceivably exist without the other. In which case there's no dependence relation of a sort that requires two really (real-ly) distinct entities. But the present point is simply the point—the simple point—that *a* field, a single field, strictly entails *a* subject, a single subject, and conversely. If you bring a single thin subject into existence at time *t* then you necessarily bring a single, unified experiential field into existence at *t*, and conversely. The singleness of the subject at *t* entails, and is in fact essentially constitutive of, the singleness of its total experiential field at *t*. So too, the singleness of the total experiential field at *t* entails the singleness of its subject at *t*, for the experiential content that is experienced is necessarily experienced in a single or unified experiential perspective (anything that is experientially there at all, in any sense at all, is automatically part of the unity, just as any paint that is added, in the painting of a picture, is immediately and automatically and wholly part of the whole picture). The point is a 'logical' one, as 'trivial' as it is important. I'll call it *Fundamental Singleness*—the 'indecomposable' unity of any experience (James 1890: i. 371). Experiencing one's experience as fragmentary at a given time doesn't put the singleness of the subject or total experiential field in question; on the contrary, it presupposes it. Experimental-psychological results that deliver a sense in which our visual field (say) is gappy have no impact on the point.

Fundamental Singleness holds true of all necessarily-subject-of-experience-involving experiential-field unities, whatever their duration, and it applies to all possible subjects of experience, however complex or primitive. This means that it is independent of Kant's relatively speaking much higher level claim that when we consider ourselves as subjects we must necessarily regard ourselves as single; his claim that 'the proposition *I am simple* [i.e. single] must be regarded as a direct expression of apperception' (1781–7: A355). For one thing, Kant's claim seems to be restricted to expressly self-conscious creatures like ourselves, whereas the present Fundamental Singleness thesis doesn't depend on the subject's having any sort of express or 'thetic' experience of itself as subject at all, let alone any such experience of itself as single, as subject. If worms have experience, their experience has Fundamental Singleness, at any given time, and not just by being very simple.

It may be said that the unities in question (unity of subject, unity of experiential field) are 'merely functional' unities, in some sense, but it's not clear what 'merely' can mean, given that what are in question are actual, concretely existing phenomena, i.e., a concretely existing total experiential field, and a concretely existing subject for whom that field is an experiential field. And whatever it may mean, it's quite unclear how it could detract in any way from these unities' claim to be true metaphysical unities. Even if we can find a sense in which they're functional unities, it can't touch the fact that we have to do with concretely existing unities, genuine metaphysical unities, unbeatable examples of strong activity-unities that have, as such, an unbeatable claim to TOSity. And by the time we have *processualized* the notion of a TOS in the way we have to if it's to retain any place in fundamental metaphysics, and have rejected the idea that TOSs are entities that stand in fundamental ontological contrast with instantiated properties, there will be no grounds for supposing that these unsurpassable examples of concretely existing unity—these experiential-field unities, these thin-subject experiencer unities—have less claim to be TOSs than paradigmatic examples of strong activity-unities, such as u-fields, or indeed good old-fashioned immaterial souls.

It may now be objected that Fundamental Singleness is a 'merely experiential unity' and so not a real metaphysical unity. The first target of this objection is likely to be the claim that a total experiential field is itself a true or objective metaphysical unity—the objection being that this unity is really only an appearance: that it is only from a certain point of view that the total experiential field presents as unified. The objection may then be aimed directly at the (thin) subject of the experience, the objection being that the unsurpassable unity of thin subject, too, is, somehow, 'merely experiential'.

It's true that the unity of the total experiential field of an experience is essentially, and if you like 'merely', an *internal experiential* or *IE* unity, whatever else it is or isn't. It's true that it is a unity considered just in respect of its internal experiential character, a unity considered from the point of view of its subject, a unity, indeed, that is constituted as such by the existence of the point of view of its subject.[23] It's also true that there's a crucial sense in which its fundamental-unity characteristic is wholly a matter of its experiential being (when we consider the existence of the experience non-experientially, we find millions of u-fields in a certain complex state of interaction, on the smallest hypothesis). All true. But it is at the same time an objective fact that subjective experience exists, and it's an objective fact that it has the character it does. That is: the experiential fact that one of these IE unities exists is itself an objective metaphysical fact, a fact about the world. That is, it's a fact that stands as a fact from a perspective external to the perspective internal to the IE unity. The reason why we're right to judge an IE unity to be a fully metaphysically real unity when considering it externally, from the outside, objective point of view, is nothing other than the fact that it is indeed a strong internal experiential unity, a unity constituted as such by an internal subjective point of view. But there's nothing odd about the sense in which subjective phenomena can be objective facts. This is part of any minimally sensible realism about the subjective (pain is real!). All that's added here is the slightly

---

[23] However unreflective the subject, however little 'thetic' apprehension it has of the fact that the unity in question is a unity.

more specific point that the existence of an IE unity—an IE unity that is the experiencing of a total experiential field by an experiencing subject at a given moment—is itself an objectively existing real unity (experience is real!), both in its single-subject aspect and in its single total-experiential-field aspect (which may at bottom be the same thing). The statement that this unity exists and is wholly metaphysically real holds true outside the perspective of the subject in question, although the unity in question is nothing other than the phenomenon of the existence of that subject having that experience, with the content that it has, at the time in question.[24]

If this is right, then both (a), the occurrent experiential content (the total-experiential-field content) that we find in any given living moment of experience, and (b), the subject for whom that experiential content is experiential content, have the strong-activity-unity characteristic to an apparently unsurpassable degree. They are therefore, so far, prime candidates for being TOSs, although they're not (given smallist materialism) absolute metaphysical simples in the way that the ultimate constituents of physical reality (or immaterial souls) are sometimes supposed to be.

—The claim that minimal subjects possess the strong-activity-unity property depends, so far, on what we find when we consider them in the living moment of experience. But while it may be easy to specify synchronic unity conditions (or identity conditions), it may not be nearly so easy to specify diachronic unity conditions (identity conditions). But you must do so if minimal subjects are going to have a chance of qualifying as TOSs.

Here are two possible solutions. The first is that time is discrete and that living moments of experience are one chronon long (perhaps 10^{43} seconds). The second is that experience comes in discrete units of a neurophysiologically detectable size (whether time is discrete or dense in the specified sense), say 25 ms. These solutions take questions about the diachronic identity conditions of minimal subjects to be empirical questions that we may or may not be able to answer.

A third and more sweeping reply: it's already enough if we have found strong activity-unity in the living moment of experience. This is sufficient proof that we have found a TOS, and we just needn't worry about how long it lasts. On this view, minimal subjects have, knowably, the strong activity-unity sufficient for TOSity. They also have genuine temporal extent (given that time is real), because nothing can exist only at an instant. We don't need to think further. We can judge a phenomenon to be a TOS on the basis of inspection at a given moment, merely on the basis of the quality—the strong-activity-unity quality—of its mode of being at that moment.

---

[24] There need be no distinctive experience of unity on the part of the subject of the IE unity, inasmuch as the necessary unity in question is simply the fact already mentioned: the trivial fact that any subject necessarily experiences all the material it experiences at any given time in a single experiential perspective.

—On your view mere patches of experiential content come out as prime candidates for being TOSs, in addition to subjects of experience. This is a *reductio* of the idea that strong activity-unity is all that matters when it comes to TOSity—to say nothing of the idea that the object/property distinction is not a fundamental and categorial ontological distinction.

I have no difficulty with the TOSity of what you call 'patches of experiential content', given Fundamental Singleness. As for the standard object/property distinction, I think it's past saving (see n. 5 above).

9. THE PHYSICALITY OF MINIMAL SUBJECTS

The Fundamental Singleness point adds to our understanding of the nature of the minimal subject (of any subject considered in the living moment of experience). But what exactly is the minimal subject, given that materialism is true? What is its physical being?

It is best, perhaps, to ask first what experience is, given that materialism is true. I've assumed that it's wholly a matter of brain activity. There's a great deal of brain activity in Louis, in the Louis-reality, and some of it, I take it, is experience (what-it's-likeness), although this doesn't show up when the brain is inspected by neurophysiology or physics.

This assumption puts me at odds with some versions of EEE thinking, if they hold, as they seem to, that Louis's experience is located or realized in his whole body, or at least in more than his brain. Fine—the question is empirical. It's a question about what Louis's experience (what-it's-likeness) actually is, physically speaking—a question about which u-fields in his body, in which state of activation, actually are his experience (I use 'is' for clarity, in preference to 'constitute' and 'consist in'). My bet is that the site or location of his experience is wholly in the brain, although I don't want to rule out the possibility that brain prostheses ('wetware' or not) that exhibit phase-locked activation of the sort characteristic of the brain may one day realize experience outside the brain (see e.g. Clark 2009). So too, I take it that the existence of a minimal subject is wholly a matter of brain activity. This, I propose, is what we have to do with when we have to do with a minimal subject as it is present and alive in the living moment of experience.

Consider a particular living moment of experience, a particular temporal interval t, and consider the experience going on during t, which I'll call e. The proposal is that e is a large number of brain-constituting u-fields in a highly complexly structured state of interaction, a complexly structured portion of neural process-stuff,[25] a *neural synergy* of process-stuff, which I'll call n^e

---

[25] The word 'process-stuff' builds temporality into the superficially static notion of a portion.

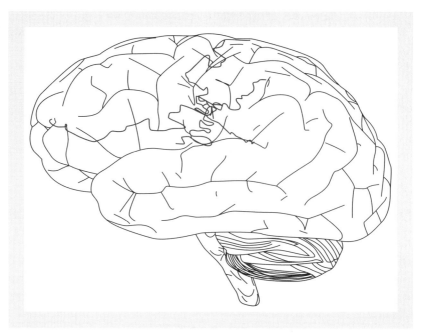

Figure 10.1 Experience *e*

(remember that the term 'u-field' is officially neutral between different ontological categories or modes of being) The phenomenon n^e, then, is identical with the phenomenon e, and one perspicuous name for this phenomenon is $[n^e = e]$.

One might represent $[n^e = e]$ schematically by the added squiggles in Figure 10.1. Given that $[n^e = e]$ exists at t, a minimal subject exists at t, because $[n^e = e]$ is experience, and experience can't exist without a minimal subject of experience existing. I'll call the minimal subject of e 's', and I'll confine my attention to human minimal subjects.

We know that s exists at t, given that e exists, because (again) experience can't exist without a subject of experience existing, and indeed without a minimal subject existing, and s is the name we've given to the minimal subject of e independently of any view about its ontological category. The existence of s, like that of e, is the existence of a synergy of neural process-stuff n^s, so that $[n^s = s]$, for I've assumed that everything that concretely exists is either a u-field or a number of u-fields in a certain spatiotemporal relation, and the present suggestion is simply that the existence of s is the existence of a number of u-fields in the brain and isn't something smaller or simpler or less closely spatiotemporally related than anything that could reasonably be called a neural *synergy* (e.g. a single-u-field-sized portion of neural process-stuff, or a non-synergetic set of single-u-field-sized portions of neural process-stuff). s is a synergy subject: $[n^s = s]$.

10. What is the Relation between E and S?

[$n^s = s$] certainly exists, given that [$n^s = e$] exists. What is the relation between them? What, in other words, is the relation between e and s?

Before considering this question, let me say that the basic picture of the minimal subject is in place, and that this is one possible point to stop reading (what follows is more exploratory).

In the normal course of things the existence of e depends on the existence of many other things. e occurs in a living human being, and is, perhaps, experience of a castle. In this case it depends causally on the aliveness of the human being, the castle, photons, the operation of the optic nerve, and so on. But these things are not part of what e is, considered in itself. One can put the point by saying that a god could conceivably create a neural synergy qualitatively indistinguishable from [$n^e = e$] without creating anything else (it would in so doing create a subject of experience $s^* \neq s$ whose experience $e^* \neq e$ was qualitatively identical to s's experience e).

I've assumed that the existence of s, like the existence of e, is nothing more than the existence of a neural synergy, and I take it, unsurprisingly, that e and s are in the same brain. The question is then this. Is s either entirely distinct from e, or do they overlap? Is [$n^s = s$] a proper part of [$n^e = e$], or is [$n^e = e$] a proper part of [$n^s = s$], or are they somehow (mysteriously) identical?

The portion of process-stuff s, existing at t, is the actual subject or haver of e, existing at t, which is itself a portion of process-stuff. I take it that s, a portion of process-stuff, can't possibly exist at any other time, or be any other activity of u-fields than the activity of u-fields it is; and that the same goes for e. They are as it were 'time-stamped'; they can't have any being other than their actual being (not just because they consist partly of virtual particles, which—plausibly—can't possibly exist at any time or place other than the time and place at which they do exist). s and e can't vary under counterfactual speculation, given that they actually exist, although we can say that they might not have existed at all.

Can we say that s might have existed although e didn't, or conversely? Only if they are entirely distinct. Any overlap puts them both in place, existing exactly as they do—as surely as their being identical does. Can they be entirely distinct, in such a way that one could possibly exist without the other? No, because e is experience, actual experiencing, a necessarily-subject-involving phenomenon. The property of being necessarily-subject-involving is already given just with e, the portion of process-stuff that is e, and since s is the actual subject of e, i.e., part (or all) of the necessarily-subject-involving-ness of e, e, the actual portion of process-stuff e, can't possibly exist without s existing. So too, s can't possibly exist without experience existing (by definition of 'minimal subject'), and since s is actually the subject of e, s, actual s, can't possibly exist without e existing. s and e can't possibly come apart under counterfactual speculation (a device that is often misused in philosophy). e couldn't possibly have had some other subject $s^* \neq s$, and s couldn't possibly have had some other portion of experience $e^* \neq e$.

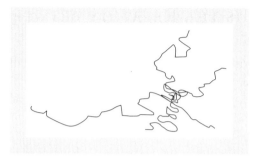

Figure 10.2 $e = s$

Figure 10.3

At the very least, the portion of process-stuff s and the portion of process-stuff e overlap. Are they in fact—somehow—identical? I'm inclined to think so, as already remarked, in which case there is nothing more to the existence of s than the existence of e as depicted in Figure 10.2.

This, though, is a difficult idea, and it may be said that there must be more to s than e, as indicated by the thicker lines in Figure 10.3, although s and e are partly overlapping, partly constituted of the same u-fields or process-stuff.

This can't be an adequate depiction of things, in fact, given that the squiggles represent e, an actual experiencing whose existence is sufficient for the existence of s whether or not anything else exists, but the question of which process-stuff s is is in any case a straightforward question of fact. Its status as a question of fact, a question for science, is straightforward even if it is a very difficult—perhaps impossible—question to answer.

11. PROBLEMS WITH E

—Many other questions arise before this one. For one thing, all portions of process-stuff have non-experiential being, whatever their size, and whether or not they also have experiential being. So when single-u-field-sized portions of process-stuff form part of an experience like *e*, and therefore have experiential being, they must also have non-experiential being. But their non-experiential being can't directly constitute the experiential being of *e*, given the definition of 'experience' in section 1. So one can't in fact refer just to *e* in referring to neural synergy n^e. In referring to neural synergy n^e one inevitably refers also to the non-experiential being of n^e. So, at the very least, you're going to have to say that one refers only to certain *properties* of n^e, in referring to *e*; in which case one doesn't refer to a TOS at all, on your terms.

A first reply is that something may come out as a matter of properties on your metaphysical scheme without failing to be a full fledged TOS on mine; all it has to do is to be a strong activity-unity. The object/property distinction doesn't cut reality at any real joints, only at conventional joints that are useful and natural for many human purposes.[26] This has been known for a long time, in fact, and there's pressure on the object/property distinction from science, not just philosophy.

A second reply is that I'm not worried about the TOSity of *e* so long as the TOSity of *s* is secure. I'm going to put this reply aside, though, on account of my fondness for the Experience/Experiencer Identity Thesis, which has the consequence that anything that is a problem for *e* is a problem for *s*.

A third reply invokes panpsychism. There are impressive reasons for thinking that the most tenable form of real materialism should not only be panpsychist, in holding that all matter *sive* mass/energy is experience-*involving*, but pure panpsychist, in holding outright that all mass/energy is experience, experientiality, necessarily-subject-of-experience-involving experientiality: the energy or activity whose nature we capture in part in the structure-revealing equations of physics is in fact experientiality. On this view, the problem raised by the non-experiential being of process-stuff disappears, for it has none.[27]

Pure panpsychism is fully compatible with current physics, because it simply carries out a 'global replace' on the conventional conception of the mass/energy as non-experiential, replacing it by a conception of mass/energy as experientiality. All the phenomena remain fully correctly characterizable by physics (or a completed physics) within the limits of physics's powers of characterization. Nothing that physics can possibly get right, given its expressive power, either is or can be put in question by pure panpsychism.

You're reaching for Occam's razor, but it may not do what you want. To hold on to the conventional view that physical reality is in its fundamental nature entirely non-experiential, while remaining a real materialist, is to take on the colossal problem of how it is that certain spatiotemporal arrangements of entirely non-experiential phenomena can be experiential phenomena.[28] Faced with this problem, Occam's

---

[26] For some purposes: there's a sense in which the object/property distinction is not even part of ordinary thought. See n. 5 above.

[27] Other problems remain. See e.g. James 1890: i. 158–62.

[28] I argue for this in Strawson 2006.

razor cuts away irreducibly *non*-experiential phenomena, leaving panpsychism. Perhaps the energy that is physical reality is partly experiential but also partly non-experiential in its fundamental nature? Again Occam's razor slices away the irreducibly non-experiential in favour of pure panpsychism, which is more parsimonious than this hybrid view in denying a fundamental dualism.

Some think I sail off the map at this point. I'm sure I'm still on the map, if the terrain (or ocean) is the metaphysics of the self or subject of experience. My continued use of the terms 'materialism' and 'physicalism' may seem intolerable, but it's fully in accord with treating these terms as the natural-kind terms they are or should be. Twenty years' advocacy of the natural-kind-term use of 'physical' and 'material' has shown me that it isn't going to catch on, however,[29] and I retain the terms only to emphasize the important point that the present view is (i) a view about the actual nature of the concrete reality that physics deals with, (ii) a view that allows—takes it—that physics may have got a very great deal right about the (ultimate) nature of reality, and (iii) a view that takes it that the existence of experience and the subject of experience is wholly a matter of brain activity.

Some cite the fundamental 'repugnance' of consciousness and space as a reason why the global replacement can't be carried out (see e.g. McGinn 1995). This move seems weak, because we've known for a long time that *space—extension*—can't be anything like we ordinarily suppose it to be, and the pressure exerted on anything resembling the ordinary idea of space by recent developments in science goes way beyond the already extraordinary pressure that stems from its absorption into the space-time of relativity theory around 100 years ago. 'Space', we may say, is a natural-kind term. It refers to a certain concrete structural reality, but we can't have any confidence that we can know anything more about its nature, considered as a concrete reality, than what we can know about its mathematically characterizable structural features or 'abstract dimensionality'.[30]

Given that the concrete real must have dimensionality (*Existenzraum*, as it were) of some sort, we may say the following: existing conceptions of space or space-time are conceptions of the nature of the dimensionality of the concrete real that fit with existing conceptions of the nature of the concrete real as good old-fashioned non-experiential physical stuff—mass/energy-stuff. To suppose instead that the concrete real is experientiality is to suppose that the dimensionality of the concrete real, although not understood by us, is something that fits with the nature of the concrete real conceived of as experientiality, experiential energy-stuff, in the same general way as the way in which space/space-time—which is certainly not

[29] It's incompatible with the terms of the conventional debate, which distinguishes between materialism, mentalism, idealism, dualism, and so on.
[30] Kant is useful here (see e.g. Kant 1781–7: A358–60, 379–80). See also Greene 2004: 472–91; Lockwood 1989: ch. 10; Strawson 2003: 58–9.

understood by us—fits with the nature of the concrete real conceived of as good old-fashioned non-experientially propertied physical stuff.

A fourth reply puts panpsychism aside. It retains an affection for traditional materialism, holding (*a*) that the being of all portions of physical process-stuff always involves non-experiential being. It is at the same time a real materialist view (section 3), fully realist about experience, as any remotely plausible materialist view must be, and it therefore allows (*b*) that the being of some portions of physical process-stuff involves experiential being at least some of the time. It then moderately proposes (*c*) that the being of portions of physical process-stuff only ever involves experiential being when the process-stuff in question is part of the brains of certain animals, thereby embracing the first and perhaps most popular form of real materialism.

Having taken these moderate steps, it's ready for its positive suggestion—a radicalization of the dissolution of the object/property distinction. The supposed problem is that all portions of process-stuff have non-experiential being. The conclusion drawn is that if the being of *e* is the being of a synergetic portion of process-stuff, *e* must have non-experiential being. But *e* has no non-experiential being by definition. So the being of *e* can't be the being of a synergetic portion of neural process-stuff. So what can it be? It seems that the best we can say is that the being of *e* is the being of certain *properties* of a synergetic portion of neural process-stuff *n*, and not simply of the being of *n* considered as a whole. But this presumably means that we can't think we have a TOS if we have *e*, because we only have property-stuff, as it were. But *e* has already been hailed as an unbeatable example of a TOS.

One of the consequences of the collapse of the traditional object/property distinction, however, is that TOS individuation need be no respecter of traditional TOS boundaries (we're back at the first reply). It can, relative to that tradition, be extremely fine grained, and seem wildly cross-categorial. The fundamental criterion of TOSity, once again, is simply strong activity-unity, nothing more or less. Any phenomenon which seems that it must have the strong activity-unity property, considered in itself, is *ipso facto* as good a candidate as anything else for being a TOS. This is so however odd its metaphysical 'shape' may seem from some perspectives, and even if we're initially and traditionally inclined to identify it as a 'mere' property of something else, for example, or as a bitty collection of aspects of some other phenomenon we naturally think of as a TOS or some other phenomena we natural think of as TOSs.

The proposal is that this may be true of *e*, where '*e*' is as always taken to refer to something wholly experiential. The proposal is that *e* may have the strong-activity-unity characteristic to a very high degree, a degree that suffices to establish its claim to TOSity against all metaphysical schemes that disallow this claim.

—What if it can be shown that the existence of wholly experiential phenomenon *e* (and so of *s*) metaphysically requires the existence of some wholly non-experiential phenomenon *x*?

This is compatible with the ontological separateness of e and x in many metaphysical schemes, where by ontological separateness I mean that e and x have no u-fields (process-stuff) in common, so that a god could conceivably create e without creating x. And in this case e's claim to being a TOS, in spite of the fact that it is wholly experiential being, can stand untouched.

—Suppose there's no such ontological separateness; suppose that the ground of non-experiential x's necessity for experiential e is that x is a part of e, or that e is an inseparable part of x, or indeed that e and x are identical?

This is impossible in almost all existing metaphysical schemes. Wholly non-experiential x can't be identical with, or a part of, wholly experiential e, nor can wholly experiential e be a part of wholly non-experiential x; not at least until we allow that an existent like e can be experiential through and through, i.e. in every aspect, as e is by definition, and at the same time non-experiential in some aspect, and thereby (so it seems) give up the law of non-contradiction. But even if reality is this way, no problem arises for the present argument/description. For in this case, too, the Fundamental-Singleness-based claim that s-involving e is a TOS can stand untouched.

A fifth conciliatory reply simply changes the definition of 'experience' in section 1, allowing that all experience (what-it's-likeness) may after all have irreducible non-experiential being in addition to experiential being. It then argues that the Fundamental Singleness of e (which entails, by being essentially dependent on, the Fundamental Singleness of s) remains secure given the nature of its experiential being. Many difficulties lurk here, though, and I'm still attracted by the idea that what may look like a partial patchwork of the properties of something (i.e. not even the total propertiedness of something) from one standard metaphysical perspective, may from another and more fundamental metaphysical perspective seem as good a candidate for being a TOS as anything else. So let me make one more attempt to satisfy those who hold that e alone can't be a good candidate for being a TOS, because e is a neural synergy of process-stuff and all process-stuff has non-experiential in addition to experiential being.

It seems clear that we can, forsaking all other things, take e and e alone as a legitimate individual *object of thought*, and that we can do this even though e is, by the definition in section 1, absolutely nothing but experiential being. Such is the power of thought. This obviously doesn't show that e can also be taken to be a genuine TOS: e can't be inferred to be a genuine TOS merely on the basis of the fact that it can be taken as a legitimate individual object of thought. The proposal, then, is that e can be known to be a TOS just so long as it can be seen—shown—to fulfil the strong activity-unity requirement even when it and it alone is taken as a legitimate individual object of thought. In this case (the proposal goes), the cut which that thought makes when it considers e and e alone and finds Fundamental Singleness can be, and can be known to be, a genuine metaphysical and indeed TOS-yielding cut, not just a thought-cut.[31] Even if the portion of process-stuff that has to exist if *e* exists contains non-experiential being, still *e*, which by definition has no non-experiential being, can qualify as a TOS. Even if it seems impossible to deny the suitability of a way of putting things according to which we're picking out some *property* or *properties* of a neural synergy *n*, to the exclusion of other properties of *n*, when we pick out *e* as a candidate TOS, still *e* can qualify as a TOS. What other and better criteria of TOSity are there?

—Criteria supplied by physical theory. Leave TOSity to physics.

I would if I could, but physics is experience-blind. It has no way to detect experiential strong activity-unity. As a real materialist, I take it that an ideal extension of our physics would find TOSity, on its own physical-theory terms, wherever there is experiential strong activity-unity. This, though, would involve a coinciding of distinct criteria, given that this physics would still be experience-blind.

Peter's smile can be picked out as a legitimate object of thought even if it can't possibly exist apart from Peter, or can't at least exist apart from more of Peter than his smile alone. The present claim for consideration is, again, that *e* can not only be radically singled out as a legitimate object of thought, but also, given the strong-activity-unity property that it can be seen to have when it is so singled out, as a legitimate candidate for being in itself a TOS—even if there is something (other than itself) which it can't exist apart from. This may seem very unsatisfactory, but the power of the Fundamental Singleness point suggests that the unsatisfactoriness derives from rejecting the third reply, i.e., clinging to the view that there is non-experiential being, a view that has, in fact, now and forever, zero evidence to support it.

I wonder whether this last point (about zero evidence) will ever be widely accepted by analytic philosophers.[32] One barrier lies in the common belief that experience or consciousness is essentially defined, at least in part, by adaptive function. On this view, experience/consciousness can't exist at all unless it has such a function, and this makes it seem wildly implausible that mass/energy (or the subject matter of physics) is nothing but experientiality, given that it has been around since the 'Big Bang'. In fact the common belief incorporates a basic mistake about the theory of evolution, because experience/consciousness has to exist before evolution can shape it into adaptive forms, just as body has to exist before evolution can shape it into adaptive forms. But even if the belief is discarded, the conviction that there is irreducibly non-experiential being is unlikely to weaken.

---

[31] This claim has a certain resemblance to Descartes's claim to know that he had grasped the mind completely or as a complete thing in conceiving of it as something that had nothing corporeal about it. Since Descartes's claim was unwarranted, I have to do better.

[32] Unlike many, I make no appeal to the idea that matter is inconceivable, which has been popular at least since Berkeley's time (see e.g. Berkeley 1710; Foster 1982; Robinson 1982; Sprigge 1983).

12. S

It's hardly a separate matter, but let me end by asking how *s* deals with the objection that all portions of process-stuff have non-experiential being, whatever their size, and whether or not they also have experiential being. One common conception of the subject of experience is unruffled, because it holds that subjects in themselves have no experiential being at all, although they have experience. I reject this, because I hold that there's no real distinction between the existence of *s* at any time, and the existence of its propertiedness, of which *e* is at least a part, at that time. Nevertheless this 'no real distinction' position appears to leave open the possibility that *s* has both experiential and non-experiential being, which can't be true of *e*, given that *e* is defined in such a way that its existence is only and wholly the existence of experience, living experiencing. It can't be true of *s* either, if the Experience/Experiencer Identity Thesis is true—if the existence of *s* is identical with the existence of living experiencing *e*. But why should anyone wish to endorse the Experience/Experiencer Identity Thesis? Well, I have my reasons. Doing so opens *s* up to all the problems faced by *e*, but the solutions offered for *e*'s problems become available for *s* . . .

There is more to say. Here I'll conclude with the claim that minimal subjects certainly exist, and are neural synergies, and qualify as TOSs if any phenomena do. Timothy Sprigge writes that 'each of us, as we are at any one moment, is most essentially a momentary centre of experience or state of consciousness with the duration of the specious present' (2006: 474), and I'm sympathetic to this view, suitably adapted to the living moment of experience. We shouldn't, though, deny that there's a sense in which we're human beings, things that last considerably longer than the living moment of experience, and have many properties that can't be ascribed to minimal subjects.[33]

References

Berkeley, G. (1710/1998). *Principles of Human Knowledge*, ed. J. Dancy (Oxford: Oxford University Press).

——(1713/1998). *Three Dialogues between Hylas and Philonous*, ed. J. Dancy (Oxford: Oxford University Press).

Chun, M., and Marois, R. (2002). 'The Dark Side of Visual Attention', *Current Opinion in Neurobiology*, 12: 184–9.

---

[33] I attempt to solve the problems that arise from the combination of these claims in Strawson 2009: parts 6–8 (among other things, I attempt to explain why Leibniz's Law can't ground a valid objection).

CLARK, A. (2009). 'Spreading the Joy? Why the Machinery of Consciousness is (Probably) Still in the Head', *Mind*, 118/472: 963–93.

DAINTON, B. (2008). *The Phenomenal Self* (Oxford: Oxford University Press).

DESCARTES, R. (1648/1976). *Conversations with Burman*, tr. with a philosophical introduction and commentary by J. Cottingham (Oxford: Clarendon Press).

DU BOIS-REYMOND, E. (1872/1974). 'On the Limits of the Knowledge of Nature', in *Vorträge über Philosophie und Gesellschaft* (Hamburg: F. Meiner).

DUNNE, J. (forthcoming). 'Reflexivity and Subjectivity: Views from Dharmakīrti and his Successors'.

FOSTER, J. (1982). *The Case for Idealism* (London: Routledge).

FREGE, G. (1918/1967). 'The Thought: A Logical Inquiry', in *Philosophical Logic*, ed. P. F. Strawson (Oxford: Oxford University Press).

GREENE, B. (2004). *The Fabric of the Cosmos* (New York: Knopf).

HUME, D. (1739–40/1978). *A Treatise of Human Nature*, ed. L. A. Selby-Bigge and P. H. Nidditch (Oxford: Oxford University Press).

——(1748–51/1999). *An Enquiry Concerning Human Understanding*, ed. T. L. Beauchamp (Oxford: Oxford University Press).

JAMES, W. (1890/1950). *The Principles of Psychology*, 2 vols (New York: Dover).

KANT, I. (1772/1967). Letter to Marcus Herz, 21 Feb. 1772 in *Kant: Philosophical Correspondence 1759–99*, ed. and tr. Arnulf Zweig (Chicago: University of Chicago Press).

——(1781–7/1933). *Critique of Pure Reason*, tr. N. Kemp Smith (London: Macmillan).

LEVINE, J. (1983). 'Materialism and Qualia: The Explanatory Gap', *Pacific Philosophical Quarterly*, 64: 354–61.

LOCKE, J. (1689–1700/1975). *An Essay Concerning Human Understanding*, ed. P. Nidditch (Oxford: Clarendon Press).

LOCKWOOD, M. (1989). *Mind, Brain, and the Quantum* (Oxford: Blackwell).

MCGINN, C. (1995/2004). 'Consciousness and Space', in *Consciousness and its Objects* (Oxford: Oxford University Press), 93–115.

MONTAGUE, M. (2009). 'Perceptual Experience', in A. Beckermann and B. McLaughlin (eds), *Oxford Handbook in the Philosophy of Mind* (Oxford: Oxford University Press), 494–511.

PESSOA, L., and DE WEERD. P. (2003). *Filling-In: From Perceptual Completion to Cortical Reorganization* (Oxford: Oxford University Press).

ROBINSON, H. (2002). *Matter and Sense: A Critique of Contemporary Materialism* (Cambridge: Cambridge University Press).

RUSSELL, B. (1927/1995). *An Outline of Philosophy* (London: Routledge).

SHOEMAKER, S. (1986). 'Introspection and the Self', in P. A. French, T. E. Vehling and H. K. Wettstein (eds), *Studies in the Philosophy of Mind* (Minneapolis, Minn.: Midwest Studies in Philosophy, Vol. 10), 101–120.

SIMONS, D. J., and LEVIN D. T. (1997). 'Change Blindness', *Trends in Cognitive Sciences*, 1: 261–7.

SPINOZA, B. DE (1677/1985). *Ethics*, in *The Collected Works of Spinoza*, ed. and tr. E. Curley (Princeton: Princeton University Press).

SPRIGGE, T. L. S. (1983). *The Vindication of Absolute Idealism* (Edinburgh: Edinburgh University Press).

——(2006). *The God of Metaphysics* (Oxford: Oxford University Press).

STONE, J. (1988). 'Parfit and the Buddha: Why there are No People', *Philosophy and Phenomenological Research*, 48: 519–32.

——(2005). 'Why there Still are No People', *Philosophy and Phenomenological Research*, 70: 174–92.

STRAWSON, G. (2003). 'Real Materialism', in L. Antony and N. Hornstein (eds), *Chomsky and his Critics* (Oxford: Blackwell).

——(2006). 'Realistic Monism: Why Physicalism Entails Panpsychism', in A. Freeman (ed.), *Consciousness and its Place in Nature* (Thorverton: Imprint Academic), 3–31.

——(2008a). 'The Identity of the Categorical and the Dispositional', *Analysis*, 68/4: 271–82.

——(2008b). 'What is the Relation between an Experience, the Subject of the Experience, and the Content of the Experience?', in *Real Materialism and Other Essays* (Oxford: Oxford University Press), 151–87.

——(2009). *Selves: An Essay in Revisionary Metaphysics* (Oxford: Oxford University Press).

TYNDALL, J. (1874). *Address Delivered Before the British Association Assembled at Belfast, With Additions* (London: Longmans, Green, & Co.).

VAN INWAGEN, P. (1990). *Material Beings* (Ithaca, NY: Cornell University Press).

WILSON, R. (2004). *Boundaries of the Mind: The Individual in the Fragile Sciences* (Cambridge: Cambridge University Press).

CHAPTER 11

THE NO-SELF
ALTERNATIVE

THOMAS METZINGER

WHENEVER popular or academic debates about 'the self' flare up again, we can
often observe an embarrassing fact: Just because—quite obviously, and in many
cultures—there is a folk-metaphysical and a folk-phenomenological *concept* of 'the
self', and just because someone has put this concept back on the agenda, many
participants automatically assume that an *entity* like 'the self' must actually exist
and that a relevant and well-posed set of scientific and theoretical questions relates
to this entity. However, there seems to be no empirical evidence and no truly
convincing conceptual argument that supports the actual existence of 'a' self.
Nothing forces us to make this assumption. Therefore, many debates of this type
are threatened by a certain shallowness right from the very beginning and, due to
their endorsement of an unwarranted existence assumption, run the risk of triviality.
As it turns out, the 'no-self alternative' may not be an alternative at all—it could
simply be the default assumption for all rational approaches to self-consciousness
and subjectivity.

In the first part of this short chapter, I will differentiate a number of possible
claims regarding the non-existence of 'the self' and will also try to at least sketch
one typical argument for each thesis. In the second part, I will offer some new ideas
on why all such arguments will always remain counterintuitive for many of us.

I am indebted to Jennifer M. Windt and Adrian J. Smith for a number of a number of helpful
critical comments and for their help with the English version of this chapter.

1. ANTI-REALISM ABOUT 'THE SELF'

Ontological anti-realism about 'the self'

The standard way to be an anti-realist about selves is to deny that selves are *substances*:

(ARS$_0$) The self is not a substance.

A substance is an entity that can 'stand in existence' all by itself, even if all other existing entities were to disappear. It is 'ontologically self-subsistent', because it can sustain its own existence. It endures over time and is an ontologically *fundamental* entity, because it belongs to the basic building blocks of reality. Of course, there is a highly differentiated universe of metaphysical theories about 'substancehood'. But, given this simple working definition, the thesis of ARS$_0$ amounts to the claim that selves are not self-subsistent entities: they do not endure over time and they do not belong to the basic building blocks of reality.

There are two well-established ways in which one can argue for this sort of ontological anti-realism about 'the self'. The first strategy is to confine discussion to the target phenomenon of self-consciousness and related folk-phenomenological discourse, including its unwarranted metaphysical assumptions. The second strategy is to deny the existence of *all* substances or individuals on theoretical grounds, *tout court*. Here the obvious traditional example is the anti-substantialist metaphysics of Buddhist philosophy (see Siderits 2003, 2007, Chapter 12 below; for examples of recent discussions, cf. Albahari 2007; Westerhoff 2009). In addition, current debates in the theory of science—particularly, in the philosophy of physics—have long made it obvious that our standard views about individuals, intrinsic properties, and relations are obsolete. Instead, an ontic form of *structural realism* seems to be the most promising candidate in modern metaphysics, proposing that relations are all that exist. Said relations do not hold between objects with intrinsic properties, but even the relata themselves can be decomposed into sets of relations, with structure always being more ontologically fundamental than objects or 'substances' (for a paradigm example, see Ladyman and Ross 2009). In a certain sense, this would lead us into an 'unfounded universe', because the ultimate reality would then be the nomological structure of the world, where even the identity and individuality of objects would depend upon this (relational) structure.

Just as current physics is fully compatible with the view that quantum-objects are non-individuals, the corresponding metaphysical underdetermination of cognitive neuroscience certainly makes it tenable that mental, psychological, or phenomenological entities like 'the self' are not proper individuals at all: they simply possess no clearly specifiable identity criteria. In some contexts, classical objects, as well as 'selves', are useful heuristic posits, but nonetheless ontologically dispensable entities. If this is correct, we should rather search for an alternative metaphysics that renders the predictive success of our empirical theories intelligible without committing us to theoretical terms referring to individual entities in the world (like 'the self'), or to the truth of certain statements in which these terms appear.

Let us now confine discussion to a sketch of the *first* strategy mentioned above, considering only the target phenomenon of self-consciousness and the related folk-phenomenological discourse. Why should we assume the existence of selves in the first place? The main problem, according to ARS$_0$, is that in our widespread and naively realistic manner of speaking about 'the self' we introduce an individual, making an existence assumption which typically is not backed up by independent argument.

What are selves? If not 'nuggets of reality', what else could they be? Selves could be unobservable entities, perhaps conceptual fictions—although in an interesting sense they are also phenomenological 'everyday objects'. As robust elements of the phenomenal ontology applied by our brains (cf. Metzinger and Gallese 2003), they play a leading role in the everyday phenomenology of our experiential *Lebenswelt* and the pre-scientific folk-psychology it gives rise to. How are we to interpret this fact on the level of philosophical metaphysics? Let us briefly look at the three main theoretical options.

If we wanted to establish selves as proper individuals, our first option could be to take a sober and straightforward approach: we could try to be old-fashioned scientific realists, and, for example, identify them with their position in space and time, turning them into single, countable entities by means of the physical properties they share with no other physical object. With Leibniz (1646–1716) we would then say that individuality simply amounts to distinguishability, adopting the Principle of the Identity of Indiscernables. However, only *bodies* can be fully individuated in this way—but selves are not to be taken as bodies or biological organisms *simpliciter*.

If we wanted to find a metaphysical representation of our pre-scientific, phenomenological intuitions about selfhood, then the second theoretical option would be to posit some special sort of *haecceitas* in the sense of Duns Scotus (1266–1308): a property of primitive 'thisness' or self-identity, a transcendent property of selves that grounds their intrinsic individuality as well as their numerical identity. For example, there could be a uniquely instantiable, non-qualitative property of (say) being identical with Shaun Gallagher, responsible for the irreducible individuality and the numerical identity of the very person who is the editor of this *Handbook*. The haecceity approach has a certain prima facie appeal, because it may actually capture something phenomenologically important, whereas, metaphysically, it is less convincing. On the one hand, introducing a 'primitive thisness' constituting individual substances is, of course, a pure hypostatization. It is a philosophical move that does not explain anything but just introduces a further, unobservable property without argument or potential empirical evidence. On the other hand, I believe that we may have overlooked an important phenomenological fact, one that could usefully serve as a constraint on a more comprehensive theoretical account. There is a distinct *phenomenology of singularity*, a non-sensory phenomenology of 'thisness'—for example, in the phenomenology of meditation, but also in bodily self-consciousness. If we look closely enough, we can discover the phenomenology of primitive 'thisness' in our own subjective experience. It is particularly distinct in certain non-conceptual layers of self-awareness (their content has a non-perceptual but nevertheless 'demonstrative' character), and it certainly is a feature that requires careful attention in the phenomenology of self-consciousness. But phenomenological structure *per se* will never determine metaphysics.

The third option then would be to develop a theory of 'the self' as a mere collection of properties. A typical example of anti-substantialist and anti-individualist approaches to 'the self' are so-called 'bundle theories'. I have already mentioned Buddhist philosophy above; the most prominent Western representative, perhaps, is David Hume (1711–76). Hume would have said that we typically solve the conflict between experienced sameness across time and the succession of change, between the phenomenology of identity and that of diversity, by conjuring up a substance: 'the imagination is apt to feign something unknown and invisible, which it supposes to continue the same under all these variations; and this unintelligible something it calls a substance, or original and first matter' (T 220). Conceptually, bundle-theorists analyze substances as some sort of, possibly complex, relation between properties (which, however, could in turn either be conceived of as universals or as tropes, i.e. individual property instantiations). Selves would just be collections of properties.

The open question now becomes what principle *exactly* is responsible for the establishment of the complex relation just mentioned—what turns all the features comprising the self into a coherent whole? Empirically, one could say that selves (or other entities previously described as substances) are just collections of properties, which, as a matter of fact, we happen to mentally represent *as* individual entities. From the perspective of present-day cognitive neuroscience, this would be a scientifically plausible strategy: Our brains segment scenes and constitute multimodal, consciously perceived perceptual objects (e.g. one's own body as a whole) not by attaching properties to some more basic entity, but by a dynamic, bottom-up process of self-organization called 'feature-binding' (see e.g. Singer and Gray 1995). All technical details aside, what is new today is that science offers conceptually clear models of functional mechanisms which could parsimoniously explain the *integration* of individual property-representations into a unified self-representation. This theoretical model requires no transcendental subject to stand behind the appearance of 'a' self as consciously represented, because it gradually emerges out of the self-organizing interaction between a large number of simpler components. This possibility—the appearance of ordered structures without external interaction or a well-defined and highly specific initial state—simply was not available to thinkers in the past; it is a novelty in the history of ideas. Therefore, dynamical self-organization is a new theoretical option for the bundle theorist, in metaphysics as well as in phenomenology (see Metzinger 1995, 2003; Parfit 1982 and Chapter 18; Thompson 2007).

To sum up, the general point about substances, individuals, and identity criteria is that none of the currently available scientific data determine our metaphysics in such a way as to make the assumption of the existence of 'a self' necessary. Moreover, the principle of parsimony demands that we try to find a *simpler* metaphysical representation of our current knowledge about self-consciousness, of its causal history and its constitutive conditions, than what we have traditionally assumed to be the self-as-substance.

Before proceeding to a short sketch of epistemological, methodological, and semantic variations on the no-self alternative, let us briefly pause to look at the wider context in which such discussions take place. The first strategy mentioned above often emphasizes simply that no empirical evidence could ever ground a substantialist metaphysics of selfhood. This more modest approach would refrain from making any general metaphysical claims about the possibility of substances *per se*, but would only demonstrate the irrationality of positing a special sort of *individual* substance, namely, 'the self'. Although our very own naturally evolved cognitive structures (our inbuilt 'naïve physics') almost seem to make it a functional necessity for us to use substance-concepts like the notions of an enduring particular or an individual substance, which then work as carriers of properties, nothing in the brain or the self-conscious biological organism as a whole could even remotely count as a substance in any philosophically interesting sense. We just don't find a substantial self anywhere in the world and nothing on the level of scientific facts determines our metaphysics in this way.

What we do find, however, is the *phenomenology* of substantiality, on the level of introspective experience: subjectively, we often experience ourselves exactly as self-subsistent, enduring entities forming non-exchangeable and irreducible parts of reality. Moreover, the deeper core of our theoretical problem might lie in the more subtle fact that our phenomenal experience of selfhood not only expresses an aspect of 'reality' (i.e. the factual *realness* of the self), but also an aspect of 'metaphysical necessity' (i.e. the *impossibility* of non-existence, across all conceivable scenarios). I will return to these points below, and for two reasons. First, all deflationary or so-called 'weaker' theories of the self (for examples see Ghin 2005; Legrand 2005) typically miss the mark, by failing to explain what could ground the phenomenology of the self-as-substance and what the causal history or the biological function of this illusion of substantiality could have been. Second, the phenomenal self is *the* proto-object as such. If anything grounds our naive-realistic world-view that reality is composed out of individual substances possessing intrinsic, context-invariant properties and standing in certain relations to each other, it is exactly the phenomenology of selfhood. Cognitively, the conscious experience of selfhood leads directly to the metaphysical prototype of 'objecthood' and to the idea of an *individual* substance. This observation implies the interesting conclusion that many of our irresistible theoretical intuitions about substancehood are ultimately anchored in the conscious experience of selfhood. With this wider context in mind, let us now return to our brief sketch of theoretical options.

Epistemic anti-realism about 'the self'

For those who cannot resist the intuition that individual substances like selves exist, the obvious move will be to posit the existence of unknowable individuals possessing an unknowable intrinsic nature:

(ARS$_E$) The self is part of an unknowable realm of individuals, possessing an unknowable intrinsic nature.

Just as with the unknowable nature of the Kantian *Ding an sich* (thing in itself), we could posit an unknowable self pulling the strings behind the observable behavior of self-conscious agents and underlying the introspective phenomenology of selfhood. Consequently, all we could ever know would be the *structure* of the self—for example, its form of interaction with other selves and the laws and regularities guiding its cognitive and bodily behavior. Its *nature* (the sort of entity it really *is*) would remain epistemically inaccessible to us. Epistemological anti-realism treats the self as an unobservable entity, but derives no specific metaphysical position from its central claim. We can view it as a form of agnosticism.

However, there is at least one specific problem, which arises in the context of 'selves' as objects of knowledge. If they really are unknowable individual substances or have an unknowable intrinsic nature, then self-consciousness can no longer be seen as a process that provides us with a direct and epistemologically relevant form of *acquaintance* with ourselves. On this view, substantive forms of self-knowledge are no longer possible: in introspection and in phenomenal self-awareness, we never grasp our own true nature—it may well be that we have an essence, but this essence will forever remain inaccessible to us. Therefore, the distinct, characteristic, and Cartesian *phenomenology of certainty* which accompanies self-consciousness is an illusion. Furthermore, as the phenomenology of certainty is not about the existence of some merely objective, historical person, but about the indubitable ontological status of oneself *as self*,[1] epistemic anti-realism renders the self not only epistemologically irrelevant, but also leaves us with no further metaphysical issue to be resolved.

---

[1] This type of phenomenological first-person certainty is intimately related to the capacity of thinking Cartesian I*-thoughts of the form [I am certain that I* myself exist]. In other words, Descartes claimed that he was certain that he* (he *himself*) existed, not that he was certain that Descartes existed. Lynne Baker has made this point very clear in Baker 1998, 2007.

Methodological anti-realism about 'the self'

It is perhaps on this level that we find the most straightforward and convincing argument for the elimination of the concept of 'a' self:

(ARS$_M$) Nothing in the scientific investigation of self-consciousness commits us to assume the existence of individual selves.

As already noted in my discussion of ontological anti-realism above, there are no strong empirical data whatsoever supporting the existence of selves. There are first-person reports, and as such they may function as data-points, but of course there are no first-person *data* in any more rigorous sense.[2] More importantly, the process of generating and testing new hypotheses in empirical research programs investigating self-consciousness, agency, social cognition, etc. simply does not *require* the assumption of a theoretical entity by the name of 'the self'. Science can achieve its predictive success, describe and explain the available data, and integrate them into a larger evolutionary or neuroscientific framework without assuming that there is a mysterious thing called 'the self' which is represented in self-consciousness, initiates actions, or engages in social cognition related to other mysterious individuals called 'selves'. Prediction, testing, and explanation can take place in a much more parsimonious conceptual framework, for instance by introducing the concept of a 'transparent self-model' (Metzinger 2003*a*, 2006, 2008, 2009).

Semantic anti-realism about 'the self'

We refer to ourselves using the word 'I'. But what, exactly, is the meaning of the linguistic expression 'I'? If—as seems obvious—it doesn't *refer* to a specific part of reality in an object-mode of reference, what exactly is its logical or semantic

---

[2] Seriously assuming the existence of 'first-person data' rests on an extended usage of a concept that is well defined in another (namely, scientific) context. First, the whole concept of a 'first-person perspective' is just a visuo-grammatical metaphor, without a theory to back it up—currently, we simply don't know what that could be, 'a' first-person perspective (for a first conceptual differentiation, see Blanke and Metzinger 2009). Second, 'data' are extracted from the physical world by *technical* measuring devices, in a *public procedure*, which is well-defined and well-understood, replicable, and improvable; and which is necessarily *intersubjective*. Therefore, speaking of 'first-person data' would rest on an extended usage of a concept which is only well-defined in another context of application. 'Data' are typically (though not always) gathered with the help of technical measuring devices (and not individual brains) and by groups of people who mutually control and criticize each other's methods of data gathering (namely, by large scientific communities). In particular, data are gathered in the context of rational theories aiming at ever better predictions, theories that—as opposed to phenomenological reports—are capable of falsification. Autophenomenological reports themselves can be treated as data, the experience itself cannot (for a dissenting view, cf. Thompson 2007: 474 and 338 n. 10). All of this is not to deny that what are sometimes called 'first-person methods' could have an enormous impact on our way towards a rigorous, empirically based theory of self-consciousness.

function? In order to be semantic realists about 'I', we would have to assume that it reliably connects us to an irreducible, elementary aspect of reality. Semantic anti-realism denies this:

(ARS$_s$) The indexical expression 'I' does not refer to any entity that is ontologically fundamental.

A lot of excellent philosophical work has been done with regard to the semantics of the indexical term 'I' (see e.g. Boër and Lycan 1980; Castañeda 1966, 1967; Perry 1979, 1993; Recanati 2007). Does 'I' refer to some sort of invisible object, like some other linguistic expressions do? Does 'I' refer to a Cartesian Ego? Does it perhaps refer to some sort of 'objective self' (see Nagel 1986: ch. 4), because sentences like 'I am Thomas Metzinger' always possess a second reading, a second set of truth-conditions superseding the trivial, purely objective self-identification with a particular, historical person? Is the object of reference for 'I' always a *person*, that is, an entity which is ontologically basic and which simultaneously possesses mental and physical properties (Strawson 1959)? But how, then, do we explain the particular structure of self-consciousness—is it perhaps best characterized by a specific *mode of presentation*, perhaps an 'EGO-mode' of internally presenting information (Newen 1997; Perry 1979; Recanati 1993)? Or does 'I' simply not refer at all—at least not to a 'self', but simply to an organism that has gained knowledge about itself (Anscombe 1975)?

Clearly there is a distinct, fourth strategy the anti-realist about 'the self' can adopt: she can investigate the semantics and the logical deep structure of *linguistic* acts of self-reference. Employing her prescribed theory of meaning, she can then deny the referential nature of our uses of 'I'. Yet again, every single act of linguistic self-reference is accompanied by a distinct phenomenology, which, although it locally supervenes on functional properties of our central nervous systems, transports exactly those intuitions that turn us into naive realists and make us doubt any anti-realism about 'the self'. In uttering an 'I*'-sentence, we often actually *do* have the feeling of directly referring to something deep and real, to an invariant and substantial core of our own being. If anything could be a paradigm case for direct acquaintance or immediate epistemic access, then it is the phenomenology of non-conceptual self-representation, in which such linguistic (or even purely cognitive) acts of seemingly 'direct' self-reference are anchored: we feel infinitely close to ourselves. And any philosophical anti-realism about 'the self' can only succeed if it complements its theoretical strategy with a convincing account of the phenomenology that gives rise to our Cartesian intuitions, to our enduring feeling that some sort of self simply *must* exist.

Therefore, having briefly sketched the four main variants of the no-self alternative and some of the arguments supporting them, we must now take a closer look at the role of intuitions and their relationship to the metaphysics of selfhood. This will be done in the second, and last, part of this chapter.

WHY IS ANTI-REALISM ABOUT 'THE SELF' COUNTERINTUITIVE?

Intuitiveness

Intuitiveness is a property of theoretical claims or arguments, relative to a class of representational systems exhibiting a specific functional architecture. Conscious human beings are one example of such a class. The brains of human beings are naturally evolved information-processing systems, and when engaging in explicit, high-level cognition they use specific representational formats and employ characteristic styles of processing. Whenever we try to comprehend a certain theory, an argument or a specific philosophical claim, our brains construct a *mental model* of this theory, argument, or claim (Johnson-Laird 1983, 2008; Knauff 2009). This mostly automatic process of constructing mental models of theories possesses a phenomenology of its own: some theories just 'feel right', because they elicit subtle visceral and emotional responses, some claims 'come easily' and some arguments (including implicit assumptions they make in their premises) seem 'just plain natural'.

There are two overarching reasons for this well-known fact. First, such theories exhibit a high degree of 'goodness of fit', in regard to our network of explicit prior convictions, and further, in optimally satisfying the constraints provided by our conscious and unconscious models of reality as a whole. These latter represent both the totality of the knowledge we have acquired during our lifetime, as well as certain assumptions about the causal deep structure of the world that proved functionally adequate for our biological ancestors. Theories that immediately feel good because they are characterized by a high degree of intuitiveness maximize internal harmony. What we introspectively detect is a high degree of consistency, but in a non-linguistic, subsymbolic medium. Therefore we could also replace the term 'intuitiveness' by a notion like 'intuitive soundness' or 'introspectively detected consistency'. In principle it ought to be possible to spell this point out on a mathematical level, by describing the underlying neural computations and their properties in a connectionist framework, or utilizing the conceptual tools provided by dynamical systems theory.

The second major causal factor underlying the conscious experience of 'intuitive soundness' simply is the amount of energy it takes to activate and sustain a mental model of a given theory, plus the amount of energy it would take to permanently *integrate* it into our pre-existing model of reality. Our mental space of intuitive plausibility can be described as an energy landscape: claims that 'come easily' do so because they allow us to reach a stable state quickly and easily; theories that 'feel good' are theories that can be appropriated without a high demand of energy. Theories that *don't* feel good have the opposite characteristics: they 'don't add up', they 'just don't compute', because they endanger our internal harmony and functional coherence, and it would take a lot of energy to permanently integrate them into our overall mental model of reality. They are costly.

Obviously, the no-self hypothesis simply is *the* paradigm example of a theory that just 'doesn't compute' for beings like us. However, what does or does not compute is a contingent fact determined by the functional architecture of our brain, shaped by millions of years of biological evolution on this planet, and—to a much lesser degree—by our individual cognitive history and a given cultural/ linguistic context. The phenomenology of intuitive soundness—the fact that some arguments seem 'just natural'—ultimately is a biological phenomenon, with a short cultural history supporting it as well. However, the inner landscape of our space of intuitive plausibility is not only contingent on our evolutionary history and on certain physical and functional properties of our brains—it was optimized for *functional adequacy* only. It serves to sustain an organism's coherence and physical existence, but this does not mean that the *content* of intuitions is epistemically justified in any way. The no-self hypothesis therefore becomes the paradigm example of an almost insurmountable obstacle, a major challenge to our intellectual honesty: It demands that we investigate a claim even if it contradicts our deepest intuitions, something that somehow is 'just too radical', way too costly, likely to be self-damaging, and cries out for a more moderate, weaker version because it just 'doesn't compute'. The no-self alternative is a theoretical construct, which nicely exemplifies the point made at the very beginning of this section: 'intuitiveness' and counterintuitiveness are *functional properties* that depend on the way in which a theoretical construct is encoded in a given class of systems with a given internal structure. We also see how any philosophical methodology that just tries to make our 'deepest intuitions' explicit in a conceptually coherent way immediately turns into a rather trivial enterprise. At best, it just charts our intuition space; at worst, it confuses failures of imagination with insights into conceptual necessity ('philosopher's syndrome', according to Dennett 1991: 401).

Maybe there is another, perhaps even better, way to put the point. Philosophers sometimes like to speak of sets of 'logically possible worlds', of 'nomologically possible worlds', or even of 'metaphysically possible worlds', and then proceed to investigate relations of epistemic access between such sets of worlds. We could refine our definition of intuitive soundness by introducing the notion of a 'phenomenologically possible world': every world that can be mentally simulated on the level of conscious experience by a given class of systems realizing a specific set of functional constraints is a phenomenologically possible world. For example, some worlds are close neighbors to our current perceptual world-model, others are more distant from it (but still are possible conscious experiences, representing something that could, phenomenologically, *be the case*), and still others are strictly phenomenologically impossible. For certain conscious cognitive agents, some theories will be false—will feel false—in all possible phenomenal worlds. Here is the central point: the no-self hypothesis describes an impossible scenario, because it cannot be *actively* simulated and embedded—the property of cognitive agency itself would have to be dissolved (see the next section). For beings like us, it is therefore not a phenomenologically possible world. But of course 'phenomenal possibility' is relative to the functional architecture that a certain class of systems contingently happens to have.

There are not many interesting relations of epistemic access pointing from the space of intuitive possibility to other sets of possible worlds. Epistemologically speaking, 'phenomenal possibility' is a rather irrelevant notion: logically inconsistent scenarios could always *appear* as possible phenomenal experiences to certain cognitive systems; nomological necessities could be encoded as contingent (because there is at least one possible phenomenal world in which, for this kind of system, they are false); a claim that turns out to be false in the actual world could be simulated as true in all possible phenomenal worlds, as metaphysically necessary, and so on.

The counterintuitive nature of the no-self alternative

We should now ask, 'Why is anti-realism about 'the self' counterintuitive?' It would be good to have an empirically grounded answer to the following question: what, in systems like us, determines the *phenomenology of actual existence* and what determines the *phenomenology of metaphysical necessity*? Let me explain. If we want to know why anti-realism about the self is counterintuitive, it would be helpful to understand how realism about the self comes to be intuitive in the first place. It would be good to understand how something must be experienced as 'definitely real', and sometimes also as necessarily existing.

First, we must clearly separate the phenomenology of 'realness' and the phenomenology of 'metaphysical necessity'. One phenomenological constraint that clearly has been neglected too much in most current work on consciousness is the 'realness constraint'. One and the same phenomenal content—a visually perceived object, or, say, the bodily self—can appear as more or less real, while the content itself remains stable: the content of subjective experience can vary along a dimension of realness. There are well-documented psychiatric conditions like derealization and depersonalization in which the core of the problem is that either the environment or the content of the patient's self-model appear as less and less real (Hunter *et al.* 2004; Simeon and Abugel 2006). Different parts of phantom limbs in congenital aplasia appear as more or less real depending on the respective subregion of the body-model, and all of them are less real than representations of actually existing body-parts, and so on. For example, a recent case study by Brugger and colleagues introduced a vividness rating on a seven-point scale that showed highly consistent judgments across sessions for their subject AZ, a 44-year-old university-educated woman born without forearms and legs. For as long as she remembers, she has experienced mental images of forearms (including fingers) and legs (with feet and first and fifth toes)—but these were not *as* realistic as the content of her non-hallucinatory self-model (cf. Brugger *et al.* 2000: 6168; Metzinger 2008).

Then we have conditions during intense religious experiences or under the influence of psychoactive substances where the specific content of phenomenal experience is held constant while everything becomes *more* real than normal. On the representational level of analysis, the phenomenology of realness can be captured by the intensity constraint for presentational content (Metzinger 2003*a*: section 3.2.9) and by the transparency constraint (ibid., section 3.2.7). On the functional and neuroscientific levels of description, plausible correlates are sheer stimulus strength, the general level of arousal, and the temporal coherence of neural responses.

Then there is the phenomenology of 'metaphysical necessity'. It means that we experience something—for example, the self—not only as real, but as something *of which it is not possible that it could not exist*. To consciously represent something as 'metaphysically necessary' (in this purely phenomenological sense) means that it is not possible that the thing in question could *not* be real. Phenomenologically, there is not a single possible world in which this could actually be the case, actual non-existence is inconceivable, only centered worlds exist. 'Inconceivability' here means 'phenomenal impossibility' as explained above. We confuse the apparent phenomenal necessity of the self with metaphysical necessity.

Of course, we can all construct conscious mental models of worlds in which we ourselves do not exist—for instance, because we have not yet been born or because we have already died. But what the no-self hypothesis demands is something else: In order to appear as intuitively sound, we should be able to conceive of the *actual* world—i.e. *given* the ongoing phenomenology of substantial selfhood, of ontological self-subsistence, and transtemporal identity—minus our own existence. We should be able to imagine a selfless world, but *from a first-person perspective*. For beings like ourselves, however, this is at least a functional impossibility: we cannot mentally simulate the conscious experience of a world in which we are not present as selves, but which we nevertheless experience from a first-person perspective. This fact is a contingent fact about the causal structure of our brains, about the functional architecture underlying our conscious minds. Here, I will make no stronger claim to interpret this fact in terms of conceptual necessities or possibilities—perhaps selfless first-person perspectives can be coherently described. The intriguing question, lying outside the scope of this entry, is whether there could be *epistemic* first-person perspectives without *phenomenal* selves as constituting factors.

So why does anti-realism about 'the' self seem counterintuitive? After having clearly separated the phenomenology of 'realness' and the phenomenology of 'metaphysical necessity' we can now proceed to the core of the problem: conscious mental agency. A lot of empirical research demonstrates how the experience of global control is intimately linked to the experience of selfhood. However, global control connotes not only bodily agency but also the focus of attention and (in some cases) the focus of high-level, conceptually mediated cognition. A completely selfless mental model of reality cannot be *actively* simulated, because the property of cognitive agency itself would then have to be dissolved. Reality-models in which the no-self alternative is true are of course possible, but what is not possible is a first-person phenomenal simulation of such a world. In particular, the 'first-personness' of the simulation itself, the ongoing activity of the cognitive self, could not be mapped onto such a world.

We can illustrate the point by briefly looking at the fallacy underlying Thomas Nagel's beautiful but failed argument for the existence of an 'objective self' (Nagel 1986: ch. 4). What Thomas Nagel terms the *objective self* is a conceptual reification of an ongoing misrepresentational process. This process takes place within a perspectivally structured model of reality, in the conscious mind of his readers experimenting with the *View from Nowhere*. This is what happens to you when reading Nagel: propositional input activates a chain of phenomenal mental models in your brain. As a cognitive agent, you try to understand his argument by constructing a mental model. In particular, you now simulate a non-centered reality *within* a centered model of reality. Under Nagel's description, this non-centered 'conception' of the world also contains all experiences and the perspective of Thomas Nagel as well:

Essentially I have no particular point of view at all, but apprehend the world as centerless. As it happens, I ordinarily view the world from a certain vantage point, using the eyes, the person, and the daily life of TN as a kind of window. But the experiences and the perspective of TN with which I am directly presented are not the point of view of the true self, for the true self has no point of view and includes in its conception of the centerless world TN and his perspective among the contents of that world. (Nagel 1986: 61)

But this description is false: *this* inner experience, the current *View from Nowhere* as initiated and executed by the cognitive agent TN is *not* contained in the 'centerless conception of the world'. The *last* phenomenal event—namely, the intended shift in perspective—is not contained in the centerless conception, because this would lead to an infinite regress. However, it must obviously be contained in Nagel's autobiographical self-model—otherwise it would not be reportable. The current perspective is not part of reality as non-perspectivally seen by the true self Nagel postulates. Logically speaking, the threat of infinite regress is blocked by an object-formation, by introducing a metaphysical entity—the objective self. Technically, the fallacy is an act—object equivocation: What we have is not a thing, but a process.

Here is what *really* happens. A conscious, self-modeling system internally simulates a non-centered reality. This simulation is opaque (i.e. phenomenally experienced *as* a form of mental content), and it is embedded in the currently active phenomenal self-model: at any time you know that this is only a thought-experiment, and you know that *you* are carrying it through. Anything else would either be a manifest daydream or a full-blown mystical experience—and this certainly is not the phenomenology Nagel describes. In this phenomenally simulated reality there is a model of a person, TN (or, respectively, yourself), enriched by all the properties until then only known under the phenomenal self-model, as your *own* properties. This person-model forms the object-component of your consciously experienced first-person perspective; it is part of a comprehensive simulational process. Following Nagel's implicit instruction, you generate the simulation of an 'inner third-person perspective', namely by forming a model of yourself, which is *not* a self-model, but the model of yourself as if you were only given to yourself through indirect, external sources of knowledge. It is a model of a person alone in oceans of space and time, '*a momentary blip on the cosmic TV-screen*' (Nagel 1986: 61).

This process is fully reversible: In a second step you can now *reintegrate* the simulated person with the transparent partition of your phenomenal self-model, which, of course, has been there all along. Like a monkey or a dolphin recognizing himself in a mirror, as it were, you discover yourself in the *internal* mirror of your ongoing phenomenal simulation of a centerless world, by discovering a strong structural isomorphism to one of the persons contained in this world. To this representational event you can linguistically refer by exclaiming sentences of the type 'I am TN!' in their second, 'philosophical' reading. But there is no second set of truth-conditions, there is no additional 'perspectival fact' to be expressed,[3] and

---

[3] There are a number of problems here, if one looks more closely. First, the logical structure of the alleged perspectival fact is never clearly stated (see Lycan 1987: 78; 1996: 50; Metzinger 1993: 233; 2003). Second, the *objective self*—which is more similar to Husserl's notion of a 'transcendental ego' in his later philosophy than to the Wittgensteinian subject as forming the border of the world—in being used in Nagel's ubiquitous visual metaphor of the 'taking' of perspectives immediately creates distal objects as its counterparts. In its conceptual interpretation this then leads to persisting act–object equivocations, to the freezing of phenomenal *events* into irreducible phenomenal individuals. Again, see Lycan 1987: 79; 1996: 51. Thirdly, at a closer look, Nagel's concept of an 'objective self' is inconsistent. It is not a mental object any more, because the concept of mentality was *introduced* via the notion of a perspective, as referring to subjective points of view and their modifications (see Nagel 1986: 37). 'Self', however, is a mentalistic term *par excellence*. Norman Malcolm has pointed out how an aperspectival objective self would be a 'mindless thing' because in its striving for objectivity it would have distanced itself so radically from the point of view of the *psychological* subject that now it could itself not be grasped by any mental concept any more. See Malcolm 1988: 158. The most important mistake, however, consists in using 'I' as a designator and not as an indicator in the 'philosophical' reading of the relevant identity-statements. There are no criteria of identity offered for the individual in question. As Malcolm (1988: 154 and 159) puts it: 'Does this make any sense? *It would if there were criteria of identity for an I.* [emphasis TM] . . . When we are uncertain about the identity of a person, sometimes we succeed in determining his identity, sometimes we make mistakes. But in regard to the identity of an *I* that supposedly occupies the point of view of a person, we could be neither right nor wrong. After a bout of severe amnesia Nagel might be able to identify himself as TN—but not as *I*. "I am TN" could announce a discovery—but not "I am I". . . . An important source

there is no homunculus that was briefly united with the transcendental ego (Nagel's *objective self*) and is now hurled back into the empirical subject.

The *View from Nowhere* is a phenomenal simulation, but one in which the phenomenal properties of selfhood and cognitive agency never disappear—it is only a thought experiment carried out by a cognitive agent, always accompanied by an intact phenomenal self comfortably seated in the proverbial armchair. Therefore, it generates only a 'small' version of the *View from Nowhere*. The 'big' version would be a full-blown mystical experience, a phenomenal model of reality in which the property of selfhood is instantiated in no form whatsoever. We might interestingly view this type of conscious reality-model as the counterpart of the no-self hypothesis on the level of the brain's internal ontology. In conceptually interpreting Nagel's 'small' armchair version of the *View from Nowhere*, realism about the purported objective self creeps in at the very moment one forgets about the processuality (i.e. the event-character and the sustained agency-component of the ongoing phenomenal simulations described), and the phenomenal opacity (i.e. the subjectively experienced *representational* nature characterizing the overall process).[4]

CONCLUSION

The no-self alternative comes in a variety of different flavours and strengths, each being supported by a number of ontological, epistemological, methodological, and semantic arguments. One may well view it as the default assumption for all rational, data-driven approaches to self-consciousness and subjectivity. Its central problem is its radically counterintuitive nature.

Intuitiveness is a property of theoretical claims or arguments, relative to a class of representational systems exhibiting a specific functional architecture. Our intuition that 'the self' *exists* and that it *must* exist therefore is grounded in three different factors. First, it is a functional feature of our own mental architecture that any attempt to consciously simulate a world in which the no-self hypothesis turns

of confusion in Nagel's thinking is his assumption that the word 'I' is used by each speaker, to *refer* to, to *designate—something*. But that is not how "I" is used. If it were, then "I am I" might be false, because "I" in these two occurrences had been used to refer to different things. Nagel's statement, "I am TN", could also be false, not because the speaker was not TN, but because Nagel had mistakenly used "I" to refer to the wrong thing. If Nagel had not assumed that "I" is used, like a name, to designate something, he would not have had the notion that in each person there dwells an *I* or *Self* or *Subject*—which uses that person as its point of viewing.'

[4] For a concise definition of the terms 'phenomenal opacity' and 'phenomenal transparency', plus their role in cognitive self-reference, cf. Metzinger 2003*b*.

out to be true generates the phenomenology of mental agency, cognitive control, and therefore selfhood. Second, in describing this phenomenology, we are prone to act–object equivocations, because we turn a process into a thing, hypostatizing a phenomenal individual where there is only an intermittent chain of events, using 'I' as a designator where it only is an indicator. Third, evolution has shaped our brains in a specific way. We have a strong inbuilt tendency to interpret a functionally grounded phenomenal necessity as a metaphysical necessity. But of course the fact that we simply cannot consciously imagine a certain state of affairs has no implications for the deeper structure of reality. Metaphysics is underdetermined by phenomenology.

At the outset, I pointed out that we have no empirical evidence and no truly convincing conceptual argument that supports the actual existence of 'a' self. Consequently, debates about 'the self' can easily degenerate into merely ideological disputes, turning into projection screens for metaphysical desires and hopes. There are two ways this can happen. One is the endorsement of the no-self hypothesis for purely ideological reasons, because it seems to lend support to a metaphysical world-view, which is grounded in tradition, organized religion, a specific creed or faith, and so on. The obvious example here is what I would like to term 'ideological Buddhism'. The other standard case is the rejection of the no-self hypothesis for equally ideological reasons, and here the obvious examples are all principled and purely ideological forms of anti-reductionism, as we find them in some forms of philosophical phenomenology or any substantialist metaphysics of the 'soul', for example, in Western religions. I believe that for anyone with a more serious interest in epistemic progress on self-consciousness in all its aspects, the first task will consist in effectively protecting more rigorous philosophical discussions and scientific research programs from degenerated debates of this kind.

REFERENCES

ALBAHARI, M. (2007). *Analytical Buddhism: The Two-Tiered Illusion of Self* (New York: Palgrave Macmillan).

ANSCOMBE, G. E. M. (1975). 'The First Person', in Samuel Guttenplan (ed.), *Mind and Language* (Oxford: Clarendon Press).

BAKER, L. (1998). 'The First-Person Perspective: A Test for Naturalism', *American Philosophical Quarterly*, 35: 327–46.

——(2007). 'Naturalism and the First-Person Perspective', in G. Gasser (ed.), *How Successful is Naturalism? Publications of the Austrian Ludwig Wittgenstein Society* (Frankfurt am Main: Ontos-Verlag), 203–26.

BLANKE, O., and METZINGER, T. (2009). 'Full-Body Illusions and Minimal Phenomenal Selfhood', *Trends in Cognitive Sciences*, 13/1: 7–13.

BOËR, S., and LYCAN, W. (1980). 'Who, Me?', *Philosophical Review*, 89: 427–66.

BRUGGER, P., KOLLIAS, S. K., MÜRI, R. M., CRELIER, G., HEPP-REYMOND, M.-C., and REGARD, M. (2000). 'Beyond Re-membering: Phantom Sensations of Congenitally Absent Limbs', *Proceedings of the National Academy of Science USA*, 97: 6167–72.

CASTAÑEDA, H.-N. (1966). '"He": A Study in the Logic of Self-Consciousness', *Ratio*, 8: 130–57.

——(1967). 'Indicators and Quasi-Indicators', *American Philosophical Quarterly*, 4: 85–100.

DENNETT, D. C. (1991). *Consciousness Explained* (Boston: Little, Brown & Co.).

GHIN, M. (2005). 'What a Self could be', *Psyche*, 11(5): www.theassc.org/files/assc/2617.pdf.

HUME, D. (1740). *A Treatise of Human Nature* (Oxford: Oxford University Press, 1967 edn).

HUNTER, E. C. M., SIERRA, M., and DAVID, A. S. (2004). 'The Epidemiology of Depersonalization and Derealization: A Systematic Review', *Society for Psychiatry and Psychiatric Epidemiology*, 39: 9–18.

JOHNSON-LAIRD, P. N. (1983). *Mental Models* (Cambridge, Mass.: MIT Press).

——(2008). 'Mental Models and Deductive Reasoning', in L. Rips and J. Adler (eds), *Reasoning: Studies in Human Inference and its Foundations* (Cambridge: Cambridge University Press).

KNAUFF, M. (2009). 'A Neurocognitive Theory of Deductive Relational Reasoning with Mental Models and Visual Images', *Spatial Cognition and Computation*, 9: 109–37.

LADYMAN, J., and ROSS, D. (2009). *Every Thing Must Go: Metaphysics Naturalized* (Oxford: Oxford University Press).

LEGRAND, D. (2005). 'Transparently Oneself', *Psyche*, 11(5): www.theassc.org/files/assc/2616.pdf.

LYCAN, W. G. (1987). *Consciousness* (Cambridge, Mass., and London: MIT Press).

——(1996). *Consciousness and Experience* (Cambridge, Mass.: MIT Press).

MALCOLM, N. (1988). 'Subjectivity', *Philosophy*, 63: 147–60.

METZINGER, T. (1993). *Subjekt und Selbstmodell* (Paderborn: mentis; 2nd edn. 1999).

——(1995). 'Faster than Thought: Holism, Homogeneity and Temporal Coding', in T. Metzinger (ed.), *Conscious Experience* (Thorverton: Imprint Academic; Paderborn: mentis), 425–61.

——(2003a). *Being No One: The Self-Model Theory of Subjectivity* (Cambridge, Mass.: MIT Press).

——(2003b). 'Phenomenal Transparency and Cognitive Self-Reference', *Phenomenology and the Cognitive Sciences*, 2: 353–93.

——(2006). 'Conscious Volition and Mental Representation: Towards a More Fine-Grained Analysis', in N. Sebanz and W. Prinz (eds.), *Disorders of Volition* (Cambridge, Mass.: MIT Press).

——(2008). 'Empirical Perspectives from the Self-Model Theory of Subjectivity: A Brief Summary with Examples', in Rahul Banerjee and Bikas K. Chakrabarti (eds), *Progress in Brain Research*, 168 (Amsterdam: Elsevier), 215–46.

——(2009). *The Ego Tunnel: The Science of the Mind and the Myth of the Self* (New York: Basic Books).

——and GALLESE, V. (2003). 'The Emergence of a Shared Action Ontology: Building Blocks for a Theory', in G. Knoblich, B. Elsner, G. von Aschersleben, and T. Metzinger (eds), 'Self and Action'. Special issue of *Consciousness and Cognition*, 12/4 (Dec.): 549–71.

NAGEL, T. (1986). *The View from Nowhere* (New York and Oxford: Oxford University Press).

NEWEN, A. (1997). 'The Logic of Indexical Thoughts and the Metaphysics of the ' "Self" ', in W. Künne, A. Newen, and M. Anduschus (eds), *Direct Reference, Indexicality and Propositional Attitudes* (Stanford, Calif.: CSLI).

PARFIT, D. (1984). *Reasons and Persons* (Oxford: Oxford University Press).

PERRY, J. (1979). 'The Problem of the Essential Indexical', *Noûs*, 13: 3–22.

——(1993). *The Problem of the Essential Indexical and Other Essays* (New York: Oxford University Press).

RECANATI, F. (2007). 'Content, Mode, and Self-Reference', in S. L. Tsohatzidis (ed.), *John Searle's Philosophy of Language: Force, Meaning and Mind* (New York: Cambridge University Press), 49–64.

SIDERITS, M. (2003). *Personal Identity and Buddhist Philosophy: Empty Persons* (Aldershot: Ashgate).

——(2007). *Buddhism as Philosophy: Empty Persons* (Aldershot: Ashgate).

SIMEON, D., and ABUGEL, J. (2006). *Feeling Unreal: Depersonalization Disorder and the Loss of the Self* (New York: Oxford University Press).

SINGER, W., and GRAY, C. (1995). 'Visual Feature Integration and the Temporal Correlation Hypothesis', *Annual Review of Neuroscience*, 18: 555–86.

STRAWSON, P. (1959). *Individuals: An Essay in Descriptive Metaphysics* (London: Routledge).

THOMPSON, E. (2007). *Mind in Life* (Cambridge, Mass.: MIT Press).

WESTERHOFF, J. C. (2009). *Nagarjuna's Madhyamaka. A Philosophical Investigation* (Oxford: Oxford University Press).

....

CHAPTER 12

BUDDHIST NON-SELF

THE NO-OWNER'S MANUAL

....

MARK SIDERITS

THE Buddha claimed to have discovered a path to liberation from suffering. In this he was not alone. A number of such paths were developed in early classical India. All share the belief that sentient beings suffer because of ignorance about their true identity: we are trapped on the wheel of *saṃsāra* because we identify with things that are not the true self. What set the Buddha's teachings apart from those of other Indian doctrines of liberation is that the Buddha denied there is a self. On his analysis, our ignorance about our identity consists in our holding that there is such a thing as 'I' and 'mine'. Instead, everything is non-self.

In modern discussions of the Buddha's teachings one sometimes finds it claimed that the Buddha only denied the existence of an empirical self, and not the existence of a self that transcends all possible experience.[1] And it is true that his arguments for non-self typically canvass just the five groups of psycho-physical elements (*skandhas*), all of which are possible objects of sensory experience. When, for instance, the Buddha points out that all the psychophysical elements lack the sort of permanence that a self would require, this proves that there is no self only

---

[1] Albahari 2007 is a recent instance.

given the additional premise that there is no more to the person than the empirically given elements. And the Buddha seems not to have argued for such a premise. So one might suppose that the Buddha only meant to deny that the self is an empirical element, and not deny outright that there is such a thing as the self. This would bring the Buddha's teachings more in line with the views of some of the Brahmanical schools, such as Sāṃkhya and Vedānta. But this is not how the Buddhist philosophical tradition understood the Buddha's teachings. They took the doctrine of non-self to mean that there is no self *tout court*. What I shall discuss here is their philosophical articulations of this understanding of non-self.

Among the various schools that make up Indian Buddhist philosophy, the most widely accepted understanding of non-self is what I call Buddhist Reductionism. Its formulation involves the introduction of a distinction between the terms 'self' and 'person'.[2] If we think of possible views as to what the word 'I' might denote, we can say that broadly speaking there are two sorts: those that take 'I' to refer to some one part of the psychophysical complex that is its essence; and those that take 'I' to denote a whole made up of the psychophysical elements. By 'self' we shall here mean the one part that is the essence. And by 'person' we shall mean the psychophysical complex as a whole. Then Buddhist Reductionism can be formulated as the two claims:

1. There is no self.
2. The person is a conceptual fiction, something that is only conventionally and not ultimately real.

Of these two claims, it is the second that requires the most explanation. But I shall begin with a brief discussion of the first.

The notion that the self is some one simple part from among the parts making up the psychophysical complex is the consensus view of those (non-Buddhist) Indian philosophers who are realists about the self. The view that this is what 'I' denotes is not as counterintuitive as it might seem.[3] We know that our use of 'I' extends beyond the loss of various psychophysical elements: I believe that I would survive the loss of a kidney or the replacement of my heart; I believe that I once existed lacking certain commitments that I now consider central to my existence; and so on. If, like most classical Indian philosophers, we believe that there is

---

[2] This distinction is not always honored; in some cases the term *ātman* (which is usually translated as 'self') is used for both. But making such a distinction is required in order to formulate the thesis of the Pudgalavāda school (about which more below), according to which the self is not ultimately real but the person (*pudgala*) is ultimately real. Where the term *ātman* is used for both, a distinction is still drawn between the sense of 'I' had by ordinary people—which corresponds to the concept of a person—and the philosophers' notion of a simple, eternally enduring *ātman*.

[3] Of course, that a given view about persons is counterintuitive would not count as an objection to that view for most of the Indian philosophers in question. Since they held that most people lack knowledge of their true identity, our intuitions about our nature are not to be treated as reliable evidence. Being in the wisdom business, Indian philosophers are quite cheerfully revisionist.

rebirth, this phenomenon becomes all the more striking, since between death and rebirth all my body and typically all my psychological makeup are replaced. It then becomes quite tempting to suppose that there is some one part the continued existence of which is necessary for the continued existence of this 'me'. And since this entity must endure over extremely long durations, it is equally tempting to suppose that it is simple or impartite. For if transitory entities come into and go out of existence through the rearrangement of parts, it follows that simple entities must be eternal. There was considerable debate about how else to characterize the self. Some saw it as both cognizer and agent, others held it to be just the subject of experience; some took it to have moral properties, others thought it is nothing but a witnessing consciousness; etc. But all agreed that it is in some sense simple, and that it endures.

The most common Buddhist argument for the non-existence of the self is the argument from impermanence. The Buddha formulated this argument in terms of a survey of the five kinds of psychophysical element: each being impermanent, none could be the self. Later Buddhist philosophers sought to prove that no existing thing could be permanent. One strategy involved the point that a simple entity could not undergo any sort of change, as this would require that one part of the entity change while another part remain the same, and simples have no parts. But since an enduring thing can bring about a change in other things only by itself undergoing some sort of change, it follows that a simple enduring thing could not be causally efficacious. But, it was claimed, for something to exist is just for it to be causally efficacious. Hence there can be no simple enduring entities, and therefore there can be no self.

If there is no self, though, and nothing about us persists even a single lifetime, why does it seem to us as though we are enduring entities? Buddhist Reductionists answer this question by claiming that the person—the whole constituted by the psychophysical elements—is a mere fiction, albeit a useful one. This is what they mean when they say that the person is only conventionally and not ultimately real: our talk of persons is a mere façon de parler, but one that we have come to take altogether too seriously. The defense of this claim is relatively complex and will require careful consideration. What one should keep in mind in the course of this investigation is that it is meant to steer a middle course between, on the one hand, the view that there is some real entity that 'I' denotes, and on the other the utter rejection of our concept of the person. The Buddhist Reductionist view of persons is in some respects compatible with views of the self that have recently been discussed in philosophy and cognitive science (and are represented in other contributions to this volume). For instance, a Buddhist Reductionist might welcome a narrative view of the self (the view that we see ourselves as the authors of self-constituting narratives) as one that gives important insights into how the concept of the person serves a useful function. But they would insist that this convergence should not blind us to the fact (as they see it) that the concept of the person is useful only up to a point, beyond which its employment leads to existential suffering. The Buddhist formulation of Reductionism is meant to show how we can continue to reap the very real benefits that come with our deployment of this concept while not falling into the difficulties that come with complete acquiescence.

Their formulation and defense of the claim that the person is a mere conceptual fiction is grounded in a thoroughgoing mereological reductionism, according to which all partite entities in our common-sense ontology are only conventionally and not ultimately real. As this terminology suggests, Buddhist Reductionism employs a two-tier ontology, according to which only some of the things we take to be real belong in our final ontology, while others are relegated to the status of mere back-benchers. Among the latter are, in addition to persons, such things as chariots, pots, trees, mountains, fires, rivers, hands, and minds. Our folk ontology contains both entities such as these, and the ultimate parts of which they are composed: in the case of macrophysical objects, atoms;[4] in the case of complex mental entities, simple psychological events such as pains and occurrent desires. But there is good reason not to allow both the wholes and their parts into our final ontology. If, for instance, we count both the pot and the atoms of which it is composed as equally real, then we must say whether the pot is identical with those atoms or distinct from them. Among the reasons against saying they are identical are the fact that the pot is one while the atoms are many; that it is only when those atoms are arranged pot-wise that they are taken to compose one thing and not just be a many (why the prejudice against the same atoms when they are smeared into several odd-shaped mono-molecular films?); and that it is indeterminate at what point the pot ceases to exist as we remove randomly selected atoms from it one at a time.[5] Among the reasons for denying that pot and atoms are distinct are the fact that they occupy the same space at the same time, and the fact that the pot has no autonomous causal powers (the alleged effects of the pot turn out to be just effects of the atoms).[6]

There being good reasons to deny that the pot and the atoms are equally real, one or the other must go. And we have reason to suppose that the atoms are real: they possess autonomous causal powers. So the pot must go. Still it would be odd

[4] The atoms that belong in our final ontology are, of course, the philosophers' atoms, not the so-called atoms of current physics, which are misnamed. Both 'atom' and its Sanskrit equivalent (*paramāṇu*) were intended to refer to impartite physical entities. It is because physicists in the 19th century. jumped the gun that what we today call atoms are misnamed. What the real atoms might be we do not yet know.

[5] The last sort of consideration, appealing to the *sorites* difficulties that arise when whole and parts have the same ontological status, was not among those Buddhist Reductionists appealed to in defending their view about wholes.

[6] Van Inwagen 1995 and Merricks 2001 both give sophisticated and subtle arguments for mereological reductionism about macrophysical objects. But both resist applying the view to persons.

to suppose that the pot is utterly unreal, like the golden mountain or the son of a barren woman. One who believes there to be a golden mountain will inevitably be disappointed in their schemes, while one who believes there to be a pot will have success in storing their honey. It thus seems sensible to grant the pot a kind of provisional or conventional ontological status as a conceptual fiction, something we take to be real only because of our employment of a useful concept as a part of our going theory. As the term 'reductionism' is commonly understood, a reductionist about pots would be one who holds that a pot *just consists in* atoms arranged pot-wise. The two-tier ontology of Buddhist Reductionism helps us understand what this means: that while pots do not belong in our final ontology, a theory that commits us to their existence turns out to be useful given what is in our final ontology (such as atoms arranged pot-wise) and what our interests and our cognitive limitations are (we need containers for our honey, and we're bad at keeping track of individual atoms). To call pots conventionally real is to steer a middle path between realism about pots and outright eliminativism about pots.

All this can be expressed quite neatly if we introduce two distinct truth-predicates, 'ultimately true' and 'conventionally true', with the former applying to sentences that depict how the ultimately real things are, and the latter to sentences that depict how the conventionally real things are. Then when 'There is a pot on the table' is conventionally true, there will be some ultimately true sentence that says there are atoms arranged in such-and-such a way. There is one important caveat here, though: no statement employing *convenient designators* (words for partite entities, such as 'pot') is ultimately truth-apt. In effect this bans all talk of conceptual fictions from our ultimate discourse. This is because if such talk were permitted then we could raise the question whether the pot is identical with or distinct from the atoms arranged pot-wise, and such talk would lead to paradox in short order.[7] Now it is an open question whether Buddhist Reductionists would want to similarly ban talk of ultimately real entities from the conventional discourse; the texts are silent on this matter. To do so (to make the semantic barrier between the two truths two-way) would mean, for instance, that *sorites* paradoxes could not arise in conventional truth: since one could not then speak of the pot and its constituent atoms in the same breath, one could not ask the embarrassing question at what precise point the pot ceases to exist as one removes randomly selected atoms. Since Buddhist Reductionists think conventional truth is deceptive in important respects, they might see no reason to install such a barrier at the conventional level. Still the conventional truth (i.e. those of our going theories

---

[7] One can, however, say things about the word 'pot' at the ultimate level of truth, for instance that the word is a convenient designator (and hence does not designate anything real). This is how Ābhidharmikas avoid paradox while asserting what we might more incautiously put as 'Pots are not ultimately real'. One can keep the ultimate truth contradiction-free by using this sort of meta-linguistic strategy.

that involve commitment to wholes) is useful, and this is difficult to explain if it contains paradoxes. Moreover, there are advantages to be realized if we limit conventional discourse to just talk of conceptual fictions. We can then see how novel predicates can arise at the conventional level for which no algorithm can be given for translation into ultimate discourse, without inviting the mystery-mongering of emergentism. For we can then see how the aesthetic properties of a pot might supervene on the properties of the constituent atoms even though we cannot give a precise formula for arranging atoms so as to produce beautiful pots.

The real payoff from this semantic dualism comes with its application to the concept of the person. We take ourselves to be entities that endure at least a lifetime. Ultimately there are only impersonal impermanent entities making up distinct causally connected series. None of these entities lasts a lifetime. And the series that they constitute, being wholes made of parts, are not ultimately real. But given the facts about such entities and their causal interactions, it turns out to be useful to carve the world up into aggregations that correspond roughly to distinct causal series of psychophysical elements. This in turn makes it conventionally true that we are persons, things that endure at least a lifetime. The personhood concept is a useful fiction.

Our personhood concept carries with it such important features as interest in one's survival, responsibility for one's past actions, and concern about one's future states. Here is an illustration of how such a concept might be a useful fiction. Persons typically take the stance of appropriation toward the past and future states in the causal series: they take those states to be 'me' or 'mine'. Suppose this disposition is the product of early childhood socialization.[8] Why might it be useful to socialize the child into taking such a stance? Consider the case of brushing one's teeth, something that children typically do not enjoy. The child can have a motive to brush their teeth only if they identify with those future elements that are spared the occurrence of the pain of tooth decay. Only if the child learns to think of that future dental patient as themselves will they see a reason to do something that brings no present pleasure and some minor present discomfort. To instill the concept of the person in this causal series is a way of equipping it with resources that turn it into a center for local enhancement of overall welfare. There is less overall pain and suffering and more overall pleasure and happiness in the world when the child learns to think of itself as a person.

Buddhist Reductionists deny that ultimately there is anything that endures in the way in which we take ourselves to endure. This is sometimes thought to have the consequence that we are not enduring entities. And this in turn would mean that we can have no reason to feel concern about the future states in this causal series. But Buddhist Reductionists call this view about the future 'annihilationism', and

---

[8] Buddhist Reductionists typically say that the disposition to engage in appropriation stems from habits acquired in the beginningless series of past lives. We say more about this below.

they consider it one of the two extreme views about ourselves that are to be avoided (the other being the non-Reductionist view that we are separately existing, enduring selves, a view they call 'eternalism'). They advocate what they call a 'middle path' between these two extreme views. Semantic dualism is what makes such a middle path possible. The question 'Am I something that endures?' concerns the temporal properties of a complex entity. Among the presently occurring psychophysical elements, there is no individual element that could take up the first-person stance on its own. The referent of this 'I' could only be something complex. Consequently the question is semantically ill-formed at the ultimate level. No answer to this question could be ultimately true, or ultimately false either. For it concerns something partite, and partite entities can only be referred to at the conventional level. The question only makes sense at that level. And given the facts about the causal series of psychophysical elements, the answer that is conventionally true is that I am something that endures. So the personhood feature of concern about one's future states holds in the only way that it could—conventionally. Likewise for the other important personhood features.

Moreover, if the semantic barrier between the two truths is two-way, there cannot be any incompatibility between the ultimate truth concerning the causal series and the conventional truth about us. Suppose, for instance, that all occurrences of psychophysical elements obey deterministic causal laws. It is then ultimately true that all the elements are causally determined. Might this be incompatible with the statement that persons bear moral responsibility for their actions? For two statements to be incompatible, the truth of one must entail the falsity of the other. And for the entailment relation to hold, the statements in question must be such as to be either true or false in the same way. 'All the elements are causally determined' is, we are supposing, ultimately true. 'Persons bear moral responsibility for their actions' is (for reasons given in the last paragraph) conventionally true. On the hypothesis that the semantic barrier is two-way, neither statement can be true or false in the way that the other is true. So the two statements cannot be incompatible. The claim that determinism is incompatible with the sort of freedom required for moral responsibility cannot be true.[9]

Buddhist Reductionists hold it to be conventionally true that we are persons, things that endure, have concern about their future states, and have the other personhood features. This is conventionally true because things turn out better—there is more overall pleasure and happiness and less overall pain and suffering—when the personhood theory is adopted and employed. But this holds only up to a point. For when we come to think of ourselves as persons, this sets the stage for existential suffering. It gives rise to the feelings of alienation, frustration, and despair that inevitably arise when we confront the fact of our own impermanence. It would be better if we could

---

[9] For a more complete discussion of this see Siderits 2008. For a defense of the alternative view that Buddhist Reductionists are committed to hard determinism see Goodman 2002.

reap the benefits of thinking of ourselves as persons—by, for instance, avoiding actions that yield minor present pleasure in exchange for greater long-term pain— while recognizing this for just the useful fiction that it is. The ideal state, they hold, is one in which we continue to behave like persons but cease taking ourselves quite so seriously. This is how, in their view, overcoming our ignorance about our identity can lead to liberation from suffering.

Not all schools of Indian Buddhism espoused Buddhist Reductionism. One clear exception is the school (or group of schools) known as the Personalists (Pudgala-vādins).[10] While Personalists agree that there is no self, they hold that the person— understood as a whole that is conceived in dependence on the psychophysical elements—is no mere conceptual fiction. It is not entirely clear just what ontological status they wish to assign it, but they are committed to the claim that the person is neither identical with nor distinct from the elements, as well as that it somehow exists separate from the elements. This suggests a kind of emergentism, the view that in certain cases something genuinely new emerges when sufficiently many entities enter into sufficiently complex interrelations. The most common form of emergent-ism is property-emergentism, which has it that what emerges is a novel property of the system composed of the more basic entities. The vitalist view that the properties of living systems emerge from the assembly of inanimate material particles is an example of this sort of emergentism.[11] But one might also espouse a substance-emergentism, according to which what emerges is a new kind of substance altogeth-er.[12] And this would seem to be what the Personalists had in mind. They agree with Reductionists that the person is conceptualized in dependence on the psychophysi-cal elements, and that the person cannot be said to be either identical with or distinct from the elements. But they reject the claim that the person is thought to exist only because of the useful role the personhood concept plays in our going theory. Their alternative view might be couched in the current parlance as the claim that the person non-reductively supervenes on the psychophysical elements.[13]

[10] For a thorough discussion of the school, its literature, and the difficulties in its interpretation, see the first seven chapters of Priestley 1999. (It should be noted that the interpretation Priestley develops beginning in the eighth chapter is highly speculative.)

[11] There is likewise a dispute among Buddhists as to whether there exists anything like a vital force in sentient beings. But this concerned the question whether it is some single ultimately real entity that explains the continued life of a sentient being, or instead that the 'vital force' is a mere conceptual construction reductively supervening on the powers of the being's material components. Neither view represents a kind of property-emergentism. For this dispute see Cox 1995: 291–2.

[12] For a recent formulation and defense of substance emergentism with respect to persons see Hasker 1999.

[13] For an account of the dispute over non-reductive supervenience in the philosophy of mind see Kim 1998. Buddhist Reductionists claim that the person reductively supervenes on the elements. Their disagreement with the Personalists has to do with whether or not there remains any explanatory work to be done once all the facts about the elements and their arrangement are taken into account. The Personalist view would thus count as an instance of what Parfit calls the 'further-fact' form of Non-Reductionism. See Parfit 1984: 210.

Personalists give several reasons for their claim about persons. Some of these rely on appeals to the Buddha's authority. But Personalists also argue that theirs is the only view that can account for the occurrence of such moral properties as desert. They agree with Buddhist Reductionists that there is no self, so an enduring self cannot be what bears the property of deserving to be rewarded or punished for one's past deeds. But, they claim, if the person were a mere conceptual fiction then it could not do the job either. Buddhist Reductionists obviously disagree, and from what was said earlier we can see how they respond to this objection. But perhaps the greatest challenge for Personalism lies in explaining just how the non-reductive supervenience they claim holds between person and elements is supposed to work. The most sustained attempt to do this comes with their fire-fuel analogy. The idea seems to be that by 'fuel' is meant just those material elements that make up wood and the like, and that fire occurs when certain of those elements are arranged in a certain way. In this case we can say that since fire is one while the elements of which it is composed are many, fire can be neither identical with nor distinct from those elements. But something else is needed if fire is not to be reducible to the elements. Fire must be shown to exert 'downward' causation: it must be the case that the occurrence of fire brings about changes among the elements that cannot be explained on the basis of facts about the elements alone. And this turns out to be singularly difficult to show.[14] Failing such a demonstration, Ockham's razor (known to Indian philosophers as the principle of 'lightness') rules in favor of reducing fire to the elements. For if all that happens at the base level can be explained in terms of facts about the entities at that level, there is no reason to suppose that higher-level entities exist apart from our ways of conceptualizing aggregates of base-level entities. So it is not clear that Personalism constitutes a viable alternative to Buddhist Reductionism.

It is sometimes claimed that, in addition to the Personalists, the Prāsaṅgika Madhyamaka school of Indian Buddhist philosophy also rejects Buddhist Reductionism.[15] This seems plausible given that the simples that Buddhist Reductionism requires for its ultimate ontology are said to be things with intrinsic natures (svabhāva), and the central claim of Madhyamaka is that nothing has intrinsic nature. Since Madhyamaka thus rejects the kind of privileged ontology required for semantic dualism, it seems reasonable to suppose that it repudiates the reductive analysis of persons into impersonal elements. But this conclusion may be premature, for it is difficult to reconcile with what Candrakīrti says in commenting on Nāgārjuna's discussion of non-self in Mūlamadhyamakakārikā XVIII. 1–5 (Katsura and Siderits 2008: 32–4) and Mūlamadhyamakakārikā XXVII. 3–20 (Katsura and Siderits forthcoming). The arguments there are just the ones that Buddhist

---

14 The example is discussed at *Abhidharmakośabhāṣya*, 462, translated in Duerlinger 2003: 74–6.

15 Each of the following makes this claim about Candrakārti in a slightly different way: Duerlinger 1993; Ganeri 2007; Perrett 2002.

Reductionists typically give for their view. Moreover, if Candrakīrti held a Minimalist view of persons, as Perrett (2002: 378) claims, he should acquiesce in our common-sense concept of persons and the normative commitments it brings with it. Instead Candrakīrti famously likens our ordinary sense of 'I' to having a nest of snakes in the walls of one's house, and he calls realization of non-self the 'magic charm' that destroys all sense of 'I'.[16] These are things a Reductionist might say, but not a Minimalist.

What may have led some to view Candrakīrti as anti-Reductionist is the way he argues for the claim that the person can be neither identical with nor distinct from the elements. Arguing against the view that 'I' denotes all the psychophysical elements in the series (so that the person is identical with the elements) he points out that on one occasion 'I' will denote one subset of those elements, while on another occasion it denotes a distinct subset. There being no single set of elements that my use of 'I' always denotes, the person cannot be identical with any such set. Now this can be taken as an anti-Reductionist argument only if one takes reduction to require full translatability between the two discourses. But Buddhist Reductionism, with its semantic barrier between conventional and ultimate truth, rejects this requirement. This is the point of the commonly cited example of 'The tree bears fruit'. On any given occasion what makes a sentence using the word 'tree' true will be some set of parts in the causal series of elements that constitute an arboreal life history. And among those elements are fruits (assuming for the moment that fruits are ultimate parts). Still they cannot be among the elements involved in assessing the contribution of 'tree' to the sentence 'The tree bears fruit', lest the sentence turn out to be uninformative. Indeed we can appreciate why it would be important that there not be a precise mapping of convenient designators onto ultimately real entities. Such convenient designators as 'tree' and 'pot' are convenient precisely because they are highly tolerant and flexible: they have, as it were, a large margin of error. Given that we have an interest in referring to aggregates with functions like producing fruit and holding honey, and that there are hugely many possible aggregations of particles that can perform these functions, and that our sense organs are macroscopes and not microscopes, and that our computational powers are rather limited, it is in our interest that 'tree' and 'pot' not be identified with any determinate set of particles in any determinate arrangement. This is why Buddhist Reductionism puts semantic barriers between the two truths.[17]

---

[16] See *Madhyamakāvatāra* 6. 141 for the snake analogy, *Madhyamakāvatāra* 6. 145 for the claim about the magic charm. For an English translation see Padmakara Translation Group 2002: 88.

[17] Various logical and semantic strategies have been proposed to circumvent the *sorites* difficulties that would result if terms from the ultimate discourse could be introduced into the conventional discourse (i.e. if the semantic barrier were only one-way). For a brief survey and general discussion see Keefe and Smith 1997: 52–7; also Parsons 2000. In Siderits 2003: 77–85 I suggested that Buddhist Reductionism might be developed in such a way as to yield a semantics for vague terms that employed a degree-theoretic truth-predicate. While I still believe such an approach can be made to work, I am

The example of 'The tree bears fruit' also illustrates a way in which Buddhist Reductionism might be used to explain why we believe that persons have selves. The case of the tree involves taking the set of all the parts in the series and dividing it into two distinct subsets, one taking subject role and the other taking object role. We do something similar with persons, particularly with respect to actions, as in 'I raised my right hand'. This can give rise to the sense that there is some core set of parts that constitutes the control center. But a part that goes in the object slot on one occasion might fall on the subject side on another, as in 'I steered the car around the pylon', where my right hand seems to count as among the entities that are involved in the exercise of control. And we seem capable of exercising some degree of control over all the parts (not on any one occasion, of course, but on successive occasions). This can give rise to the illusion that the control center must be something existing separately from the empirically accessible parts. It can lead to a sense of the self as a 'center of narrative gravity'.[18] It is an illusion, this sense of a transcendent yet contentful self, yet we can see how it would be useful and so would come to play an important role in the common-sense core of our going theory.

Among the many objections that have been raised to Reductionism, those that charge it with circularity are especially important. One such objection is that there cannot be conventional truth without persons to establish the conventions. Since Buddhist Reductionism claims that persons are constituted by the conventions that make up our going theory, it is circular. This objection is easily answered through appeal to selectionist explanations. One can suppose that processes of natural selection yielded aggregate systems of the sort that make up what we are here calling causal series of psychophysical elements. And then, one can suppose, processes of cultural selection yielded groups of such series that shared the conceptual practices making up the personhood theory.[19] To say that it is conventionally true that we are persons is to say that the personhood theory better serves our interests than any of the other readily available theories of what we are. In that case, those social groups in which the theory arose would have outperformed those in which some other conceptual practice arose, leading to the present-day universal acceptance of the personhood theory.

A rather more interesting answer to this objection comes from the Buddhist Reductionist. Buddhists claim that *saṃsāra* is beginningless: there is no first life in the series of lives that has this life as its latest member. (That there may be an end to

now inclined to think that Buddhist Reductionists would reject the modifications of classical logic that introduction of such a truth-predicate requires. This is why I now think they would insist that the semantic barrier be two-way.

18 See Dennett 1992. See also Flanagan 2002: 213–64. Note though that Flanagan appears to endorse a kind of non-reductive supervenience view of the narrative self (217).

19 Of course the development of culturally encoded systems of representation requires that there already be proto-conceptual resources in place at the level of the individual. For an example of such bootstrapping see Carey 2004.

this series is the promise of the Buddha's third noble truth, that there is *nirvāṇa* or the cessation of suffering.) If there is no first life in any series of lives, then there need not have been a time before which there was no social structure capable of bringing about socialization into the theory that we are persons. Of course it will be said that the regress cannot be benign, for the time required runs out at the Big Bang. As long as each life lasts for some finite amount of time, there can only be a finite number of lives in a series that began sometime after the Big Bang. But classical Indian cosmologies typically see this universe as just the latest in a beginningless series, the collapse of each sowing the seeds for the start of another. On this view, the Big Bang that started our universe was the effect of a Big Crunch with which the immediately preceding universe ended. One might be highly skeptical about the very hypothesis that there is rebirth. But it is not obvious that this answer to the circularity objection is incoherent.

A second sort of circularity objection is not so easily answered. This can be put as the point that successful reduction requires the existence of experiencing subjects, and Reductionism implicitly calls the existence of such subjects into question. In general, reductionisms seek to show how, given what does exist, it would seem to us as if there is something extra. To reduce heat to mean kinetic energy it is not enough just to show a correlation between judgments of heat and high mean kinetic energy. We need to be convinced both that there is something there for the high mean kinetic energy to be correlated with, and that this something is somehow less than robustly real. The target of the reduction, we say, *just is* certain 'more basic' things. We pull off this trick of making the reduction target something real, but not too real, by making it subjective, a mere appearance, but reliably so. The tangible property of heat is how high mean kinetic energy will seem to systems with sense organs and interests of a certain sort. We can understand how, given our needs and the nature of our cognitive capacities, it would seem to us that there are pots when there are really just atoms arranged pot-wise. But, the objection goes, is it really coherent to assert, as the Reductionist does, that it seems to us as though we are persons when there are really just psychophysical elements arranged person-wise? For then to whom do these appearances appear?

This, it should be noted, is not your garden-variety circularity objection. The complaint is not that the *explanandum* occurs in the *explanans*. That sort of complaint is often lodged against Reductionism, since Reductionist explanations sometimes appeal to the interests served by the personhood concept, and interests would seem to be adjectival on persons. To answer that complaint the Reductionist must show how their explanations can be de-homuncularized, and selectionist stories are one way to do this. But the present objection is different. Its target is not the explanation but the consumer of the explanation. To find a Reductionist explanation plausible I must see my way clear to taking a third-person stance on my own first-person stance. And doing so seems to require my taking a first-person stance. How, the opponent asks, can it seem to me as if I am a person if there is no 'me' for whom things seem this way?

While those classical Indian philosophers who were realists about the self raised a variety of objections to Buddhist Reductionism, it is interesting that this circularity objection was not among them. The reason may be that there was something in the ultimate ontology of Buddhist Reductionism that could be proposed as the subject of experience without being taken for a self. This is consciousness (*vijñāna*), the fifth of the five types of psychophysical element posited by the Buddha. Consciousness is described as that which is aware in general;[20] it is another type of psychophysical element, perception (*saṃjñā*), that is said to perform the task of identifying the object of awareness. This makes consciousness look rather like a subject of experience. Great stress is placed, however, on the point that consciousness is impermanent. For instance, the Buddha argues that consciousness originates in dependence on sense–object contact, so that experience across different sense modalities involves distinct consciousnesses.[21] Since it is one consciousness that serves as the subject of the experience of seeing the mango and another consciousness that serves as the subject of the experience of tasting the mango, consciousness cannot be thought of as a self that serves to unify these distinct experiences. There is, Buddhist Reductionists claim, nothing that unifies these experiences. The appearance of unification arises because of the causal connections that obtain among these and other psychophysical elements in a causal series, plus our use of the convenient designator 'person'.[22] So the objection that Reductionism requires an experiencing subject is answered with the claim that the experiencing subject, being momentary, is thoroughly impersonal in nature.

But not all Buddhist Reductionists were happy with this answer. Early in the development of the Yogācāra school of Mahāyāna Buddhism we find a concern to banish all traces of the subject–object dichotomy, including the distinction between conscious subject and object of experience within an individual experience-event.[23] This concern eventually manifests itself in the claim of Dignāga, founder of the school of Buddhist epistemology, that a cognition has two forms, that of the object and that of itself as something that cognizes. This claim is directed against the naive realist view of cognition, according to which cognitions only have the single nature of cognizing, the form of the object being located in an object that is wholly distinct from that which cognizes. Dignāga is here

[20] See, for instance, the definition of *viññāna* (consciousness) given at *Milindapaha*, 62, tr. at Rhys Davids 1965: 95.

[21] See, for instance, Horner 1954: 314–15.

[22] This is the subject of the second half of Vasubandhu's 'Refutation of the Theory of the Person', the ninth chapter of *Abhidharmakośabhāṣya* (the first half being taken up with the investigation of Personalism). For translations and discussion see Duerlinger 2003; Kapstein 2001: 367–75.

[23] See Vasubandhu's commentary on *Vimśatikā*, 10, Sthiramati's commentary on *Trimśikā*, 21cd in Levi (1925).

representing the view of the representationalist and the subjective idealist, for both of whom what one is directly aware of in cognition is in some sense immanent to the cognizer. But it is open to the representationalist and the idealist to hold that the form of the object occurs in a mental image, and that awareness of that form occurs through the relation of the image to a distinct consciousness event that cognizes the image. Dignāga's claim that both forms are in a single cognition reflects the Yogācāra concern that any type of subject–object dichotomy, even one based on a distinction among momentary mental events, can serve as a breeding ground for a sense of 'I' and thus lead to suffering. This claim would give the Buddhist Reductionist one way to answer the present circularity objection, which in effect charges the Reductionist with trying to reduce everything to the third-person stance of objectivity through appeal to the subjective and the first-person perspective. Dignāga would reply that the subject–object dichotomy is merely a useful conceptual construction, one that a proper (Reductionist) understanding of the nature of cognition helps us transcend.

One might wonder whether this reply can be made to work. But perhaps a more important question here is what reason there is to hold that cognitions have two forms. Dignāga argues that if a cognition only had one form, either the form of the object or the form of itself as something that cognizes, then we would be unable to distinguish between the cognition of a pot (c_1) and the cognition of the cognition of a pot (c_2). For if a cognition is characterized only by the form of its object, then c_1 and c_2 would both have the nature of the form of a pot, P; while if a cognition is only characterized by its own form C, then once again c_1 and c_2 would share the same form. But this difficulty only arises if we assume that what is cognized by a cognition must be immanent to that very cognition. This assumption is rejected by direct realists, who claim that a cognition always cognizes something distinct from itself. They argue that to say otherwise is to hold that a cognition can cognize itself, something we know to be no more possible than that an acrobat can stand on their own shoulders. One can then distinguish between c_1 and c_2 on the basis of the fact that while c_1 and c_2 both have C as their nature, c_1 has something P-natured as its object while c_2 has something C-natured as its object.

Dignāga would reply by defending the claim that cognition cognizes itself, which is supported by the analogy of light that illuminates both the object and itself. He also argues that the alternative view, that consciousness is irreflexive, suffers from two major difficulties. First, it leads to an infinite regress: if a second cognition is required in order to cognize my cognition of a pot, then a third is required to cognize the second, etc. Second, the notion that cognition is itself cognized by a distinct act of introspection is incoherent. Presumably the introspective cognition occurs after the cognition that it takes as object. But this turns introspection into a kind of remembering: to be aware of the cognition of a pot is to remember cognizing the pot a moment earlier. And, points out Dignāga, one cannot remember what one did not oneself experience. So I cannot introspectively cognize an earlier cognition if that cognition was not itself something I was aware of at the time it occurred. Given that we can be aware of our own cognizing, it must be the case that cognition cognizes itself as well as the form of the object. So the argument for cognition's having two forms goes through.

This defense can be questioned. First, the analogy of the light that illuminates itself is problematic. True, when we shine a torch we may say that we see not just the objects in the room but the light as well, and this without some second light that illuminates the first. But when we see a beam of light it is actually illuminated dust motes that we see. Second, the infinite regress argument presupposes what it tries to prove. Just as other-illumination (the view that a cognition is only illuminated by another cognition) means that cognition of c_1 requires a subsequent c_2, so the cognition of c_2 would require yet another cognition c_3. But why should this mean that on that view the cognition of a pot would require an infinite number of cognitions? On the other-illumination view, apperception is always optional: one can cognize a pot without cognizing the cognition that cognizes the pot. The alleged infinite regress arises only if one assumes that a cognition cannot cognize its object unless it cognizes itself. Third, the argument from memory is effective only against that form of other-illumination view that sees apperception as introspection. According to the form of other-illumination view espoused by the (Brahmanical) Bhāṭṭa Mīmāṃsā school, a cognition is cognized only through a kind of abductive inference. This view is formulated based on the assumption that a cognition can never be directly cognized. Our awareness of our cognition comes about instead through an inference to the best explanation: the pot now having the property of cognizedness, there must have occurred a cognition taking the pot as its object. It thereby avoids the objection from memory by in effect accepting the claim that cognition could be directly cognized only if it were reflexive, but denying that cognition is directly cognized. Finally, questions can be raised about the metaphysics of the claim that cognition has two forms, which comes perilously close to the substantialist view all Buddhist Reductionists reject.

Given these difficulties, it might be worth seeing what other options are open to the Buddhist Reductionist. Not all Buddhists accepted Dignāga's claim that consciousness is reflexively aware; some held the other-illumination view. But I know of no surviving text that defends this view and discusses how it could be used to answer the circularity objection we have been considering. So what follows must be somewhat speculative. Suppose we wished to say that our awareness of our own cognition comes about through a kind of abductive inference. We would then be claiming that awareness is something I posit in order to explain the cognizedness I experience in the pot and the like. But now the question arises how one can be aware of cognizedness in the object without being aware of cognition. Cognizedness looks like a relational property, and one can be aware of relational properties only if one can be aware of the relata: one can be aware of Jill's property of being taller than Jack only if one can also be aware of Jack and his height. To this objection some Bhāṭṭas reply that the property of cognizedness is a property the pot has just by virtue of its being available for action and speech.[24] The difficulty with this response is that it runs the risk of turning cognition into a mere empty place-holder. To see why, consider the case of blind-sight, where the patient successfully navigates around all the obstacles in the path while sincerely claiming to see nothing. We think of this as a case of 'unconscious seeing' precisely because visual input is going directly to the action-control system without being made available to other systems like speech and memory. This suggests that for the normally sighted subject the obstacle has the property of cognizedness just by virtue of visual input being available to several different systems. And if the distinct property of cognizedness is not found in blind-sight, where there is just the one input–output path, why suppose that such a distinct property emerges where there are several paths possible? To a Buddhist Reductionist this will look like a case of reifying what is merely a convenient designator. The upshot is that if the other-illumination theorist goes the abductive inference route to account for our aware-ness of our own awareness, consciousness turns into a conceptual construction and not something ultimately real.

Buddhist Reductionists would be loath to accept this consequence. First, the Buddha seems to have considered consciousness to be a psychophysical element, so calling it a conceptual construction is tantamount to calling the Buddha's authority into question. Second, the practice of meditation looks like nothing so much as the disciplined investigation of consciousness, and meditation is supposedly effica-cious in producing liberation, so this might raise doubts about the Buddhist path to nirvāṇa. Still I think the other-illumination approach might help the Buddhist Reductionist answer the circularity objection. The first point to make here is that to take this approach is not necessarily to embrace eliminativism about conscious-ness. The claim is that consciousness, while not part of our final ontology, is posited by a theory we use in coping with reality. Both a reductionist and an eliminativist would accept this claim; their disagreement concerns whether the theory is useful or useless. Just as Buddhist Reductionists claim the theory that we are persons is useful, so they could claim a similar status for the theory that posits consciousness as a psychophysical element. Buddhist Reductionists could say that consciousness is conventionally real.

More importantly, this strategy would give the Buddhist Reductionist a response to the circularity objection that does not rely on the notion of reflexive awareness. The objection was that Reductionism cannot remove the source of the sense of 'I am' in the guise of the experiencing subject (even if that subject is only momentary). The response is that consciousness as cognizer is constructed in the interest of achieving conceptual economy. There are just the causal paths linking

---

[24] There is an interesting parallel here with the notion of global availability discussed in Metzinger 2003: 31.

input and output; consciousness is what we call the situation of there being a multiplicity of open paths. Of course it will be objected that we can never be persuaded that this is true, since being persuaded would require an occurrence of the what-it-is-like-ness characteristic of the (conscious) state of conviction. To this, two responses are possible. The first is that some illusions are not dispelled by knowledge of their sources. One can know perfectly well that the lines in a demonstration of the Ponzo illusion are of equal length, yet one will continue to see some as longer than others. The sense that there is the subjective or perspectival, it might be said, is just such an illusion. Of course this must count as the mother of all illusions, since without it there could be no gap between how things seem and how things are. But it nonetheless makes sense to speak of it as an illusion, since it leads the system in which it occurs to misrepresent its environment. There is no what-it-is-like-ness for the thermostat, yet we speak naturally of our fooling the thermostat into taking the room to be warmer than it is by holding a candle nearby. So we might say that the psychophysical system misrepresents its environment as containing a subject to which things seem a certain way. One's grasping of this point may include an instance of just such a seeming. But this need not be paradoxical. Once we see how the illusion is generated, and why it persists (due to its utility for systems like these), we can understand that it is a misrepresentation, and why such a misrepresentation occurs.

A second possible response is that this is among those illusions that are dispelled by knowledge of their sources. In certain Buddhist accounts of the fully enlightened being we glimpse the possibility of what might be called a state of total blind-sight. According to the teachings of Mahāyāna Buddhism, the fully enlightened being works ceaselessly to help the unenlightened overcome suffering. On some accounts the enlightened being does this without cognizing those being helped. We might dismiss accounts of such a 'Robo-Buddha' as no more than devotionalist hyperbole. But another possibility is suggested by a perfectly sane piece of Buddhist epistemological doctrine: the claim that while reliably caused perception in familiar circumstances generates knowledge immediately, reliably caused perception in a novel setting results in knowledge only after subsequent confirmation. The idea is that in the familiar setting there is no need to run the fact-checker routine, one simply acts in accordance with the input and one's interests, while in unfamiliar circumstances there is a need to reflect on the sources of the input. Such reflection takes the form of treating the input as an internal state of the system, something made available to multiple sub-systems of the organism. So the suggestion is that the positing of cognition as an inner state occurs when we don't know our way about. Robo-Buddhas, having developed their skills at exercising compassion through countless eons of training, do know their way about. I am not such a being. But being thirsty, and having quenched my thirst hundreds of times at the water fountain in front of me, I act effortlessly on my present visual stimulation. There is no need to treat my visual stimulation as an inner cognitive state. Were I asked if

I was aware of seeing the fountain I would doubtless say yes. But this judgment is retrospective. The suggestion is that I say this only because often I do not know my way about, and so have to check up on the credentials of my sensory stimulations. Robo-Buddhas, being fully enlightened and so always knowing their way about, are able to act directly on their sensory stimulation without making it available to other systems. Having total blind-sight, for them the illusion of consciousness is dispelled. There being nothing for which things appear a certain way, there is no longer the basis for a sense of 'I am'. There is just a causal series of psychophysical elements, interacting with its environment in such a way as to maximize overall welfare.

References

ALBAHARI, MIRI (2007). *Analytical Buddhism: The Two-Tiered Illusion of the Self* (New York: Palgrave Macmillan).

CAREY, SUSAN (2004). 'Bootstrapping and the Origins of Concepts', *Daedalus*, 59–68.

COX, COLLETT (1995). *Disputed Dharmas* (Tokyo: International Institute for Buddhist Studies).

DENNETT, DANIEL C. (1992). 'The Self as a Center of Narrative Gravity': http//ase.tufts.edu/cogstud/papers/selfctr.htm (accessed July 2010).

DUERLINGER, JAMES (1993). 'Reductionist and Non-Reductionist Theories of Persons in Indian Buddhist Philosophy', *Journal of Indian Philosophy*, 21: 79–101.

——(2003). *Indian Buddhist Theories of Persons: Vasubandhu's 'Refutation of the Theory of a Self'* (London: RoutledgeCurzon).

FLANAGAN, OWEN (2002). *The Problem of the Soul* (New York: Basic Books).

GANERI, JONARDON (2007). *The Concealed Art of the Soul* (New York: Oxford University Press).

GOODMAN, CHARLES (2002). 'Resentment and Reality', *American Philosophical Quarterly*, 39: 359–72.

HASKER, WILLIAM (1999). *The Emergent Self* (Ithaca, NY: Cornell University Press).

HORNER, L. B. (tr.) (1954). *The Collection of Middle Length Sayings* (Majjhima-Nikaya) (London: Pali Text Society).

KAPSTEIN, MATTHEW (2001). *Reason's Traces: Identity and Interpretation in Indian and Tibetan Buddhist Thought* (Studies in Indian and Tibetan Buddhism; Boston: Wisdom).

KATSURA SHORYU and SIDERITS, MARK (tr.) (2008). *Mūlamadhyamakakārikā* XI–XXI, *Journal of Indian and Tibetan Studies (Indogakuchibettogaku Kenkyū)*, 12: 170–221.

——and ——(tr.) (forthcoming), *Mūlamadhyamakakārikā* XXII–XXVII.

KEEFE, ROSANNA, and SMITH, PETER (eds) (1997). *Vagueness: A Reader* (Cambridge, Mass.: MIT Press).

KIM, JAEGWON (1998). *Mind in a Physical World: An Essay on the Mind-Body Problem and Mental Causation* (Cambridge, Mass.: MIT Press).

LEVI, SYLVAIN (ed.) (1925). *Vijnaptimatratasiddhi: Deux traites de Vasubandhu:* Vimsatika (La vingtaine) accompagnee d'une explication en prose, et Trimsika (La trentaine) avec le commentaire de Sthiramati (Paris: Champion).

MERRICKS, TRENTON (2001). *Objects and Persons* (Oxford: Clarendon Press).

METZINGER, THOMAS (2003). *Being No One* (Cambridge, Mass.: MIT).

Padmakara Translation Group (2002). *Introduction to the Middle Way* (Boston: Shambala).

PARFIT, DEREK (1984). *Reasons and Persons* (Oxford: Clarendon Press).

PARSONS, TERRENCE (2000). *Indeterminate Identity* (Oxford: Clarendon Press).

PERRETT, ROY (2002). 'Personal Identity, Minimalism and Madhyamaka', *Philosophy East and West*, 52: 373–85.

PRIESTLEY, LEONARD (1999). *Pudgalavada Buddhism: The Reality of the Indeterminate Self* (South Asian Studies Papers, 12; monograph 1; Toronto: Centre for South Asian Studies).

RHYS DAVIDS, T. W. (tr.) (1965). *The Questions of King Milinda* (Delhi: Motilal Banarsidass).

SIDERITS, MARK (2003). *Personal Identity and Buddhist Philosophy: Empty Persons* (Farnham: Ashgate).

——(2008). 'Paleo-Compatibilism and Buddhist Reductionism', *Sophia*, 47: 29–42.

VAN INWAGEN, PETER (1995). *Material Beings* (Ithaca, NY: Cornell University Press).

CHAPTER 13

UNITY OF CONSCIOUSNESS AND THE PROBLEM OF SELF

DAN ZAHAVI

Lilly tried to force me to drink some brandy. I bit hard on the rim of the glass, seeing the ceiling light through the moist glass, spots overlapping spots, my dizziness got worse and I felt nauseated. . . . Lilly pushed the brandy glass between my teeth again. The warm liquid shook my tongue and slid down my throat. The ringing in my ears filled my whole head. . . . Sweat ran down my neck, and Lilly wiped the cold sweat for me.

This short passage from Ryū Murakami's novel *Almost Transparent Blue* can serve as an example of something all of us should be familiar with, namely the fact that experiences never occur in isolation, and that the stream of consciousness is an ensemble of experiences that is unified both at and over time, both synchronically and diachronically.

According to a classical view, we need to appeal to a self in order to account for this diachronic and synchronic unity. To think of a simultaneous or temporally dispersed plurality of objects is to think of myself being conscious of this plurality, and this requires an undivided, invariable, unchanging me. On such an account, the unity of self is taken to be something with explanatory power rather than something that itself is in need of an explanation. The classical term for this principle of organization and unification is *transcendental ego*.

It shouldn't come as a surprise, though, that not everybody has been willing to accept the existence of such a principle. As Thomas Wakley, long-time editor of the British medical journal *The Lancet* wrote in one of his editorials (25 March 1843):

From the fact that the philosophy of the human mind has been almost wholly uncultivated by those who are best fitted for its pursuit, the study has received a wrong direction, and become a subtle exercise for lawyers and casuists, and abstract reasoners, rather than a useful field of scientific observation. Accordingly, we find the views, even of the most able and clear-headed metaphysicians, coming into frequent collision with the known facts of physiology and pathology. For example, that 'consciousness is *single*' is an axiom among the mental philosophers, and the proof of *personal identity* is made by those gentlemen to rest chiefly on the supposed universality or certainty of that allegation. But what would they say to the case of a somnambulist who evinced what is regarded as double consciousness . . . (Quoted in Hacking 1995: 221)

Wakley is not the only one who has used psychopathological findings as an argument against the existence of a unitary and unifying self. A similar fascination with cases of double consciousness can be found in French intellectuals such as Hippolyte Taine and Théodule Ribot later in the nineteenth century. Both figures were opposed to the idea of an autonomous, persisting, freestanding self—something distinct from the diversity of transient sensations, memories, ideas, perceptions, conceptions—and took cases of double consciousness to disprove the existence of a transcendental ego. As Ribot, who held the chair of experimental and comparative psychology at the Collège de France, wrote in his book *Les Maladies de la mémoire*: 'To conceive of the self as an entity distinct from states of consciousness is a useless and contradictory hypothesis, which takes as simple that which appears simple, and which postulates instead of explaining' (Ribot 1883: 82–3).

If one moves forward in time and examines contemporary discussions of the relation between consciousness and self, one will also come across various references to neurological and psychiatric cases; just think of the frequent appeals to split-brain patients or to cases of schizophrenic thought-insertion.

Whether neuro- and psychopathological findings can serve to disprove philosophical claims regarding the nature of self is a question worthy of its own extensive treatment. It is, for instance, not clear whether pathological disturbances create new experiential phenomena, whether they are the exceptions that prove the rule, or whether they involve breakdowns of more complex functions thereby disclosing more primitive features of normal experience. But these are not issues I will focus on in this chapter. Rather I will address the relation between unity and self from a somewhat different angle. As I started out by indicating, one way to defend the existence of the self is by arguing that our mental life would collapse into unstructured chaos if it were not buttressed by the organizing and unifying function of a pure ego. Some critics however have accepted the underlying assumption, but have then gone on to argue that if the diachronic and synchronic unity of consciousness were not conditioned by a distinct self, the latter would lose its *raison d'être*, and there would no longer be any reason to uphold the reality of the self.

In the following I will consider a few accounts of consciousness that all explicitly deny that the unity of consciousness is guaranteed or conditioned by a distinct self. The question I then want to discuss is what conclusion we should draw if we accept these arguments.

1. THE ILLUSORY SELF

My point of departure will be a recent book by Miri Albahari entitled *Analytical Buddhism: The Two-Tiered Illusion of Self.* Drawing on literature from Western philosophy, neuroscience, and in particular Buddhism, Albahari's basic aim is to argue that the self is an illusion. What notion of self is she out to deny? She initially provides the following definition: the self should be understood as a unified, happiness-seeking, unbrokenly persisting, ontologically distinct conscious subject who is the owner of experiences, the thinker of thoughts, and the agent of actions. What is interesting about Albahari's proposal is that whereas many advocates of a so-called no-self doctrine have denied that consciousness is characterized by unity, unbrokenness, and invariability, and taken the denial of these features to amount to a denial of the reality of the self, Albahari considers all three to be real features of consciousness, but she nevertheless considers the self to be illusory (Albahari 2006: 3).

To get clearer on why she thinks this is the case let us look closer at a distinction she introduces between different forms of ownership, namely *possessive ownership*, *perspectival ownership*, and *personal ownership*. We can ignore possessive ownership, which in this context is of less interest, since it merely denotes the fact that certain objects (a car, a pair of trousers, etc.) can be regarded as mine by right of social convention. But what is the difference between personal ownership and perspectival ownership? Personal ownership is a question of identifying oneself as the personal owner of an experience, thought, action; it is a question of appropriating certain experiences, actions, thoughts etc. as one's own, that is, a question of either thinking of them as being *mine* or apprehending them as being part of *me* (and this is something that can occur either pre-reflectively or reflectively). By contrast, for a subject to own something in a perspectival sense is simply for the experience, thought, or action in question to present itself in a distinctive manner to the subject whose experience, thought, or action it is. So the reason I can be said to perspectivally own my thoughts or perceptions—if one will excuse this slightly awkward way of talking—is because they appear to me in a manner that is different from how they can appear to anybody else. When it comes to objects external to the subject, what will be perspectively owned isn't the object, but the specific manner through which the object appears to the subject (Albahari 2006: 53).

Albahari argues that there is a close link between having a sense of personal ownership and having a sense of self. When the subject identifies certain items as being itself or being part of itself, it will harbor a sense of personal ownership towards the items in question. But this very process of identification generates the sense of a self–other distinction. It constitutes a felt boundary between what belongs to self and what doesn't. Thereby the self is cast as a unified and ontologically distinct entity—one that stands apart from other things (Albahari 2006: 73, 90). In this way, the subject understood as a mere point of view is turned into a substantial personalized entity (ibid. 94). To put it differently, for Albahari, there is more to being a self than being a point of view, than having perspectival ownership.

One way to bring out the difference between perspectival and personal ownership is to point to possible dissociations between the two. Pathology seems to provide some examples. In cases of depersonalization, we can come across thoughts, feelings, etc. which are perspectively owned, that is, which continue to present themselves in a unique manner to the subject, without however being felt as the subject's own (Albahari 2006: 55). Thus on Albahari's reading, the process of identification fails in depersonalization and, as a consequence, no sense of personal ownership regarding the experience in question will be generated (ibid. 61).

Let us now consider Albahari's self-skepticism. What does it mean for the self to lack reality? What does it mean for the self to be illusory? On Albahari's account, an illusion involves a conflict between appearance and reality. X is illusory if x does not have any appearance-independent reality, but nevertheless purports to have such reality, that is, we are dealing with an illusion if x purports through its appearance to exist in a particular manner without really doing so (Albahari 2006: 122). One obvious problem, however, with such a definition is whether it at all makes sense to apply it to the self. Does the self really purport to exist outside of its own appearance, or is the reality of the self rather subjective or experiential? This consideration leads Albahari to redefine the notion of illusion slightly. If the self purports to be what she calls unconstructed, that is, independent from the experiences and objects it is the subject of, and if it should turn out that it in reality depends, even if only partially, on perspectivally ownable objects (including various experiential episodes), then the self must be regarded as being illusory (ibid. 130).

Albahari also emphasizes the need for a distinction between self and sense of self. To have a sense of x doesn't necessarily entail that x exists. Indeed whereas Albahari takes the sense of self to exist and to be real, she considers the self itself to be illusory (2006: 17). Contrary to expectations, our sense of self is not underpinned by an actually existing ontological independent self-entity. Rather, all that really exists is the manifold of thoughts, emotions, perceptions, etc. as well as a pure locus of apprehension, which Albahari terms *witness-consciousness*. It is the experiential flow in conjunction with this locus of apprehension that generates the sense of self. But if this is so, the self lacks an essential property of selfhood, namely ontological independence (ibid. 72). In short, the illusory status of the self is due to the fact that the self does not have the ontological status it purports to have. Thoughts appear to be owned and initiated by an independently existing unified self, but rather than preceding the experiences, rather than thinking the thoughts, it is in reality the other way around. It is not the self that unifies our thoughts and experiences, they do so themselves with some help from the accompanying witness-consciousness (ibid. 130–2). To repeat, although it might seem to the subject as if there is a pre-existing self which identifies with various intentional states, the reality of the matter is that the self is created and constructed through these repeated acts of identification (ibid. 58).

As I mentioned in the beginning, an interesting aspect of Albahari's proposal is that she considers many of the features traditionally ascribed to the self to be real, it is just that they—in her view—become distorted and illusory if taken to be features of the self (2006: 74). For instance, Albahari takes our conscious life to be characterized by an intrinsic but elusive sense of subjective presence; one that is common to all modalities of awareness, that is, one that is common to seeing, hearing, thinking, feeling, introspecting, etc. (ibid. 112, 144, 156). What does this subjective presence amount to? It includes the experience of being the perspectival owner of various experiences. It also includes diachronic and synchronic unity. Although we experience various objects, although the objects we experience might change from one moment to the next, there still appears to be an unbroken consciousness that observes the change without itself changing (ibid. 155). Indeed, while from a first-person perspective it certainly makes sense to say that I have various experiences, we automatically feel them to belong to one and the same consciousness. For Albahari, all these features are properly ascribed to the witness-consciousness, and she is adamant that we have to distinguish witness-consciousness from self. Whereas the latter on her definition involves felt boundaries between self and non-self, the former doesn't.[1]

Let me recapitulate. For Albahari, one can be aware without being presented to oneself as an ontologically unique subject with personalized boundaries that distinguish a me from the rest of the world. One can be aware without being aware of oneself as a personal owner, a thinker of thoughts, an agent of actions. Examples that come to mind are cases of pathology. Albahari asks us to consider both the real-life case of epileptic automatism and the hypothetical case of global

---

[1] I think one can find various defenders of self, who would dispute its bounded nature, and for instance deny that there is always a clear division to be made between self and environment. As a case in point, consider Neisser's notion of ecological self. I will, however, postpone a more extensive criticism of the notion of bounded self to some other occasion.

depersonalization. In both cases, the person or patient would be awake and responsive to the environment, so there would be awareness present. But there would be no sense of a bounded individual self, there would be a complete lack of personal ownership, there would be no sense of me or mine (Albahari 2006: 171, 177). Albahari suggests that such a state of mind might not only be encountered in pathologies, but also in newborn infants, and in primitive organisms. And as she then points out in the conclusion of her book, and this is of course where her Buddhist orientation becomes evident, if we were to attain enlightenment, we would move from consciousness-plus-self-illusion to consciousness-*sans*-self-illusion, and the latter condition, although strictly speaking not identical with global depersonalization—after all, it correlates with highly advanced cognitive capacities—might nevertheless be compared to it (ibid. 161, 207).

2. PHENOMENOLOGICAL CONSIDERATIONS

Having discussed Albahari's position in some detail, let me now turn to two other thinkers who have also questioned the unifying role of the self, but whose theoretical orientation and affiliation differ somewhat from hers.

Husserl

In the *Logical Investigations*, Husserl explicitly denied that the unity intrinsic to our experiential life was conditioned or guaranteed by any ego. Indeed, on his view whatever synthesizing contribution the ego could have made would be *superfluous* since the unification had already taken place in accordance with intra-experiential laws. To put it differently, on Husserl's early view, the stream of consciousness is self-unifying, and in order to understand its unity, we do not have to look at anything above, beyond, or external to the stream itself. In fact, since the ego, properly speaking, is the result of this unification, it couldn't be something that preceded or conditioned it (Husserl 1984: 364).

Husserl's early reasoning was partly motivated by his aversion to any kind of ego-metaphysics. As he wrote in a letter to Hans Cornelius in 1906: 'The phenomenological investigation is not at all interested in egos or in states, experiences, developments belonging to or occurring in egos' (Husserl 1994: 27). However, Husserl's general view on the ego was subsequently to change. In *Cartesian Meditations* for instance, Husserl claimed that the phenomenological task of explicating the monadic ego ultimately included all constitutional problems, and that the phenomenology of self-constitution coincided with phenomenology as a whole (Husserl 1950: 103). It would lead too far afield to explain precisely what Husserl meant by these statements. Rather, for our purposes the point of interest is that, even at this late stage, Husserl still held onto some of the claims he had originally made in *Logical Investigations*.

Contrary to a widespread misunderstanding, Husserl did not overlook the problem of passivity in his phenomenological investigations. On the contrary, he dedicated numerous analyses to this important issue. Although our starting-point might be conscious episodes that involve an active position-taking by the subject, that is, acts in which the subject is comparing, differentiating, judging, valuing, wishing, or willing something, Husserl was quick to point out that whenever the subject is active, it is also passive, since to be active is to react to something (Husserl 1952: 213, 337). And as he ultimately would say, every kind of active position-taking, indeed every activity of the ego, presupposes a preceding *affection*, an affection by something that escapes the control of the ego, an affection by something foreign to the ego (ibid. 336). Indeed, for Husserl, intentional activity is founded upon and conditioned by an obscure and blind passivity, by drives and associations. Husserl considered the most fundamental constitutive synthesis of them all, the very process of temporalization, to be a synthesis taking place in pure passivity. He took it to be regulated by strict and rigid laws and he repeatedly denied that it was initiated, influenced, or controlled by the ego (Husserl 1966: 72, 235, 323; 1950: 125). If we look at the painstaking analysis of its structure that we find in the famous *Lectures on the Phenomenology of the Consciousness of Internal Time* we will find no reference to the ego as the ultimate unifying or synthesizing agent. In fact, Husserl occasionally suggested that an in-depth investigation of temporality would lead to a pre-egological level, that is, to a level of egoless streaming. As he wrote in *Zur Phänomenologie der Intersubjektivität III*:

The analysis of the structure of the primal present (the persisting living streaming) leads us to the ego-structure and to the continual substratum of the *egoless streaming* that founds it, and thereby, through a consistently carried out regressive inquiry (*Rückfrage*), back to that which makes even this sedimented activity possible and which this sedimented activity presupposes: the radically pre-egoic. (Husserl 1973: 598)

So although Husserl is frequently considered an ardent defender of an egological account of consciousness, he obviously did not envisage the ego or self as the big unifier. But what is the implication of this? That the ego is ultimately illusory? Husserl would never have drawn that conclusion. If we take a closer look at Husserl's analysis, we will somewhat surprisingly also find him stating that the ego is present *everywhere* in the living present, and that even the anonymous stream of consciousness would be unthinkable without an original ego-pole as the center of action and affection (Husserl 1973: 350). Husserl's simultaneous reference to the egoless and egological character of the stream of consciousness makes it clear that some equivocation is at play. My proposal is as follows. When Husserl speaks of an egoless streaming, the term 'egoless' does not refer to the absence of self, rather the term 'pre-egological' is meant to indicate that the ego is not participating in or contributing to the (self-)constitution of this fundamental process in any *active* way. Thus, Husserl is mainly referring to the passivity of the streaming, which is beyond the influence of the ego (Husserl 1974: 293). It is not the ego which unifies the experiences. This is taken care of by the very process of temporalization. But although the passive syntheses are not initiated by me, they still happen to me, not to somebody else or to nobody.

Sartre

Let us next turn to France, and to Sartre's early work *The Transcendence of the Ego*. As Sartre pointed out at the beginning of the text, many philosophers have considered the ego a formal principle of unification. Many have argued that our consciousness is unified because the 'I think' might accompany each of my thoughts. It is because I can say *my* consciousness that my consciousness is different from those of others (Sartre 1936: 16, 20). But is this really true, or is it rather the 'I think' which is made possible by the synthetic unity of our thoughts? To put it differently, is the ego an expression rather than a condition of unified consciousness? Sartre's own view is clear. On his account, the nature of the stream of consciousness does not need an exterior principle of individuation, since it is *per se* individuated. Nor is consciousness in need of any transcendent principle of unification, since it is, as such, a flowing unity. Thus, a correct account of time-consciousness will show that the contribution of a transcendental ego is unnecessary and it consequently loses its *raison d'être* (Sartre 1936: 21–3).

In addition, Sartre argued that a correct phenomenological description of lived consciousness will simply not find any ego, whether understood as an inhabitant in or possessor of consciousness. As long as we are absorbed in the experience, *living* it, no ego will be present. The ego emerges only when we adopt a distancing and objectifying attitude to the experience in question, that is, when we *reflect* upon it. Even then, however, we are not dealing with an I-consciousness, since the reflecting pole remains non-egological, but merely with a consciousness *of* I. As Sartre put it, the appearing ego is the object and not the subject of reflection.

However, whereas Sartre in *The Transcendence of the Ego* characterized pre-reflective consciousness as *impersonal*, he described this view as mistaken both in *Being and Nothingness* and in his important 1948 article 'Consciousness of Self and Knowledge of Self'. Why did he change his mind?

Sartre famously argued that intentional consciousness is *for-itself* (*pour-soi*), that is, self-conscious. An experience does not simply exist, it exists for it-self, that is, it is given for itself, and this self-givenness is not simply a quality added to the experience, a mere varnish; rather for Sartre it constitutes the very *mode of being* of consciousness (Sartre 1948). When speaking of self-consciousness as a permanent feature of consciousness, Sartre was however not referring to what we might call reflective self-consciousness. Reflection (or higher-order representation) is the process whereby consciousness directs its intentional aim at itself, thereby taking itself as its own object. By contrast, Sartre considered the self-consciousness in question to be pre-reflective. It is not an addendum to, but a constitutive moment of, the original intentional experience.

Although no ego exists on the pre-reflective level, Sartre eventually came to realize that consciousness, far from being impersonal and anonymous, must be said to possess a basic dimension of selfhood—which Sartre termed *ipseity* (from the Latin term for self *ipse*)—precisely because of its ubiquitous self-givenness. As he wrote, 'pre-reflective consciousness is self-consciousness. It is this same notion of *self* which must be studied, for it defines the very being of consciousness' (Sartre 1943: 114).

3. SUBJECTIVITY AND THE EXPERIENTIAL SELF

It is time to return to Albahari's arguments for the illusory nature of the self. As we have seen, Albahari considers invariability, unbrokenness, and subjective presence to be real features of consciousness. What she is opposed to is the notion of an ontologically independent self-entity. On Albahari's view, the self purports to be ontologically independent, independent from the experiences and objects it is the subject of, and since it doesn't really possess this status, since it consequently lacks what she considers to be an essential property of selfhood, it must ultimately be regarded as illusory (Albahari 2006: 72).

How should we appraise this argument? Frankly, I don't find it convincing. I think Albahari is committing the same mistake that I take Metzinger to have made in his *Being No One*. In that book, Metzinger took the self to be a process-independent ontological substance that might exist all by itself, that is, in isolation from the rest of the world (Metzinger 2003: 577, 626), and since he denied the existence of such an entity he concluded that no such things as selves exist. But the only reason to accept his and Albahari's conclusion would be if their respective notions of self were the only ones available, and that is precisely what I would deny. To put it differently, my worry is that many self-skeptics are implicitly endorsing a very traditional reified understanding of what a self is. They seem committed to the view that a self—if it exists—must be some kind of ontologically independent invariant *principle of identity* that stands apart from and above the stream of changing experiences. But such a view of the self has by and large been abandoned, not only by most empirical researchers currently interested in the development, structure, function, and pathology of selves, but certainly also by most figures in twentieth-century French and German philosophy. Consider for instance Ricoeur's notion of *narrative self*. He has occasionally presented this notion as an alternative to the traditional dilemma of having to choose between the Cartesian notion of the self as a principle of identity that remains the same throughout the diversity of its different states and the positions of Hume and Nietzsche, who held an identical subject to be nothing but a substantialist illusion (Ricoeur 1985: 443). Ricoeur suggests that we can avoid this dilemma if we replace the notion of identity that they respectively defend and reject with the concept of narrative identity. As he writes, the identity of the narrative self can include changes and mutations within the cohesion of a lifetime. Indeed, Ricoeur explicitly rejects the attempt to account for and define the self in terms of what he calls idem-identity, that is, the identity of the same.

But let me postpone a further discussion of Ricoeur's position for some other occasion, and instead return to Husserl and Sartre. The reason why I chose to spend some time presenting their respective views was not only in order to show that one can find thinkers who maintain a belief in the reality of the self while denying that it possesses the unifying role it traditionally is ascribed.[2] The point was also to show that both operate with a notion of self which is very different from the one employed by Albahari, but which, as we shall see, nevertheless bears a striking resemblance to a dimension of consciousness the reality of which she is prepared to accept and defend.

For both Husserl and Sartre, an understanding of what it means to be a self calls for an examination of the structure of experience, and vice versa. In other words, their claim would be that the investigations of self and experience have to be integrated if both are to be understood. Indeed for both of them the self referred to is not something standing beyond or opposed to the stream of experiences but is rather a crucial aspect of our experiential life. To quote the central passage from Sartre once again: 'pre-reflective consciousness is self-consciousness. It is this same notion of *self* which must be studied, for it defines the very being of consciousness.'

---

[2] I would reject the view—and so would Husserl and Sartre—that it is the self or ego which unifies the stream of consciousness. Does this rejection entail a rejection of the notion of a transcendental ego? This is how Sartre would reason, though it is crucial to understand that he upholds the belief in the existence of a constituting transcendental consciousness. His point is merely that the transcendental dimension is pre-personal and non-egological (Sartre 1936: 18–19). But in fact, I don't think we need to reason like him. Contrary to a widespread misunderstanding, the notion of a transcendental ego is not bound up with an idea of an autonomous sovereign free-standing ego. To defend the existence of a transcendental ego is to be committed to the view that the first-person perspective is a necessary condition of possibility for manifestation. It neither commits one to the idea that it is a sufficient condition of possibility, nor does it necessarily involve a failure to recognize the role of passivity.

Or, as Michel Henry would later put it, the most basic form of selfhood is the one constituted by the very self-manifestation of experience (Henry 1963: 581; 1965: 53).

To better understand the guiding idea,[3] consider the following example:

I have climbed the spire of Our Saviour's Church together with my oldest son. Holding onto the railing, I see Copenhagen spread out before me. I can hear the distant noise from the traffic beneath me and feel the wind blow against my face. Far away, I can see an airship. My attention is drawn to something that is written on its side, but despite repeated attempts to decipher the text, I cannot read it. My concentration is suddenly interrupted by a pull in my hand. My son asks me when we are supposed to meet his mother and brother for cake and hot chocolate. I look at my watch and embarrassingly realize that we are already too late for our appointment. I decide to start the descent immediately, but when rushing down the stairways, I stumble over an iron rod and feel pain blossom up my shin.

A careful analysis of this episode will reveal many differences. If we compare perceptual experiences, voluntary movements, passivity experiences, social emotions, the experience of pain, effortful concentration or decision-making etc., we will not only encounter a phenomenal complexity, but also a diversity of qualitatively different experiences of self. There is for instance a vivid difference between the kind of self-experience we find in embarrassment and the kind of self-experience we have when our body is moved by external forces. Despite these differences, however, there is also something that the manifold of experiences has in common. Whatever their character, whatever their object, all experiences are subjective in the sense that they feel like something *for somebody*. They are subjective in the sense that there is a distinctive way they present themselves to the subject or self whose episodes they are.

Some might object that there is no property common to all my experiences, no stamp or label that clearly identifies them as mine. But this objection seems misplaced in that it looks for the commonality in the wrong place. When consciously seeing the moon, imagining Santa Claus, desiring a hot shower, anticipating a forthcoming film festival, or remembering a recent holiday in Sicily, all of these experiences present me with different intentional objects. These objects are there *for me* in different experiential modes of givenness (as seen, imagined, desired, anticipated, recollected, etc.).[4] This *for-me-ness* or *mineness*, which seems inescapably required by the experiential presence of intentional objects and which is the feature that really makes it appropriate to speak of the *subjectivity* of experience, is obviously not a quality like green, sweet, or hard. It doesn't refer to a specific experiential content, to a specific *what*, nor does it refer to the diachronic or synchronic sum of such content, or to some other relation that might obtain between the contents in question. Rather, it refers to the distinct givenness or *how*

[3] For a more extensive discussion see Zahavi 1999, 2005.

[4] Pace various representationalist approaches to phenomenality it makes little sense to claim that this aspect of experience is simply a property of the represented object.

of experience. It refers to the first-personal presence of experience. It refers to what Albahari calls *perspectival ownership*. It refers to the fact that the experiences I am living through are given differently (but not necessarily better) to me than to anybody else. It could consequently be claimed that anybody who denies the for-me-ness or mineness[5] of experience simply fails to recognize an essential constitutive aspect of experience. Such a denial would be tantamount to a denial of the first-person perspective. It would entail the view that my own mind is either not given to me at all—I would be mind- or self-blind—or present to me in exactly the same way as the minds of others.[6]

But who or what is this self that has or lives through the experiences? The account I favor denies that the self under consideration—and let us just call it the experiential core self—is a separately existing entity, but it would also deny that the self is simply reducible to any specific experience or (sub)set of experiences. If we shift the focus from a narrow investigation of a single experience and instead consider a diachronic sequence of experiences, it should be obvious that each successive experience doesn't have its own unique for-me-ness or mineness—as if the difference between one experience and the next experience was as absolute as the difference between my current experience and the current experience of somebody else—but that the for-me-ness or mineness can on the contrary preserve its identity in the flux of changing experiences. If I compare two experiences, say a perception of a blackbird and a recollection of a summer holiday, I can focus on the differences between the two, namely their respective object and mode of presentation, but I can also attend to that which remains the same, namely the first-personal character of both experiences. To put it differently, we can distinguish the plurality of changing experiences from the abiding *dative of manifestation*. The latter has a certain transcendence *vis-à-vis* the former. The self does not exist in separation from the experiences, but nor can it simply be reduced to the sum of or connection between the experiences. An informative way of describing it is consequently as a *ubiquitous* dimension of first-personal givenness in the multitude of changing experiences. This way of presenting matters tallies well with Husserl's observation that the ego cannot simply be identified with our experiences, since the former preserves its identity, whereas the latter arise and perish in the stream of consciousness, replacing each other in a permanent flux (Husserl 1952: 98; 1974: 363). But as Husserl then goes on to emphasize, although the ego must be distinguished from the experiences in which it lives and functions, it cannot in

---

[5] And whereas the dative suggests a structural feature, the genitive suggest a qualitative feature—both aspects are important.

[6] I wouldn't consider the latter option a successful way of addressing the problem of other minds. It wouldn't solve the problem; it would dissolve it by failing to recognize the difference between our experience of self and our experience of others.

any way exist independently of them. It is a transcendence, but in Husserl's famous phrase: *a transcendence in the immanence* (Husserl 1976: 123–4).[7]

Let me stress that although the self in question can be described as an ubiquitous dimension of first-personal self-givenness, this is not meant to imply that genuine self-experience requires the experience of something invariant or identical, as if one had necessarily to be conscious of one's overarching identity as the subject of different experiences in order to be self-conscious. We certainly need to distinguish the case where I reflect on myself as the one who in turn deliberates, resolves, acts, and suffers and the case where I simply consciously perceive a table, but even the latter is an experience of something for someone; even that experience entails a pre-reflective sense of self.[8]

On this view, there is no pure experience-independent self. The self is the very subjectivity of experience and not something that exists independently of the experiential flow. Moreover, the experiences in question are world-directed experiences. They present the world in a certain way, but at the same time they also involve self-presence and hence a subjective point of view. In short, they are of something other than the subject and they are like something for the subject. If we want to study the self, we should consequently not turn the gaze inwards; rather we should look at our intentional experiences. I experience myself in what I do and suffer, in what confronts me and in what I accomplish, in my concerns and disregards. I am acquainted with myself when I am captured and captivated by the world. Just as the self is what it is in its worldly relations, self-acquaintance is not something that takes place or occurs in separation from our living in a world. On the contrary, self-experience is the self-experience of a world-immersed self, or, to put it differently, our experiential life is world-related, and there is a presence of self when we are worldly engaged.

On the present account, there is obviously no experiential self, no self as defined from the first-person perspective, when we are non-conscious. But this does not necessarily imply that the diachronic unity of self is threatened by alleged interruptions

---

[7] For comparison consider the relation between an object and its profiles. The object is not merely the sum of its profiles—had that been the case, we would never see the object as long as we merely saw one of its profiles, but only part of the object, and that doesn't seem right—but rather an identity in and across the manifold of profiles. This doesn't mean that the object stands in opposition to or is independent of its profiles.

[8] One might add though that experiences never occur in isolation, and that there will always be a tacit experience of synchronic and diachronic unity. But even if we grant that, the tacitly experienced unity will differ from the identity we disclose when we explicitly compare different experiences in order to isolate that which remains the same. Moreover, this also confronts us with the tricky issue of how to individuate experiences. When does an experience stop and a new one start? When are we dealing with a complex experience and when with a set of distinct experiences? If our gaze wanders over our desk by taking in, one after the other, the computer, the keyboard, the books and papers, the empty coffee cups, are we then confronted with one complex perceptual experience or with a multiplicity of perceptual experiences, each with its own distinct object?

of the stream of consciousness (such as dreamless sleep, coma, etc.), since the identity of the self is defined in terms of givenness rather than in terms of temporal continuity. Whether two temporally distinct experiences are mine or not depends on whether they are characterized by the same first-personal character; it is not a question of whether they are part of an uninterrupted stream of consciousness. In that sense, it is a category mistake to liken the relationship between my present and my past experience to the relation between two different beads on one and the same string of pearls, since the two beads would be part of the same necklace only if they were in fact joined by an uninterrupted string.

Given what has been said so far, it could be argued that there is indeed some relation between self and unity after all. The self doesn't actively unite disparate bits of experience, nor is the self an extra element that must be added to the stream of consciousness in order to ensure its unification. The point is rather that all experiences that share the same primary presence or first-personal character are mine. To put it differently, experiential (diachronic and synchronic) unity is constituted by first-personal character.[9]

Hopefully, it should by now have become clear that the notion of self defended by Husserl and Sartre is very similar to the invariable but elusive subjective presence that Albahari also wants to retain and defend. Albahari takes ontological independence—or to use one of her own technical terms 'unconstructedness'—to be an essential property of selfhood, and since she denies the reality of this feature, she claims that the self is illusory.[10] As I have tried to show, many other thinkers

---

[9] At the same time, however, it should also be obvious that there are clear limitations to what this notion of self can explain and account for. Consider for instance the case of a man who early in life makes a decision that proves formative for his subsequent life and career. The episode in question is however subsequently forgotten by the person. He no longer enjoys first-person access to it. If we restrict ourselves to what can be accounted for by means of the experiential core self, we cannot speak of the decision as being his, as being one he made. Or take the case where we might wish to ascribe responsibility for past actions to an individual who no longer remembers them. By doing that we postulate an identity between the past offender and the present subject, but the identity in question is again not one that can be accounted for in terms of the experiential core self. However, on the account I favour, we need to realize that the self is so multifaceted a phenomenon that various complementary accounts must be integrated if we are to do justice to its complexity. In short, we ultimately need to adopt a multilayered account of self. We are more than experiential core selves, we are for instance also narratively configured socialized persons. And we continue to remain so even when non-conscious. So even if there is no experiential self (no self as defined from the first-person perspective) when we are non-conscious, there are various other aspects of our self that remain, and which make it perfectly legitimate to say that *we* are non-conscious, i.e. that we persist even when non-conscious.

[10] It is by the way remarkable that Albahari although denying unconstructedness to self ascribes it to witness-consciousness. As she puts it at one point, 'awareness must be shown to exist in the manner it purports to exist. Awareness purports to exist as a witnessing presence that is unified, unbroken and yet elusive to direct observation. As something whose phenomenology purports to be unborrowed from objects of consciousness, awareness, if it exists, must exist as *completely unconstructed* by the content of any perspectively ownable objects such as thoughts, emotions or perceptions. If *apparent* awareness . . . turned out to owe its existence to such object-content rather than to (unconstructed) *awareness itself*, then that would render awareness constructed and illusory and hence lacking in

would refute this definition of self. They would insist that selfhood, rather than being something that stands apart from and above the stream of consciousness, is on the contrary a crucial aspect of its phenomenality, and therefore something that in no way could exist in separation from our experiential life. As a consequence, they would in no way feel compelled to draw the same conclusion as Albahari does regarding the illusory character of self.

4. OWNERSHIP AND IDENTIFICATION

Let me end by considering an obvious rejoinder. It could be argued that the contentious issue rather than being metaphysical is a semantic one. When is it appropriate to call something a self? Albahari might very well agree with a strong emphasis on first-personal character, but might simply deny that first-personal character, that is, the subjectivity of experience, equals a minimal form of self. In short, she might insist that the minimal notion of experiential core self I wish to defend is too deflationary and revisionary.[11] Another way to press this objection is as follows. It could be argued that there is something like subjectivity of experience, but that too much focus on this trivial truth will belittle a significant difference, namely the one existing between experiences that so to speak are mere happenings in the history of my mental life and experiences that are my own in a much more profound sense. To put it differently, it could be argued that, although it is undeniably true that an experience, that is, a conscious thought, desire, passion, etc., cannot occur without an experiencer (see Chapter 10 above), since every experience is necessarily an experience for someone, this truism will mask crucial distinctions. Consider, for instance, thoughts that willy-nilly run through our heads, thoughts that strikes us out of the blue, consider passions and desires that are felt, from the first-person perspective, as intrusive—as when somebody says that, when he was possessed by anger, he was not in possession of himself—or take experiences that are induced in us through hypnosis or drugs, and then compare these cases with experiences, thoughts, and desires that we welcome or accept at the time of their occurrence. As Frankfurt argues, although the former class might indeed be conscious events that occur in us, although they are events in the history of a person's mind, they are not that person's desire, experience, or thought

independent reality' (2006: 162). This seems to commit one to viewing awareness as an ontological independent region. It is not clear to me why one would want to uphold such a view of consciousness in the first place.

[11] In fact, this is a rejoinder that Albahari has made in personal correspondence. I am grateful to her for several helpful comments on an earlier version of this chapter.

(Frankfurt 1988: 59–61). According to Frankfurt, a person is not simply to be identified with whatever goes on in his mind. On the contrary, conscious states or episodes that we disapprove of when they occur might not be ours in the full sense of the word (ibid. 63). To disapprove of or reject passions or desires means to withdraw or distance oneself from them. To accept passions or desires, to see them as having a natural place in one's experience, means to identify with them (ibid. 68). Frankfurt concedes that it is difficult to articulate the notion of identification at stake in a satisfactory manner, but ultimately he suggests that when a person decides something without reservations,

the decision determines what the person really wants by making the desire on which he decides fully his own. To this extent the person, in making a decision by which he identifies with a desire, *constitutes himself*. The pertinent desire is no longer in any way external to him. It is not a desire that he 'has' merely as a subject in whose history it happens to occur, as a person may 'have' an involuntary spasm that happens to occur in the history of his body. It comes to be a desire that is incorporated into him by virtue of the fact that he has it *by his own will*.... Even if the person is not responsible for the fact that the desire *occurs*, there is an important sense in which he takes responsibility for the fact of having the desire—the fact that the desire is in the fullest sense his, that it constitutes what he really wants—when he identifies himself with it. (Ibid. 170)

Frankfurt's basic point, that the identification in question amounts to a specific form of ownership which is constitutive of self, fits neatly with Albahari's notion of personal ownership (though, of course, there is nothing to suggest that Frankfurt would agree with Albahari's metaphysical conclusion, i.e., her self-skepticism), and also with her suggestion that the constitution of a sense of self is closely linked to the issue of emotional investment. Not only do emotions such as guilt, fear, and disappointment help constitute our sense of being a temporally extended numerically identical self (Albahari 2006: 141), but, according to Albahari, emotions generally involve boundaries between self and desired/undesired scenarios and thereby help construct a bounded self. Indeed on her account emotional concern for one's own welfare is a major contributor to the construction of a sense of self (ibid. 171, 178–9). Frankfurt's point also tallies rather well with points made by Ricoeur and Taylor. For Ricoeur, to be a self is a question of adopting certain norms as binding; to be bound by obligation or loyalty. It is to remain true to oneself in promise keeping. It is to be somebody others can count on. It is to assume responsibility for one's past actions and for the future consequences of one's present actions (Ricoeur 1990: 341–2). As Ricoeur already pointed out back in his 1950 *Philosophie de la volonté*:

I form the consciousness of being the author of my acts in the world and, more generally, the author of my acts of thought, principally on the occasion of my contacts with an other, in a social context. Someone asks, who did that? I rise and reply, I did. Response-responsibility. To be responsible means to be ready to respond to such a question. (Ricoeur 1950: 55)

As for Taylor, he has argued that the self is a kind of being that can only exist within a normative space, that being a self is to stand in an interpretative and evaluative relation to oneself, and he therefore claims that any attempt to define selfhood through some minimal or formal form of self-awareness must fail, since such a self is either non-existent or insignificant (Taylor 1989: 49). Again, let me stress that Frankfurt, Ricoeur, and Taylor would distance themselves from the metaphysical conclusions drawn by Albahari, but they all share the view that the mere subjectivity of experience is insufficient for selfhood.

How might one respond to this criticism? There are several moves available. One possibility would be to say that subjectivity of experience although being insufficient for selfhood is nevertheless a necessary condition for selfhood, there is no self without it, and that it consequently is something that any plausible theory of self must consider and account for. To put it differently, any account of self which disregards the fundamental structures and features of our experiential life is a non-starter, and a correct description and account of the experiential dimension must necessarily do justice to the first-person perspective and to the primitive form of self-reference that it entails. Moreover, to claim that the subjectivity of experience is trivial and banal in the sense that it doesn't call for further examination and clarification would be to commit a serious mistake. Not only would it disregard many of the recent insights concerning the function of first-person indexicals (the fact that 'I', 'me', 'my', 'mine' cannot without loss be replaced by definite descriptions) and ascriptionless self-reference (the fact that one can be self-conscious without identifying oneself via specific properties), but it would also discount the laborious attempt to spell out the microstructure of lived subjective presence that we find in Husserl's writings on time. As Husserl would argue, given the temporal character of the stream of consciousness, even something as apparently synchronic as the subjective givenness of a present experience is not comprehensible without taking the innermost structures of time-consciousness into account. Indeed, Husserl's investigation of inner time-consciousness was precisely motivated by his interest in the question of how consciousness manifests itself to itself. His analysis of the interplay between protention, primal impression, and retention is consequently to be understood as a contribution to a better understanding of the relationship between selfhood, self-experience, and temporality.

Another possibility would be to maintain that the subjectivity of experience amounts to more than merely an indispensable and necessary prerequisite for any true notion of self, but that it rather in and of itself is a minimal form of self. Ultimately, however, the distinction between these two options (considering subjectivity of experience as a necessary but insufficient vs. necessary and sufficient condition for selfhood) might be less relevant than one should initially assume, since we—with the possible exception of certain severe pathologies, say, the final stages of Alzheimer's disease—will never encounter the experiential core self in its purity. It will always already be embedded in an environmental and temporal horizon. It will be intertwined with, shaped, and contextualized by memories, expressive behaviour, and social interaction, by passively acquired habits, inclinations, associations, etc. In that sense, a narrow focus on the experiential self might indeed be said to involve an abstraction. Nevertheless, and this would be my own view, although one must concede that such a minimal notion is unable to accommodate or capture all ordinary senses of the term 'self', and although it certainly doesn't provide an exhaustive understanding of what it means to be a self, the very fact that we employ notions like *first-person* perspective, for-*me*-ness, and *mine*ness in order to describe our experiential life, the fact that it is characterized by a basic and pervasive reflexivity and pre-reflective self-consciousness, is ultimately sufficient to warrant the use of the term 'self'.

It is intriguing that Frankfurt, while defending the importance of identification and commitment for the constitution of self, at the same time accepts that consciousness does entail a basic form of self-consciousness. As he writes:

what would it be like to be conscious of something without being aware of this consciousness? It would mean having an experience with no awareness whatever of its occurrence. This would be, precisely, a case of unconscious experience. It appears, then, that being conscious is identical with being self-conscious. Consciousness *is* self-consciousness. (Frankfurt 1988: 1612)

As Frankfurt makes clear this claim is not meant to suggest that he endorses some version of a higher-order theory of consciousness. The idea is not that consciousness is invariably dual in the sense that every instance of it involves both a primary awareness and another instance of consciousness which is somehow distinct and separable from the first and which has the first as its object. Rather, and this constitutes a clear affinity with a perspective found in phenomenology,

the self-consciousness in question is a sort of *immanent reflexivity* by virtue of which every instance of being conscious grasps not only that of which it is an awareness but also the awareness of it. It is like a source of light which, in addition to illuminating whatever other things fall within its scope, renders itself visible as well. (Ibid. 162)

For Frankfurt, however, self-consciousness doesn't amount to consciousness of a self. Rather, the reflexivity in question is merely consciousness's awareness of itself (ibid.). Couldn't this be the fall-back option of the self-skeptics? Just as they might concede that there is a subjectivity of experience without thereby accepting the existence of self, they might accept that consciousness is characterized by a fundamental reflexivity without thereby seeing themselves as being committed to the reality of self.

On the face of it, it is quite true that self-consciousness doesn't have to be understood as a consciousness of a separate and distinct *self*; it might simply refer to the awareness which a specific experience has of *itself* (cf. Gurwitsch 1941). It is a mistake, however, to suggest that we in the latter case would be dealing with a non-egological type of self-consciousness, one lacking any sense of self. The very distinction between egological and non-egological types of (self-)consciousness is ultimately too crude and fuelled by a too narrow definition of what a self amounts to. As I have argued above, there is subjectivity of experience and a minimal sense of self, not only when I realize that *I* am perceiving a candle, but whenever there is perspectival ownership, whenever there is first-personal presence or manifestation of experience. It is this pre-reflective sense of self which provides the experiential grounding for any subsequent self-ascription, reflective appropriation, and thematic self-identification. Had our experiences been completely anonymous when originally lived through, any such subsequent appropriation would become inexplicable.

Thus, rather than saying that the self does not exist, I think the self-skeptics should settle for a more modest claim. They should qualify their statement and instead deny the existence of a special kind of self.

REFERENCES

ALBAHARI, M. (2006). *Analytical Buddhism: The Two-Tiered Illusion of Self* (New York: Palgrave Macmillan).

FRANKFURT, H. (1988). *The Importance of What We Care About: Philosophical Essays* (Cambridge: Cambridge University Press).

GURWITSCH, A. (1941). 'A Non-Egological Conception of Consciousness', *Philosophy and Phenomenological Research*, 1: 325–338.

HACKING, I. (1995). *Rewriting the Soul: Multiple Personality and the Sciences of Memory* (Princeton: Princeton University Press).

HENRY, M. (1963). *L'Essence de la manifestation* (Paris: PUF).

——(1965). *Philosophie et phénoménologie du corps* (Paris: PUF).

HUSSERL, E. (1950). *Cartesianische Meditationen und Pariser Vorträge* (Husserliana, 1; The Hague: Martinus Nijhoff).

——(1952). *Ideen zu einer reinen Phänomenologie und phänomenologischen Philosophie, ii. Phänomenologische Untersuchungen zur Konstitution* (Husserliana, 4; The Hague: Martinus Nijhoff).

——(1966). *Analysen zur passiven Synthesis: Aus Vorlesungs- und Forschungsmanuskripten 1918–1926* (Husserliana, 11; The Hague: Martinus Nijhoff).

——(1973). *Zur Phänomenologie der Intersubjektivität: Texte aus dem Nachlass, iii. 1929–1935* (Husserliana, 15; The Hague: Martinus Nijhoff).

——(1974). *Formale und transzendentale Logik: Versuch einer Kritik der logischen Vernunft* (Husserliana, 17; The Hague: Martinus Nijhoff).

——(1976). *Ideen zu einer reinen Phänomenologie und phänomenologischen Philosophie I* (Husserliana, 3/1–2; The Hague: Martinus Nijhoff).

——(1984). *Logische Untersuchungen, ii. Untersuchungen zur Phänomenologie und Theorie der Erkenntnis* (Husserliana, 19; The Hague: Martinus Nijhoff).

——(1994). *Briefwechsel II* (Husserliana Dokumente, 3/1–10; Dordrecht: Kluwer Academic Publishers).

METZINGER, T. (2003). *Being No One* (Cambridge, Mass.: MIT Press).

RIBOT, TH. (1883). *Les Maladies de la mémoire* (Paris: Librairie Germer Baillière).

RICOEUR, P. (1950). *Philosophie de la volonté*, i. *Le Volontaire et l'involontaire* (Paris: Aubier).

——(1985). *Temps et recit*, iii. *Le Temps raconté* (Paris: Éditions du Seuil).

——(1990). *Soi-même comme un autre* (Paris: Seuil).

SHOEMAKER, S. (1996). *The First-Person Perspective and Other Essays* (Cambridge: Cambridge University Press).

SARTRE, J.-P. (1936). *La Transcendance de l'ego* (Paris: Vrin).

——(1943/1976). *L'Être et le néant* (Paris: Tel Gallimard).

——(1948). 'Conscience de soi et connaissance de soi', *Bulletin de la Société Française de Philosophie*, 42: 49–91.

TAYLOR, C. (1989). *Sources of the Self* (Cambridge, Mass.: Harvard University Press).

ZAHAVI, D. (1999). *Self-Awareness and Alterity: A Phenomenological Investigation* (Evanston, Ill.: Northwestern University Press).

——(2005). *Subjectivity and Selfhood: Investigating the First-Person Perspective* (Cambridge, Mass.: MIT Press).

PART IV

PERSONAL IDENTITY, NARRATIVE IDENTITY, AND SELF-KNOWLEDGE

CHAPTER 14

PERSONAL IDENTITY

JOHN CAMPBELL

1. WHY ARE THERE PROBLEMS ABOUT PERSONAL IDENTITY?

In this chapter my aim is not to propose a resolution of the problems of personal identity, but to look at what makes the problems of identity in this case so difficult. After all, there are problems about the identities of concrete objects generally, and problems about the identities of abstract objects such as numbers. But in the case of persons, we seem to have the problems of object identity generally, and in addition to have difficult issues that are specific to this case.

I think there are two broad sources of difficulty. One is the causal complexity of persons. Questions about the identities of concrete objects and questions about their causal structure have often been observed to be connected, and I will review two ways of explaining the connection. The causal complexity of persons has to do with the way in which their physical and psychological lives can seem each to have their own causal structure. This means that we face the difficult question of which, if either, should be given more weight in resolving questions of identity. I will suggest a way of addressing this question below, in section 4.

The second source of difficulty is the relation between personal identity and the first person. Questions about personal identity can typically be framed in terms of the first person, and often have their sharpest formulations in those terms. For example, you can state Locke's example of the Prince and the cobbler by saying, 'Suppose I, a humble cobbler, wake up occupying an unfamiliar body, the body of a Prince, surrounded by people I have never seen . . .' This kind of imagining seems comprehensible, and its intelligibility seems to destabilize the idea that persons are biological organisms, since a biological organism could not change bodies.

In section 3 I will try to identify what it is about the first person that contributes so much to our puzzlement about the identity of the self, over and above the problems raised by the causal complexity of persons. I begin, though, by outlining the connection between causality and the identities of concrete objects generally, and how specifically it applies to the case of persons.

2. IMMANENT CAUSATION

Before making any comment on the connection to identity, I remark first on the kind of causality that is internal to an object. We tend to think of causality as involving interactions between objects. For one thing to strike another, affecting both, is our prototype of causation. Suppose a car strikes a lamppost, bending it. The way the lamppost is after the collision depends in part on the kind of thing that struck it, and how that thing was behaving at the time of the collision. But it also depends in part on the properties of the lamppost itself, which bear on how it will behave through the collision. The way the lamppost was before the collision will affect how it is after the collision. Its earlier properties are one of the determinants of its later properties. So here we have a kind of causality that is, as it were, internal to the object. And this internal or 'immanent' causality ticks away within the object even when it is not engaged in collisions or any interactions with other objects. If the object is stable, the reason it has its later properties is that it had those properties earlier. If the object is unstable, still its having the properties it does later is a consequence of its having had the properties it did earlier. In general, an object's later properties are causally affected by its earlier properties (cf. Shoemaker 1984a).

Similar points apply to the physiologies of persons. You watch your health because what you do now affects how you will be later. Interventions on your diet and exercise now will make a difference to how you are in a year's time. In those terms, the same points apply to the immanent causation that ticks away within persons at the physical level. But it is also true that psychological interventions on you now will affect how you are later, psychologically. As Shoemaker in effect pointed out, we can regard perception as a matter of the world intervening on the mind, and making a difference to which memories are formed. What perceptions you have now affects what memories you form later. Of course, we by no means have a clean separation between psychological and physical causal structures. Your diet now may make you very unhappy later. The incidents you witness now may affect not just your later memories, but also your later blood pressure. Still, Locke's case of the Prince and the cobbler may suggest we can make something of the two coming apart. If the Prince and the cobbler do swap bodies, the later psychological states of the person inhabiting the body of the Prince will causally depend on how it was with the cobbler earlier. But the earlier physical life of the cobbler may make no differences to the later physical life of the person occupying the body of the Prince, other than those that are implicated in the psychological connections between the early cobbler and the person later occupying the body of the Prince.

In these terms, what does it take for an object to be internally causally connected? For O's earlier condition to be a cause of its later condition is for intervening on O's earlier condition to be a way of intervening on O's later condition. So what we want is that there should be correlations between O's earlier condition and its later condition, under interventions on the earlier condition. We need the counterfactual to be true: had there been an intervention on O's earlier condition, there would have been a difference in O's later condition (for more on the notion of intervention here, see Campbell 2007).

To put it like this leaves it seeming that we know well enough what a physical object is, in advance of having the conception of it as internally causally connected. Many philosophers who have written on the identity of physical things, however, have taken it that the internal causal connectedness of a concrete object is central to its identity; mere spatiotemporal continuity in the absence of causal connectedness, were such a thing possible, would not be enough for sameness of object.

One thing more we might expect, then, is an account of the kind of causal dependence of later on earlier that is distinctive of a physical object. One possibility is that we could try to give a reductive account of physical objects, in interventionist terms. That is, we would define a set of relations among variables the holding of which would be constitutive of the existence of a concrete object at a particular place. For this to work the variables would evidently have to be defined over places rather than things. Then knowing of the existence of a particular object would be a matter of knowing what would happen under various interventions at a particular place.

We might suspect, though, that we will have to take the notion of a concrete object for granted in defining our variables—perhaps basic volumetric notions like size and shape, and perhaps even color predicates, are initially defined for concrete things. It may also be true that we can make nothing of psychological terms except as predicates of concrete objects. In that case there will be no possibility of reducing the existence of concrete objects to the possibilities of intervention at places. But we might still look for an account of the patterns of dependence of later on earlier that are distinctive of a single concrete thing. For example, we might suspect that it will typically be a family of properties of a single object that is responsible for a single tendency it has to behave thus-and-so in future interactions. And it might be further that there is nothing more to be said about the identity conditions of a concrete object than spelling out the kind of causal structure that the object has, what immanent connections there are between its earlier possession of properties and its later possession of properties.

When we think of the connection between causality and identity in these terms, one source of the problems of personal identity seems plain enough. The difficulty is the complexity of the causal structure that we find in persons. Centrally, we do not know:

(a) Whether the causal structure associated with the psychological properties of the person can be regarded as specifying the identity conditions of a thing, or if we find an autonomous causal structure only when we consider the broader class of physical properties of the person,

(b) Suppose psychological properties and physical properties do turn out to specify relatively autonomous causal structures, as the case of the Prince and the cobbler may seem to suggest. Which one should be given greater weight in specifying the identity conditions of the person?

There are evidently far-reaching questions associated with both of those topics. Philosophers who emphasize the embodied or embedded nature of the psychological life, for example, are likely to find barely intelligible the idea of autonomous causal structures for the psychological and physical lives of a person. Philosophers who think that persons are simply biological organisms, on the other hand, may argue that the physical life of a person defines the only causal structure relevant to specifying the identity conditions of a person. However, I do not want to try to resolve these questions here.

I want to point rather to two further sources of difficulty about the specification of the identity conditions of persons. One, that I will discuss in section 4 below, has to do with a further dimension to our notion of causation: the idea of mechanism, and the notion that concrete objects are the prototypical mechanisms for transmitting causal influence from place to place. As we will see, this way of thinking of the connection between causation and the identities of objects puts a great deal of pressure on the notion of a purely psychological self, to the point of making it seem that there could be no such thing. The second further source of difficulty about the specification of the identity conditions of persons has to do with our understanding of the first person. This seems to bring in a set of issues that are different to the problems relating to the causal structure of person. I turn now to these questions about the first person.

3. THE AUTONOMY OF THE FIRST PERSON

The complexity of the causal structure of persons is certainly one central factor making it possible for there to be real uncertainty about what persons are, how to characterize their conditions of identity. But it is hardly enough to explain how there can be such radical uncertainty as we encounter in the philosophical literature. In many cases when we are talking about objects of one type or another, it is not even possible to refer to the object at all without having a firm grasp of what you are talking about. For example, someone talking about elementary arithmetic, talking about numbers and elementary operations performed on them, can hardly be struck by wonder and ask, well, could it be after all that I am talking here about trees, or sub-atomic particles? Equally, someone engaged in a discussion of types of coffee can hardly find a basis for uncertainty as to whether they might after all be referring here to distant galaxies. There are some cases, of what we might call 'dependent' reference, in which this kind of uncertainty is possible. For example, I might frame a descriptive specification such as 'whatever Sally is thinking about' and that might specify anything from the law of tort to a blade of grass. But in that kind of case there is always available a further specification of the reference, and grasping that further specification is not consistent with radical uncertainty as to what is being referred to. Moreover, in this kind of case the 'further specification of the reference' is more fundamental than the original specification, in the following sense. Predications of the object referred to in general are understood and explained in the context of identifications of the object in context of the further specification. Suppose that what Sally is thinking about is the number 5. Predications of the number 5 such as 'is odd' or 'is prime' cannot be first understood and explained in the context of propositions such as 'what Sally is thinking about is odd'. If you have no idea what 'odd' means, it takes you no further forward to be told that what Sally is thinking about is odd. What would help are uses of the predicate in the context of numerical statements: propositions such as '1 is odd, 3 is odd, 5 is odd, 7 is odd, and so on . . .'

The problem about 'I' is that it does not seem to be a dependent form of reference, but an understanding and use of the term does seem to be consistent with radical uncertainty about what is being referred to. People who grasp the first person perfectly well do in fact dispute whether it refers to a body, a soul, or something else. Or perhaps it does not refer at all. This does not seem to be because 'I' is a dependent form of reference. But it has no parallel with most cases of reference to concrete objects. If we are not considering a case of dependent reference, then you can hardly be uncertain as to whether you are referring to a war between nations or a pickled onion. If you had not made up which of those you meant to identify, you would not yet be in a position to refer to either.

How does it happen that this uncertainty is possible in the case of the first person? We might begin on diagnosis by remarking that the first person is a token-reflexive. That is, the use of 'I' in English is governed by some such rule as:

Any token of 'I' refers to whoever produced it.

Now since 'I' is governed by this rule, anyone who uses the term cannot help but refer to a particular person. If the speaker is not reckoning into account any connection the term might have to some more basic way of identifying persons, then you can use 'I' as a referring term without having settled any of the familiar uncertainties as to which thing the term is referring to. In contrast, other terms referring to concrete objects are not governed by any such systematic rule.

The problem is exacerbated by the fact that our understanding of the notion of a 'person' is ordinarily achieved only by way of our understanding of the first person. That is, there are not two stages here: achieving an understanding of 'person' and then, subsequently, using that understanding of 'person' to achieve an understanding of 'I', grasped as subject to the token-reflexive rule. Rather, your understanding of 'person' is correlative with your understanding of 'I'. A 'person' is whatever uses of 'I' refer to. And x is the same person as y if and only if x's uses of 'I' refer to the same thing as y's uses of 'I' refer to. The notion of a person does not give any grip on the identities of persons, independent of our understanding of the first person. Of course, there is more to be done to make the concept of a person explicit; you might, for example, argue that for the concept to be true of someone they must have some capacity for autobiographical memory, perhaps some grasp of psychological predicates and some capacity for social interaction. But these further aspects of the concept of a person do not provide us with a full grasp of the identity conditions of persons.

You might argue that the use of token-reflexives does depend on there being some more fundamental way of identifying the objects in question, a level of thought about the objects that will make it manifestly determinate what their identity conditions are. Suppose we consider a language whose speakers are intelligent and articulate, but the terms of the language simply do not include token-reflexives. Suppose, for instance, that we find a people who, though intelligent and possessed of a common language, do not have the first person, or anything like it. They do, however, have ways of identifying individual humans. They may give various humans names, and they may use demonstrative terms like 'that one' to refer to particular humans. They also have a range of predicates that they use to describe humans. For example, they may comment on one another's physical characteristics, though let us suppose that they do not as yet have any psychological predicates. And suppose we now suggest to them that they could introduce a new term to their language, 'H', governed by the rule:

Any token of 'H' refers to the human that produced it.

After the community has gained a certain facility in the use of 'H', they may use it to express a lot of facts about themselves. They may say things like, 'H weighs 167.5 pounds', 'H is bleeding', and so on. But this use of 'H' will be entirely dependent on the underlying, pre-existing level of thought about humans, using names and demonstratives. The situation is parallel to the introduction of terms like 'the number of the planets' used to identify numbers. It is of course possible to make remarks like, 'the number of the planets plus the number of the trees on earth is greater than the number of the rivers on earth'. But your understanding of what it takes for such a proposition to be true depends on your understanding of how it relates to a more basic level at which the numbers are identified using the numerals. Similarly, when you encounter the remark 'H is F' you understand it by knowing that it is true, if it is true, in virtue of the truth of propositions using some more basic way of identifying humans, such as names and demonstratives. This will be so even for your own uses of 'H'. Now given this way of using 'H', there is as yet no reason to think that there is any particular uncertainty attaching to what it refers to. Of course, given the causal complexity of actual humans, there will be some problems about what it takes for us to have the same human later as we had earlier. We might expect, for example, that there may be disputes between those who think that a human ceases to exist at the time of death, and those who think the human breathing earlier is identical to the present corpse. And there may be subtler issues. But there will be nothing like the radical uncertainty that attaches to the way we presently think about persons.

Is our ordinary understanding of 'I' just like these people's use of 'H'? The theoretical situation would be a great deal clearer if they were similar. The point about 'H' is that it is plainly a dependent form of reference, in the following sense. The predicates that one uses in conjunction with 'H' were all themselves first introduced and explained using ways of identifying humans, names, and demonstratives, and so on, that do not themselves depend on an understanding of 'H'. So questions about identity-conditions are not best stated in terms of 'H'. It is better, rather, to formulate questions about identity directly at the lower level of uses of names and demonstratives to refer to humans. The trouble is that in just this respect 'H' does not seem to be a good model for our use of 'I'. In the case of ordinary use of the first person, we have a whole complex family of predicates that are first introduced and explained at the level of uses of the token-reflexive itself. These are psychological terms—terms such as 'sees Vienna', 'reads a newspaper', and so on. These terms are typically introduced and explained in the context of first-person statements, such as 'I am in pain'. Although we do have third-person uses of these statements, such as 'She is in pain', they are characteristically grasped as equivalent to first-person statements made by the other person, 'I am in pain'.

In consequence of this, first-person present-tense ascriptions of psychological state to oneself are typically, in Shoemaker's phrase, 'immune to error through misidentification'. That is to say, suppose I form the judgment, 'I am in pain'. I will typically not have done this by first establishing some third-personal proposition, 'She is in pain', and then, taking that person to be myself, coming to the conclusion, 'I am in pain'. If that were the procedure I followed, then there would be circumstances in which I could hold on to my right to the claim that someone is in pain, but selectively question whether it is I that is in pain. But as Shoemaker (1984b) pointed out, that kind of doubt seems to make no sense in the ordinary case of current judgments to the effect that 'I am in pain'. Usually, however it happens that I have the right to the judgment 'there is pain', I have by the same lights the right to the judgment 'I am in pain'. There is no rational basis on which I could hold fast to my right to the claim that there is pain, but question only whether it is I who has it. This is what I meant by saying earlier that the first person is not a dependent mode of reference; there is a large family of predicates, the psychological predicates, that are first introduced and explained in the context of the first person.

It is quite different with 'H'. As I have described it, there is no family of predicates that is first introduced and explained in the context of 'H'. Uses of 'H' to report an individual's possession of one physical property or another are truly subject to error through misidentification. To establish that, as you would say, 'H is bleeding', you would first have to establish that 'that man is bleeding' and then accept that that man is H. You could be challenged at this second point: it could turn out you had make a mistake there, and that while it is true that that man is bleeding, that man is not H. Using this kind of talk it seems quite evident that at no point are we talking about anything other than ordinary humans, and the uncertainties we might experience are no more than the experiences one might have in talking about ordinary humans. When we reflect on the ordinary use of the first person, though, the landscape is quite different. Our understanding of the first person in the context of psychological statements does seem to be autonomous. And that is what makes it so very difficult for us to establish just what the referent of the term is, and to secure agreement on whatever conclusion we think we have reached.

4. OBJECTS AS MECHANISMS

There is one final source of difficulty in our ordinary understanding of personal identity. Earlier I spoke of the complexity of the causal structure of persons. And I characterized this complexity in terms of the kinds of properties persons have, and the kinds of correlations we find between how a person is later and how they were earlier, under various interventions on different properties. But there is more to our idea of a continuing object than the idea of a range of correlations between variables under various potential interventions. In the case of ordinary physical things, we think of sameness of physical object as the reason why an intervention on one variable now, changing the color of the thing, for instance, will mean there is a difference in its color later. I want to remark on this feature of our ordinary understanding of the causal significance of sameness of object, before asking whether any version of it applies to our ordinary thinking about persons.

One way to bring out the point is to ask how it happens that causal influence can be transmitted from place to place. It is really basic to our understanding of ourselves as spatially located that what happens at one place can have repercussions for what happens at other places. Places are not causally insulated from one another. But we also resist the idea of action at a distance: we have difficulty with the notion that what goes on at one place could immediately affect what goes on at some distant place. So how is causal influence transmitted from place to place?

If you think about the surface of a pond, you might think of waves fanning out from one place to another set of locations, and causal influence being transmitted in that way. But that is not how we ordinarily think. Usually, we would think that the movement of objects transmits causal influence from place to place. I light an oil heater in the garden and then find it is cold indoors, so I bring the heater in. Because of the movement of the heater, my intervention, my lighting of the gas at one place, makes a difference to the temperature at another place. We would be baffled by the idea that my lighting the heater outside could have made a difference to the temperature of the room without the heater having been moved, unless of course we appeal to some other story about heat waves or the motion of molecules. That is what we are ruling out when we rule out action at a distance. The movement of the physical thing, the oil heater, explains how it is that my intervention outside is making a difference to the temperature inside. This implies:

(*a*) there is more to the movement of a physical object than there being correlations under interventions between what goes on at one place and what goes on at another, and

(*b*) this further sameness of physical object at one place with physical object at another place is what explains the existence of those correlations between what goes on at one place and what goes on at the other, under interventions on one of the places.

We could sum all this up by saying that there is more to our ordinary concept of causation than the truth of counterfactuals about what would happen to the values of some variables when there are interventions on the values of other variables. In addition to the fact that an intervention on one variable makes a difference to the value of another, we think there must a mechanism by which this happens. Ordinary physical objects are just the very simplest examples of such mechanisms. An intervention at one location can make a difference at another location; and movement of the object from one location to another is the mechanism by which this transmission of influence from one location to another is achieved.

Now earlier I talked about the causal structure of persons as a matter of there being correlations between the values of certain variables under interventions on others. For example, I said that in perception the world intervenes on the beliefs of the person, so that later there are differences in the memories that the person has. And of course, earlier physical interventions on the person, making a difference to diet or exercise, may make a difference to how the person is later. I emphasized the complexity in the structure of these sets of correlations between the later characteristics of the person and what happens in earlier interventions. But another dimension in our understanding of the causal structure of a person emerges when we ask what the mechanism is by which causal influence is transmitted from earlier to later. So long as we think of relatively mundane cases of physical influence, it seem innocuous enough to say that sameness of person is the mechanism by which causal influence is transmitted over time. But suppose we think once again about the case of the Prince and the cobbler. In ordinary imagining or in literature, it seems plain enough what is supposed to be happening here. The earlier psychological states of the cobbler are affecting the later psychological states of the person in the Prince's body. Were there to have been interventions on those earlier psychological states of the cobbler, there would have been differences in the later psychological states of the person in the Prince's body. But what is the mechanism by which this happens? How does it come about that the earlier interventions on the psychological life of the cobbler are making a difference later to the psychological states of the person in the Prince's body? There may be no physical continuity between the cobbler's body and the Prince's body; the two may never have so much as touched. So if we are to think of sameness of person as the mechanism by which causal influence is transmitted from the early cobbler to the later person in the Prince's body, we cannot think of the mechanism in question as the physical continuation of an ordinary physical body. Rather, we must be dealing with some para-physical analogue of the continuation of an ordinary physical body. This is where we see the connection between dualism and the idea that the cobbler has come to inhabit the body of the Prince. There is on the face of it nothing specifically dualist about the idea that the psychological attributes earlier associated with this body may be making a difference to the psychological attributes later associated with that body. The link to dualism emerges when we ask: what is the mechanism by which these earlier and later attributes are connected? And since on the face of it there is no physical mechanism connecting the two, we are bound to consider the possibility that causal influence is being transmitted through the persistence of a non-physical, para-mechanical mechanism: that is, a soul.

I do not think that there is any inescapable commitment here to the idea of a soul, on the part of one who thinks that there is a psychological structure that has been transmitted from the earlier cobbler to the person who later inhabits the body of the Prince. If we want to resist the idea of the soul at this point, we would have to say that sameness of person is not here the mechanism that transmits the causal structure from earlier to later. Rather, obviously, the mechanism is not sameness of physical body either, since there is no sameness of physical body. It may be, however, that there could be a multiplicity of fine-grained physical mechanisms at work, mediating between the earlier psychological states of the cobbler and the later psychological states of the Prince, so that there is no causal influence here without a mechanism, even though the mechanism is not being constituted by the persistence of any one physical or immaterial object, but by a multiplicity of more fine-physical particles or waves. The trouble is that we would not ordinarily expect to achieve reference to such an abstract, complex causal structure by means of a device of simple reference, such as the unstructured use of 'I'. We would expect that such unstructured referential devices themselves can delineate only prototypical physical mechanisms, or, at any rate, quite simple causal structures. So it is a surprise to be told that our ordinary use of 'I' is managing to delineate this abstract, complex causal structure. If we do not want to embrace the soul, the alternative is to deny that the scenario of the cobbler and the Prince is after all possible.

5. ELIMINATING THE FIRST PERSON

In *Reasons and Persons* (1984) Derek Parfit maintains that 'we could give a complete description of reality without claiming that persons exist'. He advertises his view as being revisionist of our ordinary ways of thinking (also see Chapter 18 below). Admittedly we do make references to people in our ordinary thought and talk; but, Parfit thinks, it would be beneficial if we eliminated those references. On his view, it is not just that we could eliminate the talk of persons when giving some speculative philosophical account of the fundamental constituents of the world; we would benefit by eliminating talk of persons from our ordinary thinking as agents, the kind of thinking that we engage in every day when deciding what to do about this or that. The closest we would come to talking about persons would be to talk about the sequences of experiences which are causally dependent on one or another physical body. The great advantage of this way of talking, according to Parfit, is that it would let us get a better focus on some of our most basic concerns, such as the concern to survive, which we ordinarily formulate using the first person, 'I', a term which refers to persons; the concern to survive, we ordinarily think, is a concern that I should survive. If we eliminate the use of the first person here, and substitute a concern that 'the sequence of experiences causally dependent on this body should be prolonged for as long as possible', it seems apparent that there is something arbitrary about the concern. It is hard to invest quite the same uncritical passion in a concern to prolong the sequence of experiences causally dependent on this body that it is natural to invest in a concern that I should survive. Parfit sums up the intended effect of his revision like this:

When I believed my existence was . . . a further fact, I seemed imprisoned in myself. My life seemed like a glass tunnel, through which I was moving faster every year, and at the end of which there was darkness. When I changed my view, the walls of my glass tunnel disappeared. I now live in the open air. There is still a difference between my life and the lives of other people. But the difference is less. Other people are closer. I am less concerned about the rest of my own life, and more concerned about the lives of others. (1984: 281)

This is the effect you get if, in your practical deliberations, you replace the use of 'I' with references to 'the series of experiences of which this experience is one', or 'the series of experiences which is causally dependent on this body'. Questions such as 'What's in it for me?' seem all too readily intelligible. But Parfit aims to take away the vocabulary in which such concerns are expressed, leaving us only with the talk about series of experiences. And a strong concern with one rather than another such series of experiences cannot but seem arbitrary: what is so special about the series of which this experience is a member, or the series which causally depends on this body? When we have abandoned the use of the first person, and moved to a vocabulary in which this arbitrariness in evident, the walls of the tunnel simply do fall away. That's the idea, at any rate.

It is natural to wonder, though, whether this elimination of the first person is possible at all. Ascriptions of psychological states involving the first person have often been thought to be essential to the explanation of action. In a famous example, John Perry wrote:

I once followed a trail of sugar on a supermarket floor, pushing my cart down the aisle on one side of a tall counter and back the aisle on the other, seeking the shopper with the torn sack to tell him he was making a mess. With each trip around the counter, the trail became thicker. But I seemed unable to catch up. Finally it dawned on me. I was the shopper I was trying to catch. (Perry 1993: 33)

Perry's whole point is that the appearance of the first person in the thought, 'I am making a mess' is essential to its having the explanatory value it does. He will not try to clear things up until he has the thought, 'I am making a mess'. Contrariwise, when the shopper does try to clear things up, you can explain what he is doing only by ascribing to him the thought, 'I am making a mess'. That is why, in Perry's formulation, the indexical 'I' is essential.

If we accepted Parfit's conceptual revolution, though, we would not be able to use the first person in our thinking at this point. The moment of revelation for the shopper would have to be expressed by some such formulation as 'The series of experiences, of which this experience is a member, is causally dependent on a body which is causing a mess to be made', or 'the series of experiences which is causally dependent on this body is dependent on a body which is causing a mess to be made'. These thoughts seem quite different to the thought, 'I am making a mess'. The impersonal thoughts seem to give no particular reason to feel responsible for what is happening. Having identified a body which is causing a mess, why should the shopper feel any more responsibility for what that body is doing than he does for what any other body is doing? As we would unreconstructedly say, why is it his problem to clear things up? It is not an accident that we have this distancing of the shopper from the actions he observes. It is the same distancing that loses us the most elementary sense of responsibility as loses us the urgency of the concern to survive. It is the same distancing that explains the loss of concern about the sugar as explains the loss of the concern to survive.

REFERENCES

CAMPBELL, JOHN (2007). 'An Interventionist Approach to Causation in Psychology', in Alison Gopnik and Laura Schulz (eds), *Causal Learning: Psychology, Philosophy and Computation* (Oxford: Oxford University Press), 58–66.

LOCKE, JOHN (1975). *An Essay Concerning Human Understanding*, ed. P. H. Nidditch (Oxford: Oxford University Press).

PARFIT, D. (1984). *Reasons and Persons* (Oxford: Oxford University Press).

PERRY, JOHN (1993). 'The Problem of the Essential Indexical', in *The Problem of the Essential Indexical and Other Essays* (Oxford: Oxford University Press).

SHOEMAKER, SYDNEY (1984a). 'Identity, Properties and Causality', in *Identity, Cause and Mind* (Cambridge: Cambridge University Press), 234–60.

——(1984b). 'Self-Reference and Self-Awareness', in *Identity, Cause and Mind* (Cambridge: Cambridge University Press), 6–18.

CHAPTER 15

··

ON WHAT WE ARE

··

SYDNEY SHOEMAKER

I

··

In the opening chapter of his recent book *What Are We?* Eric Olson (2007) takes personal identity theorists to task for not addressing the question that serves as his title, or for confusing it with different questions—for example, the question of what constitutes our persistence, or the persistence of persons, through time. The question he wants answered is not the question 'What are persons?'—for his question is about the nature of beings of our own kind, human persons, and he is open to the possibility that there are persons who are not of our kind. And it is not the question 'What constitutes our persistence through time?'—for he thinks that an answer to that question will not by itself tell us what we are, and that an account of what we are will not by itself tell us what our persistence conditions are. He considers a number of answers to his question: that we are animals, that we are things constituted by animals, that we are brains, that we are temporal parts of human animals, that we are bundles of mental states and events, and that we are souls. He finds difficulties with all of these; but his sympathy is clearly with the view that we are animals, and his criticism of the other answers often includes the complaint (sometimes directed at me in particular) that these answers deny the obvious truth that animals can think.

Earlier versions of this chapter were presented at the University of Girona, Spain, at the Australian National University, and at Melbourne University. I am grateful to audiences on those occasions for their comments.

In this chapter I will address Olson's title question. I will suggest that it is much closer to the truth than he allows that saying that what our persistence conditions are tells us what we are—what sort of things we are. But I will do more than answer the question of what *we* are. I will sketch a general account of what determines the nature of any sort of persisting thing, and then apply it to persons and to our kind of persons. My account will imply that in one sense of 'animal' animals cannot think, but will suggest that there is a different sense of 'animal' in which animals can think and in which we ourselves are animals. But I do not think that saying that we are animals in this second sense, supposing it is allowed to exist, provides a satisfactory answer to the question of what we are. I don't think that any of the answers Olson considers does that. Answering that question cannot consist in finding some common noun or noun phrase N such that we can say 'We are Ns'. It is doubtful if there is any such phrase other than 'human person' and obviously 'We are human persons' does not give us an answer of the sort Olson is looking for.

II

The guiding idea behind the account I will offer is that properties are individuated by causal profiles and that there is an internal relation between the causal profiles of properties and the identity conditions of the things that have them. The causal profile of a property consists of its forward-looking causal features, the aptness of its instances to cause or contribute to causing certain effects, and its backward-looking causal features, its being such that its instantiation can be caused by certain things. I now believe that the forward-looking causal features determine the backward-looking ones, so all we really need in the account is the forward-looking causal features. In saying that properties are individuated by causal profiles I mean that, in any given world, properties having the same causal profile are identical. This is weaker than the claim, which I in fact hold but do not assume here, that having a certain causal profile is both necessary and sufficient for being a given property, and that causal profiles are essential to the properties that have them. In speaking of the identity conditions for a kind of thing I mean two kinds of unity relations—synchronic unity relations that hold amongst the different property instances that occur in a thing at a particular time, and diachronic unity relations that hold amongst the different property instances that occur in a thing's career at different times and constitute its persistence over time.

Let's first see how it is that the causal profiles of properties are internally related to the synchronic unity of the things that have them. For the most part, the instantiation of a property causes an effect, or bestows a causal power, only in conjunction with other properties that are coinstantiated with it, that is, are instantiated in the same thing at the same time. So a full specification of a forward-looking causal feature of a property would say that when it is coinstantiated with such and such properties its instance and the instances of those properties jointly produce certain effects under certain conditions, or jointly confer certain powers. But arguably there is an entailment that goes in the opposite direction as well: if property instances are so related that they jointly produce certain effects under certain circumstances, then the properties belong to the same thing, that is, are synchronically unified. This of course does not mean that whenever property instances combine to produce an effect they belong to the same thing—obviously property instances in different things frequently contribute to the production of certain effects. Only when an effect is of a kind such that it belongs to the causal profiles of the instantiated properties that their coinstantiation produces an effect of that kind does the production of such an effect imply that the property instances are synchronically unified. So, for example, if an instance of sharpness, an instance of hardness, and an instance of a certain mass jointly result in a piece of wood being cut when pressure is applied to it, these instances will all belong to a single thing, namely that (say a knife) by which the pressure is applied. Or to take a psychological example, if a belief and a desire jointly give rise to an action they jointly make rational, they belong to the same subject. Here I assume that it belongs to the causal profiles of the belief and desire that when they are co-personal, that is, belong to the same person, they will give rise to such an action. So, in the central case, what constitutes the synchronic unity of different property instances is their being so related that they jointly produce the effects, or jointly bestow the powers, which it is the nature of the instantiated properties to produce or bestow when coinstantiated. Because the synchronic unity relation is transitive, this permits pairs of property instances that lack joint effects to be synchronically unified. There is nothing that is an obvious candidate for being something jointly caused by my mass and my complexion. But instances of mass and instances of shape jointly cause certain effects, and so do instances of shape and instances of complexion (e.g. effects on the experiences of observers, and on cameras). If an instance of mass and an instance of complexion are such that each is related to an instance of shape in such a way as to make them synchronically unified with it, then the instance of mass and the instance of complexion will themselves be synchronically unified.

Whereas the synchronic unity of two property instances has to do, in the central case, with their propensity to jointly produce certain effects, the diachronic unity of two property instances has to do, in the central case, with one of them being the cause or partial cause of the other. The reason for the second occurrence of 'in the central case' is that property instances occurring at different times in the career of a thing won't always be causally related. They may be diachronically unified because they are synchronically unified with other property instances that are causally related. My height yesterday and my complexion today are not causally related; but the first is synchronically unified with my weight yesterday and the second is synchronically unified with my weight today, and my weight yesterday and my weight today are causally related. So diachronic unity relations include not only causal relations between property instances but also instances of the relation *being synchronically related to property instances that are causally related.*

Again, this doesn't mean that whenever property instances occurring at different times are causally related they are diachronically unified. Whether causally related property instances are diachronically unified depends on the causal profiles of the properties. Among the causal features in the causal profile of a property will be its aptness to contribute to the production of what I will call 'successor states', later states of the same thing. This is most obvious in the case of dispositional properties like elasticity. A thing that is elastic will be disposed to change its shape in response to certain forces imposed on it, and then revert to its original shape when those forces are removed. It, that same thing, will first have one shape, then a different one, and then the first shape again. If a thing is malleable, it will be disposed to change its shape in response to forces imposed on it, but not to revert to its original shape when the forces cease to be applied to it. In both cases the disposition is specified in terms of effects on the future career of its possessor. But what goes for dispositional properties also goes for the properties that ground or realize them. Many properties have among their causal features a tendency to perpetuate themselves; an instantiation of such a property in a thing at a time will tend to result in that same property being instantiated in the thing at subsequent times. Of course, the extent to which this is true of a property will depend on what other properties are coinstantiated with it; if we give a certain shape to a piece of steel we can be pretty sure it will have that shape the next day, but if we give it to a piece of wax that may be exposed to heat we should not be so sure of this. In all of these cases we can say that the subsequent stages in the career of an object are related by 'immanent causation', causation that works within the career of a thing—although in many cases this is supplemented by 'transeunt' causation involving causal interaction with other things. And arguably this immanent causation is an important part of what constitutes the persistence of an object over time. If a property instance contributes to the immanent causation of a later property instance, the property instances will stand in the diachronic unity relation, and will be parts of successive stages in the career of a single persisting thing. Here, as in the case of synchronic unity, we have implications in two directions. If a property has a causal profile with certain sorts of forward-looking causal features, its instantiation in certain circumstances will cause the existence in the same thing of a successor state of a certain sort. And if in those circumstances the instantiation of a property with that causal profile causes a state of that sort, then that state and the instance of the property will stand to one another in a relation of diachronic unity and will belong to the same persisting thing.

III

But while the causal profiles of all properties contribute equally to bestowing relations of synchronic unity, properties differ in the extent to which their causal profiles contribute to the existence of relations of diachronic unity. Properties of persisting things can be classified as either thick or thin.[1] Thin properties are properties that can be shared by things of different kinds—or, equivalently, by things having different persistence conditions. They include shape, size, mass, electric charge, and a number of other properties. Thick properties are properties that can only be instantiated in things of a certain kind. I will later contend that mental properties are thick. Presumably biological properties are thick. So also are automotive properties, like being in first gear or having power steering, and computer properties like being connected with the internet or having a floppy drive. It is primarily thick properties whose causal profiles are such that their successive instantiations generate the diachronic unity relations that constitute persistence through time.

This is not to deny that knowing what thin properties a thing has at a time often gives one information about what properties that same thing will have at later times. Most property instances, including instances of thin properties, tend to be self-perpetuating at least in the short run. And there are cases in which it is predictable that the thin properties of something will change in certain ways over time, what thin properties the thing has at a later time being a function of, among other things, what its thin properties were at an earlier time. This is true when the properties are the shapes and sizes of a growing tree. But here, of course, it is because we are dealing with an object of a certain sort, one having certain persistence conditions, that the thin properties change systematically in the way they do. The persistence of the tree consists in there being a career whose successive stages are united by the relations of diachronic unity generated by the instances of biological properties occurring in them, and the shape and size instantiated in that career at a time are the joint effects of what shapes and sizes were instantiated in it earlier and the biological properties instantiated in it earlier. And there can, of course, be sudden and drastic changes in the size and shape of a tree, as when it is struck by lightning or high winds, which reduce its size by more than half and drastically change its shape. Things of other kinds, cars for example, will not survive the sudden removal of more than half their matter. That trees can do so reflects the kind of persistence conditions they have. And these are determined by the causal profiles of their biological properties—that is, their thick properties.

---

[1] It may be that properties can vary in their degree of thickness, but here I will keep things simple and assume a dichotomy of thick and thin.

IV

On the account I am developing, the existence of a persisting thing is constituted by the existence of a set of property instances united by relations of synchronic and diachronic unity. Or, more exactly, by a set of property instances the simultaneous members of which are united by relations of synchronic unity and the non-simultaneous members of which are united by relations of diachronic unity. But this is not a bundle theory. It does not identify a persisting thing with such a set; it merely says that where there is such a set, there is a persisting thing. And it does not dispense with substances, qua subjects of property instantiations. The property instances it speaks of can be thought of as states of affairs, or what are sometimes called Kim-events, consisting in the possession of a property by a thing at a time. What the account says is that when the members of a set of property instances are related in the way indicated, the things involved in them are all one and the same. It also says that when a persisting thing exists, there is a set of property instances related in the way indicated.

We can say something similar about the existence of persisting things of particular kinds. A persisting thing of a given kind exists just in case there is a set of property instances related in the way indicated above, *and* the thick property instances involved are of a certain sort, generating diachronic unity relations and persistence conditions of a specific kind. On this account the modal properties of a kind, its being such that its members can or cannot survive the loss of certain properties, can or cannot acquire certain properties, etc., are determined by the causal profiles of the thick properties whose instances figure in the careers of things of that kind.

V

I think we are now in a position to say what constitutes a persisting thing's being of a certain kind. What kind of thing something belongs to is fixed by what properties it is capable of having, and in particular what thick properties it can have. What thick properties a thing can have determines its persistence conditions, and these determine what properties, including thin properties, it can acquire.

When we ask concerning some things, for example ourselves, what kind of things they are, there may or may not be some generic common noun or noun phrase that can be used to give the answer. Maybe, as Olson suggests, the term 'person' doesn't give the answer to the question of what we are, because there can be persons that are not of our kind. We can stipulate that we are *human* persons; but if we ask what kind of thing human persons are there may be no more general term that provides the answer. On the animalist view the term 'animal', or 'organism', may serve, but on the psychological view there is no term in common parlance that will do the job. If, as I assume, our properties include physical ones, and the instantiations of all of them are physically realized, then we are material beings. But 'material beings' does not pick out a kind of objects in the relevant sense, for there is no set of thick properties that is specific to material beings—'material being' is too general a term to have a particular set of persistence conditions associated with it. Maybe there is a larger category, other than *person*, to which we can be said to belong. But we don't need that in order to say what kind of thing we are. We can do that by saying what sorts of properties we have and, what is most important, what our thick properties are.

The account I favor is the neo-Lockean account that says that our thick properties are psychological ones. This goes with the view that persistence of persons consists in psychological continuity. Historically an important source of support for this view has been change of body thought experiments. Locke imagined the soul of a prince, carrying with it consciousness of the prince's past life, being transferred to the body of a cobbler, and said that in such a case the post-transfer cobbler-body person would be the same person with the prince—not because he would have his soul but because he would have the consciousness, that is, memory, of his past life of which the soul was assumed to be the carrier. A contemporary version of this example has what is transferred be a brain, or cerebrum, rather than a soul, and stresses that the result would be not just that the brain or cerebrum recipient would remember the past of the donor but that his mental life would be in a variety of ways continuous with the past mental life of the donor. A common intuition, the 'transplant intuition',[2] is that in such cases the soul or brain recipient would be identical with the donor, despite having a different body, and that this identity would somehow consist in the psychological 'continuity and connectedness' linking the pre-transfer and post-transfer states.

In the remainder of this chapter I will work with the version of the example in which what is transplanted to a different body is a cerebrum rather than a whole brain. This is because of a point made by Eric Olson in his earlier book *The Human Animal*. He points out that allowing that a brain-transplant could be person-preserving does not automatically establish the psychological view and refute animalism. For the whole brain includes the brainstem, which is, he says, the biological control center of the person. And an animalist could hold that a brain transplant could be person-preserving because the recipient has the same brainstem as the donor and is for that reason biologically continuous with him. What

---

[2] The term is due to Eric Olson (1997), who thinks the intuition is mistaken.

the animalist denies is that, if only the cerebrum is transferred, and so the only continuity preserved in the transfer is psychological continuity, then the transfer is person-preserving.

VI

As I have said, a common intuition is that the psychological continuity is person-preserving. We need to look into the source of this intuition. It seems obvious, to begin with, that mental properties are thick properties. To anticipate a point that will be important later on, the mental properties of a person are not shared by an entity coincident with the person but not identical with it, namely the person's body. Further, if we look at what is involved in the possession of certain mental properties, it seems central to their causal profiles that their instantiation causes or contributes to causing successor states of certain sorts in the future career of the same person. It is characteristic of many mental states that they leave memories of themselves. Beliefs give rise, in reasoning, to other beliefs to which they give deductive or inductive support. Beliefs and desires give rise to intentions, and intentions give rise to decision and actions. In all these cases the successor states belong to the same subject as the states that give rise to them, and it seems central to the concepts of these states that this should be so. This makes plausible the view that if a series of mental states, or mental property instances, consists of states so related that the successor states which members of the series should produce, given their causal profiles, are in fact produced and are themselves later members of the series, then the states in the series will all belong to the same person. Or as we might put it, if we have a series of mental states the simultaneous members of which all stand in relations of synchronic unity and the successive members of which stand in what, given their causal profiles, should be relations of diachronic unity, then the series constitutes the mental history of a single person over the interval in question. This supports the claim that mental properties are thick properties whose causal profiles determine the persistence conditions of person.[3]

---

[3] Eric Olson tries to undermine the plausibility of this view by pointing out that in a case of fission, e.g. the case in which the two hemispheres of someone's brain are transplanted into different bodies, there will be two series of mental states of this description—one consisting of the states of the original person and those of one of the fission products and one consisting of the states of the original person and those of the other fission product—in each of which the later (post-fission) states belong to a different person than the earlier (pre-fission) states (Olson 2007: 34). But it is easy to accommodate this point. The claim can be that such a series will be the mental history of a single person if the series is non-branching.

This gets further support from the role of mental properties in our concept of a person. Locke defined person as 'a thinking intelligent being, that has reason and reflection, and can consider itself as itself, the same thinking being in different times and places, which it does only by that consciousness which is inseparable from thinking, and it seems to me essential to it' (Locke 1975: 335). Certainly we conceive of persons as creatures that have, and in some sense necessarily have, mental or psychological properties. Of course, an animalist can hold a version of this view; when the person becomes a human vegetable, entire devoid of mentality, the animalist can say that it ceases to be a person but does not thereby cease to exist. On such a view Locke's definition only gives us the nominal essence of persons. One might think that the nominal essence reading is recommended by Locke's claims about the unknowability of real essences. But the rest of what Locke says in this chapter goes better with the view that it is necessary *de re* of persons that they are beings that satisfy his definition, that is, are thinking, intelligent beings, etc. And that, suitably qualified, seems to me an intuitively plausible view.

But it is plausible that persons, at least persons of our sort, are also essentially subjects of physical properties. What, given this, makes having mental properties more central to their nature than having physical properties? Of course, most physical properties are not thick properties in my sense. We have already seen that there is a case for saying that mental properties are thick properties. And I think it will strengthen the case for this if we can show that when physical properties belong to a person they do so in virtue of how their instances are related to instances of mental properties belonging to the person. This, if it is the case, shows that while persons of our sort are essentially subjects of physical properties, they are in the first instance subjects of mental properties.

Assuming physicalism, as I am doing, mental properties are physically realized. A subject of mental properties will at least have properties that are physical realizers of those mental properties. There is of course a good sense in which one has the mental properties because one has their physical realizers. But if we ask what makes a particular physical realizer a property of a particular person, the answer seems to be that it belongs to that person because it is a realizer of a mental property of that person. This gives us a sense in which one has the physical property in virtue of having the mental property. But by itself this doesn't get us very far, for these realizer properties, which will be complex neural properties of whose nature we are largely ignorant, are of course not the physical properties we ascribe to persons in everyday discourse—properties like height, weight, a certain complexion, etc.

It is natural to speak of the latter properties as properties of the person's body, and it might seem that if we can explain what it is for a person to have a body we will thereby have explained how it is that the person has the properties of that body. There is a natural account of what it is for a subject of mental properties to have a particular body as its body. Something is the body of a certain subject in virtue of there being an intimate relation between physical goings-on in the body and mental states of the person. Perceptual states of the person are caused by inputs to the sense organs of the body, movements of the body are caused by volitional states of the person, and sensations of the person are caused by states of the body and are felt as located in the body. If a person is related in these ways to a body, that body is the body of that person (see Shoemaker 1976). But to say this much is not yet to explain how it is that the person can be said to have the properties of the body. If a person's body has a certain weight, the person will certainly have the relational property of having a body with that weight. And perhaps on a Cartesian view, or on the view that we are brains, our ascriptions of height and weight to ourselves have to be understood as the ascriptions of such relational properties. Cartesian souls and brains cannot have among their intrinsic properties the heights and weights that bodies have, but they can have such relational properties. On such views, the same *predicates* can be true of a person and her body, but the *properties* ascribed are different; those ascribed to the body are intrinsic, while those ascribed to the person are relational. But intuitively, and contrary to the view that we are souls or brains, height and weight are intrinsic properties of persons, not relational ones. How can the subject of mental properties have these?

Part of the answer comes from considerations about action. One's body is essentially involved in one's actions. Its mass contributes to determining the consequences of one's actions, and the performance of actions of a given sort constitutively involves changes in the spatial properties of one's body. If one performs an action, and what performs it must have mass and spatial properties, then one must oneself have mass and spatial properties. And if one has these, one must have other bodily properties whose instances are synchronically unified with instances of them.

I mentioned earlier the view, which a Cartesian account would seem to be committed to, that the only way a person, qua subject of mental properties, can satisfy physical predicates is by having relational properties of a certain sort. Could it be held that the property of performing a certain action is really a relational property that one has in virtue of having a body that is behaving in certain ways as the result of one's volitions? Perhaps that is what a Cartesian should hold. But if my volitional states, along with my other mental states, are physically realized, then instances of their realizers will stand in relations of synchronic unity to instances of other bodily properties, including the property of having a muscular and nervous system capable of implementing the actions produced by those volitional states, and these in turn will stand in relations of synchronic unity to instances of properties like mass and shape.

But in order to defend the view that persons are in the first instance subjects of mental properties it is not really necessary to establish that physical predicates that are true of persons ascribe intrinsic physical properties to them rather than relational properties. It is enough to show that physical predicates are true of a person in virtue of the person's being in physical states that are related in certain ways to the mental states of the person, and that will be true whether or not the predicates turn out to be relational. It will be true in virtue of the points I have mentioned that some physical properties belong to a person in virtue of being realizers of the person's mental states, and that a body belongs to a person, and its states are parts of the truth-makers for the application of physical predicates to the person, in virtue of its relation to the mental states of the person.

In any case, it is arguable that in one way or another physical predicates are true of a person in virtue of relations of instances of physical properties to that person's mental properties. But if mental properties are primary, it is to be expected that features of the causal profiles of mental properties that pertain to diachronic unity will play a central role in determining the persistence conditions, or identity conditions, of persons. And this coheres with the widespread intuition that in the hypothetical case of a cerebrum transplant, where the cerebrum is the carrier of psychological continuity, the person goes with the cerebrum and the person acquires a different body. Of course, the recipient body's becoming the body of that person will consist in its coming to stand to it in the relations I earlier said determine body ownership—it will become the body whose sensory inputs cause the person's perceptual and sensory states, and whose behavior is the product of the person's volitional states.

Here I should clarify what I think the neo-Lockean view should say about the hypothetical cerebrum transplant case. So far I have spoken as if the neo-Lockean, the psychological theorist about personal identity, is committed to the view that cerebrum transplants and the like could be person-preserving. But what the neo-Lockean is committed to holding is really something weaker than this. The commitment is to a *conditional* proposition: that *if* a cerebrum transplant were to result in full psychological continuity between donor and recipient, it would result in a person's coming to have a different body. And it is this conditional proposition that animalists deny. In discussion of this issue it is usually assumed on both sides that if the recipient of a cerebrum transplant had any psychology at all, it would be one continuous with that of the donor—that the recipient would have seeming memories of the donor's past, would inherit her beliefs, desires, and intentions, would have her personality and character traits, and so on. But while this seems plausible, it is not guaranteed a priori that it is true. It could be that, contrary to what is usually assumed, much more of a person's body than the cerebrum is involved in grounding the person's psychology. It might even be that the physical realizations of the person's mental states are distributed throughout the person's body in such a way that there is no proper part of the body which could be transplanted to a different body in such a way as to result in full psychological continuity between donor and recipient. I don't think this is true, but it is compatible with the neo-Lockean view that this should be true. For its truth is compatible with the truth of the conditional that, if the transplant of the cerebrum were to result in full psychological continuity, the person would go with the cerebrum. The truth of that conditional is all the neo-Lockean needs, and that conditional could be true even if its antecedent is always false. About the possible case in which the physical realizers of a creature's psychological states are distributed throughout the body, the neo-Lockean will say that while in that case the identity of the biological animal is sufficient for the identity of the person, this is because in that case biological continuity is sufficient for psychological continuity, it being the psychological continuity that constitutes the persistence of the person.

VII

As I have already mentioned in passing, proponents of the animalist view of personal identity reject the claim that persons are essentially subjects of mental properties. They can allow that being a subject of mental properties belongs to the 'nominal essence' of persons, but they hold that being a person is a 'phase sortal', not a 'substance sortal', and that what is a person at one time can cease to be a person without ceasing to exist. So, on this view, what is a person can lose all of its mental properties, and even the capacity for having mental properties, and continue to exist as a 'human vegetable'. They also hold that what is a person can begin its existence as a non-person, namely in the fetal stage where there is no psychology. This of course challenges the view that the things that are persons, for example, ourselves, are in the first instance subjects of mental properties. We need to look at what animalists say against the psychological view.

If a person's body can continue to exist after the person's death, the person is arguably not identical with that body, even on the animalist view. But on the psychological view the person is also not identical with the biological animal constituted by that body. If the cerebrum of a person is transplanted to a different body, in such a way that the recipient is psychologically continuous with the original person, the psychological view says that the person goes with the cerebrum. But it seems out of the question that the biological animal goes with the cerebrum. If the soul or cerebrum of Locke's prince is transferred to the body of his cobbler, that doesn't make the resulting cobbler-body person the same *animal* as the former prince—which is probably why Locke said, implausibly, that he is not the same *man* as the prince, although he is the same person.[4] Persons of our sort are human beings, and it seems a truism that human beings are a kind of animal. One

---

[4] Locke 1975: 340. Locke thought that the word 'man', unlike the word 'person', refers to a kind of animal.

objection to the psychological view is that it seems to involve the denial of that truism. It also seems to involve the denial of Eric Olson's truism that animals can think.

But we need to ask what these truisms are. If we take biological animals to be creatures having biological persistence conditions, then it seems clearly correct to deny that in the cerebrum transplant case the biological animal goes with the cerebrum. But it is not clear that the truism that persons are animals should be equated with the claim that persons are biological animals in this sense. Unquestionably, wherever there is a human being there is a biological animal in this sense, just as wherever there is a human being there is a human body. But just as we can say that the body is not identical with the human being, but only coincident with it, it is open to us to say that the biological animal is not identical with the human being, but only coincident with it. To combine this with allowing that it is a truism that human beings are animals, we must hold that 'animal' has a sense other than 'biological animal'. And I think this is plausible. It is questionable, to say the least, whether ordinary folk, in using the term 'animal', intend to be referring to things with biological persistence conditions; very likely, any ideas they have about the persistence conditions of the things referred to are extremely vague.[5] What they are referring to are certainly things whose existence is constituted by the existence of biological animals. But it is compatible with this that animals in this sense are not identical with the biological animals that constitute them—just as, on the psychological view, persons are not identical with the biological animals that constitute them, and just as, on both the psychological view and the animalist view, persons and animals are not identical with the bodies that constitute them. It is with animals in this sense that persons can be identified. And animals in this sense can certainly think. This reply will of course not satisfy those who question the coherence of supposing that numerically different things can coincide and share their matter. I will discuss doubts about this later on.

A similar reply can be made to another difficulty. I have claimed that mental properties of persons are thick properties whose causal profiles determine their persistence conditions. But biological properties are thick properties of biological animals whose causal profiles determine their persistence conditions. And persons have both mental properties and biological properties. But this seems to imply that persons have both psychological persistence conditions and biological persistence conditions, which should imply the absurd consequence that in a cerebrum transplant the person should both go with the cerebrum and stay behind as a human vegetable. Now it is compatible with the neo-Lockean view that some

---

[5] It might be suggested that ordinary speakers defer to experts in their use of terms, and that here utterances by ordinary speakers containing 'animal' might have biological truth conditions of which those speakers are ignorant. This might be so if 'animal' were a term whose original home was in scientific discourse and which has migrated into ordinary discourse. But that is not the case.

biological properties are essential to persons, or at any rate persons of our kind. These would include the property of being a mammal and the property of being a vertebrate. There is no danger of these being lost in a person-preserving cerebrum transplant. Where there may seem to be a problem is in the case of biological properties that can be acquired and lost. Many predicates ascribing biological properties of this kind that are applicable to biological animals are also applicable to persons. But it is compatible with this that the properties ascribed with these predicates are somewhat different in the two sorts of applications. The properties are different because their causal profiles are slightly different. The biological animal can be described as anemic and immune to smallpox, and so can the person. But if the person's cerebrum is transplanted to a different body the person may lose the properties of being anemic and being immune to smallpox (perhaps the recipient body was never vaccinated), while the human vegetable that is left behind will retain them. This reflects a difference in the causal profiles of the non-essential biological properties of persons and the biological properties of biological animals that have the same names, a difference that makes these different properties. We can say that such biological properties of biological animals are thick properties while those of persons are not.

But my reply to the objection that the psychological view denies the truism that persons are animals leaves part of the animalist objection untouched. It allows us to say that there is a sense of 'animal' in which we are animals, and so a sense in which animals can think. But it doesn't allow us to say that we are biological animals, and it implies that either biological animals cannot think or there are always at least two thinkers where there should be only one. The animalist claim that it is a truism that biological animals can think loses force if it is allowed that there is a sense of 'animal' in which animals can think and in which it does not refer to biological animals. But there is a prima facie plausible argument that the psychological view is committed to holding that biological animals can think—more generally, that they have whatever psychological properties persons have. The psychological view holds that persons coincide with biological animals, and share their matter. It seems to follow from this that a biological animal has whatever physical properties the coincident person has. Assuming physicalism, and the supervenience of psychological properties on physical ones, it should follow that the biological animal has whatever psychological properties the person has. On the Lockean definition of *person*, this should imply that the biological animal is a person, which contradicts the psychological view, given that the persistence conditions of biological animals are biological rather than psychological. But it is bad enough if the view has the consequence that every person shares its space with a psychological duplicate. This is what I have elsewhere called the 'too many minds' objection (Shoemaker 1999).

There is an *ad hominem* response to this objection if it is offered in support of animalism. Even the animalist must allow, it can be argued, that the person, held by him to be a biological animal, is not identical with, but only coincident with, the person's body. For the body can survive death, as a corpse, while the biological animal can't. But if that is so, the same argument will show that the body, sharing the physical properties of the person/biological animal, must share as well its mental properties. And this has the unacceptable consequence that there are too many minds and too many persons. Animalists try to avoid this argument by denying that there is any genuine persisting entity distinct from a person that is referred to by expressions like 'Jones' body' (see Olson 1997: e.g. 150). But it is hard to deny that if we see a scar or tattoo on someone's corpse we can say that it is the result of something that happened to *it*, that same body, at some time prior to the person's death. And it is not open to the animalist to say that the corpse *is* the biological animal, and so the person, given that the life processes that constitute the identity of the biological animal ceased when it became a corpse.

But we need more than an *ad hominem* reply to the too many minds argument. We need to explain how we can avoid the conclusion that the biological animal that shares a person's matter, and also the body that shares this matter, are themselves subjects of mental states, and are themselves persons. Fortunately we already have available a distinction that enables us to do this. This is the distinction, drawn earlier, between thick and thin properties. The too many minds argument goes wrong in assuming that coincident entities must share all of their physical properties. What is true is that they must share all of their physical thin properties. But it is not thin properties that determine the mental properties of the subject. It is not the thin properties on which the mental properties of a person supervene, and it is not the thin properties that realize mental properties. The physical properties on which mental properties supervene, and are their realizers, are thick properties, and these belong only to the person, not to the coincident biological animal and human body.

The thickness and thinness are thickness and thinness of causal profile. The causal profiles of thick properties are richer than the causal profiles of thin properties, and their additional richness has to do with what sorts of successor states their instantiation causes or contributes to causing. Thin properties have some such features, but the ones they have are not specific to particular kinds of things. Take the property of having a certain mass. It is a consequence of something's having this property that as long as it has it the application of certain forces will cause a certain amount of acceleration. This will be true of things of very different sorts that have that mass, and it will be true equally of a person, the person's body, and the biological animal that is coincident with the person. Contrast this with a mental property like having a certain belief. Here the causal features of the property that have to do with producing or contributing to producing successor states are specific to particular kinds of things, namely subjects of mental properties. And the diachronic unity relations that obtain in virtue of exercises of these features are constitutive of the persistence through time of things of that kind, in a way those that are conferred by the causal features of thin properties are not.

I said above that it is not the thin properties of a subject that determine its mental properties. This is not to deny that the distribution of thin properties in the world determines the distribution of mental properties. That there are instantiated where I am the thin properties I share with my body and my coincident biological animal determines that there are instantiated here psychological properties of the sort I have. The instantiation of these determines that there is *something* here having those psychological properties; but their instantiation in a particular thing does not determine that *it* is that something, as is evident from the fact that there are three things here that instantiate them and only one thing that has the psychological properties. In determining the distribution of mental properties the distribution of thin properties in the world also determines the distribution of thick physical properties that are realizers of mental properties; but, again, the instantiation of thin properties in a particular thing does not determine that it is the subject of any particular thick properties. (How it is that the distribution of thin properties in the world determines the distribution of thick properties will be discussed in the next section.)

VIII

My account assumes that there can be coincident entities, numerically different things that occupy the same space and are composed of the same matter. In particular, it assumes that persons, their bodies, and their biological animals are such coincident entities. Many philosophers find the idea that there can be coincident entities implausible or worse. In this section I will first show that the possibility of coincident entities is a natural consequence of a physicalist view about how properties of macroscopic things are realized, and then show how we can answer one sort of objection that is raised against the possibility of coincident entities.

Assuming physicalism, instances of properties of macroscopic things are realized in microphysical states of affairs. These states of affairs consist in micro-entities being propertied and related in certain ways. A microphysical state of affairs will realize a property 'instance' in virtue of being of a type having a causal profile that matches in a certain way the causal profile of the instantiated property. The career of a macroscopic thing will consist in a series of synchronically and diachronically unified property instances, and so will be constituted by a series of synchronically and diachronically unified microphysical states of affairs that realize these instances. But the same micro-entities can be involved in the realization of different property instances in virtue of different ways in which they are propertied and related. So there can be two or more series of property instances which are such that at each moment of time it is the very same micro-entities that are involved in the realization of the property instance occurring in those series at that time. And there is no reason why the property instances in each of these series cannot be synchronically and diachronically unified. In other words, there is no reason why the different series cannot be different careers, and so careers of different macroscopic objects that are composed at each moment of time of the same micro-entities.

This explains how it is that the distribution of thin properties in the world determines the distribution of thick properties. Corresponding to any microphysical state of affairs there will be a property, a thin property, that something has at a time just in case it is composed of micro-entities so configured as to constitute a state of affairs of that sort. So the totality of thin property instantiations determines the totality of microphysical states of affairs. But some of these microphysical states of affairs will be realizers of thick properties—states of affairs whose existence entails the existence of a thick property of some sort.

I said that the same micro-entities can occur in the micro-realizations of the property instances that make up the careers of different but coincident entities. It is also true that the same microphysical state of affairs will occur in careers of different coincident entities. These will realize instances of what I call thin 'MSE properties' (microphysical states of affairs embedding properties), that are possessed by a thing simply in virtue of the fact that some of its constituent micro-entities are configured in a way that constitutes the existence of a certain state of affairs. But in some cases the shared state of affairs will realize an instance of a certain thick property in one of the coincident entities, but not in the other. Consider the microphysical state of affairs that realizes in me an instance of a mental property, say thinking of Vienna. This microphysical state of affairs will also occur in the career of my body and in the career of the biological animal I am coincident with, but in them it does not realize such a mental property instance; though it does realize an instance of a thin property that also occurs in me.

How is it that the occurrence of a state of affairs that is a thick property realizer in one thing can bestow on that thing an instance of the thick property while its simultaneous occurrence in a coincident thing bestows a thin property on that thing but does not bestow that thick property on it? The answer is that it realizes a thick property instance if it is embedded in a certain way in a career of a certain sort, and so bestows a thick property instance on a particular thing only if the thing has a career of that sort. Letting SA be our state of affairs and TP the thick property instance it realizes, the career must be one in which the causal relations of SA to other states of affairs that are realizers of property instances in that career match the causal relations TP has to those other property instances—the causal relations that constitute its synchronic and diachronic unity with them. SA will stand in these causal relations in virtue of the nature of its causal profile, and it is this that will make it a realizer of TP. If the state of affairs SA is a realizer of an instance of TP it will have to be embedded in this way in some career of this sort, but it may also occur in careers that are not of this sort, and in these it does not bestow TP, although it does bestow a thin property that is shared by the possessor of TP.

Now let's consider an objection to the idea that there can be coincident objects—an objection of a kind that is often raised. An often discussed putative case of coincidence involves a statue and the piece of clay that constitutes it. Arguably these are not identical, since the piece of clay may have existed before the statue did and may survive its destruction, and the statue could survive the replacement of some of its parts while the piece of clay could not. One objection raised against the idea of coincidence is that counting the statue and the piece of clay as different things has the embarrassing consequence that if a fifty pound statue falls and breaks my foot, the breaking of my foot is due to the impact on it of *two* fifty pound objects, one being the statue and the other being the piece of clay. Doesn't that mean that a hundred pounds of force were exerted on my foot? And isn't that clearly false?

I noted above that different instances of thin properties in coincident objects can have the same microphysical state of affairs as a realizer. Because property instances are individuated in part by their possessors, the instance of weighing fifty pounds that occurs in the statue is different from the instance of weighing fifty pounds that occurs in the piece of clay. But property instances cause what they do in virtue of their microphysical realizers causing what they do; and, weight being a thin property, the microphysical realizers of these property instances are identical. One and the same microphysical state of affairs realizes the statue's weighing fifty pounds and the piece of clay's weighing fifty pounds. That is why the force exerted on my foot is fifty pounds rather than a hundred pounds, even though two fifty pound objects fall on it.

IX

But there is still a version of the thinking animal objection to the psychological view that needs to be considered. Persons are not the only creatures that think—or at any rate, that have mental states. It is generally thought that chimpanzees, dolphins, and dogs, among other species, have mental states of various sorts. These creatures are certainly animals. And if they are biological animals, their existence contradicts the thesis that biological animals cannot think.

We do not have for creatures of other species names and concepts that have the close connection with mentality that the word 'person' and its associated concept have. There is no word for dogs that has a definition similar to Locke's definition of 'person', one that would lead one to expect a psychological account of their persistence conditions. Still, brain transplants involving such creatures are imaginable. And the conditional proposition that neo-Lockeans are committed to in the case of persons, namely that if such a transplant resulted in full psychological continuity between donor and recipient the transfer would be mental-subject-preserving, seems plausible here as well. If a dog's brain is transplanted into a different canine body, and the recipient, after recovering from the operation, recognizes the owners of the original dog and fawns on them just as that dog did, knows its way around their house and neighborhood, knows the tricks they taught the donor dog, digs for bones where the donor buried them, etc., it would be hard to deny that it is the old dog in a new body. If we accept this, we can say that dogs are animals, in the same sense persons are, but can deny that their persistence conditions are biological rather than psychological, and so can deny that they are biological animals. Dogs, like persons, will coincide with biological animals, and will be constituted by them, but they will not be identical with them. The same will go for chimpanzees, dolphins, and the rest. If this seems hard to swallow, we should remember that 'biological animal' is a term of art, and that all that common sense is committed to is that these creatures are animals, which is not here being denied.

X

My answer to the question of what we are is in part that we are creatures having certain kinds of mental properties as the thick properties whose causal profiles determine their persistence conditions. But what distinguishes us from other sorts of persons, if there are such, is that we are constituted by biological animals—so my account is a version of what Eric Olson calls constitutionism. Olson's chief objection to constitutionism is that it denies that animals can think, holding that thinking occurs only in creatures constituted by animals. My response to this is twofold. First, there is a legitimate sense of 'animal' such that we are animals in that sense and, therefore, animals in that sense can think. Second, while the account denies that biologically individuated animals can think, it holds that the careers of such animals contain the states of affairs that realize thoughts—it is just that the thoughts they realize occur in the persons they constitute rather than in the biological animals themselves.

REFERENCES

JOHNSON, W. E. (1964). *Logic, Part III, The Logical Foundations of Science* (New York: Dover).

LOCKE, J. (1975/1689). *An Essay Concerning Human Understanding*, ed. P. H. Nidditch (Oxford: Oxford University Press).

OLSON, D. (1997). *The Human Animal* (Oxford: Oxford University Press).

——(2007). *What are We?* (Oxford: Oxford University Press).

SHOEMAKER, S. (1976). 'Embodiment and Behavior', in A. Rorty (ed.), *The Identities of Persons* (Berkeley and Los Angeles: University of California Press), 109–37.

——(1979). 'Identity, Properties and Causality', *Midwest Studies in Philosophy*, 4: 321–42.

——(1999). 'Self, Body and Coincidence', *Aristotelian Society Supplementary Volume*, 72: 287–306.

——(2007). *Physical Realization* (Oxford: Oxford University Press).

CHAPTER 16

ON KNOWING
ONE'S SELF

JOHN PERRY

1. INTRODUCTION

I believe that I live in Palo Alto—a rather dull case of self-belief.[1] But what do I believe, when I believe *that*? It seems the content of my belief should be just what has to be the case, for it to be true. My belief is true, if and only if a certain person, John Perry, lives in Palo Alto. So that must be what I believe. If so, it is the same thing I believe when I believe that John Perry lives in Palo Alto. But are these beliefs really the same?

It seems I might believe that John Perry lives in Palo Alto, without believing that I do. In a few years, when I am even more senile than I am now, I may wander off, forgetting my name and where I live. Finding his driver's license with a Palo Alto address, I may be quite sure that John Perry lives in Palo Alto. But that really isn't *self*-knowledge, only knowledge about the person I happen to be. I might wonder if I live there too, but think it doubtful. It seems that what I would be doubtful of, that I live in Palo Alto, is one thing and what I would be sure of, that John Perry lives there, is another.

---

[1] 'Self-knowledge' is a common and rather mellifluous phrase, usually thought to stand for a virtue; none of this can be said for 'self-belief'. But this chapter is mainly about self-belief; not much attention is paid to what makes some of it knowledge.

In this case, would it be correct to say 'John Perry believes that he lives in Palo Alto'? According to Hector-Neri Castañeda, it depends on whether 'he' is functioning simply as an anaphoric pronoun, picking up the reference of the subject term, or instead as what he calls a 'quasi-indicator' (Castañeda 1969/1994). If the first, the report would be true. But if 'he' is functioning as a quasi-indicator, the report would be false. It would require something more of the belief than simply that it is about the subject. It would describe the sort of case where the subject would use the first person to express the belief, and so it would not describe the case we are imagining.

There appears to be more to self-belief than having a belief about the person one happens to be. I can believe, or imagine, or hypothesize, that John Perry lives in Palo Alto without believing, imagining, or hypothesizing that I live there. What is the difference?

2. FREGE

We seem to have here a special case of Frege's problem about identity (1892). Where A and B are different singular terms, 'A = A' seems to have quite different 'cognitive significance' than 'A = B' even if 'A = B' is true. The problem is not restricted to identity statements. Given the identity, any two statements 'A is so and so' and 'B is so and so' will predicate the same condition of the same object. But they may not have the same cognitive significance.

The experiences that lead to the beliefs expressed by the statements may differ. I may learn that Tully was a Roman senator by reading texts that contain the name 'Tully', without learning that Cicero was a Roman senator. Even if I believe that Tully was a Roman senator and I also believe that Cicero was a Roman senator, the beliefs themselves may be different. I can acquire them at different times, from different sources. They may be altered or extinguished independently. And the different beliefs motivate different actions, most clearly what I infer and what I say. In the imagined situation, my belief that Tully was a Roman senator explains why I write 'true' next to '*True or False*: Tully was a Roman orator' on my mid-term, inferring from my belief that he was a senator that he was probably an orator. In all of these ways, the statement 'John Perry lives in Palo Alto' might have a different cognitive significance for the senile me than 'I live in Palo Alto'.

When late in Frege's career his attention turned to indexicals and particularly the word 'I', he said, 'Now everyone is presented to himself in a particular and primitive way, in which he is presented to no one else' (1918/1967: 25–6). One way to read Frege's remark is to suppose that for each person there is a primitive property ψ, both uniquely instantiated by that person and unobservable to anyone else, and by 'I' the person means 'the ψ'. Something like this reading may be required to make Frege's treatment of 'I' fit into his general theory of sense, modes of presentation, and reference. But it isn't very plausible to suppose that for each person there is such a private property that only that person instantiates, and that he associates with 'I' (Perry 2000: ch. 1).

The remark is more plausible if we reverse the quantifiers: there is a particular and primitive way of being presented to a person, in which each person is presented to himself but to no one else. Or perhaps: there are methods of knowing facts about a person that are available to every person, and are, for any given person, methods of picking up information about that very person, but not ways for that person to learn about anyone else. This seems quite plausible. There is a method for knowing whether one has a headache, the same method for each of us, that won't work to find out if anyone else has a headache. There is a way of finding out whether one is hungry that won't work to find out if anyone else is hungry. There is a way to find out if one needs to go to the bathroom that won't work to find out if anyone else needs to go to the bathroom. There are ways of finding out what we feel, and believe, and worry about that we each can use to find out about ourselves, but not about others. These are not always more reliable than other methods. Parents are often better at knowing when their two-year-olds need to go the bathroom than the two-year-olds. There may be vexed issues about what is going on when we apply these methods, and the word 'methods' may have misleading connotations, but something along these lines seems beyond doubt. We all use these same methods to find out things about ourselves, but can't use them to find out about others. I'll call these *self-informative* ways or methods of knowing. So we might interpret Frege's idea as coming to this: we are each uniquely presented to ourselves and to no one else *as* the person we find out about with self-informative methods.

Still it seems a bit odd to say in many such cases that *we* are *presented* to ourselves at all. As Wittgenstein notes in *The Blue and Brown Books*: 'there is no question of recognizing a person when I say I have a tooth-ache. To ask, "are you sure it is *you* who have pains?" would be nonsensical' (1958: 66–7). When you see that someone *else* has a toothache that person is presented to you; you see a certain person, perhaps rubbing their gums and complaining, 'My tooth hurts'. The person is presented to you in perception; the toothache is not presented but inferred. What is characteristic about one's own case is that the owner isn't really presented at all—just the toothache.

3. IMMUNITY

In 'Self-Reference and Self-Awareness' Sydney Shoemaker begins by considering Wittgenstein's remark. He develops Wittgenstein's point with the concept of *immunity to error through misidentification relative to the first person pronoun* (1968/1994). If, while wrestling, I perceive a bloody foot and think 'I am bleeding', I may be wrong, because although someone is bleeding, the someone is not me. In contrast, if I see a canary, and, on the basis of visual experience say 'I see a canary', it cannot turn out that I was right that someone was seeing a canary but wrong that it was me doing the seeing. In the bleeding case we don't have first-person immunity, in the seeing case we do.

Shoemaker and Anscombe (1975/1994) both suggested the problem we are considering might provide philosophers grounds for thinking that when a person thinks or asserts 'I am so and so', the word 'I' doesn't refer to the person himself or herself, but a closely related object, a Cartesian Ego—a conclusion they both reject. Anscombe, but not Shoemaker, thinks the only way to avoid this conclusion is to give up the whole idea we refer with 'I'. Like Shoemaker, she holds that in cases where we have first-person immunity, we are aware of an occurrence of some property F in a special way that does not require identification or recognition of the possessor of the property, and entitles us to say, 'I am F'. If 'I' refers, then we will have referred to ourselves. But she maintains that we should not say that 'I' refers at all. Her thinking echoes Lichtenberg's criticism of Descartes: 'We should say *it thinks*, just as we say *it lightens*. To say cogito is already to say too much as soon as we translate it I think. To assume, to postulate the I is a practical requirement' (Lichtenberg 2000: notebook K #18, p. 190.)

If I have a toothache, not in the throes of Cartesian doubt, but while communicating with others, it seems worthwhile to note, as a 'practical requirement', that I know of the toothache directly, not in the way that I learn of the toothaches of others. Perhaps this is all that 'I' really does; it connotes an absence rather than referring to a presence. If we take this line, Anscombe argues, we can avoid an argument for Cartesian egos based on the special features of the first-person pronoun.

Anscombe reconstructs Cartesians as being impressed by two things about the first person. The first is that when I say or think 'I', I can be sure that what I refer to exists, but I may not be in a position to know that any person in the ordinary sense, a flesh and blood being, exists. Descartes was sure that when he thought 'I exist' that he was referring to something, although he wasn't sure, at least according to Anscombe, that the person Descartes existed. The second is that when I say 'I', I am immune to referring to some being other than the one I intended to refer to. The seductive idea is that Cartesian Egos are the sorts of things with respect to which one wouldn't need to have either of these worries. Since we don't have them when we say 'I', we must be referring to Egos. Anscombe thinks that the only way to avoid the Cartesian conclusion is to give up the idea that 'I' refers, but that seems like a rather heavy price to pay; it is, as Evans says, 'an extraordinary conclusion' (Evans 1982/1994: 190n.).

But Cartesian Egos wouldn't solve our problem about 'I'. Suppose we each have a Cartesian Ego, and when each person uses 'I' that use refers to his or her own Cartesian Ego. Still, it seems that if there are Cartesian Egos, they can be named. Call mine 'JP'. If one can forget one's own name, one can also forget the name of one's Cartesian Ego. If I find a copy of this chapter, after turning senile, I may read it and learn that there once was a fellow named 'John Perry', the author of the chapter, who named his Cartesian Ego 'JP'. If my use of 'I' refers to my Cartesian Ego, then my statements ''I am JP', 'I am I', and 'JP is JP' would all be true. But I might be as certain as that 'I am I' and 'JP is JP' are true, but be quite convinced that 'I am JP' is false. The problem about the difference between 'I am I' and 'I am JP' isn't affected by whether we take ourselves to be referring with 'I' and 'JP' to Cartesian Egos, or to a quite ordinary persons. The problem appears to be with the difference in ways of referring, not in the nature of what is referred to.

In one clear sense, I *can* be wrong about the reference of my use of 'I', whether 'I' refers to me or to my ego. Suppose that in my senility, I not only forget that I am John Perry, but come to believe that I am John Searle: years of admiration morph into delusion. I may then think I am referring to John Searle when I say, 'I live in Berkeley': I think that I am referring to John Searle *by* referring to myself. The move to egos makes no difference. Call John Searle's Cartesian Ego 'JS'. I may think that I am referring to JS *by* referring, with 'I', to my own Cartesian Ego. Since Cartesian Egos do not eliminate our problems, our problems do not motivate the postulations of Cartesian Egos.

Anscombe thinks that our paradigms of reference, proper names and demonstratives do not provide the guarantee of existence and the immunity from misidentification that 'I' does, and so that the whole idea that 'I' refers is fishy. Shoemaker argues more plausibly that we simply need to appreciate that 'I' refers in a different way, putting different cognitive demands on the user, than do descriptions, names, or even demonstratives. With 'I' there is no issue of identifying the thing designated as meeting certain further criteria.

With demonstratives there is a sort of immunity. I might refer to a cup I see and hold in my hand as 'this cup'. If I am not thinking of it as some cup I have previously encountered, or the cup that someone else has asked about, but simply as the cup I see and hold at that moment, there is no issue of being wrong about *which* cup I refer to. Still, there may be other candidate cups around. The words 'this' or 'that' permit us to refer to different salient cups, depending on our intention. But if I am using 'I' with its ordinary meaning, there is no additional intention that is needed or can make any difference: I refer to myself.[2]

---

[2] For a discussion of the role of intentions with demonstratives; see Perry (2009*a*).

Evans notes that on these issues there is a closer fit with other indexicals—'here' for example, and especially 'now' and 'today'—than with descriptions, names, or demonstratives (Evans 1982/1992). Just as there is immunity to misidentification of persons relative to 'I' there is also immunity to misidentification of times relative to the word 'now' or 'today'. Suppose the time of my hunger pangs and of my utterance is July 4. Still, 'I am hungry *on July 4*' is not immune to error in the way that 'I am *now* hungry' and 'I am hungry *today*' are. I *might* be wrong about what day it was, and think that my hunger was occurring on July 4 when it was really occurring on July 3. The phenomenon of hunger presents itself in a certain way; when it does so, I can be sure that the 'owner' of the hunger is *me*, and the time of the hunger is *now*; but neither the owner nor the time seem to present themselves as further objects.

This suggests that the nature of the immunity that attaches to 'I', 'now', and 'today' has to do with what they have in common in the *way* they refer.

Indexicals differ from names and descriptions in that they are associated, by their meanings, with what I shall call *utterance-relative roles*. The object that occupies the role, relative to a given utterance of an indexical, is the object to which the indexical refers; unlike the case of demonstratives, a further intention, beyond using language in the normal way, is not required.[3] An utterance of 'I' refers to the *speaker* of the utterance; an utterance of 'now' refers to the *time* of the utterance; an utterance of 'here' designates the *place* of the utterance. Indexicals are assigned to roles, because the rule of reference that governs them is *reflexive*. An utterance of the word 'I' refers to the speaker of *that very utterance*. An utterance of the word 'now' refers to the time of *that very utterance*. In contrast, the rule of reference for a name is not relative to the utterance, at least on most theories. Rather than an utterance-relative role for the referent to play, a property for the referent to have, independently of any particular utterance of it, seems assigned to the name as its meaning. On a popular theory, the rule of reference is something like this: an utterance of the name 'N' refers to the object to which 'N' has been assigned by convention. Descriptions, at least those that do not themselves include indexicals or demonstratives as components, are also not utterance-reflexive: an utterance of 'the ψ' denotes x, if x is the unique object that has the property assigned by the lexical and compositional rules of the language to ψ.

Can the utterance-reflexivity of 'I' shed light on our problem? Anscombe thought not: 'we are inclined to think that "It's the word each one uses in speaking of himself" explains what "I" names, or explains "I" as a "referring expression". It cannot do so if "He speaks of himself" is compatible with ignorance, and we are

---

[3] I actually believe things are somewhat more complicated, so that intentions can play some role with respect to 'now' and 'here', in determining the extent of time or space referred to. If we reflect on time-zones and long-distance calls, we can even find role for intentions to play with 'today'. See Perry (2009*b*: ch. 4).

using the reflexive pronoun, in both cases, in the ordinary way' (142). To use the reflexive pronoun 'himself' in the ordinary way is to mean no more than this:

(I) For each *x*, when *x* uses 'I', *x* refers to *x*.

The other way of using 'himself' is as a quasi-indicator. Then the rule requires more than that the user and the person referred to are one and the same, more than (I) does. It would require that the user is thinking of himself in the way appropriate for using 'I'. But, so conceived, the rule only gets at the meaning of 'I' in a circular way.

Pace Anscombe, I do think this simple rule (I), and in particular its reflexive nature, does explain what is special about the first person, why it is apt for expressing self-beliefs, and provides a clue to the difference between self-beliefs and beliefs merely about the person one happens to be. The key point is that the rule assigns a role to the word, and roles play a central role in thought and action that self-reference and self-belief require us to recognize.

4. ROLES

Consider 'today'. The rule of reference for 'today' is more or less this: an utterance of 'today' refers to the day on which the utterance was made. The conditions for being the referent of an utterance of 'today' are 'utterance-bound'. The day has to stand in a certain relation to the utterance, to play a certain role *vis-à-vis* the utterance. In contrast, the reference-conditions provided by 'July 19, 2009' are not utterance-bound. Whether an utterance of those words occurs before that date, or on that date, or after that date makes no difference. Whenever the utterance occurs, it refers to the nineteenth day of the seventh month of the ninth year of the third millennium.

Now consider the methods we have for finding out about the current day—that is the day we will refer if we say, 'today'. 'If you want to know whether the sun is shining on a given day, look into the sky. If you want to know whether it is raining, look out the window.' These methods are not *utterance*-bound, for one can learn a lot using them without uttering anything. But they are *inquiry*-bound. They are methods for knowing about the day on which the inquiry is conducted. Adapting a slightly modified version of Frege's formula, we can say that there is a way information about each day is presented to us, on that day, a way in which information about that day never was presented to us before, and never will be again.

Other methods of inquiry are not inquiry-bound, or, more carefully, less inquiry-bound. Once July 19th is in the past, one can no longer find out about it by looking at the sky or out the window. But you can look at your diary, or go the library and find the *New York Times* for that day and find out a lot about it.

I will say that a method of reference, or a method of finding out about an object, is *role-based* if the object referred to, or the object about which information is obtained by using that method is one that plays a certain role *vis-à-vis* the act of reference or act of inquiry. I'll say that such methods are *property*-based, if the object is determined by some property that it has or lacks independently of the act of reference or inquiry. So, at least arguably, proper names, definite descriptions that are free of indexicals and demonstratives, and dates give us methods of reference that are property-based rather than role-based.[4]

Role-based methods of reference and inquiry belong to a wider class of role-based ways of acting. When we move our limbs or body so as to have a direct effect on an object, *which* object we have an effect on will be determined by the relation it stands in to us. There is a certain way of picking up a cup of coffee that is a way of picking up the cup of coffee in front of us. It will work for any person, and any cup of coffee, as long as that cup of coffee is in the right relation to—plays the right role in the life of—the person at the time of action. And of course there are ways of finding out about the cup that are similarly bound to the act of inquiry. By opening your eyes and looking in front of you, you can find out more about a cup that is in front of you. By sticking your finger in it, you can find out if the coffee in it is hot. By bringing it to your lips and tilting it, you can find out how the coffee in it tastes.

This example illustrates that many of the roles that objects play in our lives at a certain time are *architecturally bound*. Facts about how the world works, about how we are built, and about how things are built and arranged, insure that the object that plays one role in our lives at a certain time will also play many others. The cup of coffee I can see by directing my glance in a certain way is the one I can pick up by moving my hands and arms in a certain way.

If you live a temporally simple life—live day to day, as we say—never making appointments for more than a few hours ahead of time, having no calendars, basing what you do each day on what it is like and what happens that day—you really don't seem to need the term 'today'. You don't need to think, 'It's cloudy today.' You can just think, 'It's cloudy'. You don't need to think, 'I have an appointment today at 4 p.m.', you can just think 'I have an appointment at 4 p.m.' If you think 'It's cloudy' on a certain day, your thought will be true or false based on

<hr/>

[4] Again, I think things are actually a bit more complicated. Ultimately all activity including all thought and all use of language connects to the world in role-based ways, but the roles can be of quite different sorts, and less and less dependent on the features of the particular episode and more and more on external features that are the same at different times and places and for different people, and thus approximate to being property-based. See Perry (2009*b*).

what it is like on that day. But that dependence needn't be reflected in an articulated component of your thought. One can imagine simple folk who find out about each day in the way we do, and base what they do on what they find out, but who don't really think about *days* at all. Of such folk, I will say that their thoughts and language *concern* the present day, the day on which their inquiries and discourse and other actions occur, even though there is no word in their vocabulary or idea in their minds specifically charged with *standing for* the present day. That the truth-conditions of their thoughts and discourse have to do with the day on which they occur is determined by the fact that the methods of inquiry they use provide information about that day, and the success of the actions these thoughts motivate is determined by how things are on that day. It is their *form of life* that ties their thought and language to the present day, rather than any word like 'today' (see Perry 2000: ch. 10). If one found such folks using the word 'today', one might wonder if it really referred, or simply served redundantly to register the methods they were using to find out about cloudiness, rain, and the like.

5. THE SELF

Being the present day is an example of an important role. Such roles are architecturally bound with others that permit one to get information about the objects that play them in certain ways, and determine how such objects affect the results of one's action. The present day is the one I refer to with 'today', the day I can find out about by looking out the window, the day whose weather will determine whether lying on the beach will make me tan or burnt or cold or wet. I'll say that such roles 'support' role-based methods of inquiry, and role-sensitive ways of accomplishing things. This latter phrase includes the fact that we have ways of acting that affect the objects that play the role, and ways of acting whose success is dependent on the attributes of the objects that play the role, although not affecting them in the ordinary sense. If I say 'The coffee in that cup is cold', the truth or falsity of my statement will be sensitive to the cup I refer to, although I don't really affect the cup by referring to it and saying something about it.

Selves are persons; *Self* is a role persons play. One's self is like today or one's home or one's father; a perfectly ordinary object, thought of in virtue of its relation to the thinking agent. The relation associated with 'self' is just identity. That is,

If x is y's self, then $x = y$

There are self-based methods of inquiry, and self-sensitive ways of accomplishing things. Reflection and introspection and perception are all self-based methods of inquiry. Perception is doubly role-based. I find out about the objects seen and touched. And I find out about the seer and toucher. All basic ways of acting are similarly doubly role-based. I have an effect on objects that play a certain role in my life at that time: the cup I see and pick up; the telephone I talk into; the person at the other end of the line connected to the phone I talk into, and the further results of my action depend on their properties. But the actions are also ultimately self-sensitive; the effect of one's actions depends on how things stand in relation to oneself. A certain movement will result in *my* head being scratched: it affects me. Another movement will result in the cup in front of *me* being moved across the table; or the phone *I* am dialing being connected to the phone whose number I dial, or the person who answers that phone being distracted from some more important task. By moving my lips in a certain way, I can tell the person on the phone with *me* that I'm sorry for dialing the wrong number; I don't need to know anything about who they are except that they stand in this relation to me.

Philosophers, worried about the metaphysics and epistemology of consciousness and the specter of skepticism, and charged with recruiting future generations of philosophers by working yearly through the *Meditations* with undergraduates, focus on self-informative methods, like introspection, that seem to be *necessarily* self-informative. There is a much wider class of normally self-informative methods, architecturally and contingently guaranteed to be self-informative. There is a way of finding out about your own feet, looking straight down and inspecting the feet you see, but distorting glasses, or very bad posture, could make them methods of finding out about the feet of the person next to you. Looking in a small mirror held close is a way of finding out about one's own nose, lips, and beard, but if we had large donut-shaped heads it might be a way of finding out about what was happening behind us. Ordinarily the metaphysically guaranteed and the merely architecturally guaranteed self-informative methods function as a seamless whole; we think of ourselves as the occupants of a bundle of roles bound together.

We might ask what justifies us in thinking, say, that the being that is aware of *this* toothache is the same as that which is aware of being aware of the toothache (McTaggart, 1921–7: §386). H. P. Grice once proposed solving this problem by introducing the self as a logical construction; the relation of possible co-awareness by a single act of introspection is used to define a 'total temporary state'; then a version of Locke's memory theory is constructed to bind the total temporary states into a single self or person (Grice 1941). But, as with most attempted logical constructions, there is a heavy dependence on counterfactuals, that seem to rely on causation, and ultimately suggest that the unity that holds the various aspects of our selves together has to do with dependence on a single continuant like a brain or a body (Perry 2008*b*). At any rate, the question doesn't usually arise; I am the one who feels this toothache, and the one who owns these hands I see before me, and the one whose feet I can move at will, and the one who is looking at the things I see. I don't have to decide which really captures my sense of self, any more than I have to decide whether the car I drive is the one I sit in, the one I steer, the one I brake, or the one whose windshield I see through.

When we investigate the objects around us, in virtue of applying role-based methods of inquiry, we pick up information that motivates role-sensitive methods of acting. I learn that a cup I see contains hot coffee by employing role-based methods of inquiry; I pick it up and drink from it by using role-based methods for picking up a cup and drinking from it. But there being a cup of hot coffee there isn't sufficient motivation for so acting; the act would be irrational unless I was thirsty, or needed caffeine, or both, and unless I knew that the cup was in front of *me*. So my beliefs need to reflect those facts about me, for my act to be properly motivated.

In this case, it suffices that I have beliefs that *concern* me. My beliefs can be like Lichtenberg and Wittgenstein and Anscombe have in mind, of the sort we might express with 'Hot coffee in that cup in front; there is thirst and caffeine deprivation; so drink.' We can imagine animals, cognitively sophisticated enough to perceive the world in terms of objects having properties and standing in relations, and perhaps even to reidentify objects perceived at different times, with no need to appreciate *themselves* as objects. Their beliefs concern them, but do not represent them in the way that they represent other objects.

Such an animal picks up and acts on the basis of information about itself in spite of not having an idea that stands for itself—much less a first-person pronoun. It gets information about how things are around *it*, and this influences which self-sensitive actions it takes. I'll say such an animal has *primitive* self-knowledge, gained by methods that are self-informative, and motivating actions that are self-sensitive. And we are like such animals when we are young enough, and revert to this more primitive level of thought in cognitively undemanding situations (and, oddly enough, in the rather more demanding situation of trying to follow Descartes in methodical doubt). Lichtenberg's insight is that in the situation of the Second Meditation, where Descartes is (we are to suppose) not only meditating, but withholding assent from the very idea that there is anyone else to communicate with, he has no real need for 'I'.

The use of the particle 'self' in 'self-informative methods' may give the impression of circularity. I can learn that I have mustard in my beard in a self-informative way, by looking in a small mirror held right in front of my face. Or I can learn in a way that others can use—perhaps my face and mustard-soaked beard appear on the Jumbo-Tron above the outfield at a Giants baseball game, and I see it, and learn about myself, in the same way that everyone else learns about me. In both cases John Perry learns something about John Perry—about *himself*, in what Anscombe calls the 'ordinary'—that is, not quasi-indicative—use of the reflexive pronoun. The difference is that with the first method of knowing, but not the second, the known is always, or at least normally, the knower. Marking the difference doesn't require any appeal to an antecedent or underlying self, or any use of quasi-indication, and is not circular.

6. THE PERSON ONE HAPPENS TO BE

Most of us, even if we would like to live only in the present day, can't manage it. In addition to our role-based ways of thinking and talking about days, we have an elaborate property-based way of thinking about them. Calendars embody this. I have a large calendar on my refrigerator, where I make notes about appointments and projects. In the 'July 21' box, there is a note, 'John has dental appointment'. The notation in the box amounts to a statement that is true if I go to dentist on July 21, false if I don't. It expresses the same proposition on May 1, when the appointment was made and noted on the calendar, as it does on July 21, when I will or won't go, and as it will when that date is long past.

Our system of dates gives us a property-based way of referring to and thinking about days that is independent of when we are doing the referring and thinking. It is useful because the world we live in provides us ways of forming well-grounded beliefs about days other than the present one. And the world also provides us with structures so that our actions can have predictable results on days other than when we perform them. When the dentist's secretary and I agree on the July 21 appointment, we come to have well-grounded beliefs about July 21: that I will show up, that the dentist will be ready to look at my teeth, and the like. When, on May 1, I write a note about the appointment in the July 21 box on my calendar, my action, if things go right, will have its intended effect on July 21, when seeing the note will lead me to drive to the dentist.

The calendar doesn't have any boxes marked 'today'. But I have a little red magnet that I move each morning to the appropriate box. Something like this happens automatically with calendars on computers. What is the point of that? What information will I add to the 'July 21' box on the calendar when I place the magnet there that morning? It is not the magnet, but the fact that the magnet is there on a certain box on a certain day, that carries the information. If my habits are regular enough, the magnet's presence in a box on the calendar will carry the information that the day *when* I am doing the looking is the very day the box stands for. The box I see the magnet on has notations from which I can discover what is supposed to happen on the day the box stands for, and the magnet tells me I can find out more about that by looking out the window. It is the day on which I will do the things I do today. I know how to go to the dentist—get in the car and drive up Channing to his office—but the method I use is a method for getting to the dentist on the whatever day that I use it. There is no specific method for getting to the dentist on July 21. To do that, I need to deploy the role-sensitive method, on the day when my little magnet is on the same box as 'John has an appointment at the dentist'; that is when July 21 occupies the 'today' role.

To navigate around the more complex informational world that dates and calendars enable to me to live in, I do need the word 'today' and the thoughts I can think with it. I need to be able to make inferences like: 'I go to the dentist July 21 (what the calendar tells me); today is July 21 (what the magnet tells me); so I go to the dentist today'. All the calendars in the world won't make me into a well-organized and punctual person, if I can't convert the property-based references provided by the dates, into my inquiry- and action-bound ways of thinking of the present day.

The world also supplies property-based ways of referring to me and thinking about me, most prominently my name. I'll call these *nominal* ways of referring and thinking. This in turn makes possible ways of gaining information about me, and acting in ways that affect me, or whose success is sensitive to my facts about me, in ways that are not self-sensitive. If someone knows my name, she can look up my phone number in the directory, find out how much I owe on my property taxes at the County Hall of Records, and, in the age of the internet, no doubt find out endless number of other things about me by Googling my name (although this is mostly a way of finding out about John Perry Barlow, the Grateful Dead lyricist and cyberlibertarian). Although the County is nice enough to send me a bill, once I open it I use the same method as anyone else to find out what my property taxes are: I look for a notation where the name 'John Perry' is linked with an amount due. If I forget my own phone number, I will find out what it is in the same way anyone else would, by looking it up in the directory. And each quarter I look in the class schedule to find out when and where my class meets, just as the students do.

When I am senile, and forget my own name, I will still be able find out about myself by reading about John Perry in various directories and schedules, and hearing his name in conversation. This won't be what we ordinarily think of as self-knowledge. What is lacking is the ability to get the knowledge thus gained tied to knowledge of myself gained in self-informative ways. Someone who was stuck in a Lichtenbergian language, with no first-person way of referring and thinking, would be similarly disabled. To make use of these public, non-self-informative methods of finding out about people, in order to gain self-knowledge, I need a way of thinking about and referring to myself that is associated with self-informative ways of knowing and self-sensitive ways of acting, but can also be linked to nominal methods. I need to be able to look at the time schedule, and infer: 'John Perry teaches in the Philosophy Department Seminar Room at two p.m.; I am John Perry; so I teach in the Philosophy Department Seminar Room at two p.m.'

So, perhaps surprisingly, it is the availability of methods of gaining information about ourselves in non-self-informative ways that makes having a first person crucial. In an informationally simpler world, where there are no such methods, we wouldn't need a first person any more than those who live in the present moment, or at least in the present day, would need 'today'.

We need to be careful here, however. It is not really the first person that is needed. It is the function that the first person performs that is important. A name could perform it, and often does with children (Perry 2000: ch. 3). If Eloise is the only child with that name in her household, so that every remark she hears that uses the name 'Eloise' is about her, and every time she hears a shout 'Eloise!' it is she that is summoned or chastised, then hearing the name 'Eloise' is a self-informative method of gaining information for her, and she can use 'Eloise' in asking for things in much the way she will use 'I' later on: 'Eloise wants a cookie.' The word 'I' is suited by its meaning to perform this function for every English speaker, and Eloise will need to learn it to get cookies when she starts interacting with other Eloises, and people who don't know her name.

7. IDEAS, NOTIONS, AND BUFFERS

It may be helpful to develop an admittedly oversimple model of cognition that organizes the ideas discussed so far. I'll assume we have *beliefs*, which are particular states. Beliefs have causal roles and contents, which *mesh*. Our ordinary way of identifying beliefs is by their contents, for example my present belief *that my shirt is badly coffee-stained*. The content is a proposition, that my shirt is badly coffee-stained; a proposition is an abstract object that encodes truth-conditions. How we think of propositions, as sets of possibilities, or structures of objects and properties, won't matter much so long as they encode truth-conditions in one way or another.

The belief I have about my shirt was caused by a self-informative perception. I look down and see my shirt with some big coffee-colored splotches on it. My perception has content, that the shirt had coffee-colored splotches on it. My perception, plus some background beliefs and memories (of spilling coffee) led to the conclusion that my shirt is badly coffee-stained. When we say the perception led to the belief, we have in mind two things. First, the perception was a cause of my acquiring the belief. Second, the content of the belief makes sense given the content of the perception, together with the contents of background beliefs and memories. That's part of what I mean by saying the cognitive and causal roles *mesh*. We also get meshing when we look forward. My belief that my shirt is coffee-stained, together with my desire to appear reasonably well-kempt when my wife and I go out to dinner, together with a number of other beliefs, such as that I have a clean shirt upstairs in the closet, will motivate me to go upstairs and change my shirt.

That is, it will cause me to execute a number of bodily movements, which will get me upstairs in front of my closet, and then result in getting a fresh shirt out of the closet and putting it on. The results these movements will have, *if* my beliefs are true, are that I will have changed my shirt, and will have a cleaner shirt on than I do now, and will appear considerably more kempt. And these results will promote the satisfaction of my desire, to appear well-kempt when we go out for dinner, although of course they will not absolutely guarantee it, as there will be more opportunities to spill things on myself. So that is another part of the idea of meshing. The result of the actions a complex of beliefs and desire cause should promote the satisfaction of the desires, if the beliefs are true.

My beliefs have structure; they are made up of ideas. Ideas contribute to the causal roles and contents of beliefs of which they are components. And they are common components of many beliefs. My idea of a university is a common component of my belief that Stanford is a University, my belief that UC Riverside is a university, and many others. My idea of Stanford is a common component of my belief that Bratman teaches at Stanford, that CSLI is located at Stanford, and many others. And so forth. I'll just call ideas of the sort we associate with general terms, verbs, prepositions, and the like 'ideas'. I'll call ideas associated with particular things—people, places, things, universities, and, although it's a bit of a stretch to call them 'things', days—'notions'. A notion, plus all of the ideas associated with it in belief, makes up a *file*. The file associated with a given notion determines the conception, or a conception, that a person has of the object the notion is *of*.

Finally, among notions, I'll distinguish between *buffers* and *standing notions*. A buffer is typically tied to a perception, or series of perceptions, of an object. It is the basis of a sort of temporary file, used to keep track of the object while one stays in more or less steady perceptual contact with it. More generally, buffers are tied to roles and bundles of roles that a given object plays in our lives for a while.

Standing notions are more or less permanent notions that we use to store information about objects we are not perceiving or otherwise epistemically attached to; objects that are not currently (as far as we know) playing any informative or action-affording roles in our lives. I have a standing nominal notion of, say, Joseph Biden, our vice-president. I've never met him; I've read about him; I've used nominal-methods to acquire information about him. Perhaps some day I will go to a Democratic Party fundraiser, and will see a distinguished, silver-haired, rather loquacious fellow, and form a new buffer. Eventually I accumulate enough information in the buffer about how this fellow looks, his opinions, his demeanor, and the like, to infer that he must be Joe Biden; that is, I recognize him; I pool the information in the buffer and the standing notion. Now I have a belief that Joe Biden, the vice-president, is across the room from me. This combines with the long-standing desire to shake hands with Joe Biden, so I cross the room, and so on.

What notions contribute to the contents of the beliefs of which they are components is what they stand for, what they are *of*, not the conceptions associated with the notions. The object an agent's notion is *of* need not be a good fit for his conception of it. It's nice if the ideas associated with a notion pretty much accurately depict the object the notion is of, but it is in no way guaranteed. Perhaps I wrongly believe that Biden is a former Senator from Pennsylvania. My *conception* of Biden, the complex condition determined by my Biden file, doesn't *denote* anyone, for no one is both vice-president and a former senator from Pennsylvania.

The point of introducing this machinery is to allow us to focus on what's special about what I call 'the *self*-notion'. I assume that all normal humans past a certain age have a *self-notion*, an idea that is dedicated to dealing with information about themselves. This is the notion that controls the use of the first person; that is, beliefs of mine with my self-notion as a component I will express with 'I' or 'me', even after, in my senility, I have forgotten my name. It is the notion with which all of the information picked up in self-informative ways is associated, and the beliefs associated with this notion motivate self-sensitive actions.

Normally our self-notions will not only be associated with ideas picked up in normally self-informative ways, but all sorts of additional information, about our telephone numbers, salaries, class-schedules, doctor's appointments, and lots of other things, that we have learnt about ourselves by hearing or reading our name in various letters, on various lists, announcements, and the like, and hearing others says things about us. That is, for one who knows his own name, one's self-notion will also serve as a standing notion, a nominal-notion associated with one's own name. The information we get about ourselves using nominal methods and our own names, as when we look up our own phone numbers, is pooled with the information we get in normally self-informative ways, and the combined information guides our actions.

The semantics of the self-notion is very simple: it is *of* the person it belongs to. Beliefs with the self-notion as a component are *about* the person it belongs to, whether the beliefs were acquired in self-informative ways or not. From one's self-notion we can retrieve one's self-conception, what one takes oneself to be. This is quite relevant to one's psychology, but irrelevant to the semantics of one's beliefs. Psychologists tell us it is unlikely to be completely accurate. But for most of us, it is quite extensive and detailed, and gets a lot of things right. I know my own height, weight, salary, age, and the middle names of my parents. I don't think I know all of that about anyone else. But my self-notion would still be *of* me, even if it were wildly inaccurate.

Self is an extremely special role. And it has some very special features. Most importantly, it is played permanently by the same person. One's self never changes, in the sense that only one person ever occupies that role. The occupant of the self-role, unlike the occupant of the person-I-am-talking-to role, or the today-role, or the here-role, never gets replaced. This means that one can use one's self-buffer as one's standing notion for oneself. One doesn't need a little magnet to keep track of whom one refers to with 'I'.

The self-buffer isn't unique in this respect. For most of us, the same planet will play the role of the planet-I'm-standing-on-or-flying-above our whole life. For many generations of people, millennia-I-live-during was a role occupied by the second millennium throughout their entire life. These roles are, or were, only contingently guaranteed to be occupied by the same thing. Universe-I-am-a-part-of seems metaphysically secure. And, as Ken Taylor once pointed out, nothing is quite so immune from error through misidentification as the occupant of the role possible-world-we-are-in is under the phrase, 'the actual world'.

Philosophers have sometimes tried to give simple role-based analyses of our sense of self: 'the being having *this* experience', perhaps. But in fact we play many roles relative to episodes of thought, perception, and action. I am the person seeing *these* things; the person having *these* sensations; the person performing *these* actions; the person experiencing *these* emotions, the person having *this* inchoate background of bodily feeling, and much else besides. Descartes maintained a sense of self, while doubting that he had a body; the special access he had to his own ideas seemed to suffice. Some schizophrenics think that their own thoughts are not their own; they nevertheless maintain enough sense of self through connections to actions and the physical world around them to think the thought that some of their thoughts are not their own. In 'Where Am I', Dan Dennett prises apart the structure of roles bound together in our ordinary sense of self, until we have no idea where we are, and only the barest sense of who we are (Dennett 1981).

8. SELF-BELIEF

Let's return to the problem of section 1. How can I have a belief that John Perry lives in Palo Alto, without believing that I live there? What more is required for self-belief?

The current dominant view of the semantics of names and indexicals is that they are *directly referential*, in David Kaplan's sense (Kaplan 1989). This means that they contribute the objects referred to, rather than any modes of presentation of those objects, to the *contents* of the statements containing them. This means that the statements 'I live in Palo Alto', spoken by me, and 'John Perry lives in Palo Alto' have the same content, that is, express the same proposition. If we are referential-ists, then we must admit that at the level of content we lose track of the differences between the ways that indexicals and names refer, and the differences between the beliefs that might lead to using one rather than the other.

The direct reference picture does not imply that there are no special modes of reference associated with indexicals. As Kaplan notes, the rules of reference for indexicals, what he calls *characters*, do supply something very much like the modes of presentation Frege appeals to in his theory. The difference is that for the referentialist, these modes do not become constituents of the propositions expressed.[5]

The conclusion we should draw from this, however, is not that my statements, 'I live in Palo Alto' and 'John Perry lives in Palo Alto', have the same cognitive significance, but rather that, if we embrace referentialism, we should not expect to find differences in cognitive significance at the level of content. When we want to see how the truth-conditions of our statements and thoughts, the information we pick up in perception, and the results we expect to achieve in action, all *mesh* in a coherent way, we cannot lose track of the modes of reference and presentation involved. The place to look for cognitive significance is in the whole structure of the statements (and the beliefs that lead to them), the way in which the meaning of the sentence used interacts with the context to determine that content.

In particular, we need to look at what I will call the *conditions of truth*. This is a condition that the utterance or statement itself has to meet, in order to be true, that incorporates, rather than loses track of, the way reference is achieved.

Consider statements of 'I live in Palo Alto', by a group of diverse people. These statements all have something important in common. Each statement is true if and only if the person who makes *it* lives in Palo Alto. Each statement *s* will have to meet the same reflexive condition of truth:

If *s* is an utterance of 'I live in Palo Alto', *s* is true iff the person who makes *s* lives in Palo Alto.

On the other hand, they each have something important that is not in common, and corresponds to the referentialist theory of content. My statement will be true iff John Perry lives in Palo Alto. Debra Satz's statement will be true iff Debra Satz lives in Palo Alto. John Searle's statement will be true iff John Searle lives in Palo Alto. And so forth. Each statement will express a different proposition, once we fix to whom the utterance of 'I' in it refers.

---

[5] For Kaplan, the reference of a term is *indirect*, if the referent of a term depends on some reference-determining aspect of the proposition that a statement using the term expresses. This is Frege's picture. The proposition expressed doesn't depend on the referent of the term; the referent of the term depends on the proposition, in particular that aspect of it contributed by the sense of the term, an identifying condition. This aspect, plus facts about the world, determines the referent. On Kaplan's picture of direct reference, the character of the term and certain aspects of the world, the context, determine the referent, and the referent determines (along with the rest of the statement) which proposition is expressed. The route from utterance through character and context to referent may be quite complex and in that sense indirect, but that's not the sense Kaplan has in mind.

Now consider everyone in the group saying, 'John Perry lives in Palo Alto'. Assume they are all employing the same convention C associated with 'John Perry'. Then we can say:

If s is an utterance of 'John Perry lives in Palo Alto', s is true iff the person associated by C with the name 'John Perry' lives in Palo Alto.

This is not a reflexive condition of truth; the variable s does not occur on the right side of the 'iff'.

Unlike referential contents, conditions of truth keep track of the roles objects must play, or the properties they must have, in order to be referred to. This is required if we are to understand how the truth-conditions of the statements one makes mesh with the beliefs that lead one to make them.

Each sincere person who says 'I live in Palo Alto' will be motivated by a belief consisting of his self-notion and the idea of living in Palo Alto. Such a belief is true, iff the owner of the self-notion, the thinker of the thought, lives in Palo Alto. In normal circumstances the role of being the thinker of a thought, and being the speaker of words motivated by the thought, are tightly bound. The use of the word 'I' to refer to oneself is just one example of a self-sensitive action; the person the agent refers to is the agent. Each sincere person who says, 'John Perry lives in Palo Alto' will be motivated by a belief consisting of a nominal notion associated with the name 'John Perry' and the idea of living in Palo Alto. In normal circumstances (and putting aside the complexities due to multiple conventions for the same name), using a name N is a way of expressing a belief involving a nominal notion associated with N.

Until I become senile and forget my name, my self-notion will serve as a nominal notion associated with the name 'John Perry'. So, until then, my statements 'John Perry lives in Palo Alto' and 'I live in Palo Alto' will not only have the same referential content, but will be motivated by the same belief, the association of my self-notion with the idea of living in Palo Alto. This belief won't be the total motivation, otherwise we couldn't explain when I said one and when I said the other. How I express the belief on a given occasion will depend on what I take the conversational situation to be. If I am with some people who don't know my name, but are interested in Palo Alto, I might volunteer, 'I live in Palo Alto'. They will learn from this that they are talking to someone who ought to know something about the place, and can direct questions at him; I couldn't achieve the same result with 'John Perry lives in Palo Alto'. If I am at a Pomo bar in Berkeley and have overheard a conversation in which some mean-looking people have said many negative things about analytical philosophers and Palo Alto, and am asked, 'Do you know of any analytical philosophers who live in Palo Alto?' I might say, 'John Perry lives in Palo Alto', and leave it at that.

Suppose now I have forgotten my name, but still remember that I live in Palo Alto. I keep running into references to John Perry and believe that he lives there too. Then my statements will still have the same referential content, but not express the same belief. And, finally, when I have forgotten where I live, it will be correct to say, using the 'he' quasi-indicatively, 'John Perry believes that John Perry lives in Palo Alto, but John Perry doesn't believe that he lives in Palo Alto.' What I lack is a belief that has the referential content that John Perry lives in Palo Alto in virtue of having my self-notion as a component.

9. Self-Notions and Cartesian Egos

Apart from being metaphysically more plausible (I hope), does the theory of self-notions fare any better with our problem than the theory of Cartesian Egos? Let 'JP' now stand not for my Cartesian Ego, but for my self-notion. Senile me might doubt that I live in Palo Alto, but be quite certain that JP's owner lives in Palo Alto. So what have we gained, as far as our original problem goes?

Self-notions are objects, and there are many ways to think about and refer to any object. Senility isn't even required for the envisaged situation. Suppose that Krista Lawlor is giving a lecture on self-knowledge at 10 a.m., and considers my theory among others. For the sake of argument, let's even assume she accepts the theory. To illustrate it she says, 'Let's name Perry's self-notion "Bruno".' She writes 'Bruno is a self-notion' on the board, where she also writes, 'Bruno belongs to a Palo Alto resident.' Since she accepts the theory, and knows I live in Palo Alto, she believes both statements.

At the end of class Lawlor uncharacteristically doesn't erase the board. I teach in the same room at 11, and want to talk about self-notions. I see that 'Bruno' is clearly the name of a self-notion. So I just start talking about Bruno. I refer to my own self-notion with 'Bruno', but I don't know it. I have no idea whether the statement on the board, 'Bruno belongs to a Palo Alto resident', is true or false.

This all isn't a problem for the theory of self-notions. Referring to Bruno is one thing, having Bruno as a component of one's beliefs is another. Lawlor's beliefs have her nominal notion *of* Bruno as a component; they are thus *about* my self-notion; it is part of their subject matter. Bruno is a constituent of the referential content of her belief and of the statements she wrote on the board. But it is *not* a component of her thought. It is not a notion that is a structural part of her belief, but a notion her belief is about.

The belief I express with 'I live in Palo Alto' does have Bruno as a component, but it is not about Bruno; Bruno isn't part of its subject-matter. The thought is not *about* Bruno, but about me. On the other hand, the belief I express with 'Bruno's owner lives in Palo Alto', like the thought Lawlor expresses with that sentence, does not have Bruno as a component; that is, it does not have my self-notion as a component, even though it is about it. It has a nominal notion *of* Bruno as a component, but not Bruno itself. If I were to assert, 'Bruno's owner is no doubt a profound thinker', that would not show that I was immodest, for it would not show that I had a belief whose condition of truth is that the owner of that very belief is profound. The fact that I can think and talk *about* my self-notion without knowing that I do so is not a problem.

On the theory on offer, the differences between my senile thoughts, 'I live I Palo Alto' and 'John Perry lives in Palo Alto' are: (*a*) at the level of what goes on in my mind, that the first has my self-notion as a component, and the second has a nominal notion of me as a component; (*b*) at the level of content, even though both beliefs have the same referential content, the structures whereby they come to have that content are quite different. The first has a reflexive condition of truth, and is about me and is about me in virtue of a role I play in the life of the believer, namely identity; the second has a non-reflexive condition of truth, and is about me because of a property I have, namely being the person assigned to 'John Perry' by the relevant convention.

REFERENCES

ALMOG, JOSEPH, PERRY, JOHN, and WETTSTEIN, HOWARD (eds.) (1989). *Themes from Kaplan* (New York: Oxford University Press).

ANSCOMBE, G. E. M. (1975/1994). 'The First Person', in Samuel Guttenplan (ed.), *Mind and Language* (Oxford: Oxford University Press, 1975). Repr. in Cassam (1994: 140–59). Page references to reprint.

CASSAM, QUASSIM (1994). *Self Knowledge* (Oxford: Oxford University Press).

CASTAÑEDA, HECTOR-NERI (1969). 'On the Phenomeno-logic of the I', *Proceedings of the 14th International Congress of Philosophy*, iii (Vienna: University of Vienna). Repr. in Cassam (1994: 160–6). Page references to reprint.

DENNETT DAN (1981). 'Where Am I?', *Brainstorms* (Cambridge, Mass.: MIT), 310–23.

DESCARTES, RENE (1641/1984). *Meditationes de prima philosophia*, tr. as *Meditations on First Philosophy* in *The Philosophical Writings of Descartes*, tr. J. Cottingham, R. Stoothoff, and D. Murdoch (Cambridge: Cambridge University Press, 1984).

EVANS, GARETH (1982/1994). 'Self-Identification', *The Varieties of Reference* (Oxford: Oxford University Press, 1982), 205–33. Repr. in Cassam (1994: 184–209). Page references to reprint.

FREGE, GOTTLOB (1892/1960). 'Über Sinn und Bedeutung', *Zeitschrift für Philosophische Kritik*, NF 100 (1892), 25–30. Tr. by Max Black as 'On Sense and Reference', in *Translations from the Philosophical Essays of Gottlob Frege*, ed. and tr. P. Geach and M. Black (Oxford: Basil Blackwell, 1960), 56–78.

——(1918/1967). 'The Thought: A Logical Inquiry', in *Philosophical Logic*, ed. P. F. Strawson (Oxford: Oxford University Press, 1967), 17–38. This translation, by A. M. and Marcelle

Quinton, originally *Klogische Untersuchung*, appeared in *Beiträge zur Philosophie des deutschen Idealismus I* (1918), 58–77. Page references are to the Strawson volume.

GRICE, H. P. (1941). 'Personal Identity', *Mind*, 50. Repr. in Perry (1975: 73–95).

KAPLAN, DAVID (1989). 'Demonstratives', in Almog *et al.* (1989).

LICHTENBERG, GEORG CRISTOPH (2000). *The Waste Books.* tr. with an introduction by R. J. Hollingdale (New York: New York Review of Books).

McTAGGART, JOHN, and McTAGGART, ELLIS (1921–7). *The Nature of Existence* (Cambridge: Cambridge University Press).

PERRY, JOHN (2000). *The Problem of the Essential Indexical* (expanded edn. Stanford, Calif.: CSLI Publications).

——(2001). *Knowledge, Possibility and Consciousness* (Cambridge, Mass.: MIT Press).

——(2002). *Identity, Personal Identity and the Self* (Indianapolis: Hackett Publishing).

——(ed.) (2008*a*). *Personal Identity* (2nd edn. Berkeley and Los Angeles: University of California Press).

——(2008*b*). 'Personal Identity, Memory, and the Problem of Circularity', in Perry (2008*a*: 135–55).

——(2009*a*). 'Directing Intentions', in Joseph Almog and Paolo Leonardi (eds.), *The Philosophy of David Kaplan* (New York: Oxford University Press).

——(2009*b*). *Reference and Reflexivity* (2nd edn. Stanford, Calif.: CSLI Publications).

SHOEMAKER, SYDNEY (1968/1994). 'Self-Reference and Self-Awareness', *Journal of Philosophy* (1968), 555–67. Repr. in Cassam (1994: 80–93). Page references to reprint.

WITTGENSTEIN, LUDWIG (1958). *The Blue and Brown Books* (Oxford: Oxford University Press).

CHAPTER 17

THE NARRATIVE SELF

MARYA SCHECHTMAN

IF the person sitting next to you on a long plane trip suddenly launches into the story of his life you may be amused, or annoyed, or simply glad for the distraction. Whatever your reaction, you are unlikely to be *surprised* that he has a story to tell. The idea that our lives are in some sense story-like runs deep in our everyday thought. This idea has also been widely explored in more formal academic studies of the self. While there is broad (but by no means universal) assent to the view that the self is narrative in form, there is little consensus on just what this means or what implications it has.

This chapter investigates the narrative approach to self found in philosophy and related disciplines. The first section provides a provisional picture of the content of the narrative approach. This approach is not monolithic, but includes views that use different conceptions of narrative in different ways to illuminate different aspects of the self. This section provides overviews of some of these views. The second section highlights significant commonalities and differences among the views described in section 1, seeking to get clear both on the wide range of narrative views and on the commonalities that define the approach as a whole. The third section considers some important objections that have been raised to the narrative approach and what the responses to these objections reveal about this approach. Each section will provide further insight into the fundamental claims of the narrative approach as well as uncovering outstanding questions and pointing to directions for future development.

1. The Views

Narrative views of the self all draw some kind of link between narrative and selfhood, but the links drawn vary widely. In this section we consider some of the most commonly held and important conceptions of the connection between narrative and self. I divide these into two basic categories, but this is a somewhat tentative distinction. As the discussion develops we will see that there are important differences between views within the same categories and important similarities that cross categorical boundaries. It is also important to be clear that the views described here do not exhaust the space of existing narrative views. This section should thus be taken as providing an overall feel for the range of claims that are made about the relation between narrative and self rather than as providing a firm and complete taxonomy of existing narrative views.

Selves are constituted by narratives

Perhaps the most basic kind of narrative view, and the one that draws the strongest connection between narrative and self, holds that selves are inherently narrative entities. There are usually two elements of this claim. One is that our *sense of self* must be narrative, the other that the *lives* of selves are narrative in structure. These two elements are not considered to be completely distinct, but seen rather as two sides of the same coin. Selves, on this view, are beings who *lead* their lives rather than merely having a history, and leading the life of a self is taken inherently to involve understanding one's life as a narrative and enacting the narrative one sees as one's life.

This kind of claim is seen in three of the philosophers most readily associated with the narrative approach—Alisdair MacIntyre, Charles Taylor, and Paul Ricoeur.[1] Although these theorists differ from each other, they also overlap in many significant respects. I will call the kind of narrative view they hold the 'hermeneutical' narrative view because it conceives of selves as fundamentally self-interpreting beings and because its proponents are inspired by hermeneutics theory. The basic features of the hermeneutical view are most easily explicated by looking at the strong connections it draws between selfhood, narrative, and agency. Selves are fundamentally agents on this view, and agency requires narrative. To be agents we must be intelligible to ourselves and to others; our actions must be meaningful and significant in a way that cannot be captured in purely naturalistic terms, but requires that we interpret our behaviors in the context of a narrative.

---

[1] Psychologist Jerome Bruner (e.g. Bruner 1990) and philosopher Anthony Rudd (2007) provide other examples of this approach.

This insight is perhaps expressed most directly by MacIntyre. He points out that a particular behavior might be characterized with 'equal truth and appropriateness' as digging, gardening, taking exercise, preparing for winter, or pleasing one's wife (MacIntyre 1984: 206). In order to say what an agent is doing when he displays this behavior, we need to understand how these different answers are related to one another and which one captures the agent's primary intentions. To know this we need to be able to place the behavior in the context of intersecting stories—stories about households and domestic arrangements, about the cycles of the seasons, about gardening and the story of the actor's life. 'Intentions', MacIntyre says, 'need to be ordered both causally and temporally and both orderings will make references to settings' (1984: 208). This ordering is a narrative, and so 'narrative history of a certain kind turns out to be the basic and essential genre for the characterization of human action' (MacIntyre 1984: 208). To identify an occurrence as an action, he says, is to 'identify it under a type of description which enables us to see that occurrence as flowing intelligibly from a human agent's intentions, motives, passions, and purposes' (1984: 209), that is, to tell a narrative that explains it. This narrative account of action must, moreover, have certain characteristics. To be intelligible, action must be aimed at some end or *telos*. This requires that narrative explanation include a normative or evaluative dimension which, according to MacIntyre, applies not just to individual actions but to our lives as a whole. To *lead* a life is to search for and aim toward the good. 'The unity of a human life', he therefore concludes, 'is the unity of a narrative quest' (1984: 219).

Taylor offers similar analysis arguing against a particular kind of naturalistic or reductionist view that implies that our lives can be lived without any particular relation to a tradition or to the good. To the contrary, he claims, selfhood and the good 'turn out to be inextricably intertwined themes' (Taylor 1989: 3). As did MacIntyre, Taylor concludes that this intertwining means that the self must be narrative in form. He endorses MacIntyre's characterization of human life as a quest, and describes the specific nature of this quest in terms of 'frameworks', background traditions which define the fundamental terms by which we evaluate our lives and our world. A framework 'incorporates a crucial set of qualitative distinctions' and provides the sense that some action or way of life is 'incomparably higher than the others which are more readily available to us' (Taylor 1989: 19). For Taylor, as for MacIntyre, the intelligibility of action requires that our lives be narrative in form.

Ricoeur's view falls into this same general category by suggesting that our lives must be narrative in form if we are to make sense of human agency. It is, however, an extremely intricate view, and differs from MacIntyre's and Taylor's in many important details which I will not be able to recount here. I limit myself to noting one salient difference flagged by Ricoeur himself. While Ricoeur, like Taylor, endorses MacIntyre's view of our lives as a quest narrative, he is keen to emphasize discontinuities between life and literature in a way that MacIntyre does not

(Ricoeur 1994: 158–63). This difference turns out to be one that makes a difference, and I will discuss it in more detail later.

The hermeneutical views are not the only views that see selves as inherently narrative in form. An extremely famous narrative view quite different from the ones just discussed is found in Daniel Dennett's account of the self as a 'center of narrative gravity'. For Dennett, the self is a fiction, but a useful fiction, like the notion of a center of gravity as it occurs in physics. There is no such *thing* as a center of gravity, Dennett says, 'but it is a fiction that has a nicely defined, well delineated, and well behaved role within physics' (1992: 103). This is because it can be used to explain and predict and to manipulate objects; it is a fiction that does work. The self, he says, has similar ontological status. Selves, as he conceives them, are characters in the narratives we humans spin. Key to Dennett's view is the distinction he draws between the entity that generates an autobiographical narrative and the protagonist depicted within it. Though Melville begins *Moby Dick* 'Call me Ishmael' we would be making a mistake to think that we are supposed to call *Melville* Ishmael. Melville is the author of the narrative; Ishmael is a character within it. Selves are, Dennett says, relevantly like Ishmael. Human brains are narrative-generating machines and selves are the protagonists of the narratives they generate.

Neither the narrating brain nor the human organism within which it operates—both of which are real things—are selves on Dennett's view; they are Melville to the self's Ishmael. We tend to conflate the two because the narratives our brains spin generally depict the movements of the human being from which they emanate. Nevertheless it remains a mistake, Dennett says, to identify the author of a narrative with its protagonist. To show this he tells a story of his own involving a 'novel-writing machine'—a computer that generates novels. Suppose this machine spits out a novel that begins 'Call me Gilbert' and takes the form of an autobiography of someone named Gilbert. Gilbert is the protagonist of this story, but there is no temptation to say that Gilbert, the subject of the autobiography, is actually the clanking computer sitting on the table.

But now suppose, Dennett continues, that we put this machine into a robot on wheels with a television eye. It begins its novel 'Call me Gilbert' and creates a narrative with the form of an autobiography, but this autobiography incorporates the information coming in through the television eye so that soon 'we will be unable to ignore the fact that the fictional career of the fictional Gilbert bears an interesting resemblance to the "career" of this mere robot moving through the world' (Dennett 1992: 108). Nevertheless, Dennett argues, we will still not be tempted to think that the machine has become a self just by being placed into a mobile robot (he stipulates that the machine is not conscious). Gilbert is not the robot; Gilbert is still a fictional protagonist in a story spun by a machine. Similarly, our brains are narrative-generating machines but they are not selves; brains don't *know* anything. For this reason, he says, 'it is a category mistake to start looking around for [selves] in the brain' (Dennett 1992: 109). He bolsters this argument by looking at cases of Multiple Personality Disorder, which he glosses as a circumstance in which a single brain generates multiple, non-intersecting narratives, each of which has its own protagonist, none of whom can be exclusively identified with the narrating human.

For Dennett, the self is constituted through human narration just as it is for the hermeneutical theorists, but there are important differences as well. Dennett's idea of narrative does not necessarily involve any strong form of evaluation or a quest for the good; it is more a matter of keeping track of the history of the body in which the narrating brain resides. Rather than constituting ourselves as selves as the hermeneutical view has it, in Dennett's view the brain constitutes a fictional protagonist by telling a story. On the former view, there are genuine human selves whose self-conception and mode of life constitute their selfhood; on the latter there are no such things.

I have also defended a view of the self as narrative in form—'The Narrative Self-Constitution View' (NSCV) (Schechtman 1996). It is in some ways in-between the hermeneutical view and Dennett's. The NSCV says that we constitute ourselves as selves by understanding our lives as narrative in form and living accordingly. This view does not demand that we explicitly formulate our narratives (although we should be able, for the most part, to articulate them locally when appropriate) but rather that we experience and interpret our present experiences not as isolated moments but as part of an ongoing story. The experience of winning the lottery will, for instance, be a different experience for someone immensely wealthy, someone who has lived a life of crushing poverty, and someone who has struggled unsuccessfully with a gambling addiction. The difference is the difference in the background narrative against which winning is interpreted. Having a narrative, and so being a self, on this view is primarily a matter of keeping track of this background and responding accordingly. The NSCV is like the hermeneutical view, then, in that it sees the self as real and constituted by a narrative. It is more like Dennett's, however, in that it does not emphasize agency so strongly as the hermeneutical view does, nor does it insist on an overall ethical orientation or thematic unity to the life of a self.

Selfhood and narrative capacity

The views we considered above see selves as the protagonists of human-generated narratives; characters in the stories we spin. Another kind of narrative view links selfhood to the capacity to think in narrative terms and to offer narrative explanations. These views differ from the ones just considered in that they do not require a narrative of one's whole life. They do not focus on the *story* of a life, identifying the self with a character in that story, but rather on the fact that selves employ the kind of logic found in stories when they describe, explain, and choose their own behavior.

Views of this kind are found frequently in developmental and evolutionary psychology. In this context the mastery of basic narrative competency is taken to be an important developmental milestone. Narrative ability allows us to understand ourselves as extended over time and to draw more robust distinctions between self and other. It also supports the development of autobiographical memory and contributes to a host of the complicated cognitive capacities that are characteristic of human selves. An example of this kind of view from the perspective of evolutionary psychology can be found in the work of Merlin Donald (1991, 2001). Here I will concentrate on an example from developmental psychology by looking at the work of Katherine Nelson.

Nelson explores 'the hypothesis of a new level of consciousness that emerges in early childhood together with a new sense of self situated in time and in multiple social realities' (Nelson 2003: 17). She describes the increasingly complex kinds of self-awareness that can be identified during the normal development of a human infant and sees the emergence of a 'new subjective level of conscious awareness, with a sense of a specific past and awareness of a possible future, as well as with new insight into the consciousness of other people' that develops in the late preschool years (Nelson 2003: 33). This level of consciousness is linked to the development of the ability to tell simple narratives about one's life, and so she finds a 'close connection between narrative and the emergence of a specifically human level of consciousness' (Nelson 2003: 22).

Nelson's idea is that as children enter into language they learn, with the help of their caregivers, to narrate the events in their lives. At first this involves nothing much more than describing things that happened to them in sequence and offering rudimentary evaluations (e.g. 'Mommy and I went to visit Daddy at work in a big building. We looked out a high window. It was fun.'). At the beginning even these very basic narrations require a great deal of prompting and reminding from adults. Gradually, however, children learn to do this work themselves, and when they do they enjoy qualitatively new kinds of experiences and are able to participate in new forms of social interaction. Nelson describes the dramatic transformation this brings about: 'This level of self understanding integrates action and consciousness into a whole self, and establishes a self-history as unique to the self, differentiated from others' experiential histories. . . . [I]t adds . . . a new awareness of self in past and future experiences and the contrast of that self to others' narratives of their past and future experiences' (Nelson 2003: 7).

Nelson's view is, in many ways, continuous with some of the views described in the previous section. Like the views described above Nelson's focuses on the importance of self-conception in the constitution of selfhood and the way in which a narrative sense of self is crucial to selfhood. While the narratives she sees as marking our entrance into selfhood are quite rudimentary and local, the idea is that ultimately we will come to think of ourselves as persisting individuals with a single life story. Moreover, even these very basic narratives include some measure of evaluation. One way of thinking about the difference between the views described earlier and views like Nelson's is in terms of the specific questions they ask. The former take adult human selves with the full complement of human-specific capacities and seek to define what is required to be such a self. Evolutionary and developmental psychologists, on the other hand, are interested in the emergence of self and the threshold that must be crossed in order for full-blown selfhood to begin to develop. These theorists thus investigate the basic cognitive accomplishments that initiate this development.

Another example of a view that links self to narrative capacity is David Velleman's view of the self as narrator. Velleman's view is developed as a reply to Dennett, arguing that Dennett's thought experiment does not, when properly interpreted, show what he says it does. Velleman accepts the basic outlines of Dennett's account of the making of the self through narrative, but believes that if we follow this account to its logical conclusion we will see that the self that emerges from the narrative activity of the human brain is real and not fictional. To make this point, Velleman returns to Dennett's story about the narrating robot who weaves the story of Gilbert. In Dennett's case, you will recall, the narrative of Gilbert follows events in the history of the robot—for example, if the robot gets locked in a supply closet, the narrative will involve Gilbert having been locked in the supply closet. Velleman rightly points out that if this kind of connection can be formed retrospectively, there is no reason to think that it cannot be formed prospectively. A narrating machine that can notice that the robot in which it sits was locked in a closet and thereafter generate 'I went into the closet and was locked in there' should be able to generate 'I am going to the closet' and then alter the path of the robot so that it does so.

Dennett does not describe his robot in this way but, as Velleman points out, he does attribute this capacity to human brains in his discussion of Multiple Personality Disorder. In discussing the case made famous in the book *Sybil* Dennett describes the patient as generating multiple narratives and says she 'engaged the world' with the self whose narrative was active. Presumably this means that Sybil lived as her narration suggested rather than simply narrating what had already been lived. 'If a self-narrator works in both directions,' Velleman concludes, 'then the self he invents is not just an idle fiction, a useful abstraction for interpreting his behavior. It—or more precisely his representation of it—is a determinant of the very behavior that it's useful for interpreting' (Velleman 2006: 212). According to Velleman, this ability ultimately makes the narrator an agent. The narrator's pronouncements about what will happen next give him *reasons* to follow the course he has announced. In making such pronouncements he is thus choosing among different possible continuations of the story and this gives him, in Velleman's view, 'as much free will as a human being' (2006: 218).

What this all means, Velleman concludes, is that in the narrative of Gilbert 'Gilbert' 'is not the name of a self; it's the name of a unified agent who *has* a self, in the form of an inner locus of agential control' (Velleman 2006: 220–1). So Gilbert is a real self, where a self is understood as something that an agent has by virtue of its agency. Velleman is quick to point out, however, that this understanding of self points to an important difference between his view of the relation of narrative to self and Dennett's. Dennett conceives of a self-narrative as trying to unify an entire life making 'all of our material cohere into a single good story' (Dennett 1992: 114). Velleman, on the other hand thinks of narratives as extremely local. In his view 'we tell many small, disconnected stories about ourselves—short episodes that do not get incorporated into our life-stories' (Velleman 2006: 222). Self-narration takes place in units 'as small as the eating of a meal, the answering of a phone, or even the scratching of an itch' (Velleman 2006: 222). In this respect, Velleman's view is very different not only from Dennett's, but from all of the views discussed in the first section. Here, even more than in Nelson's view, it is very clear that selfhood has to do with being able to use the devices of narrative to account for what one does, and not with weaving a narrative of one's life as a whole.[2]

2. COMMONALITIES AND DIFFERENCES

The last section provided a provisional picture of some of the ways in which narrative has been used to investigate and explain the self. In order to get a true

[2] The views we have discussed so far in one way or another claim that narrative is essential to selfhood. In addition to these there are a great many different kinds of views that see narrative as a particularly useful tool for understanding some crucial aspect of human selves. These views have a great deal to tell us about narrative and the self. In the remainder of this discussion I will put them to one side and focus on views that see narrative as a defining feature of persons. Before moving on it is, however, worth at least mentioning some of these views to give an idea of the range of the work on the narrative self. Hutto (2008) offers the 'Narrative Practice Hypothesis' to explain how humans become adept 'mind readers' using folk psychology to explain and predict the behavior of others. Goldie (2007a, 2007b) describes how novels help us develop the capacity to take an 'external perspective' on others—allowing us to engage with them more effectively—and on ourselves, aiding us in coming to terms with our pasts and planning for our futures. Lindemann Nelson (2001) considers the way in which the narratives that others tell about us can interfere with our autonomy, and how our counter-narratives can help us to regain it, and Lloyd (1993) offers a rich exploration of self and identity in literature and philosophy. There has also been interesting work bringing together narrative perspectives and empirical work. Several theorists have used narrative in discussing pathologies of the self, shedding light on both the pathologies and the nature of the self (e.g. Gallagher 2007). Damasio's (1999) theory of selfhood and consciousness relies heavily on narrative, and Hardcastle (2008) has brought empirical work and narrative theory together to illuminate the mechanisms behind the narrative self. These are just a few examples of views that see narrative as an important concept in understanding the self without holding that selves are intrinsically narrative entities, views that are too many and too complex to explore in a single essay.

appreciation of what the narrative approach has to offer, it is necessary both to respect the very real differences among these views and to recognize what they have in common. This section will draw on the discussion of the last, articulating some of the important similarities and differences that emerged there. The picture of the relations among these views that develops here will be deepened in the next section, where we consider objections to this approach.

Emphasis on meaning and intelligibility

A general commitment of the narrative approach is the idea that the lives of selves cannot be fully described or explained in mechanical or even biological terms. A different kind of explanation is required to capture the truth about selves. More specifically, the lives of selves must be described in ways that make the events and actions in them *meaningful* or *significant* in ways that naturalistic, reductive descriptions cannot. Meaning and significance of the relevant sort are humanistic concepts, not scientific ones, and are related to human goals and projects. This emphasis is front and center in the hermeneutical views, but it is found even in Nelson's preschoolers where, for example, a series of movements is not just a series of movements but a trip to see (for the purpose of seeing) Daddy at work. This emphasis on meaning is a common theme in the narrative approach because narrative is a particularly good way of capturing this dimension of human experience. Events in a story have a kind of meaning that comes from their place in the narrative as a whole, and cannot be completely captured outside of that context, and so narrative produces meaning of the appropriate sort.

There are, however, some important differences in the expression of this theme in different narrative views. Most notably, the notions of 'meaning' and 'significance' are not the same in all of them. The *meaning* of life as hermeneutical theorists understand it is a weighty matter, a question, to use Taylor's term, of whether our lives have 'spiritual significance' (Taylor 1989: 18). It is the kind of meaning someone seeks while embroiled in an existential crisis. In most of the other views, however, 'meaning' has the more mundane sense of intelligibility. In these views meaning need not apply to a life as a whole, but rather to the bits of behavior that make it up—the behavior of MacIntyre's gardener or of Gilbert the robot when he enters the closet. Even in the NSCV and in Dennett's view, where the required narrative spans an entire life and the meaning of individual events comes from the whole of one's life, there is no claim that the life itself, taken as a whole, has some further meaning.

While I have distinguished the grander type of meaning found in hermeneutical views from the mundane intelligibility required by other narrative theorists, defenders of hermeneutical theories would reject this distinction. They hold that the more mundane notion of intelligibility rests upon the stronger one. If there is no ultimate purpose, they say, nothing that it is all about in the end, then our more mundane purposes are illusory and even the more basic kinds of intelligibility are threatened. In order for our actions to be intelligible at all on this view, we need to find significance in our lives as a whole. This is, naturally, a contentious claim. Most narrative theorists would hold that human action and experience can be made intelligible by being put into a more basic kind of narrative and do not see a need for a life to have an overarching theme or purpose. We may be alienated and unhappy if we think that mundane meaning is all the meaning there is (or we may not), but the act of pulling weeds to keep the garden nice is fully *intelligible* even if we do not think that the garden signifies anything at all in the grand scheme of things.

It is difficult to adjudicate this dispute; in many ways it seems to come down to two fundamentally different pictures of human existence, with some truth in each. It seems obvious that we need not explicitly think of our lives as having overall purpose to find our actions basically intelligible—someone who finds life purposeless or ultimately absurd may still understand that he is walking north to catch the train that will take him to work, even if he does not quite know why he bothers to go. At the same time, there does seem to be some legitimacy to the claim that any local purpose can always be challenged with a further 'why' question. (Why is he pulling those plants? To get his garden in shape. Why? To please his wife. Why?, etc.). Mundane intelligibility does seem to require placement in ever broader contexts to produce real intelligibility, and this is something that deserves to be explored and addressed in more detail than it usually is by most narrative theorists.

Normativity, evaluation, agency

Another theme found in almost all narrative views is that selfhood and the narratives that make us selves must involve some level of evaluation and normativity. This theme is directly connected to the one we just discussed. Intelligibility requires an aim or purpose at which action is directed, but purpose requires evaluation—a valued outcome we hope to bring about. Because of this connection, the expression of the demand for an evaluative component of self-narratives varies in something like the way emphasis on meaning did, with hermeneutical narrative theories calling for a stronger form of evaluation than the other views.

In hermeneutical views, ethical orientation is at the heart of selfhood, and the narrative life of the self must be a quest for the good. Other narrative theories allow a much broader understanding of the relevant kind of evaluation, one which is not necessarily tied to ethics or morality in any traditional sense. Velleman, for instance, says Gilbert the robot's announcement that he is going to the closet gives him *reasons* to go to the closet, since doing so is necessary to keeping his narrative coherent. This makes him an evaluator, a being who can view some courses of action as preferable to others in a principled way, long before any question of ethics or the good life is brought in. Evaluation enters into the NSCV in much the same way as in Velleman's view. In Nelson's account, simple evaluation is a part of what makes up the narratives of preschoolers, and something that is learnt along with temporal sequencing from listening to the narratives of adults. The trip to visit Daddy is described as 'fun'—an evaluation to be sure, but quite far from any developed consideration of the good.

The dispute described above about whether mundane meaning is possible without deeper meaning is recapitulated in obvious ways with respect to evaluation, and it is similarly inconclusive.[3] Still, we see in each version of the narrative approach an emphasis on evaluation, and this is an important characteristic of the approach as a whole. It shows that a core element of the narrative view is an emphasis on choice, value, and agency. However this is understood, it distinguishes the narrative conception from a more Cartesian picture of self as a basically passive experiencing subject. On this approach practical reasoning of some sort is an essential feature of selfhood, and of the meaning that inheres in the lives of selves.

Embeddedness, embodiedness, interactions with others

A feature related to emphasis on evaluation which is also found throughout the narrative approach is an emphasis on the fact that selves are embodied creatures, embedded in a social context in which they interact with others. The idea that selves are agents brings with it the idea that selfhood is something that emerges in a community, further distinguishing the narrative conception of self from the Cartesian picture of an isolated and independent thinking subject. This feature, too, is expressed differently in the different versions of the narrative approach, but in this case the differences may be somewhat more superficial than with the other features.

In the hermeneutical views, we see this feature in the stress put on the necessity of placing oneself in a tradition. There can no more be private meaning in the sense requisite for selfhood, according to these theorists, than there can be a private language according to Wittgenstein, and for many of the same reasons. 'To be a subject of a narrative', MacIntyre says, is 'to be accountable for the actions and experiences which compose a narratable life. It is, that is, to be open to being asked to give a certain kind of account of what one did or what happened to one' (1984: 103). The narrative structure of selfhood also means that one can ask others for an account of what they have done or suffered and expect to receive one. Without such accountability narratives 'would lack the continuity required to make both

---

[3] There is a weaker reading of hermeneutical theories according to which they, also, can allow a broader conception of value or meaning than I have described here. This reading, however, has a cost that we will see when we consider objections to the narrative approach.

them and the actions that constitute them intelligible' (ibid.). Taylor also emphasizes this feature of narrative. A narrative requires a moral framework, and to have these frameworks we must place ourselves in a historical tradition, even if only to react against it. It is for this reason that he says that 'one is a self only among other selves. A self can never be described without reference to those who surround it', adding that 'this obviously cannot be just a contingent matter' (Taylor 1989: 35).

The NSCV places two constraints on self-constituting narratives; the 'articulation constraint', which involves the capability to articulate one's narrative locally where appropriate, and the 'reality constraint', which demands that our narratives fit with the basic conception of reality shared by those in our community (it probably cannot e.g. involve being able to get from Paris to Chicago in one minute). The justification for these constraints is precisely that selfhood requires the ability to engage in certain kinds of characteristic human interactions and this in turn requires that we master our community's understanding of what the life of a self looks like and apply it to ourselves. Selfhood is an essentially social concept here as well. This basic idea is also present in Velleman's view, since it is fundamentally an account of self as agent. This emphasis on embeddedness takes a somewhat different form in Nelson's account, but one that is connected closely with the other views. Nelson emphasizes the need for social scaffolding in developing narratives, and concludes that

narrative emerges from and belongs to the community, but in the individual lives of children it is a vehicle through which consciousness of both self and the wider social and temporal world becomes manifest and gradually emerges as a new subjective level of conscious awareness, with a sense of a specific past and awareness of a possible future, as well as with new insight into the consciousness of other people. (Nelson 2003: 33)

Narrative thus comes from the community and serves as the vehicle through which an individual can interact with it.

In all of these views we see an insistence that one can be a self only by distinguishing oneself from, and interacting with, other selves. One important implication of this embeddedness, as we have seen, is that it puts constraints on our self-narratives. We are not composing the stories of our lives in a vacuum, but in a world where there are others with their own stories about themselves and about us. If narration is going to produce meaning in the way it must for selfhood we need somehow to negotiate the multiple narratives in which we are involved. It is this that leads MacIntyre to caution that: 'we are never more (and sometimes less) than the co-authors of our own narratives. Only in fantasy do we live what story we please' (MacIntyre 1984: 99). Both because our narratives must make reference to the stories available to us from the traditions in which we find ourselves and because they must interact with the realities of the world in which we live and the narratives of others, our narratives must be understood as embedded in a world of other selves.

How do we tell our narratives?

So far we have looked at themes common to all narrative views and highlighted differences in their expression. Here we find a commonality linked to a common unclarity. The unclarity is associated with the question of whether and how we tell our self-narratives. Narratives are, in the first instance, stories told to an audience. If selves are narrative in structure, we may reasonably ask whether their narratives are told, and if so how, and to whom. Narrative theories seem to differ in their answers to these questions, but because none of them presents an entirely clear answer, it is not obvious how deep these differences run. To see this, consider the question of how our narratives should be expressed as it would be answered by the views we have been discussing.

Hermeneutical theorists see selfhood as consisting in a self-conscious quest for the good. This suggests that the fundamentals of our narratives must be something that we at least tell ourselves. We may not explicitly describe our lives as a narrative or a quest, but if we are not aware of the active attempt to move our lives in the direction of the good we would not, I presume, be selves on this view. Moreover, since the values that underlie our lives as a whole are used in explaining ourselves to others, we must at least sometimes articulate them to these others. Hermeneutical theorists also say that we must enact our narratives; we do not so much *tell* them as live them by engaging in purposive activity that strives for a unified good. So it seems as if, according to these theories, we must explicitly understand our whole lives as a quest for the good, sometimes articulate the values and themes that guide this quest to others, and always express them in our actions. But this is still sketchy and it is not evident what it amounts to in practice. It is not that these theorists do not say anything on this score, only that it is hard to get a clear picture of what they are saying. MacIntyre, for instance, rather unhelpfully tells us that 'the only criteria for success or failure in a human life as a whole are the criteria of success or failure in a narrated or to-be-narrated quest' (1984: 219), but does not tell us anything about what the status 'to-be-narrated' entails.

Dennett presents narratives as something explicitly told. Gilbert the robot either says or writes everything that happens, just as Melville writes down all of the events that make up Ishmael's story. It is by no means evident, however, that Dennett envisions narration being similarly articulated in human lives. In his discussion of Sybil, as we have seen, he suggests that one's narrative can be expressed in action as well as in words. It is clear that Dennett sees our brains as spinning narratives, but it is less clear just how and when (or if) these narratives are told and to what audience. Velleman's reinterpretation of Dennett is similarly mysterious. Who, for instance, is the audience of my narrative of my scratching an itch or eating a meal? Presumably narratives are enacted in life for Velleman, but since reason-giving often involves explicit narration, there must be some of that as well.

For Nelson self-narrations are explicit, but this is an artifact of the experimental set-up that tests children for their capacity to offer narrative accounts. The inability to verbally reproduce any part of one's history in narrative form would certainly be taken as evidence that a child has not mastered the necessary cognitive skills, but it is not clear exactly what kind of narration, if any, is supposed to be happening when the child is not telling her story to others. Finally, the NSCV requires that one be able to articulate one's narrative locally where appropriate, but sees narration as a largely implicit process that manifests itself mostly in the quality of our experience and the choices that we make.

It seems safe to say that no narrative view requires that we compose explicit and complete autobiographies in speech, writing, or thought, but that all of them require that we be able at least occasionally to explicitly narrate at least some portion of our lives. Much of our self-narration is expressed in the way we think, the way we live, and the kinds of explanations we feel called upon to give to others. Beyond this, however, it is hard to say anything much more specific about how self-narration is supposed to work. This is, I think, a common frustration with the narrative view, and one to which I will return in discussing objections in the next section.

3. Objections to the Narrative Approach

As the narrative approach has become more widely accepted there has naturally been an increasing number of detractors. Here I will focus on some prominent objections to this approach. They are not the only objections that have been offered, but they are important objections that connect with some of the insights generated in the previous sections.

Strawson's episodic nature and Zahavi's minimal self

Galen Strawson, one of the most famous opponents of narrative views, identifies two strands of the narrative approach. There is what he calls the 'psychological Narrativity thesis', which holds as a 'straightforwardly empirical, descriptive thesis' that ordinary humans experience their lives in narrative form, and what he calls the 'ethical Narrativity thesis', which holds that it is a good thing to experience one's life as a narrative—'essential to a well-lived life, to true or full personhood' (Strawson 2004: 428). Strawson rejects both theses. The psychological thesis is, on his view, false, while the ethical thesis is pernicious. Narrative theorists, he surmises, have based their views on introspection, assuming that the way they arrange their experiences is the way everyone else does or that the kind of life that works well for them will work well for everybody. This assumption is unwarranted, Strawson argues, and he offers himself as a counterexample to universalized narrative claims about the self. Describing himself as an 'Episodic' he says that he has 'absolutely no sense of [his] life as a narrative with form, or indeed as a narrative without form. Absolutely none.' He asserts, moreover, that he is able to live a perfectly rich, full, and meaningful life without such a narrative and suggests that views that demand that everyone strive for a narrative self-experience, 'close down important avenues of thought, impoverish our grasp of ethical possibilities, needlessly and wrongly distress those who do not fit their model, and are potentially destructive in psychotherapeutic contexts' (Strawson 2004: 429).

In explicating this claim Strawson draws a distinction between 'one's experience of oneself when one is considering oneself principally as a human being taken as a whole, and one's experience of oneself when one is considering oneself principally as an inner mental entity or "self" of some sort' (Strawson 2004: 429). Strawson uses self* (and the corresponding I*, you*, he*) to designate this inner mental entity. He recognizes that he* has a special relation to the other selves that have inhabited the body of Galen Strawson (GS), but sees himself* as a different experiencing subject: 'I'm well aware that my past is mine in so far as I am a human being, and I fully accept that there is a sense in which it has special relevance to me* now. At the same time I have no sense that I* was there in the past, and think it is obvious that I* was not there, as a matter of metaphysical fact' (Strawson 2004: 434). His self, he holds, is episodic in nature, and not part of any ongoing narrative.

Much of Strawson's account of his episodic nature is a denial that his life has any overall theme or moral unity of the sort required by the hermeneutical narrative view. Since this analysis does not apply to all versions of the narrative view, it is most useful to think of Strawson's challenge as presenting a dilemma for narrative theorists. The dilemma is roughly this: either narrative views are too demanding to be plausible or they are not 'narrative' in any interesting sense. That is, either the narrative view really demands that our lives and self-understandings are like literature in some strong sense or it does not. If it is the former Strawson's Episodic self serves as a counterexample; if the latter, it risks triviality. As Strawson puts it, 'if someone says, as some do, that making coffee is a Narrative that involves Narrativity, because you have to think ahead, do things in the right order, and so on, and that everyday life involves many such narratives, then I take it the claim is trivial' (Strawson 2004: 439).

Hermeneutical theorists obviously fall on the first horn of the dilemma. A possible response for these theorists is to claim that Strawson's Episodic nature does not, in fact, serve as a counterexample to the narrative view because episodicity as he depicts it is in fact narrative. In describing himself as an Episodic, these theorists might argue, Strawson precisely tells us something about his deeper nature and the values that shape his life as a whole. He asserts, for instance, that 'truly happy-go-lucky, see-what-comes-along lives are among the best there are, vivid, blessed, profound' (Strawson 2004: 449). 'Blessed' and 'profound' certainly sound like ethical terms. These theorists might thus argue that Strawson has misunderstood the nature of narrative in claiming that his life is non-narrative. The free spirit is a recognizable character from literature, as Stawson himself reveals by using the character Tom Bombadil from *The Lord of the Rings* as an example of such a being (Strawson 2004: 449 n. 49). Looking to be free from stifling thematic unity is something that the hermeneutical view can recognize as a quest. The NSCV can follow a similar strategy, arguing that the way in which Strawson recognizes all of the actions and experiences of GS as having implications for how things are for him* and for what he must do is all that is required for a self-narrative.

Strawson might argue that these replies throw these theorists to the other horn of the dilemma. If Strawson's episodic orientation and his recognition of certain facts about his connection to the history of GS qualify as having a narrative, he might say, then a narrative is something we cannot help but have and the claim that it is something we must have if our lives are to be meaningful seems to lose much of its force. This in itself is not a problem since most narrative theorists would accept the claim that we cannot but have a narrative; in some ways that is their very point. But if any set of preferences counts as an ethical orientation or a quest for a good, the claim that someone has a self-narrative in even the strongest sense proposed seems to collapse into a claim that selves have some set of characteristics and need a basic understanding of the unfolding of events, and this does seem trivial.

This brings us to the second horn of the dilemma. If we are going to allow that a self-narrative need not have the characteristics of a literary work we have to explain in what sense it is a *narrative*, and to do so in a way that makes the claims of the narrative approach non-trivial. Narrative theorists do have something to say in response here. As we have seen, the claim that selves are narrative in structure is minimally a claim that there is a form of explanation necessary to describing human lives that does not reduce to physical or biological explanation and gives events and actions significance. There is a way in which human actions hang together that is characteristic and purposive. As Anthony Rudd puts it in his response to Strawson, the claim 'that the understanding of even simple human actions must take a narrative form is, I would suggest, by no means a trivial point, given the continuing influence of rival, scientist models of action-explanation' (Rudd 2009: 63).[4] It is by no means obvious that the claims of narrative theorists

---

[4] Rudd goes on to claim that he thinks that the real concern is with whether these mundane narratives imply that one's life as a whole is narrative in form. He argues that they indeed do, employing the kind of strategy described earlier of claiming that local intelligibility ultimately requires broader context.

become trivial as soon as they allow life narratives to deviate from literary form. Still, as our earlier discussion already revealed, and as I shall discuss further below, it would be useful for the approach as a whole to have a clearer expression of what characterizes narrative and how it differs from other explanatory forms.

There is, I think, another kind of disagreement between Strawson and narrative theorists that stands behind the differences already described. It seems sometimes less as if Strawson and narrative theorists disagree on how to explain the phenomenon of self, and more that they disagree on what that phenomenon is. For Strawson self is defined in terms of subjectivity alone; the entire dimension of agency and embeddedness is left out of the equation (see Chapter 10 above). This points to a whole new set of questions for the narrative theorist. Self-consciousness, reflexivity, and the capacity to know oneself as oneself are crucial elements of the self on the narrative approach, but it is not always evident where the brute phenomenological experience of oneself as a self distinct from others fits into the whole picture, and this is another lacuna.

This concern also emerges in Dan Zahavi's complaint that narrative theories are incomplete because they fail to recognize a core component of selfhood, namely the fundamental, given mineness that is part of the structure of all experience. This 'primitive self', described in the work of phenomenologists, is 'conceived as the invariant dimension of first-personal givenness in the multitude of changing experiences' (Zahavi 2007: 189). Zahavi does not deny that narrative organization of experience can be very important to us and is part of our selfhood but it cannot, he says, be all of selfhood. Without narrative we can still have brute first-personal experience, but without the phenomenology of the first-personal there is no narrative. 'None of the narrative theories . . . even come near to being able to explain how first-personal givenness could be brought about by narrative structures but', he says, 'this failure is not really surprising, since the reverse happens to be the case' (Zahavi 2007: 200). The claim that narrative is not required for selfhood, found in both Strawson and Zahavi, can thus be seen as the claim that what narrative adds (complex interactions with others, meaningful experience) are at most enrichments of an already existing self. A self, on this view, is a self-conscious entity that is the kind of thing that might care about the nature of its life and interactions, and narrative comes in after the self already exists.

One way to respond to these worries is to allow that there are many uses of the term 'self' and that narrative theorists are defining only one of these. There is, however, a much more interesting line of response. A narrative theorist might argue that the kind of phenomenological self-consciousness that makes a self is a qualitatively different *kind* of consciousness than the brute first-personal awareness we presumably share with many animals, and that this different kind of consciousness requires narrative. The idea would be that the character (and not just the content) of first-personal experience is different for self-narrators than for non-narrators. Something like this is suggested, for instance, in Nelson's talk of a new level of self-consciousness that emerges when we learn to narrate. This is an intriguing possibility, and I believe that the empirical work in evolutionary and developmental psychology has much to offer in considering whether it is defensible.[5]

Strawson and Zahavi thus do not offer completely devastating criticisms of the narrative approach; narrative theorists can respond to most of their objections. Nevertheless, they do point out important places where narrative theorists are unclear about the exact nature of their claims and points where the approach could be further developed. In particular, we have seen a need to get clearer on the essential features of narrative explanation and on the role of phenomenology and self-consciousness in the narrative approach.

Lamarque and literary narrative

A second major objection comes from Peter Lamarque who argues that narrative theories of the self take the analogy between life and literature too seriously in a way that threatens to mislead us about both. A core feature of literature, he says, is that the manner in which a story is presented is of the utmost importance. When we are trying to understand a piece of literature we look at the language in which the story is told. We assume that the details of the story—the color of a hair-ribbon, a seemingly accidental encounter—are serving some artistic purpose, and we look for symbolism, foreshadowing, and other literary devices in interpreting their meaning. To think of our lives as genuinely like literature we thus need to do one of two things; either we must reduce literature to plot and character—as if the details of presentation do not really matter—or we must think of our lives as full of purpose and meaning at every turn—as if the accidents and coincidences that befall us are really by design. 'The more we try to restore the distinctively literary features of [canonical literary] narratives the more remote they become from real life', he says. 'Indeed a stronger point can be made. To the extent that literary features are brought to bear on real-life narratives they have a distorting and pernicious effect on the self-understanding that such narratives are supposed to yield' (Lamarque 2007: 119).

---

[5] I have also suggested such a connection (see e.g. Schechtman 1996: 149–62; 2004). More recently I have offered a response to Strawson, acknowledging that the NSCV equivocates on whether the unity of self consists in a strong phenomenological connection of the sort Strawson sees as constituting the self and a weaker kind of narrative connection of the sort that unifies his understanding of the continuity of the life of GS. But I also explore the possibility that there are deeper connections between these two notions than may at first appear. While this is not exactly on the point of whether the quality of self-consciousness is affected by narrative, it is not unrelated (Schechtman 2007).

To underscore this point, Lamarque looks at how literary critics work. These critics dissect the language and details of presentation in a novel, showing how literary devices are employed by authors to communicate the themes and insights that lie behind the events of narratives. It is not even clear what it would mean to take a similar stance with respect to one's own life, he points out. Lives just have a different logic than constructed works of fiction because they are not works of art. If we take 'the great literary works to be models for our self-directed narratives,' he thus concludes, 'we are prone to two serious mistakes' (Lamarque 2007: 132). The less serious is 'to suppose that literary works are simply stories about people like you and me, a species of real life narratives'. The more serious and potentially dangerous mistake is 'to suppose that our own life narratives are mini-works of literature complying with the principles of literary appreciation'. This mistake is potentially dangerous because it invokes a 'false image of ourselves as kinds of fictional characters, whose identity rests on narrative description and whose actions are explicable in functional, teleological or thematic ways' (Lamarque 2007: 132).

Lamarque's concerns, like Strawson's, apply most straightforwardly to the hermeneutical narrative views. Still, insofar as all narrative views make the claim that the lives of persons are characterized by meaning, and insofar as Lamarque's claim is that the kind of significance events in our lives have is vastly different from the kind that events in narratives do, his criticism applies to them all. I will begin by considering how defenders of hermeneutical views might reply, and from there we will be able to see how this response can be more broadly applied.

It is important to note first that the question of the correspondence of life to literature is one about which hermeneutical theorists are themselves divided. MacIntyre allows some differences between life and literature (the fact that we can at most co-author our lives), but is clear that he sees them as essentially the same in structure. As we have seen, Ricoeur differs from MacIntyre on this issue, seeing differences between life and literature very like those Lamarque does (Ricoeur 1994: 159–61). Ricoeur does not see these differences as undermining the narrative approach, however. These difficulties, he says, 'do not seem to me to be such as to abolish the very option of the *application* of fiction to life. The objections are valid only in opposition to a naive conception of *mimēsis*.' He goes on to say 'these are less to be refuted than to be incorporated in a more subtle, more dialectical comprehension of *appropriation*' (ibid. 161–2). Ricoeur's suggestive response to the differences between life and literature is to define selfhood in terms of the negotiation of these differences.

Using Ricoeur's basic insight as inspiration, we can devise a strategy for responding to Lamarque that both illuminates the narrative approach and points to a direction for further development. To begin, let's separate three different roles with respect to narrative: those of character, author, and critic (or reader). In discussing the difference between life and literature, Lamarque focuses most directly on the perspective of the critic. He suggests that a critic looking at a piece of literature should assume she is dealing with an artifact whose meaning is best determined by presupposing that the details are non-accidental and therefore all potentially significant.[6] This is so because it is assumed that the author, who builds the narrative out of whole cloth, chooses each detail for some aesthetic purpose—to symbolize a major theme, move the plot along, develop characters, and so on. From the point of view of the author, then, decisions about what to include must be made with such purposes in mind. From the point of view of the characters in a novel, on the other hand, there are plenty of accidents and contingencies, as Lamarque himself points out in discussing the accident at the beginning of *Tess of the d'Ubervilles*. If the question is what caused Tess's accident 'the answer, within the fictional world, is that she fell asleep and was run into by the mail-cart' (Lamarque 2007: 125). From the perspective of the literary critic, on the other hand, the answer is that the accident lays out the themes of the entire novel.

Lamarque's complaint is that our lives are not everywhere filled with purpose and design, but are rather driven by accident, contingency, and coincidence. We might put this by saying that narrative theorists, on his view, suggest we should take the perspective of the critic and/or author on our own lives, when in fact the only accurate perspective is that which would be taken by a character within a fictional world. The kinds of explanations that apply to our lives are the kind Tess would give of her accident, not the kind a critic would, and only the latter is rife with the kind of significance narrative theorists are after. But we may ask if narrative theorists really do suggest that we take only the attitude of critic. The version that comes closest to doing so is, again, that offered by hermeneutical theorists, and even they do not say we should take the perspective of critic or even author to the *exclusion* of the perspective of character. It is perhaps better to think of these views as saying, as Ricoeur implies, that what is unique to selves is that they must take all of these perspectives.

We must view our lives on the level of a character internal to a fictional world insofar as successful selfhood requires us to acknowledge that we are at best co-authors of our own lives and that we are constrained by the facts about the social and natural world in which we find ourselves. But we must also take the perspective of authors because we are not just moved about by causal forces and there is no author outside of us who will directly push our story forward. While we do not make our lives up out of nothing, finding ourselves in the world we are also confronted with the question of what to do next. We cannot always decide any way we wish, and we are never guaranteed that things will go as we plan, but we must think of ourselves as authors of our lives insofar as we must make decisions

---

[6] I will not engage in disputes about the nature of criticism, which are not directly germane to the central point here, but will operate with the view I take to be Lamarque's.

and these must involve reasons or purposes. Insofar as we are agents, we are partial authors of our lives. We are also critics, reflecting on our lives. When we do take the role of critic in our own life, however, we must do so with an understanding of the kind of authorship involved, looking for significance of an accident, for instance, in the choices that led to it and the responses it engenders, rather than in the fact that it occurred.

The three roles we have been describing are only artificially separated in human life. As critics we interpret what has happened so far in a way that impacts the future authorship of our lives, and as characters we enact those choices and have the experiences that generate the significance we appreciate as critics. For narrative theorists we are beings who generate meaning in our own lives by finding meaning in the unfolding of events, intending actions we find meaningful, and living according to the meanings we have found. We enter into ongoing stories, stories we must interpret and continue, and these functions are in constant interaction with one another. Life is different from literature because we write it as we live it and engage in criticism as we go along rather than after the fact, and because this forces us to take on different roles and perspectives. The creative act in narrative self-constitution is thus neither to produce a tidy and meaningful story out of whole cloth nor to take accidents and contingencies and arbitrarily interpret them as meaningful. It is rather to carve out a meaningful life trajectory by appreciating the contingencies, considering how to respond to them meaningfully, and directing life so much as possible in the direction of that meaning.

This, I think, is why these theorists have so much difficulty giving a clear account of exactly how narration occurs in actual lives; it occurs in different ways at different levels all at once. Having seen this we may wonder whether some of the differences among narrative views might be largely attributable to different levels of emphasis on the different roles. Views that think of the self in terms of mundane narratives that track the events that befall one emphasize the way in which we are characters in our narratives and, to a lesser extent, critics. Velleman's view of selves as agents emphasizes our role as authors, but of course we must be characters and critics to be agents in this way as well. The hermeneutical views emphasize our role as critics more than some of the other views do, and Nelson's view is more concerned with how we gain the basic capacities necessary to negotiate the different roles. The proponents of these views might well reject this suggestion. It is, nevertheless, an intriguing possibility to see the fundamental insight of the narrative approach as the claim that selves are beings who negotiate the roles of character, author, and critic in their own lives, and that the unique kind of meaning or significance found in human lives comes from just that fact.

4. Conclusion

We have seen that the narrative approach is made up of a wide array of different kinds of views addressed to different questions. We have also seen that perhaps at bottom these views share a similar insight—namely that the complexity of selves is to be found in the multiple perspectives on our lives that we negotiate in living them, a complexity best understood in narrative terms. This is a promising insight at many levels, but much work remains to develop its full potential. The chief difficulties facing narrative theories revolve around making the idea that the self is narrative concrete—What, exactly, counts as a narrative in this context? Where do self-narratives reside, how explicitly must they be articulated, and to whom? Where do the phenomenological aspects of selfhood fit in?

Thinking about the narrative self in terms of the interplay between the three narrative roles provides a strategy for beginning to answer these questions and the promise of a more fleshed-out narrative view, one with the potential to define a being complex enough to appear contingently in the seat next to you on a long plane flight, to amuse, distract, or annoy you with the stories of his life, and in so doing to alter the course of your own.

References

BRUNER, JEROME (1990). *Acts of Meaning* (Cambridge, Mass.: Harvard University Press).

DENNETT, DANIEL (1992). 'The Self as a Center of Narrative Gravity', in Frank S. Kessel, Pamela M. Cole, and Dale L., Johnson (eds), *Self and Consciousness: Multiple Perspectives* (Hillsdale, NJ: Lawrence Erlbaum Associates), 103–15.

DAMASIO, ANTONIO (1999). *The Feeling of What Happens: Body and Emotion in the Making of Consciousness* (New York: Harcourt Brace & Co.).

DONALD, MERLIN (1991). *Origins of the Modern Mind: Three Stages in the Evolution of Culture and Cognition* (Cambridge, Mass.; Harvard University Press).

——(2001). *A Mind so Rare: The Evolution of Human Consciousness* (New York: W.W. Norton & Co.)

GALLAGHER, SHAUN (2007). 'Pathologies in Narrative Structures', in Daniel Hutto (ed.), *Narrative and Understanding Persons* (Cambridge: Cambridge University Press), 203–24.

GOLDIE, PETER (2007a). 'Dramatic Irony, Narrative, and the External Perspective', in Daniel Hutto (ed.), *Narrative and Understanding Persons* (Cambridge: Cambridge University Press), 69–82.

——(2007b). 'Narrative Thinking, Emotion and Planning', *Journal of Aesthetics and Art Criticism*, 67/1: 97–106.

HARDCASTLE, VALERIE GREY (2008). *Constructing the Self* (Amsterdam: John Benjamins Publishing Co.).

HUTTO, DANIEL (2008). *Folk Psychological Narratives: The Sociocultural Basis of Under-standing Reasons* (Cambridge, Mass.: Bradford Books).

LAMARQUE, PETER (2007). 'On the Distance between Literary Narratives and Real-Life Narratives', in Daniel Hutto (ed.), *Narrative and Understanding Persons* (Cambridge: Cambridge University Press), 117–32.

LINDEMANN NELSON, HILDE (2001). *Damaged Identities, Narrative Repair* (Ithaca, NY: Cornell University Press).

LLOYD, GENEVIEVE (1993). *Being in Time: Selves and Narrators in Philosophy and Literature* (London: Routledge).

MACINTYRE, ALASDAIR (1984). *After Virtue* (2nd edn. Notre Dame, Ind.: University of Notre Dame Press).

NELSON, KATHERINE (2003). 'Narrative and the Emergence of a Consciousness of Self', in Gary D. Fireman, Ted E. McVay, Jr., and Owen J. Flanagan (eds), *Narrative and Consciousness* (New York: Oxford University Press).

RICOEUR, PAUL (1994). *Oneself as Another*, tr. Kathleen Blamey (Chicago: University of Chicago Press).

RUDD, ANTHONY (2009), 'In Defence of Narrative', *European Journal of Philosophy*, 17/1: 63.

SCHECHTMAN, MARYA (1996). *The Constitution of Selves* (Ithaca, NY: Cornell University Press).

——(2004). 'The Case of Self-Interested Reasons', in Maureen Sie, Marc Slors, and Bert Van Den Brink (eds), *Reasons of One's Own* (Aldershot: Ashgate), 107–28.

——(2007). 'Stories, Lives, and Basic Survival: A Refinement and Defense of the Narrative View', in Daniel Hutto (ed.), *Narrative and Understanding Persons* (Cambridge: Cambridge University Press), 155–79.

STRAWSON, GALEN (2004). 'Against Narrativity', *Ratio*, 17/4: 428–52.

TAYLOR, CHARLES (1989). *Sources of the Self* (Cambridge, Mass.: Harvard University Press).

VELLEMAN, J. DAVID (2006). 'The Self as Narrator', in *Self to Self: Selected Essays* (Cambridge: Cambridge University Press), 203–23.

ZAHAVI, DAN (2007). 'Self and Other: The Limits of Narrative Understanding' in Daniel Hutto (ed.), *Narrative and Understanding Persons* (Cambridge: Cambridge University Press), 179–202.

PART V

ACTION AND THE MORAL DIMENSIONS OF THE SELF

CHAPTER 18

THE UNIMPORTANCE OF IDENTITY

DEREK PARFIT

WE can start with some science fiction. Here on Earth, I enter the teletransporter. When I press some button, a machine destroys my body, while recording the exact states of all my cells. The information is sent by radio to Mars, where another machine makes, out of organic materials, a perfect copy of my body. The person who wakes up on Mars seems to remember living my life up to the moment when I pressed the button, and he is in every other way just like me.

Of those who have thought about such cases, some believe that it would be I who would wake up on Mars. They regard teletransportation as merely the fastest way of travelling. Others believe that, if I chose to be teletransported, I would be making a terrible mistake. On their view, the person who wakes up would be a mere replica of me.

This essay originally appeared in Henry Harris (ed.), *Identity: Essays Based on Herbert Spencer Lectures given in the University of Oxford* (New York: Clarendon Press, 1995), 13–45. It appears here with minor revisions. Some of it draws from part III of Parfit 1984.

I

That is a disagreement about personal identity. To understand such disagreements, we must distinguish two kinds of sameness. Two billiard balls may be qualitatively identical, or exactly similar. But they are not numerically identical, or one and the same ball. If I paint one of these balls a different colour, it will cease to be qualitatively identical with itself as it was; but it will still be one and the same ball. Consider next a claim like, 'Since her accident, she is no longer the same person.' That involves both senses of identity. It means that *she*, one and the same person, is *not* now the same person. That is not a contradiction. The claim is only that this person's character has changed. This numerically identical person is now qualitatively different.

When psychologists discuss identity, they are typically concerned with the kind of person someone is, or wants to be. That is the question involved, for example, in an identity crisis. But, when philosophers discuss identity, it is numerical identity they mean. And, in our concern about our own futures, that is what we have in mind. I may believe that, after my marriage, I shall be a different person. But that does not make marriage death. However much I change, I shall still be alive if there will be someone living who will be me. Similarly, if I was teletransported, my replica on Mars would be qualitatively identical to me; but, on the sceptic's view, he wouldn't *be* me. *I* shall have ceased to exist. And that, we naturally assume, is what matters.

Questions about our numerical identity all take the following form. We have two ways of referring to a person, and we ask whether these are ways of referring to the same person. Thus we might ask whether Boris Nikolayevich is Yeltsin. In the most important questions of this kind, our two ways of referring to a person pick out a person at different times. Thus we might ask whether the person to whom we are speaking now is the same as the person to whom we spoke on the telephone yesterday. These are questions about identity over time.

To answer such questions, we must know the *criterion* of personal identity: the relation between a person at one time, and a person at another time, which makes these one and the same person.

Different criteria have been advanced. On one view, what makes me the same, throughout my life, is my having the same body. This criterion requires uninterrupted bodily continuity. There is no such continuity between my body on Earth and the body of my replica on Mars; so, on this view, my replica would not be me. Other writers appeal to psychological continuity. Thus Locke claimed that, if I was conscious of a past life in some other body, I would be the person who lived that life. On some versions of this view, my replica would be me.

Supporters of these different views often appeal to cases where they conflict. Most of these cases are, like teletransportation, purely imaginary. Some philosophers object that, since our concept of a person rests on a scaffolding of facts, we should not expect this concept to apply in imagined cases where we think those facts away. I agree. But I believe that, for a different reason, it is worth considering such cases. We can use them to discover, not what the truth is, but what we believe. We might have found that, when we consider science fiction cases, we simply shrug our shoulders. But that is not so. Many of us find that we have certain beliefs about what kind of fact personal identity is.

These beliefs are best revealed when we think about such cases from a first-person point of view. So, when I imagine something's happening to me, you should imagine its happening to you. Suppose that I live in some future century, in which technology is far advanced, and I am about to undergo some operation. Perhaps my brain and body will be remodeled, or partially replaced. There will be a resulting person, who will wake up tomorrow. I ask, 'Will that person be me? Or am I about to die? Is this the end?' I may not know how to answer this question. But it is natural to assume that there must *be* an answer. The resulting person, it may seem, must be either me, or someone else. And the answer must be all-or-nothing. That person can't be *partly* me. If that person is in pain tomorrow, this pain can't be partly mine. So, we may assume, either I shall feel that pain, or I shan't.

If this is how we think about such cases, we assume that our identity must be *determinate.* We assume that, in every imaginable case, questions about our identity must have answers, which must be either, and quite simply, Yes or No.

Let us now ask: can this be true? There is one view on which it might be. On this view, there are immaterial substances: souls, or Cartesian Egos. These entities have the special properties once ascribed to atoms: they are indivisible, and their continued existence is, in its nature, all or nothing. And such an Ego is what each of us really is.

Unlike several writers, I believe that such a view might be true. But we have no good evidence for thinking that it is, and some evidence for thinking that it isn't; so I shall assume here that no such view is true.

If we do not believe that there are Cartesian Egos, or other such entities, we should accept the kind of view which I have elsewhere called *reductionist.* On this view

(1) A person's existence just consists in the existence of a body, and the occurrence of a series of thoughts, experiences, and other mental and physical events.

Some reductionists claim

(2) Persons just *are* bodies.

This view may seem not to be reductionist, since it does not reduce persons to something else. But that is only because it is hyper-reductionist: it reduces persons to bodies in so strong a way that it doesn't even distinguish between them. We can call this *identifying* reductionism.

Such a view seems to me too simple. I believe that we should combine (1) with

(3) A person is an entity that has a body, and has thoughts and other experiences.

On this view, though a person is distinct from that person's body, and from any series of thoughts and experiences, the person's existence just *consists* in them. So we can call this view *constitutive* reductionism.

It may help to have other examples of this kind of view. If we melt down a bronze statue, we destroy this statue, but we do not destroy this lump of bronze. So, though the statue just consists in the lump of bronze, these cannot be one and the same thing. Similarly, the existence of a nation just consists in the existence of a group of people, on some territory, living together in certain ways. But the nation is not the same as that group of people, or that territory.

Consider next *eliminative* reductionism. Such a view is sometimes a response to arguments against identifying reductionism. Suppose we start by claiming that a nation just is a group of people on some territory. We are then persuaded that this cannot be so: that the concept of a nation is the concept of an entity that is distinct from its people and its territory. We may conclude that, in that case, there are really no such things as nations. There are only groups of people, living together in certain ways.

In the case of persons, some Buddhist texts take an eliminative view. According to these texts

(4) There really aren't such things as persons: there are only brains and bodies, and thoughts and other experiences.

For example:

Buddha has spoken thus: 'O brethren, there are actions, and also their consequences, but there is no person who acts. . . . There exists no Individual, it is only a conventional name given to a set of elements.'[1]

Or:

> The mental and the material are really here,
> But here there is no person to be found.
> For it is void and fashioned like a doll,
> Just suffering piled up like grass and sticks.[2]

Eliminative reductionism is sometimes justified. Thus we are right to claim that there weren't really any witches, only persecuted women. But reductionism about

---

[1] Vasubandhu, quoted in Stcherbatsky (1919: 845).
[2] The *Visuddhimagga*, quoted in Collins (1982).

some kind of entity is not often well expressed with the claim that there are no such entities. We should admit that there are nations, and that we, who are persons, exist.

Rather than claiming that there are no entities of some kind, reductionists should distinguish kinds of entity, or ways of existing. When the existence of an X just consists in the existence of a Y, or Ys, though the X is *distinct* from the Y or Ys, it is not an *independent* or *separately existing* entity. Statues do not exist separately from the matter of which they are made. Nor do nations exist separately from their citizens and their territory. Similarly, I believe,

(5) Though persons are distinct from their bodies, and from any series of mental events, they are not independent or separately existing entities.

Cartesian Egos, if they existed, would not only be distinct from human bodies, but would also be independent entities. Such egos are claimed to be like physical objects, except that they are wholly mental. If there were such entities, it would make sense to suppose that they might cease to be causally related to some body, yet continue to exist. But, on a reductionist view, persons are not in that sense independent from their bodies. (That is not to claim that our thoughts and other experiences are merely changes in the states of our brains. Reductionists, while not believing in purely mental substances, may be dualists.)

We can now return to personal identity over time, or what constitutes the continued existence of the same person. One question here is this. What explains the unity of a person's mental life? What makes thoughts and experiences, had at different times, the thoughts and experiences of a single person? According to some non-reductionists, this question cannot be answered in other terms. We must simply claim that these different thoughts and experiences are all had by the same person. This fact does not consist in any other facts, but is a bare or ultimate truth.

If each of us was a Cartesian Ego, that might be so. Since such an ego would be an independent substance, it could be an irreducible fact that different experiences are all changes in the states of the same persisting ego. But that could not be true of persons, I believe, if, while distinct from their bodies, they are not separately existing entities. A person, so conceived, is not the kind of entity about which there could be such irreducible truths. When experiences at different times are all had by the same person, this fact must consist in certain other facts.

If we do not believe in Cartesian Egos, we should claim

(6) Personal identity over time just consists in physical and/or psychological continuity.

That claim could be filled out in different ways. On one version of this view, what makes different experiences the experiences of a single person is their being either changes in the states of, or at least directly causally related to, the same embodied brain. That must be the view of those who believe that persons just are bodies. And we might hold that view even if, as I think we should, we distinguish persons from their bodies. But we might appeal, either in addition or instead, to various psychological relations between different mental states and events, such as the relations involved in memory, or in the persistence of intentions, desires, and other psychological features. That is what I mean by psychological continuity.

On constitutive reductionism, the fact of personal identity is distinct from these facts about physical and psychological continuity. But, since it just consists in them, it is not an independent or separately obtaining fact. It is not a further difference in what happens.

To illustrate that distinction, consider a simpler case. Suppose that I already know that several trees are growing together on some hill. I then learn that, because that is true, there is a copse on this hill. That would not be new factual information. I would have merely learnt that such a group of trees can be called a 'copse'. My only new information is about our language. That those trees can be called a copse is not, except trivially, a fact about the trees.

Something similar is true in the more complicated case of nations. In order to know the facts about the history of a nation, it is enough to know what large numbers of people did and said. Facts about nations cannot be barely true: they must consist in facts about people. And, once we know these other facts, any remaining questions about nations are not further questions about what really happened.

I believe that, in the same way, facts about people cannot be barely true. Their truth must consist in the truth of facts about bodies, and about various interrelated mental and physical events. If we knew these other facts, we would have all the empirical input that we need. If we understood the concept of a person, and had no false beliefs about what persons are, we would then know, or would be able to work out, the truth of any further claims about the existence or identity of persons. That is because such claims would not tell us more about reality.

That is the barest sketch of a reductionist view. These remarks may become clearer if we return to the so called 'problem cases' of personal identity. In such a case, we imagine knowing that, between me now and some person in the future, there will be certain kinds or degrees of physical and/or psychological continuity or connectedness. But, though we know these facts, we cannot answer the question whether that future person would be me.

Since we may disagree on which the problem cases are, we need more than one example. Consider first the range of cases that I have elsewhere called the *physical spectrum*. In each of these cases, some proportion of my body would be replaced, in a single operation, with exact duplicates of the existing cells. In the case at the near end of this range, no cells would be replaced. In the case at the far end, my whole body would be destroyed and replicated. That is the case with which I began: teletransportation.

Suppose we believe that in that case, where my whole body would be replaced, the resulting person would not be me, but a mere replica. If no cells were replaced, the resulting person would be me. But what of the cases in between, where the percentage of the cells replaced would be, say, 30, or 50, or 70 per cent? Would the resulting person here be me? When we consider some of these cases, we won't know whether to answer Yes or No.

Suppose next that we believe that, even in teletransportation, my replica would be me. We should then consider a different version of that case, in which the scanner would get its information without destroying my body, and my replica would be made while I was still alive. In this version of the case, we may agree that my replica would not be me. That may shake our view that, in the original version of the case, he *would* be me.

If we still keep that view, we should turn to what I have called the *combined spectrum*. In this second range of cases, there would be all the different degrees of both physical and psychological connectedness. The new cells would not be exactly similar. The greater the proportion of my body that would be replaced, the less like me would the resulting person be. In the case at the far end of this range, my whole body would be destroyed, and they would make a replica of some quite different person, such as Greta Garbo. Garbo's replica would clearly *not* be me. In the case at the near end, with no replacement, the resulting person would be me. On any view, there must be cases in between where we could not answer our question.

For simplicity, I shall consider only the physical spectrum cases, and I shall assume that, in some of the cases in this range, we can't answer the question whether the resulting person would be me. My remarks could be transferred, with some adjustment, to the combined spectrum.

As I have said, it is natural to assume that, even if *we* can't answer this question, there must always *be* an answer, which must be either Yes or No. It is natural to believe that, if the resulting person will be in pain, either I shall feel that pain, or I shan't. But this range of cases challenges that belief. In the case at the near end, the resulting person would be me. In the case at the far end, he would be someone else. How could it be true that, in all the cases in between, he must be either me, or someone else? For that to be true, there must be, somewhere in this range, a sharp borderline. There must be some critical set of cells such that, if only those cells were replaced, it would be me who would wake up, but that in the very next case, with only just a few more cells replaced, it would be, not me, but a new person. That is hard to believe.

Here is another fact, which makes it even harder to believe. Even if there were such a borderline, no one could ever discover where it is. I might say, 'Try replacing half of my brain and body, and I shall tell you what happens'. But we know in advance that, in every case, since the resulting person would be exactly like me, he would be inclined to believe that he was me. And this could not show that he *was* me, since any mere replica of me would think that too.

Even if such cases actually occurred, we would learn nothing more about them. So it doesn't matter that these cases are imaginary. We should try to decide now whether, in this range of cases, personal identity could be determinate. Could it be true that, in every case, the resulting person either would or would not be me?

If we do not believe that there are Cartesian Egos, or other such entities, we seem forced to answer No. It is not true that our identity must be determinate. We can always ask, 'Would that future person be me?' But, in some of these cases,

(7) This question would have no answer. It would be neither true nor false that this person would be me.

And

(8) This question would be *empty.* Even without an answer, we could know the full truth about what happened.

If our questions were about such entities as nations or machines, most of us would accept such claims. But, when applied to ourselves, they can be hard to believe. How could it be neither true nor false that I shall still exist tomorrow? And, without an answer to our question, how could I know the full truth about my future?

Reductionism gives the explanation. We naturally assume that, in these cases, there are different possibilities. The resulting person, we assume, might be me, or he might be someone else, who is merely like me. If the resulting person will be in pain, either I shall feel that pain, or I shan't. If these really were different possibilities, it would be compelling that one of them must be the possibility that would in fact obtain. How could reality fail to choose between them? But, on a reductionist view,

(9) Our question is not about different possibilities. There is only a single possibility, or course of events. Our question is merely about different possible descriptions of this course of events.

That is how our question has no answer. We have not yet decided which description to apply. And, that is why, even without answering this question, we could know the full truth about what would happen.

Suppose that, after considering such examples, we cease to believe that our identity must be determinate. That may seem to make little difference. It may seem to be a change of view only about some imaginary cases, that will never actually occur. But that may not be so. We may be led to revise our beliefs about the nature of personal identity; and that would be a change of view about our own lives.

In nearly all actual cases, questions about personal identity have answers, so claim (7) does not apply. If we don't know these answers, there is something that we don't know. But claim (8) still applies. Even without answering these questions, we could know the full truth about what happens. We would know that truth if we knew the facts about both physical and psychological continuity. If, implausibly, we still didn't know the answer to a question about identity, our ignorance would only be about our language. And that is because claim (9) still applies. When we know the other facts, there are never different possibilities at the level of what happens. In all cases, the only remaining possibilities are at the linguistic level. Perhaps it would be correct to say that some future person would be me. Perhaps it would be correct to say that he would not be me. Or perhaps neither would be correct. I conclude that in *all* cases, if we know the other facts, we should regard questions about our identity as merely questions about language.

That conclusion can be misunderstood. First, when we ask such questions, that is usually because we *don't* know the other facts. Thus, when we ask if we are about to die, that is seldom a conceptual question. We ask that question because we don't know what will happen to our bodies, and whether, in particular, our brains will continue to support consciousness. Our question becomes conceptual only when we already know about such other facts.

Note next that, in certain cases, the relevant facts go beyond the details of the case we are considering. Whether some concept applies may depend on facts about other cases, or on a choice between scientific theories. Suppose we see something strange happening to an unknown animal. We might ask whether this process preserves the animal's identity, or whether the result is a new animal (because what we are seeing is some kind of reproduction). Even if we knew the details of this process, that question would not be merely conceptual. The answer would depend on whether this process is part of the natural development of this kind of animal. And that may be something we have yet to discover.

If we identify persons with human beings, whom we regard as a natural kind, the same would be true in some imaginable cases involving persons. But these are not the kind of case that I have been discussing. My cases all involve artificial intervention. No facts about natural development could be relevant here. Thus, in my physical spectrum, if we know which of my cells would be replaced by duplicates, all of the relevant empirical facts would be in. In such cases any remaining questions would be conceptual.

Since that is so, it would be clearer to ask these questions in a different way. Consider the case in which I replace some of the components of my audio-system, but keep the others. I ask, 'Do I still have one and the same system?' That may seem a factual question. But, since I already know what happened, that is not really so. It would be clearer to ask, 'Given that I have replaced those components, would it be correct to call this the same system?'

The same applies to personal identity. Suppose that I know the facts about what will happen to my body, and about any psychological connections that there will be between me now and some person tomorrow. I may ask, 'Will that person be me?' But that is a misleading way to put my question. It suggests that I don't know what's going to happen. When I know these other facts, I should ask, 'Would it be correct to call that person me?' That would remind me that, if there's anything that I don't know, that is merely a fact about our language.

I believe that we can go further. Such questions are, in the belittling sense, merely verbal. Some conceptual questions are well worth discussing. But questions about personal identity, in my kind of case, are like questions that we would all think trivial. It is quite uninteresting whether, with half its components replaced, I still have the same audio-system. In the same way, we should regard it as quite uninteresting whether, if half of my body were simultaneously replaced, I would still exist. As questions about reality, these are entirely empty. Nor, as conceptual questions, do they need answers.

We might need, for legal purposes, to *give* such questions answers. Thus we might decide that an audio-system should be called the same if its new components cost less than half its original price. And we might decide to say that I would continue to exist as long as less than half my body were replaced. But these are not answers to conceptual questions; they are mere decisions.

(Similar remarks apply if we are identifying reductionists who believe that persons just are bodies. There are cases where it is a merely verbal question whether we still have one and the same human body. That is clearly true in the cases in the middle of the physical spectrum.)

It may help to contrast these questions with one that is not merely verbal. Suppose we are studying some creature which is very unlike ourselves, such as an insect, or some extra-terrestrial being. We know all the facts about this creature's behaviour, and its neurophysiology. The creature wriggles vigorously, in what seems to be a response to some injury. We ask, 'Is it conscious, and in great pain? Or is it merely like an insentient machine?' Some behaviourist might say, 'That is a merely verbal question. These aren't different possibilities, either of which might be true. They are merely different descriptions of the very same state of affairs.' That I find incredible. These descriptions give us, I believe, two quite different possibilities. It could not be an empty or a merely verbal question whether some creature was unconscious or in great pain.

It is natural to think the same about our own identity. If I know that some proportion of my cells will be replaced, how can it be a merely verbal question whether I am about to die, or shall wake up again tomorrow? It is because that is hard to believe that reductionism is worth discussing. If we become reductionists, that may change some of our deepest assumptions about ourselves.

These assumptions, as I have said, cover actual cases, and our own lives. But they are best revealed when we consider the imaginary problem cases. It is worth explaining further why that is so.

In ordinary cases, questions about our identity have answers. In such cases, there is a fact about personal identity, and reductionism is one view about what kind of fact this is. On this view, personal identity just consists in physical and/or psychological continuity. We may find it hard to decide whether we accept this view, since it may be far from clear when one fact just consists in another. We may even doubt whether reductionists and their critics really disagree.

In the problem cases, things are different. When we cannot answer questions about personal identity, it is easier to decide whether we accept a reductionist view. We should ask: Do we find such cases puzzling? Or do we accept the reductionist claim that, even without answering these questions, if we knew the facts about the continuities, we would know what happened?

Most of us do find such cases puzzling. We believe that, even if we knew those other facts, if we couldn't answer questions about our identity, there would be something that we didn't know. That suggests that, on our view, personal identity does *not* just consist in one or both of the continuities, but is a separately obtaining fact, or a further difference in what happens. The reductionist account must then leave something out. So there is a real disagreement, and one that applies to all cases.

Many of us do not merely find such cases puzzling. We are inclined to believe that, in all such cases, questions about our identity must have answers, which must be either Yes or No. For that to be true, personal identity must be a separately obtaining fact of a peculiarly simple kind. It must involve some special entity, such as a Cartesian Ego, whose existence must be all-or-nothing.

When I say that we have these assumptions, I am *not* claiming that we believe in Cartesian Egos. Some of us do. But many of us, I suspect, have inconsistent beliefs. If we are asked whether we believe that there are Cartesian Egos, we may answer No. And we may accept that, as reductionists claim, the existence of a person just involves the existence of a body, and the occurrence of a series of interrelated mental and physical events. But, as our reactions to the problem cases show, we don't fully accept that view. Or, if we do, we also seem to hold a different view.

Such a conflict of beliefs is quite common. At a reflective or intellectual level, we may be convinced that some view is true; but at another level, one that engages more directly with our emotions, we may continue to think and feel as if some different view were true. One example of this kind would be a hope, or fear, that we know to be groundless. Many of us, I suspect, have such inconsistent beliefs when we think about the central themes of metaphysics: God, the Self, consciousness, time, and free will.

II

I turn now from the nature of personal identity to its importance. Personal identity is widely thought to have great rational and moral significance. Thus it is the fact of identity which is thought to give us our reason for concern about our own future.

And several moral principles, such as those of desert or distributive justice, presuppose claims about identity. The separateness of persons, or the non-identity of different people, has been called 'the basic fact for morals'.

I'll address only one of these questions: what matters in our survival. I mean by that, not what makes our survival good, but what makes our survival matter, whether it will be good or bad. What is it, in our survival, that gives us a reason for special anticipatory or prudential concern?

We can explain that question with an extreme imaginary case. Suppose that, while I care about my whole future, I am especially concerned about what will happen to me on future Tuesdays. Rather than suffer mild pain on a future Tuesday, I would choose severe pain on any other day. That pattern of concern would be irrational. The fact that a pain will be on a Tuesday is no reason to care about it more. What about the fact that a pain will be *mine*? Does *this* fact give me a reason to care about it more?

Many people would answer Yes. On their view, what gives us a reason to care about our future is, precisely, that it will be *our* future. Personal identity is what matters in survival.

I reject this view. Most of what matters, I believe, are two other relations: the psychological continuity and connectedness that, in ordinary cases, hold between the different parts of a person's life. These relations only roughly coincide with personal identity, since, unlike identity, they are in part matters of degree. Nor, I believe, do they matter as much as identity is thought to do.

There are different ways to challenge the importance of identity.

One argument can be summarized in this way:

(1) Personal identity just consists in certain other facts.
(2) If one fact just consists in certain others, it can only be these other facts which have rational or moral importance. We should ask whether, in themselves, these other facts matter.

Therefore

(3) Personal identity cannot be rationally or morally important. What matters can only be one or more of the other facts in which personal identity consists.

Premise (1) is reductionism; (2) we might call 'reductionism about importance'.

Mark Johnston (1992) criticizes this argument. He calls it an *argument from below*, since it claims that, if one fact just consists in certain others, it can only be these other lower-level facts which matter. Johnston replies with what he calls an *argument from above*. On his view, even if the lower-level facts do not in themselves matter, the higher-level fact may matter. If it does, the lower-level facts will have a derived significance. They will matter, not in themselves, but because they constitute the higher-level fact.

To illustrate this disagreement, we can start with a different case. Suppose we ask what we want to happen if, through brain damage, we become irreversibly unconscious. If we were in this state, we would still be alive. But this fact should be understood in a reductionist way. It may not be the same as the fact that our hearts would still be beating, and our other organs would still be functioning. But it would not be an independent or separately obtaining fact. Our being still alive, though irreversibly unconscious, would just consist in these other facts.

On my argument from below, we should ask whether those other facts in themselves matter. If we were irreversibly unconscious, would it be either good for us, or good for others, that our hearts and other organs would still be functioning? If we answer No, we should conclude that it would not matter that we were still alive.

If Johnston were right, we could reject this argument. And we could appeal to an argument from above. We might say:

It may not be in itself good that our hearts and other organs would still be functioning. But it is good to be alive. Since that is so, it is rational to hope that, even if we could never regain consciousness, our hearts would go on beating for as long as possible. That would be good because it would constitute our staying alive.

I believe that, of these arguments, mine is more plausible.

Consider next the moral question that such cases raise. Some people ask, in their living wills, that if brain damage makes them irreversibly unconscious, their hearts should be stopped. I believe that we should do what these people ask. But many take a different view. They could appeal to an argument from above. They might say:

Even if such people can never regain consciousness, while their hearts are still beating, they can be truly called alive. Since that is so, stopping their hearts would be an act of killing. And, except in self-defense, it is always wrong to kill.

On this view, we should leave these people's hearts to go on beating, for months or even years.

As an answer to the moral question, this seems to me misguided. (It is a separate question what the law should be.) But, for many people, the word 'kill' has such force that it seems significant whether it applies.

Turn now to a different subject. Suppose that, after trying to decide when people have free will, we become convinced by either of two compatibilist views. On one view, we call choices 'unfree' if they are caused in certain ways, and we call them 'free' if they are caused in certain other ways. On the other view, we call choices 'unfree' if we know how they were caused, and we call them 'free' if we have not yet discovered this.

Suppose next that, when we consider these two grounds for drawing this distinction, we believe that neither, in itself, has the kind of significance that could support making or denying claims about guilt, or desert. There seems to us no such significance in the difference between these kinds of causal determination; and we believe that it cannot matter whether a decision's causes have already been discovered. (Note that, in comparing the arguments from above and below, we need not actually accept these claims. We are asking whether, *if* we accepted the relevant premises, we ought to be persuaded by these arguments.)

On my argument from below, if the fact that a choice is free just consists in one of those other facts, and we believe that those other facts cannot in themselves be morally important, we should conclude that it cannot be important whether some person's choice was free. Either choices that are unfree can deserve to be punished, or choices that are free cannot. On a Johnstonian argument from above, even if those other facts are not in themselves important—even if, in themselves, they are trivial—they can have a derived importance if and because they constitute the fact that some person's choice was free. As before, the argument from below seems to me more plausible.

We can now consider the underlying question on which this disagreement turns.

As I have claimed, if one fact just consists in certain others, the first fact is not an independent or separately obtaining fact. And, in the cases with which we are concerned, it is also, in relation to these other facts, merely a conceptual fact. Thus, if someone is irreversibly unconscious, but his heart is still beating, it is a conceptual fact that this person is still alive. When I call this fact conceptual, I don't mean that it is a fact about our concepts. That this person is alive is a fact about this person. But, if we have already claimed that this person's heart is still beating, when we claim that he is still alive, we do not give further information about reality. We only give further information about our use of the words 'person' and 'alive'.

When we turn to ask what matters, the central question is this. Suppose we agree that it does not matter, in itself, that such a person's heart is still beating. Could we claim that, in another way, this fact does matter, because it makes it correct to say that this person is still alive? If we answer Yes, we are treating language as more important than reality. We are claiming that, even if some fact does not in itself matter, it may matter if and because it allows a certain word to be applied.

This, I believe, is irrational. On my view, what matter are the facts about the world, given which some concept applies. If the facts about the world have no rational or moral significance, and the fact that the concept applies is not a further difference in what happens, this conceptual fact cannot be significant.

Johnston brings a second charge against reductionism about importance. If physicalism were true, he claims, all facts would just consist in facts about fundamental particles. Considered in themselves, these facts about particles would have no rational or moral importance. If we apply reductionism about importance, we must conclude that nothing has any importance. He remarks: 'this is not a proof of Nihilism. It is a reductio ad absurdum.'

Given what I've said today, this charge can, I think, be answered. There may perhaps be a sense in which, if physicalism were true, all facts would just consist in facts about fundamental particles. But that is not the kind of reduction which I had in mind. When I claim that personal identity just consists in certain other facts,

I have in mind a closer and partly conceptual relation. Claims about personal identity may not mean the same as claims about physical and/or psychological continuity. But, if we knew the facts about these continuities, and understood the concept of a person, we would thereby know, or would be able to work out, the facts about persons. Hence my claim that, if we know the other facts, questions about personal identity should be taken to be questions, not about reality, but only about our language. These claims do not apply to facts about fundamental particles. It is not true for example that, if we knew how the particles moved in some person's body, and understood our concepts, we would thereby know, or be able to work out, all of the relevant facts about this person. To understand the world around us, we need more than physics and a knowledge of our own language. We need chemistry, biology, neurophysiology, psychology, and much else besides.

If we are reductionists about importance, we are not claiming that, whenever there are facts at different levels, it is always the lowest-level facts which matter. That is clearly false. We are discussing cases where, relative to the facts at some lower level, the higher-level fact is, in the sense that I have sketched, merely conceptual. Our claim is that such conceptual facts cannot be rationally or morally important. What matters is reality, not how it is described. (So this view might be better called *realism* about importance.)

I have now briefly described reductionism about persons, and reductionism about importance. These together imply that personal identity is not what matters. Should we accept that conclusion?

Most of us believe that we should care about our future because it will be *our* future. I believe that what matters is not identity but certain other relations. To help us to decide between these views, we should consider cases where identity and those relations do not coincide.

Which these cases are depends on which criterion of identity we accept. I shall start with the simplest form of the physical criterion, according to which a person continues to exist if and only if that person's body continues to exist. That must be the view of those who believe that persons just are bodies. And it is the view of several of the people who identify persons with human beings (see e.g. Ayers 1999; Snowdon 1995; Chapter 5 above). Let's call this the *bodily criterion*.

I discuss this view for a special reason. As we shall see there is another argument for the unimportance of identity, which appeals to Wiggins's imagined case of division. But those who accept the bodily criterion reject one premise of that other argument. To persuade these people that identity is not what matters, my only argument is reductionism about importance.

Suppose that, because of damage to my spine, I have become partly paralysed. I have a brother, who is dying of a brain disease. With the aid of new techniques, when my brother's brain ceases to function, my head could be grafted onto the rest of my brother's body. Since we are identical twins, my brain would then control a body that is just like mine, except that it would not be paralysed.

Should I accept this operation? Of those who assume that identity is what matters, three groups would answer No. Some accept the bodily criterion. These people believe that, if this operation were performed, I would die. The person with my head tomorrow would be my brother, who would mistakenly think that he was me. Other people are uncertain what would happen. They believe that it would be risky to accept this operation, since the resulting person might not be me. Others give a different reason why I should reject this operation: that it would be indeterminate whether that person would be me. On all these views, it matters who that person would be.

On my view, that question is unimportant. If this operation were performed, the person with my head tomorrow would not only believe that he was me, he would seem to remember living my life, and be in every other way psychologically like me. These facts would also have their normal cause, the continued existence of my brain. And this person's body would be just like mine. For all these reasons, his life would be just like the life that I would have lived, if my paralysis had been cured. I believe that, given these facts, I should accept this operation. It is irrelevant whether this person would be me.

That may seem all important. After all, if he would not be me, I shall have ceased to exist. But, if that person would not be me, this fact would just consist in another fact. It would just consist in the fact that my body will have been replaced below the neck. When considered on its own, is that second fact important? Can it matter in itself that the blood that will keep my brain alive will circulate, not through my own heart and lungs, but through my brother's heart and lungs? Can it matter in itself that my brain will control, not the rest of my body, but the rest of another body that is exactly similar?

If we believe that these facts would amount to my non-existence, it may be hard to focus on the question whether, in themselves, these facts matter. To make that easier, we should imagine that we accept a different view. Suppose we are convinced that the person with my head tomorrow *would* be me. Would we then believe that it would matter greatly that my head would have been grafted onto this other body? We would not. We would regard my receiving a new torso, and new limbs, as like any lesser transplant, such as receiving a new heart, or new kidneys. As this shows, if it would matter greatly that what will be replaced is not just a few such organs, but my whole body below the neck, that could only be because, if that happened, the resulting person would *not* be me.

According to reductionism about importance, we should now conclude that neither of these facts could matter greatly. Since it wouldn't be in itself important that my head would be grafted onto this body, and that would be all there was to the fact that the resulting person wouldn't be me, it wouldn't be in itself important that this person wouldn't be me. Perhaps it would not be irrational to regret these facts a little. But, I believe, they would be heavily outweighed by the fact that, unlike me, the resulting person would not be paralysed.

When it is applied to our own existence, reductionism about importance is hard to believe. But, as before, the fundamental question is the relative importance of language and reality.

On my view, what matters is what's going to happen. If I knew that my head could be grafted onto the rest of a body that is just like mine, and that the resulting person would be just like me, I would know enough to decide whether to accept this operation. I need not ask whether the resulting person could be correctly called me. That is not a further difference in what's going to happen.

That may seem a false distinction. What matters, we might say, is whether the resulting person would *be* me. But that person would be me if and only if he could be correctly called me. So, in asking what he could be called, we are not merely asking a conceptual question. We *are* asking about reality.

This objection fails to distinguish two kinds of case. Suppose that I ask my doctor whether, while I receive some treatment, I shall be in pain. That is a factual question. I am asking what will happen. Since pain can be called 'pain', I *could* ask my question in a different way. I could say, 'While I am being treated, will it be correct to describe me as in pain?' But that would be misleading. It would suggest that I am asking how we use the word 'pain'.

In a different case, I might ask that conceptual question. Suppose I know that, while I am crossing the Channel, I shall be feeling sea-sick, as I always do. I might wonder whether that sensation could be correctly called 'pain'. Here too, I could ask my question in a different way. I could say, 'While I am crossing the Channel, shall I be in pain?' But that would be misleading, since it would suggest that I am asking what will happen.

In the medical case, I don't know what conscious state I shall be in. There are different possibilities. In the Channel crossing case, there aren't different possibilities. I already know what state I shall be in. I am merely asking whether that state could be redescribed in a certain way.

It matters whether, while receiving the medical treatment, I shall be in pain. And it matters whether, while crossing the Channel, I shall be sea-sick. But it does not matter whether, in feeling sea-sick, I can be said to be in pain.

Return now to our main example. Suppose I know that my head will be successfully grafted onto my brother's headless body. I ask whether the resulting person will be me. Is this like the medical case, or the case of crossing the Channel? Am I asking what will happen, or whether what I know will happen could be described in a certain way?

On my view, I should take myself to be asking the second. I already know what's going to happen. There will be someone with my head and my brother's body. It's a merely verbal question whether that person will be me. And that's why, even if he won't be me, that doesn't matter.

It may now be objected: 'By choosing this example, you are cheating. Of course you should accept this operation. But that is because the resulting person *would* be you. We should reject the bodily criterion. So this case cannot show that identity is not what matters.'

Since there are people who accept this criterion, I am not cheating. It is worth trying to show these people that identity is not what matters. But I accept part of this objection. I agree that we should reject the bodily criterion.

Of those who appeal to this criterion, some believe that persons just are bodies. But, if we hold this kind of view, it would be better to identify a person with that person's brain, or nervous system (see Mackie 1976: ch. 6; Nagel 1986: 40–5; Chapter 21 below). Consider next those who believe that persons are animals of a certain kind, viz. human beings. We could take this view, but reject the bodily criterion. We could claim that animals continue to exist if there continue to exist, and to function, the most important parts of their bodies. And we could claim that, at least in the case of human beings, the brain is so important that its survival counts as the survival of this human being. On both these views, in my imagined case, the person with my head tomorrow would be me. And that is what, on reflection, most of us would believe.

My own view is similar. I would state this view, not as a claim about reality, but as a conceptual claim. On my view, it would not be incorrect to call this person me; and this would be the best description of this case.

If we agree that this person would be me, I would still argue that this fact is not what matters. What is important is not identity, but one or more of the other facts in which identity consists. But I concede that, when identity coincides with these other facts, it is harder to decide whether we accept that argument's conclusion. So, if we reject the bodily criterion, we must consider other cases.

Suppose that we accept the brain-based version of the psychological criterion. On this view, if there will be some future person who is psychologically continuous with me, because he will have enough of my brain, that person will be me. But psychological continuity without its normal cause, the continued existence of enough of my brain, does not suffice for identity. My replica would not be me.

Remember next that an object can continue to exist even if all its components are gradually replaced. Suppose that, every time some wooden ship comes into port, a few of its planks are replaced. Before long, the same ship may be entirely composed of different planks.

Suppose, once again, that I need surgery. All of my brain cells have a defect which, in time, would be fatal. Surgeons could replace all these cells, inserting new cells that are exact replicas, except that they have no defect.

The surgeons could proceed in either of two ways. In *Case One*, there would be a hundred operations. In each operation, the surgeons would remove a hundredth part of my brain, and insert replicas of those parts. In *Case Two*, the surgeons would first remove all the existing parts of my brain and then insert all of their replicas.

There is a real difference here. In Case One, my brain would continue to exist, like a ship with all of its planks gradually replaced. In Case Two, my brain would cease to exist, and my body would be given a new brain.

This difference, though, is much smaller than that between ordinary survival and teletransportation. In both cases, there will later be a person whose brain will be just like my present brain, but without the defects, and who will therefore be psychologically continuous with me. And, in *both* cases, this person's brain will be made of the very same new cells, each of which is a replica of one of my existing cells. The difference between the cases is merely the way in which these new cells are inserted. In Case One, the surgeons alternate between removing and inserting. In Case Two, they do all the removing before all the inserting.

On the brain-based criterion, this is the difference between life and death. In Case One, the resulting person would be me. In Case Two he would *not* be me, so I would cease to exist.

Can this difference matter? Reapply the argument from below. This difference consists in the fact that, rather than alternating between removals and insertions, the surgeon does all the removing before all the inserting. Considered on its own, can this matter? I believe not. We would not think it mattered if it did not constitute the fact that the resulting person would not be me. But if this fact does not in itself matter, and that is all there is to the fact that in Case Two I would cease to exist, I should conclude that my ceasing to exist does not matter.

Suppose next that you regard these as problem cases, ones where you do not know what would happen to me. Return to the simpler physical spectrum. In each of the cases in this range, some proportion of my cells will be replaced with exact duplicates. With some proportions—20 per cent, say, or 50 per cent, or 70 per cent—most of us would be uncertain whether the resulting person would be me. (As before, if we do not believe that here, my remarks could be transferred, with adjustments, to the combined spectrum.)

On my view, in all of the cases in this range, it is a merely conceptual question whether the resulting person would be me. Even without answering this question, I can know just what's going to happen. If there is anything that I don't know, that is merely a fact about how we could describe what's going to happen. And that conceptual question is not even, I believe, interesting. It is merely verbal, like the question whether, if I replaced some of its parts, I would still have the same audio-system.

When we imagine these cases from a first-person point of view, it may still be hard to believe that this is merely a verbal question. If I don't know whether, tomorrow, I shall still exist, it may be hard to believe that I know what's going to happen. But what is it that I don't know? If there are different possibilities, at the level of what happens, what is the difference between them? In what would that difference consist? If I had a soul, or Cartesian Ego, there might be different possibilities. Perhaps, even if *n* per cent of my cells were replaced, my soul would keep its intimate relation with my brain. Or perhaps another soul would take over.

But, we have assumed, there are no such entities. What else could the difference be? When the resulting person wakes up tomorrow, what could make it either true, or false, that he is me?

It may be said that, in asking what will happen, I am asking what I can expect. Can I expect to wake up again? If that person will be in pain, can I expect to feel that pain? But this does not help. These are just other ways of asking whether that person will or will not be me. In appealing to what I can expect, we do not explain what would make these different possibilities.

We may believe that this difference needs no explanation. It may seem enough to say: Perhaps that person will be me, and perhaps he won't. Perhaps I shall exist tomorrow, and perhaps I shan't. It may seem that these must be different possibilities.

That, however, is an illusion. If I shall still exist tomorrow, that fact must consist in certain others. For there to be two possibilities, so that it might be either true or false that I shall exist tomorrow, there must be some other difference between these possibilities. There would be such a difference, for example, if, between now and tomorrow, my brain and body might either remain unharmed, or be blown to pieces. But, in our imagined case, there is no such other difference. I already know that there will be someone whose brain and body will consist partly of these cells, and partly of new cells, and that this person will be psychologically like me. There aren't, at the level of what happens, different possible outcomes. There is no further essence of me, or property of me-ness, which either might or might not be there.

If we turn to the conceptual level, there *are* different possibilities. Perhaps that future person could be correctly called me. Perhaps he could be correctly called someone else. Or perhaps neither would be correct. That, however, is the only way in which it could be either true, or false, that this person would be me.

The illusion may persist. Even when I know the other facts, I may want reality to go in one of two ways. I may want it to be true that I shall still exist tomorrow. But all that could be true is that we use language in one of two ways. Can it be rational to care about that?

III

I am now assuming that we accept the brain-based psychological criterion. We believe that, if there will be one future person who will have enough of my brain to be psychologically continuous with me, that person would be me. On this view, there is another way to argue that identity is not what matters.

We can first note that, just as I could survive with less than my whole body, I could survive with less than my whole brain. People have survived, and with little psychological change, even when, through a stroke or injury, they have lost the use of half their brain.

Let us next suppose that the two halves of my brain could each fully support ordinary psychological functioning. That may in fact be true of certain people. If it is not, we can suppose that, through some technological advance, it has been made true of me. Since our aim is to test our beliefs about what matters, there is no harm in making such assumptions.

We can now compare two more possible operations. In the first, after half my brain is destroyed, the other half would be successfully transplanted into the empty skull of a body that is just like mine. Given our assumptions, we should conclude that, here too, I would survive. Since I would survive if my brain were transplanted, and I would survive with only half my brain, it would be unreasonable to deny that I would survive if that remaining half were transplanted. So, in this *One-Sided Case*, the resulting person would be me.

Consider next the *Two-Sided Case*, or *My Division*. Both halves of my brain would be successfully transplanted, into different bodies that are just like mine. Two people would wake up, each of whom has half my brain, and is, both physically and psychologically, just like me.

Since these would be two different people, it can't be true that each of them is me. That would be a contradiction. If each of them was me, each would be one and the same person: me. So they couldn't be two different people.

Could it be true that only one of them is me? That is not a contradiction. But, since I have the same relation to each of these people, there is nothing that could make me one of them rather than the other. It cannot be true, of either of these people, that he is the one who could be correctly called me.

How should I regard these two operations? Would they preserve what matters in survival? In the One-Sided Case, the one resulting person would be me. The relation between me now and that future person is just an instance of the relation between me now and myself tomorrow. So that relation would contain what matters. In the Two-Sided Case, my relation to that person would be just the same. So this relation must still contain what matters. Nothing is missing. But that person cannot here be claimed to be me. So identity cannot be what matters.

We may object that, if that person *isn't* me, something *is* missing. *I'm* missing. That may seem to make all the difference. How can everything still be there if *I'm* not there?

Everything is still there. The fact that I'm not there is not a real absence. The relation between me now and that future person is in itself the same. As in the One-Sided Case, he has half my brain, and he is just like me. The difference is only that, in this Two-Sided Case, I also have the same relation to the other resulting person. Why am I not there? The explanation is only this. When this relation holds between me now and a single person in the future, we can be called one and the same person. When this relation holds between me now and *two* future people,

I cannot be called one and the same as each of these people. But that is not a difference in the nature or the content of this relation. In the One-Sided Case, where half my brain will be successfully transplanted, my prospect is survival. That prospect contains what matters. In the Two-Sided Case, where both halves will be successfully transplanted, nothing would be lost.

It can be hard to believe that identity is not what matters. But that is easier to accept when we see why, in this example, it is true. It may help to consider this analogy. Imagine a community of persons who are like us, but with two exceptions. First, because of facts about their reproductive system, each couple has only two children, who are always twins. Second, because of special features of their psychology, it is of great importance for the development of each child that it should not, through the death of its sibling, become an only child. Such children suffer psychological damage. It is thus believed, in this community, that it matters greatly that each child should have a twin.

Now suppose that, because of some biological change, some of the children in this community start to be born as triplets. Should their parents think this a disaster, because these children don't have twins? Clearly not. These children don't have twins only because they each have *two* siblings. Since each child has two siblings, the trio must be called, not twins, but triplets. But none of them will suffer damage as an only child. These people should revise their view. What matters isn't having a twin: it's having at least one sibling.

In the same way, we should revise our view about identity over time. What matters isn't that there will be someone alive who will be me. It is rather that there will be at least one living person who will be psychologically continuous with me as I am now, and/or who has enough of my brain. When there will be only one such person, he can be described as me. When there will be two such people, we cannot claim that each will be me. But that is as trivial as the fact that, if I had two identical siblings, they couldn't be called my twins.

IV

If, as I have argued, personal identity isn't what matters, we must ask what does matter. There are several possible answers. And, depending on our answer, there are several further implications. Thus there are several moral questions which I have no time even to mention. I shall end with another remark about our concern for our own future.

That concern is of several kinds. We may want to survive partly so that our hopes and ambitions will be achieved. We may also care about our future in the kind of way in which we care about the well-being of certain other people, such as our relatives or friends. But most of us have, in addition, a distinctive kind of egoistic concern. If I know that my child will be in pain, I may care about his pain more than I would about my own future pain. But I cannot fearfully anticipate my child's pain. And if I knew that my replica would take up my life where I leave off, I would not look forward to that life.

This kind of concern may, I believe, be weakened, and be seen to have no ground, if we come to accept a reductionist view. In our thoughts about our own identity, we are prone to illusions. That is why the so-called 'problem cases' seem to raise problems: why we find it hard to believe that, when we know the other facts, it is an empty or a merely verbal question whether we shall still exist. Even after we accept a reductionist view, we may continue, at some level, to think and feel as if that view were not true. Our own continued existence may still seem an independent fact, of a peculiarly deep and simple kind. And that belief may underlie our anticipatory concern about our own future.

There are, I suspect, several causes of that illusory belief. I have discussed one cause today: our conceptual scheme. Though we need concepts to think about reality, we sometimes confuse the two. We mistake conceptual facts for facts about reality. And, in the case of certain concepts, those that are most loaded with emotional or moral significance, we can be led seriously astray. Of these loaded concepts, that of our own identity is, perhaps, the most misleading.

Even the use of the word 'I' can lead us astray. Consider the fact that, in a few years, I shall be dead. This fact can seem depressing. But the reality is only this. After a certain time, none of the thoughts and experiences that occur will be directly causally related to this brain, or be connected in certain ways to these present experiences. That is all this fact involves. And, in that redescription, my death seems to disappear.

References

Ayers, M. (1999). *Locke* (London: Routledge).

Collins, S. (1992). *Selfless Persons* (Cambridge: Cambridge University Press).

Johnston, M. (1992). 'Reasons and Reductionism', *Philosophical Review*, 101: 589–618. Repr. in J. Dancy (ed.), *Reading Parfit* (New York: Wiley-Blackwell, 1997).

Mackie, J. (1976). *Problems from Locke* (Oxford: Oxford University Press).

Nagel, T. (1986). *The View from Nowhere* (New York: Oxford University Press).

Parfit, D. (1984). *Reasons and Persons* (Oxford: Oxford University Press).

Snowdon, P. (1995). 'Persons, Animals and Bodies', in J. Bermúdez, N. Eilan, and A. Marcel (eds), *The Body and the Self* (Cambridge, Mass.: MIT Press).

Stcherbatsky, T. (1919). 'The Soul Theory of the Buddhists', *Bulletin de l'Academie des Sciences de Russie*. 823–54, 937–58.

CHAPTER 19

....

SELF-AGENCY

....

ELISABETH PACHERIE

1. INTRODUCTION

....

We are perceivers, we are thinkers, and we are also agents, bringing about physical events, such as bodily movements and their consequences. What we do tells us, and others, a lot about who we are. On the one hand, who we are determines what we do. On the other hand, acting is also a process of self-discovery and self-shaping. Pivotal to this mutual shaping of self and agency is the sense of agency, or agentive self-awareness, that is, the sense that one is the agent of an action.[1]

As folk, we appear to be deeply wedded to a conception of self-agency according to which consciousness plays a pervasive role prior to acting, while acting, and after one has acted. Here's how the story goes. *Conscious* deliberation on the basis of our *conscious* beliefs and desires yields a *conscious* decision to pursue a certain *conscious* goal, leading to the formation of a *conscious* intention or volition to realize that goal. Our *conscious* intention in turn causes our action, by *consciously* initiating and *consciously* controlling it. While acting we experience our *conscious* intention as causing our action and, on that experiential basis, we are able to judge immediately after acting that we were the agent of the action. On that story, the causation of action by conscious mental states and the sense of agency for actions are but two sides of the same coin. Although not uncontested, this folk-psychological picture has been endorsed by many philosophers. Typically, their qualms have concerned less the role attributed to consciousness than the rather prodigal ontology of

---

[1] In this chapter, I will use 'sense of agency' and 'agentive self-awareness' as synonyms.

mental states the folk is content to entertain (Davidson 1980) and the difficulties involved in making room for mental causation in a physicalist framework—the infamous exclusion problem (Kim 1998). The apparently obvious link between the causation of action by conscious mental states and the sense of agency may also explain why until recently the sense of agency was a topic rather neglected by philosophers of action and philosophers of consciousness alike.

Things have changed, however, and of late the sense of agency has regained its place in the agenda of philosophers and scientists.[2] This recent explosion of interest in the topic is due in a large part to the development of psychological and neuroscientific methods that have made the phenomenology of action an object of empirical investigation and yielded results that challenge the received wisdom. On the one hand, empirical research done over the last two decades provides evidence that the role of consciousness in action production is far less pervasive than our folk-conception would have it. Many of our actions are selected, carried out, and controlled non-consciously, with conscious states playing at best a role in non-default modes of action control (such as trouble-shooting) and being at worst mere epiphenomenal by-products of something else that does the causal work. On the other hand, cognitive scientists have also developed models of how the sense of agency is generated, exploring a number of potential cues to agency and proposing several different mechanisms, ranging from high-level cognitive mechanisms to low-level sensorimotor cues.

This recent empirical work has done a lot to rekindle the interest of philosophers in these issues by suggesting that they are far more complex than previously thought. First, the sense of agency itself appears to be a complex, multifaceted phenomenon, raising questions about how its various aspects are related, what their content and structure is, to what extent they are dissociable, and whether some are more basic than others. Second, the relationship between sense of agency and conscious mental causation of action appears to be much less straightforward than the two-sides-of-the-same-coin story would have it. To the extent that some of the mechanisms involved in the generation of the sense of agency are only indirectly related to the mechanisms involved in action production, sense of agency and agency may dissociate. We sometimes have a sense of agency for actions we did not actually perform or did not consciously intend, and conversely we may lack a sense of agency for actions we did consciously intend and actually performed. This has led some to claim that the conscious will is an illusion. It isn't entirely clear what exactly this claim is supposed to mean and whether it is warranted. Certainly, however, the existence of such dissociations invites us to reconsider our conception of self-agency, of the link between self-agency and conscious mental causation, and of the role the sense of agency plays within agency.

---

[2] Useful collections of papers can be found in Roessler and Eilan (2003), Sebanz and Prinz (2006), Pockett *et al.* (2006), and Siegel (2007).

In order to introduce readers to the new terms of the debate over self-agency, I start with a brief survey of recent models of how and where in the cognitive architecture the sense of agency is generated. I also argue that these models should be seen as complementary rather than as rivals. Building on that basis, I then turn to issues concerning the contents and structure of states of agentive self-awareness. Finally, I discuss the relation between agency and sense of agency. Is the sense of agency a reliable indicator of actual agency? Does it represent agency as it really is? What role does the sense of agency play in agency?

2. How is the Sense of Agency Generated?

Empirical research on agency has explored a number of potential cues to agency, and different cognitive models for agency have been proposed, ranging from high-level cognitive mechanisms to low-level sensorimotor mechanisms.

Cognitive cues and high-level mechanisms

Some authors focus on high-level cognitive mechanisms and invoke a 'central' interpretive system to explain our awareness of our own agency. According to this approach, the sense of agency is subserved by a holistic mechanism that is concerned with narrative self-understanding. Our sense of what, if anything, we are up to is based on the operations of a high-level integrative process that draws on the agent's self-conception and tries to put the best spin on things that it can. Such a conception has strong Dennettian overtones. We turn Dennett's intentional stance inwards, and treat ourselves as entities whose behavior needs to be made sense of in light of an implicit theory of ideal agency.

Many authors have expressed some sympathy with, and in some cases whole-hearted commitment to, the narrative approach. Interpreting split-brain studies in light of Dennettian (1992) themes concerning the role of narrative in self-interpretation, Roser and Gazzaniga (2004, 2006) have argued that the left hemisphere contains an interpreter, whose job it is to make sense of the agent's own behavior. The psychologist Louis Sass has suggested that schizophrenic patients with delusions of alien control no longer feel as though they are in control of their actions because 'particular thoughts and actions may not make sense in relation to the whole' (1992: 214). Developing Sass's proposal, Stephens and Graham suggest that a 'subject's sense of agency regarding episodes in her psychological history might depend on her ability to integrate them into her larger picture of herself' (2000: 161). Peter Carruthers suggests that 'our awareness of our own will results from turning our mind-reading capacities upon themselves, and coming up with the best interpretation of the information that is available to it—where this information doesn't include those acts of deciding themselves, but only the causes and effects of those events' (2007: 199).

Holistic themes also play an important role in Daniel Wegner's influential treatment of agentive self-awareness. On the one hand, Wegner argues that the sense of agency is typically inferred from the existence of a match between a prior thought and an observed action:

The experience of consciously willing our actions seems to arise primarily when we believe our thoughts have caused our actions. This happens when we have thoughts that occur just before the actions, when these thoughts are consistent with the actions, and when other potential causes of the actions are not present. . . . In essence, the theory suggests that we experience ourselves as agents who cause our actions when our minds provide us with previews of the actions that turn out to be accurate when we observe the actions that ensue. (2005: 23)

On the other hand, he also notes that we perform many actions without the benefit of such previews and suggests that 'Even when we didn't know what we were doing in advance, we may trust our theory that we consciously will our actions and so find ourselves forced to imagine or confabulate memories of "prior" consistent thoughts' (2002: 146).

A wide array of evidence can be marshaled in support of this high-level account. When young children happen to achieve a goal by luck, they will say that they had intended the action that yielded that goal all along (Phillips *et al.* 1998). Proponents of this approach have also appealed to studies involving patients with brain damage. Patients with anosognosia for hemiplegia say that they are currently raising their arm when, in fact, their arm has not moved. When it is pointed out to the patient that his arm has not moved, he may confabulate an excuse for his inertia (Feinberg *et al.* 2000). Split-brain subjects are prone to confabulate accounts of actions that are generated by their right hemisphere (Gazzaniga and LeDoux 1978). Data from subjects in altered states of consciousness also support the narrative approach. For example, bizarre behaviors performed in response to hypnotic suggestion are often accompanied by elaborate rationalizations and confabulation on the part of the agent (Moll 1889). Finally, this approach derives support from a number of laboratory studies with normal subjects, in which it has been shown that the sense of agency can be modulated by priming and various contextual parameters (Aarts *et al.* 2005; Wegner *et al.* 2004; Wegner and Wheatley 1999).

Sensorimotor cues and low-level mechanisms

In contrast to this very high-level approach, a number of researchers have proposed that the monitoring of action execution is crucial for agency and that the sense of agency is generated by low-level mechanisms that exploit performance-related sensorimotor cues.

One possibility is that efferent signals sent to the motor system while implementing an intention provide such cues. Tsakiris and colleagues have proposed that efferent signals are used to generate accurate temporal and kinematic predictions about how and when particular body parts should move (Tsakiris and Haggard 2005; Tsakiris et al. 2005, 2006). In support of that claim, they demonstrated that self-recognition of one's own bodily movements crucially depends on efferent signals.

Another line of evidence for the role of efferent signals in generating a sense of agency involves 'intentional binding', a phenomenon in which self-produced movements and their effects are perceived as being closer together in subjective time than they actually are (Haggard and Clark 2003; Haggard et al. 2002). More specifically, when a voluntary act (e.g. a button press) causes an effect (e.g. a tone), the action is perceived by the agent as having occurred later than it did, and the effect is perceived as having occurred earlier. In contrast, when similar movements and auditory effects occur involuntarily rather than voluntarily, the binding effect is reversed and cause and effect are perceived as further apart in time than they actually are. Haggard suggests that intentional binding is best explained in terms of predictive mechanisms of action control: it depends on efferent signals since it does not occur with passive movements and it causes anticipatory awareness of action effects, a shift that suggests prediction. On this predictive account, the sense of agency would be constructed at the time of the action itself, as an immediate by-product of the motor control circuits that generate and control the physical movement itself.

Another mechanism appeals to internal forward models used for action control (Blakemore and Frith 2003; Frith et al. 2000a, 2000b). According to this proposal, forward models are fed an efference copy of actual motor commands and compute estimates of the sensory consequences of the ensuing movements. The predicted sensory consequences are compared with actual sensory feedback (reafferences). When there is a match between predicted state and actual state, the comparator sends a signal to the effect that the sensory changes are self-generated, and when there is no match (or an insufficiently robust match), sensory changes are coded as externally caused. Indirect evidence for this model comes from studies demonstrating that discrepancies between predictions and sensory reafferences affect tactile sensations (Blakemore et al. 1998, 2000) and visual perception of one's own actions (Leube et al. 2003). Direct evidence is also provided by studies demonstrating that agency is gradually reduced as these discrepancies increase due to spatial deviations and temporal delays (Fourneret and Jeannerod 1998; Knoblich and Kircher 2004; Knoblich *et al.* 2004; Leube *et al.* 2003; Sato and Yasuda 2005; van den Bos and Jeannerod 2002).

Perceptual cues and intermediate-level mechanisms

However, as several authors have pointed out (Gallagher 2007; Knoblich and Repp 2009; Pacherie 2008), the results of some of these studies are open to alternative interpretations in terms of perceptual rather than sensorimotor cues. It is well known that we have little awareness of the proprioceptive feedback associated with movements or even of the corrections we make during goal directed movements (De Vignemont *et al.* 2006; Fourneret and Jeannerod 1998). Indeed, passive movements are associated with more activity in the secondary somatosensory cortex than active movements (Weiller *et al.* 1996). Frith (2005) even suggests that lack of proprioceptive experience may be one indicator that one is performing a voluntary act. The vast majority of our actions aim at producing effects in the environment and we normally attend to the perceptual effects of our movements rather than to the movements themselves. It may therefore be that perceptual cues rather than sensorimotor cues are crucial to the sense of agency. Direct evidence for this view comes from an experiment of Fourneret and Jeannerod (1998) where subjects are instructed to move a stylus on a graphic tablet on a straight line to a visual target. Subjects cannot see their drawing hand, only its trajectory being visible as a line on a computer screen. On some trials, the experimenter introduces a directional bias electronically so that the visible trajectory no longer corresponds to that of the hand. When the bias is small ($< 14°$) subjects make automatic adjustments of their hand movements to reach the target but remain unaware that they are making these corrections. It is with larger biases that subjects become aware of a discrepancy and begin to use conscious monitoring of their hand movement to correct for it and to reach the target. These results suggest that, although discrepancies between predicted and actual sensory feedback are detected at some level since they are used to make appropriate corrections of the hand movement, they do not influence the sense of agency. Rather, their sense of agency for the action seems to rely mostly on a comparison of the predicted and actual perceptual consequences of their action. As long as the trajectory seen on the screen matches sufficiently well the predicted trajectory, proprioceptive information is ignored.

Further evidence that perceptual cues may contribute more to the sense of agency than sensorimotor cues comes from pathologies (Jeannerod 2009). For instance, schizophrenic patients are impaired in explicitly judging whether they are in control of perceptual events but not impaired in automatically compensating for sensorimotor transformations between their movements and the resulting perceptual events (Fourneret *et al.* 2002). Frontal patients, like schizophrenic patients, have a preserved automatic sensorimotor control, contrasting with impaired action awareness and conscious monitoring (Slachevsky *et al.* 2003).

Toward an integrated model of agentive self-awareness

All the models I briefly reviewed share a core idea. They appeal to a principle of congruence between anticipated outcome and actual outcome. Where they differ is on whether the cues used are primarily cognitive, perceptual, or sensorimotor and on how closely they are related to action production mechanisms and intentional processes. There is now, however, a growing consensus that these different models should be seen as complementary rather than as rivals and that the sense of agency relies on a multiplicity of cues coming from different sources (Bayne and Pacherie 2007; Gallagher 2007; Knoblich and Repp 2009; Pacherie 2008; Sato 2009; Synofzik *et al.* 2008).

Thus, the conceptual framework I proposed (Pacherie 2008) distinguishes between three hierarchically ordered intentional levels: (1) distal intentions, where the action to be performed (i.e. goals and means) is specified in cognitive terms, (2) proximal intentions, where it is specified in actional-perceptual terms, that is terms of the action schemas to be implemented and the perceptual events that will occur as a consequence, and (3) motor intentions where it is specified in sensorimotor terms. Comparisons of desired, predicted, and actual states at each of these three levels provide different cues to agency.

This framework, as well as other similar integrative frameworks, leaves open a number of questions. What is the relative weight of cues on each of the three levels with regard to experiencing agency? To what extent can cognitive expectations overrule perceptual and sensorimotor evidence? To what extent can the relative weight of different agency cues be modulated by the nature of the task, by the attentional state of the agent, or by the agent's level of expertise? To answer those questions empirical investigations are needed. By themselves, however, such integrative frameworks may also help allay some of the controversies and perplexities surrounding the content, mode, structure, and reliability of states of agentive self-awareness.

3. CONTENT, MODE, AND STRUCTURE OF AGENTIVE SELF-AWARENESS

To have a sense of agency for an action is to be aware of oneself as the agent of the action. But what form(s) does this awareness take? To answer this question, several dimensions of agentive self-awareness must be considered. A first dimension along which states of agentive self-awareness can be located concerns their representational contents. A second, closely related, dimension concerns their mode. A third concerns their structure, what the direction of fit is supposed to be between these states and the world. A fourth important dimension is the temporal dimension: states of agentive self-awareness may differ according to whether one is about to act, one is in the process of acting, or one has already completed the action. As we will see, these dimensions are not strictly orthogonal; rather they interact in a variety of ways. I start with agentive content and mode.

Agentive content and mode

Agentive contents can range from the 'thin' to the 'thick'. At the thin end of the spectrum, one can experience oneself as acting and as acting more or less effortfully. For instance, one can be aware of one's bodily movements as active rather than passive. Moving up the spectrum, agentive content can include not merely the representation of a movement as one's own action, but also a representation of its effects in the world as effects one brought about. Moving even further up, agentive content can include a representation of the kind of action one is performing and one's reasons for performing it. One can be aware of oneself as opening a door, and as opening a door in order to (say) leave a building (as opposed to showing someone how to open the door). At the thicker end of the spectrum, some authors argue that agentive contents represent our mental states as causing our actions (Hohwy 2004). They might say, for instance, that I am aware not just that I am opening the door in order to leave the building, but that I am aware of my opening the door as caused by my intention to leave the building. Or, in the self-referential variant endorsed by Searle (1983) and Mossel (2005), that states of agentive self-awareness represent themselves as causing the target action.

Not all theoreticians agree that agentive contents can display such richness. Some hold onto an austere conception that only allows for thin contents. One way to make sense of their reticence is in terms of a second important dimension of agentive self-awareness. Bayne and Pacherie (2007) distinguish between agentive judgments and agentive experiences. Gallagher (2007) draws a similar distinction between two levels of the sense of agency, contrasting them in terms of first-order phenomenal experience of agency and higher-order, reflective attribution. Some states of agentive self-awareness take a judgmental (or doxastic) form. Normally, one's awareness of the kinds of actions that one is performing—making a cup of coffee, writing a paper—takes the form of belief. Yet, the 'vehicles' of agentive self-awareness are often more primitive than judgments. Consider what it is like to push a door open. One might *judge* that one is the agent of this action, but this judgment is not the only way in which one's own agency is manifested to oneself. Instead, one *experiences* oneself as the agent of this action. Such states are no more judgments than are visual experiences of the scene in front of one or proprioceptive experiences of the current position of one's limbs.

It seems that proponents of an austere conception of agentive content have agentive experiences in mind. It is very much an open question how rich the contents of agentive experience can be. Arguably, there are restrictions on the kind of properties that can be experientially encoded. A strong case can be made for thinking that the contents of agentive experience can go beyond merely representing oneself as actively moving, and may also include information about the degree of control one has over the movement and the degree to which the action is effortful. But it is less clear to what extent the intentional content of an action or one's aims in performing the action can also be encoded in agentive experience. Insofar as matches and mismatches between perceptual predictions and feedback appear to be important cues to agency, I am inclined to consider that agentive experience can partake of the richness of perceptual experience. Similarly, Gallagher (2007) suggests that the sense of agency as a first-order experience includes not just sensorimotor content linked to bodily movement but also perceptual information linked to the effects of the action in the world.

Whatever the constraints on the contents of agentive experiences, there are no obvious restrictions on cognitive content; almost any property can be represented in cognition. Insofar as agentive judgments have cognitive contents, there are therefore not obvious limits to their richness. Thus, as long as one is willing to countenance both agentive experiences and agentive judgments as complementary forms of agentive self-awareness, the debate about agentive content shouldn't really be about how rich it is possible for it to be. Rather, the debate is about how this content is distributed between agentive experience and agentive judgment and about how experience and judgment relate.

With respect to the distribution of agentive content, one important issue beyond those already considered concerns the cognitive penetrability of agentive experience. One aspect of agentive experience—our moment-by-moment sense of ourselves as the agents of various movements—is largely based on sensorimotor cues from low-level, comparator-based systems. These low-level systems are largely modular and as such presumably rather impervious to top–down influences. Thus, Fried and colleagues (1991) reported that electrical stimulation of the supplementary motor area could elicit in their patients a subjective 'urge' to perform a movement in the absence of overt motor response. Furthermore, at some sites where these subjective experiences were elicited, stimulation at higher current evoked an overt motor response. Subjects in these experiments had all the reasons to judge that they were not the agents of their movements as they knew these were caused by the electrical stimulation applied to their brain; yet they felt the urge to move and when they actually moved had an experience of actively moving.

Yet, as we saw in section 2, there are reasons to think that perceptual cues may contribute more to agentive experience than sensorimotor cues. Now there's a better case to be made for cognitive penetrability of perceptual content. In one of the classic papers of New Look psychology, Bruner and Goodman (1947) found that poorer children perceived coins as bigger than rich children do. This study suggests that high-level information can affect the contents of visual perception. Similarly, it might be possible for cognitive expectations to exert a top–down influence on agentive experience at least around the margins.

Conversely, one may ask how strong the dependence of agentive judgments on agentive experience is. Agentive judgments are typically grounded in and justified by agentive experiences. In the normal case, we judge that we are the agent of a particular action on the grounds that we enjoy an agentive experience with respect to it; here, our agentive judgments are simply endorsements of our agentive experiences. Correlatively, we normally judge that we are not the agent of a particular event because we lack an agentive experience with respect to it. In light of this, pathologies of agentive self-awareness in which the agent denies that one of their actions is their own are likely to be grounded in pathologies of agentive experience. The aetiological account of such pathologies would, on this approach, be primarily a matter of accounting for disturbances in the agent's experience of their own agency (Pacherie *et al.* 2006).

Yet, our agentive judgments are often more than just endorsements of our agentive experiences. Although my agentive experience might tell me that I performed a certain action, it may not tell me what kind of action it was or what my reasons were for performing it. The job of agentive judgments would then be to provide an interpretation of the action in the light of one's self-conception. They may do so, as Wegner suggests, by either linking the action to some consistent prior thought we had or, if need be, by confabulating reasons for the action.

Furthermore, our agentive judgments are not beholden to our agentive experiences. Not only can we deny that we are the authors of events towards which we have an agentive experience, we can also assert that we are the authors of events for which we lack such an experience. The agent's narrative self-conception and cognitive expectations might place rich and substantive constraints on whether or not the contents of agentive experiences are to be accepted. In general, experiential states do not compel assent, and there is no reason to think that matters are any different with respect to agentive experiences. It might be the case that agents evaluate their agentive experience (or lack thereof) in light of their narrative self-conception. Agentive experience for an action may be overridden by certain holistic constraints, in instances where the action makes no sense with regard to our narrative self-conception. Or, conversely, we may self-attribute an action despite lacking an experience of agency for that action, if the action makes perfect sense in light of our narrative self-conception. The latter may actually be quite common, as there is reason to think that in many cases the agent won't have any information about agentive experience to draw on in forming agentive judgments. Such experiences are likely to be labile and short-lived; leaving no trace in long-term memory unless attentional resources are used to probe and consolidate them. Given their short life-span, our agentive experiences may well have been obliterated by the time we make an agentive judgment. Such 'gaps' between agentive experience and agentive judgment might be large enough for processes of narrative reconstruction to exploit, allowing an agent's narrative self-conception to restructure their agentive self-awareness.

Structure and time course

Bayne (2008) distinguishes four possible conceptions of the structure of states of agentive self-awareness. As a first possibility one may think of them as having a descriptive structure. On this view, they are supposed to say how things are, have a mind-to-world direction of fit, a world-to-mind direction of causation, and veridicality conditions. Alternatively, one may hold that states of agentive self-awareness have a directive structure, representing how the world is to be changed and having a world-to-mind direction of fit and a mind-to-world direction of causation. On the directive account, then, these states would have conditions of satisfaction but not veridicality conditions. The third account holds that states of agentive self-awareness are akin to Millikan's *pushmi-pullyu* representations (Millikan 1995), having at once a mind-to-world and a world-to-mind direction of fit and thus being both descriptive and directive. According to the fourth and final account, states of agentive self-awareness would lack intentional content altogether, involving only raw phenomenal feels. As pointed out by Bayne, although Searle (1983) did much to put the directive account on the table, the descriptive account seems to be the majority view,[3] while the 'pushmi-pullyu' and the raw feels accounts have not been developed in any detail.

   In my view, all these accounts have some merits. Yet, given the complex nature and the many facets of agentive self-awareness, it is unlikely that a single account should hold across the board. Let us first consider the distinction between agentive experience and agentive judgment. Clearly, the only plausible account of the structure of agentive judgments is the descriptive account. Agentive judgments have a mind-to-world direction of fit and veridicality conditions. Thus, it is only when one focuses on agentive experiences that there is room for debate. Second, we should also note that specific temporal constraints apply to states with directive structure, while no particular temporal constraints on their contents are imposed on states in virtue of their having a descriptive structure. For instance, my beliefs can be about past, present, or future states of affairs. When temporal constraints apply, they do apply not in virtue of the state having a descriptive structure but in virtue of features of its mode (as in regret that can only concern past states of

---

[3] For recent defenses of the descriptive account, see Bayne (2010) and Proust (2003).

affairs). In contrast, there are temporal constraints on the contents of states with a directive structure. I can intend to do something now or to do something tomorrow, but I cannot intend to do something yesterday. These constraints stem from the fact that these states have a mind-to-world direction of causation and from the time-asymmetry of causation: effects cannot precede their causes. For agentive experiences to have a directive structure, it would therefore be necessary, although not sufficient, that they satisfy those temporal requirements. In other words, it would be necessary that these experiences occur before the state of affairs they are about.

Among the cues contributing to agentive experiences that we discussed in section 2, some but not all satisfy these requirements. Matches between desired and actual (sensory or perceptual) effects as well as between predicted and actual effects are thought to provide cues to self-agency, but for there to be such matches, the actual effects must have been brought about already. So the agentive contents contributed by these cues cannot have a directive structure. There are other cues to self-agency, however, that seem to have the right temporal characteristics. Efferent signals (Tsakiris and Haggard 2005; Tsakiris *et al.* 2005) and matches between desired and predicted effects both provide cues to agency in advance of actual movement, thus tagging the forthcoming event as being 'mine'. Yet, this does not suffice to vindicate the directive account. There should also be a mind-to world direction of causation. Obviously, efferent signals contribute to the production of the action, but what about matches between desired and predicted states? In computational models of the motor system (Miall and Wolpert 1996) the comparison of predicted and desired states is seen as a final check before the gates to action execution are opened, suggesting indeed that signals arising from that comparison process control the gates to action execution. The signals would thus underlie the sense that one is initiating an action.

So we have signals that appear to both play a role in action production and function as cues to self-agency. Is the directive account thereby vindicated? Not quite. The phrase 'X is a cue to self-agency' can be understood in two different ways: as meaning that X is a constituent of agentive experience (the constitutive reading) or as meaning that X plays a causal role in bringing about the agentive experience (the causal reading). Only the constitutive reading is consistent with the directive account; the causal reading would belong with a descriptive account. I find it hard to tell how much this is an empirical as opposed to a conceptual issue. Following Bayne (2008), we could say that the constitutive reading would rule out the possibility of a person experiencing herself as initiating an action she is not actually initiating, whereas the causal reading would allow it, suggesting this is at least in part an empirical issue. In practice, however, it may prove extremely difficult to completely separate out the various components of agentive experience and thus test for such a dissociation.

Finally, even if we opt for the constitutive reading, we are not yet out of the woods. The directive account, like the descriptivist account, is representationalist in spirit. But do the relevant signals carry intentional content accessible to consciousness? Pure efferent signals may be thought to be responsible for raw feelings of activity and effort, amenable to a raw feelings account rather than to the directive account. Signals arising from the comparison of desired and predicted states present us with better prospects, for obviously the states compared carry intentional content. Yet it is unclear whether we have access to the contents of the states compared or simply to the result of their comparison. As we saw in section 2, empirical evidence indicates that we are largely unaware of the nature of our movements. This suggests that, at the sensorimotor level at least, we have no conscious access to the contents of sensorimotor representations of desired and predicted states or to contents encoding the nature of the possible discrepancies between them. Rather we may simply have access to information that there is or there isn't a match. The agentive experience would then have very thin content indeed, something we may paraphrase as 'Ok, let's go' or 'Wait, not ready'. Comparisons of desired and predictive effects made at the proximal level may however provide more glamorous agentive content, for here empirical evidence suggests that we normally have precise conscious expectations regarding the perceptual events our action is to bring about. So, something like 'Let there be light!' may enter the content of our agentive experience when about to press a switch.

Experiences with agentive content based on predictive signals may then constitute the most convincing case for the directive account. However, given the dual role predictions play in motor control, they may also be amenable to a pushmi-pullyu interpretation. On the one hand, comparisons of desired with predicted states control the gates to action execution; on the other hand, comparisons of predicted with actual states signal either completion or the need for corrections. With respect to their former function, they seem to have a directive structure, with respect to the latter a descriptive structure. That a single representation might have two opposite directions of fit may appear paradoxical. This air of paradox may be somewhat alleviated if one considers the time-course of these representations. They would seem to have a directive structure in the early stages of action, but a descriptive structure in its late stages. When all goes well and action execution proceeds without impediment, the intentional content of predictions remains the same, but their direction of fit gradually changes from directive to descriptive.

In a nutshell, each of the four accounts of the structure of agentive self-awareness distinguished by Bayne may have some plausibility for at least some components of agentive self-awareness. The descriptive account is certainly the one with the widest scope. All the components of agentive self-awareness that are judgmental in form have descriptive structure and so do many experiential components of agentive self-awareness. If one considers, however, that agentive experience is not a point-like experience but an experience extended in time and evolving as the action unfolds, one should be open to the possibility that some components of this experience have a directive or a pushmi-pullyu structure. Finally, the brute efferent component of agentive experience may be responsible for raw phenomenal feels of activity and effort.

4. Agency and Sense of Agency

How reliable is the sense of agency?

This question takes different forms depending on what we take the structure of states of agentive self-awareness to be. If one holds that states of agentive self-awareness have a descriptive structure, the question whether they are reliable becomes the question whether or not they tend to be veridical. If one holds that (at least some) states of agentive self-awareness have directive structure, reliability will be cashed out in terms of success rather than truth. On a directive account, states of agentive self-awareness are reliable to the extent that they tend to bring about the state of affairs they represent. If one favors a raw feels account, the question of reliability simply does not arise. Phenomenal feels are not about anything and have no satisfaction conditions; they are simply present or absent.

Given that the debate over the reliability (or lack thereof) of states of agentive self-awareness has mostly been conducted within a descriptive framework, in what follows I will keep to that framework. The question of how reliable states of agentive self-awareness are may yield different answers depending on how much we pack into their contents. The more agentive content includes, the more possibilities for error are created. This question may also yield different answers depending on how closely we take the mechanisms involved in the generation of agentive self-awareness to be related to the mechanisms of action production.

In sections 2 and 3, we discussed evidence that agentive experience exploits performance-related sensorimotor cues. These would be highly reliable cues to self-agency insofar as they have very direct links to action production (efferent signals) and exploit proprioceptive information that is immune to error through misidentification (proprioceptive information can only be information about oneself). If agentive experiences were based only on efferent-cum-proprioceptive information they would be very reliable indeed, as it is hard to see how one could experience oneself as actively moving when one isn't. Yet, as we also discussed, these cues contribute rather thin agentive content mostly concerned with active bodily movements, the body parts involved, and the timing of their movements.

Perceptual cues largely contribute to enriching the contents of agentive experience. We do not just experience ourselves as moving but also as producing effects in the world. Matches between the predicted perceptual effects of our movements and perceptual events in the world may thus play a central role in agentive experience. Yet, perceptual events resulting from one's own and others' actions are not qualitatively different and keeping them apart is not trivial. Reliance on perceptual cues therefore opens the possibility of errors that can be either false positives as when we have an experience of agency for events actually produced by someone else's action or false negatives as when we lack an experience of agency for an event we actually brought about. The latter kind of error can also happen because we sometimes fail to correctly predict the perceptual consequences of our action. If I press a switch expecting the light to go on and it doesn't, I may fail to notice that by pressing the switch I turned the ventilator on and thus lack a sense of agency for that event.

We can act and lack an experience of agency for perceptual effects that our action brought about or have an experience of agency for perceptual effects that were actually produced by someone else's action. But can we have a sense of agency when we do not act at all? Experimental work suggests that indeed we can. For instance, Wegner and colleagues (2004) devised a 'helping hands' experiment, where participants watched themselves in a mirror while another person behind them, hidden from view, extended hands forward on each side where participants' hands would normally appear. The hands performed a series of movements. When participants could hear instructions previewing each movement, they reported an enhanced sense of agency for the action compared to those cases where the instructions did not match the hand movement or followed it. These results suggest that when sensorimotor cues and perceptual cues are in conflict, the latter might dominate and trump the former.

However, reliability does not require infallibility and in normal environments such errors may not be systematic enough as to make agentive experiences generally untrustworthy. Those who contend that the sense of agency is deeply flawed tend to attribute richer content to states of agentive self-awareness. Thus, Wegner's claim that the conscious will is an illusion comes with a high-loaded view of what agentive content includes. As several commentators have noted (Bayne 2006; Carruthers 2007), he seems to have a number of different illusions in mind. The experience of freedom and the experience of conscious mental causation appear to be his main targets.

To evaluate claims that these are illusory, one must consider several issues. What exactly are these contentious contents? Are they really the contents of agentive experiences or rather the contents of agentive judgments that interpret agentive experiences? If the latter, are they part and parcel of the folk-psychological conception of agency and thus presumably widely shared, or rather the products of philosophical interpretations of folk-psychological notions? Finally, what is the empirical evidence relevant to their assessment?

Free agency

Let us start with the experience of freedom. Here, Wegner's contention seems to be that we experience ourselves as acting freely, but that for this experience to be veridical we would need metaphysically free will, understood as an uncaused cause of action. Libet's experiments (Libet 1985; Libet *et al.* 1983), however, showed that conscious intentions to act (W-judgments) are first experienced on average 200 milliseconds before movement onset but are reliably preceded by several hundred milliseconds by a negative brain potential, the so-called 'readiness potential'. Either the readiness potential causes the action directly and causes the conscious experience of willing as a mere epiphenomenal accompaniment, or it causes the conscious experience which in turn causes the action. But either way, the conscious will doesn't initiate the action and thus the action isn't performed freely. Recent experiments (Soon *et al.* 2008*a*, 2008*b*) also showed that, although subjects who had to decide between two actions reported having made a conscious decision on average 1000 ms before action onset, the outcome of their decision was encoded in brain activity of prefrontal and parietal cortex up to 10 s before it entered awareness. Following the same line of reasoning, one could say once again that since the conscious decision follows specific unconscious brain activity rather than precedes it, it cannot be free. Therefore, according to Wegner, the experience of freedom is illusory.

Let us note first that it is very doubtful that the experience of freedom, if there is such a thing, includes such a metaphysically loaded notion of freedom. It may well be that what we call the experience of freedom is something much more modest. One may attempt a negative characterization of the experience of freedom and suggest that to experience oneself as acting freely is *not* to experience oneself as compelled to act, in the way that people suffering from obsessive compulsive disorder (OCD) seem to be experiencing their compulsive actions. Indeed, if we take the phenomenology of compulsive actions to be the negative image of the phenomenology of freedom, what seems central is not the felt causal origin of the action but its uncontrollability or unstoppability. People with OCD acknowledge their compulsive actions as originating within their own mind (and not as imposed by outside persons as in delusions of control), but they experience them as uncontrollable—however hard they try to resist performing them, they fail in their attempts. If one's experience of freedom is at bottom the experience that one has control over the actions one performs, can stop an action one is about to engage in, or correct or abort if need be an ongoing action, the experience of freedom does not appear to qualify as a systematic illusion. Indeed, even Libet acknowledges that we can veto actions and, apart from ballistic actions that cannot be stopped or corrected once started, we are normally able to exert control over our ongoing actions.

But here we are a far cry from the metaphysically loaded notion of freedom that is under attack. We might not err so much in our experiences of freedom as in the interpretations of these experiences that transpire in our agentive judgments. Perhaps, then, our folk notion of freedom is incompatibilist and we spontaneously interpret the actions we experience as free as caused by conscious decisions or intentions that are themselves uncaused. This, of course, presupposes that we are natural incompatibilists. But is it really the case? Philosophers working in the field of experimental philosophy have begun using methods borrowed from psychology to probe ordinary intuitions concerning freedom in a controlled and systematic way. But results so far have not been clear-cut (Feltz *et al.* 2009), with some studies suggesting that we are natural compatibilists (Nahmias *et al.* 2005, 2006) and others that we are natural incompatibilists (Nichols and Knobe 2007). From reading this literature, one gets the impression that what people really care about is moral responsibility, for which they take freedom to be necessary, and that they are willing to embrace either compatibilism or incompatibilism as long as their doing so helps preserve moral responsibility.

If, rather than hardcore incompatibilists or compatibilists, people are merely metaphysical opportunists with respect to freedom, their agentive judgments that they are acting freely need not be metaphysically loaded one way or the other and therefore need not be systematically mistaken.

Conscious mental causation

Another target of Wegner's claim that the conscious will is an illusion is the idea that we have an experience of conscious mental causation. While it is doubtful that a specific metaphysical conception of freedom is part and parcel of our folk-psychology, it is beyond doubt that the idea of conscious mental causation is a core element of our folk-psychology: we firmly believe that our own distinctly mental properties are causally efficacious in the production of our behavior. As pointed out by Hohwy (2004), however, the conception of mental causation that people are so firmly attached to often seems rather poorly articulated. Hohwy usefully distinguishes two sets of aspects in our conception of mental causation. Elements in the first set constitute what he calls the narrow conception of mental causation: we believe in mental causation because we successfully explain and predict behavior in the mental state terms of common-sense folk-psychology and this success is best explained if these mental states are causally efficacious (reasons as causes), that is, if events can be causes in virtue of being instantiations of mental properties. These features of the narrow conception of mental causation do not fully explain the attraction that the idea of mental causation exerts on us. To understand this attraction one must consider a broader conception of mental causation that appeals to phenomenal features.

According to Hohwy (2004), we further believe that our beliefs and desires and their contents are current triggering causes of our behavior (*here and now causation*), that we are often aware of the mental property that was causally efficacious in causing bodily behavior (*awareness of mental causation*), that we voluntarily select, or endorse, which mental properties are going to cause behavior and control how they do it (*voluntary selection/endorsement and control of mental causes*); and finally that we generally reliably judge that there is mental causation when there is mental causation (*reliable tracking of mental causation*). In other words, we do not just believe in mental causation, we believe in conscious mental causation.

It is this latter set of features of our conception of mental causation that appear to be the immediate target of Wegner's skepticism. But are our beliefs in the existence of these features themselves grounded in our agentive experience? Do our agentive experiences include an experience of mental causation that is simply endorsed by these beliefs? Are the beliefs best seen instead as interpretations of agentive experiences in the light of our folk-psychological conception of mental causation, committing us to more than what our basic agentive experiences actually contain? Opinions are divided. Some theorists, including Hohwy (2004), seem happy to countenance experiences of mental causation, that is, experiences of one's actions as caused by one's conscious mental states. Others (Horgan *et al.* 2003; Wakefield and Dreyfus 1991) strongly deny experiencing their actions as caused by their mental states. Instead, they claim that they experience their actions as caused by themselves or as having their sources in themselves. We may well judge that our actions are caused by our mental states, but such judgments would be more than simply endorsements of agentive experiences. If we allow that we enjoy experiences of mental causation and Wegner's criticisms are warranted, then our agentive experience itself is deeply flawed. If we deny the existence of experiences of mental causation, our agentive judgments regarding mental causation may be shown to be systematically in error, without this affecting the probity of our agentive experiences.

Among Wegner's arguments, the argument from automaticity is perhaps the most successful in casting doubt on conscious mental causation. Automaticity is pervasive in our life. In many cases, cognitive goals are triggered by environmental features and our behavior is controlled by automatic mental processes that bypass consciousness (Bargh and Chartrand 1999; Bargh and Ferguson 2000). Furthermore, automatic activation of goals creates a state that is functionally very much like conscious activation of goals; motivating behavior and higher mental processes involved in goal-directed behavior, such as maintaining the goal active and monitoring its progress (Bargh and Chartrand 1999; Custers and Aarts 2005).[4] If automaticity is pervasive, subjects will often misidentify the reasons they acted as they did, or fail to identify any reasons at all, because those reasons are activated without being consciously accessed.

As pointed out by Hohwy (2004), automaticity poses no threat to the idea of mental causation, insofar as activated goals are mental representations that, when activated, produce their effect qua being mental properties. Automaticity, however, poses a threat to conscious mental causation and to the broad conception of mental causation according to which we are generally aware of the mental states that cause our actions and exert voluntary control on mental causation. How serious the threat is depends on how pervasive automaticity is. It is certainly fairly widespread but could it really be the case that all mental causation is automatic? Wegner is certainly right that we overestimate the role conscious mental causation

---

[4] Recent studies (Aarts *et al.* 2009) also provide evidence that mechanisms underlying nonconscious goal pursuit promote experiences of self-agency through the same kind of matching processes that conscious goal pursuit does.

plays in our life. But are we also hopelessly wrong in thinking that conscious mental causation even exists? Indeed, we could turn the argument from automaticity on its head and argue that automaticity is what makes conscious mental causation possible. Conscious processes are known to be slow, resource-demanding, and to have limited capacity compared to automatic processes. We would accomplish very little if we had to rely entirely on conscious processing. Instead, automatic processes make us free to apply our precious conscious resources to issues that matter to us. Perhaps, indeed, one reason we overestimate the role played by conscious mental causation generally is that conscious mental causation is at play in matters we really care about.

5. Conclusion

On our folk-psychological conception of ourselves as agents, we are conscious agents both in the sense that our actions are caused by conscious mental states that we voluntarily select and control and in the sense that we have a conscious experience of agency for our actions. Indeed, on this picture conscious agency as conscious mental causation of action and conscious agency as conscious experience of ourselves as agents are really two sides of the same coin: conscious agency in the latter sense is taken to be an experience of oneself as a conscious agent in the former sense.

Empirical work casts a heavy shadow on this portrait of the self as an agent. On the more radical interpretation of these empirical findings, there is simply no such thing as conscious mental causation. Our self-portrait is in effect a vanity picture and our experience of self-agency a systematic illusion, the result of an elaborate hoax our mind plays on us. More plausibly, I think, empirical findings demand that we seriously retouch this self-portrait, not that we shatter it altogether. On the one hand, they show that conscious mental agency, understood as conscious mental causation, is neither the unique nor the most common form human agency takes. On the other hand, they also suggest that the folk-psychological depiction of the conscious experience of agency as the experience of conscious agency is misleading. In many cases, the experience of agency is something more basic. We may experience an action as ours, without *experiencing* it as caused by conscious mental states and done for this or that reason, although we can readily *interpret* it in that way.

With this touched-up portrait, we may also see the link between agency and consciousness of agency in a new light. On the folk-psychological picture of agency as conscious mental causation, the link is constitutive. Indeed, on this picture it is unclear why there should be conscious experiences of agency over and above agency. If agency is by definition conscious, what is the need for an extra-layer of consciousness—a *conscious* experience of *conscious* agency? On the radical reinterpretation of agency Wegner sometimes seems to advocate, we are also left to wonder why we should bother weaving a fictitious conscious story, when actual agency operates quite independently of consciousness. But if human agency is characterized by the interplay of automatic and conscious processes, experiences of agency may play an important role in their integration. If we lacked altogether even a minimal sense of agency for automatically triggered actions, our agentive selves would be but fragmented islands on a sea of automaticity.

REFERENCES

AARTS, H., CUSTERS, R., and WEGNER, D. (2005). 'On the Inference of Personal Authorship: Enhancing Experienced Agency by Priming Effect Information', *Consciousness and Cognition*, 14/3: 439–58.

BARGH, J., and CHARTRAND, T. (1999). 'The Unbearable Automaticity of Being', *American Psychologist*, 54: 462–79.

——and FERGUSON, M. (2000). 'Beyond Behaviorism: On the Automaticity of Higher Mental Processes', *Psychological Bulletin*, 126/6: 925–45.

BAYNE, T. (2006). 'Phenomenology and the Feeling of Doing: Wegner on the Conscious Will', in S. Pockett, W. Banks, and S. Gallagher (eds), *Does Consciousness Cause Behavior?* (Cambridge, Mass.: MIT Press), 169–85.

——(2008). 'The Phenomenology of Agency', *Philosophy Compass*, 3/1: 182–202.

——(2010). 'The Sense of Agency', in F. Macpherson (ed.), *The Senses* (Oxford: Oxford University Press).

——and PACHERIE, E. (2007). 'Narrators and Comparators: The Architecture of Agentive Self-Awareness', *Synthese*, 159/3: 475–91.

BLAKEMORE, S., and FRITH, C. (2003). 'Self-Awareness and Action', *Current Opinion in Neurobiology*, 13/2: 219–24.

——WOLPERT, D., and FRITH, C. (1998). 'Central Cancellation of Self-Produced Tickle Sensation', *Nature Neuroscience*, 1: 635–40.

————and —— (2000). 'Why can't you Tickle Yourself?', *Neuroreport*, 11/11: R11–R16.

BRUNER, J., and GOODMAN, C. (1947). 'Value and Need as Organizing Factors in Perception', *Journal of Abnormal and Social Psychology*, 42/1: 33–44.

CARRUTHERS, P. (2007). 'The Illusion of Conscious Will', *Synthese*, 159/2: 197–213.

CUSTERS, R., and AARTS, H. (2005). 'Positive Affect as Implicit Motivator: On the Nonconscious Operation of Behavioral Goals', *Journal of Personality and Social Psychology*, 89/2: 129–42.

DAVIDSON, D. (1980). *Essays on Actions and Events* (New York: Oxford University Press).

DENNETT, D. (1992). 'The Self as a Center of Narrative Gravity', in F. Kessel, P. Cole, and D. Johnson (eds), *Self and Consciousness: Multiple Perspectives* (Hillsdale, NJ: Erlbaum), 103–15.

DE VIGNEMONT, F., TSAKIRIS, M., and HAGGARD, P. (2006). 'Body Mereology', in G. Knoblich, I. Thorton, M. Grosjean, and M. Shiffrar (eds), *Human Body Perception from the Inside Out* (New York: Oxford University Press), 147–70.

FEINBERG, T. E., ROANE, D. M., and ALI, J. (2000). 'Illusory Limb Movements in Anosognosia for Hemiplegia', *Journal of Neurology Neurosurgery and Psychiatry*, 68/4: 511–13.

FELTZ, A., COKELY, E., and NADELHOFFER, T. (2009). 'Natural Compatibilism versus Natural Incompatibilism: Back to the Drawing Board', *Mind and Language*, 24/1: 1–23.

FOURNERET, P., and JEANNEROD, M. (1998). 'Limited Conscious Monitoring of Motor Performance in Normal Subjects', *Neuropsychologia*, 36/11: 1133–40.

——DE VIGNEMONT, F., FRANCK, N., SLACHEVSKY, A., DUBOIS, B., and JEANNEROD, M. (2002). 'Perception of Self-Generated Action in Schizophrenia', *Cognitive Neuropsychiatry*, 7/2: 139–56.

FRIED, I., KATZ, A., McCARTHY, G., SASS, K. J., WILLIAMSON, P., SPENCER, S. S., and SPENCER, D. D. (1991). 'Functional Organization of Human Supplementary Motor Cortex Studied by Electrical Stimulation', *Journal of Neuroscience*, 11/11: 3656–66.

FRITH, C. (2005). 'The Self in Action: Lessons from Delusions of Control', *Consciousness and Cognition*, 14/4: 752–70.

——BLAKEMORE, S., and WOLPERT, D. (2000*a*). 'Abnormalities in the Awareness and Control of Action', *Philosophical Transactions of the Royal Society of London, B Biological Sciences*, 355/1404: 1771–88.

——and ——(2000*b*). 'Explaining the Symptoms of Schizophrenia: Abnormalities in the Awareness of Action', *Brain Research Reviews*, 31/2–3: 357–63.

GALLAGHER, S. (2007). 'The Natural Philosophy of Agency', *Philosophy Compass*, 2/2: 347–57.

GAZZANIGA, M., and LeDOUX, J. (1978). *The Integrated Mind* (New York: Plenum Publishing Corporation).

HAGGARD, P., and CLARK, S. (2003). 'Intentional Action: Conscious Experience and Neural Prediction', *Consciousness and Cognition*, 12/4: 695–707.

————and KALOGERAS, J. (2002). 'Voluntary Action and Conscious Awareness', *Nature Neuroscience*, 5/4: 382–5.

HOHWY, J. (2004). 'The Experience of Mental Causation', *Behavior and Philosophy*, 32/2: 377.

HORGAN, T., TIENSON, J., and GRAHAM, G. (2003). 'The Phenomenology of First-Person Agency', in S. Walter and H.-D. Heckmann (eds), *Physicalism and Mental Causation: The Metaphysics of Mind and Action* (Exeter: Imprint Academic), 323–40.

JEANNEROD, M. (2009). 'The Sense of Agency and its Disturbances in Schizophrenia: A Reappraisal', *Experimental Brain Research*, 192/3: 527–32.

KIM, J. (1998). *Mind in a Physical World* (Cambridge, Mass.: MIT Press).

KNOBLICH, G., and KIRCHER, T. T. J. (2004). 'Deceiving Oneself about Being in Control: Conscious Detection of Changes in Visuomotor Coupling', *Journal of Experimental Psychology, Human Perception and Performance*, 30/4: 657–66.

——and REPP, B. H. (2009). 'Inferring Agency from Sound', *Cognition*, 111/2: 248–62.

——STOTTMEISTER, F., and KIRCHER, T. (2004). 'Self-Monitoring in Patients with Schizophrenia', *Psychological Medicine*, 34/8: 1561–9.

LEUBE, D., KNOBLICH, G., ERB, M., GRODD, W., BARTELS, M., and KIRCHER, T. (2003). 'The Neural Correlates of Perceiving One's Own Movements', *NeuroImage*, 20/4: 2084–90.

LIBET, B. (1985). 'Unconscious Cerebral Initiative and the Role of Conscious Will in Voluntary Action', *Behavioral and Brain Sciences*, 8/4: 529–39.

——GLEASON, C., WRIGHT, E., and PEARL, D. (1983). 'Time of Conscious Intention to Act in Relation to Onset of Cerebral Activity (Readiness-Potential): The Unconscious Initiation of a Freely Voluntary Act', *Brain*, 106/3: 623.

MIALL, R. C., and WOLPERT, D. M. (1996). 'Forward Models for Physiological Motor Control', *Neural Networks*, 9/8: 1265–79.

MILLIKAN, R. G. (1995). 'Pushmi-Pullyu Representations', *Philosophical Perspectives*, 9: 185–200.

MOLL, A. (1889). *Hypnotism* (London: Walter Scott).

MOSSEL, B. (2005). 'Action, Control and Sensations of Acting', *Philosophical Studies*, 124/2: 129–80.

NAHMIAS, E., MORRIS, S., NADELHOFFER, T., and TURNER, J. (2005). 'Surveying Freedom: Folk Intuitions about Free Will and Moral Responsibility', *Philosophical Psychology*, 18/5: 561–84.

————————and ——(2006). 'Is Incompatibilism Intuitive?', *Philosophy and Phenomenological Research*, 73: 28–53.

NICHOLS, S., and KNOBE, J. (2007). 'Moral Responsibility and Determinism: The Cognitive Science of Folk Intuitions', *Noûs*, 41/4: 663–85.

PACHERIE, E. (2008). 'The Phenomenology of Action: A Conceptual Framework', *Cognition*, 107/1: 179–217.

——GREEN, M., and BAYNE, T. (2006). 'Phenomenology and Delusions: Who Put the "Alien" in Alien Control?', *Consciousness and Cognition*, 15/3: 566–577.

PHILLIPS, W., BARON-COHEN, S., and RUTTER, M. (1998). 'Understanding Intention in Normal Development and in Autism', *British Journal of Developmental Psychology*, 16: 337–48.

Pockett, S., Banks, W. P., and Gallagher, S. (eds) (2006). *Does Consciousness Cause Behavior?* (Cambridge, Mass.: MIT Press).

PROUST, J. (2003). 'Perceiving Intentions', in J. Roessler and N. Eilan (eds), *Agency and Self-Awareness* (Oxford: Oxford University Press), 296–320.

Roessler, J., and Eilan, N. (eds) (2003). *Agency and Self-Awareness: Issues in Philosophy and Psychology* (Oxford: Clarendon Press).

ROSER, M., and GAZZANIGA, M. (2004). 'Automatic Brains: Interpretive Minds', *Current Directions in Psychological Science*, 13/2: 56–9.

——and ——(2006). 'The Interpreter in Human Psychology', *The Evolution of Primate Nervous Systems* (Oxford: Elsevier).

SASS, L. (1992). *Madness and Modernism: Insanity in the Light of Modern Art, Literature, and Thought.* (New York: Basic Books).

SATO, A. (2009). 'Both Motor Prediction and Conceptual Congruency between Preview and Action-Effect Contribute to Explicit Judgment of Agency', *Cognition*, 110/1: 74–83.

——and YASUDA, A. (2005). 'Illusion of Sense of Self-Agency: Discrepancy between the Predicted and Actual Sensory Consequences of Actions Modulates the Sense of Self-Agency, But Not the Sense of Self-Ownership', *Cognition*, 94/3: 241–55.

SEARLE, J. (1983). *Intentionality: An Essay in the Philosophy of Mind* (Cambridge: Cambridge University Press).

Sebanz, N., and Prinz, W. (eds) (2006). *Disorders of Volition* (Cambridge, Mass.: MIT Press).

SIEGEL, S. E. (2007). 'Symposium on the Phenomenology of Agency', *Psyche*, 13/1.

SLACHEVSKY, A., PILLON, B., FOURNERET, P., RENIE, L., LEVY, R., JEANNEROD, M., and DUBOIS, B. (2003). 'The Prefrontal Cortex and Conscious Monitoring of Action: An Experimental Study', *Neuropsychologia*, 41/6: 655–65.

SOON, C. S., BRASS, M., HEINZE, H. J., and HAYNES, J. D. (2008*a*). 'Unconscious Determinants of Free Decisions in the Human Brain', *International Journal of Psychology*, 43/3–4: 543–5.

————and ——(2008*b*). 'Unconscious Determinants of Free Decisions in the Human Brain', *Nature Neuroscience*, 11/5: 543–5.

STEPHENS, G., and GRAHAM, G. (2000). *When Self-Consciousness Breaks: Alien Voices and Inserted Thoughts* (Cambridge, Mass.: MIT Press).

SYNOFZIK, M., VOSGERAU, G., and NEWEN, A. (2008). 'Beyond the Comparator Model: A Multifactorial Two-Step Account of Agency', *Consciousness and Cognition*, 17/1: 219–39.

TSAKIRIS, M., and HAGGARD, P. (2005). 'The Rubber Hand Illusion Revisited: Visuotactile Integration and Self-Attribution', *Journal of Experimental Psychology, Human Perception and Performance*, 31/1: 80–91.

————FRANCK, N., MAINY, N., and SIRIGU, A. (2005). 'A Specific Role for Efferent Information in Self-Recognition', *Cognition*, 96/3: 215–31.

——PRABHU, G., and HAGGARD, P. (2006). 'Having a Body versus Moving your Body: How Agency Structures Body-Ownership', *Consciousness and Cognition*, 15/2: 423–32.

VAN DEN BOS, E., and JEANNEROD, M. (2002). 'Sense of Body and Sense of Action Both Contribute to Self-Recognition', *Cognition*, 85/2: 177–87.

WAKEFIELD, J., and DREYFUS, H. (1991). 'Intentionality and the Phenomenology of Action', in E. LePore and R. Van Gulick (eds), *John Searle and his Critics* (Cambridge, Mass.: Blackwell), 259–70.

WEGNER, D. (2002). *The Illusion of Conscious Will* (Cambridge, Mass.: MIT Press).

——(2005). 'Who is the Controller of Controlled Processes', in R. R. Hassin, J. S. Uleman, and J. A. Bargh (eds), *The New Unconscious* (Oxford: Oxford University Press), 19–36.

——and WHEATLEY, T. (1999). 'Apparent Mental Causation: Sources of the Experience of Will', *American Psychologist*, 54/7: 480–92.

——SPARROW, B., and WINERMAN, L. (2004). 'Vicarious Agency: Experiencing Control over the Movements of Others', *Journal of Personality and Social Psychology*, 86/6: 838–48.

WEILLER, C., JUPTNER, M., FELLOWS, S., RIJNTJES, M., LEONHARDT, G., KIEBEL, S., MULLER, S., DIENER, H. C., and THILMANN, A. F. (1996). 'Brain Representation of Active and Passive Movements', *NeuroImage*, 4/2: 105–10.

CHAPTER 20

....

SELF-CONTROL IN ACTION

....

ALFRED R. MELE

PHILOSOPHERS use the term 'self-control' in a variety of different ways. Daniel Dennett (1984), for example, uses it to mean roughly what some other philosophers (Mele 1995) mean by 'autonomy'. And Jeanette Kennett distinguishes among three senses of 'self-control': in one sense, it is a sort of control required for any intentional human action (2001: 126); in another sense, it is manifested specifically in careful thought about one's actual desires and 'which action would best serve those desires *overall*, in circumstances where those desires are in danger of being forgotten or where a lesser immediate satisfaction beckons bright' (p. 127); and in a third sense (discussed below under her heading 'orthonomous self-control', p. 141), it requires a commitment by the agent to 'the rule of reason' (p. 129).

One current philosophical use of the term 'self-control'—the primary use in this chapter—is linked to Aristotle, who tells us that self-control (*enkrateia*) and its contrary (*akrasia*) 'are concerned with that which is in excess of the state characteristic of most men; for the [self-controlled] man abides by his resolutions more and the [akratic] man less than most men can' (*Nicomachean Ethics* 1152a25–7). The philosophical project of understanding self-control, construed along broadly Aristotelian lines, has its roots in ancient efforts to explain intentional actions. In *De Motu Animalium* (701a7–8), Aristotle asks: 'How does it happen that thinking is

A draft of this chapter was written during my tenure of a 2007–8 NEH Fellowship. (Any views, findings, conclusions, or recommendations expressed in this chapter do not necessarily reflect those of the National Endowment for the Humanities.)

sometimes followed by action and sometimes not, sometimes by motion, sometimes not?' A proper answer requires understanding, among other things, how it happens that we sometimes act in accordance with the conclusions of our reasoning about what it is best, on the whole, to do and sometimes fail to do so, pursuing instead courses of action at odds with those conclusions.

In Plato's *Protagoras*, Socrates says that the common view about seemingly commonplace intentional actions that clash with agents' beliefs or judgments about what it is best to do is that 'many people who know what it is best to do are not willing to do it, though it is in their power, but do something else' (352d). In disputing this view, Socrates raises (among other issues) a central question in philosophical work on akratic action. Is it possible to perform uncompelled intentional actions that, as one recognizes at the time of action, are contrary to what one judges best, the judgment being made from the perspective of one's values, principles, desires, and beliefs? More briefly, is *strict* akratic action possible (Mele 1987: 7)? Relevant judgments include judgments in which 'best' is relativized to options envisioned by the agent at the time. In instances of strict akratic action, agents do not need to judge that a course of action *A* is the best of all possible courses of action. They may judge that *A* is better than the alternatives they have envisioned—that it is the best of the envisioned options. If, nevertheless, in the absence of compulsion, they do not do *A*, and instead intentionally pursue one of the envisioned alternatives, they act akratically. (For stylistic purposes, it is useful to have a label for the kind of judgment against which an agent acts in strict akratic action. I dub it a *decisive judgment*.) It is a truism that a perfectly self-controlled agent would never act akratically. So strict akratic action, if it is possible, exhibits at least imperfect self-control. The question whether strict akratic action is possible and, if so, how, therefore raises a parallel question about imperfect self-control.

Aristotle understands self-control and *akrasia* as character traits (*Nicomachean Ethics* 7. 1). There is a middle ground between them, and not all akratic actions must manifest *akrasia*. Someone who is more self-controlled than most people in a certain sphere may, in a particularly trying situation, succumb to temptation in that sphere against his decisive judgment. If his intentional action is uncompelled, he acts akratically—even if his action manifests, not *akrasia*, but an associated imperfection. Similarly, a person with the trait of *akrasia* may occasionally succeed in resisting temptation and act in a self-controlled way. In the recent philosophical literature, akratic and self-controlled *actions* have received considerably more attention than the character traits. In this chapter, I follow suit. Because theories about the two kinds of action at issue are tightly interconnected, I discuss both akratic and self-controlled actions in this chapter; but my emphasis is on the latter.

1. THE SELF OF SELF-CONTROL AND THE SCOPE OF SELF-CONTROL AND *AKRASIA*

Although, in this chapter, I follow Aristotle in understanding akratic and self-controlled action as two sides of the same coin, I depart from him on a pair of pertinent issues. One is the nature of human beings and, accordingly, the nature of the *self* involved in a proper conception of self-control. The other is the sphere of akratic and self-controlled actions.

Aristotle views the self-controlled agent as a person whose 'desiring element' is 'obedient' to his 'reason' or 'rational principle', though less obedient than the virtuous person's (*Nicomachean Ethics* 1102b26–8). A human being 'is said to have or not to have self-control', Aristotle writes, 'according as his reason has or has not the control (*kratein*), on the assumption that this is the man himself' (1168b34–5). Given his contention that 'reason more than anything else is man' (1178a7; also see 1166a17, 22–3; 1168b27 ff.; and Plato, *Republic* 588b–592b), Aristotle's identification of self-control with control by one's 'reason' is predictable.

On an alternative, holistic view of human beings of the sort I favor (Mele 1987, 1995, 2003), the self of self-control is identified with the whole human being rather than with reason. Even when one's passions and emotions run counter to one's decisive judgment, they often are not plausibly seen as alien forces. A conception of self-controlled individuals as, roughly, people who characteristically are guided by their decisive judgments even in the face of strong competing motivation does not commit one to viewing emotion, passion, and the like as having no place in the self of self-control. Self-control can be exercised in support of decisive judgments partially based on a person's appetites or emotional commitments. In some cases, our decisive judgments may indicate our evaluative ranking of competing emotions or appetites.

I turn to the second issue. Aristotle limits the sphere of *enkrateia* and *akrasia*, like that of temperance and self-indulgence (*Nicomachean Ethics* 3. 10, 7. 7), to 'pleasures and pains and appetites and aversions arising through touch and taste' (1150a9–10).[1] However, self-control and *akrasia* have come to be understood much more broadly. Self-control, as it is now conceived, may be exhibited in the successful resistance of actual or anticipated temptation in any sphere. Temptations having to do with sexual activity, eating, drinking, smoking, and the like are tied to touch and taste. But we may also be tempted to work less or more than we judge best, to gamble beyond the limits we have set for ourselves, to spend more or less on gifts than we believe we should, and so on. We can exercise self-control in overcoming such temptations or akratically succumb to them.

---

[1] For other restrictive features of Aristotle's notion of *enkrateia*, see Charlton 1988: 35–41.

Self-control and *akrasia* are not manifested only in overt behavior, but also in some purely mental behavior (Mele 1987: ch. 4; 1995: chs. 5 and 7). People may accept principles concerning the acceptance, rejection, and modification of their beliefs, emotions, values, preferences, or desires. Acceptance of such principles may sometimes take the form of judgments. For example, Ann may judge it best to assess her desires and preferences from an impartial perspective, Bob may judge it best to monitor his values with a view to keeping them in line with those of his spiritual leader, and so on. Relevant mental actions of people who are self-controlled in these spheres will accord with the principles they accept. If, for example, Ann is self-controlled regarding evaluative reasoning about her preferences, she reasons about them impartially.

There is ample evidence that motivation often exerts a biasing influence on what we believe, as in cases of self-deception (Kunda 1999; Mele 2001). Suppose Ann assents to the principle that it is best not to allow what she wants to be true to determine what she believes is true. She may be in a position to exercise self-control in resisting a natural tendency toward motivationally biased belief. Out of a concern to be an unbiased believer about important issues, Ann may endeavor to scrutinize relevant data in an objective way, seek out the advice of experts, and so on.

It is generally recognized that we have some control over whether particular emotions result in action. However, there is also room for self-control in bringing our emotions themselves into line with relevant decisive judgments (Mele 1995: ch. 6). We may stem an embarrassing flow of sympathy for a character in a film by reminding ourselves that he is *only* a character. The man who regards his anger at his child as destructive may dissolve or attenuate it by vividly imagining a cherished moment with the child. The timid employee who believes that he can muster the courage to demand a much-deserved raise only if he becomes angry at his boss may deliberately make himself angry by vividly representing injustices he has suffered at the office. These are instances of *internal* control. Many emotions are subject to *external* control as well—control through one's overt behavior. Ann defeats moderate sadness by calling her brother. Bob overcomes modest fears by visiting his coach for an inspirational talk.

Self-control may be either regional or global, and it comes in degrees (Rorty 1980). A scholar who exhibits remarkable self-control in adhering to the demanding work schedule that he judges best for himself may be akratic about eating. He is self-controlled in one 'region' of his life and akratic in another. And some self-controlled individuals apparently are more self-controlled than others. Agents possessed of global self-control—self-control in all regions of their lives—would be particularly remarkable if, in every region, their self-control considerably exceeded that of most people.

In normal agents, a capacity for self-control is not a mental analog of brute physical strength. We learn to resist temptation by promising ourselves rewards for doing so, by vividly imagining undesirable effects of reckless conduct, and in countless other ways. Our powers of self-control include a variety of skills—and considerable savvy about which skills to use in particular situations.

What I term *orthodox* exercises of self-control serve the agent's decisive judgment (Mele 1995: 32). As I understand self-control, there are also unorthodox exercises of it (Mele 1987: 54–5; 1995: 60–4). Young Bruce has decided to join some friends in breaking into a neighbor's house, even though he judges it best on the whole not to do so. Experiencing considerable trepidation, Bruce tries to steel himself for the deed. He succeeds in mastering his fear, and he proceeds to pick the lock. Seemingly, Bruce exercised self-control in the service of a decision that conflicts with his decisive judgment.

The existence of unorthodox exercises of self-control does not preclude there being a tight connection between self-control and decisive judgment (Mele 1995: ch. 4). Donald Davidson (1985) argues that any interpretable human agent is largely rational, in the sense that his beliefs, intentions, and the like generally cohere with one another and with his behavior. If this is true, we should expect this rationality to manifest itself in the purposes people have in exercising self-control. Even if the frequency with which self-controlled agents attempt to exercise self-control in support of their decisive judgments were not to exceed that of other agents, the former agents, owing to their greater powers of self-control, would tend to succeed more often. To be sure, owing to their greater powers, self-controlled agents may also have a greater rate of success in *unorthodox* exercises of self-control. But given the presumption that every interpretable agent is generally rational in Davidson's sense, interpretable agents who make attempts at self-control will tend to do so much more often in support of their decisive judgments than in opposition to them. As a little arithmetic would show, greater success in the more limited domain of unorthodox self-control is insufficient to counterbalance the effects of greater powers of self-control in the much broader domain.

Some philosophers understand self-control in such a way that unorthodox exercises of it are conceptually impossible. Edmund Henden contends that self-control can only be exercised in the service of 'what one takes oneself to have most reason to do' (2008: 73–4, 85). In his view, young Bruce exercises 'will-power'—but not self-control—in mastering his fear (p. 85).

Jeanette Kennett contends that what she calls *orthonomous self-control* 'best answers to the common-sense notion of self-control' (2001: 134). Exercises of orthonomous self-control are restricted to bringing 'the agent's actions into line with her view about what is, all things considered, desirable in the circumstances' (p. 133). Thus, in mastering his fear, young Bruce is not exercising orthonomous control.

Whether Kennett is correct in claiming that orthonomous self-control 'best answers to *the common-sense notion* of self-control' seemingly cannot be settled from the armchair. Psychologists and experimental philosophers have studied a host of folk (or common-sense) concepts by presenting nonspecialists with brief scenarios and asking them, in effect, whether a given concept does or does not apply to these scenarios (Knobe and Nichols 2008). I know of no such studies of the folk concept (or concepts) of self-control. In any event, various senses of 'self-control' can be defined, and philosophers can look for interesting theoretical questions about self-control understood in various ways and seek to ascertain how the questions should be answered. When a conception of self-control is associated with interesting phenomena, philosophers can try to shed light on those phenomena.

I close this section with a brief discussion of a theoretical question about self-control that has received considerable philosophical attention. In some cases, exercising self-control in support of one's decisive judgment is unproblematic. Ann thinks that she spends entirely too much time playing solitaire on her office computer and she believes that it would be best, on the whole, not to play the game at work. At the moment, after another bout of game-playing at work, her motivation to bring it about that she no longer plays the game in her office is stronger than her motivation not to bring this about, and she removes the game from her computer. But consider Ian, who is now more strongly motivated to continue watching a golf tournament on television than he is to do anything else. Even so, he judges it best to turn off the television and get back to work (Mele 1987: 69–72). Is Ian in a position to exercise self-control in support of his decisive judgment? It may seem that, given that his motivation to continue watching golf is stronger than his motivation to get back to work, his motivation *not* to exercise self-control in support of his getting back to work is stronger than his motivation to exercise self-control for that purpose. Accordingly, it may seem that Ian's motivational condition at the time precludes his exercising self-control in support of his decisive judgment.

Some philosophers argue that exercising self-control in support of his decisive judgment is not an option for Ian (Pugmire 1994; for a reply, see Mele 1995: 47–55). Even philosophers who maintain that this is a possibility for Ian have disagreed about *how* it is possible (see Alston 1977; Kennett 2001: 135–47; Kennett and Smith 1996, 1997; Mele 1987: ch. 5; 1995: ch. 3; 2003: ch. 8). The argumentation is intricate. I lack the space to review it here.

2. AKRATIC ACTIONS

Attention to akratic actions and how they may be caused sheds light on self-control. A feature of paradigmatic strict akratic actions that typically is taken for granted and rarely made explicit is that the judgments with which they conflict are *rationally* formed. In virtue of their clashing with the agent's rationally formed decisive judgment, such actions are subjectively irrational (to some degree, if not without qualification). There is a failure of coherence in the agent of a kind directly relevant to assessments of the agent's rationality. (On failures of coherence, see Arpaly 2000 and Harman 2004.) Accordingly, the literature on self-control tends to associate it with rationality.

To the extent that one's decisive judgment derives from one's motivational attitudes, it has a motivational dimension.[2] That helps explain why some philosophers regard strict akratic action as impossible (Socrates in Plato's *Protagoras*; Hare 1963: ch. 5; Pugmire 1982; Watson 1977) or at least as theoretically perplexing. How, they wonder, can the motivation associated with a judgment of this kind be outweighed by competing motivation, especially when the competing motivational attitudes—or desires, broadly construed—have been taken into account in arriving at the judgment?

In Mele 1987 (where various arguments for the impossibility of akratic action are evaluated), I defend an answer to this question that rests partly on two theses, both of which I defend there.

1. Decisive judgments normally are formed at least partly on the basis of our evaluation of the 'objects' of our desires (that is, the desired items).
2. The motivational force of our desires does not always match our evaluation of the objects of our desires (Santas 1966; Smith 1992; Stocker 1979; Watson 1977).[3]

If both theses are true, it should be unsurprising that sometimes, although we decisively judge it better to *A* than to *B*, we are more strongly motivated to *B* than to *A*. Given how our motivation stacks up, it should also be unsurprising that we *B* rather than *A*.

Thesis 1 is a major plank in a standard conception of practical reasoning. In general, when we reason about what to do, we inquire about what it would be best, or better, or 'good enough' to do, not about what we are most strongly motivated to do. When we ask such questions while having conflicting desires, our answers typically rest significantly on our assessments of the objects of our desires—which may be out of line with the motivational force of those desires, if thesis 2 is true.

Thesis 2, as I argue in Mele 1987, is confirmed by common experience and thought experiments and has a foundation in empirical studies. Desire-strength is influenced not only by our evaluation of the objects of desires, but also by such factors as the perceived proximity of prospects for desire-satisfaction, the salience of desired objects in perception or in imagination, and the way we attend to desired

---

[2] This is not to say that motivation is 'built into' the judgment itself.

[3] For opposition to the idea that desires vary in motivational strength, see Charlton 1988; Gosling 1990; Thalberg 1985. For a reply to the opposition, see Mele 2003: ch. 7.

objects (Ainslie 1992; Mischel and Ayduk 2004; Rorty 1980). Factors such as these need not have a matching effect on assessment of desired objects.

A few hours ago, Al decisively judged it better to A than to B, but he now has a stronger desire to B than to A. Two versions of the case merit attention. In one, along with the change in desire strength, there is a change of judgment. For example, last night, after much soul-searching, Al formed a decisive judgment favoring not eating after-dinner snacks for the rest of the month and desired more strongly to forego them than to indulge himself; but now, a few hours after dinner, Al's desire for a snack is stronger than his desire for the rewards associated with not snacking, and he decisively judges it better to have a snack than to refrain. In another version of the case, the change in relative desire strength is not accompanied by a change of judgment. Al retains the decisive judgment favoring not eating after dinner, but he eats anyway. Assuming that Al eats intentionally and is not compelled to eat, this is a strict akratic action.

Empirical studies of the role of representations of desired objects in impulsive behavior and delay of gratification (reviewed in Mele 1987: 88–93; see Mischel *et al.* 1989 for an overview) provide ample evidence that our representations of desired objects have two important dimensions, a motivational and an informational one. Our decisive judgments may be more sensitive to the informational dimension of our representations than to the motivational dimension, with the result that such judgments sometimes recommend courses of action that are out of line with what we are most strongly motivated to do at the time. If so, strict akratic action is a real possibility—provided that at least some intentional actions that conflict with agents' decisive judgments at the time of action are not *compelled*.

A discussion of compulsion would lead quickly to the issue of free will, which is well beyond the scope of this chapter. Fortunately, it is a truism that, unless a desire of ours is irresistible, it is up to us, in some sense, whether we act on it. Of course, a proper appreciation of the extent of irresistible desires would require an analysis of irresistible desire.[4] It may suffice for present purposes to suggest that, often, when we act against our decisive judgments, we could have used our resources for self-control in effectively resisting temptation.[5] Normal agents apparently can influence the strength of their desires in a wide variety of ways (Ainslie 1992; Mischel and Ayduk 2004; Mischel *et al.* 1989). For example, they can refuse to focus their attention on the attractive aspects of a tempting course of action and concentrate instead on what is to be accomplished by acting as they judge best. They can attempt to augment their motivation for performing the action judged best by

---

[4] See Mele 1992: ch. 5, for an analysis of irresistible desire.

[5] This is not a necessary condition for strict akratic action. There are Frankfurt-style cases (Frankfurt 1969) in which, although one A-ed akratically and without any external interference, if one had been about to resist temptation, a mind-reading demon would have prevented one from doing so (see Mele 1995: 94–5).

promising themselves rewards for doing so. They can picture a desired item as something unattractive—for example, a chocolate pie as a plate of chocolate-coated chewing tobacco—or as something that simply is not arousing. Desires typically do not have immutable strengths, and the plasticity of motivational strength is presupposed by standard conceptions of self-control. Occasionally we *do not* act as we judge best, but it is implausible that, in all such cases, we *cannot* act in accordance with these judgments (Mele 1987: ch. 2; 1995: ch. 3; 2002; Smith 2003). At least sometimes, our being able to act in accordance with these judgments depends on our being able to exercise self-control.

3. SELF-CONTROL AND VANISHING AGENTS

Some philosophers claim that any causal theory of action-explanation and any causal analysis of action is inconsistent with there being any actions at all—that the causal views make agents *vanish*. A. I. Melden writes: 'It is futile to attempt to explain conduct through the causal efficacy of desire—all *that* can explain is further happenings, not actions performed by agents. . . . There is no place in this picture . . . even for the conduct that was to have been explained' (1961: 128–9). Thomas Nagel voices a similar worry:

The essential source of the problem is a view of persons and their actions as part of the order of nature, causally determined or not. That conception, if pressed, leads to the feeling that we are not agents at all. . . . *my doing* of an act—or the doing of an act by someone else—seems to disappear when we think of the world objectively. There seems no room for agency in [such] a world . . . there is only what happens. (1986: 110–11)

David Velleman expresses a variant of Nagel's worry. He contends (1) that standard causal accounts of action and its explanation do not capture what 'distinguishes human action from other animal behavior' and do not accommodate 'human action *par excellence*' (Velleman 1992: 462; see Velleman 2000: ch. 1). He also reports (2) that his objection to what he calls 'the standard story of human action' (1992: 461), a causal story, 'is not that it mentions mental occurrences in the agent instead of the agent himself [but] that the occurrences it mentions in the agent are no more than occurrences in him, because their involvement in an action does not add up to the agent's being involved' (p. 463). Velleman says that this problem would remain even if the mind–body problem were to be solved (pp. 468–9), and, like Nagel (pp. 110–11), he regards the problem as 'distinct from the problem of free-will' (p. 465 n. 13).

A significant capacity for self-control is plausibly regarded as a crucial ingredient in the sort of agency exhibited in what Velleman calls 'human action *par excellence*'.

In cases of such action, as Velleman sees it, 'the agent's concern in reflecting on his motives [is] to see which ones provide stronger reasons for acting, and then to ensure that they prevail over those whose rational force is weaker' (1992: 478). Indeed, an important virtue of his position, he contends, is that it accounts for the truth of the plausible idea that 'a person sometimes intervenes among his motives because the best reason for acting is associated with the intrinsically weaker motive, and he must therefore intervene in order to ensure that the weaker motive prevails' (p. 480). One wonders how the weaker motive can prevail. Velleman's proposed solution is that the agent intervenes by throwing 'his weight behind' this weaker motive (motive W) and this consists in the weaker motive's 'being reinforced by' the agent's desire to act in accordance with reasons (desire R); 'the two [i.e., W and R] now form the strongest combination of motives' (p. 480).

Velleman's formulation of his solution is awkward. On his view, one prominent role for an agent's desire to act in accordance with reasons (desire R) in human action *par excellence* is to motivate the agent to reflect 'on his motives' (1992: 478). So R is present even before the agent throws his weight on the side of the weaker motive (motive W), and perhaps the strength of R plus the strength of W was already greater than that of the motive that opposes W. If so, then, even before the agent throws his weight around, there is a sense in which R and W 'form the strongest combination of motives'. In that sense, however, the two motives are combined only artificially, in somewhat the way that the coins in my pockets and those in yours combine—add up—to fifty cents. What is needed is a *relevant* combination, if one wants to speak in terms of combinations.

An argument from Mele (1990: 55–6) for the thesis that an agent's having self-control as a trait of character requires his having a desire like R points to a way of filling the gap. I reproduce the argument (with some minor stylistic changes) in the following three paragraphs.

A person who has developed remarkable powers of self-control may, owing to a personal tragedy, lose all motivation to exercise them. A man who recently lost his family in a fatal plane crash may no longer care how he conducts himself, even if, out of habit, he continues to make decisive judgments: he may suffer from *acedia*. As a partial consequence, he may cease, for a time, to make any effort at self-control, even when he recognizes that his preponderant motivation is at odds with his decisive judgments. He may simply act in accordance with whatever happens to be his strongest motivation, without being at all motivated to exert an influence over how his motivations stack up. If, as seems plain, we are unwilling to describe such an agent at the time in question as a self-controlled person, we must include a motivational element in an account of what it is to be a self-controlled agent. A self-controlled person cares how he conducts himself—he is a practically concerned individual—and he is appropriately motivated to exercise self-control.

Exercise it in support of what? Notice that although normal (and, hence, largely rational) human agents do care how they conduct themselves, they do not care *equally* about all of their projects, nor the objects of all of their hopes and desires. Practical concern is not egalitarian in this way. What one cares most about, if one is largely rational, are the things one deems most important. In a largely rational individual, this variegated system of concerns is reflected in the agent's decisive judgments. This reflection may be collective rather than individual. An occasional decisive judgment may miss the mark, but, on the whole, what an agent judges best indicates what he cares most about. And if it is his lack of practical concern that leads us to withhold the epithet 'self-controlled person' from our unfortunate man, we should expect the presence of such concern in the same man to manifest itself partly in motivation to attempt to make things go as he judges they should go, and to exercise his powers of self-control in support of his decisive judgments when they are challenged by competing motivation. Given the discriminativeness of practical concern, the self-controlled individual's motivation to exercise self-control will typically be aimed at the support of his decisive judgments. A largely rational person who does not care equally about the objects of all of his desires will not be uniformly motivated to exercise self-control in support of each of them. Because he is for the most part internally coherent, his motivation to exercise self-control will generally fall in line with his *decisive judgments*.

The self-controlled person's motivation to exercise self-control, as I am understanding it, is associated with his practical concern—that is, with his caring how he conducts himself, with his not being a victim of *acedia*. *Because* he cares how he conducts himself, and because practical concern is discriminative in the way explained, he is disposed to see to it that his behavior fits his decisive judgments and to intervene into his own motivational condition when competing motivation threatens to render his better judgments ineffective. This disposition's manifestations include desires for specific exercises of self-control on particular occasions. Such a disposition, I should think, is present to some degree in all normal adult human agents.

That is the argument from Mele 1990. What does it suggest about human agency *par excellence*, on the assumption that a significant capacity for self-control is central to such agency? If the argument is on target, being a self-controlled person—that is, having self-control as a trait of character—entails caring how one's life goes, the caring being manifested partly in motivation to do what it takes to bring one's conduct into line with one's decisive judgments. Such motivation can take the form of something describable as *a desire to act for superior reasons*. Now, largely rational, mature human beings are very likely to have learnt—and hence to believe, at least tacitly—that things tend to go better for them if, when faced with relatively important practical issues, they give the matter some thought and then act in accordance with the reasons they deem superior. Rational agents who believe this and care how their lives go are very likely to be disposed to desire, when facing relatively important practical issues, that they reflect on what it would be best—or at least 'good enough'—to do and then act in accordance with their conclusions about this. On a traditional conception of standing desires, the disposition to desire this is a standing desire, and it may be dubbed 'a standing desire to act for superior reasons'. I have no need to count so-called standing desires as desires. The point to emphasize for present purposes concerns desires that are manifestations of the disposition in which the so-called standing desire consists. These desires include desires of a sort that are well-suited for playing an important role in accounting for practical reasoning that takes the form of reasoning about what it is best to do, or about what it is good enough to do—namely, desires to do whatever is best in the circumstances and desires for acceptable courses of action (see Mele 2003: ch. 4). These desires themselves may reasonably be described as desires to act for superior reasons.

The desires just identified—manifestations of a disposition to desire to act for superior reasons—can play the causal roles Velleman highlights. They can help explain why an agent assesses his reasons for action, and they can contribute to the motivational strength of desires for particular courses of action (Velleman 1992: 478–9; see Velleman 2000: 11–12), courses of action that one takes oneself to have superior reasons to pursue. What I call the *positive motivational base* of a desire 'is the collection of all occurrent motivations of the agent that make a positive contribution to the motivational strength of that desire' (Mele 1987: 67). When agents take themselves to have superior reasons to A it is easy to see how a desire to act for superior reasons can enter into the positive motivational base of their desires to A.

I should add that I myself do not believe that agents vanish in all but their self-controlled actions. As I see it (Mele 2003: ch. 10), Velleman runs together two separate issues. Human agents may be involved in some of their actions in ways that chimps and tigers are involved in many of their actions. Scenarios in which human agents vanish are one thing; scenarios in which actions of human agents do not come up to the level of human action *par excellence* are another. Proponents of causal accounts of what intentional actions are and of causal theories about how actions are to be explained—causalists, for short—should complain that Velleman has been unfair to them. In his description of 'the standard story' (1992: 461), he apparently has in mind the sort of thing found in the work of causalists looking for what is common to all (overt) intentional actions, or all (overt) actions done for reasons, and for what distinguishes actions of these broad kinds from everything else. If some nonhuman animals act intentionally and for reasons, a story with this topic *should* apply to them. Also, human action *par excellence* may be intentional action, or action done for a reason, in virtue of its having the properties identified in a standard causal analysis of these things. That the analysis does not provide sufficient conditions for, or a story about, human action *par excellence* is not a flaw in the analysis, given its target. If Velleman were to believe that causalism lacks the resources for accommodating human action *par excellence*, he might attack 'the standard story' on that front, arguing that it cannot be extended to handle such action. But Velleman himself is a causalist. Moreover, causalists have offered accounts of kinds of action—for example, free action, autonomous action, and action exhibiting self-control (see e.g. Fischer and Ravizza 1998; Mele 1995, 2006)—that exceed minimal requirements for intentional action or action done for a reason. It is not as though their story about minimally sufficient conditions for action of the latter kinds is their entire story about human actions.

4. Implementation Intentions and Self-Control

In the present section I turn to some empirical work that bears importantly on self-control. A large body of work on 'implementation intentions' (for reviews, see Gollwitzer 1999; Gollwitzer and Sheeran 2006) provides encouragement concerning our prospects for self-control. Implementation intentions, as Peter Gollwitzer conceives of them, 'are subordinate to goal intentions and specify the when, where, and how of responses leading to goal attainment' (1999: 494). They 'serve the purpose of promoting the attainment of the goal specified in the goal intention'. In forming an implementation intention, 'the person commits himself or herself to respond to a certain situation in a certain manner'.

In one study of subjects 'who had reported strong goal intentions to perform a BSE [breast self-examination] during the next month, 100% did so if they had been induced to form additional implementation intentions' (Gollwitzer 1999: 496). In a control group of people who also reported strong goal intentions to do this but were not induced to form implementation intentions, only 53 per cent performed a BSE. Subjects in the former group were asked to state in writing 'where and when' they would perform a BSE during the next month.

Another study featured the task of 'vigorous exercise for 20 minutes during the next week' (Gollwitzer 1999: 496). 'A motivational intervention that focused on increasing self-efficacy to exercise, the perceived severity of and vulnerability to coronary heart disease, and the expectation that exercise will reduce the risk of coronary heart disease raised compliance from 29% to only 39%.' When this intervention was paired with the instruction to form relevant implementation intentions, 'the compliance rate rose to 91%'.

In a third study reviewed in Gollwitzer 1999, drug addicts who showed symptoms of withdrawal were divided into two groups. 'One group was asked in the morning to form the goal intention to write a short curriculum vitae before 5:00 p.m. and to add implementation intentions that specified when and where they would write it' (p. 496). The other subjects were asked 'to form the same goal intention but with irrelevant implementation intentions (i.e., they were asked to specify when they would eat lunch and where they would sit)'. Once again, the results are striking: although none of the participants in the second group completed the task, 80 per cent of the subjects in the first group completed it.

Many studies of this kind are reviewed in Gollwitzer 1999, and Gollwitzer and Paschal Sheeran report that 'findings from 94 independent tests showed that implementation intentions had a positive effect of medium-to-large magnitude . . . on goal attainment' (2006: 69). Collectively, the results provide evidence that the presence of relevant distal implementation intentions significantly increases the probability that agents will execute associated distal 'goal intentions' in a broad range of circumstances. In the experimental studies that Gollwitzer reviews, subjects are explicitly asked to form relevant implementation intentions, and the intentions at issue are consciously expressed (1999: 501). (It should not be assumed, incidentally, that all members of all of the control groups lack conscious implementation intentions. Indeed, for all anyone knows, most members of the control groups who executed their goal intentions consciously made relevant distal implementation decisions.)

Research on implementation intentions certainly suggests that one useful technique for mastering anticipated motivation not to do what one decisively judges it best to do later—for example, conduct a breast self-examination next month, exercise next week, or finish writing a CV by the end of the day—is simply to decide, shortly after making the judgment, on a very specific plan for so doing (and to make a record of that decision). Of course, what works against relatively modest motivational opposition might not work when the opposition is considerably stronger. Stronger opposition of a specific kind is featured in the following section.

5. ADDICTION AND SELF-CONTROL

Although addicts are often viewed as victims of irresistible desires, this view has met with significant opposition (Bakalar and Grinspoon 1984; Becker and Murphy 1988; Heyman 1996: Peele 1985, 1989; Szasz 1974). This section explores some theoretical issues surrounding a strategy for self-control of potential use to addicts on the assumption that their pertinent desires *fall short* of irresistibility.

Most desires have more than a momentary existence. If there are irresistible desires, desires that are irresistible at some times may be resistible at others. The guiding assumption of this section has at least two distinct interpretations. In articulating them, some shorthand will prove useful: I use 'a-desires' as shorthand for 'desires characteristic of addicts'. On a strong reading, the assumption is that no

SELF-CONTROL IN ACTION 479

a-desire is irresistible at any time. On a weaker reading, it is assumed that every *a*-desire is resistible at some time or other. Imagine a crack cocaine addict who has exhausted his supply and wants to use more crack as soon as he can. Suppose that, owing partly to this desire, he drives to his brother's house and steals some crack. His driving where he does is motivated by this desire, and the desire is still in place when he steals the drug. On the strong reading of the assumption, this desire is not irresistible even when he gains possession of the drug. On the weak reading, it might be. If the desire is irresistible now, then even though the addict might have been able successfully to exercise self-control in resisting it earlier, there is no longer any chance of that. I leave both readings of the assumption open here.[6]

Work by George Ainslie on self-control and its contrary sheds light on the behavior of addicts and their prospects for self-control, on the assumption just discussed. In early work, Ainslie marshals weighty evidence for a view that I summarize in Mele 1987 (p. 85) as follows:

1. 'The curve describing the effectiveness of reward as a function of delay is markedly concave upwards' (Ainslie 1982: 740). That is, a desire for a 'reward' of a prospective action, other things being equal, acquires greater motivational force as the time for the reward's achievement approaches, and after a certain point motivation increases sharply.
2. Human beings are not at the mercy of the effects of the proximity of rewards. They can bring it about that they act for a larger, later reward in preference to a smaller, earlier one by using 'pre-committing devices', a form of self-control ...(Ainslie 1975, 1982).[7]

These ideas in Ainslie 1975 and 1982 are developed more fully in Ainslie 1992 and 2001. Later, I will apply them specifically to addiction. A broader focus is useful for introductory purposes.

In Ainslie's view, 'personal rules are the most flexible and acceptable precommitting device' (1992: 154). He opens a discussion of hyperbolic discount functions and personal rules with the following claim:

It is possible to deduce a mechanism for willpower from the existence of deeply concave discount curves...if we assume only that curves from multiple rewards combine in an additive fashion. In brief, choosing rewards in aggregates rather than individually gives later, larger rewards a major advantage over smaller, earlier ones; and the perception of one's current choice as a precedent predicting a whole series of choices leads to just such aggregations. (1992: 144–5)

---

[6] Notice that even the weaker reading is quite strong. Consider a crack addict's desire to use some crack *now*, a desire he just acquired. If that desire is resistible at some time, the relevant time is now. Incidentally, even the much less demanding assumption that *some* desires characteristic of addicts are resistible suffices for present purposes.

[7] For further discussion, see Mele 1987: 84–6, 90–3; 1992: ch. 4. Also see Elster 1984 on imperfect rationality and precommitment.

Consider Beth. She judges it best to adopt a certain exercise routine as a means of losing weight, but she knows that she has a record of violating her exercise resolutions. If Beth has come to believe the following assertion, *P*, about herself, she might enjoy more success in the future: (*P*) Whatever choice I make and execute the first time I am tempted to violate my new exercise routine is the choice I will uniformly make and execute on subsequent occasions of temptation. This assertion is not absurd: after all, given that the temptations are similar, how she chooses and acts on the first occasion is evidence about how she will choose and act on relevant subsequent occasions. Believing *P*, Beth should regard herself now, at time *t*, as faced with a choice between the following two items: (1) the series of 'rewards' to be obtained should she *not* abide by the exercise plan, both on the first occasion of temptation and on all subsequent occasions, and (2) the series of 'rewards' to be obtained by *abiding by* this plan on the first and all subsequent occasions of temptation. If, at *t*, Beth deems the latter series of rewards better, on the whole, than the former, she should choose 2 over 1 (if she can).

Regarding temptation, Ainslie writes: 'The crucial time at which preference between . . . two whole series of rewards changes [is the time, t_i] at which the value V' of the series of larger rewards equals the value V of the series of smaller ones', the time of 'indifference' (1992: 145). 'If the choice is made before [t_i], it will favor the series of larger, later rewards, and if it is made after [t_i], it will favor the series of smaller, earlier rewards' (p. 145).

If, at *t*, Beth chooses the series of 'larger, later rewards' to be obtained by abiding by her plan, she thereby adopts a *personal rule* about exercise. 'The force of a personal rule', Ainslie writes, 'is proportional to the number of delayed rewards that are perceived to be part of the series at risk' (1992: 174). 'In principle, personal rules make it possible for a person never to prefer small, early alternatives at the expense of the series of larger, later ones. He may be able to keep temptations close at hand without succumbing to them' (p. 193).

On Ainslie's view, some personal rules are, as I wish to put it, more *self-protective* than others, in virtue of certain properties of the rules themselves. The term 'self-protective' should be understood in a double sense: protective of the *rule*, including both its persistence or survival and its not being violated; and protective of the person whose rule it is, or, more precisely, of the person's prospects for maximizing reward. Ainslie summarizes the major self-protective features of rules as follows:

To be cost-effective, a personal rule must be drawn with three characteristics: (1) The series of rewards to be waited for must be long enough and valuable enough so that it will be preferred over each impulsive alternative. (2) Each member of the series and its impulsive alternatives must be readily identifiable, without ambiguity. (3) The features that exclude a choice from the series must either occur independently of the person's behavior or have such a high intrinsic cost that he will not be motivated to bring them about just for the sake of evading the rule. (1992: 162)

Relatively precise rules—rules with 'bright lines'—that one has explicitly endorsed (pp. 163–73) are harder to ignore than vague impressions about how one ought to conduct oneself. Rules that one views as serving the maximization of reward, that are precise enough to leave little room for doubt about their application to particular cases, and that are explicitly formulated with a view to excluding the voluntary production of conditions that satisfy the rules' escape clauses, are in virtue of these very properties—less likely to be violated, other things being equal, than rules lacking one or more of these features.[8] If Ainslie is right, Beth may benefit from adopting an exercise rule with these features.[9]

On Ainslie's view, like Plato's (*Protagoras* 355e–357e), the perceived *proximity* of a reward tends to exert a powerful positive influence on the strength of an agent's motivation to pursue it, an effect that pre-commitment strategies of self-control, including the tactic of personal rules, are designed to counter. He contends that 'it is in the *addictive* behaviors that the influence of proximity on the temporary preferences is especially evident: For instance, an alcoholic may plan not to drink, succeed if he keeps sufficiently distant from the opportunities, become overwhelmingly tempted when faced with an imminent chance to drink, but later wholeheartedly regret this lapse' (1992: 98; my emphasis). He says, in the same vein, that 'the behaviors that seem best to fit the description "temporarily preferred" are often called addictions. They have a clear phase of conscious though temporary preference, followed by an equally clear period of regret' (p. 97). On Ainslie's view, 'Acts governed by willpower evidently are both diagnostic and causal. Drinking too much is diagnostic of a condition, alcoholism out of control, but it causes further uncontrolled drinking when the subject, using it to diagnose himself as out of control, is discouraged from trying to will sobriety' (p. 203).

Merely choosing (or deciding, or intending) to refrain from a certain kind of tempting activity indefinitely (for example, cocaine use) is not sufficient for using the tactic of personal rules. To use the tactic, one must view what is to be gained by resisting as a series of rewards stretching out over a considerable time. Ainslie contends that people who take this long view of things will tend to do better at resisting relevant temptations than people who do not; for, other things being equal, the longer the series of similar rewards one has in view, the more strongly motivated one will be to actualize the series.[10] The point about motivation is

---

[8] I set aside the technical question what, exactly, would count as violating (or not violating) a vague or ambiguous rule.

[9] An additional alleged feature of personal rules is that behavior guided by them tends to increase the probability that the agent's relevant subsequent behavior will also be guided by them.

[10] Among the relevant 'other things' are subjective probabilities. In some cases, a lengthening of a series might include a significant decrease in one's subjective probability of achieving its rewards and a net decrease in motivation. For some people, a New Year's resolution (personal rule) like 'Don't eat between meals this month' might be more effective in the long run than a resolution

plausible; how often the resultant motivation will be enough to sustain resistance is an empirical matter.

The success of the tactic of personal rules also depends on how well-tailored one's rules are to oneself. A sedentary, middle-aged man concerned about his deteriorating physical condition might envision a lengthy series of rewards associated with daily exercise. But if he deems it highly unlikely that he would abide by a daily exercise routine, a rule requiring exercise three days a week may prove more beneficial. Given that one's motivation to follow a rule is partly a function of the subjective probability that one will succeed in following it and achieve the associated rewards, the man may be more motivated to pursue the less demanding routine, even though he believes that the daily routine would yield greater rewards were he to follow it faithfully. Some failures by agents who employ the tactic of personal rules may be attributable, not to any flaw in the tactic itself, but to their setting their sights unrealistically high.

Whether the tactic of personal rules works, and how reliably it works, are empirical matters, of course. If we can satisfy ourselves, independently of their succeeding in resisting temptation, that a group of people are employing the tactic, we can wait and see how well they fare in resisting temptation. And we can see how well they fare relative to people who judge it best to resist but do not employ this tactic.

6. AN ENERGY MODEL OF SELF-CONTROL

Roy Baumeister writes: 'If it were up to me to set national policy in psychological matters, I would recommend replacing the cultivation of self-esteem with the cultivation of self-control' (2002: 130). 'Self-control', as he understands it, 'refers . . . to conscious efforts to alter [one's own] behavior, especially restraining impulses and resisting temptations' (p. 129). Baumeister produces evidence that 'self-control operates on the basis of a limited resource, akin to energy or strength, that can become depleted through use' (p. 130). His 'energy model' of self-control predicts that 'performance at self-control would grow worse during consecutive or continuous efforts, just as a muscle becomes tired' (p. 131).[11]

---

never again to eat between meals. A person who succeeds for a whole month in this endeavor might then be in a much better position consistently to abide by the latter personal rule.

[11] For a philosophical discussion of self-control that benefits from Baumeister's work, see Holton 2003.

This prediction of 'ego depletion' (Baumeister *et al.* 1998) has been confirmed. For example, in one study (Muraven *et al.* 1998), subjects who regulated their emotions (either by amplifying or suppressing them) while watching a sad video clip gave up faster in a test of physical stamina than a control group that watched the same clip. In another study (Baumeister *et al.* 1998), hungry subjects instructed to eat radishes rather than tempting chocolates and cookies gave up much faster on a puzzle than people in the control groups. One control group was allowed to eat the tempting desserts, and the other saw no food. 'A mere five minutes of resisting the temptation to eat cookies and making oneself eat radishes instead reduced subsequent persistence on difficult puzzles from 21 minutes to 8 minutes' (Baumeister 2002: 133).

Baumeister and his colleagues also tested the hypothesis that our capacity for self-control improves with practice. Subjects who exercised self-control in various ways over a two-week period later displayed significantly more self-control than a control group (Muraven *et al.* 1999). This is encouraging news.

Baumeister reports that 'Muraven (1998)...showed that the effects of ego depletion could be resisted if the stakes were high enough' (2002: 134). A substantial monetary award for successful performance on the second self-control task results in good performance. After an initial self-control task, 'new challenges are apparently evaluated for their importance. If they are not highly important, the self holds back from exerting itself, but when something important does arise, the self is willing to expend more of its remaining resources' (Baumeister 2002: 134).

Money and other rewards are not alone in this regard. Thomas Webb and Paschal Sheeran (2003) have produced evidence that implementation intentions can help to overcome ego-depletion. In one study, ego-depleted subjects were given a Stroop task. They were instructed to name as quickly as possible the ink color of each word they were presented with (e.g., the green color in which the word 'red' was printed). Subjects in the implementation intention group 'were asked to tell themselves: "As soon as I see the word I will ignore its meaning (for example, by concentrating on the second letter only) and I will name the color ink it is printed in"' (p. 281). 'Ego-depleted participants who formed implementation intentions performed significantly better than similarly depleted participants who did not form implementation intentions'; and the ego-depleted subjects in the implementation intention group performed about as well on the Stroop task as nondepleted controls (p. 284).

7. PARTING REMARKS

Aristotle distinguishes self-control (*enkrateia*) not only from *akrasia* but also from temperance (*sophrosune*), a virtue. Both self-controlled and temperate agents are disposed 'to do nothing contrary to the rule for the sake of bodily pleasures'; but the former, unlike the latter, must occasionally struggle against 'bad appetites' (*Nicomachean Ethics* 1151b34–1152a3). The desires and feelings of temperate agents are in perfect agreement with their 'rational principle' (1102b13–31); and because the moral virtues imply the presence of the *right* rule or principle (1144b26–7), the desires and feelings of these agents never miss the mark. Temperate individuals desire the pleasures *that* they ought, *when* they ought, and *as* they ought. Self-controlled agents are typically successful in *resisting* temptation; temperate individuals are not even *subject* to temptation.

Perhaps this helps to explain why Peter Geach reports that temperance 'is a humdrum common-sense matter' and the considerations that recommend the trait 'are not such as to arouse enthusiasm' (1977: 131). Self-control, too, is at least partly a common-sense matter; but without a capacity for it, we would be in serious trouble. Self-controlled action has not aroused the theoretical enthusiasm of philosophers to the extent to which akratic action has. Even so, understanding either kind of action would seem to require understanding the other kind; and self-controlled action is interesting in its own right. An account of self-controlled action is an essential part of any comprehensive philosophy of action.

References

AINSLIE, G. (1975). 'Specious Reward: A Behavioral Theory of Impulsiveness and Impulse Control', *Psychological Bulletin*, 82: 463–96.

——(1982). 'A Behavioral Economic Approach to the Defense Mechanisms: Freud's Energy Theory Revisited', *Social Science Information*, 21: 735–80.

——(1992). *Picoeconomics* (Cambridge: Cambridge University Press).

——(2001). *Breakdown of Will* (Cambridge: Cambridge University Press).

ALSTON, W. (1977). 'Self-Intervention and the Structure of Motivation', in T. Mischel (ed.), *The Self: Psychological and Philosophical Issues* (Oxford: Basil Blackwell), 399–409.

ARISTOTLE (1915a). *De Motu Animalium*, in *The Works of Aristotle*, ed. William Ross (London: Oxford University Press), v.

——(1915b). *Nicomachean Ethics*, in *The Works of Aristotle* ed. William Ross (London: Oxford University Press), ix.

ARPALY, N. (2000). 'On Acting Rationally Against One's Best Judgment', *Ethics*, 110: 488–513.

BAKALAR, J., and GRINSPOON, L. (1984). *Drug Control in a Free Society* (Cambridge: Cambridge University Press).

BAUMEISTER, R. (2002). 'Ego Depletion and Self-Control Failure: An Energy Model of the Self's Executive Function', *Self and Identity*, 1: 129–36.

——BRATSLAVSKY, E., MURAVEN, M., and TICE, D. (1998). 'Ego-Depletion: Is the Active Self a Limited Resource?', *Journal of Personality and Social Psychology*, 74: 1252–65.

BECKER, G., and MURPHY, K. (1988). 'A Theory of Rational Addiction', *Journal of Political Economy*, 96: 675–700.

CHARLTON, W. (1988). *Weakness of Will* (Oxford: Basil Blackwell).

DAVIDSON, D. (1985). 'Deception and Division', in E. LePore and B. McLaughlin (eds), *Actions and Events* (Oxford: Basil Blackwell), 138–48.

DENNETT, D. (1984). *Elbow Room* (Cambridge, Mass.: MIT Press).

ELSTER, J. (1984). *Ulysses and the Sirens* (Cambridge: Cambridge University Press).

FISCHER, J., and RAVIZZA, M. (1998). *Responsibility and Control: A Theory of Moral Responsibility* (New York: Cambridge University Press).

FRANKFURT, H. (1969). 'Alternate Possibilities and Moral Responsibility', *Journal of Philosophy*, 66: 829–39.

GEACH, P. (1977). *The Virtues* (Cambridge: Cambridge University Press).

GOLLWITZER, P. (1999). 'Implementation Intentions', *American Psychologist*, 54: 493–503.

——and SHEERAN, P. (2006). 'Implementation Intentions and Goal Achievement: A Meta-Analysis of Effects and Processes', *Advances in Experimental Social Psychology*, 38: 69–119.

GOSLING, J. (1990). *Weakness of the Will* (London: Routledge).

HARE, R. (1963). *Freedom and Reason* (Oxford: Oxford University Press).

HARMAN, G. (2004). 'Practical Aspects of Theoretical Rationality', in A. Mele and P. Rawling (eds), *The Oxford Handbook of Rationality* (Oxford: Oxford University Press), 45–56.

HENDEN, E. (2008). 'What is Self-Control?', *Philosophical Psychology*, 21: 69–90.

HEYMAN, G. (1996). 'Resolving the Contradictions of Addiction', *Behavioral and Brain Sciences*, 19: 561–610.

HOLTON, R. (2003). 'How is Strength of Will Possible?', in S. Stroud and C. Tappolet (eds), *Weakness of Will and Practical Irrationality* (Oxford: Clarendon Press), 39–67.

KENNETT, J. (2001). *Agency and Responsibility* (Oxford: Oxford University Press).

——and SMITH, M. (1996). 'Frog and Toad Lose Control', *Analysis*, 56: 63–73.

——(1997). 'Synchronic Self-Control is Always Non-Actual', *Analysis*, 57: 123–31.

KNOBE, J., and NICHOLS, S. (eds) (2008). *Experimental Philosophy* (Oxford: Oxford University Press).

KUNDA, Z. (1999). *Social Cognition* (Cambridge, Mass.: MIT Press).

MELDEN, A. (1961). *Free Action* (London: Routledge & Kegan Paul).

MELE, A. (1987). *Irrationality* (New York: Oxford University Press).

——(1990). 'Errant Self-Control and the Self-Controlled Person', *Pacific Philosophical Quarterly*, 71: 47–59.

——(1992). *Springs of Action* (New York: Oxford University Press).

——(1995). *Autonomous Agents* (New York: Oxford University Press).

——(2001). *Self-Deception Unmasked* (Princeton: Princeton University Press).

——(2002). 'Akratics and Addicts', *American Philosophical Quarterly*, 39: 153–67.

——(2003). *Motivation and Agency* (New York: Oxford University Press).

——(2006). *Free Will and Luck* (New York: Oxford University Press).

MISCHEL, W., and AYDUK, O. (2004). 'Willpower in a Cognitive-Affective Processing System', in R. Baumeister and K. Vohs (eds), *Handbook of Self-Regulation* (New York: Guilford), 99–129.

——SHODA, Y., and RODRIGUEZ, M. (1989). 'Delay of Gratification in Children', *Science*, 244: 933–8.

MURAVEN, M., BAUMEISTER, R., and TICE, D. (1999). 'Longitudinal Improvement of Self-Regulation through Practice: Building Self-Control Strength through Repeated Exercise', *Journal of Social Psychology*, 139: 446–57.

——TICE, D., and BAUMEISTER, R. (1998). 'Self-Control as a Limited Resource: Regulatory Depletion Patterns', *Journal of Personality and Social Psychology*, 74: 744–89.

NAGEL, T. (1986). *The View from Nowhere* (New York: Oxford University Press).

PLATO (1953*a*). *Protagoras*, in *The Dialogues of Plato*, tr. Benjamin Jowett (Oxford: Clarendon Press).

——(1953*b*). *Republic*, in *The Dialogues of Plato*, tr. Benjamin Jowett (Oxford: Clarendon Press).

PEELE, S. (1985). *The Meaning of Addiction: Compulsive Experience and its Interpretation* (Lexington, Mass.: Lexington Books).

——(1989). *Diseasing of America: Addiction Treatment Out of Control* (Lexington, Mass.: Lexington Books).

PUGMIRE, D. (1982). 'Motivated Irrationality', *Proceedings of the Aristotelian Society*, 56: 179–96.

——(1994). 'Perverse Preference: Self-Beguilement or Self-Division', *Canadian Journal of Philosophy*, 24: 73–94.

RORTY, A. (1980). 'Akrasia and Conflict', *Inquiry*, 22: 193–212.

SANTAS, G. (1966). 'Plato's Protagoras and Explanations of Weakness', *Philosophical Review*, 75: 3–33.

SMITH, M. (1992). 'Valuing: Desiring or Believing?', in D. Charles and K. Lennon (eds), *Reduction, Explanation, and Realism* (Oxford: Clarendon Press), 323–59.

——(2003). 'Rational Capacities, or: How to Distinguish Recklessness, Weakness, and Compulsion', in S. Stroud and C. Tappolet (eds), *Weakness of Will and Practical Irrationality* (Oxford: Clarendon Press), 17–38.

STOCKER, M. (1979). 'Desiring the Bad', *Journal of Philosophy*, 76: 738–53.

SZASZ, T. (1974). *The Myth of Mental Illness: Foundations of a Theory of Personal Conduct* (New York: Perennial Library).

THALBERG, I. (1985). 'Questions about Motivational Strength', in E. LePore and B. McLaughlin (eds), *Actions and Events* (Oxford: Basil Blackwell), 88–103.

VELLEMAN, J. D. (1992). 'What Happens When Someone Acts?', *Mind*, 101: 461–81.

——(2000). *The Possibility of Practical Reason* (Oxford: Oxford University Press).

WATSON, G. (1977). 'Skepticism about Weakness of Will', *Philosophical Review*, 86: 316–39.

WEBB, T., and SHEERAN, P. (2003). 'Can Implementation Intentions Help to Overcome Ego-Depletion?', *Journal of Experimental Social Psychology*, 39: 279–86.

···

CHAPTER 21

MORAL RESPONSIBILITY AND THE SELF

···

DAVID W. SHOEMAKER

Every person is conscious, that he is now the same person or self he was, as far back as his remembrance reaches; since, when any one reflects upon a past action of his own, he is just as certain of the person who did that action, namely himself, the person who now reflects upon it, as he is certain that the action was at all done.

(Joseph Butler)

Consider . . . a sculptor who has created a particular sculpture. [It] has a set of features relevant to its aesthetic evaluation. . . . But it is a quite different question to ask what exactly we value in the artist's creative activity. . . . [I]t is that he has engaged in a certain sort of artistic self-expression. Similarly, the good or ill will of the agent as evinced in the relevant action might be the feature of the action pertinent to one's reactive attitudes: and yet the value of the agent's acting in such a way as to be fairly held morally responsible derives from a different feature of the action—that it is a certain sort of self-expression.

(John Martin Fischer)

My thanks to Sean Foran, Michael McKenna, Matt Talbert, and the members of my Spring 2009 graduate seminar on moral responsibility and the self at Bowling Green State University for their help in the preparation of various aspects of this chapter.

It is thought to be a platitude that 'one can be morally responsible only for one's own actions'. Call this *The Platitude*. It is my aim in this chapter to explore both the meaning of The Platitude as well as its application conditions. In so doing, I will be discussing two significant ways in which moral responsibility is thought to be relevant to the self, namely, as it pertains to (*a*) personal identity, and (*b*) self-expression. Talk of the first leads naturally to talk of the second, so that will be the order in which this chapter is constructed. In what follows, I intend to argue that the question of what makes an action *one's own* (in the sense relevant to The Platitude) is not addressed by standard investigations into personal identity; it is, rather, a matter of *practical* identity.

1. RESPONSIBILITY AND IDENTITY

Introduction to the issues

For an agent to be morally responsible for an action A, it seems necessary for the agent to bear some sort of intimate relation to A. But what is this intimate relation? For many philosophers working in the field, to understand the relation we begin with The Platitude, which is then taken to entail the philosophical slogan that 'moral responsibility presupposes personal identity', that is, in order for someone to be morally responsible for A, that person must be the same person as the agent of A. Call this *The Slogan*.[1] If the entailment obtains then one ought to be able to provide an analysis of the intimate relation between the agent and A by offering the correct theory of personal identity as the proper account of what makes an action one's own. In other words, if some past action is mine *in virtue of the fact* that I was the person who performed that action, then whatever makes me identical to that past person is what makes 'his' actions mine for purposes of responsibility. In order to illuminate a key component of moral responsibility, then, it looks like we need to explore the nature of personal identity. Specifically, we are looking for whatever criterion of personal identity most plausibly fills in the following blank: *what makes an action one's own is_____.*

---

[1] Philosophers who have accepted or advocated this entailment include Butler 1736: e.g. 104; DeGrazia 2005: 88–9; Glannon 1998: 231; Haksar 1980: 111; Locke 1694; Madell 1981: 116; Parfit 1984: 323–6 (on the Extreme Claim); 1986: 837–43; Reid 1785: 116–17; Sider 2001: 4, 143, 203–4; Schechtman 1996: e.g. 14.

The Lockean approach

John Locke was the trailblazer for this sort of general methodology, and he filled in the blank as follows: what makes an action one's own is *that one has consciousness of it*, where 'consciousness' is typically taken to be synonymous with 'memory'.[2] As he puts it:

[C]onsciousness, as far as ever it can be extended ... unites existences and actions, very remote in time into the same person, as well as it does the existences and actions of the immediately preceding moment: so that whatever has the consciousness of present and past actions, is the same person to whom they both belong. (Locke 1694: 45)

And later he writes:

This personality extends itself beyond present existence to what is past, only by consciousness, whereby it becomes concerned and accountable, owns and imputes to itself past actions, just upon the same ground and for the same reason that it does the present.... [And at the 'great day' of the last judgment, when 'the secrets of all hearts shall be laid open'], [t]he sentence shall be justified by the consciousness all persons shall have, that they themselves, in what bodies soever they appear, or what substances soever that consciousness adheres to, are the same that committed those actions, and deserve that punishment for them. (Locke 1694: 51)

The idea, then, is that one is responsible ('accountable') only for those actions of which one has consciousness, insofar as that consciousness is what renders those actions one's own, imputable to oneself.

This view, while perhaps initially plausible, is susceptible to some persuasive counterexamples, however, which suggest that consciousness/memory is neither necessary nor sufficient for the kind of ownership that is itself necessary for moral responsibility. On the one hand, the actions of a drunk man belong to his hungover self the next morning, even if he blacked out and has no recollection of those actions. Consciousness is thus not necessary for ownership. On the other hand, if a memory trace of my having performed some action were copied into your brain, such that you had consciousness (a 'quasi-memory'[3]) of it, that action would surely not belong to you thereby. Consciousness is thus not sufficient for ownership.

Locke's view is inadequate to the task of explicating the intimate relation between agent and action for purposes of moral responsibility. But this may seem to be because of the problematic nature of his theory of personal identity. After all, it is now commonly understood that I may forget certain parts of *my* past, and one memory does not identity make. For these reasons, then, perhaps we

---

[2] See Locke 1694. Whether or not Lockean 'consciousness' is synonymous with 'memory' is a matter of some controversy, however. See Schechtman 1996: 106–14.

[3] For talk of quasi-memories, or q-memories, see S. Shoemaker 1970; Parfit 1984.

should simply look to a more plausible theory of identity to preserve and defend The Slogan.

The biological approach

One way to avoid the first counterexample to Locke is by adopting a biological criterion of personal identity (also known as 'animalism'), according to which a person at one time is identical to an individual at any other time if and only if the former's biological life is the latter's. What I am essentially on this view is a human animal, a biological creature, and so what preserves my identity is the preservation of that biological creature's life. This means that I am one and the same thing as the pre-conscious fetus from which I grew, and that I could well be one and the same thing as the post-conscious vegetable into which I might lapse (see e.g. Olson 1997; DeGrazia 2005).

Applying this account of identity to the criterion of ownership of actions, then, we get that what makes an action one's own is *that it was performed by an organism with whom one is biologically continuous*, that is, an entity with the same biological life as oneself. And this view easily accounts for the case of the drunk/hungover man, for even if this morning I don't remember what happened last night, those drunken actions are still mine, and on the present account this would be because I'm biologically continuous with that drunken performer last night. The view also accounts for the memory trace transplant case, for even if you become able to (quasi-)remember an action I performed, it would not be *your* action insofar as you are not biologically continuous with the person who originally performed the action.

Nevertheless, the account stumbles over other cases. Suppose I commit some crime and then my entire cerebrum is transplanted into a cerebrum-less head, such that the resulting person has a different body from me but is exactly like me psychologically, someone who seems to remember the bank robbery, cherishes my bank-robbing values, anticipates getting away with the crime, and so forth. The application of the biological criterion implies that, insofar as he will not be me (he doesn't have my biological life), my actions are not his, but this seems the wrong answer, which implies biological continuity isn't necessary for ownership. My actions do belong to him, we want to say, which is the necessary condition for his being morally responsible for them.

Consider a less science-fiction case. Suppose Johann enters a fugue state for two years during which he calls himself 'Sebastian'. In this state, he disappears from home and wanders around the country picking up odd jobs and committing various petty crimes. One day Johann wakes up having no idea where he is or where he's been. He eventually reconnects with his family and never remembers what happened during the fugue state, despite having been shown pictures of himself culled from various surveillance cameras during that period. On the application of the biological criterion, the Sebastian-actions would have to be Johann's, given their shared biological life, but again this seems wrong. Biological continuity isn't sufficient for ownership.[4]

More generally, though, ownership of actions doesn't seem to have anything significant to do with biological relations in the first place. Instead, what makes some action my own seems obviously to be a *psychological* matter: actions involve the execution of intentions (where this may or may not involve any physical activity), purported ownership generally involves possible endorsement or rejection of the various attributions, and ownership pertaining to responsibility involves susceptibility to various assessments, that is, hearing, being receptive to, and responding to expressions of praise or blame, as well as rendering judgments about the fairness of such appraisals and experiencing various emotions in their wake. But these are all psychological states, so it's no wonder that biological continuity seems fairly irrelevant to ownership. (Cf. Olson 1997: 57–8.)

The psychological approach

Accordingly, many have taken considerations of moral responsibility to favor a psychological criterion of identity, according to which a person X at one time is identical to a person Y at a later time if and only if Y is uniquely psychologically continuous with X.[5] This is a Lockean theory insofar as it (*a*) points to a relation, rather than a substance, as preserving diachronic identity, and (*b*) points to a *psychological* relation as that identity preserver. The main difference with Locke comes from the psychological criterion's dependence on a wider range of psychological relations than just memory. The psychological criterion is about psychological continuity, which consists in overlapping chains of sufficient numbers of direct psychological connections. These connections include, beyond memories, intentions fulfilled in action, persisting beliefs, desires, and goals, and similarities of character. These connections together constitute psychological continuity, such that even if I have no direct connections to some distant past self, that self may still

---

[4] Note that I'm not saying here that biological continuity isn't sufficient for *moral responsibility*. The intuition pump is only about ownership. Again, the theorists at issue have the following slogan in mind: personal identity is a necessary condition for moral responsibility. What allegedly mediates identity and responsibility is ownership, but it's a complicated relationship: identity is thought to be a *criterion* for ownership (i.e. it provides the necessary and sufficient conditions for ownership), and ownership is then thought to be only a necessary condition for responsibility. Insofar as we are examining the first relationship—identity as criterion of ownership—it's perfectly legitimate to point to cases where identity is *insufficient* for ownership, which is what the Johann/Sebastian case reveals.

[5] There are too many advocates of the psychological criterion to cite. I draw the version in the text from Parfit 1984.

be *me* in virtue of the fact that there are overlapping chains of strong direct connections between us.

When the psychological criterion is inserted into the criterion of ownership, we get the following: what makes an action one's own is *that it was performed by a person with whom one is uniquely psychologically continuous.* This view once again improves upon its predecessor. It of course handles the drunk/hangover case, for the hungover person is psychologically continuous with the drunk, even if he doesn't remember his actions. It also handles the single memory trace case, for a single memory isn't sufficient to generate psychological continuity and thus identity.

Furthermore, it is an improvement over the insertion of the biological criterion insofar as it handles both the cerebrum transplant and fugue state cases with ease: my actions belong to the person who inherits my cerebrum insofar as he is uniquely psychologically continuous with me, while the Sebastian-actions during the fugue state are not properly attributable to Johann insofar as Johann is not psychologically continuous with Sebastian.

Notwithstanding these successes, though, there are still some troublesome cases for this application of the psychological criterion. Consider first a variation on the fugue state case. Suppose that Johann's transformation into Sebastian occurs not suddenly but gradually: Johann's brain grows a tumor, say, that after several weeks yields Sebastian yet all the while preserves psychological continuity. And after two years, once the tumor is discovered, it is gradually destroyed, so that the transformation from Sebastian back to Johann is once again gradual and preserves psychological continuity. In such a case, it seems the Sebastian-actions still don't belong to Johann: they were the actions of someone with a very different character as well as very different beliefs, desires, goals, and values, and they strike Johann himself as the actions of a complete stranger. Nevertheless, inserting the psychological criterion into the criterion of ownership directly implies that the Sebastian-actions *do* belong to Johann, given that he is psychologically continuous with him (despite not being psychologically connected with him). This case then suggests that psychological continuity is not sufficient for ownership.

It is also not necessary. Consider a variation on the drunk/hangover case. Suppose this person while drunk assaults a child and then is beaten up badly by a bystander, a beating which causes severe psychological discontinuity. The person who wakes up in the morning thus has an insufficient number of psychological connections to render him continuous with the person from the night before, but nevertheless suppose he does have a memory of assaulting the child and he persists in having a small number of beliefs, desires, and character traits that were essential to his being motivated to perform and enjoy the assault. Here we likely want to say that the assault belongs to him, despite his lack of psychological continuity with the assaulter.

What these cases indicate is that perhaps ownership of actions is drawn from only a certain *subset* of psychological relations, ones towards which one has a particular attitude. In other words, it looks like psychological continuity both incorporates too many relations and is also too objective in its assignment of weight to those relations.

The narrative approach

To this point we have been investigating applications of various criteria of *numerical* identity to the criterion of ownership of actions. These are criteria purporting to answer a *reidentification* question, telling us what makes X at a time one and the same individual or person as Y at another time. However, some have thought that, when we are attempting to articulate the relation between identity and our practical concerns (e.g. responsibility), something other than the reidentification question—and thus numerical identity—is more relevant, namely, the *characterization* question: what makes various experiences and actions occurring at different times those of one person (Schechtman 1996; Chapter 17 above)? The sense of 'identity' taken to be relevant to answering this question is essentially that of an 'identity crisis', which involves an uncertainty about who one really is, about which experiences and psychological features, say, truly belong to one.

The narrative identity theorist is someone who answers the characterization question as follows: what makes various experiences, features, and actions attributable to one person is that they are 'part of a single identity-constituting narrative' (Schechtman 1996: 136). Think of the idea in the following way. Suppose there were a human subject of experiences, an entity to which various experiences merely happened over time. What distinguishes this subject of experiences from a *person*, on the view under discussion, is that the experiences and actions of the latter's life are unified as all *belonging* to her, the experiences and actions of one person. And what provides this unity is the entity's subjective attitude towards, and the story she tells about, those experiences and actions. As Marya Schechtman puts it, 'What it means for an action to be part of someone's narrative is for it to flow naturally from the rest of her life story—to be an intelligible result of her beliefs, values, desires, and experiences' (1996: 159). One's narrative identity, then, is a function of the incorporation of such features into one coherent storyline, the biography of a person.

Inserting this account of identity into the criterion of ownership, then, yields the following: what makes an action one's own is *its being correctly included as an event in the self-told story of one's life*.[6] This view seems an improvement over the purely third-person psychological approach when it comes to both the fugue variation and the drunken assault cases just discussed. Despite Johann's psychological

---

[6] See e.g. DeGrazia 2005: 83. The 'correctness' condition is typically included to provide some plausible constraints on the storytelling allowed. I can't e.g. talk about myself as continuing the life of Napoleon. See DeGrazia 2005: 85–6; Schechtman 1996: 119–30.

continuity with Sebastian, for instance, there are certain features of his life that simply don't fit coherently into his self-told story, as flowing intelligibly from his beliefs, values, desires, and experiences. So the Sebastian-actions don't properly belong to Johann, and as a result Johann is not morally responsible for them. And even though the hungover person who wakes up after the beating isn't psychologically continuous with the drunken assaulter of the night before, his memories of the incident, combined with the fact that it flowed directly from the small number of beliefs, desires, and character traits that still persist in him, should easily be sufficient to establish his narrative identity with the assaulter. In both cases, the sheer number of psychological connections involved is less relevant than which of the connections that obtain actually *matter* to the narrator. The subjective importance assigned to various experiences and actions thus determines (subject to the minimal accuracy constraints) both ownership and, to a great extent, moral responsibility. This is also why narrative identity theorists are fond of talking about narrative identity being a matter of *identification*, and this terminology makes it easy to talk about both cases: Johann simply doesn't identify with the earlier (Sebastian-)actions, while the morning-after assailant still does.

Setting aside its vagueness, the narrative identity view flees too far in the subjective direction to account for ownership and responsibility. It's quite possible, for instance, that Johann comes to embrace the Sebastian-actions as his own by weaving them into the story of his life. Perhaps what was now *his* ordeal increases the value of autonomy in his life, or perhaps it helps explain why he now volunteers his time to fight against domestic terrorism. Nevertheless, the fact that Johann claims to have *taken on* ownership in this way doesn't yet render the Sebastian-actions his in the way relevant to moral responsibility. We are just as likely to judge the Sebastian-actions as *not* his as we were in the scenario in which Johann feels himself to be alienated from them. In other words, Johann's subjective attitude toward the actions seems fairly irrelevant to whether or not he genuinely owns them. An event's being incorporated into someone's narrative identity thus seems insufficient for ownership.

It also seems unnecessary. In telling the story of my life, I may leave out lots of relevant actions, as a product of self-deception, forgetfulness, or editing (e.g. I deem them unimportant).[7] Nevertheless, some of these omitted events could well be those I own for purposes of moral responsibility. This will be the case, for instance, in the original drunken assaulter example, for the hungover person can't even remember the assault, and so can't incorporate it into his life story, yet it is still clearly his action.

---

[7] Notice that this sort of editing doesn't violate the accuracy constraint of the theory either, that the events in my narrative be 'correctly included', for this is a condition on events that are *included*, namely, that they be accurate to reality. There is no requirement that *every* event be included, nor even that every event that *matters* be included.

The mistake is in thinking that the identification that renders an action one's own is a product of first-personal active reflection, that various actions become my own only when I *gather them up* via my active storytelling. But this ignores the fact that much of the time our selves are constructed passively, that we *find* ourselves identified with various experiences, psychological features, and actions independently of any active reflection or narration.

For instance, a police officer who has been studying Buddhism for a time may wonder whether or not he is, at his core, a cop or a Buddhist (given that they conflict in their views on the necessity of violence), and he may well *discover* the truth at some point, perhaps when he is called upon to shoot a suspect and finds that he can no longer bring himself to do so. As he discovers in that moment, he is identified with his Buddhism. And we may make such discoveries about ourselves in a variety of less dramatic circumstances.

Identification with actions may often be passive as well. Suppose that our hungover assailant, even when presented with the visual evidence of his assault on YouTube, denies that action a place in his narrative, actively rejecting ownership of it. But as he goes about the living of his life, he notices little things about himself he hadn't noticed before, that he is quick to anger, that his fists clench during tense conversations, that his fantasies often involve violence against others. He then eventually comes to recognize that he *does* identify with that assailant on YouTube, indeed, *that he had all along*, and that it was exactly the action one should have expected from him when alcohol had lowered his inhibitions. He now incorporates this event into the story of his life. But notice that this incorporation involves no new, active identification with the action; rather, it is an acknowledgment of his pre-existing (but unaware) identification with it.

Of course, the narrative theorist might reply that this man's drunken assault now *does* fit into an intelligible narrative, making narrative identity necessary to his identification with the action. But this reply misses the point, which is that just because an intelligible narrative can be provided about the relation between various actions and events, it is not the narrative which *makes* an action one's own, something with which one is identified. Instead, these narratives point out *pre-existing patterns*, a tale often about antecedent identifications, not a creation of them. Thus we still don't have an adequate account of the relation between identity and responsibility.

Fission and four-dimensionalism

With the exception of narrative identity, all of the theories of identity discussed thus far have been theories of numerical identity. And while narrative identity purports to be about a sense of 'identity' very different from numerical identity, it actually presupposes it. That is, the various experiences of *one and the same* subject of experiences are alleged to be gathered up into the life of one person (more or less successfully) via that subject's narrative. Further, a person cannot continue as a narrator unless that person also continues to exist (DeGrazia 2005: 114). But theories that are directly about, or that presuppose, numerical identity all run into difficulty dealing with the case of fission.

Suppose that I split down the middle and then each half of my body grows a copy of its missing half, resulting in two people exactly similar to me in all of their physical and psychological features (call this *physical fission*). What has happened to me? There are three possibilities: I survive as both people, I survive as only one person, or I do not survive. The first option is impossible: there are two people in existence, and two doesn't equal one. The second option is implausible: what possible non-arbitrary reason could there be for why I'm one and not the other? The third option is thus the only viable option: I have ceased to exist, and there are two new people now in existence. My ceasing to exist is due only to the logic of identity, however, for the identity-relation must obtain uniquely, whereas the relation between me and the resulting people is one–many. Thus the relation between us cannot be one of numerical identity.

But now suppose that just prior to physical fission I stole some money without justification. Both fission products now seem to remember stealing the money, they both delight in the crime, and they both intend to spend the money on beer and baubles. If numerical identity is what provides the criterion of ownership, then neither fission product owns my action because neither is me. And further, if ownership were necessary for moral responsibility, then neither fission product would be morally responsible (to any degree) for what I did. But this seems the wrong answer. Surely my action *does* belong to both, which establishes the very plausible possibility that both are (to some extent) morally responsible for it. Consideration of the fission case thus suggests that numerical identity is actually irrelevant to ownership, and thus responsibility.[8]

Nevertheless, there may be a different solution to the fission case, namely, the possibility that *there were two people all along*. This is the answer given by a four-dimensionalist metaphysics, according to which persons have not only spatial but also temporal parts. On this view, then, two (or more) distinct persons might have spatially overlapping temporal stages, just as two distinct roads might have overlapping spatial

[8] I should be clear that the three reactions to the fission case are the *only* options only for those who believe that identity is always *determinate*, that for every possible permutation there is always a 'yes' or 'no' answer to the question of whether or not some person is me. One might think, though, that sometimes there just is no fact of the matter about identity, and so one might also think in the fission case that it is indeterminate whether or not one or the other fission products is me. On a view in which identity provides the criterion of ownership, then, this would imply that it is indeterminate whether or not the fission products own my actions. Nevertheless, I think the intuition that both products own my actions is fairly strong, which suggests this indeterminacy option is implausible. Thanks to Sean Foran for helpful discussion of this point and the four-dimensionalist option below.

stages for a stretch (see e.g. Lewis 1976 and Sider 2001). In the fission case, then, according to such a view, my two fission products overlapped pre-fission: they spatially coincided up until the point of fission when they were finally spatially separated. This means both fission products are two distinct persons—each one numerically identical only with himself—who share a common part. One might think, then, that actions performed by the shared person stage would belong to *both* persons (both when they overlap and when they don't), a result in line with our intuitions. If so, numerical identity could still provide the ownership relation between agents and those held responsible for their actions. This view thus seems to preserve the alleged entailment of The Slogan by The Platitude.

It is very important to note, though, that four-dimensionalism is not itself what we have been thinking of as a criterion of numerical identity. Rather, it is simply a view about the nature of material objects, asserting that they have both spatial and temporal parts (Sider 2001: p. xiii). This means that if X refers to a temporal stage of a person at t1 and Y refers to a temporal stage at t2, these are just distinct temporal stages (they have different temporal properties, at the very least), which renders the standard reidentification question of numerical identity—what makes X one and the same individual as Y?—a kind of category mistake. Instead, there are myriad distinct space-time worms—four-dimensional objects—that are numerically identical *with themselves*. It is wrong, then, to say of their parts—their various temporal stages—that they are *identical* with one another; rather, the various temporal stages are *unified* with one another as part of one and the same space-time worm. The reidentification question must be asked in a different form, therefore, to the four-dimensionalist: what makes the various temporal stages of one and the same space-time person-worm part of that ontological object? Call the criterion produced in answer to this question the *unity relation* for persons.[9]

This fact reveals a problem for our purposes, though, namely that four-dimensionalism itself implies nothing whatsoever about the nature of that unity relation (see Sider 2001: 194). It could consist in biological continuity, psychological continuity, or narrative identity; nothing about the four-dimensionalist story itself favors any of these possibilities. But surely any viable application of identity into the criterion of ownership relevant to moral responsibility, were it to rely on a four-dimensionalist ontology (in order, perhaps, to avoid the fission objection), would have to include a plausible story about the relation *unifying* persons' various temporal stages. Otherwise, the application would be empty, providing nothing at all to *explicate* the nature of ownership or moral responsibility, which is precisely the point of the enterprise.

But if a viable application of a four-dimensionalist understanding of identity to the criterion of ownership still must rely on one of the standard stories about

---

[9] This is also known as the 'genidentity relation' or the 'I-relation'. See e.g. Lewis 1976 or Sider 2001: 194.

numerical identity (cashed out in terms of a unity relation), it will fall prey to the counterexamples we have already discussed to each of them. So while some have taken four-dimensionalism's facility in handling the fission and moral responsibility case as providing a powerful consideration in favor of the theory (see e.g. Sider 2001: 4), it seems instead that, because of the antecedent need for an adequate unity relation to explicate the relation between identity and *ownership*, advocates of four-dimensionalism have been far too quick in claiming support from such a case.

Responsibility without identity

We can explain responsibility and ownership in the fission-type cases—and all our other cases as well—without having to rely on four-dimensionalism *or any specific theory of identity at all* once we come to appreciate a serious methodological mistake at the heart of the enterprise thus far. The most succinct formulation of The Platitude allegedly entailing The Slogan is that 'a person can only be held responsible for her own actions' (Schechtman 1996: 14). But this claim doesn't entail the Slogan—that responsibility presupposes identity—simply because, while responsibility presupposes ownership, *ownership doesn't entail identity*.

As a matter of logical entailment, this seems uncontroversial: there is no contradiction in supposing that some action A belongs to me where I am not identical with the agent of A. The source of this non-contradiction is that the two relations—identity and ownership—just have two different sets of relata. The relata of the personal identity relation are persons (or human individuals) at different times; the relata of the ownership relation are persons and *actions*. It's unsurprising, then, that one might have the latter without the former with no contradiction.

It is not enough, though, to point out the logical gap between ownership and identity, for there may, nevertheless, be no *conceptual* gap. Do we have, then, any positive reason to believe that ownership is conceptually distinct from identity? It turns out that we do.

One reason to think so stems from an analogy to property ownership. It is true that I can be taxed, say, only on my own property. Nevertheless, this fact doesn't imply that all property that's mine is mine *exclusively*. I am a joint owner of the house I live in, for example, as is my wife: the ownership relation I bear to the house also obtains between my wife and the house. But of course my wife and I are not identical. Thus because identity is one–one, and property ownership may be one–many, property ownership doesn't presuppose identity.

Indeed, this is how things seem to be in the physical fission case as well. If I commit some immoral action and then undergo fission, it seems plausible to say that both my fission products own my actions, even though neither is me, for I am only one person, they are two people, and one doesn't equal two (and there's no non-arbitrary reason why I would be one and not the other). Thus because identity is one–one, and action ownership may be one–many, action ownership doesn't presuppose identity.

There are two worries one might have about the analogy, though. First, one might think that, while property ownership is a conventional matter, action ownership isn't, so the fact that ownership obtains one–many in the former implies nothing whatsoever about how it might obtain in the latter.[10] It's quite unclear, however, that action ownership *isn't* conventional. What counts as ownership relevant to responsibility may well be a product of our practices and traditions, a thought rendered more plausible by reflection on the myriad ways in which the conventional practices of *legal* responsibility have bled over into assessments of moral responsibility (e.g. with respect to the insane or the mentally retarded).[11]

Nevertheless, the analogy may be blocked in a different way by the advocate of four-dimensionalism. On such a view, both identity and ownership could remain one–one, even in the fission case, for each fission product would, on this ontology, be identical to the original (pre-fission) agent of the action and so each could own the original's actions *exclusively*.[12] Of course, it is as yet unclear just which particular *unity* relation obtains between pre- and post-fission agents, but that's not directly relevant to motivating the disanalogy here.

We can sidestep both worries altogether, though, if we can find cases of joint ownership in the realm of actions, where even a four-dimensionalist ontology won't be able to preserve exclusivity of ownership. As it turns out, there are many such examples, called *joint* or *shared cooperative actions*. For example, singing a duet, winning a (team) game, having sex, performing a play, building a house, and engaging in a class action lawsuit are all actions that, while presupposing individual contributions, are nevertheless irreducibly joint.[13] These are actions only a *we* performs, and so the actions are attributable at the time to the joint agent. And so as individual members of the joint agent, you and I share ownership of the original action, and so may be assessed thereby. But the key point is this: just because I share ownership of some action, that doesn't mean that I'm numerically identical to the original agent of the action, simply because that original agent was a *we*, not an *I*.[14] If my ownership of some action entailed my numerical identity to the original agent, then I would have to be numerically identical to the joint agent,

---

[10] Thanks to Peter Barry and Steve Wall for pressing me to address this point.

[11] See e.g. Wolf 1987. Matt Talbert suggests (in correspondence) that it might actually be that, in certain instances, the order of influence has run in a different direction, from moral responsibility to legal responsibility, that widely-shared intuitions about moral responsibility have bled over into the legal world. This may well be true, but the larger point I'm making remains, which is that action ownership is informed by our responsibility practices (legal or moral), which are to some extent conventional.

[12] Does this mean there were actually *two* actions performed originally, then? It's unclear precisely how the treatment here might go.

[13] For these sorts of examples and more, see Bratman 1992.

[14] I am grateful to Steve Wall for insightful discussion of this point.

which, by transitivity, would have to render me numerically identical with all other contributors to that joint agency, which clearly I am not.

Now consider a different sort of case. Suppose a general orders his soldiers to 'take the bridge'. When the soldiers do so, that action—the taking of the bridge—is the general's; it belongs to him. When the action is praised, therefore, (much of) the praise will be directed to the general. This will be true despite the fact that the general himself performed *none* of the individual actions contributing to the action that he owns and for which he is praised.

Both of these examples positively illustrate the main point, then, which is that responsibility doesn't necessarily presuppose personal identity. I may be responsible only for my own actions—only for actions that belong to me—where, first, that ownership relation isn't exclusive, as the numerical identity relation must be: my ownership in cases of joint agency is shared with the other individual contributor(s) to the joint act. Second, my ownership relation to the action may be exclusive without my being involved in the performance of the action at all, as is the case with the general. Here identity with some agent is clearly unnecessary to ownership of that agent's actions.

What really undercuts The Slogan is the fact that responsibility merely presupposes ownership, which is just a relation between an agent and an *action*. Identity, by contrast, is a relation between an agent and an *agent*. No wonder, then, that the various attempts to insert a criterion of identity into the criterion of ownership fail: they are inserting the wrong kind of relation into the formula. This is also why the move to four-dimensionalism in the fission case is unmotivated (at least with respect to responsibility): both fission products bear the right sort of ownership relation to the original action, so the question of their identity with the original agent is just *irrelevant*.

Once we have set aside the question of a relation between identity and responsibility, though, we are still left with the question of the relation between ownership and identity. What, after all, is the right criterion of ownership here? And what does ownership have to do with the self? It is to this second topic that we now turn.

2. RESPONSIBILITY AND IDENTIFICATION

Introduction to the issues

The Platitude states that ownership is a necessary condition of moral responsibility. Insofar as ownership has been prised apart from identity, not only is it possible that some action may belong to me even if I wasn't its agent, but also it is possible that some action may not belong to me even if I *was* its agent. This could well be true in the fugue case: what Sebastian did does not belong to Johann, even if Johann *is* Sebastian (on the correct criterion of personal identity). But it could also be true in less dramatic cases, cases in which one is *alienated* from what one actually does.

This sort of talk will likely sound familiar to many, and it jibes well with our earlier discussion of the narrative view, according to which ownership is really about *identification*. On this understanding, an action genuinely belongs to me to the extent that I identify—or am identified—with it (or at least I identify with the will on which it depends). An action with which I identify, then, has a special kind of authority, for it in effect *speaks for me*; it is an expression of my self in the world, and so it is something for which my self may be (and may be held) responsible.

This has struck a number of theorists as quite a plausible understanding of the relation between ownership and responsibility, and it will be the subject of this section. In particular, I will examine so-called *Real Self* theories of responsibility, which maintain in general a kind of 'self-expression' view: one is morally responsible only for those actions that flow from one's deepest or truest self. Along the way, I will discuss the many challenges that face such a view, and whether or not a version of the view is worth preserving in light of these challenges.

Identification, appetites, and reason

Virtually all investigations into the nature of this sort of identification have their roots in the pioneering work of Harry Frankfurt (e.g. Frankfurt 1971, 1976, as well as the later versions of the view in Frankfurt 1987, 1992). In 'Freedom of the Will and the Concept of a Person', Frankfurt articulates a hierarchical picture of persons that remains deeply influential. The idea is by now familiar. Many creatures may be said to have *first-order desires*, or desires about what to do (some of which might conflict). Persons, however, are those self-reflective creatures who have, in addition to second-order desires (desires about which first-order desires to have), second-order *volitions*, that is, desires about which first-order desires are to constitute their wills. For persons, it matters which of their first-order desires actually wins out in action, and so they typically take sides in any first-order conflicts and in so doing *identify* with one or another first-order desire through the formation of a second-order volition. This volitional move renders that first-order desire more truly their *own*, and it also consists in the withdrawal of persons away from the losing first-order desires, which, if they are still effective in motivating the person, produce actions which can't properly be said to belong to their agent (Frankfurt 1971: 18).

The opposing account has become equally familiar, grounded in Gary Watson's early critique of Frankfurt (Watson 1975). Because second-order volitions are themselves just desires, why think their second-order status gives them any special sort of authority in identification? Just because some psychological element is higher up in the hierarchy, that doesn't mean it is any more representative of one's *self*. After all, wantonness—failing to care about which of one's desires is effective—is possible at any order. What Watson suggests instead, then, is an account of identification according to which the self is essentially located in one's faculty for practical, evaluative judgments (one's valuational system), such that one identifies with a *course of action* (and not a first-order desire) whenever one judges it to be most worth pursuing (Watson 2004: 28–30).

The basic disagreement (one which persists in competing accounts of identification to this day) is over the proper location of the self. Is it to be found, to use Platonic language, in Reason or in Appetite, in the rational or in the irrational part of the soul?[15] For our purposes, though, this question takes a back seat to a more fundamental question, namely, what relation purportedly obtains between identification—*whatever* it consists in—and moral responsibility?[16] We will now explore a theory that explicitly attempts to tie the two together, one that has produced a fascinating thread of discussion for more than twenty years.

The deep/real self view

In 1987, Susan Wolf wove what she took to be the common elements of Frankfurt's, Watson's, and Charles Taylor's (1975) views of freedom and identification into a general theory about moral responsibility. On Wolf's analysis, all three are attempts to articulate just how one's true self may or may not be expressed in action, such that 'if we are responsible agents, it is not just because our actions are within the control of our wills, but because, in addition, our wills are not just psychological states *in* us, but expressions of characters that come *from* us, or that at any rate are acknowledged and affirmed *by* us' (Wolf 1987: 49; emphasis in original). This expression is filled out in different ways by the various authors, but the basic structure for all three is allegedly the same: for someone to be responsible for her actions, they must be governed by her will/superficial self, and her will must be governed by her deep self. Wolf called this general theory of responsibility the *deep-self view*.

---

[15] In addition to ongoing work by Frankfurt, there are many others working in one or the other tradition. Here's a very short list: Bratman 2007; D. Shoemaker 2003; Stump 1996; Velleman 2000 and 2002.

[16] Indeed, the pioneering theories of identification just discussed were originally attached simply to theories of *free agency*, not moral responsibility. Frankfurt is explicit about this point, noting that he is articulating the conditions for freedom of the will and that, while such freedom has been 'generally supposed' to be a necessary condition for moral responsibility, he believes this to be false (Frankfurt 1988: 23). Note later how Wolf 1990 ignores this point in her discussion.

In later work (Wolf 1990), Wolf fleshed out her discussion of the view and in so doing changed its general label (for reasons described below) to the *Real Self View*.[17] Compatibilists typically maintain that determinism is compatible with moral responsibility insofar as it is only certain sorts of causes that undermine responsibility, namely, those causes that *constrain* an agent in some way. For many early compatibilists, the relevant constraints are those external to the agent, outside forces that prevent the agent from executing her will. The agent is, on this view, alienated from her action. Nevertheless, certain cases reveal the insufficiency of such an analysis, namely, kleptomania and hypnosis. In a genuine case of kleptomania, for instance, the agent isn't in fact prevented from executing her will, but she seems non-responsible nevertheless, and the reason is that the formation of her *will* has been constrained, and it has been constrained, furthermore, from the *inside*. This leaves her alienated from her own will. The remedy for many compatibilists, then, has been to articulate a view of responsibility according to which it attaches to unalienated selves. When (and only when) an action is ultimately dependent on the agent's real (unalienated) self, it is an action for which she is morally responsible.

More formally, the view may be stated as follows:

The Real Self View (RSV): an agent is morally responsible for X if and only if X is attributable to the agent's real self, that is, if and only if (*a*) the agent has a real self, (*b*) the agent is able to govern X on the basis of her will, and (*c*) the agent is able to govern her will on the basis of her valuational system. (Wolf 1990: 28–35)

There are a few things to note about this criterion. First, Wolf's understanding of a valuational system is broader than Watson's, for it includes not just judgments of good but also all the things that the agent cares about—the things that *matter* to her—where this still allows for the key distinction between desires and values (Wolf 1990: 31). Second, this is what's known as a structural view, otherwise known as a *mesh* view (see e.g. Fischer and Ravizza 1998: 184–5). All that matters for responsibility, on this view, is that there is a mesh between different sources (or locations in a hierarchy) of one's preferences, a harmony between one's valuational system and one's will. Anytime (and only when) this structural relation is achieved, one is morally responsible for the result. Third, and relatedly, this is a non-historical view of moral responsibility: it doesn't matter what the causal history of one's current will is; all that matters is what that will's particular structure now consists in.

On this view, the real self is 'the self with which the agent is to be properly identified' (Wolf 1990: 30). Is this a plausible criterion of moral responsibility?

---

[17] The change to a capitalized label from a lower-case label is in keeping with Wolf's own typography.

Problems with the real self view

The basic idea behind the RSV, and the reason it is relevant for our discussion, is that an action is properly attributable to me—it is mine, I identify with it—for purposes of moral responsibility if and only if it is governed ultimately by my real self (where my real self is defined essentially by my broadly construed valuational system). There have been at least five attacks on this account of responsibility, however, some of which are quite powerful. The first two are based on Wolf's own objections to the sufficiency condition, while the rest are objections to the necessary condition.

(1) *Responsibility for selves*

There are cases in which we may fully attribute some action to an agent's real self while nevertheless thinking him to be not morally responsible insofar as we believe him to lack responsibility *for* that self. In other words, we may believe it's not his fault that his real self is the way it is. This will be true for the insane, those subjects of thoroughgoing psychological conditioning (e.g. brainwashing), and those from severely deprived or traumatic childhoods (Wolf 1990: 37). We may also include here the more generally cited worries about 'external manipulation': one's current 'real' self may simply have been externally implanted, in which case various actions may flow from it without the agent's being deemed morally responsible for them, insofar as he bears no responsibility for the real self that is producing them.[18]

(2) *Superficial responsibility*

Attribution of an action to a real self seems to involve nothing more than attributing a bad (or good) act to a bad (or good) *act-maker*. This is primarily just to hold the agent *causally* responsible for an event that, depending on our interests, has positive or negative value. 'But', according to Wolf, 'when we hold an individual morally responsible for some event, we are doing more than identifying her particularly crucial role in the causal series that brings about the event in question' (Wolf 1990: 40–1). Instead, we are holding *her* responsible, 'judging the moral quality of the individual herself in some more focused, noninstrumental, and seemingly more serious way' (Wolf 1990: 41). This is *deep responsibility*, and insofar as it is what genuine *moral* responsibility must be about, the RSV is an insufficient account of it.

---

[18] See e.g. Fischer and Ravizza 1998: 196–201, 230–6; D. Locke 1975; Stump 1988.

(3) *Negligence*

Suppose I fail to salt down the ice on my front steps prior to my dinner party this evening, and when you arrive you slip and get injured. I am morally responsible, it seems, despite the fact that I performed no action, formed no will, and engaged in no self-reflective evaluation whatsoever. Such cases suggest, then, that none of the conditions of the RSV are actually necessary to moral responsibility.

(4) *Whims*

Suppose that as I'm wandering through a crowded store I suddenly decide to steal something, an action that upon any reflective consideration I would not have performed. Here we have a case in which my will operates independently from my valuational system—it's a will with which I neither identify nor disidentify—but it nevertheless produces an action for which I would be deemed morally responsible, again suggesting that governance by the real self is unnecessary for moral responsibility. (See e.g. Lippert-Rasmussen 2003.[19])

(5) *Inverse akrasia*

When Huck Finn can't bring himself to turn in the slave Jim, despite the fact that he judges it the right thing to do, he takes himself to be a moral failure. We, however, see him as praiseworthy, and so as clearly morally responsible for his actions. This is true despite the fact that the action he performs doesn't look to be governed by his valuational system, which again seems to reveal the conditions of the RSV as unnecessary for moral responsibility. (See e.g. Arpaly and Schroeder 1999.)

This is an intimidating block of objections.[20] To reply sufficiently to them all would require far more space than I have here. Nevertheless, I will at least try to gesture at how one might *begin* an answer in each case, and then spend some more time on two of them.

The necessary condition

The Platitude with which we began was that one can be morally responsible only for one's own actions, that is, ownership is a necessary condition for responsibility.

---

[19] Another relevant example here might be Watson's 'perverse cases', wherein I fully embrace as my own some action that runs counter to my evaluative judgments, perhaps because it will be more fun or stress-free. See Watson 1987 in Watson 2004: 169.

[20] Wallace 1994 has also mentioned or discussed one or more of these objections to versions of the Real Self View.

We have been working under the assumption that the most plausible account of ownership (identification) comes from the RSV, according to which an action is one's own just in case it is governed by a will that is itself governed by one's valuational system. But if real-self-governance is unnecessary for moral responsibility—as it is according to objections (3)–(5)—then ownership is unnecessary as well. But The Platitude is, well, a *platitude*. To preserve it in light of these objections, then, it seems like we must deny that the RSV is the right account of ownership and moral responsibility.

This is too quick, however. Essential to the RSV is that one have the *ability* to govern one's actions with one's real self, whereas implicit in objections (3) and (4), for instance, is the thought that one *in fact* did not govern one's actions with one's real self. To act on a whim is to act in accordance with one's 'superficial self', we might say, without the actual imprimatur of one's deeper self, but this isn't yet to say that one's deeper self is *unable* to exercise the appropriate oversight.[21] Similarly, the fact that I was negligent in failing to salt the steps doesn't mean my action (or inaction) wasn't governable by my real self; indeed, we might say that my negligence here *did* flow from my real self, that of a genuinely inconsiderate person.[22]

The inverse *akrasia* case involves something different, perhaps. We might just stipulate, for instance, that Huck was indeed *unable* to govern his actions with his real self: his real self is found in the valuational system producing the judgment that turning in Jim is the right thing to do, but he is ultimately too 'weak' to render that judgment his will. Nevertheless, in finding him praiseworthy, we seem to deny the necessity of the RSV, for we deem him responsible regardless of the fact that his actions aren't governable by his real self.

This is a clever and interesting case, but it by no means establishes the irrelevance of the RSV. One line of response, for instance, would be to deny that Huck's action doesn't flow from his real self. Of course, not much has been said to this point to give a precise account of the nature of the 'real self', but on the broad suggestion mentioned earlier, there's no reason it can't include not only one's evaluative judgments *but also* one's nexus of cares, that is, the set of emotional commitments one has that are indicative (or perhaps even constitutive) of evaluative importance.[23] On a suitably detailed story like this, then, one might be able to explain

---

[21] Lippert-Rasmussen 2003 considers and rejects this reply, but for a very odd reason. As he puts it, 'Suppose an agent whose will is constituted by a whimsical desire is psychologically unable to so govern her will because she considers the issue too trivial to engage her values. In such a case we would not deny that the agent in question is responsible when she acts on a whimsical desire' (p. 372). This is to conflate two senses of 'unable,' however. One might be unable insofar as one just can't *rouse* oneself to engage with the issue without thereby being *incapacitated* from doing so. Surely the latter is the sense relevant for undermining responsibility.

[22] There is clearly more to say about this sort of case, though, and I will do so in my discussion of Angela Smith's work below.

[23] This is, for instance, the way I explicate my own view of autonomy in D. Shoemaker 2003.

why someone's evaluative judgments may occasionally be *un*representative of his real self (due to self-deception or indoctrination, say), despite what he thinks, which would be a story about the phenomenon of *passive* identification mentioned earlier. On this sort of account, then, Huck may indeed be passively identified with his action, despite his own conscious judgments to the contrary, and such a story would allow the conditions of the RSV still to be necessary for moral responsibility.

As I said, much more is needed to fill in fully adequate responses to these objections. The more worrisome objections, though, are (1) and (2), for it seems initially compelling to think that, even if some of the actions for which I'm morally responsible do not flow ultimately from my deep self, surely on the occasions when they do I must be morally responsible for them. After all, if some action is fully representative of *me*, one that flowed from a will I fully authorized, how could I not be responsible for it?

Responsibility for selves and normative competence

According to the first objection, nevertheless, I might not be responsible in cases where my real self was insane, brainwashed, or the product of serious deprivation, trauma, or manipulation. There might be various replies offered here, depending on how the cases are fleshed out, including a denial that the agent in question still has a real self, a denial that the identified 'real self' is the agent's *actual* real self, or a bullet-biting denial that the agent is non-responsible.[24] But none of these approaches initially seems very plausible, and that's because the RSV as it stands focuses exclusively on how the self is related to its actions, independently of how that self is or is not related to the world and the people around it. But as Watson puts it, 'Holding people responsible is not just a matter of the relation of an individual to her behavior; it also involves a social setting in which we demand (require) certain conduct from one another and respond adversely to one another's failures to comply with these demands' (Watson 2004: 262). What's missing from the RSV, in other words, is the condition of *normative competence*.[25]

This seems to me to be correct in one sense. It is indeed true that what is essential to being *accountable to others* is not just that one's actions are self-determined but that one also has the capacity to determine those actions in light of the moral demands of others. A fully self-determined psychotic remains outside the boundaries of our moral community. Of course, what counts as normative competence is a matter of some controversy. For some, it involves a facility for grasping and applying moral reasons (e.g. Wallace 1994); for others, it involves in addition a certain sort of emotional capacity (D. Shoemaker 2007*b*). But at any rate it is still

---

[24] See e.g. Frankfurt 1975: 52–4, for the first and third of these approaches.
[25] On this terminology, see Benson 1987, as well as Watson 1996.

possible that certain actions could be one's own—those with which one identifies, that are properly attributable to one's self—without one's being *accountable* for them, and so without one's necessarily having the requisite normative competence. This conclusion is still compatible with The Platitude, of course, which claims only that ownership is a necessary condition for moral responsibility. The question, then, is whether or not accountability is the whole of moral responsibility.

Two faces of responsibility

Watson says No, and it is in his development of this answer that he responds to Wolf's second objection above (Watson 1996). Recall that objection: merely to attribute some bad action to a self is really just to hold that self *causally* responsible for the bad action, which is responsibility only in a superficial sense. Deep responsibility, truly *moral* responsibility, it is implied, consists only in the kind of *holding accountable* that requires the aforementioned normative competence, a proper orientation to and facility with the moral world.

Watson, however, defends the sort of attributability Wolf derides as a distinct, but nevertheless deep, face of true moral responsibility. On this face—called variously 'responsibility as attributability', or 'aretaic appraisal', or 'the self-disclosure view'—to make the relevant assessment of someone is to attribute an action, say, to some character trait—good or bad—in the agent. So if I risk my life in saving someone, that action is traceable to my character: *I* am courageous. My action was expressive of my ends and values, and insofar as *that* is the target of others' attributive judgments, it is surely sufficiently deep: 'To adopt an end, to commit oneself to a conception of value in this way, is a way of taking responsibility', for it is an expression of one's *practical* identity, and as such it has 'ethical depth in an obvious sense' (Watson 2004: 271).

The RSV, therefore, might best be construed as simply a view of responsibility as attributability, and not (or not necessarily) as a view of responsibility as accountability. One is eligible for a judgment of responsibility on the former face when one's action is ultimately dependent on—and thus properly attributable to—one's real self. And this could be the case even if one lacked a robust sort of normative competence: a psychopath's actions could be judged cruel, or manipulative, even if he lacked the ability to truly grasp or apply moral reasons and be accountable to us thereby.[26]

Does this account thwart Wolf's objection to the RSV? Is a judgment of attributability—an assignation of a moral predicate—to someone a sufficiently robust form of moral responsibility? Angela Smith (2008) thinks a severe ambiguity runs throughout the account, preventing it from being a successful way for an RSV

---

[26] On this point, see Watson (forthcoming) and D. Shoemaker (2009).

advocate (like herself) to fend off Wolf's attack. Watson is attempting to articulate a conception of responsibility that falls in between the 'praise and dispraise' model of mere good and bad action-making (causal responsibility) and full-throated moral blame (Smith 2008: 377). At some points, though, the conception he articulates sounds like nothing more than the former, and at other points like nothing less than the latter, according to Smith.

To explain, Watson suggests that what's involved in responsibility as attributability is the assignation of various moral predicates. But to call someone's behavior 'shoddy', say, or 'cruel' or 'manipulative' is either to express censure or it isn't. If it does express censure, then it doesn't seem distinct from an accountability assessment, for it is a form of blaming activity Watson reserves only for those assessments the targeted agent had a fair opportunity to avoid (Watson 2004: 276). And Smith insists it is difficult to see this as anything but censure: '"Shoddy"... implies a certain meanness or contemptibility, a despicable lack of concern for the interests of others; one cannot apply such an epithet to a person's conduct, it seems, without expressing some degree of condemnation for it' (Smith 2008: 377). This seems false, though. I may be quite callous and bet you (an equally callous person) that someone we both know will treat his girlfriend in a shoddy manner at dinner. When he does, I am delighted (for I've won the bet). That his behavior was shoddy we both agree on, yet neither of us may express any condemnation whatsoever for it.[27]

Continuing with Smith's analysis, though, if there is no censure expressed in such an assessment, then how is it anything more than dispraise, a judgment that simply reports on how the agent's conduct stands with respect to some moral standard without bringing with it 'any further implications of fault or discredit' (Smith 2008: 377), a mere grading evaluation? Calling someone 'shoddy' or 'cruel' would simply be akin to calling him 'ugly' or 'near-sighted'. But if this is all that's going on with judgments of attributability, it is hard to see how such assessments are deep in any interesting sense at all.

There is a difference, though, between the judgments of our callous countertypes above and the judgments of this sort that most of us actually make. Smith is right to some extent: for *most* people, a judgment of shoddiness is attached to a negative attitude, typically condemnation. Does this attitude make the judgment *censure*, though, an accountability assessment? Not quite. But it is also more than mere grading. Consider the latter point first. When I judge your behavior to be cruel, say, I am typically finding fault with *you*, and not just finding that your behavior falls below some standard of excellence. I am tracing this behavior to a flaw in your character, tracing it to your self. And accompanying this judgment is also typically a negative attitude (more on just what these attitudes are in a moment).

[27] Cf., the series of cases introduced in McKenna and Vadakin 2008.

This isn't necessarily yet an accountability assessment, though, insofar as a judgment of this sort doesn't necessarily *hold* its object *to account*, that is, an expression of the judgment doesn't yet constitute any form of moral address, censure, or sanction. Relatedly, responsibility as accountability (on the negative side) is most often marked by the familiar set of reactive attitudes, led in particular by resentment (by those wronged), indignation (by those witnessing or aware of wrongs to others), and guilt (by those doing the wronging) (Strawson 1962). But while there are negative attitudes that typically accompany aretaic appraisals, they don't seem culled from this 'accountability set'. Instead, the attitudes associated with negative attributability judgments include horror, disgust, scorn, hatred, embarrassment, and even a kind of stunned bewilderment ('How could you *do* such a thing?!'). And on the positive side of the map, whereas the reactive attitudes associated with assessments of accountability include gratitude, love, and respect, the attitudes associated with assessments of attributability include admiration, pride, and a head-shaking sort of wonder.

Attributability-responsibility is necessary for accountability-responsibility on Watson's picture (Watson 2004: 263), and often the two are concurrently deployed.[28] This may actually be why Smith thinks the attitude associated with judgments of shoddiness is condemnation, then, for one also typically holds to account the person whose behavior one judges to be shoddy, and this is often expressed as a form of censure. Nevertheless, it is possible to imagine making such judgments about someone without offering the additional moral address to her that is constitutive of accountability.[29] In such a scenario, the attributability-attitudes I've pointed to are nevertheless likely to be present: alongside a judgment of cowardice often comes embarrassment (for the target agent); alongside a judgment of cruelty comes horror or disgust; alongside a judgment of insensitivity comes a recoiled cringe.[30]

A dramatic way to see this point is to consider psychopaths, agents who, absent any developed emotional capacities, are deaf to the appeal of moral reasons.[31]

---

[28] Is attributability actually necessary for accountability? I'm not so sure. It seems possible to be accountable for actions that don't express one's ends or reflect one's stand-taking evaluative self, as in, perhaps, the earlier-explored case of whims, Watson's own 'perverse cases' (wherein I judge X to be best but do Y—without compulsion—because it's more fun or stress-free), and cases of the mildly mentally retarded (who may have the emotional capacities to grasp the relevant accountability reasons but may lack the deductive capacities to express their ends in concrete actions—see D. Shoemaker 2007*b* and 2009 for discussion of this last sort of case).

[29] Either one might call the former sort of appraisal non-blame and only the latter appraisal blame, or one might call both sorts blaming appraisals, just of different kinds. I remain neutral on what the best labels might be.

[30] I leave open whether or not the latter in each case actually precedes and/or spurs the former.

[31] The literature on psychopathy is vast. For some excellent philosophical discussions, see Deigh 1995; Duff 1977; Fingarette 1967; Greenspan 2003; Haksar 1965; Kennett 2001; Murphy 1972; Nichols 2004; Talbert 2008. I also discuss psychopathy at length in D. Shoemaker 2007*b*.

Given the fact that they are either unable to grasp or unable to respond to such reasons, they cannot sensibly be held accountable for their actions: if the expression of resentment qua blame, say, is a form of moral address, address which presupposes the intelligibility of such address to the intended audience in order to have a point, and psychopaths find such address unintelligible, then blaming a psychopath for his behavior is pointless.[32] Nevertheless, psychopaths aren't completely off the hook, for various predicates and attitudes clearly seem to apply to them: they can be cruel, manipulative, and just plain old sons of bitches (see e.g. Watson forthcoming), and accompanying these judgments (for those who are aware they're dealing with a psychopath) will be attitudes such as disgust or horror. These responses and attitudes position the psychopath between animals and full-fledged moral persons: they are different from the former insofar as our judgments of their attributability-responsibility are more robust than mere judgments of causal or 'grading' responsibility, but they remain different from the latter, perhaps, insofar as they can't sensibly be held accountable for their actions.

There are less dramatic cases in which this is true as well, for it is not as if the coward or the spendthrift are in any important sense *accountable to us* for that behavior. Nevertheless, they remain the targets of judgments of attributability-responsibility, a kind of moral responsibility that once again seems anything but superficial.[33] The RSV, therefore, has the means within its disposal to resist Wolf's complaint about depth.

Responsibility for attitudes

Despite her objection to Watson about the ambiguity of responsibility as attributability, Smith is also a RSV theorist. What she and like-minded theorists (e.g. Adams 1985; Scanlon 1998; Sher 2006) really take issue with, however, are the two will-based conditions of the view as stated, namely, that for X to be responsible for Y, (1) Y must be governed by X's *will*, and (2) X's *will* must be governed by X's real self. For sometimes, the thought goes, X is responsible for Y where X's will had nothing whatsoever to do with Y. Several cases illustrate the point. Suppose I forget a close friend's birthday, or I am quite insensitive to someone's feelings, or I fail to notice the likes and dislikes of my spouse (all discussed in Smith 2005). In each case I am morally responsible, it seems, despite the fact that what I'm responsible

[32] For this sort of talk of moral address, intelligibility, and the point of expressions of accountability, see Watson 1987b; McKenna 1998.

[33] It seems obvious from these sorts of cases as well that attributability-responsibility isn't necessarily restricted to straightforward *moral* assessments: being a coward or a spendthrift may be purely prudential assessments (or perhaps even *aesthetic* assessments). My only point here, though, is just that when our attributability assessments *are* about moral flaws, the level of responsibility attached surely has significant depth.

for—my forgetting, my insensitivity, and my failure to notice—aren't governed by or otherwise the product of my will at all. They are, in other words, *nonvoluntary*.[34]

Smith's focus is on the *attitudes* for which one may be responsible, attitudes which are beyond one's voluntary choice or control. The cases are indeed compelling, and insofar as attributability is assumed to require control, it might look like so much the worse for attributability as a condition of moral responsibility. But there is a clear reply: why assume attributability requires control? Why think, in other words, that in order for something to be properly attributable to me it must be governed by my will? After all, my insensitivity or my forgetfulness seems just as much *mine*, still bearing as much of an essential relation to my moral self, as some action I performed because I genuinely wanted to. In both cases one may be called on for *justification*, to answer for what one has done or expressed, and in both cases the various reactive attitudes involved in a breach of the moral demand may be identical in both kind and force.

What one may do, then, is preserve the RSV by altering the central conditions to more accurately reflect the reality of our responsibility practices. So instead of focusing solely on actions, the view can incorporate attitudes as well. And instead of requiring the item for which one is morally responsible to be subject to one's voluntary control (i.e. governed by one's will), one could formulate a more expansive condition, one that explains both the appropriate relation between the actions/attitudes and one's self as well as how one can be answerable for attitudes outside of one's control. In proceeding in this way, for example, Scanlon replaces the condition of control with a requirement that one's attitudes, say, be judgment-sensitive (Scanlon 1998: ch. 6); Sher requires instead that one's attitudes be expressive of one's character or go to make up the person one is (Sher 2006: 298–301); and Smith herself proposes that a mental state is properly attributable to someone when it directly reflects, or is governable by, her evaluative judgments and commitments (Smith 2005: 250–64). But at any rate, it seems clear that one can adjust the RSV in some fashion to account for these cases while preserving the central insight that moral responsibility is grounded in facts about the self-expression of agents.

The question, though, is whether or not making this move eliminates the need to preserve a distinction between responsibility-as-attributability and responsibility-as-accountability. Smith says yes. She takes the ordinary sense of moral responsibility

---

[34] George Sher details three general sorts of case that also fit the nonvoluntary-but-nevertheless-responsible bill, cases wherein the responsible agent does something wrong as a result of (*a*) being forgetful or having a lapse of attention (e.g. leaving one's dog in a hot car to the point of death when one is distracted at the store); (*b*) displaying poor judgment (e.g. giving a colicky baby vodka to get it to sleep); or (*c*) lacking moral insight (e.g. telling an offensive joke) (Sher 2006: 286–91).
In all these sorts of instances, argues Sher, the agent is responsible for having done something wrong that she nevertheless does not *recognize* as wrong, and so if will-governed (voluntarily controlled) action requires such conscious awareness, X's moral responsibility for Y does not require governance of or by X's will at all.

to be about accountability, and she insists that her version of the RSV (what she calls 'the rational relations view') 'is working with full-blooded notions of moral apprais-al, blame, and criticism' (Smith 2008: 379–80). This is because these accountability notions (*a*) 'imply something about our *activity* as rational agents' (Smith 2008: 380; emphasis in original), and (*b*) address moral demands for justification to their targets. On a view like hers, then, to morally criticize someone is to assess her in light of what flows from her practical agency, which is an agency that ranges over not only the choices one makes but also one's 'rational judgments and assessments quite generally' (Smith 2008: 381). This means not only that one's actions and attitudes are subject to moral appraisals but also that the appraisals in both cases are *accountability* appraisals. It looks, then, as if responsibility-as-attributability isn't a face of respon-sibility distinct from accountability after all (Smith 2008: 377).

This is too quick, however, for it leaves us without a response to the psychopath. The psychopath is, in some sense, a rational agent, engaged in rational activity (e.g. he has ends he is concerned to advance efficiently), but he is not an appropriate subject of our moral demands insofar as he is incapable of grasping or responding to moral reasons. He is more than an animal but less than a fully moral self. So while it is pointless to hold him to account, he nevertheless may aim to do us harm and is capable of cruelty, manipulativeness, and so forth. It is hard to see how Smith might account for this case. We certainly do assess psychopaths as responsi-ble at times (e.g. in legal contexts) and we may well express certain sorts of reactive attitudes and related responsibility judgments about them. But it remains pointless to censure them or subject them to robust moral criticism insofar as they're incapable of hearing or replying to such a moral demand. If, on the RSV, there is no relevant distinction between attributability-assessments and full-fledged accountability-assessments, then the view has no room for an attributability assess-ment of the psychopath *sans* an accountability assessment, which is precisely what seems required. There may be good reason, then, to preserve the distinction, and if we remind ourselves of the fact that attributability judgments may be quite robust and deep themselves (and come equipped with their own set of reactive attitudes), the motivation for eliminating the distinction may be undermined altogether.[35]

CONCLUSION

It is time to weave together the disparate threads of this dialectic into a coherent whole. We began with The Platitude: one can be morally responsible only for one's

---

[35] For more on this sort of distinction as applied to the psychopath, see Watson forthcoming and Shoemaker 2009.

own actions. Our aim was to discover just what The Platitude means and what the conditions of its application are. Here is what we have found.

1. The Platitude is not about personal identity, either numerical or narrative. Many philosophers have taken The Platitude to entail The Slogan—that moral responsibility presupposes personal identity—and they have appealed to The Slogan to provide a plausibility check on various competing theories of personal identity, such that if an application of a theory into the criterion of action ownership met with counterexamples, the theory was rendered worse off. This methodology yields serious problems for *all* theories of personal identity, however. The best move methodologically, then, is to cease applying theories of identity to the criterion of ownership. But not only is this the best argumentative strategy, it is also, more importantly, warranted by the conceptual gap found between ownership and identity, a point illustrated by consideration of joint actions and actions dependent on the will of another (e.g. the general and his troops). The most that's entailed by The Platitude, then, is that moral responsibility presupposes *ownership*: for me to be morally responsible for some action, it must be attributable to me, and this may be true regardless of whether or not I'm identical with the person who performed the action. The key to understanding the nature of The Platitude, then, is to understand the nature of attributability.

2. Attributability seems less about identity, then, than identification: an action is mine just in case I identify with it or the psychic elements from which it flows. When this idea is incorporated into The Platitude, therefore, we get the view that one is morally responsible only for those actions (that depend on psychic states) with which one identifies. This sort of view has an important problem, however. Suppose that identification is taken to be (as most take it to be) only an *active* process, wherein one consciously endorses or embraces some action or psychic element as one's own. If so, then it seems there are cases in which one may be morally responsible for an action with which one doesn't identify—that attributability of this sort is in fact *not* necessary for moral responsibility—because an action may be properly attributable to one without one's conscious endorsement of it (or even despite one's conscious endorsement of a contrary action/element). This is true, for instance, in cases of negligence, whims, and inverse *akrasia*.

One answer, however, is to point out that identification is not exclusively an active process; there may well be cases of passive identification. So in acting on a whim or in being negligent, I may well be passively identified with my indulgent or insensitive traits, those that give rise to the action (or inaction). And in acting *akratically* (inverse or otherwise), I may be passively identified with my action or the psychic element(s) on which it depends insofar as it is grounded ultimately in my nexus of cares (i.e. emotional commitments), regardless of any active judgments or endorsements made. Given our experience with our own selves, it should be obvious that what we think or judge our real selves to consist in may have little (or even no) overlap with what our real selves actually consist in.

3. Encouraged by the fact that attributability qua identification does seem necessary for moral responsibility, then, one might attempt something more ambitious by holding that it is also *sufficient* for moral responsibility. This is just what the advocates of the RSV attempt. Against this move there is a powerful objection, viz., that attributability on its own provides only a very superficial sort of responsibility, one that is neither moral nor particularly interesting (as it is essentially about just causal responsibility). In response, one may mark a distinction between two faces, or senses, of responsibility, and then maintain that while the RSV isn't about the accountability face of responsibility, it is nevertheless about the attributability face, which itself may be moral and is sufficiently deep. One way I have suggested this position may be advanced is by considering the sorts of reactive attitudes that are expected and appropriate in light of various actions, attitudes distinct from, and responding to different features of agents than, the set of reactive attitudes typically associated with the accountability face. Another way is to consider the case of the psychopath, who lacks the requisite conditions for accountability but who nevertheless seems an appropriate target of attributability-judgments. Responsibility-as-attributability thus seems a legitimately deep form of moral responsibility in its own right. It is not demand-based, as is responsibility-as-accountability, but its judgments involve more than mere gradings.

4. In sum, then, to say that one can be morally responsible only for one's own actions may be taken to mean that one is eligible for judgments of *attributability-*responsibility only for those actions with which one is identified (note the passive construction), where this refers to those actions flowing ultimately from one's real self, itself constituted by one's various evaluative commitments.[36] Indeed, one might say that The Platitude is less about *personal* identity than it is about *practical* identity. And insofar as the relevant sort of identification involved in one's practical identity is not restricted by considerations of numerical or narrative identity, it remains possible that one may be identified with the actions of *other* people, a point which may have implications for questions of collective responsibility. In addition, The Platitude as it stands may well be expanded in two ways. First, one could, it seems, have it incorporate not only actions but *attitudes*: insofar as these may flow as well from my real self, the expanded Platitude could account for the judgments of responsibility we have in response to them. Second, a version of The Platitude restricted to just responsibility-as-attributability might advance a stronger claim, namely, that one is morally responsible (on this face) for *all and only* one's own actions. Whether this change is worth making depends on the RSV's

---

[36] While I haven't really discussed this last aspect of Smith's Real Self View, I think it's crucial that 'evaluative commitments' include emotional commitments, i.e. carings, as well as judgments of value.

success in fending off various important challenges, a task I have undertaken only briefly here but which does have, I believe, genuine promise.

References

ADAMS, ROBERT M. (1985). 'Involuntary Sins', *Philosophical Review*, 93: 3–31.

ARPALY, NOMY (2003). *Unprincipled Virtue: An Inquiry into Moral Agency* (Oxford: Oxford University Press).

——and SCHROEDER, TIMOTHY (1999). 'Alienation and Externality', *Canadian Journal of Philosophy*, 29: 371–87.

BENSON, PAUL (1987). 'Freedom and Value', *Journal of Philosophy*, 84: 465–86.

BRATMAN, MICHAEL E. (1992). 'Shared Cooperative Activity', *Philosophical Review*, 101: 327–41.

——(2007). *Structures of Agency* (Oxford: Oxford University Press).

BUSS, SARAH, and OVERTON, LEE, eds. (2002). *Contours of Agency: Essays on Themes from Harry Frankfurt* (Cambridge, Mass.: MIT Press).

BUTLER, JOSEPH (1736). 'Of Personal Identity', *The Analogy of Religion*. Repr. in Perry (1975: 99–105).

Dancy, Jonathan (ed.) (1997). *Reading Parfit* (Oxford: Blackwell).

DeGRAZIA, DAVID (2005). *Human Identity and Bioethics* (Cambridge: Cambridge University Press).

DEIGH, JOHN (1995). 'Empathy and Universalizability', *Ethics*, 105: 743–63.

DUFF, ANTONY (1977). 'Psychopathy and Moral Understanding', *American Philosophical Quarterly*, 14: 189–200.

FINGARETTE, HERBERT (1967). *On Responsibility* (New York: Basic).

FISCHER, JOHN MARTIN (2006). *My Way: Essays on Moral Responsibility* (Oxford: Oxford University Press).

——and RAVIZZA, MARK (1998). *Responsibility and Control: A Theory of Moral Responsibility* (Cambridge: Cambridge University Press).

FRANKFURT, HARRY (1971). 'Freedom of the Will and the Concept of a Person', *Journal of Philosophy*, 68: 5–20. Repr. in Frankfurt (1988: 11–25).

——(1975). 'Three Concepts of Free Action', *Proceedings of the Aristotelian Society*, suppl. vol. Repr. in Frankfurt (1988: 47–57).

——(1976). 'Identification and Externality', in Rorty (1976: 239–51), repr. in Frankfurt (1988: 58–68).

——(1978). 'The Problem of Action', *American Philosophical Quarterly*, 15: 157–62. Repr. in Frankfurt (1988: 69–79).

——(1987). 'Identification and Wholeheartedness', in Schoeman (1987: 27–45), repr. in Frankfurt (1988: 159–76).

——(1988). *The Importance of What we Care about* (Cambridge: Cambridge University Press).

——(1992). 'The Faintest Passion', *Proceedings and Addresses of the American Philosophical Association*, 66; repr. in Frankfurt (1999: 95–107).

——(1999). *Necessity, Volition, and Love* (Cambridge: Cambridge University Press).

——(2002). 'Reply to Michael E. Bratman', in Buss and Overton (2002: 86–90).

GLANNON, WALTER. (1998). 'Moral Responsibility and Personal Identity', *American Philosophical Quarterly*, 35: 231–49.

GREENSPAN, PATRICIA (2003). 'Responsible Psychopaths', *Philosophical Psychology*, 16: 417–29.

HAKSAR, VINIT (1965). 'The Responsibility of Psychopaths', *Philosophical Quarterly*, 15: 135–45.

——(1980). *Equality, Liberty, and Perfectionism* (Oxford: Oxford University Press).

JOHNSTON, MARK (1989). 'Fission and the Facts', *Philosophical Perspectives*, 3: 369–97.

——(1992). 'Reasons and Reductionism', *Philosophical Review*, 101: 589–618.

——(1997). 'Human Concerns without Superlative Selves', in Dancy (1997: 149–79), repr. in Martin and Barresi (2003: 260–91).

KENNETT, JEANNETTE (2001). *Agency and Responsibility* (Oxford: Oxford University Press).

LEWIS, DAVID (1976). 'Survival and Identity', in Amelie Oksenberg Rorty (ed.), *The Identities of Persons* (Berkeley, Calif.: University of California Press).

LIPPERT-RASMUSSEN, KASPER (2003). 'Identification and Responsibility', *Ethical Theory and Moral Practice*, 6: 349–76.

LOCKE, DON (1975). 'Three Concepts of Free Action: I', *Proceedings of the Aristotelian Society*, suppl. 49: 95–112.

LOCKE, JOHN (1694). 'Of Identity and Diversity', *Essay Concerning Human Understanding*, in Perry (1975: 33–52).

McKENNA, MICHAEL (1998). 'The Limits of Evil and the Role of Moral Address: A Defense of Strawsonian Compatibilism', *Journal of Ethics*, 2: 123–42.

——and VADAKIN, ARON (2008). 'Review of George Sher's *In Praise of Blame*', *Ethics*, 118: 751–6.

MADELL, GEOFFREY (1981). *The Identity of the Self* (Edinburgh: Edinburgh University Press).

MARTIN, RAYMOND, and BARRESI, JOHN (eds) (2003). *Personal Identity* (Oxford: Blackwell).

MURPHY, JEFFREY (1972). 'Moral Death: A Kantian Essay on Psychopathy', *Ethics*, 82: 284–98.

NICHOLS, SHAUN (2004). *Sentimental Rules* (Oxford: Oxford University Press).

OLSON, ERIC T. (1997). *The Human Animal: Personal Identity without Psychology* (Oxford: Oxford University Press).

PARFIT, DEREK (1984). *Reasons and Persons* (Oxford: Oxford University Press).

——(1986). 'Comments', *Ethics*, 96: 832–72.

PERRY, JOHN (ed.) (1975). *Personal Identity* (Berkeley, Calif.: University of California Press).

REID, THOMAS (1785). 'Of Mr. Locke's Account of Our Personal Identity', *Essays on the Intellectual Powers of Man*, in Perry (1975: 113–18).

RORTY, AMELIE OKSENBERG (ed.) (1976). *The Identities of Persons* (Berkeley, Calif.: University of California Press).

SCANLON, T. M. (1998). *What we Owe to Each Other* (Cambridge, Mass.: Harvard University Press).

SCHECHTMAN, MARYA (1996). *The Constitution of Selves* (Ithaca, NY: Cornell University Press).

SCHOEMAN, FERDINAND (ed.) (1987). *Responsibility, Character, and the Emotions* (Cambridge: Cambridge University Press).

SHER, GEORGE (2006). 'Out of Control', *Ethics*, 116: 285–301.

SHOEMAKER, DAVID W. (2003). 'Caring, Identification, and Agency', *Ethics*, 114: 88–118.

——(2007*a*). 'Personal Identity and Practical Concerns', *Mind*, 116: 317–57.

——(2007*b*). 'Moral Address, Moral Responsibility, and the Boundaries of the Moral Community', *Ethics*, 118: 70–108.

——(2009). 'Responsibility and Disability', *Metaphilosophy*, 40: 438–61.

SHOEMAKER, SYDNEY (1970). 'Persons and their Pasts', *American Philosophical Quarterly*, 7: 269–85.

SIDER, THEODORE (2001). *Four-Dimensionalism* (Oxford: Oxford University Press).

SMITH, ANGELA M. (2005). 'Responsibility for Attitudes: Activity and Passivity in Mental Life', *Ethics*, 115: 236–71.

——(2008). 'Control, Responsibility, and Moral Assessment', *Philosophical Studies*, 138: 367–92.

STRAWSON, PETER (1962). 'Freedom and Resentment', *Proceedings of the British Academy*, 48: 1–25.

STUMP, ELEONORE (1988). 'Sanctification, Hardening of the Heart, and Frankfurt's Concept of Free Will', *Journal of Philosophy*, 85: 395–420.

——(1996). 'Persons: Identification and Freedom', *Philosophical Topics*, 24: 183–214.

TALBERT, MATT (2008). 'Blame and Responsiveness to Moral Reasons: Are Psychopaths Blameworthy?', *Pacific Philosophical Quarterly*, 89: 516–35.

TAYLOR, CHARLES (1976). 'Responsibility for Self', in Rorty (1976: 281–99).

VELLEMAN, J. DAVID (2000). *The Possibility of Practical Reason* (Oxford: Oxford University Press).

——(2002). 'Identification and Identity', in Buss and Overton (2002: 91–123).

WALLACE, R. JAY (1994). *Responsibility and the Moral Sentiments* (Cambridge, Mass.: Harvard University Press).

WATSON, GARY (1975). 'Free Agency', *Journal of Philosophy*, 72: 205–20. Repr. in Watson (2004: 13–32).

——(1987*a*). 'Free Action and Free Will', *Mind*, 96: 145–72. Repr. in Watson (2004: 161–96).

——(1987*b*). 'Responsibility and the Limits of Evil: Variations on a Strawsonian Theme', in Schoeman (1987: 256–86). Repr. in Watson (2004: 219–59).

——(1996). 'Two Faces of Responsibility', *Philosophical Topics*, 24: 227–48. Repr. in Watson (2004: 260–88).

——(2004). *Agency and Answerability* (Oxford: Oxford University Press).

——(forthcoming). 'Psychopathic Agency'.

WOLF, SUSAN (1987). 'Sanity and the Metaphysics of Moral Responsibility', in Schoeman (1987: 46–62).

——(1990). *Freedom within Reason* (Oxford: Oxford University Press).

PART VI

SELF PATHOLOGIES

CHAPTER 22

THE STRUCTURE OF SELF- CONSCIOUSNESS IN SCHIZOPHRENIA

JOSEF PARNAS

LOUIS A. SASS

INTRODUCTION

Then something odd happens. My awareness of myself, of my father, of the room, of the physical reality around and beyond us instantly grows fuzzy. Or wobbly. I think I am dissolving, I feel—my mind feels—like a sand castle with all the sand sliding away in the receding surf... Consciousness gradually loses its coherence. One's center gives way... [it] cannot hold. The 'me' becomes a haze, and the solid center from which one experiences reality breaks up... There is no longer a sturdy vantage point from which to look out, take things in, assess... No core holds things together, providing the lens through which we see the world. (Saks 2007: 12)

This first-person account of anomalous self-experience, at the age of 7 years, is taken from a recent autobiography, *The Center Can Not Hold*, written by Elyn Saks, who has suffered from schizophrenia for most of her life. It presents in a dramatic way the anomalies of self-consciousness that occur in schizophrenia (and other schizophrenia spectrum conditions) and that are the topic of this chapter. An attempt will be made to present characteristic phenomenological features of abnormal self-experience that occur already during the early, pre-psychotic stages of schizophrenia.

The presentation and interpretation of self-pathology—and its philosophical implications—will be rooted in a phenomenological reflection on the nature of the self, self-consciousness, and phenomenality. Here, the term 'phenomenology' is used in its standard continental philosophical sense—to refer to the study of 'lived experience' or the *subjective* dimension of mental disorders. Our purpose is dual: to gain a better grasp of the phenomenology of the self in general and also of the psychopathological architecture of disordered self in schizophrenia in particular. Psychopathology will serve here as a means to validate phenomenological claims regarding the structure of self-consciousness. In the phenomenological psychiatric tradition, it is generally assumed that psychopathology, especially of schizophrenia, may help to inform us about normally tacit, taken-for-granted features and structures of experience and its conditions of possibility.

Addressing phenomenology and the nature of self-pathology in psychiatric disorders must meet certain constraints; here we will mention but one. This is that theoretical contributions must do descriptive justice to the investigated anomalous experiential phenomena. Descriptive and theoretical effort must consider potential links to other, co-occurring abnormal experiences, rather than focusing exclusively on a single, atomized feature that happens to fit with a selected theoretical model. The patient's subjective experience is the ultimate arbiter of validity. For this reason, there is always 'something fragile about phenomenology: it requires a kind of living contact with thinking and clinical experience to be at its best' (Owen 2009). As an example of this problem, we will mention the symptom of 'thought insertion'. This symptom has been widely written about in the theoretical literature (following the publication of Frith 1992, whose illustrative case vignette is reiterated in countless articles), yet without recognizing or accounting for various crucial phenomenological aspects of 'thought insertion': namely, that it is a part of an experiential continuum with variable phenomenological profiles (ranging from a vague sense of alienation to frank delusion); that it frequently co-occurs with other, related phenomena, especially thought broadcasting, other passivity phenomena, and *Gedankenlautwerden* (thoughts-aloud); and that it is usually accompanied by diminished self-presence (Nordgaard *et al.* 2008)—the topic that we address below. The point highlights the importance of the richness and representative nature of the psychiatric data used for philosophical reflection.

SELF AND SCHIZOPHRENIA: HISTORICAL ASPECTS

From the very introduction of the concept of schizophrenia, it has been recognized that this illness involves profound transformations of the self. But although both founders of this diagnostic category (the psychiatrists Emil Kraepelin and Eugen Bleuler) considered pathology of self as quite essential in defining schizophrenia, they presented no concrete and systematic, clinical descriptions of anomalous *self-experience*. It seems correct to say that they *inferred pathology of the self* from a symptomatic picture marked by manifold forms of internal contradiction, disorganization and dissociation. Emil Kraepelin (1919/1971) spoke of 'loss of inner unity of consciousness' and 'devastation of the will' ('orchestra without a conductor') as *core* features of schizophrenia. Eugen Bleuler (1911/1950: 143) wrote that the patient's ego tends to undergo 'the most manifold alterations', for example, splitting and loss of the directedness of thinking. Only occasionally do we find in these texts any reference to *phenomenal anomalies of self-consciousness*, such as *Bennomenheit* (diminished clarity) or 'transitivism', an experience of diminished privacy of one's mental states ('loss of ego-boundaries'). Thus, on the whole, disorder of self was not conceived as a particular domain or species of experience but more as a *construct*, something *inferred* from the characteristic psychotic disintegrations of thinking, feeling, perceiving, and willing.

Excellent clinical descriptions of anomalies of self-experience were, however, published by several French authors toward the end of nineteenth and beginning of the twentieth centuries, for example, Janet, Hesnard, and Blondel.[1] The concept of schizophrenia was slow, however, in finding a solid foothold in the French classification system, a historic circumstance that weakened potential diagnostic (nosological) impact of these studies. The descriptions of experiential anomalies as an essential component of the schizophrenia spectrum did however appear regularly in the continental phenomenological psychiatric tradition, for example, in the work of Berze (1914), Kronfeld (1922), Minkowski (1927), Binswanger (1956), Conrad (1957), Blankenburg (1971), and Kimura Bin (1992). Except for a few excerpts and one excellent anthology (Cutting and Shepherd 1987), these studies are untranslated into English and are basically unknown in the English-speaking world (for English-language discussion of these contributions, see Parnas and Bovet 1991; Sass 2001).

In 1914 Joseph Berze, a Viennese psychiatrist, published a unique, extensive monograph with rich phenomenological descriptions of anomalies of experience

---

[1] The relative thematic prominence of subjectivity in the French psychiatric literature is largely due to a strong influence of Henri Bergson, whose doctoral dissertation on the structures of consciousness was widely read in psychology and psychiatry. Bergson's friend William James was not comparably influential in Anglophone psychiatry.

in schizophrenia. Berze concluded that the primary disorder in schizophrenia resided in *diminished*, unstable, or *waning* states of awareness, suggesting the term '*hypo*-phrenia' instead of *schizo*-phrenia. Beginning in the 1960s, Berze's descriptive project was reactivated in Germany by a group of researchers who set out systematically to map the anomalies of experience in schizophrenia (the so-called 'basic symptom' approach of Huber 1983).

The concept of self is not mentioned in the current diagnostic criteria for schizophrenia of either DSM IV or ICD 10. Depersonalization is listed as one optional feature among many defining the schizotypal disorders.

RECENT EMPIRICAL FINDINGS

The contemporary systematic empirical work on self-disorders was motivated by clinical experience accumulated during several years' work in a Danish psychiatric unit dedicated to diagnosis and treatment of young, first-contact patients suspected of suffering from a schizophrenia-spectrum disorder. It was striking that the main complaints of these patients, taken at face value, monotonously circled around the themes of lacking immersion in the world, weakened sense of being a self-present subject, and various other, quite general deformations of experience. What they described was not solely a change in the *contents* of consciousness (e.g. ruminations). Rather, their complaints seemed to point to the disruptions of *formal* or *structural* aspects of subjectivity as well.

Two subsequent, pilot assessments of consecutively admitted patients with beginning schizophrenia, independently conducted in Norway and Denmark (Møller and Husby 2001; Parnas *et al.* 1998), confirmed these clinical intuitions in a systematic manner.

These initial findings were subsequently replicated in a study comparing residual schizophrenia and bipolar illness in remission (Parnas *et al.* 2003), and a longitudinal, five-year follow-up study of 155 first admitted patients (two-thirds with a schizophrenia spectrum disorder) (Parnas *et al.* 2005). In the latter study, self-disorders recorded at first admission not only strongly discriminated spectrum from non-spectrum diagnoses, but were, moreover, predictive of subsequent incident (new) cases of schizophrenia-spectrum disorders (Vollmer-Larsen 2008). The analyses of a large genetic sample ($n = 305$) with ninety persons with a schizophrenia-spectrum diagnosis (Raballo *et al.* 2009) showed that self-disorders discriminated strongly between spectrum conditions and other, non-spectrum psychiatric disorders. Notably, self-disorders were *nearly absent* in the individuals without any psychiatric diagnosis. The reliability of the measures of anomalies of experience employed in these studies was highly satisfactory (Vollmer-Larsen *et al.* 2007). Recently, we published a psychopathological, phenomenologically oriented instrument for recording the qualities of self-disorders and their intensity (EASE: Parnas *et al.* 2005*b*).

Collectively, these studies demonstrate that self-disorders (1) aggregate significantly and *selectively* in the schizophrenia-spectrum disorders (schizophrenia and schizotypal disorder), (2) have a tendency to persist, (3) occur in adolescents considered to be at risk of future psychotic mental disorder, and (4) are detectable before the onset of the syndromatic phases of the illness.

SELF-CONSCIOUSNESS: SENSE OF SELF, FIRST-PERSON PERSPECTIVE, AND PHENOMENALITY

We will try to sketch the phenomenological structure of first-person presence with its inchoate, substantial sense of embodied subjectivity. This structure merits the label of 'minimal or 'core' self' (Zahavi 2005), for it refers to a minimum of what must be the case for an experience to be considered 'subjective' at all. (It can also be referred to as 'ipseity'; see Parnas 2000; Sass and Parnas 2003, 2007.) Minimal self is a necessary foundation for the articulation of a richer or sophisticated, *reflective*, language-bound, narrative selfhood, with its representational elements and dispositions. Yet, saying that the minimal self is *necessary* may be conductive to an erroneous assumption that it is a sort of prior foundation, the pre-existing ground for the *subsequent* stages in a diachronic development. In reality, the ontogenetic development of selfhood is likely to be complex from the very outset, in the sense of being dependent on the infant's or child's bodily needs, structure, and dispositions, and co-constituted through intersubjective interactions (see Chapter 2 above).

Self-consciousness and self-reference

The notions of self and self-reference logically presuppose self-consciousness. We will start by looking at the distinctions between self-consciousness, first-person perspective, and awareness *of* self. Self-consciousness refers to the fact that experience is familiar with *itself* or *knows itself*, or that consciousness is in some sense *intrinsically* reflexive. For instance, in looking at a landscape, I am not only aware of the objects in my visual field but am also aware, in a tacit way, of the fact that I am, in fact, *seeing* something (and not e.g. hearing it) and that I exist, in some sense, as a kind of subjective presence. It can be argued that self-consciousness, in this case the *self-presence of seeing*, is, in fact, a condition of the appearance of the visual object. As the French phenomenological philosopher Michel Henry puts it, 'self-manifestation is the essence of manifestation' (1973: 143). Without such self-manifestation of seeing, that is, without some implicit awareness *of* our seeing, we could not, in fact, be said to see or to be conscious of the visual object or visual field present to our awareness. Self-consciousness of seeing is thus not some *extra* consciousness added on to the (independent) appearance of the object; it is not something lurking 'in the background', margins of awareness,[2] or just beyond the attentional focus. Rather, this consciousness is, in a sense, everywhere and no-where: it '*is at the very center—but not object*' (Fasching 2008: 474; emphasis added).

One's awareness or sense of self—of *the subjective sense of presence* and of *the presence of a self*—involves an awareness or intuition of existing as a singular, unified, temporally persisting subject (Albahari 2006). A key question to ask is whether we are dealing here with a fundamental *belief* (formed, in some sense, after the fact) or whether this experience of subjecthood is, rather, inherent—an *integral and necessary part of experience* itself (hence the term 'sense of'). Our claim here is that self-consciousness blends *experientially* into self-reference; in other words, that the implicit self-consciousness pervading experience ultimately feeds into or leads to more explicit forms of consciousness *of the self* as an embodied subject. On the level of first-order experience (e.g. as when gazing at a landscape), I simply *am* this self-present subject in a tacit and immediate manner.

First-person perspective

The structure of self-consciousness is linked to my first-personal predicament. My perception of the landscape is given visually to me; with a 'me' that is an (*elusive*) *perspectival source* of my seeing. The first-person perspective itself *is never given to me as an object* to which I can attend while simultaneously living in my first-person perspective. In other words, *a subject cannot simultaneously be given as his own object*. The subject is *elusive*: each time we try to grasp it through a reflective move and objectify it, it withdraws one step behind. Our sense of being a subject is therefore said to be *intrinsically elusive*: there is always a blind spot at the very origin of my subjectivity. True, we can objectify this elusive source *in reflection*, grasping it intellectually and describing it verbally as a center of my various (past) thoughts and perceptions, as a sort of residual or assumed necessary center of a

---

[2] Such expressions as 'margin' or 'background' (of consciousness) imply a subject–object epistemic structure, because they entail the notion of center or focus of attention, which assumes the presence of a subject.

previous multitude of conscious acts, for example, thoughts, perceptions, etc. (which Husserl called the 'ego's transcendence in immanence'). This, in fact, is precisely what we have been doing in the previous sentence. Yet in this very act of reflection, in one's attempt to grasp the 'me', the living or functioning source of one's present, first-person perspective retreats once more, a further step behind, and retains its elusive status.

Self-consciousness and the sense of self seem, then, to be linked in ways that can seem confusing and even paradoxical. A self may well seem, after all, to be something that must be experienced, something that could not possibly exist in the absence of some kind of self-conscious awareness. Yet as we have just noted, the sense of self seems also to be, in some sense, *incompatible* with self-consciousness, or at least with certain *forms* of self-consciousness.

The question is now: is it possible to flesh out the first-person perspective in a way that would help to account for the obvious yet, in some ways, mysterious link between self-consciousness and the sense of self? A closely related question asks whether the elusive nature of basic self-experience implies that such selfhood is an instance of absence or pure void, something that has no phenomenal presence whatsoever, or perhaps, whose presence is precisely that of an absence (as Sartre often implies). An alternative view (which we endorse) is that, although basic selfhood is not in fact given as an object, there is nonetheless a positive sense of subjective presence, a self-presence that has a certain experiential (phenomenal) thickness.

One famous view (associated with Kant, among others) considers first-person perspective to be a pure transcendental *form*, a structural basis of experience that has no direct, phenomenal presence, and therefore defies any further *phenomenological* description. Authors who try to describe it in more detail usually end with formulations such as 'the experience's givenness for me', 'intrinsic self-referentiality', or 'intrinsic ego-centricity', 'in my experiential field', etc. Zahavi (2005) proposed here the use of the term 'mineness', suggesting that, in the first-person perspective, all experience is characterized by a specific phenomenal character, namely its configuration 'for me'. Albahari (2006)[3] distinguishes between two terms: '*perspectival* ownership' and '*personal* ownership' of experience. The former term refers to an intrinsic *form* or mode of givenness of all experience, namely that all experience has always this 'for me' character—*first-person perspective*. Personal ownership, on the other hand, refers to a form of experience that is more complex and richer in content; it arises from *identifying* perspectival ownership with

---

[3] Albahari's goal is to determine which aspects of self-hood are 'real' in a specific Buddhist metaphysical sense, which is not our concern here. Albahari mentions depersonalization (2006: 172–4), claiming that experience retains 'perspectival' and partly 'personal' ownership: after all, the depersonalized person still experiences herself as a subject. As we argue, however, depersonalization in schizophrenia is associated with unstable 'perspectival ownership'.

particular mental contents, which are then felt as 'mine'. Albahari considers the 'perspectival' type of ownership to be more 'real' than the 'personal' type, and argues that only the latter type is vulnerable to the Buddhist critique of the illusory nature of selfhood (see Chapters 9, 12, and 13 above). We need now to address briefly the notion of 'perspective' in order to determine whether Albahari's distinction is viable. At a superficial descriptive level, at least, the first-person perspective seems to articulate itself differently in different modes of experience.

In perception, the givenness of a *perceptual* object is always partial, *perspectival,* always seen, heard or felt from a particular 'here'.[4] In Husserl (1907/1970), we find a thorough description of the co-constitution of the perceptual 'from-where' of the embodied subject and of the ever-changing, perspective-driven, adumbrating givenness of the intentional object. Husserl offers a metaphor modelled upon ocular optics: the picture of a centrally located ego-subject who sends out a cone-shaped, centrifugal mass of 'intentional rays', and is subjected to converging centripetal affections coming from the world. This *cone-like image* of first-personal perspective is quite persuasive and easy to grasp, and endows the notion of perspective with a spatial character and embodiment. In particular, the uniqueness of one's location is obvious: nobody else can simultaneously witness the world from the very same spatial position that I, for example, am occupying in the now.[5] The first-person perspective in perception is thus not a free-floating, experiential configuration but a function of the lived body, moving in space. This form of embodiment helps to constitute the *sense of self,* of being a substantial (spatial) subject.

Yet the cone-like image does *not* fit *all* experience. If we examine the nature of first-person perspective present in the case of *thinking,* for instance, the 'cone-like image' will seem to apply only to a certain (hyper)-reflective introspective stance, or perhaps to some meta-cognitive states. The first-person perspective inherent in most instances of thinking (in 'first order' thinking) is simply the quality of 'me-ness' or 'as me' that imbues the thinking itself. It is the 'me' that inhabits the thoughts, guaranteeing their subjectivity, providing my thinking (or, as we claim, any intentional mode) with its first-person perspective. But then there seems to be *no distance* between myself and my thoughts, no breach sufficient for slipping in and justifying the concept of 'ownership' or other form of *relation.*

In other words, the first-person perspective is not only a pure form. It is not only a sort of abstract reference to the mere existence of an apprehending, subjective pole in experience. Indeed, it is our claim that experience normally includes *a certain phenomenal sense* of this pole. The 'for-me-ness' of experience

---

[4] A more comprehensive analysis of the 'from where'—understood as a mobile *perspectival source*—would have to take into account embodiment, dispositions, the sedimentation of habits, and, in the case of exteroception, the self-specifying aspects of the appearing world.

[5] This is why a solipsistic claim that 'the world is my world' is, in a sense, simply trivial or vacuous.

has, in this sense, a kind of substantiality that is part and parcel of the experience itself. This phenomenal variant of self-consciousness is not a reflective consciousness of an objectified 'I', an explicit sense of existing as a persisting, invariable bounded entity. It is, rather, a *tacit self-presence* that is a condition of the possibility of any such reflective self-identification. This tacit or *pre-reflective self-presence*[6] is the ongoing self-affection of a living organism, and the affectivity so understood is the fundamental dimension of embodiment. This is the dimension that Michel Henry elaborates throughout his philosophical work. For Henry, this sense of 'me-ness' (as *ipseity* or self-affection) is our sense of subjective vitality and self-presence, a self-presence that cannot be isolated from experience and that permeates experience as its phenomenalizing first-personal source. On Henry's account, affectivity, as self-affection, is to be found in every fibre of perception, feeling, cognition, willing, and action. Our subjective life attests itself as a self-presence or form of ipseity in each experience, without mediation or distance; it is not something we have initiated but occurs in the form of a radical passivity to which we are given and that is a condition of any active 'spontaneity'.

This 'self-feeling of self', then, is *not* intentional, either in the (everyday) sense of being volitional or in the (philosophical, Brentanean) sense of being an *object* of experience. Basic self-feeling is not a product or object of *observation* or reflection, of an '*inner perception*' understood as a form of introspection. Rather, it is a peculiar, non-relational 'relation' inherent in experience, in which the '*what*' and the '*for whom*' constitute a single, inseparable term: 'the genitive and the dative of appearance [being] is one and the same' (Hart 2009).

All appearance, says Michel Henry, presupposes this immanent self-manifestation as a source of phenomenality. In his view, the intentional manifestation of the world (otherness) is founded on the self-luminosity of immanent self-affection, on a kind of subjecthood or selfhood. Henry's interpretation of the famous expression 'transcendence in immanence' is the claim that all 'external', transcendent, *ekstatic*, or other-directed manifesting of the world requires, as its grounding medium, the phenomenality of immanent self-affection.

---

6 Pre-reflective self-consciousness is not a matter of conceptualizing oneself or attending to oneself. Rather, it is a kind of implicit acquaintance with oneself, a self-familiarity, always permeating the world-engaged consciousness. It is a subtly manifested phenomenal consciousness. Recently, Schear (2009) complained of insufficient phenomenological evidence for accepting such a notion. We will mention two simple examples. (1) When one is severely depressed, with slowness, sadness, a sense of inability and oppressive burden, and so forth, one is not *only* depressed when one self-consciously reflects on one's condition and thinks *that one is depressed*; rather, one is and one feels continuously depressed. The depression does not become *unconscious* when one stops thematizing it in an explicit manner. (2) When one is in a cinema watching a fascinating movie, and all one's attention is invested in the screen, one may suddenly be stunned or scared by a horrific scene. One's pulse jumps, one's throat is dry, etc. It would be wrong to say that one *awoke* to self-awareness. Self-awareness has been there with one all along.

Phenomenality

The concept of phenomenality is close to the notion of consciousness understood as an ontological domain, even a kind of 'stuff' or 'phenomenological substance' (Henry 1990 speaks of *matiére phénomenologique*)—a dimension in which appearing occurs.[7] The term 'phenomenality' refers then to the 'givenness of the given', *the very fact* that something articulates itself as 'manifestation'. Phenomenality is the *appearing* of appearances, the condition for the manifestation of objects. This is not to say, however, that consciousness is *exhausted* by the appearance of intended *objects* or *contents* (the phenomenality of minimal self is not object-like). It is thus a constitutive feature of experience, including experiences that are non-thematic, 'first-order', or pre-reflective. As a *medium*, as the *self-presence of presence*, phenomenality is primordial and a condition for the emergence of any phenomenal *structure* whatsoever (Fasching 2008: 472–3). The 'hard problem' of neuroscience and philosophy of mind is to account for phenomenality.

How can we be cognizant or aware of the dimension of phenomenality, given that, as a kind of omnipresent medium, it is necessarily invisible? In a certain sense, of course, we are always aware of the being of phenomenality *through* the brute fact *that objects appear* or are *manifest* (that there is experience). In seeing a book lying on a table, our consciousness is directed to the book. Phenomenality or consciousness is not some additional feature that is somehow added on. Yet one can say that phenomenality shines *through* and *in* this *appearance*; it is attested to by the object's *manifest* 'thereness', its existence not as an autonomous 'in-itself' but as something that presupposes and thus includes (or is included within) consciousness and experience (Fasching 2008). The notion of phenomenality seems to be closely linked to the notion of first-person perspective (see Chapter 13 above). If we agree that all experience is necessarily *someone's* experience (i.e. that experience is always subjective) and so deny the possibility of anonymous free-floating experiences, then all appearing is, at bottom, always articulated as subjective.

We will follow two tracks to address this issue. We will first proceed by using certain elements of the Buddhist tradition recently presented by Albahari (2006)[8] and then will look to the tradition of phenomenological philosophy.

---

[7] In his 'General Psychology' (1912/2007) Paul Natorp used the term *Bewusstheit*, to indicate the givenness of presence. He considered *Bewusst-heit* (appearing that allows appearance) to be a more elemental term than *Bewusst-sein* (consciousness), for the latter always alludes to some kind of *relation* involved in *being*-conscious. *Bewusstheit* (in French *consciosité*) is simply *phenomenality*, linking the appearance (object) with its subject.

[8] Albahari tries to show, in accord with a Buddhist perspective, how certain components of the ordinary human sense of being a subject are indeed 'real', i.e. *natural aspects of consciousness* (which itself is real). These include unity, invariability-persistence, perspective, elusiveness of the subject [the subject is necessarily excluded from its own focally attentive purview]. By contrast, other features— such as boundedness (a sense of being a delimited, spatiotemporally demarcated entity) and a sense of

Buddhist thought operates with a notion of consciousness/phenomenality as a kind of substance, a primordial 'stuff' (like physical 'matter') that possesses a kind of ontological autonomy and persistence. 'Witnessing' or 'witness-consciousness', according to Albahari, is the appropriate term for consciousness, because it picks up a necessary and essential feature of the notion of consciousness, namely that some form of *apprehending* always takes place, no matter how passive or minimal that apprehending might be (Albahari, 2006; also see Chapter 12 above). The notion of 'witness-consciousness' includes all phenomenal apprehension, all percipience and knowing; it subsumes all forms of experiencing, feeling, perceiving, thinking, introspecting, and so forth. 'Witness-consciousness' is endowed with intrinsic self-reflexivity in the sense of being self-aware or self-luminous. To characterize consciousness, Albahari offers metaphors of light and illumination. As she notes, light is indeed necessary to illuminate objects, yet the light beams are not themselves visible, unless 'hitting the eye, whether directly or by means of reflection from something else such as a cloud of dust'. Nevertheless, she notes, the beams 'exist as *a potential source of visible illumination*' even when they are not in fact visible; 'Nothing about the light *intrinsically* alters with the addition or subtraction of dust [existence of the object]' (Albahari 2006; 39, addition in brackets). With this metaphor, Albahari conveys the view that consciousness has a kind of ontological autonomy and self-subsistence. A phenomenological version of the light metaphor is the luminosity of a flame (Hart 2009). The minimal *self* is, in fact, like a flame: self-illuminating but, simultaneously, also illuminating the objects surrounding it. The source of phenomenality is *consciousness as subjectivity*; alternatively we might say that the subject is the *agent of manifestation* (for extensive discussion see Hart 2009: ch. 1). For Michel Henry 'the invisible [here he is referring to the immanence of subjective presence] in its opposition to the visible . . . [he is referring to the manifestation of objects of awareness] is determined not as a concept of a separated essence, but in the fluidity of the passage wherein it [subjective presence] constantly constitutes itself as that which hides itself there' (1973: 446). It is important to note that phenomenality can have degrees of *intensity*. As Kant noted, 'even consciousness has always a degree, which admits of being diminished' (in Henry 1973: 445). One may also describe variations of phenomenality by speaking of degrees of 'transparency' or 'opaqueness' of consciousness—as a way of capturing the extent to which awareness of consciousness-as-such intrudes itself in our experience of worldly objects. The question of phenomenality and subjective presence was central to the French author Antonin Artaud, who suffered from schizophrenia (spending the last nine years of his life in asylums). Artaud seems to have been referring to the core dimension of human existence as a vital, subjective presence when he spoke of what he called 'the

unconstructedness (being an authentic autonomous soul)—are in her perspective 'illusory', mere upshots of desire-driven complexifications of consciousness.

essential illumination' and the 'phosphorescent point' (thereby adopting the light metaphor). He equated this illuminating centre-point with the 'very substance of what is called the soul', and described it as a prerequisite for true, conscious experience of the world, thus for avoiding what he called 'constant leakage of the normal level of reality' (Artaud 1976a: 169, 82; 1965: 20; Sass 2003).

MINIMAL SELF AND ITS DISORDERS IN SCHIZOPHRENIA

Our central claim regarding schizophrenia is that this psychiatric condition is associated with disorders *that affect the articulation and functioning of minimal or core self*. To speak of a 'self-disorder' in schizophrenia is not to say that the patient is *bereft* of any subjective perspective or existence, or that minimal self effaces itself completely. The notion indicates, rather, that 'minimal self' is fragile, constantly threatened, and *unstable* (recall the introductory quotation from a patient).[9] It seems that the normally smooth, pre-reflective sense of self loses its automaticity and transparency. The minimal self seems to be affected in its phenomenological aspects: phenomenality, first-person perspective, and self-presence. In a recent contribution, we summarized our position in the following way (Sass, Parnas, Zahavi forthcoming):

The core abnormality in schizophrenia is a particular kind of disturbance of consciousness and, especially, of the sense of self or ipseity that is normally implicit in each act of awareness. (*Ipseity* derives from *ipse*, Latin for 'self' or 'itself.' Ipse-identity or ipseity refers to a crucial sense of . . . existing as a subject of experience that is at one with itself at any given moment . . .) This self- or ipseity disturbance has two main aspects or features that may at first sound mutually contradictory, but are in fact complementary. The first is hyper-reflexivity—which refers to a kind of exaggerated self-consciousness, that is, a tendency to direct focal, objectifying attention toward processes and phenomena that would normally be 'inhabited' or experienced as part of oneself. The second is diminished self-affection—which refers to a decline in the (passively or automatically) experienced sense of existing as a living and unified subject of awareness.

It is obvious that the articulation of what might be termed the *narrative* self is not untouched by disorders of minimal self. However, the specificity of the clinical

---

[9] Such instability may be associated with a characteristic feature of schizophrenia known as 'dialipsis'—a term denoting brief, intermittent drops in performance as e.g. during eye-tracking or other cognitive tasks (Matthysse *et al.* 1999).

picture of the schizophrenia spectrum in particular seems to lie in the instability of *minimal* self.

In the majority of cases, schizophrenia evolves in an incremental (but not necessarily linear) manner, with the onset of illness taking place in late adolescence or young adulthood. The pre-psychotic stages ('premorbid', referring to habitual behavioural deviations, and 'prodromal', i.e. with symptoms that herald the onset of psychosis) are characterized by increasing isolation, alienation, eccentricity, diminished energy and initiative, and, often, a serious decline in functioning (Parnas 1999). There is a panoply of anomalies of subjective experience, anxiety, and lowering of mood. In the schizotypal disorders, the patient does not develop a long-lasting frank psychosis, yet manifests the essential non-psychotic features also found in schizophrenia.

Naturally, patients vary with respect to their willingness and ability to describe the details of their condition. Suspiciousness or indifference may be pronounced; and it requires time, effort, and skill to conduct a detailed phenomenological exploration of the patient's subjective life. Another problem is linked to a potential ineffability of anomalous experience, which may affect pre-reflective and formal aspects of experience that are difficult to express in a propositional form. The vocabulary at our disposal did not, after all, evolve for the purpose of describing or expressing the subtleties of subjective states (Parnas and Handest 2003). Patients will frequently complain of being simply unable to describe their experiences, or they may use metaphors and other analogies that require effort to be understood. In addition, self-disorders themselves typically have an inherent tendency to undermine one's ability to express oneself, since they disturb any stable point of view and disorganize the field of consciousness. In cases with rapid initial progression, discursive abilities are especially disrupted. The patient's *Weltanschauung* and mood may become especially difficult to gain access to and grasp. Often, a thorough interview session, focused on subjective anomalies, may give the patient at least a temporary feeling of relief; it can be reassuring to realize that the psychiatrist or psychologist is *familiar* with her (often terrifying) experiences, which she had assumed were uniquely her own and did not dare to reveal to others.[10]

Below we will briefly present self-disorders grouped along three axes of normal self-experience: self-presence, perspective, and phenomenality. These are not independent, object-like features, nor can they be considered as mutually independent *symptoms* in accord with the medical model. They are better understood as interdependent aspects of a single whole, considered from different viewpoints. They co-occur, overlap, and imply each other, forming together a certain psychopathological *Gestalt* that, we have claimed, influences the subsequent symptomatic

---

[10] Certain psychiatric symptoms, such as hallucinations or compulsions, are items of popular knowledge, and are certainly mentioned in conversations in a psychiatric ward.

evolution (Sass and Parnas 2003, 2005, 2007; Parnas and Sass 2008). This presentation is not, of course, an exhaustive account, either in a phenomenological or a clinical sense. Here we only address issues of self and, briefly, of intentionality, leaving out important developments pertaining (for example) to intersubjectivity and temporality. For a clinical-descriptive catalogue of self-disorders, see Parnas *et al.* (2005).

Self-presence

A frequent complaint, which often has its onset in early school-years, is a strong and disturbing feeling of being different from others. This feeling is not associated with relatively superficial issues, such as one's social status or attractiveness, or even the stigma of a chronic psychiatric illness. The feeling in question, which is quite profound and distinct, seems to be linked to a diminished or altered sense of self-presence, of one's very existence as subjectivity. The patient complains, for instance, of unstable fullness or reality of his self-awareness. He feels that something profound is afflicting him, something that cannot easily be expressed in propositional terms. The phrasings may range from such a simple statement as 'I don't feel myself' or 'I am not myself' to 'I am losing contact with myself', 'I have a strange ghostly feeling as if I was from another planet. I am almost nonexistent' or 'I am becoming a monster', 'I am turning inhuman'. The patient may speak of an 'inner void' or, as one put it, a 'lack of inner nucleus'. One patient reported that in his secondary school years (gymnasium) he set for himself difficult, effort-demanding goals (e.g. high marks) in order to 'achieve human dignity'. On a closer exploration, he explained that his term, 'lacking dignity', actually meant lacking a sense of 'existing as a *spiritual* being', a subject. He 'felt like a physical object, e.g. like a refrigerator'.

Some of these experiences are associated with abnormalities of the normal sense of embodiment: the patient may feel his body to be a mere thing; she may have a sense of extreme separation between mind and body, or may feel amazement *to be a body* at all. Such experiential anomalies suggest a diminishment or alteration of a kind of fundamental self-familiarity, that is, of the immediate, non-observational sense of being me that is the foundation of all other senses of identity (ipseity). The patient may dwell on the question of 'who he is'. He may closely examine his own mirror reflection, finding it alien and frightening, or inspecting facial features (especially the eyes) in a search for change.

It is typical for patients with such experiences to describe their feelings of differentness through self-representations that are personally appropriate and age- and culture-dependent. The person may secretly consider herself to be a time-traveller or an extra-terrestrial. She feels *ontologically different* from others, and therefore alone. This, in fact, is a frequently reported reason for suicidality

(Skodlar *et al.* 2008; Skodlar and Parnas 2010). Feelings of solipsistic grandiosity are another possible reaction. The social isolation, listed as a diagnostic feature in both DSM and ICD, seems to be, in large measure, an outgrowth *from within*, from this inner sense of profound ontological solitude.

Perspective

Our introductory quote from Elyn Saks (2007) describes something that nearly defies description: an obliteration of the first-person perspective in perception. Such moments of total or near-total obliteration seem to be rare, or perhaps are underreported because of their nearly ineffable character. More frequently, the patient will report a kind of spatial shift in the location of her perspective on the world, her 'from where': 'Sometimes my point of view seems to move two centimetres to the back (or sinks a little)'. Other patients report changes in visual perception that may reflect perspectival instability: for example, objects or the entire visual field may seem skewed, with strange spatial proportions, as if seen from another angle or from far away.

As described above, the first-person perspective in thinking is the quality of 'me-ness' in thinking—the sense that there is an 'I' or 'me' who inhabits one's ongoing thinking, providing a kind of 'zero point of orientation'. Even when the stream of thoughts is choppy, the sense of subjectivity will normally seem uninterrupted, rendering it the same stream. In a given temporal segment, the constituent contents of the stream (e.g. thoughts, images, sensations) are co-conscious in the sense of being united and interacting mutually in a kind of experiential whole. In normal experience the sense of 'me-ness' typically permeates this whole, imbuing it with first-personal perspective: in this sense *there is normally no distance between my thoughts and myself.* By contrast, one schizophrenia patient, suffering from painful introspective states, complained of '*having* thoughts rather than *being* thoughts'. As she explained, 'being thoughts is equal to *filling them up as "me"*, saturating them'. In the 'having' state, by contrast, 'the thoughts are *delimited*; you can hear or see them, but they are not spread out in the body; they are incomplete, they are not real'.

This patient described what appears to have been a fundamental, hyper-reflexive mutation in the stream of consciousness, a change involving a sense of *experiential fissure* between the sense of subjectivity and the contents of awareness. In such patients, the thinking process seems to lose its sense of vital self-affection. Smooth, first-order thinking is undermined by a kind of ongoing introspection that imposes itself on the patient, but that may also be taken up by the patient as a more active project. As a result, mental contents appear increasingly objectified and spatialized (thinking may e.g. be felt localized to specific parts of the head).

This experiential fissure is also at the root of the formation of *Gedankenlaut-werden*, the symptom of 'hearing thoughts aloud', which may range from private, non-psychotic experiences to a clearly hallucinatory and delusional condition. Here, the inner speech that normally serves as a medium for thinking loses its expressive unity of content (signified) and vehicle (signifier) (Husserl 1913/1970). In normal experience, it is not necessary to inspect or *listen* to one's thoughts in order to know *what* one is thinking; meaning is simply given in a direct or unmediated fashion through the (typically unnoticed) medium of inner speech. Patients with *Gedankenlautwerden* may, however, feel rather as if they are *witnessing* their thoughts, or as if they need to listen in order to know what they are actually thinking. This of course is hardly conducive to the spontaneous flow of thought and speech. In a postcard Artaud (1976*b*; see below) complained of being deprived of a necessary 'minimum of absorption of my thought within my thought', of lacking 'that fusion...of the expression with the thought, that instantaneous forgetting which is given to all men and allows them convenience of expression' (1976*b*: 210).

The feelings of diminished self-presence and waning first-person perspective are, on this view, the expression of a self-disorder, best described as a disorder of self-affection. And this self-disorder is at the root of the disturbed relationship to objects and the world that is typical of schizophrenia. Self-affection is, after all, the very condition for the experience of appetite, vital energy, and point of orientation. It is what grounds human motivation and organizes our experiential world in accordance with needs and wishes, thereby giving objects their significance for us as obstacles, tools, objects of desire, and the like (see below: intentionality). In the absence of this vital self-affection and the lines of orientation it establishes, the structured nature of the worlds of both thought and perception will be altered or even dissolved. For then, there can no longer be any clear differentiation of means from goal; no reason for certain objects to show up in the focus of awareness while others recede; no reason for attention to be directed outward toward the world rather than inward toward one's own body or processes of thinking (see below: intentionality).

Phenomenality

Schizophrenia is associated with several, often paradoxical, changes in the processes of manifestation or phenomenality. Normal experience is an ever-changing flux of appearing appearances, a living and dynamic interplay involving interpenetration between theme and background, the distant and the proximal, the pre-reflective and the reflective-thematic, the opaque and the transparent. Ordinary experience is intentionally directed to, or absorbed in, the world. It is invested in daily affairs and social interactions, with a self-presence that subsists as a pre-reflective, tacit medium and framework of intentional directedness—though this directedness and tacit quality may of course be interrupted during occasional moments of introspective self-reflection. In the early phases of schizophrenia, there is often a radical transformation, leading to an enduring, rigidly *hyper-reflexive configuration of awareness.* The patient becomes trapped *in a prison* of his own interiority that *does not recede,* not even when orientation toward the external world is called for and would be appropriate. Many patients complain of 'living only in the head', being unable to reach out and become immersed in the world. There might be an ongoing 'simultaneous introspection',[11] where the patient suffers from a constant, reflective self-scrutiny that disrupts his or her intentional dealings with the world.

The hyper-reflexivity found in schizophrenia is not, at its core, an intellectual, volitional, or 'reflective' kind of self-consciousness—though such kinds may certainly occur. More basic to schizophrenia is a kind of 'operative' hyper-reflexivity that occurs in a largely passive, automatic fashion. The field of experience and action is disturbed by an automatic popping-up or popping-out of phenomena and processes that would normally remain tacit in the pre-reflective framework of awareness (where they serve as a medium of implicit self-affection), but that now come to be experienced in an objectified and alienated manner. Phenomenally speaking, hyper-reflexivity can be manifest as an emergence or intensification of experience *as such,* or as prominence (or opaqueness) of proximal over distal aspects of stimuli (see e.g. Sass 1992, re 'phantom concreteness'), including focal awareness of kinaesthetic bodily sensations, inner speech, or the processes or presuppositions of thinking (Sass 1992). Phenomena that would normally function as the very *medium* of self-awareness come to be experienced, rather, as reified, spatial-like entities (spatialization of experience) or even as externalized objects. Trapped in the enclosure in his interiority, the normal world directedness becomes disrupted and impeded, and immersion in the world is impossible.

It makes little sense, incidentally, to characterize our self-disorder view by using a simple opposition between 'too much' versus 'too little' self-experience (as do Lysaker and Lysaker 2008: 32) or to apply the 'positive–negative' symptom dichotomy, also based on a similar too-much, too-little, reasoning (Sass 2003). On our view, there is a sense in which the person with schizophrenia has *both* too little awareness of self (diminished self-presence or self-affection) *and* also too much self-consciousness (hyper-reflexivity). This means that a certain heightening of phenomenality of self-consciousness (increased focal awareness of the normally 'inner') is intimately bound up with a failure to experience the normally implicit foundations of self-presence, namely self-affection (that is, to *inhabit* one's kinaesthetic sensations or inner speech).

---

[11] Considered as highly characteristic of schizophrenia in Japanese psychiatry e.g. in the work of Kimura Bin (Bin 2001; Sass 2001).

As an expression of disruption of the processes of manifestation, hyper-reflexivity (a kind of phenomenality) and diminished self-affection or self-presence are best conceived as being two aspects of the *same* process that is simply being described in different terms. Whereas the notion of hyper-reflexivity emphasizes the way in which something normally tacit becomes focal and explicit, the notion of diminished self-affection emphasizes a complementary aspect of this very same process: the fact that what once *was* tacit is no longer being inhabited as a medium of taken-for-granted selfhood.

Some quotations from Artaud illustrate this duality of diminished self-presence together with exaggeration of forms of self-consciousness. Artaud frequently describes both *lacking the sense of truly existing as a vital center-point* of experience (diminished self-affection) *and also* experiencing various forms of *intensified self-consciousness* (hyper-reflexivity). Thus, for example, he complains of undergoing a 'central collapse of the mind', a kind of erosion, both essential and fleeting' that afflicts both thought and feeling (Artaud 1965: 10–11) and prevents him from being 'validly and lastingly aware of who I am . . . from becoming aware and staying aware of myself' (p. 292). This lacking sense of self-presence was typically accompanied by tendencies to focus attention on background assumptions and also on bodily sensations that would normally be unnoticed—thus leading to feelings of alienation from both his thinking and his lived body. 'I felt the ground under my thought crumble,' he writes in one passage, 'and I am *led* to consider the terms I use without the support of their inner meaning, their personal substratum. And even more than that, the point at which this substratum seems to connect with my life suddenly becomes strangely sensitive and potential' (Artaud 1976: 94; emphasis added).

Some patients complain directly of alterations in the phenomenal quality of self-consciousness whereby the very luminosity or phenomenality of experience is compromised. The patient continues to be aware, yet does not feel fully awake or fully conscious and present; as if his self-experience or self-awareness were diminished: 'I have no consciousness', 'My consciousness is not as whole as it should be', 'I am half awake', 'I have no self-consciousness', 'My feeling of consciousness is fragmented', 'It is a continuous universal blocking' (see also our introductory quote from Elyn Saks). One patient described his condition as 'a constant feeling as if the head was filled with fog', hastening to add that the fog metaphor was only a poor verbal simile for describing this inner state that was, in truth, beyond description.

Intentionality

The schizophrenia patient's dominant or most typical experience of the world and other people—his existential style—may be described as one involving perplexity, ambivalence, and mistrust. It derives from a certain deficiency in the normally automatic pre-understanding of meaning of objects, situations, and others (Min-kowski 1927; Blankenburg 1971; Parnas and Bovet 1991; Parnas *et al.* 2002). This deficit affects interpersonal relations as well as perception of non-human objects. The interpersonal and impersonal cannot, in fact, be neatly separated because all perception happens in practical space, always already pregnant with intersubjective, symbolic elements (Sartre, Heidegger). The following verbatim reports from patients with schizophrenia are extracted from Blankenburg's seminal monograph 'Loss of Natural Evidence' (see also Parnas and Bovet 1991). The pervasive complaint here is some indefinable (personal) deficiency or lack, preventing the patients from living fully and affecting all domains of her life:

What is it that I really lack? Something so small, so comic, but so unique and important that you cannot live without it . . .

What I lack really is the 'natural evidence' . . . It has simply to do with living, how to behave yourself in order not to be pushed outside, outside society. But I cannot find the right word for that which is lacking in me . . . *It is not knowledge; it is prior to knowledge.* It is something that every child is equipped with. It is these very simple things a human being has the need for, to carry on life, how to act, to be with other people, to know the rules of the game. . . .

[Another patient writes to his friend:] For your happiness, your lenience and your safety, you can thank 'a something' of which you are not even conscious. This 'something' is first of all that which makes lenience possible. It provides *the first ground.* (Blankenburg 1971; emphasis added)

It seems that, in such cases, the full and automatic constitution of meaning fails because of an inability to grasp objects in their contextual significance. Phenomenological psychiatry used here the terms of 'autism', 'crisis of common sense', or a 'loss of natural evidence' (Blankenburg). What is at stake in the *sensus communis* is not a question of a sufficient stock of explicit or implicit knowledge (i.e. dispositional beliefs) that are expressible in propositional terms: for example, 'I know *that* one has to stop the car at the red light' or 'I know *that* one says hello to greet the others'. Rather, it is the ability to see things in the appropriate perspective, to have an *implicit, non-conceptual grip* of the 'rules of the game', a *sense of proportion*, and a taste for what is adequate and appropriate, likely and relevant (Tatossian 1979). This requires a pre-epistemic or non-reflective *indwelling* in the intersubjective world, which is a necessary condition for a fluid grasp of context and background and thus of the significance of objects, situations, events, and other people, and for any articulation of thematic meaning. A number of more contemporary terms—such as 'background capacities' (Searle 1992), 'skilful coping' (Dreyfus and Dreyfus 2000), and 'habitus' (Bourdieu 1980/1990)—overlap the concepts of common sense and natural evidence. The significance in question is never a fixed entity but something enacted and constantly moulded and remoulded by the subject's ongoing actions. The lack of 'common sense' that is associated with the isolation and loneliness of psychotic stages is thus not a mere absence (e.g. a shrinking social network) but has a more constitutive significance. As Rümke puts it, 'loneliness so to say grows up within [the patient] as the way of being in a new *changed world* which has become adequate to him. It is [. . . the] *determining constitutive moment* of his *world, in itself radically lonely*' (1951: 186; emphasis added).

One way in which the characteristic deficiency of common sense can be manifest is as the 'interrogative attitude' (Minkowski 1927). The patients wonder about features of the world or situations that others simply take for granted as self-evident or beyond or beneath explanation. Why, they ask themselves, is the grass green? Why do people say hello? Why is a cat called a 'cat'? The cognitive/perceptual style in question is hyper-reflexive, highly focused, and detail-oriented, tending to miss the forest for the trees. As one of our patients explained: 'I have no ability to *go directly to the objects* and get involved . . . For me it is always a process of a distant, stepwise composition [of whole from details] . . . In school [working as a teacher], I was unable to notice or anticipate an approaching moment when a playful contest between school boys turns into a serious fight . . .' This hyper-reflexive style—elaborated in detail by Sass (1992)—is to be considered as an alteration of intentionality *and* of self-consciousness, that is, as a hyper-reflexive disorder of minimal self. Though obsessive in some respects, it is, ultimately, quite different from the habitually focused, rigid cognition in some obsessive personalities, whose world-orientation is stably analytic and detail-bound (Shapiro 1965). Obsessive conditions do not display the same kind of fundamental destabilization of the field of awareness and self-consciousness; nor is there the same paradoxical interplay between volition and affliction. As we have emphasized above, a fundamental hyper-reflexivity in schizophrenia is not, at its core, an intellectual, volitional, or 'reflective' self-consciousness ('hyper-reflectivity') but, rather, what we call an 'operative' hyper-reflexivity, a structural alteration of the processes of phenomenalization. The net result is a loss of the sense of spontaneity, easiness, and lenience in the involvement with life and other people. One of Minkowski's patients summed it up in the following way: 'I can reason quite well, but only in the absolute, because I have lost contact with life' (Minkowski 1927).

SELF-DISORDER AS A GENERATIVE DISORDER (*TROUBLE GÉNÉRATEUR*)

We argue that the above-described disorder of minimal self is, in fact, the core feature of schizophrenia, a '*trouble générateur*' of this complex and heterogeneous illness. The term *trouble générateur* comes from a seminal figure in phenomenological psychopathology, the early twentieth-century French psychiatrist Eugene

Minkowski. Minkowski (1927/1997) equivocates as to whether the *trouble généra-teur* is to be understood as primary—in a causal/pathogenetic sense—or as the-matically central. Thus he describes the *trouble générateur* of schizophrenia as 'not a consequence of other psychical disturbances, but an essential point [or state] *from which spring*, or at least *from which it is possible to view in a uniform way* all the cardinal symptoms' (1927/1997: 8/; emphasis added). According to the former interpretation ('from which spring'), the core feature would in some way *give rise to* the other prominent symptoms; according to the latter interpretation ('view in a uniform way'), the *trouble générateur* would constitute the *essential defining feature* of the condition.[12]

Elsewhere we have argued that our own proposal on self-disorders in schizo-phrenia can help to 'explain' schizophrenia in both these senses, and account for three major conventional domains of symptoms—positive, negative, and disorga-nized (Sass and Parnas 2003, 2007; Sass in press).

In *one* sense of the term 'explanation', the notion of self-disorders helps to show how seemingly distinct features of conscious experience (such as the symptoms of apathy and of 'thoughts aloud', for instance) may in fact be mutually interdepen-dent in the sense of being different aspects of the same experiential whole involving a disorder of minimal selfhood. We refer to this type of relationship as one involving 'phenomenological implication' (on the analogy of logical implication). The key phenomena of self-disorders as we have described them so far—disorders of self-presence, of first-person perspective and of phenomenality—are themselves 'equiprimordial' in the sense of being aspects of the same fundamental structural alteration of self-consciousness. Another example of an implicative relationship is that which often exists between the *content* of a delusion in schizophrenia (e.g. the 'influencing-machine' delusion) and the underlying disturbance of basic self-expe-rience (e.g. fading sense of privacy of one's interiority) that such a delusional belief seems to *express* and perhaps to rationalize. In *another* sense of the term 'explana-tion', phenomenology can help one to understand (and also to explain) how one form of experience might *lead into* another form. On this view, certain symptoms of schizophrenia may be viewed as consequences, and others as compensatory, coping attempts.

There is a long tradition of dismissing abnormal experience and action in schizophrenia as being utterly psychologically incomprehensible, beyond the realm of mental causation. Karl Jaspers (1963) believed that the essential defining feature of schizophrenia was, in fact, its incomprehensibility; presumably this distinguished it from the affective psychoses, which involved exaggerations of normal states of mind that were *not* beyond the pale of empathic comprehension.

---

[12] Similar notions are to be found in German literature. Thus Gruhle (1929) speaks of self-disorders as *Grundstimmung* of schizophrenia. Kronfeld (1922) considers the disorder of self-consciousness as the 'basic psychotic symptom'.

It is certainly true that the clinical picture in schizophrenia may be complex, unpredictable, and beyond everyday understandability of straightforward psychological connections (e.g. a depression following a death of spouse). Yet, as we have tried to show, the subjectivity of a patient with schizophrenia can in fact be understood to a considerable extent, so long as one recognizes the nature of certain altered structures of subjectivity that underlie their anomalous forms of experience and expression.

CLOSING COMMENTS

Contemporary practice in Western psychiatry has increasingly come to rely on pre-formed, highly structured interview schedules; intimate acquaintance, especially long-term acquaintance, with patients has become exceedingly rare. This has meant a mounting simplification of our understanding of psychopathological phenomena and widespread ignorance of the rich tradition of psychopathology (Andreasen 2007). The result, in our view, has been a serious decline in our ability to grasp the underlying nature of schizophrenia, its clinical demarcation, and its aetiology and pathogenesis.

Schizophrenia certainly includes a very heterogeneous set of symptoms that can seem difficult or even impossible to comprehend within any encompassing interpretive or explanatory framework. There is, in fact, a strong and understandable temptation to deny any unity whatsoever to what Eugen Bleuler originally termed 'the group of schizophrenias'. But various as they are, the subtypes and symptom groups are not, in fact, so easily separated. Indeed, repeated attempts to divide schizophrenia into reliable subtypes have never been very successful or intellectually satisfying. We believe that a phenomenological approach, in particular one centred on disorders of self-experience, offers the possibility of capturing the elusive yet distinctive, unifying features of the schizophrenic disorders.

In this chapter, we have tried to describe the essential structures associated with the minimal self, as well as the disorders of these aspects of self-experience that are central to schizophrenic psychopathology. The notion of a disorder of minimal self, a disturbance of the basic, lived sense of subjectivity, offers one, highly promising, way of understanding the core features of this condition and of addressing several issues of relevance to both clinical practice and scientific research on this important disorder.

If taken seriously, the hypothesis of a disorder of minimal self should lead to a clinical reorientation towards the patient's own lived experience and its abnormalities, perhaps especially in first-contact situations. Since the necessary interview for mapping such disorders demands an empathic doctor–patient conversation, the interest in self-disorders has the potential to rehumanize aspects of clinical practice.[13] Clinical knowledge of these disturbed and distressing states of mind or forms of subjectivity may assist psychotherapeutically oriented interventions, both by suggesting new ways of understanding the deficiencies of current interventions and by generating promising new approaches. Self-disorders, considered as a core of schizophrenia, may also constitute essential 'phenotypic' markers that can help to define the boundaries of the schizophrenia-spectrum disorders and thereby improve our classificatory systems. Researchers and clinicians have often pointed to a characteristic and specific psychopathological *Gestalt* in schizophrenia— which, however, was extremely elusive or resistant to operationalization through a listing of symptoms or symptom combinations (Parnas *et al.* 2002). We believe that the profound changes in the structures of consciousness described above, perceived but not thematized by the clinician, are co-constitutive of this elusive *Gestalt*. Another important point is that self-disorders seem to be persisting features of schizophrenia that occur well before the onset of psychosis. This makes them highly relevant for ongoing projects of early-illness detection and intervention in populations considered to be at increased risk for psychosis. A final point is that self-disorders may be crucial for biological research in providing phenotypes that are closely associated with the basic neural-disease correlates.

REFERENCES

ALBAHARI, M. (2006). *Analytical Buddhism: The Two-Tiered Illusion of Self* (New York: Palgrave Macmillan).

ANDREASEN, N. C. (2007). 'DSM and the Death of Phenomenology in America: An Example of Unintended Consequences', *Schizophrenia Bulletin* 33/1: 108–12.

ARTAUD, A. (1965). *Antonin Artaud Anthology*, ed. J. Hirschman (San Francisco: City Press).

——(1976a). *Antonin Artaud: Selected Writings*, ed. S. Sontag, tr. H. Weaver (Berkeley, Calif.: University of California Press).

——(1976b). *Œuvres complètes*, i. *Textes surrealistes, lettres* (Paris: Gallimard).

BERZE, J. (1914). *Die primäre Insuffizienz der psychischen Aktivität: Ihr Wesen, ihre Erscheinungen und ihre Bedeutung als Grundstörungen der Dementia Praecox und der hypophrenen überhaupt* (Leipzig: Frank Deuticke).

——and GRUHLE, H. W. (1929). *Psychologie der Schizophrenie* (Berlin: Springer).

BIN, K. (2001). 'Cogito and I: A Bio-Logical Approach', *Philosophy, Psychiatry, and Psychology*, 8: 331–6.

---

[13] This restitution of a comprehensive psychiatric interview, comprising history-taking and exploration of the patient's subjective experience through an empathic, semi-structured, interview at the patient's very first clinical-psychiatric contact, will likely increase the accuracy of differential diagnosis and thus improve early detection of schizophrenia-spectrum conditions.

BINSWANGER, L. (1956). *Drei Formen Misglückten Daseins: Verstiegenheit, Verschrobenheit, Manieriertheit* (Tübingen: Niemeyer).

BLANKENBURG, W. (1971). *Der Verlust der Natürlichen Selbstverständlichkeit* (Stuttgart: Ferdinand Enke Verlag).

BLEULER, E. (1911/1950). *Dementia Praecox or the Group of Schizophrenias*, tr. J. Zinkin (New York: International Universities Press).

BOURDIEU, P. (1980/1990). *The Logic of Practice*, tr. R. Nice (Oxford: Blackwell).

CONRAD, K. (1957). *Dis begienende Schizophrenie* (Stuttgart: Thieme Verlag).

CUTTING, J., and SHEPHERD, M. (1987). *The Clinical Roots of the Schizophrenia Concept* (Cambridge: Cambridge University Press).

DREYFUS, H., and DREYFUS, S. (2000). *Mind over Machine* (New York: Free Press).

FASCHING, W. (2008). 'Consciousness, Self-Consciousness and Meditation', *Phenomenology and Cognitive Sciences*, 7: 463–83.

FRITH, C. D. (1992). *The Cognitive Neuropsychology of Schizophrenia* (Hove: Lawrence Erlbaum).

GRUHLE, H. (1929). 'Schizophrene Grundstimming (Ich-Störrung)', in J. Berze and H. Gruhle, *Psychologie der Schizophrenie* (Berlin: Springer Verlag), 86–94.

HART, J. (2009). *Who One Is*, i. *Meontology of the 'I': A Transcendental Phenomenology* (Berlin: Springer Verlag).

HENRY, M. (1973). *The Essence of Manifestation*, tr. G. Etzkorn (The Hague: Martinus Nijhoff).

——(1990). *Phénoménologie matérielle* (Paris: Presses Universitaires de France).

HUBER, G. (1983). 'Das Konzept substratnaher Basissymptome und seine Bedeutung für Theorie und Therapie schizophrener Erkrankungen', *Nervenarzt*, 54: 23–32.

HUSSERL, E. (1907/1970). *Ding und Raum: Vorlesungen 1907*, ed. U. Claesges (The Hague: Martinus Nijhoff).

——(1913/1970). *Logical Investigations*, i, tr. J. N. Findlay (London: Routledge & Kegan Paul).

JASPERS, K. (1963). *General Psychopathology*, tr. J. Hoenig and M. W. Hamilton (Chicago: University of Chicago Press).

KRAEPELIN, E. (1919/1971). *Dementia Praecox*, ed. G. M. Robertsen (New York: Robert E. Krieger Publishing Co.).

KRONFELD, A. (1922). 'Über schizophrene Veränderungen des Bewustsseins der Aktivität', *Zeitschrift für die gesamte Neurologie und Psychiatrie*, 74: 15–68.

LYSAKER, P. H., and LYSAKER, J. T. (2008). 'Schizophrenia and Alterations in Self Experience: A Comparison of Six Perspectives', *Schizophrenia Bulletin*. Advanced Electronic Publ. doi:10.1093/schbul/sbn077

MATTHYSSE, S., LEVY, D. L., WU, Y., RUBIN, D. B., and HOLZMAN, P. (1999). 'Intermittent Degradation in Performance in Schizophrenia', *Schizophrenia Research*, 40: 131–46.

MINKOWSKI, E. (1927). *La Schizophrènie: Psychopathologie des schizoïdes et des schizophrènes* (Paris: Payot).

——(1928/1997). 'Du symptome au trouble générateur' (originally in *Archives suisses de neurologie et de psychiatrie*, 22), in *Au-delà du rationalisme morbide* (Paris: Éditions L'Harmattan).

MØLLER, P., and HUSBY, R. (2000). 'The Initial Prodrome in Schizophrenia: Searching for Naturalistic Core Dimensions of Experience and Behavior', *Schizophrenia Bulletin*, 26: 217–32.

NATORP, P. (1912/2007). *Psychologie générale selon la methode critique*, tr. É. Dufour and J. Servois (Paris: Vrin).

NORDGAARD, J., ARNFRED, S. M., HANDEST, P., and PARNAS, J. (2008). 'The Diagnostic Status of First-Rank Symptoms', *Schizophrenia Bulletin*, 34/1: 137–54.

OWEN, G. (2009). 'Review of "Philosophical Issues in Psychiatry" (KS Kendler and J Parnas eds.)', *Psychological Medicine*, 39: 1923–5.

PARNAS, J. (1999). 'From Predisposition to Psychosis. Progression of Symptoms in Schizophrenia', *Acta Psychiatrica Scandinavica* (suppl. 395), 99: 20–9.

——(2000). 'The Self and Intentionality in the Pre-Psychotic Stages of Schizophrenia', in D. Zahavi (ed.), *Exploring the Self: Philosophical and Psychopathological Perspectives on Self-Experience* (Amsterdam: John Benjamin), 115–47.

——(2005). 'Self-Disorders in Schizophrenia: A Clinical Perspective', in T. Kircher and A. David (eds), *The Self and Schizophrenia: A Neuropsychological Perspective* (Cambridge: Cambridge University Press), 115–47.

——and BOVET, P. (1991). 'Autism in Schizophrenia Revisited', *Comprehensive Psychiatry*, 32: 7–21.

——and HANDEST, P. (2003). 'Phenomenology of Anomalous Self-Experience in Early Schizophrenia', *Comprehensive Psychiatry*, 44: 121–34.

——and SASS, L. A. (2008). 'Varieties of "Phenomenology": On Description, Understanding, and Explanation in Psychiatry', in K. Kendler and J. Parnas (eds), *Philosophical Issues in Psychiatry: Explanation, Phenomenology, and Nosology* (Baltimore: Johns Hopkins University Press), 239–77.

——BOVET, P., and ZAHAVI, D. (2002). 'Schizophrenic Autism: Clinical Phenomenology and Pathogenetic Implications', *World Psychiatry*, 1/3: 131–5.

——HANDEST, P., JANSSON, L., and SÆBYE, D. (2005). 'Anomalous Subjective Experience among First Admitted Schizophrenia Spectrum Patients: Empirical Investigation', *Psychopathology*, 38: 259–67.

——————SÆBYE, D., and JANSSON, L. (2003). 'Anomalies of Subjective Experience in Schizophrenia and Psychotic Bipolar Illness', *Acta Psychiatrica Scandinavica*, 108: 126–33.

——JANSSON, L., SASS, L. A., and HANDEST, P. (1998). 'Self-Experience in the Prodromal Phases of Schizophrenia: A Pilot Study of First Admissions', *Neurology, Psychiatry and Brain Research*, 6: 107–16.

——MÖLLER, P., KIRCHER, T., THALBITZER, J., JANSSON, L., HANDEST, P., and ZAHAVI, D. (2005). 'EASE: Examination of Anomalous Self-Experience', *Psychopathology*, 38/5: 236–58.

RABALLO, A., SÆBYE, D., and PARNAS, J. (2009). 'Looking at the Schizophrenia Spectrum through the Prism of Self-Disorders', *Schizophrenia Bulletin* (open access electronic publication).

RÜMKE, H. C. (1951). 'Significance of Phenomenology for the Clinical Study of Sufferers of Delusion', in F. Morel (ed.), *Psychopathologie des Délires* (Congrès International de Psychiatrie, Paris 1950) (Paris: Herman & Cie), 174–205.

SAKS, E. (2007). *The Center Can Not Hold: Memoirs of My Schizophrenia* (London: Vargo).

SASS, L. (1992). *Madness and Modernism* (New York: Basic Books).

——(2001). 'Self and World in Schizophrenia: Three Classic Approaches', *Philosophy, Psychiatry, and Psychology*, 8: 251–70.

——(2003). 'Negative Symptoms, Schizophrenia, and the Self', *International Journal of Psychology and Psychological Therapy*, 3: 153–80.

——(2010). 'Phenomenology as Description and as Explanation: The Case of Schizophrenia', in S. Gallagher and D. Schmicking (eds), *Handbook of Phenomenology and the Cognitive Sciences* (Berlin: Springer Verlag), 635–54.

——and PARNAS, J. (2003). 'Schizophrenia, Consciousness, and the Self', *Schizophrenia Bulletin*, 29: 427–44.

——and ——(2007). 'Explaining Schizophrenia: The Relevance of Phenomenology', in M. C. Chung, K. W. M. Fulford, and G. Graham (eds), *Reconceiving Schizophrenia* (Oxford: Oxford University Press), 63–95.

————and ZAHAVI, D. (in press). 'Phenomenological Psychopathology and Schizophrenia: Contemporary Approaches and Misunderstandings', *Philosophy, Psychiatry, Psychology*.

SCHEAR, J. K. (2009). 'Experience and Self-Consciousness', *Philosophical Studies*, 144: 95–105.

SEARLE, J. (1992). *The Rediscovery of Mind* (Cambridge, Mass.: MIT Press).

SHAPIRO, D. (1965). *Neurotic Styles* (New York: Basic Books).

SKODLAR, B., TOMORI, M., and PARNAS, J. (2008). 'Subjective Experience and Suicidal Ideation in Schizophrenia', *Comprehensive Psychiatry*, 49: 482–8.

—— and PARNAS, J. (2010). 'Self-disorder and Subjective Dimensions of Suicidality in Schizophrenia', *Comprehensive Psychiatry*, 51(4): 363–6.

TATOSSIAN, A. (1979). *Phénoménologie des psychoses* (Paris: Masson).

VOLLMER-LARSEN, A. (2008). 'The Course and Outcome in Schizophrenia Spectrum Disorders: A 5-Year Follow-Up in Copenhagen Prodromal Study', University of Copenhagen, Ph.D. dissertation.

——HANDEST, P., and PARNAS, J. (2007). 'Reliability of Measuring Anomalous Experience: The Bonn Scale for the Assessment of Basic Symptoms', *Psychopathology*, 40/5: 345–8.

ZAHAVI, D. (2005). *Subjectivity and Selfhood: Investigating the First-Person Perspective* (Cambridge, Mass.: MIT Press).

CHAPTER 23

....

MULTIPLE SELVES

....

JENNIFER RADDEN

INTRODUCTION

....

The trope of multiple selves—of distinct individuals or persons successively or even simultaneously housed in the same body—comes to us from works of the imagination, psychopathological case histories, and postmodernist writing, as well as analytic philosophy. In some of these multiplicity occurs as little more than a vivid metaphor, or a casual *façon de parler*; others present it as a metaphysical fact of the matter. Thinking about multiple selves, my particular concern has been descriptions of cases from psychopathology, that is, heterogeneity so extreme as to seemingly transgress norms of mental health. It has also been to question and clarify those norms, however. With their mixed minds, changes of course, forgetfulness, entrenched ambivalence, and the like, normal people are far from simple unities. So what degree of self-fracture should be judged incompatible with a healthy psyche? (Indeed, even as ideals, how much unity and singularity are desirable?) To guide this normative inquiry I examine the way multiplicity has been depicted, and or implicated, in some recent philosophical discussions, where alternative conceptions bring differing criteria by which multiple selves are to be determined, and ascribe different grounds for positing such multiplicity.

The development of these ideas was enhanced by a seminar-workshop on personal identity at the University of Dortmund, Germany, in Feb. 2008. I am grateful to Professor Logi Gunnarsson and his graduate students, as well as to other guests Stephen Braude and Carol Rovane, for the help they provided.

This exploration has two outcomes. First, a modest degree of self unity is rightly valued, and appropriately recognized as emblematic of mental health (a finding derived not from metaphysical conceptions of personhood but from our society's normative preferences). And second, if real phenomena correspond to the extremes of multiplicity reported from the clinic, then—with certain caveats—they are apt for unifying treatment.

To provide general background, I sketch shifts of emphasis within philosophical writing on personal identity from the last decade of the twentieth century (section 1). Three contrasting discussions that yield definitions and criteria are introduced in section 2: those of Stephen Braude (1991), Carol Rovane (1998), and my own (Radden 1996). Some of the grounds for positing and or attributing multiple selves as they are found in these three analyses are discussed in section 3. Section 4 raises questions of value: the desirability of self-unity understood as a norm of mental health. Finally in section 5, I approach the implications of these conclusions for treatment, and consider the warrant for therapeutic intervention in the cases of radical multiplicity reported from the clinic.

1. CHANGES IN THINKING ABOUT PERSONAL IDENTITY

The post-Parfit era has seen changes in the interest persons and personal identity have held for philosophers. New areas of focus include the part played by *embodiment* in identity, the implications of a greater acknowledgment of *agency* and the first-person perspective, and the *characterization identity* that is allied to identity politics and to conceptions of a narrative self. Each of these foci, in its own way, eschews earlier traditions attributing identity to the continuity of phenomenological states. Each turns away from that tradition's mentalist (and dualistic) associations, its emphasis on the psychic elements of memory and consciousness—even, to some extent, the central place assigned to numerical identity. And each must be kept in mind as we consider the possibility of multiple selves or persons (the terms are used as rough equivalents in this discussion), whether construed as separate identities successively housed in the same body, or as separate identities and perhaps even separate centers of awareness or agency, simultaneously coexisting in that body.

Many thinkers have stressed the significance of the embodied point of view (Korsgaard 1989; Rudder Baker 2000; Mackenzie and Atkins 2007).[1] The link

---

[1] This view has sometimes been taken to support and/or been expressed as 'animalism' (persons are human animals).

between embodiment and self or personhood, it is pointed out, has been at worst denied entirely (in the errors of Cartesian dualism), and at best neglected.[2] Although persons are not reducible to their embodiment, they are necessarily embodied, and the continuity of the first-person perspective provided by that embodiment is *what makes them persons*. A person's personal life has been said to 'encompass' her organic life (Rudder Baker 2000).[3] And embodiment is required for the sense of identity and personhood in which we reflect about what we intend to do, and then act.[4] The body is required for 'practical identity', oneself understood as a *doer*.

While they suggest that embodiment is required for personhood, none of these assertions reduces personhood to embodiment, or personal identity to bodily identity.[5] More would be required to show that, if there is one body, there *can only* be one self or person. A number of identities may be able to succeed one another in the self-same body, even if embodiment is required for and constitutive of self or personhood. (We speak this way, for instance, when there is radical personal transformation as the result of 'life-changing' events, such as religious or ideological experiences.) Of course, this is only the tamest kind of multiplicity. Whether such claims about embodiment would permit a body to *simultaneously* house more than one center of phenomenal awareness, or of agency, remains to be seen. If the self or person is understood as a center of awareness reliant on (bodily) sensory apparatus, the body and psyche may be inextricably fused—in which case, arguably, there could be but one self or person at a time. Whether phenomenal awareness could be synchronically fractured this way may to some extent depend on empirical matters, although thus far, evidence of 'offline' processing of sensory input seems more to support than to preclude the possibility of such sensorial duality. At worst, perhaps, the facts about human embodiment might be supposed to allow that the surface only *appears* fractured and multiple.

That fractured surface is the focus of the present chapter, however. Arguments about embodiment take as their starting-point certain familiar features of our human constitution.[6] None of these, I believe, is sufficient to decisively establish

---

[2] Not all would agree. See Strawson 1999, for example.

[3] 'There are not two different lives, but one integrated personal life . . . a human person has a single life that incorporates organic life . . . We are not human organisms plus something else: I am not a person *and* an animal; I am a person constituted by an animal' (Rudder Baker 2000: 18–19).

[4] 'You are a unified person at any given time because you must act, and you *have only one body with which to act*' (Korsgaard 1989: 111; emphasis added).

[5] Not all would agree; see Williams 1973; Olson 1997.

[6] Embodiment seems to ensure a kind of everyday agency, or intentional control, so that my impulse to clench my fist has direct dominion, if at all, over the muscles of my hand, not yours. Yet the domain of our intentional control extends to our use of tools, and of legal devices (Rovane 1998). Then again, motor control is often privileged as the source of 'basic actions'—thus, it has been argued that embodiment involves a kind of intentional control that is more fundamental and

claims about the necessary unity of the person that would prevent us from speaking of multiple selves.

Emphasis on the *experiencing subject*, the continuity of whose conscious states is taken to have explained identity in earlier accounts, has also been widely replaced by emphasis on *agency*.[7] As persons we must see ourselves as actors, capable of choice, deliberation, and practical reason (see Chapters 19 and 21 above). On Christine Korsgaard's analysis, for example, the self is a center of practical identity. Rather than phenomenological continuity, the 'rational agency' of intention and action links the parts of the self at any particular time to provide their synchronic unity, and through stretches of time, ensuring diachronic unity. If you understand yourself as an agent, implementing something like a particular plan of life requires you to *identify* with your future, 'in order to be *what you are even now*' (Korsgaard 1989: 113–14).

As coherent phenomenological report (synchronic) subjective experience is by its nature unified; agendas, by contrast, *need not be*. Counting several simultaneous agendas per bodily person, then, is quite different from acknowledging more than one contemporaneous awareness or phenomenal consciousness per bodily person. If our subselves are construed more as agents than as the subjects of phenomenological states, it seems possible to accept their being units smaller than the body. This is the position adopted by Carol Rovane, whose work is explored in the next section. Rovane's normative analysis of personal identity, she insists, makes appeal neither to bodily identity nor phenomenological unity (Rovane 1998: 203). When self-consciousness is construed as the capacity to reflect upon and know one's reasons for action, we can readily countenance multiple subselves simultaneously sharing the same body (Rovane 1998: 68).[8]

This loosely sketched conceptual landscape will need to be filled in when we have examined particular claims about multiple selves and evaluated the contexts in which those claims are put forward. But before that, let me make a few preliminary remarks about the third shift noted above, that towards identity as characterization, and as the product of a narrative self.

The beliefs, values, desires, and other psychological features making a person the person that (as we say) *she is*, is sometimes known as 'characterization'

more direct than these other kinds. (See Whiting 2005.) Whether these seemingly contradictory aspects of our human nature and constitution show that questions about the relationship between embodiment and personal identity are unanswerably indeterminate, as has sometimes been asserted, I will not discuss. (See Sider 2001; Gendler 2002; Eklund 2004.) At least they leave open the possibility of one body housing more than one self or person as sketched above.

[7] This account oversimplifies the many earlier analyses, such as Parfit's, I believe. (See Radden 1996.) Nonetheless it has been widely adopted.

[8] In addition, Rovane concludes that suitably 'like minded' centers of agency can be attributed to units comprising *more than one such body*.

identity. Here, identity is merely a psychological construct: the attributes comprising individuals' own unique self-concepts—or *who they are*.[9] When identity is understood as characterization identity, any constraints on the number of possible identities simultaneously housed in one body will be imposed by social norms, not metaphysics, and they seem likely to be less stringent. Although perhaps giving rise to internal conflicts, the variety of social roles and personal facets in most lives make simultaneous multiple selves of this kind a commonplace. And nothing very significant appears to rest on whether we say the chess-playing home-body and the stand-up comic who dreams of a stage career comprise one rather complex and perhaps conflicted characterization identity, or two such separate identities simultaneously housed within a single body.

Characterization identity is rarely introduced without reference to how such identity came to be formed, however. And while characterization identity may not preclude multiplicity, the narrative, self-authored characterization identity proposed by some arguably presupposes a unitary self. On such an account, Marya Schechtman speaks of a person's identity as 'constituted' by the content of her self-narrative, so that 'the traits, actions, and experiences included in it are, by virtue of that inclusion, hers' (Schechtman 1996: 94; Chapter 17 above).[10] When the active self-creation of identity is thus emphasized, the process of authoring the so-called self-narrative is depicted as one of selecting, arranging, and unifying disparate parts to construct a single whole, when both the whole produced, and the 'author' are one, not several. (See e.g. Wollheim 1984.) This model can accommodate *sequential* authors of the self-narrative, successively housed in the same body but not, perhaps, *simultaneous* co-authors. (Because other spatiotemporally distinct people are often seen as essential contributors to this project, they may also be viewed as 'co-authors', but their separate embodiment makes them co-authors in a different sense.)

Summing up then: emphasis on embodiment might preclude the possibility of multiple selves *simultaneously* inhabiting the same body on certain accounts, while not the possibility of separate ones doing so, each successively embodied—as characterization identity appears to do when linked to the narrative self of contemporary theorizing. By contrast, emphasis on selves as rational agents seems compatible with multiplicity understood both as coexisting, simultaneous selves and as successive ones.

---

[9] 'Identity' is something of a misnomer here, it has been pointed out (Quante 2007). Yet its association with the self-characterizations of identity politics makes it an unavoidable term, I believe.

[10] For an important critique of this set of ideas see Strawson 1999.

2. WAYS OF ATTRIBUTING AND DEFINING COEXISTING MULTIPLE SELVES

Braude

Stephen Braude's efforts are directed at a degree of multiplicity that bespeaks pathology. He thus employs a sense of multiplicity sufficient to distinguish these extreme cases from the more ordinary heterogeneities within what we are accustomed to think of as single selves.[11] Persuaded that multiple personality disorder is a real phenomenon that has been brought about when early psychic trauma results in the formation of dissociative barriers, Braude appeals to a transcendental unifying principle to explain why, despite their apparent multiplicity, even those suffering this disorder must finally be regarded as one person, rather than many (Braude 1991).[12]

In the spirit of eschewing any alleged underlying unity in favor of the fractured surface, the latter claim can be set aside. And Braude provides us with a way to characterize such cases of (apparent) personal multiplicity. A state is *indexical* when a person believes it to be her own state; a state is *autobiographical* when she experiences it as her own. Those suffering multiplicity to the point of disorder (and only them) comprise distinct *apperceptive centers*—the autobiographical and indexical states of each self are (respectively) largely non-autobiographical and non-indexical for other selves. Although not sharply separated, these differences among indexical and autobiographical states admit of clear cases, Braude insists. A clearly indexical, autobiographical claim might be 'I know I've seen him before'; a clearly non-indexical, non-autobiographical one 'My friend misses her mother.' And multiples alone, among related dissociative phenomena such as depersonalization and hypnotic states, comprise distinct *apperceptive centers*.

As well as serving to identify apparently extreme and pathological cases of multiplicity, Braude's criteria are distinguished by their exclusive appeal to the subjective report of the persons involved. And in this respect, we shall see, they differ from multiplicity criteria that have been adopted by other theorists.

---

[11] As a diagnostic category, Multiple Personality Disorder (or Dissociative Identity Disorder) is described as the apparent presence of fairly well-developed personalities alternating control of the same body, at least one of which is ignorant of at least some of the states and activities of another through a process of psychogenic amnesia, or dissociation.

[12] Braude offers two arguments for these claims. His capacities argument asserts that the functional capacities shared by alters are too protean in their manifestations to provide differentiation; and the 'compositional reversibility' argument claims that earlier and general fragmentation cannot be inferred from the evidence of later psychic fracture. (See Braude 1991.)

Rovane

Among thinkers whose interest in personal identity has led them towards *agency* as such, rather than agency that is linked to embodiment, these questions of multiplicity have been raised in the work of Rovane. For Rovane, as we saw, more than one 'person' can inhabit the same body. The rational point of view of multiple persons within the same human being would involve, as she puts it: 'separate practical commitments within a single human being to many different, smaller-scale, unifying projects' (Rovane 1998: 174). Thus, 'a single human being with a single unified consciousness could be the site of multiple persons, each of which has a normative commitment to achieving overall rational unity just within its own distinct rational point of view'. The important point about multiple persons, she goes on to explain, is that: 'they are not rationally required to regard either their cohabitation in the same human body or their shared consciousness as a reason to achieve overall rational unity together. That is why these persons have separate rational points of view, rather than a single rational point of view in common' (ibid. 132).

Whether stress is placed on agency as an expression of a rational point of view, or on agency as embodied practical identity, focus is on the relation between cognitive states (my intention to X) and their realization (my subsequent doing of X), when the cognitive states are understood more as dispositions to act than as phenomenological occurrences within conscious awareness. And as she herself asserts, Rovane can accommodate both kinds of multiplicity identified earlier: when multiple persons succeed one another, and when the same human being comprises several such multiple persons simultaneously, each with his or her own 'different, smaller scale unifying projects'. The minimal conditions for distinct rational points of view within a single human being are for Rovane that each multiple person within the same human being would (1) have to regard some of the intentional episodes that figure in the life of that human being as constituting its distinct rational point of view, and (2) have to be committed to achieving overall rational unity just within the set of intentional episodes that constitute its own rational point of view (ibid. 173).

This is a less robust sense of multiplicity than Braude's, obviously. Rovanean subselves need not possess the distinct apperceptive centers required by Braude's criteria. Two Rovanean subselves may thus be 'co-conscious', that is, the recipients of a single, unified set of sensory and phenomenal experiences resulting from their embodiment, possessing a single strand of phenomenal continuity. Moreover, Rovane's subselves need have no experiences that lack an autobiographical quality and or indexicality. When their apparently disparate or even contrary agendas are revealed, they might explain (and believe): 'This is another side of me', 'Ah, my alter ego', 'Didn't I ever tell you I was also a stand-up comic?' The distinctness of such subselves rests solely in what Rovane calls their separate 'points of view', that is, the agentic patterns and projects that distinguish and separately unite their separate sets of intentions, values, and goals. We shall return to the reasoning by which Rovane reaches this position in section 3. First, though, I want to introduce a further contrast by sketching the sense of multiplicity employed in my own earlier work.

Radden

Like Braude's, my particular interest in multiplicity has been as evidence of selves (or persons) sufficiently disunified to seem in need of unifying treatment. This will require a more robust sense of multiplicity than Rovane's, one that separates these extreme cases from everyday personal heterogeneities. Normal persons comprise a miscellany of short-term, separable, unified projects along the lines described by Rovane, after all, and they require no unifying treatment. This account of multiplicity shares features of both Braude's and Rovane's and thus provides of the three the most demanding standard for the ascription of separate selves or persons coexisting within a single body (Radden 1996, 1998).

'Agentic' conditions of the sort Rovane relies on make up an important part of this multiplicity. As long as we are postulating anything more than fleeting self fragments, one condition of multiplicity will be separate 'agentic patterns', that is, separate sets of beliefs, values, goals, desires, and responses that find their expression in distinguishable patterns of motivation and behavior. In addition to these, however, I have introduced other criterial features. One of these is distinguishing personality traits: physical and emotional style, temperament, gender and cultural identity, moral disposition, idiosyncratic history, and self concept—indeed, the sort of features comprising 'characterization' identity. Agentic patterns accommodate much of what is captured in these traits, it is true. A person's intentions and actions—her 'practical identity'—tell us a great deal about her personality. Other aspects of personality do not reveal themselves in this straightforward way, however: those that are habits more of mind than behavior, for example, or are aspects of emotional style. Separate, identifying patterns of personality are not entirely reducible to agentic patterns.

Reference to *patterns* here highlights the point that we could not establish the presence of a second self, distinguished in terms of either agency or personality, unless we saw repeated instances of its presence. Like 'person', 'personality', and 'character', 'self' is a dispositional or trait term. To attribute a self to its attendant body is to refer to a tendency to respond in certain ways over stretches of time. This is true also of the attributes of agency and personality. They reveal themselves in patterns, and take time to do so: to attribute them is to presuppose the possibility of more than one temporally separated occasion at which they will be exhibited. Thus, in addition to these characteristics of separate agency and personality, separate selves will have some considerable *continuity*.

Finally, we come to the epistemic features of the psychic life of the multiple on which Braude's criterion is focused. Braude captures these, we saw, in terms of two attributes discovered through subjective report: the phenomenological feel of psychic states (non-autobiographical), and the content of beliefs held (non-indexical), by separate subselves, that together distinguish them as separate apperceptive centers. In a psyche as fractured as those described in the clinical literature, epistemic or amnesic barriers often interfere with introspective awareness. At least until these barriers are reduced through therapeutic intervention, one, some, or several separate subselves are prevented from introspecting the contents of consciousness in the normal way, namely, effortlessly, immediately, and completely. Not only immediate experiences but also memories are included in those contents, note, and indeed, retrospectively understood, disordered awareness results in or becomes disordered memory. This yields a condition that, while it will serve to capture the same epistemic deficiency as do Braude's criteria, is not ascertained exclusively through subjective report. The disordered awareness condition is that: disordered awareness on the part of at least one subself will result in abnormally disordered memory.

Summing up then the four parts of my own, more stringent characterization of the conditions required for us to speak of (simultaneously occurring) multiple selves: a *separate agency condition* asserts that separate selves will have separate agendas; a *separate personality condition* requires that separate selves exhibit distinct, non-agential personality traits; a *continuity condition* ensures that separate selves will persist through time, and a *disordered awareness condition* states that disordered awareness on the part of at least one subself will result in abnormally disordered memory.

Whichever multiplicity criteria we adopt, the fictional character of Jekyll and Hyde offers us a paradigmatic case. The differences between these three accounts become evident when we turn away from such 'textbook' examples. (The considerable skepticism over whether there are *actual* clinical cases is noted later in this chapter. It is sufficient for our purposes that these case descriptions appear to be coherent and realistic.)

The fact that the attributes we have been looking at all admit of degree accounts for some, although not all, of the uncertainty here. There will be greater and lesser separations between subselves in terms of agentic pattern, personality, and disordered awareness; the continuity condition requires us to arbitrate over when passing states and lacunae are sufficiently stable and recurring to be deemed patterns. Moreover, intermediate cases, such as those introduced below, will fulfill some but not all of the separate criteria in multi-criterial accounts such as Braude's and my own. All three sets of criteria are beset by similar vagueness, then—although this will be a feature of more and less concern to their authors.[13]

[13] In particular, given the role of multiplicity in Rovane's analysis and the way her argument proceeds, this will be unlikely to trouble her.

Aside from fictional characters, cases of multiples can be found in the records of the criminal courts, and the matter of differentiating the separate subselves or 'alters' of those diagnosed with Dissociative Identity Disorder has often thwarted attempts to assign criminal responsibility. (These responsibility questions are not dealt with in the present chapter.[14]) In the simplest cases, at least some among several subselves are apparently oblivious of the states of mind of one another, protected by dissociative barriers, as Dr Jekyll was from Mr Hyde. In a more complex relationship, some subselves are depicted as aware, but powerless to prevent, the actions of one another. Such a case is that of a defendant known as John Woods.

Case 1: John/Donnie

John Woods, a college student who killed two women, was examined after the crime. Woods proved to comprise two subselves. The examining clinician's report includes exchanges between herself and these separate subselves, and one of these, named Donnie, is portrayed as having been an innocent 'bystander' during the commission of the crime by John. Donnie is said to have 'watched' the crime, although he did not do it. In Donnie's account, he 'was watching throughout most of the attack [by Woods on the women]', although 'he was unable to describe much of what happened because he was too scared to think. He felt as if he were back in his childhood, where everything was "wild and confused"; he had wanted to leave, but was trapped.' (Reported by Armstrong 2001.)

As *agents* John and Donnie are sufficiently differentiated, even in this brief description, to be deemed separate subselves by Rovane's criterion: the actions taken by John were alarming and abhorrent to Donnie. Although unable to prevent them, he would have not intended them. Moreover this seems to suggest that John and Donnie are also distinguishable by personality traits. But the case illustrates the difficulty of applying epistemological criteria that rely on disorders of awareness, whether subjectively determined or not. Aware of the attack by John, trapped in the body that perpetrated it, panicked and confused, Donnie is arguably an unreliable witness as to the indexical and autobiographical aspects of his experience at the time of the crime. Only by inference from what we know of his seemingly separate agentic patterns and personality, perhaps, can we conclude that Donnie neither believes these deeds to be his, nor experiences them that way. Whether a disorder of awareness and subsequent memory can be ascribed to Donnie seems equally difficult to establish. Moreover, whether 'bystander' memory such as Donnie's qualifies as autobiographical at all remains an unresolved aspect of this criterion. (It is explored in Case 4, below.)

---

[14] But see Radden 1996; Saks 1997; Braude 1996; Bayne 2001; Kennett and Matthews 2003; Eklund 2004; Radden 2006; Sinnott-Armstrong and Behnke 2002; Matthews 2003; Gunnarsson 2009.

Here, then, the criteria introduced earlier suggest differing conclusions about whether Donnie and John are one or two selves or persons. By Rovane's criterion, they are two; according to Braude's and Radden's, they may not be. In contrast, the following case presents a considerable degree of self-fracture while meeting none of the three kinds of criteria.

Case 2: Arthur at work and at home

Arthur has spent his working lifetime in the employ of an exacting, tyrannical boss. Throughout his long days his demeanor must be subservient and self-effacing, a role he has been forced to perfect through many years of practice. Returning home to his grown daughter each evening, he himself takes on something of the role of the tyrant: he becomes demanding, dictatorial, and intolerant. Arthur wants to keep his job, do his duty, and provide a home for his daughter.

Arthur displays two radically different sides to his character, we might even say that he exhibits different 'personalities' in his two very different roles. The distinct personality style would certainly be sufficient for both inter-psychic and interpersonal identification and reidentification. Yet the larger contours of Arthur's life plan and intentional profile seem to form a seamless, coherent whole. He is one Rovanean person, not two subselves.

Arthur's duality also fails to meet thicker standards for multiplicity. He believes himself to be, and experiences himself as, a unified whole. He is apparently without disorders of awareness or memory any greater than the next person's. Whatever contrasts he experiences between life at work and life at home, he likely puts down to the contrast in settings and roles involved rather than to any changes or conflicts within himself. Despite his two distinguishable facets, Arthur seems to be one person, not two, on each of our criteria.

Case 3: Beth/Felicity

In clinical writing, a division of labor is often attributed to multiples. 'Specialized alters' are described as performing tasks such as schoolwork, selling illicit drugs, dancing in strip clubs, cleaning bathtubs, dealing with in-laws, holidays, weddings, and funerals (Piper and Merskey 2004: 679). One account reports that a separate subself 'handles sex' with the multiple's husband (Bliss 1986: 146). From this we can construct the following: Beth aims to be, and is, an exemplary wife in many respects but finds her husband's sexual demands impossible to meet for reasons to do with her own early sexual abuse; Felicity's sexual appetites are a match for the husband's. Otherwise never appearing, Felicity 'handles' sex, and dissociation allows Beth to avoid it.

If Beth is prevented from experiencing Felicity's activities by amnesic barriers that are sufficiently strong, then arguably Beth/Felicity represents a multiple according to Braude's criteria. Autobiographically and indexically, Beth is distinct from Felicity, of whose presence she remains unaware. If Beth is sufficiently differentiated from Felicity in personality, the composite Beth/Felicity also fulfills Radden's conditions of personality differentiation and disordered memory. Criteria involving separate agendas or projects (Rovane's and Radden's) are more difficult to apply here, however. Even if Felicity's only appearances are in the bedroom, the contrast between Beth and Felicity in their respective plans and proclivities suggests two separate subselves. Yet, the way the notion of 'specialized alters' has often been interpreted in clinical writing (whether rightly or wrongly) prompts another analysis. In a case such as this it seems almost impossible not to attribute a long-term goal, shared by Beth and Felicity—namely, *to fulfill the role of 'good wife' while avoiding what is abhorrent to Beth.* An underlying, unified 'executive' self may be attributed on the basis of this analysis. Alternatively, though, we can say that Beth's and Felicity's agendas and projects are *congruent.* Either way, it is unclear whether, on such agency-based criteria, the composite Beth/Felicity is multiple.

Case 4: Erika/Manfred

The case is that of a 'bi-gendered' identity who alternates masculine and feminine presentations, self-concept, and appearances.[15] (The bodily characteristics are hermaphroditic and sexual tastes, androgynously eclectic.) As a self-employed artist living in a tolerant community, Erika/Manfred may exist this way with some freedom, and with few, if any, social costs. Based on Erika's first-person account, it seems that some days she wakes up 'feeling like' Manfred, other days more like Erika. After many years of switching between these two personae, the rest is easy: a choice of masculine or feminine clothing triggers an effortless, unselfconscious, and thoroughgoing shift from one identity to the other.

Erika reports remembering Manfred's experiences and inner states as completely and accurately as she does her own, even while recognizing the more masculine cast through which they present themselves. Thus, for example, Erika remembers that on seeing the attractive woman in the elevator Manfred briefly imagined reaching a hand down her low-cut blouse. Erika would not want to have done that, but recognizes how it felt for Manfred to have been affected that way.[16]

[15] Reportedly, this is an actual case. It may be a rare one: certainly the recent literature on transgender and identity places little stress on such examples. Closest are discussions of transvestism. (See Stryker and Whittle 2006; Hayes 2007.)

[16] The category of bi-gendered person challenges our culture's strong expectation that gender is a quality assigned at birth and invariant through the person's lifetime. For some, then, including some within psychiatry, Erika/Manfred's divisions are somehow pathological, regardless of whether they transgress other social norms. Ascriptions of pathology based on such presumptions and role expectations are set aside in the present discussion.

This case readily meets Rovane's criterion for multiplicity: Erika and Manfred are distinct subselves; they also meet criteria based on personality differentiation. Ambiguity arises with the other criteria, however. No obvious interruption of awareness or memory interferes. Nonetheless, Manfred's experiences are not indexical for Erika—they are his, not hers. Whether Erika's memory of Manfred's experiences counts as appropriately autobiographical is another matter, and exposes one difficulty applying criteria such as Braude's which rely on phenomenological report. Erika seems to have remembered the experience in the elevator *as Manfred's rather than her own*. She remembers it from within, and that includes something very intimate, she remembers *how it felt to Manfred*.

Can this rightly be judged an instance of autobiographical memory? It can, I believe, for Erika describes remembering Manfred's experience as we all sometimes remember the experience of our younger selves. A grown woman recalls how it felt to be a little girl with her beloved doll. She remembers the yearning, the delight, the excitement and pleasure—yet from the perspective of an adult who has long lost all interest in such toys. The remembered experience will not be indexical for her. But this is an autobiographical memory. We remember being ourselves when we were different selves. And given that such childhood memories seem to form part of what we mean by normal *autobiographical memory*, Erika may be said to have autobiographical memory of Manfred's experience, alien as it is to her and to her 'gender identity', and despite its status as non-indexical.

Erika/Manfred may not possess separate apperceptive centers then, since Braude's criteria are not fully met.[17] (The more public, non-phenomenological evidence for separate apperceptive centers, as I have argued elsewhere, seems weak and open more to plausible explanations (Radden 1999: 347–50).[18])

These four ambiguous cases have served to illustrate the difficulty of applying any of the multiplicity conditions we have looked at to actual case descriptions. They have also shown, as we'd expect, that judgments over how to characterize

[17] The application of multiplicity criteria that place reliance on first-person accounts presents further, more general difficulties. The introspective reports on the basis of which distinct apperceptive centers of awareness are solely established (the indexical 'I am not X' and autobiographical 'This does not feel like me') resemble the assertions of severely psychotic patients, who speak of experiencing thoughts and feelings that are not their own. ('These thoughts are not mine,' they say. 'Someone is putting beliefs into my mind.') Whether rightly or wrongly, such assertions are standardly dismissed as delusional, rather than acknowledged to be accurate or veridical claims. Thus, e.g. recent accounts posit that delusions involve hallucinated 'beliefs'—imaginings that are mistakenly taken to be beliefs. (See Coltheart and Davies 2000; Bayne and Pacherie 2005.) The similarity between these phenomenological claims seems to raise the same question of validity for Braude's method of determining the separateness of apperceptive centers.

[18] Two kinds of evidence for separate apperceptive centers, or as it is sometimes known 'co-consciousness', are offered by Braude: shared knowledge (the non-reigning self is in possession of knowledge acquired by the reigning self), and observable 'waverings' interrupting the progress of the reigning self that are taken to indicate interference from a cognizant but non-reigning self. For my critique, see Radden 1998: 662.

such psychic fractures correspond to reasoning and presuppositions that differ considerably.

3. GROUNDS FOR POSITING AND/OR ATTRIBUTING MULTIPLE SELVES

The purpose of criteria such as Braude's and my own is to identify and define the limits of extreme (and pathological) multiplicity. And although Braude insists that every multiple must finally be seen as possessing a kind of underlying unity, yet he believes that multiplicity is rightly attributed in these cases, demanding acknowledgment as a scientific phenomenon and not a mere artifact of the clinical setting or of an overactive imagination.

The clinical evidence yields a more guarded inference, on my assessment. Although such dissociative disorders were widely diagnosed during the last decades of the twentieth century, their status as iatrogenic conditions has since been raised (Hacking 1995; McHugh 1995; Merskey 1992; Piper and Merskey 2004). And rather than a distinct disorder, studies suggest, this alleged syndrome merges into a range of less sharply defined dissociative states (Saxe *et al.* 1993). If there are any actual cases of the multiplicity captured in the four-part criterion, I believe, then because of the value we place in a certain degree of self-unity, such cases will rightly be judged to transgress mental health norms, and deserve therapeutic attention. (The nature of that attention and the philosophical issues it raises are explored in the conclusion of this chapter.)

Rovane's argument for multiplicity shares none of these presuppositions or concerns. The unity of rational points of view, she believes, represents a normative ideal to which we should all strive. From this position she concludes that multiple selves in the sense allowed by her account of multiplicity are possible—and that humans without the requisite rationality (children, for example) are not persons. Having agency involves having a rational point of view and reasons on which to act, and every exercise of agency 'ought to be directed at realizing the universal goal of agency, and is so directed insofar as it is fully rational' (Rovane 1998: 87) Theorizing about personal identity has often drawn inferences from facts of the matter, but the implications of these facts of the matter are less than conclusive.[19] In starting where she does, Rovane offers a metaphysical position *revised in light of values.*

---

[19] This view, outlined in n. 3, is sometimes expressed in terms of the indeterminacy of the concept of personhood.

4. THE DESIRABILITY OF SELF-UNITY

The normal self is never simple and rarely entirely 'single-minded' in its goals and attributes. Moreover, there are variations among normal people in respect to self-unity. Some lives comport with Kierkegaard's definition of purity of heart—to will one thing. But circumstances, disposition, and talents direct other lives towards contrasting goals and projects, severally embraced. Some people, it has been observed, are great planners, and 'knit up their lives with long-term projects'. Others 'merely go from one thing to another. They live life in a picaresque or episodic fashion. Some people make few plans and are little concerned with the future. Some live intensely in the present, some are simply aimless' (Strawson 1999: 15)[20]

Rovane will acknowledge this heterogeneity. For her, as for other thinkers who believe that rational unity dictates the nature of persons, the self-unity of single-mindedness is not a description of actual selves—rather, it functions as an *ideal*[21] (see also Frankfurt 1999). And for Rovane, at least, it is an ideal that can be approached by several subselves coexisting, or succeeding one another within one body, each with their separate projects and goals.

I am less attracted than Rovane to the kind of rationality she depicts. As an ideal, perfect self-unity of this kind, whether sought by one self or several subselves, seems to bespeak something more akin to divine or artificial than to human intelligence. The confusion and complexity found in the usual psyche are a valuable part of human nature, suited to the moral categories and social institutions we cherish—and encompassed, I believe, within less stringent conceptions of rationality. The individual variation between those who knit up their lives with long-term projects, and those who live life in a more picaresque or episodic fashion, enriches human experience, as does that between lives devoted to a single goal and those involving many different ones.

But Rovane's sort of rational unity contains another implication I find troubling. In increasing the total number of rational points of view and so adding value to the world beyond that offered by a single rational point of view, it seems to imply, multiplicity must be *preferred to singularity*. Whether multiplicity is

---

[20] See also Whiting (2005: 408), who speaks of 'a human being who fails to undertake any commitments to persons, projects, ideals and so on and simply drifts through life, doing and believing whatever it feels like doing and believing at any given time, indifferent to the consistency of these things with what it remembers having done and believed at other times or anticipates doing and believing in the future', and asks—are these not also persons?

[21] Thus 'Rather than the claim that every exercise of agency is in fact directed at realizing the universal goal of agency, we must claim instead that every exercise of agency ought to be directed at realizing this goal, and is so directed insofar as it is fully rational' (Rovane 1998: 87).

preferable to singularity could depend, for Rovane, on the value of the substantive projects involved. One project may be substantively superior to an assortment of valueless separate ones. But it could depend on nothing else: there are for her no other reasons why (singular, embodied) human beings should strive to achieve overall rational unity. No failure of rationality occurs when whole human beings are not rationally unified, as she puts it (Rovane 1998: 168). Whether this uncompromising refusal to privilege the whole human person's rational unity could preclude endorsing the multiplicity depicted in some clinical cases, such as that of John/Donnie or perhaps Beth/Felicity, above—unless on the grounds that their substantive projects were wanting—is not clear. Evidence of such extremes of multiplicity might be expected to temper our enthusiasm for multiple rational points of view for the very good reason that the quality of their projects would likely be poor or insufficient. But as long as they were distinguished by a greater number of worthwhile substantive projects (Erika/Manfred, perhaps) then multiples will have to be judged not only as good as, but preferable to, whole human persons. (Rovane comes closest to recognizing this sort of concern when she is defending against critics who would privilege the rational unity achieved by whole human beings. In response to the suggestion that '*more* rational unity is *better*', she replies that if so, 'that... would entail a commitment to integrating into one single *group* person who comprised all human beings' (Rovane 1998: 181; my emphasis.) The reasoning here, that more rationality would be achieved through a group person, seems to ignore the possibility that the multiplication of rational unities through separate subselves may achieve a comparable increase, and that even if it did not, it may still exceed the rational unity achieved through privileging whole human beings.)

Although Rovane's appeal to normative considerations reaches conclusions over which I am doubtful, I do believe this is a way to proceed. I have previously spoken of the normative 'tug' of individualism to describe the valued categories and concepts that seem to depend on some, admittedly modest, degree of human personal unity. Those categories and concepts justify our preference for whole human beings over subparts, even if those subparts multiply the number of rational points of view and worthwhile projects in the world (Radden 1996).

A range of moral concepts, categories, and principles have long been taken to depend on personal oneness or cohesion. The idea can be found, for example, in Thomas Reid's assertion that the identity of persons forms 'the foundation of all rights and obligations, and of all accountableness' (Reid 1785: 112). Examples include our central moral notions, like responsibility, obligation, culpability, promise-keeping, and individual rights, as well as our sense of ourselves as voluntary, goal-directed agents; those time-spanning emotional attitudes and responses such as pride, gratitude, regret, guilt, remorse, contrition, and shame, that involve self-assessment; the goods associated with friendship; the attitude of (judicious) trust, that is implicated both in the moral life and in epistemic practices, and the conception of character essential to everyday moral assessment in terms of vices and virtues. We can imagine a world without some of these, although it would not be an attractive one. Without others, such imagined worlds are radically and abhorrently depleted—nasty and brutish, as Hobbes illustrates, where trust is missing; mechanical and empty in any 'brave new world' without acknowledgment of agency, as Huxley depicted.

A different kind of normatively based appeal, then, looks not at rationality as an ideal, but at the value of singularity when construed as a precondition for other goods.

These arguments have been used, by and since Reid, to confirm the *metaphysical necessity* of not only self-unity but the numerical identity of the person. But the appeal to the normative blandishments of relatively unified selves or persons is better suited, in my opinion, to establishing more limited conclusions. Only if the sense of ourselves and our moral lives captured in such concepts and categories and the societal institutions supporting them are cherished will a degree of personal unity have this kind of value.

I do not mean to suggest that relinquishing these goods could be a matter of individual decision, or even easy. (Some of postmodernism's rejection of the unified self recognizes these links to traditional conceptions of agency and rationality and on that very basis argues to jettison those values (agency and rationality), although I believe it does so without due regard for the implications of such a move.[22]) Nor could such revision be impossible. Values and the social practices embodying them are always potentially open to revision. Were such re-evaluation to occur, the particular normative weight placed on some limited degree of self-unity might alter.

In this one respect, then, my interest in self-unity is similar to Rovane's. As purely normative considerations, both Rovane's and my reasons will have sway only to the extent that they comport with the concepts, institutions, and practices we and others hold dear. Those lacking enthusiasm for perfect rational unity as a normative ideal, or for the sort of concepts, institutions and practices that seem to rest on some modest degree of self-unity, might remain unmoved by either Rovane's or my accounts of selves or person.

---

[22] For a critique along the lines just indicated, see Mackenzie and Atkins (2007). Social norms and cultural traditions can sometimes be oppressive and disabling, she points out, but 'the solution is not to dismiss the notion of normative agency as necessarily "normalizing," to regard our subjectivities as mere effects of the operations of power, to claim that the "self" is an illusion, or to suggest that identities are performative and to advocate a subversive "playing around" with one's identity' (Mackenzie and Atkins 2007: 16).

5. UNIFYING TREATMENT: WHOLE TO PART ISSUES IN CONSENT, SUFFERING, AND DYSFUNCTION

Some psychic heterogeneity is normal and may even be desirable, we saw; it will be entirely compatible with mental health. Extreme multiplicity, however, will not. It appears inimical to many other values we hold dear, and thus may indicate the desirability of unifying treatment. A full evaluation of the ethics of such treatment cannot be embarked on here.[23] But features of the whole to part relations involved when we countenance multiplicity have direct bearing on this ethical issue, and these will be noted in relation to consent, as well as to the attributes appealed to as justifications for therapeutic intervention, suffering, and dysfunction.

First, consent. When imposed on normally unified persons diagnosed with personality disorders, conditions such as Multiple Personality Disorder that *only respond to* treatment undertaken voluntarily, employing some form of persuasion, have been characterized as *moral* rather than *medical* conditions (Charland 2004).[24] Because Multiple Personality is classified as a personality disorder, we may better speak not of treatment for mental disorder but of 'moral' treatment, or re-education (on the desirability of becoming more unified). Whichever way we characterize the intervention, however, it is difficult to imagine how unification could be imposed without the willing participation of at least some of the constituent parts.[25] And certainly, no forms of *wholly* involuntary treatment, even if possible, could be warranted *ethically*. But how many subselves' approval would constitute collective consent to intervention? Need all subselves be willing participants before such intervention could be warranted?

Ostensibly, when one or some but not all of the subselves seek help, there are everyday parallels. Another (spatiotemporally distinct) person may employ persuasion in the face of my ambivalence, or when I am, as we say, of two minds. In dissuading me from some action about which I am unresolved, for example, you throw your weight on the side of one perspective at the expense of the other, talking me into the option you regard as preferable. However, where the intervention imposed might be unsought, resisted, and even 'involuntary' from the perspective of one or several of the subselves, the notion of a partial or fractured willingness

[23] For some further discussion of these issues, see Radden 1996: 212–15; Quante 2007.
[24] Charland's work is directed towards one subgroup of personality disorders only; nonetheless, his general principle seems to be applicable here.
[25] The nature of the unification process remains somewhat opaque, even after detailed clinical and 'autobiographical' descriptions (Putnam 1989; Kluft and Fine 1993; Chase 1987); its effectiveness has also been questioned (Bateman and Fonagy 2000).

introduces a moral hazard not encountered in the everyday case.[26] It seems likely that without unanimous consent to treatment from all the subselves, such interventions will always be unacceptable.[27]

The same complexities arising from the whole to part relationship noted above recur when extremes of multiplicity are considered in terms of the suffering and dysfunction standardly appealed to in justifying intervention.

As it presents itself in the clinic, extreme multiplicity is often the source of suffering, and in this respect, it falls within some of our culture's more settled ideas about mental disorder and its treatment. When such disorder brings personal distress, clinical intervention to help alleviate that distress is in the eyes of many not only warranted, but obligatory.[28] Generalizations about the suffering wrought by extremes of multiplicity must be made with caution, nonetheless. Fractured selves may seek clinical attention *only when*, and *because*, their condition results in suffering or distress, it has sometimes been speculated. Other multiples (Erika/Manfred, perhaps) will live on, outside the clinic, either without experiencing significant disadvantage from the condition, or, as in the case of Beth/Felicity, seemingly helped to *avoid* distress by their multiplicity. So the actual extent to which multiplicity might enhance or detract from suffering can be determined neither a priori, nor from clinical records alone.[29] Within the clinic if not outside it, though, whole to part questions remain over the unit to which such suffering is ascribed. One or several of these subselves may suffer without all doing so, case records seem to demonstrate. This suggests another prescriptive conclusion. For intervention to be warranted might require the attribution of suffering to all and every subself, in the same way that, we saw, it probably requires unanimous consent to treatment.

The presence of *dysfunction* reflects the other norm over which there is some broad, societal consensus when it comes to judging unhealth severe enough to warrant intervention. Yet attributions of dysfunction introduce further puzzles, for the whole to part relationship that we saw complicates the attribution of other traits to multiples, also confounds an ascription of dysfunction to them.

[26] In some clinical descriptions the achievement of unification occurs through 'killing off' certain, reluctant subselves (Prince 1906; Yalon 1989). Other accounts emphasize the importance of enlisting the willing participation of *all* subselves (Dell and Eisenhower 1990; Ross *et al.* 1995).

[27] Bayne has reached this same conclusion through appeal to the full moral status he believes must be accorded to such subselves, selves by dint of their possession of certain psychological properties (Bayne 2001). The vulnerability of this approach resides in the factual claim, for others have stressed the depleted and comparably 'thin' set of psychological properties possessed by subselves (Braude 1995; Kennett and Matthews 2002).

[28] This is not to imply that treatment is imposed on unwilling subjects, but rather that the healer has a positive duty.

[29] Social scientists have tools for assessing the incidence of disorders in the community, so I do not mean to suggest that the accurate epidemiological picture could not be sought, although I know of no data presently available on these numbers.

The ascription of psychological dysfunction is today often linked to evolutionary psychology. There, it has several distinguishable interpretations, including the idea that something prevents a psychological module from performing its (evolutionary) function, and the very different idea that the psychological function has become maladaptive *in relation to* the changed environment surrounding it.[30] These different explanatory models need concern us in only one respect: the first attributes dysfunction within the (whole human) person, while in the second, dysfunction is attributed on the basis of a relationship between two terms, the person and her environment. The forms of dysfunction identified within the clinic reflect this contrast. Inner conflicts, contradictions, and memory lapses suggest a malfunctioning psyche; the more social disadvantages they bring, involving behavior, plans, goals, and relationships, suggest a mismatch between the broader social environment and the individual within it.

As we would expect, whole to part issues complicate that picture also. Some subselves (Beth, for example) seem to function successfully *because of* the presence and activities of others, even if the resulting whole human being, the composite Beth/Felicity, is dysfunctional in some respects (prey to troubling blackouts, memory lapses, and communicative difficulties, for example, as well as problems about self 'identity').

On analogy with the above analysis of suffering, we might suppose that only if all separate subselves exhibit *separate* dysfunction could such a norm ground therapeutic intervention with multiples. But dysfunction is attributed to systems, and there are several systems involved here, including the subself system (Beth's one, Felicity's another), the system encompassing the whole human being (the composite Beth/Felicity's); and that of the broader social setting within which the whole human being is situated (Beth/Felicity's lifeworld). More holistic in these ways than attributions of suffering, attributions of dysfunction can and often do take as their subject the whole, or composite human being, *rather than any or all of its component parts*. But the functioning of the whole human being cannot be detached from the broader setting in which it occurs. Dysfunction in the whole human person brings difficulties in the broader system surrounding that person—dysfunction in relation to other persons, societal institutions, and practices.

This broad and far-reaching *social dysfunction* often guides diagnosis and intervention in the clinic. And the norms around social function and dysfunction link to earlier remarks about the desirability of a degree of self-unity (see above). When multiplicity stands in the way of valued qualities such as those enumerated there (agency, trust, certain moral categories, and relationships), there will be

---

[30] These are not proposed as incompatible models, it should be pointed out; they seem likely to provide complementary explanations. For additional models and a fuller discussion see Murphy and Stich 2000; Murphy 2004.

dysfunction in the most holistic system identified above—that including the full social surround. And only then, perhaps, is unifying intervention rightly recommended.

Summing up then: a certain degree of self-unity is rightly recognized as emblematic of mental health, and if actual phenomena correspond to the extremes of multiplicity reported from the clinic, unifying treatment will be appropriate—warranted, however, not by timeless and abstract conceptions of personhood, but by our society's normative preferences. As actual attributes and as ideals, self-unity and singularity are preconditions for other valued qualities, traits, and practices. Granted, the case for aligning self-unity with mental health would diminish if and to the extent that those other goods, and the institutions they support, ceased to be valued. But it is because these goods *are* valued that social dysfunction is disvalued, and that we have justification for privileging the whole person over its separate parts, and preferring oneness to radical personal fracture. *Within our present culture* extremes of multiplicity are rightly understood as dysfunction in the whole, socially embedded human being.

CONCLUSION

This chapter began by placing the notion of multiplicity within some broader, recent, philosophical theorizing. Three accounts of multiplicity and rationales for countenancing its possibility, some solely focused on the extreme cases reported from the clinic (Braude's and my own) and one not (Rovane's), were then introduced—none without ambiguity, it was shown, when applied to particular, borderline cases. Rather than appealing to metaphysical conceptions of personhood, emphasis was placed on normative accounts such as Rovane's and my own.

My focus here has been to clarify and explain our apparent societal preference for self-unity that assigns to conditions of extreme multiplicity the status of psychopathology. This has involved two separate explorations: saying how and why we might find undesirable the extremes of multiplicity reported from the clinic, and inquiring into how the whole to part relationships introduced by those extremes affect the ethics of therapeutic intervention. There is justification for privileging the whole person over its separate parts and preferring oneness to radical personal fracture, it is concluded. But the further step of engaging in unifying treatment will likely require that such treatment be willingly entered into by all subselves; that suffering from the multiplicity is endured by all, and/or that social and not merely intra-psychic dysfunction is present. At least as we can understand multiple selves from clinical description, such conditions will not always, and perhaps not often, be met.

REFERENCES

ARMSTRONG, J. (2001). 'The Case of Mr Woods', *Southern California Interdisciplinary Law Journal*, 10: 205, 207–16.

ARMSTRONG, J. C., and LOEWENSTEIN, R. J. (1990). 'Characteristics of Patients with Multiple Personality and Dissociative Disorders on Psychological Testing', *Journal of Nervous and Mental Diseases*, 178/7: 448–54.

BATEMAN, A. W., and FONAGY, P. (2000). 'Effectiveness of Psychotherapeutic Treatment of Personality Disorder', *British Journal of Psychiatry*, 177: 138–43.

BAYNE, T. J. (2001). 'Moral Status and the Treatment of Dissociative Identity Disorder', *Journal of Medicine and Philosophy*, 27: 87–105.

——and PACHERIE, E. (2005). 'In Defence of the Doxastic Conception of Delusions', *Mind and Language*, 20/2: 163–88.

BEHNKE, S., and SINNOTT-ARMSTRONG, W. (2000). 'Responsibility in Cases of Multiple Personality Disorder', *Action and Freedom, Philosophical Perspectives*, 14 (Malden, Mass.: Blackwell).

BLISS, E. (1986). *Multiple Personality, Hypnosis and Allied Disorders* (New York: Oxford University Press).

BLOCH, J. P. (1991). *Assessment and Treatment of Multiple Personality and Dissociative Disorders* (Sarasota, Fla.: Professional Resources Press).

BRAUDE, S. E. (1991). *First Person Plural* (New York: Routledge).

——(1995). 'Multiple Personality and Moral Responsibility', *Philosophy, Psychiatry and Psychology*, 3: 37–54.

BRAUN, B. G. (ed.) (1986). *Treatment of Multiple Personality Disorders* (Washington, DC: American Psychiatric Press).

BROWN, M. T. (2001). 'Multiple Personality and Personal Identity', *Philosophical Psychology*, 14/4: 435–47.

CHARLAND, L. (2004). 'Moral Treatment and the Personality Disorders', in Jennifer Radden (ed.), *The Philosophy of Psychiatry: A Companion* (New York: Oxford University Press), 64–77.

CHASE, T. (1987). *When Rabbit Howls* (New York: E. P. Dutton).

COLTHEART, M., and DAVIES, M. (eds.) (2000). *Pathologies of Belief* (Malden, Mass.: Blackwell).

DELL, P. F., and EISENHOWER, J. W. (1990). 'Adolescent Multiple Personality: Preliminary Study of Eleven Cases', *Journal of the American Academy of Child and Adolescent Psychiatry*, 29/4: 359–66.

EKLUND, M. (2004). 'Personal Identity, Concerns, and Indeterminacy', *The Monist*, 87/4: 489–511.

FRANKFURT, H. (1999). *Necessity, Volition and Love* (Cambridge: Cambridge University Press).

GUNNARSSON, L. (2009). *Philosophy of Personal Identity and Multiple Personality* (New York: Routledge).

GENDLER, T. (2002). 'Personal Identity and Thought Experiments', *Philosophical Quarterly*, 52: 34–54.

HACKING, IAN (1995). *Rewriting the Soul: Multiple Personality and the Sciences of Memory* (Princeton: Princeton University Press).

HAYES, C. (2007). *Self Transformations: Foucault, Ethics, and Normalized Bodies* (New York: Oxford University Press).

KENNETT, JEANETTE, and MATTHEWS, S. (2002). 'Identity, Control and Responsibility: The Case of Dissociative Identity Disorder', *Philosophical Psychology*, 15/4: 509–26.

KLUFT, R., and FINE, C. (eds) (1993). *Clinical Perspectives on Multiple Personality Disorder* (Washington, DC: American Psychiatric Press).

KORSGAARD, C. (1989). 'Personal Identity and the Unity of Agency: A Kantian Response to Parfit', *Philosophy and Public Affairs*, 18 (Spring): 101–32.

——(1996). *The Sources of Normativity*, ed. O. O'Neill (Cambridge: Cambridge University Press), chs. 1–4.

McHUGH, P. (1995). 'Multiple Personality Disorder is an Individually and Socially Created Artifact', *Journal of American Academy of Child and Adolescent Psychiatry*, 34/7: 957–9.

MACKENZIE, C., and ATKINS, K. (eds) (2007). *Practical Identity and Narrative Agency* (New York: Social Philosophy and Policy).

MATTHEWS, S. (2003). 'Establishing Personal Identity in Cases of DID', *Philosophy, Psychiatry and Psychology*, 10/2: 143–51.

MERSKEY, H. (1992). 'The Manufacture of Personalities: The Production of Multiple Personality Disorder', *British Journal of Psychiatry*, 160: 327–40.

MURPHY, DOMINIC (2004). 'Darwinian Models of Psychopathology', in Jennifer Radden (ed.), *Philosophy of Psychiatry: A Companion* (New York: Oxford University Press), 329–37.

——and STICH, S. (2000). 'Darwin in the Madhouse: Evolutionary Psychology and the Classification of Mental Disorders', in P. Carruthers and A. Chamberlain (eds), *Evolution and the Human Mind* (Cambridge: Cambridge University Press), 62–92.

OLSON, E. (2007). *The Human Animal* (New York: Oxford University Press).

PIPER, A., and MERSKEY, H. (2004). 'Persistence of Folly: Critical Examination of Dissociative Identity Disorder', *Canadian Journal of Psychiatry*. 49: 678–83.

PRINCE, M. (1906). *The Dissociation of Personality: A Biographical Study in Abnormal Psychology* (New York: Longmans, Green & Co.).

PUTNAM, F. (1989). *Diagnosis and Treatment of Multiple Personality Disorder* (New York: Guilford Press).

QUANTE, M. (2005). 'Personal Identity between Survival and Integrity', *Poiesis Prax*, 4: 145–61.

——(2007). 'Dimensions of Personhood', *Journal of Consciousness Studies*, 14/5–6: 56–76.

RADDEN, JENNIFER (1996). *Divided Minds and Successive Selves: Ethical Issues in Disorders of Identity and Personality* (Cambridge, Mass.: MIT Press).

——(1998). 'Pathologically Divided Minds, Sychronic Unity and Models of the Self', *Journal of Consciousness Studies*, 5/5–6: 658–72.

——(2001). 'Am I My Alter's Keeper? Multiple Personality Disorder and Responsibility', *Southern California Interdisciplinary Law Journal*, 10/2: 253–66.

REID, THOMAS (1785). *Essays on the Intellectual Powers of Man*. Repr. in John Perry (ed.), *Personal Identity* (2nd edn, Berkeley, Calif.: University of California Press, 2008), 107–18.

ROSS, C. A., ANDERSON, G., HEBER, S., and NORTON, S. R. (1990). 'Dissociation and Abuse among Multiple Personality Patients, Prostitutes and Exotic Dancers', *Hospital Community Psychiatry*, 41: 328–30.

ROVANE, C. (1998). *The Bounds of Agency* (Princeton: Princeton University Press).

RUDDER BAKER, L. (2000). *Persons and Bodies: A Constitution View* (New York: Cambridge University Press).

SAKS, E., and BEHNKE, S. (1997). *Jekyll on Trial: Multiple Personality Disorder and Criminal Law* (New York: New York University Press).

SAXE, F. N., VAN DER KOLK, B., BERKOWITZ, G., et al. (1993). 'Dissociative Disorders in Psychiatric Inpatients', *American Journal of Psychiatry*, 150: 1037–42.

SCHECHTMAN, MARYA (1996). *The Constitution of Selves* (Ithaca, NY: Cornell University Press).

——(2005). 'Experience, Agency and Personal Identity', *Social Philosophy and Policy*, 22/2: 1–24.

SIDER, T. (2001). 'Criteria for Personal Identity and the Limits of Conceptual Analysis', *Philosophical Perspectives*, 15: 189–209.

SINNOTT-ARMSTRONG, W., and BEHNKE, S. (2002). 'Responsibility in Cases of Multiple Personality Disorder', *Noûs*, 34/14: 301–23.

STRAWSON, G. (1999). 'The Self', in S. Gallagher and J. Shear (eds), *Models of the Self* (Thorverton: Imprint Academic), 1–24.

STRYKER, S., and WHITTLE, S. (eds) (2006). *The Transgender Studies Reader* (New York: Routledge).

WILLIAMS, B. (1973). *Problems of the Self* (Cambridge: Cambridge University Press).

WHITING, JENNIFER (2005). 'Review of Rovane's *The Bounds of Agency*', *Philosophical Review*, 114/3: 399–410.

——and MARTIN, R. (1998). *Self-Concern: An Experimental Approach to What Matters in Survival* (Cambridge: Cambridge University Press).

WOLLHEIM, R. (1984). *The Thread of Life* (Cambridge: Cambridge University Press).

YALON, I. (1989). *Love's Executioner, and Other Tales of Psychotherapy* (New York: Basic Books).

CHAPTER 24

AUTISM AND THE SELF

PETER R. HOBSON

INTRODUCTION

One source of insight into the nature of the self and the varieties of self-experience is the academic discipline of developmental psychopathology. The principle of this approach to research is simple, namely to study typical and atypical development in relation to one another. Through the study of children who follow an atypical path of development, it is possible to discern unexpected dissociations among features of mental functioning that seem to be intertwined in the typical case. From a complementary viewpoint, the study of typical development helps us to understand the nature and developmental implications of psychological dysfunction early in children's lives.

Developmental psychopathology may present a further, more radical challenge to our customary ways of thinking about the mind and its development. If one's aim is to encompass typical and atypical development within a single explanatory scheme, then it may prove necessary to re-examine and reformulate the concepts in terms of which current, more restricted explanations are framed. It is especially but not exclusively here that the approach of developmental psychopathology has the potential to inform and be informed by philosophical considerations.

This chapter is concerned with one particular disorder of childhood, early childhood autism. I shall be summarizing clinical descriptions and controlled studies of children and adolescents with autism that promise to deepen our thinking about the nature and development of self-experience. This will entail consideration of diverse manifestations of selfhood and, in particular, aspects of self–other relatedness such as propensities to imitate and to experience 'social emotions', both non-verbal and verbal expressions of self-consciousness, facets of language that include the use of personal pronouns, and, last but not least, linguistically formulated understandings of oneself and others as persons with minds.

From a theoretical perspective, four themes weave through this account. First, as already indicated, special interest is attached to evidence that what had seemed complementary aspects of unified phenomena of the self decompose into dissociable components of self-development. From a complementary viewpoint, we may discover that some familiar components of mental life—for example, supposedly separable cognitive and affective contributions to social experience and understanding—may originate as indissoluble *aspects* of coherent forms of social relatedness (Hobson 2008*a*). In this latter case, what had seemed to be constructed or assembled in the course of development may instead turn out to be unitary in nature, and foundational in its developmental role. Second is the theme of connectedness and differentiation. How are we to characterize the forms of relation that exist between an individual infant or toddler or older person and the social and non-social world? Thirdly, and already implicit in the two themes already outlined, is that of development. What is the appropriate conceptual framework for tracing the developmental continuities and discontinuities in what we can observe in the behaviour of typically developing infants on the one hand, and atypically developing young children with autism on the other, with what become older children's (and adults') linguistically expressed self-experience and self/other-understanding? Fourthly, what are the conditions that provide the basis for establishing a shared form of life (Wittgenstein 1958) which serves as the backdrop for interpersonal communication and language?

I shall begin by summarizing clinical descriptions of children with autism. I do so in order to illustrate how there is strong case for considering autism as a disorder not only in self–other relations but also self-awareness.

CLINICAL DESCRIPTIONS OF AUTISM

In the final sentence of the very first description of the syndrome of autism, Kanner (1943: 250) expressed his view that the group of children he studied had 'inborn autistic disturbances of affective contact'. He noted how 'people, so long as they left the child alone, figured in about the same manner as did the desk, the bookshelf, or the filing cabinet' (p. 246). Kanner's case descriptions provide vivid illustration of these children's qualities of self-awareness as well as their lack of connectedness with others. Their seeming imperviousness to other people sometimes extended to a marked failure to respond to others calling the child's own name, or an insensitivity to others' attitudes to the self. For example, Paul G. (Case 4) 'rarely responded to any form of address, even to the calling of his name . . . It made no difference whether one spoke to him in a friendly or harsh way' (pp. 227–8). Kanner noted how such abnormality extended to self-expressions in language, for example when Donald T. (Case 1) stumbled and nearly fell, and said of himself: 'You did not fall down'; or as reported by the mother of Frederick W. (Case 2): 'When receiving a gift, he would say of himself: "You say Thank you."' Kanner remarked how it was around the sixth year of life that the children he studied gradually learnt to speak of themselves in the first person and the person addressed in the second person. Earlier in life, they appeared to lack comprehension of what it meant to be an 'I' in relation to a 'you'.

Alongside these features, Kanner recorded abnormalities in non-verbal aspects of self/other awareness. For example, Elaine C. (Case 11) was said to move among other children 'like a strange being, as one moves between the pieces of furniture in a room' (p. 241). He also described a number of instances in which the children related not to what another *person* had just done, but to the hand that was in the way or the foot that stepped upon the child's blocks (Donald T., Case 1, and Paul G., Case 4), or the pin that had pricked or hand that took away a book (Barbara K., Case 5, and Charles N., Case 9). Yet when it came to the children's attitudes towards objects, it seemed to Kanner that, typically, the autistic child 'is interested in them, can play with them happily for hours. He can be very fond of them, or get angry with them . . . When with them, he has a gratifying sense of undisputed power and control' (p. 246). Such wilfulness was stressed by the mother of Frederick W. (Case 2), who stated 'He was stronger-willed that I was and held out longer'. Kanner also noted how the children took pleasure in achievements such as completing puzzles. Yet such pleasure was also notable for something else: of Frederick W., Kanner wrote: 'He blew out a match with an expression of satisfaction with the achievement, but did not look up to the person who had lit the match' (p. 224), and of Barbara K. (Case 5): 'she showed no interest in test performances. The concept of test, of sharing an experience or situation, seemed foreign to her' (p. 229). So whatever feelings accompanied the children's achievements, these appeared to lack an orientation towards other people's appreciation of what they had achieved.

The philosophically inclined writings of Bosch provide an insightful gloss on such clinical descriptions (which, incidentally, should not be taken to represent *all* children with autism, especially those who are older and more able). Bosch attempted to delineate 'the particular mode of existence of an autistic child'

(Bosch 1970: 3). He remarked on the children's difficulty in interpreting the emotional expressions of others, and illustrated how the children often seem to lack a sense of possessiveness as well as self-consciousness and shame, to be delayed in 'acting' on others by demanding or ordering, and to be missing something of the '"self-involvement", the acting with, and the identification with the acting person' (p. 81). As a reflection of this, a 'delay occurs in the constituting of the other person in whose place I can put myself . . . [and] in the constituting of a common sphere of existence, in which things do not simply refer to me but also to others' (p. 89). In these ways, Bosch framed his account of self- and other-awareness with reference to attitudes implicated in interpersonal involvement and relational stances, agency, and possession. Such attitudes are striking for their presence in typically develop-ing toddlers, but (Bosch suggested) relatively lacking in those with autism.

In order to find a very different, yet in some ways complementary, perspective on the self in autism, one might turn to a contemporary first-hand account of self-experience from the writings of a professional woman with autism, Temple Grandin (1992). Grandin wrote that, even in adulthood, she 'had an odd lack of awareness of my oddities of speech and mannerisms until I looked at videotapes' (p. 113). Here it is striking that only when confronted with herself depicted on videotape, rather than apprehending herself through the attitudes of others, could she become aware of her mannerisms. Moreover, as Happé (1991) has noted, Grandin's accounts are remarkable for their lack of emphasis on her own emotional or family life, and for their portrayal of autism as an abnormality of perceptual processing and cognitive style. On the face of it, this seems to reflect not only her (probable) unengagement with others, but also her unengagement with her*self*-as-unengaged with others. This suggests that we may need to characterize qualities of relatedness that exist not only between affected individuals and the personal and non-personal world, but also between the children or adults and themselves as 'selves'. Only partly is this a matter of whether they have concepts of self, and with what content; it is also a matter of whether they have a coherent sense or senses of self, and whether they care about, feel responsible for, attempt to exercise restraint on, or otherwise engage with themselves.

Now I turn to some controlled studies of children and adolescents with autism. These have value in determining whether the kinds of abnormality in self–other relations and experience already described are specific to children with autism, and not (for example) a reflection of severe learning difficulties that also occur among children without autism. Such studies also have the potential to illuminate the qualities of self–other relations and understanding that are impaired in autism, and to contrast these with other kinds of self-awareness that appear to be relatively intact.

CONTROLLED STUDIES OF CHILDREN
AND ADOLESCENTS WITH AUTISM

Relational self/other-awareness

An appropriate place to begin is with a controlled study involving parent report. Wimpory *et al.* (2000) interviewed parents of children between two and a half and four years old who were referred with difficulties in relating to and communicating with others. It was only after a series of such interviews had been conducted that ten children who subsequently received the diagnosis of autism were compared with ten of the children, matched for age and developmental level, who did not have autism. The focus of the interview was upon the first two years of the children's lives. Group differences emerged in manifestations of both person-to-person relations such as showing intense eye gaze, greeting, turn-taking, or directing feelings of anger and distress towards people, and person–person–world relations such as giving or showing objects to others.

A point to stress here is that very young children with autism tend not to orientate to and engage intensely with what is expressed by bodily endowed people in person-with-person exchanges, as well as in settings of joint attention. As one example from the above list, children with autism tend not to direct their anger and distress *towards people*. Their attitudes are not other-person-centred in the way that is the norm in typical development.

Experimental studies corroborate these descriptions of the children. Although there is little research that has made *direct* quantitative assessments of primary intersubjectivity among children with autism—a method that, by necessity, entails human raters making judgements of the quality of engagement between participants and other people, and achieving inter-rater reliability in doing so—there have been two such studies with children and adolescents that suggest how intersubjective deficits persist as a feature of the syndrome. In the first of these, Hobson and Lee (1998) studied spontaneous greetings and farewells of children and adolescents with and without autism relating to an unfamiliar person. There were group differences in measures that included eye contact and smiling, and in addition, fourteen participants without autism but only two with autism were judged to engage 'strongly' when greeting the adult, and only two without autism but thirteen with autism were rated as 'hardly engaged' at all. If at first blush these results seem less than startling, it is worth reflecting on the implications of giving centre-stage to 'strength of interpersonal engagement' (rather than, say, 'co-ordination of expressive behaviour') in our account of what distinguishes children with and without autism.

A predecessor to our second study on self–other engagement and communication appeared to yield contradictory findings. Capps *et al.* (1998) studied nonverbal communication in videotaped conversations between verbal young people and an interviewer, and reported that, surprisingly, participants with autism smiled and displayed appropriate affect as frequently as comparison children and did not differ in nodding and shaking their heads to respond to yes/no questions, even though they were less likely to nod while listening to their partners talk. García-Pérez *et al.* (2007) pursued a similar methodology but added ratings of two *relational* characteristics: participants' degree of affective engagement with the interviewer, and the flow of the dyadic exchange. Again there were only subtle group differences in measures of the behavioural components of nonverbal communication, yet the participants with autism were rated as significantly lower in interpersonal-affective engagement and even more markedly discrepant from the control group in the smoothness of their exchanges. As in the study by Capps *et al.* (1998), interestingly, participants with autism often showed an absence of head-shakes/nods when the conversational partner was talking, even though the group difference was *not* significant when the participants were talking; and in addition, the interviewer *also* showed less head-shaking/nodding specifically when the participant was talking, even though he did not look significantly less to these participants, nor was he lacking in smiles. We interpret these results as reflecting a specific difficulty for individuals with autism when they needed to accommodate to and connect with *someone else's* stance-in-talking. The children without autism not only nodded in accord with their own conversational input, but they also nodded in accord what they identified-with (and assimilated to their own stance) when listening to the utterances of their conversational partner. In addition, the interviewer's lack of head nods seemed to reflect *his* difficulty in identifying with moment-to-moment shifts in linguistically expressed stance manifested by the participants with autism. Here one could see how for individuals with autism *and* their partner in conversation, there were subtle nonverbal expressions of abnormality in self–other connectedness-with-differentiation associated with movements in psychological stance.

When it comes to studies of person–person–world relations (secondary intersubjectivity), there is evidence that young children with autism are relatively insensitive to the feelings of other people as the others' feelings, not only in settings that might elicit empathy but also those involving social referencing towards a shared environment. Sigman *et al.* (1992) videotaped thirty young children with autism who had a mean age of under four years, together with matched children without autism, in the presence of an adult who appeared to hurt herself by hitting her finger with a hammer, simulated fear towards a remote-controlled robot, and pretended to be ill by lying down on a couch for a minute, feigning discomfort (and see Charman *et al.* 1997, for similar events involving twenty-month-olds). In each of these situations, children with autism were unusual in rarely looking at or relating to the adult, or being affected by the adults' attitudes to the robot. When the adult pretended to be hurt, for example, children with autism often appeared unconcerned and continued to play with toys. These observations not only confirm the relative lack of emotional connectedness between young children with autism and other people, but they also illustrate the children's lack of engagement with other people's attitudes towards a shared world—a world that, amongst other things, contains themselves.

Such abnormalities in social relatedness may be contrasted with an aspect of the children's relationships that seems relatively intact, namely their attachment to a significant caregiver. There are several published studies that indicate how young children with autism *do* respond to separation from and reunion with their caregivers, at least in the short term (e.g. Rogers *et al.* 1991; Shapiro *et al.* 1987; Sigman and Mundy 1989). Many (not all) two- to five-year-old children with autism are like matched learning disabled children in showing somewhat variable mood changes such as fretting when their caregiver leaves them, and upon reunion they tend to spend more time alongside the caregiver than a stranger. Therefore the children's *relationship* with their caregivers is clearly special, even though their qualities of *relatedness* are atypical. This raises the question whether attachments to significant others might be organized by principles that differ from those that are critical for the kinds of other-person-centred engagement and perspective-shifting considered earlier.

Linguistic expressions of self/other-awareness

If a child is to adjust his or her language according to situational and communicative context as construed by conversational partners, then that individual needs to coordinate linguistic expressions with what he or she interprets to be the perspectives expressed and anticipated by the partner. More than this, he or she needs the propensity to *engage with* the other's perspective in such a way as to make the appropriate adjustments, a motivational as well as a cognitive matter. Therefore it is to be expected that children with autism who are relatively unengaged with other people's attitudes will be limited in sensitivity to pragmatic aspects of language.

One especially revealing detail of this picture is the difficulty that children with autism encounter in the use of personal pronouns. From his observations of children with autism, Kanner concluded that personal pronouns '*are repeated just as heard*, with no change to suit the altered situation' (1943: 244). One result of the child's tendency to 'echo' other people is that pronouns become misplaced, for example when the autistic child says, 'Do you want a bath?' to express his desire to have a bath, and this has led some to suppose that this tendency to echolalia amounts to a sufficient explanation of pronoun confusions. However, as Bosch (1970) pointed out, pronouns may also be used incorrectly in non-echolalic utterances, and sometimes the autistic child may make third-person self-references by naming himself or calling himself 'he', or may substitute passive constructions for what would normally be expressed in assertive first-person statements. This suggests that there is something unusual about the child's experience of himself *as* a self *vis-à-vis* others. Indeed, echolalia might arise from limitations in self–other differentiation and/or self-conception (Hobson 1990, 1993*a*, 1993*b*). Instead of relating the other person's utterance to that person's attitude and then identifying with the other person's stance, children with autism tend to adopt speech forms that correspond with *their* experience of the circumstances in which the words are uttered, and therefore to repeat utterances as heard (Charney 1981). This represents a failure to recognize and assume the other person's attitude-in-speaking.

Evidence compatible with this account of atypical self- and other-reference comes from studies by Jordan (1989) and Lee *et al.* (1994), where in settings such as being the object of a puppet's tickling, or when referring to photographs of themselves, children with autism would sometimes give proper names to themselves or the experimenter sitting alongside, rather than using the pronouns 'me' or 'you'. We interpreted our own study as indicating that participants with autism had a relatively detached, almost third-person attitude to photographs of themselves and the experimenter. In contrast, children without autism seemed to identify with the depictions of themselves, and to see and care about the photographed person as 'me'. The images were infused with individuals' *sense* of identity as well as formal identity. It is also of note that in a study by Loveland and Landry (1986), correct production of I/you pronouns by autistic children was related to the number of their spontaneous initiations of joint attention with an experimenter. This suggests that correct usage may reflect a special quality of engagement and co-reference between self and other. Although it is possible that additional cognitive and perhaps grammatical limitations contribute to the children's difficulties with personal pronouns (Fay 1979), it is plausible that this abnormality stems from their difficulties in recognizing and investing in self and other *as* selves who can occupy reciprocal roles in discourse.

Alignment between self and other through imitation

The reason that so much attention has been paid to young children's developing propensities and abilities to imitate other people is that here we may find not only reflections of developing self–other awareness, but also pointers to the mechanisms through which new levels of self–other understanding might be achieved. There is a complex and in part conflicting literature on this topic. On the one hand, there are many clinical and experimental reports to indicate that the children find it hard and/or are rarely moved to imitate a range of emotional expressions, bodily movements, and pantomimed actions of other people (e.g. DeMyer *et al.* 1972; Rogers *et al.* 2003). On the other hand, children with autism are able to copy the goal-directed actions of someone else (e.g. Charman and Baron-Cohen 1994), and are prone to 'echo' the behavior of others. Moreover, several studies have reported how children with autism show responsiveness to being imitated, so that they often become more socially engaged and interactive when an adult imitates their actions (Dawson and Adams 1984; Dawson and Galpert 1990). Therefore the specific qualities of the children's imitative deficits may betray something about the basis for their limitations in self–other awareness, and the specific qualities of their imitative *abilities* illuminate how they develop some forms of self-consciousness and self-concept.

Two aspects of imitation are especially revealing insofar as they appear to tap the process of identifying with someone else. Hobson and Lee (1999) tested matched groups of children with and without autism aged between 9 and 19 years (and verbal mental ages between 4 and 13 years) for their ability to imitate a person demonstrating four novel goal-directed actions on objects in two contrasting 'styles'. In one condition, the demonstrator made a toy policeman-on-wheels move along by pressing down on its head *either* with his wrist cocked *or* with extended index and middle fingers. In other conditions, he showed either gentle or harsh styles of action. The results were that children with autism were perfectly able to copy the demonstrator's actions, for example in pressing down the policeman's head to make him move, but contrasted with control participants insofar as very few adopted the demonstrator's style of acting upon the objects. Instead of adopting the wrist or two-finger approach to activating the toy, for example, most of them pressed down on the policeman's head with the palm of a hand. Here there appeared to be a contrast between children's ability to observe and copy intended actions *per se*, relatively intact in autism, and the propensity to identify with and thereby imitate a *person's* expressive mode of relating to objects and events in the world. Secondly, when the demonstrator held a pipe-rack against his own shoulder in order to strum it with a stick, a substantial majority of the control participants positioned the pipe-rack against their own shoulder before strumming it, but most of the children with autism positioned the pipe-rack at a distance in front of them, on the table. Again with respect to self-orientation, the children with autism did not identify with the other and perform the actions from a person-centred perspective.

Subsequent studies have confirmed this lesser propensity to adopt the self/other anchored orientation of actions, for example manifest in the demonstrator rolling a wheel either close-to-self or close-to-other (Meyer and Hobson 2004). Moreover, a study by Hobson and Hobson (2007) yielded evidence that the propensity to adopt the demonstrator's self/other-orientation was specifically related to one form of joint attention, namely that involving 'sharing looks' (but not other forms of person-to-person looking, such as checking-out looks) between participant and demonstrator of a kind that conveyed personal involvement. Thus two aspects of social engagement that *appear* to be quite distinct—forms of sharing experience, as reflected in sharing looks, and the adoption of other-centred-stances when imitating—turn out to be intimately related to one another. This adds force to the suggestion that, in each case, what one observes is a quality of intersubjective engagement that implicates a degree of identification with the person related to.

Finally, two studies have had the aim of analysing the role of identification in communicative settings. Hobson and Meyer (2005) devised an original methodology called the Sticker Test and demonstrated that whereas children without autism would often point to *themselves* to communicate that a tester should place a sticker on *herself*, this was much less frequently the case among children with autism. Here the children without autism appeared to identify with the tester in assuming that she would interpret the child's self-orientated action as one with which she should identify, in order to place the sticker on her own (i.e. the tester's) body. Participants with autism seldom adjusted their communication in this mutually coordinated, person-anchored way. In the second study, Hobson *et al.* (2007) created a setting in which participants had the task of observing an investigator who demonstrated an action, and then communicating to another tester who only subsequently entered the room that he should complete the same action. There were six actions demonstrated, and for each in turn, the demonstrator's instruction was: 'Get Pete to do this'. As predicted, the results were that participants with autism contrasted with matched participants without autism in showing lesser degrees of (*a*) emotional engagement with the testers, (*b*) forms of joint attention that implicate sharing of experiences, (*c*) communication of styles of action, and (*d*) role-shifting from that of the learner to that of the teacher. When these measures were combined in a composite index of identifying with someone else, the two groups were almost completely distinct. This illustrates how 'identifying with' someone else is a motivational as well as an emotional process: one person is drawn or moved to assume another's psychological orientation.

Self-conscious emotions

Feelings such as coyness, embarrassment, guilt, pride, jealousy, or shame are sometimes called 'social' or even 'complex' emotions, on the grounds that they seem to entail sophisticated understandings of self and other people along with relatively high levels of self-consciousness. However, it is far from clear that this heterogeneous group of feelings are 'social' in the same respects, nor that they are all 'complex' in the sense that they implicate relatively sophisticated thinking, nor that they are all bound up with a similar kind of self-consciousness. Indeed, controlled studies of social emotions and self-conscious feelings among individuals with autism challenge each of these presumptions.

Here it is worth returning to what parents say about their children with autism. Hobson *et al.* (2006) interviewed parents of children with and without autism who were aged between approximately 6 and 13 years and matched for verbal ability (roughly that of typically developing 3 to 9 year olds). Parents felt they could recognize in their children with autism not only emotions such as anger and fear, but also emotional responsiveness to other people's mood states, as well as shyness, non-person-directed pride, and jealousy. Yet they could seldom cite clear instances of other-person-centred emotions such as guilt, shame, pity, empathic concern, or embarrassment. One parent who gave a convincing account of her child's jealousy said this about his expressions of concern: 'He might be worried but he doesn't have that empathy sort of concern—he doesn't show that at all. . . . Empathetic sadness isn't there.'

These reports from parents dovetail with what may be gleaned from self-reports elicited from verbally fluent children and adolescents with autism. For example, Kasari *et al.* (2001) described how high-IQ children with autism reported feeling guilt, but only 14 per cent of participants with autism (versus 42 per cent of those with typical development) spoke of guilt over physical harm to others, and none referred to emotional harm such as hurting someone's feelings. Instead they were more likely (73 per cent of instances) to describe situations of rule-breaking, disruptiveness, or property damage. When speaking of embarrassment, fewer participants with autism explicitly mentioned an audience (also Capps *et al.* 1992). In 'self-understanding interviews' conducted by Lee and Hobson (1998), children with autism were not only restricted in the feelings they expressed about themselves, but also failed to mention friends or being members of a social group. And Bauminger and Kasari (2000) described how children with autism spoke of loneliness but failed to refer to the more affective dimension of being left out of close intimate relationships. Therefore it is not merely that children and adolescents with autism *seem* to have difficulty in responding to another person's feelings or attitudes as belonging to that person (and at times shaping their own feelings), but it is also that this limitation is apparent in their own descriptions of what they feel.

Finally, there is evidence from quasi-experimental studies such as that conducted by Kasari *et al.* (1993), who tested young autistic and non-autistic retarded children (mean age 42 months) and MA-matched typically developing children (mean age 23 months). Each participant completed a puzzle, and the investigator and parent reacted neutrally; then the child completed a second puzzle, and after three seconds, both adults gave praise. Although children with autism were like mentally retarded and typically developing children in being inclined to smile when they succeeded with the puzzles, those with autism were less likely to draw attention to what they had done or to look up to an adult, and less likely to show pleasure in being praised. Their pride assumed a strangely 'asocial' form. It seems that pride has two components, namely pride in accomplishing something—a feeling that is not 'social'—and pride before other people.

In a very recent study of our own on anticipatory concern (Hobson *et al.* 2009), children witnessed one adult tearing another (non-responsive) adult's drawing. In contrast to children without autism, who expressed dismay, questioned the perpetrator, and showed concern towards the victim, most children with autism showed very little indication of *feeling for* the person whose drawing it was. For example, few responded to the sight of the adult tearing the drawing by giving an immediate look to the victim, a reaction that was not only very common among those without autism, but also seemed to reflect how swiftly they identified with and anticipated the hurt the person would feel. The victim had shown no overt expression, yet the children without autism immediately orientated towards, and showed concern for, this person.

So, too, Hobson *et al.* (2006) contrived situations in which participants might feel pride, guilt, and coyness/embarrassment. Again children with autism were relatively less likely than matched participants without autism to manifest other-person-directed expressions of the feelings. For example, when they felt responsible for the leg falling off a doll, they were less likely to show a 'guilty looks' pattern of orientation towards the tester that included expressions of relief when the tester reassured them that the doll was already broken; and when they received the attentions of a cuddly toy wielded by a playful tester, they rarely showed 're-engagement looks' that give coyness a specially intimate quality. This was despite the fact that the participants with autism showed many signs of being aware when they were the focus of attention. It seemed that there was a dissociation between these participants' self-consciousness in being observed, and their ability to be affected by and engaged with the attitudes of a particular embodied other person. Or again, there appears to be a contrast between the ability of children with autism to remove rouge from their faces when they perceive themselves in a mirror, and their relative lack of coyness in that same context (Dawson and McKissick 1984; Neuman and Hill 1978; Spiker and Ricks 1984).

IMPLICATIONS FOR THE DEVELOPMENT OF SELF

The evidence from clinical observations and recent research on autism suggests that children with this syndrome show abnormality in a propensity that configures self–other interaction among typically developing young children, namely that of identifying with the attitudes of other people (Freud 1955/21). Through identification, the self not only responds to another individual's bodily expressed orientation from that other person's stance, but also assimilates that orientation so that it becomes a possible mode of relating for the self. Importantly, therefore, what is perceived in the other is apprehended to have otherness in virtue of its grounding in the other person's body. For example, infant-style episodes of affective sharing have a dyadic structure in which the child experiences such events as essentially linked with a special kind of thing in the world, namely the other person with whom the sharing is occurring (albeit not yet conceptualized as such). So, too, the developmental implications of social referencing depend not only on the infant's adjustments in attitude through responsiveness to another person's bodily expressed attitudes, but also upon the infant experiencing this shift as occurring through another source of attitudes, that is, another person. It is critical for developments in social understanding that the infant should register the shift *as* a shift across perspectives, not merely as a change in the meaning of objects at the focus of referencing, if the infant is to come to understand what it means to hold a perspective. The fact that, at the end of the first year, infants are showing or pointing out things to other people betrays their engagement with others as separate sources of attitude to objects and events in the world. Then around the middle of the second year of life, the child acquires the abilities to conceptualize what it means for people to have their own 'selves' and psychological stances, to exercise self-reflective awareness, and to introduce (originally person-anchored) perspectives to new objects in symbolic play.

The claim is *not* that individuals with autism are completely lacking in these abilities; rather, they appear not to have the powerful pull towards, nor fully organized experience of, relations that have the other-person-centred qualities that identification affords. This means that the quality of their engagement with others, and more specifically their ability to apprehend, be moved by, and have feelings configured by, other-person-centred attitudes is compromised. There appear to be essential links between such abnormalities and these children's ability to attend, respond, and adjust to the attitudes of others as these are directed to a shared world—and, importantly, to experience and understand themselves as selves in relation to other people with selves of their own (also Frith and Happé 1999). They are compromised in the ability to occupy a 'form of life' that is held in common with others (Wittgenstein 1958; and Hobson 2008*b*, on the relevance of Wittgenstein's ideas for autism). It is very probable that this set of deficits underlies the children's limited propensity to make adjustments in pragmatic aspects of language, and to adopt multiple co-referential attitudes to objects and events in symbolic play (e.g. Hobson 1993*a*, 2002; Hobson *et al.* 2008).

Central to this account is the claim that within human forms of sharing experience—forms of sharing that appear to be a feature of typically developing infants' social relations, at least from the age of about two months—one person has affective engagement with the attitudes of another in such a way that the otherness of the embodied other is encompassed within the experience. In the typical case, relating to this other-centred stance as a stance-towards-the-world is something that develops over the first year, and understanding what it is for a self to hold or adopt a stance-towards-the-world emerges in the second year. Concern and guilt are manifestations of affective engagement with other people as centres of subjectivity with whom one is linked and from whom one is differentiated. Self/other role-reversals and adjustments support the acquisition of context-sensitive language and communication as well as more specific expressions of deixis such as personal pronouns.

What follows for our account of how children acquire a concept of self? A condition of having the concept of something is that one needs to know what it is to relate to that something in ways that are appropriate to the object or event in question (Hamlyn 1974, 1978). In the case of self–other understanding, this means that in order to acquire concepts of self and other, one needs to have a grasp of the kinds of relations that are fitting between selves and other selves. If one had *no* experience of these kinds of personal relations, and for example always perceived persons as pieces of furniture, then one could not derive concepts of self and other, because it is part of what we understand selves to be that they engage in personal forms of self–other relations. If one had only partial experience of the appropriate kinds of relation—and this seems to be the case for people with autism—one would acquire only a partial concept of self. The importance of this is that concepts of self and other, and with this, concepts of mental states that are properties of self and other, are grounded in preconceptual forms of experience of relations with embodied, and bodily expressive, other people.

As Strawson (1962) argued, it is in the nature of concepts that they are generalizable and applicable to more than one instance of whatever they pick out. Therefore to conceptualize the self is also to conceptualize other selves: concepts of self and other are logically intertwined (which is not the case for all *senses* of self). Moreover, like the concept of persons, the concept of self has intrinsically self-ascriptive and other-ascriptive uses, and to learn what 'self' means is to learn that it applies to oneself and to other selves. According to the present account, both self and other are prefigured in forms of sharing that appear early in infancy, and that might be viewed as reflecting the most primitive kinds of identification (see Chapter 2 above). The developmental path is towards increasing 'distancing' between self and other, as Werner and Kaplan (1984, originally 1963) described, and this is achieved in part by infants perceiving and identifying with other people's manifest attitudes towards a shared world that includes themselves. When the child acquires concepts in the second year, therefore, there is no need for a new mechanism or process to establish linkage and differentiation between concepts of self and other: self and other are already linked and differentiated within experience.

Expressions of self–other relatedness and self-awareness among children with autism highlight the importance of these considerations. Children with autism have restricted experience of engagement with the bodily expressed attitudes of others and, more specifically, a limited ability to experience the world as peopled by human beings with whom they can identify and towards whom they feel concern, guilt, embarrassment, and so on. Identifying with the attitudes of others is a primary way to establish a connection between first-person phenomenological experience of, say, feelings of distress or possessiveness or agency, and other people's experiences of these kinds (Barresi and Moore 1996). Through movements across self/other perspectives—that is, shifts in person-anchored perspectives that occur through pre-conceptual, non-inferential processes of identification—young children come to understand what it is for a self to have a perspective, and to acquire the form of explicit (symbolic) representation needed for concepts of self and other. It is difficult to conceive how these developments would take place without some awareness of self-agency and others' agency, of self-as-having versus other-as-having (or perhaps, appropriating), as well as a diverse set of relational patterns of feeling in which the infant experiences something of the other's attitudes (e.g. the other's anger) alongside their own attitudes (e.g. distressed) in response. Structures of self/other awareness are foundational for, and not merely the products of, concepts of self and other (Bråten 1998; Reddy 2003).

Because a child's experience of affectively patterned personal relatedness is constitutive of that child's understanding of the nature of persons with minds (Hobson 1993b), children with autism acquire only a 'thin' notion of selves with minds of their own. Yet, as we have seen, (many) children with autism have *some* concept of self and *some* capacity to acquire self-reflection (although there are no studies on whether this ability is hard-won and achieved relatively late in childhood). Their concepts of self and their range of self-directed attitudes are limited in virtue of their abnormality in some, but only some, of several dissociable lines of development that contribute to the typical development of self.

Within the domain of social relations, children with autism have the propensity and ability to read intentions and goal-directed actions in other people's behavior, but they relatively lack the propensity and ability to read and respond to the attitudes of others (e.g. Hobson 1995; Moore *et al.* 1997). They can copy goal-directed actions, but tend not to identify with the person whose actions those are and thereby to assume the other person's physically grounded orientation-in-acting. They are affected by expressions of feeling in others in a rather ill-focused manner, but are seldom affected (through identification) by the other person's feelings *as* the feelings of another self with whom they are engaged. Frith and de Vignemont (2005) suggest that people with Asperger syndrome suffer from a disconnection between a strong naive egocentric stance, where the other person is represented in relation to the self, and an allocentric stance detached from interactions with people, where the existence or mental states of other people need to be represented as independent from the self. The present account promises to explain why, even when they do acquire the ability to reflect upon themselves, individuals with Asperger syndrome appear to be restricted to an egocentric perspective, and at the same time experience themselves as an onlooker towards relations among others. So, too, a restricted ability to identify-with-oneself in the past and future is relevant for explaining phenomena such as delayed self-recognition (Lind and Bowler 2009) and impaired autobiographical memory (e.g. Bowler *et al.* 2000) in persons with autism.

Through autism, then, we learn something new about the underpinnings of self/other-awareness in typical development and, more specifically, the ways in which identifying-with introduces structure to self–other relatedness. The phenomenology of such forms of relatedness has a special quality, most simply expressed in terms of sharing experiences with another, but also extended to events where the participants' attitudes are complementary or otherwise coordinated (e.g. when a child identifies with an angry parent and at the same time feels fear). As John Campbell (2005: 288) has expressed this for the special case of joint attention: 'joint attention is a primitive phenomenon of consciousness. Just as the object you see can be a constituent of your experience, so too it can be a constituent of your experience that the other person is, with you, jointly attending to the object.' As Freud proposed for melancholia and intimated for other states such as fellow-feeling or empathy, the phenomenology of certain mental states may depend upon configurations of identification.

It may be worth adding a brief postscript to this account. Evidence from neuroscience, and more specifically functional MRI scanning that has had a focus upon the operation of 'mirror neurones' or other reflections of self–other psychological connectedness and correspondence in interaction (see Minio-Paluello et al. 2009, for a recent study of empathy, together with secondary references), has given us a picture of how something like identification may operate on neurofunctional level (see for discussion, Decety and Chaminade 2003; Gallese 2001). There is also evidence, both from fMRI findings (Dapretto et al. 2006) and EEG patterns of mu frequency suppression (Oberman et al. 2005), that such functioning may be atypical among children with autism (Williams et al. 2001). It would be premature to attribute a causal role to such indications of neurological dysfunction among people with autism—they could just as easily reflect the developmental outcome of diverse deficits in social engagement—but they have generated welcome interest in the structure of *inter*personal perception and experience.

Some Final Considerations on Self-Conscious Emotions

Cognitive-developmental theory has posited that concepts of self are *necessary* if a child is to feel and express so-called social emotions. For example, Lewis (2003: 286) has suggested that 'In the case of jealousy, envy, empathy, embarrassment, shame, pride, and guilt ... the elicitation of this class of emotions involves elaborate cognitive processes, and these elaborate cognitive processes have, at their heart, the notion of self, agency, and conscious intentions.' Yet it is not clear that 'elaborate cognitive processes' are either necessary or sufficient for the experience of the feelings in question. Just as experience of personal relations is constitutive of the concept of persons with minds, so experience that is *seemingly* complex in its cognitive structure may be constitutive of concepts of self and other.

There are three points to stress here. First, the phenomenology of a variety of socially embedded feelings may be difficult to characterize without using a lot of words, but this does not mean that such feelings are built up out of components that correspond with the words we use (also Frijda 1993). They might be primitive in nature. In particular, they may not require concepts. Secondly, it is difficult to see how *concepts* of self and other would explain much about the emergence of phenomenological qualities of, say, guilt or shame. Why should concepts transform supposedly simpler emotions into such distinctive and powerful new feelings? The third point is complementary to the first two, and concerns the basis for acquiring concepts of self and other. The question here is what structure and content such concepts would have, if there were not *already* a rich set of attitudes with which an infant could identify in order to establish the developmental bases (e.g. movements in attitude through others) for the emergence of these concepts around the middle of the second year? If both the acquisition of conceptual thinking and the content of concepts of self and other depend on experience of self–other relations, one should beware of supposing that too much by way of interpersonal relatedness is concept-dependent.

Of course, there are important changes in children's ways of experiencing themselves and others once they begin to conceptualize self and other, and changes also take place in how they behave in response to what they feel (see e.g. Lewis 2004). When they acquire a concept of self, children take a major step towards experiencing more grown-up forms of responsibility that go with more sophisticated kinds of guilt. Yet (to repeat) it could also be that an unconceptualized sense of responsibility is part of what gives rise to the concept of self in the first place, just as it may contribute to the phenomenology of guilt. If the concept of self derives much of its content from an individual's experience of self–other relations, then infantile experience of such relations as those that implicate early forms of concern, pride, jealousy, perhaps guilt, appropriation, embarrassment, coyness, and so on, might be critically important for the development of the concept at all.

We are led to question a second premise of much thinking in contemporary cognitive developmental psychology, namely that seemingly complex forms of psychological functioning are constructed from cognitive, affective, and motivational components. If one considers interpersonal engagement, or indeed a process such as that of identifying with the attitudes of someone else, what one encounters is a phenomenon with cognitive, affective, and motivational *aspects* (Hobson 2008a). Again it seems plausible that the relative separation of cognition, affect, and conation is a developmental achievement, not its starting-point. According to the social-developmental account presented here, for example, it is no surprise that children with autism appear to lapse in the motivation to apply whatever understandings of self and other they acquire.

To conclude: if one steps back and considers the range and quality of the children's abnormalities in their self–other relations, including those implicated in empathy and social emotions, one is struck by how children with autism have a relative dearth of engagement with other people's feelings *as* located in the other people *and* of importance for themselves in one way or another. This importance might either take the form of concern for the other, or for themselves in the eyes of the other, or indeed for what the world means for the other and therefore what it might mean for the self. Prime facie, it appears probable that these are among the abnormalities that constrain the development of such feelings as concern and guilt. From a complementary perspective, it is not possible to consider an emotion 'social', unless the individual experiencing that emotion has some awareness of other persons. At minimum, such awareness might be constituted by having an emotion of the kind that establishes or reflects personal relatedness; that is, the emotion might establish what is social, rather than require a pre-existing awareness of persons. The lesson for typical human development is that a great deal (but not everything) in the development of interpersonal relations and social understanding depends upon self–other structure to social experience from very early in life.

REFERENCES

Barresi, J., and Moore, C. (1996). 'Intentional Relations and Social Understanding', *Behavioral and Brain Sciences*, 19: 107–54.

Bauminger, N., and Kasari, C. (2000). 'Loneliness and Friendship in High-Functioning Children with Autism', *Child Development*, 71: 447–56.

Bosch, G. (1970). *Infantile Autism*, tr. D. Jordan and I. Jordan (New York: Springer-Verlag).

Bowler, D. M., Gardiner, J. M., and Grice, S. (2000). 'Episodic Memory and Remembering in Adults with Asperger's Syndrome', *Journal of Autism and Developmental Disorders*, 30: 305–16.

Bråten, S. (1998). 'Infant Learning by Altercentric Participation: The Reverse of Egocentric Observation in Autism', in S. Bråten (ed.), *Intersubjective Communication and Emotion in Early Ontogeny* (Cambridge: Cambridge University Press), 105–26.

Campbell, J. (2005). 'Joint Attention and Common Knowledge', in N. Eilen, C. Hoerl, T. McCormack, and J. Roessler (eds), *Joint Attention: Communication and Other Minds* (Oxford: Clarendon Press), 287–97.

Capps, L., Kehres, J., and Sigman, M. (1998). 'Conversational Abilities among Children with Autism and Children with Developmental Delays', *Autism*, 2: 325–44.

——Yirmiya, N., and Sigman, M. (1992). 'Understanding of Simple and Complex Emotions in Non-Retarded Children with Autism', *Journal of Child Psychology and Psychiatry*, 33: 1169–82.

CHARMAN, T., and BARON-COHEN, S. (1994). 'Another Look at Imitation in Autism', *Development and Psychopathology*, 6: 403–13.

——SWETTENHAM, J., BARON-COHEN, S., COX, A., BAIRD G., and DREW, A. (1997). 'Infants with Autism: An Investigation of Empathy, Pretend Play, Joint Attention, and Imitation', *Developmental Psychology*, 33: 781–9.

CHARNEY, R. (1981). 'Pronoun Errors in Autistic Children: Support for a Social Explanation', *British Journal of Disorders of Communication*, 15: 39–43.

DAPRETTO, M., DAVIES, M. S., PFEIFER, J. H., SCOTT, A. A., SIGMAN, M., and BOOKHEIMER, S. Y. *et al.* (2006). 'Understanding Emotions in Others: Mirror Neuron Dysfunction in Children with Autism Spectrum Disorders'. *Nature Neuroscience*, 9: 28–30.

DAWSON, G., and ADAMS, A. (1984). 'Imitation and Social Responsiveness in Autistic Children', *Journal of Abnormal Child Psychology*, 12: 209–26.

——and GALPERT, L. (1990). 'Mother's Use of Imitative Play for Facilitating the Social Behavior of Autistic Children', *Development and Psychopathology*, 2: 151–62.

——and MCKISSICK, F. C. (1984). 'Self-Recognition in Autistic Children', *Journal of Autism and Developmental Disorders*, 14: 383–94.

DECETY, J., and CHAMINADE, T. (2003). 'When Self Represents the Other: A New Cognitive Neuroscience View on Psychological Identification', *Consciousness and Cognition*, 12: 577–96.

DEMYER, M. K., ALPERN, G. D., BARTON, S., DEMYER, W. E., CHURCHILL, D. W., HINGTGEN, J. N., BRYSON, C. Q., PONTIUS, W., and KIMBERLIN, C. (1972). 'Imitation in Autistic, Early Schizophrenic, and Non-Psychotic Subnormal Children', *Journal of Autism and Childhood Schizophrenia*, 2: 264–87.

FAY, W. H. (1979). 'Personal Pronouns and the Autistic Child', *Journal of Autism and Developmental Disorders*, 9: 247–60.

FREUD, S. (1955/1921). 'Identification', in *The Standard Edition of the Complete Psychological Works of Sigmund Freud*, ed. J. Strachey (London: Hogarth), xviii. 105–10.

FRIJDA, N. H. (1993). 'The Place of Appraisal in Emotion', *Cognition and Emotion*, 7: 357–87.

FRITH, U., and DE VIGNEMONT, F. (2005). 'Egocentrism, Allocentrism, and Asperger Syndrome', *Consciousness and Cognition*, 14: 719–38.

——and HAPPÉ, F. (1999). 'Theory of Mind and Self-Consciousness: What is it Like to be Autistic?', *Mind and Language*, 14: 1–22.

GALLESE, V. (2001). 'The "Shared Manifold" Hypothesis: From Mirror Neurons to Empathy', *Journal of Consciousness Studies*, 8: 33–50.

GARCIA-PÉREZ, R. M., LEE, A., and HOBSON, R. P. (2007). 'On Intersubjective Engagement in Autism: A Controlled Study of Nonverbal Aspects of Conversation', *Journal of Autism and Developmental Disorders*, 37: 1310–22.

GRANDIN, T. (1992). 'An Inside View of Autism', in E. Schopler and G. B. Mesibov (eds), *High-Functioning Individuals with Autism* (New York: Plenum Press), 105–26.

HAMLYN, D. W. (1974). 'Person-Perception and our Understanding of Others', in T. Mischel (ed.), *Understanding Other Persons* (Oxford: Basil Blackwell), 1–36.

——(1978). *Experience and Growth of Understanding* (London: Routledge & Kegan Paul).

HAPPÉ, F. G. E. (1991). 'The Autobiographical Writings of Three Asperger Syndrome Adults: Problems of Interpretation and Implications for Theory', in U. Frith (ed.), *Autism and Asperger Syndrome* (Cambridge: Cambridge University Press), 207–42.

HOBSON, J. A., and HOBSON, R. P. (2007). 'Identification: The Missing Link between Imitation and Joint Attention?', *Development and Psychopathology*, 19: 411–31.

——Harris, R., Garcia-Pérez, R., and Hobson, R. P. (2009). 'Anticipatory Concern: A Study in Autism', *Developmental Science*, 12: 249–63.

Hobson, R. P. (1990). 'On the Origins of Self and the Case of Autism', *Development and Psychopathology*, 2: 163–81.

——(1993a). *Autism and the Development of Mind* (Hove: Erlbaum).

——(1993b). 'The Emotional Origins of Social Understanding', *Philosophical Psychology*, 6: 227–49.

——(1995). 'Apprehending Attitudes and Actions: Separable Abilities in Early Development?', *Development and Psychopathology*, 7: 171–82.

——(2002). *The Cradle of Thought* (London: Macmillan; repr. New York: Oxford University Press, 2004).

——(2008a). 'Interpersonally Situated Cognition', *International Journal of Philosophical Studies*, 6: 377–97.

——(2008b) 'Wittgenstein and the Developmental Psychopathology of Autism', *New Ideas in Psychology*, 2: 243–57.

——Chidambi, G., Lee, A., and Meyer, J. (2006). 'Foundations for Self-Awareness: An Exploration through Autism', *Monographs of the Society for Research in Child Development*, 284/71: 1–165.

——and Lee, A. (1998). 'Hello and Goodbye: A Study of Social Engagement in Autism', *Journal of Autism and Developmental Disorders*, 28: 117–27.

——and ——(1999). 'Imitation and Identification in Autism', *Journal of Child Psychology and Psychiatry*, 40: 649–59.

——Lee, A., and Hobson, J. A. (2008). 'Qualities of Symbolic Play among Children with Autism: A Social-Developmental Perspective', *Journal of Autism and Developmental Disorders*, 39: 12–22.

——————and ——(2007). 'Only Connect? Communication, Identification, and Autism', *Social Neuroscience*, 2: 320–35.

——and Meyer, J. A. (2005). 'Foundations for Self and Other: A Study in Autism', *Developmental Science*, 8: 481–91.

Jordan, R. R. (1989). 'An Experimental Comparison of the Understanding and Use of Speaker-Addressee Personal Pronouns in Autistic Children', *British Journal of Disorders of Communication*, 24: 169–79.

Kanner, L. (1943). 'Autistic Disturbances of Affective Contact', *Nervous Child*, 2: 217–50.

Kasari, C., Chamberlain, B., and Bauminger, N. (2001). 'Social Emotions and Social Relationships: Can Children with Autism Compensate?', in J. A. Burack, T. Charman, N. Yirmiya, and P. R. Zelazo (eds), *The Development of Autism* (Mahwah, NJ: Erlbaum), 309–23.

——Sigman, M. D., Baumgartner, P., and Stipek, D. J. (1993). 'Pride and Mastery in Children with Autism', *Journal of Child Psychology and Psychiatry*, 34: 352–62.

Lee, A., and Hobson, R. P. (1998). 'On Developing Self-Concepts: A Controlled Study of Children and Adolescents with Autism', *Journal of Child Psychology and Psychiatry*, 39: 1131–41.

——and Chiat, S. (1994). 'I, You, Me and Autism: An Experimental Study', *Journal of Autism and Developmental Disorders*, 24: 155–76.

Lewis, M. (2003). 'The Development of Self-Consciousness', in J. Roessler and N. Eilan (eds), *Agency and Self-Awareness* (Oxford: Clarendon Press), 275–95.

——(2004). 'The Emergence of Human Emotions', in M. L. Lewis and J. M. Haviland-Jones (eds), *Handbook of Emotions* (2nd edn. New York: Guilford), 265–92.

LIND, S., and BOWLER, D. M. (2009). 'Delayed Self-Recognition in Children with Autism Spectrum Disorder', *Journal of Autism and Developmental Disorders*, 39: 643–50.

LOVELAND, K. A., and LANDRY, S. H. (1986). 'Joint Attention and Language in Autism and Developmental Language Delay', *Journal of Autism and Developmental Disorders*, 16: 335–49.

MEYER, J. A., and HOBSON, R. P. (2004). 'Orientation in Relation to Self and Other: The Case of Autism', *Interaction Studies*, 5: 221–44.

MINIO-PALUELLO, I., BARON-COHEN, S., AVENANTI, A., WALSH, V., and AGLIOTI, S. M. (2009). 'Absence of Embodied Empathy during Pain Observation in Asperger Syndrome', *Biological Psychiatry*, 65: 55–62.

MOORE, D., HOBSON, R. P., and LEE, A. (1997). 'Components of Person Perception: An Investigation with Autistic, Nonautistic Retarded and Normal Children and Adolescents', *British Journal of Developmental Psychology*, 15: 401–23.

NEUMAN, C. J., and HILL, S. D. (1978). 'Self-Recognition and Stimulus Preference in Autistic Children', *Developmental Psychobiology*, 11: 571–8.

OBERMAN, L. M., HUBBARD, E. M., McCLEERY, J. P., ALTSCHULER, E. L., RAMACHANDRAN, V., and PINEDA, J. A. (2005). 'EEG Evidence for Mirror Neuron Dysfunction in Autism Spectrum Disorders', *Cognitive Brain Research*, 24: 190–8.

REDDY, V. (2003). 'On Being the Object of Attention: Implications for Self–Other Consciousness', *Trends in Cognitive Sciences*, 7: 397–402.

ROGERS, S. J., HEPBURN, S. L., STACKHOUSE, T., and WEHNER, E. (2003). 'Imitation Performance in Toddlers with Autism and Those with Other Developmental Disorders', *Journal of Child Psychology and Psychiatry*, 44: 763–81.

——OZONOFF, S., and MASLIN-COLE, C. (1991). 'A Comparative Study of Attachment Behaviour in Young Children with Autism or Other Psychiatric Disorders', *Journal of the American Academy of Child and Adolescent Psychiatry*, 30: 483–8.

SHAPIRO, T., SHERMAN, M., CALAMARI, G., and KOCH, D. (1987). 'Attachment in Autism and Other Developmental Disorders', *Journal of the American Academy of Child and Adolescent Psychiatry*, 26: 485–90.

SIGMAN, M., and MUNDY, P. (1989). 'Social Attachments in Autistic Children', *Journal of the American Academy of Child and Adolescent Psychiatry*, 28: 74–81.

——KASARI, C., KWON, J. H., and YIRMIYA, N. (1992). 'Responses to the Negative Emotions of Others by Autistic, Mentally Retarded, and Normal Children', *Child Development*, 63: 796–807.

SPIKER, D., and RICKS, M. (1984). 'Visual Self-Recognition in Autistic Children: Developmental Relationships', *Child Development*, 55: 214–25.

STRAWSON, P. F. (1962). 'Persons', in V. C. Chappell (ed.), *The Philosophy of Mind* (Englewood Cliffs, NJ: Prentice-Hall; originally publ. 1958), 127–46.

WERNER, H., and KAPLAN, B. (1984/1963). *Symbol Formation* (Hillsdale, NJ: Lawrence Erlbaum Associates).

WILLIAMS, J. H. G., WHITEN, A., SUDDENDORF, T., and PERRETT, D. I. (2001). 'Imitation, Mirror Neurons and Autism', *Neuroscience and Biobehavioral Reviews*, 25: 287–95.

WIMPORY, D. C., HOBSON, R. P., WILLIAMS, J. M., and NASH, S. (2000). 'Are Infants with Autism Socially Engaged? A Study of Recent Retrospective Parental Reports', *Journal of Autism and Developmental Disorders*, 30: 525–36.

WITTGENSTEIN, L. (1958). *Philosophical Investigations*, tr. G. E. M. Anscombe (Oxford: Blackwell).

....

CHAPTER 25

THE SELF

GROWTH, INTEGRITY, AND COMING APART

....

MARCIA CAVELL

I will not make poems with reference to parts. But I will make poems with reference to ensemble.

(Walt Whitman)

The philosophical literature on the self is enormous; and equally so for psycho-analysis. I am trusting that many of the issues related to the self will be discussed elsewhere in this volume, so that I may concentrate on just a few. The key issues in the literature are as follows. What is the self? Or is there no such thing? Is it present from the beginning of life? Or is it something that comes to be? When we speak of 'the lost self', or of 'finding one's self', what do we mean? What are the conditions under which the self may fall apart? What does 'falling apart' mean? Is the self continuous, or discontinuous? Are there many selves, or just one? Does the self have anything essential to do with other selves? I will address all these questions, though none in the depth they deserve.

An artist friend spoke of a chronic problem he has: 'What I'm trying to do', he said, 'is to get something inside my mind, something subjective, out onto the canvas so that it becomes a vision I can share with other people.' 'Isn't that true of any art?' I asked. So we talked about the way in which any artist must find a way of going from inner subjectivity to outer expression, a state in which he does not give up this true innerness but is also responsive to the objective world, including other people, and able to incorporate it in his work. The musician tries to translate the sounds in his head into music heard; and so with poetry; and ordinary speech, which we take so much for granted that we are not aware of the spontaneous creativity it involves. It was Plato's idea about the value of dialogue. In the exchange of views, the mutual questioning and self-questioning, Plato argued, you find that your thought or your vision becomes clearer. Furthermore, we often find that, in trying to express ourselves, what we are trying to express changes. And once the artist has made the necessary translation, he is then able to communicate with others. We were then led to the thought that just in that transition between the unformed 'inner' vision and the vision that can be shared with others is where creativity lies.

This, I remarked, is one of the ways that psychoanalytic therapy works. The struggle for expression helps create the thing to be expressed; the mind comes to know what it means in the act of trying to be understood, or misunderstood.

Speaking of a teacher and his students, David Denby (1996: 326) writes: 'They would grow in order to read the books, they would create a self, and in the end, they would make him [the teacher] obsolete.' The self, then, is the kind of thing that does grow. Growth often happens as one reaches beyond oneself, towards a goal that changes in the process. A middling pianist wants to play the *Wanderer Fantasy*. She can play it, but not well. She has a lot of work to do. She decides that she will tackle first the difficult scale and arpeggio passages. She succeeds in mastering them. This change provides a new stability against which new change will be measured. And so on. Finally she can play it very well. She had the piece in mind all the time, she thought. It was what provided her goal. She thought she heard it well enough. But she discovers that as she comes to play it better, she hears it better. And the other way around. During her practice, furthermore, she has developed her own interpretation. This is an instance of continuity against which growth can be measured. Without the continuity we cannot measure the growth.

Here again are analyst and patient. The patient has moments of fleeting illuminations, memories, bits of earlier fantasies, feelings that make no sense in the present context, or so she thinks. She and the analyst increasingly gain some feel for how they all fit together, and a growing ability to put them into words. Together they work to bring out sense and the map (the phantasy) that provides the frame. However, as Mark Solms claimed in an important paper on the emotions (on 6 October 2009, to the New York Psychoanalytic Society) 'the talking cure' is a misnomer; it leads people to think that talk and only talk is the stuff of analytic therapy, thus generating the puzzle: how can talk change anything? It can't. What happens first is feeling, Solms said; and then again and again, talk about feeling. It was the last thing he said, underlining its importance.

In the early days of psychoanalysis, the analyst was 'the authority who knows'. It was a 'one-person' model of the therapeutic process, accompanied by the idea that the patient's mental content is retrieved from the unconscious, which is itself unknowable. In the current 'two-person model', the analyst is not an authority; and both minds change in the continuing dialogue. To the extent that this is so, the analyst does not have to guess what is going on in the mind of the other because he and his patient have formulated it together, partially dispelling in such moments the problem of other minds. Of course my depiction of the two models is exaggerated, for surely every analyst uses both.

To return to my friend's question: the artist knows that unless his work has an objective quality, it remains a private phantasy, an illusion; that it is like garbled sounds rather than speech. I speak of art, but everything I have said about art is true also of human action.

D. W. Winnicott talks about growth in terms of creativity: 'It is creative apperception more than anything else that makes the individual feel that life is worth living. Contrasted with this is a relationship to external reality which is one of compliance' (1971: 67). This is what Winnicott means by 'the False Self'. For example, the child is asked to mirror the mother, to show her what she looks like, rather than feeling encouraged to look at the world through his own eyes, to form his own judgments and own values, to feel and register what he is feeling, thus beginning to form the True Self. For the child, this can happen only in the presence of other people, namely, a loving mother. Of course some compliance is necessary: crossing the street, going to bed at a certain time, learning how and where to go to the toilet. Winnicott is concerned with a kind of relationship between mother and child that begins to form his self-image, which is based on her ability to reflect his needs and moods. I think it is clear that Winnicott does not mean this to be an absolute dichotomy. To be a false self one must have some awareness of what one's true self would be, and that can only be gained through action. The false self betrays his true self and knows it. That is why he is feels like such a phoney. The 'true self' does not present a paradox, merely an impossibility. A true self that were true forever would be one whose values and self-presentation were always consistent with one's values, and so on. Such is what we might call an angel.

Other analysts also make creativity central to the development of the self: Heinz Kohut writes: 'If the mother rejects the self just as it begins to assert itself as a center of creative-productive—then the child's self will be depleted and he will abandon the attempt to attain the joys of self-assertion and will' (1977: 67). 'The self' is a misleading term. It suggests that there is such a thing, essentially enclosed, a child in a garden with no gates and a high wall. But in the picture of many of us, a self is not born, but made. The earliest mind grows slowly into a self only through its communications with other people. The child identifies with other people, and these identifications become part of her self-image. She needs other people for concept maturation and for learning to speak, and for virtually every other human capacity. 'The self', then, is embedded from the beginning in a social world, which changes as the child grows.

My central claim in this chapter is that, by definition, the self, or whatever we want to call it, grows; and is continuous; we are not born as selves. But it can also fragment, in both a pathological and a creative sense.

GROWTH

Every reader of this chapter will be familiar with Descartes's elegant one-liner (1984): 'I think, therefore I am' (or, more pointedly, 'I doubt, therefore I am'). Nevertheless we need to go through it again, quickly, and together, since the average knower may not have taken in its implications, and because it still haunts contemporary philosophy as well as psychoanalytic theory. It is elegant because it seems to prove so much in just three words (*cogito ergo sum*). It seems to prove that each of us is a self, immortal, beyond change and time. But the 'I' whose existence Descartes proves is not the bodily 'I'; nor the I that manifests itself in agency in the public world. It is not the subject that speaks. The 'I' that thinks is a totally inner I, disengaged from the body and its actions in the world. This I is invisible and unknowable, the ghost in the machine to which Gilbert Ryle's famous phrase alludes. And note that Descartes's argument works only on a particular occasion of use. It tells us nothing about what happens to the 'I' in between, if there is an in-between. Nor does it tell us anything about what an 'I' is. I cannot infer from your use of the word 'I' that you know your mind as I know mine, nor even that you have a mind.

Without intending to, some contemporary psychoanalysts have taken up Descartes's axiom that the mind is unitary, forever unknowable, unchanging, hidden behind the behavior of the body and its antics. For example, Kohut writes: 'We cannot know the self apart from its manifestations' (1977: 34). Manifestations of what? The use of the word suggests that there is some metaphysical entity behind the sensible appearances.

Responding to Descartes, the eighteenth-century empiricist David Hume said that his own experience yielded no such thing as a subject of experiences but only the experiences themselves (1951). That is, no subjects, only mental objects. It is an exact reversal of Descartes's position. Hume seems right in that no one is aware of herself as a subject behind all her experiences. He continues:

The mind is a kind of theatre, where several perceptions successively make their appearance; pass, re-pass, and glide away, and mingle in an infinite variety of postures and positions. There is properly no *simplicity* in it at one time, nor *identity* in difference. The comparison of the theatre must not mislead us. They are the successive perceptions only that constitute the mind; nor have we the least idea where these scenes are represented, or of the materials of which it is composed. (253)

As Hume admits, the metaphor is problematic. Who is watching this show? Who is putting it on? Who is the writer? The director? (Joyce McDougall, as reported by Mitchell 1991, invokes the same metaphor, the mind as a theatre.) How are these scenes connected? What makes my narrative *mine*, and yours *yours*? But without that connection we have lost the idea of personal identity as surely as Descartes.

Philosophers speak of 'I' as belonging to a logical class of what we call syncategorematic expressions, expressions that have no content in themselves. Think of 'here', now', 'then' 'you', 'it'. There is no such thing as a *now*, or a *then*, nor an *it*; nor can we infer that there is any such thing as a mind or a self. These expressions are mere pointers, the object of which depends on who is pointing and in what particular life situation. This fact about 'I' may be one of the things that trips people up when they try to understand what *the self* is.

The philosopher Richard Wollheim claims that the idea of the self as 'a collection of events spread over time is exactly wrong' (1984: 11).

Something ties these events together, such that we can say that a person in an important sense is individuated from other persons, and coherent to the extent that this something holds. The search for an accurate analysis of the concepts of person and self is a dead end. (p. 22)

Let's substitute the idea of a creature who *leads a life*. (p. 15; my emphasis)[1]

I return to Wollheim shortly.

Because it beautifully illustrates some of the points I will be making, I am going to quote at length from Virginia Woolf's novel *To the Lighthouse* (1981). At the beginning of the book, Mr. Ramsey is trying to complete what he hopes will be his philosophical *magnum opus*. He is stuck. The narrator comments: 'It was a splendid mind. For if thought is like the keyboard of a piano, divided into notes, or like the alphabet is arranged in twenty six letters all in order, then his splendid mind has no sort of difficulty in running over those letters, one by one, firmly and accurately, until he has reached, say, the letter Q' (pp. 33–4). His aim is to get to the next letter, 'R' (his name? himself?), which he does not, even at the end of the novel.

Woolf's praise of Ramsey's mind is of course ironic. Of all people, she knew that the creative mind does not work this way, stepping along a prescribed path onto stones of equal size, towards a prescribed goal. In this portrayal of the mind, states and goal are entirely given from outside; the mind has nothing to do but trace the pattern correctly.

---

[1] This chapter was heavily influenced by Richard Wollheim. We were friends in the Berkeley philosophy department for a number of years, but I hadn't yet discovered him as a philosopher. I am very sad that a lovely man, a wonderful philosopher, and a teacher from whom I could have learnt much, has died.

Lily Briscoe, a painter and the Ramseys' houseguest for the summer, is also stuck. She has been trying to complete a portrait of Mrs Ramsey, seated in a window with her little boy, James, the beautiful summer garden just beyond. Lily muses:

'Like a work of art', she repeated, looking from her canvas to the drawing room steps and back again. She must rest for a moment. And resting, looking from one to the other vaguely, the old question which traversed the sky of the soul perpetually, the vast, the general question, which was apt to particularize itself at such moments as these, when she released faculties that had been on the strain, stood over her, paused over her, darkened over her. 'What is the meaning of life?' That was all—a simple question; one that tended to close in on one with the years. The great revelation had never come. The great revelation perhaps never would come. Instead there were little daily miracles, illuminations, matches struck unexpectedly in the dark: here was one. This, that and the other . . . this was of the nature of a revelation. . . . In the midst of chaos there was shape; this eternal passing and flowing. She looked at the clouds going and the leaves shaking and was struck into stability. (p. 161)

Later, with another guest:

He turned, with his glasses raised to the scientific examination of her canvas, the question being one of the relation of masses, of lights and shadows, which, to be honest, he had never considered before—he would like to have it explained—what then did she wish to make of it? And he indicated the scene before them. She looked. She could not show him what she wished to make of it, could not see it even herself with her brush in her hand. . . . She took up once more her old painting position . . . becoming once more under the power of that vision which she had once seen clearly and must now grope for among hedges and houses and mothers and children—her picture, It was a question, she remembered, how to connect this mass on the right hand with the branch across so; or break the vacancy in the foreground by an object. But the danger was that by doing that the unity of the whole might be broken. (p. 53)

No work of art will yield to a scientific examination. Of course you could map the different pigments, just where they are placed, and so on; but from that you can't deduce the beauty of the canvas, nor even what it represents, if anything.

Lily too has not yet reached her goal.

On my view, any adequate view of the self must make room for growth, one aspect of which is reaching a goal that one has set for herself. The self can grow, it can come to know itself in the process of growing. But it can also diminish, as my discussion below of coming apart is meant to show. The self is not, then, that timeless, unchanging, ineffable, Cartesian something behind appearances.

How does Hume account for the apparent continuity of the self? He says that the connection between ideas is causal, and it is that, the sequence of causal connections, that makes for a kind of unity. But this is a confused idea. Take Lily's musings. What, in each case, is doing the causal work? Causal connection presumes causal laws, generalities under which cause and effect can be subsumed. But that is impossible here. Particulars like the lighthouse are causally connected to what? Previous experiences of lighthouses? Unlikely, since it is the context in which the lighthouse is embedded that is the element to be explained. And the same for Lily's illuminations. Or is it the whole thing at any one moment that is to be connected to some other whole thing? But surely there can be no causal laws for any of these. Without some idea of just what experiences are causally connected, the claim is empty.

The multiplicity of philosophic views about the self is matched in psychoanalytic theory. Mitchell writes:

The most striking thing about the concept of self within current psychoanalytic thought is precisely the stark contrast between the centrality of concern with self and the enormous variability and lack of consensus about what the term even means. The self is referred to variably as an idea or set of ideas in the mind, a structure in the mind, something experienced, something that does things, one's unique life history, even an idea in someone else's mind. Kahn, whose central concern has been the self, admits that no one has defined the 'self experience' successfully, and even Kohut, whose theory is named after the term 'self', acknowledged difficulty in clearly defining what he meant by it. Why is something so important so hard to grasp? (1992: 12)

One answer is that 'self' is deeply ambiguous: it can mean 'person', 'the I', 'the subject'. Another is that there is disagreement about the issues with which 'the self' is entangled. For example, is there a self at the start (Melanie Klein), or only after the infant has gone through many developmental stages (Anna Freud)? And third, 'self' is a core concept in our conceptual scheme, as are 'truth', 'knowledge', 'reality'. Core concepts cannot be defined, since other concepts are defined in terms of them. That does not mean, however, that we are unable to say some interesting things about them.

It is tempting to say, with Kant and Wittgenstein, that the self isn't anything. That is certainly true if we hear it as 'the self isn't any *thing*'. But it doesn't touch the large questions of what sort of creatures we are that can puzzle about ourselves, grow, form life projects, deceive ourselves, and so on.

Of everything I have read about the self, Wollheim's suggestion, that rather than trying to define 'self' we speak of one who is leading a life, seems the most illuminating. Except with tongue in cheek—perhaps saying something like 'My dachshund leads the life of Riley'—we wouldn't speak of dogs and cats or most mammals as leading a life. To lead a life means to have something like a conception of a life, one's own life, projects, goals, and moral values. Wollheim's idea implies that 'person' is not a mere descriptive term, but also an evaluative one. A self can be 'whole' (rather than in parts, or divided against himself). Such a person can be true to himself, and reliable for others. Only a creature who is focused on the present, enriched by the past, and headed toward the future, is leading a life. He is not passive; or to the extent that he is, he is in the process of losing his life. To have integrity is to have unified oneself to the extent that he has a coherent set of values on which he is able to act. Unfortunately, Wollheim does not give us any graceful way to speak in this alternative language; so I shall continue to speak of 'the self'.

Freud thought that the valuing capacity comes into its own with the waning of the Oedipal Complex, which begins to happen when the child is around the age of 5. I suggest that we substitute for Freud's ego, and for 'I', all the circumstances that finally allow a child to say 'I' in the appropriate circumstances, with understanding, shame, and pride, and love for the 'you' and the 'they' that 'I' implies. 'I' emerges with the painful understanding that you and I are separate. For better and for worse, I now have accepted the fact that you cannot lead my life (if we ever do). She can now speak truly for herself, acknowledging a 'you' whom she addresses. Freud speaks of this as the consolidation of the ego. But one does not have to believe in Freud's theories about this in order to see that values arise largely from within, out of hate and love, the ability to see others in terms of their needs, and out of the capacity to punish oneself by standards he has to a large extent made his own.

The self as moral agent is not a single thing. Nor is it something behind its manifestations. It is woven together from such capacities as I have spoken of. There is no essence to know. There is only a creature who develops such that he becomes a moral agent, a creature who can lead a life, one of the characteristics of which is the ability to make choices and to act on them.

Goncharov's Oblomov is often taken as an example of someone who makes no choices, to which the response is that of course he does. He has decided to do nothing with his life. It's a choice, and his choice is passivity. In choosing it, Oblomov has chosen to lose his life. The person whose actions are guided by old fears and phantasies that have nothing to do with the real present—or by unreal phantasies of the future—by anxieties that the phantasies are meant to deny, is being ruled by the past, and that is precisely *not to lead a life*, which looks forward. Susan Nieman writes:

Reasoning . . . is something you do. Thus reason became the central Enlightenment goal, which Kant called growing up. It's easier to be passive than active. Which is why we're all too happy to let other people run the world that circumscribes our lives . . . Growing up means taking our lives out of others' hands and into our own. (2009: 206–7)

This, in my terms, is becoming a self.

Leading a life describes what is unique to us, and on this account, no questions about continuity or discontinuity, mind and body, arise. Wollheim's idea builds temporality, memory, the freedom from that part of the past that is constricting, the ability to envision the future, contact with present reality, the valuing capacity, into the very idea of what we often call the 'self'. Without valuing, rather than merely wanting, there are babies longing for their mothers, Midas willing to do anything for more and more money, kleptomaniacs, madmen, but not selves. An accomplished 'self' is capable of 'whole-hearted valuing' (R. Frankfurt)—that is, a valuing in which one's different values have been weighed and bound together such that they allow for one overall value on which one can act—and, importantly self-knowledge. That process begins to happen as someone lets go of the phantasies that defend him from past anxieties, phantasies that continue to put a defensive screen between himself and the world.

The moral sense has precursors, which are a complex of a number of object relations (personal relations) and internal relations to them, the interplay between love and hate, identification, fear, guilt, that Freud (1923) calls 'the Ego' (*das Ich*). It is a structure that has been long in the making, virtually since the beginning of life. The ego is a structure, meaning that many elements make it up and that it endures, and that the elements can change in relation to each other and in themselves, but only with difficulty. Freud's story is at once about the constitution of the self, the nature of the self as conflicted and self-contradictory, guilt as a feature of being human, our vulnerability to coming apart, our capacity for delusion but also for self-knowledge.

Like the self, self-knowledge exists along a spectrum as an aspect of growth. It is incompatible with single-minded self-interest. Phillips and Taylor (2009: 13) write: 'The notion of self-interest implies that we always know what we want, by knowing what the self is and what its interests are. It forecloses discovery.'

INTEGRITY

Knowing oneself is a process in which we learn what we want, and take the other person's interests into account in reflecting on our own. This last goes back to my early claim that the infant is social from the start. Self-knowledge is a slow process that changes the selves we are. I am thinking of the painter who didn't know how to put his subjective self on the canvas, revealing and making his public self. In the process his self has changed, and so has what he wants to say. And similarly with Lily and David Denby's students.

Again the psychoanalytic process: people who don't know much about it wonder how self-knowledge can change the patient. What is the connection between self-knowledge and change? You discover that you hated your father. So what? But such facts do not count as the kind of self-knowledge that is mutative. That rather lies in the creative process of getting there, emotionally understanding its implications. There is no way of prescribing how that happens, nor even any notion of what it might mean for any particular person to know himself. But most important, the psychoanalytic neophyte is in error about the kind of knowledge in question. To learn that you hated your father is only the first step. Self-knowledge is really self-discovery and it never ends.

What states of mind foreclose it? For one, the arrogance of thinking that you know yourself already. This is what *Oedipus the King* is about. He insists that he has self-knowledge; and that presumption leads him to the most ghastly self-discovery.

My general thesis in this section is that integration of the self as a kind of wholeness, or the mind in health, and integrity as a moral condition, are two sides of the same phenomenon. As the self comes apart, self-knowledge becomes more and more difficult, and moral agency diminishes.

Mitchell says: 'We are all composites of overlapping, multiple organizations and perspectives, and our experience by an illusory sense of continuity' (1991: 5). There is a conflation here of complexity with discontinuity. But in my view, in the healthy mind, phantasies, memories, traumatic experiences, growth experiences, continually weave themselves through each other in a process of self-reflection or therapeutic dialogue. It is the continuity of the weaving, each thread changing in its interactions with the others, that is the process of change. Change also is not the same as discontinuity. If it were, what would it mean for Jenny to play the *Wanderer Phantasy* better and better?

About Virginia Woolf, Lehrer writes:

> She shows us our fleeting parts, but she also shows us how our parts come together. The secret, Woolf realized, was that the self emerges from its source. While her characters begin as a bundle of random sensations, echoing about the brain's electrical membranes, they instantly swell into something else. (2008: 180)

'Emergence' seems to me just the right word. There is no self at first. Melanie Klein has it exactly wrong. According to her there is a self or an ego at the beginning, and then, motivated by various conflicts, the ego begins to split. A more useful model, it seems to me, is that there is nothing we can call an 'ego' from the start; there are only feelings, longings, perceptions, instincts, that slowly come together in certain vital ways and slowly yield a self. According to Freud, the moral sense is founded along a web of faults. By the age of 4 or so, the child's cognitive responses to the world are subtly refined by his possession of a large conceptual repertoire, and as this has grown, so have the capacities for honesty and deceit, integrity, but also self-deception and self-division. There is no such thing as integrity before this psychological moment (by 'moment' I mean a developmental process that takes place in time and has special importance). To be human is to be divided within oneself, self-deceived, torn by love, self-hatred, and guilt. The self is continuous and one, in something like the sense that a painting or a piece of music is one.

COMING APART

Self-deception, denial, dissociation, and repression are among the chief psychological moves that undermine integrity. Each of them divides the self. Philosophers usually regard self-deception as paradoxical: how can one both believe and not believe the same proposition at the same time? Their task, the philosophers then think, is to resolve the paradox. My argument is that, understood correctly, there is no paradox. I begin with self-deception, both because it is the phenomenon with which even the layman is familiar, and because all the elements of the other forms of coming apart are here.

In interpersonal deception, A believes that *p*, but wants B to believe that *not-p*. A sets about to persuade B of what he, A, considers a falsehood. It doesn't matter, by the way, whether *p is* true, only that A believes it is. If A is successful, then B comes to believes that *not-p*. When Iago seeks to deceive Othello about Desdemona's chastity, Iago believes she is chaste, but wants Othello to believe that she is not. Iago thinks about how to deceive him, and how to enlist other people in his plan. Nothing is puzzling here because A and B are two different, separate people.

To treat self-deception on this model, one ends up trying to find a way in which two minds can be one mind, or one mind two. And as is not the case in interpersonal deception, 'A' and 'B' are both in on the secret. That is, one mind holds contradictory, conscious, beliefs. These are the stumbling-blocks to taking interpersonal deception as the model for self-deception.

How, then, might we understand it differently so that, without generating paradox, we catch something of the two-person character while being true to the fact that there is only one? By including a phenomenon that decisively reveals the one-person character of self-deception, namely *intra-psychic conflict*.

There is really only a handful of concepts that are fundamental to Freud's picture of the mind: the unconscious, repression, infantile sexuality, instinct theory, the genetic hypothesis—that everything in the mind has a history—and intra-psychic conflict. Of course, all of these have changed their meaning, some drastically, since Freud first introduced them. Intra-psychic conflict is the concept with which people think they have the least trouble; but it is also the hardest to take in. Once you do, you can begin to see just how complex, but not paradoxical, self-deception can be. Trying to fit it to the two-person model misses the phenomenon at its heart. In both, the attempt is not to satisfy two desires but to dissolve two sets of anxiety, each of which is exaggerated by the other.

Roskolnikoff, a complex, self-loathing character, hates his landlady and resolves to murder her. The desire is buried in other desires and anxieties which make him feel guilty, and which remain opaque to him because of his effort not to understand them. He kills her and instead of dissolving his anxiety, the murder increases it. He justifies his action by thinking of her as vermin who deserved to be killed. But he does not really believe this, and it only increases his guilty sense that he is the vermin. The trouble with self-deception is that it is not a matter of changing your mind, nor of successfully veiling what it is you want to deny. You remain aware of, if only dimly.

A banker, Mr Madison, decides to join a group of his colleagues in a project that will make them rich, but at the expense, they know, of impoverishing their clients. Increasingly they distance themselves from the immorality of the act by saying to themselves that there are other people who are doing the same thing, so why shouldn't they? Or that they deserve more money. Or that their clients are rich and won't be harmed by the financial loss they will experience. Or that their behavior enriches the company, which they take as their moral guide. These excuses are the self-deceptive moves that generate anxiety and that may also be generated by it.

None of these little stories remotely resembles interpersonal deception, because the phenomena turn out to require that there be only one person.

Repression describes a mental event or feeling or episode that for the moment is lost to consciousness. Whether it is truly beyond recovery is a difficult question. I am inclined to think that, at the moment, the neurologists can do a better job with this one than the psychoanalysts. In any case, if the material is truly repressed, the agent has no responsibility for it, though the self is drastically compromised.

In dissociation, the content is conscious but denied as one's own. The person who is dissociating is not lying, even to himself. But he is in a state of willed, but not fully conscious, confusion. What is denied is the connection between the dissociated thoughts and oneself, so that the phenomena seem to float free, or even to belong to someone else. In multiple personality, the links between these 'selves' are denied. Even the analyst may be seduced by one or two of the 'multiples', forgetting that they are embedded in conflict with the other 'selves'. Analysts pay more attention these days to dissociation than to repression, but they hold that it does not replace it. Repression is vertical, so to speak, dissociation is horizontal. Dissociation describes a state in which one alienates oneself from a part of an idea, an action, a feeling, an experience, a memory. 'That action is not mine' (which it is), 'I did not do it' (which she did). It is the connection between action and actor, and between the multiples, that serves a defensive function and so must be brought into conscious awareness and owned as one's own.

There are some sorts of dissociation that are not defensive, a cover for anxiety, but creative. Philip Bromberg regards dissociation as essential to selfhood. He says: 'self-states are what the mind comprises. Dissociation is what the mind does. The relationship between self-states and dissociation is what the mind is. It is the stability of that relationship that enables a person to experience himself as an "I"' (2006: 2). And quoting an artist named Clemente, Bromberg continues: 'Because fragmentation is an inevitable part of the creative process, there are gaps between the fragments. And in those gaps something happens' (pp. 10–11).

And similarly with a kind of dissociation. Fragments of ideas just come to Lily. They don't seem like her own. She can live with periods of chaos, not anxiously searching for the threads that string them together.

The neurotic unconscious I spoke of a moment ago is the opposite of self-knowledge. But there is a very useful move in current psychoanalytic thinking to revise the traditional concept of the unconscious as timeless in favor of one that is open to change and time. Quoting Lancelot Law Whyte, Bromberg writes:

the antithesis conscious/unconscious may have exhausted its utility ... It may be wrong to think of two *realms which interact*, called the conscious and the unconscious. There may exist, as I believe, a single realm of metal processes ... of which certain transitory aspects or phases are accessible to immediate conscious attention. (3)

I think of Virginia Woolf's metaphor of the lighthouse. The light steadily swings across the landscape, illuminating one shadowed strip after another. The land beyond the beam is not in total darkness but in the wings, waiting its turn to be illumined by the beam. The dichotomy, darkness/light, would precisely miss this phenomenon. The lighthouse is a metaphor for the goal which helps define what it means to lead a life, and I take it as a metaphor for the relation between conscious and less than conscious as well. In the beginning of the novel the goal is divisive, pitting the children and Mrs Ramsey against her remote husband. But in the course of the novel the meaning of the lighthouse changes for them all, and the goal which earlier set them apart now brings them together. Mrs Ramsey died some years ago, and it is a goal that earlier Mr Ramsey saw as a reason to mourn. Now it is a goal that redefines him. Mr Ramsey is off with his now grown children to keep the promise he had made and broken at the beginning of the novel. His callous 'No' with which we are introduced to him hangs balefully over the novel. Now, with Mrs Ramsey and one son dead, the trip is finally happening. He thought his life's goal was to complete his philosophical masterpiece; now it is to make what amends he can to the surviving children. He wants to bind his family, to take something nice to the men who work there, and of course to make amends to his grown children. The lighthouse establishes the continuity of self through change. The novel ends with Lily's reaching her goal:

Quickly, as if she were recalled by something over there, she turned to her canvas. There it was—her picture. Yes, with all its greens and blues, its lines running up and across, its attempt at something ... With a sudden intensity, as if she saw it clear for a second, she drew a line there, in the center. It was done, It was finished. Yes, she thought, laying down her brush. I have had my vision. (pp. 208–9)

I have spoken at length about growth as a central characteristic of being human. I don't mean that only human beings grow, but if the creature doesn't have the capacity for growth, spiritual and moral, it isn't a self. Growth happens only to a creature who is continuous and who moves through time. Change implies stability against which change can be measured. But as I argued above, the stability in question does not mean 'unchanging'.

There are other important adjectives in human discourse that have meaning only as applied to a creature who is continuous through time. For a beginning: *Happiness.* The point rests on distinguishing *happiness* from *pleasure*, from *ecstasy*, from *delight*. One can feel pleasure just for a short while. Even a seriously depressed person can take brief pleasure, or delight, in seeing her grandchild eating a favorite dish. One might feel ecstasy for an evening, but never before nor again. This could not be the case with happiness. One can be temporarily delighted by a surprising gift. But we don't call a person happy if the equanimity, pleasure, relative self-satisfaction, love has not been present and growing, for a long time.

Self-Knowledge and Self-Discovery. I have spoken about this already.

Wisdom. One might manifest intelligence, or knowledge, for a brief period, but not wisdom, for it is implicit in its meaning that it is acquired through hardship, reflection, and long studies in empathy and self-knowledge.

'The self' is the primary theme in the first movement, an Andante, gathering resonances, changing tempo and key, as it moves forward.

REFERENCES

BROMBERG, P. (2006). *Awakening the Dreamer* (Mahwah, NJ: Analytic Press).

DENBY, D. (1996). *Great Books* (New York: Simon & Schuster).

DESCARTES, R. (1984). *Philosophical Writings of René Descartes*, i, tr. J Cunningham *et al.* (Cambridge: Cambridge University Press).

FRANKFURT, H. (1988). 'Identification and Wholeheartedness', in *The Importance of What we Care about* (Cambridge: Cambridge University Press).

FREUD, S. (1923). *The Ego and the Id*, in *The Standard Edition of the Complete Works of Sigmund Freud,* ed. J. Strachey, *et al.* (London: Hogarth Press), xix. 3–63.

HUME, D. (1951). *A Treatise of Human Nature* (Oxford: Clarendon Press).

KOHUT, H. (1977). *The Restoration of the Self* (New York: International Universities Press).

LEHRER, J. (2008). *Proust was a Neuroscientist* (Boston and New York: Houghton Mifflin).

MITCHELL, S. A. (1991). 'Contemporary Perspectives on Self: Toward an Integration', *Psychoanalytic Dialogues*, 1: 121–47.

NIEMAN, S. (2009). *Moral Clarity* (Princeton: Princeton University Press).

PHILLIPS, A., and TAYLOR, B. (2009). *On Kindness* (New York: Farrar Strauss).

Psychodynamic Diagnostic Manual, 2006, Alliance of Psychoanalytic Organizations.

SOLMS, M. (2009). 'Discussion of Brian Koehler on "Neuropsychoanalysis and Psychosis"'. Neuropsychoanalysis Lecture Series, New York Psychoanalytic Institute, 6 June.

WINNICOTT, D. W. (1971). *Playing and Reality* (New York: Basic Books).

WOLLHEIM, R. (1984). *The Thread of Life* (Cambridge: University of Cambridge Press).

WOOLF, V. (1981). *To the Lighthouse* (New York and London: Harcourt, Inc.).

PART VII

··

THE SELF IN DIVERSE CONTEXTS

··

CHAPTER 26

....

OUR GLASSY ESSENCE

THE FALLIBLE SELF IN PRAGMATIST THOUGHT

....

RICHARD MENARY

Proud man, dressed in a little brief authority, most ignorant of what he is most assured, his glassy essence.[1]

(Shakespeare, *Measure for Measure*, 2. 2)

INTRODUCTION

....

Pragmatism begins by assaulting the Cartesian image of the thinker as infallibly assured of his own essence. This is reflected in the famous speech of Isabella in Act 2 of *Measure for Measure* which casts doubt, and not a bit of scorn, on 'the angry ape' who pictures himself at one with the immortals. The Cartesian picture of the self as

---

[1] An abbreviated version of this quotation was used by Peirce to describe his view of a characteristically Cartesian account of the self.

a thinking thing that is infallibly certain of its own nature, by the God-given light of reason, is to be contrasted with the pragmatist account of the self as fallible, embodied, and developed through social interaction. Our glassy essence is no essential thing at all. If there is a self, it is what we do (including what we think). Therefore what we do is not to be thought of as distinct from what we are.

The classical pragmatists—Peirce, James Dewey, and Mead—all had important things to say about the self and there are clear continuities in their thought. Since little work has been done to connect them up, in this chapter I trace these continuities and begin to assemble a picture of a pragmatist conception of the self. The picture that emerges is strikingly modern and original and has much to offer contemporary accounts of the self.

I shall develop four interconnected themes that illuminate the concept of the fallible self as found in the work of the classical pragmatists:

(1) the fallible self as non-Cartesian;
(2) the fallible self as dynamically aware;
(3) the fallible self as a social self;
(4) the fallible self as a moral agent.

In the concluding section I shall combine these strands into a fuller account. I shall begin by outlining the pragmatist assault on the Cartesian picture of the self and contrasting it with the fallible self of pragmatism.

1. THE FALLIBLE SELF AS NON-CARTESIAN

In 1868 the publication of two papers in the *Journal of Speculative Philosophy* (*JSP*), 'Questions Concerning Certain Faculties Claimed for Man' and 'Some Consequences of Four Incapacities', set pragmatism rolling by demolishing the central philosophical claims of Cartesian philosophy. Peirce denies that we should begin philosophy with self-evident truths directly apprehended either as clear and distinct ideas or as ideas given in experience. Descartes attempted to base knowledge of the external world on a single indubitable premise which he directly apprehended 'intuitively'. Peirce denies both that knowledge could rest on such foundations and secondly that the purely deductive method of reasoning employed by Descartes was a sound method for philosophy. Peirce replaced the Cartesian method with a fallible and self-correcting method based on that of the sciences. We begin our enquiries with all our beliefs and prejudices in place and not from some directly intuited premise. Peirce asked philosophy 'to trust rather to the multitude and variety of its arguments than to the conclusiveness of any one. Its reasoning should not form a chain which is no stronger than its weakest link, but a cable whose fibres may be ever so slender, provided they are sufficiently numerous and intimately connected' (CP 5. 265).[2] Peirce's cable is a direct ancestor of Neurath's raft.

Peirce's arguments against an intuitive faculty of self-consciousness undermine the Cartesian doctrine that knowledge of ourselves and our own minds is direct and infallible. Contrary to Descartes, Peirce holds that knowledge of ourselves and our minds is indirect (by inference) and fallible. In the next section I look at Peirce's assault on the Cartesian method and the Cartesian self that is a direct product of the application of that method. In the second section I shall briefly look at the fallibilistic method that Peirce endorses and say something about the fallible self that emerges from the application of this method. These sections lay the foundations of pragmatist thinking which recur throughout the work of the classical pragmatists. In later sections I look at Peirce's positive account of the self: the social and linguistic (or semeiotic[3]) basis of the self and his account of self-controlled and self-directed conduct, both of which hint towards future developments in the work of Dewey and Mead.

Peirce's assault on Cartesianism

Descartes distinguished between direct or non-inferential knowledge and indirect or inferential knowledge. Pragmatism is at odds with the idea of that which is directly known as infallibly known. When Cartesians speak of intuition as the direct apprehension of a premise, or uninferred truth, they stand in a tradition that goes back to Aristotle's *Posterior Analytics*. Aristotle there insists that any demonstrable knowledge must be based upon a premise which is undemonstrable and it is this undemonstrable premise that is here referred to as an intuition. Gallie describes Descartes's account of intuition in the following way: 'Every intuition is an essentially indubitable or self evident truth: something like an analytic truth. I am thinking therefore I exist, if equals be added to equals their sums will be equal' (Gallie 1952: 62). An intuition is a direct relationship between the mind and a truth (Gallie 1952). An intuition can be nothing other than a truth that is self-evident to reason; it cannot be of the form of a hypothesis or a conjecture. An intuition is true in virtue of itself; it is not made true by another thought from which it is inferred, it

---

[2] I shall follow the standard reference notations for the two major collections of Peirce's work, first the *Collected Papers of Peirce* (CP, followed by volume number and then paragraph number). Secondly the *Writings of Charles Sanders Peirce* (W followed by volume number and page number).

[3] 'Semeiotic' is Peirce's preferred spelling and helps to differentiate his work on signs from that of Saussure.

is simply clearly and distinctly true. Other truths may be inferred from it, however—
such is the role of the cogito.

There are two questions with which Peirce (1868a) is concerned in the first of the
JSP papers that are immediately pertinent:

1. Whether we have an intuitive faculty of discriminating intuitions from inferences.[4]
2. Whether we have an intuitive self-consciousness. (Whether our consciousness
   of self is intuitive or whether it is inferred.)

The answer to the first question is important for if we are not able to distinguish
intuitions from inferences then we cannot apply the Cartesian method. If we do
not have an intuitive self-consciousness, if our consciousness of self is not intuitive,
then the Cartesian picture of the self has no grounding. If Peirce's arguments
convince us that we should answer these questions in the negative, then they
have opened the way for a pragmatist account of the self.

Question 1: whether we have an intuitive faculty of discriminating intuitions from inferences

Peirce defines an intuition as 'a cognition (a thought, judgement, association or
sensation) not determined by a previous cognition of the same object, and therefore so determined by something out of the consciousness' (W 2. 193). This is to be
contrasted with a cognition that has been determined by a previous cognition, by
inference or association for example.

The question is whether we have any intuitive faculty for discriminating intuitions from inferences; can we, by thinking about it, determine that some cognitions
are intuitive? Peirce denies that there is any evidence that we do have such a faculty
(W 2. 194). He produces a variety of arguments in support of this conclusion. We
might argue that we feel that certain cognitions are intuitive; however, the weight
of the testimony depends upon being able to distinguish in this *feeling* whether it is
the result of some previous cognition, such as an association, or whether it is
intuitive. As Peirce puts it:

> it depends on presupposing the very matter testified to. Is this feeling infallible? And is this
> judgement concerning it infallible? and so on, *ad infinitum*. Furthermore, there is no
> historical agreement as to which cognitions are intuitive, yet an infallible faculty for
> distinguishing between intuitions and other cognitions ought to lead us to solid results
> on the question. (W 2. 194)

This last point is telling, for if there were an infallible faculty for distinguishing
between intuitions and inferences then there ought not to be any controversy

---

4 There are five other questions which Peirce (1868a) addresses which need not detain us here.

concerning which mental states are intuitions. There is no such agreement and there is an ongoing controversy about the very existence of intuitions, which, taken together, cast doubt on the existence of an infallible intuitive faculty.

Peirce provides an argument against the 'given' in experience in a way that will be familiar to those who have read Sellars's famous work on the myth of the given (Sellars 1956). Like Sellars, he argues that we cannot discriminate between that which is given directly in experience and that which is inferred from previous experience. In other words, we cannot tell just by examining sensations that they are directly produced in us by some object. Peirce's argument partly depends upon what we would now call unconscious inference. By simply consciously attending to a thought, we will not detect the unconscious series of inferences which produced it. Nor by attending to visual or aural experiences will we be able to determine that the experience is the result of a series of unconscious processes. This argument fits quite neatly with contemporary cognitive science, whether of a classical, connectionist, or dynamical kind.[5]

Peirce illustrates the claim with the example of a pitch of a tone as produced by a succession of vibrations which reach the ear. The sensation of the tone is produced from this rapid succession of vibrations; however, merely attending to the pitch sensation itself does not reveal the series of sensations from which it is produced. Therefore the sensation of the pitch of a tone is determined by previous cognitions of which we are unaware.

Consequently, Peirce thinks that his arguments cast sufficient doubt on the claim that we have an intuitive faculty for discriminating between intuitive cognitions and mediate cognitions.[6] Peirce's conclusion here is to cast doubt on the faculty for discrimination. He doesn't—in this argument at least—deny that there are such things as intuitive cognitions. However, the effect of the arguments across the *JSP* papers is designed to show that there are only mediate cognitions.

Question 2: whether we have an intuitive self-consciousness

Since Peirce has already argued that we do not have a faculty by which we can discriminate between intuitions and inferences, he turns his attention to the claim that we have a faculty of intuitive self-consciousness. By self-consciousness Peirce means 'the recognition of my *private* self. I know that *I* (not merely *the* I) exist' (W 2. 201).

Peirce invites us to entertain the view that the sense of self develops from birth, rather than being inborn. We might expect children to have an intuitive self-knowledge, but they don't. Gallie in discussing Peirce's argument puts it as follows:

---

[5] This is because the cognitive sciences rely upon unconscious processes which produce conscious experiences.

[6] Those cognitions inferred from previous cognitions.

'Children appear to come by the idea of themselves as unique individuals having thoughts of their own through interpreting the speech that others address to them' (Gallie 1952: 66).[7]

Since it is not self-evident that we have an intuitive self-consciousness, Peirce claims that the issue can only be determined by evidence concerning the actual functioning of known faculties. To demonstrate that we do not require an intuitive faculty to develop self-consciousness, Peirce provides a brief but compelling account of how children might develop a sense of self which does not make reference to any intuitive faculty of self-consciousness. Rather than suppose that self-consciousness is a precondition of thought, Peirce reverses the order of priority by making thought the precondition of self-consciousness—self-consciousness develops out of the child's development of cognitive capacities (Peirce, W 2. 201). Even prior to the capacity for thought is the child's attention to its body:

A very young child may always be observed to watch its own body with great attention. There is every reason why this should be so, for from the child's point of view this body is the most important thing in the universe. Only what it touches has any actual and present feeling; only what it faces has any actual color; only what is on its tongue has any actual taste. (Peirce, W 2. 201)

The child soon learns that bodily interaction with objects causes them to change; which is an important stage of development leading towards a sense of agency. Most importantly Peirce thinks that with the onset of language children learn that the testimony of others is a reliable guide to the nature of the objects with which they are already familiar. When the child is told that the stove is hot, but ignores this testimony and touches the stove anyway, she soon learns that testimony is a reliable guide to fact. The child learns of the possibility of error and ignorance and as Peirce strikingly puts it: 'Thus he becomes aware of ignorance, and it is necessary to suppose a *self* in which this ignorance can inhere' (W 2. 202–3).

Furthermore, the child's error is *his* error and is explained by the supposition of a fallible self. Peirce has already been able to convincingly explain the development of self-consciousness through the child's interaction with the world and others and through their ignorance and error. This reverses the order of priority for the Cartesian. The Cartesian holds that thought is grounded in self-consciousness. Peirce gives us a picture of the self developing out of thought, primarily out of a process of trial and error, which is the beginning of the fallibilistic method of thought, being a self-corrective form of conduct, that I will develop in the next section. If the environment turns out to be different from the way you expect it to

---

[7] This is very close to the account of the development of the self given by Mead as we shall see in section 4. It sits very happily with contemporary narrative accounts of a child's development of a sense of self (Nelson 2003; Gallagher 2006).

be, you quickly develop a sense of a self capable of error; the self out of step with its environment.

Peirce's arguments are designed to undermine the picture of the mind as one of a clearly apprehended consciousness that intuitively knows its contents, whether they be clear and distinct ideas or simple sensations. What we learn when we become self-aware is our relationship to the world, not awareness of the contents of our minds independently of the world. Peirce, through his assault on Cartesianism, has shown how the self is inferred rather than intuited: 'self consciousness may easily be the result of inference' (W 2. 204). This makes the status of introspection the same as the status of outward perception. We come to know about the external world through a series of inferences and interpretations, which are fallible, prone to error, but still aimed at the establishment of belief as habit.[8] Consequently our knowledge of the self has no higher status of certainty than our knowledge of other things we find in the world.

This is a fundamental strand of pragmatist thought about the self. Our knowledge and understanding of the self is gained by reliable, but fallible, inferential processes. Furthermore, our understanding of the self comes not from a special cognitive faculty of intuition, but from our interactions with others and our conduct in the world. The self is to be understood by external and public criteria, not by criteria that are private and internal (to some thinking substance, or a Kantian transcendental ego). Peirce avoids the scylla of an 'atemporal substantive self' and the charybdis of an abstract bundle of signs and perceptions.

In the next subsection I give an outline of the fallibilistic method that Peirce proposes as the method of pragmatism and show a little more how the application of this method gives us an account of the fallible self.

Fallibilism

Peirce models our thinking on the self-corrective practices of experimental science, rather than deduction from indubitable first premises that are directly apprehended (or intuited) by the thinking self. 'Peirce replaces self-warranting cognitions with self-corrective practices' (Colapietro 2006: 4). Therefore Peirce rejects the notion of cognitive immediacy and intuitive knowledge, which philosophy had been striving for since Plato and Aristotle. The arguments of the *JSP* series are designed to show that there are no good reasons for thinking that we have any powers of mental intuition, nor that the assumption that we do should lead us to model philosophical method on the basis that we can begin with intuited first principles that function as an indubitable basis for the future course of reasoning.

---

[8] I explore this in more detail in the next subsection.

We are born with a basic set of hardwired responses. However, for the most part actions and signs have no meaning for the newborn. Meltzoff (Meltzoff and Moore 1977) has shown that newborn infants respond to facial gesture by imitation. The evidence shows that there is an innate capacity for a primitive self-awareness at birth (Bermúdez 1996: 390; Gallagher 1996). Certainly, however, there is no evidence that something like a Cartesian self with infallible access to the contents of its own mind—an infallible self-consciousness—is present from birth (see Chapter 2 above).

We are fallible creatures right from birth and there is evidence that a fallibilistic self develops over time. As the infant grows, a certain amount of randomness and spontaneity enters into its behaviour as it begins to explore its surroundings and interact with its carers. No longer are all responses to vocal and physical communications specific and hardwired. A range of calls, gestures, and actions become generalized and habitual such that 'stimuli and responses are grouped, respectively, and take on representative functions' (Scheffler 1974: 42). Psychologists such as Stern argue that the infant begins to develop 'biases and preferences', and develops a basic capacity to 'form and test hypotheses' (Stern 1985: 41–2).

The regularity of the infant's habitual activity parallels the regularity of the environment. This is an important externalist claim for Peirce: if the environment affords regular forms of gesture, words, and facial expressions these will lead to regularized habits in the infant. However, Scheffler rightly notes that the resulting habits are not wholly rigid, such that the infant's conduct lacks any spontaneity at all; but nor does the environment become wholly predictable and stable (Scheffler 1974).

Peirce's law of mind is that feelings and ideas have a tendency to generalize; in particular Peirce presents an account of this tendency which shows that habits (in cognitive mode beliefs) are developed by the irritation produced by a stimulus that blocks action and the responses of an organism that succeed in overcoming it (Scheffler 1974: 42). Habits are laid down in response to the circumstances that produce irritation in the organism, resulting in activity that overcomes the irritation. The circumstances become more than simply physical stimuli, they take on a significant character in relation to the habituated organism.

Take Scheffler's (1974) example of a cat placed for the first time in a box with a door and a latch on it, which, when struck, opens the door. With a saucer of cream placed beyond the door and in sight of the cat, it would be unsurprising if the cat were to attempt to reach the cream. At first its actions might be random and spontaneous, being produced by the irritations presented by the circumstance: hunger, the inability to reach the cream, and so on. If the random movements of the cat were lucky enough to strike the latch and open the door then the irritation would be appeased.

Subsequently the movements of the cat would become less random and more ordered, until they became directed at manipulating the latch, and as such the cat would have acquired a habit with regards to the solution of the 'puzzle box' situation.

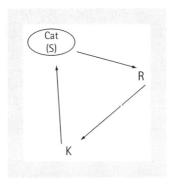

Figure 26.1 The 'Puzzle box' situation

However, this is not a simple case of stimulus response correlation; the cat has developed a habit directed at appeasing the irritation which gave rise to its behaviour in the first place. The cat's movements are *directed* at manipulating the catch to reach a desired end. As Scheffler summarizes it: 'given this situation S, with perceptual and motivational features p and m, it responds appropriately with response R, to achieve the desired and perceptible consequence K' (Scheffler 1974: 43).

Scheffler stresses the importance of the mediational role of R; it mediates between the initial source of irritation and the state that the organism reaches in which the irritation is assuaged. This provides us with a model of belief and belief fixation which is distinct from the traditional concept of belief as an intellectual state which is 'removed' from the environment. Peirce locates belief in the world as a habitual state that is teleologically tied to action. The organism's behaviour becomes self-directed and even self-controlled; this is again different from classical behaviourism where the external stimuli control the behaviour of the organism. Consequently it comes as no surprise that Peirce rejects the radical doubt of Descartes and the sensationalist empiricism of Locke (Scheffler 1974).

Thought and inquiry begin with genuinely irritating doubts that arise in a situation. The aim of inquiry is to reach a settled state of belief, which is a settled habitual state that predisposes us to act. This is clearly at odds with the Cartesian search for certain foundations that can be intuited by purely intellectual processes and which can axiomatically function as indubitable first premises. By contrast, in Peirce's fallibilistic self: 'we encounter a sign using animal, continuous with other species, denied intuitive, infallible access to reality (including what this self is *really* feeling, doing, or thinking)—an agent exposed to the possibility of error at every level' (Colapietro 2006: 25). Yet, this fallible agent is more often a reliable and competent actor and thinker in a vast array of non-identical yet overlapping situations.

Peirce's early papers published in the *SJP* are directly targeted at dismantling the Cartesian methodology of intuiting indubitable first premises and replacing that method with the fallibilistic and open-ended form of inquiry. This has two important consequences. First, if Peirce is right then he gives further armoury to the argument that we do not have direct and infallible acquaintance with *the self*. Secondly, Peirce's fallibilist methodology indicates that our self-knowledge is built up from our engagements with the world by the development of self-controlled and self-directed actions. In section 3 I link this fallibilistic method and fallible self with Dewey's work on the moral self and moral agency. I return to Peirce in the final section on the social development of the self by linking his work with that of Mead.

An important strand of pragmatist argument concerns denying the split, or gulf, between a conscious, knowing, or experiencing, subject and a world experienced. It follows that the focus of interest turns to the nature of purposive intelligent actions. Purposive and intelligent actions are the developmental soil out of which the fallible self grows. Pragmatism does not just reorientate our thinking about the self from a static spectator which is transcendent to the world; it also provides us with an account of conscious experience that is apt for an embodied, embedded, and active self.

Dewey in particular conceives of conscious experience in terms of biological embodiment. Where there is a living organism there will be experience and where there is such an organism, there will also be a complex environment in which that organism lives and develops. Dewey's conception of experience is a naturalistic one; experience is a natural phenomenon. However, experience is not the product of a passive organism, receiving information through its senses about its environment. The organism is active, constantly interacting with its environment and coping with changes in the environment from moment to moment.

Experiences are these interactions of organism and environment. Dewey's account of experience has strong affinities with recent developments in externalist accounts of cognition; particularly distributed and extended accounts of cognition (Hutchins 1995; Clark 2008) and enactive or sensori-motor accounts of perception (Noë 2004; O'Regan and Noë 2002). The importance of Dewey and Peirce's work for the nascent embodied and extended approaches to cognition has recently been made explicit by some of those working in the field. For example, Gallagher (2009) and Menary (2007) both discuss the importance of Dewey's conception of organism–environment relations as a grounding for contemporary discussions of embodied and extended mind. I will take up this theme in the final section.

2. The Fallible Self as Dynamically Aware

The classical pragmatists held that experience is continuous rather than particular. This was most famously argued for by James (1890), who denies that sensations, images, and ideas are discrete atoms of experience. He replaces them with a continuous stream of consciousness. As such, experiences are temporally extended; they are not frozen snapshots.

As we saw in section 1, the pragmatist rejects the traditional picture of the conscious subject as having indubitable direct knowledge of the mind and conscious experience, and of knowledge as an otiose transcript of experiences. Conscious subjects are primarily biological organisms. Their experiences are both of the world and in the world, that is, continuous with nature. They are embodied and embedded in their environment. The transactions between the organism and its environment are 'experiences' and experiences are not, solely, a knowledge affair. Embracing these embodied approaches to experience and being in the world leads us away from qualia type approaches to experience. However, James focused on the dynamical nature of a personal consciousness. James's famous stream of consciousness is compatible with the fallible self, but James does not take the more embodied and embedded approach to the self that we find in Peirce and Dewey. There is a tension between the more individualistic approach of James and the socially embedded approach of Peirce, Dewey, and Mead. However, as I shall go on to explain, this tension need not cause a break in the continuities found throughout the work of the pragmatists.

James: the self and the stream of consciousness

In this section I shall concentrate on James's conception of consciousness and how it relates to the self. In the *Principles* James ascribes the following properties to conscious thought:

(1) Every thought tends to be part of a personal consciousness.

(2) Within each personal consciousness thought is always changing.

(3) Within each personal consciousness thought is sensibly continuous.

(1) is simply a statement that each thought appears to be owned by someone (or some self). Indeed James asserts that 'all thought tends to assume the form of personal consciousness' (1890: 229). Since James is here talking about adult consciousness, and not providing a description of how that consciousness develops, what he says is almost a common banality. Since we know that James takes consciousness to be a dynamical stream of thoughts, it is less banal to identify that stream with a person or self.

In (2) James's main point is that no mental state recurs in an identical way. The same object is experienced time after time, but each experience is subtly different. 'No state once gone can recur and be identical with what it was before' (1890: 229). His aim here is the empiricist theory of ideas, for example Locke's simple ideas. The target is the objectification of consciousness; the same, objective, unmodified, mental atoms/molecules are combined and recombined in consciousness. Therefore, we have a notion of 'A permanently existing idea or Vorstellung which makes its appearance before the footlights of consciousness at periodical intervals, is as mythological an entity as the Jack of Spades' (1890: 138).

Consciousness is a fluid stream, but real physical objects are constant; as Scheffler puts it: 'When we read the latter constancy back into the mind, it is understandable that we must get a distorted picture' (1974: 138). It does not follow from what James is saying here that the sensation of green grass at T1 and the sensation of green grass at T2 are not both sensations of green grass; it simply follows that they are not sensations of green grass because they are the same permanently existing simple idea, *Vorstellung* or representation.

According to (3) consciousness changes in a continuous way, rather than jumping from discrete state to discrete state. Even when there are breaks in consciousness—such as being asleep—awareness of being the same person/consciousness is maintained. James is attacking the atomistic conception of conscious thought as received again from the empiricists. Rather than think of consciousness as a sequence of independent atoms of sensation or thought, James emphasized (like Peirce) the qualitative continuity of conscious experience. It is here that he famously describes consciousness as a stream. He does so by contrasting the descriptions of 'train' or 'chain' of thought with those of 'river' or 'stream'. 'In talking of it hereafter, let us call it the stream of thought, of consciousness, or of subjective life' (James, 1890: 239). This is another conception fundamental to pragmatism which all of the pragmatists share. It is a non-reductive account of conscious experience whereby thinking and experiencing are understood in terms of temporal and psychological continuities, in contrast to the atomism of empiricists and rationalists who 'chop' consciousness up into discrete states. This is also an approach that remains influential with philosophers and psychologists today.[9]

James's account of consciousness is personalized. Conscious thought is fluid, dynamical, and continuous, but it is also *my* consciousness. The self is primarily identified with the stream. He distinguishes between the self as experienced—the empirical self, or *me*—and the self as experiencing subject—the spiritual self, or *I*.

James begins with the distinction between the experienced, or empirical, selves and the experiencing self. There are different senses of self associated with the empirical selves—the material and the social. The material self is comprised of the body and at least those possessions to which one is emotionally tied. The social self is the collection of different habitualized personality traits that we project outwards onto the world. The spiritual self is that which experiences the empirical selves.

---

[9] One need only think of the radical atomism of Fodor's language of thought.

James takes a quasi-narrative stance to the collection of empirical selves, I quote James at length, since it is impossible to improve upon his prose:

I am often confronted by the necessity of standing by one of my empirical selves and relinquishing the rest. Not that I would not, if I could, be both handsome and fat and well dressed, and a great athlete, and make a million a year, be a wit, a bon-vivant, and a lady-killer, as well as a philosopher; a philanthropist, statesman, warrior, and African explorer, as well as a 'tone-poet' and saint. But the thing is simply impossible. The millionaire's work would run counter to the saint's; the bon-vivant and the philanthropist would trip each other up; the philosopher and the lady-killer could not well keep house in the same tenement of clay. Such different characters may conceivably at the outset of life be alike possible to a man. But to make any one of them actual, the rest must more or less be suppressed. So the seeker of his truest, strongest, deepest self must review the list carefully, and pick out the one on which to stake his salvation. All other selves thereupon become unreal, but the fortunes of this self are real. Its failures are real failures, its triumphs real triumphs, carrying shame and gladness with them. (1890: 309–10)

Who or what is it that identifies itself with these various empirical or objective selves? This is the problem *par excellence* of the self: what is the experiencing subject? James is clear about this:

The consciousness of self involves a stream of thought, each part of which as 'I' can 1) remember those which went before, and know the things they knew; and 2) emphasize and care paramountly for certain ones among them as '*me*,' and appropriate to *these* the rest. The nucleus of the '*me*' is always the bodily existence felt to be present at the time. (James 1890: 400)

The empirical self is 'an empirical aggregate of things objectively known' (James 1890: 400), but the I which knows them is not such an aggregate (James 1890: 400–1). It does not follow that the experiencing self, the I, is 'an unchanging metaphysical entity like the Soul, or a principle like the pure Ego, viewed as "out of time"' (James 1890: 401). The experiencing self is simply identified as the constant flow of experience over time. Far from being a selection of time slices, the self is a cumulatively changing flow of thoughts and experiences appropriating its past as a history of empirical facts. Consequently, James's account of the self as a dynamical flow of conscious experiences that coalesces into a dynamical continuity does not sound radically discontinuous with the non-Cartesian fallible self of Peirce and Dewey.

What we can take from James is the idea of consciousness as a dynamic continuity, that the self is constituted by the selective attention paid to parts of that stream—where, in particular, that selective attention becomes habituated over time. Indeed, this habituation over time might well be understood in terms of a narrative construction of self out of the flow of conscious experience. In the next section I return to the theme of the fallible self as social.

3. THE FALLIBLE SELF AS A SOCIAL SELF

Peirce makes the strongest possible identification of the self with language. Furthermore, this is not some inner and private language but the public language in which our thoughts are first formulated and expressed. He has shown us how the first glimmerings of self-consciousness arise through linguistic interaction (from which the child learns of its ignorance) and the interaction of the child with objects in its environment (from which it learns error). Peirce identifies the self with language in the following way:

1. Thoughts are signs.
2. Thinking is conducted in a series (a train of thought) where previous signs determine consequent signs - through association, inference or other forms of interpretation.
3. All signs have their origin externally (in the world, not in the private inner substance).
4. The self that I recognize as *myself* is identical with the train of thoughts of which I am conscious.
5. Therefore, an individual self is identical with this linguistic series of thoughts.

This is remarkably close to contemporary narrative approaches to the self (see Schechtman in Chapter 17). In many respects Peirce is close to Dennett (1991) and Velleman (2006), differing in that he recognizes the importance of bodily interaction in the construction of the self. Although Peirce sounds like an abstract narrativist, the self is too pragmatically anchored to the world to be so counted. We should also take seriously the claim that man is an external sign. Peirce thinks that we are nothing (qua selves) without being part of a linguistic community. The self is, therefore, thoroughly relational; it cannot exist without the other with which it converses. The self does not, therefore, exist simply as some Joycean virtual machine produced by the brain's activity. Indeed, the self is available for interpretation by others as an external linguistic sign.

Peirce denies the extreme individualism of modern philosophy. Where he finds it in James's account of the stream of consciousness he is critical: 'You think there *must* be such isolation, because you confound thoughts with feeling-qualities; but all observation is against you. There are some small particulars that a man can keep to himself. He exaggerates them and his personality sadly' (CP 8. 81). It does not follow that Peirce denies that there is absolutely no individual, just that we should not think of the individual as containing an essential inner kernel of privacy and there is a tension here in pragmatist thought between individualism and communalism. James tends towards the individualistic and Peirce towards the communalistic—they are the two poles of pragmatist thought. Dewey can be found somewhere in between the two, but Mead is Peircean through and through.

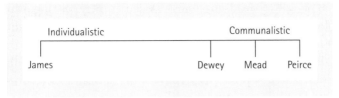

Figure 26.2 The tension between individualism and communalism in pragmatist thought

Peirce did not deny the existence of individuals (as embodied subjects), nor the subjectivity of conscious experience; however, he did deny that these 'facts' were sufficient to establish a subjective individualist account of the self and self-consciousness.

An important component of Peirce's pragmatism was continuity/synechism. Not only is the self continuous with the community to which it is related, but it is continuous with the rest of the biological and physical world as well. Far from instituting a nominalistic dualism about self and other or self and world, Peirce sees them as radically continuous. Peirce and Dewey share an approach to mind and world that I have elsewhere called the continuity thesis (Menary 2009): the continuity thesis requires that there is no deep metaphysical discontinuity between the mind and the world. Mental and cognitive capacities are not intrinsically different from other kinds of capacities found in the natural world.

I take it that Peirce here sees the self as essentially developmental and dynamic (rather than a static substance with fixed properties); it is developmental in the sense that the self is in a continuous process of development and because of this it is oriented towards the future in which it will be developed. Without this, the self is, as Colapietro puts it, a mere negation of selfhood (Colapietro 1989: 78).

Mead variations

Mead's social conception of the self holds as true a fundamental thesis that the self is a product of social interaction and the individual self is not a precondition for social interaction. Therefore, Mead's starting-point for investigating the self and mental phenomena in general is social; it is a guiding principle very much like Vygotsky's approach to developmental psychology. Again it has the hallmarks of a pragmatist approach to the mind and self: it is a primarily social phenomenon and as such there is no private individual self logically or temporally prior to the social self.

Like Peirce, Mead thinks of the self coming into being through linguistic interaction. However, Mead presents a variation on the Peircean theme: 'When the response of the other becomes an essential part in his behaviour—then the individual appears in his own experience as a self; and until this happens he does not appear as a self' (Mead 1934: 195). Mead is here distinguishing between hardwired biological responses to others, some of which we might share with other animals, and the ability to take on the symbolic gestures (linguistic responses) of others as our own. It is in this latter ability that we find the formation of the social self. This is a process, as Thayer puts it, of the 'transformation of the "biologic individual" into a "minded self". But the process originates not in private experience' (1968: 253). It originates in social activity. Infant babbling and other vocal gestures are constantly responded to by adult caregivers. Some vocal gestures are particularly praised and reinforced, and the child becomes part of an interactive community (see Chapter 2 above).

The development of language is a complicated process, but the child is nevertheless a member of a linguistic community and this influences the development of the child's linguistic abilities. It is in this membership of a social group that the self originates, not because the child has direct experience of herself, but has experience of herself indirectly through the responses elicited by her communicative acts. This is the feature of pragmatic thinking about the self that we first saw in Peirce; where the child becomes aware of itself through interaction with the world and with others.

The individual experiences himself as such, not directly, but only indirectly, from the particular standpoints of other individual members of the same social group, or from the generalized standpoint of the social group as a whole to which he belongs. For he enters his own experience as a self or individual, not directly or immediately, not by becoming a subject to himself, but only in so far as he first becomes an object to himself just as other individuals are objects to him or in his experience; and he becomes an object to himself only by taking the attitudes of other individuals toward himself within a social environment or context of experience and behaviour in which he and they are involved. (Mead 1934: 138)

The development of the self is a process of the internalization of the communicative act, such that the process of 'responding to one's self as another responds to it, taking part in one's own conversation with others, being aware of what one is saying and using that awareness of what one is saying to determine what one is going to say thereafter—that is a process with which we are all familiar' (Mead 1934: 140). Mead uses this inner communicative model of the self to develop further Peirce's idea of self-controlled conduct. However, Mead also sees that the reflexive power of language enables the self-reflexive thought required for self-controlled conduct. 'I know of no other form of behaviour than the linguistic in which the individual is an object to himself, and, as far as I can see, the individual is not a self in the reflexive sense unless he is an object to himself' (Mead 1934: 142). Language affords reflexivity and can allow for the control of behaviour by modifying and responding to behaviour as another might. I turn now to the developed self as a moral agent.

4. THE FALLIBLE SELF AS A MORAL AGENT

It is in Peirce's account of the development of self-control that we find his clearest account of the individual. 'Moreover, in order for the self to function as an agency of self-control, he or she *must* be something more than a locus of error and ignorance; he or she must be a center of purpose and power' (Colapietro 1989: 74). To accomplish this development of purpose and power the self must be oriented to an open-ended future. This is another important strand in pragmatist thought: thinking is future-oriented, not simply oriented to the recent past of experience (as in classical empiricism), but towards future experience.

Colapietro indicates that inner speech gives the capacity for 'self determination' and 'self control'. Inner speech functions in such a way that it provides a 'critical self', whose function is to provide moral direction—a kind of teleological direct-edness—by providing a critical analysis of habit, character, and conduct.

The critical self plays a corrective role in guiding conduct. However, it does so not primarily through providing feelings of guilt or unease but by critical reflection and guidance. It is a preliminary to choice which initiates action. Furthermore, the function of the critical self is not just in the choice of action; it plays a crucial role in the formation and breaking of habits. The role of critical dialogue here must be more than simply an epiphenomenal awareness of habits that structure our character. The 'modelling' of good and bad habits directly leads to the development of new habits and the curtailment of existing bad ones. But how does it achieve this? Peirce is not explicit, but if the right choices are made consistently, then, following Aristotle, we might say that a settled state of character has been developed. This links with Dewey's account of the modelling of action as a process of thought: 'Deliberation is a dramatic rehearsal (in imagination) of various competing possible lines of action . . . Deliberation is an experiment in finding out what the various lines of possible action are really like. But the trial is in imagination, not in overt fact' (1976–83 xiv. 132). Peirce is primarily interested in the development of self-control over our practices, whether linguistic or epistemic. However, if we connect up the account of self-controlled inquiry with the anti-Cartesian account of the development of a child's sense of self through interaction with the world and in particular the discovery of error, then we can see a continuation in the development of the self, not through having an innate faculty of self awareness (or an infallible faculty of intuition), but through a continuous process of gaining more control over our actions and practices through a constant interaction with the environment. This is an ecological account of the self, not a substance or ego-based account of the self. We find this account of the self put to work by Dewey in his account of the self as a moral agent.

The moral self

Dewey's primary development of a notion of the self occurs in his works on ethics. Bergmann (2005: 51) lists the following as principles of Dewey's moral psychology pertaining to the self:

1. The self is constituted, on the one hand, by its acts and habits, and on the other, by its social membership.
2. Habits may be routine, mechanistic, and closed to new experiences, or intelligent, artful, and open to revision.
3. Choice, the most characteristic activity of the self, both expresses the current self and shapes the future self.
4. The only moral 'end' or 'law' is growth of the self; the essential moral criterion is what sort of self is being furthered and formed.
5. Moral judgement requires that all selves (persons) be granted equal moral standing (the principle of impartiality, equity, fairness, or common good).

I turn first to the role of habit in the formation of moral agency.

The pragmatist concept of habit is very different from a behaviouristic model where one simply responds habitually to environmental stimuli.

Dewey's concept of the habitual self is 'that body of active tendencies and interests in the individual which make him open, ready, warm to certain aims, and callous, cold, blind to others' (1976–83: v. 234). However, the habitual self is not simply a fixed set of active tendencies, indeed far from it: the self grows and acquires new habits and reorganizes old ones. Consequently, the self is adaptable and open-ended and active habits 'are opposed to routine which marks an arrest in growth' (ibid. ix. 57–8). The ability to develop new habits is 'essentially the power to learn from experience; the power to retain from experience something which is of avail in coping with the difficulties of a later situation. This means . . . the power to *develop dispositions*. Without it, the acquisition of habits is impossible' (ibid. 49).

Since Dewey takes growth to be 'the characteristic of life' he takes the end of moral activity to be growth itself, thereby eschewing a teleological conception of ethical development with a static or ultimate end as its aim. 'Not perfection as a final goal, but the ever-enduring process of perfecting, maturing, refining, is the aim of living. . . . Growth itself is the only moral "end"' (ibid. 12. 181). Consequently the self is realized by this continuous pattern of growth; it is teleological, but the ends are not fixed habits or dispositions.

Dewey denies the separation of the self and action, whereby we might think of the act simply as a means to the formation of a moral will, or the formation of dispositions as a means to producing the right consequences. (Dewey is here thinking of Kantian and Utilitarian ethical positions). It is an error to separate the self and its acts: the key to morality is to recognize 'the *essential unity of the self and its acts*' (Dewey 1981–90 vii. 288). By analogy it would be a mistake to consider that bricks are merely a means to building a house, for those same bricks will also compose part of the house. The relationship between the self and conduct can be understood by considering the nature of choice, 'since choice is the most characteristic activity of a self' (ibid. 286).

Dewey distinguishes between a spontaneous preference, which may be organically determined, and a choice which is made deliberately and knowingly. Choices reveal the existing self and, if repeated over time, form the future self (ibid. 287). In choosing to act or choosing one object over another 'one is in reality choosing what kind of person or self one is going to be. Superficially, the deliberation which terminates in choice is concerned with weighing the values of particular ends. Below the surface, it is a process of discovering what sort of being a person most wants to become' (ibid.).

Dewey thinks of this process, in characteristically pragmatic style, as an open-ended process of 'discovery'. It is not a process which reaches a final terminus in human nature or some other kind of essentially human self. Nevertheless there is a direct and intimate connection between self and act, where the self is not merely a causal means to some end 'in the sense in which a match is the cause of fire' (ibid.). The self is revealed in its choices and the moral evaluation of an act is, by implication, also a moral judgement on the character of the actor.

Responsibility and self-control

Responsibility and freedom are dependent upon the possibility for the self to grow and change by a process of learning. New habits can be acquired and old ones changed, even if they have become 'fossilized'. This requires a remarkably flexible and adaptable notion of the self; there is no core metaphysical essence which remains unchanged. The self is made continuous by the continuity of a coherent grouping of habits. A habit is understood as a 'working capacity' (Dewey 1976–83 xiv. 21), but these are, more or less, flexible and open-ended. Freedom arises from: 'being actively concerned to keep the avenues of growth open, in the degree in which we fight against induration and fixity, and thereby realize the possibilities of recreation of ourselves, we are actually free (Dewey 1981–90: vii. 306).

Several objections can be raised here; the first: it is not clear how we know which habits require change. Second: the charge may be raised that it is precisely the opposite end that we seek from the one that Dewey presents; we seek settled and continuous habits, we do not seek nascent states of constant flux. The first charge is met by Dewey's experimental conception of education; if we are self-reflective and open to new experiences we are likely to discover them for ourselves, or at least by observing others. The second charge is more interesting and depends upon interpreting Dewey as making an overly strong claim. Dewey is emphasizing the plasticity of the self to highlight a capacity that is often overlooked, at least in philosophical discussion of the self: the capacity for change. It is not a requirement of his position that we should be constantly seeking change for change's sake; rather, if we want to be different—conduct ourselves differently—then we must look to change our habits. However, Dewey's experimentalism requires him to see the developing self (acquiring new habits, not simply changing old ones) as a better end than a static self: 'The growing, enlarging, liberated self, on the other hand, goes forth to meet new demands and occasions, and readapts and remakes itself in the process. It welcomes untried situations. The necessity for choice between the interests of the old and of the forming, moving, self is recurrent' (ibid. 307).

The growth of the self requires choice and deliberation; it requires what Peirce called critical self-control. Intelligent conduct arises from deliberation which is 'dramatic rehearsal (in imagination) of various competing possible lines of action' (Dewey 1976–83: xiv. 132). Like Peirce's critical self engaged in internal dialogue, Dewey envisages the self deliberating about competing courses of action leading to choice: 'the thing actually at stake in any serious deliberation is not a difference of quantity, but what kind of person one is to become, what sort of self is in the making. What kind of a world is making' (ibid. xiv. 150). Unlike Peirce, Dewey has given us a clear link between the choices we make and the consequent characters we develop.

5. CONCLUSION: THE FALLIBLE SELF AND CONTEMPORARY THOUGHT

The fallible self of the pragmatists finds a congenial environment in contemporary embodied and embedded approaches to the mind and narrative approaches to the self. In this final section I will say something about the support for the fallible self found in developmental psychology. I will then outline the interesting connections between the pragmatist account of the fallible self and embodied and narrative accounts of the self.

There are two strands of thought that we have found in the work of the pragmatists that I want to draw out concerning the development of the self in childhood: the fallible self and intersubjectivity; language and narrative. The fallible self begins with a primary sense of embodied agency. The sensorimotor capacities of an infant are developing right from birth. As Gallagher notes, if there is a sense of self tied to early neonate experiences then this sense of self will be tied to an embodied sense of self (Gallagher 2005: 79). Indeed, the early fallible self is really an instance of what Neisser (1988) described as the *ecological self*; a sense of self that develops from proprioception and movement in an environment. Hence, it should come as no surprise that infants develop an exploratory and open-ended method of interacting with their environment. Peirce's fallibilism grows directly out of these sensorimotor explorations of the local environment.

However, as Meltzoff's neonate imitation studies show, the infant is socially orientated from birth. Trevarthan calls the ability of an infant to respond to the communicative actions of a parent primary intersubjectivity: 'In the gentle, immediate, affectionate, and rhythmically regulated playful exchanges of proto-conversation, 2-month-old infants look at the eyes and mouth of the person addressing them while listening to the voice' (Trevarthan and Aitken 2001: 6). The infant's primary sense of embodied agency is at the same time scaffolded by constant social interactions with caregivers. Trevarthan (1979) indicates the onset of shared attention at around the one-year mark. This would be an important juncture at which the child could learn through error and have its actions corrected by a caregiver, in much the way that Peirce envisioned.

The intersubjective nature of early infant–mother interactions leads us towards the development of a sense of self that is thoroughly social and other-regarding. It leads us away from the picture of a hidden Cartesian self that is primarily orientated towards itself. The evidence of contemporary developmental psychology fits better with the embodied, embedded, and intersubjective nature of the fallible self.

Peirce and Mead argue that the sense of self is further developed through the acquisition of linguistic capacities. Children's narrative capacity appears to be developed from their conversational (or discursive) capacities, as well as autobiographical memory and other cognitive capacities (Gallagher 2006). Once children begin to be able to hold rudimentary conversations from age 2 onwards they quickly begin to engage in conversations which tell a narrative (Nelson 2003). However, very young children have only a rudimentary sense of self as actor: 'During this early developmental period language is being learned and used but it is not yet a vehicle for conveying the representation of narrative' (Nelson 2003: 245). Indeed 3- to 5-year-old children typically produce narratives that miss out on or only weakly exhibit three essential components of narrative: 'temporal perspective, the mental as well as physical perspective of self and of different others, and essential cultural knowledge of the unexperienced world' (Nelson 2003: 28).

Mead's view that the child's sense of self is mediated by the interiorization of speech still has currency. Children learn to respond to the verbal commands of adults in controlling and directing their actions (Morin 2005). They are able to perform actions with the verbal and physical support of adult caregivers. The internalization of the regulatory function of language and the self-generation of inner speech is important to developing this self-control. Kendall and Hollon (1981) give us four categories of the regulatory use of speech for problem-solving: (1) the precise definition of the problem; (2) the effective approach to the problem; (3) the focus on the problem; (4) the progress evaluation that includes praise or strategy readjustment (Morin 2005). The development of the fallible self finds a natural home in current developmental psychology. It also finds a home in current thinking about embodied and extended minds.

The pragmatists were philosophical and psychological precursors to the current embodied and extended approaches to mind and cognition. Dewey and Peirce are explicit in their externalism about thinking. Thinking does not take place in some inner mental substance, nor in some inner cognitive system. Thinking is an activity involving the interaction between an organism and its environment. The fallible method of thinking is the direction of activity to achieve some desired end. Like the cat in the puzzle-box, we learn to manipulate the environment to achieve our goals. These manipulations become habitual and we do not even notice them in the background of our cognitive lives. This just is the view that cognition is extended by our bodily manipulation of the environment (Menary 2007; Rowlands 1999). The extended mind hypothesis currently has no theory of the self, but it can find one ready-made in the form of the pragmatist's fallible self.

We have already seen how there is strong developmental evidence in support of the fallible self, and that this comes in part from the child's development of linguistic capacities. The role of language and internal dialogue in structuring the fallible self finds its corollary in the narrative approach to the self. However, as I noted above, the narrative self that we find in Peirce's work is thoroughly embodied and embedded. Peirce's narratives are what I have elsewhere called *embodied narratives* (Menary 2008).

Embodied narratives arise directly from the lived experience of the embodied subject and these narratives can be embellished and reflected upon if we need to find a meaningful form or structure in that sequence of experiences. So the fallible self links the embodied basis of the self, and its dynamical stream of conscious thought, with a narrative structuring of that stream (see James's account of the stream of consciousness above). The fallible self as embodied narrator is thoroughly intersubjective, coming to narrate by internalizing the linguistic interactions that are first shared with parents and siblings.

The pragmatists thus provide us with an account of the self which touches on many of the themes explicated in this volume:

1. How does the self originate in infancy? The fallible self originates in the infant's first intersubjective relations with its mother. The development of a sense of self is further developed by the infant's exploration of and interaction with its environment. As Peirce puts it, consciousness of a self is inferred from these initial explorations and re-enforced by intersubjective interactions with caregivers.

2. How is self related to embodiment? The fallible self is embodied and embedded: the development of self-consciousness by infant exploration of an environment could not otherwise occur. The development of the fallible self is primarily a matter

of a growing awareness of our bodily activity in an environment. However, this self-awareness does not suddenly end once we reach adulthood.

3. Is the self minimal or extended by narratives? The fallible self is intersubjective; it is extended by social interactions. Mead and Peirce make it clear that the internalization of language is an important step in the development of the fallible self.

4. The moral dimensions of the self? Dewey gives us an account of agency, self-control and responsibility which is continuous with the thought of other pragmatists, such as Peirce. His account of ethical agency does not require an ideal rational spectator that can judge the most rational course of action.

The continuities in the work of the classic pragmatists share the same pragmatic principle: that a static and essentialist image of the self is shattered once we *see* that what we do is not to be thought of as distinct from what we are.

REFERENCES

BERGMANN, R. (2005). 'John Dewey on Educating the Moral Self', *Studies in Philosophy and Education*, 24: 39–62.

BERMÚDEZ, J. (1996). 'The Moral Significance of Birth', *Ethics*, 106/2: 378–403.

CLARK, A. (2008). *Supersizing the Mind* (Oxford: Oxford University Press).

COLAPIETRO, V. (1989). *Peirce's Approach to the Self* (Albany, NY: State University of New York Press).

——(2006). 'Practice, Agency, and Sociality: An Orthogonal Reading of Classical Pragmatism', *International Journal for Dialogical Science*, 1/1: 23–31.

DENNETT, D. (1991). *Consciousness Explained* (London: Allen Lane).

DEWEY, J. (1925). *Experience and Nature* (New York: Dover).

DEWEY, J. (1976–83). *The Middle Works: 1899–1924* (15 vols. Carbondale, Ill.: Southern Illinois University Press).

——(1981–90). *The Later Works: 1925–1953* (17 vols. Carbondale, Ill.: Southern Illinois University Press).

GALLAGHER, S. (1996). 'The Moral Significance of Primitive Self-Consciousness: A Response to Bermúdez', *Ethics*, 107/1: 129–40.

——(2005). *How the Body Shapes the Mind* (New York: Oxford University Press).

——(2006). 'The Narrative Alternative to Theory of Mind', in R. Menary (ed.), *Radical Enactivism* (Amsterdam: John Benjamins).

——(2009). 'Philosophical Antecedents of Situated Cognition', in P. Robbins and M. Aydede (eds), *The Cambridge Handbook of Situated Cognition* (Cambridge: Cambridge University Press).

GALLIE, W. B. (1952). *Peirce and Pragmatism* (Harmondsworth: Penguin Books).

HUTCHINS, E. (1995). *Cognition in the Wild* (Cambridge, Mass.: MIT Press).

JAMES, W. (1890). *The Principles of Psychology* (New York: Dover).

KENDALL, P. C., and HOLLON, S. D. (1981). 'Assessing Self-Referent Speech: Methods in Measurement of Self-Statements', in P. C. Kendall and S. D. Hollon (eds), *Assessment Strategies for Cognitive-Behavioral Interventions* (New York: Academic Press).

MEAD, G. H. (1934). *Mind, Self, and Society* (Chicago: University of Chicago Press).

MELTZOFF, A. N., and MOORE, M. K. (1977). 'Imitation of Facial and Manual Gestures by Human Neo-Nates', *Science*, 198: 75–8.

MENARY, R. (2007). *Cognitive Integration: Mind and Cognition Unbounded* (Basingstoke: Palgrave Macmillan).

——(2008). 'Embodied Narratives', *Journal of Consciousness Studies*, 15/6: 63–84.

——(2009). 'Intentionality, Cognitive Integration and the Continuity Thesis', *Topoi*, 28: 31–43.

MORIN, A. (2005). 'Possible Links between Self-Awareness and Inner Speech: Theoretical Background, Underlying Mechanisms, and Empirical Evidence', *Journal of Consciousness Studies*, 12/4–5: 115–34.

NEISSER, U. (1988). 'Five Kinds of Self-Knowledge', *Philosophical Psychology*, 1: 35–59.

NELSON, K. (2003). 'Narrative and the Emergence of a Consciousness of Self', in G. D. Fireman, T. E. J. McVay, and O. Flanagan (eds), *Narrative and Consciousness* (Oxford: Oxford University Press).

NOË, A. (2004). *Action in Perception (Representation and Mind)* (Cambridge, Mass.: Bradford Books/MIT Press).

O'REGAN, J. K., and NOË, A. (2001). 'A Sensorimotor Account of Vision and Visual Consciousness', *Behavioural and Brain Sciences*, 24: 939–1031.

PEIRCE, C. S. (1868a). 'Questions Concerning Certain Faculties Claimed for Man', *Journal of Speculative Philosophy*, 2: 103–14.

——(1868b). 'Some Consequences of Four Incapacities', *Journal of Speculative Philosophy*, 2: 140–57.

——(1931–60). *Collected Papers of Charles Sanders Peirce*, ed. C. Hartshorne, P. Weiss, and A. Burks (8 vols. Cambridge, Mass.: Harvard University Press).

——(1984–93). *Writings of Charles Sanders Peirce* (Bloomington, Ind.: Indiana University Press), i–v.

ROWLANDS, M. (1999). *The Body in Mind: Understanding Cognitive Processes.* (Cambridge: Cambridge University Press).

SCHEFFLER, I. (1974). *The Four Pragmatists* (London: Routledge).

SELLARS, W. (1956). *Empiricism and the Philosophy of Mind* (Cambridge, Mass.: Harvard University Press).

STERN, DANIEL N. (1985). *The Interpersonal World of the Infant: A View from Psychoanalysis and Developmental Psychology* (New York: Basic Books).

THAYER, H. (1968). *Meaning and Action* (Indianapolis: Hackett).

TREVARTHAN, C. (1979). 'Communication and Co-operation in Early Infancy: A Description of Primary Intersubjectivity', in M. Bullowa (ed.), *Before Speech* (Cambridge: Cambridge University Press), 321–47.

——and AITKEN, K. (2001). 'Infant Intersubjectivity: Research, Theory, and Clinical Applications', *Journal of Child Psychology and Psychiatry*, 42/1: 3–48.

VELLEMAN, J. D. (2006). *Self to Self: Selected Essays* (New York: Cambridge University Press).

....

CHAPTER 27

THE SOCIAL CONSTRUCTION OF SELF

....

KENNETH J. GERGEN

IN treating the social construction of self it is first necessary to identify the boundaries of the domain. At the outset, there is the matter of the self. History has prepared us to speak of the self in many different ways, and some of these are more central to constructionist concerns than others. My particular concern in the present chapter will be with a family of uses that generally refer to a psychological or mental world within the individual. The members of this family are many and varied. We variously speak of persons as possessing mental concepts of themselves, and it is often said that these concepts are saturated with value, that they may be defective or dysfunctional, that they figure importantly in the individual's rational calculus, and that they ultimately supply resources for the exercise of personal agency. And too, many simply identify the process of conscious choice as equivalent to the individual self. Such assumptions are deeply embedded in Western culture, and provide the under-girding rationale for practices of jurisprudence, childrearing, education, counseling, and psychotherapy, among others. Further, such assumptions furnish the basis for myriad research studies in psychology and sociology. Individual self-esteem, for example, has been one of the most intensively studied topics in psychology. Indeed, the Western traditions of democracy and capitalism are both wedded to conceptions of the individual self as alluded to above.

With this particular focus on self in place, I shift attention to the matter of social construction. In this case, it is important to outline some of the major assumptions that play themselves out in contemporary constructionist scholarship. The ground is then prepared for treating issues in the social construction of the self. Here I will begin with a discussion of the ungrounded character of mental accounts in general. Following this, I will discuss major lines of inquiry into the social construction of self, along with its socio-political implications. Finally, I will introduce an alternative to traditional conceptions of self, one that emerges distinctly from social constructionist theory.

The Emergence of Social Constructionist Theory

There are many stories to be told about the development of social constructionism in scholarly worlds. I offer here but one, although one that is congenial with much common understanding. To be sure, one may trace the intellectual roots of social constructionism to Vico, Nietzsche, Dewey, and Wittgenstein, among others. And Berger and Luckmann's *The Social Construction of Reality* (1966) was a landmark volume with strong reverberations in neighboring disciplines. However, the social movements and intellectual ferment taking shape in the late 1960s in the United States and Western Europe were perhaps more influential in paving the way to social construction in psychology. Resistance to the Vietnam War and to the country's political leadership was intense; profound skepticism of the established order was voiced. Much of the academic community was deeply engaged in political protest. The context was optimal for reassessing the established rationale and practices within the sciences and other scholarly traditions. In brief, one can locate at least three major forms of broadly shared critique that resulted from such reassessment. Each of them found expression in the psychological literature. Most importantly, the amalgamation of these forms of critique—sometimes identified with postmodernism—largely serves as the basis for most social constructionist inquiry in the scholarly world today.[1]

Perhaps the strongest and most impassioned form of critique of the dominant orders has been, and continues to be, *ideological*. In this case, critics challenge various taken-for-granted realities in society and reveal the political ends that they

---

[1] For a more detailed account of these critiques within psychology, see Gergen (1994*b*). Additional accounts of social constructionist premises and potentials may be found in Potter 1996; Gergen 2009; Hacking 1999.

achieve. In effect, such analysis discloses the socio-political consequences of the sedimented accounts of reality, in the attempt to liberate the reader from their subtle grasp. Within the scholarly world more generally, such 'unmasking' has played a major role in Marxist scholarship, along with anti-psychiatry, feminist, racial, gay and lesbian, and anti-colonialist movements, among others.

The second major form of critique may be viewed as *literary/rhetorical*. With developments in semiotic theory in general and literary deconstruction in particular (Derrida 1976), attention was variously drawn to the ways in which linguistic convention governs all claims to knowledge. Thus, whatever reality posits one puts forward, they will bear the marks of the linguistic forms (including, for example, grammatical rules, narrative conventions, and binary distinctions) necessary for communication. In this sense the forms of language are not driven by reality so much as they provide the forestructure for what we take to be its nature.

The third significant critique of foundational science was stimulated largely by the 1970 publication of Thomas Kuhn's *The Structure of Scientific Revolutions*. Kuhn portrayed normal science as guided by paradigms of thought and practice shared by particular communities. In effect, the outcomes of science were not demanded by the world as it is, but are the result of communal negotiation. This social account of science was further buttressed by a welter of research in the sociology of knowledge and the history of science (see e.g. Feyerabend 1978; Latour and Woolgar 1986).[2] Although these movements largely originated within separate scholarly spheres, scholars increasingly discovered affinities among them. In effect, one could recognize the contours of a broader movement, often identified as social constructionist. Within this movement, three domains of agreement are noteworthy: the social origins of knowledge, the centrality of language, and the politics of knowledge.

The social origins of knowledge

Perhaps the most generative idea emerging from the constructionist dialogues is that what we take to be knowledge of the world and self finds its origins in human relationships. What we take to be true as opposed to false, objective as opposed to subjective, scientific as opposed to mythological, rational as opposed to irrational,

[2] It should be noted that the term *constructivism* is sometimes used interchangeably with constructionism. However, unlike social construction, early scholars tended to define constructivism in terms of cognitive processes within the individual mind. For these theorists the focus was placed on the individual's perceptions and interpretative capacities as the originating source of their constructions of the world. Recent scholarship has made it increasingly difficult to sustain the distinction between constructivism and constructionism. Constructivists increasingly view mental practices as reflections or embodiments of social process. Many now speak of social constructivism, or use the terms interchangeably.

moral as opposed to immoral is brought into being through historically and culturally situated social processes. This view stands in dramatic contrast to two of the most important intellectual and cultural traditions of the West. On the one hand is the tradition of the individual knower, the rational, self-directing, morally centered, and knowledgeable agent of action. Within the constructionist dialogues we find that it is not in the individual mind that knowledge, reason, emotion, and morality reside, but in relationships.

The communal view of knowledge also represents a major challenge to the view of Truth, or the possibility that the accounts of scientists, or any other group, reveal or approach the objective truth about what is the case. In effect, propose the constructionists, no one arrangement of words is necessarily more objective or accurate in its depiction of reality than any other. To be sure, accuracy may be achieved within a given community or tradition—according to its rules and practices. Physics and chemistry generate useful truths from within their communal traditions, just as psychologists, sociologists, and priests do from within theirs. But from these often-competing traditions there is no means by which one can locate a transcendent truth, a 'truly true'. Any attempt to determine the superior account would itself be the outcome of a given community of agreement.

To be sure, these arguments have provoked antagonistic reactions among scientific communities in particular. There remains a substantial number in the scientific community, including the social sciences, who still cling to a vision of science as generating 'Truth beyond community'. For scientists who see themselves as generating pragmatic or instrumental truths, constructionist arguments are quite congenial. Thus, for example, both would agree that while Western medical science does succeed in generating what might commonly be called 'cures' for that which is termed 'illness', these advances are dependent upon culturally and historically specific constructions of what constitutes an impairment, health and illness, life and death, the boundaries of the body, the nature of pain, and so on. When these assumptions are treated as universal—true for all cultures and times—alternative conceptions are undermined and destroyed. To understand death, for example, as merely the termination of biological functioning would be an enormous impoverishment of human existence. The constructionist does not abandon medical science, but attempts to understand it as a cultural tradition—one among many.

The centrality of language

Central to the constructionist account of the social origins of knowledge is a concern with language. If accounts of the world are not demanded by what there is, then the traditional view of language as a mapping device ceases to compel. Rather, following Wittgenstein (1953), a view of language is invited, in which meaning is understood as a derivative of language use within relationships. And, given that games of language are essentially conducted in a rule-like fashion, accounts of the world are governed in significant degree by conventions of language use. Psychological research could not reveal, for example, that 'motives are oblong'. The utterance is grammatically correct, but it is cultural nonsense. Rather, while it is perfectly satisfactory to speak of motives as varying in intensity or content, conventions of talk about motivation in the twenty-first century do not happen to include the adjective, 'oblong'. Expanding on this point, many constructionists see attempts at generating philosophical foundations for scientific study as forms of language games. For example, the long-standing question of whether and to what degree the mind has access to the external world—the central problem of episte-mology—is a problem only within a given game of language (see Rorty 1979). To play the game we must agree that there is a 'mental world' on the one hand and a 'material world' on the other (an 'in here' and 'out there'), and that the former may possibly reflect the latter. If one does not agree to play by these rules, there is no 'problem of individual knowledge'.

Of special relevance to an understanding of research methods, constructionists also tend to accept Wittgenstein's view of language games as embedded within broader 'forms of life'. Thus, for example, the language conventions for communi-cating about human motivation are linked to certain activities, objects, and settings. For the research psychologist there may be 'assessment devices' for motivation (e.g. questionnaires, thematic analysis of discourse, controlled observa-tions of behavior), and statistical technologies to assess differences between groups. Given broad agreement within a field of study about 'the way the game is played', conclusions can be reached about the nature of human motivation. As construc-tionists also suggest, playing by the rules of a given community is enormously important to sustaining these relationships. Not only does conformity to the rules affirm the reality, rationality, and values of the research community, but the very *raison d'être* of the profession itself is sustained. To abandon the discourse of the mind would threaten the discipline of psychology; to dispense with the discourse of social structure would threaten the collapse of sociology. Without conventions of construction, action loses value.

The politics of knowledge

As indicated above, social constructionism is closely allied with a pragmatic conception of knowledge. That is, traditional issues of truth and objectivity are replaced by concerns with that which research brings forth. It is not whether an account is true from a god's eye view that matters, but rather, the implications for cultural life that follow from taking any truth claim seriously. This concern with consequences essentially eradicates the long-standing distinction between *fact* and *value*, between is and ought. The forms of life within any knowledge-making community represent and sustain the values of that community. In establishing 'what is the case', the research community also place value on their particular metatheory of knowledge, constructions of the world, and practices of research. When others embrace such knowledge they wittingly or unwittingly extend the reach of these values.

Thus, for example, the scientist may use the most rigorous methods of testing intelligence, and amass tomes of data that indicate racial differences in intelligence. However, the presumptions that there is something called 'human intelligence', that a series of question and answer games reveal this capacity, and that there are separable 'races' in the world, are all specific to a given tradition or paradigm. Such concepts and measures are not required by 'the way the world is'. Most importantly, to accept the paradigm and extend its implications into policy within the tradition is deeply injurious to those people classified as inferior by its standards.

This line of reasoning has had enormous repercussions in the academic community and beyond. Drawing sustenance in particular from Foucault's (1978, 1979) power/knowledge formulations, one comes to understand that the realities, rationalities, and values created within any social enclave have socio-political ramifications. And particularly because those within a given interpretive community seldom appreciate that their realities are local and contingent, there is a strong tendency toward reification. Those who fail to share the local realities and values are thus viewed as misled, ignorant, immoral, and possibly evil. In effect, with the process of reality building set in motion, the result is often social division and antagonism. Each tradition of the real becomes a potential enemy to all those who do not share in the tradition. To illustrate, experimental psychologists are generally committed to a causal view of human action, and view the experimental method as the most valuable means of demonstrating cause–effect relations. There is little doubting these assumptions and practices; they are simply taken for granted. However, this form of life cannot accommodate the concept of human agency. To include an uncaused cause within the formulations would destroy a way of life. At the same time, to embrace the experimental way of life is to threaten the legitimacy of claims to voluntary action and thus a tradition of moral responsibility. With this background in place, we may now turn to more specific concerns with the self.

MENTAL DISCOURSE IN QUESTION

The term 'self' is employed in many different settings, and for different purposes, and in this sense is richly polysemic. On the present account, all such meanings are essentially constructed within social enclaves. However, the more difficult task is to remove the sediment sense of the real accumulating from long-standing usages. It is only when the painstaking work of denaturalizing has taken place that one is liberated from the past, and thus positioned to reformulate as conditions require. It is in this context that I wish to focus specifically on the self as a constituent member in the family of mental discourse. Over the past three centuries Western culture has developed an enormous vocabulary referring to mental states, mechanisms, processes, or conditions. Although subject to long-standing contention within philosophy (see e.g. Almoq 2005; Ryle 1949), for most people there is little doubting the existence of the world created by these terms. We readily speak of one's thoughts, desires, emotions, and motives, in the same way we refer to one's 'self-image', 'self esteem', 'self love', and 'voluntary choice'. As indicated earlier, these 'realities' are insinuated into the rationale for many of the major institutions and traditions of Western culture. In what follows I wish to outline some of the major problems inhering in the attempt to anchor the discourse of the psychological self in an independent world of existents. This brief account should move toward unsettling existing assumptions. In the following section we explore some of the major means by which the psychological self is constructed. These explorations will set the stage for considering alternatives to the psychological conception of self.

As proposed, we typically employ such terms as 'thought', 'emotion', 'motivation', and 'self-esteem' as if they referred to existing states or entities within the individual. Yet, one may ask, on what grounds do we make such references? In many domains, and science in particular, we justify the favored vocabulary through ostensive definition. In effect, we can point to what we take to be an entity and declare, 'that is a cow', or 'this is the left hemisphere of the cerebral cortex'. To be sure, such constructions may be shared only within particular traditions, but the ability to relate the vocabulary to a publicly shared world of observables can serve as a local form of grounding. In contrast, there is little way of wedding mental terms to a world of ostensively designated referents. The Western tradition does suggest two major candidates for justification: *self-observation* and *observation by others*. In the former case, we might presume that we can know with confidence about mental states such as self-esteem because we are intimately acquainted with them. As psychologists often say, we have *metacognitive* knowledge of our psychological processes. In the case of external observation, we might presume a warrant for psychological knowledge based on the reasoned inferences of neutrally positioned observers. Let us consider these possibilities further.

First, in the case of knowledge through self-observation, a scan of both philosophic and psychological analyses suggests that the very concept of internal observation is deeply flawed. To succinctly summarize some of the major problems (for a more extended summary of these arguments, see Gergen, 2009):

- How can consciousness turn in upon itself to identify its own states? How can experience become an object to itself? Can a mirror reflect its own image?
- How can one be certain that various mental processes would not obstruct the attempt to identify one's states? Could other processes (e.g. repression, defense) not prevent accurate self-appraisal?
- What are the characteristics of mental states by which one could identify them? By what criteria does one distinguish, let us say, among states of anger, fear, and love? What is the color of hope, the size of a thought, or the shape of anger? Why do none of these attributes seem quite applicable to mental states? Is it because our observations of the states prove to us that they are not? What would we be observing in this case?
- By what criterion could one determine that what one experiences as 'certain recognition' of a mental state is indeed certain recognition? Wouldn't this recognition ('I am certain in my assessment') require yet another round of self-assessments ('I am certain that what I am experiencing is certainty . . . '), the results of which would require additional processes of internal identification, and so on in an infinite regress?
- How could one identify an inner state save through an a priori agreement about what exists in the mind? Could one identify an emotion that was not already given within the prevailing discourse on emotion? Could a Westerner identify 'liget' or 'amae' (terms from non-Western cultures)?
- Could one identify one's mental states through their physiological manifestations—blood pressure, heart rate, etc.? Can one know he or she is 'thinking' by examining one's blood pressure, or that one has 'hope' through a recording of neurological activity? And, if one did have access to brain scan data, how could one know to which states such scans referred?

Of course, many contemporary psychologists (along with many psychoanalysts) are quite willing to abandon the idea of inner observation (or introspection) as a valid source of psychological knowledge. For many, it is the external observer— rationally systematic and personally dispassionate—who is ideally situated to draw valid conclusions about people's internal states. Yet, the past thirty years of poststructural and hermeneutic deliberation leave the presumption of external observation as imperiled as that of introspection. Again in abbreviated form, consider some of the major flaws:

- If we were to base our knowledge on our subjects' descriptions of their internal states (e.g. 'I am depressed', 'I am angry') how would we know to what the terms referred within their own mind/brain? We have no access to the states or conditions. What if one person's referent for 'love' was another's referent for 'anxiety'? Without access to the putative referents, there would be no means of sorting out the differences. Indeed, how could one be certain that mental terms refer to anything at all (e.g. 'my soul is anguished')?

- If we abandon introspection as the basis of knowledge, how can we trust any self-reports (e.g. 'I feel . . .', 'I aspire to . . .', 'It is my opinion that . . .') as the basis of external inference? How could the person know about these conditions, sufficient that the reports would count as inferential evidence?
- Even if self-reports converge (as in the items making up a self-esteem scale), how would we know to what (in the individual's mind/brain) the individual items referred—if anything (could we not also generate a twelve-item scale of 'soul anguish')? How could we trust the subject to know?
- How can we determine the nature of what we are observing, save through the lens of a theory already established? Could we identify 'cognitive conservation' without a theory enabling us to interpret a child's action in just this way? Could we observe aggression, moral behavior, altruism, conformity, obedience, or learning, for example, without a pre-understanding that would call our attention to certain patterns of activity as opposed to others? Can we observe a 'causal relation' without at least a rudimentary theory of cause already in place? Or, in effect, aren't our observations of psychologically relevant behavior theory determined?
- If we propose to identify psychological states through their physiological correlates (as in 'the physiology of memory'), how can we determine to what psychological states the physiology provides the underpinning? If we cannot determine when a 'memory', 'a thought', or 'an agitation of the spirit' has occurred, how are we to establish the physiological correlates?

As this brief account suggests, the discourse of the psychological self cannot be anchored in a referential base sufficient to inspire, direct, or constrain its usage. It is largely for this reason that the conception of self has been such an inviting topic of exploration for social constructionist scholars.

The Construction and Critique of Self

Inquiry into the social construction of self can roughly be divided into three categories. The first is primarily concerned with establishing the self as a social construction; the second is focused on specific social processes in which the conception of self is embedded; and the third involves critical assessments of the cultural and political repercussions of traditional beliefs in the self. I consider each in turn.

The self in historical and cultural context

One gains an acute appreciation of the extent to which one's everyday under-standings are both culturally and historically situated—and perhaps precariously so—through comparisons with commonplace beliefs in other cultures and times. In this sense, such comparisons not only illustrate the richness in human con-structions of the self, but function as well as a destabilizing device in contemporary culture. The historical and cultural literature in this case is enormous, and as these topics are relevant to other discussions in this volume, I will simply earmark here two significant lines of inquiry. On the historical side, two of the most extensive accounts of the vicissitudes in Western conceptualizations of the self are those of Charles Taylor (1989) and Jerrold Siegel (2001). Both explore this history in an attempt to locate resources for a morally or personally meaningful life. Numerous other accounts treat the emergence of particular concepts of self within cir-cumscribed historical periods (see e.g. Cary 2000; Cushman 1996; Holstein and Gubrium 2000). Much the same denaturalization of the self takes place in cross-cultural comparisons. Perhaps the major theme that pervades this work is the comparison between the individuated, bounded, and autonomous view of the self that is shared within Western culture, and the more socially or communally embedded vision of the self that may be found in many other cultures of the world (see e.g. Marsella *et al.* 1985; Becker 1995; Markus and Kitayama 1991).

The self as social accomplishment

A second significant line of constructionist inquiry builds on the first. If the self is socially constructed, one asks, how are we to understand the processes central to this achievement? Echoing the earlier discussion of the literary and rhetorical contributions to social construction, the major focus of this line of inquiry has been on discourse practices. To be sure, psycholinguistic study of the relation of mind (or cognition) to language, along with research into grammar and syntax, for example, has generated a large corpus of literature. However, within a construc-tionist frame, this tradition has not been engaging. For one, studies relating mind to language have presumed a dualism between mind and speech that many con-structionists call into question. Further, in its search for 'the truth about language', traditional research was stripped of concern with political and ideological context, and thus of little relevance for many constructionists.

Inquiry into social achievement of the self has taken two major forms. The first is concerned with the structure of language and the demands made by linguistic convention on the conception of self. The second has focused on ongoing conver-sational practices. In the case of language structure, for example, Sampson (2008) has drawn attention to the binary structure of language and its contribution to the self/other dichotomy. As Harré (1991) has also proposed, the existence of personal pronouns (e.g. I, you, he, me) contributes significantly to an ontology of separate selves. Perhaps the most prominent form of inquiry linking discursive structure to conceptions of self has centered on narrative. Drawing from a long-standing emphasis in semiotic studies on the formative influence of narrative structure, scholars have variously explored the way in which conceptions of the self are guided by a narrative forestructure. As MacIntyre (1984) cogently argued, one's conception of self, and indeed one's moral integrity, emerges from one's narrative of self. It is the form of this narrative, as shared within an interpretive tradition, that underlies one's sense of self. The work of Gergen and Gergen (1983), Sarbin (1986), Polkinghorne (1988), Rosenwald and Ochberg (1990), and Bruner (1990) has given the study of narrative a prominent place in the psychology of the self. The long-standing concern in psychology with life history has also been highly congenial to narrative study. The work of Dan McAdams (1985, 1997) has underscored the centrality of narrative not only to self-understanding but to the trajectory of one's actions. His inquiry into 'redemptive narratives' has also fired interest in the relationship of self-understanding and spiritual traditions (McAdams, 2006).

The second major line of inquiry into the self as a social accomplishment has been concerned with ongoing interaction. Such inquiry was initially stimulated by the work of Harold Garfinkel (1967) and the *ethnomethods* by which realities are constituted within conversation. The link between ethnomethodology and the psychological self was secured in Jeff Coulter's 1979 volume, *The Social Construction of Mind: Studies in Ethnomethodology and Linguistic Philosophy*. Coulter's work demonstrated the ways in which the self is continuously fashioned and refashioned as conversation unfolds. Inquiry into discursive *positioning* (Davies and Harré, 1990; Van Langenhove and Harré, 1998) offered subsequent insight into a critical aspect of this process. The concern in this case is with the way in which conversational interlocutors position each other's identity as they speak. However, while further work in discourse and conversational analysis adds depth and richness to these views, such inquiry reaches a juncture at which the specifically psychological self is no longer in focus (see e.g. Benwell and Stokoe 2006, and Buchholtz 1999). Such inquiry focuses almost exclusively on the spoken or written word, while simultaneously placing the 'conversational object' at ontological risk. Thus, analysts will demonstrate how conversational references to the self deconstruct the psychological referent. Attention is then drawn to publicly defined identity.

Critical reflection on the psychological self

For the constructionist, the realities created by people together are functionally insinuated into their daily relationships. The discursive ontologies and ethics are embedded within normal and normative practices. Or, more succinctly, the discourses of daily life are constitutive of living traditions. In this sense, scholars have been concerned with the way in which vocabularies of the self both rationalize and sustain cultural practices. It is in this vein that many constructionists have drawn sustenance from Foucault's (1978, 1979) writings on knowledge and power. Language, for Foucault, serves as a major medium for carrying out relations. Because language constitutes what we take to be the world, and rationalizes the form of reality thus created, it also serves as a socially binding force. By acting within language, relations of power and privilege are sustained. And, by engaging in the further circulation of a form of language, the array of power relations is further extended (see Rose 1985, 1990).

In particular, as many critics see it, there is a substantial dark side to constructing a world of individual and agentic selves. When a fundamental distinction between self and other is established, the social world is constituted in terms of differences. The individual stands as an isolated entity, essentially alone and alienated. Further, such a view lends itself to a prizing of autonomy—of becoming a 'self-made man', who 'does it my way'. To be dependent is a sign of weakness and incapacity. To construct a world of separation in this way is also to court distrust; one can never be certain of the other's motives. And given distrust, it becomes reasonable to 'take care of number one'. Self-gain becomes an unquestionable motive, within both the sciences (such as economics and social psychology) and the culture at large. In this context, loyalty, commitment, and community are all thrown into question, as all may potentially interfere with 'self-realization'. Such views represent an extended critique of Western individualism. (See e.g. Gelpi 1989; Hewitt 1989; Bellah *et al.* 1985; Heller *et al.* 1986; Lasch 1978; Leary 2004.)

These critiques become more pointed in their implications when self-dysfunction is considered. At the outset, an extensive literature illuminates the constructed character of the psychiatric concepts of mental illness, and points to the ideological and political interests served by diagnostic categorization. Thus, for example, scholars have explored the social construction of schizophrenia (Sarbin and Mancuso 1980), anorexia (Hepworth 1999), depression (Blazer 2005), attention deficit disorder (Divorky and Schrag 1975), post traumatic stress disorder (Quosh and Gergen 2008), and many other forms of 'mental disorder' (see e.g. Neimeyer 2000; Fee 2000). These deconstructions of illness categories have been accompanied by critical assessments of the impact on both clients and the society more generally. For example, diagnostic categories are variously seen as devices used largely for purposes of social control (e.g. client management, insurance justification), that mystify the values agendas they express, and sustain the myth of mental health practice as medical science in such a way that problems in living are increasingly treated with pharmaceutical suppressants (Kutchins and Kirk 1997; Szasz 1961). Further, by disseminating 'knowledge of mental illness' to the culture, people cease to examine the societal conditions that may favor depression or hyperactivity, for example, and increasingly come to construct themselves in these terms (Gergen 2006; Hare-Mustin 1994). Further, to be categorized as mentally ill frequently increases the anguish of those who bear the labels. To hear voices, to be hyperactive, or to be chronically sad, for example, is not inherently to possess an illness, and there are more beneficial constructions possible (Parker *et al.* 1995).

THE RELATIONAL SELF

The preceding critiques of the psychological self have brought about an active movement to reconceptualize the mind in general, and the self in particular. The attempt in this case is to construct an ontology that replaces the vision of the bounded self as the atom of the social world with relational process. From this standpoint, it would not be selves who come together to form relationships, but relational process out of which the very idea of the psychological self could emerge. As can be seen, the development of such a view follows congenially from the constructionist perspective so instrumental in denaturalizing the traditional view of the psychological self. If what we call knowledge emerges from social process, then social process stands as an ontological prior to the individual.

Relational explorations draw nourishment from a number of early lines of scholarship. Phenomenologists have long been concerned with the arbitrary character of the mind/world dichotomy. For example, Edmund Husserl (1859–1938) proposed that all experience is *intentional*, essentially directed toward or absorbed by some pattern (object, person, etc.). Thus, conscious experience is fundamentally relational; subject and object—or self and other—are unified within experience. For many psychologists George Herbert Mead's volume, *Mind, Self and Society* was the first important step toward a relational account of self. As Mead proposed, there is no thinking, or indeed any sense of being a self, that is independent of social process. For Mead, we are born with rudimentary capacities to adjust to each other, largely in response to gestures—with the hands, vocal sounds, facial expressions, gaze, and so on. It is through others' response to our gestures that we slowly begin to develop the capacities for mental symbolization; as others respond to our gestures, and we experience these responses within us, we are able to gain a sense of what the other's gesture symbolizes for him or her. 'No hard-and-fast line can be drawn between our own selves and the selves of others, since our own selves exist and enter as such into our experience only in so far as the selves of others exist and enter as such in our experience also' (Mead 1934).

The work of Lev Vygotsky (1978) also offered a bold alternative to the dominant conception of mind independent from social process. For Vygotsky, individuals are inextricably related, both to each other and to their physical surrounds. Of particular interest for Vygotsky were the 'higher mental functions' such as thinking, planning, attending, and remembering. For Vygotsky, these higher processes are lodged within relationships: 'social relations or relations among people genetically underlie all higher (mental) functions and their relationships.' In effect, mental functioning reflects social process. On the psychoanalytic front, theory has shifted toward 'object relations' (or the mental representation of others). Here therapists have become increasingly concerned with the complex relations between transference and counter-transference. As relational analysts propose, it is no longer possible to view the therapist as a neutral investigator of the client's mind, as the therapist's psychological functioning cannot be extricated from that of the client. Literary theory has also served as a vital stimulus to theorizing a relational self. Bakhtin's explorations of dialogicality in the novel have been especially significant. As Bakhtin (1981) reasons, self and other are locked together in the generation of meaning: 'Consciousness is never self-sufficient, it always finds itself in an intense relationship with another consciousness.' Or, in brief, 'To be means to communicate.'

With these resources serving as a vital background, the question emerges as to whether it is possible to eliminate entirely the 'thinker behind the words'. Wittgenstein's *Philosophical Investigations* (1953) provides the groundwork for such a venture. For Wittgenstein, language obtains its meaning and significance primarily from the way in which it is used in human interaction. Thus, for example, the meaning of 'yellow card' and 'corner kick' gain their significance from their use in the game of soccer. This same logic may be applied to the discourse of the self, and in particular, to the way in which one refers to states of mind. We may expand on the implications with the following propositions.

1. *The self as discursive action.* As we have seen, there is no viable way of understanding such utterances as 'I decided' or 'I am angry' as reports on what we presume to be an inner state of mind. We may thus relinquish the view of such discourse as a manifestation or 'outward expression of an inner world'. Rather, we may view the meaning of such discourse as dependent upon its use in relationships. Thus, to announce, 'I am unhappy' about a given state of affairs, the term 'unhappy' would not be rendered meaningful or appropriate by virtue of its manifesting the state of one's neurons, emotions, or cognitive schema. Rather, the report plays a significant social function. It may be used, for example, to call an end to a set of deteriorating conditions, enlist support and/or encouragement, or to invite further opinion. Both the conditions of the report and the functions it can serve are also circumscribed by social convention. The phrase 'I am deeply sad' can be satisfactorily reported at the death of a close relative but not the demise of a spring moth. A report of depression can secure others' concern and support; however it cannot easily function as a greeting, an invitation to laughter, or a commendation. In this sense to use mental language is more like a handshake or an

embrace than a mirror of the interior. In effect, mental terms are used by people to carry out relationships.

2. *Discourse of the self as performance.* As theorists further reason, we are not dealing here with 'mere words' used by people to 'get what they want from the other'. One's utterances are essentially performative in function. That is, in the very saying of something, one is also performing an action within a relationship. As performance, more than the felicitous use of words is required. For example, if spoken in a faint voice, eyes on the floor, and with a smile, the words 'I am angry' would constitute a failed performance. It would be culturally bewildering. In order to perform anger properly within Western culture, voice intensity and volume are essential; a stern face and a rigid posture may be required. Much is gained, then, by replacing the image of private 'feelings' with public action; it is not that one has emotions, a thought, or a memory so much as one *does* them.

3. *Discursive action as relationally embedded.* If it is reasonable to view psychological discourse as embedded within an embodied performance, one may then inquire into its origins. If there is no animating origin lying behind the action, one is then drawn to its roots within relationship. In the same way that one cannot achieve intelligibility by using a word of his own creation, one's actions will not make sense if they do not borrow from a cultural tradition. Thus, the performance of self carries a history of relationships, manifesting and extending them. One may also ask about audience; for whom are these intelligible performances? As Bakhtin (1981) pointed out, to speak is always to address someone—either explicitly or implicitly—within some kind of relationship. This is also to say that the performances are fashioned with respect to the recipient. The other enters expressions of the self in their very formulation.

The relational rewriting of self

Relational theorizing of this sort has been a significant stimulus to a range of constructionist inquiry, which together essentially reconfigures both the conception of the psychological self and its implications for practice. In one of the earliest provocations of this kind, Potter and Wetherell (1987) demonstrated the problems inhering in the supposition that attitudes in the head cause overt public actions. As they went on to demonstrate, an attitude is more fruitfully understood as a public action in itself, or essentially, a position taken in a conversation. Much the same line of argument may be applied to the concept of reason. Replacing the Cartesian view of thinking as that process establishing the very certitude of self, reasoning may be viewed as a form of public performance. As Billig (1987) has proposed, most of what we take to be rational thought is more adequately viewed as a social process of argumentation. We do not argue because we have private thoughts, but rather, private thinking comes into being through the social practice of argumentation. What we consider 'good reasoning', then, is not distinguishable from effective rhetoric.

Echoing this line of reasoning is a substantial movement focused on *communal memory*. Common conceptions of memory—and indeed the conceptions that ground most scientific study of memory—presume the existence of an interior process. Following the preceding line of reasoning, however, one may consider the word 'memory' in its performative role. It makes little sense to view the phrase 'I remember' as a report on a particular psychological or neurological condition. What kind of condition would one be reporting on, how would one be able to 'look inside' and recognize when we had a memory as opposed to a 'thought' or a 'desire'. Rather, as John Shotter has put it, 'Our ways of talking about our experiences work not primarily to represent the nature of those experiences in themselves, but to represent them in such a way as to constitute and sustain one or another kind of social order' (1990: 145). In effect, memory is not an individual act but a collective one.

In this sense, if a school child is asked 'what does three times three equal?' the answer 'nine' is not a report on an inner condition of memory, but an action that has been fashioned within a complex relational history. And when the family gathers at a reunion, the stories of yore are not pictures of their minds, but forms of conversation that have typically been incubated in a long history of conversation. In their study of how people recall political events—such as wars or revolutions—the researchers conclude, 'Every memory, as personal as it may be—even of events that are private and strictly personal and have not been shared with anyone—exists through its relation with what has been shared with others: language, idiom, events, and everything that shapes the society of which individuals are a part.' For an extended review of the literature on collective or relational memory the reader may consult Middleton and Brown (2005).

A final line of inquiry adds further dimension to this relational reconstruction of self. One tends to think of emotions as 'natural givens', simply part of one's biological makeup. We generally assume that infants are born into the world with fully functioning emotions; a child's cry is taken as a sign of anger, and a smile as an expression of happiness. Psychologists attempt to locate the physiological basis of emotion, and argue for its universality. The argument for universality is appealing on one level, as it suggests that human understanding is part of our biological makeup. We are innately prepared, for example, to appreciate another's fear or love or joy. Yet, it is also a dangerous assumption, in as much as what one assumes to be 'natural' is typically the emotions of one's own culture. What the Ifaluk call *fago* or the Japanese call *mayae*, for example, we in the West simply delete from the universal vocabulary of emotion.

In the present context, it is more helpful to view emotional expressions as relational performances. More specifically, one may employ the concept of a *relational scenario*, that is, a scripted set of interdependent actions such as one might find in a stage performance. Each action in the scenario sets the stage for that which follows; what follows gives intelligibility to that which has preceded. In effect, the performance of each actor is required to give the play its coherent unity; each performance depends on the others for its intelligibility. In these terms, one can view emotional performances as constituents of culturally specific scenarios— parts of a play in which others are required. This is to propose that the angry shout or the sluggish expression of depression only make sense by virtue of their position in a relational scenario. That is, such expressions cannot take place anywhere and anytime, but only within a culturally appropriate sequence. One cannot easily jump to his feet in the middle of family dinner and shout, 'I am so sorry'; such behavior would be unintelligible. But if accused of an implicitly racist remark, the same expression would not only seem fitting, but desirable. More generally, there are socially prescribed times and places where it is appropriate to perform an emotion.

Further, once an emotion is performed the relational scenario also prescribes what follows. Thus, if a friend announces that he fears he has a fatal disease, certain actions are virtually required by the cultural scenarios and others prohibited. One may properly respond with sympathy and nurturance, but it would be tasteless to reply with a silly joke or talk about one's vacation. Further, like good stories, many emotional scenarios also have *beginnings* and *endings*. If it is late at night and one's electric power is suddenly lost, that is the beginning of a scenario in which expressions of fear (as opposed, for example, to jealously or ecstasy) would be appropriate. In contrast, if someone is reporting one's sorrow, another may continue to give nurturance and support until the sorrow subsides. At that point the scenario is terminated.

The relational reconstruction of the self has naturally given rise to a range of criticism. Two of these critical points are most prominent. In the first case, critics charge that such relational views create a black box or empty organism, bereft of all subjective life. In reply, the relational theorist points to the desirability of abandoning dualism, and the problematic distinction between *inner* and *outer*, between self and identity. This is not to deny that one is doing something privately in one's prolonged gaze into the distance as one begins to write an essay. However, it is a mistake if it is proposed to view this silent period specifically in terms of *psychological* processes, that is, functioning according to their own autonomous demands. Rather, the relational theorist proposes, when preparing to write, one is readying oneself to put socially intelligible statements on paper, that is, preparing to engage in a social action. Thus, one may be doing something privately—which we might want to call reasoning, pondering, or feeling—but from the relational standpoint these are essentially public actions carried out in private. To illustrate, consider the actress preparing her lines for a play. The lines are essentially nonsense independent of their placement within the play; that is, they require a relationship to be intelligible. Yet, the actress can rehearse the lines in private, quietly performing the words without voicing them. We might say she was 'imagining' or 'thinking them through'. But essentially she is carrying out a public action, only without audience and full performance. In effect, they are *partial performances* (Gergen 2009).

The second significant critique is that a relational view represents an eradication of individual agency, and thus undermines long-standing traditions of moral responsibility. To this the relational constructionist replies that there is no eradication of tradition implied. The relational account is itself a construction, and not a truth posit. No traditions need be abandoned; however, all may be subjected to critical reflection. At this point, questions may be raised concerning the wisdom, and indeed the justice, of holding single individuals responsible for their actions. Not only do such practices generate alienation and resentment, but in selecting a target of scorn, they relieve those in judgment from assaying their own contribution to the unwanted outcome. In contrast, the relational theorist proposes, a relational account abandons the determinist/voluntarist antinomy of long standing, and shifts the concern with 'wrong-doing' to the collaborative practices that may be viewed as its origin. One begins to inquire into practices of justice that may sustain viable relationships as opposed to severing them.

References

Almoq, J. (2005). *What am I? Descartes and the Mind-Body Problem* (New York: Oxford University Press).

Bakhtin, M. (1981). *The Dialogic Imagination* (Austin, Tex.: University of Texas Press).

Becker, A. E. (1995). *Body, Self, and Society: The View from Fiji* (Philadelphia: University of Pennsylvania Press).

Bellah, R. N., Madsen, R., Sullivan, W. M., Swidler, A., and Tipton, S. M. (1985). *Habits of the Heart: Individualism and Commitment in American Life* (Berkeley, Calif.: University of California Press).

Benwell, B., and Stokoe, E. (2006). *Discourse and Identity* (Edinburgh: Edinburgh University Press).

Berger, P., and Luckmann, T. (1966). *The Social Construction of Reality* (New York: Doubleday/Anchor).

Billig, M. (1987). *Arguing and Thinking* (London: Cambridge University Press).

Blazer, D. G. (2005). *The Age of Melancholy: Major Depression and its Social Origins* (New York: Routledge).

Bruner, J. (1990). *Acts of Meaning* (Cambridge, Mass.: Harvard University Press).

Buchholtz, M. (1999). *Reinventing Identities: The Gendered Self in Discourse* (New York: Oxford University Press).

Capps, D., and Fenn, R. K. (1998). *Individualism Reconsidered: Readings Bearing on the Endangered Self in Modern Society* (New York: Continuum).

CARY, P. (2000). *Augustine's Invention of the Inner Self: The Legacy of a Christian Platonist* (New York: Oxford University Press).

COULTER, J. (1979). *The Social Construction of Mind: Studies in Ethnomethodology and Linguistic Philosophy* (London: Macmillan).

CUSHMAN, P. (1996). *Constructing the Self, Constructing America: A Cultural History of Psychotherapy* (New York: Da Capo).

DAVIES, B., and HARRÉ, R. (1990). 'Positioning: The Discursive Production of Selves', *Journal for the Theory of Social Behaviour*, 20: 43–63.

DERRIDA, J. (1976). *Of Grammatology*, tr. G. Spivak (Baltimore: Johns Hopkins University Press).

DIVORKY, D., and SCHRAG, P. (1975). *The Myth of the Hyperactive Child* (New York: Pantheon).

FEE, D. (ed.) (2000). *Pathology and the Postmodern* (London: Sage).

FEYERABEND, P. (1978). *Against Method* (New York: Humanities Press).

FINEMAN, M. A. (2004). *The Autonomy Myth: A Theory of Dependency* (New York: New Press).

FOUCAULT, M. (1978). *The History of Sexuality*, i. *An Introduction* (New York: Pantheon).

——(1979). *Discipline and Punish: The Birth of the Prison* (New York: Random House).

GARFINKEL, H. (1967). *Studies in Ethnomethodology* (Englewood Cliffs, NJ: Prentice Hall).

GELPI, D. L. (1989). *Beyond Individualism: Toward a Retrieval of Moral Discourse in America* (Notre Dame, Ind.: University of Notre Dame Press).

GERGEN, K. J. (1994a). *Toward Transformation in Social Knowledge* (2nd edn. London: SAGE; originally publ. Springer Verlag, 1982).

——(1994b). *Realities and Relationships* (Cambridge, Mass.: Harvard University Press).

——(2006). *Therapeutic Realities* (Chagrin Falls, Ohio: Taos Institute Publications).

——(2009). *Relational Being: Beyond Self and Community* (New York: Oxford University Press).

——and DAVIS, K. E. (eds) (1985). *The Social Construction of the Person* (New York: Springer).

——and GERGEN, M. M. (1983). 'Narratives of the Self', in T. R. Sarbin and K. E. Scheibe (eds), *Studies in Social Identity* (New York: Praeger), 254–73.

GRAUMANN, C. F., and GERGEN, K. J. (eds) (1996). *Historical Dimensions of Psychological Discourse* (New York: Cambridge University Press).

HACKING, I. (1999). *The Social Construction of What?* (Cambridge, Mass.: Harvard University Press).

HARE-MUSTIN, R. (1994). 'Discourse in a Mirrored Room: A Postmodern Analysis of Therapy', *Family Process*, 33: 199–236.

HARRÉ, R. (1991). 'The Discursive Production of Selves', *Theory and Psychology*, 1: 51–63.

HELLER, T. C., SOSNA, M., and WELLBERY, D. E. (eds) (1986). *Reconstructing Individualism: Autonomy, Individuality, and the Self in Western Thought* (Stanford, Calif.: Stanford University Press).

HEPWORTH, J. (1999). *The Social Construction of Anorexia Nervosa* (London: Sage).

HEWITT, J. P. (1989). *Dilemmas of the American Self* (Philadelphia: Temple University Press).

HOLSTEIN, J. A., and GUBRIUM, J. F. (2000) *The Self we Live by* (New York: Oxford University Press).

KUHN, T. (1970). *The Structure of Scientific Revolutions* (2nd edn. Chicago: University of Chicago Press; 1st publ. 1962).

KUTCHINS, H., and KIRK, S. A. (1997). *Making us Crazy, DSM: The Psychiatric Bible and the Creation of Mental Disorders* (New York: Free Press).

LASCH, C. (1978). *The Culture of Narcissism* (New York: Basic Books).

LATOUR, B., and WOOLGAR, S. (1986). *Laboratory Life: The Construction of Scientific Facts* (Princeton: Princeton University Press).

LEARY, M. R. (2004). *The Curse of the Self: Self-Awareness, Egotism, and the Quality of Human Life* (New York: Oxford University Press).

McADAMS, D. (1985). *Power, Intimacy and the Life Story: Personalogical Inquiries into Identity* (New York: Guilford).

——(1997). *The Stories we Live by: Personal Myths and the Making of the Self* (New York: Guilford).

——(2006). *Identity and Story: Creating Self in Narrative* (Washington, DC: American Psychological Association).

MacINTYRE, A. (1984). *After Virtue: A Study in Moral Theory* (2nd edn. Notre Dame, Ind.: University of Notre Dame Press).

MARKUS, H. R., and KITAYAMA, S. (1991). 'Culture and the Self: Implications for Cognition, Emotion, and Motivation', *Psychological Review*, 98: 224–53.

MARSELLA, A. J., DeVos, G., and Hsu, E. L. K. (eds) (1985). *Culture and Self: Asian and Western Perspectives* (Malabar, Fla.: Robert E. Krieger Publishing Co.).

MEAD, G. H. (1934). *Mind, Self, and Society from the Standpoint of a Social Behaviorist*, ed. C. W. Morris (Chicago: University of Chicago Press).

MIDDLETON, D., and BROWN, S. D. (eds) (1990). *The Social Psychology of Experience: Studies in Remembering and Forgetting* (London: Sage).

NEIMEYER, R. A. (ed.) (2000). *Constructions of Disorder: Meaning-Making Frameworks for Psychotherapy* (Washington, DC: American Psychological Association).

PARKER, I., GEORGAS, E., HARPER, D., McLAUGHLIN, T., and STOWALL-SMITH, M. (1995). *Deconstructing Psychopathology* (London: Sage).

POLKINGHORNE, D. E. (1988). *Narrative Knowing and the Human Sciences* (Albany, NY: State University of New York Press).

POTTER, J. (1996). *Representing Reality* (London: Sage).

——and WETHERELL, M. (1987). *Discourse and Social Psychology: Beyond Attitudes and Behavior* (London: Sage).

QUOSH, C., and GERGEN, K. J. (2006). 'Constructing Trauma and Treatment: Knowledge, Power, and Resistance', in T. Sugiman, K. J. Gergen, and W. Wagner (eds), *Meaning in Action: Construction, Narratives and Representations* (New York: Springer).

RORTY, R. (1979). *Philosophy and the Mirror of Nature* (Princeton: Princeton University; Cambridge: Cambridge University Press).

ROSE, N. (1985). *The Psychological Complex* (London: Routledge & Kegan Paul).

——(1990). *Governing the Soul* (London: Routledge).

ROSENWALD, G., and OCHBERG, R. (eds) (1990). *Storied Lives* (New Haven: Yale University Press).

RYLE, G. (1949). *The Concept of Mind* (London: Penguin).

SAMPSON, E. E. (2008). *Celebrating the Other: A Dialogic Account of Human Nature* (Chagrin Falls, Ohio: Taos Institute Publications).

SARBIN, T. (ed.) (1986). *Narrative Psychology* (New York: Praeger).

——and MANCUSO, J. (1980). *Schizophrenia: Medical Diagnosis or Verdict?* (Elmsford, NY: Pergamon).

SHOTTER, J. (1990). 'The Social Construction of Remembering and Forgetting', in D. Middleton and D. Edwards (eds), *Collective Remembering* (London: Sage), 142–9.

SIEGEL, J. (2001). *The Idea of the Self, Thought and Experience in Western Europe since the Seventeenth Century* (New York: Cambridge University Press).

SZASZ, T. S. (1961). *The Myth of Mental Illness: Foundations of a Theory of Personal Conduct* (New York: Hoeber-Harper).

TAYLOR, C. (1989). *Sources of the Self: The Making of the Modern Identity* (Cambridge, Mass.: Harvard University Press).

VAN LANGENHOVE, L., and HARRÉ, R. (1998). *Positioning Theory* (London: Blackwell).

VYGOTSKY, L. S. (1978). *Mind in Society: The Development of Higher Psychological Processes* (Cambridge, Mass.: Harvard University Press).

WITTGENSTEIN, L. (1953). *Philosophical Investigations*, tr. G. Anscombe (New York: Macmillan).

CHAPTER 28

THE DIALOGICAL SELF

A PROCESS OF POSITIONING IN SPACE AND TIME

HUBERT J. M. HERMANS

THE self can only be truly dialogical when the other person is seen as not purely outside, but simultaneously part of the self and even constitutive of it. Dialogicality, as a form of 'sociality' or 'intersubjectivity', is not something that is 'added' to an embodied self that, in its pre-existing state, has an existence separate from the other. The self can only be properly understood when intersubjectivity and sociality are considered as intrinsic to its embodiment in space and time. Rather than contrasting the 'internal self' with the 'external' society, the self *itself* functions as a social and societal process. As I shall argue in this chapter, the self functions as a mini-society, being part, at the same time, of the society at large.

HISTORICAL BACKGROUND

The notion 'dialogical self' is a composite concept. It weaves two notions, self and dialogue, together in such a way that a deeper understanding of the interconnection of self and other is realized. In many usages of the term, the concept of self refers to something 'internal', something that happens *within* the mind or even within the skin of the individual person, while 'dialogue' is typically associated with something 'external', a process that takes place *between* two or more people engaged in communication. The composite concept 'dialogical self' is explicitly devised to transcend this dichotomy and to bring the external into the internal and, in reverse, to infuse the internal into the external. Such a self–society interconnection allows us to abandon any conception in which the self is regarded as essentialized and encapsulated in itself. Moreover, it avoids the existence of a 'self-less society' that is deprived of the richness and creativity that the individual human mind has to offer to the renewal and innovation of existing social practices.

Dialogical self theory is not an isolated conceptual development but emerged, and is still emerging, at the interface of two traditions: American Pragmatism and Russian Dialogism. As a self theory it is influenced by James's (1890) and Mead's (1934) classic formulations on the workings of the self (see Chapter 26). As a dialogical theory, it is inspired by the fertile insights on dialogical processes as presented by Bakhtin (1973) and his colleagues (also see Chapter 27).

James's formulations on the extended and social nature of the self

To understand the social and societal nature of the self, it is helpful to refer to some of the insights proposed by James (1890) who has had a tremendous influence on the psychology of the self as it flourished during the twentieth and now the twenty-first century. His distinction between the *I* and the *Me* represents, according to Rosenberg (1979), a classic contribution to the psychology of the self. In James's conception, the *I* is equated with the self-as-knower, or the self as subject, and has three features: continuity, distinctness, and volition. The *continuity* of the self-as-knower refers to a sense of personal identity, that is, a sense of sameness through time. A feeling of *distinctness* from others, or individuality, also characterizes the subjective nature of the self-as-knower. Finally, a sense of personal *volition* is reflected in the continuous appropriation and rejection of thoughts by which the self-as-knower proves itself as an active processor of experience. Implicit in these features (continuity, distinctness, volition) is the awareness of self-reflectivity that characterizes the self-as-knower (Damon and Hart 1982).

According to James, the *Me*, as equated with the self-as-known or the self as object, is composed of the empirical elements considered as belonging to oneself. Of crucial significance for the later formulations of a dialogical self is James's insight in the gradual transition between *Me* and *mine*. He observed that the empirical self is composed of all that the person can call his or her own, 'not only his body and his psychic powers, but his clothes and his house, his wife and children, his ancestors and friends, his reputation and works, his lands and horses, and yacht and bank-account' (1890: 291). An important implication of this frequently cited quotation is that people and things in the environment, as far as they are felt as 'mine' or 'belonging to me', are, as the result of the process of appropriation, properties of an extended self. This conception implies that not only 'my mother' belongs to the self in the extended sense of the term, but also 'my critic' or 'my opponent'. Apparently, James's notion of the extended self can be contrasted with the Cartesian self which is based on a dualistic conception, not only between self and body but also between self and other (Hermans and Kempen 1993; Straus 1958). Self and other do not exclude but rather include each other. They are not exclusive but rather inclusive oppositions. With his conception of the extended self, James has paved the way for later theoretical developments in which contrasts, oppositions, and negotiations are part of a distributed, multi-voiced self.

Almost one century before postmodernist thinkers drew attention to the decentralized multiplicity of the self, James (1890) was well aware that the extended self was social enough to incorporate parts of the social environment as different constituents of the self:

Properly speaking, *a man has as many social selves as there are individuals who recognize him* and carry an image of him in their mind. To wound any one of these his images is to wound him. But as the individuals who carry the images fall naturally into classes, we may practically say that he has as many different social selves as there are distinct *groups* of persons about whose opinion he cares. He generally shows a different side of himself to each of these different groups. Many a youth who is demure enough before his parents and teachers, swears and swaggers like a pirate among his 'tough' young friends. We do not show ourselves to our children as to our club-companions, to our customers as to the laborers we employ, to our own masters and employers as to our intimate friends. From this there results what practically is a division of the man into several selves; and this may be a discordant splitting, as where one is afraid to let one set of his acquaintances know him as he is elsewhere; or it may be a perfectly harmonious division of labor, as where one tender to his children is stern to the soldiers or prisoners under his command. (p. 294)

As this quotation suggests, society is not added to the self as a purely external environment, but rather reflected *in* the extended self in terms of a multiplicity of constituents that are not only different from each other but also show different levels of organization, varying from 'discordant splitting' to 'division of labor'.

James's formulations on the self reveal a striking paradox. As a volitional being a person may *reject* his enemy as 'different from me' and in doing so the person has the subjective conviction that the enemy does not belong to his self. However, as *my* enemy the other person, defined as *Mine*, is a constituent of an extended self. This paradoxical element in James's formulations has a significant empirical correlate.

As Gregg (1991) has observed, some aspects of the self are located in the vague and ambiguous border-zone between self and non-self which can be characterized as 'identity-in-difference', that is, they belong to me and do not belong to me *at the same time*. For example, I'm aware that I'm sometimes jealous but at the same time, I do not fully admit jealousy as 'belonging to me'. I reject parts of *my* experience. This ambiguity applies also to the extended domain of the self. Particular significant others (e.g. 'my always cynical colleague', or 'my ex-husband who left me') can be disowned and subjectively defined as 'not belonging to me'. Yet, they are significant constituents of an extended self as far as they are defined as 'mine' and as such they play a recurring and affect-arousing part in one's memory, imagination, and anticipation. Apparently, the same aspect of the self can be rejected and yet be appropriated by the same self in a wider sense.

Mead's emphasis on innovation

Mead (1934), the great representative of 'symbolic interactionism' as later commentators have characterized him, has at least two views in common with James. Both theorists were interested, each in their own way, in the distinction between *I* and *Me* and in the social nature of the self. In order to demonstrate the interplay between self and society, Mead used the *I–Me* distinction, somewhat differently from James, in order to show that selves are not only representatives of society and conforming to existing institutional structures, but also able to *innovate* them. He was concerned about the problems that were raised when the social process would be limited to the internalization of social rules and conventions of the 'generalized other' into the self. Had he done so, the self would be no more than a copy of externally dictated social roles and the members of society no more than 'slaves of customs'. Societal processes would be overly repetitive and there would be no innovations that are needed for social changes and renewal of existing institutions. Against this background, Mead introduced his distinction between *I* and *Me*:

I have been undertaking to distinguish between the 'I' and the 'me' as different phases of the self, the 'me' answering to the organized attitudes of the others which we definitely assume and which determine consequently our own conduct so far as it is of a self-conscious character. Now the 'me' may be regarded as giving the form of the 'I.' The novelty comes in the action of the 'I,' but the structure, the form of the self is one which is conventional. (1934: 209)

As Mead saw it, social rules and conventions of the generalized other become part of the *Me*, whereas the *I* functions as a source of innovation. Artists, like scientists, do not only follow particular conventions but also break away from them. They certainly accept certain rules of expression but, in their urge to criticize, undermine, and modify existing forms, they also bring in new elements. Artists and scientists introduce an originality that makes their contribution unconventional.

James's and Mead's original contributions are indispensible for conceptualizing a dialogical self. Both have emphasized the intrinsic social nature of the self, arguing against a conception of an encapsulated self that is essentialized as having an existence in itself. Moreover, both theorists found in the *I–Me* distinction a necessary element in the conception of an agentic self that was necessary for a proper understanding of the connection between the self and the social environment. James did so by considering the *I* as volitional, that is, capable of appropriating or rejecting elements as constituents of a self that is, more or less, extended to the environment. Mead did so by depicting the *I* as a source of innovation and as capable of introducing new elements into a society that would otherwise engender overly conforming participants.

In bringing central elements of the two theorists together, we conclude that, as part of the *I–Me* distinction, the *I* is agentic in two ways. First, the *I* is volitional, that is, as an appropriating and rejecting agency it is able to extend an existing *Me* or *Mine* towards the social environment and take up the other as part of the self. Second, society, in the form of the (generalized) other, is part of the *Me*, with the *I* as able to innovate in society and self. While James carries the self to society, Mead brings society into the self. Despite this difference, both theorists acknowledge, each in their own way, *I* as agentic. It makes the self both volitional (James) and innovative (Mead).

Bakhtin's polyphonic novel

In James's formulations we discern several characters which he sees as belonging to the *Me* or *Mine*: my wife and children, my ancestors and friends. Such characters are more explicitly elaborated in Bakhtin's metaphor of the polyphonic novel which serves as another source of inspiration for later dialogical approaches to the self. Bakhtin introduced this metaphor in his book *Problems of Dostoevsky's Poetics* (1973) in which he elaborates on the idea that in Dostoevsky's works there is not a single author at work—Dostoevsky himself—but several authors or thinkers, characters such as Myshkin, Raskolnikov, Stavrogin, Ivan Karamazov, and the Grand Inquisitor. Rather than treating these characters as obedient slaves in the service of one author-thinker, Dostoevsky put these characters forward as independent thinkers, each with their own perspective on the world. Dostoevsky does not stand *above* his characters imposing from there his finalizing artistic vision upon his characters and enforcing them within the limiting framework of a unified objective world. Rather, the characters are standing *beside* the author, even disagreeing with him. As in a polyphonic musical work, multiple voices accompany and oppose one another in dialogical ways. Along these lines, Dostoevsky creates a polyphonic multiplicity of perspectives, portraying characters conversing with their alter egos (Ivan and Smerdyakov), with the Devil (Ivan and the Devil), and even with caricatures of themselves (Raskolnikov and Svidrigailov).

Whereas James was primarily, but not exclusively, interested in the temporal aspects of self and consciousness (e.g. his stream of consciousness and his principle of continuity), Bakhtin seemed to be more interested, certainly in his treatment of Dostoevsky's novels, in space. The notion of dialogue, open as it is, provides the possibility of differentiating the inner world of one and the same character in the form of an interpersonal relationship. The transformation of an 'inner' thought of a particular character into an utterance instigates dialogical relations to occur between this utterance 'here' and the utterance of an imagined other 'there'. This opposition was vividly exemplified in Dostoevsky's novel *The Double* in which the second hero (the double) was introduced as a personification of the interior thought of the first hero (Golyadkin). In this way, the interior thought of the main character was exteriorized in the form of a spatially separated opponent so that a fully developed dialogue between two relatively independent parties could develop. In such a dialogical narrative that is structured by space and time, space is 'upgraded' so that temporal relations are transformed into spatial relations. This leads to a construction in which temporally dispersed events are contracted into spatial oppositions that are simultaneously present. In Bakhtin's words: 'This persistent urge to see all things as being coexistent and to perceive and depict all things side by side and simultaneously, *as if in space rather than time*, leads him [Dostoevsky] to dramatize in space even the inner contradictions and stages of development of a single person' (p. 23; emphasis added). The construction of narratives as a polyphony of spatial oppositions allows Bakhtin to treat a particular thought or experience in the context of both interior and exterior dialogues, creating an interface where a multiplicity of perspectives can meet.

James and Mead with their fertile views on the self and Bakhtin with his ground-breaking views on dialogue have been significant sources of inspiration for the development of dialogical self theory as depicted in this chapter. At the same time, I want to go beyond these authors by developing a theory in which the notion of *positioning* is necessary in order to further articulate both the temporal and spatial aspects of the self. As we will see, this theoretical development provides a basis for understanding the process of *positioning and counterpositioning* as spatial aspects and the process of *positioning and repositioning* as temporal aspects of an embodied dialogical self. In the following I give a brief description of the dialogical self and then elaborate on some of its foundations and implications.

THE DIALOGICAL SELF AS POSITIONED
IN SPACE AND TIME

Inspired by the founding work of James (1890), Mead (1934), and Bakhtin (1929), Hermans *et al.* (1992) criticized the assumption that the self is organized around *one* centre or core. Rather than arguing for a self that is organized from a centralized headquarters and separated from its environment, they proposed a (partly) decentralized self that is extended to the social world with the social other as located not outside but inside the self. Instead of one centralized author with a unifying view on the world, the dialogical self was conceived in terms of a dynamic multiplicity of relatively autonomous '*I*-positions' that are organized in an imagined landscape. These *I*-positions are involved in processes of mutual dialogical relationships that are intensely interwoven with external dialogical relationships with actual others. In this conception, the *I* is always bound to particular positions in time and space but has the possibility to move from one position to the other in accordance with changes in situation and time. In this process of positioning and repositioning, the *I* fluctuates among different and even opposed positions, and has the capacity to imaginatively endow each position with a voice so that dialogical relations between positions can develop. The voices behave like interacting characters in a story, involved in a process of question and answer, agreement and disagreement, negotiations and integrations. Each of them has a story to tell about their own experiences from their own perspective. As different voices, these characters exchange information about their respective *Mes*, creating a complex, narratively structured self.

The presented view does not imply that dialogue is there always and everywhere. At least two factors prevent dialogical relationships from developing. First, as part of a multiplicity of positions, some of them are more dominant in the self than other ones. As Linell (1990) has argued, such dominance differences are partly the result of differences in relative dominance between speakers in interaction (e.g. the amount of talk), partly they are reflections of societal power differences (e.g. positions based on one's race, gender, religion, or age). The implication of these differences is that some positions and their voices are backgrounded, silenced, or even suppressed. When one position becomes highly dominant in the self, so that other positions have no chance to speak from their own needs, emotions, memories, and expectations, the relationship becomes more monological than dialogical. It should be noted, by the way, that a monological relationship is not simply undesirable. There are situations in which a monological relationship can be necessary (e.g. a quick decision of a general in an emergency situation at war) or desirable (e.g. when 'I as a smoker' is seen as obnoxious, it can be suppressed by 'I as concerned about my health' and this suppression is felt as contributing to the well-being of many other parts of the self). Second, not all positions in the self are in direct contact with each other so that dialogical relationships have no chance to develop. Some positions can function well without contact with other significant positions. For many people sex ('I as being in a sexual mood') may be a desirable position in which they find themselves well functioning, but this position has no direct contact with their functioning as an intellectual thinker. Stronger, when engaged in an intimate contact, a dialogical interchange between these positions could well disturb the well-functioning of each of them. On the other hand, there are situations in which a direct dialogical contact between positions is felt as highly desirable in order to take a 'reasonable' decision as, for example, when the person is involved in an inner conflict between her wish to reduce her working time in the service of 'I as an enjoyer of life' and her wish to work more hours in the service of 'I as making a career'. In other words, dependent on the nature of the situation and the organization of the position repertoire as a whole, positions are involved in contact with each other or not. When they are involved in contact, this can take the form of a dialogue or a monologue. The processes of positioning and counterpositioning, like the positioning and repositioning, are taking place in a self that can be described as a 'society of mind' (for a comparable view, see Minsky 1985). When dialogical relationships have a chance to develop, positions get in touch with each other and exchange ideas, emotions, memories, expectations, and plans. They learn from each other to their mutual benefit and to the benefit of the self as a whole. In other words, in the presented theory, dialogue is seen as a valuable *potential* of the self and as intrinsically bound to the process of positioning that both enables the self and constrains it.

In the proposed conception the dialogical self is seen as 'social', not in the sense that a self-contained individual enters into social interactions with other 'outside people', but in the sense that other people occupy *I*-positions in a multi-voiced self. The self is not only 'here' but also 'there' and due to the power of imagination the person can act 'as if' she *were* the other (the other-in-the-self). This is not to be equated with 'taking the role of the other' as Mead (1934) would have it, as this expression implies that the self takes the *actual* perspective of the other. Rather, I construe another person or being as an 'external position in the self' that I can occupy and that creates an alternative perspective on the world and myself. This perspective may or may not be congruent with the perspective of the actual other, can be more or less imaginary, and might be a creative construction (e.g. an artistic perception or depiction of the other). The imaginary, illusionary, or creative aspects of the other-in-the-self can be made explicit by entering into a dialogue with the actual other leading to the confirmation, correction, modification, or further development of the original position.

In psychological circles questions are often raised about the implications of the multi-voiced dialogical self for psychological health. The implicit assumption behind this question is that multi-voicedness is detrimental to the prevailing notion of the self as an indivisible unity and centred in itself. In these discussions, unity is often contrasted with fragmentation, with unity as a desirable end-state or even as a starting-point, and fragmentation as an aberration. Consequently, many scientists and professionals believe that healthy self-development requires the fostering of unity and the avoidance of fragmentation. However, the notion of *I*-position favours the *inclusive* opposition between unity and multiplicity instead of the *exclusive* opposition between unity and fragmentation. Whereas the exclusive opposition is associated with a strong evaluative connotation (unity is good, fragmentation is bad), the inclusive opposition assumes that the two principles, unity (expressed in the continuity of the *I* across positions) and multiplicity (expressed in the diversity of positions), are equivalent and even presuppose one another as complementary and dynamic aspects of a dialogical self.

A frequently discussed issue is the distinction between the normal functioning of the multi-voiced, dialogical self and the controversial clinical dysfunction, Multiple Personality Disorder (MPD) or, its more recent version, Dissociative Identity Disorder (DID) (see Chapter 23). Typically, these clinical categories refer to the serious impediments in the dialogical relationships between the 'host personality' and a diversity of 'alters', the latter ones representing rejected aspects of the original self (Carson *et al.* 1996). The difference between a multi-voiced self and dissociative phenomena, however, can only be fully grasped if one takes into account the insight that the dysfunctional aspects of MPD and DID are not primarily in the existence of 'parts' in the self but in their functioning and organization. In the dysfunctional case, the dialogical contact between the several positions is severely constrained although in some cases one personality may be co-conscious with another and different parts may even communicate with each other (Barresi 1994). As Bromberg (2004) has argued, multi-voicedness is the normal condition, but it becomes abnormal when it used for defensive purposes or for the dissociation of unbearable parts of the self. As a consequence, the different voices are not in line with the demands of the situation at hand. An adult person may behave as a child in a situation that requires the response of an adult. In the dysfunctional organization of the self, moreover, one alter tends to dominate the total experiential field, with a simultaneous impairment of the possibility to move flexibly to other alters (although some people with this dysfunction may learn to invite different alters to enter into mutual conversations). Therefore, one could agree with Watkins (1986) when she concludes that dissociative phenomena are characterized by a sequential, monological succession of parts rather than by a simultaneous, cooperative, and dialogical relationship between different subselves. (For research and treatment of a client with DID, see Hermans and Hermans-Jansen 1995: 187–95.)

The spatial nature of the self

The concepts of position and voice can only be properly understood when their spatial nature is taken into account. This nature becomes particularly manifest when one focuses on the difference between logical and dialogical relationships (Bakhtin 1973; Vasil'eva 1988). Consider two phrases that are completely identical, 'life is good' and again 'life is good'. From the perspective of Aristotelian logic, these two phrases are related in terms of *identity*; in fact, they are one and the same statement. From a dialogical perspective, however, they are considered as two remarks expressed by the voices of two spatially separated people involved in communication, who entertain a relationship of *agreement*. From a logical point of view the two phrases are identical but as utterances they are different because they are originating from two people with different positions in space. The first is a statement, the second a confirmation. Similarly, the phrases 'life is good' and 'life is not good' can be compared. Within the framework of logic, one is a *negation* of the other. However, as utterances from two different speakers, there is a relation of *disagreement*.[1]

There are not only spatial differences between two people in communication, but also between different voices of the self of one and the same person. Two voices in the self have different spatial positions and their meaning is determined not only by these positions but also by their dialogical interchange. This is quite evident when I'm involved in an imagined conversation with my father who is somewhere 'there' in my mind, located in a place in my self-space that is different from the place 'here' from which I speak to him. This spatial difference does not only apply to the imagined contact with a dear parent, understanding friend, wise adviser, or ideal lover, but also with purely imaginary figures. Referring to cultural anthropological literature, Watkins (1986) gives the example of the Batak people of northern Sumatra, who believe that a spirit who determines the character and fortune of a person is 'a man within a man'. Such a spirit does not coincide with his self and can even be considered as an opponent who is experienced as a special being within the self, with its own will and desires. Also Cassirer (1955) emphasizes that in mythical awareness a tutelary spirit is not conceived as the 'subject' of someone's inner life but as something objective, 'which dwells in man, which is spatially connected with him and hence can also be spatially separated from him' (Cassirer 1955: 168, cited by Watkins 1986).

The spatial distance and tension exist not only between the position of myself 'here' and the imagined or imaginary other who is experienced as 'there', but also

---

[1] Dialogical relationships even allow the *same* sentence to receive the *opposite* meaning, depending on a different intonation in speech. When two people leave a theatre and one says, 'This was a good performance' and the other 'repeats' the remark in a sarcastic way, 'This was a good performance!' then this meaning difference fits with a dialogical framework but not with a logical one.

between different positions in the purely internal domain of the self (e.g. 'I as open' vs. 'I as closed' or 'I as rational' or 'I as emotional'). This becomes particularly manifest when people say that they have different or even opposite 'sides' in their personality or, more dynamically, when they feel 'swept' between two impulses during an internal conflict. Spatial differences are intrinsic to different positions in which one is located and to the different voices with which one speaks. Different positions and voices are associated with different emotions, memories, aspirations, and expectations that are subjected to articulation, development, or change as originating from their different locations in the space of the self (for the notion of 'self-space' see also Jaynes 1976).

The embodied nature of the self

Although verbal language plays a crucial role in the practice of the dialogical self, it should be noted that dialogue is broader than linguistic dialogue. Much dialogue between people develops through body language, facial expression, smiling, gazing, vocalizations, intonations, and gestures. Non-verbal forms of dialogue are also expressed in dance, drum beating, music, ballet, and in other forms of artistic activity. Even actions can have a symbolical meaning as, for example, when a parent punishes a child as a sign of disapproval. Mead (1934) also was well aware of the relevance of non-verbal communication, when he introduced the notion of 'gesture' as a central element in his theory of symbolic interactionism.[2]

The body and body movements function as a physical basis for the metaphorical movements in a multi-positional self. Johnson (1987), for example, has argued that metaphors are deeply entrenched in the human mind in the form of 'image schemas', like verticality and horizontality, which find their origin in the shape of our body. We use such schemas to structure the environment and make sense of the events that take place in our surroundings. A verticality schema helps us to employ an up–down orientation. We stand 'upright' or 'lie down' and ask how tall our child is. A horizontality schema is useful to employ a here–there orientation. We 'leave a place' or push something 'away' that bothers us.

However, an image schema has a function that goes beyond a purely corporeal structure. It is employed as a metaphor for organizing our psychological

---

[2] From a neuropsychological point of view, Schore (2004) refers to the relevance of the right hemisphere for non-verbal forms of dialogue. He argues that empathy, identification with others, and more generally intersubjective processes, are largely dependent upon right hemisphere resources. In apparent contrast to the conception that linguistic processes are typically associated with the left hemisphere, Schore emphasizes the critical function of the right hemisphere for the development of a dialogical self. Early social interactions are crucial for the development of non-verbal manifestations of the self and, in turn, these events influence the later development of a more complex dialogical self.

understandings. For example, estimations of quantities are expressed in terms of verticality, as in the phrasings 'prices are going up' or 'the company's gross earnings fell'. Such statements are based on the concept that 'more is up' although we are not aware of that. Apparently, we employ a verticality schema as a physical base for our mental comprehension, although there is not any intrinsic reason why 'more' should be 'up'. Similarly, horizontal schemas are applied to structure and to understand ourselves and the surroundings. We say, 'I feel such a distance in my contact with him' or 'the project is in progress'. We are used to applying a horizontal schema to conceptualize what is happening, although there is no intrinsic reason to see improvement of a project as a form of forward movement.[3]

Apparently, an image schema emerges first as a structure of our body and is then figuratively applied at more abstract levels of understanding. Likewise, the processes of positioning and repositioning are originally movements of the body that are later used as metaphors for understanding the functioning of the self. On a vertical plane we experience ourselves as 'top-dog' or 'underdog', terms that reflect power differences as contrasting positions in the self. The verticality dimension can be seen as a metaphorical basis of the relative dominance of positions in the self. On a horizontal plane where we make (imaginary) steps towards or away from something or somebody else, we can position ourselves as 'close to' or 'far from' somebody else, in this way reflecting a psychological distance between ourselves and others. Also dialogical relationships can be portrayed as metaphorical movements. We move to the position of the other and back, going hence and forth on an horizontal plane. When we are dominant in an interchange with another or ourselves (e.g. placing ourselves above the other or looking down to ourselves in case of disrespect) we are moving up and down on a vertical plane. The horizontal and vertical planes form bodily fundaments on which processes of positioning and counterpositioning can take place both between people and within the self.

---

[3] A recent trend in psychology is studies on 'embodied cognition'. They are based on the idea that many metaphorical expressions have their literal basis in the body. For example, Williams and Bargh (2008) went with their participants into an elevator and asked them to keep, for a short time, a cup of warm or cold coffee in their hands. The participants who had felt the warm object judged afterwards a target person as having a warmer personality than did the participants who had felt the cold object. Also the metaphorical experience of 'pain' has a basis in the body. On the basis of a literature review, MacDonald and Leary (2008) describe that humans experience emotional pain as physical pain, in agreement with the finding that social animals have a warning system for socially threatening situations that has its roots in the brain areas for physical pain. Such experiments are in support of the idea that the use of metaphors has a literal basis in the functioning of the body.

Significant moments in the development of the dialogical self

For understanding the dialogical nature of the self, both space and time are basic categories.[4] From a temporal perspective, I will describe some forerunners and early manifestations of dialogical activities in order to demonstrate that verbal dialogical activity has its basis in embodied forms of intersubjectivity. I will argue that the dialogical nature of the self is rooted in prelinguistic and non-verbal forms of interaction and intersubjectivity (see Chapter 2). In order to understand the emergence of a dialogical self, and the process of positioning and repositioning in particular, insight in the bodily basis of early interactions is required.

Imitation, provocation, and inborn subjectivity

Like echoing in the auditory field, imitation in the visual field can be considered as a precursor of dialogical activity. Investigations of neonatal imitation are particularly relevant to understanding the developmental and embodied basis of a dialogical self. Neonatal imitation refers to a young infant's facial, hand, and finger movements and vocalizations as a reflection of the corresponding movements of a perceived other. Much of this research is instigated by the pioneering work by Maratos (1973) and Meltzoff and Moore (1994) who demonstrated that from birth onward infants are capable of imitating tongue protrusion as modelled by an experimenter. This phenomenon is striking as infants are able to imitate the perceived body movements of the other *before* a visual representation of the corresponding parts of their own body is available.

Studying the mechanism of neonatal imitation Nagy and Molnar (2004) discovered that newborns are not only capable of responding to tongue protrusion by an experimenter, but are also able to take *initiative* during this interaction. Apparently, there exists not only neonatal imitation but also neonatal 'provocation' as indicated by the finding that newborns spontaneously produce previously imitated gestures while waiting for the experimenter's response. Infants are not only capable of responding to a model by imitating, but also able to take the initiative to evoke an imitative response on the part of the other. As part of this study, the investigators found that the underlying physiological mechanisms of imitation and provocation were different. While imitation was accompanied by heart rate acceleration (as an index of preparatory arousal), provocation was accompanied by heart rate deceleration (as an index of orientation and attention). The investigators concluded that, 'These findings may constitute a laboratory demonstration of the first dialogue' (p. 54). Indeed, imitation, as responding to the initiative of the other, and

---

[4] In this section some developmental issues are part of a more extensive review by Hermans and Hermans-Konopka (2010: ch. 4).

provocation, as taking the initiative, can be considered as precursors of turn-taking behaviour and exchange in terms of question and answer, as typical of later dialogical processes.[5]

Pseudo-dialogues, memory, and imagination

For the development of turn-taking behaviour, so-called 'pseudo-dialogues', taking place between mother and child, are of particular interest. Studying early interactions with the use of stop-frame and slow-motion microanalysis of films and videotapes, investigators have observed that mothers and infants are involved in turn-taking behaviour from the moment the infant is born. Involved in an intimate contact with their children, mothers respond to the sucking pattern of their babies. When the baby sucks, the mother is quiet. However, when the baby pauses, she often talks to her and touches her, addressing the baby in verbal and non-verbal ways. The mother treats the baby's burst of sucking as a 'turn', responding to it with an interactional pattern. During this rhythmic process of turn-taking, the mother waits for an *imagined* response from the baby and acts *as if* the baby is involved in an actual process of turn-taking (Newson 1977).

At some later point in time, the infant actually responds with babbling and the incidence of this reaction increases dependent on the mother's responses. When the baby is approximately one year old, she is generally able to give some real responses. When there is an expectant pause in the interaction, the child is able to vocalize and pseudo-dialogues change into more developed speech acts:

Baby: (turns attention to a top)
Mother: 'Do you like that'?
Baby: 'Da'!
Mother: 'Yes, it's a nice top, isn't it'? (Newson 1977: 57)

As said earlier, at the beginning of this chapter, imagination is crucial for the functioning of a dialogical self, particularly for the development of the other-in-the-self. When children are 2 to 3 years of age, they converse not only with their parents and siblings, but also with *imagined* interlocutors. When they are on their own, they rework memories of earlier events, amuse themselves, and use language to direct their own actions. Garvey (1984) recorded a variety of vocalizations and speech from 28-month-old Sarah during a nap period and found a remarkable variety of quiet murmurs, grunts, squeals, and intoned babbles. The range included humming and snatches of songs, rhymes, and counting. Sarah had an imagined 'telephone conversation' and even described her own activities (e.g. 'I'm putting

---

[5] Imitation is not limited to physical movements but includes also affective reactions. Newborn infants at an average of 36 hours of age were able to imitate facial expressions of happiness, sadness, and surprise as a reaction to an actress who displayed these expressions (Field *et al.* 1982).

my socks on'). As these observations suggests, memory and imagination enable the child to evoke others (e.g. family members and dolls) and interiorize them as positions of their extending selves.

Joint attention and indirect self-knowledge

A crucial step in the development of a dialogical self is when the child, by 9 months of age, starts to perceive and understand others as *intentional*. The perception of the other as an intentional being is closely related with viewing the environment from the perspective of the other. When the adult, involved in a conversation with the child, points with her finger to an object in the environment, the child does not look at the finger, as it used to do earlier, but it looks in the direction to which the adult is pointing. This interactional phenomenon is described in terms of 'joint attention', highlighted as 'the nine-month miracle' (Tomasello 1993). When children are able to jointly attend, they are not just directing their attention to other individuals as separate from objects in the environment and not to objects in the environment as separated from others, but they actually start to see objects from the perspective of the other person, that is, through the eyes of the other person. The child is learning not simply *from* another but rather *through* another.

A significant developmental step is made when the joint attention between caretaker and child is directed not only to the environment, but also to the child itself, resulting in a form of *self-reflective attention*. This attention is not a direct but rather an *indirect* perception of the child of herself, that is, through the perspective of the caretaker. From now on, the child is able to learn about herself via the perception, intention, and evaluation of the other toward her (Bertau 2004; Tomasello 1993). This indirect self-knowledge is well in agreement with Mead's (1934) classic notion of 'taking the role of the other', with the difference that the position of the other-in-the-self is a complex combination of taking the position of the other and imaginative processes that construct and reconstruct the other as part of an extended self.

Joint attention is not only a cognitive process, it also has affective implications. Contingent on the frequency, intensity, and duration of the reactions of the parents, some positions become more dominant in the self than others. When the child is repetitively placed in a negative position by parents or caretakers (e.g. 'You are a bad boy'), there is a good chance that this position becomes more rooted and dominant in the self than when he is primarily placed in a positive position ('You are a good boy'). As the result of joint attention and its affective connotation, the child incorporates the (affective) view of the other towards himself, unless his self is able to develop counter-forces that compensate for this influence. Self-reflection and self-dialogue develop *via* the other and include the perceptions, intentions, and emotions of the other *and* the child's reactions to them. The process of joint attention paves the way for inclusion of the other-in-the-self as resulting from a two-way interchange between self and other.[6]

Turning points in body positions

The relationship between self and environment is highly contingent on the positioning and repositioning of the body. When Neisser (1988) proposed his concept of the 'ecological self' he had in mind the position of an embodied self in a spatial environment. The perception of objects depends directly on the information about the location of one's own body in the environment. The perception of the environment gives feedback and information about one's own position in space. On the empirical level, this view is supported by Lee and Lishman (1975) who placed an observer in a room in which the end wall recedes from the position of the observer. The discrepancy between the visual information and the position in the room then causes a loss of posture stability in the backward direction and, as a correction of this loss, the observer tends to fall forward. The opposite effect takes place when, in the reversed condition, the observer is placed in a room with an approaching wall. As such experiments suggest, one's physical position in space has direct repercussions for the way the environment is perceived and vice versa.

With reference to the ecological nature of the self, there are four moments in the development of the young child that show how the process of repositioning in space leads to dramatic differences in perspectives: rolling over, crawling, standing, and walking. By 6 months most babies are able to *roll over* from back to front and front to back, movements that give entirely different views on the environment. The front position gives the child a frontal view on the environment and from this position it can actively grasp and move objects toward the body and to the mouth in particular. The objects can be moved from 'there' to 'here' and back and, moreover, from 'not felt' to 'felt' and back on a horizontal plane. When babies, from 6 to 12 months, start *crawling*, objects that are initially out of reach can be approached and touched. Placed in a field of tension between what is reachable and what is not reachable, a dynamic and linear field is stretched between 'here' and 'there' in which the baby is able to make movements from the one to the other with the possibility to diminish or enlarge the distance between the two positions. The first attempts to *stand upright* can be observed from the time that the child is about 4 to 5 months old. Whereas crawling enables the infant to move on the horizontal plane, standing up, although frightening at the beginning due to the risk of falling, makes it possible to explore movements on a vertical plane. While crawling makes

---

[6] In dialogical self theory, the spatial foundation of the process of positioning is intimately connected with its embodied and affective nature. For an elaboration of affective processes, and the dialogical relationship between self and emotions in particular, see Hermans and Hermans-Konopka (2010: ch. 5).

it possible to play and experiment with the opposite pair of 'here' versus 'there', standing stimulates the child to explore the opposite pair of 'high' versus 'low'. The form and structure of the body and corresponding movements in the spatial environment enable the child to position and reposition himself in a physical space. This physical space provides the basis for later metaphorical forms of positioning, repositioning, and counterpositioning in the space of the self. The ecological self forms the basis for a spatially structured dialogical self.

CONNECTION BETWEEN THE SOCIAL
AND THE BODY

The infant is social and embodied from birth onward. The social and embodied foundations of the self are intensely interconnected. If one gives primacy to the social, then one is at risk of underestimating the role of the body. When, reversely, primacy is given to the body, one is confronted with the problem of neglecting the profound role of the social in human life. As the increasing interest in the role of 'embodied (social) cognition' (e.g. MacDonald and Leary 2008) exemplifies, there is not only theoretical but also empirical evidence that body and social cognition are intensely intertwined from a psychological and neuroscientific point of view.[7]

If this is so, what then is the relationship between the body and the social in the emergence of a dialogical self? In order to answer this question, the spatial and embodied nature of the self should be taken into account from the onset in order to understand the social development of the child. As soon as social processes are taking place, the child is developing, at the same time, as an embodied being and she can only be social in an embodied way. In the course of her development, the child will increasingly structure her experiences in relation to others and herself on the basis of spatial metaphors that have their roots in the form of the body and in the movements that are allowed by the body. As bodily located, the child is able to move (crawl or walk) away from the mother and to go back to her. When the spatial distance between the mother and the child increases, the child feels, at some point, unsafe and wants to return to the mother in order to feel safe again.[8] In

---

[7] See nn. 2 and 3.

[8] In order to demonstrate the pervasive influence of early mother-child interactions on the maturation of the brain, Schore (1994) refers to the ability of the self to occupy a 'multiplicity of positions' as reflecting the emergent capacity to adaptively switch between psychobiological states that are colored by different affects. When the maturing child develops a dialogical self, she is increasingly able to transcend her immediate state (e.g. distress) and to enhance 'self-solace' capacities, i.e. the child is able to make a transition from an unsafe to a safe position. She can do so also when the mother

doing so, the child is moving on a horizontal dimension that is, at some later point in time, interiorized in the self as a metaphorical dimension stretched between the polar opposites of feeling *close* versus feeling *distant* in the relationship with the mother as a significant other-in-the-self or in the relationship with oneself (e.g. feeling close to oneself or alienated from one's desires).

In summary, social and bodily dimensions are intensely intertwined in the development of the child and sign-mediated interchanges with others and oneself lead to the construction of personal and social meanings in a spatially structured and embodied self. *I*-positions are not abstract entities but emergent properties of a socially constructed and embodied self. They emerge from social processes that are structured by the form and movements of the body and its basic opposites. Analogous to Vygotsky's (1987) view that the child begins to converse with himself as he previously conversed with others, I assume that the child experiences the positions in himself that he previously experienced in his embodied relationship with the other. It should be added that, when positions emerging from social interactions are interiorized, the self is able to *respond* to these positions in the form of counterpositions. In the interplay between positions and counterpositions the agency of the self comes to its full expression.

What is Dialogical in the Self?

The preceding considerations lead us to the question of what is dialogical in the self. In order to answer this question four notions that are at the heart of the dialogical self are needed: addressivity, difference, innovation, and alterity.

Addressivity

When there is a verbal dialogue between people or groups of people, they do not simply talk about each other, but they talk *with* each other. They address each other

---

is not present ('Mammy is away now but she will come back'). The mature orbitofrontal cortex, involved as it is in homeostatic regulation, is increasingly able to adjust and correct emotional responses, given its capacity to shift between different limbic circuits and to make a transition between high and low arousal states in response to stressful alterations of external environmental conditions. The capacity of the orbitofrontal system to facilitate such transitions enables the self to maintain continuity across various situational contexts. As Schore argues, this capacity to make transitions from a negative to positive positions and to realize a certain level of adaptive continuity of the self is seriously reduced in forms of insecure attachment (1994: 373–85). (For neurological and psychological processes in the 'dialogical brain' see also Lewis 2002.)

on a level where they both are subjects involved in a social relationship. One person addresses another person as another *I*, approached in his subjectivity and intentionality. In the context of dialogue, the subject is not understood as a separate person, encapsulated in his own subjectivity or as a self-contained entity, as Sampson (1985) would have it, but as a participant in an interchange that is marked by addressivity and responsiveness. In this interchange the Jamesian levels of self-as-subject and self-as-object have to be taken into account. On the subject level different selves address and respond to each other as subjects involved in a process of verbal or non-verbal interchange. They do so from the perspective of their own positions from which they address the positions on the part of the other (e.g. the other as friend, parent, opponent). On the object level the parties involved in dialogue talk about themselves, each other, or their worlds. The two levels are not independent. The subject level has primacy over the object level. That is, the content of the object level is not fixed, stable, and materialized as a book in a library. Instead, it is fluid, changing, and modifiable as a result of the influence of the subject level on the object level. When I have a productive discussion with a friend about matters that interest us, my view on the object matter and on myself is changed under the influence of our intersubjective exchange.

Addressivity as an intrinsic feature of dialogue is not a purely individualized matter. It refers not only to productive interchanges between the voices of individuals but also between collective voices of the groups, communities, and cultures to which the individual person belongs. Collective voices speak *through* the mouth of the individual person (e.g. 'I as a psychologist', 'I as a member of a political party', or 'I as a representative of an ecological movement'). From a Bakhtinian perspective, all utterances are multi-voiced and dialogical at the same time (Skinner *et al.* 2001). They are multi-voiced not only because I can talk with different internal voices (e.g. in an internal conflict) but also because I'm part of social groups, conventions, or communities. In the act of speaking there are at least two voices: the voice of the speaking person and the voice of a social language (e.g. one's dialect, one's professional group, one's generation). As Bakhtin argued, the word in language is 'half-foreign' as the collective voice of a social group speaks through the mouth of the individual speaker. The collective voice of the group or community becomes one's own when the speaker populates it with his own intentions, intonations, and expressive tendencies (e.g. 'I speak as a psychologist, but at the same time I'm expressing my personal view or conviction'). A significant feature of collective voices is that they already exist before the individual person is born and they become deeply entrenched in particular positions in the self. Collective voices influence the content of particular positions in the self (e.g. I as a man, as white, as raised in a Western culture) and even their organization (e.g. depending on the culture in which I'm raised, some positions receive a higher place in the position hierarchy than others). Not only verbal but also non-verbal forms of collective positioning influence the content and organization of the individual position repertoire, as exemplified by collective practices like carnival festivities, funeral ceremonies, rites of passage and religious traditions, forms that can be renewed over time depending on changing circumstances and the innovative capacities of individuals and groups.

Individual selves are not only bearers of traditions but also agentic in the sense that they are equipped to give an original response to the workings of collective voices and traditions. They do so in the form of agreement or disagreement, confirmation or renewal, from a personal point of view. As Hermans (2001a) has argued, self is culture-inclusive and culture is self-inclusive. An implication of this view is that collective voices are not purely outside the individual self but a constitutive part of it. Self and others are addressing each other as a multiplicity of individual and collective voices.[9]

Difference

Dialogue can only proceed when differences between the voices are taken into account. As argued in the preceding sections, differences are in the nature of dialogue because, even when the same sentence is produced, they are different as utterances given their different positions in space. Such differences are at the heart of the dialogical self, because the mind is addressing and questioning itself without receiving an immediate answer. In a thorough analysis of the notion of dialogue, Blachowicz (1999) conceives the self in terms of a series of proposals and disposals, comparable with the interchange between a witness and a police artist cooperating in the construction of a drawing of a suspect:

I propose viewing the 'dialogue of the soul with itself' as a series of proposals and disposals similar in function to the exchange between the police artist and the witness in their collaboration. The two parties represent the independent interests of meaning and articulation. At one moment we may possess a meaning but fail to articulate it; at another moment we may possess just such an articulation, but find that its meaning fails to correspond with our intended one. We talk to our self when we think because only a

---

[9] The notion of collective voice provides a useful alternative to Mead's notion of the generalized other. As Ritzer (1993) has argued, Mead's theory represents a 'homogeneous society' metaphor, with a heavy emphasis on micro-social game-like processes. In a globalizing world that is increasingly populated by a multiplicity and diversity of contrasting and conflicting voices on the interfaces of cultures (Hermans and Dimaggio 2007), the concept of the 'generalized other' becomes more and more obsolete. At these interfaces, different and even conflicting rules that 'worked' within the boundaries of relatively isolated groups or cultures have lost their significance as general principles. Given the processes of globalization and localization as intimately related developments, world citizens are challenged by the possibility and even necessity to develop 'joint attention' to their differences and conflicts as participants in a world that is spatially compressed but populated by individuals and groups who are lacking the dialogical capacity to deal with cultural differences and conflicts.

dialogue where each side provides proposals and corrective disposals for the other can achieve a simultaneous satisfaction of these twin requirements. (1999: 182)

For a well-functioning self, it should be added that the two parts are not *entirely* different. Blachowicz (1999) is well aware of this in arguing that, in order to produce a well-functioning dialogue, the partners need some degree of each other's skills. Each should share the capacities of the other to some degree in order to make the collaboration productive. As part of a dialogue difference needs some degree of commonality. When people are cooperating in performing some kind of activity that needs coordination, such as husband and wife, employer and employee, or guide and traveller, they need some knowledge and understanding of each other's contribution to make the cooperation effective.

As involved in a process of proposing and disposing or positioning and counter-positioning, the self is confronted with its own differences and *needs* these differences in order to arrive at some point of clarity about itself. A dialogical self is based on the differences between the self and itself and therefore it is necessarily a process of positioning itself *toward* itself, including the-other-in-the-self. As Gadamer wrote: 'Because our understanding does not comprehend what it knows in one single inclusive glance, it must always draw what it thinks out of itself, and present it to itself as if in an inner dialogue with itself. In this sense all thought is speaking to oneself' (1989: 422). In this context, Gadamer referred to the 'imperfection of the human mind' in an anti-Cartesian way: 'the imperfection of the human mind consists in its never being completely present to itself but in being dispersed into thinking this or that' (1989: 425). Likewise, the dialogical self is intrinsically uncertain because it is never complete at any moment in time and is always in need of a *different* part of itself, in order to arrive at some clarity in its relation to itself and the world.[10]

Innovation

Agreement and disagreement, like question and answer, are dialogical forms. However, a question can be purely rhetorical or even coercive. And a disagreement between two people, particularly when they are defending their own point of view, can result in a two-sided monologue. A fully fledged dialogue is more than that. It implies a *learning* process that confirms, innovates, or further develops existing positions on the basis of the preceding exchange (see also the innovative potential of the *I* in Mead's (1934) view). As a learning process it has the capacity to move the self to higher levels of awareness and integration. It is an arena of individual and collective learning (see also Bohm *et al.* 1991). As such, dialogue is more specific

---

[10] Dialogue as a processing of differences is exemplified by self-criticism, self-conflict, self-agreement, and self-consultation (Hermans and Hermans-Konopka 2010).

than the broader concept of 'communication'. When a demagogic political leader is giving a speech to his audience describing another group of people as 'bad', 'evil', or 'dangerous', this is certainly a form of communication, but can it be said that he is involved in dialogue? The problem with the notion of communication is that it means 'everything' and therefore 'nothing'. In contrast, dialogue is one of the most precious learning instruments of the human mind and is valuable enough to be stimulated and developed, particularly in situations where learning is hampered by monological communication. Therefore, it is necessary that we know not only how dialogue can be stimulated but also what its constraints are. There are situations where there is no dialogue or where it is not or not yet possible (e.g. in situations in which one party believes that its power position can only be maintained by the suppression of the other party) or even not required (e.g. a rescue in an emergency situation). The crucial question is not: is the person dialogical or not? But rather: when and under which conditions is dialogue possible and how can it be fostered?

The dialogical self can be further articulated by distinguishing it from 'inner speech', usually described as the activity of 'silently talking to oneself' and discussed in the literature in the form of equivalent concepts like 'self-talk' or 'self-verbalizations' and related concepts like 'private speech' or 'egocentric speech' (for review see Morin 2005). The dialogical self is different from inner speech in at least four respects: (*a*) it is multi-voiced rather than mono-voiced, as involved in interchanges between spatially different voices from different social or cultural origin; (*b*) voices are not only 'private' but also 'collective', as they talk through the mouth of the individual speaker; (*c*) the dialogical self reflects a theoretical view that explicitly rejects any dualism between self and other: the other (individual or group) is not purely outside the self but conceptually included as other-in-the-self; (*d*) the dialogical self is not only verbal but also non-verbal: there are embodied forms of dialogue before the child is able to verbalize or use any language (Hermans and Hermans-Konopka 2010).[11]

Innovation is lacking in the phenomenon called 'rumination', where one or a few negatively experienced positions are dominating in the self (e.g. 'I as a failure', 'I as guilty', 'I as a loser', or 'I as drinking too much') to a degree that other positions that are qualitatively different have no chance to be included in the interchange. Often these positions are connected with a limited range of extended positions (e.g. 'my angry father' or 'my boss who is not satisfied about me') that evenly lack qualitative differences. In rumination the *I* is severely constrained by a cluster of positions that are easily accessible, but do not allow any exit as long as the worrying process continues. Typically, the person makes cyclic movements across these positions, again and again arriving at the same positions and becoming absorbed in their negatively coloured memories, cognitions, and anticipations. In fact, such a cluster

---

[11] See also J. Lysaker (2006) who critically discussed Wiley's (2006) view in which the dialogical self and inner speech are seen as equivalent concepts.

functions as an *I*-prison from which the person feels not able to escape. There is a tendency of becoming locked up in oneself and losing an open contact with the environment. Positive positions (e.g. 'I as optimist' or 'I has having a sense of humour') are backgrounded and not accessible so that the negative positions have no chance to change or develop as long as the self is imprisoned in rumination.

Alterity

In a dialogical conception of the self a moral stance follows from the consideration that the 'other' is an intrinsic part of an extended self. As Richardson *et al.* say: 'Dialogic relations are always fundamentally ethical because in them we always are either acknowledged or ignored, understood or misunderstood, treated with respect or coerced' (1998: 510). Not only dialogue, but also the self can be seen as a basically moral enterprise, as Taylor concludes in an exploration of the self as emerging in the history of philosophy: 'My identity is defined by the commitments and identifications which provide the frame or horizon within which I can try to determine from case to case what is good, or valuable, or what ought to be done, or what I endorse or oppose. In other words, it is the horizon within which I am capable of taking a stand' (1989: 27). Indeed, in dialogue we appear before the actual others and take a moral stance. This implies that dialogical relationships do not only require that the other person is recognized as different from oneself but is also respected and valued in his alterity.

As Cooper and Hermans (2007) have observed, there is not only an alterity in the world around us, but also inside: the positions within the self deserve attention and recognition in their otherness. Just as one can talk of the alterity of another person, it is legitimate to talk of 'self-alterity'. By introducing this concept, we proposed to go beyond Levinas's (1969) characterization of the self as 'sameness' and understand it, instead, as having an intrinsic diversity and alterity. We emphasized that self-alterity should be seen as an extension of 'other-alterity' rather than as an alternative to it. The idea was that even the most 'internal' self-experiences are infused with something non-self. Self-alterity, like other-alterity, is characterized by the recognition and evaluation of the differences, multiplicity, and changes of one's own positions in their relative autonomy.

The alterity of self and other and its realization in dialogical relationships is located in a field of tension with the notion of identity in the sense of sameness over time. It is a well-accepted view in the social sciences that the self is striving for identity, stability, and continuity because these qualities are in the service of the basic need of safety. As a result, the alterity of the other becomes subordinated to dominant identity positions in the self. Recognizing the alterity of the other implies certain 'identity costs' as it is challenging a stabilized self-identity. Therefore, in order to recognize the alterity of the other and even of the different positions in the self, a certain tolerance for uncertainty is required. This tolerance should be a central part of 'alterity-learning' (Hermans and Hermans-Konopka 2010) that invites the person to find a balance between the need for a clear and sufficiently stable (yet open) identity on the one hand and the necessity of accepting alterity as part of productive dialogical relationships on the other hand. Alterity learning is a challenging task because the need for stability and safety instigates people to remain in the 'comfort zone' of the self that refers to a set of ordinary positions that are perceived as familiar and to which one continuously tends to return. We tend to return to the same positions not only in the internal domain but also in the external (extended) domain and we do so in our memories, thoughts, and fantasies (e.g. a picture of a deceased family member on the wall or a figure who is revisited in one's fantasies). Such 'returning visits' bring order, continuity, and safety in the self. In contrast to this tendency, alterity needs some deviation from the stabilized routines of everyday life and requires a broadening and innovation of one's comfort zone. The self is able to take alterity into account only when it is open to the uncertain inputs of the less familiar aspects of both the positions of others *and* those of oneself.

SUMMARY

The 'dialogical self' is a composite concept that weaves together two notions, self and dialogue, in such a way that dialogue is brought into the self and the self into dialogue. Inspired by James (1890), Mead (1934), and Bakhtin, the proposed theoretical framework aims to transcend any dualism between self and other and, in a wider sense, between individual and society. The central thesis of this chapter is that the dialogical self is *positioned* in space and time. The notion of space was materialized by the concepts of positioning and counterpositioning whereas time was elaborated in the process of positioning and repositioning. Closely related to the spatial nature of self and dialogue, the bodily foundation of the dialogical self was explored. Referring to recent studies in developmental psychology, some precursors and developmental origins of the dialogical self were presented: imitation, provocation, joint attention, and significant turning points in the development of the body and its movements. Together these phenomena show how the spatial, embodied, and social aspects of the dialogical self go together in prelinguistic forms of contact and interchange. Finally, four key factors were discussed that are central to a full-fledged dialogical self: addressivity, difference, innovation, and alterity. As an extension of the view of Levinas (1969), the phenomenon of 'self-alterity' was presented as an acknowledgement and evaluation of the differences between positions within the self.

REFERENCES

BAKHTIN, M. (1973). *Problems of Dostoevsky's Poetics* (2nd edn., tr. R. W. Rotsel, Ann Arbor, Mich.: Ardis; original work publ. 1929 as *Problemy tvorchestva Dostoevskogo*).

BARRESI, J. (1994). 'Morton Prince and B.C.A.: A Historical Footnote on the Confrontation between Dissociation Theory and Freudian Psychology in a Case of Multiple Personality', in R. Klein and B. Doane (eds), *Psychological Concepts and Dissociative Disorders* (Hillsdale, NJ: Lawrence Erlbaum Associates), 85–129.

BERTAU, M.-C. (2004). 'Developmental Origins of the Dialogical Self: Some Significant Moments', in H. J. M. Hermans and G. Dimaggio (eds), *The Dialogical Self in Psychotherapy* (London: Brunner and Routledge), 29–42.

BLACHOWICZ, J. (1999). 'The Dialogue of the Soul with Itself', in S. Gallagher and J. Shear (eds), *Models of the Self* (Thorverton, UK: Imprint Academic), 177–200.

BOHM, D., FACTOR, D., and GARRETT, P. (1991). *Dialogue: A Proposal.* www.davidbohm.net/dialogue/dialogue_proposal.html.

BROMBERG, P. (2004). 'Standing in the Spaces: The Multiplicity of Self and the Psychoanalytic Relationship', in H. J. M. Hermans and G. Dimaggio (eds), *The Dialogical Self in Psychotherapy* (New York: Brunner and Routledge), 138–59.

CARSON, R. C., BUTCHER, J. N., and MINEKA, S. (1996). *Abnormal Psychology and Modern Life* (10th edn. New York: HarperCollins).

CASSIRER, E. (1955). *The Philosophy of Symbolic Forms*, ii. *Mythical Thought* (New Haven: Yale University Press).

COOPER, M., and HERMANS, H. J. M. (2007). 'Honoring Self-Otherness: Alterity and the Intrapersonal', in L. Simão and J. Valsiner (eds), *Otherness in Question: Labyrinths of the Self* (Greenwich, Conn.: Information Age), 305–15.

DAMON, W., and HART, D. (1982). 'The Development of Self-Understanding from Infancy through Adolescence', *Child Development*, 4: 841–64.

FIELD, T. M., WOODSON, R., GREENBERG, R., and COHEN, D. (1982). 'Discrimination and Imitation of Facial Expressions by Neonates', *Science*, 218: 179–81.

GADAMER, H.-G. (1989). *Truth and Method* (2nd edn., tr. revised by J. Weinsheimer and D. G. Marshall; New York: Continuum).

GARVEY, C. (1984). *Children's Talk* (Cambridge, Mass.: Harvard University Press).

GREGG, G. S. (1991). *Self-Representation: Life Narrative in Identity and Ideology* (New York: Greenwood Press).

HERMANS, H. J. M. (1996). 'Voicing the Self: From Information Processing to Dialogical Interchange', *Psychological Bulletin*, 119: 31–50.

——(2001*a*). 'The Dialogical Self: Toward a Theory of Personal and Cultural Positioning', *Culture and Psychology*, 7: 243–81.

——(2001*b*). 'The Construction of a Personal Position Repertoire: Method and Practice', *Culture and Psychology*, 7: 323–65.

——and DIMAGGIO, G. (2007). 'Self, Identity, and Globalization in Times of Uncertainty: A Dialogical Analysis', *Review of General Psychology*, 11: 31–61.

——and HERMANS-JANSEN, E. (1995). *Self-Narratives: The Construction of Meaning in Psychotherapy* (New York: Guilford).

——and KEMPEN, H. J. G. (1993). *The Dialogical Self: Meaning as Movement* (San Diego, Calif.: Academic Press; see also Japanese tr. by S. Mizokami, R. Mizuma, and M. Morioka, publ. by Tuttle-Mori Agency, 2006).

——and HERMANS-KONOPKA, A. (2010). *Dialogical Self Theory: Positioning and Counter-Positioning in a Globalizing World* (Cambridge: Cambridge University Press).

——KEMPEN, H. J. G., and VAN LOON, R. J. P. (1992). 'The Dialogical Self: Beyond Individualism and Rationalism', *American Psychologist*, 47: 23–33.

JAMES, W. (1890). *The Principles of Psychology*, i (London: Macmillan).

JAYNES, J. (1976). *The Origin of Consciousness in the Breakdown of the Bicameral Mind* (Boston: Houghton Mifflin).

JOHNSON, M. (1987). *The Body in the Mind: The Bodily Basis of Meaning, Imagination, and Reason* (Chicago: University of Chicago Press).

LEE, D., and LISHMAN, J. R. (1975). 'Visual Proprioceptive Control of Stance', *Journal of Human Movement Studies*, 1: 87–95.

LEVINAS, E. (1969). *Totality and Infinity: An Essay on Exteriority*, tr. A. Lingis (Pittsburgh, Pa.: Duquesne University Press).

LEWIS, M. D. (2002). 'The Dialogical Brain: Contributions of Emotional Neurobiology to Understanding the Dialogical Self', *Theory and Psychology*, 12: 175–90.

LINELL, P. (1990). 'The Power of Dialogue Dynamics', in I. Marková and K. Foppa (eds), *The Dynamics of Dialogue* (New York: Harvester Wheatsheaf), 147–77.

LYSAKER, J. (2006). 'I am Not What I Seem to Be' (commentary on Wiley). *International Journal for Dialogical Science*, 1: 41–6.

MacDONALD, G., and LEARY, M. (2008). 'Why does Social Exclusion Hurt? The Relationship between Social and Physical Pain', *Psychological Bulletin*, 131: 202–23.

MARATOS, O. (1973). 'The Origin and Development of Imitation in the First Six Months of Life', Ph.D. thesis, University of Geneva.

MEAD, G. H. (1934). *Mind, Self, and Society* (Chicago: University of Chicago Press).

MELTZOFF, A. N., and MOORE, M. K. (1994). 'Imitation, Memory, and the Representation of Persons', *Infant Behavior and Development*, 17: 83–99.

MINSKY, M. (1985). *The Society of Mind* (New York: Simon & Schuster).

MORIN, A. (2005). 'Possible Links between Self-Awareness and Inner Speech: Theoretical Background, Underlying Mechanisms, and Empirical Evidence', *Journal of Consciousness Studies*, 12: 115–34.

NAGY, E., and MOLNAR, P. (2004). 'Homo Imitans or Homo Provocans? Human Imprinting Model of Neonatal Imitation', *Infant Behavior and Development*, 27: 54–63.

NEISSER, U. (1988). 'Five Kinds of Self-Knowledge', *Philosophical Psychology*, 1: 35–59.

NEWSON, J. (1977). 'An Intersubjective Approach to the Systematic Description of Mother–Infant Interaction', in H. R. Schaffer (ed.), *Studies in Mother–Infant Interaction* (London: Academic Press), 47–61.

RICHARDSON, F. C., ROGERS, A., and McCARROLL, J. (1998). 'Toward a Dialogical Self', *American Behavioral Scientist*, 41: 496–515.

RITZER, G. (1993). *The McDonaldization of Society: An Investigation into the Changing Character of Contemporary Social Life* (Thousand Oaks, Calif.: Pine Forge Press).

ROSENBERG, M. (1979). *Conceiving the Self* (New York: Basic Books).

SAMPSON, E. (1985). 'The Decentralization of Identity: Toward a Revised Concept of Personal and Social Order', *American Psychologist*, 11: 1203–11.

SCHORE, A. N. (1994). *Affect Regulation and the Origin of the Self: The Neurobiology of Emotional Development* (Hillsdale, NJ: Erlbaum).

SKINNER, D., VALSINER, J., and HOLLAND, D. (2001). 'Discerning the Dialogical Self: A Theoretical and Methodological Examination of a Nepali Adolescent's Narrative', *Forum: Qualitative Social Research*, 2: 1–18.

STRAUS, E. W. (1958). 'Aesthesiology and Hallucinations', in R. May, E. Angel, and H. F. Ellenberger (eds), *Existence: A New Dimension in Psychiatry and Psychology* (New York: Basic Books), 139–69.

TAYLOR, C. (1989). *Sources of the Self: The Making of the Modern Identity* (Cambridge, Mass.: Harvard University Press).

TOMASELLO, M. (1993). 'On the Interpersonal Origins of Self-Concept', in U. Neisser (ed.), *The Perceived Self: Ecological and Interpersonal Sources of Self-Knowledge* (Cambridge: Cambridge University Press), 174–84.

VASIL'EVA, I. I. (1988). 'The Importance of M. M. Bakhtin's Idea of Dialogue and Dialogic Relations for the Psychology of Communication', *Soviet Psychology*, 26: 17–31.

VYGOTSKY, L. S. (1929). 'The Problem of the Cultural Development of the Child', *Journal of Genetic Psychology*, 36: 415–34.

WATKINS, M. (1986). *Invisible Guests: The Development of Imaginal Dialogues* (Hillsdale, NJ: Erlbaum).

WILEY, N. (2006). 'Pragmatism and the Dialogical Self', *International Journal for Dialogical Science*, 1: 5–22.

WILLIAMS, L. E., and BARGH, J. A. (2008). 'Experiencing Physical Warmth Promotes Interpersonal Warmth', *Science*, 322: 606–7.

CHAPTER 29

GLASS SELVES

EMOTIONS, SUBJECTIVITY, AND THE RESEARCH PROCESS

ELSPETH PROBYN

PROLOGUE

I'm in an interviewing room in a hospital for children. We've been doing focus groups with patients in an anorexia recovery program. Some are outpatients but not the small girl with long blond hair and tubes leading from her nostrils. She's the one who brightened up when I mentioned food and cooking TV shows. She said she was addicted to them and watched them as much as she could. She was embarrassed to watch them with her friends. The others soon joined in relating their favourite TV cooking programs. The objective of the research project was to compare what girls who have been diagnosed with anorexia think about media images of women and what 'normal' girls think. It wasn't an angle I would have chosen, as it tends to replicate semi-causal equations of media influence. As such research along these lines pays scant attention to the intricacies of subjectivity.

My research interest in the self and subjectivity has often intertwined with questions about anorexia. My earliest research was sparked by reading Louis Althusser's (1971) magisterial essay on Ideological State Apparatuses (ISA). At the time—in the early 1980s—everyone in cultural theory seemed immersed in Althusserian theory, or at least this was certainly the case in Montreal. As you may recall, Althusser broke with certain versions of Marxism in order to bring a subjective dimension via Lacan into Marxist debates. I immediately loved the concept of interpellation, and his explanation of how ideology hails us as subjects. Like many I was affectively interpellated by Althusser's ISAs. I had been meaning to use an Althusserian framework to analyse an important government document about identity. As I read and reread the difficult theoretical texts, my thoughts would flicker to thinking about how ISAs had interpellated me. I was quite severely anorexic when I was a young girl. Trying to figure out the nuances of how ideological structures, including the media, entered into subjectivities, I would use my own experience—my own self—as a touchstone to see whether my theoretical thoughts made sense.

I ended up doing my masters thesis on the genealogical analysis of anorexia especially in regards to how anorexia nervosa (as it was named by William Gull in 1868) had functioned historically as one way in which young women, who because of their gender positions had few resources with which to fashion a self, might elaborate anorexia as a mode of negotiating societal strictures (Probyn 1987). From there I went on to do a Ph.D. thesis about the uses of the self mainly from a Foucauldian perspective. In Foucault's final two volumes of the *History of Sexuality* I found another set of tools with which to consider closely the workings of what he calls subjectification, or the work we conduct upon ourselves.

This was then the distant background I brought to the pilot project, which I have briefly described above.[1] The project was conducted with a paediatrician intern. Unfortunately the collaboration with the doctors got off to a bad start. In the first focus group I introduced myself to the girls. It was the usual thing: what the research is about, the guarantees of anonymity, etc. I also added: 'not that I think it matters but I was diagnosed with anorexia and hospitalized when I was young'. There was a flicker of interest on some of the girls' faces. But it was no big deal. It was, however, to the supervising paediatrician who let it be known that she thought that prefacing of my own experience was unprofessional.

When I heard of her opinion anger got added to what was already a heady brew of emotions. I'll quickly flag and name some of the feelings that filled this research space. Entering the hospital I walked into painful memories. No one likes hospitals and for me a sense of claustrophobia compounded the squeamishness and unease that so often accompanies being in a hospital space. I was incarcerated when I was young in a hospital pysch ward and the clearest and still visceral memory I have was of lying in bed looking up at the low white ceilings with holes that in my boredom I would connect into patterns. That memory of being confined and subjected to the crude treatment programs for anorexia brought on a deep sadness—and panic. When I entered the interview room the

---

[1] For obvious reasons I won't give any details of the participants.

girls were there—some six or seven, all aged in between 10 and 15. They were so bright, so scared, so bored, so lost, that I nearly lost it.

Later my anger grew: an epistemological anger that burns deep, or more precisely anger at the epistemology that frames anorexia in terms of the thinnest understanding of visibility and subjectivity. Anger at the discursive formation that holds these understandings so firmly in place within institutional spaces: how did ideas first promulgated through feminism about body image come to be welded onto institutional frameworks? Anger at the ways in which young girls' bodies— and most particularly those diagnosed or presumed to be anorexic—are scrutinized, and obsessively read for proof. In a very useful new book, *Inside Anorexia*, Halse, Honey, and Boughtwood allow for girls' voices from within the experience of anorexia. Their girls attest to a dehumanizing that is part and parcel of the discursive formation. They complain they 'are treated like a stereotype'. They say of the nurses: 'You get those looks, it makes you feel less than a human being' (2008: 120).

In terms of much research on anorexia—and it seems especially feminist analysis—Rebecca Lester argues that 'the debilitating illness of anorexia nervosa is read as a text—a symbolic struggle played out in the "language" of the body—to the degree to which we begin to wonder if we are talking about real women at all' (1997: 481). This regime of visibility, which overdetermines understandings of subjectivity, has come to imprison anorexics as objects of scrutiny for several discursive institutional orders: medical, feminist, educational, academic, journalistic, and psychotherapeutic. In the evocative words of one recovering anorexic: 'sometimes I feel as if I'm made of glass—like I'm transparent. And everyone can see right into my insides. It makes me want to scream, "Get out! Get out of me!"' (cited in Lester 1997: 484).

Without losing sight of the tragic consequences, this woman's words point to the ways in which the framing, treatment, and knowledge about anorexia nervosa is a perfect exemplar of how a discursive formation grounded in the visible comes into being. Deleuze has expounded at length on how Foucault's work, especially in *The Order of Things*, *The Birth of the Clinic*, and *Madness and Civilisation*, demonstrates how knowledge is sedimentized: 'made up of things and words, of seeing and speaking, of the visible and the sayable, of zones of visibility and fields of legibility, of contents and of expressions' (1988: 40). And we all know that the hospital as well as the asylum and the prison stand as exemplars of the welding together of the visible and the sayable. 'The asylum arose as a new way of seeing and revealing the mad . . . And medicine, but also the law, regulations, literature, etc. invented a system of statements concerning unreason as a new concept' (ibid. 40). As Deleuze continues, 'there is here a "self-evidence", an historical perception or sensibility as much as a discursive system' (ibid.). This intricate system of self-evidence, of seeing and knowing, 'exceeds behaviour, consciousness and ideas since it makes them possible'.

Subjectivity, the Self, and its Discontents

A self made of glass—what an awesome image. Of course it captures the sheer vulnerability, as it speaks painfully to the sensation of being made visible, of being known. This sense of being known is one that comes through in many interviews I have conducted over the years with recovering anorexics. They talk of how hard it is at school when they have been labelled anorexic and their peers look at them and dismiss them as having bought into anorexia as a 'glamorous' thing to do, a fad, a way of drawing attention to their selves. I remember well how you have to wear people's knowledges of you as an anorexic. Pinned to one definition your subjectivity is erased, other people's knowledge of you is worn as a suffocating cloak. This is particularly galling for many anorexics who seek to disappear from view through starvation.

In her essay on Diderot's lesbian nun in his *La Religieuese*, Eve Sedgwick, in her magisterial way, drills deeper into this morass of knowing. Under the title 'Privilege of Unknowing', Sedgwick seeks to rescue ignorance from a postmodern circuit of cultural critique fascinated by knowledge and overly invested in unraveling complexity into a simple task of deconstruction. In her words:

Insofar as ignorance is ignorance of a knowledge—a knowledge that may itself, it goes without saying, be seen either as 'true' or 'false' under some other regime of truth—these ignorances, far from being pieces of the originary dark, are produced by and correspond to particular knowledges and circulate as part of particular regimes of truth. (1993: 25)

This swirling of knowing and ignorance is at the heart of Sedgwick's (1990) formulation of the 'epistemology of the closet'—the open secret, the looks of knowingness. In a different register although fueled by much the same epistemological imperative, this is, I would argue, what produces the anorexic self of glass. In other words, and taking from Rita Goldberg whom Sedgwick cites, the self here is produced within a historical process of 'the feminisation of knowing' (Goldberg, cited in Sedgwick 1990: 30). Goldberg captures this: 'It is rather as if the corpse on the table were also the doctor doing the dissection' (ibid.).

In this chapter I want to turn to the question of the foldings of the self, subjectivity, and emotion. Let me use the above description of the research project as a tableau of selves: the self of me, the researcher, in relation to the selves of the girls under study. This is an apt way to speak of the research. However it reveals it as one-dimensional and static. But I will use it in order to reflect on the dynamics of researching subjectivity—the subjectification of research as problematization, to use Foucault's term. My aim here is to think a bit more deeply about the intra- and intersubjectification that is the motor of research, that which drives research but which is often masked by ignorance.

In a generous reading of some of my previous work, Rebecca Lester writes of the model that I elaborated from Foucault's arguments about the technology of the self. She puts forward the case that I reintroduce

the possibility of agency (limited, though it may be, within the bounds of available discourses and the 'spaces' they present) by suggesting that subjects can indeed transform themselves—consciously and deliberately—through the constant perception and re-evaluation of the relationship between the 'inside' and the 'outside' and how this positions us in relation to others, particularly to other women. (1997: 483)

This is, as I said, a generous reading of my argument in *Sexing the Self* (1993). Lester's own argument is a particularly sophisticated and convincing one about the 'theory' and practice of anorexia within the process of self-tailoring.

As Lester makes clear and extends in her own work, we need to use Foucault's injunctions to think about the self in a doubled or folded way. Or, to put it more precisely, this is to consider 'attitude' as a vehicle for informing and expressing subjectivity. In Foucault's words, it is: 'A mode of relating to contemporary reality . . . a way of thinking and feeling; a way, too, of acting and behaving that at the one and the same time marks a relation of belonging and marks itself as task' (1984: 39). The challenge Foucault issues is large but also simply stated: a critical attitude demands that we work at the limits of ourselves. In other words, subjectification is a task performed on our selves by our selves and it compels an acute awareness of that work in the process of criticism: 'to recognise ourselves as subjects of what we are doing, thinking and saying' (1984: 45–6).

What I did not explicitly theorize in that earlier work is the question of the different forms of feeling that enter into this process: how feeling and thinking become intertwined in the act of problematizing subjectivity, and the processes of subjectification of one's self in relation to another's. This is not only to question what emotions do to one's self but how the emotions generated in research motivate the critical task, to take the etymology of emotion at its most basic.

ANGER AND THE SPIRAL OF THE SELF

So what do emotions do? It depends on the emotion, and as I've argued in the case of disgust and shame, each distinct emotion or affect has a distinct type of motion that it inaugurates and fuels. Analysing the different forms of affect inspired by the sight of an anorexic body and that of an obese one, I argued that images of the anorexic seek to elicit shame, whereas the obese one calls forth disgust (2000). Disgust acts to make the reader want to push away the image, to expunge the sight and the closeness of the obese person. The anorexic fills us with shame and we bow our heads before her image.

To return to my example of anger—my anger—it is clear that anger sets into motion a whirlwind of values, stances, and ideas, especially as they coalesce in one's self. It shakes up the self at a very fundamental level and lets loose an array of dispositions. Of course anger has been variously used as a force furthering different political projects, notably aimed at undoing oppressions. Anger is often framed as an appropriate response to various forms of injustice. The question of anger has especially interested feminists in part because it is seen as an excessive emotion. The blog Feminist Rage Page's motto is: 'equality never looked so pissed [off]'. In the introduction to the blog they write 'the world gives us so much to be angry about, and then tells us not to be angry'.[2]

In an experimental piece, Elizabeth Spelman writes in the voice of anger—literally in the form of a diary that anger writes. Anger and Spelman fondly recall Aristotle's thoughts about anger: 'Anyone who doesn't get angry at the right person at the right time for the right reason is a fool' (1998). Noting the put-down that is seemingly only ever directed at women ('you're so cute when you're angry'), Spelman argues that 'the fact of being angry tells us about the angry person'. Tellingly she writes that 'to be angry is to take yourself seriously'. This then connects with ways in which anger is seen as less objective than laughter: 'When one responds in helpless explosive laughter to a person or situation, it's not because one is irrational or blinded by passion but on the contrary is responding directly to what is there for all to see or notice' (1998: 3). Laughter draws attention to the self-evident whereas anger reveals and names the inner person. Spelman's argument succinctly raises the ways in which anger directs attention and implicates the being who experiences it. While she plays with laughter being seen as less subjective, all emotions, feelings, or affects will skewer the pursuit of objective knowledge. Donald Nathanson, a close follower of Silvan Tomkins, succinctly describes how 'affect is biology, feeling is psychology and emotion is biography' (1992: 50).[3]

Much of the motivation, movement, and impact of these kinds of feminist rage seem to be rhetorical. Of course the rhetorical spills over into action but it tends to

---

[2] http://community.livejournal.com/feminist_rage/, accessed Mar. 2009.

[3] As Despret writes, 'to de-passion knowledge does not give us a more objective world, it just gives us a world "without us" and therefore "without them"' (2004a: 131). Of course we must do more than merely dwell on the fact of the intersubjective transfer. As many have argued, the trick is how to translate emotions. Richard Shweder notes that emotions are interpretive systems, 'complex narrative structures that give shape and meaning to somatic and affective experiences' (1994: 37). Fred Myers, the renowned anthropologist of the Australian Aboriginal people of the western desert, has repeatedly emphasized that 'emotions are not simply reactions to what happens, but interpretations of an event, judgements' (1986: 428, cited in Abu-Lughod 1990: 26). At the heart of Myers's work as with that of others is the contention that emotions throw us into a world of entanglements as they also depict the complex relationality of the world. 'The simplicity of the us/them dyad—assumed in the flow of cultural translation from "them" to "us"—is no longer sustainable' (Myers 2006: 235).

be verbal. As a young feminist I remember raging in situations where I was the sole feminist voice. In those cases the rage and the isolation built upon each other, always threatening to shut down voices and actions.

A recent article sets out to explore the physical and the material side of rage. Kimberly Flemke and Katherine Allen describe their study of women incarcerated in prison for violence against their partners. The premise of their research proceeds from the need to differentiate 'complexities formerly overlooked within women's experience of intimate violence' (2008: 59). As they say, 'the monolithic experience of fear and terror, housed within a framework of victimhood and powerlessness ... is becoming challenged and rethought as simply one possible experience among other possibilities' (ibid.). This is a good start.

The women's descriptions of their anger are quite extraordinary. 'Priscilla' says: 'with anger, you get angry for a moment and get over it. With rage, I took a butcher knife and stabbed him (boyfriend) because he laughed at me.' 'Honey' describes: 'my hands shake, my jaw clenches together. It's like the devil is crawling up my back' (63). What rage makes some of these women do is amazing. 'Olivia' talks about how rage at her boyfriend who had hit her made her take 'his penis and balls and cut them off with a knife and the penis was cut off. It was just dangling here in my hand' (67).

Flemke and Allen are careful to differentiate rage from anger: 'Rage: A feeling that exceeds healthy anger. It overpowers normal brain functioning because it loses the rational component found within healthy anger. A person full of rage feels out of control and seeks to hurt another in a physical way' (2008: 61). But what I find intriguing about their stance is how distanced the researchers are from the women's descriptions of their rage and what it made them do. This is all the more surprising because they introduce their argument with a description of how they came to be interested in women prisoners' rage. Flemke writes about how she was in a meeting about how to treat female offenders of domestic violence and how the atmosphere became charged:

[M]any of the attendees at the meeting revealed having their own rage, but somehow they perceived themselves—unlike the female offenders of domestic violence—as having a mechanism to manage it. This undefined mechanism seemed to be the boundary that separated the people at the meeting from the 'women offenders' they were discussing and considering for treatment purposes. (Ibid. 58)

Here we can see that their research emerged out of a fraught discussion and is explicitly framed as a critique of the idea that some people have the ability to possess 'an undefined mechanism' to control their feelings and others do not. One can hazard that those who have this 'ability' are more likely than not to be middle-class professional women. But Flemke and Allen do not pursue this. Nor do they reflect on their own practices. Their article proceeds to follow the standard academic practice of separating the researchers' selves from the emotionally drenched research material they elicit from their informants.

Over the years I have continually wondered at the ability of qualitative research-ers to cordon themselves off from the visceral aspects of their research material. Years of feminists writing the personal has yet to resolve the epistemological and methodological quandary of how one researches the subjective in a deeply radical way. By this I mean the very roots of the subjective, understood as rhizomatic connections of researched, researcher, and the research material.

IMMERSION AND DEEP PROXIMITY

I've argued elsewhere that researching the affective registers takes a toll on one's body and sense of self (2005*a*). One can swallow others' emotions, breathing in and taking on together emotional registers. Taking from Georges Devereux we begin to understand how profound this may be. In the 1960s Devereux founded an area of research called ethno-psychiatry. One of his most influential books is entitled *From Anxiety to Method in the Behavioral Sciences* (1967). Having first studied physics under the tutelage of Marie Curie, he trained as a psychoanalyst after completing a Ph.D. in anthropology. His work remains important in the clinical treatment of mental disorders in non-Western countries, and has also been influential in Gilbert Herdt and Robert Stoller's anthropological work on sexuality (Giami 2001).

Devereux's ideas on how methods within social science both protect and promote anxiety in the researcher are central to my ideas here. He argues that the singularity of the social sciences is that they deal with affective material: 'the analysis of man's conception of himself'. Of the three great revolutions—Copernicus, Darwin, and Freud—he remarks that, 'It was easier to be objective about the heavenly bodies than about man as an organism, and the latter easier than objectivity about man's personality and behavior' (1967: 3). The trouble and conversely the great potential of the sciences of man (in particular, anthropology, sociology, and some branches of psychology) lies in:

The difficulty in clearly distinguishing materials that come from outside (the subject, the field) and from inside (his or her own emotional reactions). The researcher has to struggle with these emotional reactions and anxieties . . . The researcher is, in one way or another, the subject and object of the knowledge that he/she elaborates. (Giami 2001)

Devereux puts his argument bluntly: 'In short, behavioral science data arouse anxieties, which are warded off by a counter-transference inspired pseudo-methodology; this manoeuvre is responsible for nearly all the defects of behav-ioral science' (1967: p. xvii). Devereux outlines three points essential to the production of the real data of behavioral science:

1. The behavior of the subject.
2. The 'disturbances' produced by the existence and observational activities of the observer.
3. The behavior of the observer: His anxieties, his defensive manoeuvres, his research strategies, his 'decisions' (= his attribution of a meaning to his observations). (1967: p. xix)

Following from this Devereux includes as data his attempts to understand his own behavior, both as a field ethnologist and as a clinical psychoanalyst. He also demands that his colleagues take notes on their own affective behavior. He asks for and receives from his colleagues written summaries of their dreams and symptomatic reactions sparked by discussions of their research material.

Elephants and Counting Horses

How might Devereux's ideas and methods be applicable to the affective swirls of bodies and space in the study of anorexic subjectivity? Schematically the space that Devereux gestures to is created through the co-presence of the researched and the researcher but it goes beyond mere proximity to create the inter- and intra-subjective as manifest. Focusing on this intersection or interstice may allow for a break or a rupture to open in the otherwise seamless discursive formation in which the girls, the institutional practices and knowledges, and the researchers are anchored. Paying full attention to the feelings in the in-between of the subject and object, the subjective and the objective may illuminate 'the elephant in the room'.

This phrase perfectly encapsulates the question of feelings within qualitative social scientific research. Emotion as a radical part of the research process constitutes 'an important and obvious topic, of which everyone present is aware, but which isn't discussed, as such discussion is considered to be uncomfortable'.[4] To underline my argument, this is not just talking about emotions and feelings but being attuned to how they perform an attunement of bodies, of inter- and intra-subjectivity within research processes.

The idea of attunement of articulation here comes from Bruno Latour and his band of actor-network thinkers. As we well know, ANT has forged an exciting way of thinking about science. Their objective could be flatly described as debunking the scientific quest for objectivity but it goes well beyond that. In Latour's words, 'whenever you want to understand a network, go and look for actors, but whenever

---

[4] http://www.phrases.org.uk/meanings/elephant-in-the-room.html, accessed Mar. 2009.

you want to understand an actor, go and look through the net at the work it has traced' (2002: 127).

In one of the more fascinating accounts in this vein, Vinciane Despret recounts an experiment conducted at the beginning of the last century, and then retrialed in the 1960s, to test subjectivity in the scientific research process. In 1904 a group of German experts (scientists, educators, circus trainers) gathered to examine the strange case of Mr von Osten's horse, Hans. Hans was a four year old who responded to questions about multiplication, division, and square root problems. He was also asked to spell words and differentiate between colours and tones in music. Hans would tap out the answers with his hoof. As Despret tells the tale, some thought Hans was a telepathist while most dismissed it as fraud. The professor of psychology Stumpf who wrote the report said that 'no signals or tricks "which are at present familiar" seemed to be involved' (Despret 2004a: 112). This wasn't good enough for one of his assistants, Oskar Pfungst, who went back to examine the case more rigorously. After much scrutiny he finds that 'unintentional minimal movements (so minimal that they had not been perceived until now) are performed by each of the humans for whom Hans had successfully answered the questions.... And no one among them knew they were doing so, no one among them noticed that their bodies were talking to the horse, telling him when to begin and when to stop' (ibid. 113).

What an amazing scene: the experts hunched over the horse that speaks loudly of the limitations of their observation. For Pfungst, and in the history of psychology, this case became a corner-stone example of the power of subjective influence, which would become such a problem in social science. As Despret puts it, 'Influence, which was for Pfungst the best way to study how experimentally bodies can "articulate" differently, became, for modern psychologists, a menace they strove to eradicate.' The urge to remove any and all factors of influence becomes the backdrop against which Devereux had to contend when he sought to reframe intra- and intersubjective feelings as a major source of rich data. As Despret frames it, 'the horse could not count, but he could do something more interesting: not only could he read bodies, but he could make human bodies be moved and affected, and move and affect other beings and perform things without their owners' knowledge' (ibid. 113).

In the 1960s an American behavioral psychologist, Rosenthal, sought to put the question of influence to the test, and as is so often the case he used his students. He told them that they were to experiment with specially bred rats who had become 'bright' over the generations of in-breeding, as well as with 'dull' ones. The students dutifully carried out the experiment of running them through mazes and indeed they found that the bright rats were bright and the dull ones dull. Rosenthal's underlying objective was to prove 'that little things "affect the subjects to respond differently than they would if the experimenter had been literally an automaton"' (cited in Despret 2004a: 117). So he had lied to his students about the rats—they were common-or-garden-variety lab rats. But because of how he had framed the rats' abilities he had led the students to care and to be invested in 'their' rats. Rosenthal could claim that he had recreated a scene of influence, and therefore could pinpoint what needed to be eradicated. Then as now the 'little things' that needed to be got rid of in the scientific process are care, affect, emotion, attention, and bodily attunement—the multi-directional flows between researcher and researched. Despret's argument goes well beyond a suggestion that the humans were or should be anthropomorphically invested in the rats. What seemingly happened in this situation was that through Rosenthal's instructions the humans cared about what the rats did and in turn the rats sensed this—through the careful handling and attention paid to them. The rats became part of the equation of rat–human or rat-with-human, human-with-rat.

Despret draws on William James's (1983) theory of emotion, which to be succinct we can sum up as we feel the emotion because we feel its affects ('we are sad because we cry'). Despret's interpretation of James's theory is crucial: '[I]t was not to define what is felt but what makes feels, it was not to describe a passive being, but rather a being that both produces emotions and is produced by them. An emotion is not what is felt but what makes us feel' (2004a: 126). While there are now many readings of James (Massumi 2002; Redding 1999) the idea of emotions making us feel is compelling. It allows for a radical understanding of the scientific process, which as Despret says can be seen in other notable scientists such as Konrad Lorenz—the founder of ethology and the study of animal behavior. What becomes clear in her discussion of Lorenz's empathy or attunement with his animal research subject was that he profoundly relocated himself 'with' them. This goes beyond notions of sympathy or empathy. 'Empathy allows us to talk about what it is to be (like) the other, but it does not raise the question of "what it is to be 'with' the other"' (Despret 2004a: 128).[5]

What Deleuze, Devereux, Despret, Lorenz, and others such as Tobie Nathan (Devereux's follower) trace out is an alternative path within the 'human sciences'. Latour and his followers can be said to be responding to the question Deleuze takes from Spinoza—that we do not know what a body can do, we do not know the full capacities of bodies (cf. Gatens 1996; Probyn 2004). Deleuze would offer other terms, such as the agencement and assemblage of bodies—human and non-human.[6] But he might have agreed with this statement of Latour's:

[5] While there is not the space to go into an in-depth discussion I want to flag the work of Tobie Nathan in this regard. Nathan who took up the mantle of Devereux's research and is the director of the Centre Georges Devereux has a fascinating interpretation of how to conduct ethnographic research cross-culturally. Much of his interest has been in how in so-called traditional cultures people are 'possessed' by spirits. He argues for ways of respecting different claims for describing the world and uses the idea of translation across these as the movement across different but genuine theories.

[6] And of course Deleuze (1992) has his own take on Lorenz, which elsewhere I've called a rhizo-ethology (2004). But the objective remains similar in ethos and even in method. Of course Deleuze

You cannot possibly speak and say that the things you speak about are not in some ways similar to you: they express through you a sort of difference that has you, the speaker, as one of their proprietors. What looks like an impossibility for the philosophy of identity, offers no difficulty for the philosophy of 'alterity'. Possession is another way of talking about translation. (2002: 130)

BEING POSSESSED

I have departed from the example of two feminist researchers valiantly setting out to document rage and anger only to find that they reproduce the same disembodied data, as is their discipline's wont. The problem is that they deviated from their initial insight or what could be more accurately called a research attunement when they caught the anger and angst in the room amongst the clinicians faced with the immensely strong passions of the women prisoners. With all the best intentions, they veer back into using method as anesthesia—a way of dampening down any transfer or translation between and among all the bodies in the research process. There is no possibility of 'possession' here; the researched cannot haunt the researcher.[7] Given the experiments I have discussed, if students come to care about their lab rats, and if this subtly alters the research process, how strange is it to refuse to admit the feeling generated in the inter- and intra-subjective research process with other humans?

I have also departed from my discussion of my own anger. What did it do in the research process? What could it have done better? At one level it reminds me of the passion that has driven much of my work. As Sedgwick puts it so well: 'I think many adults (and I am among them) are trying, in our work, to keep faith with vividly remembered promises made to ourselves in childhood: promises to make invisible possibilities and desires visible; to make tacit things explicit' (1993: 3). In terms of the research with the anorexic girls, I may have failed a promise I made to myself. It is an unwieldy one that may not be able to be fulfilled. The rough

---

was hardly a social scientist and his objects were of a different order than the science labs of Latour (Latour and Woolgar 1979) or the financial ecologies of Callon (1998).

[7] As researchers working in the areas of Holocaust studies and trauma, such as Dominick LaCapra, have argued, empathy in the strong sense is a deeply unsettling process. LaCapra defines this as the space wherein 'the other is recognized and respected as other' (2001: 212). He points to the 'after-effects—the hauntingly possessive ghosts—of traumatic events' (p. xi). LaCapra's field is history and his attention is to how to read traumatic accounts. But his insight about empathy as 'an affective relation, rapport of bond with the other recognized as other' (2000: 67) has resonance in my argument and project. Most obviously it curtails any desire to too readily identify with the other in ways that would overtake her singularity, her affects, and emotions.

contours have to do with imparting dignity to the choices and actions that people knowingly or unknowingly undertake, to lend part of my self to those who suffer—in this case—under the burdens of an institutional framing, which leaves them little room other than to cry out: 'I feel as if I'm made of glass . . . "Get out! Get out of me!"' (cited in Lester 1997: 484)

Despret describes the research process as a continual translation, which involves 'being a squatter in the interiority of the other' (2004*b*: 269). But equally it means translating from what one imagines to be that interiority into concrete interventions into how and why some girls and boys come to be imprisoned in a glass self. This is to say that one cannot stop at the insistence that the inter- and intra-subjective and its role within research are crucial. Anger, and more precisely an anger that drives the very project of epistemology, must continually wreak havoc with the rules that seek to govern research, which push the subjective off the agenda. And it must follow insights so preciously given by our informants, those who share in the research process.[8]

I have borrowed the metaphor of the self made of glass to reflect on the ways in which sufferers of anorexia are positioned within institutional regimes. But can we turn the metaphor around—to make it into a looking glass—to reflect on the layers of researcher's self? It is clear that different forms of the self and of subjectivity are put into motion each time we enter into the research process. We bring institutional training and experience, we bring previous stories of having been cautioned not to display our selves, we carry various amounts of empathy and personal experience into research encounters. Good, bad, and sad feelings comingle with years of discipline. Complicated histories render any simple transparency impossible. And yet we persist, trying to realize that 'a realistic science of mankind can only be created by [wo]men most aware of their own humanity precisely when they implement it most completely in their scientific work' (Devereux 1967: p. xvii).

REFERENCES

ABU-LUGHOD, LILA (1990). 'Shifting Politics in Bedouin Love Poetry', in Catherine A. Lutz and Lila Abu-Lughod (eds), *Language and the Politics of Emotion* (Cambridge and Paris: Cambridge University Press and Maison des sciences de l'homme), 24–45.

ALTHUSSER, LOUIS (1971). *Lenin and Philosophy, and Other Essays* (New York: Monthly Review Press).

---

[8] One outcome of my encounter with the girls and their love of cooking shows is to pursue questions about what food and cooking means within the worlds of anorexia. See also the important work of: Warin (2009) and Boughtwood and Halse (2008).

BOUGHTWOOD, DESIREE, and HALSE, CHRISTINE (2008). 'Ambivalent Appetites: Disso-
nances in Social and Medial Constructions of Anorexia Nervosa', *Journal of Community
and Applied Social Psychology*, 18: 269–81.

BRUMBERG, JOAN JACOBS (2000). *Fasting Girls: The History of Anorexia Nervosa* (New York:
Vintage).

CALLON, MICHEL (ed.) (1998). *The Laws of the Markets* (London: Blackwell Publishers).

DELEUZE, GILLES (1988). *Foucault*, tr. Sean Hand (Minneapolis: University of Minnesota
Press).

——(1992). 'Ethology: Spinoza and Us', in J. Crary and S. Kwinter (eds), *Incorporations*
(New York: Zone).

DESPRET, VINCIANE (2004*a*). 'The Body We Care for: Figures of Anthropo-zoo-genesis',
Body and Society, 10/2–3: 111–34.

——(2004*b*). *Our Emotional Make-up: Ethnopsychology and Selfhood*, tr. Marjolijn de Jager
(New York: Other Press).

DEVEREUX, GEORGES (1967). *From Anxiety to Method in the Behavioral Sciences* (The Hague:
Mouton & Co.).

FLEMKE, KIMBERLY, and ALLEN, KATHERINE R. (2008). 'Women's Experience of Rage:
A Critical Feminist Analysis', *Journal of Marital and Family Therapy*, 34/1: 58–74.

FOUCAULT, MICHEL (1984). *The Foucault Reader*, ed. P. Rabinow (New York: Pantheon).

GATENS, MOIRA (1996). 'Sex, Gender, Sexuality: Can Ethologists Practice Genealogy?',
Southern Journal of Philosophy, 34 (suppl.): 1–19.

GIAMI, ALAIN (2001). *Counter-Transference in Social Research: Georges Devereux and Beyond*
(Papers in Social Research Methods Qualitative Series, 7; London: LSE).

HALSE, CHRISTINE, HONEY, ANNE, and BOUGHTWOOD, DESIREE (2008). *Inside Anorexia:
The Experiences of Girls and their Families* (London: Jessica Kingsley Publisher).

JAMES, WILLIAM (1983). *Essays in Psychology* (Cambridge, Mass.: Harvard University Press).

LACAPRA, DOMINCK (2000). *History and Reading: Tocqueville, Foucault, French Studies*
(Melbourne: Melbourne University Press).

——(2001). *Writing History, Writing Trauma* (Baltimore: Johns Hopkins University Press).

LATOUR, BRUNO (2002). 'Gabriel Tarde and the End of the Social', in P. Joyce (ed.), *The
Social in Question: New Bearings in History and the Social Sciences* (London: Routledge).

——and WOOLGAR, STEVE (1979). *Laboratory Life: The Social Construction of Scientific Facts*
(London: Sage).

LESTER, REBECCA J. (1997). 'The (Dis)Embodied Self in Anorexia Nervosa', *Social Science
Medicine*, 44/4: 479–89.

MASSUMI, BRIAN (2002). *Parables for the Virtual: Movement, Affect, Sensation* (Durham,
NC: Duke University Press).

MYERS, FRED (1986). *Pintupi Country, Pintupi Self: Sentiment, Place, and Politics among
Western Desert Aborigines* (Washington, DC: Smithsonian Institution Press).

——(2006). 'We are Not Alone: Anthropology in a World of Others', *Ethnos*, 71/2: 233–64.

NATHAN, TOBIE (n.d. *a*). 'Georges Devereux and Clinical Ethnopsychiatry', tr. Catherine
Grandsard, http:www.ethnopsychiatrie.net (accessed Feb. 2009).

——(n.d. *b*). 'PTSD and Fright Disorders: Rethinking Trauma from an Ethnopsychiatric
Perspective', http:www.ethnopsychiatrie.net (accessed Feb. 2009).

NATHANSON, DONALD (1992). *Shame and Pride* (New York: W. W. Norton).

PROBYN, ELSPETH (1987). 'The Anorexic Body', in M. and A. Kroker (eds), *Body Invaders*
(New York: St Martin's Press).

——(1993). *Sexing the Self: Gendered Positions in Cultural Studies* (London: Routledge).

——(2000). *Carnal Appetites: Food Sex Identity* (New York: Routledge).

——(2004). 'Eating for a Living: A Rhizo-Ethology of Bodies', in H. Thomas and J. Ahmed Shweder (eds), *Cultural Bodies: Ethnography and Theory* (Oxford and Boston: Blackwell), 215–40.

——(2005*a*). *Blush: Faces of Shame* (Minneapolis: University of Minnesota Press).

——(2005*b*). 'Sex and Power: Capillaries and Capacities', in C. Calhoun, C. Rojek, and B. Turner (eds), *The Sage Handbook of Sociology* (London: Sage), 516–29.

REDDING, PAUL (1999). *The Logic of Affect* (Ithaca, NY: Cornell University Press).

SEDGWICK, EVE K. (1990). *Epistemology of the Closet* (Berkeley, Calif.: University of California Press).

——(1993). *Tendencies.* (Durham, NC: Duke University Press).

SHWEDER, RICHARD (1994). ' "You're not sick, you're just in love": Emotion as an Interpretive System', in P. Ekman and R. Davidson (eds), *Questions about Emotion* (New York: Oxford University Press).

SKARDERUD, FINN (2007). 'Shame and Pride in Anorexia Nervosa: A Qualitative Study', *European Eating Disorders Review*, 15: 81–97.

SPELMAN, ELIZABETH V. (1999). 'Anger: The Diary', in Robert C. Solomon (ed.), *Wicked Pleasures: Meditations on the Seven 'Deadly' Sins* (Lanham, Md.: Rowan & Littlefield), 117–32.

WARIN, MEGAN (2009). *Abject Relations: Everyday Worlds of Anorexia* (Brunswick, NJ: Rutgers University Press).

....

CHAPTER 30

THE POSTMODERN SELF

AN ESSAY ON ANACHRONISM AND POWERLESSNESS

....

LEONARD LAWLOR

JEAN-FRANÇOIS Lyotard's 1979 *The Postmodern Condition: A Report on Knowledge* introduced the term 'postmodern' into philosophical discourse (see Bennington 1988; Cahoone 1996; Williams 1998). Although Lyotard 'reports' that what makes the present historical period 'postmodern' is the transformation of knowledge into information, strictly the term does not refer to a particular historical epoch (Lyotard 1991*b*: 5). What defines postmodern thinking—regardless of the epoch in which it may appear—is *anti-Platonism*. Lyotard argues that the belief in a transcendent world of forms or any transcendent domain (however this may be conceived) that exists separately from the world of appearance or of experience is no longer tenable (Lyotard 1992: 9).[1] The general characterization of postmodernism as the demise of the belief in a transcendent domain has allowed the term's scope to be expanded beyond Lyotard's work to the work of Jacques Derrida, Michel Foucault, Gilles Deleuze, and Félix Guattari, to an entire generation of French philosophers who came of age in the Nineteen-Sixties (Descombes 1980: 180–6).

---

[1] See also Deleuze (1990: 253–65); Derrida (1981: 61–172); Foucault (1998: 369–91).

In order to indicate the demise of the belief in the transcendent, these philosophers sometimes point to Gödel's discovery that logical systems cannot be totalized (Lyotard 1984: 42–3; also Deleuze and Guattari 1994: 158; Derrida 1978: 53–4). Non-totalization means that no 'meta' or transcendent position outside the system can be established. For instance, thanks to Gödel, we know that the discourse on the rules which validate knowledge claims cannot be separate from the discourse within which those knowledge claims appear (Lyotard 1984: 54–5; also Lyotard 1988: 138). *Anti-Platonistic thought is immanentist thought.* Lacking a transcendent measure to hierarchize and systematize the discourses (or genres, as Lyotard would say[2])—a transcendent measure not only like a realm of forms but also like an origin or an end (a prelapsarian principle or a final purpose)—immanence results in differences among discourses, differences which cannot be ultimately unified. In other words, there is no one genus or genre of being (there is no unifying meaning of being); there are only multiplicities of things that exist (multiplicities of beings). *The primary consequence of immanence therefore is heterogeneity.*

Heterogeneity determines how the 'postmodernist' philosophers conceive the self. The postmodernist philosophers conceive the self as heterogeneous because they recognize that self-experience is conditioned by time. Because the self is conditioned by time, these philosophers argue that the self is always differentiated into past and future. In other words, the experience of time shows that self-experience does not originate with an identical self and it does not end with an identical self. The postmodernist self therefore is defined in this way: just as there is no transcendent measure for discourses, there is no identity constitutive of the self (or of the subject). Instead of identity, I find, inside of myself, difference: 'I is an other' (Deleuze 1994: 86).[3] The other in me turns the 'I', the self, into a 'we'.[4] But this 'we' is heterogeneous, and therefore not strictly a 'we' at all.

The fact that the self is a 'we' and yet that the 'we' is absent (that is, the 'we' is a collectivity but one that lacks unity) leads to what is really at issue in the postmodern self.[5] Since Hume, after all, had already criticized the personal identity conception of a continuous self (see Deleuze 1991a; Lyotard 1988: 61–3), what is at issue is not the

---

[2] The French word 'genre' should be heard in two ways, as referring to literary genres and to genera or kinds. So, the term in Lyotard is supposed to invoke not only language games as in Wittgenstein but also Aristotle's multiple meanings of being.

[3] Deleuze is quoting one of Rimbaud's 'Letters of a Visionary' (letter of 15 May 1871 to Paul Demeny): 'Je est un autre.'

[4] See Derrida (1982: 136). The final line of this essay is 'Mais qui, nous?', 'But who, we?' See also Deleuze and Guattari (1987: 159); here they ask, 'But who is this we that is not me . . . ?' Also Merleau-Ponty (1968: 3); here Merleau-Ponty asks, 'what is this we?' The question of who we are also drives Foucault's work in *The Order of Things* (1994), esp. in the famous ninth chapter, 'Man and his Doubles'. Also Foucault (2008: 14).

[5] For the concept of absent community, see Blanchot (1988: 15). See also Deleuze and Guattari (1987: 346).

individual self, but what Lyotard calls 'the social bond' (Lyotard 1984: 11).[6] To put this as clearly as possible, *what is at issue in the postmodern self is the political subject.*[7]

How is the political subject—called 'the people'—possible when immanence makes discourses, 'selves', and, most generally, beings, heterogeneous? The recognition that beings are heterogeneous (a heterogeneity which, as we shall see, is fundamental and irreducible) is really the reason why postmodernism consists in the loss of belief in any transcendent form of identity. But in particular, the recognition of heterogeneity has made the modern (or cosmopolitical) social bond at least questionable if not impossible. No longer, it seems, are we able to constitute the identity of a universal humanity by means of a large narrative about history having an end or purpose in absolute knowledge or universal freedom. As well, it does not seem possible to return (except perhaps under the guise of nationalism) to the wild social bond, in which a primitive tribe's identity is constituted by means of a small narrative about the origin of that tribe. Instead, in the postmodern epoch of the demise of the narrative constitution of the social bond, we find that something like a bond among peoples can be constituted by means of the criteria of optimal performance and efficiency, the building up of power and time; it is what Lyotard in his 1983 *The Differend* calls 'the hegemony of the economic genre' (Lyotard 1988: 178).[8] Here the economic seems to be the sole genre or genus of being; the economic seems to be the sole genre or genus of thinking. The dominance of the economic genre is 'the victory of capitalist technoscience' (Lyotard 1992: 18). The domination of global capitalism over every other genre of thinking and being, for Lyotard, amounts to a kind of totalitarianism (Lyotard 1992: 58 and 66–7; also Deleuze and Guattari 1987: 473). And therefore what is most at issue in the postmodern self is the attempt to conceive a 'we' which is not totalitarian (Lyotard 1988: p. xiii).[9]

The purpose of this chapter consists in determining the non-totalitarian postmodern conception of the 'we'. Although Lyotard's work (in particular his work from the late 1970s to the early 1980s) will play a central role, the ideas presented here derive from the work of all of the philosophers usually associated with postmodernism. The project of determining this 'we' divides into two problems. Thanks to Kant, we are able to formulate the first problem with the question: what

[6] The French is 'le lien social', which could also be rendered in English as 'the social link'.

[7] See Rancière (2009: 274–88). Rancière (1999) has also attempted to extend Lyotard's idea of a differend (see esp. pp. xi–xii).

[8] In his 1983 *The Differend*, however, he makes a much stronger claim than the claim that heterogeneity is irreducible, saying that the event of the Holocaust (the name 'Auschwitz') permanently disrupts the teleological constitution of a 'we'. See Lyotard (1988: 97–9; also 1989: 360–92). Lyotard's reflections on Auschwitz are inspired by Adorno. But Lyotard is not alone in making a claim such as this. Deleuze and Guattari (1994: 106–7) also speak of the 'shame at being human' in light of the Holocaust. And Derrida (2008: 26) has compared the killing of animals to the Holocaust and genocide.

[9] See also Gasché (2007: ch. 11), which concerns Lyotard and the honor of thinking.

ought we to be? (Lyotard 1988: 178). More precisely, if the victory of capitalist techno-science is a kind of totalitarianism, then the first problem consists in determining a 'we' that does not totalize or homogenize all the differences into a unity and identity. In other words, can there be a people that does not do violence to singularities? Is it possible for us to imagine such a people—a people somehow bound together and yet singular?

The second problem concerns the question of imagination. We can express it in this way: if the non-totalitarian people is absent, then how are we to call it forth? More precisely, if, as Lyotard shows, the social bond is constituted by narratives, by stories, then are we able to imagine a kind of narrative, a kind of literature, that would call forth a non-totalitarian people?

At the end, I suggest solutions to these two problems. Here are the two problems again: first, the determination of the non-totalitarian people, *and* second, the imagination of a literature that would constitute the non-totalitarian people. The solutions will be respectively the friends of passage and a literature of the secret. In this chapter, however, I shall be concerned not so much with the solutions, which are not sufficient, as with establishing the 'conditions' of the problems.[10] The true problem does *not* come into view if we think that the determination of a non-totalitarian people amounts to overcoming all obstacles to consensus among heterogeneous individuals, as if the goal were a universal people. The true problem comes into view only when we recognize that totalization (a universal people) is impossible and yet the dispersion into groups is also impossible. Posed in the terms of impossibilities, we see finally that the goal and the solution have changed, but also that the problem no longer looks to be an obstacle. Now the problem is a spur for more thinking, for more writing.

What stimulates more writing can be indicated with two words: anachronism and powerlessness. As we shall see, the conditions of impossibility called anachronism and powerlessness link in an inseparable and disunified way both heterogeneity and unity, both event and repeatability. We shall be able to discover these conditions however only if we start with individual not collective experience, with the self and not the people. It is incontestable that my self-experience is, as we have already indicated, temporally conditioned. Therefore we shall begin by reconstructing the descriptions of time presented by the two philosophical movements

---

[10] Here, I am appropriating what Deleuze has written about the problem. Deleuze (1994: 159) and Deleuze and Guattari (1996: 16–17) speak of the conditions of a problem as the terms and relations which allow the problem to be posed and which allow possible solutions to be considered. They also stress that the values of true and false apply to problems. Derrida (1993: 11–12) has stressed that a problem is a kind of shield which protects an experience or an idea from attempts to master it. It is also possible that this problem is more like a riddle, and the idea of conditions for it could be explained in terms of an extraordinary language game. On the 'great riddle' and solutions, see Diamond 1991: 267–89.

that have most influenced the postmodernist philosophers: phenomenology and Bergsonism.[11]

1. PHENOMENOLOGY AND BERGSONISM: THE BEGINNINGS OF POSTMODERNISM

Throughout their works, Husserl and Bergson had placed time at a foundational level: time is the absolute.[12] Both moreover had shown that the present never appears alone, never first. The present is always, necessarily, surrounded by the past and future. While the descriptions which Husserl and Bergson give of time— temporalization and duration—overlap conceptually (time not as discrete instants but as prolongation and thickness) and historically (both descriptions appear in the early years of the twentieth century), each contributes a novel aspect which must be stressed.

First Husserl (1964, 1983): Husserl describes temporalization in terms of the present perception, the living present, in a word, in terms of presence; the 'now-phase' is, so to speak, the 'center' of the living present, its 'eye'. Yet describing the thickness of time, Husserl insists that, always conjoined with the now, there is a 'retentional phase', that is, a repetition of what is no longer present. The non-presence of the repetitive retention, so to speak, gouges out the eye, leaving behind a hole, a kind of blindness. As we shall see, this blindness will play a crucial role in our attempt to determine a non-totalitarian people.

Now Bergson (1959c: 321; 1959b: 1402, 1959a): Bergson describes the duration— the inner flow of experience—as 'a multiplicity like no other' and as 'a unity like no other'. Negatively, the duration, according to Bergson, is not a 'spatial multiplicity', in which the members of the multiplicity are homogeneous, juxtaposed, and separate from one another, and therefore countable. Positively, the duration is a 'temporal multiplicity' in which the parts interpenetrate one another (producing the unity) and yet are different from one another (making them multiple).[13] Again we shall see that this multiplicity will play a crucial role in what follows.

---

[11] It is important to keep in mind that Lyotard wrote his first book on phenomenology in 1956 (Lyotard 1991a).

[12] This chapter continues an earlier text on postmodernism (Lawlor 2003, 'The Beginnings of Postmodernism: Phenomenology and Bergsonism, Derrida and Deleuze', pp. 109–22). I argue that postmodernism flows out of the philosophy of life.

[13] Deleuze and Guattari have drawn out the important consequences of Bergsonian multiplicity. See Deleuze and Guattari (1987: 8, 249, and 470).

These abbreviated descriptions of both Bergson and Husserl's important descriptions of time are based on their respective analyses by Deleuze in his *Bergsonism* and Derrida in his *Speech and Phenomena*.[14] Both analyses attempt to show that at an upper, perhaps constructed, level the experience of time looks to be either continuity or discontinuity. But deeper, more fundamentally, there is, below the holding of the past in retention (Husserl) and below the interpenetration of moments in the duration (Bergson), an irreducible link between what we can call a repeatability and an event. Derrida of course interprets the image of above and below in terms of the idea of a dismantling, a deconstruction ('deconstruction' being a term closely associated with 'postmodernism'). But if the upper level of the experience gives way to an irreducible link between two contradictory terms (a repetition necessarily includes no event and an event necessarily includes nothing repeatable), then we can speak of the irreducible link as 'the undeconstructable itself' (Derrida 1992: 15). We are not able to dismantle the structure of the experience any further. We can speak of the undeconstructable as the secret.

The secret of the phenomenological-Bergsonian descriptions lies in the fact that time is a medium that heterogenizes, that is, a continuity that discontinues. Lyotard (to whom we shall turn in a moment) perhaps expresses the secret best, when, in *The Differend*, he says that time is a conjunction, which 'allows the constitutive discontinuity (or oblivion) of time to threaten, while defying it through its equally constitutive continuity (or retention)' (Lyotard 1988: 66). Time consists in a link that disjoins as it joins. This heterogenizing link—or bond, as in the 'social bond'——affects all experience since all experience is conditioned by time. Every experience, necessarily, takes place in the present. In the present experience, there is the kernel or point of the now, the 'eye' of present perception (Husserl). What is happening right now, insofar as it is a kind of point, must be described as an event, different from every other now ever experienced; there is alteration. Yet, also in the present, the recent past is retained and what is about to happen is anticipated. The retention and the anticipation are based in a kind of repeatability (as the 're' of retention indicates). This fundamental 'repetition' results in continuity. In other words, because the present being experienced right now can be immediately recalled, it is repeatable and that repeatability therefore motivates the anticipation that the same thing will happen again. Opening up a horizon in which what is coming must appear, what is happening right now necessarily bears certain similarities to the retained past, which make the singular status of what is coming as an event questionable. The event is, in effect, also *not* different from every other now ever experienced; they interpenetrate (Bergson).

At the same time, the present experience is an event because it is a singular now and it is not an event because the experience necessarily includes a repetition; *at the*

---

[14] Derrida (1974); Deleuze (1991). With these descriptions, we are not far away from what Gallagher (1998: 178) has called 'prenoetic temporality'. When we speak of time being out of joint this disjointure is at least related to what Gallagher calls 'inordinance'.

same time, the present experience is alteration and it is not alteration because there is continuity. This 'at the same time', this simultaneity, is the crux of the matter. Because of temporalization, we can have no experience that does not essentially contain these two forces of event and repeatability in a relation of disunity *and* inseparability. In other words, because of temporalization, we are confronted with *two necessities* (the need to repeat and the need to singularize) related in an irreducibly necessary relation. As I already indicated, Derrida would call this irreducible necessary relation the undeconstructable itself; he would also call it *anachronism*, against time, never on time, always coming at the wrong time (Derrida 1993: 65). Time is out of joint, and we are *powerless* to put it in joint: *anachronism and powerlessness* (Deleuze 1994: 88; also Derrida 1994: 21).

The undeconstructable conjunction of disunity and inseparability implies that experience contains a difference which cannot be made coincident or be closed. If we follow the absolutism of Bergsonism and phenomenology, then we must say that whatever the self is, it is based on this experience, the experience of powerlessness. In temporalization we do not find juxtaposable and countable instants and therefore we do not find calculable possibilities. Instead, we find the impossibility of stopping repetition and singularization. It is impossible to foresee all the events that will come about within repetition; it is impossible to remember all the events which are being repeated. We cannot stop the contingency, the accidents, and the supplements from clouding our vision of what is being repeated, and we cannot stop the repetitions, the reproductions, and the essences from clouding our vision of the events. We cannot see ahead into what will happen in the future and we cannot see back into what has happened in the past. We cannot see the origin or the end. If the origin is conceived—as it always has been in philosophy—as self-identical, then we must say now, in light of our descriptions, that the origin had always been already, immediately divided. If we shift our focus to the future and think about the end, then we must say that the end will always be still, immediately divided. A prelapsarian and a postlapsarian principle, both of these principles are not possible.[15]

2. Transition from the Dissolved Self to the Social Bond: Hearing oneself Speak

The two impossibilities of origin and end anticipate the two ways in which narrative attempts to constitute the social bond. We have seen the two impossibilities are

---

[15] Descombes (1980: 182) calls this impossibility 'the supposition of the eternal recurrence'.

necessitated because phenomenology and Bergsonism make time absolute. This absolutism is truly anti-Platonistic if we recognize that Platonism conceives the transcendent world of forms as atemporal. But we must also recognize that the reversal of Platonism is the reversal from the priority of objects to the priority of the subject, the reversal from the priority of form to the priority of experience. The absolutism of phenomenology and Bergsonism is also *anti-Cartesian*, but only in the sense that it denies a substantial distinction between the subject and the object, between thought and extension. It remains Cartesian insofar as it pursues the sphere which Descartes opened up (even though Descartes does not himself investigate this sphere): the sphere of the subject, the soul, the cogito.[16] Therefore as a transition to our discussion of the social bond in postmodernism, we must more thoroughly investigate the sphere of the cogito. Unlike Plato, who in the *Republic* investigates the soul on the basis of an investigation of the *polis* (ii. 368c–369b), we (anti-Platonists) investigate the *polis* on the basis of an investigation of the soul.

In Plato's *Theaetetus*, we find thinking defined by means of an interior monologue (189e–190a), that is, by means of a kind of auto-affection. Until he proves in the Third Meditation that God exists, Descartes is also engaged in a kind of auto-affection, a meditation on himself. Indeed, the Cartesian formula of 'I think therefore I am' is an expression of auto-affection, since we find the same ego on both sides of the 'therefore'. If we progress in large steps across the history of philosophy, we see then that Descartes's cogito forms the basis for the Kantian idea of autonomy. The Kantian idea of autonomy of course means that I am self-ruling; I give the moral law to myself—unlike animal life, for instance, on which nature imposes its laws. But, in order to give the law to myself, I must tell it to myself. Kantian autonomy therefore rests on the specific form of auto-affection called 'hearing oneself speak'. Hearing oneself speak seems to include two aspects. On the one hand, I seem to hear myself speak *at the very moment* that I speak, and, on the other, I seem to hear *my own self* speak and not someone or something other. Let us now examine the particular experience of hearing oneself speak.

When I engage in interior monologue—when, in short, I think—it seems as though I hear myself speak at the very moment I speak. It seems as though my interior voice is not required to pass outside of myself, as though it is not required to traverse any space, not even the space of my body. So, my interior monologue seems to be immediate, immediately present, and not to involve anyone else. Interior monologue seems therefore to be different from the experience of me speaking to another *and* different from the experience of me looking at myself in the mirror, where my vision has to pass through, at the least, the portals of my eyes.

As in the discussion of time earlier, here too we are engaged in a kind of deconstruction, exposing the essential structure below what is apparent or believed.

---

[16] See Husserl (1970: sections 17–18). See also Heidegger (1996: section 21).

So, the problem with the belief that interior monologue (in a word, thought) is different from other experiences of auto-affection is twofold. On the one hand, the experience of hearing oneself speak is temporal (like all experience). The temporalization of interior monologue means, as we have just seen, that the present moment involves a past moment, which has elapsed and which has been retained. It is an irreducible or essential necessity that the present moment comes second; it is always involved in a process of mediation. The problem therefore with the belief that interior monologue happens *immediately* (as if there were no mediation involved) is that the *hearing* of myself is never immediately present in the moment when I *speak*; the hearing of myself in the present comes a moment later; there is a *delay* between the hearing and the speaking. This conclusion means that my interior monologue *in fact* resembles my experience of the mirror image in which my vision must traverse a *distance* that differentiates me into seer and seen.[17] I cannot, it is impossible for me to, hear myself immediately. But there is a further implication. The distance or delay in time turns my speaking *in the present moment* into something coming second. The descriptions of time have shown us that the present is not an origin all alone; it is compounded with a past so that my speaking in the present moment is no longer *sui generis*. Therefore it must be seen as a kind of response to the past.

The fact that my speaking is a response to the past leads to the other problem with the belief that interior monologue is *my own*. Beside the irreducible delay involved in the experience of auto-affection, there is the problem of the voice. In order to hear myself speak at this very moment, I must make use of the same phonemes as I use in communication (even if this monologue is not vocalized externally through my mouth). It is an irreducible or essential necessity that the silent words I form contain repeatable traits. This irreducible necessity means that, when I speak to myself, I speak with the sounds of others. In other words, it means that I find in myself other voices, which come from the past: the many voices are in me. Earlier in temporalization we discovered a kind of blindness; now in the auto-affection of hearing oneself speak, we discover a kind of deafness.[18] I cannot hear myself speak, it is impossible, but the inability to hear myself speak allows me to hear other voices, to hear a multi-vocality. Others' voices contaminate the hearing of myself speaking. Just as my present moment is never immediate, my interior

---

[17] Although time (temporalization and duration) has been the principal idea so far, space (the porous limit, the hiatus, and now distance) plays an equally important role. Fundamentally the hiatus is neither time nor space.

[18] Once again, I am trying to show that what is apparent is not the case or is founded on a different process. Indeed, with these descriptions and arguments, I am trying to bring this process to light. In both the case of blindness and deafness, I am trying to show that, when the domination of my self-reflection and my self-hearing breaks up, one experiences powerlessness: I cannot see myself clearly; I cannot hear myself speak immediately. But, and this is a crucial idea for the discussions of power, when I realize that I cannot see and hear clearly, I have the power to see and hear more. That is, instead of the restricted direction towards myself, I am now unrestricted and open to the voices and views of others.

monologue is never simply my own.[19] Quoting Deleuze again (who quotes Rimbaud), we can say, 'I is an other.' Because the 'I' is always necessarily a heterogeneous and differentiated multiplicity, a kind of 'we', the social bond or link is already anticipated in it. So let us now turn to the ways in which Lyotard thinks the *social bond* may be constituted and the consequence of these constitutions, which is *totalitarianism*.

3. The Social Bond and Totalitarianism

According to Lyotard, there are two complementary ways to use narratives in order to constitute the social bond, that is, in order to constitute the criteria of evaluating what is performed or what can be performed within a given collectivity (Lyotard 1984: 19; also Lyotard 1988: 155).[20] The narratives, in short, 'legitimate', as Lyotard says, but especially they constitute the identity of a people (Lyotard 1992: 39–43). The two uses of narrative are the wild or primitive (*le récit sauvage*) and the cosmopolitical or modern (Lyotard 1988: 155; also Lyotard 1984: 38).[21]

On the one hand, the primitive narrative—Lyotard always refers to the Brazilian tribe called the Cashinahua (see D'Ans 1978)—such as myths, tales, and legends, always concerns the origin of the tribe. In particular, the myths provide the origin of names, proper names, through which one who has this name now understands his position in the society (Lyotard 1988: 153). The narratives in other words set up a world of names, the Cashinahua world. In order to hear the narrative, you have to have a Cashinahua name, and in order to recite the narrative, you have to have a Cashinahua name. According to Lyotard, the sense of the story, which recounts the origin of the names, constitutes the social bond, but so does the present act of recitation. The narratives are repetitive; each narrative begins and ends with a fixed formula: 'On this date, in that place, it happened that, etc.' (Lyotard 1984: 21–2). Through the fixed formulas, the differences between each recitation are consigned to oblivion, and therefore it seems as though the stories were told 'forever' (ibid. 20). The stories seem to be at once evanescent and immemorial, as if the origin was always present and will always be present (ibid. 22). There seems to be no hiatus between the current narrator and the ancients, there seems to be no hiatus between the narrator and the hero of the story. In this way the 'we' of the Cashinahua, the identity of this one tribe, is what it has always been. Because these myths legitimate

[19] Fred Evans (2008) has developed an important conception of the voice. See esp. pp. 144–68 and 280–2.
[20] Here Lyotard speaks of 'the bond' (*le lien*) among the Cashinahua.
[21] In *The Postmodern Condition*, Lyotard of course cites Claude Lévi-Strauss (1966).

only the one particular tribe, they are, according to Lyotard, 'small narratives' (*récits petits*) or 'little stories' (*petites histoires*) (Lyotard 1988: 155).

In contrast to the wild narratives, cosmopolitical narratives tell a 'large story' (*grande histoire*) (ibid.). Like the wild narratives, the cosmopolitical ones are also concerned with legitimation and with establishing identity. According to Lyotard, the modern or cosmopolitical narratives ask this question: 'since this x, this date, and this place are proper names [like the Cashinahua], and since proper names belong by definition to worlds of names and to specific "wild" narratives, how can these narratives give rise to a single world of names and to a universal narrative?' (ibid.). The Cashinahua little stories allow the Cashinahua to distinguish themselves or even to make themselves an *exception* in relation to other humans. The universal history of humanity however consists in the extension of particular narratives to the entire set of human communities (ibid. 157). The extension is possible because here, unlike the primitive narratives which ground legitimacy in an original founding act, legitimacy in the modern narratives is grounded 'in a future to be brought about, that is, in an Idea to realize' (Lyotard 1992: 50). In contrast to the primitive narratives, the modern narratives do not tell a story of proper names, a story of particulars. They tell the story only of a general or universal name. Following German Idealism, Lyotard says that either we have a meta-narrative of spirit—an abstract and theoretical subject above humanity—which comes to know itself by overcoming ignorance, or we have an epic in which the people—a concrete and practical subject—emancipates itself from what prevents it from governing itself. Finally, unlike the primitive narratives which are evanescent and immemorial, the modern narratives consist in memory and projection, as if the end was intended in the past and will be fulfilled in the future (Lyotard 1984: 26; also 1992: 50).

We see the distinction Lyotard is trying to make in these kinds of narratives. Primitive narratives are little, while modern are large: particular versus universal; primitive narratives concern origins while modern concern ends: myth versus history (Lyotard 1992: 41); primitive narratives concern the proper name of a tribe, while modern concern the general name of humanity; and finally, primitive narratives are evanescent and immemorial, while modern narratives are projection and memorial: panchrony (which means constantly through time) versus diachrony (which means going through time toward an end). Overall, the distinction between primitive and modern narratives is the difference between an original social identity and a final social identity.

As I noted at the beginning, when Lyotard was making his report on knowledge, near the end of the twentieth century, the belief in the modern, cosmopolitical large narratives was in decline: postmodernism is arising. Since the 1980s (*The Differend* was originally published in 1983), perhaps we have seen as well the return of primitive narratives under the heading of a revitalized nationalism (for example, in the Balkan states). But more clearly, as Lyotard himself notes, and here he coincides with Deleuze and Guattari and with Derrida, we have seen the rise, after the dissolution of the Soviet Union, of global capitalism (Lyotard 1988: 179; also Deleuze and Guattari 1987: 492; Derrida 1998: 42–3). Becoming global, capitalism makes the economic genre hegemonic over all other genres or kinds of discourse, over all other modes of thought, over all other genera of beings. By means of globalization, the economic genre seems to be universal; it seems to form a kind of unity among peoples since now there seems to be a universal way of speaking, of thinking, of being (Lyotard 1988: 177). What becomes universal with the economic genre is the criterion of optimal efficiency or optimal performativity (Lyotard 1984: 41–7 and 64). This criterion allows 'the tribunal of capitalism' to resolve all disputes and to resolve them as efficiently and as quickly as possible.

The criterion of efficiency indicates that the economic genre has a specific relation to time (ibid. 61). For Lyotard, the work that goes into production does not expend energy; it expends time. Work 'stocks up time' in the product (Lyotard 1988: 174). It is then the amount of stocked-up time which determines the value of the product. As well, money amounts to stocked-up time since it is or ought to be the more or less faithful equivalent of the product's values (i.e. the faithful equivalent of the time incorporated in the product). But having more capital means having more time and having more time means having the ability (or power) to gain more time. Time is here not the experience of temporalization and duration which I analyzed above, temporalization and duration always including the heterogeneity and contingency of the event, its incalculability and unforeseeability. Here time must be countable, a quantity about which we can calculate. What follows from Lyotard's definition of value in terms of countable time is that exchange of products consists in the attempt to recover or, better, 'to cancel' the time lost in work (Lyotard 1988: 175). However, the more delays there are in the process of exchange, the more time is lost. So, as Lyotard says, 'we see what the ideal is: to make up time *immediately*' (ibid. 176; my emphasis). The ideal is to have the smallest hiatus or distance in between the exchange. The goal of economic genre is to get time back as quickly as possible. If the small primitive narratives are panchronic and the large modern narratives are diachronic, then the economic genre is *ortho-chronic*, that is, it aims at traversing time as quickly as possible so that the payment is paid back never at the *wrong* time, always at the *correct* time, *on time. The economic genre demands that there must be no anachronism.*

And yet the economic genre is *hyper-chronic* insofar as it wants to gain as much time as possible: not just equal to the quantity of lost time, but *more time.* Because of this 'more', always more, the economic genre seems to resemble universal history: everyone is making progress toward having more time for doing things, more time for adventures (Lyotard 1988: 178). But in fact, the aim of gaining time is nothing but a quasi-aim since the economic genre never asks the question of what we ought to be. Global capitalism therefore shifts the emphasis from ends (from finality) to means (Lyotard 1984: 37; also 1988: 179). The question constantly being asked in the economic genre is: what are the most efficient means to gain more time (that is, to gain more capital)? In order to find answers to this question, the economic genre engages in stories, simulations (which are really calculations) of possibilities, probabilities, and improbabilities (Lyotard 1988: 148). The economic stories however are only exercises in hypothetical thinking. The only concern of the economic genre lies in the possibility of gaining more time: *power and hyper-chronism*. We can see already that with its quasi-end of gaining time, the economic genre is totalitarian (or global): 'the complete hegemony of the economic discourse' (Lyotard 1992: 58).

For Lyotard, however, the two narrative modes of constituting the social bond are also totalitarian.[22] We have seen that the tradition of the Cashinahua myths about the origin legitimate obligations and prescriptions through the authority of the Cashinahua name. The legitimation is total since it is based in the totality of life instituted by the narratives. But more importantly, for Lyotard, any event, human or natural, for which there is no Cashinahua name has no authority to exist since it is not part of the whole of life set up by the Cashinahua myth of the origin of names. The myths therefore allow the Cashinahua to see themselves as the exception among peoples: again, they are the 'the true men' (Lyotard 1992: 46). There is no question of the final identity of the 'we', an identity to be accomplished in the future, since the Cashinahua narrative always says that we ought to be what we are—Cashinahua (ibid. 49). Importantly, Lyotard shows how the primitive narrative function has a modern significance. He extends the myth of origin legitimation to the Nazis who developed the fabulous stories of the 'Aryan ancestors'. In the Nazi myths, the Aryans are the 'true men', the exception among peoples, and just as in the Cashinahua myths there is no question of a future 'we' to be accomplished: 'We ought to be what we are—Aryan.' In the myth of Aryan origin, other peoples then do not participate in the vital principle of the Aryans; therefore all that remains to be done is finish them off, *exterminate* them (ibid. 51–2).

Now let us turn to the large modern narrative function. So, in contrast to the primitive myths of origin, the modern large myths are myths of a future to be brought about, an idea to be realized: the idea of universal freedom or enlightenment. For this idea to come into realization, it must be the case that a singular people's identity passes through an identity crisis, that is, its identity must decompose or fissure (ibid. 52). In other words, the proper name of this people must be questioned, turning the people into a mass or a crowd (Lyotard 1992: 56; also Deleuze and Guattari 1987: 33).[23] Then the mass asks itself what they ought to be. But this self-questioning opens up an equivocation in the concept of the people. This equivocation is perhaps Lyotard's greatest contribution to political philosophy.

[22] Here I am relying on Lyotard's 1984 essay called 'Memorandum on Legitimation' which is found in Lyotard (1992).
[23] Deleuze and Guattari cite Elias Canetti (1966).

With the concept of the people, one does not know whether what is being invoked is based on the tradition of a narrative of origin or on a tendency toward the idea of freedom. In other words, the name of a people—the French people, for example, in the 1789 Declaration of the Rights of Man—encompasses at once the singularity of a contingent community and the incarnation of a universal sovereignty (Lyotard 1992: 53; also 1988: 97 9).[24] The equivocation implies that the ideal community already seems to be real; the people already seem to know how to name themselves. For Lyotard, the equivocation in the concept of the people leads once more to the Nazis. In the 1930s, the Nazi cure for the German community's identity crisis consisted in presenting (in their 'festivals') the Aryan myths as the exceptional people (*das Volk*) who imparts its name to the end pursued by human history. The Nazis do not simply say, 'Let us become what we are—Aryans'; they say, 'Let the whole of humanity be Aryan' (Lyotard 1992: 56). For the Nazis, the imparting of this name to everyone led to the violence of a world war. Therefore, as Lyotard shows, because of the equivocation in the concept of the people, the modern myths are different from the primitive myths only in terms of the size of their domination. Both are totalitarian insofar as they produce an identity that dominates an entire collectivity such as a tribe ('the Cashinahua') or an identity that dominates all humans ('the Aryans'): 'the true men'. These myths however are totalitarian in a more dangerous sense: they exterminate anything heterogeneous or contingent, the non-exceptional singularities, that might disturb the identity.

4. CONCLUSION: THERE WILL NEVER BE ENOUGH WRITTEN

In Lyotard's writings, the term 'postmodern' has four registers. First, the term refers to an epoch, the twentieth century, and now, Lyotard would say, the twenty-first century. Second, the term 'postmodern' refers, within current times, to the decline of belief in the large narratives of humanity making progress toward the purpose of universal freedom and absolute knowledge. The third and fourth registers derive from the decline of the belief that history has a purpose or end. So, third, the term 'postmodern' refers to what replaces the belief or what is victorious over the belief: capitalist techno-science. Here knowledge must be transformed into information and processed as rapidly as possible in order to gain time. In this third register, postmodernism refers to the aim of the stocking up of time (countable units of

---

[24] Balibar (2009) discusses Lyotard's discovery of this equivocation.

time) and therefore of calculable possibilities: hyper-chronism and power. In this case, what defines postmodernism is the hegemony of the economic genre, its kind of totalitarianism. But then fourth, what contests the hegemony of the economic genre is immanentist thinking,[25] a genre of thinking that revolves around two problems. In fact, these two problems define the most positive sense of postmodernism. If the social bond is what the postmodern self truly concerns, then two problems define the postmodern self. The two problems concern the constitution of a non-totalitarian 'we'. We shall conclude by suggesting solutions to them.

At the beginning we were able to formulate the first problem with Kant's help, his question of what we ought to be. But now we are able to formulate the problem more precisely with this question: is a social bond possible which does not bind in a totalitarian way—as we have seen both the small primitive narratives and the large modern narratives are totalitarian—and more precisely does not bind by means of the aim of gaining more time and having more calculable possibilities, which does not succumb to the economic goal of power? The condition for this problem lies in time. By means of panchronism, diachronism, and hyper-chronism, these modes of constituting the social bond aim to shelter the social identity from contingency and heterogeneity. Yet, as we have seen, the absolute of temporalization or duration necessarily includes contingency and heterogeneity. Therefore, anachronism always persists despite and below these other chronisms (Lyotard 1988: 144).

We are able therefore to formulate a solution to this problem by reflecting more on anachronism. Time is fundamentally ana-chronic because time temporalizes or endures by means of two forces, the force of repetition and the force of singularization, the force of universality and the force of event. The necessity of these two forces is so strong that we are powerless *not* to obey their command. But if we are unable not to obey, *then we are able.* We are subjected to the two forces, but they also enable us. If we are unable to stop repetition and if we are unable to stop singularization, we are able to be unable. In other words, our powerlessness gives us a kind of power. Unable to stop repetition, we are able to let it happen; unable to stop singularization, we are able to let it happen. Instead of calculable possibilities, our ability to be unable opens up an incalculable and uncontrollable potentiality. Therefore, unlike the economic genre which calculates in order to make the hiatus pass as quickly as possible, we devote ourselves to the passing of time, letting the hiatus take the time it needs, stretching the link out as long as possible. We devote ourselves, which takes time, to being blind and deaf, a blindness to what cannot be seen: totality, homogeneity, and identity—in order to see better, in order to see heterogeneity, to see difference, and contingency; a deafness to what cannot be heard: my own or own voice—in order to listen better, to hear the multi-vocality of

---

[25] In *The Postmodern Condition*, Lyotard calls this genre of thinking 'paralogy'. See Lyotard (1988: 61).

all living things. This ability to be unable amounts to a new sensitivity, a sensitivity that turns away from the molar and majoritarian forms toward the micro and minor informalities. Taking up the equivocation in the concept of the people which Lyotard has pointed to, we contest the singularity of a people in order to make it pass into universality, in order to pass over the limit and become otherwise; we contest the universality of a people in order to make it pass into singularity, in order to pass over the limit and become otherwise. There would be no consensus here just as there would be no dispersion. This would be a people who does the least violence to singularities because it is unified around powerlessness. So far, I have only used a negative name for this 'we' who are bound together by the power of powerlessness: non-totalitarian. Now, I am able to give it a positive name: *the friends of passage*. Friends however require names, proper names, and the question of the name brings us to the second problem.

How are we able to call forth these friends of passage? Lyotard has shown that the social bond of a people is based in narratives, in stories or histories, in literature in a broad sense. But he has also shown that both the primitive myths of origin and the modern myths of end constitute a people who are totalitarian. He has pointed out as well that even the economic genre, which is totalitarian in its own way, makes use of stories insofar as it simulates hypothetical possibilities, foreseeable future outcomes of possible means. We must therefore try to imagine a literature that differs from all of these kinds of stories. As we have seen, the anachronism of time implies that there is no experience that does not include a repetition. The primacy of repetition means that there is no original identity or original presence being repeated. In other words, if repetition is necessarily first, then we are never able to know what is being repeated. Likewise, anachronism shows that there is no experience that does not include an event; if an event is necessarily last, then we are never able to know what is going to happen. Due to this inability to know, we can suddenly imagine a kind of story. It would concern *a secret*. Throughout the story two questions would remain unanswered because they are unanswerable: what happened and what is going to happen?[26] No calculation of means and ends would be possible here. This literature would recount the unrememorable and the unforeseeable. In the story, perhaps there would be a central character with a proper name; or perhaps the story would be recounted in a letter addressed to someone with a proper name. The proper name would not indicate a self in the traditional sense, a singular identity. No, it would indicate a singular potentiality. Unable to find the answers to the questions of what happened and what is going to happen, being deaf and blind, this person or persons would hear and see better. They would hear and see better the others within themselves, allowing them to become otherwise. And then their proper names would no longer be appropriate. They

---

[26] This discussion is based on Plateau 8 (Deleuze and Guattari 1987); also see Deleuze and Guattari (1986). Also Derrida's work on friendship and the name (1997; 1995: 89–127).

would no longer know what name is proper to them. Other names would be needed and therefore other letters addressed to other addressees. In the end we would have neither the small narrative of one proper name (the Cashinahua) nor the large narrative of one proper name (the Aryans), but an ever-changing cloud of stories calling forth these friends whose proper names are never able to be appropriate because they are letting others pass.[27] However, as I said a moment ago, friendship is not possible without knowing the other person's proper name. Therefore this friendship will never be present, this people will never be complete. The people will always be in the future and still coming, which means that whatever we write, *it will not be sufficient*.[28] We must continue to write more: never will there be enough written in the name of passage.[29] Writing more, we recognize that the self (either individual or collective) is always absent (there is no original identity) and always to come (there is no final purpose). Writing more, we recognize (we postmodernists) that the problem of the self is more than an obstacle. It is a spur to thinking.[30]

REFERENCES

BALIBAR, E. (2009). 'Derrida and "The Aporia of Community"', *Philosophy Today*, 53: SPEP suppl. 'Continental Philosophy: Between Past and Future (Selected Studies in Phenomenology and Existential Philosophy)', vol. 34): 5–18.

BENNINGTON, G. (1988). *Lyotard: Writing the Event* (New York: Columbia University Press).

BERGSON, H. (1959a). *Essai sur les données immédiates de la conscience*, in *Œuvres* (Édition du Centenaire; Paris: Presses Universitaires de France). English tr. F. L. Pogson, *Time and Free Will* (Mineola, NY: Dover Publications, 2001).

——(1959b). 'Introduction à la métaphysique', in *Œuvres* (Édition du Centenaire; Paris: Presses Universitaires de France). English tr. T. E. Hulme, *Introduction to Metaphysics* (New York: Palgrave Macmillan, 2007).

——(1959c). *Matière et mémoire*, in *Œuvres* (Édition du Centenaire; Paris: Presses Universitaires de France). English tr. N. M. Paul and W. S. Palmer, *Matter and Memory* (New York: Zone Books, 1994).

BLANCHOT, M. (1988). *The Unavowable Community*, tr. P. Joris (Barrytown, NY: Station Hill Press).

CAHOONE, L. (ed.) (1996). *From Modernism to Postmodernism* (Oxford: Blackwell Publishers).

CANETTI, E. (1966). *Crowds and Power* [original German title: *Masse und Macht*], tr. Carol Stewart (New York: Viking Press).

---

[27] Lyotard makes use of the image of a cloud. See Lyotard (1988: pp. xxiv and 64).

[28] This entire chapter extends ideas I formulated in Lawlor (2007).

[29] This sentence alludes to something that Deleuze and Guattari say: 'In short, we think that one cannot write sufficiently in the name of an outside' (1987: 23).

[30] This sentence indicates the great debt that postmodernism has to Heidegger (see Heidegger 1968). It is Deleuze (1988: 116) who most stresses this question.

D'Ans, M.-A. (1978). *Le Dit des vrais hommes* (Paris: Union générale d'éditions).

Deleuze, G. (1988). *Foucault*, tr. S. Hand (Minneapolis: University of Minnesota Press).

——(1990). *The Logic of Sense*, tr. M. Lester, with C. Stivale (New York: Columbia University Press).

——(1991*a*). *Empiricism and Subjectivity*, tr. C. V. Boundas (New York: Columbia University Press).

——(1991*b*). *Le Bergsonism*, tr. Hugh Tomlinson and Barbara Habberjam (New York: Zone Books).

——(1994). *Difference and Repetition*, tr. Paul Patton (New York: Columbia University Press).

——and Guattari, F. (1986). *Kafka: Toward a Minor Literature*, tr. D. Polan (Minneapolis: University of Minnesota Press).

——and ——(1987). *A Thousand Plateaus*, tr. B. Massumi (Minneapolis: University of Minnesota Press).

——and ——(1994). *What is Philosophy*, tr. H. Tomlinson and G. Burchell (New York: Columbia University Press).

Derrida, J. (1974). *Speech and Phenomena*, tr. David B. Allison (Evanston, Ill.: Northwestern University Press).

——(1978). *Edmund Husserl's Origin of Geometry: An Introduction*, tr. John P. Leavey, Jr. (Stony Brook, NY: Nicolas Hays Ltd.).

——(1981). *Dissemination*, tr. Barbara Johnson (Chicago: University of Chicago Press).

——(1982). *Margins of Philosophy*, tr. Alan Bass (Chicago: University of Chicago Press).

——(1992). 'Force of Law: The Mystical Foundation of Authority', tr. Mary Quaintance, in Drucilla Cornell, Michael Rosenfeld, and David Gray Carlson (eds), *Deconstruction and the Possibility of Justice* (New York: Routledge).

——(1993). *Aporias*, tr. T. Dutoit (Stanford, Calif.: Stanford University Press).

——(1994). *Specters of Marx*, tr. P. Kamuf (London: Routledge).

——(1995). *On the Name*, ed. T. Dutoit (Stanford, Calif.: Stanford University Press).

——(1997). *Politics of Friendship*, tr. G. Collins (London: Verso).

——(1998). 'Faith and Knowledge', tr. Samuel Weber, in Jacques Derrida and Gianni Vattimo (eds), *Religion* (Stanford, Calif.: Stanford University Press).

——(2008). *The Animal that Therefore I am*, tr. David Wills (New York: Fordham University Press).

Descombes, V. (1980). *Modern French Philosophy*, tr. L. Scott-Fox and J. M. Harding (Cambridge: Cambridge University Press), 180–6.

Diamond, C. (1991). *The Realistic Spirit: Wittgenstein, Philosophy, and the Mind* (Cambridge, Mass.: MIT Press).

Evans, F. (2008). *The Multivoiced Body: Society and Communication in the Age of Diversity* (New York: Columbia University Press).

Foucault, M. (1994). *The Order of Things* (New York: Vintage).

——(1998). 'Nietzsche, Genealogy, History', tr. Donald F. Bouchard and Sherry Simon, in *Essential Works of Foucault 1954–1984*, ii. *Aesthetics, Method, and Epistemology* (New York: New Press), 369–91.

——(2008). *Le Gouvernement de soi et des autres* (Paris: Gallimard Seuil).

Gallagher, S. (1998). *The Inordinance of Time* (Evanston, Ill.: Northwestern University Press).

Gasché, R. (2007). *The Honor of Thinking* (Stanford, Calif.: Stanford University Press).

HEIDEGGER, M. (1968). *What is Called Thinking*, tr. J. Glenn Gray (New York: Harper Colophon).

——(1996). *Being and Time*, tr. J. Stambaugh (Albany, NY: SUNY Press).

HUSSERL, E. (1964). *The Phenomenology of Internal Time-Consciousness*, tr. James Churchill (The Hague: Martinus Nijhoff Publishers). French tr. H. Dussort, *Leçons pour une phenomenology de la conscience intime du temps* (Paris: Presses Universitaires de France, 1964).

——(1970). *The Crisis of European Sciences and Transcendental Phenomenology*, tr. D. Carr (Evanston, Ill.: Northwestern University Press).

——(1983). *Ideas Pertaining to a Pure Phenomenology and to a Phenomenological Philosophy: First Book*, tr. Fred Kersten (The Hague: Martinus Nijhoff Publishers). French tr. P. Ricoeur, *Idées directrices pour une phenomenologie* (Paris: Gallimard, 1950).

LAWLOR, L. (2003). *Thinking through French Philosophy: The Being of the Question* (Bloomington, Ind.: Indiana University Press).

——(2007). *This is Not Sufficient: An Essay on Animality and Human Nature in Derrida* (New York: Columbia University Press).

LÉVI-STRAUSS, C. (1966). *The Savage Mind* (Chicago: University of Chicago Press).

LYOTARD, J.-F. (1984). *The Postmodern Condition*, tr. Brian Massumi (Minneapolis: University of Minnesota Press).

——(1988). *The Differend*, tr. Georges Van Den Abbeele (Minneapolis: University of Minnesota Press).

——(1989). 'Discussions, or Phrasing "After Auschwitz"', in *The Lyotard Reader*, ed. Andrew Benjamin (Oxford: Blackwell Publishers), 360–92.

——(1991*a*). *Phenomenology*, tr. B. Beakley (Albany, NY: SUNY Press).

——(1991*b*). *The Inhuman*, tr. Geoff Bennington and Rachel Bowlby (Stanford, Calif.: Stanford University Press).

——(1992). *The Postmodern Explained*, tr. Don Barry, Bernadette Maher, Julian Pefanis, Virginia Spate, and Morgan Thomas (Minneapolis: University of Minnesota Press).

MERLEAU-PONTY, M. (1968). *The Visible and the Invisible*, tr. A. Lingis (Evanston, Ill.: Northwestern University Press).

RANCIÈRE, J. (1999). *Disagreement: Politics and Philosophy*, tr. J. Rose (Minneapolis: University of Minnesota Press).

——(2009). 'Should Democracy Come? Ethics and Politics in Derrida', in P. Cheah and S. Guerlac (eds), *Derrida and the Time of the Political* (Durham, NC: Duke University Press).

WILLIAMS, J. (1998). *Lyotard: Toward a Postmodern Philosophy* (Cambridge: Polity Press).

....

SELF, SUBJECTIVITY, AND THE INSTITUTED SOCIAL IMAGINARY

....

LORRAINE CODE

> On ne naît pas femme: on le devient.
> One is not born, but rather becomes, a woman.
>
> (Beauvoir 1989: 267; 1949: i. 285)

While the Anglo-American ('liberal') tradition tends to speak about the 'self', the French tradition tends to speak about the 'subject'...The concept of 'self' is closely tied to the notion of property. I speak of 'my'self. In the English tradition, the notions of 'self' and 'property' are inseparable from the notion of 'rights'....The French tradition, derived most importantly from Descartes's 'I think, therefore I am', centers on the importance of reason or thought as the foundation of (human) being. Where the 'self', as property, resembles a thing, the 'subject', as reason, resembles a grammatical function. . . . in the sentence 'I think, *therefore* I am,' what is posited is that it is *thinking* that gives the subject being.

(Johnson 1993: 3)

I

How a female infant becomes a woman, a self; how she enacts her subjectivity, is no simple matter of growing freely and unfettered into adult womanhood, but rather of learning her place—and continuing throughout her life to find, define, and occupy a place—in and within, or on the fringes and in defiance of, a social imaginary where the very possibilities of being and becoming are enshrined. Starting from the quotations I have cited, and reading Johnson's reference to Descartes through a reconstructed Cartesianism, where 'thinking' and grammaticality expand to encompass discursive practices, actions, and relationships constitutive of becoming,[1] I will examine some effects of the tension between self and subjectivity in feminist philosophy in the early twenty-first century. Johnson observes: 'while Descartes saw a *coincidence* of human thinking with human being, Lacan sees a *disjunction*... an illusion of the stable self [that] motivates a lifelong attempt to "catch up" to the image'. In a Foucauldian disciplinary society, she notes, this subject becomes 'a function of what a given society defines as thinkable' (1993: 6). Here I will approach the self-subjectivity tension as productive, not aporetic.

The subject—the knowing subject, the moral-political subject—has often, and indeed variably along the lines Johnson draws—been invisible in philosophy, as the unaddressed and unspecified presence behind or within analyses of knowing, being, and acting. Yet theories of knowledge, ethical theories, political theories all (if tacitly) work from and are constituted in their background assumptions and their substance by sedimented, often merely taken for granted, conceptions of subjectivity that inform their descriptive and normative substance. Thus theories of knowledge for which 'the knower' is merely a vehicle through which information passes on the way to becoming public knowledge work with a thin conception of infinitely replicable knowers who could be anyone or no one; it matters neither way to the substance of the theory or the knowledge produced. Indeed, the worry is that if subjectivity or individuated selves were allowed to matter, objectivity would be compromised. Analogously, ethical theories for which it matters not who the moral agent is, for she or he is a mere place-holder in the formal structure of the moral judgement, work with a thin conception of human selves as interchangeable in the sense that their particularity, their specificity, is of no account. It should be kept out of the picture if moral principles are to be impartially enacted, moral agency is to be impartially performed, and good is to be done. In this chapter, I contest these assumptions, and interrogate the social imaginary that holds them in place.

[1] Consider Debra Bergoffen's comment in a different context that, following Maurice Merleau-Ponty, she sees humanity 'as a species that transforms itself through its linguistic practices' (Bergoffen 2006: 11).

I propose that a viable feminist analysis has to start from a recognition that selves/ subjects are always embodied and situated—always gendered, raced, and otherwise multiply identified—and details of their specificity and positioning are germane to understanding how they are, as human selves/subjects, thrown together and thrown into a complex, rich, challenging, often intractable world, both human and other-than-human. Taking subjectivity into account is crucial for making viable epistemological and moral-political theories and acting according to their principles.[2]

It would oversimplify the issue to propose that conceptions of the self in feminist philosophy, whether at the beginning of the second wave or now, in the early twenty-first century, fall neatly into one of the conceptual frames Barbara Johnson designates: the Anglo-American self or Francophone-derived subjectivity. It would be implausible to suggest that they, together or separately, offer the only available options or that they have ever been so neatly compartmentalized. But Johnson's division, read with and against Beauvoir's famous dictum, opens a way into reading and evaluating the implications of feminist interpretations of the self in English-language philosophy: it suggests some paths to follow, some threads to trace.

The liberal conception of the unified self—ideally self-sufficient, self-making, secure in its self-ownership and transparent to itself, striving for individual rational autonomy and defending its rights—functioned as a human ideal for many white affluent Anglo-American feminists of the early second wave. This implicitly male self, derived in large measure from post-Kantian and liberal ethical-political theory, stood as an exemplar of the rights and possibilities feminists who argued for equality sought to achieve. In these strivings, the symmetrical structure of equality tended to disappear from view in arguments for women's equality with men, which they would realize by emulating that very autonomous liberal self and participating in its achievements. That goal has continued, albeit with variations, to play a regulative part in liberal feminist theory into the twenty-first century, and its achievements are not to be dis- counted. But recognition that such putatively autonomous self-realization has in practice been available only to a very specific class of men in white affluent societies initially took second place to its idealization as a universal human achievement which feminists must strive to realize. Its limited scope notwith- standing, this conception has exerted descriptive and normative force in uphold- ing a (descriptive) exemplar of what human beings can be, and conveying strong (normative) directives as to what they should be. This same liberal political- moral ideal has played a constitutive part in mainstream theories of knowledge, setting standards for how knowing subjects ought to be and how they can and

---

[2] See my 'Taking Subjectivity into Account', in Alcoff and Potter (1993); Code (1995).

should know, and enshrining a regulative conception of objectivity, cleansed of situational and subjective specificity. Some version of this idealized masculine self shaped early versions of feminist epistemology, confirming that received conceptions of self-or-subjectivity and ethics, epistemology, political philosophy are reciprocally constitutive and need to be analysed and understood accordingly. Their reciprocal influence is apparent in how the epistemic injunctions a theory of knowledge instantiates attest to deeply sedimented, if often merely tacit, beliefs about the 'nature' and capacities of knowing subjects, as ethical-political injunctions attest to analogous assumptions about human capacities for realizing the 'oughts' that comprise their substance. Despite his invisibility in epistemological and moral-political normative principles, this abstract moral-political-epistemic agent with his capacity for autonomous, self-sufficient being, doing and knowing is the presumptive 'self' whose intellectual and practical potential is taken for granted in theories and practices where he occupies the subject position. Such theories are tailor-made to fit the presumed scope and limits of his imagined subjectivity.

There are numerous points of entry into considering how this self has come to be. Revisiting Johnson's reference to 'the importance of reason or thought as the foundation of (human) being', I begin by rereading Genevieve Lloyd's landmark text *The Man of Reason*[3] to show how the character ideals she traces from the ancient Greeks through to Simone de Beauvoir were formative in establishing the regulative conceptions of self, subjectivity, and rational agency that have, often tacitly, informed and shaped philosophical thought in the European intellectual tradition. Here I am reading Lloyd's text as a nuanced *diagnostic-genealogical investigation* whose achievement is less to chart historically evolving necessary and sufficient conditions for thought and/or knowledge 'in general' than to unmask, expose hitherto 'unthought' conditions that have held certain instituted social-epistemic imaginaries in place, with their emblematic figures and governing ideals of subjectivity, objectivity, and agency, even as they have suppressed, discredited, or silenced other contenders. From *his* emblematic figurations as Lloyd portrays them, there can be no doubt that the man of reason—the book and the man himself—count among the pre-eminent enabling conditions for illuminating the intricate interconnections between and among the ideals and enactments of subjectivity, rationality, and hegemonic epistemic character ideals in Western philosophy. Lloyd's approach, charting the reciprocally constitutive effects of theories of knowledge, rationality, morality, and character ideals against one another (within the historically specific then-going imaginary, so to speak), opens the way to exploring a range of issues about the self with which feminists continue to work.

---

[3] See Lloyd (1994). These thoughts are drawn from Code (2006*b*).

So familiar are feminist and other philosophers, now, with *The Man of Reason*—
the book and the 'character'—that it is easy to underestimate one of its most
striking innovations. From its title and through its readings of the history of
philosophy, the text *introduces* the thinker, the reasoner, the *man* who neither
figures as an invisible yet interchangeable place-holder in a formula for articulating
the claims of reason, nor as just any philosopher who happens to advance ideas that
were already there for the taking, for everyone else. Often, translated into today's
language, the text opens ways of recognizing him as *the knowing subject*: indeed as a
'situated knower'[4] who, in his thinking and knowing, embedded within the gender-
inflected sociality, materiality, values, prohibitions, and possibilities of his time and
place, becomes an exemplar for how reason and knowledge are figured in their
inclusions and exclusions; how their regulative principles are produced and reproduced in the reasoning of specific knowers; how it was for a thinker, a reasoning
'self', to live and know well, *then and there*, rationally, capably, creatively, responsibly—or otherwise. Thus Lloyd highlights the salience of posing a hitherto 'unthought' question: asking *who* rather than *what* a thinker is, where asking *what*
preserves mere place-holder status, while asking *who* catches more of that self, that
knowing subject, in a sense I owe to Adriana Cavarero, who wryly observes:

Philosophers themselves—servants of the universal—are the ones who teach us that the
knowledge of Man requires that the particularity of each one, the uniqueness of human
existence, be unknowable... *What* Man is can be known and defined, as Aristotle assures
us; *who* Socrates is, instead, eludes the parameters of knowledge as science, it eludes the
truth of the *episteme*. (2000: 9)

I am suggesting that a sometimes tacit, but always insistent '*who?*' question
animates Lloyd's encounters with the men (and occasional women) of reason
whose works frame her inquiry. Her readings engage with the particularities, the
uniqueness, and the commonalities of human selves and subjectivities in and for
their time and place, in ways that are crucial to feminist and other post-colonial
projects, even as they resist and seek to counter an implausible individual*ism* that
has been the hallmark of post-Cartesian, post-Kantian philosophy. These readings
can be enlisted, also, to infuse moments of recognition that afford standpoint and
other 'situated knowledge' projects a point of entry.[5]

As Lloyd shows, the symbolisms and metaphorics that hold the man of reason in
place accomplish their inclusions and exclusions in repudiations of the feminine,
tacitly hypostasized as a '*what*', if indeed it is *thought* at all. To cite just two passages:
'The obstacles to female cultivation of Reason spring to a large extent from the fact
that our ideals of Reason have historically incorporated an exclusion of the

---

[4] The reference is to Donna Haraway, "Situated Knowledges': The Science Question in
Feminism and the Privilege of Partial Perspective', in Haraway (1991).
[5] Lloyd was not alone in making these moves possible. Also in the 1980s, Evelyn Fox Keller
(1985) and Susan Bordo (1986, 1987) addressed subjectivity in ways that pose the 'who?' question.

feminine, and that femininity itself has been partly constituted through such processes of exclusion' (p. xix); 'The metaphors do not merely express conceptual points about the relations between knowledge and its objects. They give a male content to what it is to be a good knower' (p. 17). The point is as normative in its force as it is descriptive in its formulation. Woman cannot simply enter the domain of reason and expect to find a place there.

In thus underscoring the *maleness* of reason throughout historically evolving conceptions of masculinity and rationality, Lloyd anticipates her readings of Michèle Le Dœuff's insistence that 'there is no intellectual activity that is not grounded in an imaginary' (2003: p. xvi). The power of an instituted imaginary to legitimate or silence the workings of reason plays a central part in the diagnostic-genealogical investigations *The Man of Reason* initiates: effects which Lloyd pursues as an 'unthought'[6] in subsequent writings. She observes: 'features of the male–female distinction *as it operated in their cultural context* became part and parcel of understanding what it is to be rational. Those assumptions about relations between the sexes were thus an "unthought" element in the philosophical imaginary that can now be unmasked' (Lloyd 2000b: 42; emphasis original). Here I am rereading *The Man of Reason* alongside figurations of the repudiated feminine in Le Dœuff's *The Sex of Knowing*, to emphasize how femininity, female subjectivity, becoming woman, in its various modalities has been constituted, historically, in processes of exclusion. The issue (recalling Cavarero) is not about *what* Woman is in her epistemic elusiveness, but about *who* the women were/are who have sought, in the particularity of their circumstances and relationships—as situated would-be thinking and acting subjects—to negotiate possibilities of intellectual subjectivity and agency within an imaginary that rendered them universal Man's complement: the second sex. Women's uneasy positioning in the hegemonic imaginary, their need to conduct themselves defiantly (Le Dœuff cites the virago and bluestocking), or with a compromised docility despite their intellectual prowess, confirms the imaginary in its tenacity.

'Discoveries' of forgotten intellectual women, or 'add women and stir' techniques without systemic, structural analysis, can do no more than introduce token women into an instituted imaginary amply equipped to downgrade 'the feminine' as merely '"complementary" . . . to male norms of human excellence' (Lloyd 1994: 104), or to absorb them into masculine models of viable selfhood/subjectivity. But reading such figures, as Lloyd and Le Dœuff variously do, within lived implications of the social imaginary where gendered ideals of reason prevail, exposes lacunae in its putative seamlessness, reveals its structural flaws and its contingency, shows how a society living under its sway is incongruous with itself, with scant reason for self-satisfaction. Such readings prepare the way for what Cornelius Castoriadis (1994)

---

6 The French reads: 'ce qui n'aurait pas été encore pensé' (Le Dœuff 1998: 70).

calls an 'instituting social imaginary': a vehicle of radical social critique which, albeit gradually, slowly, can begin to unsettle the hegemony of the old. (Recall Michel Foucault, 'Genealogy is gray, meticulous, and patiently documentary': 1977: 139.)

What spaces, then, do the temporally-historically specific analyses Lloyd develops open for rethinking how selves/subjectivities have participated in the making of objectivity? How have the figures who hover in the shadows, unthought behind their thought which passes untouched through their minds, configured philosophical projects? How does thinking *with them*, in their circumstances, *re*configure such projects, where the '*who*?' may also be fictional, as in Lloyd's (2000*a*: 116–17) reading of the character Pat Barker models on Siegfried Sassoon or of Virginia Woolf's Katherine Hilbery with her secret, unfeminine, passion for mathematics (Lloyd 1994: 74)? In Lloyd's work, the thinking, the struggles of historical and fictional figures are quite particularly theirs and of *their* time and place; yet she shows, with consummate subtlety, how their ways of responding to, embracing, railing against, stoically accepting, or drawing scarcely perceptible resources from their situations contribute to engaging thoughtfully with female subjectivity in *our* time, and to opening space for deconstructing the grammatical structures of which the man of reason is the uncontested subject.

That said, it is crucial to recall that reason as it has infused conceptions of self and subjectivity in Western philosophy and culture has not instantiated a generic masculinity, any more than it has excluded a generic femininity. Feminists and other Others have amply demonstrated the derivation of that idealized masculine self from the circumstances of an elite race, class, and otherwise privileged group of Western men who were free to act and judge as they did. Although the feminine/masculine division Lloyd traces through the history of Western philosophy unifies femininity and masculinity along lines other post-colonial theorists would contest, and rightly so, this homogeneity is a consequence of her chosen domain: the texts that comprise the Western philosophical canon. Hence her analysis attests, also, to the local character of hegemonic Reason and to its connections with specific conceptions of self, subjectivity, and practical-political circumstances. It is an exemplary instance of local inquiry, peculiar to the symbolic events that have shaped Western philosophy—and to their 'trickle-down' social-political effects.[7] Yet her analyses of the gendered 'unthought' open spaces for revisiting other erasures and exclusions integral to orthodox ethics and epistemology: prohibitions that block a range of genealogical routes toward understanding situated gendered, raced, class, and other specificity-informed constructions of self, subjectivity, knowledge, and imagination.

---

[7] Lloyd has gone on to examine other sites of privilege and exclusion, notably in her essay 'No One's Land: Australia and the Philosophical Imagination' (2000*c*).

Reason, then, is discursively constructed in symbols and metaphors that shape and are shaped by historically, culturally dominant ideals of masculinity. Its association with ideal masculinity stakes out a rational domain inaccessible, or accessible only uneasily, to those whose positionings have not fostered the characteristics of ideal masculinity. Well into the late twentieth century, and for many white Western philosophers still in the twenty-first century, the abstract autonomous rational agent has stood as the social ideal of mature, effective human selfhood and citizenship, just as he has stood as the hero of philosophical moral, political, and epistemological discourse: the person—more accurately, the *man*—whose conduct and attributes are exemplary, descriptively and normatively, for establishing standards of epistemic, moral, social, and political conduct and agency. He is the invisible subject whose presumptively generic modes of being give content to dominant conceptions of subjectivity and self: of the individual, self-sufficient abstract masculinity enacted by *homo economicus* together with the universal rationality that has informed the epistemologies of mastery that have grounded the rise of scientific supremacy, the nation-state, and the liberal individual who is the principal character in all of their enactments. Hence it is not surprising that feminists of both the first and the second waves, perceiving his successes, should extol and seek to emulate these seemingly quintessential human achievements from which they had systematically, systemically, and conceptually been excluded. From Mary Astell, Mary Wollstonecraft, and Harriet Taylor through to the initially path-breaking work of Carol Gilligan and others in the early years of second-wave feminism, variations on the eighteenth-century liberal conception of the autonomous self prevailed as the model of self-realization many white Anglo-American feminists sought likewise to achieve.

Gilligan's research stands as a pivotal moment in thinking about feminism and the self in the USA. Although it was less influential in the United Kingdom, Australia, and 'the French tradition', in the 1980s and 1990s its effects were path-breaking for white liberal North American feminists' rethinking of autonomy's veneration as a mark of rational, moral maturity and hence as an overarching ideal of human subjectivity. A psychologist working with Lawrence Kohlberg's scale for measuring developmental stages toward moral maturity, Gilligan was puzzled to find that female subjects, both children and young adults, tended to score consistently lower than male subjects. Hence her principal contribution to the deconstruction of autonomous subjectivity was to intervene at the level of what philosophers of science would see as the context of discovery. Contesting the universal validity and gender-neutrality of the scale itself and thence also the evidence-filtering assumptions that informed it, she reread the scores to demonstrate the contingency of deeply entrenched psychological and more widespread social convictions that achieved, detached autonomy is the 'natural' *telos* of generic human maturation. From her research, the regulative function of autonomy-centred moral decisions emerges as a product of an instituted social imaginary—of local cultural values, imagery, and ideologies—which is specific to its time and place, and could have been otherwise.

Gilligan found, in effect, that the girl children and young female adults in the groups she studied had been elaborately socialized toward more collaborative, dialogic, 'second person' modes of cooperative interaction and deliberation than their male counterparts, hence that detached, putatively autonomous, and mono-logic ways of dealing with complex dilemmas and situations were often not, for them, self-evidently right or indeed intelligible. Frequently, their styles of delibera-tion and judgement departed from both utilitarian and Kantian models of impar-tial, detached distancing to move toward a pattern akin to Aristotelian practical reasoning, where the concern is less with formal principles or consequences, and more with the implications and effects of certain exemplary conduct, ways of thinking, and motives, both for those to whom one is accountable and who are affected by or implicated in these actions, and for oneself. To discern these implications, a moral agent has to position her- or himself critically within a situation, in relation to as many of its aspects as he or she can discern, so as to take imaginative account of its multiple implications while neither erasing nor paralysing her capacity to act. Such stances attest to a conception of self and agency that diverges markedly from the detached deliberative self required of an orthodox Kantian or utilitarian. Although Gilligan does not take her analysis in this direc-tion, such a stance may also, as Simone de Beauvoir suggests, allow feminists and others to acknowledge and work with an 'irreducible ambiguity ... [that] charac-terizes human existence ... which demands a response through concrete human actions ... that can in no way dispel or diminish the ambiguity, but which allow us to *live* this ambiguity in meaningful ways'.[8] It is my sense that a cultivated and constantly renewed capacity to live the ambiguities of human existence is integral to what Johnson calls the '*thinking* that gives the subject being'; nor need it reduce to pernicious relativism or to unprincipled, casual decision-making. But this thought anticipates a direction my discussion will take.

Although Gilligan's analyses address *moral* deliberation and have thus been particularly relevant for feminist ethics and its attendant-constitutive conceptions of the self, they are analogously pertinent to issues of knowledge, epistemology, styles of reasoning as these have also, in the philosophical mainstream, worked with a conception (again often merely tacit, invisible) of an infinitely replicable self/ knowing subject who could be everyone and no one, details of whose specificity are, can, and *should be* irrelevant to knowledge properly so called. Such an autonomous knower endeavours to transcend the specificities of situation, circum-stance, and sociality to arrive at purely objective, neutral, and detached knowledge claims verifiable or falsifiable by anyone in the same (controlled) situation. Feminist

---

[8] The quotation is from Gail Weiss (1995: 45). Her reference is to Simone de Beauvoir (1976).

epistemology in its various modalities and to varying degrees aims to demonstrate that taking subjectivity and epistemic situation into account in making, evaluating, and circulating knowledge is integral to making available a wider range of conditions for the possibility of knowledge than the formalisms of the tradition allow, and exposing the structures of dominance and subjugation that tell for or against uptake in epistemic circumstances. In these endeavours, analogously to feminist ethics and political theory, it eschews the conception of the autonomous impersonal knower for a more complex analysis of the subjectivities at work in the construction and circulation of knowledge.

Annette Baier's thinking of persons as 'second persons' initiates a radical reconception of self and subjectivity in Anglo-American philosophy, consonant to some degree with Gilligan's view. Baier famously writes: 'A person, perhaps, is best seen as one who was long enough dependent upon other persons to acquire the essential arts of personhood. Persons essentially are *second* persons.'[9] Her claim is as significant for epistemic as for moral agency: indeed in knowing as in acting 'the good and hopeful aspects of our condition, as much as the evils, stem from the fact of interdependence' (1985: 231). For Baier, human selves/subjectivities are social all the way down: philosophical analyses that suppress, deny, and disdain interdependence in favour of an isolated, detached individualism rely on conceptions of 'the self' so remote from how human beings are or *can be* that their capacity to foster intelligibility is seriously truncated. Yet it is also worth noting that 'second personhood', for Baier, is no saccharine, cloyingly good conception of dyadic human 'togetherness': hers is a realistic challenge to the overarching esteem accorded to abstract individualism in the Anglo-American tradition, together with a plea for recognition of how even the 'purest' autonomous subjectivity and the most 'impure' anti-social self is realized only in circumstances of human and circumstantial interdependence, whether benign or malign. Her second-person analysis opens the way toward conceptions of *relational* autonomy that have come to occupy a central place in feminist ethics.[10] It paves the way, too, for work in social epistemology that acknowledges and reclaims the significance of testimony in much of what 'we' come to know.[11] While both of these points may appear to be more descriptive than normative, their normative significance is far-reaching if theories of knowledge and action are to yield principles realizable by real knowers-doers in real circumstances. Admittedly, they sacrifice a level of ideality that it has been philosophers' aim to articulate; but that loss is compensated by an enhanced capacity to address situation-specific issues that instantiate a more plausible

---

[9] Annette Baier, 'Cartesian Persons' (1985: 84). I examine the implications of second personhood for epistemology in Code (1991: ch. 2 and elsewhere).

[10] See e.g. the essays in Mackenzie and Stoljar (2000).

[11] See in this regard Lackey and Sosa (2006), Fricker (2007), and Code (2010).

conception of epistemic agency than has been on offer from formal epistemology and ethics.

In social epistemology, the bare fact of epistemic interdependence works to contest the disdain for *testimony* produced by the presumed self-reliance, self-sufficiency of the subject in classical empiricist-positivist theories of knowledge. Elizabeth Fricker aptly observes: 'one may question whether the supposed ideal figure of the autonomous knower, who refuses ever to trustingly accept another's testimony, a fortiori will never allow her own judgement to be corrected by another's, is really such an ideal after all' (2006: 239). The question highlights the urgency of reconceiving the epistemic and ethical self/subject presupposed in Anglo-American philosophical analysis, particularly through the twentieth century, if epistemology is to address and adjudicate the concerns of real knowers. It pushes practices of taking subjectivity into account toward recognizing how the ideal self-protecting 'buffered self' of modernity (to borrow Genevieve Lloyd's apt phrase[12]) has in fact blocked philosophical inquiry into the *who* who has eluded the truth of the *episteme* (recalling Cavarero) and in consequence has circumscribed the scope, the potential, of the *episteme* itself.

Challenges to the orthodox conception of ethical subjectivity such as Gilligan and others propose, and to the epistemic subject such as feminist and anti-racist social-naturalized epistemology propose, highlight the inadequacy of these at-tenuated conceptions of self to engage with the questions a viable philosophical analysis that starts from real-world situations has to address. Elizabeth Fricker's plea for testimony acknowledges as much.

Returning, then, to Barbara Johnson's contrast, it is worth noting that Beauvoir, a philosopher in 'the French tradition' whose influence in feminist thinking about self and subjectivity has been profound, works with interdependence as a given of human being in the world. In *The Ethics of Ambiguity* through *The Second Sex* and beyond she sustains the position that 'no existence can be validly fulfilled if it is limited to itself. It appeals to the existence of others' (1976: 67). The thought persists, with no assumption that such 'appeals' are presumptively benign: the Othering that represents woman as the second sex results, also, from 'the existence of others as a freedom [that] defines my situation and is even the condition of my own freedom' (1976: 91). Beauvoir's account of the transition in her thought from individualism to a quintessentially social conception of self is illuminating for my argument here. In *The Prime of Life*, reflecting on the position she had taken in *Pyrrhus and Cinéas*, she writes:

I do not disapprove of my anxiety to provide existentialist morals with a material content; the annoying thing was to be enmeshed with individualism still, at the very moment I thought I had escaped it. An individual, I thought, only receives a human dimension by recognizing the existence of others. Yet, in my essay, coexistence appears as a sort of accident that each individual should somehow surmount; he should begin by hammering out his 'project' in a solitary state, and only then ask the mass of mankind to endorse its validity. In truth, society has been all about me from the day of my birth; it is in the bosom of that society . . . that all my personal decisions must be formed. (1962: 549–50)

This acknowledgement of the ineluctable sociality of human lives (which need not, I think, be read as question-begging) exposes the implausibility of autonomous subjectivity as an overriding ideal or an achievement.

II

In her 'Introduction.' to *The Oxford Amnesty Lectures 1992* from which I quote at the beginning of this essay, Barbara Johnson writes that contributors to the 'Freedom and Interpretation' lecture series were invited to 'consider the consequences of the deconstruction of the self for the liberal tradition', to think about whether the self 'as construed by the liberal tradition still exist[s]', and if it does not, 'whose human rights are we [= we Amnesty activists] defending?' (1993: 2). They were to address an apparent conflict, then, between the defence of human rights at the core of Amnesty International's mandate, and postmodern and other deconstructions of humanistic subjectivity which contest the very idea of the unified, autonomous, self-reliant rights-bearing self whom 'rights talk' commonly presupposes, and thus of a moral-political agent responsible for respecting or entitled to claim those rights, or positioned to make reparation for violating them. Because, as I have noted, the self of the liberal-Enlightenment moral-political tradition is the self-same self who is the taken-for-granted knowing subject in orthodox Anglo-American theories of knowledge; and because fulfilling its own mandate requires Amnesty to know, responsibly and well, the persons for whom and the situations in which it intervenes, these issues are as epistemologically significant as they are morally and politically urgent. They pose a range of equally complex questions about the intricacies of situated epistemic subjectivity: of subjects knowing and subjects known, whose epistemological implications I explore more fully in *Ecological Thinking* (2006a). In revisiting them my intention is to underscore the importance of recognizing that, continuous with the liberal self-conceptions that inform her research, a tacit assumption persists in Gilligan's work that the selves whose moral decision-making she studies are situated in reasonably 'normal', polite circumstances and lives. The Amnesty question stands as a reminder that this assumption, which circumscribes the reach of her conception of self, is open to interrogation.

As influential as Gilligan's *In a Different Voice* was for white liberal feminists of the 1980s who were working with conceptions of 'the self as construed by the liberal tradition' was Jean Baker Miller's *Toward a New Psychology of Women* (1976) in which, contributors to a 2008 symposium on her work contend, Miller 'sought to challenge the emphasis that developmental models of psychology placed on separateness, power, and hierarchy, replacing them with a model that emphasized mutual respect and the building of community'.[13] Contributors to the symposium show that Miller's contribution to feminist theories of the self is at once path-breaking and contentious: I am reading it as forming a bridge between fixed assumptions about the liberal self and the implications of its putative 'deconstruction'. Although Miller's analysis remains firmly within the liberal tradition, she begins to contest the implicit individualism of its focus on the patriarchal construction of women's identities, opening that analysis out to connect identity to 'women's work orientations', as Aída Hurtado (2008: 344) notes. Despite stark personal and academic differences from Miller, especially with respect to her failure to take class, race, or sexual orientation into account, Hurtado commends Miller's courage in breaking away from an established model of female subjectivity to open space for a 'method of *relational dovetailing* in intellectual production' that bypasses 'the destructive effects of adversarial knowledge production' (ibid. 342). Even in dissociating her own stance from the white liberal middle-class position that informs Miller's work, Hurtado evinces respect for its riskiness in its time and place in concentrating on 'women's work orientations', through which, as she reads it, it foreshadows 'the work of African American feminists who urge us to adopt multiple epistemologies to fully grasp the experiences of African American women in particular and of women in general . . . to expand our definitions of desirable subjectivities and our ways of relating to others' (ibid. 344). Other contributors to the symposium are less kindly disposed. To cite a second example by way of moving further toward the 'deconstruction' of the self, Catriona Macleod (2008: 348) deplores Miller's 'narrow model of the self which leads to a narrow politics based on the heterosexual relationship with the nuclear family as backdrop, and her naivety around the temporary nature of some inequalities'. This 'self' is, if implicitly, a white middle-class North American woman for whom gender inequities are the principal social disparities with which she struggles, and most of whose struggles take the form of self-directed or therapy-assisted striving for individual self-realization in a social world where such a possibility has been open only to men, also presumptively white, and middle-class. Macleod is critical of a

---

[13] Quoted from the Editors' Introduction by Zeedyk and Greenwood (2008: 321).

conception of self that sees gender differences as the fundamental human differences, given that it homogenizes women and thus fails, as South African and other not-white, not-American feminists must, to see 'the multiplicity of gender relations' (ibid. 350), while separating the self 'from the activities in which the person engages' (ibid. 351), which, by implication, are constitutive of self and subjectivity. Feminist conceptions of self that emerge 'out of women's engagement in national liberation struggles' (ibid. 355) require an analysis sensitive to a complex history of social circumstances which are by no means captured by—or indeed visible in— the polite pictures of liberal democratic society within which Miller's women strive to achieve authentic selves and to fulfill 'their needs'.

Miller's work does not simply echo Gilligan's, but in the exclusions it effects, it tacitly poses the very question Amnesty poses, if from a different direction. Both in what it includes that was absent from previously dominant North American conceptions of the self, and in what it excludes, it shows that theories of 'the liberal self' are, in effect, self-defeating. I base this claim, in part, on the aggregation, the reification effected by the conception of subjectivity they enact: a conception which can adequately be addressed only piecemeal and *in medias res*, by appealing to *who* and not merely *what* such a subject is, and to *how* it is in its relationships and actions. I base it also, in part, on how this self-contained human subject appears to be devoid of feeling, affect—perhaps owing to its origins, as Lloyd depicts them, in a conceptual frame for which feeling was so particular, and indeed also so irrational, as to elude philosophical analysis. Hence one must ask what, then, becomes of the self as vulnerable, the self as multiple, the self as rejoicing or suffering, the self as affiliative, the self as ecological? These are only some of the modalities missing from liberal conceptions of the self as property: as 'mine alone'.

'The self' in the liberal theories I have discussed is depicted with a certain quotidian integrity, in bland, affectless circumstances which are rarely specified. It is as if this self moves—and can readily move—through its life as a self-contained whole, untouched in its salient ontological and ethical-epistemological aspects by experiences and circumstances that would, in other conceptual frameworks, be recognized as constitutive of the very possibility of the *episteme* and of the *who* who achieves selfhood/subjectivity within its purview. Because situations make different aspects of subjectivity possible while thwarting others, the partiality of presumptively unfettered, benignly rational selfhood has to be contested in situations and analyses where none of these settled assumptions can be assumed to hold fast. Selves are never not situated, nor are they presumptively impervious to the vagaries of situation and circumstance, whose effects both benign and malign are constitutive of the scope and limits of 'self-realization', subjectivity, and agency. Recall Johnson's observation that for Foucault, the subject becomes 'a function of what a given society defines as thinkable' (1993: 6). Examples come readily to mind: the unthinkability of a woman voting, attending university, gaining a Ph.D., counting as a reliable witness; of a black man or woman being elected president of the USA, claiming professional status, gaining a Ph.D., also counting as a reliable witness. Patricia Williams observes: 'I could not but wonder . . . what it would take to make my experience verifiable. The testimony of an independent white bystander?'[14] And Charles Mills notes: 'During slavery, blacks were generally denied the right to testify against whites, because they were not seen as credible witnesses' (2007: 32). These are just some of the modalities of subjectivity certain given 'modern' societies have defined as unthinkable.

The examples recall Miranda Fricker's observation, in *Epistemic Injustice*, to the effect that in acts of testimonial injustice, where a putative knower's testimony is discounted, contradicted, or discredited because of who he or she is, that person is harmed in her/his very sense of self; is treated as 'less than a full epistemic subject' (2007: 145). The capacity of systemic events of this kind to destabilize a person's sense of self in ways that liberal conceptions of unfettered autonomy and injunctions about 'pulling oneself up by one's bootstraps' fail to address in their full ontological—as well as moral and political—implications is well known, and cannot justifiedly be dismissed. Fricker notes, when the 'driving prejudicial stereotype involves the idea that the social type in question is humanly lesser [as a woman, a black, a member of a marginalized class or group]' . . . 'the dimension of degradation qua human being is not simply symbolic; rather it is a literal part of the core epistemic insult' (ibid. 45). 'Testimonial injustice', Fricker concludes, 'denies one access to what originally furnishes status as a knower . . . [it] can carry a symbolic weight to the effect that the speaker is less than a full epistemic subject' (ibid. 145). These are some of the ontological implications of going against the grain of what a given society defines as thinkable.

Even in theories about the self as property, in the English tradition, 'the body' figures (implausibly) as a standardized, generic body; and the Cartesian 'thinking thing' maintains a principled distance from physicality and, a fortiori, from emotion and feeling. Thus it is as incongruous and as politically immobilizing, I suggest, to conceive of the self as property as it is to represent thinking as the practice that gives the subject being. By contrast, the ecological subject, who is the central protagonist in *Ecological Thinking*, is both more and other than a rights-bearing thinker, even though it is both of these as well. It is, as Annette Baier (1995: 316), following Montaigne, puts it, 'marvellously corporeal', ineluctably embodied: its spatially and temporally situated corporeality are as constitutive of the modalities of its being as are its thinking, feeling, knowing, and other 'inner' processes.

Barbara Johnson's question about whether the self of the liberal tradition (the morally and epistemically autonomous bearer of rights, the rational self-conscious agent, and thence the orthodox empiricist knower) *still* exists is question-begging in its assumption that he has ever been more than a fictive creature and an

---

[14] Williams (1991: 47, 48). I discuss this example more fully in 'Incredulity, Experientialism, and the Politics of Knowledge' in Code (1995).

implausible fiction at that. Thus Elizabeth Fricker wonders in the remark I cite earlier whether the supposedly ideal figure of the autonomous knower is a worthy ideal after all, epistemologically, ontologically, or morally. In my view, he has existed only in narrowly conceived theoretical places, abstracted and isolated from the exigencies, vulnerabilities, and multiple vagaries of human lives. In philosophical-political theory, he has been presumptively male, white, privileged, able-bodied, articulate, and educated, 'buffered' against the inconvenient practical implications of corporeality, and insulated against having to participate in events that obtrude insistently in everyday matters of vulnerability and trust, and/or in trauma and crisis. The deconstruction of the self in postmodern thought is matched if not exceeded by ordinary and extraordinary contestations of the very possibility of integrated subjectivity and self-ownership, occurring routinely below the polite surface of the liberal tradition, for which 'autonomous man' is emblematic of everything humanly admirable, and personal-social-material-ecological circumstances are uniformly so benign as to require no mention in analyses of rights-enabling or thwarting projects.

In short, Amnesty's question confines the knowings it problematizes to deconstructions and fragmentations of selves more abstractly theoretical, less experientially basic than the climate of oppression, torture, abuse, and rape its mandate requires it to address, where victims/survivors and others who attempt to know them and their circumstances well must deal with systemic assaults on 'the self' far more radical than theoretical deconstruction, and people are more vulnerable than autonomous man ever seems to be. Everyday vulnerability and extraordinary experiences of trauma make *owning* one's capacities, emotions, and actions less matter-of-course than the liberal self-sufficient self-as-property assumes; yet, phenomenologically, such experiences are as central to human being as autonomy. Thus, for example, discussing Simone de Beauvoir's conflicted political engagement in the case of Djamila Boupacha, a young Muslim woman and rape victim of the Algerian war, Sonia Kruks aptly observes: 'In the face of her privileges, Beauvoir addresses questions about the responsibility and complicity of a situated self, a self that is not autonomous and that makes decisions while dwelling in a world not fully of its own making' (2005: 195; see also Kruks 2001). The larger idea, consonant with Johnson's point about what a given society defines as thinkable, is that our selves are not really our own, and never so unequivocally of our own making as the liberal tradition supposes. Nor, I want to propose, are they enabled or confined only by conditions of what is thinkable, knowable, for again, on such an assumption, selves as feeling, as confident and vulnerable, as joyous or sorrowing, as loving or hating, are erased from the conceptual frame, where such experiences are not merely accretions to an underlying self-in-neutral, but are constitutive of who and how it is. Such would seem to be Sandra Bartky's worry when she expresses regrets that 'few theorists have examined closely enough the emotional dimension that is part of the search for better cognitions or the affective taste of the kinds of intersubjectivity that can build political solidarities' (1997: 180). Bartky reminds her readers, as does the idea that thinking gives the subject being, that so narrow an emphasis on rationality, on cognition, produces a reductive, diminished conception of human selves in its erasure of the affective repertoire as essential to intersubjective engagement as to the political activism that is at the core of feminist work. The goal, in her view, is not disengaged, abstract, epistemic self-reliance but rather 'a knowing that transforms the self who knows, a knowing that brings into being new sympathies, new affects as well as new cognitions and new forms of intersubjectivity. The demand, in a word, is for a knowing that has a particular affective taste' (ibid. 179). Such a demand is consonant, I suggest, with Baier's claim that persons are essentially second persons even as it moves that idea into a phenomenological register where its lived potential is more fully apparent.

Often, as for the Amnesty essayists, it is neither the self as one-time rights bearer nor the self as theoretically dispersed who pushes most urgently at the boundaries of received, objectivist knowledge, but the embodied, injured subject, struggling to construct or reconstruct a liveable way of being out of systemic oppression, grief, trauma, or despair. Its dispersal puts the affective-imaginative self-certainties of would-be (humanistic) knowers into question just when those putatively more 'stable' selves encounter urgent demands to maintain a constancy that can allow them to know well enough to act responsibly, intelligently, effectively. Suppose, then, inquiry into feminist conceptions of self and subjectivity were to start from the question: how would it be to enter theory and practice from a place where human subjects are imagined not as rational, self-sufficient agents, whose prototype is the Enlightenment 'man of reason', but as vulnerable creatures who can live their vulnerabilities well only in climates of recognition, mutual responsibility, and trust? How could vulnerability—specific vulnerabilities—claim the attention that contortions around preserving an overblown autonomy ideal have claimed in the hegemonic social imaginary of the Western world, to the peril of the vulnerable: of all of us?

Prompted, I believe, by just such questions, Debra Bergoffen in her article 'February 22, 2001: Toward a Politics of the Vulnerable Body',[15] revisits the 2001 UN war crimes trial at The Hague, where three Bosnian soldiers were found guilty of *crimes against humanity* for raping and torturing Muslim women and girls. For Bergoffen The Hague decision is a landmark event whose pronouncements could generate the momentum to unsettle the social imaginary in which autonomous man, invulnerable, transparent, and infinitely replicable, has been the main player. She reads the court's judgment that women have a basic human right to sexual integrity as initiating a linguistic practice with the capacity to transform women's vulnerability 'from a symbol of men's power to a sign of our shared humanity . . . [as] inaugurating

---

[15] Bergoffen (2003: 117). The decision is known as the Kunarac, Kovac and Vukovic judgement. It is with reference to this decision that she refers to humanity 'as a species that transforms itself through its linguistic practices', in Bergoffen (2006).

a politics of the vulnerable body which challenges current understandings of evil, war crimes, and crimes against humanity' (2006: 11). Whether or not these hopes are realizable, they extend beyond the extremity of separate or collective acts of rape, murder, and sexual violence to require theorists to engage at the level of the *instituted social imaginary* that holds them in place and often condones these acts by casting them as ordinary events in women's lives, to be evaluated according to what a woman has or has not 'asked for'.

The Hague decision, Bergoffen argues, shows that 'we cannot forget that human bodies are abused when their intentionalities, specifically the intentionalities of integrity, are violated' (2003: 121). So dramatic a move away from equating 'self integrity with the integrity of the unmarked autonomous self' (ibid. 127) points toward a breakthrough that could *denaturalize* male violence against women, which is too often 'naturalized' as a dominant social-structural effect of inflated figurations of autonomy, derived from autonomous man's 'normative "neutral" body'. (Recall Susan Brison's ironic reminder that 'the every-dayness of sexual violence . . . leads many to think that male violence against women is *natural*'; even though 'they simultaneously manage to deny that it really exists': 1993: 7; my emphasis; also see Brison 2002.) It is here, if Bergoffen's idea is plausible, that complacent beliefs need to be dislodged from their illusory self-certainty: beliefs in the orderliness of a society so privileged as to enable (some of) its citizens to imagine violence—and other 'unfortunate events'—as mere blemishes on an otherwise unsullied social surface. Such beliefs affirm the tenacity of the liberal model with the polite imaginings integral to its standard repertoire; and traumatic, albeit 'ordinary', events of sexual violence in women's lives count merely as extraordinary for an imaginary nourished to uphold such expectations, which relegate evidence of women's (and other Others') vulnerability to the aberrant, to places where a woman may have 'asked for it' in failing to play by the rules. An ecology of incredulity maps standard responses to such episodes, sustaining a dream of andro-centred safety, evidence to the contrary notwithstanding. It conceals a whole fabric of ignorance.

The disruption The Hague court initiates works to interrogate a complex of moral, ontological, legal, and other social-structural significations, thereby unsettling Western philosophy's self-presentation as a neutral, universally applicable, yet detached and dislocated inquiry. Sonia Kruks observes:

> To exist is to be one's body; and this is to be a 'body-subject,' or a 'sentient' subject, and not the rational, autonomous consciousness so central to the Western tradition. . . . consciousness and materiality, subjectivity and the world of 'things' are coextensive and co-constitutive. Such a relationship may be experienced as supportive and affirming of the self, but also as threatening and negating. (Kruks 2007: 30)

Kruks reminds 'us' that structurally/phenomenologically a focus on vulnerability is always already there in the *Lebenswelt*: it would require no argument to accord it recognition were it not for the overweening power of liberalism's autonomy obsession, also naturalized, which makes working toward a politics of the vulnerable body more onerous than it need be. Anglo-American philosophy's principled disdain for the material-corporeal specificities of human lives is an intransigent theoretical obstacle, consequent on and constantly reinforcing this excessive veneration of autonomy. In received social-political and legal discourse, that disdain is directed to 'experiential stories', 'anecdotal evidence'—derogatory labels reserved for 'testimony'—and commonly discredited as 'special interest' pleading. Thus, orthodox epistemology and moral-political theory work to conceal practices and processes—such as rape and other egregious 'crimes against humanity'—casting them as deviant episodic disturbances and thence discrediting their tellers as unreliable witnesses to the stories of 'their own' lives. Because the autonomy-of-reason presumption sustains a politics of unknowing around events about which an affluent white Western 'public' cannot bear too much truth, creating spaces where The Hague decision might animate reconfigurations of deliberation, democratic principles, and 'our' lives is neither an easy nor a conflict-free endeavour. But 'general interest' in these and other war crimes and harms against persons is relatively thin on the ground, deflected, paradoxically, by the very ordinariness *and* extraordinariness together in which violent acts in 'other' places tend, for white Western folk, to be shrouded ('ordinary' because that is just how people in those places act; 'extraordinary' because it is so outrageous that 'we' cannot imagine anything of that order happening here, so we need not think about it).

In her essay 'The Question of Social Transformation', Judith Butler declares that 'keeping our notion of the 'human' open to a future articulation . . . [is] essential to the project of a critical international human rights discourse and politics'. She rereads her own *Gender Trouble* to address sexual difference in its ontological, political, ethical, and oppressive dimensions, cautioning her readers that taking entrenched modalities of human intelligibility for granted can result in failure 'to think critically—and ethically—about the consequential ways that the human is being produced, reproduced, deproduced'. She 'cannot imagine a "responsible" ethics or theory of social transformation' operating without such critical inquiry (2004: 222). Questions about who and what counts as 'real', Butler reminds her readers, are questions about knowledge and power, for 'power dissimulates as ontology' (ibid. 215). Issues of gender dysphoria prompt her analyses: questions of how, in regimes of hetero-normativity, refusals of gender norms expose the refusers to losing their 'job, home, the prospects for desire, or for life' (ibid. 214). In societies governed by such norms, ontological congruity—indeed, recognition as 'real'—is achievable only through conformity: Hence, for example, 'the ways in which women are said to "know" or to "be known" are already orchestrated by power precisely at that moment in which the terms of "acceptable" categorization are instituted' (ibid. 215).

Butler's questions are not Bergoffen's; but their analyses are mutually illuminating. Butler takes some inspiration from Cavarero who, in work that also accords a
central place to recognition, departs from a Kantian emphasis on an autonomous,
rights-bearing 'I' to focus instead on an Arendtian-derived politics of '"the who" in
order to establish a relational politics . . . in which the exposure and vulnerability of
the other makes a primary ethical claim upon me'. For Cavarero, in Butler's
reading, 'we are beings who are, of necessity, *exposed* to one another in our
vulnerability and singularity. . . . [O]ur political situation . . . consists in part in
learning how best to handle—and to honor—this constant and necessary exposure' (Butler 2005: 31–2). Cavarero's emphasis on natality (drawn from Hannah
Arendt) is a reminder to her readers that recognizing ourselves *as* beings who are
exposed to one another is a reminder that we come as vulnerable creatures into a
world where autonomy is held up as a character achievement realized in separating
and dissociating itself from that vulnerability: an overcoming, perhaps something
of a promise, that encourages and rewards denials of vulnerability. One way to
pursue the 'thrown-ness' metaphor, then, is to acknowledge that we come into the
world as fragile creatures, given over into each other's keeping. Autonomy-driven
lives are forever involved in not just overcoming this fragility—which would
indeed in some of its modalities be a worthy project—but in denying it, attempting
to avoid accommodating it within the other psychic and social structures that
determine those lives: withdrawing from that primordial keeping and holding.
Hence the pertinence of Cavarero's reminder of how 'every existent, from its birth,
is *exposed*'.

None of this is simple. Butler's reference to 'exposure' counts also as a reminder
that bringing women's vulnerabilities into focus imports its own risks. Structurally,
vulnerability acknowledged carries a certain shame: another ontological effect of an
autonomy-veneration for which human subjects are dispassionate creatures,
moved neither by vulnerabilities nor by pleasures and desires. Hence it runs the
risk of pathologizing women's bodies and lives, opening the doors to a new
paternalism. How could this danger be countered? For a start, engaging with
these issues requires eschewing any sense that vulnerability is *either* essential (to
women or other Others) *or* merely incidental. It is a variably distributed, structural
effect of an adulation of autonomy which is ultimately oppressive; a pervasive
mode of human complexity, integral—if variously—to living in a fragmented,
multiply signifying world. 'We' are remarkably alike, and radically different, in
our vulnerabilities.

But there are precedents. For feminists the discourse of care, despite its multiple
shortcomings, offers a distant analogy: an outgrowth of Gilligan's developmental
psychology that travelled into ontology, morality, ethics, politics, critical legal
theory, and further. As that discourse has struggled—with partial success—to
affirm what was best in it, to defuse the subservient connotations that colour it,
so vulnerability *assumed* (in Beauvoir's sense) requires strategies for defusing

associations of shame, abjection, and other attendant pathologies. But it cannot develop them honourably without attending to a still greater risk: namely, that *knowing* the structural implications of (an)other(s) vulnerability can be as dangerous as it is affirming. No politics of the vulnerable body can effect social transformation(s) without bringing vulnerabilities in their specificity before the public eye—neither papering them over nor otherwise concealing them—if neither in sensationalism, nor 'merely anecdotally'. Somehow, the process requires narrating vulnerability into being; paradoxically, making it no longer exceptional while exposing the outrageousness of its particularity. But the negotiations are delicate; not least because vulnerabilities exposed—known—can generate the ironic effect of making the vulnerable more vulnerable still, their weaknesses exposed, their 'soft spots' available for damage. So the conundrum, which I have merely introduced, is how to think well within ecologies of vulnerability acknowledged, held in trust, with the responsibilities such practices must also assume: how to work toward a renewing social imaginary that pivots upon human vulnerability and hierarchies of intelligibility, while abandoning the (illusory) security promised by autonomy assumptions, and avoiding exposing vulnerabilities to greater abuse.

REFERENCES

BAIER, A. (1985). *Postures of the Mind: Essays on Minds and Morals* (Minneapolis: University of Minnesota Press).

——(1995). *Moral Prejudices: Essays on Ethics* (Cambridge, Mass.: Harvard University Press).

BARTKY, S. (1997). 'Sympathy and Solidarity: On a Tightrope with Scheler', in Diana Meyers (ed.), *Feminists Rethink the Self* (Boulder, Colo.: Westview Press), 177–96.

BEAUVOIR, S. DE (1962). *The Prime of Life*, tr. Peter Green (London: Penguin Books; original publ. 1960).

——(1976). *The Ethics of Ambiguity*, tr. Bernard Frechtman (New York: Citadel Press; original publ. 1947).

——(1989). *The Second Sex*, tr. H. M. Parshley (New York: Vintage Books; from *Le Deuxième Sexe*, Paris: Gallimard, 1949).

BERGOFFEN, D. (2003). 'February 22, 2001: Toward a Politics of the Vulnerable Body', *Hypatia: A Journal of Feminist Philosophy*. 18/1: 116–34.

——(2006). 'From Genocide to Justice: Women's Bodies as a Legal Writing Pad', *Feminist Studies*, 32:1, 11–37.

BORDO, S. (1986). 'The Cartesian Masculinization of Thought', *Signs: Journal of Women in Culture and Society*, 11/3: 439–56.

——(1987). *The Flight to Objectivity* (Albany, NY: SUNY Press).

BRISON, S. J. (1993). 'Surviving Sexual Violence: A Philosophical Perspective', *Journal of Social Philosophy*, 24/1: 5–22.

BRISON, S. J. (2002). *Aftermath: Violence and the Remaking of a Self* (Princeton: Princeton University Press).

BUTLER, J. (2004). *Undoing Gender* (New York: Routledge).

——(2005). *Giving an Account of Oneself* (New York: Fordham University Press).

CASTORIADIS, C. (1994). 'Radical Imagination and the Social Instituting Imaginary', in G. Robinson and J. Rundell (eds.), *Rethinking Imagination: Culture and Creativity* (London: Routledge), 136–54.

CAVARERO, A. (2000). *Relating Narratives: Storytelling and Selfhood*, tr. Paul A. Kottman (London: Routledge).

CODE, L. (1991). *What Can She Know? Feminist Theory and the Construction of Knowledge* (Ithaca, NY: Cornell University Press).

——(1993). 'Taking Subjectivity into Account', in Linda Alcoff and Elizabeth Potter (eds.), *Feminist Epistemologies* (New York: Routledge), 15–48.

——(1995). *Rhetorical Spaces: Essays on (Gendered) Locations* (New York: Routledge).

——(2006a). *Ecological Thinking: The Politics of Epistemic Location* (New York: Oxford University Press).

——(2006b). 'Reason, Imagination, and the Unthought: A Tribute to Genevieve Lloyd', paper presented at the American Philosophical Association Eastern Division meetings, December.

——(2010). 'Testimony, Advocacy, Ignorance: Thinking Ecologically about Social Knowledge', in A. Millar, A. Haddock, and D. Pritchard (eds.), *Social Epistemology* (Oxford: Oxford University Press).

FOUCAULT, M. (1977). 'Nietzsche, Genealogy, History', in D. F. Bouchard (ed.), *Language, Counter-Memory, Practice: Selected Essays and Interviews by Michel Foucault* (Ithaca, NY: Cornell University Press).

FRICKER, E. (2006). 'Testimony and Epistemic Authority', in J. Lackey and E. Sosa (eds.), *The Epistemology of Testimony* (Oxford: Oxford University Press), 225–50.

——(2007). *Epistemic Injustice: Power and the Ethics of Knowing* (Oxford: Oxford University Press).

HARAWAY, D. (1991). *Simians, Cyborgs, and Women: The Reinvention of Nature* (New York: Routledge).

HURTADO, A. (2008). 'Superserviceable Feminism: Revisiting *Toward a New Psychology of Women'. Feminism and Psychology*, 18/3: 341–6.

JOHNSON, B. (ed.) (1993). *Freedom and Interpretation: The Oxford Amnesty Lectures 1992* (New York: Basic Books).

KELLER, E. F. (1985). *Reflections on Gender and Science* (New Haven: Yale University Press).

KRUKS, S. (2001). *Retrieving Experience: Subjectivity and Recognition in Feminist Politics* (Ithaca, NY: Cornell University Press).

——(2005). 'Simone de Beauvoir and the Politics of Privilege', *Hypatia: A Journal of Feminist Philosophy*, 20/1: 178–205.

——(2007). 'Merleau-Ponty and the Problem of Difference in Feminism', in D. Olkowski and G. Weiss (eds.), *Feminist Interpretations of Merleau-Ponty* (University Park, Pa.: Penn State University Press), 29–47.

LACKEY, J., and SOSA, E. (eds.) (2006). *The Epistemology of Testimony* (Oxford: Oxford University Press).

LE DŒUFF, M. (1998). *Le Sexe du Savoir* (Paris: Aubier).

LE DŒUFF, M. (2003). *The Sex of Knowing*, tr. Kathryn Hamer and Lorraine Code (New York: Routledge).

LLOYD, G. (1993). *The Man of Reason: 'Male' and 'Female' in Western Philosophy* (2nd edn. London: Routledge; originally publ. 1984).

——(2000a). 'Individuals, Responsibility, and the Philosophical Imagination', in C. Mackenzie and N. Stoljar (eds.), *Relational Autonomy: Feminist Perspectives on Autonomy, Agency, and the Social Self* (New York: Oxford University Press), 112–23.

——(2000b). 'Le Dœuff and the History of Philosophy', in Max Deutscher (ed.), *Michèle Le Dœuff: Operative Philosophy and Imaginary Practice* (New York: Humanity Books), 33–59.

——(2000c). 'No One's Land: Australia and the Philosophical Imagination', *Hypatia: A Journal of Feminist Philosophy*, 15/2: 26–39.

——(2008). *Providence Lost* (Cambridge, Mass.: Harvard University Press).

MACKENZIE, C., and STOLJAR, N. (eds.) (2000). *Relational Autonomy* (New York: Oxford University Press).

MACLEOD, C. (2008). ' "Who? What?": An Uninducted View of *Towards a New Psychology of Women* from Post-Apartheid South Africa', *Feminism and Psychology*, 18/3: 347–57.

MILLER, J. B. (1976). *Toward a New Psychology of Women* (Boston: Beacon Press).

MILLS, C. (2007). 'White Ignorance', in S. Sullivan and N. Tuana (eds.), *Race and Epistemologies of Ignorance* (Albany, NY: State University of New York Press), 13–38.

WEISS, G. (1995). 'Ambiguity, Absurdity, and Reversibility: Responses to Indeterminacy', *Journal of the British Society for Phenomenology*, 26/1: 43–51, 45.

WILLIAMS, P. J. (1991). *The Alchemy of Race and Rights: Diary of a Law Professor* (Cambridge, Mass.: Harvard University Press).

ZEEDYK, M. S., and GREENWOOD, R. M. (2008). 'Reflections on the Work of Feminist Theorist Jean Baker Miller', *Feminism and Psychology*, 18/3: 321–5.

INDEX

·················